Nineteenth-Century Literature Criticism

Guide to Gale Literary Criticism Series

For criticism on	Consult these Gale series
Authors now living or who died after December 31, 1999	*CONTEMPORARY LITERARY CRITICISM (CLC)*
Authors who died between 1900 and 1999	*TWENTIETH-CENTURY LITERARY CRITICISM (TCLC)*
Authors who died between 1800 and 1899	*NINETEENTH-CENTURY LITERATURE CRITICISM (NCLC)*
Authors who died between 1400 and 1799	*LITERATURE CRITICISM FROM 1400 TO 1800 (LC)* *SHAKESPEAREAN CRITICISM (SC)*
Authors who died before 1400	*CLASSICAL AND MEDIEVAL LITERATURE CRITICISM (CMLC)*
Authors of books for children and young adults	*CHILDREN'S LITERATURE REVIEW (CLR)*
Dramatists	*DRAMA CRITICISM (DC)*
Poets	*POETRY CRITICISM (PC)*
Short story writers	*SHORT STORY CRITICISM (SSC)*
Black writers of the past two hundred years	*BLACK LITERATURE CRITICISM (BLC)* *BLACK LITERATURE CRITICISM SUPPLEMENT (BLCS)*
Hispanic writers of the late nineteenth and twentieth centuries	*HISPANIC LITERATURE CRITICISM (HLC)* *HISPANIC LITERATURE CRITICISM SUPPLEMENT (HLCS)*
Native North American writers and orators of the eighteenth, nineteenth, and twentieth centuries	*NATIVE NORTH AMERICAN LITERATURE (NNAL)*
Major authors from the Renaissance to the present	*WORLD LITERATURE CRITICISM, 1500 TO THE PRESENT (WLC)* *WORLD LITERATURE CRITICISM SUPPLEMENT (WLCS)*

ISSN 0732-1864

Volume 105

Nineteenth-Century Literature Criticism

Excerpts from Criticism of Various
Topics in Nineteenth-Century Literature,
including Literary and Critical Movements,
Prominent Themes and Genres, Anniversary
Celebrations, and Surveys of National Literatures

Edna M. Hedblad
Editor

**Jessica Menzo
Russel Whitaker**
Associate Editors

GALE GROUP

THOMSON LEARNING

Detroit • New York • San Diego • San Francisco
Boston • New Haven, Conn. • Waterville, Maine
London • Munich

STAFF

Janet Witalec, Lynn M. Zott, *Managing Editors, Literature Product*
Kathy D. Darrow, Ellen McGeagh, *Content-Product Liaisons*
Edna M. Hedblad, *Editor*
Jessica Menzo, Russel Whitaker, *Associate Editors*
Mark W. Scott, *Publisher, Literature Product*

Maikue Vang, *Assistant Editor*
Jenny Cromie, *Technical Training Specialist*
Deborah J. Baker, Joyce Nakamura, Kathleen Lopez Nolan, *Managing Editors, Literature Content*
Susan M. Trosky, *Director, Literature Content*

Maria L. Franklin, *Permissions Manager*
Debra Freitas, Shalice Shah-Caldwell, *Permissions Associates*

Victoria B. Cariappa, *Research Manager*
Sarah Genik, *Project Coordinator*
Tamara C. Nott, Tracie A. Richardson, *Research Associates*
Nicodemus Ford, *Research Assistant*
Michelle Campbell, *Administrative Specialist*

Dorothy Maki, *Manufacturing Manager*
Stacy L. Melson, *Buyer*

Mary Beth Trimper, *Composition and Prepress Manager*
Gary Leach, *Composition Specialist*

Randy Bassett, *Imaging Supervisor*
Robert Duncan, Dan Newell, Luke Rademacher, *Imaging Specialists*
Kelly A. Quin, *Editor, Imaging and Multimedia Content*
Michael Logusz, *Graphic Artist*

Library of Congress Catalog Card Number
ISBN 0-7876-5237-7
ISSN 0732-1864
Printed in the United States of America

10 9 8 7 6 5 4 3 2 1

Contents

Preface vii

Acknowledgments xi

Literary Criticism Series Advisory Board xiii

Preface

Since its inception in 1981, *Nineteenth-Century Literature Criticism* (*NCLC*) has been a valuable resource for students and librarians seeking critical commentary on writers of this transitional period in world history. Designated an "Outstanding Reference Source" by the American Library Association with the publication of is first volume, *NCLC* has since been purchased by over 6,000 school, public, and university libraries. The series has covered more than 300 authors representing 29 nationalities and over 17,000 titles. No other reference source has surveyed the critical reaction to nineteenth-century authors and literature as thoroughly as *NCLC*.

Scope of the Series

NCLC is designed to introduce students and advanced readers to the authors of the nineteenth century and to the most significant interpretations of these authors' works. The great poets, novelists, short story writers, playwrights, and philosophers of this period are frequently studied in high school and college literature courses. By organizing and reprinting commentary written on these authors, *NCLC* helps students develop valuable insight into literary history, promotes a better understanding of the texts, and sparks ideas for papers and assignments. Each entry in *NCLC* presents a comprehensive survey of an author's career or an individual work of literature and provides the user with a multiplicity of interpretations and assessments. Such variety allows students to pursue their own interests; furthermore, it fosters an awareness that literature is dynamic and responsive to many different opinions.

Every fourth volume of *NCLC* is devoted to literary topics that cannot be covered under the author approach used in the rest of the series. Such topics include literary movements, prominent themes in nineteenth-century literature, literary reaction to political and historical events, significant eras in literary history, prominent literary anniversaries, and the literatures of cultures that are often overlooked by English-speaking readers.

NCLC continues the survey of criticism of world literature begun by Gale's *Contemporary Literary Criticism* (*CLC*) and *Twentieth-Century Literary Criticism* (*TCLC*).

Organization of the Book

An *NCLC* entry consists of the following elements:

- The **Author Heading** cites the name under which the author most commonly wrote, followed by birth and death dates. Also located here are any name variations under which an author wrote, including transliterated forms for authors whose native languages use nonroman alphabets. If the author wrote consistently under a pseudonym, the pseudonym will be listed in the author heading and the author's actual name given in parenthesis on the first line of the biographical and critical information. Uncertain birth or death dates are indicated by question marks. Single-work entries are preceded by a heading that consists of the most common form of the title in English translation (if applicable) and the original date of composition.

- The **Introduction** contains background information that introduces the reader to the author, work, or topic that is the subject of the entry.

- A **Portrait of the Author** is included when available.

- The list of **Principal Works** is ordered chronologically by date of first publication and lists the most important works by the author. The genre and publication date of each work is given. In the case of foreign authors whose works have been translated into English, the list will focus primarily on twentieth-century translations, selecting those works most commonly considered the best by critics. Unless otherwise indicated, dramas are dated by first performance, not first publication. Lists of **Representative Works** by different authors appear with topic entries.

- Reprinted **Criticism** is arranged chronologically in each entry to provide a useful perspective on changes in critical evaluation over time. The critic's name and the date of composition or publication of the critical work are given at the beginning of each piece of criticism. Unsigned criticism is preceded by the title of the source in which it appeared. All titles by the author featured in the text are printed in boldface type. Footnotes are reprinted at the end of each essay or excerpt. In the case of excerpted criticism, only those footnotes that pertain to the excerpted texts are included. Criticism in topic entries is arranged chronologically under a variety of subheadings to facilitate the study of different aspects of the topic.

- A complete **Bibliographical Citation** of the original essay or book precedes each piece of criticism.

- Critical essays are prefaced by brief **Annotations** explicating each piece.

- An annotated bibliography of **Further Reading** appears at the end of each entry and suggests resources for additional study. In some cases, significant essays for which the editors could not obtain reprint rights are included here. Boxed material following the further reading list provides references to other biographical and critical sources on the author in series published by Gale.

Indexes

Each volume of *NCLC* contains a **Cumulative Author Index** listing all authors who have appeared in a wide variety of reference sources published by the Gale Group, including *NCLC*. A complete list of these sources is found facing the first page of the Author Index. The index also includes birth and death dates and cross references between pseudonyms and actual names.

A **Cumulative Nationality Index** lists all authors featured in *NCLC* by nationality, followed by the number of the *NCLC* volume in which their entry appears.

A **Cumulative Topic Index** lists the literary themes and topics treated in the series as well as in *Classical and Medieval Literature Criticism, Literature Criticism from 1400 to 1800, Twentieth-Century Literary Criticism,* and the *Contemporary Literary Criticism* Yearbook, which was discontinued in 1998.

An alphabetical **Title Index** accompanies each volume of *NCLC*, with the exception of the Topics volumes. Listings of titles by authors covered in the given volume are followed by the author's name and the corresponding page numbers where the titles are discussed. English translations of foreign titles and variations of titles are cross-referenced to the title under which a work was originally published. Titles of novels, dramas, nonfiction books, and poetry, short story, or essay collections are printed in italics, while individual poems, short stories, and essays are printed in roman type within quotation marks.

In response to numerous suggestions from librarians, Gale also produces an annual paperbound edition of the *NCLC* cumulative title index. This annual cumulation, which alphabetically lists all titles reviewed in the series, is available to all customers. Additional copies of this index are available upon request. Librarians and patrons will welcome this separate index; it saves shelf space, is easy to use, and is recyclable upon receipt of the next edition.

Citing *Nineteenth-Century Literature Criticism*

When writing papers, students who quote directly from any volume in the Literary Criticism Series may use the following general format to footnote reprinted criticism. The first example pertains to material drawn from periodicals, the second to material reprinted from books.

Kim McQuaid, "William Apes, Pequot: An Indian Reformer in the Jackson Era," *The New England Quarterly,* 50 (December 1977): 605-25; excerpted and reprinted in *Nineteenth-Century Literature Criticism,* vol. 73, ed. Janet Witalec (Farmington Hills, Mich.: The Gale Group, 1999), 3-4.

Richard Harter Fogle, *The Imagery of Keats and Shelley: A Comparative Study* (Archon Books, 1949), 211-51; excerpted and reprinted in *Nineteenth-Century Literature Criticism,* vol. 73, ed. Janet Witalec (Farmington Hills, Mich.: The Gale Group, 1999), 157-69.

Suggestions are Welcome

Readers who wish to suggest new features, topics, or authors to appear in future volumes, or who have other suggestions or comments are cordially invited to call, write, or fax the Managing Editor:

Managing Editor, Literary Criticism Series
The Gale Group
27500 Drake Road
Farmington Hills, MI 48331-3535
1-800-347-4253 (GALE)
Fax: 248-699-8054

Acknowledgments

The editors wish to thank the copyright holders of the excerpted criticism included in this volume and the permissions managers of many book and magazine publishing companies for assisting us in securing reproduction rights. We are also grateful to the staffs of the Detroit Public Library, the Library of Congress, the University of Detroit Mercy Library, Wayne State University Purdy/Kresge Library Complex, and the University of Michigan Libraries for making their resources available to us. Following is a list of the copyright holders who have granted us permission to reproduce material in this volume of *NCLC*. Every effort has been made to trace copyright, but if omissions have been made, please let us know.

COPYRIGHTED EXCERPTS IN *NCLC*, VOLUME 105, WERE REPRODUCED FROM THE FOLLOWING PERIODICALS:

American Literature, v. 62, March, 1990. Copyright © 1990 by the Duke University Press. Reproduced by permission.—*American Quarterly,* v. 19, Winter, 1967; v. 31, Summer, 1979. © 1967, 1979 Johns Hopkins University Press. Both reproduced by permission.—*Callaloo,* v. 7, Winter, 1984. © The Johns Hopkins University Press. Reproduced by permission./ v. 20, Winter, 1997. Copyright © 1997 by Charles H. Rowell. All rights reserved. © The Johns Hopkins University Press. Reproduced by permission.—*Dalhousie Review,* v. 62, Summer, 1982 for "'Our Mutual Friend' and the Test of Worthiness" by Lewis Horne. Reproduced by permission of the publisher and the author.—*Dickens Quarterly,* v. 8, September, 1991. Reproduced by permission.—*Dickens Studies Annual,* v. 18, 1989; v. 19, 1990; v. 24, 1996. Copyright © 1989, 1990, 1996 by AMS Press, Inc. All reproduced by permission.—*The Dickensian,* v. 77, Autumn, 1981 for "Boffin and Podsnap in Utopia" by Jerome Meckier; v. 86, Autumn, 1990 for "Dickens and Popular Culture: Silas Wegg's Ballads in 'Our Mutual Friend'" by Wilfred P. Dvorak. Both reproduced by permission of the respective authors.—*Early American Literature,* v. XII, Fall, 1977; v. XIII, Fall, 1978; v. XIX, Winter, 1984-85; v. XX, Spring, 1985. All reproduced by permission.—*Eighteenth-Century Life,* v. 5, Winter, 1978. Reproduced by permission.—*ELH,* v. 40, Spring, 1973. © 1973 Johns Hopkins University Press. Reproduced by permission.—*Essays in Criticism,* v. 13, July, 1963; v. 25, April, 1975. Both reproduced by permission.—*Essays in Literature*, v. 3, Fall, 1976. Reproduced by permission.—*Etudes Anglaises,* v. XXXVIII, July-September, 1985. © Didier Erudition, 1985. Reproduced by permission.—*The French Review,* v. LI, March, 1978. Copyright 1978 by the American Association of Teachers of French. Reproduced by permission.—*Journal of American Studies,* v. 9, 1975. Reproduced by permission.—*The Journal of Narrative Technique,* v. 15, Fall, 1985. Reproduced by permission.—*Journal of Narrative Theory,* v. 30, Winter, 2000. Copyright © 2000 by *Journal of Narrative Theory.* Reproduced by permission.—*Modern Philology,* v. 86, August, 1988. © 1988 by The University of Chicago. All rights reserved. Reproduced by permission.—*The New England Quarterly,* v. 64, September, 1991 for "The Nantucket Sequence in Crevecoeur's 'Letters from an American Farmer'" by Nathaniel Philbrick. Copyright 1991 by *The New England Quarterly.* Reproduced by permission of the publisher and the author.—*Nineteenth-Century Fiction,* v. 20, 1965 for "Dickens's Our Mutual Friend' and Henry Mayhew's 'London Labour and the London Poor'" by Harland S. Nelson; v. 20, 1965 for "The Motif of Reading in 'Our Mutual Friend'" by Stanley Friedman. © 1965 University of California Press. Both reproduced by permission of the publisher and the respective authors.—*Nineteenth-Century Fiction,* v. 34, 1979 for "The Education of the Reader in 'Our Mutual Friend'" by Rosemary Mundhenr. © 1979 University of California Press. Reproduced by permission.—*Nineteenth-Century Literature,* v. 49, June, 1994 for "'A Dismal Swamp': Darwin, Design, and Evolution in 'Our Mutual Friend'" by Howard W. Fulwieler. Copyright 1994 by Regents of the University of California. Reproduced by permission.—*Novel,* v. 28, Winter, 1995. Copyright NOVEL Corp. © 1995. Reproduced with permission.—*Papers on Language and Literature,* v. 30, Fall, 1994. Reproduced by permission.—*Philological Quarterly,* v. 61, Winter, 1982 for "From the Ending of 'The Professor' to the Conception of 'Jane Eyre'" by Rebecca Rodolff. Reproduced by permission of the author.—*Review of English Studies,* v. XI, May, 1960 for "The Manuscript of 'The Professor'" by M.M. Brammer. Reproduced by permission of the publisher and the author./ v. XLVII, May, 1996. © Oxford University Press 1996. Reproduced by permission.—*South Atlantic Quarterly,* v. 69, Summer, 1970. Reproduced by permission.—*Studies in American Fiction,* v. 18, Autumn, 1990. Copyright © 1990 Northeastern University. Reproduced by permission.—*Studies in the Novel,* v. 10, Summer, 1978. Copyright 1978 by North Texas State University. Reproduced by permission.—*Texas Studies in Literature and Language,* v. 13, Fall, 1971 for "Laughter in 'Our Mutual Friend'" by Ray J. Sherer. Reproduced by permission of the publisher and the author.—*Victorian Newsletter,* v. 24, Fall, 1963. Reproduced by permission of *The Victorian Newsletter* and the author.—*William and Mary Quarterly,* v. 48, April, 1991; v. 55, April, 1998. Copyright 1991, 1998 by the Institute of Early American History and Culture. Both reproduced by permission.

Literary Criticism Series Advisory Board

The members of the Gale Group Literary Criticism Series Advisory Board—reference librarians and subject specialists from public, academic, and school library systems—represent a cross-section of our customer base and offer a variety of informed perspectives on both the presentation and content of our literature criticism products. Advisory board members assess and define such quality issues as the relevance, currency, and usefulness of the author coverage, critical content, and literary topics included in our series; evaluate the layout, presentation, and general quality of our printed volumes; provide feedback on the criteria used for selecting authors and topics covered in our series; provide suggestions for potential enhancements to our series; identify any gaps in our coverage of authors or literary topics, recommending authors or topics for inclusion; analyze the appropriateness of our content and presentation for various user audiences, such as high school students, undergraduates, graduate students, librarians, and educators; and offer feedback on any proposed changes/ enhancements to our series. We wish to thank the following advisors for their advice throughout the year.

The Professor

Charlotte Brontë

The following entry presents criticism of Brontë's novel *The Professor* (1857). For information on Brontë's complete career, see *NCLC,* Volume 3; for information on *Jane Eyre,* see Volume 8; for information on *Villette,* see Volume 33, and for information on *Shirley,* see Volume 58.

INTRODUCTION

The Professor (1857), Charlotte Brontë's first novel, was unpublished until after the author's death despite repeated efforts to find a publisher. Even the popularity of *Jane Eyre* and the fame her work brought her weren't enough to entice publishers to print *The Professor* while Brontë lived. Eager for more from Charlotte Brontë's pen, readers were nevertheless unenthusiastic about *The Professor,* and it received numerous unfavorable reviews upon publication. Written from the point of view of a male narrator, the novel has been criticized as an immature effort and a failed attempt to write from the male perspective. Modern critics are primarily interested in the gender issues posed by the work and in analyzing the work's early reception, while others focus on the influence *The Professor* had on Brontë's later novels. However, Brontë's first attempt as a professional writer has consistently met with reservations from readers and critics alike.

PLOT AND MAJOR CHARACTERS

Drawn from Brontë's experiences in Brussels, *The Professor* tells the story of the orphan William Crimsworth, who seeks his future in Brussels after attempting to make a living as a clerk for his older brother, a mill owner in the north of England. Crimsworth begins the novel as a dependant, the ward of an aristocratic family. He rejects this life and the expectation that he become a clergyman in order to enter voluntary servitude to his prosperous brother. Unable to endure his brother's tyrannical nature, Crimsworth departs for Brussels to pursue a career in education. Hired to teach English at a girls' school, Crimsworth falls in love with Frances Henri, a pupil-teacher at the school. Crimsworth resists the manipulations of the deceitful Catholic headmistress, Zoraïde Reuter, who later marries the headmaster of a nearby boys' school. After resigning his position at the school, Crimsworth finds a new post, enabling him to marry Frances. His bride refuses to give up her own career as a seamstress, and together the two earn a respectable income and return to England.

MAJOR THEMES

In *The Professor,* Brontë is very much concerned with the treachery of Catholics, as was much of contemporary Victorian England. Through Mlle. Reuter and his interaction with the Catholic students at the school, Crimsworth experiences the superficial and deceptive nature of the Catholic educational system. Mlle. Reuter is characterized as duplicitous and manipulative and stands in sharp contrast to the honest Protestant Frances. Often viewed as the mouthpiece for Brontë's own views, Crimsworth offers a scornful account of "Romish wizardcraft" and its effect on the schoolgirls, who are portrayed as deceitful and shallow. Crimsworth's sexuality is explored as he is both voyeuristically fascinated and repulsed by the girls he teaches. Additionally, the novel focuses on the relationship between sexual dominance and social identity. As a dependent without any fortune or social stature of his own, Crimsworth is acutely aware of his unattractiveness to young women. Frances is also orphaned, poor, and meek in manner—a characterization that stresses the connection between inferiority of social status and the enforced repression of emotion. Through Frances, Brontë explores her concern for the predicament of women who lack wealth and social connections. Both Frances and Crimsworth combat their lack of social advantage by working hard and exhibiting self-restraint, characteristics that are ultimately rewarded with financial and domestic security.

CRITICAL RECEPTION

The contemporary view of *The Professor* was largely unfavorable. Upon its publication, many reviewers dismissed the novel as a poorly conceived first attempt of a young novelist. Brontë's characters are considered unnatural, and her style said to be less artful than in *Jane Eyre,* or *Shirley.* Additionally, many of *The Professor*'s themes were reworked into Brontë's *Villette,* which critics considered a much more successful work. The close parallels between the subject matter of these two novels led critics to dismiss *The Professor* for its inferiority. Others looked to Brontë's experience in Brussels, which had become widely known as a result of Elizabeth Gaskell's *Life of Charlotte Brontë,* to explain the overly biographical and unpolished narrative of Crimsworth. Specifically, explains twentieth-century critic Annette Tromly, Brontë's frustrations involving unrequited love resulted in her writing an "uncontrolled" novel. Tromly maintains that while Brontë may have drawn from her own life to write *The Professor,* she did so in a much more complex way than critics typically assume. Tromly goes on to examine subtle and ambiguous characterization in the work. Other critics are concerned with the gender issues Brontë investigated in *The Professor.* Ruth D. Johnston explores the narrative processes in *The Professor* that establish the feminine subject. Arguing that representation is the locus of both ideological and sexual conflict, as well as the generation of the subject, Johnston concludes that *The Professor*'s narrative processes make feminine subjectivity impossible. Also concerned with gender issues, Annette R. Federico studies the way in which female authors, including Brontë, used male narrators to understand gender relations and how these authors represented masculinity. Federico asserts that *The Professor,* with its descriptions of male dominance, voyeurism, and sexual suppression, reproduces Victorian masculinity. Federico further maintains that the novel is not concerned with attaining power but outgrowing the need for power. Like Tromly, Catherine Malone observes that appraisal of *The Professor* is typically informed by the biography published soon after Brontë's death. Surveying the criticism of the novel, Malone notes that the unappealing nature of Crimsworth's character has been attributed to Brontë's immaturity as a writer. In her assessment of Crimsworth's characterization, Malone contends that Brontë does not fail to create a convincing male protagonist, but that a male protagonist is unable to tell the story that Brontë desired to write, that is, a "history of suffering." Criticism is frequently tied to the well-known life of *The Professor*'s author, which has led Malone to argue that we have come to love Brontë more than her books. Significantly, the body of criticism is much smaller for this novel than for Brontë's other work, as even the defenders of *The Professor* acknowledge its inferiority to the genius of *Jane Eyre.*

PRINCIPAL WORKS

Poems by Currer, Ellis, and Acton Bell [by Charlotte, Emily and Anne Brontë] (poetry) 1846

Jane Eyre: An Autobiography [edited by Currer Bell] (novel) 1847

Shirley: A Tale [as Currer Bell] (novel) 1850

Villette [as Currer Bell] (novel) 1853

The Professor: A Tale [as Currer Bell] (novel) 1857

The Twelve Adventurers and Other Stories (juvenilia) 1925

Legends of Angria: Compiled from the Early Writings of Charlotte Brontë (juvenilia) 1933

Five Novelettes (novelettes) 1971

CRITICISM

The Athenaeum (review date 1857)

SOURCE: Review of "*The Professor: a Tale.* By Currer Bell." In *The Athenaeum,* No. 1546, June 13, 1857, pp. 755-57.

[*In the following essay, the critic offers a plot summary and dismisses* The Professor *as incomplete, lacking the "descriptive or womanly touches" of Brontë's other novels.*]

After nine years—the fitting Horatian interval—Currer Bell's rejected novel makes its posthumous appearance in print. The wondrous story of **Jane Eyre** has so much gratified, and the more wondrous, "ower true," and over-tragic life-drama of Charlotte Brontë so much amazed the world, that it feels disposed rather to err on the side of gentleness than rigour, and to question the justice of the criticism which refused, rather than the constructive power which was latent in the earlier tale. Accordingly friends, lovers, and biographer have moved for a new trial, and *The Professor* comes before the public with every advantage of typography, and with the best prospects of a hearing. Whether the counsel which prompted, or the love which consented, to publication was wise or considerate, is as fairly open to doubt as the friendship which is disinclined to consider a dog Diamond as on some occasions providential. The world has not gained greatly by 'The Prelude,' and perhaps we ought to be resigned to the loss of a few sheets more of 'The Opium-Eater.' That the work before us will be read and discussed by all who have read the *Life of Charlotte Brontë* is certain enough, but the interest excited will be rather curious than deep, and the impression left on the reader one of pain and incompleteness. It is a mere study for **Jane Eyre** or **Shirley,**—certainly displaying effects of the same force, the same characteristic keenness of perception, the same rough, bold, coarse truthfulness of expression, the same compressed style, offence of dialogue, preference for forbidden topics, and pre-Raphaelitish contempt for grace,—but with scarcely any relief or shadow, and with fewer descriptive or womanly touches. Unity or arrangement there is none. The sketches are carelessly left loose for the reader to connect or not, as he chooses,—a carelessness the result of a deliberate intention, as is clear enough from the Preface.—

> I said to myself that my hero should work his way through life as I had seen real living men work theirs— that he should never get a shilling he had not earned— that no sudden turns should lift him in a moment to wealth and high station; that whatever small competency he might gain, should be won by the sweat of his brow; that, before he could find so much as an arbour to sit down in, he should master at least half the ascent of 'the Hill of Difficulty;' that he should not even marry a beautiful girl or a lady of rank. As Adam's son he should share Adam's doom, and drain throughout life a mixed and moderate cup of enjoyment.

The incidents of the story are few; the principal parts are sustained by an unnatural brother, a rough manufacturer, of the type of Mr. Helstone, who interposes *ex machinâ* and rescues the hero, an obstinate but well-regulated character in difficulties. The hero, a younger son of a Yorkshire blue-dyer, is of patrician race by the mother's side, but though educated at Eton he declines to adopt the Church and the opinions of his titled uncles, and in preference offers himself as a clerk to his brother, a rich Yorkshire manufacturer, the husband of a childish-looking, *red-haired* lady, whom he terrifies by driving a restive quadruped,— "only opening his lips to damn his horse."

Here is a portrait of Mr. Crimsworth, the elder brother, and a peep into the manufacturing "concern":—

> Workpeople were passing to and fro; a waggon was being laden with pieces. Mr. Crimsworth looked from side to side, and seemed at one glance to comprehend all that was going on; he alighted, and leaving his horse and gig to the care of a man who hastened to take the reins from his hand, he bid me follow him to the counting-house. We entered it; a very different place from the parlours of Crimsworth Hall—a place for business, with a bare, planked floor, a safe, two high desks and stools, and some chairs. A person was seated at one of the desks, who took off his square cap when Mr. Crimsworth entered, and in an instant was again absorbed in his occupation of writing or calculating—I know not which. Mr. Crimsworth, having removed his mackintosh, sat down by the fire. I remained standing near the hearth; he said presently—'Steighton, you may leave the room; I have some business to transact with this gentleman. Come back when you hear the bell.' The individual at the desk rose and departed, closing the door as he went out. Mr. Crimsworth stirred the fire, then folded his arms, and sat a moment thinking, his lips compressed, his brow knit. I had nothing to do but to watch him—how well his features were cut! what a handsome man he was! Whence, then, came that air of contraction—that narrow and hard aspect on his forehead, in all his lineaments? Turning to me he began abruptly:—'You are come down to———shire to learn to be a tradesman?'—'Yes, I am.'—'Have you made up your mind on the point? Let me know that at once.'—'Yes.'—'Well, I am not bound to help you, but I have a place here vacant, if you are qualified for it. I will take you on trial. What can you do? Do you know anything besides that useless trash of college learning—Greek, Latin, and so forth?'—'I have studied mathematics.'—'Stuff! I dare say you have.'—'I can read and write French and German.'—'Hum!' He reflected a moment, and then opening a drawer in a desk near him took out a letter and gave it to me. 'Can you read that?' he asked. It was a German commercial letter; I translated it; I could not tell whether he was gratified or not—his countenance remained fixed. 'It is well,' he said, after a pause, 'that you are acquainted with something useful, something that will enable you to earn your board and lodging: since you know French and German, I will take you as second clerk to manage the foreign correspondence of the house. I shall give you a good salary—90*l.* a year—and now,' he continued, raising his voice, 'hear once for all what I have to say about our relationship, and all that sort of humbug!

I must have no nonsense on that point; it would never suit me. I shall excuse you nothing on the plea of being my brother; if I find you stupid, negligent, dissipated, idle, or possessed of any faults detrimental to the interests of the house, I shall dismiss you as I would any other clerk. Ninety pounds a year are good wages, and I expect to have the full value of my money out of you; remember, too, that things are on a practical footing in my establishment—business-like habits, feelings, and ideas, suit me best. Do you understand?'—'Partly,' I replied. 'I suppose you mean that I am to do my work for my wages; not to expect favour from you, and not to depend on you for any help but what I earn; that suits me exactly, and on these terms I will consent to be your clerk.' I turned on my heel, and walked to the window; this time I did not consult his face to learn his opinion: what it was I do not know, nor did I then care. After a silence of some minutes he recommenced:— 'You perhaps expect to be accommodated with apartments at Crimsworth Hall, and go and come with me in the gig. I wish you, however, to be aware that such an arrangement would be quite inconvenient to me. I like to have the seat in my gig at liberty for any gentleman whom for business reasons I may wish to take down to the hall for a night or so. You will seek out lodgings in X———.' Quitting the window, I walked back to the health. 'Of course I shall seek out lodgings in X———,' I answered. 'It would not suit me either to lodge at Crimsworth Hall.' My tone was quiet. I always speak quietly. Yet Mr. Crimsworth's blue eye became incensed; he took his revenge rather oddly. Turning to me he said bluntly—'You are poor enough, I suppose; how do you expect to live till your quarter's salary becomes due?'—'I shall get on,' said I.—'How do you expect to live?' he repeated in a louder voice.— 'As I can, Mr. Crimsworth.'—'Get into debt at your peril! that's all,' he answered. 'For aught I know you may have extravagant aristocratic habits; if you have, drop them; I tolerate nothing of the sort here, and I will never give you a shilling extra, whatever liabilities you may incur—mind that.'

The engagement proves unsatisfactory, and a Mr. Hunsden, who talks a language that partly recalls Mephistopheles and partly Mr. Carlyle, exhorts, if you "cannot get up to the pitch of resistance, why, God made you to be crushed, and lie down by all means, and lie flat, and let Juggernaut ride well over you." The advice takes; there is a hot quarrel between the brother and William Crimsworth,—the hero quits the works. The contrast between the hot scene in the counting-house and the cool wintry evening is in exquisite feeling.—

> There was a great stillness near and far; the time of the day favoured tranquillity, as the people were all employed within doors, the hour of evening release from the factories not being yet arrived; a sound of full-flowing water alone pervaded the air, for the river was deep and abundant, swelled by the melting of a late snow. I stood awhile leaning over a wall; and looking down at the current, I watched the rapid rush of its waves. I desired memory to take a clear and permanent impression of the scene, and treasure it for future years. Grovetown church clock struck four; looking up I beheld the last of that day's sun, glinting red through the

leafless boughs of some very old oak trees surrounding the church—its light coloured and characterized the picture as I wished. I paused yet a moment, till the sweet, slow sound of the bell had quite died out of the air; then ear, eye and feeling satisfied, I quitted the wall and once more turned my face towards X———.

With a letter from Mr. Hunsden, fifteen pounds, and a watch, our hero starts for Brussels. Here is a piece of writing that strongly reminds us of *Jane Eyre*:—

> Three—nay four—pictures line the four-walled cell where are stored for me the records of the past. First, Eton. All in that picture is in far perspective, receding, diminutive; but freshly coloured, green, dewy, with a spring sky, piled with glittering yet showery clouds; for my childhood was not all sunshine—it had its overcast, its cold, its stormy hours. Second, X———, huge, dingy; the canvas cracked and smoked; a yellow sky, sooty clouds; no sun, no azure: the verdure of the suburbs blighted and sullied—a very dreary scene. Third, Belgium; and I will pause before this landscape. * * Green, reedy swamps; fields fertile but flat, cultivated in patches that made them look like magnified kitchen-gardens; belts of cut trees, formal as pollard willows, skirting the horizon; narrow canals, gliding slow by the roadside; painted Flemish farm-houses; some very dirty hovels; a grey, dead sky; wet road, wet fields, wet house-tops: not a beautiful, scarcely a picturesque object met my eye along the whole route; yet to me, all was beautiful, all was more than picturesque.

Arrived in Brussels, we are introduced to M. Pelet, a schoolmaster in the Rue Royale, the prototype of M. Paul in *Villette,* who engages the hero as *Professor* of English and Latin at a thousand francs a year. The Professor's first essay with the class of moon-faced Flemings, who snuffle, snort, and wheeze the English tongue, is vigorous, but wanting in humour. We pass over the odd *ménage,*—quit the Professor's chamber, which has one window boarded up, *les convenances* forbidding irregular insight into a "Pensionnat de Demoiselles,"—and, along with the Professor, enter in due form the clear and bright, though somewhat chill, *salon* of Mdlle. Reuter, the fair *directrice,* a lady who wears her pretty nut-brown hair in curls, and is very quiet, interesting, and cat-like. There Mr. Creemsvort is engaged as occasional Professor, at five hundred francs a year; and we make the acquaintance of a triad that reminds us in idea of Blanche, Rose, and Violet. The morality of the school is thus sketched:—

> The first picture is a full length of Aurelia Koslow, a German fräulein, or rather a half-breed between German and Russian. She is eighteen years of age, and has been sent to Brussels to finish her education; she is of middle size, stiffly made, body long, legs short, bust much developed but not compactly moulded, waist disproportionately compressed by an inhumanly braced corset, dress carefully arranged, large feet tortured into small bottines, head small, hair smoothed, braided, oiled, and gummed to perfection; very low forehead, very diminutive and vindictive grey eyes, somewhat Tartar features, rather flat nose, rather high cheek bones, yet the ensemble not positively ugly; tolerably good

complexion. So much for person. As to mind deplorably ignorant and ill-informed; incapable of writing or speaking correctly even German, her native tongue, a dunce in French, and her attempts at learning English a mere farce, yet she has been at school twelve years; but as she invariably gets her exercises, of every description, done by a fellow pupil, and reads her lessons off a book concealed in her lap, it is not wonderful that her progress has been so snail-like. I do not know what Aurelia's daily habits of life are, because I have not the opportunity of observing her at all times; but from what I see of the state of her desk, books, and papers, I should say she is slovenly and even dirty; her outward dress, as I have said, is well attended to; but in passing behind her bench, I have remarked that her neck is grey for want of washing, and her hair, so glossy with gum and grease, is not such as one feels tempted to pass the hand over, much less to run the fingers through. Aurelia's conduct in class, at least when I am present, is something extraordinary, considered as an index of girlish innocence. The moment I enter the room, she nudges her next neighbour and indulges in a half-suppressed laugh. As I take my seat on the estrade, she fixes her eye on me; she seems resolved to attract, and, if possible, monopolize my notice; to this end she launches at me all sorts of looks, languishing, provoking, leering, laughing. As I am found quite proof against this sort of artillery—for we scorn what, unasked, is lavishly offered—she has recourse to the expedient of making noises; sometimes she sighs, sometimes groans, sometimes utters inarticulate sounds, for which language has no name. If, in walking up the school-room, I pass near her, she puts out her foot that it may touch mine; if I do not happen to observe the manœuvre, and my boot comes in contact with her brodequin, she affects to fall into convulsions of suppressed laughter; if I notice the snare and avoid it, she expresses her mortification in sullen muttering, where I hear myself abused in bad French, pronounced with an intolerable low German accent.

The story oscillates betwixt the two establishments for nearly three hundred pages,—M. Pelet or Mdlle. Reuter predominating by turns in endeavours to enlist the heart of the Professor and the interest of the reader. An Anglo-Swiss pupil-teacher, Mdlle. Frances Evans Henri, carries the day, and is dismissed in consequence. Love-making on the part of the *directrice*—jealousy on that of M. Pelet—several pages of search, and the discovery of the young lady in a cemetery weeping over her aunt's grave—a proposal—the appearance of Mr. Hunsden—and a wedding, are the chief events in the second volume. The Professor's proposal is original and Shirley-like. This is the scene:—

> Frances rose, as if restless; she passed before me to stir the fire, which did not want stirring; she lifted and put down the little ornaments on the mantel-piece; her dress waved within a yard of me; slight, straight, and elegant, she stood erect on the hearth. There are impulses we can control; but there are others which control us, because they attain us with a tiger-leap, and are our masters ere we have seen them. Perhaps though, such impulses are seldom altogether bad; perhaps Reason, by a process as brief as quiet, a process that is finished ere felt, has ascertained the sanity of the deed Instinct

meditates, and feels justified in remaining passive while it is performed. I know I did not reason, I did not plan or intend, yet, whereas one moment I was sitting solus on the chair near the table, the next, I held Frances on my knee, placed there with sharpness and decision, and retained with exceeding tenacity. 'Monsieur!' cried Frances, and was still; not another word escaped her lips; sorely confounded she seemed during the lapse of the first few moments; but the amazement soon subsided; terror did not succeed, nor fury; after all, she was only a little nearer than she had been before, to one she habitually respected and trusted; embarrassment might have impelled her to contend, but self-respect checked resistance where resistance is useless. 'Frances, how much regard have you for me?' was my demand. No answer; the situation was yet too new and surprising to permit speech. On this consideration, I compelled myself for some seconds to tolerate her silence, though impatient of it; presently, I repeated the same question—probably not in the calmest of tones; she looked at me; my face, doubtless, was no model of composure, my eyes no still wells of tranquillity.—'Do speak,' I urged; and a very low, hurried, yet still arch voice said—'Monsieur, vous me faîtes mal; de grâce lâchez un peu ma main droite.' In truth I became aware that I was holding the said 'main droite' in a somewhat ruthless grasp: I did as desired; and, for the third time, asked more gently—'Frances, how much regard have you for me?'—'Mon maître, j'en ai beaucoup,' was the truthful rejoinder.—'Frances, have you enough to give yourself to me as my wife?—to accept me as your husband?' I felt the agitation of the heart, I saw 'the purple light of love' cast its glowing reflection on cheek, temples, neck; I desired to consult the eye, but sheltering lash and lid forbade. 'Monsieur,' said the soft voice at last,—'Monsieur désire savoir si je consens—si—enfin, si je veux me marier avec lui?'—'Justement.'—'Monsieur sera-t-il aussi bon mari qu'il a été bon maître?'—'I will try, Frances.' A pause; then with a new, yet still subdued inflexion of the voice—an inflexion which provoked while it pleased me—accompanied, too, by a 'sourire à la fois fin et timide' in perfect harmony with the tone:—'C'est à dire, monsieur sera toujours un peu entêté, exigeant, volontaire?'—'Have I been so, Frances?'—'Mais oui; vous le savez bien.'—'Have I been nothing else?'—'Mais oui; vous avez été mon meilleur ami.'—'And what, Frances, are you to me?'—'Votre dévouée élève, qui vous aime de tout son cœur.'—'Will my pupil consent to pass her life with me? Speak English now, Frances.' Some moments were taken for reflection; the answer, pronounced slowly, ran thus:—'You have always made me happy; I like to hear you speak; I like to see you; I like to be near you; I believe you are very good, and very superior; I know you are stern to those who are careless and idle, but you are kind, very kind to the attentive and industrious, even if they are not clever. Master, I should be *glad* to live with you always;' and she made a sort of movement, as if she would have clung to me, but restraining herself she only added with earnest emphasis—'Master, I consent to pass my life with you.'— 'Very well, Frances.' I drew her a little nearer to my heart; I took a first kiss from her lips, thereby sealing the compact, now framed between us; afterwards she and I were silent, nor was our silence brief. Frances' thoughts, during this interval, I know not, nor did I at-

tempt to guess them; I was not occupied in searching her countenance, nor in otherwise troubling her composure. The peace I felt, I wished her to feel; my arm, it is true, still detained her; but with a restraint that was gentle enough, so long as no opposition tightened it. My gaze was on the red fire; my heart was measuring its own content; it sounded and sounded, and found the depth fathomless. 'Monsieur,' at last said my quiet companion, as stirless in her happiness as a mouse in its terror. Even now in speaking she scarcely lifted her head. 'Well, Frances?' I like unexaggerated intercourse; it is not my way to overpower with amorous epithets, any more than to worry with selfishly importunate caresses. 'Monsieur est raisonnable, n'est ce pas?'—'Yes; especially when I am requested to be so in English: but why do you ask me?'—'You see nothing vehement or obtrusive in my manner; am I not tranquil enough?'— 'Ce n'est pas cela—' began Frances. 'English!' I reminded her. 'Well monsieur, I wished merely to say, that I should like, of course, to retain my employment of teaching. You will teach still, I suppose, monsieur?'—'Oh yes, it is all I have to depend on.'— 'Bon!—I mean good. Thus we shall have both the same profession. I like that; and my efforts to get on will be as unrestrained as yours—will they not, monsieur?'— 'You are laying plans to be independent of me,' said I.—'Yes, monsieur; I must be no incumbrance to you—no burden in any way.'—'But, Frances, I have not yet told you what my prospects are. I have left M. Pelet's; and after nearly a month's seeking, I have got another place, with a salary of three thousand francs a year, which I can easily double by a little additional exertion. Thus you see it would be useless for you to fag yourself by going out to give lessons; on six thousand francs you and I can live, and live well.' Frances seemed to consider. There is something flattering to man's strength, something consonant to his honourable pride, in the idea of becoming the providence of what he loves—feeding and clothing it, as God does the lilies of the field. So to decide her resolution, I went on:—'Life has been painful and laborious enough to you so far, Frances; you require complete rest; your twelve hundred francs would not form a very important addition to our income, and what sacrifice of comfort to earn it! Relinquish your labours: you must be weary, and let me have the happiness of giving you rest.' I am not sure whether Frances had accorded due attention to my harangue; instead of answering me with her usual respectful promptitude, she only smiled and said— 'How rich you are, monsieur!' and then she stirred uneasy in my arms. 'Three thousand francs!' she murmured, 'while I get only twelve hundred!' She went on faster. 'However it must be so for the present; and, monsieur, were you not saying something about my giving up my place? Oh no! I shall hold it fast;' and her little fingers emphatically tightened on mine.— 'Think of my marrying you to be kept by you, monsieur! I could not do it; and how dull my days would be! You would be away teaching in close, noisey school-rooms, from morning till evening, and I should be lingering at home, unemployed and solitary; I should get depressed and sullen, and you would soon tire of me.'—'Frances, you could read and study—two things you like so well.'—'Monsieur, I could not; I like a contemplative life, but I like an active life better; I must act in some way, and act with you. I have taken notice, monsieur, that people who are only in each other's company for amusement, never really like each other so well, or esteem each other so highly, as those who work together, and perhaps suffer together.'—'You speak God's truth,' said I at last, 'and you shall have your own way, for it is the best way. Now, as a reward for such ready consent, give me a voluntary kiss.'

The pair open a school in Brussels, where Mr. Hunsden sends them pupils "to be polished off." In ten years they make a fortune, secure a pretty English home that lies among the moors thirty miles from X———. "The smoke of mills has not yet sullied the verdure, the waters still run pure." There is a long, green, shady lane starred with daisies, which gives a title to the house. There is a fine boy and a favourite mastiff;—and the story ends.

Miss Brontë does not exhibit her characters in critical action, or under strong temptation. Low chicane, astuteness, sensuality, and tyranny, are keenly and observantly drawn; but throughout the novel the quietness is unnatural, the level of fact too uniform, the restraint and the theory of life too plain. The principles and the art of the writer, though true, excite no corresponding sympathy on the part of the reader,—few demands being made on his softer or gentler nature. There is no Helen Burns that we can watch or weep over,—no sprightly little Adele that we can sport with. Frances may possibly be the mother of Lucy Snow, and Mdlle. Reuter and M. Pelet the co-efficients of Madame Modeste and Paul Emmanuel. Similarities of opinion respecting marriage may be traced, not as a crime, but an imbecility. Now and then there is a touch of grandiloquence that astonishes us. Words and events are utilized in a way that now, knowing the author's opportunities, appear to us remarkable. On the whole, this tale bears to Currer Bell's later works the relation which a pre-Shakespearian story does to the drama,—it is curious to an artist or psychologist. On closing this posthumous chapter, and ending Charlotte Brontë's strange literary history, we are reminded of a saying of Jean Paul's—"God deals with poets as we do with nightingales, hanging a dark cloth round the cage until they sing the right tune."

M. M. Brammer (essay date 1960)

SOURCE: "The Manuscript of *The Professor.*" In *Review of English Studies,* ns, Vol. 11, No. 42, May, 1960, pp. 157-70.

[*In the following essay, Brammer discusses the fair copy of Brontë's* The Professor, *examining the nature of the changes made to that copy by the author and her husband William Bell Nicholls.*]

Charlotte Brontë completed the fair copy of *The Professor* on 27 June 1846.[1] Her original draft, presumably finished by April of that year,[2] has not, so far as is known, survived; but the fair copy of this particular novel is of some interest. It is well known that after a series of 'ignomini-

ous dismissals' from various publishers, the manuscript was returned with a courteous and reasoned refusal from Smith, Elder and Co. Soon after their publication of *Jane Eyre,* Charlotte was contemplating a revised *Professor,*[3] but her publishers evidently advised her not to attempt it. However, little more than a year after she had completed *Shirley,* she again turned to her first novel, and some time before February 1851, when George Smith finally persuaded her to abandon the idea, she wrote a Preface 'with a view to publication'.

Alterations in the fair copy may therefore include revisions as late as 1851 as well as those made in preparation for the initial attempt at publication. It seems unlikely that alterations would postdate *Villette* (1853), in which most of the Brussels material had been re-used; and *The Professor* was locked up 'in a cupboard by himself' after his ninth and final rejection in February 1851.

The Professor was eventually published after the author's death. Mrs. Gaskell refused George Smith's suggestion that she should edit the novel, but, anxious that Kay-Shuttleworth should not be allowed to do so, she insisted that Mr. Nicholls ought to be entrusted with the task.[4] She and Kay-Shuttleworth agreed that several 'objectionable passages' should be removed, for *The Professor* was 'disfigured by more coarseness and profanity in quoting texts of scripture disagreeably' than any of her other works.[4] In the event she was very dissatisfied with the extent of Nicholls's editing. He had, nevertheless, bowdlerized *The Professor* to some extent, as an examination of the manuscript shows. His cancellations are of considerable interest.

Finally, the fact that the novel was not seen through the press by Charlotte Brontë herself meant that the printed text was not entirely accurate. A number of misreadings occur, and the author's punctuation and capitalization are sometimes seriously distorted.

I. ALTERATIONS IN THE MANUSCRIPT[5]

The 340 pages of *The Professor* manuscript contain between 270 and 280 alterations of various kinds. Many pages contain only one alteration: few have more than two or three. About fifty of the instances mentioned are insertions of words or phrases above the line of writing—most of them in ink, three apparently in pencil. Many are single word insertions (typically, the addition of an adjective to a descriptive phrase), and only about half a dozen are longer phrases of some significance.

The author made most of her alterations by crossing out a word or phrase with a single horizontal stroke of the pen, and writing the new phrase above the line. Thus the original words are usually legible. But one alteration, on MS. p. 48, is in a handwriting which one may fairly assume to be that of Nicholls—since he is the acknowledged editor and since there is a close similarity between the writing of the alteration and that of his transcript of the Preface. The heavy, black obliteration of the rejected words on p. 48 is almost certainly his doing, and it would seem reasonable to suppose that he was responsible for similar cancellations elsewhere in the manuscript. One passage, heavily inked out, has been replaced by a phrase in Charlotte Brontë's handwriting (MS. p. 47): on MS. p. 248 light diagonal strokes in her faded brownish ink are clearly visible as well as the darker cancellations of Nicholls. In both cases the original was probably of a type that Nicholls wished to cancel much more thoroughly than the author had done.

I assume therefore that it was he who so carefully inked out the word 'God' in the following passages:

> MS. p. 48 (chap. v, p. 76)
> God damn your insolence! (Altered to 'Confound . . .')
> MS. p. 141 (xiv. 235)
> God! How the repeater of the prayer . . .
> MS. p. 247 (xxii. 117)
> God confound his impudence!
> MS. p. 306 (xxiv. 206)
> Oh God! And I pitied the fellow . . .

These exclamations are provoked by themes or characters which produced a violent reaction in the author's mind. They are also part of *The Professor*'s realism: an Edward Crimsworth would have said 'God damn' rather than the petulant 'Confound'. Hunsden, delighting in provocative speech and excited by his battle of wits with Frances, would have spoken more emphatically than Nicholls allows him to do. On the other hand, it might be argued that Charlotte Brontë, in her attempt to portray masculine characters and to assume the character of a man as narrator, mistook coarseness for masculinity. 'God confound his impudence!', the professor's reflection on Hunsden's cool manner of making himself at home, is disproportionately strong; his earlier exclamation, provoked by the gabbled prayers of the Roman Catholic scholars, is hardly well chosen in a diatribe against irreverence.

Nicholls also appears to have cancelled, or to have confirmed the author's cancellation of, two longer passages. On MS. p. 129 (xii. 215) the phrase 'but when passion cooled' is followed by three very heavily cancelled lines. On MS. p. 248 (xxii. 118) after the sentence 'There is no use in attempting to describe what is indescribable' occur four heavily cancelled lines. The first passage is unfortunately quite illegible: but the ascenders and descenders of letters in the second are clear, and most words decipherable with a fair degree of certainty.[6] In the following version the words in italics are dubious: those bracketed are illegible in the manuscript: the conjectural reading is based on the apparent length and spacing of the words.

> . . . describe what is indescribable. I can only say that the form and countenance of Hunsden Yorke Hunsden Esq resembled *more* the *result* [of an amour] between Oliver Cromwell and a French grisette than anything else in Heaven above or in the Earth beneath.

The author's cancellation must have left the original text plainly legible: Nicholls therefore inked out each word so that the passage should not be read by publisher or printer.

Charlotte Brontë may have cancelled the sentence before sending the manuscript to any publisher at all, but it is conceivable that, looking over *The Professor* after the publication of *Jane Eyre,* and knowing the public reaction to her account of Rochester's amours, she decided to cut out the passage at this later stage. It should be noticed that the cancellation on MS. p. 129 occurs in a context where the word 'passion' is already a danger signal; and that, on MS. p. 180 (xviii. 6-7), where the words 'a warm, cherishing touch of the hand' have been altered, about one-third of the page seems to have been cut away—a method of excision frequently used by the author in, for example, the manuscript of *Villette,* and not necessarily to be attributed, therefore, to Nicholls.

The Cromwell passage is, I think, rather amusing: an odd quirk of Charlotte's imagination which adds one more piquant association to the already bizarre collection of associations surrounding the character of Hunsden. One regrets the loss of any detail which throws light on the way in which she imagined him. 'Oliver Cromwell and a French grisette' help to define her previous description: Hunsden has a tall figure, but his lineaments are 'small, and even feminine'; 'character had set a stamp upon each' of his 'plastic features'; 'expression re-cast them at her pleasure, and strange metamorphoses she wrought, giving him now that of a morose bull, and anon that of an arch and mischievous girl; more frequently, the two semblances were blent, and a queer, composite countenance they made' (iv. 61-63).[7] Again, the exotic comparison shows Hunsden's affinity with Zamorna; and in another sense 'Cromwell' links him with Angria, where romantic liaisons of the great Ruler with lesser mortals had been a major theme. In fact reaction against Angria and all it symbolized, rather than a desire for literary decorum, may have been the more or less conscious motive of Charlotte's cancellation.

One other cancellation is probably by Nicholls. It occurs on MS. p. 47 (v. 74) where three or four words are obliterated after 'I may work', and 'it will do no good' is inserted above the line. It is not written directly above the cancelled phrase; it begins towards the end of the cancellation and extends to the word 'but' in the following clause. The original words are by no means clear, but they may have been 'I may work *and toil and sweat*'. 'It will do no good' may replace the cancelled phrase: it may be an addition to it—no comma appears after 'work' in the manuscript, though some punctuation is obviously required. It is not unusual for the author to omit commas, and the placing of the new phrase is not very important by itself, but other considerations support the idea that she may have retained the old phrase, and that it was Nicholls who objected to it. '. . . and toil and sweat' might have offended Nicholls's sensibility, but Charlotte Brontë's was surely more robust: the phrase 'I may work, it will do no good' sounds jerky, yet other alterations show that the author was sensitive to rhythm, and made slight changes for the sake of euphony and balance, not in order to avoid it. The words are appropriate in an emphatic context, picking up the idea of 'toiling like a slave', and anticipating the Israelites 'crawling over the sun-baked fields of Egypt'. It seems unlikely that Charlotte would reject the phrase because 'sweat' is not strictly appropriate—in any case the idea of physical as well as mental fatigue is clearly present. If the author was responsible for the deletion, then one can only regret that in this instance her second thoughts entailed the loss of an apt and vigorous phrase.

It remains to consider the changes for which the author alone was responsible. Two main kinds are observable: those made primarily to affect the meaning, and those apparently dictated by a stylistic preference. The second group, as one might expect at a late stage of composition, is the larger.

Some of the meaning-changes are very minor ones. For example, 'letters' becomes the more accurate 'words' in 'my nature was not his nature, and its signs were to him like the words of an unknown tongue' (ii. 34). 'Lies' becomes 'rests' in the phrase, 'a stranger who rests half-reclined on a bed of rushes' (xvi. 266); 'luminous shadows' becomes 'luminous phantoms' (vii. 104). More interesting, and possibly more significant, is the substitution of 'visions' for 'romance' in the following passage: '. . . your aspirations spread eager wings towards a land of visions where, now in advancing daylight,—in X—daylight—you dare to dream of congeniality, repose, union' (MS. p. 46; v. 73). The contrast is one of 'Romance and Reality'; but perhaps 'a land of romance' would have been misleading—implying a world of the imagination which the dreamer would recognize to be 'unreal', not 'in this world'; whereas his 'visions' are potentially realizable. But the original shows clearly that the passage is in the main stream of Charlotte Brontë's thought in *The Professor*. All these, and many similar corrections, show the author's scrupulous concern for accuracy.

Other alterations are more fundamental. Very revealing, for instance, is an insertion in Chap. iii (p. 39) where the last sentence of the first paragraph originally ended, 'I looked weary, solitary, kept down like some desolate governess; he was satisfied' (MS. p. 28). The phrase 'tutor or' is inserted, apparently as an afterthought, above the line, before 'governess'. It looks as if Charlotte had not realized the unsuitability of her first phrase until a late stage of revision—showing at the same time how closely the professor's experiences were identified with her own, and, as many critics have said, how inadequately she realized his masculinity.

Another hardly disguised allusion to personal experience differs curiously from its first version. Charlotte originally wrote:

> Amidst this assemblage of all that was insignificant and defective, much that was vicious and repulsive (I except the two or three stiff, silent, decently behaved, ill-dressed British girls), the sensible, sagacious, affable directress shone like a steady star. . . .
>
> (MS. p. 123; xii. 206)

The alteration, 'by that last epithet many would have described' instead of 'I except', is inserted above the line. The reason for the clumsiness of expression is now clear: the writer wished to change her parenthesis without remodelling the entire sentence, and the result is an awkward compromise. The main sentence expresses, very emphatically, Charlotte's own point of view; the parenthesis suddenly twists round to the opinion of the 'many', undefined, yet presumably of the class of the 'insignificant and defective' or the 'vicious'. 'Repulsive', too, is inapt—not because it is too strong (compare the previous description of the 'daughters of Albion' and the phrase 'meeting hate with mute disdain' on p. 204 of the same chapter), but because it carries physical connotations, appropriate to the unwashed Amelia or 'swinish' Flamandes, and obviously, as the manuscript makes clear, originally intended for them and not for the 'clean and decent' English girls. Why then did Charlotte make the alteration? Partly, I think, because she wished Mlle Reuter's superiority to have its full value. The whole chapter is cleverly constructed: the charm of the 'sensible, sagacious, affable directress' is developed by contrast with her pupils and later by the romantic garden scene, only to be cruelly dispelled by her conversation with Pelet. The exception of the British girls blurs the black and white contrast which the author desired to produce, and makes the professor's infatuation less pardonable.

A third example occurs in the important opening paragraphs of Chap. vii. A new stage in William Crimsworth's life is beginning. His experiences at X—are over; and he, like Charlotte, will feel the joys and sorrows of exile in Belgium. This is the third paragraph of Chap. vii as it stands in the printed text:

> Third, Belgium; and I will pause before this landscape. As to the fourth, a curtain covers it, which I may hereafter withdraw, or may not, as suits my convenience and capacity. At any rate, for the present it must hang undisturbed. Belgium! name unromantic and unpoetic, yet name that whenever uttered has in my ear a sound, in my heart an echo, such as no other assemblage of syllables, however sweet or classic, can produce. Belgium! I repeat the word, now as I sit alone near midnight. It stirs my world of the past like a summons to resurrection; the graves unclose, the dead are raised; thoughts, feelings, memories that slept, are seen by me ascending from the clods—haloed most of them—but while I gaze on their vapoury forms, and strive to ascertain definitely their outline, the sound which wakened them dies, and they sink, each and all, like a light wreath of mist, absorbed in the mould, recalled to urns, re-sealed in monuments. Farewell luminous phantoms!

The manuscript reads as follows:

> . . . for the present it must hang undisturbed. Belgium! I repeat the name, now as I sit alone near midnight—it stirs my world of the Past like a summons to resurrection. Belgium! name unromantic and unpoetic . . .
>
> (MS. p. 64; vii. 103)

The sentence, 'Belgium! I repeat . . .' to 'resurrection.' is cancelled, but rewritten as in the printed text, after the words 'can produce'.

Various explanations are possible. The simplest would appear to be that we have an instance of haplography, caused by the repeated 'Belgium!', and that the passage was rewritten as the clearest means of rectifying the error. In this case the original full stop after 'resurrection' and possibly the slight difference in phrasing ('I repeat the *name*'), require some explanation. Or the sentence which now stands first may have been an afterthought—a rhetorical expansion which the author realized would be better placed for its cumulative effect before the climax, the grand crescendo-diminuendo of the final sentence. The third possibility is that the cancelled sentence existed in its first (manuscript) position in the original draft, and that the paragraph ended with the words 'can produce'. The manuscript punctuation supports this theory, and the 'I repeat' is still appropriate—the paragraph opens with the words 'Third, Belgium . . .'. We must then assume that the whole of the existing paragraph from 'the graves unclose' to the end is an afterthought, a flight of the imagination irresistibly aroused by the memories crowding into Charlotte Brontë's mind: partly, no doubt, carried away by her delight in the purple passage for its style's sake, but much more powerfully moved in spirit by the still vivid recollection of her life in Brussels. Her words have a poignancy more in keeping with the sad autumnal memories of Lucy Snowe than the tranquil 'sweet summer evening' of the professor.

One other instance may show her consciousness of the difficulties of first-person technique. In the sentence 'Her mission was upstairs; I have followed her sometimes and watched her' (MS. p. 320; xxv. 228), 'I have followed' replaces a cancelled, unfinished phrase, 'there she entere[d]'—as if Charlotte suddenly remembered that the 'I' of the story was not an omnipresent narrator.[8] The scene is conceived as a drama or mime (cf. 'in low soliloquy'), and the numerous parentheses are rather awkward: notice too the slight discrepancies in tense and time: 'I have followed her sometimes . . .'; 'the night I followed . . .'; 'that evening at least, and usually I believe . . .' (xxv. 228-9). This clumsiness is understandable if the interpolations were introduced at a late stage in composition.

It is noticeable that passages dealing with Hunsden often contain an especially large number of alterations, and though these may not be individually very significant, they show perhaps some of the difficulty Charlotte found in presenting this character.

For example, pages 326 to 333 of the manuscript (xxv. 237-47), which are concerned with Hunsden and the Lucia affair, contain seventeen alterations or insertions, some of appreciable length and importance; whereas a random selection of non-Hunsden passages yields results like the following:

> MS. pp. 47 to 54 (v. 75-vi. 85) (last interview with Edward): six alterations—one by Nicholls.

> MS. pp. 79 to 85 (vii. 128-38) (Pelet and his pupils; Madame Pelet): seven alterations.
> MS. pp. 144 to 149 (xiv. 240-50) (pupils and first lesson at Mlle Reuter's): four alterations—one important.
> MS. pp. 212 to 218 (xix. 58-68) (professor's first visit to Frances's room): four small alterations.

Even the carefully revised opening of Chap. vii yields only ten alterations in MS. pp. 64 to 70 (vii. 103-13), though these are admittedly fairly substantial.

The Hunsden alterations indicate, I think, that his character had not completely crystallized in the author's mind—that she was still shaping it as she revised her fair copy. Hunsden originally had a 'tall figure' and 'dark locks': the final version reads, 'a tall figure, long and dark locks . . .' (MS. p. 38; iv. 61), an addition not very appropriate to the rest of the sentence, where 'figure, voice, and general bearing' 'impressed me with the notion of something powerful and massive' in contrast to the 'small, and even feminine,' lineaments. But the Byronic (and Angrian) 'long locks' accentuate the essential romanticism of the character—a romanticism partly intentional, but possibly, as here, acting more powerfully on Charlotte's imagination than was consistent with the nature and dimensions of the character or book.

Two or three omissions affect the character of the professor. In Chap. xiv the author at first wrote, 'Once I laid my hand on her [Sylvie's] head and stroked her hair gently in token of approbation' (MS. p. 145; xiv. 242); '. . . and stroked her hair gently . . .' is cancelled. In Chap. xviii, '. . . a rare glance of interest, or a warm, cherishing touch of the hand; deep respect . . .' becomes '. . . a rare glance of interest, or a cordial and gentle word; real respect . . .' (MS. p. 180; xviii. 6). In both cases the final version deliberately avoids the warmth and physical intimacy of the original; in the first case understandably enough: contemporary readers found the professor's descriptions of his pupils unpleasant: and Charlotte herself must have realized that caresses between master and pupil were in somewhat dubious taste. In the second instance, she wishes to make physical attraction between William and Frances secondary; and there is considerable artistic value in the reserve and remoteness maintained right up to the climax of the uncontrollable 'tiger-leap' impulse in Chap. xxii. (Compare, '. . . her hand shrunk away . . .', xxii. 155.) That such exclusion is intentional seems conclusively proved by a third deletion, this time almost immediately before the 'tiger-leap'. The passage which now reads, '. . . no child, but a girl of nineteen; and she might be mine' was originally, '. . . a girl of nineteen, and I stole a look at Jane's face and shape; they pleased, they suited me, the well-formed head, the expressive lineaments, and she might be mine . . .' (MS. p. 277; xxiii. 162). The passage which follows makes it quite clear that Charlotte was not being coy or prudish in making this omission. She is merely underlining a theme important in this and in her better-known novels: the primacy of spiritual affinity. The professor's feeling is strong because it is an '*inward* glow', and remains so until its revelation can be expressed fully and without reserve. On the other hand, Charlotte has been careful not to exclude physical attraction entirely. In Chap. xiv, 'chiefly' replaces 'but' in '. . . the toil-worn, fagged, probably irritable tutor, blind almost to beauty, insensible to airs and graces, glories chiefly in certain mental qualities' (MS. p. 144; xiv. 240).

These changes in meaning do, I think, throw light on Charlotte's treatment of her own experience in this first novel, and possibly reveal some of her difficulties in dealing with certain characters or themes. It remains to consider changes in expression which seem to have been made primarily for the sake of style.

The stylistic alterations are varied in character, but a high proportion of them (about one-third) arise from the writer's desire to avoid repetition of a word or phrase. For example:

1. MS. p. 6 (i. 7): 'determined hostility' becomes 'persevering hostility'. Cf. 'determined race' (top of p. 7) and 'determined enmity' (previous sentence).
2. MS. p. 9 (i. 13): 'further intercourse' becomes 'further communication'. Cf. 'future intercourse' later in the same sentence.
3. MS. p. 9 (i. 13): 'will I think operate' becomes 'will I fancy operate'. Cf. 'I do not think' beginning the same sentence.
4. MS. p. 17 (ii. 26): 'that was passing' becomes 'that was going on'. Cf. 'we passed' and 'Workpeople were passing' on the same page.
5. MS. p. 19 (ii. 28): 'drew out' becomes 'took out'. Cf. 'drawer' in the same sentence.
6. MS. p. 23 (iii. 35): 'small fund' becomes 'slender fund'. Cf. 'small lodgings' earlier in the same sentence.
7. MS. p. 46 (v. 73) 'be found in' becomes 'be derived from [his society]'. Cf. 'find pleasure in', p. 72.

These may be taken as typical. Similar examples occur throughout *The Professor* at irregular intervals, but with no very noticeable concentration in any one part: that is, the book seems to have undergone a fairly systematic pruning at this level. In Charlotte Brontë's writing the iterative habit is unusually strong, and so natural to her style that it persists at a very late stage of composition. Often the repeated words are the key to a character or situation, for her attitudes are usually strongly defined. It is significant that she does not invariably alter the second of a pair of words. Each sentence has been carefully considered, and, as in Example 2, the first element may be changed. This seems to point to a later rather than a concurrent re-reading.

Sometimes she is unnecessarily eager to avoid recurrence. The repeated 'think' of Example 3 was natural and emphatic, more appropriate to spoken words than 'I fancy', though the whole speech is, of course, intentionally rather stilted. But one would not quarrel with most of the alterations: 'slender' and 'derived' are satisfactory, possibly preferable to the original. (The latter may indeed be purely stylistic preference: the connexion with 'find' is rather slight.) Sometimes the change is a definite improvement: the 'persevering hostility' of Example 1 is a total variation on the previous 'determined enmity'; in this, in its rhythmic quality and its formality, it is entirely in keeping with the peculiar mannered rhetoric of the whole passage.

The Preface to *The Professor* leads one to expect that stylistic changes will be away from the 'ornamented and redundant' and towards the 'plain and homely'. But one or two instances of an opposite tendency occur, and it is interesting to speculate on the motives for these.

For example, the opening chapter of the Brussels section, already in an 'ornamented' and poetic strain, has been even more refined in revision. 'My happiness possessed an edge whetted to the finest . . .' becomes 'My sense of enjoyment . . .'; '. . . he shall see a glorious sunrise . . .' becomes '. . . he shall behold . . .'; 'over a mountain horizon . . .' becomes 'over the eastern horizon . . .' and 'I mounted now a hill . . .', '. . . the hill . . .' (MS. p. 65; vii. 104-5). The very minuteness of the alterations is revealing. The author wishes to give her picture the greatest possible definition, her mood the greatest possible exultation.

Early critics remarked on the 'unchecked naturalness of expression'[9] in *The Professor*; or, if they were less favourably disposed, its 'rough, bold, coarse truthfulness of expression, . . . compressed style'.[10] The manuscript shows how often Charlotte intensified her already 'bold' style: adding a defining adverb or adjective, choosing a stronger noun or verb. 'Always' is inserted in 'Edward's letters had been such as to prevent the engendering or harbouring of delusions of this sort' (MS. p. 8; i. 11); 'Continual' in 'I will place my cup under this dropping' (MS. p. 21; ii. 32). 'Many' replaces 'some' in '. . . many called me miser at the time' (MS. p. 23; iii. 36). 'Pittance' replaces 'salary' in '. . . the master grudged every penny of that hard-earned pittance' (MS. p. 35; iv. 54). It is noticeable that most of these serve to bring out the harshness of Edward Crimsworth or the keen resentment of William against Edward.

This kind of intensification is closely linked with character, and occurs in clearly defined areas rather than in diffusion throughout the novel.

There is, however, a more general tendency to add descriptive details: X—becomes a 'mushroom' place (MS. p. 31; ii. 48); Vanderkelkov not only 'moon-faced' but 'thick-set' (MS. p. 74; vii. 120); Caroline's teeth are 'sparkling' (MS. p. 101; x. 166) (though her hair is no longer 'jetty'); and the fact that the professor 'crossed the Place royale' is a later addition (MS. p. 201; xix. 41). The impression given is one of vivid recollection of reality: Charlotte described things clearly because they were in every detail clear to her inward eye.

Examples of the opposite process—lowering of style, reduction of emphasis—are comparatively rare, and not very significant. In Chap. xxv, for example, 'the doom preparing for old Northern despotisms' becomes the tamer 'sentiments entertained by resolute minds respecting old Northern despotisms' (MS. p. 327; xxv. 239); and in Chap. xii an ornately developed metaphor is simplified: 'She laid her hand on the jewel within;' was originally, 'she laid her hand on the brooch of the cornelian [carnelian?] heart within; . . .' (MS. p. 125; xii. 208).

Minor stylistic changes abound. They are of various kinds, but on the whole show Charlotte's concern for the more closely defined as opposed to the general term. 'Observing' replaces 'seeing' (MS. p. 117; xii. 195), and 'perceived', 'saw' (MS. p. 39; iv. 60); 're-cast' for 'sported with' maintains a figure of speech in Chap. iv (MS. p. 40; iv. 63). Such changes are more noticeable towards the end of the novel.

Some alterations are made for the sake of euphony: 'innate', for example, was a rejected first term in 'redolent of native and ineradicable vulgarity . . .' (MS. p. 143; xiv. 239); 'heath' became 'moorland' in Chap. xxv; 'whose waters still run pure, whose swells of moorland preserve in some ferny glens, that lie between them, the very primal wildness of nature . . .' (MS. p. 325; xxv. 236); and 'still' became 'hushed' in 'The north was hushed, the south silent . . .' (MS. p. 204; xix. 45).

Such alterations give convincing evidence of a minute and thorough revision. It would seem that Mrs. Gaskell's famous description of Charlotte Brontë's method of writing requires qualification. She praised her 'singular felicity in the choice of words': 'One set of words was the truthful mirror of her thoughts; no others, however identical in meaning, would do. . . . She never wrote down a sentence until she clearly understood what she wanted to say, had deliberately chosen the words, and arranged them in their right order' (*Life,* Chap. xv). This may have been true of the 'pencilled scraps of paper' seen by Mrs. Gaskell: it certainly was not true of the fair copy of **The Professor.**

II. The First Edition

It is obviously important that the printed text should accurately represent the manuscript of a writer who took so much care over minute details. And on the whole Charlotte Brontë was well served by her publishers. They were careful and reliable, and she appreciated their giving her works 'every advantage which good paper, clear type, and a seemly outside can supply' (*S.H.B.,* [Shakespeare Head Brontë] ii. 149). She also thanked them for punctuating the proof-sheets of **Jane Eyre,** as she thought their 'mode of punctuation a great deal more correct and rational' than her own (*S.H.B.,* ii. 142).

One therefore expects Smith, Elder's edition of **The Professor** to be of a good standard: and comparison with the manuscript shows in fact a high degree of accuracy. There are, however, some half dozen errors that would no doubt have been corrected if the author herself had read the proofs:

1. 'cup' has been misread 'cups' in Chap. ii (MS. p. 14; ii. 22). An elaborate 'p' is responsible. The correct version is obviously preferable: 'a valley . . . held in its cup the great town of X—'

2. 'Semi-collong?' in Chap. x should be 'Simi-collong?' (MS. p. 102; x. 168).

3. Charlotte Brontë was not responsible for the incorrect use of 'perspicuity' in Chap. x. She wrote 'perspicacity' (MS. p. 105; x. 172).

4. 'Look at this little woman! . . .' should be '. . . this little real woman . . .' (MS. p. 107; x. 175).

5. 'worky-day' has been 'corrected' to 'work-day' (MS. p. 120; xii. 199).

6. It was '"inconvenant"' and not '"inconvenient"' for the professor to overlook his pupils (MS. p. 128; xii. 213).

7. The Crimsworths' maid is quite clearly 'Mimie' and not 'Minnie' (MS. p. 312; xxv. 215).

All these errors have been retained in subsequent editions, except for No. 6, corrected in the Dent edition of 1893, and its later reprints.

The printed version also gives little idea of the nature and extent of Charlotte Brontë's capitalization, which is extremely idiosyncratic. A certain amount has been retained, but this is often misleading, for it underlines some passages at the expense of others to which the author gave equal emphasis. It is also quite conventional, marking, for example, many of the personified abstracts, but reducing to normality words which for the author had a very special kind of life.

Notice, for instance, the inconsistent treatment of two similar passages—both dealing with Mlle Reuter, who often provokes this kind of analysis. In Chap. xx capitals are retained: '. . . I knew her former feeling was unchanged. Decorum now repressed, and Policy masked it, but Opportunity would be too strong for either of these—Temptation would shiver their restraints . . .' (MS. p. 231; xx. 90). Yet the personification here is less strongly realized than in Chap. xv, where the capitals are omitted. I give the manuscript version:

> . . . the fact is that as it was her nature to doubt the reality and undervalue the worth of Modesty, Affection, Disinterestedness, to regard these qualities as foibles of character; so it was equally her tendency to consider Pride, Hardness, Selfishness as proofs of strength. She would trample on the neck of Humility, she would kneel at the feet of Disdain; she would meet Tenderness with secret contempt, Indifference she would woo with ceaseless assiduities; Benevolence, Devotedness, Enthusiasm were her Antipathies; for Dissimulation and Self-Interest she had a preference—they were real wisdom in her 'eyes'—Moral and physical Degradation, mental and bodily Inferiority she regarded with indulgence . . . to Violence, Injustice, Tyranny she succumbed, they were her natural masters—. . . . (MS. p. 155; xv. 260)

In Chap. iv the original capitalization shows that words which now appear to be merely qualifying adjectives should have the force of nouns: '. . . they two should have been my household gods, from which my Darling, my Cherished-in-secret, Imagination, the tender and the mighty, should never, either by softness or strength, have severed me . . .' (MS. p. 33; iv. 52).

Capitalized words often occur in the 'visionary' passages: in Chap. v, 'you dare to dream of Congeniality, Repose, Union' (MS. p. 46; v. 73), and in Chap. vii, 'Thoughts, Feelings, Memories that slept, are seen by me ascending from the clods . . .' (MS. p. 65; vii. 103). The capitals mark these qualities as 'visions': Charlotte Brontë evidently feels and intends that we should feel them to have a palpable form. However uncongenial to modern taste, this is undeniably the mode of her imagination. Their absence, too, weakens the affinity with eighteenth-century prose and poetry which is an important element in her style. Again, capitals, by their purely mechanical function of arresting the eye, indicate a special emphasis, which would require, if the passage were spoken, a slow enunciation with marked pauses; and it is clearly most important to bring out the rhythmical qualities in, for example, an evocation of the past like that in Chap. vii, where the 'meaning' is primarily emotional.

There is plainly too much capitalization, and many instances—the characteristic marking of '"The Climax"' (MS. p. 45; v. 72) and '*The* Garden' (MS. p. 91; ix. 149), and of 'He' (Hunsden) (MS. p. 248; xxii. 118)—were considered by the printers too eccentric to be acceptable. I think, nevertheless, that a case can be made out for more than occurs in the First Edition. The original 'Master' especially can be justified, for its capitalization is a useful reminder of the centrality of the 'master' theme: at iii. 38, for example, it is Edward Crimsworth who is the 'Master' (MS. p. 24) whereas later it is, of course, William to whom Frances turns as the 'Master in all things' (MS. p. 318; xxv. 225).

We are fortunate that in **The Professor** (unlike *Villette,* where many phrases are literally cut out) so many of the author's first thoughts may be examined. The manuscript allows us to see something of the careful craftsmanship which, together with a more fortunate inspiration, helped to create **Jane Eyre, Shirley,** and **Villette.** Not least, it reveals the need for a text which shall more accurately represent the author's intentions.

Notes

1. Date given in the autograph manuscript of *The Professor,* p. 340.

2. See letter to Aylott and Jones, 6 April 1846. (Shakespeare Head Brontë [hereafter *S.H.B.*], *Lives, Friendships and Correspondence* (1932), ii. 87.)

3. Letter to George Smith, (*S.H.B.,* iii. 206-7).

4. Letter to Emily Shaen (*S.H.B.,* iv. 208).

5. A microfilm copy of the autograph manuscript has been consulted, and quotations from it are given by courtesy of the present owners of the manuscript, the Pierpont Morgan Library, New York.

6. The Pierpont Morgan Library kindly undertook to examine the passages by means of ultra-violet and infra-red photography, but the experiments were unsuccessful. The Curator writes: 'In addition to lining out the passages very heavily [? the Rev. Nicholls] also scraped through the lines (probably gutted them with a small pen knife). I fear that they are not recoverable.'

7. Quotations are taken from the First Edition of *The Professor,* 1857.

8. The episode derives from Mary Percy's visit to her children's nursery in *History of Angria,* Part 111 (29 April 1836: *S.H.B., Miscellaneous Writings,* ii. 148) where the narrator is an impersonal observer.

9. *The Critic,* 15 June 1857.

10. *Athenaeum,* 13 June 1857.

Rebecca Rodolff (essay date 1982)

SOURCE: "From the Ending of *The Professor* to the Conception of *Jane Eyre.*" In *Philological Quarterly,* Vol. 62, No. 1, Winter, 1982, pp. 71-89.

[*In the following essay, Rodolff discusses Brontë's move from the masculine narrator in* The Professor *to the feminine narrator in* Jane Eyre, *and focuses on the last two chapters of* The Professor *as the source of this transition.*]

Charlotte Brontë owed her facility in **Jane Eyre** to practice as well as to genius. Her Angria stories, written mostly in the 1830s, provided an extensive training in the art of fiction: the young author acquired technical skills and a serviceable store of subject matter by writing again and again about the same, and similar, Angrian characters, and by sometimes retelling the same stories with variations.[1] Moreover, in 1846 she completed a one-volume novel, **The Professor** (posthumously published in 1857). This "was a necessary stage" in the author's development, for it originated, as Kathleen Tillotson remarks, the use of "a bare framework of 'working one's way through life' with a 'rational mind.'"[2] Nevertheless, while the less disgressive structure and the grounding of the hero's story in Brussels put **The Professor** into a category different from that of the juvenilia, it yet remains an apprentice work in important respects.[3] For example, the Angria story of rival brothers that opens the novel is a curtain raiser rather than an integral part of the whole. And the male narrator, established during this episode as kin to a line of self-conscious, satirical Angrians,[4] continues throughout the novel to have two functions: like all her narrators, William Crimsworth is a partial projection of Charlotte Brontë's own feminine sensibility, and, like all her heroes, he asserts defiantly, even gratuitously, his masculinity.

Now *Jane Eyre,* begun only two months after the fair copy of *The Professor* was completed,[5] does not use the masculine point of view; and it shows a coherent structuring of plot and theme. Professor Tillotson suggests that these changes may owe a debt to Anne's *Agnes Grey,* with its female narrator telling a simple tale, and to Emily's passionate, intricately structured *Wuthering Heights.*[6] At the very least, their example would have exposed Charlotte's need for clarity in construction and in the use of point of view. But I want to show that her own first novel contributed similarly and still more importantly. The idea of the subject of *Jane Eyre* and of the feminine point of view—the idea, in short, of entering the soul of a retiring but inwardly passionate woman struggling for social independence and emotional fulfillment—was most likely grasped in the act of writing the end of *The Professor.* For the end of this novel can be shown to anticipate these as well as other ideas elaborated in *Jane Eyre.*

This is not to forget that there are many parallels between the whole of *The Professor* and the whole of *Jane Eyre,* just as there are many parallels between any two of Charlotte Brontë's novels (quite apart from all the parallels with the Angria works). Noticeable, for example, is a structure managed with varying authority but common to all four novels: a sort of prologue is succeeded by a love story having two main parts. *The Professor* has an English prologue followed by the story of Crimsworth's relations with Zoraïde Reuter, and the story of his relations with Frances Henri; Jane Eyre's childhood memories are followed by the story of her relations first with Rochester, then with St. John. *Shirley* (which exploits the mobility of the third-person narrator) begins with the three curates and goes on to set out the story of Caroline Helstone and then, in the second volume, to interweave the story of Shirley. In *Villette* an English prologue prepares the ground for the main story of Lucy Snowe's relations first with Dr. John and then with M. Paul.

This common over-all pattern points up, however, a way in which *The Professor* differs. For noticeable too is how abruptly *Jane Eyre, Shirley* and *Villette* come to a stop with proposals: in *Shirley,* with its two heroines, a proposal in the penultimate chapter and a second proposal in the final chapter are followed by a mere one-page epilogue, while in the autobiographies a proposal in the penultimate chapter is followed by a very short, three- or four-page "Conclusion" or "Finis." No new material which would call for explanation is introduced. By contrast, in *The Professor* two very long chapters, comprising about one-seventh of the novel, come after the proposal scene.[7] And new material is exactly what is introduced and developed here: in Chapter XXIV the professor's fiancée Frances encounters an appreciative Rochester-type, Yorke Hunsden; and in the final chapter the professor describes married life with Frances, her eventual success as the director of a school, and their retirement in England as Huns-

den's neighbors. The basic two-part story, confirmed by *Jane Eyre* and the other novels as the typical narrative structure of Charlotte Brontë's mature work, emerges twice in *The Professor.*

I shall be making two points. First, that Charlotte Brontë concludes the professor's story in the proposal scene, shifts the interest from the male narrator to the heroine, and then repeats the basic story of a principal character relating to two members of the opposite sex:[8] the Frances section constitutes a distinct story intermediate between those of Crimsworth and Jane Eyre. And second that, brief though it is, this feminine variation of the professor's story contains in embryo many of the elements developed at greater length in the novel that she began writing just a few weeks later: it specifically anticipates that use of plot, character, and theme which characterizes *Jane Eyre.*

In the opening chapters of *The Professor* William Crimsworth rises against and then escapes from an older, oppressing brother. Crimsworth then begins life anew in Brussels as an English teacher at a boys' school. Here he is so successful that Mlle Reuter engages him for the afternoons at her next-door girls' school. Now Jane Eyre also rises against a tyrannical relation; and she also later moves out of sexual isolation when she begins life anew under, not just Mrs. Fairfax (whom she at first supposes her employer), but Edward Rochester. Crimsworth and Jane are attracted, respectively, to the formidable, unconventional Mlle Reuter and Mr. Rochester. These latter are, in turn, intrigued by the discovery of the secret sensitivity and pride of the tutor and governess—so much so that Zoraïde Reuter spies on Crimsworth and Rochester spies on Jane. However, because in *The Professor* the author was anxious to establish the strength and masculinity of her male character, Crimsworth's inner nature, "the jewel within"[9] sought by Zoraïde's probing fingers, remains inviolable and consequently mysterious. The novel's treatment reveals no approval of a woman's spying on a man. More acceptable to Charlotte Brontë's imagination is, evidently, a man's spying on a woman. Indeed, Crimsworth closely observes Mlle Reuter and, later, Frances Henri. *Jane Eyre* further sanctions such scrutiny by adopting the point of view of the woman who accepts inspection.

The main points of resemblance between *The Professor* and *Jane Eyre* depend then on the narrators' common experience of oppression, while the differences depend on the reactions and defences available to each sex. Charlotte Brontë creates in the narrator Crimsworth—who re-enacts fictionally some of her personal experiences—a sensitivity and vulnerability to an oppressive society. Yet by virtue of the conventions of this very society and by virtue of a set of quite different, tougher character traits, he, as a man, easily overcomes his individual experiences of oppression (or threatened oppression). Even the unobstructed narrative line reflects the professor's greater ease in making his way, asserting his independence, and taking possession, in his own time, of the right mate. The man who succeeds with relative ease in his efforts to assert himself in his relations with a series of aggressive, morally inferior characters has still less difficulty in being regarded with respect and love by Frances. Crimsworth does not experience in his love life that active relationship, based on moral conflict, that will lend interest and urgency to Jane's relations with Rochester. In *Jane Eyre,* the plot and theme develop complexity because of Jane's evident moral superiority to her "Master." But in *The Professor* the narrator's struggle for ascendancy simply does not involve Frances.

Moreover, Frances is not only a passive foil to his success story; she is at this point relatively undeveloped. This in itself heightens the plausibility of her docility, as no possible reason for conflict is made available. The presentation of Frances at first (Chs. XIII-XVI) consists largely in her short answers to the professor's "abrupt" questions and in his efforts to interpret her character by observing her behavior. Her devoirs, it is true, serve as revelations to him (and so to us); yet we still learn little about Frances, for, though her essays indicate imaginative powers, they are otherwise impersonal. Finally, our introduction to the heroine is cut short in Chapter XVIII: not only does Crimsworth switch to summarizing their subsequent relations, but, just when Frances has "wakened to life" under her master's appreciation, Mlle Reuter dismisses her, and she retires from the story.

Like Crimsworth, then, we do not know much about Frances's inner life. Still, as a character of worth, she has become a perfect reward for the hero's perspicacity and prudence. Furthermore, union with her suggests the closure not only of his relations with Frances but also of his more active relations, for it indicates the confounding of Zoraïde, who would like to distract Crimsworth from his love, and the confounding of Hunsden, who supposes him destitute of love. Winning Frances satisfies the hero's emotional needs and completes the novel's story of his struggle in the world. It is for this reason, and because of the novel's theme and its very conservative, conventional presentation of masculine dominance, that it is unsatisfactory that any new development in the Crimsworth-Frances relationship takes place—least of all one which removes the interest from the young hero to the young, hitherto subordinate, heroine as a center of conflict and struggle.

Yet this is what happens. And this is the odder since, at the start of Chapter XXIII, Charlotte Brontë quickens the claims of Crimsworth upon our sympathy: she shows him, despite his handsome competency, in a state of "feverish" anxiety. And the author's involvement with the hero is signalled by her recourse to images (e.g., of eating inedibles, of wind and shipwreck) typically associated in the novels with her central characters in moments of strong emotion.[10] Indeed Crimsworth's situation has telling points of resemblance to the inspirational denouement of *Jane Eyre.* Like Jane before setting out to find Rochester, he spends the remaining hours walking about his room. Like Jane, he arrives possessed of independence, and is encouraged by the providential hearing of the loved one's voice. While Crimsworth stands at Frances's door, "a voice rewarded

the attention of [his] strained ear"; he overhears Frances pour out her heart to her empty room. Up to this point, a point suggestive of an imminent winding-up, the professor remains not only the novel's chief consciousness, but very much the central protagonist.

But from this point on, Frances becomes the more central and more interesting character. Now it is Frances who enacts the Brontëan habit of pacing "backwards and forwards, backwards and forwards." She is reciting a poem that, we believe with Crimsworth, expresses "the language of her own heart." And this poem, "Master and Pupil," probably written in 1843 in Brussels, also expresses the novelist's heart.[11] Charlotte Brontë's interest strays from the satisfied male narrator to the projection of herself in the still yearning, and feminine, "Pupil." She contrives to give Frances's point of view. When Crimsworth asks himself the question "what had she to do with love?" (asked in later novels by the heroines of themselves, e.g., *Jane Eyre,* Ch. XVI, and *Shirley,* Ch. X), the answer, supposed to emanate from Frances, requires some circumlocution and, in the last couple of sentences, some help from the feminine author:

> "Nothing," was the answer of her own sad, though gentle countenance; it seemed to say, "I must cultivate fortitude and cling to poetry; one is to be my support and the other my solace through life. Human affections do not bloom, nor do human passions glow for me." Other women have such thoughts. Frances, had she been as desolate as she deemed, would not have been worse off than thousands of her sex.

Moreover, it is Frances's heart, not Crimsworth's, that speaks, this time directly, in the poem. The poem has as its narrator a girl called "Jane" who must part from her beloved Master. Saying farewell to him in his room, she is passionately "snatched" by him. He murmurs "'Why will they part us, Jane?'" and at the poem's end declaims:

> "They call again; leave then my breast;
>   Quit thy true shelter, Jane;
> But when deceived, repulsed, opprest,
>   Come home to me again!"

Charlotte Brontë had, evidently, a special fondness for the name Jane. It was her favorite sister Emily's second name—and when given to Angrian characters it was associated with Emily.[12] It was a name that was likely to define a character, carrying with it well-established associations (associations seen in the teasing, yet authoritative disposition of the Angrian Jane Moore). Here, whether the name "Jane" induced associations with a jealously-loved sister or whether the poem simply induced a more personal identification with the heroine, Frances is metamorphosed.

In effect, a new novel, or rather an idea for a novel, originates. Even the need for a female narrator is intimated by the inclusion of the poem. Though Crimsworth necessarily continues as the observer, Charlotte Brontë takes as her subject a woman's "wakening to life." Now it is Frances more than Crimsworth who evinces the qualities and actions common to the author's personas. Like the Jane of the next novel, Frances indirectly invites a proposal from her Master. Crimsworth identifies Jane and the Master: "'Jane' was now at my side: no child, but a girl of nineteen; and she might be mine . . . the frost of the Master's manner might melt." He looks up to see that, "slight, straight, and elegant, she stood erect on the hearth." (Cf. Jane, who "stood erect before" Rochester when he proposed, Ch. XXIII, and "rose up and stood before" St. John during his proposal, Ch. XXXIV.) The next moment Crimsworth fulfills the dream of Frances's poem by "snatching" her: he holds her on his knee, "placed there with sharpness and decision, and retained with exceeding tenacity." Three times the agitated professor asks, "'Frances, how much regard have you for me?,'" at first holding her hand "in a somewhat ruthless grasp." (Cf. the proposal scene in the penultimate chapter of *Jane Eyre* where the heroine, also on her lover's knee, reports: "he retained me by a firmer grasp than ever.")

Frances's responses articulate her change. When Crimsworth asks her, more plainly, to marry him, she first blushes, then stalls in answering, rephrasing his proposal, giving it definition: "'Monsieur désire savoir si je consens—si—enfin, si je veux me marier avec lui?'" Then from hesitant cross-questioning she switches to confident teasing: Crimsworth remarks that a different Frances goes on "with a new, yet still subdued inflection of the voice—an inflection which provoked while it pleased me. . . . 'C'est à dire, Monsieur sera toujours un peu entêté, exigeant, volontaire—.'" Finally, pressed to give an answer (and to give it in English, which naturally curbs her new expressiveness), she ruminates, "'I like to be near you; I believe you are very good, and very superior. . . .'" Then "she made a sort of movement, as if she would have clung to me, but restraining herself she only added with earnest emphasis—'Master, I consent to pass my life with you.'" Her "restrained" answer receives wonderfully restrained acceptance: "'Very well, Frances.'" Charlotte Brontë uncovers a playful heroine who quizzes her master, but, perhaps because she is still at pains to maintain the narrator's masterfulness, the characters remain, very self-consciously, the master and pupil together.

Crimsworth, who as narrator must dwell upon his own manliness, lacks the natural spirited personality of Rochester. Nevertheless, Crimsworth is not a dull novel-character. It is because of the male narrator that *The Professor* lacks emotional force, but it is also why the novel is more comic than her mature work. Humor and irony pervade the narrator's description of his own forcefulness. He presents his youthful self, after Frances has accepted him, as blissfully content—and blissfully unaware of his betrothed's less complete contentment.

> Frances' thoughts, during this interval, I know not, nor did I attempt to guess them; I was not occupied in searching her countenance, nor in otherwise troubling her composure. The peace I felt, I wished her to feel; my arm, it is true, still detained her; but with a restraint that was gentle enough, so long as no opposition tightened it. My gaze was on the red fire; my heart was measuring its own content; it sounded and sounded, and found the depth fathomless.
>
> "Monsieur," at last said my quiet companion, as stirless in her happiness as a mouse in its terror. Even now in speaking she scarcely lifted her head.
>
> "Well, Frances?"

The knowing narrator deprives his young self of much of the reader's sympathy by describing his lack of interest in his beloved's thoughts; his complacent possessiveness and sense of being master ("my arm, it is true, still detained her"); his willingness to compare Frances in her happiness to "a mouse in its terror"; and his cool response (he goes on to tell us in a typical understatement, "it is not my way to overpower with amorous epithets"!). The passage serves both to draw humor out of Crimsworth's misconceptions and to prepare for a dramatic effect, for it increases our surprise when Frances, after having quietly, repeatedly addressed "Monsieur," finally works herself into expressing thoughts that do not at all suggest a being so contented as the innocent professor would have.

Frances announces a determination to be "'no incumbrance.'" Crimsworth, who does not understand that self-respect dictates her desire "'to get on'" (as she calls it), thinks to remove this desire by breaking the news of his own very lucrative teaching position. To us he admits, with almost disarming candor, the "flattering" satisfaction he experiences "in the idea of becoming the providence of what he loves—feeding and clothing it, as God does the lilies of the field." Crimsworth appears to be playing God rather more complacently and unattractively than Rochester, who, seen through Jane's eyes, gloats in a spirit of fun.[13] But Charlotte Brontë manages, even without the feminine point of view, to suggest that the man's anticipation of dominance is a delusion. When "Frances seemed to consider" his proposal that she stop working, he tells her, "to decide her resolution," that she "'require[s] complete rest.'" Crimsworth's concern, however, is undercut ironically by the commentary. He confesses: "I am not sure whether Frances had accorded due attention to my harangue . . ."; she does not answer "with her usual respectful promptitude." And indeed Frances's respect does not extend to recognizing her master as a "God" with a right to feed and clothe her and to be mindlessly obeyed. What is more, it transpires that she has not even been considering giving up work: she has been brooding on the discrepancy between his earning power and hers!

Frances gives in not to his argument but to the fact that the inequality "'must be so for the present.'" Crimsworth's superiority, established throughout the novel in his encounters with other characters and at last socially recognized by professional success, is humorously undermined. We discover that Frances is ambitious, in common with such other retiring Charlotte Brontë-types as Crimsworth himself and the Jane of her poem: "The strong pulse of Ambition struck / In every vein I owned." Now it is the heroine's superiority that we look forward to seeing asserted. Charlotte Brontë commits herself to continuing the novel. First, because Frances, as a character with ambitions, demands a professional future. Second, because Crimsworth's misunderstanding of Frances suggests a conflict in their personal relations which did not formerly exist.

The positions of Frances and Crimsworth, and their relationship, approach those of Jane and Rochester. However, in *Jane Eyre* the use of a female narrator allows sympathy with the spying, possessive male as well as with the heroine, because the heroine, whose point of view we share, views him with love and tolerance. Rochester's attitude to Jane is exonerated since, as viewed by Jane, his love is convincingly passionate (and since it is complicated by the existence of a mad wife). In *The Professor* the misunderstood heroine's point of view is usually indirectly conveyed, and by a use of irony that distances us from the imperceptive narrator. Nor can Crimsworth's sexual relationship to Frances temper this effect, for his sexuality has to this point been inadequately realized. Neither romantic nor sexual passion is a part of Crimsworth's background: there are no Célines or Claras, and we may wonder, when he calls Frances "a novice in the art of kissing," how it can be that he is not one himself.[14]

According to the text, only now do the physical charms making Frances a traditionally worthy object of affection become apparent to him. When Crimsworth looks at his "little lace-mender" after her successful suit to continue teaching, he feels "that she was singularly changed for me"; and he discovers, as he says, "that I too was a sensualist, in my temperate and fastidious way." Now that Frances has asserted her independence, has shown a disposition to coax and tease, and has become physically more attractive to him, she is altogether more formidable. The professor has to reckon with her personality, her passions, and her ambitions, as the sequel will illustrate. The tension that Charlotte Brontë has thus injected produces an immediate and extraordinary effect. "A horror of great darkness fell upon me," Crimsworth confesses; and he wonders why, *"now,* when my course was widening, my purpose brightening; when my affections had found a rest . . . why did hypochondria accost me now?" The answer evidently lies in his discoveries of a new Frances and of himself as "a sensualist."[15] However, this ordeal of hypochondria is a reaction better suited to such other authorial types as Jane, Caroline, and Lucy, whose sexuality is more credibly troubled, because of the social background, by inhibitions or by the possibility of losing personal independence in giving of the self. Crimsworth has claimed, even if unconvincingly, the prerogative of a man of the time, boldly outstaring women and controlling them. Again the difficulty is that Crimsworth is the novel's romantic hero as well as the first-person vehicle for the author's literary stock of feminine anxieties.

Though in the proposal chapter the narrative draws to a happy ending (an ending normal moreover to Charlotte

Brontë's other novels), a new narrative goal, based on Frances, has emerged. The new evidence of her inner life occasions the need in the story for a man sexually interested in her and for a man in conflict with her. Initially, Crimsworth takes this part, but he takes it uneasily, as we have seen. Then in the penultimate chapter the return of Crimsworth's eccentric opposite Yorke Hunsden provides a more workable foil to the heroine. In the last two chapters Frances proves herself by relating to Hunsden as well as to Crimsworth (just as Crimsworth has related to Zoraïde as well as to Frances, and as Jane will relate to St. John as well as to Rochester).

The extent of Charlotte Brontë's absorption in the possibilities of Frances's position is thus reflected not just in her continuing a novel by introducing new character traits and new narrative goals but also by her giving to this brief exposition the two-part structure characterizing all her novels. The introduction of a second admiring man confirms Frances's attractiveness, draws out further aspects of her personality, and complicates her relations with the first man. However, in *Jane Eyre,* for example, St. John and Rochester are clearly different types, just as, in *The Professor,* Zoraïde and Frances are different. But the author is not free, in her first novel, to present men from an outsider's viewpoint; it seems that when the inner self she projects is putatively that of a man, she is limited by the conception of "man" that this entails. So Hunsden is a figure exaggerating the narrator's own nature: Crimsworth's and Hunsden's boyish persiflage and gratuitous displays of manliness vie with their express femininity. True, Hunsden is established as more of an individual and a man of the world than Crimsworth; and we are more conscious of the obtruded trappings of manliness, e.g., his cigar and "impertinent" (Ch. III), unconventional speech. Still, the substitution of Hunsden for Crimsworth as a foil to Frances's ensuing development is sanctioned by the mysterious kinship of the men's personalities.

In the prologue this kinship manifests itself in their success at reading each other's thoughts and feelings. Now in Chapter XXIV, when Hunsden, back in Brussels, walks by and "grimaces," Crimsworth can interpret the communication as, on the one hand, "'So you have found your counterpart at last; there she sits, the female of your kind!'" and, on the other, a promise to call on him soon. The professor's inference is not mistaken. But Hunsden seems potentially isolated from Crimsworth by his (rather belabored) inability to assess Crimsworth's "counterpart." First, he supposes her to be Mlle Reuter. Then, when Crimsworth reveals her "caste," he jumps to the conclusion that the girl must be unrefined. Finally, when they ascend the stairs to Frances's lodging, Hunsden's move to continue on up shows plainly enough, as the professor notes with amusement, that "his mind was bent on the attics." We enjoy each blunder. Knowing something of Frances's worth, we anticipate with pleasure a repetition, in the triumph of her quiet dignity over Hunsden's rash surmises, of her relations with Crimsworth.

Crimsworth withdraws from the action to observe Frances captivate, in lively discourse, her sardonic visitor. And Frances matched with the worldly, difficult Hunsden elicits from the author not only a more vigorous heroine but a relationship that looks forward to the sparring of Jane and Rochester. In particular, Hunsden's discovery of Frances's qualities in social conversation parallels Rochester's discovery of Jane—and more closely than it parallels Crimsworth's discovery of Frances in the classroom. This is partly because Crimsworth described *his* attraction to Frances—but also because he was attracted to a less complex Frances; one who never argued with him as she does with her new acquaintance, and one who spoke very little before the proposal scene. The awakening, described generally in Chapter XVIII and illustrated in the proposal scene, is now repeated with Hunsden in the professor's role. "Animated by degrees, she began to change, just as a grave night-sky changes at the approach of sunrise. . . ." And though Frances and Hunsden are not lovers, Hunsden's reaction to her "fire" puts Crimsworth in mind of "a snake waking from torpor, as he erected his tall form, reared his head, before a little declined, and putting back his hair from his broad Saxon forehead, showed unshaded the gleam of almost savage satire." (When, early in their acquaintance, Jane roused Rochester by her "brusque" denial of his good looks, he too "lifted up the sable waves of hair which lay horizontally over his brow" [Ch. XIV].) Hunsden, unlike his friend, is protected from loving Frances by this tendency to wax satirical; still, sexual interest is yet suggested here, and "caste" is explicitly forgotten: "he was himself as Frances was herself." He is like Rochester, who is himself with Jane, claiming only the superiority of age and experience—though indeed Jane disallows even those claims. Rochester admires her bold replies, as he admires her disbelief that anyone "free-born would submit to [insolence], even for a salary"—though he disallows her "accuracy" (Ch. XIV). But then Jane and Rochester often disagree; argument lends a certain piquancy to their relations that is much appreciated by both. In *The Professor* this sparring relationship founded on mutual respect is sketched in the conversation of Frances and Hunsden. If he is "savagely satirical," he is also intrigued and admiring. He admires her for the "uncompromising" way she enunciates the word "hell," and is as stimulated and refreshed by her unconventionality as Rochester is by Jane's. "He liked something strong, whether in man or woman; he liked whatever dared to clear conventional limits." Though the heroine is not the narrator, she has become the central character, and, as in the next novel, the man's discovery of the heroine is observed, not communicated from his own point of view.

However, though the possibilities are outlined, this revelation of unconventionality and of strong independence of mind is not turned to any interesting structural use. Since Frances and Hunsden are not lovers, no conflict of passion and reason occurs, as it does in *Jane Eyre*, which affects the personal lives of the disputants. We see in Hunsden "a wish that some one did love him as he would like to be loved—some one whose love he could unreservedly re-

turn," but this becomes no more than a part of the characterization of the "inscrutable Hunsden." Similarly, their argument about the relative importance of logic and feeling is merely aired.[16] Nevertheless, here too the fact that Frances debates with great "feeling" but without, as Hunsden attests, any "logic," solidifies her Jane Eyrish qualities. We can hear Jane's voice in Frances's insistence that, even when logic tells against her she would, if her "'opinion really differed from [Hunsden's] . . . adhere to it when I had not another word to say in its defence; you should be baffled by dumb determination.'" Hunsden recognizes the accuracy of her self-analysis just as Rochester will recognize, but with a lover's trepidation, Jane's stubborn capacity to adhere to what she has determined upon as right and owing to herself. In *Jane Eyre,* in other words, the author purposely works towards and integrates the conflict of the two characters. In *The Professor* the exchange is an indication of the character-types and situations now claiming the author's interest.

In sum, then, Charlotte Brontë coalesces the Crimsworth-Hunsden and Crimsworth-Frances relationships in the penultimate chapter: the two parts Crimsworth has assumed elsewhere in the novel are taken on the one hand by Frances and on the other by Hunsden. These latter relate to each other instead of to the narrator. Yet, at the same time, Hunsden's position as Crimsworth's *alter-ego*[17] is prominently featured and Hunsden even becomes an appropriate lover for Frances. A sort of inter-changeability of the two men is realized in the penultimate chapter by means of their relationship with Frances.

Thus, when Hunsden's abuse of Switzerland provokes Frances to warn him off marrying a Swiss—for "'your mountain maid will some night smother her Breton-bretonnat, even as your own Shakespeare's Othello smothered Desdemona'"—Hunsden parries her thrust by proposing Crimsworth's "'being in my nightcap.'" This doubling of the men in the role, though not very remarkable taken on its own, carries weight by virtue of the yet more curious passage to follow. Out in the street Hunsden collars his friend and they "grapple" together after the manner of other literary doubles, if somewhat more discreetly.

> It was dark; the street lonely and lampless. We had then a tug for it; and after we had both rolled on the pavement, and with difficulty picked ourselves up, we agreed to walk on more soberly.[18]

Charlotte Brontë has re-introduced the Angrian theme of male rivalry, but she uses it as a means for exposing Hunsden's thoughts about women and, in particular, about Frances. According to him, Frances is "'too good for [Crimsworth], but not good enough for me,'" and he is jealous of Crimsworth's happiness ("'what business have you to be suited so well with a partner?'"). He cannot imagine finding his heart's repose in Crimsworth's "'Alpine peri,'" but dreams instead of a "'queen'" with "'a nobler and better developed shape than that perverse, ill-shriven child can boast.'" Hunsden's ideal, in fact, is the type that attracted the young Rochester, and in *Jane Eyre* the author will imagine Rochester having married such a woman and found disillusion. Bertha was formerly "'a fine woman, in the style of Blanche Ingram; tall, dark, and majestic'" (Ch. XXVII). But the Rochester we know scorns both his wife and that "'extensive armful'" (Ch. XXIII), the "queenly" Miss Ingram (Ch. XVII), delighting rather in his peri down from the mountains of the moon. However, such a change of opinion is merely hinted at in *The Professor*; Charlotte Brontë projects a possible romantic relationship by recording Hunsden's superfluous protestations of indifference to Frances and by merging the roles of Hunsden and Crimsworth.

A close reading of the novel's last chapter reveals that Frances continues to be more central and more intensely realized than the narrator. Even the interesting state of hypochondria is transferred to the heroine. At least, though it is not so denominated, hypochondria appears to be Frances' state. On her wedding day she is found crying by a bewildered bridegroom. Crimsworth registers his incomprehension while yet reporting her distress: "Singular to state, she was, or had been crying." When he asks if she is ready, she replies "'Yes, Monsier,' with something very like a checked sob"; and he tells us that he expressed himself "sorry to see her in such low spirits, and requested to be allowed an insight into the origin thereof." While we are told that he was sympathetic, his language, by its uncolloquial formality, and by its suggestion of uncertainty and incomprehension ("she was, or had been"; "something very like"), imposes upon us (intrigued, after all, by Frances's condition) a sense of a superior sympathy with Frances's condition. Charlotte Brontë wants to explore the woman's point of view—to review her anxieties, and in doing so she perceptibly distances herself and the reader from the male narrator. Thus, this scene is very different from its successor in *Jane Eyre,* where the heroine divulges her nightmare to a man whose sympathy she can record without detracting from her own centrality. Moreover, in *Jane Eyre* the presence of Bertha justifies the heroine's fears about marriage, whereas in *The Professor* Charlotte Brontë has not "planned ahead" for Frances's distress.

The next detailed view of Frances also shows her dissatisfied, though now her dissatisfaction has a definite, ascertainable origin. It is a year and a half later when she declares:

> "I am not satisfied . . . you are now earning eight thousand francs a year" (it was true; my efforts, punctuality, the fame of my pupils' progress, the publicity of my station, had so far helped me on), "while I am still at my miserable twelve hundred francs. I *can* do better, and I *will*."
>
> "You work as long and as diligently as I do, Frances."

Crimsworth's parenthetical agreement, suggesting as it does his acceptance of his natural right to getting on, stimulates sympathy with Frances's ambitions. Her wish is to set up a school and then, when they have "realize[d] an independency," to retire to England. Thus, we expect to see two new, specific objectives achieved before the novel's ending.

The continuing unfolding of Frances's personality is integrated with the rise of a woman against a socially-determined oppression. Crimsworth is an important, if unconscious, part of this oppression. In his eyes Frances remains, if not as frightened as a mouse, at least "as docile as a well-trained child"; and the fact that Frances prefers to call her husband "Monsieur" seems almost to justify his opinion. However, though the author continues to confirm her heroine's docility, she discloses a side of Frances that is dignified and, at still other times, elfish. Ten years later, Frances is in one sense "become another woman, though in another she remained unchanged." Crimsworth even writes that he "seemed to possess two wives." For Frances daily transformed herself into "Madame the directress, a stately and elegant woman"; then, at home, "the lady directress vanished from before my eyes, and Frances Henri, my own little lace-mender, was magically restored to my arms." It is in these moments that, occasionally, Frances would show "some stores of raillery, of 'malice,' and would vex, tease, pique" Crimsworth about his "'bizarreries anglaises.'" However, as in the proposal chapter, we do not see the lover respond to her "elfish freak" as Rochester responds to Jane's. That sort of repartee and lively disagreement occurs not in the talk of the lovers, but in the talk of Frances and Hunsden.

This vignette is particularly interesting because Charlotte Brontë so soon followed it with the extended treatment in *Jane Eyre* of Rochester's and even St. John's discovery of two women in Jane. (She cultivates a "very flinty" side with Rochester at the end of Ch. XXIV; and she changes from "absolute submission" to "determined revolt" in dealing with her cousin in Ch. XXXIV.) Interesting too for its anticipation of *Jane Eyre* is Crimsworth's description of the quality of their marriage. Theirs, he says, is an ideal union where Frances "reposed in him a confidence so unlimited that topics of conversation could no more be wanting with him than subjects for communion with her own heart." It will be noticed that, by having Crimsworth speak of himself in the third person, Charlotte Brontë contrives to advance the woman's point of view of the marriage. And it is very like the ideal marriage depicted at the close of *Jane Eyre*:

> To be together is for us to be at once as free as in solitude, as gay as in company. We talk, I believe, all day long: to talk to each other is but a more animated and an audible thinking. All my confidence is bestowed on him, all his confidence is devoted to me; we are precisely suited in character—perfect concord is the result.

These pages have centered on Frances's professional success and on new insights into her personality. There is then introduced a new subject: the idea of two types of unsuitable mate for a woman. Frances believes that a woman must "'revolt'" against a marriage that is "'slavery . . . for freedom is indispensable.'" But her opinion simply indicates something additional about her character; it is not an opinion that grows out of the novel. Frances is never tried. Crimsworth, though not exactly spontaneously caring, is not really "'a harsh, envious, careless man'" while Hunsden, though claimed as having formerly been a variety of "'a profligate, a prodigal, a drunkard, or a tyrant,'" is debarred by the plot from a role as Frances's lover. But, if one softens the epithets, this is the problem that confronts the next heroine. St. John approaches the first type, Rochester the second; and Jane, when she discovers the consequences to herself of their attitudes, avoids first the slavery of being Rochester's mistress, then the slavery of being St. John's "'useful tool'" (Ch. XXXV).

The next scene shows the Crimsworths living in England with Hunsden as neighbor. Yorke Hunsden, "still unmarried," "wanders from land to land." Like the young Rochester, he does not spend much time at his old family mansion. Like Rochester, as well as Mr. Yorke in *Shirley,* the cigar-smoking Hunsden "is a polite man in his own house"; and like the later men he has a romantic past: a passionately loved mistress. Charlotte Brontë continues interested enough to develop Hunsden's potential as a romantic figure in conjunction with Frances, and has him confess his past to the novel's heroine. "One glorious night in June," after Crimsworth "had been taunting him about his ideal bride," Hunsden stops in the moonlit glade to exhibit a miniature of the black-haired "Lucia." It is Frances's bold intuition that Hunsden "'never seriously thought of marrying her'" because Lucia flouted convention. In this way the unsuitability of Hunsden's ideal is attested to at the same time that his blindness to the novel's (only) ideal woman is underlined. Both the reason for his discontentment and the nature of its possible remedy are suggested, but only the next novel will exploit these circumstances.

The professor's narrative shifts to the present tense. Frances is preparing tea. But before closing his memoirs Crimsworth has "a word to say of Victor." This supplementary character sketch of their child Victor is so curious that, far from terminating interest in the novel world, it creates bewilderment about it. The boy who when he smiles "looks so like his mother" has a close friendship with Hunsden which recalls the relationship of the three adults.

> Victor has a preference for Hunsden, full as strong as I deem desirable, being considerably more potent, decided, and indiscriminating, than any I ever entertained for that personage myself. Frances, too, regards it with a sort of unexpressed anxiety.

Moreover, Victor has received a large faithful dog named Yorke, "after the donor"; but Yorke, bitten by a rabid dog, is shot by Crimsworth. Victor is heartbroken, believing his father could have tried curing him: "'you should have burnt the wound with a hot iron, or covered it with caustic.'" This event perpetuates the conflict between Crimsworth and Hunsden, especially since Victor, who is very close spiritually to his mother, attracts Hunsden's interest. At the novel's end, instead of "grappling" in the street with his difficult double, Crimsworth, as it were, shoots him.

Now this little episode underlines what is unsatisfactory about the last two chapters. The conflict injected into the

Frances section is cut short, but not resolved. In effect, Charlotte Brontë, stimulated perhaps by her involvement with Frances, appends a number of personal interests. She relates several real-life anecdotes which have impressed her: there is Emily's cauterizing a dog-bite, and perhaps the story of an unfortunate love-affair of Mary Taylor's father. She describes moments of intense feeling experienced by herself: e.g., hypochondria, and her love of M. Heger. She realizes her daydreams: of winning over a worldly, interesting man, of running a school with great success. And she expresses her ideas: on the need for equality in marriage, on the condition of old maids, on her love for England, on the importance of feeling. It is as if Charlotte Brontë came to the end of her story—when she found she had "so many other things to say." By contrast, during the body of the novel—after the Angrian beginning through Chapter XXIII—she sticks to her story of a variation on the Brussels experience. The treatment and the construction have their defects, but there is no material introduced that is unrelated to William Crimsworth and his experiences at the two schools. This is not true of the last chapters.

The last two chapters are unnecessary to the story of the professor, and even disrupt what unity the novel possesses. Charlotte Brontë appears to have a new interest, released by the need to express Frances's reaction to the proposal, and prompting her to indulge in sketching the development of the shyly rebellious lace-mender into an independent, lively woman. It is easy to see why, after recording the fairly straightforward progress of Crimsworth, Charlotte Brontë was absorbed by her heroine's situation. Given the author's theme, Frances's resistance to social oppression will be more difficult, more pertinent, and more moving, simply because she is a woman. And in undertaking the portrayal of a woman's rather than a man's desire for independence and equality, a more interesting story of relations between the sexes is immediately promised. The ensuing struggle will, at least in a Victorian novel, naturally enter a woman's love life. Moreover, by having a man try to act as the providence of a woman who wishes to gain independence, Charlotte Brontë provides herself with a romantic plot of great potential charm. The dilemma manifests itself in a conflict, momentary in *The Professor* and protracted in *Jane Eyre,* which ends in the woman's gaining full equality and respect, and in the man's expressed satisfaction at this outcome.

However, here at the end of the first novel the material serving to unfold Frances's character is very desultorily presented. Furthermore, in seeking to confirm her heroine's attractiveness and intelligence, the author is induced to associate Frances with the more sexually experienced Yorke Hunsden. The space devoted to describing their relationship suggests that the narrator no longer afforded an adequate testimony to Frances's qualities. Hunsden is not essentially changed, but the emphasis is now shifted from his alliance with Crimsworth to his similar appreciation of Frances and his need for a woman. In his character and in his situation, the Hunsden of the last chapters comes increasingly to resemble Rochester.

Thus a variety of tentative subjects is introduced, all of which were of compulsive interest to the author—as we know from the fact that she re-introduced them in later novels, as well as from biographical evidence. However, inevitably, Charlotte Brontë does not at the end of **The Professor** do justice to these subjects. In the later novels they are treated at greater length and are made organically part of the whole. Still, the inadequacy of the treatment should not detract from the significance of the attempt. She was sufficiently stimulated by the new subject to prolong her narrative beyond the proposal scene. Indeed, the necessarily inadequate, sketchy treatment of this new subject may even have sustained the novelist's interest, stimulating her to realize more satisfactorily the characters and events here adumbrated. The presentation in the last chapters of **The Professor** of a new story centered on the heroine forms a bridge between the body of the first novel and the next novel **Jane Eyre.** The importance of the end of **The Professor** lies in its evident influence as a corrective and as a stimulus helping to lead Charlotte Brontë to conceive her first masterpiece.

Notes

1. For information on the juvenilia see Fannie Elizabeth Ratchford, *The Brontës' Web of Childhood* (Columbia U. Press, 1941). For examples of Charlotte's work see especially the compilations *Legends of Angria,* ed. Ratchford with the collaboration of William Clyde DeVance (Yale U. Press, 1933); *The Miscellaneous and Unpublished Writings of Charlotte and Patrick Branwell Brontë in Two Volumes,* ed. T. J. Wise and J. A. Symington. (Oxford: Shakespeare Head, 1936 and 1938); and *Five Novelettes: Passing Events, Julia, Mina Laury, Captain Henry Hastings, Caroline Vernon,* transcribed and ed. Winifred Gérin (London: Folio, 1971).

2. *Novels of the Eighteen-Forties,* rev. ed. (London: Oxford U. Press, 1961), p. 285.

3. This point has been made by many critics. Earl A. Knies writes that "*The Professor,* coming seven years after the 'Farewell to Angria,' might be considered part of Charlotte's mature work, but it is really a transitional piece." *The Art of Charlotte Brontë* (Ohio U. Press, 1969), p. 88. The nature of its immaturity is well described by Tillotson, pp. 282-85 and 288; W. A. Craik, *The Brontë Novels* (London: Methuen, 1968), p. 48; and Margaret Howard Blom, *Charlotte Brontë* (Boston, Mass.: Twayne, 1977), pp. 79-82.

4. That *The Professor* resembles the Angria tales in using a male narrator is observed by both Ratchford, *Brontës' Web,* p. 171, and Tillotson, p. 293, n. 5. And both note too the lingering hold of Angria to be found in the early, English chapters of *The Professor.* See Ratchford, pp. 190-98, and Tillotson, p. 282.

5. *The Professor* was finished in April 1846 and the fair copy made by the end of June. Mrs. Gaskell states that it came back rejected from one of its outings to publishers on August 25, 1846, the day Patrick

Brontë had his cataract removed. Whether the novel was re-read before being sent out again cannot be known. But we know that *Jane Eyre* was begun during her father's convalescence. It was thus begun about two months after *The Professor* had been completed and at a time when the substance of *The Professor* would probably have been reviewed whether or not that novel was itself re-read. Moreover, since this initial effort continued "plodding its weary round in London," it was very likely periodically brought to the author's mind while *Jane Eyre* was being written. *The Life of Charlotte Brontë,* introd. Clement Shorter (London: World's Classics, 1924), p. 251.

6. Tillotson, pp. 288-89 and 293. In her discussion of *Agnes Grey* W. A. Craik also makes interesting comparisons between these three works, pp. 203-06.

7. The last chapter is the longest in the novel. The penultimate chapter (XXIV) is one of the longest: only Chs. XII, XIX, XXII, and XXIII are longer. This last, it will be noticed, is the proposal chapter and is itself lengthened by the introduction of new material (as I show in my text).

8. Cynthia A. Linder describes *The Professor* as tracing Crimsworth's economic, then emotional progress, this last ending "when he has reached his goal—that of marriage to Mlle Henri." My point is that, while William's growth ends with marriage, Charlotte Brontë does not end the novel there; she continues it, concentrating on Mlle Henri's development. In fact, a comment by Linder suggests this—though it is not followed up—for she writes of "the puritanical exterior hiding a strong spirit, which is what we see developing in Mlle Henri after her marriage." *Romantic Imagery in the Novels of Charlotte Brontë* (London: Macmillan, 1978), pp. 27 and 28.

9. My references are to the Everyman ed., introd. Margaret Lane (London: Dent, 1964). I use the Penguin *Jane Eyre,* ed. Q. D. Leavis (Harmondsworth, Middx., 1966). Subsequent chapter references will be given in my text.

10. On Charlotte Brontë's use of metaphors see Margot Peters, *Charlotte Brontë: Style in the Novel* (U. of Wisconsin Press, 1973), Ch. 4.

11. In *The Complete Poems of Charlotte Brontë,* ed. Clement Shorter, with bibliog. and notes by C. W. Hatfield (London: Hodder and Stoughton, 1923), the poem "Master and Pupil" is reprinted with the note that it was written "in an exercise-book used by Charlotte Brontë in Brussels, 1843," p. 215.

12. In her 1834 "My Angria and the Angrians" she has Patrick Benjamin Wiggins—a study of Branwell— name his sisters as Charlotte, *Jane,* and Anne. *Miscellaneous and Unpublished Writings,* II, 11. Brian Wilks's *The Brontës* (London: Hamlyn, 1975), in which he remarks that Emily was the only daughter christened with two names (p. 69), reproduces draw-

ings and writings by Emily that show she signed herself Emily Jane Brontë. See pp. 55, 73, 105, and 113.

13. In Ch. XXI Rochester, Jane tells us, "chuckled over" her poverty.

14. Indeed, Crimsworth's cool observations and his analyses of the women around him suggest that he does not like women (see especially Ch. X, XI, and XII). Unlike Rochester, he is debarred from expressing enjoyment with the company of women because, for one thing, he is responsible as narrator for our understanding of the women introduced.

15. Margot Peters thinks that the language expresses a correspondence between the mental depression described and a reaction against sexuality, p. 82. This is why the description comes after his engagement to Frances and immediately after his discovery that he "was a sensualist." For Linder, in this passage "Charlotte Brontë comes as close to stating as Victorian propriety will allow, that William's attack of morbidity is the result of suppressed sexuality," p. 14.

16. Yet if we remember how important this subject is, from the beginning when Jane is sent to the Red Room through her talks with Helen Burns and with Rochester, and also in her own internal debates, merely to have the conflict of passion and reason aired here is significant.

17. Charlotte Brontë was fully aware of her reliance on such relationships. In a very interesting passage at the end of her 1834 story "The Spell" she refers to Zamorna's twin brother Valdacella as his *"alter-ego." The Spell: Ane Extravaganza,* ed. George Edwin MacLean (1931; rpt. London: Folcroft Library Editions, 1972), p. 144.

18. Margaret Blom finds here an acting out of "William's victory over the evil within himself; he has fought and thrown his personal devil," p. 77. But a re-reading of the passage shows that Crimsworth does not throw his *alter-ego.*

Annette Tromly (essay date 1982)

SOURCE: "*The Professor.*" In *The Cover of the Mask: The Autobiographers in Charlotte Brontë's Fiction,* University of Victoria, 1982, pp. 20-41.

[*In the following excerpt, Tromly reviews the contemporary reception of Brontë's* The Professor *and surveys the plot, characterization, and imagery in the novel.*]

From its earliest reviews onward, critics have accorded *The Professor* the same reception which greeted the return of Milton's Satan to Hell: "a dismal universal hiss." Only one voice has disturbed this reassuring critical certitude; and the dissenting voice has belonged to the person who is apparently least qualified to speak. Charlotte Brontë her-

self seems not to have faltered in her commitment to her first novel. She tried nine times to get *The Professor* published (it originally was rejected by six publishers), renewing her effort each time one of her other novels was more sympathetically received.[1] Brontë even attempted to use *Jane Eyre*'s popularity as a coat-tail by which her earlier narrative might be introduced to the reading public. Her efforts failed; it was not until after her death that George Smith decided to publish *The Professor*—only because he realized that nothing else was forthcoming.

Brontë described, in the "Biographical Notice of Ellis and Acton Bell," written for the 1850 edition of *Wuthering Heights, Agnes Grey,* and selected poems, her bitter disappointment at the book's reception: "Currer Bell's book found acceptance nowhere, nor any acknowledgment of merit, so that something like the chill of despair began to invade his heart."[2] The consensus that *Jane Eyre* was far superior to *The Professor* she took adamant exception to. The middle and latter portions of *The Professor,* she insisted, contained "more pith, more substance, more reality" than much of *Jane Eyre.*[3] But if Brontë's defence of *The Professor* was fervid, critics' attacks have been equally so. They have either disregarded Brontë's opinions, or, in one telling instance, denounced them. Referring to Brontë's statement about the novel's value, one critic has declared that the author is "in certain ways, as much of a hypocrite as William Crimsworth," the novel's narrator.[4]

Lying behind the animadversions against the book (in varying degrees of explicitness) are assumptions about its relation to Brontë's biography. First, critics have generally seen this maiden, unpublishable novel as a product of Brontë's artistic immaturity, the "work of a beginner."[5] (As a result, the need to make judgments about the novel—to locate signs of Brontë's apprenticeship—has too often taken precedence over the desire to understand it.) More specifically, some critics have seen the author as incompletely detached from her book, compromising its moral vision by her personal entanglements with the characters. Thus they believe that William Crimsworth, a "wholly decent young man,"[6] makes his way in a tough world by voicing directly the opinions of Charlotte Brontë.[7] Even those critics who have attempted to detach Crimsworth from Brontë (and have seen him as an essentially unreliable narrator) have not found credible artistic reasons for his limitations.[8] And similarly, Frances Henri has been seen as an idealized projection of Brontë herself.[9] Inevitably, most critics have fallen back on the shibboleth of Brontë's biography to dismiss what they consider to be *The Professor*'s shortcomings. Charlotte must have been, in the last year of correspondence with Heger, exorcising the frustrations of an unrequited love;[10] as a result, she wrote an uncontrolled novel.

No one would want to deny that traces of Charlotte Brontë's private world are present in the novel. In certain sections, particularly the chapters on Belgium, Brontë renders the raw materials of her own experience intensely.

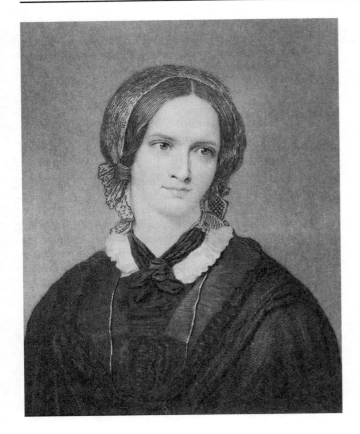

Charlotte Brontë, 1816–1855.

first place? Why is he clearly more interested in telling his story than in communicating with Charles? Surely Brontë is asking her reader, from the book's first moments, to be aware of the centrality of the narrative voice. William Crimsworth, writing from his study at Daisy Lane, is meant to be an emphatic presence.

Throughout the novel Brontë continues to obtrude Crimsworth onto the reader's attention; the narrator's handling of events continually calls attention to his shaping presence. In a number of instances Crimsworth, by means of brief or oblique allusions, passes over or underplays significant events in his life. Thus toward the end of the book he inserts the birth of his only son as an afterthought. Similarly, he downplays his rescue of Jean Baptiste Vandenhuten (who is introduced only as a means of explaining his progress in the search for employment), and skips completely his own professional experience throughout the years of his marriage. But perhaps the most tantalizing of these manipulations of significant events is his allusion to having once observed a "modern French novel":

> Now, modern French novels are not to my taste, either practically or theoretically. Limited as had yet been my experience of life, I had once had the opportunity of contemplating, near at hand, an example of the results produced by a course of interesting and romantic domestic treachery. No golden halo of fiction was about this example, I saw it bare and real, and it was very loathsome. I saw a mind degraded by the practice of mean subterfuge, by the habit of perfidious deception, and a body depraved by the infectious influence of the vice-polluted soul. I had suffered much from the forced and prolonged view of this spectacle; those sufferings I did not now regret, for their simple recollection acted as a most wholesome antidote to temptation.[13]

We hear no more of what must have been a formative experience for Crimsworth. His reticence about this and other matters points to a mind which is deliberately shaping its story. The reader is forced to wonder just what Crimsworth's principles of inclusion are.

If Crimsworth can de-emphasize the important experience, he can also inflate the unimportant. Under his pen the story of his life often unfolds as a series of significant inner moments struck into high relief largely by the force of his narrative determination. After leaving his job in Bigben Close, for example, he describes his walk into the country. He designates a fastflowing river as his symbol-for-the-moment, and takes pains to impress it on both his memory and ours: ". . . I watched the rapid rush of its waves. I desired memory to take a clear and permanent impression of the scene, and treasure it for future years" (194). At other times the meanings Crimsworth imposes on his experience are more difficult to achieve. When he thinks he has lost Frances through the machinations of Zoraïde Reuter, he offers a long disquisition which begins with the proper sphere of the novelist, passes through the dangers of sensual indulgence, glances quickly at suffering, and finally alights on the consolation of Religion to

But if she appropriated certain materials from her life, she did not do so in any simple way. *The Professor* is not, above all, Brontë's unmediated autobiography. It is, however, William Crimsworth's autobiography. A careful examination of *The Professor* reveals a primary interest in the motives and processes of self-presentation; the book is informed by its exploration of the issue. By means of a thoroughly obtrusive and essentially unreliable narrative voice, Brontë explores the reasons and the ways that an autobiographer presents himself to the world. Decades after Brontë's death, Leslie Stephen observed that "distortions of the truth belong to the values of autobiography and are as revealing as the truth."[11] *The Professor* is a novel about these distortions.

The beginning of *The Professor* has always been an irritant to critics. William Crimsworth's letter to "Charles"—who neither answers the letter nor receives it, and does not appear again in the novel—certainly seems arbitrary and contrived. It is not surprising that one critic has called the letter a "clumsy piece of narrative technique."[12] Yet in being both clumsy and irritating, Crimsworth's letter, sent to nowhere, serves its purpose well. The reader does not get very far into the novel before he is forced to ask questions about the teller of the tale. What kind of person would begin his autobiography by quoting himself at length? Why does he adopt such a self-absorbed and callous tone to his old friend? Why does he write the unsolicited letter in the

the hopeless man (277-78). And all of this, he instructs the reader, so that we might infer that—being a reasonable man—he was able to control his grief. The sheer energy Crimsworth expends in imposing a rationale on his life suggests that we should be wary of sharing his perceptions.

Crimsworth's significant moments most often take the form of inner conflicts between moral abstractions. He regrets having resigned his teaching job, for example, when he realizes that he is not in a position to approach the now-employed Frances. But Conscience helpfully intervenes:

> "Down, stupid tormentors!" cried she; "the man has done his duty; you shall not bait him thus by thoughts of what might have been; he relinquished a temporary and contingent good to avoid a permanent and certain evil; he did well. Let him reflect now, and when your blinding dust and deafening hum subside, he will discover a path."
>
> (305)

Shortly afterward, on the night that he longs to give in to his desire to see Frances, Imagination is the "sweet temptress" which he manages to repel. There are many such moments in the novel. It is difficult to imagine that, had **The Professor** been illustrated,[14] Crimsworth would not have been represented with demons on one shoulder and angels on the other; his moral universe is thoroughly dichotomized.

Brontë presents her narrator, then, as the central problem of the novel. William Crimsworth the autobiographer is everywhere present, giving shape and emphasis to his story. And Crimsworth's autobiographical manipulations become morally questionable because of his pronounced tendency to self-inflation. The abstractions through which he filters his inner conflicts, for example, impart a self-serving suggestiveness to the events of his life. He elevates his personal significance by means of the patterns he imposes.

If, however, Crimsworth's version of his life gratifies the autobiographer, it suggests something quite different to the reader. What we note in Crimsworth's account—in his omissions, emphases, and interpretations of events—is its decided simplification of complexities. If Crimsworth expands his life's meaning in his own eyes, he contracts it in ours. His act of writing becomes an act of enclosure, an act of imposing a personal mythology upon a life. And through a network of images in the novel, Brontë further undercuts Crimsworth's self-portrait. Images of physical enclosure echo the mental enclosure which lies behind Crimsworth's autobiographical impulse.

I. CRIMSWORTH: AN ISRAELITE IN BROBDINGNAG

Fastidious, hypersensitive William Crimsworth (the name has a Dickensian aural appropriateness) expends a great deal of energy guarding himself against assault: assault by

other people, assault by his own impulses, assault by all the untidy circumstances that disrupt a remarkably quotidian existence. Enclosure is his characteristic way of dealing with a world too threatening for his insecure psychic constitution. Crimsworth assumes a defensive self-protectiveness against most of his associates. He finds satisfaction in hiding his real self from his tyrannical brother's gaze: ". . . I felt as secure against his scrutiny as if I had had on a casque with the visor down . . ." (176). Similarly, he handles his students with dispatch: "In less than five minutes they had thus revealed to me their characters, and in less than five minutes I had buckled on a breast-plate of steely indifference, and let down a visor of impassible austerity" (223). When uneasy, Crimsworth seeks places which are small and closed-in; after most events of consequence, he walks in "narrow chambers," or shuts out "intruders" (including, at times, the reader). By shutting himself up, or the world out, then, he manages to maintain a fragile state of equilibrium.

Just how fragile this state is, however, becomes most clear when the intruder is one of his own feelings. The scene mentioned earlier, in which he copes with his grief for the lost (misplaced) Frances, is a good example:

> being a steady, reasonable man, I did not allow the resentment, disappointment, and grief, engendered in my mind by this evil chance, to grow there to any monstrous size; nor did I allow them to monopolise the whole space of my heart; I pent them, on the contrary, in one strait and secret nook. In the daytime, too, when I was about my duties, I put them on the silent system; and it was only after I had closed the door of my chamber at night that I somewhat relaxed my severity towards these morose nurslings, and allowed vent to their language of murmurs; then, in revenge, they sat on my pillow, haunted my bed, and kept me awake with their long, midnight cry.
>
> (278)

Crimsworth's fear that without his "strait and secret nook" his feelings will grow monstrous is a consequence of his repression; the syndrome has become common coinage in the psychological currency of our day. And as familiar is the ironical result: the sheer act of forceful control defeats its own purpose. The feelings are unearthed in a more painful way—transformed to a morbid state. The strained, hyperbolical, frenzied language in which Crimsworth describes the revenge of his "morose nurslings" is apt. He is clearly so out of touch with his feelings that he can deal with them—and enjoy them—only when they are dressed up in elaborate metaphor. Most of Crimsworth's psychic life can be characterized in terms of a similar tension: an excessive need for control along with its inevitable opposite.

Other enclosure images emphasize Crimsworth's unwholesome emotional obsessions. Sitting "alone near midnight" writing his autobiography at Daisy Lane, he attempts to capture his past. His memories rise before him like ghosts in a graveyard:[15]

Belgium! I repeat the word, now as I sit alone near midnight. It stirs my world of the past like a summons to resurrection; the graves unclose, the dead are raised; thoughts, feelings, memories that slept, are seen by me ascending from the clods—haloed most of them—but while I gaze on their vapoury forms, and strive to ascertain definitely their outline, the sound which wakened them dies, and they sink, each and all, like a light wreath of mist, absorbed in the mould, recalled to urns, resealed in monuments. Farewell, luminous phantoms!

(201)

As his griefs are pent in a "strait and secret nook," so his memories have been sealed in urns; both images represent a mind which immures the spacious potential of emotional experience. And in spite of this allusion to sinking phantoms, Crimsworth will never realize how thoroughly unsuccessful he is at resurrecting his past. As we shall see, his autobiography does not succeed in liberating his sealed memories; their forms will always remain indistinct to him.

As Crimsworth embalms his memories, so he enshrines his love:

I loved the movement with which she confided her hand to my hand; I loved her as she stood there, penniless and parentless; for a sensualist charmless, for me a treasure—my best object of sympathy on earth, thinking such thoughts as I thought, feeling such feelings as I felt; my ideal of the shrine in which to seal my stores of love. . . .

(285)

The woman he chooses is an "object" to contain his love; and he can describe his "ideal" only in terms of the gratifications she will provide for him. Crimsworth's brand of idealism, then, is as constricted as his repressed desires, his love enclosed as tightly as his grief and his memories. As we shall see, this strange person, whose thoughts are avowedly turned heavenward, becomes capable of the grimmest kind of mean-mindedness.

Crimsworth's tendency to enclose is so thoroughgoing that it undermines his perceptions altogether. He perceives his world as a series of pictures; his reliance on the visual arts is the most persistent peculiarity of his language. He consistently represents places (such as Belgium and the river in Grovetown mentioned above) as pictures. And virtually all the people he meets, from an anonymous Flemish housemaid who reminds him of "the female figures in certain Dutch paintings" (202-03) to his good friend Yorke Hunsden, whose "features might have done well on canvas but indifferently in marble" (186) are subjected to the scrutinizing eye of a self-conscious artist. Crimsworth takes great pains when presenting his pictures; they are often overloaded with descriptive minutiae. His efforts at verisimilitude, however, reveal more about the artist than his subjects. Rather than rendering faithful images of the people he describes, Crimsworth avoids or distorts the issue of who they really are. Preoccupation with physical

characteristics sometimes permits him to avoid more significant attributes of character. But more serious, perhaps, is his tendency to create simple equations between the outer person and the inner character. His student Eulalie is an example:

Eulalie was tall, and very finely shaped: she was fair, and her features were those of a Low Country Madonna; many a 'figure de Vierge' have I seen in Dutch pictures exactly resembling hers; there were no angles in her shape or in her face, all was curve and roundness—neither thought, sentiment, nor passion disturbed by line or flush the equality of her pale, clear skin; her noble bust heaved with her regular breathing, her eyes moved a little—by these evidences of life alone could I have distinguished her from some large handsome figure moulded in wax.

(222)

Crimsworth submits Eulalie to a process of reduction in several ways. First, by associating her with works of art he is able to distance himself from her. Second, in relying on the stock associations of a type of painted figure, he is forcing Eulalie into an easy and pre-existent category. And finally, the blandness of character he attributes to her on the basis of her physical type is predicated on a questionable relation between the inner and the outer person. Interpreting people as works of art enables Crimsworth to categorize his world far too neatly. Once enclosed in frames, his images become easier to control.

Crimsworth depicts himself as well as others. Even as the novel opens, he is speaking (in the letter to Charles) of his own "portrait." And in the most explicit summary he gives us of his past, his life becomes a gallery:

Three—nay four—pictures line the four-walled cell where are stored for me the records of the past. First, Eton. All in that picture is in far perspective, receding, diminutive; but freshly coloured, green, dewy, with a spring sky, piled with glittering yet showery clouds; for my childhood was not all sunshine—it had its overcast, its cold, its stormy hours. Second, X———, huge, dingy, the canvas cracked and smoked; a yellow sky, sooty clouds; no sun, no azure; the verdure of the suburbs blighted and sullied—a very dreary scene.

Third, Belgium; and I will pause before this landscape. As to the fourth, a curtain covers it, which I may hereafter withdraw, or may not, as suits my convenience and capacity. At any rate, for the present it must hang undisturbed.

(200)

In deliberately figuring his past as a gallery of pictures, Crimsworth, characteristically, claims an inflated meaning for his private experience. He presents his past, by analogy, as something that partakes of the heightened significance of paintings. Yet as he inflates, he also deflates. The frames around his past, like the urns that hold his memories, are enclosures. Even the gallery itself is a claustrophobic, four-walled cell. And Crimsworth chooses a curious kind of picture to represent his life. Each painting in the gallery might be titled "A Portrait of the Artist as a Young Landscape"; missing from the canvas is Crimsworth himself. Eulalie, then, is not the only figure who is dehumanized and regarded with detachment; Crimsworth also maintains a disturbing distance from himself. The mysterious fourth, curtained, picture is never alluded to again.[16] But as we shall see, despite Crimsworth's secrecy, it does not hang undisturbed.

From time to time Crimsworth reminds the reader that the pictures he is framing as he tells his story are corrected versions of the inaccurate pictures of his youth. An interesting dynamic develops as Crimsworth the Autobiographer, writing from Daisy Lane, enjoys contemplating his formerly callow perceptions:

> This is Belgium, reader. Look! don't call the picture a flat or a dull one—it was neither flat nor dull to me when I first beheld it. When I left Ostend on a mild February morning, and found myself on the road to Brussels, nothing could look vapid to me. My sense of enjoyment possessed an edge whetted to the finest, untouched, keen, exquisite. I was young; I had good health; pleasure and I had never met. . . . Well! and what did I see? I will tell you faithfully. Green, reedy swamps; fields, fertile but flat, cultivated in patches that made them look like magnified kitchen-gardens; belts of cut trees, formal as pollard willows, skirting the horizon; narrow canals, gliding slow by the road-side; painted Flemish farmhouses; some very dirty hovels; a gray, dead sky; wet road, wet fields, wet house-tops: not a beautiful, scarcely a picturesque object met my eye along the whole route; yet to me, all was beautiful, all was more than picturesque.
>
> (201-02)

Yet behind Crimsworth's gentle irony against his younger self is a much tougher irony which the narrator fails to see. Brontë would have us note that in correcting the perceptions of his younger self, Crimsworth often encloses himself more tightly into a set of highly inadequate attitudes.

We see these ironies operating in Crimsworth's feelings about the students of Zoraïde Reuter's school. Noticing that the window in his room which opens onto the girls' garden is boarded up (an enclosure image of his young blindness), he feels a strong desire to see behind the boards. He imagines the ground in the garden to be "con-secrated," a paradise where angels play. When he is finally hired to teach at the girls' school, he is delighted. "'I shall now at last see the mysterious garden: I shall gaze both on the angels and their Eden'" (216). All the humour of the delusion is enjoyed by Crimsworth the narrator. He describes his process of disillusionment with the girls:

> Daily, as I continued my attendance at the seminary of Mdlle. Reuter, did I find fresh occasions to compare the ideal with the real. What had I known of female character previously to my arrival at Brussels? Precious little. And what was my notion of it? Something vague, slight, gauzy, glittering; now when I came in contact

with it I found it to be a palpable substance enough; very hard too sometimes, and often heavy; there was metal in it, both lead and iron.

> (231)

But the quasi-objective tone of Crimsworth's voice of experience immediately gives itself the lie. He offers to "open his portfolio" (231) to sketch a few students, and proceeds to reveal his barely suppressed disgust and rage at the girls. His three pictures "from the life" (234) are painted by a vengeful, moralistic hand. One girl he refers to as an "unnatural-looking being," "Gorgon-like," who practises "panther-like deceit" (232). He seems capable of only the crudest kind of adversary relationship with the girls (the way they look at him is their "artillery" [233]), and falls back on his oversimplified moral abstractions in order to place them within his scheme ("Mutiny" and "Hate" are graved on Juanna's brow [234]). When Crimsworth physically confines one of the girls (locks her up in a cabinet), he is only echoing the mental confinement that his descriptions reflect.

What his attitude toward the girls reveals, then, is the constriction of Crimsworth's ostensibly maturing perceptions. Crimsworth approaches his students with naïve idealism; when forced to adjust, he castigates the real rather than tempering the ideal. As we shall see, his ideal remains intact—pent, perhaps, in another strait and secret nook—waiting only for the appropriate woman to be forced into its contracted boundaries.

Before turning to a consideration of the other main characters in the book, it would be useful to note a final pair of images which corroborates the idea of Crimsworth's mental enclosure. As I have noted, the pictures Crimsworth frames of his world are idiosyncratic—a personalized way of imposing a rationale on a perplexing life. Crimsworth is aware of the differences between himself and other people. Early in the novel, he reveals his feelings of separateness to Hunsden with a certain smug satisfaction: "'I must follow my own devices—I must till the day of my death; because I can neither comprehend, adopt, nor work out those of other people'" (198). Crimsworth's image for himself in the novel's early chapters is as an Israelite in Egypt. Orphaned, confined to drudgery in the counting-house of his unsympathetic brother Edward, he characterizes his work as a "task thankless and bitter as that of the Israelite crawling over the sun-baked fields of Egypt in search of straw and stubble wherewith to accomplish his tale of bricks" (190). The image is apt in several ways. His work is futile; he lives in bondage. But most important, Crimsworth is elevating his separateness into the virtue of a martyr. As an Israelite, he is not only victim, but chosen one. A large part of his self-delusion pertains to a puritanical notion of himself as an anti-sensualist in a world of flesh-pots. Beginning with a reference to his wealthy cousins in the letter to Charles, Crimsworth sets himself apart from women whose attractions he considers himself above. Not for him are the base sexual yearnings of the normal man.[17] (The pronounced element of twisted sexuality in his accounts of his students is an ironic contradiction of his high-mindedness.) But his attitude toward women is only one important element in Crimsworth's Israelite conception of himself. The notion of his own special nature exists in Crimsworth's mind as a means by which to exempt himself, with self-congratulatory glibness, from the humbling exigencies of self-knowledge.

Set off against the Israelite in Crimsworth's mind is a parallel image in the reader's. Brontë very delicately introduces an association between Crimsworth and another literary figure, one not quite so sombre as the Israelite in Egypt. When Crimsworth refers, while observing the Belgian landscape, to a "Brobdignagian [sic] kitchen-garden" (282), we realize that he is not so unlike another fellow-traveller. Associated with Gulliver's innocence, sexual repression, fastidiousness, and, above all, pride, William Crimsworth becomes a figure considerably less elevated than the Israelite. Like Gulliver's, Crimsworth's innocence is not ennobling, but constricting—his pride not a source of dignity, but of self-aggrandizement. The two images coexist, then, as suggestively ironic pieces in the puzzle of Crimsworth's character. Lurking just on the surface is Brontë's suggestion that Crimsworth's idea of his separateness may transform him from his own sublime into the reader's ridiculous. Crimsworth leaves England—his Egypt—in search of the Canaan which he not only feels he deserves but also can use to vindicate his uniqueness. But the reader has discovered that the Israelite's bondage was considerably more than physical.

II. HUNSDEN, REUTER, AND FRANCES HENRI:
PORTRAIT AND PENTIMENTO

Although he enjoys portraying his life as a series of pictures, William Crimsworth remains oblivious to the pentimento which complicates his literary self-portraiture. The personal myth he constructs seems to the reader to be superimposed upon a life which is far less tidy than Crimsworth himself will acknowledge. Presented with the official Crimsworth, we remain constantly aware—though the outlines are never distinct—of the traces of a second image beneath. In the portraits of the other main characters in the novel—Hunsden, Zoraïde Reuter, and Frances Henri—the pentimento is equally pronounced, and equally indistinct. We are presented with their images as seen through the eyes of Crimsworth; yet the shadows of images that Crimsworth does not see flicker always before us.

Although Hunsden Yorke Hunsden is a friend of long standing (he is the only character besides Crimsworth to exist all the way through the novel), Crimsworth's attitude to him is always acrimonious. He presents Hunsden as a presumptuous, eccentric person—a person who seems not to know that he is meant to be of secondary importance in the Crimsworth autobiography. The man who seems irritatingly idiosyncratic to Crimsworth, however, strikes the reader as ironically appropriate. For, viewed in relation to Crimsworth, Hunsden is a running commentary on the protagonist's limitations. Like Crimsworth, he has both the tradesman and the aristocrat in his lineage—but unlike Crimsworth, he is at home in the world. Like Crimsworth, he is a mixture of masculine and feminine characteristics—but unlike Crimsworth, he has the confidence to address aggressively a challenging world. Where Crimsworth is fastidious and constricted, Hunsden is generous and expansive (though the misanthropic directness of Hunsden's speech seems to Crimsworth to be far less kindly than his own minced words). Like Crimsworth, Hunsden has a feminine ideal—but unlike Crimsworth, his ideal coexists with a strong strain of practicality. He can live enthusiastically with the ideal unfulfilled. And finally, like Crimsworth, Hunsden is unique—but whereas Crimsworth's uniqueness exists only in his mind, as a means of separating himself from a tawdry world, Hunsden's uniqueness is palpable. Perhaps that is why he defies even Crimsworth's self-confident descriptive powers: "There is no use in attempting to describe," says Crimsworth, "what is indescribable" (308). The close similarities—and awesome differences—between the two men explain why Crimsworth is so perpetually vulnerable to his friend.

Hunsden is responsible for almost all the good fortune in Crimsworth's career; but he can also be called Crimsworth's nemesis. For reasons which are not quite clear, his early interest in Crimsworth abides throughout the novel. He precipitates the release from Edward's tyranny, makes the crucial referral for a teaching job in Belgium, and buys the only one of Crimsworth's pictures which is ever really important—that of his mother—as an unsolicited gift. But Hunsden's generosity is always resented by Crimsworth. In an interesting juxtaposition of scenes, Brontë demonstrates the ease with which Crimsworth can accept favours from another benefactor, Victor Vandenhuten, as compared with the bitterness that Hunsden's help always elicits. From Crimsworth's description of Vandenhuten, we infer the cause: "in short our characters dovetailed, but my mind having more fire and action than his, instinctively assumed and kept the predominance" (317). With Hunsden, Crimsworth can never keep the predominance; something within him must realize that his friend represents the authentic product of which he is himself only an unconvincing reproduction. The ironic connections between the two men are never completely brought to the consciousness of Crimsworth the narrator—nor, as we shall see, is the implicit threat that Hunsden poses to the autobiographer's happy ending.

Crimsworth's first love, Zoraïde Reuter, is also a victim of his misanthropy. The process of disillusionment which Crimsworth underwent with his students is echoed with Reuter. And echoed as well are the aging Crimsworth's sage amusement at the naïveté of his younger self, and the reader's distance from both narrators. Even at her best, Reuter hardly resembles the Angels in their Eden; she taxes even Crimsworth's ability to idealize. Yet, with great effort, the young man manages to rationalize his love. At their first meeting, he is patronizingly amused by the business talent of a young woman. He must be growing wiser, he feels, since he can admire the "crafty little politician" (226). And if Reuter does not quite fit the "female character as depicted in Poetry and Fiction" (226), she is only a more interesting challenge. When pressed for a rationale by which to justify himself, young Crimsworth is ingenious enough to fall back on religious prejudice: "She has been brought up a Catholic: had she been born an Englishwoman, and reared a Protestant, might she not have added straight integrity to all her other excellences? Supposing she were to marry an English and Protestant husband, would she not, rational, sensible, as she is, quickly acknowledge the superiority of right over expediency, honesty over policy?" (240). The scene in which Crimsworth conveys his strongest moment of infatuation takes place in that touchstone of his romantic imagination, the garden of the Pensionnat:

> In another minute I and the directress were walking side by side down the valley bordered with fruit-trees, whose white blossoms were then in full blow as well as their tender green leaves. The sky was blue, the air still, the May afternoon was full of brightness and fragrance. Released from the stifling class, surrounded with flowers and foliage, with a pleasing, smiling, affable woman at my side—how did I feel? Why, very enviably. It seemed as if the romantic visions my imagination had suggested of this garden, while it was yet hidden from me by the jealous boards, were more than realised; and, when a turn in the alley shut out the view of the house, and some tall shrubs excluded M. Pelet's mansion, and screened us momentarily from the other houses, rising amphitheatre-like round this green spot, I gave my arm to Mdlle. Reuter, and led her to a garden-chair, nestled under some lilacs near. She sat down; I took my place at her side. She went on talking to me with that ease which communicates ease, and, as I listened, a revelation dawned in my mind that I was on the brink of falling in love.

(238)

Writing from Daisy Lane, Crimsworth contrives the scene of his young delusion neatly. In retrospect, he sees the garden as the perfect location for the growth of his younger, callow self from innocence to experience.[18] For the reader, however, the garden is yet another enclosure, reflecting ironically upon both the young lover and his wiser, older self. And the author's irony becomes more stringent when, after the inevitable disillusionment, young and old Crimsworth agree in their interpretation of the event.

Appropriately, the disillusionment takes place in the same garden. Crimsworth, dreaming of Reuter at his now unboarded window, hears voices below. It is Reuter and Pelet, talking of their wedding plans, and of him. Neither the old nor the young Crimsworth understands the inadequacy of his response to his disillusionment. The love arose solely from Crimsworth's romantic mind. Yet both Crimsworths view the overheard conversation as an act of treachery, strong enough to extinguish all "faith in love and friendship" (242). The shared vision of old and young Crimsworth is demonstrated through the mixing of past and present tenses:

> Not that I nursed vengeance—no; but the sense of insult and treachery lived in me like a kindling, though as yet smothered coal. God knows I am not by nature vindictive; I would not hurt a man because I can no longer trust or like him; but neither my reason nor feelings are of the vacillating order—they are not of that sand-like sort where impressions, if soon made, are as soon effaced. Once convinced that my friend's disposition is incompatible with my own, once assured that he is indelibly stained with certain defects obnoxious to my principles, and I dissolve the connection.

(242-43)

Also echoed here are the familiar tones of Crimsworth's moralism: his castigation of whatever fails to live up to his mind-forged ideals, and his claims to a special, exalted nature. As we would expect, he calls on an abstraction—Reason—to be his physician after suffering the blow. Regardless of what his older self may think, Crimsworth has not learned much; his mind remains as sealed off as Mlle Reuter's "allée défendue."

Thenceforward, Crimsworth's bitterness and distrust regarding Zoraïde Reuter are extreme. Though Reuter continues to be crafty and manipulative, she apparently falls in love with Crimsworth and is treated very cruelly indeed. (The garden again becomes an emblem of Crimsworth's constricted perceptions.) By the time Reuter fires Frances Henri (probably with at least some justification), Crimsworth's disdain for the directress has turned into loathing. He has successfully reduced a complicated woman to the status of a bad angel.

In Crimsworth's mind, Reuter is an unattractive foil for his heart's desire, Frances. He sees Reuter as fully engaged in her world, Frances as an outsider; Reuter as manipulative, Frances as passive; Reuter as hardened, Frances as tender; Reuter as contrived, Frances as natural; Reuter as self-protective, Frances as vulnerable. Yet the novel suggests that as telling as the differences between the two women are their similarities. First, their careers are parallel: Frances, like Reuter, will become the directress of her own school. But more important, Reuter makes guarded suggestions of deeper similarities between them. "'Her present position,'" she says, "'has once been mine, or nearly so; it is then but natural I should sympathise with her . . .'" (254). Within this enigmatic comment, and also within the feelings of animosity between the two women, lurks the possibility, borne out by more direct evidence elsewhere, that Frances Henri is not what Crimsworth believes her to be.

Although critics have tended to see only Crimsworth's romanticized portrait of Frances, there is ample evidence in *The Professor* that Brontë's portrait, which lurks behind Crimsworth's, is meant to be considerably more subtle, complicated, and ambiguous. First, there are a number of hints that Frances may not always have lived the sheltered, virginal life which Crimsworth complacently assumes she has. Early in their acquaintance, Frances describes her life in Switzerland as being "'in a circle; I walked the same round every day'" (266). She speaks of knowing something of the "'bourgeois of Geneva'" and of Brussels (266). And echoing the suggestiveness of these remarks is Reuter's; the older woman says of Frances that she does "'not like her going out in all weathers'" (276). Later, Frances mentions the frustrations of "'people who are only in each other's company for amusement'" (328-29). And on several occasions she calmly entertains Crimsworth in her apartment alone.[19]

The evidence for Frances' questionable past is not obtrusive. Rather it is composed of delicately suggestive allusions which only hint at something Crimsworth cannot see. Whether or not she has had a sexual past, though, Frances certainly has had some kind of experience in her life that Crimsworth has not. Both her pronounced independence and her unmistakable emotional separateness from him do not correspond to Crimsworth's portrait of her. The very moment she accepts his proposal of marriage, for example, Frances asks to be allowed to continue teaching (327-28). This hard-headed practicality, as well as her tears on her wedding day (342), indicates that for Frances the choice to marry is far from simple. Although Hunsden may be able to live successfully on his own, Frances does not have the male option of a completely independent life; she must know that spending life alone would mean abandoning her career ambitions. It is clear, then, that Frances' view of the marriage has complications that Crimsworth does not dream of; it is likely that she accepts the marriage proposal as the most attractive of several very limited options open to her.

Frances' "Jane" poem indicates that her need for a "master"—the side of her which Crimsworth emphasizes—is a substantial part of her nature. But as Brontë skillfully demonstrates through suggestive details, the deluded Crimsworth never understands the intricacies of his wife's position. He places her on the conventional pedestal, a pedestal which fits nicely into the myth he is creating of his own "successful" life. Yet Frances knows much more of the world than does her "master." When Crimsworth says of her that "I knew how the more dangerous flame [of passion] burned safely under the eye of reason" (285), he speaks as a puritan; he has no notion of how clearly that eye of reason really sees.

Part of what makes Frances particularly suitable to Crimsworth's autobiographical designs is the fact that she is as homeless as he. Their mutual rootlessness enables Crimsworth to circumvent a certain kind of social definition; it is another means by which Crimsworth can define himself as a man outside—and above—the rest of the world. He delights in Frances' *devoir* about the emigrant and is sensitive to her expressed desire for her own Canaan. The Israelite image which he adopted in the early chapters is appropriately transformed. Crimsworth's Egypt (England) becomes Frances' Canaan, and by means of a letter from Hunsden, the entire notion is ironically reversed. Hunsden imagines Crimsworth as an Israelite in Belgium, not England: "'sitting like a black-haired, tawny-skinned, long-

nosed Israelite by the flesh-pots of Egypt'" (302). The implication is that Crimsworth would be a displaced Israelite wherever he lived; for him, exile is a state of mind. In choosing Frances, Crimsworth can cling to his feelings of being unique, and therefore special. As he speaks of Hunsden's knowledge of him, this need is apparent: "nor could he, keen-sighted as he was, penetrate into my heart, search my brain, and read my peculiar sympathies and antipathies; he had not known me long enough, or well enough, to perceive how long my feelings would ebb under some influences, powerful over most minds; how high, how fast they would flow under other influences, that perhaps acted with the more intense force on me, because they acted on me alone" (312).

If Frances' homelessness is a convenience for Crimsworth, so too is her role as his student. Brontë's frequent use of the teacher-student relationship has prompted many critics to suggest a questionable equivalence between the art and the life. Thus Inga-Stina Ewbank has called the teaching situation "an image of the ideal relationship" for Brontë.[20] In *The Professor,* however, teacher-student relationships are far from ideal: they are based, for the most part, on tyranny. As I have mentioned, Crimsworth relates to his students as an adversary: through his descriptions of the girls in Reuter's school he reveals both his constricted sexual nature and his related need for power. The same kind of problem is a factor in his relationship with Frances. Her status as a social and educational inferior provides easy superiority for Crimsworth; it enables him, through his autobiographical myth, to enclose her emotions into an even smaller nook than his own. There are several scenes when Crimsworth, forcing Frances to speak English with the ostensible purpose of benefiting her language development, becomes almost sadistic in his treatment of her. (And one such scene is the proposal scene.) The kind of dominance over Frances that Crimsworth seems to need is ironically undercut both by the specifics of their relationship and by the echoes of earlier student relationships.

Frances Henri, then, is just what Crimsworth needs. She has—on the surface, at least—precisely those qualities which enable him to impose a gratifying rationale on his life story. She is socially inferior, educationally disadvantaged, and rootless; a difficult life has made her both tractable and desperate for security. But complications arise for Crimsworth. In order to create the picture of his life in the way which gratifies him most, he must do something very earnest, very real: he must take a wife. The shaky foundations of his psychosexual nature catch up with him only moments after he proposes to Frances. His attack of hypochondria is one of Brontë's most interesting ways of revealing the irony of his mental enclosure.

In reading *The Professor* as a straightforward success story, most critics have had difficulty accounting for Crimsworth's bout of hypochondria. Robert Martin, for example, finds it to be "without any apparent relevance," and objects to its coming at a time when "Crimsworth's psychic health has never been better."[21] And Inga-Stina Ewbank reverts to Brontë biography to justify the scene: "Powerful in itself, this passage has no justification in plot or character; there is nothing either before or after to suggest such nervous sensibilities in the very sensible hero. His breakdown here is introduced, it would seem, only to give an excuse for what is a welling-up from the suppressed ego of the author."[22] These critical discussions, however, leave out what seems to me to be Brontë's major effort in the novel. Crimsworth is telling his own story, or, rather, presenting his own myth. While ostensibly creating art which will reflect his life, he is in reality moulding the life to fit the art. But, as Roy Pascal has observed about autobiography, "Consistent misrepresentation of oneself is not easy."[23] Like the other loose ends which Brontë insinuates before us, Crimsworth's attack of hypochondria qualifies his personal mythology. It represents, in Pascal's terms, a "gap" in his self-portrait, or, in James' terms, a "leakage" in his ostensibly watertight scheme. The attack of hypochondria may seem inconsistent to Crimsworth, but for the reader it is part of the pentimento.

Crimsworth's myth about himself, as I have mentioned, is based largely on his feelings of being different from others. An essential part of this difference is his view of himself as an anti-sensualist (a view which the reader has always discredited on the basis of his descriptions of his students). But just after proposing to Frances, he discovers that he is in fact strongly attracted physically to her. As he confesses to the reader: "It appeared then, that I too was a sensualist in my temperate and fastidious way" (329). Crimsworth's acceptance of his own sexual nature is followed immediately by the attack of hypochondria. Apparently his righteous self-delusions do not die easily. It is appropriate that the attack is described as claustrophobic, and as sexual. Crimsworth is imprisoned by hypochondria, who has the bony arms of a death-cold concubine:

> She had been my acquaintance, nay, my guest, once before in boyhood; I had entertained her at bed and board for a year; for that space of time I had her to myself in secret; she lay with me, she ate with me, she walked out with me, showing me nooks in woods, hollows in hills where we could sit together, and where she could drop her drear veil over me, and so hide sky and sun, grass and green tree; taking me entirely to her death-cold bosom, and holding me with arms of bone.
> . . .
>
> I repulsed her as one would a dreaded and ghastly concubine coming to embitter a husband's heart towards his young bride; in vain; she kept her sway over me for that night and the next day, and eight succeeding days.
>
> (330-31)

Crimsworth's amazement that the attack should come at this point in his life—"why did hypochondria accost me now?" (331)—is not shared by the reader. Having abandoned the safety of his clearly-defined self-image, he is bound to suffer greatly. Marriage to Frances (who is surely represented in part by the concubine) will of necessity involve psychic and physical realities which he has never before had to face.

If Crimsworth's pre-marital forebodings are complex, those of his new bride are even more so. During the early descriptions of their relationship, as I have noted, the reader continually senses that Crimsworth is not telling the entire story about Frances. Frances' behaviour strengthens this doubt. Perhaps the height of the reader's wonder about her comes in the remarkable scene when she meets Hunsden. Crimsworth takes a seat on the periphery of the room, thus characteristically removing himself and framing the participants in the spectacle. As he watches in supercilious amusement, his deferential, resigned, often vapid Frances suddenly becomes, as she converses with Hunsden, vital, daring, even sexual.

> Animated by degrees, she began to change, just as a grave night-sky changes at the approach of sunrise: first it seemed as if her forehead cleared, then her eyes glittered, her features relaxed, and became quite mobile; her subdued complexion grew warm and transparent; to me, she now looked pretty; before, she had only looked ladylike.
>
> She had many things to say to the Englishman just fresh from his island-country, and she urged him with an enthusiasm of curiosity, which ere long thawed Hunsden's reserve as fire thaws a congealed viper. I use this not very flattering comparison because he vividly reminded me of a snake waking from torpor, as he erected his tall form, reared his head, before a little declined, and putting back his hair from his broad Saxon forehead, showed unshaded the gleam of almost savage satire which his interlocutor's tone of eagerness and look of ardour had suffered at once to kindle in his soul and elicit from his eyes: he was himself, as Frances was herself, and in none but his own language would he now address her.
>
> (335)

Strangely, Frances' metamorphosis into a person of warmth, relaxation, and beauty does not threaten the complacent Crimsworth. Neither does the vitality of Hunsden who, imaged as a snake who is tempted by Frances, both ironically undercuts the couple's allegedly invulnerable love and also foreshadows their peculiar future. The scene closes with two literary references, both of which serve a purpose similar to that of the passage above. First, a reference to *Othello* reinforces the delicate suggestions of a love (between Frances and Crimsworth) built on a shaky foundation. And second, Hunsden's Byronic farewell, and Frances' positive response to it, emphasize again the potential she has for stepping outside the rigid frame in which Crimsworth has enclosed her.

Throughout the Crimsworths' married life, Brontë continues her intimations that Frances' feelings differ from her husband's. What Crimsworth describes is his pleasure at Frances' continual deference to him, his pride in his own generosity (in allowing Frances to open her school), and his delight at playfully subduing her spirit when he "frequently dosed her with Wordsworth" (348). But though Frances' surface reactions may be just as Crimsworth sees them, they indicate, by now, a great deal more to the reader than they do to Crimsworth. Perhaps the clearest signals Brontë sends to the reader in the novel's final chapters come through the passages about young Victor. When Frances leaves Crimsworth's side to visit her sleeping baby, she "abandons" him. When Victor's dog Yorke is exposed to rabies, Crimsworth coldly shoots it, leaves the body for his young son to find, and then describes the entire scene with sanctimonious relish. As he turns away from Victor's grief, it is Frances who comforts their distraught child. And finally, when Crimsworth discusses his son's treatment at the hands of his gentle mother, we feel the full force of his puritanical rage:

> though Frances will not make a milksop of her son, she will accustom him to a style of treatment, a forbearance, a congenial tenderness, he will meet with from none else. She sees, as I also see, a something in Victor's temper—a kind of electrical ardour and power—which emits, now and then, ominous sparks; Hunsden calls it his spirit, and says it should not be curbed. I call it the leaven of the offending Adam, and consider that it should be, if not *whipped* out of him, at least soundly disciplined; and that he will be cheap of any amount of either bodily or mental suffering which will ground him radically in the art of self-control . . . for that cloud on his bony brow—for that compression of his statuesque lips, the lad will some day get blows instead of blandishments—kicks instead of kisses; then for the fit of mute fury which will sicken his body and madden his soul; then for the ordeal of merited and salutary suffering, out of which he will come (I trust) a wiser and a better man.
>
> (357-58)

Crimsworth contemplates his son's suffering with chilling complacency. Frances, though she hides it from her husband, clearly has an independent relationship with—and independent opinions on—the boy. Frances seems, then, to have the same wider vision at the end of the novel that she has had throughout. She evidently goes through the motions of living up to Crimsworth's happy ending—but were she to tell the story, we feel certain that her version would be vastly different.

If the relations of the three Crimsworths to each other are ambiguous at the end of the novel, the relations of all of them to Yorke Hunsden are even more so. Hunsden is a strange presence in the Crimsworth family; Hunsden Wood, with its "winding ways," would seem to be a suggestive image of the tangled relations that may exist there. At several points, for instance, Crimsworth refers to the mutual affection between his son and Hunsden. Toward the end of the novel, he observes the two together:

> I see him now; he stands by Hunsden, who is seated on the lawn under the beech; Hunsden's hand rests on the boy's collar, and he is instilling God knows what principles into his ear. . . . Victor has a preference for Hunsden, full as strong as I deem desirable, being considerably more potent, decided, and indiscriminating, than any I ever entertained for that personage myself.
>
> (358)

As Crimsworth looks on at his son and Hunsden, apparently not deeply threatened when he witnesses their strong bond, we are reminded of the earlier scene in which he observed Hunsden and Frances with a similar complacency as they engaged in animated, almost sexually provocative, conversation. Earlier, Hunsden played the role of lover to Frances; in this scene, he would seem to be acting, at least metaphorically, as father to Victor. Indeed, the reader—accustomed by now to the alternative possibilities which lurk beneath Crimsworth's narrative—might even wonder whether the father-son relationship between Hunsden and Victor is only metaphorical. Perhaps, unbeknownst to Crimsworth, there is another family tree in Hunsden Wood in addition to his own. But whatever the actual relationships among Victor, Frances, and Hunsden may be—and no doubt we are not meant to be certain—Hunsden continues to be a dominant presence for all three members of the Crimsworth family. And, characteristically, Crimsworth continues to be oblivious to the complexities that surround him.

The moral universe of *The Professor* is decidedly postlapsarian. Crimsworth is the innocent of the novel; all the other characters are at home in a world of compromised ideals and limited expectations. Yet—realist that she was—Brontë does not castigate her characters for being less than perfect. It is Crimsworth's brand of innocence, which refuses to recognize the mixed state of humankind and retreats into complacency, that receives the sharpest blows. Only gradually does the reader realize that the novel's moral landscape borrows much of its dark tone from the short-sighted eyes through which it is perceived.

III. THE FOURTH PICTURE: A "GOLDEN HALO OF FICTION"

In the novel's final moments, Crimsworth stops framing pictures; instead, he paints one. Although he makes no explicit reference to the fourth picture in the gallery of his life, the final pages in fact represent its unveiling. Crimsworth's fourth picture completes his presentation of his autobiographical myth. He construes an image of his life at Daisy Lane as his final Eden—the family living in an unsullied region, in a "picturesque and not too spacious dwelling" (351), surrounded by roses and ivy. Having discovered, as he thinks, the pitfalls of artificial gardens[24] and the snares of false delusions, he can now envisage his married life as the real paradise. In evoking his ostensible paradise, however, Crimsworth intensifies the dehumanizing natural images he has used throughout the novel's latter sections of his wife and son; they become birds, plants which he tends, or fruit. He had earlier enjoyed characterizing Frances to Hunsden as "an unique fruit, growing wild," tantalizingly natural in contrast to his friend's "hot-house grapes" (313). Now, having transplanted Frances into a rural setting, he revels in the appropriateness of the pastoral life he has created for his "dove," his "butterfly," his "precious plant."

Brontë's ironic manipulation of prelapsarian imagery did not begin with *The Professor.* In one of the earlier novelettes (*Caroline Vernon,* 1839), her unhappy heroine is banished to Eden-Cottage, near Fidena. For Caroline, the cottage becomes a prison; she flees from Eden into the unscrupulous arms of Zamorna.[25] Though not so extreme a torture, Daisy Lane must be for Frances considerably less Edenic than it is for her husband.

The love between Frances and Crimsworth began with the teacher finding his lost student mourning her aunt's death in a cemetery. Leading her from the graveyard, Crimsworth saw himself as effecting a rebirth—a victory over the forces of poverty, death, and an antagonistic world. But after rescuing Frances from the walled-in cemetery, Crimsworth merely substitutes one enclosure—his doubtful Paradise—for another. The thought of Frances and her lifelong partner is unsettling; Brontë might have been describing a Crimsworth when she wrote to Ellen Nussey that "a man with a weak brain, chill affections and a strong will—is merely an intractable fiend—you can have no hold of him—you can never lead him right."[26] With a husband, then, whose illusions require great tact to maintain, a son whose equilibrium is constantly threatened, and the emphatic figure of the serpent-like Hunsden lurking about the "winding ways" of the forest, Frances must find life at Daisy Lane considerably less spacious.

Such is not the case for Crimsworth. The final enclosure he creates—the pastoral life at Daisy Lane—fulfills his need for an autobiographical rationale as satisfactorily as have all his other techniques for containing experience. Virtually every critic who has written on **The Professor** has commented on Crimsworth's growth during the course of the novel.[27] Yet Crimsworth has not changed essentially since the letter to Charles; only his situation is different. The ironic thrust of Crimsworth's success story is based upon the tension between worldly success and personal delusion. Crimsworth's need to superimpose his mental enclosures onto the world around him has resulted in appalling insensitivity. In the world of **The Professor,** innocence can be considerably darker than experience.

Midway through the novel, in a passage often used to characterize **The Professor,** Crimsworth states his opinion on the kinds of pictures novelists should paint:

> Novelists should never allow themselves to weary of the study of real life. If they observed this duty conscientiously, they would give us fewer pictures chequered with vivid contrasts of light and shade. . . .
>
> (277)

Brontë's success in giving us real life is achieved by means of Crimsworth's failure; in spite of himself, he manages nothing but a "golden halo of fiction" (299). As he ends his story, art appropriately catches up to life, and in fact overtakes it. Crimsworth writes his last page at the moment he lives it; the presence by his side of Frances, who is waiting tea for him, is as pleasant, he says, "as the perfume of the fresh hay and spicy flowers, as the glow of the westering sun, as the repose of the midsummer eve are

to my senses" (359). We are not surprised to find Crimsworth so much more engaged in the appearance on his page than in the reality at his elbow. At the penultimate moment, as throughout the tale, art is more real to him than life. "But Hunsden comes." As this familiar intruder forces his presence into the room which frames the family ("disturbing," as Crimsworth writes, "two bees and a butterfly"), we note once again the instability of the autobiographer's smug portrait of blissful domesticity. Crimsworth's hackneyed ending, like all his autobiographical efforts, defeats its own purpose.

Notes

1. See [Tom Winnifrith, *The Brontës* (New York: Collier, 1977)] p. 88.

2. Quoted in [Elizabeth Gaskell, *The Life of Charlotte Brontë,* ed. Alan Shelston (Harmondsworth, England: Penguin, 1975)] p. 305.

3. [*The Brontës: Their Lives, Friendships & Correspondence in Four Volumes* (Oxford: Shakespeare Head Press, 1932), hereafter as *LFC*] II, 161.

4. Winnifrith, p. 101.

5. W. A. Craik, *The Brontë Novels* (London: Methuen, 1968), p. 48.

6. [Robert Martin, *The Accents of Persuasion* (London: Faber and Faber, 1966)] p. 34.

7. Martin, p. 41.

8. See, for example, the chapters on the novel in Winnifrith and [Lawrence Jay Dessner, The Homely Web of Truth: A Study of Charlotte Brontës Novels.

9. See Margaret Blom, *Charlotte Brontë,* Twayne's English Authors Series (Boston: G. K. Hall, 1977), p. 79.

10. Winifred Gérin advances this argument quite explicitly. See *Charlotte Brontë: The Evolution of Genius* (Oxford: Clarendon, 1967), pp. 316-32.

11. Quoted in [Roy Pascal, Design and Truth in Autobiography (London: Routledge and Kegan Paul, 1960)], p. 62.

12. Winnifrith, p. 90.

13. Charlotte Brontë, *The Professor,* ed. Phyllis Bentley (London: Collins, 1954), p. 299; hereafter cited in the text.

14. See *LFC,* II, 161, for Brontë's comments to W. S. Williams about illustrating her novels: ". . . I hope no one will be at the trouble to make portraits of my characters." Considering the intentional ambiguities in Brontë's conception of her characters, it is fortunate that drawings were not done; visual images would necessarily have oversimplified the characters. Smith, Elder and Co. honoured Brontë's wishes in their 1875 edition of the *Life and Works of Charlotte*

Brontë and her Sisters: they illustrated only landscapes and houses.

15. The notion of memories sealed in urns has at least two notable historical precedents which may have implications for Brontë's use. Sir Thomas Browne, in his "Urne-Buriall" ("Hydriotaphia," in *Sir Thomas Browne: The Major Works,* ed. C. A. Patrides [Harmondsworth, England: Penguin, 1977], pp. 261-315), emphasized the vanity of earthly memorials and the futility of man's hopes for immortality by means of these memorials. And John Locke, in his *An Essay Concerning Human Understanding* (ed. Raymond Wilburn [London: Dent, 1947]), discussed, using the same image, the fallibility of memory: "Thus the ideas, as well as children, of our youth, often die before us: and our minds represent to us those tombs to which we are approaching; where, though the brass and marble remain, yet the inscriptions are effaced by time, and the imagery moulders away" (p. 56). Brontë's self-deluded autobiographers, all of whom bury and hope to resurrect their pasts, partake of both the vanity which Browne deplores and the faulty recollection of the past which Locke attributes to all men.

16. Robert Martin sees the absence of further reference to the fourth picture as a flaw in the novel: "The author's red herrings succeed only in calling unproductive attention to herself and in distracting the reader from his involvement in the novel" (p. 38).

17. Lawrence Dessner discusses Crimsworth's psychosexual impulses as they are manifested in a number of his relationships (pp. 49-63).

18. Cynthia A. Linder, in her *Romantic Imagery in the Novels of Charlotte Brontë* (London: Macmillan, 1978), discusses Crimsworth's movement from Reuter's artificial garden to Daisy Lane's natural one (pp. 25ff.). In my opinion, Linder's discussion of this image and others neglects the novels' ironies. As I attempt to demonstrate, there are often discrepancies between the autobiographers' figurative purposes and the author's.

19. F. T. Flahiff has suggested that the several references in the novel to things that are green (such as the doormat by Frances' flat and her carpet) allude to her possible promiscuity.

20. *Their Proper Sphere: A Study of the Brontë Sisters as Early-Victorian Female Novelists* (London: Edward Arnold, 1966), p. 200.

21. Martin, p. 40.

22. Ewbank, p. 188.

23. Pascal, *Design and Truth in Autobiography,* pp. 189-90.

24. See Linder's discussion of nature imagery in the novel (pp. 29ff.).

25. Charlotte Brontë, *Five Novelettes: Passing Events, Julia, Mina Laury, Captain Henry Hastings, Caroline Vernon,* ed. Winifred Gérin (London: The Folio Press, 1971).

26. *LFC,* II, 136.

27. For example, Tom Winnifrith, whose position on the question of Crimsworth's development is more cautious than most, argues that "Crimsworth is a pitiful creature at the beginning of the novel and is perhaps unduly complacent at the end, but at any rate, *The Professor* traces some pattern of spiritual growth" (p. 96). Elsewhere (p. 51) Winnifrith notes that the Crimsworth of Daisy Lane is much changed from his former self.

Ruth D. Johnston (essay date 1989)

SOURCE: "*The Professor*: Charlotte Brontë's Hysterical Text, or Realistic Narrative and the Ideology of the Subject from a Feminist Perspective." In *Dickens Studies Annual: Essays on Victorian Fiction,* Vol. 18, edited by Michael Timko, Fred Kaplan, and Edward Guiliano, AMS Press, 1989, pp. 353-80.

[*In the following essay, Johnston uses Lacanian theory to examine* The Professor *and discusses the possibility of constructing feminine subjectivity within a realistic framework.*]

The essay which follows explores the construction of sexual identity *in* representation. I argue that the realistic notion of identity as a particular temporal/spatial structuration is assumed (if modified) in the psychoanalytic account of the constitution of the subject, which means that both the theory and aesthetic practice consequently furnish a model of subjectivity that is exclusively masculine. In this context I examine Charlotte Brontë's *The Professor* as a hysterical text, by which I mean a text that interrogates the possibility of constructing a feminine subjectivity in realistic signifying practices, the narrator's biological sex in this novel serving to render the repression of the feminine explicit. In addition, I choose this novel as an exemplary hysterical text because it also makes explicit the relation (actually the complicity) of retrospective narration and geometrical perspective (that is, literary and pictorial realism), a relationship which I also explore in my definition of realism, to which I now turn.

I regard temporal structure (which includes questions of enunciation and address) to be the fundamental feature of the nineteenth-century novel.[1] Time in a realistic narrative is conceived as a continuous and consistent medium stretching to infinity, which means that the significant distinction is past vs. present. (Contrast the medieval notion of time as discontinuous and its corollary that meaning derives from the opposition between earthly time and eternity.) Realistic time is thus analogous on the one hand to the definition of space in the Renaissance perspective system and on the other to the conception of nature in Western scientific thought in the post-Renaissance era. Such art and such science belong to an empirical epistemology, which presents knowledge as a process occurring between an already-constituted subject and object and consisting in the extraction of an essence from the real object.[2]

This knowledge process depends on temporal and spatial consistency to support the empiricist/realistic notion of identity as cumulative. Any appearance of an object is understood as only partial, making it necessary to compare a whole series of views in order to detect which elements are repeated. The "sameness" that emerges from such an examination and that enables us to recognize a structure is an abstraction that constitutes the object's identity. Note further that subject and object are constituted in relation to one another insofar as successive views are compared in relation to a single, fixed viewpoint. In fact, subjectivity is a product of this system of representation.[3] However, because the knowledge operation consists in the discrimination between the real (the essence) and the inessential (the purely accidental), a distinction which already exists in the structure of the real object, both the object and process of knowledge are thought to inhere in the real object. In short, what the empiricist concept of knowledge suppresses is the notion of knowledge as production (Althusser 36-38).

In literary realism, *dis*covery of identity is actually *recov*ery, for the process or temporal order to which a particular manifestation belongs can be apprehended only through the operation of memory, that is, retrospection. The identity of a person or object cannot be perceived immediately and independently but must be *recognized* through placement in the context of the whole system: memory must supply all the previous states which help to define that identity but which are not evident at present. In realistic narrative, memory operates on two levels: first, the characters' individual acts of recall, which are subordinated to/ encompassed by the second level, the retrospection of the narrator. As a result, the narrative continuously superimposes two viewpoints insofar as every moment is shown as concrete, occurring in the "present" (of the characters), and simultaneously as part of a process that occur*red* in the narrator's past, which explains why literary realism presupposes past-tense narration.

The narrating consciousness in a realistic narrative, which determines the temporal relations among events as it records them in some unspecified future, is the analogue of the implied spectator whose vision coordinates all spatial relations within the frame in a three-dimensional painting. The location of the narrator/spectator/subject *outside* the diegesis insures the continuity of space and time as well as the validity of the system beyond the scope of the text. But the price of such uniformity is the subject's alienation from concrete existence; for the focus of this disembodied consciousness is not the particulars in themselves but their relationship. This definition of focus in turn clarifies the designation of realism as mimesis; for what is imitated is not the concrete object but the system to which it belongs. It is the perpetuation of a particular logic or organization that is at stake—retrospective narrative in the case of literature, geometrical perspective in the case of painting. Thus realism refers to a system that is self-reflexive.

It is precisely this empiricist concept of knowledge which supports realism that Lacan regards Freud as having transformed by a Copernican revolution. Lacan conceives of psychoanalysis as a theory of the subject and quite explicitly states that his notion of the subject both assumes and differs from the Cartesian subject of consciousness (*Fundamental Concepts* 44). His elaboration proceeds from a linguistic analysis of the *cogito* in which he distinguishes two levels—that of enunciation (the moment of speaking) and that of the statement. (The difference between these two levels corresponds to the distinction mentioned above between the narrator's discourse and the character's discourse in literary realism, with exceptions noted below.)

Even though the present-tense verb invites us to conflate the speaking subject (of the enunciation) and the subject in the statement or proposition, Lacan insists that the two levels of the "I think" are irreducible. His distinction makes it clear that the subject of consciousness (of empiricism) "who thinks he can accede to himself by designating himself in the statement" necessarily regards himself as an object (*Écrits* 315). In Lacan's reading, however, the *cogito* takes its place at the level of enunciation, and the subject is inscribed in the vibration between the two levels. That is, the pronoun "I" in the statement is a signifier which in linguistics is called a "shifter" because it is unstable; it refers only to a function at the moment of utterance. Since it can only "designate," not "signify," the speaking subject, that subject is therefore reduced to a "punctuality of being" (*Écrits* 298; *Fundamental Concepts* 140).

This fragility of being is pushed to the extreme in Lacan's theory and becomes the "fading" of the subject, which is bound up with its splitting: the first division involves the distinction of self and sign, which results in another division between conscious and unconscious processes in discourse (*Fundamental Concepts* 141). Consequently, Lacan re-writes Descartes's *cogito* as Freud's *"Wo es war, soll Ich werden,"* which he translates as follows: "I am not wherever I am the plaything of my thought [that is, on the statement level, where the 'I' is taken as object of thought by the subject of consciousness]; I think of what I am where I do not think to think [the unconscious]" (*Écrits* 166).

This "fading" of the subject thus implies a disjunction between knowledge and consciousness (*Écrits* 302) insofar as the unconscious discourse (the locus of knowledge) erupts in the gaps of conscious discourse. This interference introduces a pulsative (radically discontinuous) temporal dimension into psychoanalytic epistemology: as in realism/empiricism, the Freudian subject also emerges from "where it was," but Lacan argues that the verb tense in Freud's *"Wo es war"* should not be taken as the aoristic but as "a distinct imperfect" which vascillates between "an extinction that is still glowing and a birth that is retarded," from which the subject emerges as it disappears from what is said (*Écrits* 300). Lacan calls this flickering process a dialectic but emphatically distinguishes it from Hegelian dialectic, which remains caught in the "mirage of consciousness" (*Écrits* 126).

Not only does Lacan's linguistic analysis of the *cogito* suggest a rewriting of the narrative structure that organizes literary realism, but his alignment of the Cartesian subject ("which is itself a sort of geometrical point, a point of perspective" [*Fundamental Concepts* 86]) with the subject constituted in the Renaissance perspective system (which is monocular, addressed to *one* eye only) implies a rewriting of pictorial realism as well.

Lacan argues that this geometrical system is not concerned with vision *per se* but with the rationalization of space (*Fundamental Concepts* 94) in relation to which the conscious subject is reduced to a "punctiform object," a "point of vanishing" (*Fundamental Concepts* 83). This geometrical dimension suggests the following empiricist schema of pictorial mimesis: I (the conscious subject of representation reduced to the punctiform from which perspective is grasped) am presented with an image beyond which is the object itself (*Fundamental Concepts* 106).

In this schema, what is elided in the illusion of consciousness—or seeing oneself see oneself—is the function of the gaze: the organization that governs the production, necessarily unconscious, of the subject in the visible (*Fundamental Concepts* 83). Therefore, in Lacan's rewriting, it is the subject that is turned into a picture or is "photo-graphed" (that is, inscribed in the visible). Thus Lacan superimposes on the empiricist schema another that inverts it in which the gaze (or point of light) is situated outside (in the place of the "beyond" of the object above) and determines the subject through the mediation of the screen (the mask that represents the subject in the visible and is situated in the place of the image in the schema above). The screen, unlike geometrical space, is not transparent but opaque. The gaze thus presents a play of light and opacity in which, if the subject figures at all, it is only as screen (*Fundamental Concepts* 96). In other words, Lacan locates the relation of appearance and being not between the image and the object as in the empiricist schema, but between the subject and the screen or mask. Mimesis in this sense can be compared with animal mimicry, which reveals that there is no "*itself* that is behind." Rather, in mimicry there is only the *effect* of camouflage, which is "not a question of harmonizing with the background but, against a mottled background, of becoming mottled" (*Fundamental Concepts* 99). In Lacan's mimesis there is not a mastery but a subjection to the background.

Lacan's emphasis on the production of the subject in discourse is extremely important for feminist theory in general insofar as it posits sexual identity as a cultural/linguistic effect, *not* a biological/natural given. And his articulation of the question of subjectivity in relation to geometrical perspective and linguistic/fictional structures makes his work indispensable to the consideration of the operation of ideology in literary and pictorial texts. But his theory stalls precisely in accounting for the production of feminine subjectivity because of his assumption that the phallus—the "privileged signifier" of division in language—"inaugurates" the procedure in both sexes (*Écrits* 287, 288). More specifically, Lacan insists on the distinction between the penis and the phallus, even criticizing their equation as merely "an imaginary effect" that results in a crude reduction of sexual difference to a visible perception (which does not, however, prevent this "mystification" from becoming culturally normative). Nevertheless, for Lacan this "imaginary function of the phallus" becomes "the pivot of the symbolic process that completes *in both sexes* the questioning of the sex by the castration complex" (*Écrits* 198, Lacan's italics). That is to say, the symbolic process (in contrast to the imaginary process that posits one-to-one correlations between image and reality) puts sexuality *per se* in question insofar as it entails the recognition of the phallus *qua* signifier, which means a recognition that it has no *natural* referent, that its status is that of a mark: arbitrary. Henceforth two different relations to this signifier of lack—a lack in being and a lack in having—will distinguish the sexes.

The problem here is the double function of the phallus—as signifier of lack *in* both sexes and of sexual difference *between* them. Vis-à-vis the second function, what is missing from the account is an explanation of why the little girl imagines herself as castrated, or why she also equates the penis with the phallus and sees herself from a masculine perspective that is already installed at this supposedly "inaugural" moment. For clearly, this moment involves the interpretation of a sight, and elsewhere Lacan insists that the imaginary and symbolic orders are *not* sequential stages in the development of the subject but processes that operate synchronically, dialectically (*Écrits* 54, 55; also *Fundamental Concepts* 63). Yet here, Lacan treats this "imaginary effect" or "pivot" as a condition of the symbolic, an origin or given which defines difference as a *natural* perception. Applying his own terms to the account, we can say that he himself elides the gaze here, the production of difference in the visible. In so contradicting his own theory of the subject, Lacan reverts to the very empiricist/idealist ideology he is at such pains to criticize, thereby ironically completing his return to Freud by repeating the naturalization of the scene of castration in the essay "Some Psychological Consequences of the Anatomical Distinction Between the Sexes."

There Freud describes the little boy's knowledge as retrospective, hence deriving from a constructed, temporalized process:

> . . . when a little boy catches sight of a girl's genital region, he begins by showing irresolution and lack of interest; he sees nothing or disowns what he has seen,

he softens it down or looks about for expedients for bringing it into line with his expectations. *It is not until later,* when some threat of castration has obtained a hold upon him, that the observation becomes important to him: *if he then recollects or repeats it,* it arouses a terrible storm of emotion in him and forces him to believe in the reality of the threat which he has hitherto laughed at.

(187, italics mine)

Is this not "emotions recollected in tranquility"? That is, significance for the boy subject depends on the temporal separation of the look and the threat (castration), perception and consciousness. His understanding involves a retrospective interpretation or reading of events instead of immediate perception, much as in realistic art the visible figure is separate from its full meaning or identity.

The little girl, on the other hand, when she notices the penis of a brother or playmate "makes her judgement and her decision in a flash. She has seen it and knows that she is without it and wants to have it" (187-88).[4] In contrast comprehension for the little girl apparently coincides with perception; her knowledge is described as immediate in the sense of unmediated, unconstructed. What this "immediacy" of vision glosses over is that the little girl in this scenario (necessarily) adopts a masculine perspective. The opposition retrospective/immediate sets up an illusory difference which in no way affects the interpretation of the sight; it merely obscures the circularity of the reasoning. For in the argument the only constructed vision or perspective is defined as masculine, and the little girl is "by nature" excluded from this structure of seeing, yet she sees exactly what the little boy sees, thereby grounding his constructed vision of her supposed inferiority *in nature,* in a sensory perception.

No wonder that in re-viewing the castration scene, Luce Irigaray argues that "the gaze is at stake from the outset" (*Speculum* 47), which in her view implies that the little girl's castration does not initiate the scene; rather, the scene accomplishes her castration by closing off the possibility of a different interpretation—of difference itself. For the little girl presents "the possibility of *a nothing to see.*" But instead of offering a challenge to an imaginary that privileges vision, her having nothing to see is defined "as her *having* nothing" (*Speculum* 48). In short, Irigaray questions not only why the little girl should see herself as a little boy, but also the predominance of vision over the other senses.

Notice too Irigaray's alignment of visual dominance with the imaginary, her insistence that the gaze is implicated from the "outset." In another essay she associates the subject with the imaginary:

any theory of the subject has always been appropriated by the "masculine." When she submits to (such a) theory, woman fails to realize that she is renouncing the specificity of her own relationship to the imaginary.

(*Speculum* 133)

Her argument is an indictment not of psychoanalytical theory as a whole but of its failure to investigate fully the implications of the theory, especially as regards the sexual determination of its discourse (*This Sex* 72-73). Irigaray specifically challenges Lacan's painstaking distinction between the imaginary order (which he associates with the ego or consciousness and its identifications) and the symbolic (the order of language, the unconscious, which determines the subject). Irigaray implies that the supposed difference between the two registers is illusory, that the theory does not begin to entertain the notion of heterogeneity, that it only offers more of the Same.

Her procedure entails a re-interpretation of the text that brings to the surface the complicity of the two orders "from the outset." Thus Lacan describes the effects of the mirror stage, in which the *infans* accomplishes the discrimination of discrete form, as pre-sexual: he locates the agency of the ego, "before its social determination," in a fictional direction that may approach but never coincide with the emergence of the subject (*Écrits* 2). Irigaray, on the other hand, argues that this ego is already socially determined as masculine insofar as the mirror stage marks the entry into the visible world, whose laws and values— symmetry, unity, identity—are alien and already exclusive of the feminine.

In other essays as well, Irigaray's procedure serves to reveal and to disrupt the dichotomies that serve to organize discourse in our culture, "including the one between enunciation and utterance," precisely because (and in direct contradistinction to Lacan) it makes possible the organization of the subject in that discourse in terms of yet another "onto-theo-logical" dichotomy: the subject-object relation (*This Sex* 78, 79, 80).

As we have seen, these dichotomies are crucial to Lacan's rewriting of the Cartesian *cogito*; he insists that they are operative even though the use of the shifter and the present tense verb obscure their function, and he situates his subject in the difference between the oppositional terms. Compare Irigaray's response to the question "Are you a woman?," which suggests how these dichotomies serve to reduce the idea of difference so that there is no place for the woman:

A man's question? I don't think a woman—unless she had been assimilated to masculine . . . models—would ask me that question.

Because "I" am not "I" [neither subject nor object, which means that quotation marks always surround the pronoun when the woman speaks], I *am* not [cannot exist in current discourse], I am not *one* [not one, coherent, identical, identifiable . . .]. As for *woman* try and find out . . . In any case, in this form, that of concept and of denomination, certainly not.

(*This Sex* 120)

Irigaray also interrogates linearity in reading, which although not in itself a dichotomy, similarly imposes a hierarchical organization upon the text. A consequence of phonetic writing, linearity organizes the text to move in a single, irreversible direction (which makes it "teleological") and enforces the principle of non-contradiction by subordinating all the elements (the word, the utterance, the sentence, even the phoneme) to retroactive interpretation, which means that its temporality is that of consciousness, the very retrospection (founded upon the opposition past/present) that divides the perceptible from the intelligible (at least for the little boy in Freud's castration scenario).

To sum up, if Lacan's theory enables us to look for *what* is repressed in realistic systems of representation, namely the division/production of the subject in representation, Irigaray's interrogation of psychoanalytic theory suggests *why* that production is repressed: in order to obscure the procedures whereby difference is reduced to the masculine model.

It is in these terms that I will now attempt a re-reading of *The Professor*: to discover the narrative processes that constitute the subject and to discover how these processes render feminine subjectivity impossible.

The fact that the narrator of *The Professor*, William Crimsworth, is male is not *in itself* significant. Insofar as all of Brontë's novels are retrospective, all her narrators are designated as masculine in their relations to language and structures of knowledge, and their biological sex serves only to make these relations either explicit or implicit in the event of a shift in position. Initially, therefore, *The Professor* seems not unlike many other first-person nineteenth-century novels, aside from Brontë's, in which the doubling of mature and young perspectives of the protagonist is analogous to the more usual doubling of omniscient narrator's and protagonist's consciousnesses, for this temporal distance suffices to create an emotional distance that situates the narrator outside the fictional world in a position of control of the diegesis. In fact, this is so much the case in *The Professor*, at least on the surface, that Terry Eagleton argues that "it is really in a sense a third-person narration. Crimsworth delivers his success-story externally, judiciously, treating himself as an admirable object of his own narration" (77).

Such a description invites a comparison between Crimsworth and another male narrator who is (literally) present to himself as a third person, Henry Esmond. But what emerges from this juxtaposition is precisely that the great difference between the autobiographical narratives can be accounted for in terms of their very different temporal structures. For Esmond writes as if he had moved "outside of time." He frequently states that young Esmond felt this way or remembered such a thing to the last day or last hour of his life.[5] While it is true that by the end of his narrative Crimsworth distances himself from the action level to such an extent that the "evenings passed in that little parlor" with Frances resemble "a long string of rubies," each gem "unvaried" (218), far more frequently in the novel, especially in the two middle sections, Crimsworth is literally and figuratively near-sighted, a deficiency which threatens his control over his own story. In these instances he can be said to assume a "feminine" position in relation to language and to knowledge. It is here where Crimsworth's biological sex comes into play, raising the question of the relation between biology and representation and making explicit the manner in which realistic narrative constitutes the "feminine" only as a deficient version of the masculine.

The connection between narrative control and the temporal structure is registered at the beginning of the Belgian section when William-narrator conceives of his autobiography as a series of four pictures hanging in the cell where he keeps his records, each representing a stage of his life. The last picture, which is draped, he may choose not to reveal. (But in saying so, he reveals that he has a choice; he displays his mastery.) He does, however, describe the three unveiled paintings, and each picture has a spatial perspective that corresponds to, is a metaphor for, the temporal structure that organizes the respective portion of William's narrative. The Eton picture, for instance, "is in far perspective, receding, diminutive" (45), which means that this part of his life is viewed from the mature narrator's temporally distant perspective and as such accords with the way his early youth is verbally represented in the letter to Charles which prefaces his narrative. Not only its status as preface and as letter, but also its texture sets it apart from the subsequent narrative. Thus while several critics, Charles Burkhart among them, call William's introductory letter "Charlotte's nod to the past, the earlier epistolary style of Richardson" (51), it is most *un*-Richardsonian because it becomes an instrument for strong control over the past via retrospection and summary rather than immediacy, as well as over the reader via extreme discretion, even disdain, rather than confidentiality.

The insufficiency of temporal distance and consequent lack of mastery which are more characteristic of the middle sections of the narrative are made evident in the second picture hanging in William's cell, which represents his life at X—. It is a picture of unmitigated lack of differentiation. It shows unrelieved bleakness in "a yellow sky, sooty clouds; no sun, no azure; the verdure of the suburbs blighted and sullied—a very dreary scene" (45). This picture also lacks any spatial perspective which figuratively places this stage temporally in relation to the narrator. Whereas the figures in the Eton picture are diminutive, here the canvas itself is "huge." And there appears to be no retrospective filter through which its unmixed hues/emotional tones are recalled. Significantly, the description is merely a series of nouns and adjectives; there are no verbs here to express temporal relationships. (In contrast, William says the Eton picture "*is* in far perspective," relating it to the narrator's time level, while his childhood "*was* not all sunshine," the past tense serving to distance the events recorded in the pictorial representation.) Furthermore, besides being "huge," the canvas of the X—picture itself is said to be "dingy," "cracked and smoked"

(45). Inasmuch as the canvas becomes part of the scene represented on it, the distinction between reality and its representation dissolves and along with it that between subject and object.

The third picture hanging in William's record chamber, this one of Belgium, complicates the relation of subject and object in another way by transforming the spectator into an auditor. No visual image of this landscape is provided; instead, William describes the emotions which the sound of the word "Belgium" evokes in him. The switch from the visual to the aural thus signals yet another model of retrospection, the evocation of the past as echo, which is more ephemeral and more immediate than any fixed visual representation, even one which collapses the distinction between object and image as the second picture does. Thus on the one hand, "Belgium" represents a past that is not so remote as Eton: it continues to affect the narrator emotionally, for he says, using the present tense, "*whenever uttered has* in my ear a sound, in my heart an echo, such as no other assemblage of syllables, however sweet or classic, can produce" (45, italics mine). And this sense of presence is reenforced by the use of such terms as "resurrection" and "ghosts" to designate these memories. On the other hand, insofar as the resurrection is tied to the sensation which evokes it, it defies permanent as well as definitive (pictorial or verbal) formulation, which impermanence William suggests when he laments the difficulty of articulating such emotions:

> but while I gaze on their vapoury forms, and strive to ascertain definitely their outline, the sound which wakened them dies, and they sink . . . like a wreath of mist, absorbed in the mould, recalled to urns, resealed in monuments.
>
> (45)

It is tempting to interpret this sound-picture as a model for a feminine signifying practice, not only because of William's positive response to it (in contrast to his negative attitude toward the second picture) but also because in some feminist theories feminine writing is described in terms of closeness to voice, which is a version of the supposed privileged relation between the woman and the pre-Oedipal phase. For the voice is conceived as the voice of the mother and in terms of proximity to the body, in opposition to vision, which creates distance. Hélène Cixous, for example, argues that women's privileged relation to the imaginary affords them a privileged (but not exclusive) relation to writing, which she associates with voice:

> The Voice sings from a time before law, before the Symbolic took one's breath away and reappropriated it into language under its authority of separation.
>
> (*The Newly Born Woman* 93)

Julia Kristeva furnishes an interesting counter-example: she substitutes the term *semiotic* for Lacan's imaginary and associates it with pre-Oedipal oral and anal processes whose articulation she designates the *chora,* a pulsative modality that precedes figuration and is analogous only to

"vocal or kinetic rhythm" and which interacts with the symbolic in the signifying process (24-28). Kristeva, however, refuses to associate the semiotic specifically with the feminine on the grounds that such an identification defines the feminine as essence. She thereby pinpoints the problem with any idea of feminine writing such as the one advanced by Cixous. At the same time, Kristeva's own theory can be criticized because it fails to distinguish women's oppression from that of other marginal and dissident groups, as though the male avant-garde writers whom she always cites as her examples can represent the oppression of women, Blacks, the working class, and so forth.

In this connection, Mary Ann Doane's caveat that as a challenge to the existing hierarchical power structure of the senses investment in the voice risks recuperation either as some form of essentialism or as a form of romanticism is very apropos ("Voice in the Cinema" 48-49). And indeed, the model of retrospection offered in the third picture can be described as an evanescent revival of a Wordsworthian "picture of the mind." As such it forms a sequence with the other two paintings that recapitulates in miniature the narrative tradition which Brontë inherited. The Eton picture designates a model of distant retrospection that evokes but exaggerates the narrative structures appropriated from spiritual autobiography (for example, by Defoe) to impose a providential pattern on the protagonist's experience; the picture of X—recalls Richardson's "writing to the moment" pushed to extreme limits. Like the other two pictures, the Wordsworthian model is also exaggerated so as to make explicit its procedures and assumptions.

For recall that Wordsworth's retrospective narratives are poems, which means that they imitate spoken rather than written discourse. (No doubt that is why we refer to the "narrator" as the "speaker.")[6] Accordingly, the poems actualize both the speaker and the instance of uttering more than other texts—specifying to a greater degree the speaker's intonation and gestures by means of meter, spacing, punctuation, typography, and particularizing the speaker's spatial and temporal location (as the realistic narrator's is not) as well as that of the person addressed (for example, the speaker's sister in "Tintern Abbey" as opposed to the unspecified reader of a realistic text)—all in an effort to create the illusion of presence.

But it is only an illusion, for the poet is not present, and the poem is not spoken but re-cited in accordance with written instructions furnished in the text. The illusion functions to suppress the operation of reproductive mechanisms that regulate sound (harmonize it, impose a rhythm on it, modulate the pitch) and govern its transformation into language. The reference to "echo" in connection with the third picture of Brontë's text, therefore, makes evident the hidden repetition to which sound is subjected in such recitation. As Irigaray observes, the echo is a representation which presupposes a single speaker and depends on the intervention of neutral blanks and silences in order to permit "words and their repetition to be discriminated and separated out and framed"; in this doubling process, the hiatus divides the present from the past, which it defines "as a present which has taken place" (*Speculum* 257).

Applying this notion of echo to Wordsworth's poems (staying with "Tintern Abbey" as our exemplary model), we can say that the relation between the text or script and the speech act that it imitates, exactly duplicates the relationship *within* the poem between the speaker's memory and his past sensory perception, which he never recaptures, only re-constructs, although the poem creates the illusion of temporal continuity through superimposition—of the speaker's memory ("the picture of the mind") and a revival of that picture on the one hand; of the speaker's current relation to the past and his sister's repetition of that relation in the future on the other hand. Superimposition is a device that depends on/insures the preservation of the distinction between past, present, and future in order to create the illusion of continuity between the speaker's present and past selves; it indicates the speaker's investment in an empiricist notion of identity. Hence romanticism can be regarded as a *qualified* form of realism.

In Brontë's text, on the other hand, the proximity articulated in terms of the perspectives organizing the middle two pictures is manifested in William's narrative account of these stages of his life as *disruptions* of the retrospective temporal structure. Although the narrative is related in past tense for the most part, the present tense being reserved to designate the narrator's time zone, certain other present-tense insertions close the temporal gap between protagonist and narrator and make it difficult to distinguish the two time zones. One such disruption occurs when William-narrator portrays some of his students at Mlle. Reuter's pensionnat. Incidentally, he calls these descriptions "sketches" taken from his portfolio, and in fact pictures are used throughout the narrative to objectify his consciousness of other characters. However, because these are portraits, the perspective system is not specified as it is in the landscapes cited above. Instead, he uses scientific discourse to set them at a distance: he calls them "specimens," which he is careful to locate as to "genus" and "class." Furthermore, the descriptions follow a deductive order, moving from placement in a class or country to more specific, individual traits, most of which are selected according to the principles of the science of phrenology. Despite the use of scientific discourse, however, the first sketch, that of Aurelia Koslow, is given in present tense, which might be rationalized by locating the "sketch" in the narrator's time zone. However, even the account of her habitual behavior in class, which follows the description, is given in present tense: "The moment I enter the room, she nudges her next neighbor and indulges in a half-suppressed laugh. As I take my seat on the estrade, she fixes her eye on me . . ." (85). It is difficult to account for the present tense here except as William-narrator's failure to subordinate the past to the present, in other words his immersion or absorption into/by the past, because in the parallel sketch of the second student, Adèle Dronsart, he uses *past* tense to describe *her* habitual behavior in class: ". . . when I looked along the row of young heads, my eye generally stopped at this of Adèle's; her gaze was ever waiting for mine; and it frequently succeeded in arresting it" (86-87). It is unnecessary to discuss his sketch of the third student, Juanna Trista, except to say that it is given entirely in the past tense and therefore resists correlation with either one of the patterns established by the first two sketches.

Because the narrator's perspective is so close to the protagonist's, indeed at times collapses into it, it is especially significant that within the diegesis William-protagonist also occasionally experiences difficulties in separating the object from its representation. His response to his mother's portrait on the occasion of Edward Crimsworth's birthday party registers just such a confusion. William's lack of introduction to any of the young ladies present at the celebration thwarts his desire to dance with them. So though "tantalised,"[7] he instead seeks out his mother's picture and proceeds to relate to it in a manner that merges desire and identification, which is to say substitutes a narcissistic relationship that represents the unresolved masculine version of the Oedipus. Specifically, William recognizes that his "heart grew to the image" because it is "a softened and refined likeness" of himself. Interestingly, this Oedipal configuration is immediately balanced by the "feminine" version, for the narrator uses a simile that compares William's pleasure in looking at the portrait to that of fathers who find in their daughters' faces "their own similitude . . . flatteringly associated with softness of hue and delicacy of outline" (18).

Notice that both versions similarly align sexual difference with subject-object positions: the subject is always male (son or fathers), the object female (mother or daughters). On the other hand, a reversal in the subject/object opposition insofar as it refers to genealogy is suggested by the transposition of generations (offspring looks at parent; parents look at offspring), which not only subverts chronology but further implies, since the offspring is the image of the parent and vice-versa, that neither is the original. Moreover, insofar as the figure compares biological and artistic modes of reproduction, it also blurs the distinction between reality and its representation: the mother's *portrait* and *real* daughters are equated in that they evoke similar responses. But since the fathers and daughters are part of a simile, they exist only figuratively in contrast to the "reality" of William and his mother's picture. In Lacan's terms, the experience may therefore be said to belong to the Imaginary register. But in this imaginary, sexual difference is already operative in that feminine subjectivity is foreclosed regardless of the inversions that occur.

If the mother's portrait is a sort of mirror image because William both desires and identifies with it and so implicitly jeopardizes his subject position, when he literally looks in the mirror, he sees himself quite specifically as an object of desire. On his way to his first interview with Mlle. Reuter he says,

I remember very well that before quitting my chamber, I held a brief debate with myself as to whether I should change my ordinary attire for something smarter. At last I concluded it would be a waste of labour. . . . And off I started, cursorily glancing sideways as I passed the toilet-table, surmounted by a looking glass: a thin, *ir*regular face I saw with sunk, dark eyes under a large, square forehead, complexion *destitute* of bloom or attraction; something young, but *not* youthful, *no object to win a lady's love, no* butt for the shafts of Cupid.

(65, italics mine)

William is here relating to himself as women habitually relate to themselves. He is seeing himself as *someone else* would see him, while he identifies with the object. And this position occurs "at the cost of [his]self being split into two."[8] At the same time, the fact that there is a *literal* mirror in this instance and that he is *literally* (biologically) male makes explicit (1) that his designation as "feminine" is purely a construction of the process of looking and refers only to a position in relation to the image; (2) that the position is constructed in negative terms as the forfeit of subjectivity. Both these "mirror images" are, moreover, significant as analogues within the diegesis to William-narrator's project of writing his autobiography, a literary exercise that is conventionally described as looking at oneself to paint a self-portrait.

The passages above suggest a problematic relation to the symbolic order, hence to signifying systems. This dis-ease accounts for the distrust of language registered in a number of ways throughout the narrative. First, Brontë's characters use an idiom which may be described as highly formal, oratorical, or dramatic. These extremities of language suggest how the characters must strain to imbue speech with emotional tones that ordinary words lack.

The narrator as well as the protagonists finds ordinary language inadequate to articulate the feelings and attitudes he wishes to describe. Frequently he inserts self-conscious explanations about his choice of words which call attention to the process of writing. Furthermore, a tension marks the estrangement of the narrator from his language. This tension is revealed in the violent metaphors and the tendency to describe things by their opposites, that is, negatively (Kroeber 191). For instance, Chapter 19 opens with a rejection of extremes of emotion as inappropriate in a realistic representation: if novelists conscientiously studied real life, says the narrator, "they would give us fewer pictures chequered with vivid contrasts of light and shade . . ." (140). Despite this prescription, the narrator proceeds to specify what will be excluded, precisely those agonies of men "who have plunged like beasts into sensual indulgence," who then are "wrung together with pain, stamped into the churchyard sod by the inexorable hell of despair." Moreover, these agonies are not discernably less intense than the pain of "the man of regular life and rational mind," described in paragraph 2 in terms of "acute pain" which "racks him," "writhing limbs," Death which "roots up and tears violently away" what he loves. In

short, extremes of emotion are presented (negatively) even as they are overtly rejected. This incomplete sublimation makes evident the contradictions that are ordinarily rationalized in the realistic text, which in turn exposes realism as a homogenizing process.

Another signal of the distrust of language consists in the use of phrenology and physiognomy, which constitutes an attempt to transform physical characteristics into fixed signs indicating inner qualities, giving access to the reality hidden beneath the surface appearance, which is seen as a disguise. Even in the classroom context, which disposes of social, economic, and class roles, outward behavior provides no clear index of true motives. For instance, Pelet is discovered to hide his "flint or steel under an external covering of velvet" (58). And even William's professorial role is a mask which disguises his own vulnerability and lack of confidence in his relations with his students. Thus he acts (in both senses of the word) quite haughty and contemptuous on his first day in M. Pelet's school because his French is not quite good enough to go into lengthy explanations at this point (52-53). One might say that his students' latent rebelliousness and lack of interest in their studies force William to assume such a mask. Yet he also wears the "garb of austerity" in dealing with Frances, his eager and beloved pupil, to "cloak" a "kindness as mute as watchful" (131). William's sternness, therefore, is not a simple deception; it defies consistent interpretation.[9] Hence the use of these two sciences in physical description is an attempt to objectify inherent mental qualities and bypass the surface manifestation of ordinary intercourse, in short, to pin down meaning.

Yet the antagonism towards language within the novel goes even further: finally, the characters resort to nonverbal communication as the most direct and truthful. While words often disguise true motives, the body, especially the eye, speaks for those who can read. For example, in the exchange between Hunsden and William following the latter's loss of position, William refuses to express in words his gratitude to Hunsden for precipitating a confrontation with William's brother, Edward. William perversely pretends that Hunsden has lost him the job he wanted. But,

I could not repress a half-smile as I said this. . . .

"Oh! I see!" said he, looking into my eyes, and it was evident he *did* see right down to my heart.

(41)

William and Mlle. Reuter also communicate through eye language. After his first class she asks him about the three unruly girls who sit in the front row. His words are dismissive, and she ceases to question him,

but her eye—. . . showed she was even with me; it let out a momentary gleam, which said plainly, "Be as close as you like, I am not dependent on your candour; what you would conceal I already know."

(75)

And, of course, such non-verbal communication occurs throughout the novel between William and Frances, who begin to speak eye language immediately when William reads the appeal in Frances's eye to dictate more slowly on her first day in class (107).

Note that in each of these instances the characters may bypass the word through the exchange of looks, but insofar as William-narrator translates such exchanges, the narrative discourse does not similarly eschew verbalization. The recourse to eye language, then, merely exaggerates and thereby reveals the gap that always divides the perceptible (the characters' actions) from the intelligible (the narrator's interpretation) in the realistic text. However, just because that gap is so obvious here, the translation that spans it appears farfetched: just *how* does a "momentary gleam" say all that? Certainly not "plainly." Again, the strain put upon the translation process exposes it *qua* process (as does the recourse to a fixed code of interpretation in the case of physiognomy).

On other occasions, however, the text offers no interpretation; it just registers. Examples include William's mysterious bout of hypochondria following his marriage proposal to Frances and the strange wrestling match that William and Hunsden engage in upon leaving Frances's house after Hunsden's first meeting with her. Critics repeatedly complain about the irrelevance of the hypochondria to the plot (see Martin 40; Ewbank 188). Even Crimsworth asks, "Why did hypochondria accost me now?" (203). But the incident's significance derives precisely from this irrelevance: it indicates the existence of material so complex and contradictory that it defies rationalization by the narrative discourse. So does the second incident. True, the struggle occurs in part as a result of William's having misled Hunsden about Frances's supposed social inferiority. During their meeting Hunsden has learned the enormous insufficiency of her description as a mere lacemender. (In other words, the physical struggle is sparked by a statement that is *literally* accurate.) However, this explanation of the incident is no more adequate than the description of Frances that ostensibly prompts it. After all, the two men end up rolling over the pavement: their conflict is too fierce to be regarded as a mere response to William's teasing. Moreover, William "*grappled* [Hunsden] round the waist" (215), which means that however fierce, the struggle is also an embrace.[10] Neither incident, then, is thoroughly integrated into the narrative. Consequently, the text forces the reader as well to strain against the limits of discourse in an attempt to apprehend these strange relationships, even at the risk of alienating him/her. Eagleton's criticism of Crimsworth's defiance of the reader makes it clear that this risk is not negligible:

> Not even the reader must be allowed to slip under his guard; and this is why in reading his narrative we have the exasperated sense that he is telling us only what he wants us to know . . . he treats the reader with something like the stiff, wary circumspection with which he handles Mdlle. Reuter.
>
> (79)

I do not happen to share Eagleton's exasperation because for me this defiance is a mode of interrogating certain dominant narrative conventions. And the antagonism to language expressed by the violent metaphors, the negative presentation of characters and events, the use of phrenology and physiognomy, and the attempt to replace speech with extra-verbal communication ultimately ties in with the use of pictures, especially the portrait, throughout the narrative to designate material (that is, undischarged emotion) which cannot be contained by the narrative discourse or accommodated by the plot. Geoffrey Nowell-Smith, writing on melodrama, has suggested an analogy between eruptions of such excesses in the narrative text and the

> mechanisms of "conversion hysteria": in hysteria, the energy discharged by an idea that has been repressed is displaced onto the bodily symptom. The hysterical moment of the melodramatic text, which otherwise adheres to the principles of realistic representation, occurs at precisely those points where the displacement of emotion ruptures the realistic conventions.
>
> (117)

Now the notion of the hysterical text is particularly interesting in light of the classic correlation between hysteria and femininity, which requires further elaboration at this point. Recent feminist theory demonstrates that the hysterical character is merely an exaggeration of the feminine norm, that the case histories of Anna O. and Dora simply present extreme pathological versions of that norm. Freud himself suggested as much: "In a whole series of cases the hysterical neurosis is nothing but an excessive overaccentuation of the typical wave of repression through which the masculine type of sexuality is removed and the woman emerges" ("Hysterical Attacks" 157).

The reason for the correlation between hysteria and femininity is the twofold prohibition imposed on the woman. Like the little boy, she must give up the mother to accommodate a third person, but this renunciation is problematic for her because she can neither substitute the father as the object of her desire nor identify with him. The either/or opposition is transformed in her case into a neither/nor, and she is twice barred from assuming the position of subject of desire. (The little boy's Oedipal itinerary, on the other hand, enables him to exchange his passive relation to the mother for the possibility of a different, active kind of sexual pleasure.) The hysterical symptom can be viewed, then, as an effect on the woman of this double-bind situation because as a sign, the symptom bypasses consciousness and ordinary language as it registers on the body the clash between the impulse to signify desire and the multiple cultural injunctions that block her access to the place and means of its articulation (Freud, "Hysterical Phantasies" 150).

It is tempting to consider this symptom as an alternative mode of signifying in view of the fact that the "cure" for hysteria is talking—the translation of unconscious wish into conscious discourse. However, insofar as such translation forces the hysteric to assume a position that conforms more closely to the culturally defined norms, certain distortions accompany the conscious articulation of the wish, which indicate that the hysteric is more the victim than the perpetrator of the "duplicity" that characterizes the hysteric's discourse. More specifically, the commonly reported scenarios of seduction by the father, which Freud only later identified as "the expression of the typical Oedipus complex in women" ("Femininity" 106), transpose fantasy into fact and invert the subject-object relation through the use of the passive voice so that her desire *for* the father is transformed into her seduction *by* him (Laplanche 33-34). It is only through recourse to such distortion that desires so socially unacceptable can surface in consciousness (which, incidentally, clarifies why Crimsworth's Oedipal relation to his mother's portrait is explicitly compared to fathers' pleasures in looking at their daughters). Thus the talking cure may alleviate the symptom but does not at all address the cultural imperatives that precipitated the disease in the first place. As Freud explained to his patients, he could help them only to transform their "hysterical misery into common unhappiness" (*Studies on Hysteria* 305).

For this reason, it is quite interesting that in so many cases of hysteria the treatment was not completed.[11] The instance of Dora is just the most famous of these. Peggy Kamuf argues that although Freud regarded this patient's abrupt termination of the sessions as an act of revenge designed to rob him of satisfaction in the success of his therapeutic efforts, it is possible, if we view the interruption from Dora's perspective, to see it as a protest or resistance to the submissive silence and passivity she could anticipate as the effect of her total cure and return to the norm (55).

Of course, this is mere speculation with regard to Dora, since in fact her perspective is not represented in Freud's case history. But it raises the issue of whether and how we can regard the hysterical symptom as a form of protest. Just what kind of resistance does it offer? Not a refusal of normative "feminine" identity in favor of some "other" sexuality, as perhaps Freud's references to the hysteric's bisexuality imply (see "Hysterical Phantasies" 150, 151). For the only "other" option offered by bisexuality is identification with a masculine position (as in the explanation of Dora's homosexual love for Frau K).

Resistance should rather be understood in the sense of questioning the interpretation that is imposed on the symptom, interrogating the ideology of the interpretation (Irigaray, *This Sex* 137). This means interrogating sexual identity *per se* by retraversing the history of the "feminine" subject as represented by the hysterical symptom, which Freud called a "memory symbol" because its particular form corresponds to some detail of the repressed phantasy ("Hysterical Phantasies" 149). An investigation of the relation between symptom and memory in Freudian theory might then be brought to bear on the analysis of a retrospective narrative like *The Professor.*

Freud observed that the correlation between the symptom and the repressed phantasy becomes obscured through the symptom's

representing several phantasies simultaneously by means of the same material, that is, through *condensation.* . . . The phantasies thus made to coincide are often of quite different kinds, for instance, a recent wish and the re-activation of an infantile impression. . . .

("Hysterical Attacks" 153-54)

Also, symptoms can have several meanings in succession (*Dora* 70).

No wonder, then, that Freud found hysterics incapable of producing precise histories of their illness: their memories left gaps; connections remained incoherent; the sequence of events was uncertain. He regarded this impaired memory as *"a necessary correlate of the symptoms and one which is theoretically requisite"* (*Dora* 32, Freud's italics). He further maintained that the talking cure was designed to restore the memory:

> It is only towards the end of the treatment that we have before us an intelligible, consistent, and unbroken case history. Whereas the practical aim of the treatment is to remove all possible symptoms and to replace them by conscious thoughts, we may regard it as a second and theoretical aim to repair all damages to the patient's memory. These two aims are coincident. When one is reached, so is the other; and the same path leads to them both.[12]

(*Dora* 32)

But, in fact, this promise of total recall is never realized first of all because the pre-Oedipal phase of mother-attachment, deemed critical to the account of the hysteric's bisexuality, "has in analysis seemed . . . so elusive, lost in a past so dim and shadowy, so hard to resuscitate, that it seemed as if it had undergone some specially inexorable repression." This phase has been obscured insofar as the women Freud has analyzed "have been able to cling on to that very father-attachment in which they took refuge from the early phase," rendering insight into the pre-Oedipus phase "comparable in another field with the effect of the discovery of the Minoan-Mycenaean civilization behind that of Greece" ("Female Sexuality" 195, 196). Actually, the emphasis on the archaic quality of the relation to the mother is just a decoy. For the phase is *not* problematic simply or primarily for that reason. (As Irigaray demonstrates, the pre-Oedipal phase is already sexually inflected to privilege the masculine model.) Moreover, Freud fails to distinguish the connection between the phase and the etiology of hysteria from the relation of *all* women to the phase of mother-attachment. Thus his assertion that "both the phase and the neurosis . . . are characteristically feminine" ("Female Sexuality" 196) merely implies that all women are hysterical by some inherent predisposition: it explains nothing.

As for that relatively more accessible father attachment, it too resists total recall because it is not exempt from the operation of *Nachträglichkeit* or *deferred action*, even if Freud seems to repress its function in the quotation above which promises complete restoration of memory. As

Laplanche and Pontalis remark, the English translation of the term is somewhat misleading. The term does not refer to the intervention of a time-lapse between stimulus and response but to a reworking or revision of psychic material at a later time and therefore to a complex temporal logic which undermines the linear determinism implicit in any straightforward narration of events (*Language of Psycho-analysis* 112-14). The notion is described in a number of Freud's texts, but it receives one of its fullest elaborations in the 1895 "Project for a Scientific Psychology," where it is associated with Freud's formulation of the concept of trauma as part of his seduction theory, which is also a theory of repression.

According to the theory, the symptom refers to an experience that was never present, not only because the existence of so many instances of actual seduction is doubtful, but also, and more importantly, because only the memory of the scene or event gives rise to the affect.[13] More specifically, in the "Project" Freud recounts two scenes brought to light in the analysis of a hysteric he calls Emma. In the earlier scene an adult (a shopkeeper) makes a sexual overture to the eight-year-old child, which she does not understand. (Hence the scene is not sexual *for her.*) The second scene, which is nonsexual but bears some incidental resemblance to the first (two shop assistants laugh at her clothes), activates the memory of the earlier scene, now understood because she has reached puberty in the interval. On this occasion she experiences a sexual release, which turns into anxiety and which is followed by her totally forgetting (repressing) the first scene. Freud writes,

> it is a highly noteworthy fact that [the sexual release] was not linked to the assault when it was actually experienced. Here we have an instance of a memory exciting an affect which it had not excited as an experience, because in the meantime changes produced by puberty had made possible a new understanding of what was remembered.
>
> Now this case is typical of repression in hysteria. We invariably find that memory is repressed which has only become a trauma *after the event.*
>
> (*Origins* 413, Freud's italics)

In other words, the notion of deferred action means that trauma cannot be located in a specific event because it is suspended between two temporally separated events as well as two registers of meaning: perception and consciousness. Freud thus assumes a psychical apparatus structured by a process of stratification, which renders any linear conception of causality untenable.[14] Trauma, therefore, does not refer to the cause of the symptom in the form of a simple experience; rather, it is the after-affect of a process of interpretation. In short, *Nachträglichkeit* puts in question the primacy of event over significance (in the case of Emma, sexual *meaning* must be available to her in order for her to *experience* sexual release); indeed, it subverts the very idea of original event or primal scene.

The "Project," therefore, rules out any simple causal association of hysterical symptom with the pre-Oedipus (in the sense of pre-sexual) because it undermines the notion of simple causal relations on the one hand and specifies the hysterical symptom as the *deferred* effect of a *seduction* scenario on the other. It is perhaps significant that at the time of writing the "Project" Freud had not yet identified such seduction scenes with the feminine Oedipus complex nor predicated the special significance of an archaic relation of the daughter to the mother. Possibly because his theory of feminine sexuality was *not* at stake, he was able to elaborate the knowledge process that constitutes the feminine subject.

Interestingly, it is the very same retrospective procedure that produces castration anxiety in the little boy (for example, in the castration scene described in "Some Psychological Consequences of the Anatomical Distinction Between the Sexes") and marks his entry into the symbolic order and consciousness. It is this process which constructs the feminine subject as hysteric, which is to say impossible, because for her it is primarily a process of repression. The difference between *his* consciousness and access to language and *her* repression can be aligned with two different notions of cause in these scenes. Recall that in the castration scenario a cause is designated in the form of a sight that inaugurates the boy's castration anxiety; but in the hysteria scenario delineated in the "Project," the cause is missing insofar as trauma is conceived as a *relation* between events: trauma is not the cause but the *effect* of consciousness.

For Lacan the significance of this absence of cause in trauma is that it reveals the function of the real in relation to the symbolic as encounter "in so far as it is essentially the missed encounter," that is, as that which is "unassimilable." Lacan thus conceives of the real as *"en souffrance,"* a phrase that means "pending" or "in abeyance" as well as "in pain." Hence Lacan's definition of the real as "impossible" (*Fundamental Concepts* 55-56). Thus Lacan detaches the significance of trauma from the hysteria scenario and generalizes its application, which is to say that he assimilates the concept of trauma to the masculine model. (Significantly, most of his references are to the traumatic primal scene elaborated in the Wolfman case history.)

For Irigaray, on the other hand, hysteria is *not* displaced by the "real" in general as the "privileged place for preserving—but 'in latency,' 'in sufferance'—that which does not speak" (*This Sex* 136). Nor does she overlook the crucial distinction between the castration and hysteria scenarios; for her, the absence of cause in the latter indicates that the woman's relationship to the origin has been appropriated, the hysteria scenario thereafter being "condemned as so many 'bad' copies or gross caricatures of a 'good,' and valuable and valid, relationship to origin" (*Speculum* 60). For Irigaray it is feminine sexuality, not some generalized "real," that is "impossible": she demonstrates not *that* Lacan is ultimately wrong about the significance of trauma in the hysteria scenario but *how,* once again, he overlooks the sexual determination of that scene.

In this context, the hysterical moment in the text, specifically **The Professor,** clearly does not refer to the "return of the repressed" in the sense of a feminine essence that emerges in the content or a specifically feminine signifying practice that correlates with a particular literary form. Rather, the hysterical moment refers to those knots which cannot be comprehended by the realistic narrative system, which resist assimilation to consciousness and which therefore render totalization impossible. Invoking the logic whereby the exception proves the rule, the moment of hysterical rupture exposes the self-reflexive processes of realistic representation as processes that foreclose feminine subjectivity.

Surely it is not necessary to rehearse at this point the various strategies noted in the analysis of **The Professor** that bring to the surface the sexual determination of its procedures—the collapse of the oppositions whose implicit hierarchical organization insures the continuity of time, of space, of identity; the presentation of material that cannot be accommodated by the narrative discourse, and so on. But there is one aspect of the process that does require another word: the resistance of the reader.

The reader's function is crucial in realistic representation: all the reflexive structures within the text function to perpetuate the system by re-producing the same model of subjectivity—the masculine model. The reader is that subject. But what kind of subject/reader is constituted in **The Professor**? The reader, no less than the characters, becomes temporally disoriented on those occasions when the use of the present tense makes it difficult to discriminate past from present, narrator from protagonist.

Furthermore, in this novel the reader is denied omniscience first of all because his/her knowledge is subject to the limitations and fallibilities of Crimsworth's experience and memory. Of course, those limits apply to all autobiographical narrators (which is why there can be no simple correlation between narrative form and gender), but Crimsworth seems more unable than most to provide a smooth history (for example, the hypochondria incident). Secondly, this limitation is not strictly just a matter of the narrator's fallible memory and circumscribed experience: it also involves the reader's alienation. For the narrator's deliberate withholding of information keeps the reader at bay. Thus the identification mechanisms, which realism so heavily depends upon for the perpetuation of ideology and which can sometimes offer a distinct pleasure to compensate for the reader's limited access to knowledge, are here disrupted.

Disoriented, denied knowledge, denied identification—the reader's access to subjectivity is thus twice barred in this text. The reader's resistance to this foreclosure (evident, for example, in the harsh criticism leveled at the novel as noted above) is the measure of his/her determination by precisely those procedures in other, more realistic, representations. Paradoxically, then, the hysterical text alienates the reader only to implicate him/her more fully in the process of representation—especially its operation *in other texts* and contexts. For finally, the hysterical text shatters the frame that seals off the text and renders it an aesthetic object. The hysterical text reveals representation as the site of ideological/sexual conflict and production of the subject.

Notes

1. My summary account of the premises of realism is based on Elizabeth Deeds Ermarth's excellent book-length study of the subject in *Realism and Consensus in the English Novel,* esp. 5, 10, 33-34.

2. This broad definition of empiricism, elaborated by Louis Althusser, includes Cartesian rationalism, eighteenth-century sensualist empiricism, and Hegelian idealism; despite differences in the status of the subject and the object which account for the formal differences among these philosophical strands, the basic structure remains the same: these variants all confuse the object of knowledge with the real object, whether through the conceptualization of the real as the result of thought (as in Hegel's speculative idealism) or through the reduction of thought about the real to the real itself (as in empiricist idealism) (Althusser 35).

3. In contrast, works of art that are not similarly arranged by a single, fixed viewpoint, for example Chinese or medieval painting, represent the essential qualities of objects as discrete from one another. Since form and position are not relative but absolute, such systems force the perceiver to relate to the various objects in the field individually yet simultaneously, thus producing at best a fragmented, discontinuous subjectivity.

4. My analysis of this essay is indebted to Mary Ann Doane's discussion of it in "Film and the Masquerade," 79.

5. See J. Hillis Miller 21, 22 for a discussion of temporal distance between protagonist and narrator in *Henry Esmond.*

6. My discussion of Wordsworth assumes Barbara Herrnstein Smith's elaboration of mimesis in poetry.

7. The word "tantalise" appears in the text (17) and explicitly defines William's difficulty in expressing desire as a matter of the distance imposed by vision. The word means "to torment with the sight of something desired but out of reach." The distance between William and the young ladies is too great for him to negotiate; he can relate only to objects that are close, like the portrait of his mother.

8. In addition to this specific quotation (46) I am indebted to John Berger's entire chapter in *Ways of Seeing* on the European tradition of nude painting and the conventions by which women are seen as spectacles appealing to masculine spectators.

9. This resistance to interpretation is precisely why the function of the mask (elaborated in Lacan's schema

of the subject's determination in the visible by the gaze) corresponds to the function of the pronoun "I" in the verbal field. The inconsistency of meaning is also what distinguishes the subject's mask from the animal's camouflage in animal mimicry (*Fundamental Concepts* 107).

10. Recall that the dreaded hypochondria also embraces William, "taking [him] entirely to her death-cold bosom, and holding [him] with arms of bone" (202).

11. In his Letter to Wilhelm Fliess (21 September 1897) Freud complained of "the continual disappointment of my attempts to bring my analyses to a real conclusion, the running away of people who for a time had seemed my most favorably inclined patients . . ." (*Origins of Psychoanalysis* 215).

12. The account of the treatment of Anna O. describes more specifically how a controlled form of retrospection is being substituted for a hysterical representation of the memory (although the case history fails to report that this treatment was incomplete, that it was followed by Ann's hysterical pregnancy):

> Each individual symptom in this complicated case was taken separately in hand; all the occasions on which it had appeared were described in reverse order, starting before the time when the patient became bed-ridden and going back to the event which had led to its first appearance. When this had been described the symptom was permanently removed.

(*Studies on Hysteria* 35)

13. Jean Laplanche, *Life and Death in Psycho-analysis*, 40. I am indebted to Chapter 2 as a whole for my account of Freud's seduction theory.

14. In a letter to Fliess (6 December 1896) Freud described this process of stratification:

> the material present in the shape of memory traces is from time to time subjected to rearrangement in accordance with fresh circumstances—is, as it were, transcribed. Thus, what is essentially new in my theory is the thesis that memory is present not once but several times over, that is registered in various species of "signs."

(*Origins of Psychoanalysis* 173)

Works Cited

Althusser, Louis and Etienne Balibar. *Reading Capital.* Trans. Ben Brewster. London: New Left Books, 1970.

Berger, John. *Ways of Seeing.* London: BBC & Penguin, 1972.

Brontë, Charlotte. *The Professor.* London & New York: Dent & Dutton, 1910.

Burkhart, Charles. *Charlotte Brontë: A Psycho-Sexual Study of Her Novels.* London: Gollancz, 1973.

Cixous, Hélène and Catherine Clement. *The Newly Born Woman.* Trans. Betsy Wing. Minneapolis: University of Minnesota Press, 1986.

Doane, Mary Ann. "Film and the Masquerade: Theorizing the Female Spectator." *Screen* 23 (Sept./Oct. 1982): 74-88.

———. "The Voice in the Cinema: The Articulation of Body and Space." *Yale French Studies* 60 (1980): 33-50.

Eagleton, Terry. *Myths of Power: A Marxist Study of the Brontës.* New York: Barnes & Noble, 1975.

Ermarth, Elizabeth Deeds. *Realism and Consensus in the English Novel.* Princeton, N.J.: Princeton University Press, 1983.

Ewbank, Inga-Stina. *Their Proper Sphere: A Study of the Brontë Sisters as Early Victorian Novelists.* London: Arnold, 1966.

Freud, Sigmund. *Dora: An Analysis of a Case of Hysteria.* Ed. Philip Rieff. New York: Collier, 1963.

———. "Female Sexuality." *Sexuality and the Psychology of Love.* Ed. Philip Rieff. New York: Collier, 1963.

———. "Femininity." *New Introductory Lectures in Psychoanalysis.* Trans. James Strachey. New York: Norton, 1965.

———. "General Remarks on Hysterical Attacks" (1909). *Dora: An Analysis of a Case of Hysteria.* Ed. Philip Rieff. New York: Collier, 1963.

———. "Hysterical Phantasies and their Relation to Bisexuality" (1908). *Dora: An Analysis of a Case of Hysteria.* Ed. Philip Rieff. New York: Collier, 1963.

———. *The Origins of Psychoanalysis: Letters to Wilhelm Fliess, Drafts and Notes: 1887-1902.* Trans. Eric Mosbacher and James Strachey. New York: Basic Books, 1954.

———. "Some Psychological Consequences of the Anatomical Distinction Between the Sexes." *Sexuality and the Psychology of Love.* Ed. Philip Rieff. New York: Collier, 1963.

———, and Joseph Breuer. *Studies on Hysteria: Standard Edition of the Complete Psychological Works.* Trans. James Strachey et al. Vol. 2. London: Hogarth, 1955.

Irigaray, Luce. *Speculum of the Other Woman.* Trans. Gillian C. Gill. Ithaca: Cornell University Press, 1985.

———. *This Sex Which Is Not One.* Trans. Catherine Porter. Ithaca: Cornell University Press, 1985.

Kamuf, Peggy. *Fictions of Desire: Disclosures of Héloise.* Lincoln: University of Nebraska Press, 1982.

Kristeva, Julia. *Revolution in Poetic Language.* Trans. Margaret Waller. New York: Columbia University Press, 1984.

Kroeber, Karl. *Styles in Fictional Structure: The Art of Jane Austen, Charlotte Brontë, George Eliot.* Princeton, N.J.: Princeton University Press, 1971.

Lacan, Jacques. *Écrits: A Selection.* Trans. Alan Sheridan. New York: Norton, 1977.

———. *The Four Fundamental Concepts of Psycho-analysis.* Trans. Alan Sheridan. New York: Norton, 1977.

Laplanche, Jean. *Life and Death in Psycho-analysis.* Trans. Jeffrey Mehlman. Baltimore: Johns Hopkins University Press, 1976.

———, and J.-B. Pontalis. *The Language of Psycho-analysis.* Trans. Donald Nicholson-Smith. New York: Norton, 1973.

Martin, Robert B. *The Accents of Persuasion: Charlotte Brontë's Novels.* London: Faber & Faber, 1966.

Miller, J. Hillis. *The Form of Victorian Fiction: Thackeray, Dickens, Trollope, George Eliot, Meredith, and Hardy.* Notre Dame: University of Notre Dame Press, 1968.

Nowell-Smith, Geoffrey. "Minelli and Melodrama." *Screen* 18 (Summer 1977): 113-18.

Smith, Barbara Herrnstein. "Poetry as Fiction." *New Literary History* 2 (Winter 1971): 259-81.

Heather Glen (essay date 1989)

SOURCE: Introduction to *The Professor,* by Charlotte Brontë, edited by Heather Glen, Penguin Books, 1989, pp. 7-31.

[*In the following essay, Glen disputes earlier critics' claims that* The Professor *is an amateur or apprentice work, arguing instead that it provides a "coherent imaginative interrogation of values and assumptions" regarding masculinity and society.*]

The Professor was the first of Charlotte Brontë's four novels to be written. It is also by far the least known. Completed, probably, at some time in 1846, it was one of the 'three distinct and unconnected tales' that the Brontë sisters, as 'Currer, Ellis and Acton Bell', began in that year to send out to publishers as 'a work of fiction in 3 vols'. But unlike the other two of those tales, *Agnes Grey* and *Wuthering Heights,* it failed to appear in its author's lifetime. Nine times, in all, it was rejected by publishers: the rejections continued even after the success of *Jane Eyre* had made Charlotte Brontë a household name. And when, in 1857, her widower prepared the manuscript for publication, it was with some misgivings and in a slightly bowdlerized form.

For *The Professor* is not a novel to which readers have been indifferent. It has generally been adjudged an unpleasant and oddly disquieting book. Mrs Gaskell, reading it for the first time in manuscript, was uneasy: '[it] is disfigured by more coarseness—& profanity in quoting texts of Scripture disagreeably than in any of her other works'. On its first publication, an anonymous reviewer in the *Ath-*

enaeum found that 'the impression left on the reader' was 'one of pain and incompleteness': subsequent critics have concurred in finding it the least satisfactory and certainly the least attractive of Charlotte Brontë's novels. The usual explanation is that this novel is merely a piece of prentice-work, written before its author found her mature fictional voice. Thus, early reviewers—indeed, Charlotte Brontë's publisher himself—saw *The Professor* as an abortive draft of *Villette,* cruder, clumsier, less finished. More recent critics have taken up this theme, often tracing the novel's 'flaws' to the fact that it is the only one of Charlotte Brontë's published works to adopt the point of view of a male narrator. The similarity between the main events of Crimsworth's story—the journey to Brussels to become a teacher, the struggle for economic independence, the longed-for love affair between master and pupil—and some of the facts of Charlotte Brontë's life has led them to see *The Professor* as a rather clumsy fictionalization of auto-biographical concerns—concerns to which Charlotte Brontë later gave more successful expression through the female voices of Jane Eyre and Lucy Snowe.

Yet Charlotte Brontë herself did not see it thus. In December 1847, two months after the publication of *Jane Eyre,* she replied to her publisher's request for a second, serial novel with the suggestion that she should 'recast' *The Professor*:

> the middle and latter portion of the work, all that relates to Brussels, the Belgian school etc. is as good as I can write; it contains more pith, more substance, more reality, in my judgment, than much of *Jane Eyre.* It gives, I think, a new view of a grade, an occupation, and a class of characters—all very common-place, very insignificant in themselves, but not more so than the materials composing that portion of *Jane Eyre* which seems to please most generally—.

For several years after she had become a famous, indeed, a best-selling novelist, she continued to work over the manuscript with a view to publication. She drafted two prefaces. And when, in February 1851, her publishers Smith, Elder & Co. for a third time responded unenthusiastically, she humorously but definitively refused their suggestion that they take custody of the manuscript, and once again spoke up for her much rejected work:

> of course my feelings towards it can only be paralleled by those of a doting parent towards an idiot child. Its merit—I plainly perceive—will never be owned by anybody but Mr Williams and me; very particular and unique must be our penetration, and I think highly of us both accordingly. You may allege that that merit is not visible to the naked eye. Granted; but the smaller the commodity—the more inestimable its value.

It seems unlikely that the novelist who had written, only six months before (in reply to the critics who had seen *Wuthering Heights* as 'an earlier and ruder attempt of the same pen which had produced *Jane Eyre*'), that 'that writer who could attempt to palm off an inferior and immature production under cover of one successful effort, must indeed be unduly eager after the secondary and sordid result of authorship, and pitiably indifferent to its true and honourable meed'[1] should thus re-work and defend and endeavour to publish a novel that she herself regarded as immature, or as superseded by her own later achievement.

Was this merely authorial partiality? Is *The Professor* the assured and achieved work of art that Charlotte Brontë believed it to be? Or is it of interest today merely because it is a relatively unknown work by a major and much loved novelist? In this introduction I wish to argue that the charge of 'unpleasantness' that has so often been brought against this novel provides a more important clue to its nature than does the patronizing judgement that dismisses it as an immature failure. For much in *The Professor* that appears 'unpleasant' is in fact significant: part of a coherent imaginative interrogation of values and assumptions, which Charlotte Brontë is often assumed to have shared.

It is, perhaps, worth considering how *The Professor* would have appeared to early Victorian readers had it been published in 1846, when Charlotte Brontë first submitted it, and not as it appeared from the perspective provided by those later, more obviously compelling works, *Jane Eyre* and *Villette,* and by that most haunting of literary biographies, Mrs Gaskell's *Life of Charlotte Brontë.* For to see *The Professor* simply as an earlier (or, as Terry Eagleton has argued, a 'more dishonest and idealized') version of *Villette,* or as a clumsy attempt to explore its author's own experiences through the awkward disguise of a male narrator, is essentially to fail to see the kind of thing it is. In one respect, at least, it is very different from *Villette.* For it is offered to the reader less as the confessional autobiography of a peculiar individual than as a fictional example of a quite distinct and influential contemporary genre— that of the exemplary biography of the self-made man. Such lives, usually in shorter versions, would have been very familiar by the middle years of the 1840s. In 1829 the Society for the Diffusion of Useful Knowledge had launched its Library of Entertaining Knowledge with the publication of George Lillie Craik's *The Pursuit of Knowledge Under Difficulties,* a compendium of biographies of scientists, scholars, engineers and inventors, intended to serve as models for those without birth or connections who wished to make their way in the world. Craik's volume went into several editions (one re-cast 'with female examples') in the 1830s and 1840s, and was well known enough to be mocked by Thackeray in *Vanity Fair* (Chapter 37). Similar 'lives' quickly become popular in periodicals such as *Chamber's Edinburgh Journal* and the *Penny Magazine.* It was not until 1859 that the genre reached its peak, with the publication of the phenomenally best-selling *Self-Help* by one of Craik's more admiring readers, Samuel Smiles. But the origins of *Self-Help* lay in the 1840s. The lectures that formed the basis of that classic were first delivered to a young men's mutual improvement society in Leeds in 1845—the year following that in which the Brontë sisters, only a few miles away, had produced the prospectus for the boarding-school that they had hoped

would make them independent, and the year in which, very probably, Charlotte Brontë began to write this novel.

Many features of Charlotte Brontë's narrative may be paralleled in the writing of Smiles and his precursors. The commitment to sober realism announced in her preface—'I said to myself that my hero should work his way through life as I had seen real living men work theirs'—reads like a description of their subject-matter: 'the ordinary business and pursuits of common life . . . examples of conduct and character drawn from reading, observation and experience'. Like the heroes of Craik and Smiles, of *Chamber's Journal* and the *Penny Magazine,* her Crimsworth succeeds not because of birth or good fortune but despite handicaps, and through his own unaided efforts. The values he invokes are the classic values of the *Self-Help* tradition— industry and perseverance, self-reliance and independence, self-respect and self-control. And his story—the story of a young man who must make his own way in the world, who labours first as a clerk and then as a school-master, who works his way up until he owns his own school, and in the process makes a suitable marriage (rejecting a less prudent sexual adventure)—seems to be one in which those virtues are demonstrated and vindicated. When one sets it within this context, *The Professor* seems less a clumsy attempt to hide its author's 'real', feminine concerns behind the mask of a male narrator than a fictional imitation of a genre that (despite Craik's 'female examples') was overwhelmingly masculine.

Yet, unlike the classics of that genre, it failed—and has continued to fail—to win popularity. For, as generations of readers have noted, there is something oddly disagreeable, even repellent, about Crimsworth's story. It seems altogether more disturbing than one might expect of a simple tale of obstacles surmounted and victory won—full of suggestions of a barely suppressed violence, a peculiarly sadistic sexuality. And Crimsworth himself is a more disquieting character than the heroes of the *Self-Help* tradition—anxiously watchful, coolly domineering, a prey to 'Hypochondria'. There seems to be a curious disjunction between his own self-image, of independence and success, and the overall effect of his narrative.

One way of accounting for this has been to cite Charlotte Brontë's inexperience as a novelist, the uncertainty she must have felt in the use of the masculine voice. Yet the reality, I think, is altogether more interesting than this. And here, once again, her preface provides a clue. For in the opening sentence of that preface she takes pains to deny that this is in any way 'a first attempt', and announces that 'the pen which wrote it had been previously worn a good deal in a practice of some years'. And if one turns to what survives of that 'practice', to the extraordinary body of childhood and adolescent writings that were her contribution to the Brontë children's shared fantasy world, one sees a kind of literary experimentation which dispels the notion that the author of *The Professor* was an inexperienced amateur, clumsily seeking expression for her own personal concerns. For fifteen years before she came to write this novel, Charlotte Brontë had been playing with different kinds of narrative voice. The majority of her early stories are told from the points of view of male narrators, narrators who are themselves often seen with a highly sophisticated irony. A favourite, for instance, is Lord Charles Wellesley, a bombastic but uncertain, cynical but vulnerable, world-weary would-be Byronic hero: even as he swaggers and postures, his pretensions are exposed and mocked and his insecurities revealed. The voice of the first person in these tales is not simply one of special pleading, but is itself objectified and questioned. From a very early age, Charlotte Brontë seems to have been using the male narrator not as a 'disguise' but as a means of exploring the logic and the limitations of a particular kind of contemporary masculine stance.

To look at **The Professor** from the perspective provided by these writings is to begin to see a novel rather different from the awkward piece of prentice-work it has often been taken to be. The oddities of Crimsworth's narrative cannot, it seems, be attributed simply to Charlotte Brontë's inexperience in handling the masculine voice. Rather, they appear to be part of an astute and highly critical exploration of the nature and the implications of the existential stance he exemplifies—that existential stance which in mid-Victorian England was enshrined and celebrated in the tradition of *Self-Help*.

The first chapter of **The Professor** consists of a letter, which, the narrator explains, was 'sent by me a year since to an old school acquaintance'; thereafter, the epistolary form is abruptly abandoned for a straight first-person narrative. But this apparent false start does not seem to be the result of authorial ineptness. For its effect is distinctive and powerful; and it is reinforced and elaborated in the novel that follows. We learn at the end of the first chapter that no answer to this letter was ever received; that by the time it arrived, its intended recipient had departed the country: 'What has become of him since, I know not.' The confidence and intimacy usually assumed by the first-person form thus receives a curious check at the outset of this narrative. Crimsworth announces, at the end of the chapter, that he will now 'dedicate' his tale to 'the public at large': but the opening image of the unreceived and unanswered letter to the now-vanished friend remains as a pendant to the rest. And as one examines the novel more closely, this seems less an awkward incongruity than an exact and ironic pointer to the import of the whole.

For the world that is introduced in this opening chapter is one in which there seems to be no possibility of positive human interaction at all. The first paragraph of Crimsworth's letter recalls and reconstructs the relation between himself and his friend in a prose whose insistent negativism suggests not expressive interrelation but unceasing defensive opposition:

> What animal magnetism drew thee and me together I know not; certainly I never experienced anything of the Pylades and Orestes sentiment for you, and I have reason to believe that you, on your part, were equally free

from all romantic regard to me . . . your sardonic coldness did not move me. I felt myself superior to that check *then* as I do *now*.

(p. 39)

'I felt myself superior . . . *then* as . . . *now*': the assertion of an unchanging and antagonistically 'superior' self against the threat that even a friendly other presents prefigures what is to follow. This, in a sense, is what this curious and chilling narrative of self-help *is*. And the final image, of separation and dead end, points towards some of the most peculiar features of that narrative.

From the very beginning, Crimsworth's story is framed in imagery of opposition, of antipathy, of rejection and resistance. The marked negativism of the prose is accompanied by a constant emphasis on refusal and denial: 'his daughters, all of whom I greatly dislike', 'I declined both the Church and matrimony', 'I had had no thoughts of the sort', 'I do not think that my turn of mind qualifies me to make a good tradesman', 'my uncles did not remonstrate; they and I parted with mutual disgust', 'a resolution no more to take bread from hands which had refused to minister to the necessities of my dying mother', 'an irreparable breach', 'I repressed all—even *mental* comment on his note', 'I anticipated no overflowings of fraternal tenderness', 'my refusal of their proposals will, I fancy, operate as a barrier against all future intercourse'. These quotations are taken from the opening pages of the novel, but they are entirely characteristic of the whole. Not merely the narrator but all whom he meets habitually oppose, reject, repulse, resist, deny. Even supposedly non-hostile encounters are portrayed in terms of opposition and combat, from the first glimpse of Crimsworth's brother and his wife—'she *chid* him, half playfully, half poutingly, for being late . . . Mr Crimsworth soon *checked* her animated *scolding* with a kiss . . . She and Edward talked much, always in a vein of playful *contention* . . .' (p. 45, my italics)—to the closing portrait of the relation between Crimsworth and his son. The world of the novel is one in which awareness of difference leads not to interaction but to antagonism, rejection, separation. 'Once convinced', says Crimsworth, 'that my friend's disposition is incompatible with my own, once assured that he is indelibly stained with certain defects obnoxious to my principles and I dissolve the connection.' Teaching is a battle: the task of the teacher is not to respond to her pupils but 'to enter into conflict with this foreign will to endeavour to bend it into subjection to her own'. And the pupils thus confronted are 'marked by a point-blank disregard of all forbearance towards each other or their teachers; an eager pursuit by each individual of her own interest and convenience; and a coarse indifference to the interest and convenience of every one else'.

Even the courtship between Frances and Crimsworth is imaged as a struggle for power. Thus, when he praises her work she appears to him not gratified but 'triumphant'—a triumph that he feels impelled to check by 'reproof'. The scene of his proposal to her is marked by a barely suppressed violence. He holds her in 'a somewhat ruthless grasp' and insists that she speaks his language rather than hers: she, for her part, is 'as stirless in her happiness as a mouse in its terror'. And the moment in which the marriage 'compact' is 'framed' and 'sealed' is a moment not of intercommunion, or even of emotional expressiveness, but one that confirms the fundamental separateness of each:

> she and I were silent, nor was our silence brief. Frances' thoughts, during this interval, I know not, nor did I attempt to guess them; I was not occupied in searching her countenance, nor in otherwise troubling her composure. The peace I felt, I wished her to feel; my arm, it is true, still detained her; but with a restraint that was gentle enough, so long as no opposition tightened it. My gaze was on the red fire; my heart was measuring its own content; it sounded and sounded, and found the depth fathomless.
>
> (p. 249)

The only 'peace' that Crimsworth can offer is one of relief from his 'troubling' attention. His 'content' is a private treasure, to be reckoned and hoarded up within himself.

Again and again, and in a variety of ways, the novel emphasizes the absence of anything like positive feeling for others within the world projected by Crimsworth's narrative. Where such feeling is envisaged, its nature is suggested by the word that is several times applied to it— 'forbearance': it is seen as depending on the suppression, rather than the expression, of impulse. Throughout the novel, rare moments of accord are marked by comments such as 'I agreed with him, but did not say so', 'I put no obstacle in her way.' Good will is either so arbitrary, so inexplicable, as to appear to be a kind of perversity (Hunsden's assistance to Crimsworth is presented thus), or it is part of the universal, self-interested struggle to maintain 'the advantage' (M. Vandenhuten assists Crimsworth because he is desirous of 'discharging the obligation under which he affirmed I had laid him'). Such concord between individuals as there is seems simply an extension of egotism. Crimsworth and his wife, Frances, become a joint financial and educational enterprise; she describes patriotism approvingly as that which 'spreads man's selfishness in wider circles'. The pervasive image of human relations is of conflict or, at best, friction between self-defensive and self-seeking individuals.

Yet if there is little positive interaction between them, the people in this world are far from impervious to one another. One and all watch each other continually. Charlotte Brontë's carefully structured prose—very different from the colourless prose of the self-help narratives—charts a pervasive process not merely of aggressive opposition but of constant mutual surveillance. Almost as prominent in the novel as its imagery of antagonism is its imagery of looking and being looked at. The account that Crimsworth gives of his employment as a clerk is in fact an account of others' attempts to find him out (the taskmaster's watchfulness, his brother's inquiries, his landlady's speculations,

Hunsden's curiosity) and his own efforts to evade them: 'I was guarded by three faculties—Caution, Tact, Observation; and prowling and prying as was Edward's malignity, it could never baffle the lynx-eyes of these, my natural sentinels.' The school to which he goes is a place of staring eyes—'when I glanced around, behold all the boarders . . . were congregated within a yard or two of my desk, and stood staring with eyes and mouths wide open'—in which his central strategy is to watch more sharply and from a more 'commanding' position than they. 'I carefully and deliberately made these observations before allowing myself to take one glance at the benches before me . . . I found myself cool enough to admit of looking calmly up and gazing deliberately about me.' Interaction with others is a process of watching and counter-watching. Thus, Crimsworth's power struggle with Mlle Reuter begins with looks—'Her look of affright I answered with one of composure'—and continues in the same manner:

> her eye, fastened on my face, demanded of every feature the meaning of my changed and careless manner. 'I will give her an answer,' thought I; and, meeting her gaze full, arresting, fixing her glance, I shot into her eyes, from my own, a look, where there was no respect, no love, no tenderness, no gallantry.
>
> (p. 142)

And his 'war' with the students is conducted in similar terms: 'I found pleasure in answering the glance of vanity with the gaze of stoicism.'

But, more often, looking appears less as a mode than as a refusal of interaction. Again and again, at moments when another threatens in some way to impinge upon Crimsworth, that other is turned into an object of observation. Thus, as the 'disgust' inspired by his brother threatens his self-composure,

> I looked at him: I measured his robust frame and powerful proportions; I saw my own reflection in the mirror over the mantelpiece; I amused myself with comparing the two pictures . . . As an animal, Edward excelled me far; should he prove as paramount in mind as in person I must be a slave . . . his cold, avaricious eye, his stern, forbidding manner told me he would not spare.
>
> (p. 49)

The interview in which Hunsden challenges his efforts to become a tradesman stirs him deeply; but instead of betraying himself to this other he employs himself in 'a rapid scrutiny of his physiognomy', reading the signs of character in his face and lineaments. When Hunsden appears unexpectedly in his room in Belgium, his first act— even before speaking to his visitor—is to polish his spectacles and examine the other's 'mien and countenance': 'I was sitting in the window-seat, with my back to the light, and I had him *vis-à-vis*: a position he would much rather have had reversed; for, at any time, he preferred scrutinizing to being scrutinized.' 'Her gaze was ever waiting for mine, and it frequently succeeded in arresting it,' he says of Adèle, his 'Gorgon-like' pupil: but rather than allowing himself to be petrified by that gaze, he turns the face before him into an object of physiognomical observation— 'Suspicion, sullen ill-temper were on her forehead, vicious propensities in her eye, envy and panther-like deceit about her mouth.'

The objectifying language of physiognomy recurs throughout the novel. Even, or especially, when Crimsworth is moved by passion, this is his strategy. Admitting that he is 'on the brink of falling in love' with the fascinating Mlle Reuter, he decides to renew his 'observations' of her, and marvels at 'how calm she is under scrutiny': he spies on her, secretly, from the vantage-point of the window whose unboarding he has requested. Such imagery reaches its climax in his account of his developing relation with his future wife. At first she appears as a shadowy figure, of whom 'I never had more than a passing glimpse . . . consequently I had no opportunity of studying her character, or even of observing her person much'; then she becomes a physiognomical specimen, whose 'sentiments' he attempts to 'decipher in her countenance'. She looks at him; and his response is to scrutinize her—'I saw the new pupil was puzzled at first . . . once or twice she looked at me with a sort of painful solicitude . . . She looked at me; her eye said most plainly, "I cannot follow you"'—and to turn away when communication is threatened—'I disregarded the appeal.' And these preliminaries are succeeded by a series of scenes in which Crimsworth spies on Frances, watching her grief in the cemetery, 'eavesdropping' on her landing before their marriage, observing her first encounter with Hunsden from 'my position [from which] I could see them both', following and watching as she bids her son goodnight years afterwards.

This imagery of looking and being looked at runs throughout the novel, chillingly replacing any more intimate conception of human interaction. And it points not merely to a peculiar strategy of the individual, Crimsworth, but to the essential nature of the world through which he moves. In an extraordinarily precise and consistent way, Charlotte Brontë seems to be exposing and articulating the logic of a whole society—a society whose essential dynamics are the same as those that Jeremy Bentham had sought to enshrine and objectify in his great plan for a 'Panopticon' some fifty years before. The Panopticon, it will be recalled, was an exemplary institution—a school or a madhouse, a factory or a prison—in which the inmates would be completely separated from one another within individual cells, and in which each would be clearly visible from a central inspection tower. It thus provides a peculiarly exact architectural image for those strategies of control through observation, through objectification of the other, that seem to dominate Crimsworth's world of individualistic achievement. As Michel Foucault, arguing for the centrality of such strategies in late eighteenth- and early nineteenth-century French and English society, puts it: 'The Panopticon is a machine for dissociating the see/being seen dyad: in the peripheric ring, one is totally seen, without ever seeing; in the central tower, one sees everything without ever

being seen.'[2] This principle is evident, of course, in the institutions depicted in this novel: in Edward's factory counting-house with its vigilant 'taskmaster', in the schoolroom with its disciplinary surveillance. But, as her 'autobiographical' form suggests, Charlotte Brontë is not primarily concerned with institutions. Rather, with an often quite chilling acuteness, she charts the operation of such strategies in the most intimate recesses of the personality. And, in doing so, she exposes their disquieting implications.

The fundamental assumption of Crimsworth's narrative—an assumption embedded in that informing imagery of controlling observation—is the primacy of the antagonistic individual perspective, a perspective opposed to rather than shaped or modified by that of others. And, as Charlotte Brontë carefully shows, the individual who defines himself thus is a problematic entity. For even the most ordinary situations in this avowedly 'plain and homely' novel are charged, in Crimsworth's telling, with a peculiar tension. Thus he describes his first day as a clerk in his brother's counting-house:

> A sentiment of keen pleasure accompanied this first effort to earn my own living—a sentiment neither poisoned nor weakened by the presence of the taskmaster, who stood and watched me for some time as I wrote. I thought he was trying to read my character, but I felt as secure against his scrutiny as if I had had on a casque with the visor down—or rather I showed him my countenance with the confidence that one would show an unlearned man a letter written in Greek; he might see lines, and trace characters, but he could make nothing of them; my nature was not his nature, and its signs were to him like the words of an unknown tongue. Ere long he turned away abruptly, as if baffled, and left the counting-house . . .
>
> (p. 53)

Ostensibly, the moment is one of some satisfaction; of 'keen pleasure', even of victory. Yet that 'keen pleasure'—a pleasure less in the employment itself than in the fact that it is an 'effort' to become self-subsistent—is scarcely admitted before it seems to be threatened by the only other present, the watching 'taskmaster'. Thus, even positive feeling takes on the character of an antagonism— 'neither poisoned nor weakened'. The taskmaster becomes first an enemy whose 'scrutiny' is like a military threat; and then an inferior, an 'unlearned man' who cannot read the signs of the speaker's nature. The self in this encounter is hidden, defended, watching but indecipherable; and the confrontation ends, like most confrontations in this novel, with an abrupt turning away.

Yet if Crimsworth asserts his impregnable superiority, the prose registers an altogether more disquieting state of affairs. For the paragraph and the chapter end not with an account of the narrator's feelings, or of the work he pursues in such superior isolation (such as might be expected if the novel were to take his own view of himself, of his 'pleasure' and 'security'), but with an almost obsessive concentration on the actions of the antagonistic other in this scene:

he returned to it but twice in the course of that day; each time he mixed and swallowed a glass of brandy-and-water, the materials for making which he extracted from a cupboard on one side of the fireplace; having glanced at my translations—he could read both French and German—he went out again in silence.

(pp. 53-4)

The embattled, defensive self has shrunk to a mere watching point of consciousness; more concerned, it seems, with that which threatens it than with its own activity. And the next chapter begins as this ends, with a description of the efforts of those about to find him out:

Mr Crimsworth watched sharply for defects, but found none; he set Timothy Steighton, his favourite and head man, to watch also. Tim was baffled . . . Mr Crimsworth made inquiries as to how I lived, whether I got into debt . . . Mr Crimsworth employed Tim to find out whether my landlady had any complaint to make on the score of my morals; she answered that she believed I was a very religious man, and asked Tim, in her turn, if he thought I had any intention of going into the Church some day . . .

(p. 55)

The essential drama has become not the development of, or even the choices facing, the self, but the activity of these others and the strategies of the self to evade them.

What we see in this passage we see in the novel as a whole. Crimsworth's story, on one level a tale of self-respect vindicated, of self-sufficiency affirmed and rewarded, of individual success, is on another level—one that is carefully articulated through syntax, through imagery, through narrative structure—a tale not of triumphant achievement but of thwarting and conflict, not of security arrived at but of continuing and irresolvable unease. It is a tale not of competence and independence but of a self unable to change the world through which it moves and antagonistically bound to that which it would reject. And if it is a tale of 'self-control', it is one in which 'self-control' is exposed as a process of radical, indeed violent, self-division.

Thus, as Crimsworth sits in self-contained silence, awaiting his first meeting with his brother Edward and anticipating (he avows) 'no overflowings of fraternal tenderness', his hand—'so utterly a stranger to the grasp of a kindred hand'—clenches itself 'to repress the tremor with which impatience would fain have shaken it'. Thus, on the morning after his discovery of the liaison between Mlle Reuter and M. Pelet, he has to rise at dawn and take a cold bath before he can greet the latter with 'an unchanged and tranquil countenance', without betraying 'the sense of insult and treachery [which] lived in me like a kindling though as yet smothered coal'. Thus, Mlle Reuter, disappointed in her attraction to Crimsworth, adopts a demeanour towards him that is 'deficient neither in dignity nor propriety'; but her former feelings have not disappeared. 'Decorum now repressed, and Policy masked it, but Opportunity would be

too strong for either of these—Temptation would shiver their restraints.' The emphasis is less on the surface of propriety and indifference than on the processes of repression and denial by which it is produced.

In one way, the negation of impulse appears as an assertion of choice and control. Thus Crimsworth, the penniless foreigner, discovering that the woman he desires is secretly 'affianced' to his employer, adopts a position of lordly self-restraint. 'I had no intention of getting up a scene with M. Pelet, reproaching him with perfidy, sending him a challenge, or performing other gambadoes of the sort.' To reject and deny is to exercise power—over one's actions, over one's feelings, over others. It is the primary assertion of individual separateness; that which enables a public mask to be different from the private self. Yet, as Freud has famously argued, and as the example just given demonstrates, the use of the negative exposes a self-division that is the reverse of 'integrity', or individual wholeness: to deny an intention is to reveal its unconscious presence. In literature, alone among the arts, that which is negated can be given its full imaginative weight. And here, in this novel dominated by negatives, Charlotte Brontë exploits this fact to striking effect. The repeated use of the negative, here and throughout Crimsworth's narrative, gives a peculiar fictional life to that whole seething drama of denied impulse that it is the function of 'self-control' to conceal. Thus, Mlle Reuter presents an impassive façade to the world:

she said nothing, and her face and forehead, clothed with a mask of purely negative expression, were as blank of comment as her lips. As neither surprise, pleasure, approbation, nor interest were evinced in her countenance, so no more were disdain, envy, annoyance, weariness.

(p. 177)

But the effect of this description is the reverse of quiescent. The reader is invited to entertain and reject a whole succession of conflicting impulses; and Mlle Reuter appears less as a coherent individual than as a mass of warring and suppressed potentialities. Thus Hunsden rebukes Crimsworth's apparent passivity:

'What are you then? You sit at that desk in Crimsworth's counting-house day by day and week by week, scraping with a pen on paper, just like an automaton; you never get up; you never say you are tired; you never ask for a holiday; you never take change or relaxation; you give way to no excess of an evening; you neither keep wild company, nor indulge in strong drink.'

(p. 67)

And the sequence of negatives opens up a series of rejected possibilities, enacting in miniature that strategy of denial, of repression of impulse and refusal of expressiveness through which Crimsworth defines and maintains his social identity. It is not simply that he has a series of violent impulses that he restrains. In the peculiar centrifugal prose of his story, self itself appears to be held together by violence.

And if 'integrity' is thus imaginatively questioned, so too is that other cornerstone of the *Self-Help* tradition, the desired end of individual 'independence'. For Crimsworth, as for those about him, self-reliance—not being in any way dependent on, or indebted to, others—is not merely the key to success: it is essential to his whole mode of being. The words that he uses to describe this ideal state—key-words of early Victorian economic individualism—carry this resonance within them. To be economically self-sufficient is to have a 'competency'—not merely enough to live on but also the capacity to act, the power to be. To have an income is to have 'an independency'—not just money but freedom and autonomy as well. When Crimsworth is penniless, his plight presents itself in both economic and existential terms as 'a pang of *mortification* at the humility of my position, and the inadequacy of my means; while with that pang was born a strong desire to do more, earn more, *be more,* possess more' (my italics). Yet within the world he describes, economic self-sufficiency depends, paradoxically, on self-denial:

> as it had ever been abhorrent to my nature to ask pecuniary assistance, I had early acquired habits of self-denying economy; husbanding my monthly allowance with anxious care, in order to obviate the danger of being forced, in some moment of future exigency, to beg additional aid.
>
> (p. 55)

The image is less one of freedom and autonomy than of anxious defence against constantly present threat. Analogously, on an existential plane, the self whose mode of existence is one of rejection and denial is the reverse of expressively self-actualizing or freely self-determining. For far more powerfully present than that which it is, or does, is that which it is not, or cannot, or will not do. The repeated entertainment of denied possibility by which Crimsworth's narrative proceeds does not merely challenge his own self-image of 'straight integrity': it complicates the onward thrust of his story with a constant, undertowing awareness of energies choked off and repressed. And the negatives and denials by which he defines himself produce a sense of self as neither separate nor superior but as inextricably bound to that which it seeks to reject. The 'independent' individual appears as ineluctably social, the product of a whole constellation of active, antagonistic relationships.

The contradiction around which Charlotte Brontë's imagination is working and the sharpness with which she realizes it in this novel might perhaps be focused by considering the ways in which she plays upon the opposing meanings of a single word: that 'propriety' which emerges as a dominant value in the world she presents. In one key passage, Crimsworth praises the 'British English' in the girls' school where he teaches for their 'native propriety and decency'; 'by this last circumstance alone', he says, 'I could at a glance distinguish the daughter of Albion and nursling of Protestantism from the foster-child of Rome.' And the surrounding imagery all emphasizes a primary,

and now obsolete, meaning of 'propriety', that of 'property'; and a second, now rare, that of 'essence or individuality'. The self is here a private possession to be defended against attack and preserved in its inviolable distinctiveness:

> proud, too, was the aspect of these British girls . . . they *warded* off insult with *austere* civility, and met hate with mute *disdain*; they *eschewed company-keeping,* and in the midst of numbers seemed to dwell *isolated.*
>
> (p. 132, my italics)

But this constellation of meanings is almost the opposite of that which the word had come to bear by Charlotte Brontë's time and that which she emphasizes, equally tellingly, elsewhere in the novel. Thus of Hunsden's first meeting with Frances, Crimsworth remarks,

> I thought I had never seen two such *models* of propriety, for Hunsden (thanks to the *constraint* of the foreign tongue) was *obliged to shape* his phrases, and *measure* his sentences, with a *care* that *forbade any eccentricity.*
>
> (p. 259, my italics)

Here the context stresses not individuality but its reverse; not self-possession but conformity to others' rules and requirements. In both cases the restraint of free expressiveness is the same, as is the word that is chosen to describe it—'propriety'. The sense of self as isolated, inviolate, the ultimate piece of private property, thus appears inextricable from its opposite—the sense that the self is inexorably bound by others' conventions and prohibitions, that it has no independent existence at all. Unobtrusively but exactly, Charlotte Brontë seems to be highlighting a fundamental contradiction within that early Victorian philosophy of self-sufficient individualism that Crimsworth, in his tale of successful self-help, seeks to affirm.

For if *The Professor* is not a disguised autobiography of its author, neither is it merely an exploration of the psychology of a peculiar individual. In choosing to cast this, her first novel written for publication, as the story of a self-made man, Charlotte Brontë was appropriating a form which, in a quite naked and archetypal way, embodied and celebrated some of the central ideological assumptions of her society. Through her presentation of Crimsworth's narrative she offers not merely an exposure of the shortcomings of this particular teller but a coherent imaginative interrogation of those assumptions, and a disturbingly intimate exploration of their experiential implications. Like the lyrics of Blake's *Songs of Experience,* this finely articulated dramatization of a representative monologic voice embodies as acute a vision of the logic of a whole society as do many more obviously sociological analyses.

And that logic, as it is elaborated here, is very bleak indeed. For if the novel's insistent negatives delineate a field of conflicting possibilities, those possibilities are all denied. The energy is that of deadlock: no movement beyond it is envisaged. Although Crimsworth's is a linear narrative, in which effort leads to success, the novel's imaginative structure is claustrophobically circular. It begins with a description of a 'friendship' fuelled by antagonism and of a family divided by hostilities; and it ends with a similar, if more ambiguous set of images. Frances, we are told, loves her English professor 'too absolutely to fear him *much*' (my italics). Their domestic idyll is shot through with a kind of amorous antagonism: she, he says, 'would vex, tease, pique me', and he responds with a 'chastisement', which 'instead of correcting the fault . . . seemed to encourage its renewal'. The only fruit of this union is the suggestively named Victor; he, like his father, is to be sent away to Eton, where he will be 'soundly disciplined' and given a radical grounding in 'the art of self-control'. Crimsworth's story is ostensibly one not merely of success but also of requited love. But it ends as it began, with an isolated, watching individual: with a man who spies on his wife and relates to his child by trying to break his will. The feeling is less of the boundaries of the self being expanded than of the anxious separateness of the original self being confirmed.

In the private sphere, as it appears here, there seems little possibility of creative interaction between individuals. And similarly, such images of the larger society as there are are images of exclusion and conflict. The England of the novel is a place of competitive enterprise, in which 'Concern' has a one-dimensionally economic meaning; of domineering masters and resentful 'slaves'. Belgium is a place of 'Popish' duplicity and suspicious watchfulness, in which 'getting on' means gaining and maintaining 'the advantage' over others. One is reminded of a famous passage from Carlyle's *Past and Present,* published three years before this novel was written:

> We call it a Society; and go about professing openly the totalest separation, isolation. Our life is not a mutual helpfulness; but rather, cloaked under due laws-of-war, named 'fair competition' and so forth, it is a mutual hostility.[3]

Instead of Dickens's great metaphors of circulation and stoppage and George Eliot's of the social web, Charlotte Brontë offers images simply of repression and repulsion; instead of a connecting energy, she shows the tense balancing of denied impulse. The energies that animate Crimsworth's world seem, indeed, to work *against* anything we might call social bonding. His tale is one of successful self-help, but there is no sense of a supportive context for this achievement. The world of business is a world of ruthless competition, in which individuals such as Edward Crimsworth fail and make fortunes in seemingly arbitrary ways. The reasons, the processes, are not imagined. But if the individual life-trajectory remains the focus, this seems less the result of Charlotte Brontë's failure to imagine a social world than the expression of the logic of her vision. For what she suggests, with an exactitude that echoes Carlyle's more out-spoken protest, is that in a fundamental sense a society composed wholly of competing self-interested individuals has nothing but violence to hold it together at all.

The world of *The Professor* is a world of ominous instability. And nowhere is this more apparent than in the final chapter, where Crimsworth gives a picture of the success to which his efforts have led. The closing pages of the novel are full of apparently unconnected images of insecurity and violence. The narrator interrupts his portrait of married bliss to interrogate his wife as to 'what she would have been had she married a harsh, envious, careless man—a profligate, a prodigal, a drunkard, or a tyrant'. Their friend Hunsden suddenly tells a story of thwarted love for a woman who looks as if she 'once wore chains and broke them'. Crimsworth shoots his son's rabid dog, and Victor is repelled by his 'cruelty'. The picture of the child lying on the dog's grave is succeeded by one of the 'utter wretchedness' he will have to suffer when he is sent to Eton, and the misery the parents feel at the prospect of this 'fearful operation'. Within the Edenic haven of Daisy Lane the serpent lurks, in the shape of the provoking Hunsden. Victor's affection for this unpredictable friend causes his mother 'unexpressed anxiety': while he is by, 'she roves with restless movement round, like a dove guarding its young from a hovering hawk'. And as the novel closes, the 'hawk' enters to disrupt domestic peace: 'But Hunsden comes; I hear his step, and there he is, bending through the lattice, from which he has thrust away the woodbine with unsparing hand, disturbing two bees and a butterfly.' (p. 290)

Like the unanswered letter of the opening chapter, these final images are more integrally related to the rest of the novel than might at first appear. For they articulate a disquiet that has, in fact, been present throughout—a sense of something volcanic and subversive, which constantly threatens to disrupt the uneasy stasis achieved by 'self-control', something whose violence can be held in check only by an answering violence. Beneath the surface of Crimsworth's tale of successful self-help lies another world, an 'infernal world' (the phrase is one of Charlotte Brontë's names for her childhood fantasy world) of untrusted impulse and barely controllable feeling, a world far more 'strange, startling and harrowing' than that of the 'romance' that the preface announces this novel is not. The manifestations of that world are disruptively various: the unexplained tears that Frances sheds on the morning of her wedding day, or the 'eccentric vigour' she occasionally, disconcertingly, displays; the 'hypochondria' that 'accosts' and 'tyrannizes' Crimsworth; the peculiar, half-repressed sensuality that disrupts his descriptions of Mlle Reuter; the 'electrical ardour and power—which emits, now and then, ominous sparks' from Victor. Yet if they disturb the coherence of Crimsworth's narrative, that is perhaps their point. For the social world of the novel is one in which spontaneous feeling cannot be creatively expressed, one that offers no context of 'reason or love' within which it can safely be entertained. When such feeling appears it is as a 'fierce revolt', which must be subdued by violence, not merely by the inner violence of 'self-restraint' but by an external violence whose nature is focused and objectified in Crimsworth's reflections on his son's education.

The presence of Victor in the concluding pages of the novel provides a suggestive indication of the nature of Charlotte Brontë's interest in her subject: an interest not merely in Crimsworth's individual life-trajectory but in how the world he inhabits is sustained and reproduced. For here the myth of the self-made man is interrupted by a disturbing image, an image of the human being not as 'self-made' but as shaped in social relations, not as an 'independent' adult with feelings held under tight control but as a dependent and defenceless child in the grip of un-controllable feeling. Such an image has no place in the classic self-help narrative. Childhood there is dealt with perfunctorily, as preliminary to, rather than part of, the real business of life. In this novel, Crimsworth barely mentions his own childhood: it is only towards the close of his story, when describing his 'Hypochondria', that he admits that he was 'lonely' as well as 'parentless'. Yet his treatment of his son Victor, exactly mirroring his own self-suppression, is an external image of that violence of inner 'self-control' that has been evident throughout. And in thus presenting it, Charlotte Brontë does not merely offer an acute analysis of a psychological mechanism that has in recent years begun to be exposed and explored—the vio-lence of the process whereby the authoritarian personality is produced and reproduces itself.[4] She also suggests, very powerfully, that it is in its treatment of childhood that the essential nature of a whole society is revealed. The rarely smiling Victor must, Crimsworth says, be separated from his mother; for 'she will accustom him to a style of treat-ment, a forbearance, a congenial tenderness, he will meet with from none else'. Within the family, Victor may be 'subjugated' by love. But love is a poor preparation for life in this society. For, as Crimsworth asks, with a bleak directness that irradiates not merely his own assumptions but the world that sustains and is shaped by them, 'will reason or love be the weapons with which in future the world will meet his violence?' Thus the novel concludes: not with an affirmation of that individual self-sufficiency its narrator seeks to celebrate but with a disconcerting im-age of the 'infernal' violence, both within and without, on which that achievement is based.

And it is with a shock that one realizes that it was with the same resonant image—the image of the rebellious, 'subjugated' child—that Charlotte Brontë began her next, very different novel, **Jane Eyre.** There the focus is on 'the need of being loved' rather than on the drive towards inde-pendence, on a woman's experience rather than on a man's. Yet the juxtaposition is suggestive. And it indi-cates, I think, something of the importance of **The Profes-sor** within Charlotte Brontë's total *œuvre*. For this, her first, stubbornly defended novel, poses a distinctive chal-lenge to the still common view that she is, essentially, a novelist of autobiographical 'special pleading':[5] one who used her fiction as a vehicle for the indirect but powerful expression of her own 'hunger, rebellion, and rage'[6]—her longing for the love of an impossibly idealized man, her desire to affirm women's right to self-sustaining indepen-dence. **The Professor** suggests that her imaginative explo-ration of the presuppositions of her society was more searching, more flexible, more disinterestedly intelligent than this. For here, through a distinctively literary interro-gation of the premises of the classic self-help narrative, she offers a disquieting vision of the construction and the cost of masculinity in that society and a chilling critique of some of its most cherished values. Here successful manhood appears not as charismatically powerful but as blinkered and crippled, the ideal of independence not as desirable but as fundamentally flawed. To read the later novels from the perspective provided by this is to perceive a rather different set of emphases in them from those that they have customarily been made to bear. And to read this, her first and least regarded novel, with a full alertness to the sophisticated literary intelligence that is manifest in its pages is to discover a different Charlotte Brontë from the unreflective novelist of private love and longing that she is all too often taken to be.

Notes

1. *Biographical Notice of Ellis and Acton Bell,* Septem-ber 1850.

2. Michel Foucault, *Discipline and Punish: The Birth of the Clinic,* trans. Alan Sheridan, Harmondsworth, Middlesex, 1977, p 202.

3. 'Gospel of Mammon', *Past and Present,* Book Three, Chapter Two.

4. See, for example, Alice Miller, *For Your Own Good: The Roots of Violence in Childrearing,* translated by Hildegarde and Hunter Hannum, London, 1983.

5. Raymond Williams, *The English Novel from Dickens to Lawrence,* London, 1970, p. 73.

6. Matthew Arnold, in a letter to Mrs Forster, 14 April 1853.

Irene Tayler (essay date 1990)

SOURCE: "*The Professor, Jane Eyre, Shirley.*" In *Holy Ghosts: The Male Muses of Emily and Charlotte Brontë,* Columbia University Press, 1990, pp. 159-99.

[*In the following excerpt, Tayler describes the fluctuation of gender and sex roles that Brontë's characters experi-ence, linking their struggles with Brontë's own desires for gender equality in society and a deeper sense of balance between the male and female qualities within herself.*]

Charlotte's work with her sisters in getting out their joint volume of poems still left her time to undertake her first novel specifically conceived and intended for publica-tion—**The Professor.** In her "Author's Preface" Charlotte characterized the progress of her thoughts on literary method: "I had got over any such taste as I might once have had for ornamental and redundant composition, and come to prefer what was plain and homely." Her work would now stick close to the unadorned realities of life—pursue no more Angrian sunsets, worship no more false gods.

But the novel nonetheless mixes fantasy with fact in suggestive and revealing ways. Its immediate topic was Charlotte's Brussels experience, but with a twist: for Charlotte here casts herself in a double role.[1] She is both halves of the couple whose love story the novel tells: both William Crimsworth and Frances Henri. William is a young Englishman who goes to teach English in Brussels at a school whose male and female divisions are directed by a M. Pelet and Mlle. Reuter. At the school William falls in love with a young pupil-teacher, Frances Henri, and, despite the jealous interventions of Mlle. Reuter (a fictionalized Mme. Heger), he eventually marries her. Together they run a successful school and finally return to England, where they have a son and live in a vine-covered cottage retreat.

William Crimsworth is lineal descendent of the Sir William who propositioned Elizabeth Hastings, and retains something of the edgy arrogance inherited from their joint forefather, Charles Wellesley, Charlotte's earliest mouthpiece and by extension still her narrator in this novel. But he now expands to include also certain elements of M. Heger, in being Frances' beloved "master" who fulfills Charlotte's wishful fantasy of being loved by her Belgian teacher. This "master" does not send away his gifted pupil, but rather repudiates all connection with her rival, Mlle. Reuter, seeks out the bereaved Frances at the grave of the aunt who had been a mother to her, and—in a marked new development for Charlotte—takes her to his heart forever.

Frances, in turn, descends from Miss West and Elizabeth Hastings. Miss West had been a "little dusk figure" beside her showy pupils; Elizabeth Hastings was a "dim dusk foil" to hers. As humble lace mender Frances Henri is at first an even more downtrodden and shadowy figure than they; but like them she harbors brilliant inner fires, and under William's encouraging support her fires kindle and flash even more than Miss West's or Elizabeth's had done.

The novel opens in a thinly disguised Angrian setting, with characters recognizable even by name: the brothers Edward and William Crimsworth are the old Edward and William Percy. Even the Angrian Percy's minion Timothy Steighton is present in this novel as Edward Crimsworth's minion of the same name; and William's odd friend, the hostile yet protective truth teller Hunsden Yorke Hunsden, descends from the prophetic Warner Howard Warner of Angria. (Hunsden and Warner, and later Mr. Yorke of *Shirley,* are all modeled to some extent on Mary Taylor's father, whose family business at the Hunsworth Mills contributed to the names of both Hunsden and Crimsworth.)

The grinding oppression under which William struggles in the opening chapters loosely parallels Charlotte's hard years as teacher and governess, when the sense that she was doing her duty was her only real-life pleasure. As if in reference to this autobiographical period, Crimsworth is said to appear "weary, solitary, kept-down—like some desolate tutor or governess";[2] he even compares his situation to that of the Israelites enslaved in Egypt. But William's departure for Brussels and his job at the Pensionnat are drawn far more literally from Charlotte's life, with details changed only as necessary to account for the shift in gender. Doubtless partly because he is male and must incorporate elements of M. Heger, William is never a student in Brussels, as Charlotte herself had been; he is teacher only, and the role of pupil is assigned to Frances.

Ever since childhood Charlotte had been interested in exploring the implications of gender reversal—not only in assuming as author a male persona, but also in assigning character and role within her fictions. Charlotte seems to have been probing the problem of how gender relates to fate: must it always be the women who are swallowed up? Could Zamorna, with all his dangerous glamour, take female form? Before going any farther into *The Professor,* we must glance briefly at the history of Charlotte's interest in this question. Its issues are central to all her mature work.

To the early love story of Zamorna and his first wife, Marian, Charlotte attached a curious plot complication whose main purpose seems to have been to test the boundaries of gender. In **"The Secret,"**[3] written in November 1833, we learn that there had been a childhood engagement between Marian and a third Percy brother, Henry, whom Charlotte apparently invented for this purpose. Marian and young Henry had not been in love; their engagement was rather the result of youthful friendship and the dying wishes of their mothers. Accordingly, when Henry was drowned at sea three years later in the wreck of *The Mermaid* (a ship commanded by the same Steighton who appears in *The Professor*), Marian felt regret at his death, but no deep loss. And soon thereafter she fell passionately in love for the first and only time of her life—or course with Zamorna. Just as plans for their marriage were going forward, however, Marian was told that her youthful fiancé was not dead after all, and the marriage was held up until Henry's wraith appeared supernaturally, assured her that he really was dead, and released her from all obligation. Of the several wraiths to appear in Charlotte's stories after **"Albion and Marina,"** Henry's most nearly prefigures that of the drowned woman in **"Gilbert"** (like hers, Henry's rises "wet and dripping" from the sea). But Henry's message is helpful rather than vengeful: "fear not that I shall return. Death and the waters of a vast deep chain me to my place; be happy and think of your first love no more." To be sure, Henry had no grounds for vengeance: Marian had neither seduced nor abandoned him. She did not even meet Zamorna until well after *The Mermaid* had gone down with her young betrothed. Still, Marian's new attachment bears implicitly on Henry's fate; and her metaphoric destiny (ocean tomb and sea-sand pillow) mirrors his literal one.

Charlotte finished **"The Secret,"** in 1833; but apparently she felt that she had not yet finished exploring the implications of Henry's story, for in 1834 she returned to the topic in a long poem entitled **"Stanzas on the Fate of Henry Percy"** (#95).[4] In this new, expanded version, Marian is still not explicitly responsible for Henry's death. But her passion for Zamorna is now directly implicated, and the narrator assures Henry that she will suffer just as he has:

> . . . thy love, so strong, so unreturned,
>   Shall be avenged, on earth her time is brief
> The radiant Form, for whom, her spirit burned
>   Shall smile awhile then leave her bowed with grief[.]

Near the end of the poem Charlotte shifts her meter to signal a shift in narrative perspective. Henry is now dead, and the speaker addresses us rather than him: Henry "never from that vision woke," we are told; "coral banks" now "pillow" his head, and "tangled seaweeds wet with brine / Are garlanding his hair." Although "how he died no tongue can tell," still "dark . . . rumors" suggest that Percy, Henry's "awful father!" may have had Steighton kill the boy. Meanwhile Henry's rival in love, the successful Zamorna, basks in public adulation. In familiar figure, he is a wild and stormy but "enkindling" power.

Marian is in this poem less an independent agent than a middle figure caught between the two men. As she is swept by "passion's waves of conflict" in her love of Zamorna, Henry in turn drowns loving her. But the critical point has been established: men as well as women may drown in love. And this point is reinforced by the water imagery that consistently links love with death. Marian's eyes shine "like mirrored stars that glassed in dark waves lie"; her love for Henry disappears in the "rapid burning tide / That flows" from Zamorna's eyes. And of course the implications of stormy and engulfing water are literalized in Henry's drowning. The narrative hints that it was the sight of Marian's defection that really killed Henry: having once envisioned her burning for the "radiant form" of Zamorna, Henry "never from that vision woke." But Percy too may have had a hand in it. A father figure's treachery would be for Charlotte an entirely consistent element of the emotional blow of loss.

That Henry's ship is called *The Mermaid* is a point of central significance to this issue of gender inversion. As early as 1830 Charlotte had written in a poem titled **"A Serenade"** (#57) of the dangerous mermaid whose "still, sad music"—not "of humanity," as in Wordsworth, but of inhumanity—lures sailors to their death:

> It is the maiden of the sea, that sings within her cell
>   . . .
> And when her, monstrous form is seen swift-gliding
>   o'er the deep
> The Blood within the sailors veins, in frozen streams
>   doth creep[.]

This same mermaid is still a topic in *Shirley,* when Shirley and Caroline, planning a voyage, imagine encountering some mermaid with a "preternatural lure in its wily glance." "Were we men," Shirley observes, "we should spring at the sign, the cold billow would be dared for the sake of the colder enchantress; . . . Temptress terror! monstrous likeness of ourselves!" Caroline objects that the mermaid is "not like us: we are neither temptresses, nor terrors, nor monsters"; but Shirley reminds her that "Some of our kind, it is said, are all three. There are men who ascribe to 'woman,' in general, such attributes."[5] In her lethal attractiveness the mermaid is Charlotte's version of a female Zamorna; this is her meaning in Henry Percy's story, where *The Mermaid* bears Henry to his love death. But her added association in *Shirley* with the gentle Caroline, whose hair is "long as a mermaid's" (p. 112) and whose face is in the mermaid "style" (p. 276), suggests that Charlotte thought that any woman, even the least offensive, might have some mermaid characteristics.

The mermaid as dangerous siren stands for men's fear-induced misapprehension of women; Charlotte has Shirley assert that even "the acutest men are often under an illusion about women . . . they misapprehend them, both for good and evil: their good woman is a queer thing, half doll, half angel; their bad woman almost always a fiend" (p. 395). But mermaids also represent a certain truth about women. Women provide within their own bodies the amniotic sea that we all left behind in being born. The man who is lured to his death by a mermaid is in effect lured by woman-as-mother, in whom reside both the ocean of his origins and the life-long model of all his objects of sexual desire. His watery plunge, and the consequent loss of masculine separateness that he undergoes in responding to the mermaid's seductive appeal, is the male analogue of the infantilization and loss of identity that Charlotte feared from the submerging embrace of the false father.

We may pursue the parallel even further. As the male God redeems man from eternal death in the great "mother" whose dangers the mermaid emblemizes, so for Charlotte the female Divinity—Hope, the moon-mother, etc.—helps woman defend herself from the seductive father. Recall Zamorna's siren call to Caroline Vernon: "he knew how to give a tone, an accent . . . which should produce ample effect . . .—there was something protecting & sheltering about it as though he were calling her home." He is calling her in fact to his fatherly bosom and her doom. "When Zamorna kissed her & said in that voice of fatal sweetness . . . 'Will you go with me,'" Caroline, lacking a mothering conscience, is as lost as any succumbing sailor at sea.[6]

This dark version of the family romance is dramatized at least twice in *The Professor.* Just after William has wooed and won his cherished pupil, he falls briefly but helplessly prey to "hypochondria." As Charlotte associated woman's experience of hypochondria with being folded in the submerging bosom of an infantilizing father-lover, so William's hypochondria is personified as a woman who takes him "to her death-cold bosom" and holds him "with arms of bone." Though no mermaid, this figure is symbolically related: a "sorceress," she draws William to the brink of death's "black, sullen river." Because what she embodies is Charlotte's fear that the sexual plunge taken in marriage may be fatal, William rightly sees his hypochondria as the rival of his love: "I repulsed her as one would a dreaded and ghastly concubine coming to embitter a husband's heart towards his young bride." It may be that she frightens rather than attracts William partly because (though a man) he has already seen and been strengthened by the goddess Hope.

In another startling image Frances too encounters the pull of a love that is crossed with death. Having just agreed to marry her beloved "maître," she pauses in rapt contentment: "as stirless in her happiness as a mouse in its terror" (p. 224). What terrifies her, of course, is the possibility that she has gained her heart's desire at the price of being swallowed up. She weeps at the approach of her wedding; more ominously, perhaps, she shows herself after it "as docile as a well-trained child" (p. 247). It is her attendant capacity for "firmness"—chiefly shown in her insistence on retaining her professional occupation—that saves her from a Mary's fate.

Charlotte's interest in gender inversions, her awareness that both sexes may be seduced as well as seducing, helps explain why in **The Professor** she appropriates the roles of both male and female protagonists. She was struggling to imagine a sexual relationship in which both members might prosper; in which, because both are versions of herself, neither need be a "siren" luring the other to doom. As William is Charlotte's persona, a version of the voice she had been using for years, so the name "Frances" too emphasizes the ambiguities of gender—especially so since the M. Pelet who marries Frances' rival, Mlle. Reuter, is named "François" (p. 110). And Frances Henri's surname is of course a link back to Henry Percy. Although in her effort to make William convincingly masculine Charlotte attributed to him characteristics that are traditional in her domineering males—overbearing aloofness, touches of sadism—she studied the characteristics from the inside, providing motivation, exploring, as if it were her own, the need or desire out of which such behavior might arise. William flings open the classroom door and strides in masterfully just the way M. Paul will. But William offers a practical reason: "I had found that in entering with aplomb . . . consisted the grand secret of assuring immediate silence" (p. 118). He takes on the hard and indifferent character of "a rigid pillar of stone" not because it is innate to him as it will be to Brocklehurst, but in response to Mlle. Reuter's behavior: "Servility creates despotism" (p. 129).

Several critics have remarked on the feminine imagery that attaches to William. Not only is he "kept down like some desolate tutor or governess," a detail from Charlotte's own experience, but there are several slips into gender-inappropriate metaphor, as when Hunsden remarks that "Any woman, sinking her shaft deep enough, will at last reach a fathomless spring of sensibility in thy breast, Crimsworth" (p. 93), or when Mlle. Reuter's addresses to him are couched in the figurative language of male seduc-tion or rape: "her finger, essaying, proving every atom of the casket—touched its secret spring, and for a moment—the lid sprung open, she laid her hand on the jewel within . . ." (p. 105).

In **The Professor** Charlotte's pattern of sinking and rising is experienced by both William and Frances. Frances' experience is given in two versions: it is encapsulated in the poem ostensibly written by Frances, said to be "not exactly the writer's own experience," but suggested by "portions of that experience" (p. 217), and it is recounted in the plot. The poem was actually, of course, Charlotte's own wish-fulfilling fantasy, composed on leaving Brussels and later published among her poems under the title "Master and Pupil" (#205). In the poem the young speaker "Jane" falls ill at a school closely modeled on the Pensionnat Heger; but when visited at her bed by her beloved Professor, who places his hand on hers "with gentle stress" and says "God—she *must* revive!" she feels "The sense of Hope" begin its "healing work." Then as she convalesces the Professor continues to show a tender solicitude for her, and when at the end of the poem she must depart, he urges his "foster child" to "come home to me again." Thus as Jane sinks, her Professor is a mothering figure bringing hope (another gender inversion, of course, and as such it looks forward to the healing role of Caroline's mother in **Shirley**), even as he also offers the fatherly "home" that Charlotte's heroines have been learning to refuse in the interests of survival and achievement.

The other version of Frances' rising is an alternate wish fulfillment. She sinks in having lost all who love her: her aunt has died, her rival has dismissed her from the job that gave access to her Master, whom she expects never to see again. In her despair, she retreats to the fetal harbor of the graveyard "nook" where her aunt lies buried. There William discovers her and raises her into the sunshine of love, work, and a happy marriage.

This time Charlotte's old opposition between love and achievement is partly resolved by the fact that William is less a "father" than a male version of the author. But it is resolved only partly; for Frances is the *female* version of the author, and Frances splits in two after her marriage. "I seemed to possess two wives," marvels William. The first is the achieving "Madame the Directress" of their school, "a stately and elegant woman, bearing much anxious thought on her large brow," but the second—a lovable, adoring little pupil—takes her place at six o'clock. "I then came home, for my home was my heaven—ever at that hour, as I entered our private sitting-room—the lady-directress vanished from before my eyes, and Frances Henri, my own little lace-mender, was magically restored to my arms; much disappointed she would have been if her master had not been as constant to the tryste as herself" (pp. 251-52). Frances is in fact Charlotte's first heroine to keep alive both her sexuality and her intellectual ambition. The cost is high—a compartmentalization that verges on dissolution. But the gain is crucial too.

William's experience of sinking and rising provides the novel's basic story line. He is first rather attracted to Mlle.

Reuter but then meets the far worthier Frances and begins to take joy in her—the first real joy he has known in life. But suddenly she disappears; and William compares his loss and prospect of recovery with that greatest falling and rising, death and resurrection. Then he finds Frances in the graveyard nook, recognizes their mutual love, and sees the goddess "Hope." Here complications enter, in the form of additional variations on the theme of collapse and recovery. These variations seem necessary not to the plot but to the author, allowing her to recur to favorite themes.

The first of these variations is William's odd encounter with hypochondria, which we have discussed already. But more curious by far is William's relationship with his friend Hunsden, who now returns to the story. Hunsden is another ambiguous parent figure—hostile and teasing, but ultimately supportive. Though modeled in part on Mary Taylor's father, Hunsden is (like his handwriting) "neither masculine nor exactly feminine" (p. 192). As observed earlier, his Angrian original was the religious and prophetic Warner Howard Warner, who had actually been called a hermaphrodite. Hunsden's return to the story is initiated by a compressed allusion to the Old and New Testament themes of Egyptian bondage and Christian salvation. He warns of his approaching visit with a letter in which he teasingly imagines William "sitting like a black-haired, tawny-skinned, long-nosed Israelite by the flesh-pots of Egypt," and tells his friend to be ready for him: "Be on the look-out, for you know neither the day nor hour when your———(I don't wish to blaspheme, so I'll leave a blank) cometh" (p. 193). The unspoken "Redeemer" is part Hunsden himself, part the gift that he brings—a portrait of William's mother, which William has longed for but never hoped to possess, and which Hunsden makes him "pay" for through a species of humiliating teasing. Here, as throughout the novel, Hunsden is characterized by a strange perversity, evident here in both the near-blasphemy and the combination of kindness with cruelty. But perhaps this perversity, too, may be explained as a function of Charlotte's experiments with gender. The hero and heroine of *The Professor* are both explicitly parentless. Hunsden seems meant to fulfill the roles of a mother who supports and urges forward and a masculinely tough and satiric father. Thus he catapults William somewhat roughly out of the Egyptian slavery of Edward's millworks (like a masculine mother) and later descends on him bearing his mother's portrait, as a "Redeemer" (like a female father). In all of this Hunsden is not a very successful creation, but Charlotte's conception of him was certainly ambitious.

We can see the way William and Frances each reflect Charlotte's view of her own self and history. William represents Charlotte not only in that he is the oppressed "slave" of his brother, and then a teacher in the Pensionnat schoolroom; but also in his physical similarity to his sadly sensitive dead mother, in his susceptibility to hypochondria, in his vision of the goddess "Hope." In short, even though William is a man, he speaks from Charlotte's experience, both inner and outer.[7]

Frances, meanwhile, has Charlotte's gender as well as her small stature and delicate features; she is literally banished (as Charlotte had felt figuratively banished) by a powerful rival for her "master's" heart (Zoraide Reuter is an unflattering portrait of Zoë Parent, M. Heger's wife). Frances' difficulties in achieving authority as a teacher were evidently Charlotte's; she offers her "master" the "charms" that Charlotte felt she could offer Heger—"application, love of knowledge, natural capacity, docility, truthfulness, gratefulness" (p. 120)—and, like Charlotte, she differs from the Belgian girls in being "of a race less gifted with fulness of flesh and plenitude of blood, less jocund, material, unthinking" (p. 122). Like Charlotte, Frances knows the power of her intellectual gift. Though she does not respond in words to her teacher's praise, her "radiance" and "frank and flashing glance" communicate the self-confidence of genius, something Charlotte herself must often have felt: "Do you think I am myself a stranger to myself? What you tell me in terms so qualified, I have known fully from a child" (p. 137). And, as Charlotte had regarded Belgium so Frances regards England as "the promised land." Like Charlotte, "a little affection, ever so little, pleased her better than all the panegyrics in the world" (p. 147). Like Charlotte she feared for her eyesight (p. 191). And finally, the fact that Frances has no real home, but lives in "Rue Notre Dame aux Neiges" (the Street of Our Lady of the Snows), looks forward to the virginal Lucy Snowe into whom Frances will develop in Charlotte's final novel.

But the mutual growth of love between Frances and her "master"; their rediscovery of one another, after cruelly imposed separation, at a "mother's" grave; the calm courtship, happy marriage, successful joint careers—all of these are the stuff of Charlotte's wishful fantasy, even though muted to the terms of what she imagined to be workaday marital realism.[8]

The marriage of William and Frances is thus at one level a model of the marriage Charlotte dreamed she might have had with Heger, had Fate only arranged things differently. But at a deeper level—the level of her profoundest hopes and fears—this is no marriage at all, but rather a metaphor for the union of elements within Charlotte herself, of her male narrator and female self-representation. The way is prepared for Jane Eyre, the first of Charlotte's heroines to write her own life.

Notes

1. Ewbank, observing this split, describes it well: the hero and heroine "have natures and careers so similar as to make them one character distributed over two sexes" ([Ewbank, Inga-Stina. *Their Proper Sphere: A Study of the Brontë Sisters as Early-Victorian Female Novelists*. Cambridge, Mass.: Harvard University Press, 1968.], p. 157). Keefe makes a similar point in [Keefe, Robert. *Charlotte Brontë's world of Death*. Austin: University of Texas Press, 1979], p. 85.

2. [Brontë, Charlotte. *The Professor*. Ed. Margaret Smith and Herbert Rosengarten. Oxford: Clarendon

Press, 1987], p. 23. Further page references will be given in the text.

3. This tale is printed in [Holz, William, ed. *Two Tales by Charlotte Brontë: "The Secret" and "Lily Hort."* Columbia: University of Missouri Press, 1978].

4. The numbering of Charlotte's poems follows [Neufeldt, Victor A., ed. *The Poems of Charlotte Brontë.* New York: Garland Press, 1985]. All quotations from her poetry are from this edition.

5. [Brontë, Charlotte. *Shirley.* Ed. Herbert Rosengarten and Margaret Smith. Oxford: Clarendon Press, 1979.], p. 276. Further page references will be given in the text. The social and psychological implications of the mermaid as metaphor for woman (as she is feared and disparaged by men) are suggestively explored by Dinnerstein, [Dorothy. *The Mermaid and the Minotaur.* New York: Harper and Row, 1976.] and her summary of the implications of this fishwoman is remarkably apt for Charlotte's use of the figure. The treacherous mermaid who lures voyagers to their death, writes Dinnerstein, is the "seductive and impenetrable female representation of the dark and magic underwater world from which our life comes and in which we cannot live" (p. 5).

6. [Brontë, Charlotte. *Five Novelettes: Passing Events, Julia, Mina Laury, Captain Henry Hastings, Caroline Vernon.* Ed. Winifred Gérin. London: Folio Press, 1971.], "Caroline Vernon," pp. 352, 354.

7. For one further, oddly obtrusive example, note that Crimsworth voices Charlotte's judgment on Branwell, whose affair with Mrs. Robinson resulted in his being sent home in disgrace from Thorpe Green in July 1845. Crimsworth speaks: "Limited as had yet been my experience of life, I had once had the opportunity of contemplating, near at hand an example of the results produced by a course of interesting and romantic domestic treachery . . . it was very loathsome. I saw a mind degraded by the practice of mean subterfuge, by the habit of perfidious deception, and a body depraved by the infectious influence of the vice-polluted soul. I had suffered much from the forced and prolonged view of this spectacle . . ." (p. 187). The account is entirely gratuitous, except as it evidently relieved Charlotte's personal feelings.

8. Even the name Charlotte chose for Frances' and William's child—Victor—serves this fantasy in echoing the name of the Hegers' fifth child, Victorine (a girl), born shortly before Charlotte's final departure from Brussels.

Bettina L. Knapp (essay date 1991)

SOURCE: "Charlotte Brontë: 'If You Knew My Thoughts. . . .'" In *The Brontës: Branwell, Anne, Emily, Charlotte,* Continuum, 1991, pp. 133-82.

[*In the following excerpt, Knapp examines the hatred between brothers Edward and William Crimsworth in* The

Professor *and discusses the impact this has upon William's anima and his relationships with women.*]

Written with the grace and charm of many a Victorian novel, *The Professor* also possesses a psychologically fascinating quality of its own. Unlike *Wuthering Heights,* neither the happenings nor the characters emanate from the author's archetypal depths; they are not, therefore, mythical in stature. More like *Agnes Grey,* **The Professor** is a structured and rationally conceived work, an attempt on the author's part to perfect and restrain the formerly effulgent style of her juvenilia.

The writing of **The Professor** may have served as a means to clarify Charlotte's thoughts concerning the art of the novelist. Every move and thought of the protagonists, within a set framework and ambiance, gives the impression of having been churned and rechurned, sifted, fleshed out, and evaluated in the author's logical mind and within the preconceived plot line. Although spontaneous events do occur at strategic moments in the novel, they are designed to illuminate the characters' own weaknesses and foibles, thus giving them another chance to pursue the best and most righteous of courses. As in *Agnes Grey,* integrity and forthrightness are uppermost in the outlook of hero and heroine. Nevertheless, the power of passion pulsates, albeit in diminished and most always controlled sequences. Although hatred, jealousy, anger, and the purest and most naive of notions are interwoven in the very fabric of **The Professor,** these emotions are used as literary strategies designed to heighten or slacken suspense. So thought out is **The Professor** that the feelings motivating the protagonists' actions give the impression of having been built into the very lining of their personalities, thus divesting them of any authenticity. Still, the touches of morbidity and the sequences focusing on the male protagonist's sexual awakening are sufficiently complex to give the reader pause.

Like Marcel Proust who, in *Remembrance of Things Past,* transformed many a male into a female character and vice versa, thus enabling him to conceal certain anomalies, so Charlotte, unwilling to lay bare tendencies embedded within her own psyche that could possibly be offensive to Victorian readers, altered the sexual identities of her characters. She seemed to feel greater ease using a male protagonist as spokesman to disclose her feelings and thoughts than a female.

Most arresting in **The Professor** is the in-depth psychological study of hatred existing between two brothers, Edward and William Crimsworth. So understanding is the author of the problems involved, so sensitive is she to the nuances of their needs and motivations that one is inclined to consider them somewhat auto-biographical in nature. Is the seething antagonism implicit in **The Professor** a manifestation of her relationship with Emily and Anne? Or are the two brothers to be viewed as doubles—concretizations of polarities buried within her own psyche? The theme of the double is not without precedent, as, for example, Poe's "William Wilson," Dostoyevsky's *The Double,* and Gogol's *Diary of a Madman.*

BROTHER HATRED: AN OPERATIVE SHADOW

The first part of **The Professor,** which takes place in England, focuses on the bitter enmity existing between Edward and William Crimsworth. Such hostility, viewed psychologically, occurs when a shadow projection is operative.

The shadow is that part of the unconscious personality containing inferior characteristics that the individual is unwilling or as yet unable to recognize as his own and, therefore, projects onto another or others. William, the narrator, is oblivious to the fact that the "evils" he condemns in his brother are the very ones he detests and seeks to annihilate in himself. Condemning Edward freely and without any self-examination, William maintains his own sense of integrity and righteousness on the surface at least. More serious is the fact that the longer he attributes to his brother characteristics he cannot or is unwilling to accept as his own—allowing hatred, rage, and antagonism to be meted out freely to Edward—there can be no increase in self-knowledge on his part.

What is the basis of the hatred existing between the two brothers? Both are orphans. Their father, having failed as a mill owner, died six months before William's birth; the mother succumbed in childbirth. Having been repudiated by their wealthy and aristocratic maternal family, who had never forgiven Mrs. Crimsworth for having married beneath her station, the brothers were brought up with the minimum of charity by their father's uncles. Only by dint of threats from other members of the family does William receive support and go to Eton. Unwilling to enter the church upon his graduation, the twenty-year-old William opts for a business career. To this end, he seeks out his thirty-year-old brother, Edward, who through hard work, ingenuity, and a good marriage, has become a successful mill owner at Bigben Close in the North of England. Jealous of William's Etonian education, Edward harbors no warmth for his brother, and offers him a relatively low job—a second clerkship—for someone so well educated.

Although both brothers had been orphaned, Edward was ten when his parents died, and had suffered most grievously from their loss, while William had never really known them. On the other hand, Edward had benefited from his mother's love, whereas William, deprived of all maternal feeling, had been divested of all sense of belonging, warmth, and well-being. Did Edward unconsciously consider William a murderer, blaming him for his mother's demise, since she died in childbirth?

Edward's overtly destructive responses to William may be viewed as projections of negative characteristics lodged deeply within William and not necessarily contents belonging to the wealthy mill owner. It may be suggested that both Edward and William are split-offs of *one* person—the shadow side of each juxtaposed to the positive aspects of the other. Since Edward is the more emotional of the two, and affects usually emerge when adaptation is weakest, his uncontrollable behavioral patterns disclose an inability to cope with his sense of inferiority.[1]

The day after his first visit to Crimsworth Hall, Edward's "Good Morning" to William was abrupt, after which he "snatched" a newspaper from the table and began reading it "with the air of a master who seizes a pretext to escape the bore of conversing with an underling." There was no dialogue between the two. William repressed his hurt. As he was cogitating about how best he could endure his brother's insults while maintaining, at least on the outside, a courteous stance, he happened to see Edward's reflection in the mirror. But was it actually Edward's countenance that he had viewed? Or was he in fact looking upon those secret and unacceptable qualities within his own self that he had projected onto his brother? But then, William rationalized, the qualities in which his brother excelled were merely physical or "animal." As an intellectual, the younger brother considered himself superior to the business man, and has decided to "force" his mind to learn to cope with the situation at hand. As a thinking person, he was determined to force his will to dominate any emotional encounter and any unconscious pulsations that might spin off from their meeting. To assess his brother's personality might yield positive results; it would not only give William the key to his future comportment, but would help him extricate himself from an unpleasant present situation. For example, he understood that he could expect no "lion-like generosity" from his brother; nor did Edward's stern and forbidding manner augur well for the birth of any kind of relationship between the two. The consideration of both brothers as dual aspects of a *single* personality, foretells incompatibility within that one individual.

Because "Caution, Tact, Observation" determined William's behavioral patterns, his life became increasingly solitary. His practice of self-analysis, however, encouraged him to *question* his motives, needs, and desires, and to listen to his inner voice for "a clear notion" of what he was, what he wanted, and how much unhappiness he would be able to endure. He came to understand finally that were he to remain for any length of time in his brother's employ, he would not only not derive any emotional compensation from his work, but would, on the contrary, stagnate and even regress. Neither warmth nor understanding nor even a texture of friendship could be expected. The psychological condition of stasis he was suffering is reflected in the iciness of his rented room, in which the maid always forgot to light an evening fire. Without fire, an agent of transformation, no feelings or love could be born. Only rigidity.

Two factors intervened encouraging William to change his course. The first was William's chance meeting with Mr. Hunsden, a manufacturer and mill owner who saw how diligent a worker he was and how ill-treated he had been by his brother. In Hunsden's rooms, the "bright grate was filled with a genuine—shire fire, red, clear, and generous." It was Hunsden, a fire principle, who advised William to strike out on his own. What career would be to his liking? was the question. Teaching was the answer. Whereupon, Mr. Hunsden wrote a letter of introduction to a well-placed man in Brussels, who might be in a position to offer William a post as a teacher. The second event precipitating

William's departure was his brutal and unjust dismissal by Edward whose wrath had been aroused by the rumor that William had spoken ill of him.

Only one object had arrested William's attention during the three months he spent working for his brother: the portrait of his mother hanging at Crimsworth Hall. So important had it become for him that it symbolically pointed to the next step in his maturing process: the seeking out of the *mother* image, the carrier and embodiment of the feminine principle—known as anima in the male.

ANIMA AS FEMININE PRINCIPLE

The personification of the feminine principle, the *anima,* as previously defined, is "an autonomous psychic content in the male personality"; an inner woman, or the "psychic representation of the contrasexual elements in man."[2] When a man's anima is projected onto a living woman, it leads him to fall in love. If he is involved with a willful, devouring, and demonic type, and if his projection is unconscious, his ego may be submerged by the power she has over him and reduce him to a state of paralysis or childlike obedience to her. If, on the other hand, he is conscious of his anima, and his ego is sufficiently developed, she may lead him to know a meaningful and profound relationship.

A NEGATIVE ANIMA

Upon his arrival in Brussels, and thanks to Hunsden's intervention, William obtains a post as English and Latin teacher in a boy's school directed and owned by a M. Pelet. Although surprised by the mediocre intellectual level of the students, William enjoys his new post and earns respect and confidence. He pleasures in Mr. Pelet's company and is able to relate to this "clever and witty" Frenchman.

One of the windows of William's room overlooked the garden of the girl's school opposite, and decency had dictated that it should be boarded to prevent a prying eye from peering into feminine mysteries. Utterly naïve in matters of sex or anything remotely identified with womankind, William was excited about the very thought of such an interdict. When alone, he tried to find some chink or hole in the boarded-up window that might allow him to "peep at the consecrated ground." Although his efforts were to no avail, the thought of the *"allée defendue"* aroused sexual awareness in him. How much he would have enjoyed spying on these forbidden delights is conveyed metaphorically—as a beautiful garden with flowers and trees, somewhat reminiscent of a Garden of Eden.

So one-sided was William's upbringing, so identified was he with the spirit rather than with anything relating to the human sphere, that when Mr. Pelet's mother invites him to *goûter,* he is convinced that she seeks to make love to him! Mrs. Pelet's invitation is, however, business-oriented, and leads to the contrived offer to William of a position as English teacher at the "Pensionnat des demoiselles" adjacent to Mr. Pelet's academy. "I shall now at last see the mysterious garden, I shall gaze both on the angels and their Eden," William thinks.

Zoraide Reuter, director of the girls' pensionnat, was an anima figure: a seductress capable of leading William step-by-step into the world of feminine mysteries. Bewitching by her demeanor from the very outset, she, like the goddesses of antiquity, aroused in William hitherto unknown sensations of love.

In reality, Zoraide was an illusion-creating anima figure who sought, perhaps unconsciously at first, then with open determination, to envelop, embrace, and devour her prey. A negative feminine principle, she represented danger to the naïve, deception to the morally sound, and suffering to the gullible. It was only a matter of time before William would be caught in her web, and left there to strangle helplessly.

Unaware of her power over him, however, William blithely became enticed by Zoraide's bewitching feminine charm. Each time he returned from the girl's school, happiness rather than his usual somberness was imprinted on his features and his confidence and competence as a teacher also improved.

Mr. Pelet, aware of William's naïveté in terms of the opposite sex, was quick to point out to him that "any woman, sinking her shaft deep enough, will at last reach a fathomless spring of sensibility in thy breast." Believing that God's light was shining upon him and Zoraide, William was all the more unprepared for the cruel deception that was forthcoming: leaning out of his window one evening to look down on the very spot that had witnessed the first and most delectable discussion with his ladylove, he overheard a conversation between her and Mr. Pelet, which revealed that they were secretly engaged and had encouraged his infatuation simply for amusement. So deeply shocked is William that he swears to maintain henceforth a stone-cold countenance toward Zoraide.

Perplexed, because she cannot account for the sudden change in William's behavior, Zoraide becomes attracted to his invulnerability and impassibility. Using her wiles, she does her best to soften his hostility; and to impress him with her altruism, she tells of her kindness toward a poor young English-Swiss seamstress in the school's employ, Frances Evans Henri.

A POSITIVE ANIMA

If Zoraide may be considered a negative anima type, interested only in gratifying her own desires and calculating how best to ensnare and then devour her prey, Frances Evans Henri was her antithesis. Natural, innocent, methodical, and candid, she also possessed a certain winsomeness. Although spiritually oriented, she was firmly rooted to this earth, but had no illusions about life or people. She conformed to expectations both as an employee in the school and in the city, but being ambitious, she sought to improve her command of the English language and eventually gain access to better employment.

As anima, she embodied William's suprapersonal values or ideal. Like the *femme inspiratrice,* she would unconsciously play an indispensable role in his world, knowing instinctively how to focus on her own goals, and at the same time help William to function at his best under dismal circumstances. As anima, her qualities reflected his own rich unconscious feminine side.

Frances would not only play the role of the beloved, but also that of a nourishing and kindly mother figure. She would fill the void in William's heart, which had been created when he looked so longingly at the portrait of his mother hanging in Edward's home. Coincidentally, it was this very painting that Mr. Hunsden, on a visit to Brussels, had brought to William, telling him that he had bought it at an auction sale following Edward's bankruptcy.

William becomes increasingly impressed by Frances's intelligence and her beautiful character traits. Unspoiled, demure, even shy at times, she is endowed with perseverance, a sense of duty, and an extraordinary ability to contend with life's difficulties. Her integrity is antipodal to the moral unsoundness of Zoraide who, now jealous of Frances, summarily dismisses her. The "perfidious" vamp, dominated by a "vice-polluted soul," resorts to the lie, telling William that the little seamstress employed by the school has resigned her post and left no forwarding address.

Fruitlessly, William makes inquiry everywhere hoping to discover Frances's whereabouts. Finally resigning his teaching post, he sets out in search of her in the city, visiting even the Protestant cemetery in Brussels. It is there that he finds her, beside the grave of her last living relative, her recently departed aunt. Although William realizes he is in love with Frances, he cannot propose to her until he finds a new situation. Disheartening weeks follow. Finally, thanks to the father of one of his former students whom he had saved from drowning, he obtains a fine teaching position, proposes to Frances, and is accepted.

Accustomed to supporting herself in life, Frances—a good feminist—is determined to keep on working as a lace-maker and mender, even after marriage, despite William's wish that she remain a homebody. Her determined refusal is quiet but steadfast. No human power could bend her will. "Think of my marrying you to be kept by you, Monsieur! I could not do it—and how dull my days would be!" By dint of the couple's hard work, in ten years time they amassed sufficient capital to enable them and their son, Victor, to retire to England, Frances's "Promised Land."

Charlotte's expository discourse in *The Professor* concludes without being judgmental. She succeeded in cutting open the bruised soul of her protagonist—a manifestation of her own—but she did not know how to express the

workings of the masculine psyche. William's needs and ideations seem contrived, awkward, and conveyed in stilted language, and, as the reviewer for the *North British Review* wrote:

> It is quite obvious to any reader who attends to the sketch of the character of the Professor, that the Professor is a woman in disguise, . . . for she is quite properly stripped of her male costume . . . There is a shyness, a sulky tenderness, and a disposition to coquet manifest in the Professor's relations with his friend . . . which betrays to us at once that the picture is drawn from a lady's experience of her friendship with the other sex.[3]

Notes

1. C. G. Jung, *The Portable Jung,* p. 145.

2. Edward Edinger, "An Outline of Analytical Psychology," p. 10.

3. Earl A. Knies, *The Art of Charlotte Brontë.* From "Novels by the Authoress of 'John Halifax,'" *North British Review,* 29 (1858), pp. 474-475.

Annette R. Federico (essay date 1994)

SOURCE: "The Other Case: Gender and Narration in Charlotte Brontë's *The Professor.*" In *Papers on Language and Literature,* Vol. 30, No. 4, Fall, 1994, pp. 323-45.

[*In the following essay, Federico discusses Brontë's use of a male narrator in* The Professor.]

Male novelists who use female narrators have been praised for their insights into "feminine psychology," yet we seldom expect women writers to represent masculinity from a male point of view. In her recent work on feminism and narratology, Susan Lanser considers "the social properties and political implications of narrative voice," claiming that "female voice"—the grammatical gender of the narrator—"is a site of ideological tension made visible in textual practice" (4-5). This tension is conspicuous in novels published in the nineteenth century: a strict literary double-standard reflects a cultural double-standard that devalues feminine discourse in the public sphere. Like everything else, narrative voice corresponds to the cultural needs of Victorian society, and so an age comparatively rich in literary heroines (and in women writers) still finds the masculine voice more representative, and, supposedly, more rational, more "objective." Because narrative voice carries the burdens of Victorian gender polarization—in its representation of male or female language and the expectations it raises about masculine or feminine plots[1]—grammatical gender in a Victorian novel is as ideologically constructed as the gendered body inhabited by the author.

If narrative voice is a site of ideological tension, it is even more difficult to construe when a male voice is adapted self-consciously by women writers who call themselves

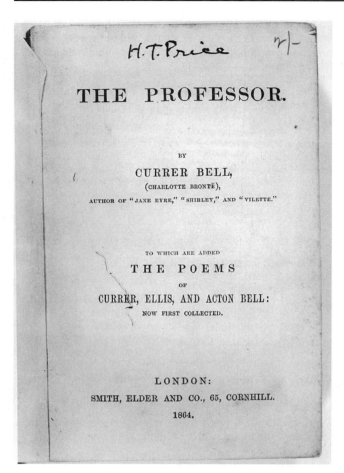

"Currer Bell" or "George Eliot." Indeed, because narrative authority conforms to rather than challenges "hierarchical, patriarchal norms" (Cohan & Shires 146) we can gain insight into the ways women who use male narrators understand gender relations, and how they reproduce masculinity—and with it, dominant discourse—in the choice of male language, preoccupations, and pursuits.

In her first novel, *The Professor,* Charlotte Brontë uses a first-person male narrator, and, as I will discuss, critics have tended to see this as both an artistic error and an elision of her feminist voice. But whether she takes a male or female narrator, Brontë is no less intent on examining the encoding of gender in nineteenth-century discourse. Specifically, the male voice provides an opening to confront a central issue for Brontë—power—which is different from her explorations of powerlessness in her later heroine-centered novels. In *The Professor,* she is learning what it is to have the power of authorship, and therefore it is consistent that she should go inside the system to attempt to represent the source of that power.[2]

Many psychoanalytic approaches to *The Professor* accept the "feminization" of the male narrator as the woman writer's personal experience of subordination translated into a pseudo-male voice. Though this helps in understanding biographical issues and the so-called "female imagina-

tion," such readings tend to overlook how the appropriation of the male voice may challenge a tradition of androcentric narrative and Victorian patriarchal hegemony. As Terry Eagleton explains, one interpretation of feminism "is not just that women should have equality of power and status with men; it is a questioning of all such power and status. It is not just that the world will be better off with more female participation in it; it is that without the 'feminization' of human history, the world is unlikely to survive" (150). Brontë engages this concern by using an intrinsically authoritative male voice to tell a story that is not about a heroine's traditional growth into power, but instead authorizes a masculine growth out of power by asserting the need to temper male authority with "feminine" social virtues, usefully defined by Susan Morgan as "gentleness, flexibility, openness to others, friendship, and love" (19). At the same time, however, Brontë describes the practical and psychological obstacles to this "feminization" for men who are subject to ideological constraints, particularly the insistence on sexual difference. For as Mary Poovey has persuasively argued, "[M]en were too thoroughly ensnared in the contradictions that characterized this ideology to be charged with being simple oppressors" (22). William Crimsworth, the hero-narrator of *The Professor,* represents a view of masculinity that differs entirely from Brontë's later portraits of attractive and powerful men who threaten the heroine's autonomy. In her first novel, Brontë attempts to be the autobiographical male, to imagine what he imagines, even to have a male body[3]—in other words, to treat the burdens of sex from the male point of view, and thereby explore the social consequences of her culture's constructions of gender.

Critics tend to speak summarily about *The Professor,* written in 1846 and published posthumously in 1857. It is "a rehearsal for *Villette*" (Lane vii) or an early "failed" attempt to create a heroine like Jane Eyre (Basch 68-9). In *A Literature of Their Own,* Elaine Showalter mentions *The Professor* only briefly as an example of how "women writers internalized the values of their society" (136-7). Even critics who turn their full attention to the novel, such as Helene Moglen and Sandra Gilbert and Susan Gubar, are conscious of a tendency to make excuses for its flaws. Moglen sees Brontë's choice of a male narrator as evidence that she is still "bound to the ambivalent attitudes of adolescence," unable to associate a female voice with authority; Crimsworth's voice is the novel's most "crucial problem" (86-8). In *The Madwoman in the Attic,* Gilbert and Gubar concede that to discuss the novel as they have done "in terms merely of roles and repressions is . . . to trivialize the young novelist's achievement in her first full-length book" (335). Their description of *The Professor* as an extension of Brontë's "exotic 'male'" Angrian tales full of "obsessive and involuntary" characterizations (313-15), and as a "pseudo-masculine *Bildungsroman,*" "literary male-impersonation," and "male mimicry" (318-19) suggest that the novel's difficulties or flaws are linked to Brontë's handling of gender, especially the use of a male narrator. Instead of dismissing the narrator as a clumsy mistake by a young writer, Gilbert and Gubar at least try to make sense of the masculine voice, explaining that "by pretending to be a man, [the woman writer] can see herself as the crucial and powerful Other sees her" (317). To put it differently, by pretending to be male, Brontë can better analyze what really concerns her: being female.

Gilbert and Gubar make a similar argument about the male narrator in George Eliot's novella, *The Lifted Veil* (1859), a text that, like *The Professor*, has been either ignored or dismissed as an unsuccessful attempt by a relatively inexperienced writer of fiction.[4] Claiming Eliot's debt to Charlotte Brontë and Mary Shelley, Gilbert and Gubar see *The Lifted Veil* as a dramatization of Eliot's "internalization of patriarchal culture's definition of the woman as 'other'" (466). The clairvoyant male narrator, Latimer, who finds women both fascinating and repulsive, is an expression of Eliot's divided consciousness and represents her attempt to survive "in a male-dominated society by defining herself as the Other" (476). "Like Charlotte Brontë's early male persona . . . Latimer reflects his author's sense of her own peculiarity" (447). In both *The Professor* and *The Lifted Veil,* then, the woman writer with the masculine pseudonym engages her own status as female Other by assuming the voice, the authority, and the privileged position of the male subject. In this interpretation, Brontë and Eliot are not concerned with the experience of the narrator as a man or the representation of masculinity; authorial voice is still tied to female "schizophrenia," a "dis-ease with authority," self-hatred, and internalization (Gilbert and Gubar 444-5, 449).

Such readings are useful in their focus on the whole problem of "otherness" for Victorian women writers. But to claim that a woman chooses a male voice in order to work out her ambivalence about being female narrows the ideological implications of otherness, as well as the revisionist possibilities of these texts. Indeed, the resonance of "otherness" in these interpretations, with its suggestions of psychological oppression, indicates the problem inherent in women's writing, so that female subjectivity and feminist discourse is necessarily undermined by the constraints of man-made language.

The fact that the Brontës' books were called "masculine" by contemporary reviewers and George Eliot's quasi-dramatized narrators arrogate masculine authority[5] suggests how well the language and voice of the male subject can serve the cause of sexual equality. "In order to be a complete individual, on an equality with man, woman must have access to the masculine world as does the male to the feminine world, she must have access to the *other*" (de Beauvoir 761). For Brontë and Eliot, as for many Victorian women, such access was not always possible. Brontë admitted as much in a letter to James Taylor written in 1849: "In delineating male characters, I labour under disadvantages; intuition and theory will not adequately supply the place of observation and experience. When I write about women, I am sure of my ground—in the other case I am not so sure" (Shorter 30). For Brontë, men occupy a world that is closed to her observation; masculine psychol-

ogy and motivation are mysterious, impenetrable. He is truly "the *other* case." Yet if one accepts Carolyn Heilbrun's claim that "No woman writer struggled as [Brontë] struggled against the judgments of sexual polarization" (78), *The Professor* may be read as Brontë's earliest effort to confront the ideology of separate spheres. To tell a man's story is to insist on access, to insist on her complete individuality as a person and as an artist. Indeed, Brontë's interest in socialized gender roles, for boys in particular, is evident in a letter written to Miss Wooler just a year before she began *The Professor*:

> You ask me if I do not think men are strange beings. I do, indeed—I have often thought so; and I think too that the mode of bringing them up is strange, they are not sufficiently guarded from temptations. Girls are protected as if they were very frail and silly indeed, while boys are turned loose on the world as if they, of all beings in existence, were the wisest and the least liable to be led astray.
>
> (Shorter 315)

By using the voice of one of these "strange beings" in *The Professor,* Brontë examines with a mixture of irony and compassion the moral and emotional immunity built into Victorian constructions of masculinity. As "a tale of socialisation[,] of becoming masculine" (Boumelha 47), *The Professor* is attentive to the costs of being indoctrinated into patriarchy, and of naturalizing characteristics Victorian society admired in men, such as fixity, dominance, exclusion, competition, and stoicism.

The voice of William Crimsworth, far from sounding "curiously androgynous" (Gilbert & Gubar 319), is aggressively masculine throughout his narrative, locked into a socially sanctioned tone of superiority. There is no feminine apologizing, no womanly code of docility. His voice approximates the literary qualities assigned to men, which Showalter has identified as "power, breadth, distinctness, clarity, learning . . . shrewdness, knowledge of life, and humor," along with "masculine faults," such as "coarseness and passion" ("Double Standard" 340). In other words, Brontë, who aspires to professional status as a novelist, is writing as a professional—that is, as a man. Although Crimsworth tells the reader "I always speak quietly," and he is an idealistic young man, his language has a feel of license which for Brontë probably defined male discourse: "to scout myself a privileged prig" (77), or "'Stuff! I have cut them'" (41). If the voice comes across as false machismo, it may be because Brontë felt permitted to be extreme. Crimsworth has a man's right to say what he wants, for the basis of his character is his relative power and his uneasy participation in various systems of oppression. Despite his physical weaknesses (he is nearsighted, and describes himself as thin and slight) and his temporary status as a dependent, Crimsworth's voice resonates with confidence. As it should. Simone de Beauvoir has claimed that "One of the benefits that oppression confers upon the oppressors is that the most humble among them is made to *feel* superior. . . . The most mediocre of males feels himself a demigod as compared with women" (xxviii). It is precisely this assumption of male power that Brontë seems to question. For Crimsworth *does* feel a demigod compared with women. He is not one of Brontë's feminine heroes, a man who "must learn how it feels to be helpless and to be forced unwillingly into dependency" (Showalter, *Literature* 152). For one thing, he has an Eton education.[6] He also has a choice of professions, and obtains some influential male friends—Hunsden, Brown, and Vandenhutten—who write letters of recommendation and advise him about his investments. The material conditions of his life are not unbearable, and unlike the heroine of *Villette* in a similar situation he can at least walk down the streets without being harassed.[7] If gender in the novel is a semantic symbol denoting power, as Moglen suggests (89), Crimsworth's masculinity automatically confers social and psychological advantages over, for example, Jane Eyre or Lucy Snowe. He does possess, at least to some degree, four qualities which define power in Victorian society: education, money, mobility, and autonomy (Newton 7).

Nevertheless, Brontë begins **The Professor** with Crimsworth as a victim of male exploitation: his wealthy maternal uncles had refused to aid Crimsworth's dying mother, and for this (after accepting the ten years at Eton), Crimsworth denies any future aid. He is then pitted against the tyranny of his elder brother, Edward, who employs him as a clerk in his mill. He resents being treated as an inferior by other men ("I hate to be condescended to" [19]), and loathes being his brother's "slave"—a word Brontë applies almost obsessively to his situation in the first five chapters of the novel. Again, one is reminded of Brontë's heroines—particularly Jane and Lucy—when they suffer similar privations; although Jane longs for a new servitude, for example, the language of Brontë's heroine is nothing compared to the fierce resentment of her hero. According to Susanne Kappeler, "The status of the slave . . . is not in itself objectionable or dehumanizing, it is only so in the context of a male being held a slave, that is to say, held like a woman" (154). Crimsworth has been thoroughly emasculated, and Brontë understands this. By allowing himself to be treated as a slave, "kept down like some desolate tutor or governess" (17), he is obeying a feminine code of passivity which is mocked by his acquaintance Yorke Hunsden, who further insults his masculinity by telling him the only way he'll get ahead in the world is through a woman's agency: "your only chance of getting a competency lies in marrying a rich widow, or running away with an heiress" (31). Yet the apparent extremity of his situation does not approximate that of a governess, "disconnected, poor, and plain" (**Jane Eyre** 190), as much as it does that of any middle-class woman, who must rely on the charity of those in power for security.[8] But Crimsworth's position fails to call out the reader's sympathy because it is described in the self-satisfied tones of masculine authority; his superior attitude, as a man and an aristocrat, only invites us to objectify the desolate governess as the lowest of the low. The fact that the hero has been a victim of male oppression (his brother even whips him) does not quicken his sympathies for the oppressed; he seeks to exert his prerogative and find someone—and why

not a woman?—to exploit in return. If he cannot do this materially, he will do it verbally in his narrative by, for example, privately abusing "'That slut of a servant'" who neglects to light his grate (24). Crimsworth is disinherited and strange-looking, and he is brought low; obviously he is an example, along with Jane Eyre and Lucy Snowe, of Brontë's misunderstood misfits. But the voice of this novel is never really conscious of being perceived as less than fully human, which is the female experience of otherness; he always maintains the privilege of the masculine subject. Even after Brontë drops the artificial, epistolary opening with its male interlocutor, one has the feeling throughout the novel that the narratee is also male.[9] The absence of feminine consciousness contributes to this, of course, but there is also the narrator's complete failure of imagination when it comes to female experience, and his persistent distancing from and objectification of women.

For example, in the blighted industrial town where he goes to work "with other slaves" (31), Crimsworth's tendency is to view the feminine element with aloofness. He would deem it "like a night-mare" to marry one of his six cousins, and especially abhors "the large and well-modelled statue, Sarah." The "young, tall, and well-shaped" (7) wife of his rich brother is dismissed as childish, and the other "tall, well-made, full-formed, dashingly dressed" young ladies (sexually mature women clearly make him uncomfortable) are totally uninteresting: "I considered them only as something to be glanced at from a distance; their dresses and faces were often pleasing enough to the eye: but I could not understand their conversation . . . When I caught snatches of what they said, I could never make much of it" (181). Brontë did not approve of the accepted standards of female attractiveness—tall and full-figured, vain, coquettish—any more than she approved of the social ideal of masculinity. But she is even-handed enough to give the lie to Crimsworth's attitude of superiority. Yorke Hunsden tells the hero that it is his own fault if women do not find him interesting, for he is too narrow-minded to find *them* interesting: a man who only perceives otherness is deprived of the *pleasures* of equality. "There are sensible as well as handsome women . . . women it is worth a man's while to talk with, and with whom I can talk with pleasure," says Hunsden (181). Instead, Crimsworth is drawn to the portrait of his dead mother, whom he resembles: he has her aristocratic features, such as the "true and tender feeling" expressed in her face (8). Every man Crimsworth knows, however, treats this susceptibility to emotion as a defect (even though most of the time they discover it by examining his physiognomy, rather than in any emotional words on his part), thereby applying pressure on Crimsworth to conform to a strict gender role. After ten years at Eton, it can be supposed that Crimsworth made only one friend, and this turns out to be a "sarcastic . . . cold-blooded" man who could acceptably converse about the masters, but received Crimsworth's occasional allusions to beauty or sentiment with "sardonic coldness" (1). Hunsden judges Crimsworth's features as too like his mother's, saying "There's too much of the sen-si-tive" (19). And later, M. Pelet bluntly tells Crimsworth the "weak point" in his character is "the sentimental" (79). These indictments of male feeling or "weakness" work effectively to construct a masculine ideal that is stoic, shrewd, and masterful. The voice of *The Professor* is just such a man; that he is imbued with Charlotte Brontë's Romanticism does not really dilute her critique of sexual polarization. The "bull-like," aggressive Edward Crimsworth is a melodramatic villain, but he is also the cultural ideal of manliness, "fine-looking," "well-made," "of athletic proportions," a man with "business-like habits" (5). Brontë clearly calculates the emotional costs of a repressed sensibility in men: Edward mistreats his horse, is cruel to his brother, and eventually abuses his wife. But that he is thoroughly masculine is never questioned.

For his patient endurance of injustice, Crimsworth is labeled "'a fossil,'" "'an automaton,'" "'an essential sap, and in no shape the man for my money'" (29) by the feminine-looking Hunsden. Brontë's loose, cynical tone describes masculine banter affecting to disguise care and compassion with sarcasm and insults. The masculine expression of emotion is couched in terms of perverse indifference—for example, Hunsden's sneering generosity and Crimsworth's constant refusal to express his gratitude. At one point, after Hunsden meets Crimsworth's future wife, Frances, the two men grapple on the street:

> No sooner than we got into the street than Hunsden collared me. . . . [H]e swayed me to and fro; so I grappled him round the waist. It was dark; the street lonely and lampless. We had then a tug for it; and after we had both rolled on the pavement, and with difficulty picked ourselves up, we agreed to walk on more soberly.
>
> (215)

What seems like antagonism is more like a male version of an embrace, and points to the cultural prohibitions placed on expressions of affection between men.[10] The "feminine" qualities of solicitude and compassion, which he identifies with his mother's portrait, are driven underground by other men in the novel who are equally bound by ideological constraints. The hero's "feminization" is constantly embattled and subdued, despite his half-suppressed longing for love or the confession that, "I am my mother's son, but not my uncles' nephew" (42).

Crimsworth's voyage to Belgium initiates a psychological quest for the "mother's son," and, significantly, commences a conventional (feminine) love and marriage plot, as the hero seeks "the mother who looms in each woman for the grown-up boy" (Rich 152). In Brussels, he is forced to confront aspects of himself that both define and diminish his masculine identity. Crimsworth's tearful exclamation, "Mother!" as he gazes on her portrait, echoes two earlier raptures: the strange "reedy" and "fertile" countryside draws the breathless cry, "Belgium!" (45), followed by the equally strange "Pensionnat!" (50) as Crimsworth gazes at the walls restraining the adolescent demoiselles. His maternal legacy emanates from a foreign landscape that is totally Other—Flemish, Catholic, French-speaking—for un-

til this time, Crimsworth admits that "feminine character" was as alien to him as Brussels. At the Pensionnat de Demoiselles, he has an opportunity to consolidate as well as to modify the *pleasure* of being a man—that is, of having personal power. But as we have already seen, in doing so he relinquishes the pleasures of sexual equality—the pleasures of shared humanity. For example, Crimsworth takes a scientific pleasure in studying the "hundred specimens of the genus 'jeune fille,'" but Brontë also makes it clear that the hero must unlearn what patriarchal, and capitalist, ideology has reinforced, and "that unlawful pleasure, trenching on another's rights, is delusive and envenomed pleasure" (166).

But the habit of privilege is difficult to surrender. Even when he arrives in Belgium—a foreigner, poor, without friends or connections—he is in the position of the masculine subject, almost immediately telling the reader about a "picturesque," though "eminently stupid" Flemish housemaid, and seeking pretty faces under the bonnets of the demoiselles at the Pensionnat. Crimsworth is, in fact, virtually obsessed with knowing the mysterious female, but this may be less because Brontë is also obsessed with femaleness than with the fact that in creating a male figure she is engaged in a study of oppression from the inside. What nineteenth-century woman writer, taking a male voice, would not need to imagine how men see women? For if she doesn't know "the other case" she does know what it is like to be the object of male scrutiny.

Along with the authority that comes with his status as professor, Crimsworth reveals an insufferable snobbishness based on his nationality, his aristocratic lineage, *and* his sexual superiority. If Brontë is using a male narrator to engage in fantasies of power, she nevertheless does not make that power attractive. This sexually fastidious man assumes almost immediately, for example, that Zoraide Reuter is "an old duenna of a directress" (55) or "a stiff old maid" (65), and totally dismisses the kind Madame Pelet as "ugly, as only continental old women can be" (59). His smug curiosity about the "unseen paradise" of the demoiselles' garden reveals the degree of his unchallenged indoctrination into his rights as subject: "I thought it would have been so *pleasant* to have looked upon a garden planted with flowers and trees, so *amusing* to have watched the demoiselles at their play; to have *studied* female character in a variety of phases, myself the while sheltered from view by a modest muslin curtain" (54, my emphasis).

To handle male appropriation of the feminine from the center of masculine consciousness is crucial to Brontë's critique. Crimsworth's interest in the demoiselles as female "specimens," his sexual "mastery" over both Zoraide Reuter and Frances Henri, his critical observations of young women's bodies and faces are precise means for developing and affirming his manliness. As Kappeler has explained, what is at stake in the objectification of women is the very basis of patriarchy and of masculine selfhood: "His understanding of gender relations is at the very bottom of his understanding of himself, it informs his understanding and organization of society, and it informs his se-mantics, his symbolization of it" (155). Brontë thus makes Crimsworth's masculinity and his discourse almost entirely dependent on how he relates to women. The "sketches" of young women Crimsworth describes in close physical detail are all negatively stereotypic: viragos, coquettes, peevish brats, cool manipulators (there is one attentive student, Sylvie, who is also "the ugliest . . . in the room" [74]). The level of discomfort Crimsworth endures when confronting these womanly-looking students (72) seems particularly sexual. This is adolescent female sexuality without the "modest muslin curtain" to protect his *amour-propre*. The peep show, which would have displayed "the angels and their Eden" (64) and which protected Crimsworth from interacting with real women, has become uncomfortably confrontational. The professor who had earlier stated "I am not easily embarrassed" (66) can blush with shame when in the presence of the demoiselles:

> More obvious, more prominent, shone on by the full light of the large window, were the occupants of the benches just before me, of whom some were girls of fourteen, fifteen, sixteen, some young women from eighteen (as it appeared to me) up to twenty; the most modest attire, the simplest fashion of wearing the hair, were apparent in all; and good features, ruddy, blooming complexions, large and brilliant eyes, forms full, even to solidity, seemed to abound. I did not bear the first view like a stoic; I was dazzled, my eyes fell . . .
>
> (71)

Though disturbed by his sexual interest in young women, what is most troubling is their bold disregard for his privilege of objectifying them. "If I looked at these girls with little scruple, they looked at me with still less" (72). Their exhibitionism and their aggressive looks—"An air of bold, impudent flirtation, or a loose, silly leer, was sure to answer the most ordinary glance from a masculine eye" (84)—appalls Crimsworth.[11] He earlier has confessed how he deplores Pelet's free allusions to "le beau sexe," telling the reader, "I abhorred, from my soul, mere licentiousness" (59). Whereas these young women are abundantly female, they are not (with the exception of Frances) demurely feminine, and this is what Crimsworth both expects and requires. In fact, they are as rowdy as his male pupils: "when it came to shrieking the girls indisputably beat the boys hollow" (55). These deviants' sexual curiosity about him gives Crimsworth some relief from guilt about his voyeuristic fantasies. But finding his subjectivity challenged, he retrenches his power, he covers his emotional nakedness: "I had buckled on a breast-plate of steely indifference, and let down a visor of impossible austerity" (73). Thus psychologically armored, Crimsworth can reassert his subjective authority by repeatedly describing the now-repulsive physical features and the bold glances of his pupils (received "with the gaze of stoicism" [103]); he launches his erotic conquests over their sluggish minds instead of their bodies: "Owing to her education or her nature books are to her a nuisance, and she opens them with aversion, yet her teacher must instil into her mind the contents of these books; that mind resists the admission of grave information, it recoils, it grows restive . . ." (104). The use of the generic feminine pronoun in his discourse consolidates his subjective privilege.

This social form of power is based, of course, on the narrator's role as tutor; but it is equally based on gender (age is not much of a factor, since Crimsworth is only a few years older than his pupils) and is endowed with the eroticism that Brontë must certainly have felt simmering in the classrooms of the Pensionnat Heger, but which would have been unacceptable if described from a female point of view. Indeed, Crimsworth's insistence on his superiority to sexual temptation gives the lie to his professional disinterestedness, and only attests to the appreciable tensions of his situation. As if suspecting how impossible it is to believe a male teacher could show such self-control, he declares, "Know, O incredulous reader! that a master stands in a somewhat different relation toward a pretty, light-headed, probably ignorant girl, to that occupied by a partner at a ball, or a gallant on the promenade" (104). The incredulous (male) reader then receives privileged information about how women *really* are (or at least, how Belgian women really are). In those rare situations where prettiness and ignorance are not encouraged in order to attract male admiration, women are fully men's equals in aggressiveness and pride.

Crimsworth among the demoiselles seems an effort to correct patriarchy's appropriation and symbolization of women. At least twice Brontë deliberately calls attention to the fact that "female character as depicted in Poetry and Fiction" (76) is onesided and sentimental. Crimsworth must discover that women are not "earthly angels and human flowers" (83). It would be a misreading to suppose that here Brontë castigates her own sex as mendacious, foolish, and sensual. On the contrary, it is to insist on women's individuality and full participation in human life. "Give us back our suffering!" cries Florence Nightingale in *Cassandra* (29), meaning give us back our faults, our humanity. It could be the motto for Brontë's entire *oeuvre*.

When Zoraide Reuter, a forerunner of Madame Beck in **Villette** and a woman who uses seduction and flattery to achieve her political ends, tells Crimsworth, "men have so much more influence than women have—they argue more logically than we do; and you, Monsieur, in particular, have so paramount a power of making yourself obeyed" (112), Brontë displays her awareness of two ideological assumptions. First, that to possess power of any kind is a virtue, and second, that it is intrinsically a male privilege. Zoraide's remark is intended to appeal to Crimsworth's vanity; but it also serves to remind him of his complicity in male dominance and the unearned advantages of masculinity. Later, when she is debased by his rejection of her, Crimsworth has an important revelation about his capacity for despotism:

> I had ever hated a tyrant; and behold, the possession of a slave, self-given, went near to transform me into what I abhorred! There was at once a sort of low gratification in receiving this luscious incense from an at-

tractive and still young worshipper; and an irritating sense of degradation in the very experience of the pleasure. When she stole about me with the soft step of a slave, I felt at once barbarous and sensual as a pasha.

(162)

Brontë makes it clear that power is sexually stimulating (it is important that Zoraide is "attractive and still young"), and yet it is "irritating" to the masculine ego that he should derive pleasure from feminine submission. Nevertheless, Brontë obviously sees this intersection of power and pleasure as a defining factor in male socialization, and she is critical of the cultural myths that reinforce it, chiefly the doctrine of separate spheres and women's economic dependence. When Frances insists on giving lessons after they are married, for example, Crimsworth describes, in chivalric terms, the egotistical pleasure of controlling women: "There is something flattering to a man's strength, something consonant to his honourable pride, in the idea of becoming the providence of what he loves—feeding and clothing it, as God does the lilies of the field" (199-200). Here he does not feel a "demigod" compared with women, but God himself—"it" becomes his creation, just as "Woman" is an icon of Victorian patriarchy. Brontë, though, undermines the intense pleasure of the narrator's generosity and power: Crimsworth's God-like fantasy gives way, and he "permits" his wife to continue teaching. Physically, though, during these negotiations, Crimsworth keeps Frances on his knee with his arms tightly around her. He describes her as "a mouse in its terror" and says he holds her "with restraint that was gentle enough, so long as no opposition tightened it" (199).[12]

Allowing his wife to work is not much of a concession, given the fact that it is Frances's "pleasure, her joy to make me still the master in all things" (223). Unlike Rochester, Crimsworth does not undergo "the inevitable sufferings necessary when those in power are forced to release some of their power to those who previously had none" (Heilbrun 57). On the contrary, the "feminization" of the male narrator involves very little suffering. By the end of the narrative, Crimsworth even seems more manly and powerful than ever: he continues to conceal his emotional vulnerability, thinks of his love and his sexuality as a "gift" to confer on the "penniless and parentless" Frances (he later refers to himself as "a man of peculiar discernment" for finding a plain woman sexually appealing) and after they are married, continues to treat her as a "docile . . . well-trained child" (219). Eventually Crimsworth and Frances open a school, return to England, make sound investments, and retire with an independency. In this novel, to "feminize" the hero is clearly not to symbolically castrate him, nor have him killed during a voyage, nor have him submit to a woman's influence. Still, despite Crimsworth's mastery over his wife and his full participation in patriarchal hegemony, Brontë concludes *The Professor* with an important critique of the system that produces male privilege—produces, in effect, the disconcerting sexism of *The Professor,* a novel written only a year before Brontë's feminist manifesto, *Jane Eyre.* The real "masquerade" in the novel has not been Charlotte Brontë as William Crimsworth (Gilbert & Gubar 318), but the character of Crimsworth himself as a perfectly adjusted Victorian gentleman. Though he adopts a manly role—as master, squire, professor, husband, and, improbably, killer of rabid dogs—he finally questions the virtue of passing on a patriarchal legacy to his young son, Victor. Elaine Showalter writes, "Victor Crimsworth will learn self-mastery in an all-male world" (*Literature* 137). But Crimsworth's description of the all-male world of Eton is highly qualified, and the tone is clearly that of regret. Their neighbor, Hunsden, affirms that Victor's mother "is making a milksop"— but, Crimsworth gives us Frances's retort: "Better a thousand times he should be a milksop than what he, Hunsden, calls a 'fine lad'" (232). "'Good fellow,'" "'fine fellow,'" "'fine lad'": by placing these epithets in inverted commas, Brontë exposes the artificiality of Victorian gender roles. Despite Hunsden's praise of the boy's manly potential, Victor has the "swelling germs of compassion, affection, fidelity" (235) which threaten to undermine his development as a genuine "good fellow." But the suggestion that Eton will take care of these tendencies indicates that Brontë understands what an education in competition and mastery will produce, since after all, Crimsworth is a product of Eton, too. But Brontë also seems to understand that in a man's world such qualities are necessary to achieve material success—at the end of the novel we learn that Crimsworth's vicious older brother "is getting richer than Croesus by railway speculations" (237).

Descriptions of male mastery, voyeurism, or sexual suppression are not signs of Brontë's self-loathing, her disgust with the female body, or "a characteristically female desire to comprehend the mysteries of femaleness" (Gilbert & Gubar 321). On the contrary, the masculine voice of *The Professor* is a representation of Victorian masculinity. It is not a picture of unqualified heroism, nor is it an unqualified success as a realistic novel—I agree with those critics who find the narrator sometimes awkward, his choice of language occasionally only "the verbal equivalents of aggressiveness" (Taylor 7). But if we consider Brontë's limited experience, the novel is a fascinating transposition of her culture's construction of men as masters of their emotions, who are nonetheless driven by desires for power and sexual domination. Certain scenes seem remarkably insightful; for example, as a Victorian man who would have absorbed his culture's construction of the Other as virgin/ whore, Crimsworth is fascinated with young women, but also ambivalent towards female sexuality. The attack of "Hypochondria" he suffers after he has proposed to Frances has been interpreted both as his fear of sexual initiation (Moglen 95-6), and as "guilt for unresolved boyhood desires for his mother" (Maynard 88). But his illness could also be provoked by the loss of his voyeuristic freedom: being sexually faithful to one woman significantly curtails his right to sexually dominate many women.

The sexual tensions of *The Professor* do reflect indirectly those felt by Victorian women; but the novel also attempts to comprehend the tensions felt by Victorian men who enjoyed the privilege of cultural subjectivity. For Brontë, such pleasure, linked to the exploitation of other human beings as "specimens," were morally dangerous—"delusive and envenomed pleasure" as Crimsworth eventually concedes (166). *The Professor* is a remarkable early effort to confront how Victorian ideologies of gender both form and limit personality, for in using a male voice, Brontë uncovers how the gender of her character largely makes him who he is.

In this sense, Brontë's confidently masculine, objectifying, often misogynist voice itself embodies anxieties about Victorian sexuality. And although each of Brontë's novels confront issues of power, *The Professor* deals not with how to obtain power (the problem for Brontë's heroines), but how to outgrow the need for power. Crimsworth has the desire for power, but he also learns the terror of being powerful. It is specifically a masculine and middle-class problem, and perhaps the principle artistic inheritors of social privilege—middle-class male novelists—were unable to treat so studiously, from within a man's experience, their own complicity in Victorian society's treatment of women. Of course, it is important to acknowledge that any use of a male narrator is a reinscription of male authority and hence of male power—male narrators generally tend to be invested with authority, and this leaves the reader with the difficult question of how we evaluate a novelist's perspective on a first-person narrator. And it is certainly feasible—and probable—that Crimsworth's scorn for Belgian Catholics, for example, is an indirect expression of Brontë's feelings based on her experiences at M. Heger's pensionnat. Though these considerations are important, they do not, I think, on the whole obscure Brontë's interrogation of Victorian gender roles. The whole experience of socialized gender may have been more recognizable to women writers, who have not only felt social prejudice more acutely, but have a greater awareness of themselves as sexually defined members of society. In this sense, the mid-Victorian woman writing from the male perspective has the difficult task of reproducing a voice which trivializes her experiences, while at the same time maintaining an alternative, subtextual authority—her own—with its insider's knowledge of the conditions of women's lives. This double perspective in literature may be connected with her double consciousness as a middle-class woman living within a patriarchal, capitalist society; she is part of the dominant culture, but she occupies a place separate and inferior within it. If nothing else, because Brontë chooses in *The Professor* to negotiate, rather than ignore, this double perspective, she amplifies the importance of recognizing the gendered nature of all discourse.

Notes

1. These segregated terms seem to undercut any critique of gendered language or narrative that Brontë might have wished to engage. But a pervasive Victorian ideology of separate spheres has led modern readers quite naturally to construct readings of these texts largely based upon sexual difference. To refer to male or female language, male/quest or female/

marriage plots, male or female *Bildungsromane,* etc., is almost unavoidable. What is interesting is how some women novelists who use male narrators still produce a heroine-centered story and a female plot. George Sand's *Indiana* (1832), for example, is narrated by a man, but the book belongs to the heroine entirely, as does, to a lesser extent, Willa Cather's *My Antonia* (1918). Brontë's eponymous narrator, on the other hand, is not telling a woman's story, he is telling his own; the heroine is secondary. This is important to keep in mind in an attempt to understand Victorian attitudes towards sexual polarity, since even the title of a novel may be an attempt to raise expectations in terms of plot, literary value, and even language. George Eliot's masculine titles (*Silas Marner, Adam Bede, Daniel Deronda*) signal a male-centered story, though women are more often than not the psychological focus. Dealing with "masculine" and "feminine" language is difficult without falling into facile stereotypes. Brontë's narrator, however, uses language that is marked, sometimes exaggeratedly, as masculine according to Dale Spender's use of gender differences as described by linguists: men's speech is "forceful, efficient, blunt, authoritative, serious, effective, sparing and masterful" (*Man Made Language* 33). This is certainly the style of speech the narrator often adopts, usually as a way to hide certain "feminine" propensities.

2. Charlotte Brontë sought professional advice, and she wanted to be published. More than her sisters Emily and Anne, she wished to be a professional novelist, and "regardless of any woman writer's ambivalence toward authoritative institutions and ideologies, the act of writing a novel and seeking to publish it . . . is implicitly a quest for discursive authority: a quest to be heard, respected, believed, a hope of influence" (Lanser 7).

3. For a woman writer, to imagine what it is like to be a man seems difficult enough even today. When recently asked in an interview if she felt able to imagine what it is like to live in a male body, American novelist Mary Gordon said, "To be larger . . . Not to be afraid of being raped . . . No, I can't imagine it yet" (25; "Love Has Its Consequences," *The New York Times Book Review,* August 8, 1993: 1+). This suggests that the greatest challenge for some women writers may be imagining personal security and control of the body in a society hostile to women. As Lanser explains, "the authorial mode has allowed women access to 'male' authority by separating the narrating 'I' from the female body" (18). But Brontë seems yet unable to separate her male "I" from her female body: it is significant that Crimsworth sometimes feels sexually threatened. Penny Boumelha has pointed out that in the episode where he is invited to tea with Madame Pelet and Madame Reuter "he undergoes a fantasy of rape-seduction far more fearful and explicit than anything Brontë assigns to her female characters" (43).

4. Beryl Gray's Afterword to the 1985 Virago edition briefly summarizes the novel's reception: Henry James called it a *"jeu d'esprit,"* Marghanita Lanski a "sadly poor supernatural story," and Christopher Ricks "the weirdest fiction she ever wrote" (*The Lifted Veil* 69-70).

5. In the "Biographical Notice" to the 1849 edition of *Wuthering Heights,* Brontë wrote that she and her sisters chose pseudonyms "without at that time suspecting that our mode of writing and thinking was not what is called 'feminine.'" Most readers of *Scenes of Clerical Life* and *Adam Bede* did not doubt that "George Eliot" was a man (although Dickens was convinced the author was female), and her publisher, John Blackwood, continued to address Eliot as a man even after he knew her true identity. See Redinger, 332-4.

6. However much he despised Eton, his training there is instrumental to his status as hero, and comes in handy when the boat of one of his Flemish pupils capsizes: "I had not been brought up at Eton and boated and bathed and swam there for ten long years for nothing; it was a natural and easy act for me to leap to the rescue" (174).

7. In Chapter 7, when Lucy Snowe first arrives in the city, she is warned that it is too late "for a woman to go through the park alone"; she is subsequently followed by two insolent men whom she calls "my dreaded hunters." They pursue her until she is "out of breath . . . my pulses throbbing in inevitable agitation" (125).

8. Brontë was severely critical of women's economic dependence within marriage. She wrote to Ellen Nussey (August 9, 1846), "I do not wish for you a very rich husband, I should not like you to be regarded by any man ever as 'a sweet object of charity.'"

9. Lanser has observed that in *Jane Eyre,* the female voice is insistently and personally "in contact with a public narratee in the manner of the 'engaging' authorial narrator" (185), and I think this is true partly because, for most of the story, Jane's voice represents many voices: "Millions are condemned to a stiller doom than mine, and millions are in silent revolt against their lot . . . Women feel just as men feel . . . It is thoughtless to condemn them . . ." (141). Rhetorically, personal contact with a reader who may be sceptical or complacent is crucial in *Jane Eyre,* for Brontë wants to change the reader's way of thinking about governesses, class privilege, beauty, even novel-writing. There are addresses to the reader in *The Professor,* but they do not have the same urgency for connection with an oppressed class.

10. Ruth Johnston views this episode, in the context of Lacan's theory of the production of the subject/reader, as another way of alienating the reader by withholding knowledge and the identification necessary in realism (370-1). But the scene is accessible if we think of the pressures of Victorian manliness. Brontë may have been describing the constraints for men in expressing their affections within the polarized bounds of "male" reason and "female" emotion. Of course, the scene can also be read as homosocial bonding.

11. Beth Newman's "'The Situation of the Looker-On': Gender, Narration, and Gaze in *Wuthering Heights*" uses Lacanian theory to discuss the implicit gendering of gaze, associating the female gaze with male castration anxiety.

12. Basch (165-66) and Moglen (64-77) identify a pattern in Brontë's fiction, based on her belief in romantic love, where the woman's pleasure is derived from feeling physically overpowered at the same time that she successfully asserts her autonomy.

Works Cited

Basch, Francoise. *Relative Creatures*. New York: Schocken, 1974.

Boumelha, Penny. *Charlotte Brontë*. New York: Harvester, 1990.

Brontë, Charlotte. *The Professor*. 1857. London: Dent, 1969.

———. *Jane Eyre*. 1848. Harmondsworth: Penguin, 1988.

———. *Villette*. 1853. Harmondsworth: Penguin, 1985.

Cohan, Steven and Linda M. Shires. *Telling Stories: A Theoretical Analysis of Narrative Fiction*. New York: Routledge, 1988.

de Beauvoir, Simone. *The Second Sex*. Trans. H. M. Parshley. New York: Vintage, 1952.

Eagleton, Terry. *Literary Criticism: An Introduction*. Minneapolis: U of Minnesota P, 1983.

Gilbert, Sandra, and Susan Gubar. *The Madwoman in the Attic: The Woman Writer and the Nineteenth-Century Literary Imagination*. New Haven: Yale UP, 1979.

Gray, Beryl. Afterword. *The Lifted Veil*. By George Eliot. New York: Virago, 1985. 69-91.

Heilbrun, Carolyn. *Towards a Recognition of Androgyny*. New York: Norton, 1973.

Johnston, Ruth D. "*The Professor*: Charlotte Brontë's Hysterical Text, or Realistic Narrative and the Ideology of the Subject from a Feminist Perspective." *Dickens Studies Annual* 18 (1989): 353-80.

Kappeler, Susanne. *The Pornography of Representation*. Minneapolis: U of Minnesota P, 1986.

Lane, Margaret. Introduction. *The Professor*. By Charlotte Brontë. London: Dent, 1969.

Lanser, Susan Sniader, *Fictions of Authority: Women Writers and Narrative Voice*. Ithaca: Cornell UP, 1992.

Maynard, John. *Charlotte Brontë and Sexuality.* Cambridge: Cambridge UP, 1984.

Moglen, Helene. *Charlotte Brontë: The Self Conceived.* New York: Norton, 1976.

Morgan, Susan. *Sisters in Time: Imagining Gender in 19th-Century British Fiction.* New York: Oxford UP, 1989.

Newman, Beth. "'The Situation of the Looker-On': Gender, Narration, and Gaze in *Wuthering Heights.*" *PMLA [Publications of the Modern Language Association of America]* 105 (1990): 1029-1042.

Newton, Judith Lowder. *Women, Power, and Subversion: Social Strategies in British Fiction, 1778-1860.* Athens: U of Georgia P, 1981.

Nightingale, Florence. *Cassandra.* 1852. New York: Feminist Press, 1979.

Poovey, Mary. *Uneven Developments: The Ideological Work of Gender in Mid-Victorian England.* Chicago: The U of Chicago P, 1988.

Redinger, Ruby. *George Eliot: The Emergent Self.* New York: Knopf, 1979.

Rich, Adrienne. *Of Woman Born.* New York: Norton, 1976.

Shorter, Clement. *The Brontës: Life and Letters.* 2 vols. 1908. New York: Haskell, 1969.

Showalter, Elaine. *A Literature of Their Own.* Princeton: Princeton UP, 1977.

———. "Women Writers and the Double Standard." *Woman in Sexist Society.* Eds. Vivian Gornick and Barbara K. Moran. New York: Basic Books, 1971. 323-43.

Spender, Dale. *Man Made Language.* London: Routledge, 1980.

Taylor, Anne Robinson. *Male Novelists and Their Female Voices: Literary Masquerades.* Troy, N.Y.: Whitston, 1981.

Catherine Malone (essay date 1996)

SOURCE: "'We Have Learnt to Love Her More than Her Books': The Critical Reception of Brontë's *Professor.*" In *Review of English Studies,* Vol. 47, No. 186, 1996, pp. 175-87.

[*In the following essay, Malone explores the claim by some critics that Brontë fails to credibly produce a male protagonist in* The Professor. *Malone argues that it is not possible for a male protagonist to relate convincingly the type of suffering about which Brontë sought to write.*]

'**The Professor** appears before the public under circumstances which preclude criticism',[1] mourned the *Saturday Review* in June 1857. Smith, Elder's decision to publish Gaskell's biography and Charlotte Brontë's first written novel in close succession was clearly an astute move. On

its publication, **Jane Eyre** was condemned as immoral and unchristian,[2] as emphatically a bad book,[3] as a book not to be given to the young.[4] Less than ten years later, the *Edinburgh Review* is declaring, 'It is impossible to speak without the deepest interest and sympathy of the genius, the trials, and the fate of Charlotte Brontë'.[5] It was *The Life of Charlotte Brontë* which was responsible for the transformation into popular heroine, precipitating the gradual re-appraisal of Brontë which had begun upon her death in 1855 with the subsequent revelation of some of the circumstances of her life.

Brontë's life was now found to contain all the necessary elements for elevation to a Victorian model of womanhood: an isolated, religious childhood; literary precocity; unstimulating, unappreciated work as a governess and teacher; devotion to duty and family none the less; fortitude in the face of family deaths; reward through fame and marriage to a clergyman. Thus 1857 finds Brontë being held up as a pattern of 'the moral battle of life fought out and nobly won':

> the lives of the saints were the theology of the monasteries. In the heroines, and the confessors, and martyrs, men saw before them examples of what they, too, might become. These forms have passed away, but the substance remains; and, as little as Charlotte Bronté [*sic*] knew it, she was earning for herself a better title than many a St. Catherine, or St. Bridget, for a place among those noble ones whose virtues are carved out of rock, and will endure to the end.[6]

By the end of the decade, *Women of Beauty and Heroism* (1859), *Heroines of Our Time: Being the Sketches of the Lives of Eminent Women, with Examples of their Benevolent Works, Truthful Lives, and Noble Deeds* (1860), and *Women of Worth* (1859) all contain chapters on Brontë. In the last of these, alongside 'The Newgate Schoolmistress—Elizabeth Fry' and 'The Earnest Christian—Lady Warwick', appears 'The Worthy Daughter—Charlotte Brontë': 'Everything was against her through life—plainness of person, poverty, a solitude and sensitiveness of soul that no one could appreciate, and disappointment of almost every expectation and wish. Yet she nobly struggled on—her watchword DUTY and her reliance Heaven.'[7] Emerging as it did amid this euology, few critics castigated *The Professor* as they had Brontë's previous works.[8] The *Eclectic Review* concludes upon the biography, 'now that we have finished the strange, sad story, we have no heart for mere literary criticism . . . others may criticize her writings—we are unable to think of anything but her life.'[9]

In the long term, however, **The Professor** has perhaps suffered from the timing of its publication. Since Brontë's personal history embraced many of the components of Victorian popular fiction and was brought to the public by an acclaimed novelist, the *Life* was treated almost as a novel itself. To the *British Quarterly Review,* 'the story of this remarkable woman, told with such deep and simple pathos by her gifted and affectionate biographer, becomes as interesting as the tale of a second Jane Eyre'.[10] It was the beginning of the merging of Brontë facts and Brontë fictions. Critics were more interested in the drama of the *Life* than in the 'chastised, controlled, subdued temper'[11] of *The Professor,* and those critics who did pronounce upon the novel invariably did so in the light of the biography, endeavouring to equate the characters with those in Brontë's life or at best, with her later literary creations: 'Hunsden is an undeveloped Rochester';[12] 'the Professor is a woman in disguise,—as indeed she proves to be,—for she is quite properly stripped of her male costume, and turned into "Lucy Snowe" in *Villette*. There is a shyness, a sulky tenderness, and disposition to coquet manifest in the Professor's relations with his friend the Yorkshire manufacturer';[13] 'Into the character of the Professor himself the writer has transferred much from her own nature'.[14] An American critic, Margaret Sweat, extends the biographical interest of the novel to an influence by Emily and Anne—'its choice of material . . . reminds us of her sisters rather than of herself as we now know her'[15]— although it is difficult to imagine that she could see in Crimsworth the passion of Heathcliff, the depravity of Arthur Huntingdon, or the piety of William Weston. 'We are unable to think of anything but her life': a pattern for criticism of *The Professor* was thus established which has changed remarkably little in the twentieth century. But should the novel be so read?

Contemporary critics were bemused by the character of Crimsworth, finding him either 'dull'[16] or, after the intense engagement between narrator and reader in Brontë's other novels, aloof: 'The principles and the art of the author, though true, excite no corresponding sympathy on the part of the reader,—few demands being made on his softer or gentler nature. There is no Helen Burns that we can watch or weep over,—no sprightly little Adele [*sic*] that we can sport with.'[17] Yet both qualities, so at odds with the typical self-portrayal of an autobiographer, are central to why Crimsworth is so interesting, if not likeable, a character. Why did Brontë choose to make her hero so unengaging? The answer surely lies in the novel's form. As in *Jane Eyre* and *Villette*, Brontë plays upon the potential in autobiographic narratives for discrepancy between the narrator's and the reader's perceptions of the text. An abandoned Preface to *The Professor,* probably written in November or December 1847 when Brontë was first attempting to persuade Smith, Elder to reconsider the work for publication, highlights this aspect by having a more objective observer, a friend of Crimsworth's, introduce the manuscript:

> I had the pleasure of knowing Mr. Crimsworth very well—and can vouch for his having been a respectable man—though perhaps not altogether the character he seems to have thought he was. Or rather—to an impartial eye—in the midst of his good points little defects and peculiarities were visible of which he was himself excusably unconscious—An air—a tone of his former profession lingered over & round him—a touch of the pedagogue—unobtrusive but also unmistakeable.[18]

One of the most notable examples of Crimsworth being 'not altogether the character he . . . thought he was' is his perception of his sexuality. Crimsworth likes to believe he is set apart from other men—'"I must follow my own devices—I must till the day of my death—because I can neither comprehend, adopt nor work out those of other people"' (p. 52)—and includes his lack of interest in women as a facet of that superiority. He observes of his brother's wife's childish mannerisms, 'this lisp and expression were, I have no doubt, a charm in Edward's eyes, and would be so to those of most men—but they were not to mine' (p. 13), and of Frances, that she is 'for a sensualist—charmless' (p. 168). Yet while at the beginning of the novel he declares an interest only in women with 'the clear, cheering gleam of intellect' (p. 13), asserting that for a professor, feminine 'mental qualities; application, love of knowledge, natural capacity, docility, truthfulness, gratefulness are the charms that attract his notice and win his regard' (p. 120), the puritanical image he presents is continually undermined by his regard for physical beauty, manifest in his obsession with the boarded window in his bedroom at M. Pelet's, and his observations on his female pupils and the women with whom he has already come into contact. During the party at his brother's house, Crimsworth is not introduced to the 'group of very pretty girls' surrounding Edward and feels that he can take no part in the dancing: 'Many smiling faces and graceful figures glided past me—but the smiles were lavished on other eyes—the figures sustained by other hands than mine— turned away tantalized' (p. 24).

Similarly, it is Mlle Reuter's outer rather than inner charms which chiefly attract Crimsworth. It is he who nearly falls in love with Zoraïde and she, confident in her relationship with Pelet, who plays with his affections. Although any relationship between the two has been largely of Crimsworth's imagining, on discovering the engagement, he considers Zoraïde and Pelet's deceit an act of 'treachery' (p. 112)—one which does not just cause him momentary bitterness, shame, or embarrassment but temporarily extinguishes his entire 'faith in love and friendship' (p. 111). Within a short space of time, he has eradicated any feeling of culpability from his mind to such an extent that he is able to maintain, 'Neither could [Hunsden] suspect for an instant the history of my communications with Mdlle. Reuter; secret to him and to all others was the tale of her strange infatuation: her blandishments, her wiles had been seen but by me, and to me only were they known' (p. 205); her 'infatuation' is indeed known only to Crimsworth because it existed only in his mind. Even after he has fallen in love with and determined to marry Frances, he continues to be powerfully attracted to Zoraïde, to the point of being capable of adultery. Crimsworth is told by Pelet that he would be welcome to remain in his establishment after he has married Zoraïde, but declines the offer: 'I was no pope—I could not boast infallibility—in short—if I stayed, the probability was that in three months' time, a practical Modern French novel would be in full process of concoction under the roof of the unsuspecting Pelet' (p. 187). Since the consequence of rejecting the offer is that he must find other lodgings, he later considers the possibility that his intended step is unnecessarily severe: '"And all this," suggested an inward voice, "because you fear an evil which may never happen!" "It will happen; you *know* it will;" answered that stubborn monitor, conscience' (p. 188). That which he first poses as a 'probability' he now confesses, extraordinarily, to be a certainty. Crimsworth, then, is not a character to be taken at his 'dull' face value, on his own terms. The *Critic* was one of the few contemporary voices to express some reservations about the hero: 'Had the description of the three young Graces of the "pensionnat" come from a "bonâ fide" Professor, we certainly should refuse to recommend him for any such post for the future';[19] while to the *Literary Gazette,* the same passage is a series of 'voluptuous descriptions which, ploughing up the passions at every sentence, give occasion to much wonder'.[20]

The majority of contemporary critics ascribed Crimsworth's reserved, unappealing nature to the fact that Brontë 'had not yet attained to that powerful delineation of character which constitutes the charm of her later performances'.[21] Brontë herself confessed to a weakness in the depiction of male characters:

> You both [James Taylor and W. S. Williams] complain of the want of distinctness and impressiveness in my heroes. Probably you are right. In delineating male character I labour under disadvantages: intuition and theory will not always adequately supply the place of observation and experience. When I write about women I am sure of my ground—in the other case, I am not so sure.[22]

Many modern critics, therefore, look no further in accounting for the comparative failure of *The Professor.* However, I would argue that the failing is not that Brontë cannot convincingly create male protagonists but that a male protagonist cannot convincingly tell the type of story Brontë wanted to narrate: a history of suffering. Brontë sets out her intention for her hero in the Preface—'that whatever small competency he might gain should be won by the sweat of his brow . . . As Adam's Son he should share Adam's doom—Labour throughout life and a mixed and moderate cup of enjoyment' (pp. 3-4)—but in the event Crimsworth's life is not one of true sweat or labour because throughout the novel he is able to rely on the privileges of his sex and class. The *Economist* is representative of contemporary, and some modern, criticism in claiming, 'The rather dismal little heroine of "Villette", Lucy Snowe, is transformed here into a young man who is "the Professor" of the story'[23] but the different gender of the two characters makes for two very different novels. A typical example is each protagonist's first morning on the Continent. Crimsworth is buoyant:

> I never experienced a freer sense of exhilaration than when I sat down at a very long black table (covered however in part by a white cloth), and, having ordered breakfast, began to pour out my coffee from a little black coffee-pot. . . . [A] gentleman, after looking towards me once or twice, politely accosted me in very good English . . .

> I lingered over my breakfast as long as I could, while it was there on the table and while that stranger continued talking to me, I was a free, independent traveller . . .

(pp. 58-9)

He then walks to Mr Brown's where he presents Hunsden's letter, declines two posts as clerk and bookseller, and accepts one as teacher.

Lucy Snowe, on the other hand, feels entirely lost:

> It cannot be denied that on entering [the coffee-room] I trembled somewhat; felt uncertain, solitary, wretched; wished to Heaven I knew whether I was doing right or wrong; felt convinced it was the last, but could not help myself. Acting in the spirit and with the calm of a fatalist, I sat down at a small table, to which a waiter presently brought me some breakfast; and I partook of that meal in a frame of mind not greatly calculated to favour digestion. There were many other people breakfasting at other tables in the room; I should have felt rather more happy if amongst them all I could have seen any women; however, there was not one—all present were men.[24]

Lacking Crimsworth's education, Lucy is unable to speak French and is without his confident ease of being a man in a man's world. Crimsworth can walk freely from his hotel to Mr Brown's; Lucy is pursued by two men on her walk to Mme Beck's from the bureau where her coach stops. Here, she has no letter of introduction and, in no position to be able to turn down employment, has to plead to be accepted for the most menial of posts. When Jean Baptiste Vandenhuten nearly drowns, Crimsworth is able to save him—'I had not been brought up at Eton and boated and bathed and swam there ten long years for nothing; it was a natural and easy act for me to leap to the rescue' (p. 196)—and thus gain the valuable friendship and patronage of his father, as a woman in his position could not have. Few observations, then, could be further from the mark than the *Critic*'s description of Crimsworth as 'a Jane Eyre in petticoats'.[25] Brontë's words in the Preface—'I said to myself that my hero should work his way through life as I had seen real living men work theirs' (p. 3)—are thus fulfilled more literally than she perhaps envisaged: her hero exploits the privileges of his sex as fully as any other.

The most significant suffering in the novel is experienced rather by Frances. Contemporary critics enthused about her as a literary creation (the poet and essayist William Roscoe judges her to be 'decidedly the most attractive female character that ever came from the pen of this author',[26] Gaskell, 'the most charming woman she ever drew, and a glimpse of that woman as a mother—very lovely'[27]) but, as with Crimsworth, saw her as a mere adumbration of later characters. The *Dublin University Magazine* reads her as 'a silhouette of the Jane Eyre, afterwards so exquisitely matured',[28] *Blackwood's,* somewhat surprisingly, as 'a sort of feminine [M.] Paul'.[29] Yet Frances is an important character in her own right, both within the text and in terms of Brontë's novelistic development, and of a more ambivalent nature than Victorian critics were willing to concede. The main action in *Jane Eyre, Shirley,* and *Villette* ends, for the most part, with the proposal to the heroine, followed by a brief closing chapter. In *The Professor,* two long chapters follow the proposal scene, amounting to almost a seventh of the novel, in which Frances becomes the central focus. The implication is that Brontë felt unable to conclude the novel without articulating Frances's own perception of her history and relationship with Crimsworth, and the inclusion of Frances's first-person poem is a part of the attempt to offer a female voice. Brontë defended her first novel throughout her correspondence with Smith, Elder. Rereading it after the publication of *Jane Eyre,* she wrote to W. S. Williams, 'I found the beginning very feeble, the whole narrative deficient in incident and general attractiveness. Yet the middle and latter portion of the work, all that relates to Brussels, the Belgian school, etc., is as good as I can write: it contains more pith, more substance, more reality, in my judgment, than much of "Jane Eyre"',[30] and it is in the middle and latter portions of the novel that the interest transfers to Frances.

Crimsworth may share some circumstances and experiences with Frances but again, his sex brings an entirely different perspective to them. He defines himself not as an exile but as an 'Israelite crawling over the sun-baked fields of Egypt' (p. 41), with the additional connotations of being a chosen one of God, and he feels liberated in Belgium by the fact that he is a foreigner and without family; Frances finds the same situation restricting and isolating. Crimsworth twice chooses to hand in his notice; Frances is in effect dismissed from Mlle Reuter's. The reader's only means of learning how Frances responds to these events, however, is through the inadequate medium of Crimsworth—through a male consciousness. His method of presenting Frances to the reader mirrors his method of teaching Frances in the schoolroom: 'motioning to her to rise, I installed myself in her place, allowing her to stand deferentially at my side' (p. 138); he installs himself in her place as the narrator of her history and the reader's knowledge of the woman by his side is one of his interpretation and editing. It becomes increasingly obvious to the reader that there are complexities in Frances's character and in her relationship with Crimsworth unacknowledged by the novel's narrator. Her first conversation with Hunsden, in which she emerges as vibrant and excited, is to Crimsworth a 'display of eccentric vigour' of which he observes, 'To me, once or twice, she had in intimate conversation, uttered venturous thoughts in nervous language, but when the hour of such manifestation was past, I could not recall it' (p. 237); it is a side of Frances's personality in which he is uninterested, which he deems to be of no importance. Long before he has any thoughts of marrying Frances, he speculates on the type of wife he will choose:

> 'the idea of marrying a doll or a fool was always abhorrent to me; I know that a pretty doll, a fair fool might do well enough for the honey-moon—but when passion cooled, how dreadful to find a lump of wax and wood laid in my bosom, a half idiot clasped in my arms, and to remember that I had made of this my

> equal—nay my idol, to know that I must pass the rest of my dreary life with a creature incapable of understanding what I said, of appreciating what I thought or of sympathising with what I felt!'
>
> (p. 108)

He here reveals not only that he is capable of being swept away by passion and marrying purely for beauty, but that he conceives of his wife in terms only of how she can tend to his needs—to *his* words, thoughts, and feelings.

The most unsettling instance of Crimsworth's narrative silence or lack of curiosity with regard to Frances is his relation of their very wedding day. He comes to her lodgings to accompany her to the church:

> Singular to state, she was or had been crying—when I asked her if she were ready she said 'Yes, Monsieur,' with something very like a checked sob; and when I took a shawl, which lay on the table, and folded it round her, not only did tear after tear course unbidden down her cheek, but she shook to my ministration like a reed. I said I was sorry to see her in such low spirits and requested to be allowed an insight into the origin thereof. She only said 'It was impossible to help it,' and then voluntarily though hurriedly putting her hand into mine, accompanied me out of the room, and ran downstairs with a quick, uncertain step, like one who was eager to get some formidable piece of business over.
>
> (p. 245)

To Crimsworth, it is a 'singular' outburst which makes him not anxious or perturbed but 'sorry'. To the reader, it appears that as much as Frances loves Crimsworth, the decision to marry him, to relinquish her independence perhaps, is by no means an easy one; she has earlier speculated that '"if a wife's nature loathes that of the man she is wedded to, marriage must be slavery"' (p. 255) and her first request on accepting his marriage proposal is that she may continue to teach. Crimsworth is reluctant to grant this request because to his mind 'there is something flattering to man's strength, something consonant to his honourable pride in the idea of becoming the Providence of what he loves—feeding and clothing it, as God does the lilies of the field' (p. 225). The comparison again strikes the reader uneasily, with its suggestion that his love is as much for playing God as it is for Frances. The impression is confirmed by an earlier description of Frances: '[one] over whose expression I had such influence; where I could kindle bliss, infuse awe, stir deep delight, rouse sparkling spirit, and sometimes waken pleasurable dread' (p. 188). The reader may well wonder whether the dread is mutually pleasurable.

While Crimsworth undoubtedly loves Frances, his depictions of her have a static, passionless quality. He terms her 'my best object of sympathy on earth', 'my ideal of the shrine in which to seal my stores of love', 'silent possessor of . . . those sources of refreshment and comfort to the sanctuary of home' (pp. 168-9); more bizarrely and disturbingly, he describes her after their first embrace as being 'as stirless in her happiness, as a mouse in its terror' (p. 224). The image, together with that of her as being 'docile as a well-trained child' (p. 247) and his admission that when Mlle Reuter steals about him 'with the soft steps of a slave' he feels at once 'barbarous and sensual as a pasha' (p. 184), suggests a desire in Crimsworth for mastery. Brontë, however, allows the reader to discern the inadequacy of such descriptions and that Frances, even after they are married, has an independence from Crimsworth's conception of her. When Crimsworth jokingly concedes, in reference to Frances's roles as directress and wife, 'I seemed to possess two wives' (p. 250), his words have a greater pertinence than he realizes.

Crimsworth's autobiography could be read as an attempt to create a new self, to write as he would wish to be perceived: as a man who is independent, determined, courageous under affliction, firm in love. He alleges, 'Novelists should never allow themselves to weary of the study of real Life—if they observed this duty conscientiously, they would give us fewer pictures chequered with vivid contrasts of light and shade; they would seldom elevate their heroes and heroines to the heights of rapture—still seldomer sink them to the depths of despair' (p. 159). In complying to this doctrine, he attempts to reduce his story to a uniform sameness, passing over or ignoring 'light and shade', dwelling on the grey of what he deems 'real Life'. The result is that the reader is aware of two stories: the history Crimsworth openly narrates, and that which he endeavours to conceal or of which he is unaware—his insecurity, his jealousy of Hunsden, his limited comprehension of Frances. That Brontë did not intend Crimsworth to be an entirely sympathetic character is confirmed in references to the novel in her correspondence. When George Smith, although unwilling to publish the work, offered to keep the manuscript in London for safe-keeping, Brontë refused:

> You kindly propose to take *The Professor* into custody. Ah, no! . . . Perhaps with slips of him you might light an occasional cigar, or you might remember to lose him some day . . . No, I have put him by and locked him up, not indeed in my desk, where I could not tolerate the monotony of his demure Quaker countenance, but in a cupboard by himself.[31]

If Frances's apprehensions about marriage are apparent in the sobs on her wedding morning, Crimsworth's make a still stranger manifestation. His marriage proposal having been accepted by Frances, he returns home only to be tormented by hypochondria for ten days. He attempts to rationalize the incident to the reader: 'Man is ever clogged with his Mortality and it was my mortal nature which now faltered and plained; my nerves which jarred and gave a false sound, because the soul, of late rushing headlong to an aim, had overstrained the body's comparative weakness' (p. 228); but the abstract, impersonal language strikes the reader as an unconvincing explanation of such an intensely physical attack. Similarly, he uses biblical allusions, such as 'A horror of great darkness fell upon me' (p. 228)—

echoing Genesis 15: 12—as a convenient means of relaying his state of mind without having to enter into a detailed analysis of his psyche. Far more telling is his relation of the seizures, which he characterizes as a relationship with a lover:

> I had her to myself in secret; she lay with me, she ate with me, she walked out with me, shewing me nooks . . . where we could sit together, and where she could drop her drear veil over me . . . taking me entirely to her death-cold bosom, and holding me with arms of bone. What tales she would tell me, at such hours! What songs she would recite in my ears! How she would discourse to me of her own Country—The Grave—and again and again promise to conduct me there erelong; and drawing me to the very brink of a black, sullen river, shew me on the other side, shores unequal with mound, monument and tablet, standing up in a glimmer more hoary than moonlight. 'Necropolis!' she would whisper, pointing to the pale piles, and add 'It contains a mansion prepared for you'.

> (p. 228)

The images betray at once disgust and attraction: he goes on to repulse her 'as one would a dreaded and ghastly concubine coming to embitter a husband's heart towards his young bride' (p. 229). Although he has earlier referred to Frances as a 'novice in the art of kissing' (p. 226), he provides no evidence that he is any less of a novice himself. The novel marks his progress from a dismissal of an 'Oriental' homage to beauty (p. 13) to the confession, 'It appeared then, that I too was a sensualist, in my temperate and fastidious way' (p. 227). Crimsworth, accustomed to being the 'maître' in the relationship, must now come to terms with the fact that it is Frances who awakens the sensualist in him, who could be perceived as an object of fear as well as desire. All that can be deduced from the incident is that for Crimsworth, as for Frances, the prospect of marriage is more unsettling than he is willing to acknowledge. Moglen comments, 'The illness which lasts for two weeks is similar to the ordeals later endured by Jane Eyre, Carolyn [*sic*] Helstone, and Lucy Snowe. For all, recovery marks a psychic rebirth: an entry into a new life.'[32] I would argue that although Crimsworth may become a husband, father, and the director of a school, it is one of the many curious aspects of the attack that there is no 'psychic rebirth', barely any psychic change; for the remainder of the novel, he is as aloof, as self-absorbed, as unperceptive as ever.

It was presumably the inclusion of such disquieting scenes and biblical allusions in the novel which led to Gaskell's misgivings: 'It is . . . disfigured by more coarseness,—& profanity in quoting texts of Scripture disagreeably than in any of her other works.'[33] Each of Brontë's novels was the victim of such accusations and even *The Professor* did not entirely escape; the *Press* held its language to be 'very good, though at times tainted with that coarseness which disfigured Miss Brontë's later works'.[34] But such censures were very much an exception. The *Christian Remembrancer* remained sceptical of Brontë's Christian faith even after reading the biography—'her character was essentially unspiritual'[35]—but now that Brontë was known to have had a life punctuated by tragedy, now, more especially, that she was known to be both the daughter and the wife of a clergyman, every effort was made by the critical establishment to portray her in as favourable, even saintly, a light as possible. Any defects in the morality of *The Professor* were whitewashed or resolutely ignored. The *Saturday Review* uses the novel to defend Brontë against the charge of coarseness:

> *The Professor* also shows that . . . Miss Brontë owed to her residence in Belgium a very peculiar view of the relations of the sexes. She states, as distinctly as words enable her to state, that she found thoughts current among women of all ages in Belgium, which were strange, repulsive, and unknown to an English girl . . . *The Professor* is fuller than any of her other tales, of passages which show she was aware of this material side of love. We wish not to be misunderstood. There is not an expression or allusion that a prude could call indelicate, but there are traces, faint but unmistakeable, of a knowledge into which, happily for themselves and their country, Englishwomen are seldom initiated. We cannot doubt that Miss Brontë derived an instruction which to a less noble, unstained, and devotional mind might have been perilous, from her residence in a foreign school . . .[36]

Yet for all the new idolization of Brontë, the problem remained of reconciling her novels with the noble, unstained, and devotional character now attributed to her. Women and girls may have been encouraged to emulate Brontë's life but it by no means followed that they were encouraged to read her works. Parental censorship prevailed. The daughter of the author Elizabeth Malleson, for example, remembers being read to as a child in the 1860s: 'Our mother was a past-master in the art of skipping as she read without pause or loss of continuity anything unsuitable to our youthful ears. I remember she read us *Jane Eyre* from beginning to end entirely omitting Rochester's mad wife, and so skilfully that we noticed nothing amiss with the plot.'[37] Quite some feat. In all the hagiographic accounts of Brontë's life, therefore, remarkably little mention is made of her novels, the very reason for her celebrity. *Heroines of Our Time* alone alludes to the incongruity: 'we have learnt to love her more than her books.'[38]

The Brontë legend, then, arose with astonishing rapidity, based solely on the revelations of the *Life*. Appearing just four months after the biography, *The Professor* received the full force of the change in the critical heart. In 1853 the *Dublin Review* was by no means alone in considering the author of *Villette* an 'unpleasing and unamiable writer';[39] in 1857 the *Eclectic Review* has as much support in regarding *The Professor* as a 'legacy of Charlotte Brontë's genius' which will 'confirm the general admiration of her extraordinary powers',[40] the same powers which, after reading all four novels, have the critic and essayist Badeau bowing to 'the mysterious supremacy of genius' and crying out '"This is the finger of God"'.[41] Victorian critics, keen to reappraise Brontë, chose to forget

that Brontë was a writer and not a saint—a writer, moreover, of novels with problematic characters, problematic endings, and which raised problematic questions. To many modern critics, *The Professor* is of interest only when read in conjunction with *Villette*. The nineteenth-century eulogies may be exaggerated but the twentieth-century indifference is surely unwarranted. Something of a balance is found in the American and perhaps more objective assessment by *Harper's New Monthly Magazine*: 'As a preliminary study for the composition of *Jane Eyre* and *Villette,* it is full of interest, and in itself possesses attractions to the lover of acute psychological analysis far superior to the majority of English novels.'[42]

Notes

1. 'The Professor', *Saturday Review* (13 June 1857), 549-50 (p. 549). All reviews are anonymous, unless otherwise stated.

2. 'The Last New Novel', *Mirror,* 2 (1847), 376-80 (p. 377).

3. 'The Caxtons', *English Review,* 12 (1849), 306-7 (p. 307).

4. H. R. Bagshawe, '*Jane Eyre* and *Shirley*', *Dublin Review,* 28 (1850), 209-33 (pp. 210-11).

5. 'The License of Modern Novelists', *Edinburgh Review,* 106 (1857), 124-56 (p. 153).

6. 'Contemporary Literature', *Westminster Review,* 68 (1857), 235-314 (p. 295). Attributed in the *Wellesley Index* to Harriet Martineau, but disputed in *Harriet Martineau: Selected Letters,* ed. V. Sanders (Oxford, 1990), 144.

7. Anon, *Women of Worth: A Book for Girls* (London, 1859), 30.

8. There is, however, a comparative scarcity of known reviews of *The Professor.* Friends and Smith, Elder sent reviews to Brontë of the three novels published in her lifetime and she duly wrote to thank them, mentioning each notice by name. With *The Professor,* this source is obviously eliminated and the correspondence of Patrick Brontë, Ellen Nussey, and Elizabeth Gaskell all fail to give reviews the same careful scrupulous attention. Allott's *Critical Heritage* of the Brontës, for example, contains only four reviews; I refer to sixteen.

9. 'Charlotte Brontë', *Eclectic Review,* NS 1 (1857), 630-42 (p. 630).

10. 'The Life of Charlotte Brontë', *British Quarterly Review,* 26 (1857), 218-31 (p. 218).

11. 'Novels of the Season', *Eclectic Review,* NS 2 (1857), 54-66 (p. 64).

12. 'The Professor', *Critic* (15 June 1857), 271-2 (p. 271).

13. R. H. Hutton, 'Novels by the Authoress of "John Halifax"', *North British Review,* 29 (1858), 466-81 (p. 474).

14. 'The Professor', *Examiner* (20 June 1857), 388.

15. M. J. Sweat, 'Charlotte Bronté and the Bronté Novels', *North American Review*, 85 (1857), 293-329 (p. 326).

16. 'New Novels', *Press* (13 June 1857), 584.

17. 'The Professor', *Athenaeum* (13 June 1857), 755-7 (p. 755).

18. Repr. in Charlotte Bronté, *The Professor*, ed. M. Smith and H. Rosengarten (Oxford, 1987), 295. All page references are to this edition and will hereafter be cited in the text.

19. *Critic*, 272.

20. 'The Professor', *Literary Gazette* (20 June 1857), 584-7 (p. 585).

21. *Press*, 584.

22. Letter to James Taylor, 1 Mar. 1849 (T. J. Wise and J. A. Symington (edd.), *The Brontës: Their Lives, Friendships and Correspondence* (4 vols., Oxford, 1932; repr. in 2 vols., 1980); ii. 312—refs. are to part nos. of the 1980 edn.).

23. 'The Professor', *Economist* (27 June 1857), 701-3 (p. 701).

24. Charlotte Bronté, *Villette*, ed. H. Rosengarten and M. Smith (Oxford, 1984), 80.

25. *Critic,* 271.

26. W. C. Roscoe, 'Miss Bronté', *National Review,* 5 (1857), 127-64 (pp. 161-2).

27. Letter to Emily Shaen, 7-8 Sept. 1856 (*The Letters of Mrs. Gaskell,* ed. J. A. V. Chapple and A. Pollard (Manchester, 1966), 409-10).

28. S. A. Brooke, 'Currer Bell's "The Professor"', *Dublin University Magazine,* 50 (1857), 88-100 (p. 97).

29. E. S. Dallas, 'Currer Bell', *Blackwood's Magazine,* 82 (1857), 77-94 (p. 91).

30. Letter, 14 Dec. 1847 (Wise and Symington (edd.), *The Brontës,* ii. 161).

31. Letter, 5 Feb. 1851 (Wise and Symington (edd.), *The Brontës,* iii. 207).

32. H. Moglen, *Charlotte Bronté: The Self Conceived* (New York, 1976), 96.

33. Letter to Emily Shaen, 7-8 Sept. 1856 (*Letters of Mrs. Gaskell,* ed. Chapple and Pollard, 409-10).

34. *Press,* 584.

35. 'The Life of Charlotte Bronté', *Christian Remembrancer,* 34 (1857), 87-145 (p. 91).

36. *Saturday Review,* 550.

37. H. Malleson, *Elizabeth Malleson 1828-1916: Autobiographical Notes and Letters* (printed for private circulation, 1926), 90.

38. J. Johnson, *Heroines of Our Time* (London, 1860), 105.

39. C. W. Russell, 'The Novels of 1853', *Dublin Review,* 34 (1853), 174-203 (p. 191).

40. *Eclectic Review,* NS 2, 64.

41. A. Badeau, *The Vagabond* (New York, 1859), 165.

42. 'Literary Notices', *Harper's New Monthly Magazine,* 15 (1857), 404–5 (p. 404).

Carl Plasa (essay date 2000)

SOURCE: "Charlotte Brontë's Foreign Bodies: Slavery and Sexuality in *The Professor*." In *Journal of Narrative Theory,* Vol. 30, No. 1, Winter, 2000, pp. 1-28.

[*In the following essay, Plasa discusses the figurative representation of colonialism found in* The Professor. *The critic also explores Crimsworth's self-contained sexuality.*]

> As we look back at the cultural archive, we begin to read it not univocally but *contrapuntally,* with a simultaneous awareness both of the metropolitan history that is narrated and of those other histories against which (and together with which) the dominating discourse acts.
>
> Edward W. Said, *Culture and Imperialism* (59)

The opening chapter of Charlotte Brontë's first novel, ***The Professor*** (completed in 1846 but published only posthumously in 1857), features a "copy of a letter, sent [. . .] a year since" by William Crimsworth, the novel's first-person narrator and central protagonist, to Charles, "an old school-acquaintance" (5) whom he had known at Eton. While the letter is designed to furnish Charles with an account of its writer's post-Etonian existence, such a purpose remains unrealized. As Crimsworth explains at the end of the chapter, his missive meets with no reply because its desired. recipient is at home no longer:

> To this letter I never got an answer—before my old friend received it, he had accepted a government appointment in one of the colonies, and was already on his way to the scene of his official labours. What has become of him since I know not.
>
> (14)

Charles's silent withdrawal to an unspecified colonial margin provides Crimsworth with the opportunity to take up where the letter leaves off, regaling "the public at large" with the autobiography—in the shape of the novel itself— originally begun for the "private benefit" (14) of his mysteriously estranged correspondent. The story of his professional and personal fortunes that Crimsworth recounts has three distinct phases. The first sees him moving from the south of England to the north, where he is employed as "second clerk" in the Yorkshire textile mill owned by the entrepreneurial Edward, his elder brother and "manage[s] the foreign correspondence of the House" (18). Dissatisfied with the task of "copying and translating business-letters" and feeling victimized, in particular, by the "Antipathy" (30) his employer/brother demonstrates toward him, Crimsworth invokes the translator's prerogative, converts his linguistic mobility into geographic form, and travels to Belgium. Here he teaches English as a foreign language, first to male and then female students in boarding-schools run by Monsieur Pelet and Zoraïde Reuter, respectively. It is here, also, through a combination of endeavour and chance, that he eventually secures his financial independence. In the novel's brief final stage, Crimsworth returns to England, accompanied by his Anglo-Swiss wife and former pupil, Frances Evans Henri and their refractory young son, Victor.

For many critics, the epistolary manoeuvre with which Brontë begins *The Professor* is both artificial and clumsy. It is, they argue, the sign of an early gaucherie on the part of a would-be novelist perilously aspiring—like Charles and Crimsworth in their own spheres—to secure a professional status within the male-dominated literary establishment of mid nineteenth-century England. Yet as Brontë informs the reader in the "Preface" to *The Professor,* the faults of her "little book" should not be excused on the basis of a "first attempt [. . .] as the pen which wrote it had been previously worn down a good deal in a practice of some years" (3). The principal allusion here is to the vast and sprawling body of Brontë's Angrian writings, produced in collaboration with her brother, Branwell, between 1829 and 1839 and situated in a phantasmagoric colonial space "carved," in the words of Juliet Barker, "out of the interior of Africa" (*Juvenilia* 270). It is thus apparent that the divergence of career between Charles and Crimsworth with which *The Professor* begins at the same time enacts a certain shift, inaugurated by *The Professor* itself, in Brontë's own fictional trajectory: like Crimsworth, her novels will remain, for the rest of her career, securely located within English and/or continental borders.

Yet if colonialism is excluded as a literal presence in Brontë's post-Angrian fiction—no longer setting the "scene" for her own "official labours," as it were—it continues to return in a number of significant unofficial forms. In the case of *The Professor,* Crimsworth's practice as "English Master" (67) in Belgium "can easily be viewed," as Firdous Azim has argued, "against the class-bound and colonial tradition that accompanies the teaching of English" (163). In this respect, the severed epistolary exchange with which the novel opens is ironically inverted, as a correspondence with colonial margins is implicitly maintained: Crimsworth's supremacist assumptions about his own language and culture take their place alongside those informing the kind of colonial pedagogy beginning to emerge in the context of British expansion in India and most notoriously advocated, for example, in Thomas Babington Macaulay's "Minute on Indian Education" of 2 February 1835.[1]

Azim's reading of *The Professor* is an important one, not least because it represents the first sustained attempt to situate Brontë's novel within the archive of a colonial history. At the same time, however, there are two respects in which *The Professor* enables a development of the approach initiated by Azim. The first of these relates to the reemergence of the colonial as textual resource. The unequal power-relations that the novel charts in the contexts of class and gender are repeatedly figured in terms of a slavery only recently abolished in Britain's colonies, and still institutionalized in the American South, when the novel was first composed. In this way, it becomes evident that *The Professor*'s rhetorical operations are involved in a politics of identification that is highly problematic. The second concerns the way in which, more broadly, questions of nation and race come to be played out in the register of sexuality. As he struggles, throughout the narrative, to negotiate his own desires—and those of others—Crimsworth consistently associates sexuality with forms of foreignness, whether these be continental or Oriental, thus constituting it as something that threatens to infect and undo his sense of himself as an Englishman. Although he claims not to know "What has become" of his friend in the wake of his colonial posting, Crimsworth's own traveller's tale dramatizes fears and fantasies of contamination analogous to those entailed in the colonial project itself. *The Professor*'s use of slavery as figure implies an identification with the other whose impetus reverses, in the context of sexuality, into flight and defence.

"FALSE PROFESSIONS AND DOUBLE-DEALING": SLAVERY AND THE POLITICS OF METAPHOR

In the "Preface" to *The Professor,* Brontë records her "surprise" (3) at the unfavourable response that her novel has elicited (it was rejected nine times in total [xxiii]). Having deliberately eschewed "the ornamented and redundant in composition" in preference for the "plain and homely," and "adopted a set of principles on the subject of incident &c." (3) that is stringently realist, she discovers that the novel's prospective "Publishers [. . .] scarcely approved this system" and, it transpires, "would have liked something more imaginative and poetical" (4) than the worldly tale of self-advancement that she tells. This unexpected situation leads to a reflection on the deceptiveness of appearances in which gender-stereotypes are overturned. Herself concealed behind the masculine persona of "Currer Bell" (5), Brontë remarks:

> until an author has tried to dispose of a M.S. of this kind he can never know what stores of romance and sensibility lie hidden in breasts he would not have suspected of casketing such treasures. Men in business are usually thought to prefer the real—on trial this idea will be found fallacious: a passionate preference for the wild wonderful and thrilling—the strange, startling and harrowing agitates divers souls that shew a calm and sober surface.
>
> (4)

For Brontë's text to be judged by "Men" who are the (feminized) opposites of what they seem is oddly appropriate for, as Penny Boumelha has argued, "*The Profes-*

sor's is a world of doubleness" in which "Virtually every major character is radically divided" (38).

In changing the original title of her novel from *The Master* to *The Professor* (xxx), Brontë appears to signal this sense of "doubleness" and radical self-division. In one respect, the new title might be considered to be something of a misnomer. As Crimsworth soon comes to learn from Mr. Brown, his contact on arriving in Belgium, the appellation bestowed on him does not possess quite the same meaning—or cachet—as in England. It translates differently: "The word professor struck me. 'I am not a professor,' said I. 'Oh,' returned Mr. Brown—'Professor, here in Belgium, means a teacher—that is all'" (60). Yet if "[t]he word professor" distorts and inflates Crimsworth's standing within the pedagogical hierarchies of the schools run by Pelet and Zoraïde alike, it is, at the same time, an accurate designation. Like several of the other key figures in the text, Crimsworth is precisely a "professor" in the alternative, or non-professional, sense defined by Boumelha, repeatedly "manifesting one motive, feeling or state of mind but also privately harbouring another" (38).

Crimsworth's tendency—in that lightly pleonastic phrase—to make "false professions" (181) is evident not just in the context of the personal images that he shapes for others (as for himself) in the course of the narrative. It is also to be discerned in terms of his textual practices as an autobiographer and, in particular, his habitual use of metaphor, a trope itself traditionally linked to notions of deception and duplicity. Especially in *The Professor*'s first six chapters, metaphor functions as the figurative vehicle for the return of the colonialism seemingly jettisoned so pointedly at the novel's outset, as Crimsworth draws on a historically burdened language of mastery and enslavement in order to represent the fraternal and class conflicts in which he is initially implicated. As his unread introductory letter attests, Crimsworth is the product of a marriage that crosses class boundaries: his mother is of aristocratic descent, with a "rare [. . .] class of face" (14), while his father is a "—shire Manufacturer" who becomes "bankrupt a short time previous to his death." On the demise of his mother, "some six months" (7) after these events, Crimsworth is entrusted to the care of the affluent "maternal uncles" (6) who will later fund his education. By subsequently rejecting their patronage, he is forced to enter the realm of mercantile capitalism in which Edward is "fast making a fortune" (8). At the end of chapter 4, Crimsworth returns to his "lodgings" to prepare for the next day's labours, flooded with "regrets" (39) as to the unpromising position to which he has been relegated. He is further agitated by the repeated "goading" (37) of Hunsden Yorke Hunsden. As his palindromically shaped name suggests, Hunsden's unpredictable appearances in the text are typically marked by an enigmatic poise that contrasts sharply with the uncertainty of Crimsworth's own prospects:

> Why did I make myself a tradesman? Why did I enter Hunsden's house this evening? Why, at dawn tomorrow, must I repair to Crimsworth's Mill? All that

night did I ask myself these questions and all that night fiercely demanded of my soul an answer. I got no sleep, my head burned, my feet froze; at last the factory-bells rang and I sprung from my bed with other slaves.

(39)

The "bells" that ring here are literal and metaphorical at once. Crimsworth's participation in the routines of the factory worker is evidently for him the cue for other echoes and resonances, prompting a crossracial identification with the disciplined body of the slave.

In summoning the worker/slave to his duties, those "bells" would seem to reverberate with the promise that the capitalist order of things will be renewed and soundly maintained. Yet equally, if obliquely, they constitute a call to insurrection that finds its response, in personal if not collective terms, in the next chapter. Crimsworth's literal dawn rising, in the passage above, prefigures what he refers to as "'The Climax'" (40), the moment of his rebellion against the oppressor/brother. Violently accused of spreading slanders about Edward that are subsequently traced back to Hunsden, Crimsworth is finally moved to liberate himself from the "yoke" (59) of his brother's employ:

> "Come, Edward Crimsworth, enough of this. It is time you and I wound up accounts. I have now given your service three months' trial and I find it the most nauseous slavery under the sun. Seek another clerk—I stay no longer."
>
> "What! Do you dare to give me notice? Stop at least for your wages." He took down the heavy gig-whip hanging beside his Mackintosh.

(42-43)

Crimsworth's rebellious turning against Edward is also a linguistic one, again performing, as it does, a troping of class in terms of race, the domestic in terms of the colonial.

The presence of slavery as metaphor in *The Professor* has some curious effects, the first of which relates to Crimsworth's role as "tradesman." While his decisive altercation with Edward clearly confirms Hunsden's taunting prophecy that "*[he]'ll never be a tradesman*" (38), there is a sense in which Crimsworth's vocation as metaphorist at the same time both reinterprets and challenges Hunsden's assertion: his trade is in language, regulated by the exchange of the literal meanings of words for figurative ones. The second effect is to qualify the stylistic claims that Brontë makes in her "Preface," as the novel turns out to be much less "plain and homely" than she takes it to be. Not only is Crimsworth's narrative recurrently "ornamented," quite plainly, by a particular figure of speech, but the figure in question is one that entails a kind of departure from the "homely" also. For metaphor, as Eric Cheyfitz points out, is a rhetorical operation in which words are transferred from literal to figurative usages, travelling from familiar to foreign destinations (36).[2] If Crimsworth will, for the bulk of the novel, be an Englishman abroad, there is a sense in which such a spatial relocation only recapitulates the itinerary laid down in advance by his own language.

Even as they question Brontë's understanding of her own text, Crimsworth's rhetorical strategies cast a different kind of doubt on themselves. The essential problem with his rituals of metaphorical self-representation is that, ultimately, they can only seem like hyperbolic gestures, variously ironized by the unstated historical truths that *The Professor* encrypts within itself. To compare class relations in the north of England to slavery would seem, on the one hand, to be an effective means of underscoring the oppression and injustice to which the worker is subjected by early to mid nineteenth-century industrial capitalism. Yet, on the other hand, Crimsworth's self-figuration carries out its own injustice. The "other slaves" whom he blithely fashions out of metaphor have their counterparts in the shape of black subjects literally enslaved either in the context of the British West Indies or the American South. As several critics, from Marx to Fanon and beyond, have argued, it is the regulated bodies of these other "other slaves," so to speak, that drive the capitalist economy from which Crimsworth freely withdraws his labour.[3] In identifying himself with the figure of the slave, Crimsworth in effect performs a metaphorical colonization, or colonization through metaphor, expropriating the racial other for his own self-serving ends.

The discrepancies between Crimsworth and the slave in terms of whom he sees himself are most visible, of course, with regard to the privileges that accrue to him by virtue of what Macaulay calls the "aristocracy of skin" (qtd. in Blackburn 448)—the fact of Crimsworth's whiteness. Although he has not followed the obscure colonial career of the correspondent alluded to in the novel's first chapter, Crimsworth nonetheless shares the assumed racial superiority on which such a career is predicated. Both figures are in turn racially elevated above the white creole pupil, the 15-year-old Juanna Trista, whom Crimsworth encounters in Zoraïde's school. As a "girl [. . .] of mixed Belgian and Spanish origin" who is born "in the—Isles" (100), Juanna is not quite to be included in the same racial echelon as her "English Master." Even so, as she leaves Europe to return to her father's unnamed West Indian estate, she does so "exulting in the thought that she should there have slaves whom, as she said, she could kick and strike at will."[4] With "the legible graving of [. . .] Mutiny and Hate" on her "brow" (101), Juanna's celebration of her future role as colonial dominatrix underscores the dubious politics of Crimsworth's figurative tendencies. Its effect is to expose the realities of colonial and racial conflict that the logic of metaphor—stressing sameness over difference—threatens to efface.

Crimsworth's metaphorical identifications open up *The Professor* to the kind of contrapuntal reading proposed by Said in the epigraph above, inviting themselves to be placed and considered, for example, in relation to Freder-

ick Douglass's *Narrative of the Life of Frederick Douglass, An American Slave, Written by Himself* (1845). Douglass's text is exactly contemporary with the writing of Brontë's novel and, as one of the formative works in the African-American autobiographical tradition, centrally concerned, like *The Professor,* with processes of self-making. These processes are encapsulated in the famous liberatory chiasmus of Douglass's "You have seen how a man was made a slave; you shall see how a slave was made a man" (47). They are subsequently initiated by the pivotal physical "battle" (50) between Douglass and the "'nigger-breaker'" (42), Edward Covey. From this conflict, lasting "nearly two hours," Douglass emerges triumphant, his "sense of [. . .] manhood" both "revived" and transfigured in a "glorious resurrection, from the tomb of slavery, to the heaven of freedom" (50). Douglass's account of his experiences provides a powerful counterpoint to the terms in which Crimsworth likes to frame his own, driving his metaphors back toward their literal ground. If Crimsworth's "brazen face" fails to "blush black" (44) during the course of his brother's verbal assault, his narrative is characterized, it would seem, by rhetorical displays that are their own impertinence.

Douglass goes on to offer a more explicit corrective to the dangerous affront of slavery as trope in another context. In the course of a lecture given to a meeting in Newcastle upon Tyne on 3 August 1846, Douglass defines it as his "duty to direct [. . .] attention to the character of slavery, as it is in the United States." He proceeds to inform his audience of the urgency of his task:

> I am the more anxious to do this, since I find the subject of slavery identified with many other systems, in such a manner, as in my opinion, to detract to some extent from the horror with which slavery in the United States is so justly contemplated. I have been frequently asked, since coming into this country, "why agitate the question of American slavery in this land; we have slavery here, we are slaves here." I have heard intemperance called slavery, I have heard your military system, and a number of other things called slavery, which were very well calculated to detract from the dreadful horror with which you at a distance contemplate the institution of American slavery.

> (*Frederick Douglass Papers* 317)

Here Douglass spells out the potential ironies that attend the slave trope. The language of a domestic politics needs to be properly disciplined if it is not simultaneously to collude with, diminish and perpetuate a "horror" that, even "at a distance," seems "dreadful."

Whether the effects are "calculated" or not, *The Professor* deploys slavery as a trope in the context not only of class- but also gender-relations. At several junctures, white female figures are associated—either by Crimsworth or themselves—with rebel slaves and/or a violent blackness. This is the way, for example, in chapter 10, in which Caroline de Blémont, one of the three self-crowned "queens" in Zoraïde's school, forces herself upon her teacher's attention:

Caroline shook her loose ringlets of abundant but some-what coarse hair over her rolling black eyes; parting her lips, as full as those of a hot-blooded Maroon, she showed her well-set teeth sparkling between them and treated me at the same time to a smile "de sa façon".

(86)

In this passage (whose syntax is almost as "loose" as Caroline's "ringlets"), Crimsworth's vision is a double one. The danger embodied in white female sexuality is represented as a colonial rebellion signalled in the allusion to the "hot-blooded Maroon."[5] If the allusion is defensively misogynist in its figuring of white female sexuality in terms of slave revolt, it is at the same time racist, as the stereotypical traits of blackness slide between Caroline and "Maroon" alike. Both have "lips" described as "full," while the former has "rolling black eyes" and a characteristic "smile" that discloses, in those "well-set teeth," a cannibalistic appetite.

It is not only the sexually excessive female who comes to be identified with a rebellious blackness but the conventionally feminine Frances also. In the novel's final chapter, after Crimsworth and Frances have been married for some ten years, he speculates on what might have become of his "good and dear wife" had she married "a profligate, a prodigal, a drunkard or a tyrant." To Crimsworth's insistent pursuit of these curious possibilities, Frances responds, with an equally "strange kind of spirit in her eye": "if a wife's nature loathes that of the man she is wedded to," Frances asserts, "marriage must be slavery. Against slavery all right thinkers revolt" (255). The potential for (un)wifely revolt that Frances hints at here is still more emphatically associated with blackness in the previous chapter (Meyer 62). During an exchange concerning the merits and demerits of her native land, Frances tells Hunsden that if he were to "take a wife out of Switzerland" and subsequently impugn her nation—as he has indeed just done, for example, by "mention[ing] the word *ass* in the same breath with the name Tell"—his insolence would meet with lethal consequences: his "Mountain Maid" would "some night smother" him, "even as [. . .] Shakspeare's Othello smothered Desdemona." As if immediately to partake in the reprisal imagined against Hunsden, the future "plan" that Frances "sketche[s]" involves an attack on a figure central to Hunsden's sense of his own cultural supremacy. Frances's revisionary drama is, as he himself recognizes, "a travesty of the Moor and his gentle lady in which the parts [are] reversed" (242), as white female revenge shockingly weds the monstrosity of black male violence.

"MIXED UP IN FOREIGN HODGE-PODGE": SEXUALITY, NATION, RACE

At the beginning of chapter 3, Crimsworth recalls his time as a subject under surveillance in his brother's mill:

I served Edward as his second clerk faithfully, punctu-ally, diligently. What was given to me to do, I had the power and the determination to do well. Mr. Crim-

sworth watched sharply for defects but found none; he set Timothy Steighton, his favourite and head-man, to watch also, Tim was baffled; I was as exact as himself, and quicker: Mr. Crimsworth made enquiries as to how I lived, whether I got into debt—no—my accounts with my landlady were always straight; I had hired small lodgings which I contrived to pay for out of a slender fund—the accumulated savings of my Eton pocket-money; for as it had ever been abhorrent to my nature to ask pecuniary assistance, I had early acquired habits of self-denying economy; husbanding my monthly al-lowance with anxious care.

(22)

All the values that define a bourgeois masculinity are operating here, "faithfully, punctually, diligently" present and correct—from "industry and perseverance," in Heather Glen's taxonomy, to "self-reliance and independence, self-respect and self-control" (11). By internalizing these values, Crimsworth necessarily leaves Edward and his "head-man" "baffled": in true Foucauldian fashion, he subjects himself to the strategies of surveillance deployed against him.[6]

With regard to his own language, however, Crimsworth's powers of self-surveillance prove less efficient. Running counter to the thrift on which he prides himself is a textual excess that disturbs the studied calculus of his self-representation, as the literal spills into the metaphorical. The "accumulated savings," "habits of self-denying economy" and "husbanding" of his "monthly allowance" to which Crimsworth alludes literally refer to his talents of financial self-management. Yet at the same time, the terms he uses have a vital currency in contemporary medical discourses, where they circulate as figures for the ways in which male sexuality is ideally to be ordered. The *locus classicus* for such discourses is William Acton's *The Functions and Disorders of the Reproductive Organs in Childhood, Youth, Adult Age and Advanced Life Considered in their Physiological, Social and Moral Relations,* published in the same year as Brontë's novel. Despite the apparent comprehensiveness of its title, Acton's inquiry is, as Steven Marcus points out, almost exclusively concerned with the sexual economy of the male (13). Within this economy, Acton defines semen as a kind of inner resource that, to adopt Crimsworth's term, requires careful "husbanding" both prior to and during marriage. Sexual expenditure occurring outside marital intercourse—especially in the baleful shape of masturbation—is simply a waste. Summarizing Acton's linkage of the sexual and the financial, Marcus writes:

The fantasies that are at work here have to do with economics; the body is regarded as a productive system with only a limited amount of material at its disposal. And the model on which the notion of semen is formed is clearly that of money. Science, in the shape of Acton, is thus still expressing what had for long been a popular fantasy: up until the end of the nineteenth century the chief English colloquial expression for the orgasm was "to spend."

(22)

Given this discursive construction of male sexuality, the "anxious care" with which Crimsworth disposes of his "Eton pocket-money" takes on a new significance. The latter phrase is a covertly sexual coinage: both metonymically and metaphorically, it unites the genital and the financial.

Crimsworth's investment in the kind of sexual self-control obliquely figured in his restrained monetary "habits" is not surprising. To lose such mastery—as Acton and other medical commentators repeatedly insist—is for the male subject to become increasingly implicated in a range of moral, psychic and bodily disorders, resulting, ultimately, in madness and/or death. For Crimsworth, though, such a loss also entails something else. If Pelet's description of Crimsworth, in chapter 11, as a "cold frigid Islander!" (96) makes the connection between sexual repression and English masculinity explicit, Crimsworth, for his part, establishes an equally emphatic and complementary link between sexual licence and Pelet's identity as Frenchman:

> He was not married and I soon perceived he had all a Frenchman's, all a Parisian's notions about matrimony and women; I suspected a degree of laxity in his code of morals, there was something so cold and blasé in his tone whenever he alluded to, what he called, "le beau sexe"; but he was too gentleman-like to intrude topics I did not invite, and as he was really intelligent and really fond of intellectual subjects of discourse, he and I always found enough to talk about, without seeking themes in the mire—I hated his fashion of mentioning Love, I abhorred, from my soul, mere Licentiousness, he felt the difference of our notions and, by mutual consent, we kept off ground debateable.
>
> (70)

The "difference of [. . .] notions" between these mutually consenting interlocutors resolves itself into a difference of nations, as Crimsworth scrupulously retreats from the lavish expenditures of a continental sexuality. Yet while Crimsworth is "willing," at this point in their acquaintance at least, "to take Pelet for what he seemed" (70), he himself less frequently earns the same favours from the reader. As one whose monetary and sexual customs are marked alike by "habits of self-denying economy," Crimsworth is necessarily a subject self-divided. The self-control that he arrogates to himself throughout the novel is simultaneously a mask for and symptom of an inner split. As Sally Shuttleworth argues:

> The picture [Brontë] draws is not of an innate, assured masculinity, but rather of a social and gender identity created and sustained only through violence: the violence of self-repression and of repudiation of all who might threaten the carefully nurtured illusion of self-control.
>
> (132)

Difference between is difference within. The oppositions by which Crimsworth recognizes and defines himself—between English and continental masculinities, sexual probity and "mere Licentiousness," self and other—are the objectification of internal conflicts. These conflicts make of Crimsworth's own subjectivity a peculiarly vexed site, itself a "ground debateable." What he claims to have "perceived" in the other is, more properly, the projection, or exportation, of what he represses in himself.

For Crimsworth, a deregulated sexuality is a national scandal, as the border, or "'l'allée défendue'" (108), between English and continental masculinities is crossed and violated. Yet the self-protective stance he adopts toward Pelet is ultimately the sign of anxieties concerning racial as well as national contamination. These are manifested in the context of *The Professor*'s treatment of miscegenation, no doubt one of the "themes" Crimsworth would want to consign firmly to his "mire." Contemplating the physical charms of Caroline, Pelet treats himself to a fleeting fantasy of interracial desire in which she is Orientalized: "Ah there is beauty! beauty in perfection," he exclaims, "what a cloud of sable curls about the face of a houri! What fascinating lips! What glorious black eyes!" (95-96). Despite his own previous figuration of Caroline in terms of a furious blackness, Crimsworth predictably recoils from these imaginings, debunking them merely as the product of an artificial "enthusiasm" and hearing "something in [Pelet's] tone which indicated got-up raptures" (96). This recoil parallels a gesture originally made in chapter 1, when the fantasy of miscegenation first articulates itself. In this version of the fantasy, gender-identities are transposed across the lines of race. Introduced to his brother's "handsome young wife," Crimsworth "peruse[s] the fair page of [her] face" and finds it wanting:

> I sought her eye, desirous to read there the intelligence which I could not discern in her face or hear in her conversation; it was merry, rather small; by turns I saw vivacity, vanity—coquetry, look out through its iris, but I watched in vain for a glimpse of soul. I am no Oriental, white necks—carmine lips and cheeks, clusters of bright curls do not suffice for me without that Promethean spark which will live after the roses and lilies are faded, the burnished hair grown grey.
>
> (13)

Crimsworth's discriminatory assertion that "[he is] no Oriental" is one instance of what Glen calls the "insistent negativism" (13) of the novel's prose. But the negation operating here is not only stylistic but also psychic. It is suggestive of the kind of defensive strategy elaborated by Freud:

> To negate something in a judgement is, at bottom, to say: "This is something which I should prefer to repress." A negative judgement is the intellectual substitute for repression; its "no" is the hall-mark of repression, a certificate of origin—like, let us say, "Made in Germany".
>
> (438)

Crimsworth's revealingly fleshly claim that he has no desire for female bodies that withhold "a glimpse of soul" and are not supplemented by the classically enduring

"Promethean spark," is thus an admission of just such a desire, albeit in disguised or antithetical form. But what is particularly important about the self-cancelling logic in which Crimsworth is enmeshed is not so much the desires it discloses as where those desires are located. The sexuality he renounces is not of European origin—something "'Made in Germany,'" Belgium or France, for example— but of more exotic provenance. Sexual desire thus poses a double problem for Crimsworth. On the one hand, it threatens to make him a male counterpart to those girls whom he teaches and classifies as "continental English." These are "the daughters chiefly of broken adventures" (102), whose exilic exposure to European culture has imbued them with "an imbecile indifference to every sentiment that can elevate humanity" (103). On the other, it confronts him with the more alienating possibility of his own Orientalization.

Crimsworth's projection/exportation of his own desires onto the figures of Pelet and the imaginary "Oriental" is a process repeated in the context of his relations to the female other. The desires for the female body that Crimsworth represses return to him in the distorted form of a persecutory female sexuality. The central scene for this drama of repression and return is Zoraïde's "'Pensionnat de demoiselles'" (61), where the erotic seems thoroughly to saturate the pedagogical. Its presence is immediately registered, in chapter 10, in the prurient comedy of the preparations Crimsworth makes before introducing himself to his class for their first lesson. Entering Zoraïde's "sanctum sanctorum" (83) and noting "a large tableau of wood painted black and varnished," "a thick crayon of white chalk" and "a wet spunge," Crimsworth comments:

> having handled the crayon, looked back at the tableau, fingered the spunge in order to ascertain that it was in a right state of moisture—I found myself cool enough to admit of looking calmly up and gazing deliberately round me.
>
> (84)

What Crimsworth sees, on raising his eyes, is an array of girls and young women, aged between "fourteen" and "twenty," whose "forms [are] full even to solidity" (84). These superabundant figures are neither the prelapsarian "angels" (76), nor even "half-angels" (85), to whom he typically dedicates his "sentimental reflections" (66). Quickly "relieved" of such a "fond and oppressive fancy" (85), Crimsworth comes to view his female pupils, by chapter 12, as "a swinish tumult" (101). With the "isolated" exception of the "British English," with their "grave and modest countenances" and "general air of native propriety and decency" (103), his class becomes the object of a violent disgust:

> They were each and all supposed to have been reared in utter unconsciousness of vice—the precautions used to keep them ignorant, if not innocent, were innumerable; how was it then that scarcely one of those girls having attained the age of fourteen could look a man in the face with modesty and propriety? An air of bold,

impudent flirtation or a loose, silly leer was sure to answer the most ordinary glance from a masculine eye. I know nothing of the arcana of the Roman-Catholic religion and I am not a bigot in matters of theology, but I suspect the root of this precocious impurity, so obvious, so general in popish Countries, is to be found in the discipline, if not the doctrines of the Church of Rome. I record what I have seen—these girls belonged to, what are called, the respectable ranks of society, they had all been carefully brought up, yet was the mass of them mentally depraved.

> (98)

Here Crimsworth claims for himself a scientific or empirical objectivity—"I record what I have seen." This enables him, with seeming authority, to trace the genealogy of the hypersexualized continental female back to its twisted "root" in "Romish wizard-craft" (102). Yet Crimsworth's narrative perspective is no more reliable at this point in the novel than elsewhere. On closer inspection, the "ordinary glance" cast by the "masculine eye" seems to bear witness less to the sexual truth of women who inhabit "popish Countries," than to the "sexual paranoia" (Boumelha 41) of the Protestant subject from whom that glance first emanates. Despite his contempt for "the discipline [. . .] of the Church of Rome," Crimsworth, in this passage, is not unlike the confessor to Sylvie, "at once the ugliest and the most attentive" (87) of his students. Crimsworth hesitates to reward Sylvie's attentiveness by even the slightest physical gesture for fear that such a "token of approbation" will be subsequently "misinterpreted and poisoned" (121) by her confessor as a sign of sexual impropriety. Yet he himself engages in just such an erroneous and overcharged hermeneutics. The depravity Crimsworth claims to behold in the collective visage of the schoolgirls "under [his] eye" (97) is a reflex of the sexuality he refuses to confront in himself.

In relation to Zoraïde's schoolgirls, Crimsworth is, paradoxically, the very source of the contamination by which he feels himself to be endangered. Such a paradoxical position is similarly evident in the context of his relation to Zoraïde herself. Despite her imminent marriage to Pelet, and Crimsworth's own increasing love for Frances, Zoraïde continues in her efforts to seduce the "English Master." Just before the marriage is "solemnized" (198), Crimsworth outlines the "singular effect" that Zoraïde produces upon him:

> her presence and manner [. . .] sealed up all that was good, elicited all that was noxious in my nature; sometimes they enervated my senses, but they always hardened my heart. I was aware of the detriment done, and quarrelled with myself for the change. I had ever hated a tyrant; and behold the possession of a slave, self-given, went near to transform me into what I abhorred! There was at once a sort of low gratification in receiving this luscious incense from an attractive and still young worshipper and an irritating sense of degradation in the very experience of the pleasure. When she stole about me with the soft step of a slave—I felt at once barbarous and sensual as a pasha—I endured her

homage sometimes, sometimes I rebuked it—my indifference or harshness served equally to increase the evil I desired to check.

(184)

This passage looks back to an earlier point in the text, where Pelet speculates that Zoraïde will "leave the print of her stealing steps on [Crimsworth's] heart" (94). It also reintroduces the slave trope, while rerouting it from British colonial/American contexts into the realms of the Oriental. Zoraïde is figured here as a "slave" because she readily submits herself to her own desires, to which—as much as to Crimsworth—she is "self-given." Far from being the paragon of "abstract reason" she appears to be at first, Zoraïde is ultimately subject to the euphemistic rule of "strong propensities" (90). Yet her self-Orientalization is a means to gain mastery over Crimsworth, precisely by subjugating him to the role of "tyrant" over her. What is so "singular" about Zoraïde's "effect" is that it brings to light Crimsworth's own doubleness, as he struggles between the repression of and the yielding to desire. By the same token, it underlines the ways in which the contradictory elements of Crimsworth's "nature" are organized in terms of racial categories. If Crimsworth is "transform[ed] [. . .] into what [he] abhor[s]," the reversal in question involves not only the dissolution into "gratification" and "pleasure" of his customary "Scipio-like self-control" (119). It is also figured as the assumption of a "noxious" Oriental identity, as he becomes "at once barbarous and sensual as a pasha."

Against the sexual menace of Zoraïde—her "body depraved by the infectious influence of the vice-polluted soul"—Frances functions, for Crimsworth, as antitype or perhaps even "antidote" (187). At the same time, she elicits from her teacher/lover and eventual spouse a desire that is distinctly narcissistic. In this way, she confirms Crimsworth's belief that nothing "pleases egotistical human beings so much as a softened and refined likeness of themselves" (24). In the first of a series of doublings, Frances, like Crimsworth, subscribes openly to the bourgeois ideology of self-improvement, initially attending his lessons "in order to perfect her knowledge of English" and so "qualify herself for a higher department of education" than that of the "lace-mending" and "ornamental needle-work" (116) by which she earns her living. In the course of her "instruction in English" (which, in rapid turn, is co-opted by Crimsworth as "a channel for instruction in literature" [146]), Frances proves herself to possess "Perseverance and a Sense of duty" to "a somewhat remarkable degree" (131). In this respect, indeed, she succeeds where her teacher, during his apprenticeship as "tradesman," had failed: Frances's approach to her studies is genuinely resolute, while Crimsworth soon recognizes he is unable to "set up" even the simulacra of resolution—"the image of Duty [and] the fetish of Perseverance"—as his "household gods" (30). Her ambitions are finally rewarded when, like Crimsworth again, she becomes a successful teacher. The most significant of the doublings between the two figures occurs, finally, in terms of sexual taste. What makes Frances "for a sensualist—charmless," is what defines her,

for Crimsworth, as "a treasure" (168). As "the personification [. . .] of self-denial and self-control" (169), Crimsworth's "best object" (168) reflects back to him the qualities that are the "guardians" and "trusty keepers" of his own sexuality and integral—for a middle-class Victorian ideology—to "the sanctuary of home" (169).

As Crimsworth's double, however, Frances necessarily also reproduces, rather than resolves, the sexual contradictions by which he is beset. In her culturally hybrid status as the daughter of an English mother and a French-speaking Swiss father, she is a living embodiment of the conflict between the sexual restraint and sexual excess associated, in this text, with English and French/continental identities, respectively. Crimsworth's repeated demands, at the beginning of the first of their "conferences" (138), that Frances "Speak English [. . .]. English. [. . .] keep to English" (139), instead of lapsing into the French that is her penchant, are thus not simply the sign of a certain linguistic colonization. At the same time, they connote a drive not only to quarantine Frances from the rabidly libidinized bodies of her classmates but also rid "that Genevese girl," as she is at one point called (176), of the sexuality Crimsworth strives to exile from himself. The prosecution of such sexually repressive policies under the guise of linguistic instruction is at its clearest in the moment of Crimsworth's marriage proposal. Even as he acknowledges that French is "the language of [Frances's] own heart" (216), he nonetheless insists, once again, that his "pupil [. . .]. Speak English" when replying to the offer of his hand. By the same token, in agreeing to "pass her life" (224) with Crimsworth, Frances, in the same breath, also consents to a different kind of passing: as wife and mother, she will continue to play the role of the "well-educated lady in Essex or Middlesex" (126) for whom Crimsworth, on first hearing her voice, had (mis)taken her—even to the point, it seems, of learning "how to make a cup of tea in rational English style" (246).

By means of the disciplinary techniques of a pedagogy and courtship often indistinguishable from one another, Crimsworth would appear to have refined his "young Genevese" (252) into an ideally desexualized partner. Yet the prospect of marriage to the "serviceable" (217) Frances works, paradoxically, only to uncover the sexual degradation he both fears in himself and projects onto others. Following their betrothal, Crimsworth uncharacteristically confesses that he appreciates Frances not only because of her "mental points"—her intellectual and moral virtues—but also for "the graces of her person," even endowing her with the "well-set teeth" previously seen, in the "Maroon"-like Caroline, to be the mark of a racialized sexuality. Recognizing that he derives "a pleasure purely material" from Frances's "delicate form," he is forced into belated acknowledgement of the similarities between himself and those he otherwise detests—Pelet, his schoolgirls, Zoraïde: "It appeared then, that I too was a sensualist, in my temperate and fastidious way."

The signs of Crimsworth's sensuality are subsequently manifested in the erotic fantasies precipitated by thoughts of carnal union with Frances in marriage. Although these fantasies are textually censored, they are deducible from the nocturnal restlessness that takes hold of Crimsworth as the immediate result of securing Frances as wife. As he returns to his rooms and tries to sleep, Crimsworth discovers that the "sweet delirium" of "the last few hours" (227) will not "subside" and continues, indeed, "till long after midnight" to break his "rest" with "troubled ecstacy." What he also discovers, however, is that sleep itself is the means by which his troubles only ramify:

> At last I dozed, but not for long; it was yet quite dark when I awoke and my waking was like that of Job when a spirit passed before his face, and like him, "The hair of my flesh stood up." I might continue the parallel, for in truth, though I saw nothing yet "A thing was secretly brought unto me, and mine ear received a little thereof; there was silence and I heard a voice," saying:

> "In the midst of Life, we are in Death."

> (228)

While Crimsworth's sudden "waking" propels him into identification with the Biblical Job, the terms in which he couches his return to consciousness bring it into "parallel" with a different kind of arousal. The implication—crude but coded—is that it is not just "'The hair of [his] flesh'" but the "flesh" itself that "st[ands] up" here. The language spoken by the hallucinatory "voice" is similarly risqué in its combination of climactic pleasure with extinction. Its death-in-life ejaculation is a *double entendre,* hinting at the discharge in the "midst" of whose occurrence Crimsworth, on stirring, is alarmed to find himself located.

Crimsworth's elided dream of Frances is thus adulterated by the vagaries of the masturbatory body. This is a reading confirmed by the manner in which his nocturnal ordeals develop, as the sexual intimacies he both anticipates and prematurely enjoys effect a disruptive return of the past upon the present. In one of ***The Professor***'s strangest and most haunting sequences, Crimsworth describes how, in the aftermath to his solitary blisses, he feels his "chamber invaded by one [he] had known formerly, but had thought for ever departed." Identifying this revenant as the feminized figure of "Hypochondria," he goes on to detail their first encounters:

> She had been my acquaintance, nay my guest, once before in boyhood; I had entertained her at bed and board for a year; for that space of time I had her to myself in secret; she lay with me, she eat with me, she walked out with me, shewing me nooks in woods, hollows in hills, where we could sit together, and where she could drop her drear veil over me, and so hide sky and sun, grass and green tree; taking me entirely to her death-cold bosom, and holding me with arms of bone. What tales she would tell me, at such hours! What songs she would recite in my ears! How she would discourse to me of her own Country—The Grave—and again and again promise to conduct me there erelong; and drawing me to the very brink of a black, sullen river, shew

> me on the other side, shores unequal with mound, monument and tablet, standing up in a glimmer more hoary than moonlight. "Necropolis!" she would whisper, pointing to the pale piles, and add "It contains a mansion, prepared for you."

> (228)

As both Azim (155-56) and Shuttleworth (141-44) suggest, the "Hypochondria" that "accost[s]" Crimsworth "*now*" and "*then*" (229) is a symptom whose aetiology, in contemporary medical discourse, is frequently linked, precisely, to the practice of masturbation. Just as it is the protocol of the symptom—according to psychoanalysis—both to disguise and disclose its cause, so Crimsworth's prose might be said to operate in terms of a symptomatic logic. This is evidenced by the way that the specifically sexual nature of the hidden origin from which his condition first arises and then recurs is flagrantly exhibited by the language in which the condition itself is articulated. In both past and present incarnations, "Hypochondria" figures as mistress. As the "acquaintance, nay [. . .] guest" of Crimsworth's pubescence, she is pursued and possessed in "secret" across a range of erogenous zones. These stretch from domestic locations ("bed and board") to the wilder scenes of "nooks in woods" and "hollows in hills" that themselves map out, in Shuttleworth's phrase, "the symbolic terrain of the female body" (141). Similarly, on her subsequent advent, "Hypochondria" takes the form of "a dreaded and ghastly concubine coming to embitter a husband's heart towards his young bride." As if to underwrite the continuity between past and present, her second coming is stimulated by the anonymous "caress of a soft hand" (229). Is this the "hand" of marriage or masturbation, belonging to Frances or Crimsworth?

The Professor's own "discourse" on "Hypochondria" is consistent with contemporary medical assumptions about the deleterious effects of masturbation upon the male subject. Even as Crimsworth remembers himself as initially enjoying his symptom, "Hypochondria" is soon revealed to be an agent of destruction rather than *jouissance,* or rather destruction through *jouissance.* She is less mistress than femme fatale and, ultimately, grave-tender. The "Necropolis" to which she threatens finally to "conduct" her young charge is a concrete symbol for the terrifying dead end for which, according to Victorian sexual ideology, the self-abusive male is destined. At the same time, it functions as another site in which the novel's association of sexuality with forms of foreignness is dramatized. By describing "The Grave" over which "Hypochondria" presides as "her own Country," Crimsworth implies that the prospective burial-ground of a misspent youth is located in an alien space or *terra incognita.* His psychic geography is further exoticized by "Hypochondria"'s second visit, in which she takes the form of "concubine." In this latter guise, she seems much like one of the "oriental odalisques" (26) with whom Hunsden associates aristocratic women in chapter 3. More disturbingly, she seems, also, to resemble the Zoraïde whom Crimsworth has renounced for Frances and whose "soft step" leads out toward an Oriental space.

After some nine days of struggle against his "evil spirit," Crimsworth begins slowly to regain his equilibrium and, within a "fortnight," declares himself fit to "seek Frances and sit at her side" once more. Yet even as he resists the "sway" of his foreign cum Oriental "demon" (229), Crimsworth's married life with Frances is not quite patterned according to the symmetry of mutual restraint for which he might have hoped. Much to his chagrin, it bears a somewhat closer resemblance to the adulterous geometry of the "Modern French novel" (187) in which he suspects Zoraïde will entangle him after her marriage to Pelet. For in Frances, Crimsworth seems, as he puts it, "to possess two wives" (250). Moving from English to French, Frances simultaneously translates herself across the fragile border between sexual self-control and sexual excess. Her mimicry of Crimsworth, that "man of regular life and rational mind" (159), is also a mockery:

> Talk French to me she would, and many a punishment she has had for her wilfulness—I fear the choice of chastisement must have been injudicious, for instead of correcting the fault, it seemed to encourage its renewal. [. . .] In those moments [. . .] she would shew me what she had of vivacity, of mirth, of originality in her well-dowered nature. She would shew too some stores of raillery, of "malice", and would vex, tease, pique me sometimes about what she called my "bizarreries anglaises", my "caprices insulaires", with a wild and witty wickedness that made a perfect white demon of her while it lasted. This was rare, however, and the elfish freak was always short: sometimes when driven a little hard in the war of words, for her tongue did ample justice to the pith, the point, the delicacy of her native French, in which language she always attacked me—I used to turn upon her with my old decision, and arrest bodily the sprite that teased me. Vain idea! no sooner had I grasped hand or arm, than the elf was gone; the provocative smile quenched in the expressive brown eyes, and a ray of gentle homage shone under the lids in its place: I had seized a mere vexing fairy and found a submissive and supplicating little mortal woman in my arms. Then I made her get a book, and read English to me for an hour by way of penance. I frequently dosed her with Wordsworth in this way and Wordsworth steadied her soon.

> (252-53)

In this long passage, language is the sado-masochistic medium in which questions of sexuality, nation and race are fused. When Frances "Talk[s] French" to her husband, she disrupts the "illusion" Crimsworth has carefully built around her. On these occasions, she behaves less like the "fair-complexioned, English-looking girl" (174) of his repressive fantasies than the "arrant coquettes" (95) of the daymares suffered at Zoraïde's school. Such linguistic lapses are also implicitly sexual ones, as Frances unnervingly changes from angel in the house to "perfect white demon."

In the "war of words" between husband and wife, Crimsworth will always be the loser, not least because the language in which he recounts their struggle is—as much as

Frances and her aggressively capable "tongue"—beyond his control. This loss of linguistic mastery is marked in two ways, the first of which relates to the glaring contradiction underpinning Crimsworth's marital pedagogy. By being forced to "read English [. . .] for an hour" and "frequently dosed [. . .] with Wordsworth," Frances, Crimsworth claims, is "steadied [. . .] soon." Yet this itself is surely an extravagant assertion, since it has already been conceded that "the choice of chastisement" is "injudicious" and "correcting the fault" of Frances's linguistic and sexual orientations merely "encourage[s] its renewal." The authority of Frances's embattled "English professor" (252) is challenged, secondly, by the silent misdemeanours of allusion. While Frances earlier consciously rewrites *Othello* with "parts [. . .] reversed," Crimsworth here rehearses Shakespeare's play with the main roles more conventionally—if unconsciously—distributed, as the striking disciplinary failures of his marriage parallel those of Othello's relation to Desdemona (whose own name is half-echoed in the figuring of Frances as "demon"). According to Stephen J. Greenblatt, "rather than confirming male authority, [Desdemona's] submission eroticizes everything to which it responds," including even the "mistreatment" she receives from her husband (80). As she herself muses, confiding to Emilia: "my love doth so approve [Othello], / That even his stubbornness, his checks and frowns,— / Prithee, unpin me,—have grace and favour in them" (4. 3. 19-21). In the same way, the "punishment"—in the shape of Wordsworth—to which Crimsworth resorts simply results in further wrongdoing, making him the victim of an irony that is, in fact, Shakespearean.

In the novel's closing scenes, Crimsworth, now permanently resident with his family in England, turns his attentions—and the reader's—toward the question of his son. Victor—"soon [to] go to Eton" (265), like his father before him—is a figure stranger even than the child of a "strange hybrid race" who, as Hunsden speculates, is the potential "progeny" (203) of Zoraïde's marriage to Pelet. There is, his father complains:

> a something in Victor's temper, a kind of electrical ardour and power, which emits, now and then, ominous sparks—Hunsden calls it his spirit and says it should not be curbed—I call it the leaven of the offending Adam and consider that it should be if not *whipped* out of him, at least soundly disciplined, and that he will be cheap of any amount of either bodily or mental suffering which will ground him radically in the art of self-control.

> (266)

In figuring the "something in Victor's temper" as "the leaven of the offending Adam," Crimsworth diagnoses in his son a condition that covers a multitude of sins, ranging from the vices of a generalized carnality to the more personal falls of his own "boyhood." From this perspective, the "sparks" periodically emitted by Victor are "ominous" indeed: they are the first signs of an implicit sexual impurity that is the mark, in turn, of national and racial infections. Victor must be "soundly disciplined," body and mind, in order that his Englishness, already compromised by the line of a double-speaking mother, be insulated against further violation.

Notes

1. As Harlow and Carter observe, Macaulay's "Minute" is "a critical [. . .] contribution to the debate on the respective roles of Indian and English traditions in the issues of government and instruction" (62). For a detailed analysis of this debate and, in particular, the role of English literature as an instrument of colonial domination, see Viswanathan.

2. For further theoretical analyses of the relations between race and metaphor see Lloyd passim and Meyer 1-28.

3. See, for example, Marx's comment, in *Capital,* that "Liverpool waxed fat on the slavetrade. This was its method of primitive accumulation. [. . .] The veiled slavery of the wage-workers in Europe needed, for its pedestal, slavery pure and simple in the new world" (qtd. in Fryer 12). See also Fanon 81. The intricate relations between slavery and economic wealth in Brontë's Yorkshire—together with her own and Emily Brontë's meticulous fictional reworkings of these relations—are minutely excavated in Heywood.

4. In his Jamaican diary entry for 9 April 1818, Matthew Lewis provides a graphically non-fictional version of the kind of colonial domination to which Juanna looks forward, while at the same time making the female the object rather than agent of abuse. Refuting the opinion "that conduct so savage occurs rarely in *any* country," Lewis writes: "I have not passed six months in Jamaica, and I have already found on one of my estates a woman who had been kicked in the womb by a white book-keeper, by which she was crippled herself, and on another of my estates another woman who had been kicked in the womb by another white book-keeper, by which he had crippled the child. [. . .] and thus, as my two estates are at the two extremities of the island, I am entitled to say, from my own knowledge (*i.e.* speaking *literally,* observe), that 'white book-keepers kick black women in the belly *from one end of Jamaica to the other*'" (241).

5. The politically charged nature of the figure of the "Maroon" is noted, in a brief discussion of this passage, by Meyer 61 n.5.

6. A similar point is made by Shuttleworth 127. For a useful overview of the Foucauldian elements running through *The Professor* as a whole, see Glen 18-19.

Works Cited

Acton, William. *The Functions and Disorders of the Reproductive Organs in Childhood, Youth, Adult Age and Advanced Life Considered in their Physiological, Social and Moral Relations.* London, 1857.

Azim, Firdous. *The Colonial Rise of the Novel.* London and New York: Routledge, 1993.

Blackburn, Robin. *The Overthrow of Colonial Slavery 1776-1848.* London and New York: Verso, 1988.

Boumelha, Penny. *Charlotte Brontë.* Hemel Hempstead: Harvester Wheatsheaf, 1990.

Brontë, Charlotte. *Juvenilia 1829-1835.* Ed. Juliet Barker. Harmondsworth: Penguin, 1996.

———. *The Professor.* Ed. Margaret Smith and Herbert Rosengarten. Oxford: Oxford UP, 1987.

Cheyfitz, Eric. *The Poetics of Imperialism: Translation and Colonization from The Tempest to Tarzan.* Expanded ed. Philadelphia: U of Pennsylvania P, 1997.

Douglass, Frederick. *The Frederick Douglass Papers: Vol. 1: Speeches, Debates and Interviews.* Ed. John W. Blassingame. New Haven and London: Yale UP, 1979.

———. *Narrative of the Life of Frederick Douglass, An American Slave, Written by Himself.* Ed. William L. Andrews and William S. McFeely. New York and London: Norton, 1997.

Fanon, Frantz. *The Wretched of the Earth.* Trans. Constance Farrington. Preface by Jean-Paul Sartre. Harmondsworth: Penguin, 1990.

Freud, Sigmund. "Negation." *On Metapsychology: The Theory of Psychoanalysis.* Trans. James Strachey. Ed. Angela Richards. Pelican Freud Library. Vol. 11. Harmondsworth: Penguin, 1984. 437-42.

Fryer, Peter. *Aspects of Black British History.* London: Index Books, 1993.

Glen, Heather. "Introduction." *The Professor.* By Charlotte Brontë. Ed. Heather Glen. Harmondsworth: Penguin, 1989. 7-31.

Greenblatt, Stephen J. "Improvisation and Power." *Literature and Society.* Ed. Edward W. Said. Baltimore and London: Johns Hopkins UP, 1980. 57-99.

Harlow, Barbara and Mia Carter, ed. *Imperialism & Orientalism: A Documentary Source-book.* Oxford: Blackwell, 1999.

Heywood, Christopher. "Yorkshire Slavery in *Wuthering Heights.*" *Review of English Studies: A Quarterly Review of English Literature and English Language.* 38 (1987): 184-98.

Lewis, Matthew. *Journal of a West India Proprietor, Kept during a Residence in the Island of Jamaica.* Ed. Judith Terry. Oxford: Oxford UP, 1999.

Lloyd, David. "Race under Representation." *Oxford Literary Review.* 13. 1-2 (1991): 62-94.

Marcus, Steven. *The Other Victorians: A Study of Sexuality and Pornography in Mid-Nineteenth Century England.* London: Weidenfeld and Nicolson, 1966.

Meyer, Susan. *Imperialism at Home: Race and Victorian Women's Fiction.* Ithaca and London: Cornell UP, 1996.

Said, Edward W. *Culture and Imperialism.* London: Vintage, 1994.

Shakespeare, William. *Othello.* Ed. M. R. Ridley. London and New York: Routledge, 1987.

Shuttleworth, Sally. *Charlotte Brontë and Victorian Psychology.* Cambridge: Cambridge UP, 1996.

Viswanathan, Gauri, *Masks of Conquest: Literary Study and British Rule in India.* New York: Columbia UP, 1989.

FURTHER READING

Criticism

Anonymous review of "Currer Bell's *Professor.*" In *Dublin University Magazine* 50, No. 295, (July 1857): 88-100.

>   Discusses Gaskell's *The Life of Charlotte Brontë,* followed by excerpts from that work pertaining to Brontë's attempts to publish *The Professor* and a plot summary of the novel.

Betsinger, Sue Ann. "Charlotte Brontë's Archetypal Heroine." *Brontë Society Transaction* 19 (1989): 301-09.

>   Suggests that William Crimsworth, *The Professor*'s narrator, is not the book's character of primary interest, but that Frances Henri is the novel's heroine and becomes the model for the heroines of Brontë's later novels.

Brown, Kate E. "Beloved Objects: Mourning, Materiality, and Charlotte Brontë's 'Never-Ending Story'." *ELH* [*Journal of English Literary History*] 65, No. 2 (Summer 1998): 395-421.

>   Examines the role and influence of Brontë's juvenilia in composing *The Professor.*

Bruce, Donald Williams. "Charlotte Brontë in Brussels: *The Professor* and *Villette.*" *Contemporary Review* 254, No. 1481 (June 1989): 321-28.

>   Maintains that the plot of *The Professor,* based on Brontë's experience as a student and teacher in Brussels, was reworked with greater success in the later novel *Villette.*

Butler, Janet. "Charlotte Brontë's *Professor.*" *Explicator* 44, No. 3 (Spring 1986): 35-37.

>   Provides a brief discussion of the depression Crimsworth suffers in *The Professor* and contends that the "spectral woman" identified as "hypochondria," or depression, is representative of sexuality that is never experienced.

McIntyre, Elizabeth. "Charlotte Brontë's New Corinne: Re-Reading *The Professor.*" *Victorian Newsletter,* No. 85 (Spring 1994): 34-39.

>   Argues that *The Professor* is based more on Brontë's reading of Madame de Staël's *Corinne* (1807) than on Brontë's own life experiences in Brussels.

Morphet, Fiona. "Playing with *The Professor.*" *College Language Association Journal* 37, No. 3 (March 1994): 348-57.

>   Maintains that *The Professor* creates "playful energies of exploration and discovery" and inspires students to develop critical evaluation skills rather than simply identifying with the story in a naïve manner or revering the well-respected author.

Additional coverage of Brontë's life and career is contained in the following sources published by the Gale Group: *Authors & Artists for Young Adults,* **Vol. 17;** *Concise Dictionary of British Literary Biography, 1832-1890; Dictionary of Literary Biography,* **Vols. 21, 159, and 199;** *DISCovering Authors* **3.0;** *DISCovering Authors: British; DISCovering Authors: Canadian; DISCovering Authors Modules: Most-Studied Authors, Novelists,* **and** *Poets; Poetry Criticism,* **Vol. 8; and** *World Literature Criticism, 1500-Present.*

Michel Guillaume Jean de Crèvecoeur
1735-1813

(Wrote under the name J. Hector St. John) French-born American fiction writer and novelist.

INTRODUCTION

Michel Guillaume Jean de Crèvecoeur was a naturalized American citizen whose observations on life in pre-Revolutionary America are still read today. His most famous work, *Letters from an American Farmer* (1782), was instrumental in differentiating the life and culture of the American colonies from that of Europe, and in helping to establish an American literary tradition out of common cultural experience where none was believed to exist. He is credited with formulating the idea of America as a melting pot where "individuals of all nations are melted into a new race of men." One of the book's individual letters, "What Is an American?," has long been considered a classic articulation of the character and identity of the members of that new nation.

BIOGRAPHICAL INFORMATION

Crèvecoeur was born in Caen, France, in 1735 to Guillaume Jean de Crèvecoeur, a minor member of the Norman nobility, and Marie-Anne-Thérèse Blouet, the daughter of a banker. He was educated at the local Jesuit college, and at the age of nineteen left France, first for England and then for Canada, where he served the French colonial militia as a surveyor and cartographer. In 1758 he was commissioned as a lieutenant in the regular army of France and was wounded in the battle for Quebec the following year. He resigned his commission and left Canada for the British colonies to the south, again working as a surveyor while traveling through New York, Vermont, and the Ohio region. He was naturalized in New York as a British subject and changed his name to J. Hector St. John. In 1769, Crèvecoeur married Mehitable Tippet, the daughter of a prosperous Westchester family, and purchased a farm near the Hudson River in Orange County, New York. Within the next six years, the couple had three children, two boys and a girl. During this time, Crèvecoeur worked his farm and began writing, in English, producing but not publishing *Letters from an American Farmer*.

Although he was not sympathetic to the cause of the American Revolution, Crèvecoeur tried to remain neutral. As a result, neither side trusted him and he was imprisoned by the British for three months, after which he left for London in a British ship with his eldest son. His wife

and remaining children were left in charge of the farm. While in England, he sold *Letters From an American Farmer* to a publisher and returned in 1781 to his native France, where he resumed his French citizenship. While there, he published *Lettres d'un Cultivateur Américain* (1784), an adaptation and expansion of his earlier work.

Crèvecoeur returned to New York in 1783 as French Consul to New Jersey, Connecticut, and New York and worked to promote trade and goodwill between France and the United States. During his absence, his wife had died and his beloved farmhouse in New York had been destroyed in an Indian raid. His children, originally believed dead, were eventually found in Boston. Crèvecoeur returned to France in 1790 and lived there for the remaining twenty-three years of his life, never again visiting his adopted country. He died at Sarcelles in 1813.

MAJOR WORKS

Crèvecoeur's most famous work, *Letters from an American Farmer* occupies a unique place in American literary history. The work consists of twelve letters written by James Hector St. John, an American-born farmer of English descent. The recipient of these letters is an English gentleman, F. B., who is interested in learning more about American life and provides Farmer James with topics for the letters. The worldly and sophisticated F. B. is contrasted with Farmer James, a self-described "*tabula rasa*," (blank slate) who admits his lack of education and experience. The first three letters detail life on an American farm and contrast the opportunities abounding in the colonies as opposed to the limited options available to a poor man in Europe. The third letter, "What Is an American?," offers a statement of national identity for this new breed of man who has shed the vestiges of European feudalism and embraced the principles of agrarian democracy. This individual letter has been extensively anthologized and is considered such a definitive description of the American national character that it was included in the onboard reading material for passengers on American Airlines in the 1970s.

The middle five letters detail life on Nantucket Island and although the idyllic picture of agrarian life Farmer James favored in New York could not be applied to the rocky, barren soil of Nantucket, the letters are still optimistic. The inhabitants of Nantucket were whalers, and by extending the farming metaphor to the ocean, James suggests that even in this seemingly inhospitable region, men unfettered by restrictive government could attain an earthly paradise.

In Letter IX, the narrator leaves Nantucket for the South, and the tone of the work changes abruptly. It describes "a melancholy scene" in Charleston, South Carolina, where Farmer James discovers a slave suspended in a cage and left to die as punishment for having killed the overseer of his master's plantation. Farmer James, a slaveholder himself, expounds on the evils of slavery, but insists that his slaves are not part of the same system: "They enjoy as much liberty as their masters, they are as well clad and as well fed; in health and sickness they are tenderly taken care of; they live under the same roof and are, truly speaking, a part of our families." In the remaining letters, Farmer James's disillusionment grows as the horrors of revolution threaten his Eden, and he makes plans to flee his farm for the wilderness, an area he once denounced as savage and chaotic.

After his return to France, Crèvecoeur published *Lettres d'un Cultivateur Américain,* which is not a translation of the earlier publication, but a new composition written in French, drawing on the materials of *Letters From an American Farmer,* but consisting of sixty-four letters, rather than twelve as in the original. In 1800, again back in France, Crèvecoeur began writing *Voyage dans la Haute Pennsylvanie et dans l'État de New York,* which was published the following year. *Sketches of Eighteenth-Century America* went unpublished until 1925, two years after the manuscript was discovered in Normandy. It consists of several letters and sketches, many of which were considered too hostile to the American Revolution and too Loyalist to the British to be included in *Letters from an American Farmer.* One such sketch, "The American Belisarius," describes the persecution of a virtuous Loyalist by his pro-Revolutionary neighbors; it is balanced, though, by the portion of "Susquehanna" that was published in *Sketches* as "The Wyoming Massacre," an account of the massacre of a Patriot community by British troops.

CRITICAL RECEPTION

Of Crèvecoeur's writings, *Letters from an American Farmer* has attracted the largest share of critical attention, and debate on the work has centered on its appropriate classification and on the general tone of its author's assessment of American life. The book, published in London, gained immediate popularity there; among its admirers were Thomas Paine and William Godwin, as well as the more radical figures of Romanticism. At that time, the work was only moderately popular in America. Until the latter half of the twentieth century, the majority of critics concentrated on Letter III and thus believed the work to be optimistic, even utopian in its evaluation of life in America. In recent years, criticism has shifted considerably to assess *Letters* as a whole, as well as within the context of Crèvecoeur's other writing, particularly *Sketches of Eighteenth Century America.* These critics, among them James C. Mohr, see Crèvecoeur's work as far more sophisticated and subtle than originally believed.

Crèvecoeur's work has been the subject of extended critical debate regarding the genre within which it should be classified. Much early criticism took these letters as autobiographical, considering the author and his narrator to be one and the same. This led to charges of inauthenticity as critics focused on exposing the fact that the author/narrator was not the grandson of immigrants from England at all, but was, in fact, born in France; that he was not a naive farmer, but an educated, sophisticated gentleman. Recent criticism has treated the work as fiction and eliminated the confusion between J. Hector St. John and his fictional persona, Farmer James. In form *Letters from an American Farmer* draws on the eighteenth-century epistolary tradition, and its individual letters read like essays on the series of topics suggested by the fictional recipient of the correspondence. However, some critics classify it as a romance, while still others claim that the work anticipates the nineteenth-century novel, insisting that the letters are unified by the narrator's progression from optimism to disillusionment.

The disillusionment that characterizes the ending of *Letters from an American Farmer,* as well as the far more pessimistic view of American life presented in *Sketches of Eighteenth Century America* have led many twentieth-century scholars to focus on these apparent ambiguities in Crèvecoeur's work. Some critics insist that Crèvecoeur genuinely believed that the American colonies could provide a testing ground for Enlightenment ideals, and that his optimism and subsequent disappointment were, therefore, genuine. Others believe that the author was being ironic in the early descriptions of an idyllic agrarian democracy, and that the expressions of disillusionment that followed convey the true tone of the work. Mary E. Rucker suggests that *Letters* is actually a dialectic on Enlightenment principles between the optimistic Farmer James and the pessimistic Crèvecoeur.

Other ambiguities explored by scholars include the work's treatment of slavery where Farmer James denounces the institution in the South at the same time he endorses it in his home region. Pierre Aubéry has explored the element of racism that runs through *Letters,* and which is inconsistent with the idealized American identity that Crèvecoeur was seeking to establish. Myra Jehlen has concentrated on the apparent contradiction between Crèvecoeur's admiration for America and his opposition to the American Revolution. Stephen Carl Arch suggests that the true purpose of *Letters* was to expose the dangers of revolution in general, while David M. Larson believes that Crèvecoeur's sentimental descriptions of the war's effect on settlers was a contrast to the usual abstract Revolutionary War rhetoric which stressed political considerations over personal hardships. For Larson, Crèvecoeur's version counters the "bloodless sanitized version of the conflict which forms the stuff of popular legend."

PRINCIPAL WORKS

Letters from an American Farmer: Describing Certain Provincial Situations, Manners, and Customs, Not Generally Known; and Conveying Some Idea of the Late and Present Interior Circumstances of the British Colonies of North America. Written for the Information of a Friend in England, by J. Hector St. John, A Farmer in Pennsylvania (fictional letters) 1782

Lettres d'un Cultivateur Américain, Écrites à W. S., Ecuyer, depuis l'année 1770, jusqu'à 1781, Traduites de l'anglois par *** 2 volumes (fictional letters) 1784

Voyage dans la Haute Pennsylvanie et dans l'État de New York, Par un Membre Adoptif de la Nation Onéida. Traduit et publié par l'auteur des Lettres d'un Cultivateur Amèricain (sketches) 1801

Sketches of Eighteenth Century America: More "Letters from an American Farmer" (fictional letters and sketches) 1925

*"Landscapes" (play) 1925

†"Susquehanna" (sketch) 1925

*This play was published as part of *Sketches of Eighteenth Century America,* in 1925.

†This work was never published in its entirety; a portion of it was published as "The Wyoming Massacre" in *Sketches of Eighteenth Century America,* and the remainder was published as "Crèvecouer on the Susquehanna" in *Yale Review,* 1925.

CRITICISM

Elayne Antler Rapping (essay date 1967)

SOURCE: "Theory and Experience in Crèvecoeur's America," in *American Quarterly,* Vol. 19, No. 4, Winter, 1967, pp. 707-18.

[*In the following essay, Rapping discusses Crèvecoeur's belief that the newly settled land of America offered an opportunity to test the principles of the Enlightenment.*]

We often read that American literature developed late because we lacked a common cultural past, and meaningful conventions and symbols for describing our shared experience. But as early as 1782, with his ***Letters from an American Farmer,*** J. Hector St. Jean de Crèvecoeur discovered and made literary use of a very real imaginative past shared by Americans. For Crèvecoeur recognized that the new nation took its form from a complex of literary and philosophic ideas which came together and found expression in eighteenth-century Europe. He saw the significance of the fact that the Age of Enlightenment, in which men began to suspect they could discover rationally the laws of nature which governed an intelligible universe, was also the age in which a new nation was being established on a newly settled land, offering an opportunity to test these theories.

In a sense the new society was built from a neat theoretical model, for the one assumption which tied these ideas together was the assumption of order. According to eighteenth-century thought a benevolent intelligence governed the laws of physics, economics and moral philosophy. Man himself was a mixture of passion and reason. He was also a product of his environment, but once he discovered the laws of human and physical nature he could learn to govern himself and his environment rationally.

Given these basic assumptions, agrarian democracy was an ideal social structure, for it allowed man to live in a middle state between primitive savagery and overly complex civilization. The farmer, living close to the earth, received the moral and physical benefits of nature and escaped the corrupting influences of the city. He avoided the dangers of the wilderness as well, for he lived in a rationally organized community and earned his living by applying reason to his industry. The American continent, where land was fertile and abundant, was an ideal setting in which to bring the model to life; and so the establishment of a perfect society became an actual possibility for the first time in history.[1]

Crèvecoeur sensed the imaginative appeal of this model. He saw it as a kind of literary heritage and he used its formal structures and clearly defined terms as conventions and symbols for describing our common experience. But he also saw that these conventions and symbols were unique, for instead of growing out of a common past, they suggested an ideal for the future. Insofar as they informed the American consciousness then, the new nation would become a sort of testing ground for the hypotheses of the model.

Crèvecoeur explores the implications of this insight in his two full-length works, the ***Letters from an American Farmer*** and ***Journey into Northern Pennsylvania and the State of New York.*** He begins both works with a hypothetical acceptance of the world as the model describes it. The narrators in both works journey through the American countryside and attempt to interpret what they see in terms of the model's assumptions. But in both cases the cumulative effect of the narrative is to convince the reader, if not the narrators themselves, that the model represents a false view of the world which will not stand the test of experience. A study of the structural developments of both books will illustrate Crèvecoeur's strategy.

In the first three chapters of the ***Letters*** he gives a detailed description of the hypothetical world the model describes. In the "Introduction" the narrator, James, identifies himself as a typical American farmer writing a series of letters to a cultivated European. James describes himself as a "*tabula rasa*" uneducated and inexperienced. His correspondent, he tells us, wishes him to record his impressions of the progress of the only nation in which one may observe a newly born society, developing freely.

It is clear from the start that both James and his country are being tested against a set of theories which the European has provided. "Remember," James tells him, "you are to give me my subjects and on no others shall I write. . . . You have laid the foundation of this correspondence . . . [and you will] receive my letters as conceived, not according to scientific rules, but agreeable to the spontaneous impressions which each subject may inspire . . . [for this is] the line which Nature herself has traced for me. . . ."[2] James, then, has accepted a set of defined terms from his correspondent, the most important of which is "Nature." Only if the model's assumptions about human and physical nature prove correct will the progress of the society fulfill the expectations of his correspondent.

In James' first letter we learn what these assumptions and expectations are. Here, presumably, Farmer James is describing his own situation spontaneously and naturally as he promised. But in the first paragraph we see that he has been won over by his correspondent's theories about him, for he remarks that his new acquaintance has broadened his views of himself and that he is "happier now than [he] thought [him]self before" (p. 45). In other words James' conception of himself has already lost some of its spontaneity and taken on the attributes of the model's ideal farmer.

The description of James' life, which follows, is in perfect harmony with the model's assumptions, as we would expect. He is a freeholder working on his own land for himself and his family. The land is fertile and his reason and industry make it productive. His government demands little of him and he has no reason to covet his neighbor's things. He does acknowledge the existence of evil in man and nature but he has faith in the power of human reason to understand and control these excesses, by changing the conditions that incite them, or by mediating among warring parties in the interest of the greatest good. He compares his own successful methods of governing his cattle with the "simple and just laws" of the American government. "The law is to us precisely what I am in my barnyard" (p. 51), he says. The difference between James' cattle and the American citizens, according to the model, is the potential power of human reason. Unlike the beast whom man must govern, the American farmer can understand that his own interest is ultimately served by leading a peaceful and industrious life. Therefore, he will not forfeit the benefits of his moderate existence to indulge his baser instincts.

It is this faith in human reason, and an intelligible natural world, which informs the image of the developing nation in James' next letter. "Here . . . are no great manufactures . . . no great refinements of luxury" he says. "We are a people of cultivators . . . united by the silken bands of mild government, all respecting the laws without dreading their power because they are equitable. . . . A pleasing uniformity of decent competence appears throughout our habitations" (p. 61).

Balance and harmony are not all that is visible, of course. There are areas of wilderness where backwoodsmen live in a state of war, hunting instead of planting. The new settlers themselves are lowly wretches when they arrive, some of them hopelessly corrupt. But to James these elements of the society are less real than the orderly farm communities. He speaks as though the universal agrarian society were already a reality, and the existing evils already overcome, because he has faith in his model's predictions. He foresees "a kind of resurrection," or "metamorphosis" (p. 76) which the new settler will experience in a society whose laws are based on those of nature. This is the model's version of reality and it is fully established in James' consciousness as he moves out of his community and begins to tour the country.[3]

The movement from James' village to the communities of Nantucket and Charles Town is a movement from the world of theory to that of experience. The preceding chapters described James' past and present life as part of an abstract plan for an ideal future. Now James moves forward in time and space to demonstrate the model's universal applicability and its powers of prediction. His first testing ground, the fishing village of Nantucket, seems to be operating successfully according to the laws of nature. Self-interest is the natural basis for behavior here, and all citizens can gratify their needs and wants since they are temperate and industrious. These two qualities, in fact, are the keys to the Nantucketers' success. According to the model they are rational principles based on the conviction that moderation best serves one's interest. But in Nantucket these qualities happen to be necessary for survival, for the soil is hard and the climate cold. The truth of the hypothesis can only be ascertained, then, by transporting these same people to a richer environment. This Crèvecoeur does next.

Although the narrative demands that each of James' letters describe a portion of a single journey, Crèvecoeur is implicitly tracing the country's development over a period of time. In his first letter James told how his father first cultivated his farm, and of how he himself received the benefits of his father's struggles. He enjoyed greater security and some leisure time to invent machines to ease his labors. Such progress from generation to generation was implicit in the model. Crèvecoeur has placed the Nantucketers in an area which demands constant labor for subsistence because they represent the early generation of settlers clearing the paths for their descendants, as James' father did. Since their resources are limited, their offspring are forced to move to other areas. The first generation has acquired some knowledge of the countryside however, and they send their descendants to Carolina, where the land is fertile and they can enjoy greater security and leisure as James does. It is Charles Town in Carolina that James visits next, and there is little doubt that Crèvecoeur intended its inhabitants to represent the next generation of Nantucketers enjoying the benefits of their forebears' experience.

But it is in Charles Town that the model begins to fail, for when the inhabitants are no longer forced to practice temperance and industry they do not choose to do so. The laws in Charles Town are based on nature and the people act in their own self-interest as they did in Nantucket, but now this rational principle does not lead to moderation and good will. Instead, it leads to tyranny, for the interest of the master is not the interest of the slave and conflicts of interest are settled by power. In Nantucket, James told us, there was only one rather idle lawyer, but the wealth of Charles Town has attracted a whole class of lawyers who have used their superior knowledge of the law to serve their own interests and have become as wealthy and powerful as the aristocracy of Europe.

Farmer James becomes confused and dismayed as he tries to interpret behavior in Charles Town in terms of his model, and his confusion centers on the word "nature." While it is natural to act in one's own interest, it seems to him contrary to the "Rules of Nature" to do so tyrannically. In James' barnyard there was only one law of nature and it was easily discovered and acted upon, for Nature was in harmony with morality and with man's instincts. But here reason, self-interest and natural law lead to gross inequity and cruelty rather than peace, because human instinct is vicious instead of virtuous, and it is not controlled by reason. James' theories about man are all contradicted here for, as he now sees, "Nature has given us a fruitful soil to inhabit [but] refused us such inclinations and propensities as would afford us the full enjoyment of it. . . . She created man and . . . provided him with passions

which must forever oppose his happiness; . . . Force, subtlety, and malice, always triumph over unguarded honesty and simplicity . . . and prevent their subsequent salutary effects, though ordained for the good of man by the Governor of the universe. Such is the perverseness of human nature" (pp. 168-71).

At this point James still believes that the laws of nature are the source of moral principles which man is intended to act upon. He realizes that there are temptations and dangers in the world, but these he feels, can be avoided if one conforms to nature. The people of Nantucket presumably illustrated this. They had wisely chosen a hard climate which demanded industry and temperance, and so avoided the excesses of the savage and the decadence of the wealthy planter. But there were two conditions necessary for the survival of the Nantucket way of life. First, man had to be intellectually and morally strong enough to resist temptation; and second, nature had to provide the environment necessary for establishing and maintaining such a life. James has come to doubt the possibility of the first condition for he has seen men perversely ignore the moral principles derived from the laws of nature. Now he considers the laws themselves in the light of all human experience, and he realizes that the second condition is also impossible for nature is actively hostile to man's higher aspirations. James' prose reaches a height of frenzied emotion here which echoes the breakdown of order and reason it describes:

> Where do you conceive then that nature intended we should be happy? . . . If we attentively view this globe, will it not appear rather a place of punishment than of delight? . . . Famine, diseases, elementary convulsions, human feuds, dissensions, etc., are the produce of every climate . . . Gracious God! To what end is the introduction of so many beings into a mode of existence in which they must grope amidst as many errors, commit as many crimes, and meet with as many diseases, wants and sufferings!
>
> (p. 171)

James' whole concept of nature has somehow been reversed in Charles Town. In the model, primitive savagery and civilized tyranny were overcome when the laws of nature were institutionalized. But now nature itself is savage and tyrannical and James must abandon his theoretical point of view and the language and tone of his model to describe it.[4] He does regain his poise and continues to assert the principles he has come to believe in, but as the narrative progresses these statements often become ironic commentaries on his actual experience. The next letter illustrates this point. In it Farmer James redraws the picture of the animal world he observes in his barnyard. But this time the creatures interact with no human intervention. The farmer is now an impartial observer who finds beauty in the skill and instinct displayed in the natural processes of murder and destruction. Once again he sees harmony in the universe, but ironically, there is no mention of moral significance. If the state of nature is a state of war, it can still be described in terms of a neat theoretical model, but it can no longer be James' model for all human values must be discarded as meaningless.

After this point James never fully regains his unqualified faith in the model's version of reality. The next letter, which describes the old age of an ideal American farmer, is not even written by him. The writer is a European, traveling through America, who has brought with him all the theories and assumptions James had learned from his correspondent. Mr. Bertram's prosperity and cultivation reinforce his visitor's faith in these theories for he is not aware of the natural forces which threaten the apparent harmony. James, who has witnessed the dissolution of this harmony, could no longer have described it with confidence, and Crèvecoeur has therefore introduced a new narrator, for whom the reality of American experience does not yet exist, in order to bring the world of the model to life again. This entire interlude is, in fact, Crèvecoeur's device for rebuilding his model of America at that point in the narrative when James' experience contradicts it most strongly. It is also the hypothetical ending to James' story, for Mr. Bertram represents the future James, as the model would have him.

But in his final letter James reappears to give another version of the end of his story, based on experience rather than theory. The American Revolution has now begun and he is forced to abandon his farm and flee for safety. In this letter it becomes clear that Farmer James is Crèvecoeur's straw man. He has carefully built a world for himself on the basis of certain principles which have all proved false. The results of his reason, industry and moderation have been swept away by the greater forces of ambition and greed. His own reason is too weak to comprehend the political issues involved, but his experience has taught him that social systems based on assumptions of order in nature are doomed to fail, and he decides to give up such schemes entirely and live the truly natural life of the Indian in the wilderness.

This decision would seem to represent the final step in James' movement from complete faith to complete disillusionment with the ideals of agrarian democracy. But as he begins to elaborate on his new plans, he begins to contradict himself. The spark of hope which the wilderness suggests to him leads him back to the seductive goals of his model. He no sooner reconciles himself to hunting with the Indians than he begins to picture himself converting the "natural" Indians to the more truly "Natural" life of rational farming. Soon only the slightest suggestion of doubt remains in his renewed faith in his model. "Perhaps my imagination gilds too strongly this distant prospect," he says. "Yet it appears founded on so few and simple principles that there is not the same probability of adverse incidents as in more complex schemes." Finally he concludes his speculations with a prayer to the "Father of Nature" to look with favor on his plans (p. 219).

The narrative ends where it started, then, with a vision of an agrarian democracy. But there is irony in James' renewed faith, for his reassertion of the model's ideals take the form of prayers rather than statements, since they occur in the world of experience, where they are no longer meaningful except in terms of some ideal future. That his faith should be renewed in the world of experience, among the ruin and corruption that have just proved it absurd, is the final ironic proof of man's inability to govern himself according to reason.

In spite of the implications of this final episode, Crèvecoeur is often thought of as an uncritical spokesman for agrarian democracy.[5] According to Leo Marx, he had no sense of progress or of history, for he expressed "unqualified affirmation" of a social ideal based on a permanent balance between nature and civilization, and never thought to ask what "would happen when the new society approached that delicate point of equilibrium beyond which further change, which is to say further departure from 'nature,' would be dangerous?"[6] Crèvecoeur, however, was aware of the importance of progress in American society, although he did not see it as a threat to the "natural" aspects of life. This was because he understood that the idea of "nature" in American democratic theory involved more than a romantic belief in the healthful effects of laboring in the earth. Nature meant the "laws of nature," and man would presumedly use his rational knowledge of these laws to pursue a moderate way of life, and to develop machines and institutions for his improvement and happiness. Cultural and material progress were implicit in his model, then, and in demonstrating that man was incapable of moderation, he implicitly denied the possibility of progress as well. For if the evils of the backwoodsman were still present in the educated lawyer, then the social conditions necessary for progress could never be maintained.

Crèvecoeur's sense of history, which is implicit throughout the *Letters,* is in fact a central theme in the final episode. By this time Farmer James is no longer a *tabula rasa,* for his experience has introduced him to a wide range of possibilities for human existence, the extremes of which are represented by the symbols of the Indian and the European statesman. In deciding upon a course of action James weighs the benefits of these two extremes, denounces the evils of civilization, and endorses the primitivism of the Indian. But before he has finished he has implicitly rejected the evils of the savage too, and once more arrived at the compromise between nature and civilization which characterized his original model. When the model's definition of human nature is restated as a synthesis of two extreme conditions, however, it becomes clear that a notion of progress informs the entire model. James assumes that the original state of nature is savage, but that as human reason develops this state will give way to the more civilized condition of the farmer. But this idea of progress in human nature is denied by James' experience, for he now realizes that the similarities he observed in the backwoodsman and the lawyer have persisted over centuries of progress, from the condition of the Indian to that of the statesman. If the natural man and the civilized man are equally warlike and irrational then there has never been any human progress. As James admits this and then denies it to reassert faith in a nobler state of nature, he reveals the self-delusion at the heart of his model, for he ignores the totality of human experience.

By the end of the *Letters,* then, Crèvecoeur has added the assumption of progress to his model and the sense of history to his image of America. In the *Journey into Northern Pennsylvania and the State of New York,* he explores the implications of these additions. He begins by stating the assumptions of his model, as he did in the *Letters,* but now the importance of historic development is explicitly stated. A learned gentleman explains that the condition of the American farmer is the result of centuries of progress. The first men were savages, but at some point they became rational, learned to cultivate the land, and ultimately arrived at the state of peace and prosperity exhibited in America. The gentleman concludes on a note of confidence for the future: "The Creator has assured the permanence of civilization," he says, "by the very comparison that man would have to make some day between the rigors of his primitive state and the advantages of his later social state."[7] Progress and stability, then, are the main elements of the model society.

In the *Voyage,* Crèvecoeur's test of this model stresses long-term results rather than basic assumptions. His narrator-travelers follow a direct line of progress from the first generation of settlers on the western frontier to the wealthy urban centers of the East. Both the narrators and the first Americans they meet assume that the model's theories are already proved by the very existence of this march of progress. But Crèvecoeur sets this forward movement against the background of historical development he introduced in the *Letters,* for the nation is bordered by the Indian wilderness on the one hand and European civilization on the other. The test of American progress takes the form of a series of comparisons between the Americans and these other groups, both of whom have forfeited the benefits of progress by proving themselves too irrational either to achieve or to maintain them. At first the evidence supports the model; as the narrative progresses, however, the comparisons reveal similarities among all three groups. The Europeans are no more civilized in their behavior than the Indians, and as the Americans move closer to the positive benefits of civilized life, their behavior begins to resemble that of the warlike Europeans. Finally the overwhelming parallels between the two white societies convince the reader that disaster and regression are inevitable and the straight line of progress is a myth.

In the first volume the narrators meet many citizens who compare the progress in their country to the lack of progress among the Indians. According to them, the Indian is destined to relive his tragedies because he has learned to control neither his warlike instincts nor his environment. The white man, on the other hand, has already established a rational and permanent social system, and his reason is about to take him even further beyond the condition of the Indian, for his scientific advances are great. The ultimate goal of American progress is to approach the divine intelligence of the Creator and establish a society in which human and physical nature are rationally understood and controlled. To the citizens in this volume such an achievement seems imminent; Crèvecoeur makes this clear by introducing countless images of industrial and agricultural progress, culminating in an image of a machine which reproduces the movements of the heavens, and whose creator is compared to God himself.

In the first volume, then, Crèvecoeur has traced the American myth of progress from man's theoretically bestial origins to his equally theoretical future. The second volume is set in an area of second-generation farmers in which many enterprises begun in the earlier settlements are already thriving; they no longer seem as secure as they did at their inception, however. Natural and political forces now threaten these Americans, who begin to seem naive in their hopefulness. The narrators visit farmers who attribute their success to the benevolence of nature, as reflected in their fields; and, then, within a few miles, they encounter chaos and destruction in nature beyond man's power to control it. They also meet other Americans fleeing the civilized eastern cities to live in the wilderness as James did, because they fear political fermentations similar to those they had fled in Europe. The hints of political disaster are reinforced by the increasing number of military structures observed by the narrators. These images begin to suggest a march toward destruction running parallel to the march of progress, and the Americans' clichés begin to sound ironic in the light of this counter-evidence they choose to ignore.

These hints of war present the most serious threat to American progress, for they indicate that its goal will never be reached. But Crèvecoeur recognized that the same human defects which led to war presented a more basic threat to the perfect society. He illustrates this in the third volume in which the narrators travel to the east coast. Mr. G., the last citizen they visit, symbolizes the way of life which the model assumes all Americans will one day share. He is wealthy and cultivated, living amid the natural abundance of his estate. Like the other Americans he ignores the political problems around him and continues to view his way of life as permanent. But within the context of this hypothetical security, he reveals the contradictions in the American dream, for as he describes his situation it becomes clear that its balance is about to be destroyed, although it has just been achieved. The reason for this is that human nature, outside of his estate, is no more rational or noble than before. Mr. G.'s descendants do not choose to live in the moderate fashion he has chosen for them. His son plans to desert the family estate and return to the frontier where hardship and coarse habits will corrupt him. His nephew plans to attend college in a large city where the evils of commerce and the dissipations of the idle will tempt him. Mr. G. himself no sooner expresses regret at the slowness of American progress compared to that of Europe than he regrets the passing of the "golden age" of colonial America, when life was simple and men happy.

By the final volume of the **Voyage,** then, the two components of a successful society, progress and balance, have proved impossible, if not meaningless. In fact, what the Americans thought of as progress has turned into a movement backward to the very aspects of European civilization they had originally fled. In the first volume the hypothetically rational American was set in opposition to the Indian and the European, who shared a common irrationality. But as Crèvecoeur begins to merge the images of the two white men, he calls attention to certain qualities which distinguish the Indian from both. Throughout the book the rhythm of the white man's progress has been played against the measured prose describing the Indians' culture. At first the Indian was an anomaly to the white man. His nature seemed contradictory, for his warlike behavior could not be reconciled with his domestic virtues. But by the final volume it is the white man who is an anomaly, for his behavior is not only as vicious and contradictory as the Indians'; his rational schemes are equally contradictory and his faith in them, in view of his experience, appears to approach madness.

It is the Indian then who emerges as the more truly civilized man, for his progress has actually been greater. He too has produced complex social systems, for there are ancient ruins of mills and arsenals which testify to the similarities between the Indians' past experience and European history. But unlike the white man, the Indian has not repeated his errors. He has learned from experience to live according to the true laws of nature. He recognizes war, change and pain as natural and inevitable, and his traditions and laws are based on his adjustment to these realities. He has established a true middle state society for he understands and accepts his warlike instincts, and so can control them more successfully than the whites. His stoic resignation allows him to be realistic about his worldly fortunes and he is not prone to the extremes of hope and despair which the white man blindly accepts as the pattern of his life. Finally he is not a victim of self-delusion for he constructs no abstract theories about the essential nature of the universe.

The final movement of the book, then, like that of the **Letters,** describes a circle where the Americans had assumed a straight line of progress. In both books the implicit movement is backward to the truly natural Indian who offers a version of reality more secure, more rational and more consistent than the model's.

The life of the Indian does not of course represent a real opinion. It is another fictitious model of reality which Crèvecoeur uses for contrast in his treatment of America. Leo Marx, in his discussion of Crèvecoeur, also discusses a statement of Thomas Jefferson's about the absence of crime among the Indians. Said Jefferson, "were it made a question, whether no law, as among the savage Americans, or too much law, as among civilized Europeans, submits man to the greatest evil, one who has seen both conditions of existence would pronounce it to be the last. . . ."⁸ According to Marx, "this statement taken out of context, does

sound as if Jefferson had joined a simple-minded cult of Nature . . . [but] what appears as a preference for the primitive actually is a rhetorical device." Marx makes a good case for the literary quality of Jefferson's thought. He calls this device "the syntax of the middle landscape; a conditional statement which has the effect of stressing a range of social possibilities unavailable to Europeans." But Crèvecoeur, whom Marx considers blind to "the obvious dilemma of pastoral politics,'"⁹ and to progress and history as well, has actually explored and expanded the implications of Jefferson's "rhetorical device" and its entire "range of social possibilities" in two full-length works of literature.

Notes

1. For detailed discussions of the various aspects of this theoretical model see the following: Chester Eisinger, "The Freehold Concept in Eighteenth Century American Letters," *William & Mary Quarterly,* IV (1947), 42-59; "Land and Loyalty: Literary Expressions of Agrarian Nationalism in the Seventeenth and Eighteenth Centuries," *American Literature,* XXI (1949), 1960-78; Paul Johnstone, "In Praise of Husbandry," *Agricultural History,* XI (1937), 80-95, and "Turnips and Romanticism," *Agricultural History,* XII (1938), 224-55; Howard Mumford Jones, *Strange New World* (New York, 1964); Leo Marx, *The Machine in the Garden* (New York, 1964); Henry Nash Smith, *Virgin Land* (New York, 1950).

2. J. Hector St. John de Crèvecoeur, *Letters from an American Farmer and Sketches of Eighteenth-Century America* (New York, 1963), pp. 43-44.

3. Compare the "History of Andrew the Hebridean" in this letter, pp. 84-99, with the "Reflections on the Manners of the Americans," in the *Sketches,* pp. 250-63, for a full appreciation of Crèvecoeur's irony in the early letters. The settler in the latter episode becomes vicious and corrupt when allowed to indulge his natural instincts; and he is thoroughly successful as well.

4. For a discussion of the symbolic quality of one incident in the Charles Town episode see Marius Bewley, *The Eccentric Design* (New York, 1963), pp. 102-6. Bewley comments on the "Implicitly ironic interplay between [Crèvecoeur's] polite and measured prose reflecting the illusion of external order in the universe," and the hideous nature of the facts he describes.

5. D. H. Lawrence, "Hector St. John de Crèvecoeur," *Studies in Classic American Literature* (New York, 1923), pp. 20-33, is probably most responsible for the prevalence of this opinion. Even those who have recognized the conflict between theory and experience in the *Letters,* however, have not always attributed its effects to conscious artistry. See, for example, Albert E. Stone Jr., *"Foreword,"* Letters and Sketches, p. xviii.

6. Marx, pp. 115-16.

7. Crèvecoeur, *Journey into Northern Pennsylvania and the State of New York,* tr. Clarissa Bostelmann (Ann Arbor, 1964), p. 15.

8. Thomas Jefferson, *The Life and Selected Writings of Jefferson,* eds. Adrienne Koch and William Peden (New York, 1963), p. 78.

9. Marx, pp. 120-21.

James C. Mohr (essay date 1970)

SOURCE: "Calculated Disillusionment: Crèvecoeur's *Letters* Reconsidered," in *South Atlantic Quarterly,* Vol. 69, No. 3, Summer, 1970, pp. 354-63.

[*In the following essay, Mohr claims that the usual reading of* Letters from an American Farmer *is an oversimplification, and that Crèvecoeur's vision of America was far more subtle and complex than most critics allow.*]

In the study of the American culture J. Hector St. John de Crèvecoeur is certainly best known as the man who first posed the now famous question, "What then is the American, this new man?" Few questions are more often discussed, more often used as the introduction for a lecture, or more often reprinted than this one. At the same time probably no question evokes more stifled groans or thoughts of "not again" from audiences and readers alike. At least part of this reaction may be traced to the fact that Crèvecoeur's own treatment of this question seems largely beside the point to most of the scholars who re-pose it; they are usually too concerned with offering an answer of their own to examine the complexity of the answer developed in the *Letters from an American Farmer.*[1]

Even when Crèvecoeur's insights are not completely ignored, they are generally oversimplified. Among the reasons for this oversimplification is the fact that the essence of the *Letters* is often presented simply as the summation which appears in the same paragraph with the "What then is the American" question, or selections which closely parallel the tone of that paragraph.[2] As a result, Crèvecoeur's America is usually thought of in rather static terms as the land of free men, small farms, material abundance, and benign morality: a kind of Jeffersonian Valhalla. Americans seem to have had a long-standing desire to believe that their society was once idyllic. Apparently they do not believe that it can ever be perfect in the future if it was not once perfect in the past. And since Crèvecoeur's best-known passages are among the sources of evidence most often cited in support of a once idyllic past, Americans have been loath to see anything more than this attractive stereotype in the *Letters.* This is unfortunate, for Crèvecoeur's insights into the American culture are complex and subtle ones which are well worth reconsidering in detail.

One way to get behind the stereotyped Crèvecoeur is to reconsider the methodology of the *Letters* as a whole.

Why is such an idyllic image of America so elaborately drawn? How does Crèvecoeur use the image after he has established it? In answering this kind of question it becomes clear that the delineation of an ideal community is not Crèvecoeur's end purpose at all, but rather the first step in developing a larger pattern. The larger pattern is almost circular and involves not simply the fulfillment of social ideals but their failure as well. The idyllic image of America which Crèvecoeur develops during the first eight letters of his book becomes the dream against which the intensity of later disillusionment is measured.

Like Crèvecoeur, many Europeans saw in America a unique opportunity for the regeneration of society. In America there were no corrupt institutions, no unequal economic systems, and no established churches. These are the hopes upon which Crèvecoeur is playing in the long "What then is the American" paragraph of Letter III, the most often quoted paragraph in the book:

> Wives and children, who before in vain demanded of him a morsel of bread, now, fat and frolicsome, gladly help their father to clear those fields whence exuberant crops are to arise to feed and to clothe them all; without any part being claimed, either by a despotic prince, a rich abbot, or a mighty lord. Here religion demands but little of him; a small voluntary salary to the minister, and gratitude to God; can he refuse these?

As Tocqueville was to re-emphasize some fifty years later, Crèvecoeur also points out that Americans had the advantage of beginning over again without having to erase any of the previous attempts to build a society that had gone wrong. America, in short, was an unblemished field in which Europeans could attempt to plant their various social ideals and to make them flourish; in America, Crèvecoeur writes, "human industry has acquired a boundless field to exert itself in—a field which will not be fully cultivated in many ages!" and Crèvecoeur devotes the first eight of his *Letters* to developing a picture of transplanted Europeans successfully creating a new society. Furthermore, he manages to maintain a remarkably judicious balance between the two most prominent social ideals of his day: the rational and the romantic.

Those who wished to see in the American social experiment the fulfillment of the rational ideals of the Enlightenment were given a good deal of support by Crèvecoeur. According to this vision of the perfect society the "new man" need only follow the self-evident laws of human behavior in order to succeed. Foremost among these self-evident laws was that of enlightened self-interest, the idea which both Franklin and Tocqueville found so dear. Crèvecoeur states explicitly that "the rewards of [the American's] industry follow with equal steps the progress of his labour; his labour is founded on the basis of nature, *self-interest*; can it want a stronger allurement?" The concept of property ownership is also prominent in this rationalist version of the perfect society; America would prosper because it was free of Europe's feudal inequities. In this fee-simple paradise "indulgent laws" insured each man his due reward. The overall result was a "surprising metamorphosis" of dignity.

In the "History of Andrew, the Hebridean," Crèvecoeur dramatizes this metamorphosis of dignity. The story of Andrew is an idealization, almost an extended metaphor, yet close to the heart of any reader who believed that "the progressive steps of a poor man, advancing from indigence to ease; from oppression to freedom; from obscurity and contumely to some degree of consequence" were taken "not by virtue of any freaks of fortune, but by the gradual operation of sobriety, honesty, and emigration." Andrew's story resembles Franklin's *Autobiography* in miniature or Emerson's image of "the sturdy lad from New Hampshire" in "Self-Reliance." It is practically a preindustrial version of the Horatio Alger fables.

Throughout the first eight letters Crèvecoeur is also careful to balance this rationalist vision of the new America against a more romantically oriented one. "Instinct" is a key word in the *Letters,* and its "cultivation" becomes a significant factor in the creation of the idyllic society which Crèvecoeur elaborates. So also is the "industry" of the rational ideal, constantly balanced against the romantic notion of "genius." James, the hero of the *Letters,* is a farmer, and Crèvecoeur often allows his farmer-hero to reflect upon the harmony of nature. When he does so, the metaphors are likely to be the organic ones of romantic literature: America, for example, is several times likened to an "embrio" of potential growth. The close-knit community life is compared to a beehive. The false elegance of Europe is said to be surpassed by the clean fresh "smell of the woods." The people of Nantucket derive benefit from their contact with natural forces, even though these are not the forces of normal agriculture, for the Nantucket fishermen are essentially "farming" the sea.

This balance between the rational ideal and the romantic ideal is insured by rejecting the two symbolic extremes of American society: the city and the frontier. The former is seen to be the seat of enervating luxuries and the lair of parasitic lawyers; in other words, the city represents the rule of law and the world of materialistic rationalism gone sour. And in a like manner the frontier is seen to be the haunt of men who "appear to be no better than carnivorous animals of a superior rank"; it seems to demonstrate how the admiration of the natural and the primitive can turn into savagery. Metaphorically as well as actually, then, Crèvecoeur locates his idyllic America between the overcivilized city and the undercivilized frontier. The balance may be precarious, but the image was no doubt a glorious one for almost all of Crèvecoeur's readers.[3]

To this point, then, the methodology of the *Letters* is fairly straightforward. Crèvecoeur presents an idealized picture of American society with a subtle balance built into it which makes it wholly acceptable both to the romantic and to the rationalist. The key terms and concepts of both romantic and rationalist are purposely blended together in this idealized picture, and neither is permitted to dominate.

It is Crèvecoeur's rejection of either extreme that McGiffert points out by including in his selections from the *Letters* the passage which deprecates the frontiersman as a social type. Yet McGiffert then allows this balanced vision of an idyllic America to represent the sum total of Crèvecoeur's insights about the American culture. He neglects to explain that this idyllic vision is only the first phase of a larger methodological pattern within the *Letters* as a whole.[4] If Crèvecoeur's idealized image of America is a balanced one, it is balanced in order to attract as many readers as possible. If Crèvecoeur devotes eight letters to developing his idealized image, his purpose is to make it as effective as he can. By playing upon his readers' fondest hopes for social progress, Crèvecoeur perpetrates something of a calculated hoax. Only after he has his readers believing that America might really be like the idyllic vision does Crèvecoeur deftly begin to cloud that vision.

In the ninth letter the tone of the *Letters* shifts from fulfillment to betrayal; the possibility of disillusionment is placed in opposition to the hopeful idealism of the first eight letters. Instead of examining the "new man" of the first eight letters, Crèvecoeur begins to examine man in general, thereby suggesting that even the most balanced and the most favorable of circumstances cannot eliminate the evil inherent in the race:

> We certainly are not that class of beings which we vainly think ourselves to be; man an animal of prey, seems to have rapine and the love of bloodshed implanted in his heart; nay to hold it the most honourable occupation in society: We never speak of a hero of mathematics [a rationalist hero], a hero of the knowledge of humanity [a romantic hero], no, this illustrious appellation is reserved for the most successful butchers of the world.

If these are the traits which are inherently human, then how realistic is America's chance to begin again without erasing the old stains? Could the old stains be erased even if man tried to erase them? What becomes of Andrew's virtues in a world where "force, subtilty, and malice always triumph over unguarded honesty, and simplicity"?

The immediate occasion for these gloomy observations is the existence of slavery in the midst of supposedly idyllic America. Nor, significantly, is the slavery simply a product of the jaded city of "Charles-Town," for slavery is "overspread in the country." In other words, slavery seems to have the potential of encroaching even upon that area in which Crèvecoeur located his idealized community. "Here the horrors of slavery, the hardship of incessant toils, are unseen; and no one thinks with compassion of those showers of sweat and of tears which from the bodies of Africans, daily drop, and moisten the ground they till." And although Letters X and XI point out that slavery had thus far been primarily limited to the South,[5] the metaphorical implications of the system prompt a grim and foreboding observation.

In what may be the strongest single passage in the *Letters* Crèvecoeur simultaneously challenges both the romantic and the rational sides of his idealized vision of the new American society:

> If from this general review of human nature, we descend to the examination of what is called civilized society; there the combination of every natural and artificial want, makes us pay very dear for what little share of political felicity we enjoy. It is a strange heterogeneous assemblage of vices and virtues, and of a variety of other principles, for ever at war, for ever jarring, for ever producing some dangerous, some distressing extreme. Where do you conceive then that nature intended we should be happy? Would you prefer the state of men in the woods [the romantic ideal], to that of men in a more improved situation [the rationalist ideal]? *Evil preponderates in both.* . . . [my italics].

"Evil preponderates in both": Crèvecoeur's methodology becomes more apparent with this powerful line. No society is immune to the kind of social evils epitomized by slavery. The idealized vision of American society so skillfully developed in the first eight letters, although certainly the most famous section of the *Letters* and the section usually allowed to stand alone, may be taken as little more than an elaborate and well-calculated introduction to this foreboding observation on the pervasiveness of social evil. Without such an effective introduction the statement loses its dramatic powers of disillusionment. If Crèvecoeur's readers could not be persuaded to imagine an idyllic America, they would obviously have no feeling of betrayal when confronted with the evidence that America was, in fact, far from perfect. The sense of foreboding in Letter IX, however, is not in itself the whole point of Crèvecoeur's methodology, any more than the balanced vision was, for there is still one more step in the pattern of the *Letters.* While this final step fulfills the grim foreboding of Letter IX, it also completes something of a cycle by eventually reasserting a fresh vision of potential and a new hope of regeneration.

The circular nature of this pattern, which Crèvecoeur sees underlying and defining the American experience, is to some extent hinted at even in that most reprinted of paragraphs, the one which asks, "What then is the American, this new man?" But the hint is ambiguous, and it seems rarely to have been picked up and followed through. "Americans are the western pilgrims," Crèvecoeur writes, "who are carrying along with them that great mass of arts, sciences, vigour, and industry which began long since in the east; they will finish the great circle." Crèvecoeur seems to be suggesting that America's heritage lies inescapably in Europe, and perhaps even in the seats of more ancient civilizations still farther east. America's destiny is to carry forward the highest ideals and achievements of those previous civilizations, even though their complete realization will certainly be impossible. The "new man," this American, is a person either foolish enough or heroic enough to try to pursue such a destiny.

Letter XII, the last of the *Letters from an American Farmer,* completes the methodological pattern of the book.

In this letter the idyllic farm community elaborated in the first eight letters and then somewhat anticlimactically revived after the foreboding of Letter IX has become a scene of open civil strife as a result of the American Revolution. The external pressures generated by the political exigencies of the conflict were forcing a polarization and a disruption of James's once idyllic community. The forebodings of Letter IX were coming true even in the perfectly balanced society of the "American Farmer"; Farmer James himself was becoming as much of a slave to these new external pressures beyond his control as the Africans had been slaves to "the chosen race" in Letter IX. Indeed, Crèvecoeur's rhetoric is remarkably similar to that employed in Letter IX, only in Letter XII the "Africans" have become the "people":

> . . . how easily do men pass from loving, to hating and cursing one another! . . . The great moving principles which actuate both parties are much hid from vulgar eyes like mine; nothing but the plausible and the probable are offered to our contemplation. The innocent are always the victim of the few; they are in all countries and at all times the inferior agents, on which the popular phantom is erected; they clamour, and must toil, and bleed, and are always sure of meeting with oppression and rebuke. It is for the sake of the great leaders on both sides, that so much blood must be spilt; that of the people is counted as nothing. Great events are not achieved for us, though it is *by* us that they are principally accomplished; by the arms, the sweat, the lives of the people.

Power considerations were replacing the old vision of harmony; intolerance was replacing the old ideal of mutual co-operation. As a result Crèvecoeur's hero decides to move his family away from the once idyllic community which had now so cruelly betrayed his hopes for a more perfect society. And the place James chooses for his removal is that very same frontier which he had once described as the kind of environment which produced only a "ferocious, gloomy and unsociable" community, a society best characterized by "hostility" and "sloth." In order to rationalize his intended move, therefore, Farmer James creates for himself a whole new illusion of potential success. He recognizes that his social ideals were not capable of being sustained even under the best of circumstances. The idyllic America of the first eight letters had degenerated finally into civil war. Furthermore, he realizes that the frontier represents a profound challenge to the kind of balanced social order which he believes in. And yet, because he is an "American" farmer, James makes this seemingly impossible rationalization anyway.

However unrealistically or illogically, frontier life is changed from barbarity to tranquillity in James's mind, and the Indian is transformed from a savage into the creator of a social system which avoids civil insurrection. And perhaps the most remarkable aspect of James's mental process is the fact that he is fully aware that he is creating an unfounded illusion. In a passage half-heroic and half-tragic he admits that perhaps "my imagination gilds too strongly this distant prospect; yet it [his imaginary vision of the society which he plans to establish on the frontier] appears founded on so few, and simple principles, that there is not the same probability of adverse incidents as in more complex schemes." But of course this is untrue and he knows it:

> These vague rambling contemplations which I here faithfully retrace, carry me sometimes to a great distance; I am lost in the anticipation of the various circumstances attending this proposed metamorphosis! Many unforeseen accidents may doubtless arise. Alas! It is easier for me in all the glow of paternal anxiety, reclined on my bed, to form the theory of my future conduct, than to reduce my schemes into practice.

In short, he recognizes that he is dreaming an impossible dream. His destiny as an American drives him into carrying forth civilization's highest social ideals, while his fate as a human being dictates that such dreams will never be wholly realized. But the pattern will continue until he loses his power to dream. Symbolically at least, "the American, this new man," must continue to do as Huckleberry Finn was doing when he decided "to light out for the territory," knowing full well that life there would really be no different from the "civilization" where, as he says, he had "been before."

"I resemble, methinks," writes Crèvecoeur in a metaphorical expression of what he thought it meant to be an American, "one of the stones of a ruined arch, still retaining that pristine form that anciently fitted the place I occupied, but the centre is tumbled down; I can be nothing until I am replaced, either in the former circle, or in some stronger one." This superb simile is as close as Crèvecoeur ever comes to answering his own famous question in a single brief statement, for in a way the entire methodological pattern of the *Letters* is an attempt to explore the implications of this simile. The old forms of society had each in turn disillusioned man. Even in cases where the circumstances had seemed most favorable, the experiment had failed of complete success. Only in illusions could social ideals exist, and so Farmer James must finally turn back to illusion. The fact that he decides to do so consciously is crucial in the pattern which Crèvecoeur works out. Some would no doubt think him foolish not to try to accommodate himself to society as it stood, even though it lacked the "pristine form" of its "ancient" ideals. But to Crèvecoeur, the decision to seek the ideal was what ultimately defined James as "American."

To define the American experience as a willingness to carry forward the ideals of civilization in the face of almost certain disillusionment is quite different from defining the American experience as a stiffly idealized balance between the rational and the romantic. If the latter definition is the one most often associated with Crèvecoeur's *Letters from an American Farmer,* then this is regrettable, since the methodological pattern of the book clearly suggests the former. Crèvecoeur presents the American culture not as a static stereotype but as a dynamic process. It would be a shame to make a cliché of Crèvecoeur's fa-

mous question while at the same time either ignoring or continuing to oversimplify his own perceptive discussion of its implications.

Notes

1. J. Hector St. John de Crèvecoeur, *Letters from an American Farmer.* All references will be to the Dolphin Books reprint of the original 1782 edition (Garden City, N. Y.: Doubleday & Company).

2. Michael McGiffert, *The Character of Americans* (Homewood, Ill., 1964), is an example of the way in which Crèvecoeur is most often dealt with. I do not single out this particular book because I feel that it is weak; in fact, the exact opposite is true. I admire McGiffert's selections and I consider them the best such volume of readings to appear in some time. And precisely because the book is so well done, it serves as a convincing example of the way in which Crèvecoeur is almost invariably treated. If a less able example were cited, its treatment of the *Letters* could simply be written off as another of its weaknesses. It is interesting to note also that the "What then is the American" section of the *Letters* is even included as a short story in *An American Reader* (New York, 1967), pp. 124-26, which American Airlines distributes to its passengers when the movie machines break down!

3. Leo Marx, in his *The Machine in the Garden* (New York, 1964), argues persuasively that this idealized balance places the *Letters* in what he calls the "pastoral" tradition. I am in complete agreement with Marx insofar as his analysis concerns the first eight letters of Crèvecoeur's book, the section which I have been discussing above. As will become evident below, however, I disagree strongly with Marx's contention that Crèvecoeur's is a "simpleminded" book (*Machine,* p. 108).

4. This applies equally to Leo Marx who argues that Crèvecoeur's crucial weakness is a "failure to recognize the obvious dilemma of pastoral politics" (*Machine,* p. 116). This conclusion seems to ignore completely the methodological pattern of the book and the reasons why Crèvecoeur took such great pains to establish his pastoral ideal in the first place. I would argue that Crèvecoeur certainly does face at least one of those "obvious dilemma[s]": the fact that the pastoral vision he sets up is a precarious illusion, not a social reality.

5. Farmer James offers an unconvincing attempt to explain away the slavery which existed in the North (*Letters,* pp. 168-69).

Marcus Cunliffe (essay date 1975)

SOURCE: "Crèvecoeur Revisited," in *Journal of American Studies,* Vol. 9, No. 2, 1975, pp. 129-44.

[*In the following essay, Cunliffe explores the contrasting tone and content of Crèvecoeur's two major publications about America:* Letters from an American Farmer *and* Sketches of Eighteenth-Century America. *The first is optimistic and patriotic; the second is pessimistic and critical.*]

I

Almost every twentieth-century discussion of American history, literature, culture or character makes reference to J. Hector St John de Crèvecoeur's **Letters from an American Farmer,** a book first published in 1782. Anthologies usually find space for an excerpt from Crèvecoeur.[1] A particular favourite is the third chapter, 'What Is An American?' Here is the best-known, the most-quoted, the almost tediously familiar paragraph from that chapter:

> What, then, is the American, this new man? He is neither an European nor the descendant of an European . . . *He* is an American, who, leaving behind him all his ancient prejudices and manners, receives new ones from the new mode of life he has embraced, the new government he obeys, and the new rank he holds. He becomes an American by being received in the broad lap of our great Alma Mater. Here individuals of all nations are melted into a new race of men, whose labours and posterity will one day cause great changes in the world. Americans are the western pilgrims who are carrying along with them that great mass of arts, sciences, vigour, and industry which began long since in the East; they will finish the great circle . . . The American is a new man, who acts upon new principles; he must therefore entertain new ideas and form new opinions. From involuntary idleness, servile dependence, penury, and useless labour, he has passed to toils of a very different nature, rewarded by ample subsistence. This is an American.

A little earlier in the same chapter Crèvecoeur says:

> We are the most perfect society now existing in the world. Here man is free as he ought to be, nor is this pleasing equality so transitory as many others are.[2]

Crèvecoeur is then a standard exhibit: the man who analyzed the essence of Americanness, including the famous melting-pot, at the very period two centuries ago when the United States was in the act of achieving independence. And there are other almost equally familiar passages in Crèvecoeur's **Letters** that serve to establish him as a prime early generalizer about the United States. Again and again he conveys the liberation, the enlargement, the wonder felt by men when they arrive in the New World and enter into 'that great field of action everywhere visible'. They undergo, says Crèvecoeur, a 'resurrection'. The new land transforms them. For one thing it is amazingly fertile. 'Men are like plants, the goodness and flavour of the fruit proceeds from the peculiar soil . . . in which they grow'. If they will take off their coats and set to work they are bound to succeed.

Again, the new country is so *big*. When the European gets to America, he therefore 'suddenly alters his scale: . . . he no sooner breathes our air than he forms schemes and em-

barks in designs he would never have thought of in his own country'. Environment, it would seem, is almost everything. In Crèvecoeur's view such a settler does not lose his identity in exchanging for the tight social order of Europe the shifting, amorphous American situation. On the contrary: the settler now assumes for the first time a genuine personal identity. He is no longer a vagrant or a 'nobody', left outside the respectable enclosure of Europe; for in America he swiftly acquires a home, land, neighbours, a district, a country. *Acquires* is the proper word—an active verb. The settler gains his identity in the act of acquiring property and improving it. This is his stake in society: *his* stake, not one that he has been 'staked *to*' by somebody else. Nor does Crèvecoeur fail to distinguish between the various regions of America. He provides an affecting and gruesome account of a Negro slave, locked up in a cage in South Carolina, to die of starvation and be tormented by voracious birds and insects. Crèvecoeur has an eloquent section on the hardy, self-reliant whalers of Nantucket. He writes circumstantially and charmingly on farming in the middle states. He praises the Quakers for one kind of simplicity, and the Indians for another.

We need not dwell further on this accessible Crèvecoeur: Crèvecoeur the agrarian, the optimist, the expounder of the preordained American success story. Here, it would appear, is an eighteenth-century chronicle whose elements have been absorbed into the United States' cosier beliefs about itself. We might feel that George Washington summed up the virtues and limitations of Crèvecoeur in a letter of 1788, replying to someone who sought advice on whether to leave Europe and come to the United States. Among published guides to the new nation he recommended a treatise by Benjamin Franklin, and Thomas Jefferson's *Notes on Virginia.* Washington ended his letter by adding that the book by Crèvecoeur, a person who had 'actually resided twenty years as a farmer . . . , will afford a great deal of profitable and amusive information, respecting the private life of the Americans, as well as the progress of agriculture, manufactures, and arts, in their country. Perhaps the picture he gives, though founded on fact, is in some instances embellished with rather too flattering circumstances'.[3]

II

Crèvecoeur is however a more complicatedly dubious witness than General Washington could have realized. True, some of the artifices in his book were obvious to, and perfectly acceptable to, Americans of his day. Many of them knew, as Washington no doubt did, that the man Washington referred to as 'Mr Crevecoeur (commonly called Mr St John)', was by birth and upbringing a Frenchman. They may not have been precisely aware that he was a gentleman of Normandy, born in 1735, who had fought as an army officer in Canada under Montcalm; who had been wounded in the battle for Quebec in 1759; and who, entering the American colonies in that year, had eventually bought a farm a few miles west of the Hudson River in

Orange County, New York. Contemporaries would not have been amazed to learn that Crèvecoeur had spent some time in England, before going to Canada, and had come near to marrying an English girl. These details—or his naturalization under the name of John Hector St John, or his actual marriage to a lady in Orange County named Mehetable Tippet—were arguably of no great consequence. Perhaps it was not important that in the *Letters* he posed as a native-born Anglo-American, self-taught, ignorant of Europe, who was farming in Pennsylvania—even if these supposed 'facts' have misled some twentieth-century scholars.[4] Such expedients, including the pretence that he was writing to an acquaintance in England, did not make him a liar. He was merely adopting the common authorial devices of his era. Pennsylvania, the home of the Quakers and of the renowned Benjamin Franklin, had a greater symbolic attractiveness than New York. Exaggerating his own lack of education enabled him to heighten the literary contrast between the virtuous innocence of the American country-dweller and the somehow less virtuous sophistication of his imaginary English correspondent. Eighteenth-century readers would not have been alarmed to discover that certain passages in the book (for example on the deep South, which Crèvecoeur seems never to have visited) had been borrowed from other writers. In that epoch, plagiarism was only a minor offence and had not yet become a moral crime. For this reason they may not have thought it odd that the central themes in Crèvecoeur—such as the dislike of cities, the praise of rural life, and the sentiments on slavery—probably derived from a European work, the *Histoire philosophique et politique* by the Abbé Raynal, to whom indeed Crèvecoeur dedicated the first edition of his own book.[5]

Again, it was not exactly Crèvecoeur's fault that the book soon ceased to be popular. Tastes change, after all. So the first, London edition of 1782, brought him some fame. So did the revised French editions of 1784 and 1787 (*Lettres d'un Cultivateur Américain*). But an American edition of 1793 fell flat; and for the next hundred years Crèvecoeur dropped out of sight. In 1851, for instance, the French literary historian Philarète Chasles made only brief mention of *Lettres d'un Cultivateur,* 'un livre . . . peu connu aujourd'hui', and seemed to assume the author was an Englishman, 'Sir John Crevecoeur'.[6] The *Letters* did not come back into print again until editions (in English) of 1904 and 1912. The explanation for this revival appears to relate to the famous chapter already quoted. He had, in other words, stumbled upon the melting-pot metaphor long before it came into vogue. In the opening years of the twentieth century, at a time of polyglot mass immigration, Crèvecoeur's vision of 'individuals of all nations . . . melted into a new race of men' was suddenly apposite: and reassuring to Americans of the liberal persuasion. It had thus an accidental and rhetorical value: hence its place in the conventional anthologies of the twentieth century, as a convenient and impressive early statement of American heterogeneity.

Yet the more explanations we offer for the career of Crèvecoeur and of his book, the more we involve ourselves in

puzzle and paradox. Here is a supposedly classic text that described and predicted the shaping of the American character. Yet it was practically forgotten, on both sides of the Atlantic, throughout the nineteenth century. Crèvecoeur's book is for example not mentioned at all in Charles Sumner's *Prophetic Voices Concerning America* (Boston, 1874), though there are several pages on the Abbé Raynal, and accounts of various other 'prophets' whose names are less familiar than Crèvecoeur's to the present-day reader. Here is a man whom some commentators have taken for an American, and some for an Englishman, but who was not really either. Here is a man often cited as a sort of Founding Father of American cultural patriotism, but who also figures in specialist histories of the American Revolution as a Loyalist: that is, a person who sided not with the colonists but with the British.[7]

These mysteries are worth unravelling, both for their own sake and for things they may tell us about the whole realm of transatlantic generalizations. We can make a start with an intriguing speculation by an unfriendly English reviewer of the 1782 edition. This reviewer found *Letters from an American Farmer* so peculiarly uneven in tone that he maintained it must have been composed by two different men. His guess was perceptive, Crèvecoeur *was* two different men inside one physiognomy—at least two, if not more. As far as citizenship went, he was never an American, Crèvecoeur was naturalized in 1765 as an Englishman. He left the colonies in 1780, half way through the War of Independence, in a British ship, and made his way from London to his native France. When he returned to New York in 1783 he came as French consul, having resumed his French citizenship. In 1790 he left New York again for France, and in the remaining twenty-three years of his life never revisited the United States. Brissot de Warville, a compatriot who knew him well in the 1780s, described Crèvecoeur as a gloomy person, sometimes apparently 'appalled' rather than pleased by the success of his book. Crèvecoeur, said Brissot, behaved like a man with 'a secret which weighed down upon his soul and whose disclosure he dreaded'.[8]

Other evidence, including Crèvecoeur's own testimony, confirms that he was miserable in those consular years from 1783 to 1790. This is in a sense easily understandable. When he set foot in America at the end of the war, after a three-year absence, he had had no news for even longer than that of the family he had left behind. What he learned seemed to fit only too justly the French surname, Crèvecoeur, that he had taken up again. He learned, heartbreakingly, that his wife was dead; his children had barely survived, thanks to the kindness of a stranger; and his beloved farmhouse, Pine Hill in Orange County, had been burned down in an Indian raid. The 'American Farmer' had no more appetite for agriculture in the New World: he sold his property in 1785.

But the full force of his misery, a semi-secret misery, was not revealed until 1925, when some further literary endeavours of his, dating back to his first American sojourn, were at last released from the obscurity of a French attic and printed as *Sketches of Eighteenth-Century America.* The *Sketches* make strange reading when set beside the *Letters.* Only at the end of the 1782 book did Crèvecoeur touch upon the strife of the Revolutionary War. He declared then that he would seek refuge by abandoning his farm, in fact by renouncing civilization altogether, to go and live among the Indians. It was so fanciful a project that no casual reader could take it seriously. In fact, as D. H. Lawrence derisively noted in his *Studies in Classic American Literature* (1922), Crèvecoeur had done the exact opposite. He had retreated *into* civilization by going to Paris, where he mingled with *salon* intellectuals.

To underline the contradiction, Lawrence stressed the discrepancy between the Frenchman's real passion for nature in America, which Lawrence called 'blood knowledge', and his artificial enthusiasm for Nature in the abstract. Lawrence wrote before the publication of *Sketches.* And in any case, being magnificently egocentric, Lawrence was more interested in his own idea of Crèvecoeur than in Crèvecoeur's actual predicaments. Lawrence therefore missed the truly remarkable discrepancy between what Crèvecoeur proclaimed in print and what he inwardly felt.[9]

In the *Letters,* remember, Crèvecoeur announces: 'We are the most perfect society now existing in the world. Here man is free as he ought to be, nor is this pleasing equality so transitory as many others are.' But in the *Sketches* he speaks in another voice altogether:

> Could I ever have thought that a people of cultivators, who knew nothing but their ploughs and management of their rural economies, should be found to possess, like the more ancient nations of Europe, the embryos of these propensities which now stain our society? . . . The range of civil discord hath advanced among us with an astonishing rapidity. Every opinion is changed; every prejudice is subverted; every ancient principle is annihilated; every mode of organization, which linked us before as men and as citizens, is now altered. New ones are introduced, and who can tell whether we shall be the gainers by the exchange? . . .
>
> But why should I wonder at this political phenomenon? Men are the same in all ages and in all countries. A few prejudices and customs excepted, the same passions lurk in our hearts at all times . . .[10]

The difference of course is that in the meantime the American Revolution had begun. Worse than that, the mild, Quakerish Crèvecoeur could not bring himself to rejoice at the rebellion. His 'secret', to use Brissot's term, may have been that certain patriots had regarded him as pro-British during the conflict. Here and there surprise was expressed that the French should have appointed such a dubious person to represent them as consul, so soon after the war. Back in New York, where the courts were full of cases involving the property of former Loyalists,[11] Crèvecoeur may have lain awake worrying that some malicious enemy would denounce him as a collaborator.

Loyalist is probably too strong a word to define Crèvecoeur's position; and so is *collaborator.* His agony was

that he had no defined position. He was, rather, a *neutralist* or a *quietist,* in a situation that did not permit quiet or neutrality. He therefore got the worst of both worlds during the Revolution. His neighbours expected active proof of his support for the American cause. His oddities as a part-time man of letters aroused suspicion. Why did he shut himself up and scribble? What was he writing about, and to whom? His half-fictional, half-autobiographical essays became, one guesses, an essential release. He could not stop committing them to paper. But they now contained dangerous sentiments. He could envisage no satisfactory outcome for the Revolution. For him, living in an area of exceptionally confused allegiances, the immediate reality was violence, bloodshed, hypocrisy; the suppression of free speech; intimidation and robbery in the name of high-sounding ideals. So Crèvecoeur composed frantic sketches with titles such as 'The Man of Sorrows' and 'The American Belisarius' (an allusion to the Roman general who, having been disgraced, blinded, and deprived of all his property, was reduced to begging by the roadside). Crèvecoeur, portraying himself or his friends or his wife's Loyalist kinfolk under various disguises, poured out his soul in bitter anecdotes of persecution and confiscation. His emotion found vent too in a number of remarkable dialogues or playlets that he called **'Landscapes'.** In these the patriots are shown as sanctimonious thugs. Their victims, on the other hand, are harmless Quakers, decent farmers, upright gentlemen. One of the victims, a woman whose husband has been hunted like a wild beast, wearily observes that 'the world was created round to convince us that nothing therein is stable and permanent'. She says of a patriot colonel, who is also a deacon: 'As a county canting, religious hypocrite I had always known thee; now as Congress delegate, and in that service dost thou use thy former qualifications.'[12]

These heartbroken essays, together with some more cheerful earlier ones, accompanied Crèvecoeur to New York City at the beginning of 1779, when he at length set out to quit the colonies. Leaving was easier said than done. New York was in the hands of the British. A local official in Orange County reported: 'the people of our country are much alarmed at their apprehensions of St John's being permitted to go to New York'. The British did not quite trust him either. They opened up the little trunk in which he guarded his papers. A British officer testified that it contained 'a great Number of Manuscripts, the general purport of which appear to be a sort of irregular Journal of America, & a State of the Times of some years back, interspersed with occasional Remarks, Philosophical & Political; the tendency of the latter is to favor the side of Government and to throw Odium on the Proceedings of the Opposite Party, and upon the Tyranny of their Popular Government.'[13] In other words, two types of essay: the optimistic ones that made up the volume of *Letters from an American Farmer,* and the pessimistic ones that were to remain unprinted until the *Sketches* volume of 1925.

An anonymous informer denounced Crèvecoeur to the British authorities in New York as a patriot spy. They put him in jail—from which he was only released, after three months, on the pleading of an impeccably Loyalist friend. Some of his papers went astray. A portion of the remainder he sold to a pair of booksellers, on arrival in London. Hence the publication of the *Letters* in London in 1782—by which time Crèvecoeur was in France.

He did not think the British completely blameless for the Revolution. Perhaps, he conjectured, their appetite for conquest had disturbed the balance in North America. Crèvecoeur was much more positive that, whatever the long-distance workings of history, the Revolution was without rational justification. The colonists had no real complaint. 'It is to England', says Crèvecoeur in one of his pre-Revolutionary essays, 'we owe this elevated rank we possess, these noble appellations of freemen, freeholders, citizens; yes, it is to that wise people we owe our freedom.' In a later essay he gropes for an understanding of what has gone wrong. 'Ambition', he suggests,

> an exorbitant love of power and thirst of riches, a certain impatience of government, by some people called liberty—all these motives, clad under the garb of patriotism and even of constitutional reason, have been the . . . foundations of this, as well as of many other revolutions. But what art, what insidious measures, what . . . masses of intricate, captious delusions were not necessary to persuade a people happy beyond any other on earth, . . . receiving from Nature every benefit she could confer, enjoying from government every advantage it could confer, that they were miserable, oppressed and aggrieved, that slavery and tyranny would rush upon them from the very sources which before had conveyed them so many blessings.[14]

Consider the ironies of Crèvecoeur's situation. When he speaks in his lyrical, pre-Revolutionary writings of 'government', he means the benevolent, far-off yet powerful British government, the guarantor of the colonists' contentment. The American, 'this new man', is actually an Anglo-American; 'the new government he obeys' is actually an Anglo-American government. And when Crèvecoeur talks of government in his subsequent essays, he refers to the truculence of patriot Congressmen, or the spleen of the New York board of commissioners established in 1777 to smell out un-American activities in Orange County and elsewhere.

Before the troubles came, Crèvecoeur's dual allegiance—to old England and the New World—involved no strain. He was doing well in British America. He was writing essays, no doubt with a view to publication, that ought to gratify English citizens on both sides of the Atlantic. Then his world split apart. He still contrived to salvage the book, or some of it, and to appeal to a now-divided double audience. But when his book reached the public it was already anachronistic, and he was a changed man. *Letters from an American Farmer* glows with a ruddy optimism. The narrator is the architect of his own fortune; his latchstring is always out for visits from neighbours and strangers alike. But by 1782, as the author must have been more painfully

aware than anyone, the optimism of the *Letters* was absurd. The latchstring had proved to be out for visits from commissioners and raiders. Literally and metaphorically, the structure of Crèvecoeur's farmhouse lay in ruins.

He tried, we can see, in the later work (published eventually as the *Sketches*) to re-order his mind, to arrive at philosophical detachment, to admit irony into his mental scheme: to turn, so to speak, from Rousseau into Voltaire. The task was too difficult. He could manage only an occasional gleam of humour or a half-hearted effort at philosophical detachment. Never a systematic thinker, he wrote incoherently about the incoherence of human history.

Crèvecoeur also tried to reshape his Anglo-American into a Franco-American identity. Soon after reaching France, in August 1781, he wrote to Benjamin Franklin, expressing himself 'glad . . . as a good Frenchman and a good American to contribute my Mite towards the Success of this grand, this useful revolution'. After the Franco-American victory at Yorktown he wrote again, to congratulate Franklin as the representative of the United States on an event that must 'convulse with joy the hearts of every loyal American as well as those of every good Frenchman'. In the next couple of years things improved for Crèvecoeur. By the end of 1783 the War of Independence was over; his English edition was being discussed and on the whole applauded; he was respected among some of the *philosophes* of Paris; and he had prepared a French version of his book. But these consolations were offset. His own part in the Revolution may now have struck him as inglorious and even cowardly. He had been proved too pessimistic; and ought he to have left his family behind in America? He experienced more subtle anxieties. The London edition of the *Letters* contained no hostile comment on the mother country. The French edition, however, introduced many partisan interpolations, so as to present the English as the villains of the story and the Americans as heroes. The old dedication to the Abbé Raynal was gone: the Abbé's advanced opinions had put him out of favour with the French court. Instead, the Paris edition of 1784 was dedicated to that fashionable new Franco-American idol, the Marquis de Lafayette. Crèvecoeur, though, can hardly have forgotten the manuscripts still in his possession—unpublished and now unpublishable. In one of them, 'an American gentleman' observes:

> When the accounts of this mighty revolution arrive in Europe, nothing will appear there but the splendid effects. The insignificant cause will be overlooked; the low arts, this progressive succession of infatuations which have pervaded the whole continent will be unknown.[15]

When Crèvecoeur was installed as French consul in New York, in 1783, he discovered that nearly all his former friends and connexions had departed into Loyalist exile. Silence about those old ties was his only recourse. Then and for the rest of his days, Crèvecoeur busied himself as conscientiously as he could with Franco-American exchanges. Most of them had to do with plants, which he perhaps found safer than people to deal with. He produced pamphlets recommending the cultivation in France of the potato and the false acacia. Scientific societies elected him to membership. He refurbished some old notes to make a book of his bygone travels, *Voyage dans la Haute Pennsylvanie et dans l'Etat de New-York* (1801)—dedicated to Napoleon.[16] On the title page he described himself as an adopted member of the Oneida Indian tribe: a detail that would have amused D. H. Lawrence. Silence, and discreetly timed absences from France, enabled him to survive a second revolution there, followed by the marchings and countermarchings of the Napoleonic wars.

III

What then is this Crèvecoeur? Is he an American, or a European, or an unhappy hybrid? I described him earlier as a would-be neutralist, or quietist. Does the additional evidence make him seem more like a Vicar of Bray, one of those 'trimmers' of chameleon-like adaptability who modified their attitudes according to circumstance? It is clear that he was a romantic rather than a political ideologue. He never showed much interest in constitutions or manifestos. I think *quietist* is a fairer description than *trimmer.* He appears more bewildered than agile; he reveals anguish rather than relish when he has to change his line, and he is clumsy at covering his tracks. But perhaps in most cases a trimmer is merely a quietist who has been forced out into the open. Such sudden and cruel exposure is a feature of revolutions, civil wars and military occupation. It is not my concern to indict Crèvecoeur for inconsistency, still less for insincerity. The only charge against him, perhaps, is that the *Letters* are full of attitudinizing: that is to say, of self-deception. This argument, to which we can return later, is that Crèvecoeur adopted fashionable notions of life in the New World and convinced himself they were as powerful as a creed, when in fact they were only a conception. If so, he paid quite a heavy psychological price.

In any case, fate was fairly kind to him after the shock of the war years in America. A good many Loyalists came back to New York when peace was restored, and most of them were able to come to terms with the new régime. They were not harassed unduly; Crèvecoeur seems to have gone unscathed. He was treated as a respectable, well-informed foreign diplomat. He corresponded now and then with such American dignitaries as Thomas Jefferson. There was no disposition in Britain to attack his record. His few English critics, agreeing with George Washington, merely complained that the *Letters* painted too rosy a picture of American life, and hinted that his motive was to encourage emigration.[17] Otherwise, the British gradually forgot him. So, as we have seen, did the French. If they wanted to read about America, Chateaubriand and later Tocqueville and Beaumont were more to their taste. Crèvecoeur may have been frightened that someone would take the trouble to compare the British and the French edition of the *Letters.* It appears that nobody did. People had other things to worry about in the tumult of the time. His death in France, in 1813, went almost unnoticed.

But that is not to say he is unimportant to us. Looking behind the twentieth-century Crèvecoeur of the textbooks and anthologies, we can use him to shed light on various reactions of people who leave their own country for some other one. Such departures are either voluntary or involuntary. The voluntary leavers are usually called *settlers* or *emigrants.* The involuntary leavers are often labelled *exiles* or—in the English usage of the French word—*émigrés.* Which of these was Crèvecoeur? A mixture, I think. The mood of the *Letters* is in general that of the voluntary voyager. The mood of the *Sketches* is that of the involuntary one. But the story goes further back. For some reason his brother officers were eager to push him out of the French regiment in which he was serving in Canada in 1759. In this respect his arrival in the British colonies makes him appear an exile or émigré from France. When he came back to his native land in 1781 he had almost forgotten how to speak French.

But let us focus for the moment on the voluntary leavers. Perhaps the rather blurred association between the two categories, settler and immigrant, helps to explain why the *Letters,* though popular for a while, lapsed into obscurity and were then resurrected. It is mainly as a spokesman for emigration (to put the emphasis on *arrival*), that we read Crèvecoeur today. An immigrant—in my sense of the word—is a man who severs his connexion with the past. He transfers to another sovereignty, another flag, another loyalty, and in so doing must repudiate his previous existence. For Crèvecoeur, to come to British America probably involved a quite complete repudiation of France: of French citizenship, and possibly of the whole atmosphere of exclusion and oppression of Continental Europe. Whether this was total we cannot know. It may be significant that he named a daughter America-Francès.[18] Recalling that as a young man he lived in England and nearly married an English girl, we may regard him as an example of the Anglomania professed by various French *philosophes.*

The important point, I believe, is that if his French origins and his repudiation of them made him an immigrant to America, his Anglophile instincts made him a settler. Defining that term in a restricted sense, a settler is a person who despite his territorial movement remains under the same flag, the same dispensation. He does not swap allegiances, he amplifies them. He takes pride in the mother country *and* in its new, extended universe. So Crèvecoeur, in his celebrated chapter 'What Is an American?', pictures an 'enlightened Englishman' landing in America and delighted to find what his countrymen, even the disadvantaged and lowly, have been able to accomplish. 'They brought along with them', he says, 'their national genius. Here [the enlightened Englishman] sees the industry of his native country, displayed in a new manner . . . What a train of pleasing ideas this fair spectacle must suggest!' Crèvecoeur to some extent visualized himself as an English settler-citizen: an Englishman *and* an Anglo-American. His literary *persona,* significantly, was that of an Englishman, and the son of an Englishman, though also

American by birth. He pretends in the *Letters* that it was his grandfather who came from England to British America. Crèvecoeur, in short, intended to write as a settler, for a European audience. The twentieth century, somewhat misreading him, has interpreted him as an immigrant, writing for an American or would-be American audience.

His personal trauma was a double one. During the War of Independence he was required to affirm that he was not an Anglo-American but an American: not a settler but an immigrant. New York State demanded a loyalty oath from what it called 'persons of neutral and equivocal character'. They were to acknowledge that New York was 'of right, a free and independent state'. Crèvecoeur could not at that stage bind himself to agree. His second tragedy was to be thrust back into the dispossessed plight of the exile or émigré, and to feel that none of the possible roles was satisfactory.

Among the elements that the settler and the immigrant have in common is a disposition to be optimistic, and to think in the future tense, of what *is to be*. If, says Crèvecoeur, the new American 'is a good man, he forms schemes of future prosperity . . . He thinks of future modes of conduct'. Such men have gambled on tomorrow. Being newcomers, they are also extremely reluctant to criticize their new environment. Their enthusiasm may thus be both sincere and oddly circumspect, even artificial. In Crèvecoeur's case, he was compelled for a while to renounce this optimistic mode. As an exile or émigré, he faced the irony of having lost England as well as America, and of having to strive to renew an allegiance to France that he had almost abandoned. Far from gaining a habitation and an identity, the exile or émigré are deprived of theirs. Not the future but the past is their tense: not *I shall be* but *I was* is their avowal. It is terrible for a man to be shifted from one extreme to the other, as was Crèvecoeur's lot. 'I am no longer the old me' (*l'ancien moi*) 'that you knew in the days of my happiness and my liberty', he lamented to a friend. 'Before this fatal era', he wrote (c. 1778), 'no man was happier than I was, I . . . was full of hopes and confidence . . .' But the previous three years had brought 'nothing but . . . acrimonious reflections which have made me a very different man from what I was'.[19] *What I was* . . . Hence the almost schizophrenic difference of outlook between the genial *Letters* and the gloomy *Sketches.*

Obviously Crèvecoeur's problems were peculiar. His difficulties of national identity were compounded during the Revolution because his farm happened to be in a chaotic debatable zone between the British and the American forces. His wife's family seems to have been chiefly Loyalist. But fascinating though his story is in its own right, we can seek some broader lessons. In some respects Crèvecoeur reveals himself as a typical man of the pre-Revolutionary Enlightenment. Like a good many of his European contemporaries, he was not sure whether America was fundamentally different from Europe, or fundamentally similar; whether, that is, the effects of environ-

ment outweighed the effects of heredity. His answers are not always consistent: a comment that can also be made about Alexis de Tocqueville's *Democracy in America,* written sixty years later. In places, Crèvecoeur seems to think that, for good and for ill, America's characteristics are entirely environmental. Elsewhere, especially in the *Sketches,* the argument tends to be that human nature is everywhere the same. Elsewhere again, Crèvecoeur appears to be saying that America is a melting-pot of all nations (the assumption of his mentor Raynal), and yet that its character has been formed on the basis of the colonies' *British* origins.[20]

This range of possibilities has continued to underlie nearly all subsequent discussion of the America-Europe relationship. As a man of the Enlightenment, Crèvecoeur probably did not feel the need for any greater analytical rigour. He does not wave the flag chauvinistically for any one nation, including the United States. He attempted to deal in universals, to look upon the world with a transnational benevolence. On the whole he did not see America and Europe as distinct, rival civilizations but as societies bound by a principle of complementarity. In praising America so highly he was imparting a message of hope for mankind everywhere. The intended moral of the *Letters* was that simple prosperity was the best guarantee of human happiness, and that such a goal could be universally attainable.

Up to the time of the American Revolution, most of the big generalizations about America had come from Europe, or were identical with American formulations. In this respect, Crèvecoeur summed up two or three centuries of the more favourable kinds of comment on America, in the *Letters*: the *Sketches,* consciously or unconsciously, recapitulate some of the unfavourable views, according to which America was a disorderly, degenerate place. For a century and more after the Revolution, the America-Europe relationship tended to become polarized into a principle of stark contrast. The gentle and rather ambiguous messages of *Letters from an American Farmer,* in an era of nationalistic scholarship, failed to excite the imagination of readers on either side of the Atlantic.

The *Letters,* as we know, were given a new lease of life at the beginning of the twentieth century. Not only did they appear to describe the conditions of melting-pot America: in general the book provided a welcome additional item to augment the none too abundant shelf of early American literary sources. Crèvecoeur ministered to the cultural and academic nationalism of the twentieth-century United States, as typified by the American Studies movement. Portions of the *Letters*—the bits to be found in the anthologies—are so fitting for the purpose that one almost thinks they would have had to be invented if they did not already exist.

Such an interpretation of course depends upon a highly selective reading of Crèvecoeur. With the exception of his biographers, few scholars seem to have taken the trouble to search for the real Crèvecoeur. They are content for the most part to reproduce a few paragraphs from the *Letters,* to ignore the *Sketches,* and to accept the *persona* of the *Letters* as an essentially accurate portrait of the author.

The result is a grossly oversimplified rendering. It prevents us from recognizing that the European-American relationship contains all sorts of nuances, with a considerable element of mythologizing. Crèvecoeur's writings, the *Sketches* no less than the *Letters,* are even more relevant for the twentieth century than conventional interpretations claim. They help us to grasp the ambivalences of departure from one society and arrival in another, and therefore of the whole drama of New World settlement. Crèvecoeur also has become relevant because our time is more aware of the similarities between the New and Old Worlds than was the nineteenth century. We are once again inclined to think transnationally. In the perspective of the 1970s, the United States and western Europe, in spite of their many dissimilarities, are seen to be running on more or less parallel lines. In the context of world history, both communities are relatively rich, relatively sophisticated, relatively urbanized and industrialized. They share common heritages, though admittedly eclectic ones. The New World is in some ways now old, the Old World in some ways new. One of the many advantages to be gained from a close reading of Crèvecoeur is the realization that this interplay between Europe and America has been going on for a very long time, and that it has never been straightforward. Crèvecoeur's essays offer an excellent text for a fresh reassessment of the past, present and future of the Euro-American relationship.[21]

Notes

1. Three random mentions and excerpts out of many:

   (a) Henry S. Commager, ed., *America in Perspective: The United States Through Foreign Eyes* (New York, Mentor, 1948), p. 25. Commager reproduces the third chapter of *Letters,* and says: 'Crèvecoeur, who lived half his mature life in America, can scarcely be classified as a foreigner, and indeed . . . he knew his adopted country better than most native-born Americans did—knew it, understood it, and loved it.'

   (b) William J. Chute, ed., *The American Scene, 1600-1860* (New York, Bantam Matrix, 1964), p. 73: 'No book of readings in American history could be considered complete without Crèvecoeur's essay, "What Is An American?".'

   (c) Richard B. Morris, *The American Revolution: A Short History* (New York, Van Nostrand, 1955), p. 139: 'Embraced in the new spirit of nationalism which pervaded the Revolutionary movement was an idyllic concept of America as a land of opportunity . . . No one expressed these ideas with greater fervor nor gave a more lucid account of the effects of the melting pot on the molding of the American character than did . . . Crèvecoeur.'

2. Hector St. John de Crèvecoeur, *Letters from an American Farmer and Sketches of Eighteenth-Century America,* ed. Albert E. Stone, Jr. (New York, Signet, 1963), pp. 60-64. All subsequent quotations from *Letters* or *Sketches* are drawn from this admirable edition—the only one that prints both books in one volume. There is another paperback edition of the *Letters* (New York, Dutton Everyman, 1957) with some interesting editorial comment by Warren B. Blake. The most detailed biographies of Crèvecoeur are by Julia Post Mitchell (New York, Columbia U.P., 1916), and Howard C. Rice, *Le Cultivateur Américain: étude sur l'oeuvre de Saint John de Crèvecoeur* (Paris, Champion, 1933)—a most useful work. A good brief recent study is Thomas Philbrick, *St. John de Crèvecoeur* (New York, Twayne, 1970).

3. Washington to Richard Henderson, 19 June 1788, in *The Washington Papers,* ed. Saul K. Padover (New York, Harper, 1955), p. 358.

4. Max Savelle, in *Problems in American History,* ed. Richard W. Leopold and Arthur S. Link (Englewood Cliffs, N.J., Prentice-Hall, 2nd edn., 1957), pp. 32-3, describes Crèvecoeur as 'a Frenchman who lived for a time in Pennsylvania'. J. C. Furnas, *The Americans: A Social History of the United States, 1587-1914* (New York, G. P. Putnam's Sons, 1969), pp. 239-40, refers to Crèvecoeur as 'a middle-aged Norman . . . who had spent much of his life in the Middle Colonies . . .'

5. 'Behold, sir, an humble American planter, a simple cultivator of the earth, addressing you from the farther side of the Atlantic and presuming to fix your name at the head of his trifling lucubrations.' *Letters,* ed. Stone, pp. 29-30.

6. Philarète Chasles, *Etudes sur la littérature et les moeurs des Anglo-Américains au XIXe siècle* (Paris, 1851), p. 11.

7. See for example William H. Nelson, *The American Tory* (repr. Boston, Beacon Press, 1964), and Wallace Brown, *The Good Americans: The Loyalists in the American Revolution* (New York, Morrow, 1969).

8. 'Crèvecoeur portait partout un front sombre, un air inquiet . . . Jamais il ne se livrait aux épanchements, il paraissait même quelquefois effrayé du succès de son ouvrage, il semblait enfin qu'il eût un secret qui lui pesât sur l'âme et dont il craignait la révélation.' Brissot, quoted in Rice, p. 43n.

9. Lawrence's essay on Crèvecoeur first appeared in the *English Review* (January 1919). It is longer than the version printed in *Studies in Classic American Literature* but equally off-hand about the actual circumstances of Crèvecoeur. See Armin Arnold, *D. H. Lawrence in America* (London, Linden Press, 1958), pp. 50-3. The two sides of Crèvecoeur are well brought out in Vernon L. Parrington, *Main Currents in American Thought* (New York, Harcourt, Brace, 1927-30), vol. I pp. 140-7.

10. *Sketches,* ed. Stone, pp. 342-3.

11. See Oscar Zeichner, 'The Loyalist Problem in New York after the Revolution,' *New York History,* 21 (July, 1940), 284-302.

12. *Sketches,* ed. Stone, pp. 450-8.

13. Major-General James Pattison, quoted in Rice, pp. 57-8.

14. *Sketches,* ed. Stone, p. 399.

15. Rice, pp. 166-70; *Sketches,* ed. Stone, p. 422. This particular dialogue anticipates the complex responses to the Revolution, and to American democracy, of James Fenimore Cooper—for instance in his *Little-page Manuscripts* trilogy. See Marcus Cunliffe, *The Literature of the United States* (Harmondsworth, Penguin, 1970 edn.), pp. 68-70.

16. Available in an English edition, as *Journey into Northern Pennsylvania and the State of New York,* transl. Clarissa Bostelmann (Ann Arbor, U. of Michigan P., 1964).

17. Rice, pp. 63-6.

18. Thomas Jefferson attended the wedding of America-Francès. See *Dictionary of American Biography* (New York, Charles Scribner's Sons, 1943), IV, p. 543.

19. Quoted in Rice, p. 162.

20. Winthrop D. Jordan, *White Over Black: American Attitudes toward the Negro, 1550-1812* (Chapel Hill, U. of North Carolina P., 1968), pp. 335-41, argues that Crèvecoeur's melting-pot vision was not representative of American thinking in Crèvecoeur's own day, nor of the state of affairs in subsequent decades. His, says Jordan, was the hopeful attitude of a non-British, though distinctly Anglophile, settler. Most other works of the period, more accurately predictive than Crèvecoeur's, stressed the dominant influence of the English (or at any rate Anglo-American) culture in subjugating other cultural strains—a dominance that persisted through the nineteenth century. Jordan also detects another limitation: that Crèvecoeur's melting-pot allowed no place for the Negro American. Apart from his one chapter on the fate of the slaves in the South, Crèvecoeur refers without embarrassment to the supposedly happy and submissive blacks whom he himself owns.

21. In addition to the works cited in note 2, there are signs of a more knowledgeably sophisticated approach to Crèvecoeur in a number of recent books and articles. See for example Elayne Antler Rapping, 'Theory and Experience in Crèvecoeur's America', *American Quarterly,* 19 (1967), 707-18; and James C. Mohr, 'Calculated Disillusionment: Crèvecoeur's *Letters* Reconsidered', *South Atlantic Quarterly,* 69 (1970), 354-63.

Joel R. Kehler (essay date 1976)

SOURCE: "Crèvecoeur's Farmer James: A Reappraisal," in *Essays in Literature,* Vol. 3, No. 2, Fall, 1976, pp. 206-13.

[*In the following essay, Kehler takes issue with some twentieth-century critics who suggest that Crèvecoeur's Farmer James is merely a straw man for demonstrating the inadequacies of Enlightenment principles.*]

Recent criticism of **Letters from an American Farmer** has focused more and more closely on the gradual psychological dissolution of St. John de Crèvecoeur's paradigmatic New World Man, Farmer James, seeing in it a case study in the souring of the American Dream. The concomitant trend has been to characterize James's observations in the pre-Charles Town Letters (I-VIII) as unrealistically optimistic and as ironic by intention in the overall design of the work. One commentator has gone so far as to call James "Crevecoeur's straw man" for proving the inadequacy of "reason," "self-interest," "agrarianism," "the law of nature," and other concepts dear to Enlightenment thought as bases of social order.[1] This view assumes a "strategy" on Crèvecoeur's part of undercutting James's characteristic thought as offering a false view of the world which will not stand the test of experience and which can only serve to wither the promise of the American Garden.[2]

Certainly Crèvecoeur's literary intention is intimately bound up with the intellectual integrity of his American Farmer. If James's mind is no more than soft wax, begging uncritically to be impressed with the faddish bywords of eighteenth-century thought, then he is unworthy of our respect, and we have good reason to suspect that Crèvecoeur does not subscribe to his vision of American life. If, as I believe, James's intellectual integrity remains intact, we have far less reason to suspect huge ironies on Crèvecoeur's part. It is true that James's thoughts are often couched in familiar, even trite-sounding terms and that he makes no particular efforts at consistency. A speculatively inclined farmer whose strongest constitutional element is nevertheless his "feeling," James is no philosopher. But neither is he a "straw man" stuffed with nonsense and set up only to be knocked down. If he does not seem troubled by what may sound like contradictions (even when they are easily reconcilable), it is perhaps because the narrative mode provides scant plausible opportunity to explore them. James is writing letters not treatises.

Notwithstanding his tendency to become emotional, James, a specimen of the eighteenth-centry "man of sensibility," is at bottom a solid pragmatist. By any reasonable standards his views are neither wildly optimistic nor absurdly uninformed. He habitually looks for the good and the bad, the credible and the incredible, in any issue to which he addresses himself. It makes only marginal sense to speak of James as if he were a theoretician, for he is certainly no ideologue. Still, his ideas bear the impress of a distinct outlook and personality—his own—and unfold with discernible method from concepts and experiences that James has proved on his own pulses. This method of unfolding has much to tell us about the author's true "strategy" in the *Letters.*

To get to the core of Crèvecoeur's thematic intention it is necessary first to demonstrate James's intellectual self-sufficiency and to vindicate him from the charge of slavish adherence to the letter of contemporary doctrine; then to find the organizing thread in the web of James's thought and to show how it has been spun from his own local experience. That James (and undoubtedly Crèvecoeur, as well) eventually has reason to be disillusioned with certain aspects of American life is undeniable. But the fault is not traceable to James or to the invalidity of his beliefs, and his "distress" in the final Letter results from the misguided actions of others not from his own folly. That our own age no longer finds the blush of promise in his intellectual stock is insufficient grounds for supposing that Crèvecoeur feels the same.

Some commentators have singled out Mr. F. B., James's European visitor, as responsible for the many familiar echoes of popular eighteenth-century thought in his rhetoric.[3] Has James allowed the *tabula rasa* of his untutored mind to be scribbled upon by an educated foreigner? Some of the echoes, certainly, may be imputed to Crèvecoeur, the author, who obviously has read things the unsophisticated James has not. But if James has gotten some of his ideas from a source within the fictional scope of *Letters,* he has more likely gotten them from a source closer to home: the minister whom he seeks out for advice in the introductory Letter. Crèvecoeur pokes a good deal of benign fun at the provincial pedantry of the good minister, who clearly "has opinions" and readily expounds them to James throughout Letter I. He even offers to "help" James "whenever I have any leisure" with the composition of the letters James has agreed to write to his European friend.[4]

But to allow for a certain influence of one more educated man over another is scarcely to make a case for intellectual tyranny. The minister has a generous respect for James's native sagacity, noting that the latter often "extract[s] useful reflections from objects which present none to my mind" (p. 40). James, furthermore, absolutely assures his European correspondent that his epistolary observations "will all be the genuine dictates of my mind" (p. 43). Even when it is said that the correspondent will supply the "subjects" for James's discourse, we need not imagine that anything more than a vague prompting is being suggested: Write me a letter on the native fauna of a given region, or Write me a letter on the general situation of the American farmer. There is no reason to suppose that James has been brainwashed by anyone.

James makes clear the nature of his intellectual debt at the beginning of Letter II, when he pointedly notes that his correspondent's "observations have confirmed me in the justness of my ideas, and I am happier now than I thought myself before" (p. 45). Whatever ideas James has about man and nature are his own and existed before they were "confirmed" by the European. What James in fact says is that he is flattered at having his views endorsed by so distinguished and so cultured a personage. If the language of James's views is often on the bookish side, his characteristic form of expressing them shows how they have been arrived at: by observation of his native surroundings.

Granting the parabolic function of James's anecdotes as central to Crèvecoeur's literary purpose, we should not lose sight of the fact that they are offered as observations. Commentators often seem to assume that James tailors his observations to fit his theories. Is not the reverse at least as plausible? Certainly "nature," for example, has less reality for James as an abstraction than it has for the European correspondent. The former lived with nature long before he knew it was a subject for theoretical speculation. In his observations on Nantucket, it is not the parallel of what he sees to a preconceived model that accounts for James's favorable commentary; it is the fact that Nantucket strikes him spontaneously as resembling his own favorite kind of community, a bee-hive. Bee metaphors abound throughout Letter VII because the people of Nantucket *seem* to James to act like bees.

James's pragmatism also tempers his devotion to such eighteenth-century bywords as "reason." He never labors under the delusion that the constructs of human thought represent the highest ordering principles. Late in Letter II James notes that "the whole economy of what we proudly call the brute creation is admirable in every circumstance; and vain man, though adorned with the additional gift of reason, might learn from the perfection of instinct how to regulate the follies, and how to temper the errors which this second gift often makes him commit" (p. 56). Somewhat paradoxically, this passage has also been used as an instance of James's unreasonable optimism in fancying that natural law can always supply the pattern for human society.[5] But in pursuing his line of thought, James, speaking of the "imperfect systems of men" and of the embarrassing disparity between them and nature's perfect order, surely means us to keep this in mind, as well: nature's system is indeed perfect if by perfect one means not just and benign in every instance but comprehensive and efficient. Justice and benignity are concepts supplied by the imperfect but necessary systems of men.

In so far as reason is systematic, abstract, and divorced from the test of experience and the needs of men, James has little use for it. To him such reason is synonymous with Solon and Lycurgus and with the kind of sophistical argumentation he finds justifying slavery in Charles Town, and political oppression by the British. Sophistry, James says in speaking of the British, is the "bane of freemen" (p. 198). James's version of right reason is "plain judgment," a concept which he associates most fully with the simple folk of Nantucket, who must daily make use of it in confronting the problems of a harsh existence. Barren logic may be imposed on the order of nature, but "plain judgment," he believes (with some reservations, as we shall see later), grows from the perception of that order.

James's attitude toward "self-interest" as a basis for social order likewise shows the pragmatic order of his own thought. Certainly it is desirable that any social system satisfy as many self-interests as possible without violating the higher dictates of justice. This much James maintains. But nowhere, either before or after his southern excursion, does he claim that the pursuit of self-interest is an infallible principle of social order. On the contrary, the whole thrust of James's barnyard example of good government in Letter II is to demonstrate that where no force for justice exists, self-interest will inevitably produce injustice for the weak. That Charles Towners, moreover, justify slavery as in their *self-interest* and as rationally based on the natural principle of *self-preservation,* does not mean that the two principles in fact coincide. Obviously, slavery is not necessary to the self-preservation of Southerners or of anyone else. They have simply argued that it is. Slavery is necessary to the preservation of a certain social system, not of human life.

Even James's cherished belief in the superiority of agrarianism to industrialism as social and economic modes has its limit. James's agrarianism, like Jefferson's, is at bottom moral not economic in character, the desired goal being to produce good men rather than wealthy ones.[6] Yet James, despite his devotion to the principle of each man's natural right to ownership of the land, acknowledges from the beginning that the so-called "freehold concept" by itself guarantees no beneficial results.[7] Some, he notes in Letter III, "have been led astray by this enchanting [American] scene; their new pride, instead of leading them to the fields, has kept them in idleness; the idea of possessing lands is all that satisfies them" (p. 78). This observation is made long before the southern excursion in Letter IX and shows that James does not have to be shocked into realistic appraisals by the gross inequities of plantation life.

What commentators have generally failed to note is that Crèvecoeur's focus is less on programmatic agrarianism than on the elemental concept of property, first given a central place in social theory by John Locke. Locke's analysis profoundly influenced French and American thought throughout the eighteenth century. In his *Two Treatises of Government* (1690), Locke contends that man in a state of nature is free within the bounds of natural order but that the state of nature is an order for individuals rather than communities. The ever more complicated contact of men as a result of their impulse to labor makes a social order based only on the state of nature inadequate. Whatever a man removes from a state of nature "he hath mixed his *Labour* with, and joyned to it something that is his own, and thereby makes it his *Property.*" The rights of property become the new organizing principles for human society, principles which Locke extends to embrace "the mutual Preservation of . . . Lives, Liberties and Estates." The sanctity of property is made as much a psychological as a social necessity, a requisite of contentment as well as of order. But since it is labor that gives rise to the idea of property, labor must be its arbiter: "Nay, the extent of *Ground* is of so little value, *without labour,* that I have

heard it affirmed, that in *Spain* itself, a Man may be permitted to plough, sow, and reap, without being disturbed, upon Land he has no other Title to, but only his making use of it."[8]

The Lockean notion of the natural right to property is an eighteenth-century commonplace echoed by such American contemporaries of Crèvecoeur as George Logan, Hugh Brackenridge, and Tom Paine.[9] What is not common is the pragmatic arrangement of thought Crèvecoeur brings to the "idea of property" itself. Through Farmer James he explores the timeless contradiction of the human impulses to set boundaries and to remain uninhibited. The episode in Letter II, in which the wren attempts quite perversely to expropriate the nests of the swallow and the phoebe, indicates the depth of the conflict. James recognizes a sort of proto-instinct for property even in nature, noting as well its potential for creating disorder and injustice: "Where did this little bird learn that spirit of injustice? It was not endowed with what we term reason! Here, then, is a proof that both those gifts border very near on one another; for we see the perfection of the one mixing with the errors of the other" (p. 57). Since the wren's seemingly rational appreciation of its unjust triumph can only be ascribed to instinct, the perfection of instinct mimics the imperfection of reason. The order of nature, therefore, is patently not synonymous for James with the idea of rational justice.

This perception shows the pragmatic approach of James's thinking and further shows how the idea of property lies at the center of his thought. In this instance the touchstone of property suggests the complex relation of reason to instinct. In a state of nature, instinct and reason are virtually synonymous, and man as a creature of nature can share in that perfection. But man is also apart from nature and, thus, can be victimized by his instincts. Property, arising naturally from labor, exerts an attraction with the force of instinct, and the desire for it drives a wedge between reason, which demands justice, and instinct, which demands the gratification of desire. The French physiocrats, for instance, tend to identify reason entirely with the order of nature and refuse to admit that man's natural rights may be modified by any form of social contract.[10] James's perceptions would make both propositions unacceptable to him.

That the idea of property is essential to complete human fulfillment Crèvecoeur leaves no doubt. James pays tribute to its psychological force in noting how the "instant I enter on my own land, the bright idea of property, of exclusive right, of independence exalts my mind" (p. 48). James subscribes to the Lockean notion that freedom implies the setting of boundaries and that, therefore, the ownership of property is a necessary condition of social and political freedom. The southern slave has no property but is himself property. Such a circumstance, James finds in Charles Town, produces terrible abuses to the natural rights of life and liberty.[11] The Charles Town lawyers treat the land as the overseers treat the slaves, abstractly with no thought for justice or humanity. At this extreme, property becomes an instrument of tyranny. At the opposite extreme, however, the result can be just as gruesome. The primitive Indians of Nantucket, in the absence of *any* formal idea of property, once preyed upon one another almost to the point of extinction. Only the reasoned decision to divide their island in two, an elementary creation of property, set limits to their license and saved them from self-annihilation. Property is revealed to be a two-edged sword, a source of fulfillment and of misery. Nowhere does either Crèvecoeur or James imply a solution to this dilemma.

James's guiding principles are few and simple, embodying a practical approach to the complex problem of property. He understands that the pull of the land will, in the absence of reasoned property rights, lead to serious disorder and injustice, even as abstract property rights detached from the reality of the land will lead to tyranny and oppression. Even his beloved agrarianism must be tempered by the principles of limitation and confrontation. Like Locke, he believes that the test of property rights is use. As James sees it, a man must not have too much land—so much, that is, that he becomes more interested in possessing the land than in tending it. A man must confront the land himself, not erect systems whereby others work the land for him. The southern plantations violate both of these principles. "Place mankind where you will, they must always have adverse circumstances to struggle with" (p. 210), says James in his final Letter. This view is an outgrowth of his powers of observation and his native good sense, rather than a newfound pessimism resulting from his experiences in the South or from fear of impending revolution.

The James who reappears in the final Letter (XII) is a sad and desperate man, but far from being a hysterical fool grasping at the straws of blasted theories, he remains rational and pragmatic. Certainly there is no reason to read a strong irony into his intention to foster agriculture among the savages he intends to live with after his flight from the coming Revolution. James has already said in Letter IX that "evil preponderates in both" the woods and in more improved situations. If the vices of the latter exceed those of the former, the apparently ingrained desire to "see the earth peopled" (p. 171), of which he also takes note, redresses the balance by making flight to the wilderness a temporary escape at best from the woes of civilization. As pitiful as James's desire to hold on to the agricultural mode of existence may appear, his course of action has the wisdom of inevitability. Agriculture, historically, has been a necessary condition for a high order of culture and for the maintenance of a large, stationary population. Although James professes admiration for some aspects of Indian life, his intellectual and moral commitment is to the idea of civilization, and he understandably has no desire to raise a family of noble savages.

James's fatalism in the final Letter, while intensified by his emotional ambivalence, is likewise a facet of his normal outlook and not a symptom of intellectual defeat. As early as Letter II he notes that "we are machines fashioned by every circumstance around us" (p. 92). His surmise in the final Letter that his "fate is determined" (p. 211) by the oncoming conflict is both accurate (given his lengthy account of his reasons for being unable to take sides) and consistent with his general outlook. His fatalism in no way represents a complete reversal from the "optimism" of the early Letters. It is the mark of James's mental soundness and resiliency that the two attitudes can coexist in his mind. Like everyone, he is a mixture of the light and the dark.

Perhaps the most frequently overlooked facet of the final Letter is the strong emphasis on British oppression, a legacy perhaps of Crèvecoeur's readings in Abbé Raynal's *Philosophical and Political History.* The Abbé, to whom Crèvecoeur dedicated the first edition of **Letters,** is especially critical of British economic oppression of the colonies, foreseeing their eventual independence.[12] Farmer James hopes only for peace, but the oblique emphasis on British oppression is crucial because James's barnyard parable of good government in Letter II specifies that "the law is to us precisely what I am in my barn yard . . ." (p. 51). Now the direct interference of British political and military force circumvents this metaphorical model entirely by ignoring the customary order of things. While the King has always been the titular ruler of the colonies, James has always thought of them as a separate unit of order. Implicit in the barnyard parable is the just and benevolent supervision of the farmer-governor, adjudicating property disputes through the exercise of his moral and common sense. Such supervision cannot take place without a thorough knowledge of the barnyard, and that is precisely why James's discussion of British interference addresses the "great personage" of the King specifically.

James's implied distinction between opposing British actions in the colonies, and rebelling against the King, is firmly rooted in the social-contract theory of the day. The illegal acts of officers inferior to the King and acting in his name but without his direct instructions may be opposed at any time; the King may be opposed only if he sets himself in a virtual state of war with his own people.[13] James is sure that the cause of the present problem must be the ignorance of the King about the "circumstances of this horrid war." A "good king" would want to "spare and protect as she [Nature] does" (p. 201). If the final Letter suggests the death of New World promise, the causes are not internal—are not in any cast of mind or model of social organization that James has had foisted upon him—but are external. A farmer cannot order his barnyard from three thousand miles away.

That James is psychologically traumatized by his experiences is beyond question. Any objective estimate of Farmer James's mind and its development must recognize Crèvecoeur's intention to dramatize the New World Man's "desperate struggle," as Albert Stone has put it, "to hold" a vision of the American Eden "in the face of discord."[14] The apocalyptic atmosphere of the final Letter is real and significant. Linked with James's despair is a certain historical consciousness of the new forever being jeopardized by the old, of outworn institutions such as slavery and despotism threatening Paradise from within and from without. In this regard, James is indeed the prototypical American Adam, forced to solve his problem through flight, the characteristic expedient of this archetypal figure in American fiction. But James remains deserving of our respect throughout, and whether we subscribe to it or not, his world-view has coherence. There is no evidence that James's expulsion from Eden is a consequence of his own sins, real or figurative. Paradise has been lost not as a result of his having eaten the apple but of someone else's having shaken the tree.

Notes

1. Elayne Antler Rapping, "Theory and Experience in Crèvecoeur's America," *American Quarterly,* 19 (1968), 708-15: "it becomes clear that Farmer James is Crèvecoeur's straw man. He has carefully built a world for himself on the basis of certain principles which have all proved false" (p. 713).

2. For other recent studies treating Farmer James as an ironically conceived figure, see James C. Mohr, "Calculated Disillusionment: Crèvecoeur's *Letters* Reconsidered," *South Atlantic Quarterly,* 69 (1970), 354-63; Thomas Philbrick, *St. John de Crèvecoeur* (New York: Twayne, 1970), pp. 80-106. For Mohr, James is a rationalizing dupe, and by "playing upon his readers' fondest hopes for social progress, Crèvecoeur perpetrates something of a calculated hoax" (p. 358). Philbrick claims that James's "expulsion from the Eden of his farm is no less the result of an inner failure than was Adam's banishment" (p. 106).

3. Cf. Rapping (p. 709) and Philbrick (p. 67), in whom the assumption is implicit rather than explicit.

4. *Letters from an American Farmer & Sketches of Eighteenth-Century America* (New York: New American Library, 1963), p. 39. This edition of *Letters* is based on the London edition of 1783 with spelling and punctuation modernized. Cited hereafter by page number within the text itself.

5. Philbrick, p. 99.

6. The point has been made with reference to Jefferson by Leo Marx in *The Machine in the Garden* (New York: Oxford Univ. Press, 1964), p. 126.

7. For a rehearsal of the major tenets of the "freehold concept," see Chester E. Eisinger, "The Freehold Concept in Eighteenth-Century Letters," *William and Mary Quarterly,* 3rd Ser., 4 (1947), 42-59.

8. *Two Treatises of Government,* ed. Peter Laslett (Cambridge: Cambridge Univ. Press, 1967), pp. 306, 368, 311.

9. Eisinger, pp. 47-48.

10. Henry Higgs, *The Physiocrats* (1897; rpt. New York: Kelley, 1968), p. 142.

11. Mohr (p. 359n) calls into question James's sincerity on the matter of slavery by alluding to his "unconvincing attempt to explain away the slavery which existed in the North." Given the frequent disparity between theory and reality on the slavery issue among many great names of his day, James's remarks are as sensible as one might hope for. He looks for the time of eventual emancipation but rejoices in the relative health and liberty of those Northern slaves not yet emancipated (p. 165).

12. *A Philosophical and Political History of the Settlements and Trade of the Europeans in the East and West Indies,* trans. J. Justamond, 3rd ed. rev. (London: T. Cadell, 1777), V, Bk. 16.

13. Cf., e.g., *Two Treatises,* p. 402.

14. Albert E. Stone, "Forward" to *Letters from an American Farmer & Sketches of Eighteenth-Century America,* p. xviii.

Harold Kulungian (essay date 1977)

SOURCE: "The Aestheticism of Crèvecoeur's American Farmer," in *Early American Literature,* Vol. 12, No. 2, Fall, 1977, pp. 197-201.

[*In the following essay, Kulungian examines Farmer James's aesthetic sensibilities, which are based solely on sentiment, in an effort to better understand Crèvecoeur's* Letters from an American Farmer.]

The colonial writer famous for first formulating the "melting-pot" interpretation of America, St. John de Crèvecoeur, was, like many sons of the European Enlightenment, a many-sided man. In his famous **Letters from an American Farmer** (1782) he evinces his aptitude for "speculative inquiries" such as history, economics, philosophy, anthropology, and political science. Underlying this varied range of intellectual curiosity about the world around him, the mind of Crèvecoeur, his essential temper, was fundamentally aesthetic and contemplative.

In the **Letters** Crèvecoeur speaks through the persona of Farmer James, a naive and native-born American of English descent. This fiction was essential if Crèvecoeur was to present the experience and outlook of a broadly representative Farmer—which he himself was not—and furnish a generalized rendition of American life. In the exposition that follows, Crèvecoeur and the American Farmer are not presumed to be identical.[1]

The slightest familiarity with Crèvecoeur's biography is enough to suggest why he wrote the **Letters.** He was a cultivated gentleman with a European education, living in rural America where there was little scope for his evident literary passion. He felt a need to express himself, to essay his feelings and ideas. So he invented an imaginary correspondent to whom he could address himself directly: "You are the first enlightened European I have ever had the pleasure of being acquainted with."[2] By putting his thoughts on paper he in a measure satisfied his need for emotional relief: "the action of thus retracing them seems to lighten the burden, and to exhilirate my spirits" (p. 211).

Crèvecoeur's Farmer was ever alert and interested in things for the images, impressions, sensations and ideas they stimulated in his own mind. Indeed, he appears to have been every bit as absorbed in his own mental and emotional life as he was in the life of colonial America. This "American Farmer" was as intent upon cultivating his own sensibilities as he was with cultivating the soil—more so, if the number of pages allotted to each topic is any indication.

What are the salient characteristics of the Farmer's aestheticism, and what light does this approach shed on Crèvecoeur's major work? First of all, for Farmer James, *reason is the slave of the passions.* He readily avows: "After all, most men reason from the passions. . . . Sentiment and feeling are the only guides I know" (p. 197). His mind is always at the mercy of the objects of his contemplation. His way is to surrender himself entirely to the sensations of the moment and enjoy their stimulus to reflection. He is, in short, an essayist in the tradition of Montaigne, a radical subjectivist who exploits his own feelings.

He has been called "a man of moods"[3] of "unabashed emotionalism."[4] But those epithets scarcely illumine our reading; they suggest merely a capricious mind. D. H. Lawrence's term "sensual understanding" is much more useful.[5] It suggests the writer's own favorite doctrine: environmentalism. "Men . . . owe all their different modifications"—which include their moods, emotions and ideas—to "local circumstances" (p. 61). Again, more forcefully stated: "Our opinions, vices, and virtues, are altogether local: we are machines fashioned by every circumstance around us" (p. 73). As we shall see, this behavioristic doctrine of environmental determinism was for its advocate no mere theory but rather arose from his own experience of himself and testifies to his self-knowledge.

It is not surprising, then, that in differing aesthetic circumstances "most of the Farmer's speculations," including not only the "concept of nature," as Philbrick observes, but human nature as well, are "radically inconsistent."[6] Philbrick says: "baffling are the reversals of position in the *Letters,*" because he has not taken cognizance of the Farmer's aesthetic principle as such: "Sentiment and feeling are the only guides I know."[7]

In a passage remarkable for its critical self-consciousness of the emotional basis of his thoughts, the Farmer observes: "In the moments of our philanthropy we often talk of an indulgent nature, a kind parent. . . . She has implanted in the heart of man, sentiments which over-balance every misery, and supply the place of every want." Though

such an idea of nature is soon enough displaced by its antithesis, still "this [notion of a beneficent nature] is undoubtedly an object of contemplation which calls forth our warmest gratitude" (p. 163). He embraces such an idea when he is in the right mood, not because it is true but because it is beautiful. We ought to be grateful for our moments of idealism, for, as he asks realistically in the same paragraph, "If we attentively view this globe, will it not appear rather a place of punishment, than of delight?" This passage clearly shows the speaker to be unabashedly aware of his moody vacillations between idealism and realism. The sentimental and imaginative advantages of idealism were at times irresistible to the fundamentally realistic man of feeling. The uncritical view of an earlier generation of scholars is here belied. They had assumed with Stanley T. Williams that "His simplicity is convincing. . . . He is untouched by halting self-criticism, by introspection."[8] Crèvecoeur's style is at one and the same time apparently naïve yet deliberately artful, and this complexity has been too often ignored.

His unrestrained tendency toward idealism when in the presence of beauty is indeed the most striking characteristic of the aesthetic Farmer, who found contemplative solace in his agrarian life. "I can think as I work," he writes. "My mind is at leisure. . . . It is as we silently till the ground, and muse along the odiferous furrows . . . that the salubrious effluvia of the earth animate our spirits and serve to inspire us" (p. 12). In his daily round of toil, his idealising faculty was doubtless his greatest consolation, for it enabled him to find "a continual source of pure joy in the ordinary duties of life's workingday."[9] Here we are more apt to think of Crèvecoeur's ploughman in connection with another musing gentleman farmer, Robert Frost, rather than as "our 18th century Thoreau."

For the aesthetic man the vision of beauty is accompanied by melancholy, because beauty is a transient thing and must inevitably perish. What will become of this beautiful thing is a cause of some anxiety, anxiety which pulls the mind away from the present vision. When James contemplates his wife suckling his child, he has "moments of paternal ecstasy." These moments are too poignantly brief for the man who covets them so. "These pleasing images vanish with the smoke of my pipe," and in the next instant he says, "I fear for the health of those who are become so dear to me." Likewise, playing with his infant is for him a fundamentally aesthetic-contemplative experience: "My warm imagination runs forward, and eagerly anticipates his future" (pp. 19-20).

Apparently the contemplative Farmer appreciates his daily toil more for its aesthetic benefits than for its economic returns, which he scarcely mentions. Everything on the farm affords him "food for useful reflections." His bees stimulate "the most pleasing and extensive themes" (p. 25). Dew drops present "voluptuous ideas" (p. 29). As he sits "smoking a contemplative pipe in [his] piazza," the countryside offers him "ravishing scenes" (p. 30). Like the true aesthete, he is so immersed in beauty and rapt in thought that he can say, "I am avaricious of every moment" (p. 30).

Even in his descriptive accounts of the colonies he has visited, the Farmer's aestheticism is patent from time to time. The contemplative observer is quick to spot men of his own temper in his travels. The richest man in Nantucket, thanks to his wife's Quaker ingenuity, is able to be "altogether passive to the concerns of his family," and thus enjoys ample leisure. "He seems to be altogether the contemplative man," notes the Farmer in a congratulatory tone (p. 144). At Siasconcet he happens upon "a single family, without a neighbor" and envies their quiet seclusion. "I had never before seen a spot better calculated to cherish contemplative ideas." He is fascinated by this spot beside "the ever raging ocean," precisely because of what the ocean does for the imagination. "My mind suggested a thousand vague reflections" (pp. 148-49). His concluding observation points to the life he most prizes: "Nothing was wanting here to make this a most philosophical retreat, but a few ancient trees, to shelter contemplation in its beloved solitude" (p. 150).

Charles-Town, South Carolina, was especially interesting because the "great contrast" there of rich and poor "afforded me subjects of the most conflicting meditation" (p. 155). After witnessing the southern system of slavery, the Yankee farmer is moved to present a very pessimistic "general review of human nature" and an "examination of what is called civil society." He then proceeds to discount his own thoughts as the product of a mood, occasioned by his present environs. "The following scene will I hope account for these melancholy reflections, and apologise for the gloomy thoughts with which I have filled this letter" (p. 166). He goes on to describe the famous "scene" of the Negro in the cage suspended in a tree, a dramatic symbol of the black man's plight in America, evoked by his intense imagination.

The final and perhaps the most important characteristic of the aesthetic mind exemplified by Crèvecoeur's Farmer is a metaphysical one: the equation of experience with mental experience, with thought and contemplation. Life, for the aesthete, is the life of the mind. His happiness is the product of his mental activity: "These images . . . I always behold with pleasure, and extend them as far as my imagination can reach" (p. 21). Thus, in his last letter, on the "Distresses of a Frontier Man" at the outbreak of the Revolution, the Farmer, again idealistically, looks forward to the consolation of a new aesthetic opportunity. He will move his family into an Indian village, "seeking a refuge from the desolation of war." "There I shall contemplate nature in her most wild and ample extent; I shall carefully study a species of society, of which I have at present but very imperfect ideas" (p. 223). Contemplation and ideas will continue to sustain him, whatever the hardness of life. Similarly, wretchedness is for him in great part a mental affair: "These dreadful meditations . . . make me more miserable, by reflecting . . ." (p. 204).

The problem for Crèvecoeur's American Farmer is that there is no middle ground between beauty and the absence of it. His "sensual understanding" is entirely dependent on his environs, which either exalt or oppress him. Thus he lives at the extremes of human feeling, oscillating between ecstasy and horror, idealism and realism. "Perhaps my imagination gilds too strongly." "These vague rambling contemplations . . . carry me sometimes to a great distance" (pp. 221-22)—to the point in fact, where it was possible and necessary to make literature out of them.[10]

Notes

1. I owe this formulation to Thomas Philbrick's essay "Crèvecoeur as a New Yorker." *Early American Literature,* 11 (1976), 22-30. The historical question of how Crèvecoeur differed from his literary creation is dealt with there. My essay limits itself to a critical exposition of a matter in the text itself.

2. St. John de Crèvecoeur, *Letters from an American Farmer* (New York, 1957), p. 17. Subsequent citations will be given in text. The question of the relationship between Farmer James and his supposed English correspondent, Mr. F. B., and its import for the narrative structure, has been treated by Jean F. Beranger, "The Desire of Communication: Narrator and Narratee in *Letters From An American Farmer,*" *Early American Literature,* 12 (1977), 73-85.

3. By Percy H. Boynton in 1936, cited in Thomas Philbrick, *St. John de Grevecoeur* (New York, 1970), p. 68.

4. Philbrick, *Crevecoeur,* p. 72.

5. Cited by Philbrick, *Crevecoeur,* p. 73.

6. Philbrick, *Crevecoeur,* p. 46.

7. Philbrick, *Crevecoeur,* p. 68. Philbrick does, however, recognize that the center of the Farmer's life, "the core of his being, is the play of sensation and emotion, not the clash of ideas and the thrust of action" (p. 78). David M. Larson, "The Expansive Sensibility of Michel-Guillaume Jean De Crèvecoeur," *Exploration,* 2 (1974) 36-51, deals with this central problem in Crèvecoeur: "Although his works do not present a coherent world view they do reflect a consistent sensibility" (p. 37). Larson solves the problem by using the 'man of feeling' concept, which is virtually the same as my thesis of aesthetic environmentalism.

8. Stanley T. Williams, "Crèvecoeur as a Man of Letters," in J. Hector St. John de Crèvecoeur, *Sketches of Eighteenth Century America,* ed. H. L. Bourdin, R. H. Gabriel, and S. T. Williams (New Haven, 1925), pp. 28, 29.

9. Ludwig Lewisohn, Introduction to Ludwig Lewisohn, ed., *Letters from an American Farmer* (New York, 1904), p. xviii.

10. This paper was written while on a grant for graduate study from the Ludwig Vogelstein Foundation.

Pierre Aubéry (essay date 1978)

SOURCE: "St. John de Crèvecoeur: a Case History in Literary Anglomania," in *French Review,* Vol. 51, No. 4, March, 1978, pp. 565-76.

[*In the following essay, Aubéry examines the way in which Crèvecoeur sought to establish an idealized American identity even as his work appeared to justify the undercurrent of racism existing in America at the time.*]

Michel-Guillaume-Jean de Crèvecoeur, born in Caen on 31 January 1735, was a prolific writer. Under the pen-name of J. Hector St. John he published his *Letters from an American Farmer,*[1] which later became *Lettres d'un cultivateur américain,*[2] his own adaptation from his original English version. Far better known and appreciated in America than in Europe, this book is a classic of American literature of the colonial period. It is especially famous for the eloquent and somewhat pompous answer which it gives to the rhetorical question raised in the third letter of the collection: "What is an American?"

James C. Mohr, a recent critic of Crèvecoeur,[3] even assures us ironically that *American Airlines* makes this canonical text available to its passengers in the form of a short story when the movie machine breaks down! It would be helpful to call to mind the essential of this purple passage for readers who might have forgotten it.

> What then is the American, this new man? . . . Here individuals of all nations are melted into a new race of men, whose labours and posterity will one day cause great changes in the world. Americans are the western pilgrims, who are carrying along with them that great mass of arts, sciences, vigour, and industry which began long since in the east; they will finish the great circle. . . . Here the rewards of his industry follow with equal steps the progress of his labour; his labour is founded on the basis of nature, *self-interest*; can it want a stronger allurement? . . . The American is a new man, who acts upon new principles; he must therefore entertain new ideas, and form new opinions. From involuntary idleness, servile dependence, penury, and useless labour, he has passed to toils of a very different nature, rewarded by ample subsistance. This is an American.[4]

To what must we attribute the impact of this passage as well as the lasting vogue of a work which modestly presented itself, in 1782, as mere *"Letters from an American Farmer; describing certain provincial situations, manners and customs, not generally known; and conveying some idea of the late and present interior circumstances of the British Colonies in North America. Written for the information of a friend in England, by J. Hector St. John, a farmer in Pennsylvania"*?

Critics still wonder whether its success is due to its documentary content, its style, its composition, or to the essential questions posed about the ideology and the identity of the Americans, or even more to the attraction and the curiosity felt in Europe for this part of the New World where humanity seemed to take a new start?

. . . . .

A taste for pseudonyms seems to have characterized a number of authors of every era and evident considerations of a political order required the use of these in order to defy the censorship, tyranny and arbitrariness of the dark ages. Yet the metamorphosis, soon complete, of Michel Guillaume Jean de Crèvecœur into J. Hector St. John as well as the many voices with which he speaks in his *Letters,* brings up many questions which go beyond the level of anecdote and shed a keen light on the true ambitions of the author.

Truly reliable information either on Crèvecœur's childhood in France, his studies in England, or his beginnings in North America is not available. His biographers, following in this area the indications given by his great-grandson,[5] report that he lived in Great Britain until 1754, and that he then made his way to New France where he served under Montcalm, as a lieutenant and cartographer. After the fall of Québec, he is then said to have proceeded to the region of the Great Lakes and later to the East to become a British subject in 1764. It was then that he bought and cultivated a rather considerable farm, "Pine Hill," in Orange County, in the state of New York; on 20 September 1769, he married Mehitable Tippet, daughter of a Yonkers merchant, and soon afterwards gave himself to writing those letters which were to make him famous.

After the occupation of New France by the English, and thanks to his knowledge of their language, Crèvecœur, having emigrated a third time towards the former colonies, did his best to become assimilated. In this respect, the extent to which he had succeeded remains an open question.

Facts are unyielding and the identity of a person often resists religious conversions, changes in nationality, and even changes in surname. In reality it is only within the discourse which he gives on America that Crèvecœur was truly able totally to reject what remained French in him, in the eyes of others if not in his inner awareness of himself.

The American, "Farmer James," supposedly writing the naïve rustic letters which finally came down to us, presents himself as the son of an English immigrant who is said to have left him in full ownership of a farm of 371 acres plus a few old books of "Scotch Divinity," the *Navigation* of Sir Francis Drake and the *History of Queen Elizabeth.*

At first young James entertained some thoughts of selling his farm. The tilling of the land then appeared to him as dull, tedious, repetitive labor. But this farm was his world, the only place on the whole earth where he had sunk deep roots. When he married, his wife rendered his "house all at once cheerful and pleasing; it no longer appeared gloomy and solitary as before" (Crèvecœur's *Letters,* p. 22). Moreover, living under a liberal political system that imposes but light burdens on its subjects, enjoying the full property of his productive farm, cultivated by "tolerably faithful and happy" (p. 23) Negroes, James soon becomes a father, which causes him to "cease to ramble in imagination through the wide world" (p. 23) and concentrate fully and happily on his small domestic universe and the gorgeous nature surrounding it. As a "farmer of feelings" he thoroughly enjoys his marital bliss, a happiness which rests firmly on the ideal of private property, his fertile and well cleared and cared for land, a bliss which invites indulgence in lyrical outbursts.

Private property, good husbandry, luxuriant, generous but well trained vegetal and animal kingdoms are the empire of the American farmer. Ploughing the fields becomes a playful game in the company of his infant son, as well as an education and an inspiration.

The harmony of the American farmer's life, at one with his environment, extends far beyond the family circle and his piece of property. The animals, birds and insects around him contribute to his prosperity and recreation; bee-catching and bird-watching provide him with a most profitable kind of relaxation. The tone of these pages of Crèvecoeur is strongly reminiscent of Rousseau or rather, because of the clever naïvety of this prose, strikingly similar to that which Bernardin de Saint-Pierre will display in his *Etudes de la nature* published in 1784 but written as early as 1773, approximately during the very years when Crèvecoeur penned his ***Letters***.

Here, as elsewhere in his writings, Crèvecoeur's paradigm is not so much the experience of rural life in early America as it is of Eden: it embodies the story of man before the Fall or the anticipation of his redeemed state after the second coming of Christ. Crèvecoeur is very careful to exonerate his spokesman-character from the most arduous type of work in the new world: the clearing of the land, and the daily chores of a farmer, because James has inherited a fully operational property and has his black slaves taking care of the tiresome, heavy work. James's life on his farm seems very close indeed to Adam and Eve's enjoyment of the garden of Eden, where almost everything, including the animal population, is friendly and useful. Without excessive exertion or personal risk, man prevails over the dangerous and predatory beasts. Thanks to the fertility of the soil and the liberality of the civil government, the American can become a good, substantial, independent farmer with moderate labors. Such is at least the picture that Crèvecoeur's second letter strives to project.

In his third missive, doubtless the most often read and quoted, Farmer James develops at length his vision of what an American is. Crèvecoeur is not the first to have made an attempt to delineate a new national stereotype. Such generalizations are all too common in literature and maintain an astonishing stability over the years. The major characteristic of Crèvecoeur's portrait of *the American* is that it is, at the same time, most appealing and self-destructive and leaves the careful reader in a momentary quandary over the real purpose of the author.

Although Crèvecoeur's spokesman points out that Americans are a new race, "a mixture of English, Scotch, Irish, French, Dutch, Germans and Swedes" (p. 41), he presents the feelings and thoughts "of an enlightened Englishman when he first lands on this continent" (p. 39). He speaks of his "*national* pride" when he views the work of his *countrymen*, who brought along with them to these shores "their *national* genius." This new society is liberal, tolerant, and egalitarian. "We have no princes, for whom we toil, starve, and bleed," writes Farmer James. "We are the most perfect society now existing in the world" (pp. 40-41). Class distinctions are minimal and many more people are needed to develop this "mighty continent."

Stressing over and over again the "strange mixture of blood" to be found in this country during the latter part of the eighteenth century, James-Crèvecoeur indicates however that New England, being populated only by the direct descendants of English immigrants, is also one exception to this process of amalgamation. Many, he writes, "wish that they had been more intermixed"; not so Farmer James, who respects them "for what they have done; for the accuracy and wisdom with which they have settled their territory; for the decency of their manners; for their early love of letters; their ancient college, the first in this hemisphere, for their industry; which to me who am but a farmer, is the criterion of everything. There never was a people, situated as they are, who with so ungrateful a soil have done more in so short a time" (p. 41).

Crèvecoeur's thinking follows a clearly identifiable dialectical pattern. If the synthesis is *the American,* the thesis *the Englishman,* the antithesis is *the poor.* In the Old World a poor man could not call his fatherland "a Country that had no bread for him, whose fields procured him no harvest, who met with nothing but the frowns of the rich, the severity of the laws, with jails and punishments; who owned not a single foot of the extensive surface of this planet" (p. 42). In other words, somewhat foreshadowing the *Communist Manifesto,* James tells us that the poor, as proletarians were called then, do not have a country of their own. Where they come from is not therefore an important and relevant consideration. However it is worth pointing out that the poor who are mentioned and whose progress is described in the ***Letters*** all come from a fairly small part of Europe, primarily the Anglo-Saxon or Germanic countries of the Old World.

These rootless and starving poor, by the power of the benevolent laws of the New World, laws that "protect them as they arrive," see to it that they receive ample rewards for their labors and have free access to property of the soil, these poor become citizens, prosperous settlers, an asset to their community. The laws are not the only element to perform this regeneration of the poor. For "we are nothing but what we derive from the air we breathe, the climate we inhabit, the government we obey, the system of religion we profess, and the nature of our employment" (p. 45). On the basis of these materialist and determinist principles James-Crèvecoeur proceeds with his examination of what an American is. He is, first of all, conditioned by his habitat. "Those who live near the sea feed more on fish than on flesh," their major occupation, fishing, distracts them from the regular labors of the land, they are boisterous and love trafficking (p. 45). "Those who inhabit the middle settlements" are purified by "the simple cultivation of the earth" (p. 45). "Industry, good living, selfishness, litigiousness, country politics, the pride of freemen, religious indifference are their characteristics" (p. 46). "Near the great woods, near the last inhabited districts . . . where men are beyond the reach of government, and where the law cannot be properly enforced, discord, drunkenness, idleness often prevail; contention, inactivity and wretchedness ensue." In spite of all their vices these "offcasts of society" perform a useful role as precursors and pioneers, paving the way for more reliable settlers (pp. 46-47).

Language and religion unite to some extent the inhabitants of the Atlantic provinces no matter how diversified they are by their occupation and habitat. But Christian religions in America have lost their more unpleasant dogmatic, sectarian, belligerent characteristics. Religion becomes predominantly a form of sociability, an agent for social integration. "Thus all sects are mixed as well as all nations; thus religious indifference is imperceptibly disseminated from one end of the continent to the other; which is at present one of the strongest characteristics of the Americans" (p. 51).

By and large climate, government, religion and occupation in America tend to redeem Europe's poor. There are however many exceptions to this rule, one of the most notorious being illustrated by those that James-Crèvecœur calls the "back settlers." Living in the wilderness they soon become wild. He describes the dissolute manners of the back settlers and speculates on their causes: the lonely situation, a too rapid transition from the constraints of Europe to the unlimited freedom of the woods, the eating of wild meat which "whatever you may think, tends to alter their temper" (p. 52). Hunting as well as trading with the Indians (not always honestly) are the real villains which lead to strife and sometimes open warfare.

The evil influences exerted upon European immigrants by "the woods," "hunting," and the "Indian trade" do not affect in the same way all back settlers, for "their depravity is greater or less, according to what nation or province they belong" (p. 54). Although he carefully defends himself against being partial or harboring any national prejudice, Farmer James the narrator concedes that great national differences remain among Americans, in spite of the much touted ideology of the melting pot. The very content of the *Letters of an American Farmer* itself tends, in our opinion, to emphasize the blatant contradictions existing between this ideology and current practices. For, in the final analysis, only the New England provinces, according to the writer of the *Letters,* never knew the disorders and the corruption which troubled the backwood areas of the settled territories. And New England, as noted above, is the only part of the continent to be settled by "the un-

mixed descendants of Englishmen" (p. 41). "There is room for everybody in America," writes Farmer James; "we know, properly speaking, no strangers; this is every person's country" (p. 56), a haven, where Europeans are welcome. Is it so indeed? For, in the same paragraph we read: "No sooner does an European arrive . . . he hears his language spoke, he retraces many of his own country manners, he perpetually hears the names of families and towns with which he is acquainted" (p. 56). After a brief description of the general prosperity that the newcomer can behold, this European who feels so readily at home in North America is given his true identity and his real name: an Englishman. Then Farmer James outlines the eighteenth-century style success story that can be his if he works moderately, behaves with propriety, "acquires knowledge, the use of tools, the modes of working the lands, felling trees etc." (p. 59) and eventually purchases some land to establish himself as a freeholder and much more as a man, redeemed by work and democratic government, a naturalized American, a British subject. "This great metamorphosis has a double effect, it extinguishes all his European prejudices, he forgets that mechanism of subordination, that servility of disposition which poverty had taught him" (p. 60).

Yet, "it is not every emigrant who succeeds" (p. 61), we are warned—only the sober, the honest and the industrious will. But who are they? In his review of successful settlers, besides the English, Crèvecœur mentions only people we would call today Anglo-Saxons, those whose language is widely spoken in the country and whose manners and life-styles have a lot in common. The immigrants most likely to prosper are "the honest Germans"; they can "travel through whole counties where not a word of English is spoken; and in the names and the language of the people, they retrace Germany" (pp. 61-62). When they arrive at their destination "they hire themselves to some of their wealthy landsmen," and through rigid parsimony, and the most persevering industry, they commonly succeed in acquiring property (p. 61). Close behind them come the Scots, sober and good workers but whose women are not as vigorous as those of the Germans, who share the hardest labors and understand better than their men the work in the fields (p. 62). Finally come the Irish who are almost incapable of adaptation, not only because of their lack of familiarity with methods of contemporary agriculture, but also because of their drinking and quarrelsome temperament: "They are litigious, and soon take to the gun, which is the ruin of everything" (p. 62). According to the *Letters,* "out of twelve families of emigrants of each country, generally seven Scotch will succeed, nine German, and four Irish" (p. 62).

In spite of the repeated claim of the writer of the *Letters* that "this great continent must in time absorb the poorest part of Europe" (p. 66) those he includes among the Europeans represent a very small part indeed of the Old World's population even if we suppose that he calls *Germans* all speakers of Germanic languages regardless of their nationality. Interestingly enough, the only person believed to be a Frenchman mentioned in the *Letters* is described as having reached this country "stark naked" after however having some exposure to the English language and culture. "I think," writes James, "he was . . . a sailor on board an English man-of-war. Being discontented, he had stripped himself and swam ashore [a kind of fundamentalist new baptism by total immersion], finding there clothes and friends, he settled afterwards at Marraneck, in the county of Chester, in the province of New York: he married and left a good farm to each of his sons" (p. 67). Before reaching these shores, before being accepted and succeeding he had to "strip himself," literally and metaphorically, of his "Frenchness," which was already tempered by his service in the Royal Navy. Of the Mediterraneans and the Slavs there is no mention in the *Letters,* as if they did not constitute a sizable part of the poor of Europe!

The twelfth letter of the collection, entitled "Distresses of a Frontier Man," deals at length with the dangers and the difficult conflict of loyalties to which Farmer James is exposed at the time of the War of Independence. He feels that he is three things concurrently: a British subject, an American citizen, and a family man. These are all important parts of himself, important elements in his life, and he can no longer assume all of these roles or choose among them without, to some extent, harming himself, his reputation, his property, and his family. The time has come to make a decision, to abandon his prosperous farm and to flee to safety. But where is safety? Politically, Farmer James seems to be a fence straddler, a most uncomfortable position in times of strife. A loyal British subject by sentiment, he realizes that being a resident of an Atlantic province of America he cannot take a stand opposed to that of his neighbors and fellow citizens without compromising himself: "As a citizen of a smaller society, I find that any kind of opposition to its now prevailing sentiments, immediately begets hatred . . . I am divided between the respect I feel for the ancient connection, and the fear of innovations, with the consequence of which I am not well acquainted; as they are embraced by my own countrymen. I am conscious that I was happy before this unfortunate Revolution. I feel that I am no longer so; therefore I regret the change" (p. 202).

Whatever side he turns to he will suffer without profit for anyone. Since the small people like himself are always victimized, great historical events are not achieved for the benefit of the common man, although the common man is their unwilling and unknowing instrument. On the level of international political action, the isolated individual is hard put to tell what is right and what is wrong. In the last analysis "sentiment and feeling" are his only reliable guides (p. 203). Before being either a loyal subject of his king, or a trustworthy citizen of his province, he is a family man. James weighs the pros and cons, and vacillates considerably between "dangerous extremes of violence" (p. 210) for more than a dozen printed pages. "Self-preservation is above all political precepts and rules, and even superior to the dearest opinions of our minds; a reasonable accommodation of ourselves to the various exi-

gencies of the time in which we live, is the most irresistible precept . . . What steps should I take that will neither injure nor insult any of the parties, and at the same time save my family from that certain destruction which awaits it, if I remain here much longer?" (p. 210). Finally, he makes up his mind and decides to transport himself and his family from a very hazardous location to an Indian village in the woods "far removed from the accursed neighbourhood of Europeans," where "inhabitants live with more ease, decency and peace, than you imagine: where, though governed by no laws, yet find, in uncontaminated simple manners all that laws can afford" (p. 211).

His brooding does not come to an end with his new resolution. What will happen to his children under the influence of "the imperceptible charm of Indian education" (p. 221) and "wild" life? He wonders whether keeping them busy tilling the earth will be enough to prevent them from adopting the lifestyle that was so detrimental to the back settlers and woodsmen, as we were led to believe by the remarks on this topic in his first letters. But this hypothetical risk is nothing compared with the pernicious and corrupting influence of the military where at the same time as the handling of the musket, they would certainly learn "all the vices which are so common" there (p. 228). And Farmer James exclaims emphatically: "Great God! Close my eyes forever, rather than I should live to see this calamity [of watching his children pressed into service]! May they rather become inhabitants of the Woods." Even in this peril, Farmer James, who still entertained the hope of converting the Indians to agriculture and a sedentary life, paid lip service to the American dream of universal reconciliation and fraternity in the bosom of generous Mother Nature, rationally dominated and cultivated. This reconciliation and fraternity would, nevertheless, not go so far as the fusion of the races, since the narrator clearly points out that Nature herself made known to us her opposition to such alliances: "However I respect the simple, the inoffensive society of these people in their villages, the strongest prejudices would made me abhor any alliance with them in blood: disagreeable no doubt, to nature's intentions which have strongly divided us" (p. 224).

Now we have a better understanding of "what an American is," at least an eighteenth-century rural American according to Crèvecœur alias Farmer James, than we did after reading the broad generalizations contained in our opening citation from the *Letters.* But do we? For the proud, self-reliant, disciplined American has almost entirely vanished from Crèvecœur's pages where we now meet only with contending Europeans, "ruffians, acting at such a distance from the eyes of any superior; monsters, left to the wild impulses of the wildest nature" (p. 207).

The good government to which the prosperity of the industrious settlers was earlier ascribed has disintegrated. Rather than placing his confidence in wise and just laws, Farmer James now trusts the manners and wisdom of the Indians, who need no laws to socialize their people. He no longer dreads that the proximity of the woods and the wilderness will make him and his family wild. He seeks their shelter in order to make another attempt at returning to a happy and well balanced state of nature.

In these last pages of Crèvecœur's book we can watch the American farmer disappear beyond the horizon. His establishment has collapsed, his prosperity and security have been destroyed, but his hopes soar again; his dream of the good life, of a redeemed life, is indestructible, for the very reason that it is nothing but a dream. Farmer James is well aware of it when he writes, "Perhaps my imagination gilds too strongly this distant prospect . . . Alas! it is easier for me in all the glow of paternal anxiety, reclined on my bed, to form the theory of my future conduct, than to reduce my schemes into practice" (p. 228).

What James writes about here does not even pretend anymore to be the factual report of the experiences of a farmer's life and other observations in the field. He conveys to us the daydreams of a "farmer of feelings" in search of peace, harmony, security, friendship, rationality and many other attributes of a truly good life. The unnamed Indian village to which James contemplates retiring is obviously a figment of his imagination, a semimythical locale where dream and reality could supposedly merge, where an ideal state of nature, under the benevolent eye of the Supreme Being, could be achieved. Significantly, it is an invocation to the Supreme Being that brings to a close the *Letters of an American Farmer,* an invocation that takes the place of action and leaves the reader in a quandary over the eventual fate of the writer and his family. At any rate, his avowed distaste for politics, his refusal to commit himself one way or another and to take sides in the struggle in progress that is shaping the American society, are quite revealing. They show that Crèvecœur wishes to wrench his spokesman out of history, out of time and strife. The Indian village where he wishes to find shelter and make a new start is nothing but a metaphor for a blessed state of nature and innocence, the garden and playground of the new Adam. Farmer James seems to believe that it is by accident that history, in the shape of a Revolution, suddenly shook the foundations of his domestic peace and prosperity. Indeed he gives evidence here of the incompatibility of the imaginary world of the dreamer and the poet, a world which is stable, harmonious, happy, and the true condition of human beings living in space and time, who die and forever fail to achieve their ideal.

At this point it seems strangely irrelevant to speculate any longer on "what an American is." If we accept the fiction of Farmer James there is no doubt that he is a modern Adam, doomed forever to move westward in the vain search for the garden from which he has been expelled, a garden, moreover, which is not really of this world. The *Letters* introduce him to us in contemporary garb, and eighteenth-century readers could very well recognize in him a symbol of their hopes and a fairly coherent concrete presentation of the ideology dominant in America. This ideology, extolling self-interest and industrious habits, has not yet quite run its course and its lasting popularity prob-

ably accounts for the success of the *Letters.* However, in the latter part of the eighteenth century Crèvecœur was a real person with serious problems on his hands. It is a fact that his estate was threatened, seized, and burned by warring factions during the Revolution. But far from removing his family and whatever assets he could save to the safety of the woods, he fled alone to France at the first opportunity, leaving behind property, wife, and children to fend for themselves.

Although he chose France as a refuge, Crèvecœur the man was still obsessed with his desire to identify himself as completely as possible with the English race. Perhaps a brief look at the map of eighteenth-century America will help us to understand his motives.

At the time he was writing his manuscript, it could be said that the moving frontier of the world known to the Europeans followed the valley of the Saint Lawrence, circled around the Great Lakes and went down the watercourse of the Ohio and the Mississippi to New Orleans and the Gulf of Mexico. A chain of forts and small settlements marked it in the West. The pioneers who settled there, and the woodsmen who patronized those trading posts, were largely French and, having little taste for sedentary and agricultural life, were always more tempted to assimilate themselves with the Indians and adopt their way of life, than to till soil and round off their property. A considerable number of eyewitness accounts which attest to this fact are available. Among the most precise as well as the most pertinent is perhaps that of Volney, who visited America between 1795 and 1798. To be French in that era and in those places was, in the eyes of the English and German settlers, to be an enemy recently defeated or, at best, an uncertain ally whose allegiance remained doubtful. Prejudices against the French developed during the French and Indian Wars were but partially weakened by the French alliance during the War of Independence and considerably reinforced eventually by the events of the 1789 Revolution.

Therefore, if Crèvecœur chose the pen name J. Hector St. John, wasn't this the better to dissociate himself from his adventurous and ill-reputed countrymen, whose irregular habits and Indian wives constituted a permanent scandal in the eyes of the Puritans of the eastern provinces? Later, the aid given by their mother France to the *insurgents* embarrassed the *loyalists* with whom our author felt close ties. It further seems that he himself soon got caught up in his own game and became a prisoner of his borrowed identity. In 1781, when he was back in France and asked by Benjamin Franklin whether "the Mr. Crèvecœur who lived for a long time in America and St. John were really the same person," he broke into an explanation which would seem ridiculous if we were ignorant of the immense and childlike vanity of men of letters. Witness what he wrote to Franklin on 26 September 1781: "Yes Sir I am the Same Person whom Madame La Comtesse de Houdetot has been so kind as to mention to you,—the Reason of this mistake proceeds from the Singularity of ye French

Customs, which renders their Names, allmost arbitrary, & often leads them to forget their Family ones; it is in Consequence of *this,* that there are more alias dictios in this than in any other Country in Europe. The name of our Family is St. Jean, in English St. John, a name as Ancient as the Conquest of England by Wm. the Bastard. I am so great a Stranger to the manners of this, thou' my native Country (having quitted it very young) that I Never dreamt I had any other, than the old family name—I was greatly astonished when at my late return, I saw myself under the Necessity of being Called by that of Crèvecœur.''[6]

Aren't we here witness to a characteristic case of acute Anglomania? Our author goes so far as to affirm himself more authentically nordic than the English themselves when he presents himself as the direct descendant of the Norman family line from whence came the famous St. John family, rendered illustrious rather recently by Bolingbroke, also the author of some remarkable *Letters,* who died in 1751. A few years later, after the Revolution, Crèvecœur managed to derive a good deal of benefit from his French identity, by having himself appointed Consul General of France in the United States.

It seems to us quite obvious that Crèvecœur was not so much concerned with "Brookfarming" as with "Bookfarming," as D.H. Lawrence once pointed out. His years at "Pine Hill" were but a passing episode in his life during which he led the leisurely existence of the gentleman farmer—rather than that of the pioneer and ploughman. Country living was conducive to meditation and writing and prepared him well for his future career as a man of letters and diplomat. Perhaps it did not really matter to him that he was never actually completely able to identify himself with the Anglo-Saxon race except through his fictional character, Farmer James. His commitment to the superiority of the Englishman in all respects was a characteristic bias of the eighteenth-century French intelligentsia. Actually Anglophilia was often the French intellectuals' device for criticizing their country, its institutions, and manners but they were not taken in by the alleged virtues of the nationals of a country they were at war with for extended periods of time. Crèvecœur's literary identification with the English has other motives. It bears witness to the strong racist undercurrent that runs through the American melting pot ideology. That this current should be justified and extolled by a Frenchman was very flattering to the Anglo-Saxon Americans; and it was morally and politically safe. They could endorse and promote his book without running the risk of being accused of prejudice although it was actually strengthening some of their preconceived ideas about the ethnic hierarchies prevailing in their country. Moreover, it is doubtful that to be an American (even during the last quarter of the twentieth century) presents an identity as well defined and clear cut as that of the nationals of most Old World countries where race, nationality, citizenship and culture have been fused into an indissoluble unity by a slow historical process. Crèvecœur was a precursor and a good writer to the extent that he gave shape and substance in his narratives to something wished

for—an American identity. However, this identity which obviously did not really exist in his day, as distinct from its European roots (even at the level of the propertied, affluent, white Anglo-Saxon classes), still remains very elusive in our day among the proletarized working class population with its diverse ethnic backgrounds. These considerations alone would provide an acceptable explanation for the lasting vogue and impact of Crèvecœur's *Letters.*

Notes

1. (London: Davies & Davies, 1782).

2. *Lettres d'un cultivateur américain,* adressées à Wm. S . . . on Esqr. Depuis l'année 1770, jusqu'en 1786. Par N. St. John de Crèvecœur, traduites de l'anglais, 3 vols. (Paris: Chez Cuchet Libraire, rue et hôtel Serpente, 1787). This rambling French version differs considerably from the more concise English original edition in composition and sometimes in emphasis and point of view.

3. "Calculated Disillusionment: Crèvecœur's Letters Reconsidered," *South Atlantic Quarterly,* 59, 3 (1970), 335.

4. *Letters from an American Farmer,* Everyman's Library 640, Introduction and notes by Warren Barton Blake (London: Dent, 1912), pp. 43-44.

5. Robert de Crèvecœur, *Saint Jean de Crèvecœur: sa vie et ses ouvrages* (Paris, 1883).

6. Letter from Crèvecœur to Franklin dated Caen, 26 September 1781. Crèvecœur gives as his address: Chez M. le Mozier, Marchand, Rue St-Jean, Caen. It is reproduced in full by Warren Barton Blake in the Everyman's Library edition of Crèvecœur's *Letters,* p. 245.

Mary E. Rucker (essay date 1978)

SOURCE: "Crèvecœur's *Letters* and Enlightenment Doctrine," in *Early American Literature,* Vol. 13, No. 2, Fall, 1978, pp. 193-212.

[*In the following essay, Rucker analyzes* Letters from an American Farmer *as a dialectic between the rational and pessimistic Crèvecoeur and his emotional and optimistic narrative persona, Farmer James.*]

The laudation of British North America offered in the first eight sketches of *Letters from an American Farmer* is predicated upon several Enlightenment concepts: the ideal value of an agrarian democracy located midway between unhandseled nature and civilization; the validity of an economic system based on the pursuit of self-interest; the responsibility of government to ensure the general welfare; the deterministic force of physical and social environments; and the order, intelligibility, and benevolence of the universe. Providing the benefits to be derived from these social and philosophical precepts, the British colonies, the sketches suggest, are the single country to realize the *philosophes'* ideal social order. Several intrusive statements, however, severely qualify this dominant idyllic praise of America.

The simultaneous affirmation and denial of the *philosophes'* conception of America in general is echoed in the simultaneous affirmation and denial of other specific conceptions. Given Crèvecoeur's own emotional vacillation and his failure to develop a coherent system of thought, one may view these contradictions as no more than a consequence of the author's intellectual shortcomings. To do so, however, is to undermine an important tension that determines the conceptual fabric of the *Letters*. Whether or not Crèvecoeur here deliberately engages in a dialectic, which legitimatizes intentional inconsistencies and contradictions, he employs two opposing consciousnesses that espouse two opposing views.[1] The meaning of the *Letters* emerges from their interaction.

One consciousness, of course, is that of his persona, the ostensible author of all but Letter XI. Even though he cannot be cognizant of Enlightenment doctrines because of his confessed ignorance, the untutored, idealistic, and romantic Farmer nevertheless celebrates his social and political felicity in a manner that reflects the supposed feasibility of those doctrines. But he is first and last a "farmer of feelings" ([*Letters from an American Farmer,* hereafter *L*] p. 26)[2] whose humanitarianism is hardly more than self-indulgent sentimentality and whose approach to the natural and social orders is, because of his "very limited power of mind" (*L,* p. 2), strictly emotional. A second consciousness, antithetical and corrective, undercuts James's narrative reliability either implicitly through irony or explicitly through displacement. Whenever the *Letters* directly treats of matters and attitudes that transcend the restrictions ensuing from his characterization of the Farmer, Crèvecoeur doffs the mask of his persona and speaks in his own knowledgeable, rational, and essentially pessimistic voice. Although he may appear to support James's belief that America is a "heavenly city"—the commentary on the Quaker settlements is primarily a further development of issues that James addresses in Letter III—Crèvecoeur insists on recognizing the marplots of American and Enlightenment ideals. By allowing his persona to express contradictory notions and to rely on sentimentality rather than reason, and by testing, from his own point of view and in his own voice, the validity of certain Enlightenment theories against specific social and cosmic realities, Crèvecoeur denies the *philosophes'* conception of man, of nature, and of America.

Despite the obvious difference in tone between Letters IV through VIII and, say, Letter II, criticism accepts the work as the unified experience of the American Farmer, whose contact with slavery (Letter IX) and the Revolution (Letter XII) destroys his bucolic world (Letters I through VIII). Practically discounting both the tonal differences and the

pessimism that counters the prevalent optimism of the work, critics have attributed to Crèvecoeur the perceptions of his persona. James C. Mohr maintains that insofar as James expects to realize in the Indian village to which he flees the same social values that have proved illusory in the European settlements, he defines Crèvecoeur's conception of America's destiny—to carry forward the highest ideals of civilization despite their being illusory. Similarly, Russell B. Nye focuses on James's flight and, justifiably reading it as a quest for peace and order, asserts that "If James's commonwealth of enlightened freeholders cannot survive in the world of revolution, or if even in peace it must eventually change into another Charles-Town, a flight to the forest, Crèvecoeur seems to imply, may be the only answer." Albert E. Stone, Jr., Thomas Philbrick (both of whom judge the *Letters* an embryonic novel), A. W. Plumstead, and Elayne Antler Rapping agree that James's fleeing the settlements signifies the failure of America.[3]

The interaction of the two consciousnesses precludes James's being his creator's spokesman. Further, the implications of his flight depend to a great degree upon the invalidations of his world view that appear as an undercurrent throughout the text. Often no more than a phrase or clause the meaning of which is nearly negated by the context in which it appears, these intrusive invalidations effectively undermine the social and moral stances of the isolated and sentimental Farmer. If James and his minister laud the regenerative powers of American government and laws, Crèvecoeur, aware of the cosmic and social realities that render man's plight tragic, avouches that no environment, not even an agrarian democracy, can alter human nature. Nor is the natural world, as Crèvecoeur conceives of it, as benevolent as James and the *philosophes* hold. The animal order, like man, is at heart bellicose and predatory.

James's blindness to realities such as these makes him vulnerable to the evils of slavery and of the Revolution, which can only threaten his naive assumptions and destroy the fabrications erected upon them. Desperately attempting to preserve his erroneous *Weltanschauung* and unable to free himself from his subjectivity, James appropriates the conditions of the Revolution in order to ratify his psychic and moral inadequacies and the behavior that they dictate. For Crèvecoeur, however, slavery and the Revolution are no more than confirmations of his pessimism, and he seeks to understand them both in themselves and according to their place in the scheme of the universe. The juxtaposition of these radically opposed consciousnesses emphasizes the insubstantiality of the world that James constructs from the perspective of his freehold and, consequently, results in a negative criticism of the Enlightenment assumptions that his point of view embodies.

The criticism is potent because it hints that belief in many of the assumptions demands naiveté and psychic weakness, the determinants of James's perception of nature and of America. Basically insecure and incapable of comprehending phenomena rationally and thereby mastering them,

James must isolate himself. He has to circumscribe even his imaginary wanderings, for his tendency to rely on his sensibilities alone renders him susceptible to traumatic onslaughts of the unfamiliar. For instance, he can only surrender totally to the power of the ocean: "my eyes were involuntarily directed to the horizontal line of that watery surface. . . . My ears were stunned with the roar of its waves . . . who is the landsman that can behold without affright so singular an element . . ." (*L,* pp. 216-17). Equally overwhelming is the sight of the caged slave whom birds and insects devour: "I found myself suddenly arrested by the power of affright and terror; my nerves were convulsed; I trembled, I stood motionless, involuntarily contemplating the fate of this negro . . ." (*L,* p. 244).⁴ A victim of his acutely fragile psyche, James is compelled to center his existence on his protective freehold, where neither his easy assumptions nor his emotional security is threatened and where he can preserve the comic view of the world that his psychic and moral constitutions require.

Erroneously projecting the security, peace, and overt order of his microcosm onto the larger socio-political structure, the unfavorable conditions of which his no-nonsense wife calls to his attention in Letter I, and accepting the domestic and psychic values of his freehold as the most crucial criteria by which he judges the country, James champions American government and laws because they grant fee simple possession of land and the rights and privileges issuing therefrom. However, unlike the typical farmer whose self-interest prompts him to be politically alert and active, James boasts of the minimal demands of citizenship. The grim price of his passiveness is not exacted until the not-so-latent hostilities between England and the colonies erupt, causing his moral as well as his social and political fabrications to collapse temporarily.

Crèvecoeur typically exposes the flaws of his persona's posture in Letter II, which addresses among other topics eighteenth-century assertions of the superiority of instinct over reason and the benevolence of nature. Even though James has admitted that he is neither a philosopher nor a politician, his response to the natural world of his freehold leads him uncharacteristically to play both. Insofar as his sentimentally humanized approach to nature automatically results in a simplistic perception of its value and in a rejection of any consideration that challenges that perception, his perfunctory observations inevitably lead to contradictory statements. Through these contradictions Crèvecoeur ironically reveals both James's unreliability and the weak foundations of the glorification of instinct. When he displaces his persona to assert in his own voice the implications of James's insights, he reinforces the negation of this Enlightenment conception.

Incapable of penetrating phenomena to discover either scientific or spiritual laws, James responds to nature as a man of feeling. A myriad of insects swarming in the sun, the sagacity of his cattle, the wisdom of his bees, the freezing of rivers, the changes in seasons, the building of nests, the reproduction of chickens—each of these he finds "astonishing." When he dares to question phenomena, he clearly reveals his limited mentality. "What sort of an agent is that which we call frost?" he asks, and "What is become of the heat of the summer . . . ?" (*L,* p. 33). The propagation of short-lived insects proves equally baffling and therefore miraculous: "they were so puny and so delicate, the period of their existence was so short, that one cannot help wondering how they could learn . . . the sublime art to hide themselves and their offspring in so perfect a manner as to baffle the rigour of the season, and preserve that precious embrio of life, that small portion of ethereal heat, which if once destroyed would destroy the species!" (*L,* p. 34). Such shallow observations prove to be an inadequate basis of the social and political "philosophy" that James offers.

Comparing his exercise of control over his rapacious cattle at feeding time with the control of government, which is to protect the weak, he concludes that man, without regulation through language, would behave just as cattle do. Failing to realize that this analogy indicts both man and animal, James appropriates the conduct of certain birds as the foundation of his judging the entire animal order superior to man: "the whole œconomy of what we proudly call the brute creation, is admirable in every circumstance; and vain man, though adorned with the additional gift of reason, might learn from the perfection of instinct, how to regulate the follies, and how to temper the errors which this second gift often makes him commit" (*L,* pp. 40-41). The behavior of another bird leads, not surprisingly, to a radically different conclusion. Among the three species for which James provides shelter is a wren that, discontent with its nesting, takes material from a swallow's box. Finding this "remarkable instance of selfishness" and the wren's delight in its triumph astonishing, James asks "Where did this little bird learn that spirit of injustice? It was not endowed with what we term reason! Here then is a proof that both these gifts [reason and instinct?] border very near on one another; for we see the perfection of the one mixing with the errors of the other!" (*L,* pp. 42, 43). Because it denies the "rights" of the swallow, the wren duplicates the behavior of James's cattle, and they both give the lie to his previous claim for the moral superiority of instinct. So too does the kingbird whose consumption of bees leads to the observation that "nothing exists but what has its enemy, one species pursue and live upon the other . . ." (*L,* p. 30).

This insistence on a primal bellicosity beneath the apparent harmony of a seemingly benevolent animal order evidences a realistic and pessimistic consciousness that must be attributed to Crèvecoeur because the perception is at odds with his persona's idealism and compelling need to discern an ordered and kindly natural world. This need, which is most obvious in Letter XII, precludes James's internalizing in all its fullness any factor that points to essential malevolence and predacity. Having created a persona whose mind is governed by emotion rather than reason and whose psychic make-up causes him to deal with externals strictly in terms of his subjectivity, Crève-coeur has to by-pass that persona and insist upon the logical conclusion to which the observed data point. When speaking in his own voice, however, Crèvecoeur is often as inconsistent as his mask.

If in Letter II he displaces James to offer without qualification the unsettling fact that "nothing exists but what has its enemy" and thereby to deny the moral value of instinct and the superiority of the animal order, when he returns to the matter he will, depending upon his concern, either defend or deny it. Commenting on the early history of the Nantucket Indians, he declares that man, unlike other animals, is essentially prone to war: "behold the singular destiny of the human kind, ever inferior, in many instances, to the more certain instinct of animals; among which the individuals of the same species are always friends, though reared in different climates: they understand the same language, they shed not each other's blood, they eat not each other's flesh" (*L*, p. 144). Of course the comment in Letter XI on the warring hummingbirds and snakes, like the description of the wren, falsifies this argument. Intending to condemn the abuse of slaves, Crèvecoeur again holds that man is instinctually bellicose: his "strong and natural propensities" toward revenge and resentment (*L*, p. 232) always surface more readily than his more positive "sentiments," which must be educated. Rather than cultivate these sentiments in his slaves, the planter leaves them "in their original and untutored state; that very state where in the natural propensities of revenge and warm passions, are so soon kindled" (*L*, p. 233). Focusing on the slave and the suffering that denies his humanity, however, Crève-coeur implicitly assumes that man is instinctually benevolent and that his humaneness is just as ready to hand as his propensity toward revenge: kindness, love of family, the urge to procreate and nurture, for instance, represent "the very instinct of the brute, so laudable, so irresistible . . ." (*L*, pp. 228-29). The contradictions of these tentative explorations of the nature of human instinct do not, in the final analysis, disqualify Crèvecoeur as a critic of the Enlightenment posture, for subsequent reflections in Letters IX and XII forcefully support the negative terms of his dialectic.

Employing the same means—exposure of his persona's flaws and displacement—Crèvecoeur criticizes also eighteenth-century valuation of agrarian democracy and its alleged regenerative powers. Whereas James, like the *philosophes,* believes that the colonies have experienced unqualified social and political success, Crèvecoeur, cognizant of the woeful limitations of human nature, confirms America's participation in history, which proves the impossibility of enduring utopias. Of the rectification of social ills he writes realistically:

> The greatest compliment that can be paid to the best of kings, to the wisest ministers, or the most patriotic rulers, is to think, that the reformation of political abuses, and the happiness of their people are the primary objects of their attention. But alas! how disagreeable must the work of reformation be; how dreaded the operation;

for we hear of no amendment. . . . To what purpose then have so many useful books and divine maxims been transmitted to us from preceding ages?—Are they all vain, all useless? Must human nature ever be the sport of the few, and its many wounds remain unhealed?

(*L*, pp. 119-20)

Because he knew that "Good and evil . . . is to be found in all societies" (*L*, p. 22), Crèvecoeur rejects the popular belief that the *philosophes'* socio-political principles had, in the colonies, elicited the essential goodness of human nature and so brought into being a "heavenly city." Responding to the use of opium in the apparently utopian Quaker settlements, he asks "where is the society perfectly free from error or folly; the least imperfect is undoubtedly that where the greatest good preponderates . . ." (*L*, p. 211). Hence the cautious conclusion of a highly laudatory description of Nantucket: "had I leisure and abilities to lead you through this continent, I could shew you an astonishing prospect very little known in Europe; one diffusive scene of happiness reaching from the sea-shores to the last settlements on the borders of the wilderness: an happiness, interrupted only by the folly of individuals, by our spirit of litigiousness, and by those unforeseen calamities, from which no human society can possibly be exempted" (*L*, p. 200).

Despite its negative consequences, the government of British North America wins Crèvecoeur's approval insofar as it is designed to secure the rights of the governed, to encourage the pursuit of self-interest, and to provide for the affirmation of human dignity. These factors cause him to deem America "the most perfect society now existing in the world" (*L*, p. 50). Yet he denies neither the effect of the European past on the American present[5] nor the several flaws, especially greed and litigiousness, to which freedom and self-interest lead. His passionate outbursts in Letters IX and XII signify his anguished wavering between hope and despair and his recognition of the truth proclaimed in one of his Revolutionary essays: "Men are the same in all ages and in all countries. A few prejudices and customs excepted, the same passions lurk in our hearts at all times" ([*Sketches of Eighteenth Century America: More "Letters from an American Farmer",* hereafter *S*], p. 179). Given this attitude toward humankind and his belief in the inevitable coexistence of good and evil in all societies, neither slavery nor the Revolution will destroy Crèvecoeur's *Weltanschauung* as they do that of his morally naive and psychologically maladjusted persona.

Just as the depth of intellection and breath of subject matter treated in Letters IV through VIII indicate that Crève-coeur there most often speaks in his own voice, so do those of the bulk of Letter IX. The pessimistic questioning of the governance of the universe, of the nature of the world that man inhabits, and of man's constitution that slavery induces is undoubtedly incongruous with the mentality of the American Farmer, who has had no educative experience that would enable him to transcend the limitations revealed in Letters I and II. Because Crèvecoeur doffs his mask and more openly approaches these questions rationally and passionately, the distance between the two consciousnesses is more manifest than it is in the first three letters.

James's very real awareness of the Negro's humanity and suffering unquestionably validates his distress, but his inability to deal with abstractions severely restricts his comprehension of the enormity of the evils of institutional slavery. Totally unmindful of the crucial matters of rights and the ugly reality of bondage, for instance, and failing to realize that because he owns slaves he denies others the natural rights that he celebrates, as a man of mere sensibility James complains only of emotional and corporeal violence, which offends him. The offense seems more important than the cause, for he embraces the situation of the caged slave and slavery itself to parade his sensibility. His reference to the "showers of sweat and of tears which from the bodies of Africans, daily drop, and moisten the ground they till" and to the "cracks of the whip" under which the slave labors (*L*, pp. 225, 226) shifts attention from the reported fact to the sensitive soul that reports. Such is the case too when James comments on the violation of African families and resorts to redundancy to heighten the emotionality of his subject: "The daughter torn from her weeping mother, the child from the wretched parents, the wife from the loving husband; whole families swept away and brought through storms and tempests to this rich metropolis," where they are "arranged like horses at a fair, they are branded like cattle . . ." (*L*, p. 226). Were he a Charles-Town planter, this devotee of the pathetic confesses, knowledge of the frauds employed to entrap slaves, of the barbarous treatment to which they are subjected, and of the anguish caused by the disruption of family ties would not allow him to "rest in peace" (*L*, p. 229).

In order to provide a more thorough and convincing condemnation, Crèvecoeur displaces his persona. His own comprehensive and intellectual consciousness, capable of outrage, appropriates the assigned function of James's melodramatic sensibility and confronts the fundamentals of the institution, the indifference or hostility of nature to which it testifies, and the omnipresence of social evil. His antipathy to slavery stems in part from specific socioeconomic principles that are predicated upon natural laws and from his agrarianism. (Like the physiocrats, he believed that land is the only source of true wealth and that labor expended is the sole determinant of value.)

Insofar as a planter has no power other than force over his chattel and no right to enslave except the specious right that money bestows, Crèvecoeur argues, he violates the slave's natural right to liberty. "Strange order of things!" he exclaims. "Oh, Nature, where art thou?—Are not these blacks thy children as well as we?" (*L*, p. 227). This violation, due to the corruption of the natural law that dictates pursuit of self-interest, leads to the violation of other natural laws. For the planter abrogates the humanity that would oblige him to respond kindly to those who serve him, and the slave must abrogate the propensity to procreate and

nurture because of the additional hardship that pregnancy imposes and because his child is doomed to enslavement. In light of these contraventions of nature, Crèvecoeur can only damn man and his arrogant claim to an elevated place in the scale of being: "What then is man; this being who boasts so much of the excellence and dignity of his nature, among that variety of unscrutable mysteries, of unsolvable problems, with which he is surrounded?" (*L*, pp. 229-30).

The implication so far is that nature has abandoned the slave to hostilities for which the planter alone is responsible. But when Crèvecoeur seeks to locate the first cause not merely of slavery but rather of all evil, he finally attributes it to nature or nature's God. As Enlightenment philosophers did, he too detects the order and control of the physical universe but, significantly, fails to discern corresponding qualities of a spiritual kind: "Is there then no superintending power who conducts the moral operations of the world, as well as the physical? The same sublime hand which guides the planets round the sun . . . and prevents the vast system from falling into confusion; doth it abandon mankind to all the errors, the follies, and the miseries, which their most frantic rage, and their most dangerous vices and passions can produce?" (*L*, p. 235). Even the physical conditions of earth hint that, if there is a God to care for man, he has opted to pare his nails. Earlier professing environmentalism, Crèvecoeur delighted in hostile climates and terrains because they promote health and virtue.[6] Now in his mood of ethical nihilism he believes that the many areas of infertility and violent climate combine to make the earth "a place of punishment" (*L*, p. 238). The prevalence of natural calamities and social evils forces him to conclude that man's happiness lies neither in the state of nature, where people "often eat each other for want of food," nor in society, where "they often starve each other for want of room" (*L*, p. 242). Human lust for power and predacity suggest that "the principles of action in man, considered as the first agent of this planet, [are] poisoned in their most essential parts" (*L*, p. 236). Because nature has so ordered his constitution, man inevitably thwarts the few causes ordained for his benefit.

The evident contrast between James's sentimental humanitarianism and Crèvecoeur's outraged rationalism, which too is humanitarian, effectively undermines the validity of James's approach to experience. To the extent that he reinforces the hostility and predacity of nature and of man that he intrusively asserted in Letter II, Crèvecoeur invalidates the Enlightenment conception of an ordered, intelligible, and benevolent universe and the belief that certain sociopolitical structures could perfect human nature.

In Letter XII, which addresses the Revolution, Crèvecoeur's and his persona's consciousnesses often merge because Crèvecoeur appropriates James's plight as a means to clarify his own attitude toward the War. He assigns to the Farmer several arguments that, despite their being uncharacteristic of his intellect and irrelevant to his life style, are nevertheless apt. The appropriateness of the arguments to James's immediate dilemma prohibits, in these instances, the glaring ideational hiatus that characterizes the other relevant letters. However, when his peculiar sensibility does manifest itself, it again serves as a means by which Crèvecoeur judges Enlightenment doctrine.

Both the *Sketches* and Letter XII reflect ambivalence toward the Revolution. If Crèvecoeur at one point deems the union between England and the colonies perfect, at another he accuses England of provoking a civil war. He may contend that the patriot's rebellion is unjustifiable because of the perfect freedom and the protection that England grants the colonies, but he will argue also that it is justifiable because of her violating compact. And yet the legitimate case for rebellion is no more than a cover for tyranny and greed. Objective defense of these ambivalent attitudes is not offered, for Crèvecoeur, perhaps because his objection to war is more compelling than the causes of the Revolution, does not deal precisely and fully with matters such as charter rights and commercial policies. Nevertheless, his unwillingness to acknowledge that the evils of war can secure the very freedoms that he judges necessary to human dignity, his blind affirmation of harmony between England and the colonies, his ready denial of valid motives, and his conflicting loyalties cause him to judge both patriots and loyalists negatively.

Loyally attributing colonial success to England—the original settlers "brought along with them their national genius, to which they principally owe what liberty they enjoy, and what substance they possess" (*L,* p. 48)—Crèvecoeur virtually disregards the import of measures such as the Stamp and Townshend Duty Acts and of previous regulations such as the Felon Act, to which he alludes in Letter III. Unlike Franklin, who devoted a most caustic essay to the Felon Act, Crèvecoeur sees in it only irony: "What a strange compliment has our mother country paid to two of the finest provinces in America! . . . what was intended as a punishment, is become the good fortune of several . . ." (*L,* p. 88). Further, the hymn to Penn, also in Letter III, indicates no cognizance at all of the intense fight between the proprietary government and the Pennsylvania Assembly over the taxation of proprietary estates. But Crèvecoeur was by no means blind to the injustices of mercantilism and to England's failure to recognize colonial contribution to imperial welfare.

He holds that the typical American farmer's struggle against pests, the shortage and high cost of labor, the formidable expenditure required to clear lands, and other hardships prohibit his assuming the additional burden of European taxes, the levying of which robs the colonies of their limited financial wealth and discourages their growth. As Crèvecoeur sees it, imperial restrictions on domestic production and trade—the reference is to laws such as the Woollen, Hat, Sugar, and Navigation Acts—are a virtual tax that causes colonial wealth to center on England. Even the importation of British goods and the ban on foreign products are financially burdensome because the lack of competition encourages England to export products of low quality and because imported clothing deters domestic

manufacture, which is economically more feasible than importation. "Thus," he concludes, "one fifth part of all our labours every year is laid out in English commodites. These are the taxes that we pay" (*S,* p. 94). Like the patriots, he believes too that the profit motive and lust for power blinded George III and his parliaments to colonial benefits other than financial ones. Through establishing the dominions of North America, Crèvecoeur reasons, the colonists "enlarged the trade, the power, the riches of the mother country" (*S,* p. 89) and, as he says in the *Letters* after commenting on colonial produce, "are therefore entitled to the consideration due to the most useful subjects . . ." (*L,* p. 73).

British exploitation, however, did not outweigh fear of the issue of the rebel cause and disbelief in the efficacy of war, concerns that he blatantly confesses: "Every opinion is changed; every prejudice is subverted; every ancient principle is annihilated; every mode of organization, which linked us before as men and as citizens, is now altered. New ones are introduced, and who can tell whether we shall be the gainers by the exchange?" (*S,* p. 178). As an uncertain stay against confusion and, significantly, as a seeming absolution of noninvolvement, he adopts a fatalist position. Regardless of the justice or injustice of the causes of war, he rationalizes, the world judges its merit solely on the basis of predetermined military victory. His ignoring France and other countries that accepted the American cause as the cause of mankind and his surrendering the success of that cause to fate are obviously escapist, and they attest to the pathos of his dilemma. The truth is that Crèvecoeur was a pacifist who could not conceive of the value of war, as an ambiguous "modern simile" demonstrates: "the action of ploughing seems to be laborious and dirty; numberless worms, insects, and wise republics of ants are destroyed by the operation. Yet these scenes of unknown disasters, of unnoticed murders and ruins happily tend to produce a rich harvest in the succeeding season" (*S,* pp. 229-30). Because the destructions of plowing do indeed yield "a rich harvest," so too, analogically, should war. But the second sentence makes sense contextually only if it is interpreted ironically. *Scenes,* [*Sketches*] then, refers to the devastations of the Revolution, which do not produce "a much preferable state of existence" (*S,* p. 229).

Staunchly loyalist yet devoted to America, cognizant of British injustice yet not willing to forego union, Crèvecoeur could not embrace either faction and for this reason, I believe, compulsively denies the necessity of rebellion. He doggedly asserts that pre-war America, a society of "regular, sober, religious people, urged neither by want nor impelled by any very great distress" (*S,* p. 179), had enjoyed a happy dependence on England. Suffering no excess of misrule, American subjects were, rather, united in freedom under an indulgent crown whose generosity the patriots now exploit. Blind to domestic and imperial political felicity, they allowed themselves to be deceptively persuaded that the king and his officers denied their rights:

But what art, what insidious measures, what deep-laid policy, what masses of intricate, captious delusions were not necessary to persuade a people happy beyond any on earth, in the zenith of political felicity, receiving from Nature every benefit she could confer, enjoying from government every advantage it could confer, that they were miserable, oppressed, and aggrieved, that slavery and tyranny would rush upon them from the very sources which before had conveyed them so many blessings.

(*S*, p. 251)

Yet if he defensively discounts the legitimate case for rebellion and ignores those patriots and loyalists who did not exploit it, Crèvecoeur was painfully aware of those who did, devoting **"Landscapes"** to a portrayal of those perversions. He repeatedly affirmed, albeit with bias, that tyranny, lust for power, greed, and other corruptions—in the guise of policy, justice, patriotism, liberty, self-defense, constitutional reason, and other honorable garments—were "the secret but true foundation of this, as well as of many other revolutions" (*S*, p. 251).

Although these antipathies and ambivalences, which echo several pessimistic beliefs that Crèvecoeur intrusively affirmed earlier in the *Letters,* are attributed to James as he contemplates flight to the Indian village, they do not indicate a radical change in his mentality. Just as in Letter II he perfunctorily observed yet rejected certain aspects of nature that challenged his conception of its benevolence, so does he now voice his creator's perception of general truths without recognizing their implications for the comic world view that he ultimately reaffirms. He characteristically uses these truths as ratifications of the behavior that his psychic and moral constitutions have previously determined. These relatively rational truths notwithstanding, James still responds in terms of his sensibilities, freely acknowledging his hysteria and his subjugation to his hyperactive imagination and freely confessing that "Sentiment and feeling are [his] only guides" to conduct (*L*, p. 288). Like an animal brought to bay, he desperately seeks an out and will distort any fact in his effort to justify himself. Significantly, neither his hysteria nor his rationalizations deny the validity of his claim that the injustice of England is one reason for his flight.

Like Crèvecoeur, James too acknowledges a "fear of innovations, with the consequence of which I am not well acquainted. . . ." Further, a similar conflict of loyalties prompts him to reject the charge that while the government of the realm is "just, wise, and free, beyond any other on earth," it is "not always so to its distant conquests" (*L*, p. 287). Regardless of his acknowledged ignorance of the motive forces of the War, James not only declares them corrupt but also contends that they are designed to manipulate the weak, who matter in the great scale of events only insofar as they realize the will of the elite: "The great moving principles which actuate both parties are much hid from vulgar eyes, like mine; nothing but the plausible and probable are offered to our contemplation. The innocent class are always the victim of the

few; they are in all countries and at all times the inferior agents, on which the popular phantom is erected; they clamour, and must toil, and bleed, and are always sure of meeting with oppression and rebuke" (*L*, p. 288). Seeking to understand any possibly valid principles, he believes, is useless, for not the justice of principles but rather sheer strength, which is fated, and consequent victory will determine the merit of the War.

If Crèvecoeur here succeeds in unifying his own consciousness and that of his persona simply because of the relevance of these attitudes to his persona's situation, the merger dissolves when James directs attention to his particular plight and its effect upon his psychology. He then displays his characteristic sentimentality, psychic instability, acute subjectivity, and moral naiveté. His living on the unprotected frontier and his "chimney-corner" discussions of military devastations so exacerbate his normal fear that he irrationally accepts his children's nightmares "as warnings and sure prognostics of our future fate" (*L*, p. 286). He of course expounds upon the sufferings of his family— their loss of appetite, the disruption of their sleep, and other discomforts that make their predicament "a thousand times worse than that of a soldier engaged in the midst of the most severe conflict!" (*L*, p. 285).

James, however, cannot find relief through participation because he cannot tolerate violence and because he lacks the moral courage necessary to sustain the consequences of committing himself to the loyalist cause. Loyalism would require him "coolly, and philosophically [to] say, it is necessary for the good of Britain, that my children's brains should be dashed against the walls of the house in which they were reared; that my wife should be stabbed and scalped before my face; that I should be either murdered or captivated; or that for greater expedition we should all be locked up and burnt to ashes . . ." (*L*, p. 294). Using his own ego as the sole measure of human capabilities, he maintains that only a being who is of an order that is either superior or inferior to that of human beings and whose motive forces are either more or less refined than those that activate man can be expected to make such a sacrifice. Additionally, the idea of arming himself against his native country is unbearable. "Must I be called a parricide, a traitor, a villain, lose the esteem of all those whom I love, to preserve my own; be shunned like a rattlesnake, or be pointed at like a bear?" he asks. "I have neither heroism nor magnanimity enough to make so great a sacrifice" (*L*, p. 289). Compelled to commit himself yet unable to make a choice, thoroughly unmanned by real and imaginary fears yet under the necessity to protect himself and his family, he can only flee. The justifications of flight reveal the extent to which the War temporarily destroys the fabrications erected upon his comic assumptions about existential and transcendent reality.

American that he is, James assumes that the natural right to life, liberty, property, and not the mere pursuit but rather the attainment and maintenance of happiness is both a political and a religious principle: God asks nothing of man but that which contributes to his own and to his fellow be-ings' felicity. This facile belief of course precludes James's discerning a more substantial and inclusive happiness than that which characterized pre-War America as it manifested itself on his freehold. For, as he says in an uncollected es-say, he lacks the capacity to comprehend the actual ambi-guity of good and evil: "My feeble and unenlighten'd mind cannot reconcile the Evils occasioned by war with that degree of happiness which one wou'd Imagine shou'd be the Lott of Creatures, or else why created?"[7] Because of the centrality of felicity in his system of values and his having confined his contentment to the freehold that he must abandon, he is compelled to respond to the Revolu-tion as the factor that voids his serenity. Without the least awareness of his naiveté, he states that "I am conscious that I was happy before this unfortunate Revolution. I feel that I am no longer so; therefore I regret the change. This is the only mode of reasoning adapted to persons in my situation" (*L*, p. 287).

James assumes too that virtue will be rewarded. He de-clares that he has helped the distressed, encouraged the in-dustrious, fostered settlement, served as pastor to his fam-ily and neighbors, devoted his life to work, and, in general, been a useful and law-abiding citizen. Despite his practical morality, however, he and his family "must perish, perish like wild beasts, included within a ring of fire!" (*L*, p. 304). Their fate evinces the fickleness of virtue, which he apostrophizes: "Oh, virtue! is this all the reward thou hast to confer on thy votaries? Either thou art only a chimera, or thou art a timid useless being; soon affrighted, when ambition, thy great adversary, dictates, when war re-echoes the dreadful sounds, and poor helpless individuals are mowed down by its cruel reapers like useless grass" (*L*, p. 303). Traumatically awakened to the reality of evil, James questions not the fact of evil, as Crèvecoeur does in Letter IX, but rather its indiscriminately afflicting the morally good and the morally reprehensible. "It ought surely," he protests, "to be the punishment of the wicked only." Echo-ing Crèvecoeur's conception of man's tragic plight, James impiously decides that life is not a valuable gift, that it is "better not to be than to be miserable" (*L*, p. 298). He has neither the moral nor the psychic energy to confront evil and either endure, prevail over, or be defeated by it.

Because James has, in Letter I, admitted that he has known very little of England and because he has confined his ex-istence to his freehold, thus rejecting political involve-ment, the political motives of his flight must be attributed to Crèvecoeur. Their relevance to James's predicament, however, makes them plausible despite their being out of character. Although he previously declared devotion to En-gland, expressed appreciation of her indulgent rule, and ar-gued that patriots are arrogant dupes of sophistry, James is aware of England's treachery. England, he affirms, "first inspired the most unhappy citizens of our remote districts, with the thoughts of shedding the blood of those whom they used to call by the name of friends and brethren" and thereby provoked a civil war. He is aware too of Britain's desire for "the universal monarchy of trade, of industry, of riches, of power," and he asks "why must she strew our poor frontiers with the carcasses of her friends, with the wrecks of our insignificant villages, in which there is no gold?" (*L*, pp. 297-98). Implied here is the notion that the profit motive and a desire for tyrannical control are the sole causes of Britain's waging war upon a people who cannot enrich her. Yielding to greed, the Mother Country attacked her American subjects and thereby violated com-pact. Doing so, she forfeited their loyalty. For these rea-sons, then, James renounces the government that has be-trayed him and wills to act as the natural laws of self-defense and revenge compel him to act:

> The Creator of hearts has himself stamped on them those propensities at their first formation; and must we then daily receive this treatment from a power once so loved? The Fox flies or deceives the hounds that pur-sue him; the bear, when overtaken, boldly resists and attacks them; the hen . . . fights for the preservation of her chickens. . . . Shall man, then, provided with both reason and instinct, unmoved, unconcerned, and pas-sive, see his subsistence consumed, and his progeny ei-ther ravished from him or murdered? Shall fictitious reason extinguish the unerring impulse of instinct? No; my former respect, my former attachment vanishes with my safety; that respect and attachment was pur-chased by protection, and it has ceased.
>
> (*L*, pp. 296-97)[8]

James's particular sensibility asserts itself too in the dila-tions upon and defenses of his acting instinctually. The ar-guments propounded indicate that the farmer of feelings appropriates self-defense, revenge, and other natural laws as means to justify further his psychic, moral, and social inadequacies. Although he has said that sentiment and feeling are his only guides to conduct, he rationalizes abandonment of his (unstated) socio-political principles and adoption of instinct as a motive force. Whereas acting upon his political precepts would inevitably offend either loyalists or patriots, his following the dictates of self-defense will, if not save him, at least excuse his cowardice and allow him to protect his family. Sensing that those whose safety permits a noble concern with principles may judge his conduct negatively, James reasons that anyone confronted with the loss of property and family will quickly see that under the circumstances "the man will . . . get the better of the citizen," that political precepts vanish before the obligation and compulsion to defend family (*L*, p. 292). Ignoring those people who have the moral strength to die for a cause that is greater than them-selves and their loved ones, and abandoning "fictitious reason" and, apparently, all else that distinguishes man from other animals, he pronounces that "Self-preservation is above all political precepts and rules, and even superior to the dearest opinions of our minds; a reasonable accom-modation of ourselves to the various exigencies of the time in which we live, is the most irresistible precept" (*L*, p. 299). This appeal to nature to deny the legitimacy of man's higher faculties ironically exposes the flaws of James's reasoning and attests to Crèvecoeur's insight into the potential pitfalls of Enlightenment conceptions of in-stinct, reason, and natural laws.

On the one hand James speciously appeals to the concept of self-preservation to conclude that man is essentially nonsocial and thereby to justify his apolitical behavior. On the other hand he inconsistently pleads a need for society as an additional reason for his move to the Indian village. Despite his having alleged active citizenship, which belies his saying that his wanderings do not exceed his freehold, James now more accurately admits his failure to realize the extent to which his security and prosperity were founded upon the larger social order. Only the disruption of that order exhibits, belatedly, its benefit. Thrown on his own resources because of that disruption, he experiences acute isolation. "I resemble . . . one of the stones of a ruined arch," James writes, "still retaining that pristine form that anciently fitted the place I occupied, but the centre is tumbled down; I can be nothing until I am replaced, either in the former circle, or in some stronger one" (*L*, p. 300). In the final analysis, however, his flight is not an affirmation of community, for its primary motives are his moral cowardice and his compelling desire for self-preservation.

Allowing James to move to the village, a regressive act, Crèvecoeur comments on eighteenth-century valuation of the primitive. If in Letter III and elsewhere he boasted of the mildness and simplicity of American laws, James now hints that the settlements are encumbered with "voluminous laws" and "contradictory codes" that often gall "the very necks, of those whom they protect" (*L*, p. 300). By contrast, the simple manners and basic concord of the Indian community answer for law, provide for "all the primary wants of man, and . . . constitute him a social being . . ." (*L*, p. 301). The tendency of many Europeans to adopt Indian culture, he continues, and the Indian's rejection of European culture evince the congeniality of the red man's social bond. His freedom from care, his perfect liberty, his lack of preoccupation with sin and salvation, and his capacity to bear asperities with patient fortitude are proof that "There must be something [in his culture] more congenial to our native dispositions, than the fictitious society in which we live . . ." (*L*, p. 306). Although the Indians of this village, like the Europeans of the interior settlements, occupy the middle ground between savagery and civilization, they are closer to nature than American farmers are and hence partake more of its moral purity and consequent happiness. They are nature's "immediate children," James avers; "the inhabitants of the woods are her undefiled offspring: those of the plains her degenerated breed, far, very far removed from her primitive laws, from her original design" (*L*, p. 308). All told, no system of philosophy provides more qualifications for happiness than does Indian culture.

This sour-grapes debunking of European culture and Pollyannaish praise of Indian culture, which ironically comment on the *philosophes*' glorification of the primitive, are but still other rationalizations. James is wholeheartedly devoted to the agrarian democracy and other civilized values of which the War has deprived him. Unlike Crèvecoeur, he has never questioned until now the efficacy of the American socio-political structure—if for no reasons other than

his limited intellect and his necessary withdrawal. Actually, his undaunted faith in these ideals determines his appreciation of the loosely organized Indian village, which will permit his family to exist as an autonomous unit and to foster their social and religious values. Although his family must adopt certain aspects of Indian culture, James determines to prevent their succumbing to its charms and hence reverting to savagery, as he ultimately judges primitivism. His children will engage in husbandry, for "as long as we keep ourselves busy in tilling the earth, there is no fear of any of us becoming wild . . ." (*L*, p. 316). And to encourage the work ethic, he will arrange to pay, after the peace, in real estate for their produce. Most importantly, he will avoid miscegenation, for his daughter's fiancé is to accompany the family. If the narrator of one of the *Sketches* realizes that interracial marriages occur because "at a certain age Nature points out the necessity of union; she cares very little about the colour" (*S*, p. 195), James cares intensely about color and can appeal to nature to account for his caring—"however I respect the simple, the inoffensive society of these people in their villages, the strongest prejudices would make me abhor any alliance with them in blood: disagreeable no doubt, to nature's intentions which have strongly divided us by so many indelible characters" (*L*, p. 320).

The anguish of this and other Revolutionary essays is due in great part to failure to recognize the implications of the radical changes, detailed in Letter III, that Americanization effects. Although Crèvecoeur believed that fee simple possession of land and a government that protects natural rights cause the immigrant to become "a new man, who acts upon new principles" and that as a consequence "he must . . . entertain new ideas, and form new opinions" (*L*, p. 56), he apparently did not realize that this change would drastically affect the immigrant's attitude toward England. To be sure, he declares that *"Ubi panis ibi patria"* (*L*, p. 54) and again that one is not necessarily loyal to the country of his birth but rather to the country most responsive to his needs: "What love can he entertain for a country where his existence was a burthen to him; if he is a generous good man, the love for this adoptive parent will sink deep into his heart" (*L*, pp. 77-78). But Crèvecoeur did not consistently recognize the potential for separation implied here. Looking upon America in the comprehensive context of the march of civilization, he envisioned a continuity that entailed no rejection whatsoever of Europe: "Americans are the western pilgrims, who are carrying along with them that great mass of arts, sciences, vigour, and industry which began long since in the east; they will finish the circle" (*L*, p. 55). Elsewhere he seemed to recognize that America's destiny was, indeed, so radically revolutionary that it precluded continuity of any kind. Given its agrarianism, economy, and government, Crèvecoeur writes, America "wants nothing but Time & hands to become the great 5th Monarchy which will change the present political sistem of the world."[9]

Regardless of these hints of an inevitable transfer of loyalty and of separatism, Crèvecoeur refused to acknowledge intellectually or emotionally that love for America and its values had, for many immigrants and natives, actually displaced love for England. Closing his eyes to the many threats to imperial union, he blithely contended that the immigrant "with a heart-felt gratitude . . . looks toward the east, toward that insular government from whose wisdom all his new felicity is derived, and under whose wings and protection he now lives. These reflections constitute him the good man and the good subject" (*L*, pp. 79-80). James's renunciation of England and his subsequent flight may suggest that Crèvecoeur in some way eventually recognized the full import of the American "revolution" effected long before the Revolutionary crises; however, the reluctance to sanction the patriot cause and the virtual exoneration of England found in Letter XII imply that even in the face of the War of Independence he did not realize the consequences of his conception of Americanization and of America's destiny. If the juxtaposition of James's flight and the defenses of England, then, is viewed as a dialectic by which Crèvecoeur tested the validity of his concept of empire, the effort fails dismally.

The contrast between James's attitudes in Letters II and III, for instance, and in the early portions of Letter XII reflects a movement from illusion to disillusion, as criticism has repeatedly demonstrated. That disillusionment and consequent flight are attributed to the conflict between dream or theory and experience or reality. Through slavery and the Revolution, so the argument goes, James learns the falsity of the Enlightenment theories and the unreality of the American Dream. "James's final rejection of the society in which he once held so much confidence," Nye writes, "is an admission of failure." Crèvecoeur, he continues, "could not find in post-revolutionary America the kingdom of reason the Enlightenment expected it to be." Philbrick too interprets James's flight as "a denial of his vision of America as the asylum of the oppressed and the mother of a new and happier race." Rapping and Mohr concur: America, which the Farmer has perceived in terms of Enlightenment ideals, has betrayed his expectations. Rapping sees his reaffirming the ideals that have failed him as proof of man's inability to learn from experience and to accept reason as a guide to conduct, while Mohr sees the reaffirmation as evidence of the truth that social ideals can exist only in illusion.[10]

The tenuity of these interpretations, I believe, lies in their ignoring both the interplay of the two consciousnesses throughout the *Letters* and the obvious fact that James rejects England rather than America. His limited mentality, his social, political, and moral naiveté, and his responding to phenomena strictly in terms of his sensibilities and psychic needs preclude the knowledge, objectivity, and rationality that would render his behavior an accurate measure of the value of Enlightenment theories and of American socio-political ideals, which, judged from his point of view, are illusory primarily because of his isolation and his tendency to project the conditions of his freehold onto the larger social structure. The untutored Farmer is hardly capable of comprehending those theories as theories, even

though they underlie his comments in Letters II and III. In Letter XII he is not concerned with American politics and culture as such but rather with the perils of war and England's treachery, which disrupt his self-contained microcosm. The Revolution challenges his comic view of the world, but it does not disabuse him of his insubstantial conception of America, which he continues to champion as he temporarily leaves the settlements. His undaunted faith in the country is clearly manifest in his determination to teach his children the virtues necessary to live as farmers in white America and in his prayer that Americans "may be restored to our ancient tranquility, and enabled to fill [the new land] with successive generations . . ." (*L*, p. 329).

That America is not what James assumes it to be the reader learns from the primarily rational, objective, and hence persuasive voice of Crèvecoeur, whose resisting easy belief in Enlightenment doctrines enables him to view the American scene in its actuality and, through his persistent although often subordinate presence, to disqualify most if not all of James's comments on the natural and social orders. His inability to believe in the efficacy of the *philosophes'* doctrines and of America's agrarian democracy does not mean that Crèvecoeur did not long for their "heavenly city." He questioned their assumptions and means, not their end. Allowing his persona unwittingly to assume that several of their ideals had been realized in America—the regeneration of man through agrarianism and pursuit of his self-interest, and the establishment of a government that secured freedoms and the general welfare—he reveals through James's pathetic losses the folly of a too ready acceptance of these assumptions. But just as America has not failed the American Farmer, who renounces England rather than the colonies, neither does it fail Crèvecoeur, who throughout the *Letters* reveals his limited expectations of all social structures. He either exposes the flaws of his persona's consciousness or displaces it to affirm the malevolent aspect of nature, the unalterable quality of human nature, and the inherent flaws of agrarian democracy. This interaction between the two consciousnesses and Crèvecoeur's challenging, in Letters IV through VIII, the ideals that issue from his own point of view, make the *Letters* an exploration of American potentials and the feasibility of Enlightenment doctrines. Both Crèvecoeur and his persona end up where they began: James the incorrigible idealist and moral coward sustains the challenge to his assumptions and regains his comic view of the world; Crèvecoeur the pessimistic realist finds confirmation of his lack of faith in the benevolence of nature and in man and his social constructs.

Notes

1. For a parallel study of the voices of the work, see Jean F. Beranger, "The Desire of Communication: Narrator and Narratee in *Letters from an American Farmer*," *Early American Literature,* 12 (1977), 73-85. Beranger examines the interaction among the characters and their function in the development of James's authorship.

2. Page references are to the reprint of the original edition of *Letters from an American Farmer* (New York, 1904), designated *L,* and to the Henri Bourdin, Ralph H. Gabriel, and Stanley T. Williams edition of *Sketches of Eighteenth Century America: More "Letters from an American Farmer"* (New Haven, 1925), designated *S.*

3. James C. Mohr, "Calculated Disillusionment: Crèvecoeur's *Letters* Reconsidered," *South Atlantic Quarterly,* 69 (1970), 362; Russell B. Nye, "Michel-Guillaume St. John de Crèvecoeur: *Letters from an American Farmer,*" in *Landmarks of American Writing,* ed. Hennig Cohen (New York, 1969), p. 41; Albert E. Stone, Jr., "Crèvecoeur's *Letters* and the Beginning of American Literature," *Emory University Quarterly,* 18 (1962), 197-213; Thomas Philbrick, *St. John de Crèvecoeur* (New York, 1970), pp. 80-88; A. W. Plumstead, "Crèvecoeur: A 'Man of Sorrows' and the American Revolution," *Massachusetts Review,* 17 (1976), 292; Elayne Antler Rapping, "Theory and Experience in Crèvecoeur's America," *American Quarterly,* 19 (1967), 707-18.

4. Although the depth and scope of the subject matter of Letters IV through VIII are characteristic of Crèvecoeur's consciousness, the speaker's response to the ocean is typically that of a man of feeling. So too is the reaction to the caged Negro, although the universal truths that the sight elicits are Crèvecoeur's.

5. Crèvecoeur says that many immigrants are so conditioned by their past that they do not profit from the advantages that America offers (*L,* p. 80), that the complexity of American laws is incomprehensible to the typically unschooled farmer, who is a dupe of rapacious yet necessary lawyers (*L,* pp. 196, 224-25), and that although self-interest may be a spur to industry, it also breeds litigiousness and greed (*S,* pp. 75-77).

6. The opportunity to consider environmentalism in a context to which he is opposed allows Crèvecoeur to see not only the fallacy of valuing harsh climates and terrains in and of themselves but also the fallacy of denying man the capacity to determine his moral being independently of the external conditions of which he is a part. Focusing attention on the general effect of America upon the immigrant, Crèvecoeur declares that "We are nothing but what we derive from the air we breathe, the climate we inhabit, the government we obey, the system of religion we profess, and the nature of our employment" (*L,* p. 56). And when contemplating the meritorious attributes of the Hebrideans, he holds that "our opinions, vices and virtues, are altogether local: we are machines fashioned by every circumstance around us" (*L,* p. 105). That Crèvecoeur could not accept man's total dependence upon externals for moral and spiritual rectitude is first hinted at in his consideration of the frontiersman. Children of backwoodsmen, he says, will be as reckless and savage as their parents "except nature

stamps on them some constitutional propensities" (*L,* pp. 67-68). His intense objection to slavery prompts Crèvecoeur to abandon his environmentalism and to hope for abolition through a change in moral values: "The only possible chance of any alleviation depends on the humour of the planters, who, bred in the midst of slaves, learn from the example of their parents to despise them; and seldom conceive either from religion or philosophy, any ideas that tend to make their fate less calamitous; except some strong native tenderness of heart, some rays of philanthropy, overcome the obduracy contracted by habit" (*L,* p. 230). Here man is not a mere mechanism determined by circumstance but rather a creature endowed with capacities to shape his environment and to abide by principles that transcend immediate circumstances.

7. "Hospitals During the Revolution," ed. H. R. Bourdin and S. T. Williams, *Philological Quarterly,* 5 (1926), 158.

8. Uniformly contending that slavery and the Revolution prove so disillusioning that James rejects America and its ideals, critics have ignored his consistent conception of the country as a British dominion. Even though he speaks of the freedoms and other advantages that are uniquely American, James views them as they exist within the imperial framework.

9. "Sketch of a Contrast Between the Spanish & English Colonies," ed. H. L. Bourdin and S. T. Williams, *University of California Chronicle,* 28 (1926), 160.

10. Nye, pp. 43, 45; Philbrick, p. 87; Rapping, p. 714; Mohr, p. 362.

David M. Larson (essay date 1978)

SOURCE: "Sentimental Aesthetics and the American Revolution: Crèvecoeur's War Sketches," in *Eighteenth-Century Life,* Vol. 5, No. 2, Winter, 1978, pp. 1-12.

[*In the following essay, Larson argues that Crèvecoeur applied the conventions of the European sentimental novel to the uniquely American experiences of colonialism and revolution, with uneven and often unsatisfying results.*]

After spending decades trying to identify wholly original, indigenous characteristics of American literature, critics finally seem willing to acknowledge the impact of English and European literary movements upon our literature. With the abandonment of literary isolationism, eighteenth-century American writing, which is clearly dependent upon British models, has gained respectability and received critical attention. Commentators have identified the major elements which link later eighteenth-century American literature to the wide-ranging movement of sensibility and sentiment, and they are beginning to fill in the details of the pattern. Terence Martin has traced the influence of the ideas of the Scottish Common Sense philosophers upon American education and fiction.[1] Herbert Ross Brown has examined the impact of British writers upon the American novel and American periodical fiction.[2] Leon Howard has shown that Americans possessed a taste for the poetry of sentiment,[3] and Martin Roth has demonstrated the influence of sentimental writers, such as Laurence Sterne, upon American playwrights and essayists.[4] Roy Harvey Pearce has even suggested that eighteenth-century American diarists recorded their feelings in language patterned after that of sentimental novelists.[5]

The efforts of scholars and critics have firmly placed later eighteenth-century American literature in its proper perspective as one strain in the movement of sensibility and sentiment. A need still remains, however, to reconcile the interpretation of American literature which stresses its connections to England and Europe with the alternative vision which, emphasizing native roots, sees our literature as the product of uniquely American conditions, such as New England Puritanism, democracy, and the frontier. American literature is best viewed as neither wholly foreign and derivative nor entirely original and native. Rather, especially in its formative years, American literature is distinguished by the dynamic interplay between received ideas, attitudes, and artistic techniques and the facts of new social and economic conditions. Many of the tensions of American literature, as of America itself, spring from the attempt to convert into reality the dreams of European writers.

The literary efforts of Michel-Guillaume Jean de Crèvecoeur, the "American farmer," stand as one of the most interesting and influential examples in eighteenth-century American literature of the adaptation of received forms and ideas to new experience. As a member of a French noble family educated in England, Crèvecoeur was familiar with the literary conventions of his age. However, in 1759 Crèvecoeur shed his identity and, after exploring the northern colonies, he settled in 1769 in New York state where he spent eleven years as an American farmer.[6] Crèvecoeur's first work, the *Letters of an American Farmer* published in England in 1782 and translated and expanded in French in 1784 and 1787, established his reputation as a leading interpreter of America for his contemporaries. The *Letters* remain a minor American classic. However, the criticism devoted to Crèvecoeur's work has failed to come to terms with the nature of his achievement. He has been hailed as an original genius, a primitive Thoreau, dismissed as a fourth-rate sentimentalist, characterized as a realistic observer of life, and typed as an early romanticist.[7] More recently Crèvecoeur's work has been interpreted as prefiguring the symbolic ambiguity of later American writers.[8]

The critical confusion over Crèvecoeur's work springs from two sources. First, the letters published in *Letters from an American Farmer* were selected from a mass of manuscripts which Crèvecoeur apparently wrote during his years as an American farmer. Consequently, despite Crèvecoeur's efforts to impose some kind of shape upon the work, it remains inconsistent. More important, in selecting the letters for this book, Crèvecoeur excluded a number of contemporaneous sketches which displayed his pro-loyalist sympathies. Although these sketches have been available since 1925, they have received only cursory attention from most critics. This situation is unfortunate, because in the Revolutionary War sketches excluded from the original English edition of the *Letters,* Crèvecoeur explicitly delineates the aesthetic principles which control not only his rendering of the American Revolution but also his portrait of the American farmer. The Revolutionary War sketches reveal that most of the apparent inconsistencies in Crèvecoeur's work spring from his aesthetics. Crèvecoeur subscribes to the essential principles of the movement of sensibility and sentiment. The tensions and ambiguities of his work stem from his use of this aesthetic to interpret new experiences through conventional forms in order to make them meaningful to contemporary readers.

Crèvecoeur portrays the life of a "typical" American farmer as such a man appears when filtered through the aesthetics of sensibility and current speculations on the innate goodness of humanity and America as the future seat of a new, nobler civilization.[9] He first presents the farmer as essentially a man of sensibility who has found in America an environment which allows him to achieve an harmonious, almost ideal existence;[10] in the Revolutionary War sketches he then achieves pathos by stripping the farmer of everything which made his happiness. The first two letters of the *Letters from an American Farmer* create a fictional author and describe the world in which he lives. The persona who writes the *Letters,* one Farmer James, is essentially a man of sensibility. The correspondent to whom he addresses his letters characterizes James as the "farmer of feelings," and James' character fits this description.[11] Like the heroes of sentimental novels, James is benevolent, sympathetic, and generous. He overflows with domestic tenderness:

> When I contemplate my wife, by my fireside, while she either spins, darns, or suckles our child, I cannot describe the various emotions of love, of gratitude, of conscious pride which thrill in my heart, and often overflow in involuntary tears. I feel the necessity, the sweet pleasure of acting my part, the part of an husband and father, with an attention and propriety which may entitle me to my good fortune. It is true that these pleasing images vanish with the smoke of my pipe, but though they disappear from my mind, the impression they have made on my heart is indelible.[12]

James displays the tender heart and warm emotions appropriate to a man of sensibility contemplating his wife and family. Although his emotions are centered on his family, James' affection also embraces new immigrants to America and even the brute creatures on his farm. He is essentially a man of feeling.

Several characteristics mark James as a uniquely American version of this figure. His feelings spring directly from his nature and environment. Reading plays no part in his development. James' mind is characterized by his minister as a "*Tabula rasa,* where strong and spontaneous impressions are delineated with facility."[13] An uneducated farmer, James represents the fulfillment of man's innate potential for virtue, and, as Thomas Philbrick suggests, for Crèvecoeur the true promise of America is that it provides a society in which man may be able for the first time to live up to his promise.[14] In the new world almost complete felicity appears to be possible. Appropriately, James insists that no man is happier or freer than he. He lists the evils which he has escaped by being born an American—a tyrannous nobility, a greedy church, oppressive laws, unjust taxes, and tithes. An independent farmer, protected by a benevolent government and mild laws, James glories in his situation. He has achieved an earthly happiness of which the European peasant can only dream.

The key to James' good fortune is his status as an American freeholder. His felicity springs from his closeness to mother earth. A working rather than a gentleman farmer, James drinks virtue and contentment from the soil itself. He concretizes their relationship in a powerful scene:

> Often when I plow my low ground, I place my little boy in a chair which screws to the beam of the plow— its motion and that of the horse please him, he is perfectly happy and begins to chat. . . . I relieve his mother of some trouble while I have him with me, the odoriferous furrow exhilarates his spirits, and seems to do him a great deal of good, for he looks more blooming since I have adopted that practice; can more pleasure, more dignity, be added to that primary occupation? The father thus plowing with his child is inferior only to the emperor of China plowing as an example of his kingdom.[15]

The first two letters create a vision of the American farmer, literally cradled in the bosom of nature, growing as naturally from the earth as the crops he cultivates. Such felicity is possible because in these letters American nature appears to be almost wholly benevolent. James' farm animals obey him as instinctively as the animals did Adam before the fall. Even James' hornets are so tame that they catch flies from the eyelids of his children without stinging them. The harmony in the natural realm echoes the domestic and social tranquility which enfold James and his family.

Crèvecoeur's *Letters* are an attempt to build an adequate myth for America. Both the content of the myth and its mode of presentation are significant. At the center of Crèvecoeur's vision is not a legendary political leader, or semi-divine warrior, but an idealized portrait of the American farmer—the common man—self-sufficient, independent, devoted to his farm and his family, harmoniously intertwined with the natural world. Crèvecoeur insists that this farmer is something new in the world, and he appears to offer hope that man can be reborn. Yet as portrayed by Crèvecoeur, Farmer James is anything but an original figure. His love of the natural world smacks of Shaftesbury and Rousseau. The emphasis on the land as the source of

virtue echoes sentimental poems as well as contemporary economic theory. James' warm-hearted good nature and hyperbolic language spring directly from the sentimental novel, as do the emotional vignettes which illustrate them. Farmer James is a conventional figure who has finally found his proper place in the world. He represents what Crèvecoeur hopes America will become, and in creating him Crèvecoeur adapts a received model to a partly real, partly ideal vision of his own American experience.

Later letters describing the degeneration consequent upon the facts of slavery and the frontier modify this vision of felicity. However, for Crèvecoeur it is the Revolution which thoroughly destroys the possibility of achieving an eighteenth-century Utopia in America. The Revolution takes away everything for which the American farmer has striven—peace, security, family and farm. It transforms dream into nightmare. Forcing Crèvecoeur to confront the intrusion of violent reality into his ideal vision, the Revolution provides a crucial test of the adequacy of his sentimental aesthetics.

In his interpretation of the significance of the Revolution, Crèvecoeur follows the principles established in the early *Letters.* Although Crèvecoeur's works reflect his Tory sympathies, they do not focus on the political issues involved in the conflict. Instead his Revolutionary sketches emphasize the human and social effects of the war. He depicts families divided, harmonious communities torn into jarring factions, and the products of years of labor destroyed in hours. Believing that civil turmoil is the worst form of oppression, Crèvecoeur dramatizes the transformation of virtuous men into vicious zealots and the rise of power of self-interested, self-proclaimed patriots. As his portrait of the idyllic existence of the American farmer centered on the benevolent, cheerful emotions fostered by social and domestic tranquillity, so Crèvecoeur's picture of the Revolution stresses the human suffering of individual families trapped in a violently disordered society.

Crèvecoeur's decision to emphasize the suffering of individuals is based only in part upon his personal experience, sensibility, and ethics. Undoubtedly his own sufferings as a loyalist influenced his writing as did his florification of the American farmer. Having placed the common farmer at the center of his vision of America, Crèvecoeur naturally must reveal the effects of the war upon ordinary citizens. However, in his choice of material and techniques for portraying the Revolution, Crèvecoeur is finally guided by artistic rather than ethical or personal principles. In one of his Revolutionary War sketches, "The American Belisarius," he explicitly sets out the aesthetic which controls these works:

> Scenes of sorrow and affliction are equally moving to the bowels of humanity. Find them where you will, there is a strange but peculiar sort of pleasure in contemplating them; it is a mournful feast for some particular souls.

> A pile of ruins is always striking, but when the object of contemplation is too extensive, our divided and wea-

ried faculties received impressions proportionally feeble; we possess but a certain quantity of tears and compassion. But when the scale is diminished, when we descend from the destruction of an extensive government or nation to that of several individuals, to that of a once opulent, happy, virtuous family, there we pause, for it is more analogous to our own situation. We can better comprehend the woes, the distress of a father, mother, and children immersed in the deepest calamities our imagination can conceive, than if we had observed the overthrow of kings and great rulers.[16]

In this passage Crèvecoeur reveals both his rationale for dealing with calamities such as those provoked by the Revolution and his artistic approach to the subject. Following the principles of contemporary philosophers and the practice of sentimental novelists, he notes that suffering can produce aesthetic pleasure: it can be a "mournful feast for some particular souls." Interestingly, Crèvecoeur offers a rather advanced version of the aesthetic of suffering. Rather than arguing that the pleasure received in viewing distress arises from the observer's desire to relieve its victim, Crèvecoeur ascribes it to an emphatic response to the suffering itself. When suffering is properly distanced, vicarious participation in it can become a source of pleasure. Crèvecoeur then lays down guidelines for creating true pathos. He argues that if it is to affect the reader, the distress must not be too diffuse or it will weary the mind's faculties. He believes that in order to assist the reader in identifying with the sufferers, the writer should focus upon specific individuals and families, preferably humble ones, and he suggests that the effect will be more intense if the writer displays his protagonist's transformation from happiness to the "deepest calamities." These speculations reveal a startling familiarity, for a supposedly casually educated writer, with current psychological and aesthetic speculations of the role of pathos in literature. Whatever the ultimate source of these ideas, they firmly establish Crèvecoeur as a conscious practitioner of the literature of sensibility, and they set up the aesthetic principles he employs in interpreting the American Revolution.

The final letter in *Letters from an American Farmer,* "Distresses of a Frontier Man," embodies Crèvecoeur's most effective application of his aesthetic theory. In this letter Crèvecoeur focuses on the effect of the Revolutionary War on Farmer James and his family. Crèvecoeur's presentation of James' plight is carefully designed to evoke the reader's sympathy. He focuses on the distress of one ordinary family, that of Farmer James. He explicitly contrasts their present misery with their former happiness in order to increase the pathos of their situation. James is characterized as a man guided by sentiment and feeling. Torn between his loyalty to his king and his attachment to his rebellious neighbors, James finds himself unable to judge objectively the rights and wrongs of the conflict. He simply suffers empathetically with the war's victims and fears for the future of his family. In order to bring the situation home to the reader, Crèvecoeur details James' mental state. Expecting destruction from fire and sword, James and his family exist in a condition of constant anxiety,

bordering on hysteria. They neither eat nor sleep in peace. James describes his family situation in an emotion laden scene:

> We never sit down either to dinner or supper, but the least noise immediately spreads a general alarm and prevents us from enjoying the comfort of our meals. The very appetite proceeding from labour and peace of mind is gone; we eat just enough to keep us alive: our sleep is disturbed by the most frightful dreams; sometimes I start awake, as if the great hour of danger was come: at other times the howling of our dogs seems to announce the arrival of the enemy: we leap out of bed and run to arms; my poor wife with panting bosom and silent tears, takes leave of me, as if we were to see each other no more; she snatches the youngest children from their beds, who, suddenly awakened, increase by their innocent questions the horror of the dreadful moment. She tries to hide them in the cellar, as if our cellar was inaccessible to the fire. I place all my servants at the windows, and myself at the door, where I am determined to perish. Fear industriously increases every sound; we all listen; each communicates to the other his ideas and conjectures. We remain thus sometimes for whole hours, our hearts and our minds racked by the most anxious suspense: what a dreadful situation, a thousand times worse than that of a soldier engaged in the midst of a most severe conflict.[17]

The details of this vignette reveal its inspiration in the sentimental novel. Crèvecoeur unites stock sentimental rhetoric with specific, picturesque details in order to portray the scene visually. The mention of the children's "innocent questions" and the wife's "panting bosom and silent tears" are obviously designed to evoke pathos. In the sentence beginning "Fear industriously increases every sound," Crèvecoeur shifts from his usual formal sentence structure to a more flexible style in order to mirror the family's suspense. And to make the pathos of the scene explicit, in the last sentence the narrator breaks out in a direct, emotional comment on the situation. Crèvecoeur employs every stock sentimental device in his attempt to portray the effects of the American Revolution.

Although the "Distresses of a Frontier Man" is unsubtle and over-strained, it does convey the pathos of James' situation. The reader sympathizes with James' plight because he has vicariously shared James' earlier happiness. Also, the hyperbolic language seems appropriate because it reflects James' anticipation of disaster. It mirrors James' psychological state, expressing the fears of a man unstrung by his active imagination and strong sensibility. Despite the excesses, Crèvecoeur does effectively use his sentimental artistry to capture the shock of a dream transformed into a nightmare. Appropriately, Crèvecoeur provides an escape, for the American farmer decides to move his family beyond the frontier, James hopes to regain in the society of friendly Indians the felicity which the Revolution has destroyed. Thus the *Letters of an American Farmer* concludes with a new optimistic vision.

Crèvecoeur's portraits of families who actually experienced the evils which James anticipates are less success-

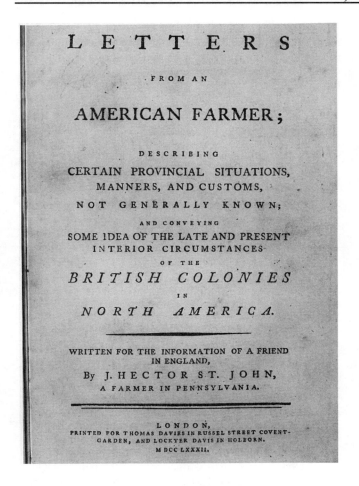

> L E T T E R S
>
> FROM AN
>
> AMERICAN FARMER;
>
> DESCRIBING
>
> CERTAIN PROVINCIAL SITUATIONS,
> MANNERS, AND CUSTOMS,
>
> NOT GENERALLY KNOWN;
>
> AND CONVEYING
>
> SOME IDEA OF THE LATE AND PRESENT
> INTERIOR CIRCUMSTANCES
> OF THE
>
> *BRITISH COLONIES*
> IN
> *NORTH AMERICA.*
>
> WRITTEN FOR THE INFORMATION OF A FRIEND
> IN ENGLAND,
>
> By J. HECTOR ST. JOHN,
> A FARMER IN PENNSYLVANIA.
>
> LONDON,
> PRINTED FOR THOMAS DAVIES IN RUSSEL STREET COVENT-
> GARDEN, AND LOCKYER DAVIS IN HOLBORN.
> M DCC LXXXII.

ful. In several sketches excluded from the original version of the **Letters,** Crèvecoeur recounts the sufferings of families destroyed by revolutionary violence.[18] These sketches flesh out Crèvecoeur's picture of the Revolution and they further develop the aesthetic principles and techniques Crèvecoeur uses in rendering human woe. As artistic works, however, they are seriously flawed.

"The Wyoming Massacre" illustrates Crèvecoeur's application of the principle that true pathos can be created only by focusing attention on the calamities suffered by individuals. In this sketch Crèvecoeur treats devastation on the grand scale. He recounts the destruction of an entire community which has provoked the anger of the British and Indians on its frontier. Because he is dealing with a "massacre," Crèvecoeur must begin by painting his portrait with broad strokes. He describes in general terms the fear, confusion, and suffering of the settlers of the Wyoming Valley during the attack. However, in order to engage his readers' sympathies he regularly narrows his field of vision to focus upon the woes of individuals. The following passage describing the retreat following the battle exemplifies his technique:

> For a considerable time the roads through the settled country were full of these unhappy fugitives, each company slowly returning towards the countries from which

they had formerly emigrated. Some others, still more unfortunate than others, were wholly left alone with their children, obliged to carry through that long and fatiguing march the infants of their breasts, now no longer replenished as before with an exuberant milk. Some of them were reduced to the cruel necessity of loading the ablest of them with the little food they were permitted to carry. Many of these young victims were seen bare-headed, bare-footed, shedding tears at every step, oppressed with fatigues too great for their tender age to bear, afflicted with every species of misery, with hunger, with bleeding feet, every now and then surrounding their mother as exhausted as themselves. "Mammy, where are we going? Where is father? Why don't we go home?" "Poor innocents, don't you know that the King's Indians have killed him and have burnt all we had? Perhaps your uncle Simon will give us some bread."[19]

In this scene, Crèvecoeur first scans the general devastation. He then narrows his focus to the mothers and children, the most pitiful members of the train, and details their sufferings. Finally he pauses on one family and recounts the naive questions of the children to their afflicted mother in order to wrench a final drop of pathos from the situation. Even in a sketch of a large-scale disaster, Crèvecoeur manipulates the point of view in accordance with the principle that the deepest pathos arises from empathy with individuals.

The painterly emphasis in this scene is a conscious, consistent element in Crèvecoeur's works.[20] Crèvecoeur often compares writing to painting, and he presents his Revolutionary War victims in carefully composed visual portraits. In most of the sketches Crèvecoeur recounts the events quickly, then pauses to describe the appearance of the sufferers at length, embellishing the description with touches of pathetic dialogue and emotional interjections by the narrator. The form of the sketches moves away from narrative and plot to emphasize pictoral scenes and the emotions they evoke. Crèvecoeur's presentation of incomplete visual and emotional fragments reflects his view of art as the expression of sensibility rather than a told story. In form as well as content, Crèvecoeur imitates the practice of such novelists as Mackenzie and Sterne.[21]

Other sketches reveal Crèvecoeur's careful, almost slavish, application of the aesthetic principles outlined in "The American Belisarius." In the aforementioned piece, he stresses the virtue and early happiness of its protagonist in order to deepen the pathos of his fall from felicity. Mr. S. K., the American Belisarius, is the most generous of men. After wresting a farm from the wilderness through unaided industry, he becomes the head of a thriving community. So benevolent is Mr. S. K. that he refuses to sell his wheat, preferring to give it to the poor, and he raises his two brothers-in-law to positions of affluence. However, during the Revolution these same brothers-in-law, leaders of the popular cause, scheme to destroy Mr. S. K.'s reputation and acquire his estates. Attainted as a loyalist, Mr. S. K. loses his son and his estates during the conflict. He ends his life in penury, living in one room of the mansion he once owned with a wife who has been driven mad by their misfortunes. Mr. S. K. and his misfortunes are designed to embody Crèvecoeur's dictum that the fall of the most virtuous individuals arouses the most empathy in the breasts of its observers.

Perhaps the gravest fault of the war sketches stems from Crèvecoeur's literal application of the principle that the deeper the calamities he portrays the more profound will be the reader's sympathy. The sketches overflow with misfortunes, and Crèvecoeur piles disaster after disaster upon his victims. In one sketch, "The History of Mrs. B.: An Epitome of all the Misfortunes which can possibly Overtake a New Settler, as Related by Herself," he carries this tendency to its logical conclusion. As the title suggests, this work recounts all of the disasters which can overtake an unlucky frontierswoman. Mrs. B. suffers through the imprisonment of her husband, a six day trek on foot with her children through the snows of winter, the division of her family during the Revolution, the death of her husband and son-in-law in the Wyoming Massacre, a retreat from the Wyoming valley impeded by a broken thigh, the death from small pox during the retreat of a son and grandson, poverty in her old age, and various minor calamities.[22] This melange of misery inevitably produces bathos rather than pathos. In slightly lesser degree, all of the sketches suffer similarly from Crèvecoeur's love of extreme situations and his taste for cliché and hyperbolic diction.

The results of Crèvecoeur's endeavor to interpret the American Revolution through the aesthetics of sensibility are very uneven. Crèvecoeur's works do bring into the foreground the much neglected ordinary citizens of the time. His aesthetic provides him with a rationale for focusing upon the experiences of the American farmer. It offers the tools for creating a vision of ideal, harmonious felicity and for portraying the Revolution as a nightmarish destruction of that dream. Sentimental aesthetics, with their emphasis on individual sensibility and experience, also provide a justification for minimizing the importance of political issues in favor of an emphasis upon the human effects of the war—the suffering which civil turmoil causes for those caught up in it. As seen by a man of sensibility, the American Revolution becomes a war like any other war. Crèvecoeur's vision corrects the sanitized, bloodless versions of the conflict which form the stuff of popular legend, and it serves as a useful counter to abstract economic and political studies.

However, for a writer as fond of extremes as Crèvecoeur, the sentimental tradition also encourages extravagant emotional flights. For an uncertain stylist such as Crèvecoeur, the language of sensibility can be a trap, for its stock diction readily becomes absurd in the hands of an imitative writer. Only a master of the genre could succeed in using the aesthetics of sensibility to create a wholly satisfactory portrait of the American experience. Crèvecoeur is not such a master. Too often his letters and sketches substitute borrowed rhetoric and stilted posturing for felt emotion. Yet Crèvecoeur's works remain interesting despite their flaws. They do embody, albeit in imperfect form, a human myth of America, and they stand as important examples of the complex interplay of received aesthetic theory and original experience in eighteenth-century American literature.

Notes

1. Terence Martin, *The Instructed Vision: Scottish Common Sense Philosophy and the Origins of American Fiction,* Indiana University Humanities Series, No. 48 (Bloomington, 1961).

2. Herbert Ross Brown, *The Sentimental Novel in America* (Durham, 1940); "Elements of Sensibility in the Massachusetts Magazine," *AL* [*American Literature*] 1 (Nov. 1929): 286-96; "Richardson and Sterne in the Massachusetts Magazine," *NEQ* [*New England Quarterly*] 5 (1932): 65-82.

3. Leon Howard, "The American Revolt Against Pope," *SP* [*Studies in Philology*] 44 (1952): 48-65.

4. Martin Roth, "Laurence Sterne in America," *Bulletin of the New York Public Library* 74 (1970): 428-36.

5. Roy Harvey Pearce, "Sterne and Sensibility in American Diaries," *MLN* [*Modern Language Notes*] 59 (1944), 403-7.

6. Thomas Philbrick, "Crèvecoeur as New Yorker," *EAL* [*Early American Literature*] 11 (Spring, 1976): 22-3. The motives behind Crèvecoeur's decision to adopt a new identity and break his ties with France remain a matter of controversy. Most biographers believe Crèvecoeur was disgraced in the battle of Quebec. See Julia Post Mitchell, *St. Jean de Crèvecoeur* (New York, 1916); Howard C. Rice, *Le Cultivateur Américain: Etude sur L'Oeuvre de Saint John Crèvecoeur* (Paris, 1932); and Thomas Philbrick, *St. John de Crèvecoeur* (New York, 1970.)

7. For examples of the controversy see Stanley T. Williams, "Crèvecoeur and His Times," intro. to *Sketches of Eighteenth Century America: More "Letters from an American Farmer,"* eds. Henri Bourdin, Ralph H. Gabriel and Stanley T. Williams (New Haven, 1925), pp. 25-29; Norman A. Plotkin, "Saint-Jean de Crèvecoeur: Critic or Panagyrist," *FHS* [*French Historical Studies*] 3 (Spring 1964): 390-404; Percy G. Adams, "Crèvecoeur—Realist or Romanticist," *The French American Review* 3 (July-Sept. 1949): 115-135; Jack Babuscio, "Crèvecoeur in Charles-Town: The Negro in the Cage," *JHS* [*Journal of Historical Studies*] (Winter 1969-70): 283-6.

8. See for examples James C. Mohr, "Calculated Disillusionment: Crèvecoeur's *Letters* Reconsidered," *SAQ* [*South Atlantic Quarterly*] 69 (Summer 1970): 354-63; Thomas Philbrick, *St. John de Crèvecoeur*; and Elayne Antler Rapping, "Theory and Experience in Crèvecoeur's America," *AQ* [*American Quarterly*] 19 (Winter 1967): 707-718.

9. The *sources* of Crèvecoeur's ideas have been explored. As Philbrick suggests, Crèvecoeur was obvi-

ously familiar with most of the conventional ideas of the enlightenment, but it remains a matter of debate whether his knowledge springs from reading the originals or derivative compilations. See Philbrick, pp. 44-46.

10. I discuss this issue in broad terms in my article, "The Expansive Sensibility of Michel-Guillaume Jean de Crèvecoeur," *Exploration* 2 (Dec. 1974): 36-51.

11. Michel-Guillaume Jean de Crèvecoeur, *Letters from an American Farmer* (Gloucester, Mass., 1768), reprint 1782 ed., p. 29.

12. Crèvecoeur, *Letters,* pp. 29-30.

13. Crèvecoeur, *Letters,* p. 21.

14. Philbrick, p. 51.

15. Crèvecoeur, *Letters,* p. 31.

16. Crèvecoeur, "The American Belisarius," *Sketches of Eighteenth-Century America: More "Letters from an American Farmer,"* eds. Henri L. Bourdin, Ralph H. Gabriel, and Stanley T. Williams (New Haven, 1925), p. 228.

17. Crèvecoeur, *Letters,* pp. 205-6.

18. These *Sketches* appear to be contemporaneous with the later *Letters.* It is not clear why they were excluded from the original *Letters from an American Farmer.* Altered versions of some of them appeared in the later French translation and expansion, *Letters d'un Cultivateur Americain* (1784, 1787), but they were published in English only in the twentieth century and then in fragmentary form.

19. Crèvecoeur, *Sketches,* p. 205.

20. Significantly the one sketch cast in dramatic rather than narrative form is entitled "Landscapes."

21. Leo Braudy, in "Sentimental Novels," *Novel* 1 (Fall 1973): 5-13, has argued that it is the form rather than the content which truly defines the sentimental novel. He writes, "Structure in the sentimental novel strives to imitate feeling rather than intellect and to embody direct experience rather than aesthetic premeditation." Although I think he undervalues the importance of the content of sentimental novels and overemphasizes the "artlessness and sincerity" of their effect, Braudy is certainly persuasive in demonstrating the ways in which the form of the sentimental novel reflects its emphasis on the primacy of individual experience. Interestingly Crèvecoeur, interpreting historical experience, conforms in part to this tendency. Philbrick discusses from a somewhat different perspective Crèvecoeur's relationship to the sentimental novel. See Philbrick, p. 92.

22. Crèvecoeur, *Sketches,* pp. 207-220.

Myra Jehlen (essay date 1979)

SOURCE: "J. Hector St. John Crèvecoeur: A Monarcho-Anarchist in Revolutionary America," in *American Quarterly,* Vol. 31, No. 2, Summer, 1979, pp. 204-22.

[*In the following essay, Jehlen analyzes the apparent contradiction between Crèvecoeur's admiration for America and his opposition to the American Revolution.*]

The author of **Letters from an American Farmer** boasted that in America "we have no princes, for whom we toil, starve and bleed: we are the most perfect society now existing in the world."[1] But he opposed the American Revolution and remained loyal to the English crown, though his French origin alone should have made him its opponent. Before the war he had declared that immigrants to America could never be expected to remain committed to European societies that condemned them to "involuntary idleness, servile dependence, penury, and useless labour." His dignity as well as the fruits of his labors secured here, the new American must inevitably "love this country much better than that wherein he or his forefathers were born." (p. 50) It was only natural and right for a man to owe his first loyalty to the land that he tilled. But having thus argued, and in the process provided perhaps the best known definition of "the American," J. Hector St. John Crèvecoeur then found himself, overnight, pleading with hostile neighbors to be allowed to return to France. His lands expropriated and his family scattered, Crèvecoeur fled the New World in September 1780. How did this come about, and why?

His sincerity and loyalty to America were beyond question. The cited passages were written before the confiscation of his farm, but he published them afterwards nonetheless, in 1781-82, when he was back in France and helping American prisoners escape across the Channel, to return home. Thomas Jefferson praised the **Letters** enthusiastically, and recognizing their remarkable propaganda value, endorsed their agrarian vision as altogether in accord with his own. In Europe Crèvecoeur was dubbed "The American Farmer." By the close of the war, the country he had left as an ignominious fugitive honored him on his return as French consul.[2] But this reinstatement should not be taken to mean that his loyalism had been a mere misunderstanding. Crèvecoeur's opposition to the Revolution was as serious and principled as his commitment to America. Making sense of this requires that we distinguish between two historical developments usually treated as one: the achievement of national independence on one hand, and the evolution of American democracy on the other.

These two developments have been linked through an interpretation of the Revolution that tends toward the teleological, in viewing it as fought essentially to achieve nationhood. This view was bolstered for a long time by the general agreement that "American society in the half century after 1775 was substantially what it had been in the quarter century before."[3] In the absence of significant social change in the new nation, it was reasonable to suppose that the Revolutionaries were politically motivated and sought independence from external control rather than any internal resolution or transformation. But recent studies have uncovered more social flux and conflict in colonial America than had been suspected, and rather less consensus about the overall national purpose. It is in this context of closer attention to the internal complexities and contradictions of early American society that I will be attempting to explain Crèvecoeur's political decision against the Revolution. In coming to this decision, however expressive it was of larger principles, Crèvecoeur responded specifically to his local experience in rural Pennsylvania.[4]

In the period before the Revolution, that society seemed to Crèvecoeur very nearly a paradise which, best of all, anyone could enter. For this is what he valued above all about America, the opportunity he saw it providing everyone to achieve abundant self-sufficiency, and the dignity of equal status among his neighbors and before the law. In America, he wrote, society "is not composed, as in Europe, of great lords who possess everything, and of a herd of people who have nothing." Here is "no invisible power giving to a few a very visible one." (p. 46) Instead everyone had equally complete control of his life, and none had power over another's. The early *Letters* celebrate the resurrection of Europe's wretched, hopeless poor, to whom America promised:

> "If thou wilt work, I have bread for thee; if thou wilt be honest, sober and industrious, I have greater rewards to confer on thee—ease and independence, . . . the immunities of a freeman. . . . Go thou and work and till; thou shalt prosper, provided thou be just, grateful and industrious."

> (p.73)

One such happy story, the ascent of Andrew the Hebridean from emigrant to American, was a New World *Pilgrim's Progress,* depicting "the progressive steps of a poor man, advancing from indigence to ease; from oppression to freedom, from obscurity and contumely to some degree of consequence—not by virtue of any freaks of fortune, but by the gradual operation of sobriety, honesty, and emigration." (p. 74) This was a parable for the aspiring middle class of course; "the rich," Crèvecoeur noted, "stay in Europe, it is only the middling and the poor who emigrate." (p. 63) But "for men of middle stations or labourers," America held out infinite possibilities; this was the familiar vision which has endured down to today, and Crèvecoeur articulated its ethic with notable precision: "we are all animated with the spirit of an industry which is unfettered and unrestrained," he exulted, "because each person works for himself." (p. 46)

That all this constituted a revolution in the politics of the individual and society was something which Crèvecoeur both understood and applauded. The American, he proclaimed, "is a new man, who acts upon new principles; he must therefore entertain new ideas and form new opinions." (p. 50) Then why not a new nation? Curiously, given his enthusiasm over the newness of the New World and what must have been the currency of such speculations, this question seems not even to have occurred to Crèvecoeur until the Revolution was upon him. In other respects he was as visionary as any, rhapsodizing, for instance, that "Americans are the western pilgrims, who are carrying along with them the great mass of arts, sciences, vigour, and industry which began long since in the east; they will finish the great circle." (p. 49) So his failure to imagine America's future as a separate nation is the more striking. Indeed, in retrospect, Crèvecoeur himself wondered how he could have ignored the larger issues of state and society for so long: "I lived on, laboured and prospered, without having ever studied on what the security of my life, and the foundation of my prosperity were established: I perceived them just as they left me." (p. 204) Amid the ruins of that prosperity, he saw that he had given too little thought to its external guarantees. His personal life had occupied all his energies, because for him only the private world mattered. "The instant I enter on my land," he had written in happier days, "the bright idea of property, of exclusive right, of independence exalt my mind." (p.30) Too late, he came to ask himself, "what is man when no longer connected with society; or when he finds himself surrounded by a convulsed and a half dissolved one?" But even as he expanded on this awakening social consciousness, he revealed in the terms by which he sought to define community why he had earlier overlooked it.

Man "cannot live in solitude," Crèvecoeur explained, because "men mutually support and add to the boldness and confidence of each other; the weakness of each is strengthened by the force of the whole." (p. 204) But he still missed the point, able to envision a social model only as inorganic arithmetical linkage. Because personal worth for him was measured by autonomy, any area of mutual definition amounted to a sort of entail on the self. Thus all relations between free men were properly foreign relations and society had to do only with external affairs.

The problem of reconciling individual independence with mutuality was not Crèvecoeur's alone. It occupied his entire century and, for that matter, the next; we are still not clear what the concept of community means in a society of individualists. Moreover, this is an ontological question, and not merely an ethical one. For Crèvecoeur, the private citizen need be neither selfish nor unsociable. He himself was apparently the most benevolent of men. "I have at all times generously relieved what few distressed people I have met with," (p. 217) he reported, judging this one of his proudest achievements. He considered neighborliness not only desirable but absolutely necessary. The Andrew parable in the third *Letter* cites prominently the unstinting aid of already established farmers. One of these employed the immigrant until he worked out his indenture, while at the same time disinterestedly preparing him for the day he would have his own farm; then others leased him land, lent tools and seeds, raised his barn, transported his crops.

Andrew could not and should not have done it alone; like Jefferson, Crèvecoeur valued farming for the social bonds as well as for the independence it fostered. It is when Andrew is made overseer of the county road and serves on petty juries that we know he was successful. He had arrived at his goal himself only when the land surrounding his farm was also finally settled; "instead of being the last man towards the wilderness, [he] found himself in a few years in the middle of a numerous society." And the process was to continue, for "he helped others as generously as others had helped him." (p. 90)

For Crèvecoeur, loners, as opposed to self-reliant individualists, threatened civilization itself. He condemned as the dregs of American society those isolated inhabitants of the wilderness become idle, licentious hunters who hated their neighbors and, living alone far from churches and schools, had themselves become wild, "ferocious, gloomy and unsociable." (p. 57) Neither a Rousseau nor a Chateaubriand, Crèvecoeur sought to disabuse his European readers of romantic notions about man in the state of nature. In the backwoods of America, he told them, there reigns "a perfect state of war";

> that of man against man . . . that of man against every wild inhabitant of these venerable woods, of which they are come to dispossess them. There men appear to be no better than carnivorous animals of a superior rank, living on the flesh of wild animals when they can catch them . . .
>
> (p. 52)

and on pilfering from each other when they can't. So that when he regretted his insufficient attention earlier to the social connection, he did not mean that he had ever thought that men should or could live alone. Far from it: isolation had always been for him not merely inconvenient, but a threat to his identity as a rational civilized being. Finding himself cut off from his community by the advent of the Revolution, he would become aware that the houses in his settlement lay "at a considerable distance from each other," (pp. 204-5) and that the wilderness, the "hideous wilderness," (p. 222) was all about. In the contemplation of this wilderness he wrote poignantly, "I feel as if my reason wanted to leave me, as if it would burst its poor weak tenement." (p. 204)

To be human, one needs human ties; to be a man, one must be entirely independent. Crèvecoeur resolved this paradox to his own satisfaction through his family. Having found farming dull in his youth, he came with maturity to appreciate its solid virtues. He reported having for a time considered leaving the land, but then

> I married, and this perfectly reconciled me to my situation; my wife rendered my house all at once cheerful and pleasing; it no longer appeared gloomy and solitary as before; when I went to work in my fields I worked with more alacrity and sprightliness; I felt that I did not work for myself alone, and this encouraged me much. My wife would often come with her knitting in her hand, and sit under the shady trees, praising the straightness of my furrows, and the docility of my horses; this swelled my heart and made everything light and pleasant, and I regretted that I had not married before.
>
> (p. 28)

It is not what is included in this idyll that is striking, so much as what it leaves out, which is any suggestion of going outward from the familial nucleus, of ties or activities beyond the family. Instead, the economic sphere for one is subsumed to the domestic; Crèvecoeur's wife is more often pictured coming out to the fields than he home to her, the metaphorical point of these meetings being to project the structure of his world and to measure its extent, which world is amply co-extensive with his family. Ideally society could be made up of such families related to each other by analogy and proximity while remaining separate and self-defined. To achieve this ideal state, those who are already established have a social duty, which works also in their own interest, to help others through temporary and reversible familial relations to achieve equal status, one mature family aiding another weak or fledgling as a father would his son. Such aid is a recurrent motif in the *Letters.* Andrew rises by being raised by parental figures who educate, equip, and stake him as he will do equally for the next "generation" of immigrants and for his sons. For America's brightest promise to the worthy is prosperity for their children, which "to every good man . . . ought to be the most holy, the most powerful, the most earnest wish he can possibly form, as well as the most consolatory prospect when he dies." (p. 73)

Therein lay Crèvecoeur's social vision of a benevolent America which nurtured each immigrant to a fulfilled manhood he then manifested by nurturing his children in turn. It is important that this fusion of private and public realms in one code of personal behavior not invoke medieval associations. If there were signs in the eighteenth century of a feudal revival in America, Crèvecoeur would have had none of it.[5] For him, the private and the public came together not in any external common domain, but in the inner man, whence they were projected into a politics of private morality generalized. So the excellent Bertram of the eleventh letter, a botanist exemplifying Crèvecoeur's notion of the social good as validated by nature, is a kindly but firm father to his brood of children, women, and blacks, all of whom he will try to raise to fulfill their potentials. Conversely when the Revolution seemed to have destroyed all hope of peace and order, Crèvecoeur's survival plan was, by his lights, less quixotic than it might appear. Gathering his distraught wife and children, taking with him husbands for his daughters, he planned to settle among the Indians and there, reconstituting his family and even ensuring its descendance, he would regenerate a micro-civilization. Civilization, in short, was the family writ large.

The contrast with Robinson Crusoe is compelling: when Defoe wanted to recreate society, he provided Crusoe with his man Friday; Crèvecoeur took a wife. Though there is a certain analogy between the captive worker and the subservient wife, the difference between them nonetheless has significant ideological implications. For Defoe, the world was a marketplace organized around the basic relation of propertied and propertyless whose hired labor enriches the former and maintains them in their status. Thus property owners benefit from the relative poverty of the lower classes. To put it simply, if Friday's share were to grow as fast as, or faster than Crusoe's profits, Crusoe would lose by it. He extends his holdings only when Friday gets back less than the wealth he generates. However productive, and whether or not beneficial for Friday or for society as a whole, this is an intrinsically competitive situation. But Crèvecoeur's relationship to his wife was not so overtly competitive. Indeed for his part, he perceived the relation as entirely complementary, between himself and just another aspect of himself. (How his wife saw it, of course, may be another story, or another history.) By the shift in Crèvecoeur's eighteenth-century world from the extended family to the individual as the unit of social identification, married women became more than ever identified with and through their husbands. It never occurred to Crèvecoeur that his wife might have interests other than his own, let alone competing interests. Thus there is a profound difference within middle-class thinking, between defining society in familial or in economic terms. In Defoe's world view, the economic model was all pervasive and defined family relations well. But as a projection directly of the family, in the way Crèvecoeur envisioned society, that model appeared far less competitive, if also less dynamic, than it did either on Addison's Royal Exchange or in the shops of Franklin's Philadelphia. Both Exchange and shops, as well as Crusoe's island, would have appalled Crèvecoeur, whose social ideal reigned instead on another island, in peaceful, quiet, and cooperative Nantucket.

For a book about farmers, the *Letters* spends a surprising amount of time on Cape Cod. Five of the twelve are about Nantucket and Martha's Vineyard, and their repetitiveness suggests that their real meaning for him may have lain deeper than Crèvecoeur could quite articulate. Overall, he seems to have seen Nantucket as the essence of Americanness, as it abjured the corruption and decadence of Europe. "How happy are we here, in having fortunately escaped the miseries which attended our fathers," he exclaimed in the opening of the Cape Cod letters. He predicted that as the tyrants of Europe raged on, "this country, providentially intended for the general asylum of the world, will flourish by the oppression of their people; they will every day become better acquainted with the happiness we enjoy, and seek for the means of transporting themselves here. . . ." Now, if the theme is already familiar from other contemporary writings, its treatment was somewhat unusual, for Crèvecoeur's "asylum" was a rocky sand-bar "barren in its soil, insignificant in its extent, inconvenient in its situation, deprived of materials for building. . . ." The significant point is that he regretted none of these shortcomings, on the contrary seeing them as the source of Nantucket excellence. It seemed to him that the

island had "been inhabited merely to prove what mankind can do when happily governed." With "freedom . . . skill . . . probity . . . and perseverance," by their own "vigorous industry," unhindered but unaided, the people of Nantucket "have raised themselves from the most humble, the most insignificant beginnings, to the ease and the wealth they now possess." Crèvecoeur insisted on the arduousness of their effort, appearing gratified even that poor soil had kept them from farming. Instead of a nurturing earth, "they plough the rougher ocean, they gather from its surface, at an immense distance, and with Herculean labours, the riches it affords; they go to hunt and catch that huge fish which by its strength and velocity ought to be beyond the reach of man."

What they have shown is that nothing is beyond the reach of men free to pursue their dreams. This was Crèvecoeur's creed:

> Give mankind the full rewards of their industry, allow them to enjoy the fruits of their labour under the peaceable shade of their vines and fig-trees, leave their native activity unshackled and free like a stream without dams or other obstacle. . . .
>
> (pp. 94-98)

Such eloquence is far from his usual style, however, and he was at his most reserved in describing those rewards. Then he spoke of "decent plainness" (p. 119), neatness, and simplicity, several times describing the dress and houses of Nantucket's Herculean labourers as "simple, useful and unadorned." (p. 116) Earlier he had praised, as a happy contrast to the showy luxury of European houses, "the pleasing uniformity of decent competence [that] appears throughout our habitations." (p. 46) Finally, this insistence on plain living comes to exceed the standards of middle-class prudence and we begin to realize that he objected not only to spending but to having as well: only the process of getting aroused his enthusiasm, the labor more than its fruits. He had no interest in superabundance, or in accumulation *per se,* were it of goods or profits; "living with decency and ease" in "plentiful subsistence" (p. 95) was the decidedly limited goal of Crèvecoeur's model American, and his own:

> I have never possessed, or wish to possess any thing more than what could be earned or produced by the united industry of my family. I wanted nothing more than to live at home independent and tranquil, and to teach my children how to provide the means of a future ample subsistence, founded on labor, like that of their father.
>
> (p. 217)

Thus despite unlimited willingness to work, and his rejection of any external limits to the self, Crèvecoeur might almost be said to have lacked ambition. He had enlarged his definition of subsistence and ease to the American scale, but he neither looked nor aspired much beyond the strict fulfillment of necessity. In speaking of the unceasing activity he saw all around him, Crèvecoeur referred to it approvingly as "restless industry" (p. 19), a phrase with no progressive implications, projecting only continual hard work. With his family as his world rather than a home-base for forays *into* the world, Crèvecoeur's was a truncated, partial kind of middle-class ethos. According to this ethos, individualism manifests itself through independence and self-assertion but not (yet) in social power or accumulated wealth. (We should recall Crèvecoeur's context among Pennsylvania farmers whose sense of equality sprang from respective self-sufficiency, to appreciate how resonant this distinction between self-assertion and social power may have been.)

In Crèvecoeur's logic, equality had egalitarian implications, for how could a man be independent if he were not actually as well as potentially equal? But for all its idealism, this primitive individualism was necessarily transitory, for it became impractical in even the most fledgling of market societies. Indeed Crèvecoeur found all markets repugnant. They were inevitably theaters for theft: "if it is not (in that vast variety of bargains, exchanges, barters, sales, etc.,) *bellum omnium contra omnes,* 'tis a general mass of keenness and sagacious action against another mass of equal sagacity, 'tis caution against caution. Happy when it does not degenerate into fraud against fraud!" I cited earlier his description of the wilderness as a "perfect state of war . . . of man against man."

In any case, the hustle and bustle of the marketplace had no charms for him, as his essay on "Manners of the Americans" makes very clear. It was not published in the *Letters* but with the more ambivalent *Sketches of Eighteenth-Century America.* Like the first letters, it depicts the evolution of an American settler from initial step into the wilderness to prosperous establishment as a foremost citizen of the region. But unlike Andrew and his kind, this farmer acts alone; no paternal neighbors help him and he has no intention of helping others. When he arrives at the point of selling crops or leasing land, he will drive the hardest bargain he can and not balk at a little cheating. He gouges interest and forecloses on mortgages; eventually he expands to become a general merchant, and "this introduces him into all the little mysteries of self-interest, clothed under the general name of profits and emoluments."

> He sells for good that which perhaps he knows to be indifferent because he also knows that the ashes he has collected, the wheat he has taken in may not be so good or so clean as it was asserted. Fearful of fraud in all his dealings and transactions, he arms himself, therefore, with it.

Crèvecoeur would have had difficulty with our nostalgia for the country-store. "Very probably," he warned, the farmer-merchant will be "litigious, overbearing, purse-proud," and irreligious because religion is neither convenient nor useful; he cares only about himself, and in this setting, even his devotion to his family takes on an equivocal character. "To him," Crèvecoeur wrote, "all that appears good, just, equitable has a necessary relation to himself and his family."[6] He would have reversed the formula

in describing farmer James or Andrew the Hebridean: all that was related to the welfare of their families *was* good, just, and equitable. The difference seems to lie between the self and the family in the non-competitive, egalitarian terms of farming, and the same concepts qualified by the necessities of a mercantile context.

The figure of the farmer-merchant retrospectively highlights a peculiar aspect of the yeoman hero in the earlier letters. One wonders whether Crèvecoeur then had excluded all trading and market activities from his account of the farmer's life in order not to taint his ideal vision. Otherwise the lack of any commerce in the agrarian idylls of the *Letters,* where neighbors exchange goods and services but never seem to sell them, remains puzzling. The issue is not money, which we would expect to be scarce in a rural economy, but profit. Crèvecoeur's model farmers achieve ease and plentiful subsistence, they gain respect and standing in the community, they earn their way, but they do not earn profits: for Crèvecoeur, this would have amounted to profiteering.

Thus anyway he argued in a sketch called "The American Belisarius," significantly written after the outbreak of the Revolution. The original Belisarius rose from the rank of servant to become the Emperor Justinian's chief general. He enjoyed something of a vogue in the late eighteenth century and was said by Sir William Temple to have been one of seven men in history who were worthy to be monarchs but weren't. The victim of endless intrigue, he reportedly refused to abuse his power to punish his enemies, while maintaining an unswerving loyalty to his Emperor. Gibbon was not certain whether the patience with which Belisarius endured his rivals' insults proved him more or less than a man; but for Crèvecoeur, the Roman's endurance and loyalty and withal the inherent superiority he refused to exploit—so that he lost his home and fortune finally without ever losing his temper—clearly made him the *beau idéal* of the American Loyalist.[7] His worthy American counterpart, S. K., had gone out to the frontier as a young man and built up a remarkably flourishing farm. As he grew rich, he did not forget his family, and duly settled his two brothers-in-law on neighboring lands where, with his help, they too were soon thriving. "Their prosperity, which was his work, raised no jealousy in him," wrote Crèvecoeur, finding it all a "pastoral and edifying spectacle: three brothers, the founders of three opulent families, the creators of three valuable plantations, the promoters of the succeeding settlements that took place around them." Here was the fulfillment of Crèvecoeur's ideal, the family generating a community of equals who progress through the kind of mutual assistance which leaves each one freely possessive of his own home and hearth. With the coming of more settlers to the region, however, certain complications do develop. "It was not to be expected that they could all equally thrive. Prosperity is not the lot of every man; so many casualties occur that often prevent it." How can the familial model deal with such casualties? What can a democratic society do with its inevitable inequalities? S. K. again points the righteous way. In hard times he opens his granary to his neighbors:

he lends them hay; he assists them in whatever they want; he cheers them with good counsel; he becomes a father to the poor of this wilderness. They promise him payment; he never demands it.

For Crèvecoeur what was most telling is his not demanding payment, for this is the touchstone of S. K.'s morality. He refuses to enter the marketplace. He has the largest stock of grain in the area, prices are soaring and traders approach him with tempting offers, but he rejects them saying,

> "I have no wheat . . . for the rich, my harvest is for the poor. What would the inhabitants of these mountains do were I to divest myself of what superfluous grain I have?"[8]

We will pay you at once, they argue, while these poor will make you wait indefinitely. He answers that he cannot let his neighbors starve.

If S. K. will not sell, neither does he buy. At harvest time he requires no hired help, for the grateful folk come from all around to gather in the "patriarchal harvest." S. K.'s patriarchism is in no sense feudal though Crèvecoeur's use of traditional terms to suggest the deeper validity of this moral code may obscure its anti-aristocratic assumptions. But just as the Roman Belisarius was a model *because* he was born a commoner, S. K. is called "princely" only to suggest that none on earth is more deserving of the title than a "good substantial independent American farmer," such as he is and remains to the end. His aim in helping his indigent fellows is not to earn their fealty but their friendship, by freeing them into self-sufficiency. He is no better than his neighbors except in the sense that he represents their common type at its best, and when he rejects the merchants' offer, it is not out of a sense of *noblesse* but of common humanity. There is nothing contradictory to democratic thought in this stance as such. Familial patriarchs after all are as congruent with middle-class societies as a patriarchal nobility was with the feudal system, the modern family being essentially a small fiefdom, as the old adage has it that proclaims a man's home as his castle. What *is* unusual about S. K. is that he plays the role of noble father not only to his family but to the community at large. In this way he represents Crèvecoeur's democratic familialism, whose ennobling patriarchism had neither the source nor the purpose of the feudal aristocratic variety. In modern terms, the alternative of such a kindly father would be neither wicked king nor faithless lord, but just such a gouging, thieving merchant as the one featured in "Manners of the Americans."

Indeed, Crèvecoeur's earlier list of the European evils that America has averted included, in addition to aristocrats, kings and bishops, "great manufacturers employing thousands." (p. 46) The old aristocracy was not the only one that he deplored. In a discussion of the unfortunate spread of tea drinking in America (when native herbs are plentiful and better for you), he shook his head over a newer breed of lords:

It was necessary that our forefathers should discover and till this country in order that their prosperity might serve to enrich a parcel of London merchants who though but citizens in England, yet are nabobs in India; who though mighty fond of liberty at home for themselves and their children, yet do not choose that other people should enjoy these great benefits in their Indian dominions. The idea of merchants becoming sovereigns, lords and tyrants . . . but a poor American farmer must not say all he thinks.[9]

What he saw as best about America—or more to the point, what had been best about it before the Revolution—was that a good man could become wealthy without engaging in imperialism or even commerce: without having to deprive his equals of the substance he acquires.

Crèvecoeur's agrarianism may have been based on the view that only farming could produce wealth without exploitation. Like the Physiocrats by whom he was influenced, he believed that only the land produces value, so that all other means of acquiring it must amount to theft—hence the fraudulent merchant. Quesnay and the Physiocrats envisioned a stable, rationalized France of cultured farmers who leased their lands and derived a comfortable subsistence, with enough over to feed the minority necessarily engaged in non-agricultural tasks. But in the American context of expansion and open-ended growth, even the modest Crèvecoeur sensed that something more was needed. Though his aspirations were limited, they were still grander than those of his European counterparts. He recognized as much with satisfaction. He therefore modified the Physiocrat program by having American farmers eventually own their land, explaining that Europe was crowded and its lands long since taken up, but that the New World remained accessible to all.

But he knew too that this concept of "equal divisions of the land offered no short road to superior riches." To speak to the American situation, he needed to represent a possibility for even larger expansion which would still remain free of the mercantile taint. That is why Nantucket was so important to him. It seemed to embody a solution to the otherwise pervasively corrupting paradox of equality and competition. For the sailors who "plough the rougher ocean," do have thereby a "short road to superior riches," which is as free from fraud as is agriculture. Like a plentiful harvest too, the sudden windfall of a good catch neither derives from nor generates pernicious social inequalities. Among the people of Nantucket,

> the gradations [of wealth] are founded on nothing more than the good or ill success of their maritime enterprises, and do not proceed from education; that is the same throughout every class, simple, useful, and unadorned like their dress and their houses.

But having an equal start and maintaining a relatively equal lifestyle does not yet comprise the fundamental equality which Crèvecoeur was after. He realized that this had to do more with the structure of the economy itself than with the way individuals entered into it. Not only do the free men of Nantucket begin their accumulation of property as equals, none having significantly more than any other, but the property they seek is such that it is continually accessible to each of them. The "necessary difference in their fortunes" does not cause among Nantucketers "those heart burnings, which in other societies generate crime," because "the sea which surrounds them is equally open to all, and presents to all an equal title to the chance of good fortune." (pp. 116-17) They get their riches from the sea, not from each other, so that no one person's income, however large, in any way lessens another's. Moreover, by using the limitless ocean to represent capital, Crèvecoeur avoided all the implications of scarcity, and could reconcile the inequalities generated by the unregulated individualistic enterprise that he considered the expression of freedom, with his moral conviction that the means for such enterprise must be equally available. In Nantucket one doesn't need to engage in fierce competition in order to grow rich; one grows rich beside one's neighbors, working hard privately but in harmony with them.

This unique instance of transcendent enterprise, however, only underlined Crèvecoeur's general rejection of the commercial nexus. For him the marketplace did not make for a better product, but for the ferocities of the jungle. Just such a jungle (to return to the case of the unhappy American Belisarius) was what the Revolution seemed to Crèvecoeur to be creating in America. The story of S. K. ends sadly. Having rejected the blandishments of usurious commerce, and having sought only to mind his farm and to assist others in minding theirs, that good man still tries to keep his private counsel when the fighting breaks out. But privacy is no longer allowed; "as a citizen of a smaller society," Crèvecoeur wrote in the throes of the war, "I find that any kind of opposition to its now prevailing sentiments, immediately begets hatred." (p. 207) The envious and greedy gather, S. K.'s brothers-in-law see an opportunity to vent their jealousy, local merchants want to see him forced to buy and sell, less advantaged farmers just want his land. Eventually he is driven from his burned-out farm into the wilderness. The leaders of the Revolution may have had more inspired motives, Crèvecoeur speculated, but the effect of their bid for freedom was to enslave everyone else. Shortly before he is totally despoiled, S. K. receives a group of local yeomen who come as usual to ask him for help over the long winter. Among them he recognizes some who have been persecuting him. They haven't wanted to, they explain, but what could they do? The weakness which has brought them to his door also makes them subject to all the petty tyrants the war has unleashed. S. K. understands their plight, and distributes the last of the grain.

What *we* come to understand is the necessity for a strong overall authority, equally restrictive of all to keep each man free of his equals. Crèvecoeur had hoped once that a benevolent environment would render its inhabitants equally benevolent. He had thought then that men might live together virtually without external authority. Again

Nantucket represented the best of all governments, one which simply left people alone:

> solemn tribunals, public executions, humiliating punishments, are altogether unknown. I saw neither governors, nor any pageantry of state; neither ostentatious magistrates, nor any individuals cloathed with useless dignity: no artificial phantoms subsist here either civil or religious; no gibbets loaded with guilty citizens offer themselves to your view; no soldieries are appointed to bayonet their compatriots into servile compliance.
>
> (p. 115)

The positive advantages of such governance are all negative, and Crèvecoeur would rather have done without it altogether. Unfortunately, even in the New World, many men have remained like those cattle who, "conscious of their superior force, will abuse it when unrestrained by any law, and often live on their neighbors' property." (p. 237) Therefore, "the law is to us precisely what I am in my barn yard, a bridle and check to prevent the strong and greedy, from oppressing the timid and weak." (p. 34) In Nantucket as everywhere, there are times when the weak must be protected from the strong, and thus "the law at a distance is ever ready to exert itself in the protection of those who stand in need of its assistance." (p. 115)

"At a distance": the phrase was all-important to Crèvecoeur, it was the key to his outlook. If we recall that he defined personal identity entirely in terms of self-possession and property, it becomes evident that he must have viewed external authority per se as inevitably problematical. It had to be all-inclusive and absolute; it also had to be non-interfering, indeed non-engaging. Across a dangerous ocean, thousands of miles away, the crown of England was the best solution imaginable. It was "the law at a distance" incarnate.

Earlier Crèvecoeur had made the ideal explicit:

> Where is that station which can confer a more substantial system of felicity than that of American farmer, possessing freedom of action, freedom of thoughts, ruled by a mode of government which requires but little from us. . . .
>
> (pp. 28-9)

Pre-revolutionary America, therefore, enjoyed the "general Happiness" which "proceeds from a government which does everything for us and requires little or nothing in return."[10] And Crèvecoeur's personal situation represented that blissful state perfectly: "I owe nothing, but a peppercorn to my country, a small tribute to my King, with loyalty and due respect." (p. 28) If the Whigs found English intrusion in America unbearable, Crèvecoeur clearly did not share their view. A few taxes seemed to him to mean relatively little compared to the secure freedom of the Nantucket sailors who ply the seas as they will:

> a collector from Boston is the only King's officer who appears on these shores to receive the trifling duties which this community owe to those who protect them,

and under the shadow of whose wings they navigate to all parts of the world.

(p. 117)

His ideal government had little impact on the local activities of individuals; its role was global, and on that scale, absolute.

This notion that maintaining equal freedom requires a strong central authority did not originate with Crèvecoeur, of course. The case had long since been made by Hobbes, among others, whose account of man in the state of nature Crèvecoeur essentially echoed, while capturing also in his barnyard image the flavor of Hobbes' view of civilized man. Moreover, Hobbes was not alone in believing that this authority was best embodied in an absolute monarch. In the next century and in another country Giambattista Vico considered it only logical that societies desiring to institutionalize "natural equity" would be ruled typically by

> monarchs who have accustomed their subjects to attend to their private interests, while they themselves have taken charge of all public affairs and desire all . . . subject to them to be made equal by the laws, in order that all may be equally interested in the state.[11]

These founding theoreticians of modern liberal society thus projected a concept of monarchy which was neither that of feudalism nor the Renaissance. This monarchy is subject-centered, justifying itself as the guarantor of the subjects' rights. Such a concept in no way precludes liberal democracy. On the contrary, the extent of that democracy—its potential for including more and more people like Andrew the Hebridean, who work their way from indenture to a full-fledged property-owning selfhood—seems to depend on the monarch's being altogether absolute, and thus out of reach of manipulation: hence Crèvecoeur's enthusiasm for King George.[12]

It was Locke who introduced the possibility that a democratic society might instead govern itself. The base of that governance would rest on the ordering force of the market, now conceived as an arena of class rather than of purely individual activity. Having accepted the accumulation of larger amounts of property than one could use on the grounds that its translation into capital and subsequent reinvestment redounded to the general welfare, Locke foresaw this process generating a consensus among the investors which might be institutionalized contractually, and generalized into government. The participants in this consensus should be able to agree on the rules of the game.

This is where one sees the relationship between S. K.'s refusal to deal with the grain merchants and his vulnerability to the greedy mob. Crèvecoeur himself was only vaguely aware of this relationship, not quite seeing that S. K. needs the King but that the merchants do better without him, their rights safeguarded by contracts, and by a contractual society whose law and order is suited to their entrepreneurial needs. Crèvecoeur's failure to understand the func-

tion of local laws and contracts was expressed more clearly in his hatred of lawyers. "What a pity," he exclaimed, "that our forefathers who happily extinguished so many fatal customs, and expunged from their new government as many errors and abuses, both religious and civil, did not also prevent the introduction of a set of men so dangerous." (p. 146) They plagued America like the clergy did Europe. This was an acute comparison, lawyers being the interpreters of the new order as the clergy were of the old. Crèvecoeur, who had hoped that the world might at last be free of all impingements of personal freedom, but for a small set of permanent injunctions, saw lawyers reweaving entanglements all around.

The crux, then, of his disaffiliation with the Lockean compromise so well represented by the American Constitution was his rejection of the ethic of the marketplace. For the American revolutionaries, enlightened self-interest reflected the natural moral order, but to Crèvecoeur its mercantile expression was little better than theft. The sort of economic order he envisaged instead was evident in his appeal to American farmers to recognize the benefits of monarchy. Secure in your holdings and master of its fruits, he reminded the yeoman,

> thou needs't not tremble lest the most incomprehensible prohibitions shall rob thee of that sacred immunity with which the produce of thy farm may circulate from hand to hand until it reaches those of the final exporter.[13]

Once again, he defined freedom as being left alone; the right to trade is a "sacred immunity" from restraint. So might any merchant argue against restraints, but he would not do so just to have his product "circulate": what he would be after would be an increase in value at each transition, that *increase* not to be limited by "incomprehensible prohibitions." This view of the farmer's stake in the national economy translated the patriarchal-familial ethic into a paradoxical ideology we might term "monarchoanarchism." Crèvecoeur was an anarchist in the sense that he carried the notion of the political integrity of the individual to its logical conclusion. His definition of self-determination was thus more radical or more absolute than that which is commonly implied by democracy, because he could see in the accommodations of majority rule no advantages but only a loss of freedom for each individual.

Both in this libertarian aspect and in its egalitarianism, Crèvecoeur's thinking reflected his eighteenth-century agrarian experiences, but it might be seen also as a sort of pre-history to one important strain of nineteenth-century dissent. Populism invoked the yeoman ideal as the core of its program, associating the vision with Jefferson as powerful validation of its Americanism; but a loyalist Frenchman the Populists had probably never heard of would have been far more sympathetic both to their resentment of the rich and their conviction that markets were where the rich became ever richer. Although historians of the United States' War of Independence have long recognized that the patriots differed sharply among themselves about even the basic definition of democracy, by and large they have assumed that, as a group, those who favored the Revolution were more democratically inclined than those who opposed it.[14] The case of Crèvecoeur puts this assumption in doubt, and highlights such findings as those of Jackson Turner Main, that the largest single group of Loyalists were, like Crèvecoeur, small independent farmers.[15] Yet these were the same "self-reliant, honest and independent" yeomen who became "the backbone of Jeffersonian democracy" and later "the common man of Jacksonian rhetoric."[16] Though such yeomen also swelled the Patriot ranks, some significant number of them rejected Jefferson's promise of a country of their own and, if Crèvecoeur is at all representative, they did so because they feared it would be less free than colonial America, at least for their kind.

What all this indicates, I think, is a need to reconsider the structure of the Revolutionary debate that now represents the winners' assumptions. Crèvecoeur's usefulness lies in his accepting none of these and yet still making perfect sense. As a result he raises basic questions about the component values and ideas which the successful Revolution fused into one apparently organic whole. Crèvecoeur was independent while refusing to compete; a seeker after plentiful subsistence who rejected profits, and a supporter of the King because monarchy was for him the corollary of social equality. His opposition to the American Revolution was grounded in the principle that all men are created equal—and that so should they remain.[17] It was a basically localist, familial impulse which committed him to absolute monarchs. In these ways, he may be seen as representing an intermediate stage in the evolution of America's liberal political philosophy, or as a case in point for its paradoxical nature at any stage.

Notes

1. J. Hector St. John Crèvecoeur, *Letters from an American Farmer,* (Garden City: Dolphin, n.d.), 46-7. Subsequent references to the *Letters* appear parenthetically in the text.

2. See the biography by Julia Post Mitchell, *St. Jean de Crèvecoeur* (New York: AMS Press, 1966).

3. Rowland Berthoff and John M. Murrin find this to be the general historical consensus in their seminal essay, "Feudalism, Communalism and the Yeoman Freeholder," in Stephen G. Kurtz and James H. Hutson, eds., *Essays on the American Revolution* (Chapel Hill: Univ. of North Carolina Press, 1973), 261.

4. Despite his protestations to the contrary in the first letter, or rather because of the very language in which these are couched, it is clear that Crèvecoeur was no simple farmer, but a highly educated gentleman whose social and intellectual connections extended far beyond Pine Hill. But if his observations were thus unusually well-informed, this does not mean they were not as linked to the realities of Pine Hill and its environs as those of farmers who knew little of the world beyond. It is an interesting problem

whether the greater sophistication of one member of a community undermines his representativeness, or perhaps heightens it, by enabling him to articulate what his neighbors may only feel.

5. Such a revival, interrupted by the Revolution, is discussed by Berthoff and Murrin, "Feudalism, Communalism and the Yeoman Freeholder," 264-76. Indeed the experience of this revival and his opposition to it may well have contributed to Crèvecoeur's loyalism, for, led in Pennsylvania by Benjamin Franklin, the opponents of feudalism sought to persuade the English crown to rule the colony directly in lieu of large proprietors: thus would the monarchy protect the equality of its subjects.

6. Crèvecoeur, *Sketches of Eighteenth-Century America* (New York: Signet, 1963), 260-63.

7. William Smith, ed., *Dictionary of Greek and Roman Biography and Myth* (Boston and London, 1849), 479-80.

8. *Sketches,* 384-86.

9. Ibid., 308-09.

10. Ibid., 253.

11. *The New Science of Giambattista Vico,* translated from the Third Edition (1744) by Thomas Goddard Bergin and Max Harold Fisch (Ithaca: Cornell Univ. Press, 1970), 8.

12. James Henretta has made the interesting suggestion that another model for Crèvecoeur's notion of a distant monarch might be found in contemporary Deism. Again the issue addressed by the model is the assurance of order without intrusive controls.

13. *Sketches,* 259.

14. This seems to be the assumption even of those scholars such as Jesse Lemisch in his essay, "Jack Tar in the Streets: Merchant Seamen in the Politics of Revolutionary America," *William and Mary Quarterly,* 3 (July 1968), 371-407, who challenge the view that such men as Washington and Jefferson represented a revolutionary consensus that included all classes. The discovery that certain groups dissented from this consensus and sought to change the character of the Revolution to better represent their interests and social vision might suggest the possibility that some who felt misrepresented by its leadership may have demurred from the Revolution altogether.

15. Jackson Turner Main, *The Sovereign States, 1775-1783* (New York: New Viewpoints, 1973), 272-73. For a more complete treatment of the Loyalists see Chap. V, "The Tory Rank and File," in William H. Nelson, *The American Tory* (Boston: Beacon Press, 1971). Nelson argues that "Taking all the groups and factions, sects, classes, and inhabitants of regions that seem to have been Tory, they have but one thing in common: [being neither unusually rich, nor En-

glish, nor colonially connected] they represented conscious minorities, people who felt weak and threatened." (p. 91)

16. *Essays on the American Revolution,* 276.

17. What Crèvecoeur feared from the Revolution, what he had hoped America would never become, is just that Yankee society Richard L. Bushman describes emerging in Connecticut and setting the scene for the coming Revolution. It was a society in which "the avid pursuit of gain" had become an acceptable goal of life, which "found an honorable place for self-interest in the social order," and which interpreted that order as orderly competition. See Bushman, *From Puritan to Yankee: Character and Social Order in Connecticut, 1690-1765* (New York: Norton, 1970), 287.

Robert P. Winston (essay date 1984)

SOURCE: "'Strange Order of Things!': The Journey to Chaos in *Letters from an American Farmer,*" in *Early American Literature,* Vol. 19, No. 3, Winter, 1984, pp. 249-67.

[*In the following essay, Winston analyzes* Letters *as a romance, suggesting that such an analysis helps explain the apparent contradiction between the early optimistic letters and the pessimistic letters that appear at the end of the work.*]

When Hector St. John de Crèvecoeur first published *Letters from an American Farmer* in England in 1782, an advertisement described the letters as "the genuine production of the American farmer whose name they bear. They were privately written to gratify the curiosity of a friend and are made public because they contain much authentic information little known on this side of the Atlantic: they cannot therefore fail of being highly interesting to the people of England at a time when everybody's attention is directed toward the affairs of America" (27). For the next one hundred and seventy-five years the American reading public—at least that portion that remembered *Letters* at all—viewed Crèvecoeur's work largely as a straightforward natural and social history of young America. Such an attitude is, however, the product of a distorted view of *Letters*: it stresses the early, optimistic epistles at the expense of the bleaker closing sections of the work, and it fails to distinguish between Crèvecoeur and his protagonist, Farmer James.

More recent critics have come to understand the complex—and darker—nature of this supposedly simple work.[1] Among the richest suggestions made are the largely undeveloped claims by Albert Stone, Jr., that *Letters* is a "prototypical romance" (208) and by Harry B. Henderson III that it is "an epistolary romance of ideas" (4). Crèvecoeur's work *is,* in fact, a germinal romance and needs to

be examined as such. To make such a claim is not, of course, to argue that Crèvecoeur was necessarily fully conscious of romance archetypes as he wrote. Nevertheless, those points of contact between the structure and devices of *Letters* and those of romance in general will help explain more clearly the tension between Farmer James's early positive dreams and the final, darker vision against which those hopes are balanced.

To begin, a review of some of the most important features of romance is in order. In *The Secular Scripture: A Study of the Structure of Romance,* Northrop Frye argues that romance "moves from one discontinuous episode to another, describing things that happen to characters, for the most part, externally" (47) instead of creating a group of characters and building a plot from them:[2]

> The characterization of romance is really a feature of its mental landscape. Its heroes and villains exist primarily to symbolize a contrast between two worlds, one above the level of ordinary experience, the other below it. There is, first, a world associated with happiness, security, and peace; the emphasis is often thrown on childhood or on an "innocent" or pre-genital period of youth, and the images are those of spring and summer, flowers and sunshine. I shall call this the idyllic world. The other is a world of exciting adventures, but adventures which involve separation, loneliness, humiliation, pain, and the threat of more pain. I shall call this the demonic or night world. Because of the powerful polarizing tendency in romance, we are usually carried directly from one to the other.
>
> (53)

That these two worlds exist in *Letters from an American Farmer* is painfully obvious to James, to Crèvecoeur, and to the reader. Moreover, the epistolary structure of the work enables Crèvecoeur to switch abruptly from episode to episode, from the idyllic to the demonic. One need only examine the optimistic ending of Letter 8, the final letter in the Nantucket series, and contrast it to the deeply disturbing description of Charles Town and slavery in the very next letter to understand these shifts.

In generalizing further about literature, and especially romance, Frye notes: "There are four primary narrative movements. . . . These are, first, the descent from a higher world; second, the descent to a lower world; third, the ascent from a lower world; and fourth, the ascent to a higher world" (97). As an examination of the general patterns of *Letters* makes clear, Crèvecoeur's work partakes of more than one of these movements. The book opens with a discussion of whether the project of corresponding with Mr. F. B. should be undertaken at all. It moves to a presentation of America as idyll, a place where the European may begin again, may be redeemed from "demonic" Europe, and this process is demonstrated in Letter 3 with the example of Andrew the Hebridean. Letters 4-8 further illustrate the possibilities of America through an examination of Nantucket and Martha's Vineyard. With Letter 9, "On Charles Town and Slavery," the reader confronts the "demonic" side of America. This confrontation continues through the sequence about the snakes and hummingbirds in Letter 10, which offers further examples of cruelty and violence, this time in nature. With Letter 11 the work rises to the possibility of the idyll once again, but here a European traveler, not James, is the author. In the last letter, James returns to insist that he can once again enjoy life in America despite the Revolution. When he suggests that he and his family will escape to the West to begin again, he reaffirms his own hope for the ideal. The work ends only on a neutral note, however, because James's dream is constantly qualified by the intrusion of such realities as Indian attacks and the possible "Indianization" of his children.

A closer examination of the structure of **Letters** as a whole is necessary, however, in order to appreciate fully the ways in which romance elements structure this work. In Letter 1, Crèvecoeur establishes the fitness of both his narrator, Farmer James, and his subject matter, America. James is an appropriate narrator because he is a representative, practical American. He functions, in the language of Henry James, as a central consciousness, a locus for observation and understanding, but he does not select his own topics for discussion.[3] As the man of action, the doer, the farmer, James is carefully dissociated from learning and sophistication; instead, his European correspondent, Mr. F. B., must select the subjects: "Remember that you have laid the foundation of this correspondence; you well know that I am neither a philosopher, politician, divine, or naturalist, but a simple farmer" (43). By removing the onus of selection from James, Crèvecoeur retains his own freedom to control his work's structure while allowing his "simple farmer" to seem free from artifice. If James, the artless tiller of the soil, dwells too long on a particular aspect of American life, he is not to blame; it is not James's interests that are being consulted but those of a European with relatively little American experience. If, on the other hand, James is so disturbed by something that he seems to initiate a letter on his own, thereby violating his carefully established relationship with Mr. F. B., the reader should recognize Crèvecoeur's hand, pointing to the importance of some moral issue by manipulating his protagonist.[4] That is, by controlling the questions to which James responds, Crèvecoeur is able, in John C. Stubbs's words, "to order the random happenings of experience into artful patterns so that the reader [can] *comprehend* the experience—either intellectually or emotionally," much as the major American romancers of the nineteenth century would do (6).

In short, Crèvecoeur, the sophisticated literary craftsman, presents his materials in a studiedly unsophisticated form in order to ensure his reader's engagement and understanding. This can be seen, for example, when James insists repeatedly that in his letters he can write only as a humble planter: "It is true I can describe our American modes of farming, our manners, and peculiar customs with some degree of propriety because I have ever attentively studied them; but my knowledge extends no farther" (33). In fact, James's knowledge does extend further than this; he is a man with keen powers of observation and a highly curious mind. After all, when asked to talk about Nantucket and Martha's Vineyard, he is able to do so for five letters. Nonetheless, this insistence on James's limited knowledge constantly separates him from the learned European and confirms him as a kind of American Everyman, typical of his class and his nation. In this sense Crèvecoeur, in creating his protagonist, foreshadows that group of "historical romancers," described by Michael Davitt Bell, "who took their art seriously [and] tended to develop their materials symbolically. Perhaps 'representatively' would be a better word (as the Emersonian hero was to be a 'representative man'); characters and events, in historical romance, really *are* a part or example of what they represent, since history was itself regarded as, in a sense, a *representation* of moral truth" (6).

Just as James is established as an appropriate narrator, so America is shown as a fit subject. The New World, unlike the Old, is progressive, constantly presenting the American with both novel challenges and the materials to meet them. Rather than looking to someplace like Italy "to trace the vestiges of a once-flourishing people now extinct," James should look to America since there "everything would inspire the reflecting traveller with the most philanthropic ideas; his imagination, instead of submitting to the painful and useless retrospect of revolutions, desolations, and plagues, would, on the contrary, wisely spring forward to the anticipated fields of future cultivation and improvement, to the future extent of those generations which are to replenish and embellish this boundless continent" (36-37). In short, it is in America that James can "record the progressive steps of this industrious farmer throughout all the stages of his labours and other operations [rather] than examine how modern Italian convents can be supported without doing anything but singing and praying" (37).

In terms of romance structure, Letter 1 functions to establish the everyday world. That is, America as a subject for literature is delineated, but America as idyllic or demonic has yet to be presented. In Letter 2, "On the Situation, Feelings, and Pleasures of an American Farmer," the portraying of America as ideal place begins. The letter is devoted to James as representative American man. Although James begins by noting that "Good and evil . . . are to be found in all societies" (45), Letter 2 is really a treatment of why America is the best of all possible worlds for him. It quickly becomes clear that the farmer's happiness depends upon ownership of property (his farm) and a stable, secure environment, as he himself indicates when he asks, "What should we American farmers be without this distinct possession of that soil? It feeds, it clothes us; from it we draw even a great exuberancy, our best meat, our richest drink; the very honey of our bees comes from this privileged spot" (48). James realizes that he must contribute to his own security, and he describes the efforts he makes to regulate his barnyard, pointing out that it is a process analogous to the process of governing men: "the law is to us precisely what I am in my barnyard, a bridle and check to prevent the strong and greedy from oppressing the timid and weak. . . . Thus, by superior knowledge

I govern all my cattle, as wise men are obliged to govern fools and the ignorant" (51). At the same time that James presents this kind of governance as a positive image, the reader apprehends an implied danger. Crèvecoeur suggests here that James's entire system of living can be endangered if rule by wise men is overturned, as the coming Revolution will demonstrate. And, as we see later, James has no real defense against instability; once his farm is endangered, and thus made insecure, he is plunged helplessly into the chaotic night world of romance.[5]

The central illustration that James employs in Letter 2, the anecdote of the kingbirds and the bees, demonstrates precisely this problem and, in so doing, presents a microcosmic version of the larger patterns of ascent and descent that structure *Letters from an American Farmer*. James's loving, and in many ways idealized, description of his farm leads him to the tale of some of his bees that, by forsaking a group defense (a "military array") and "disband-[ing]" themselves (50), allow themselves to be captured and eaten by a marauding kingbird. Crèvecoeur thus shows that even within this idyllic world the demonic can suddenly intrude. In order to save his honey, James intervenes, killing the bird and rescuing his bees. While earlier critics like D. H. Lawrence have cited this passage as "a parable of the American resurrection" in which the democratic bees escape the kingbirds of Europe, the author actually foreshadows the "neutral" ending of *Letters* as a whole (27-28); after all, only 54 of the 171 bees James rescues from the stomach of the bird survive the attack, and, as James himself has pointed out, "nothing exists but what has its enemy" (49). When James is cast in the role of the bees by the events of the Revolution, when he must flee his beloved farm, there is no beneficent protector who can rescue him.[6] Moreover, when he finally strikes out on his own to save himself and his family, an action clearly parallel to that of the bees, his chances for success must be heavily qualified: the majority of the bees died.

In this episode, then, Crèvecoeur demonstrates the patterns of ascent (the establishment of the idyllic world of the farm) and descent (the intrusion of the destructive kingbird) that ultimately balance one another in the closing pages of *Letters from an American Farmer*. Therefore, while the prospects for James's future, and thus the future of the America he represents, are bright at this point, conflicts that foreshadow the appearance of a demonic world are already present. In Letter 3, the famous "What is an American?," however, the stress is even more on the positive. This section of *Letters* is really the apotheosis of the American farmer, a description of, to use Henry Nash Smith's phrase, "the heroic figure of the idealized frontier farmer armed with that supreme agrarian weapon, the sacred plow" (123). James traces the American farmer's success from the moment the immigrant lands in America, and the crucial point he makes again and again is that in America the immigrants find that "Everything has tended to regenerate them." In America "they are become men" while "in Europe they were as so many useless plants" (62-63).

But if all men have felt some regeneration, not all have attained what is for James the highest possible station, that of husbandman. Those who live along the coastline tend to be bold and enterprising; though they largely neglect the land and earn their livelihood from the sea, they tend to be good, honest men. For example, in Letters 4-8, a rather lengthy description of the life and customs of Nantucket and Martha's Vineyard, James portrays the residents as generally embodying the moral rectitude, industry, and selflessness that he describes as central to his life. Those who live along the frontier are entirely different, however, for "There men appear to be no better than carnivorous animals of a superior rank, living on the flesh of wild animals when they can catch them, and when they are not able, they subsist on grain" (66). For those men there is very little in the way of hope; they are outcasts from every society. The heart of James's America is, of course, the farmland between the sea and the frontier: "Those who inhabit the middle settlements, by far the most numerous, must be very different; the simple cultivation of the earth purifies them, but the indulgences of the government, the soft remonstrances of religion, the rank of independent freeholders, must necessarily inspire them with sentiments, very little known in Europe among a people of the same class. What do I say? Europe has no such class of men" (65).

In fact, the tripartite structure that Crèvecoeur sees shaping American landscape is roughly equivalent to the romance worlds defined by Frye. For example, while the sea coast is essentially positive, it is clearly not as beneficial to men as the middle landscape. That is, the coastline is like the everyday world of Letter 1, a new world of challenge and opportunity that is the first step on the road to the idyllic. In fact, in Letter 7 James even points out that large numbers of Nantucketers have emigrated both to New Garden in North Carolina and the Kennebec in what is now Maine, there establishing fruitful communities that seem to approach the ideal of his farm (139-42). The central area of husbandry seems equivalent to the idyllic world of romance. However, the fact that not all immigrants are successful here allows for the descent into the demonic or night world of the frontier where men constantly war with neighbors and with nature. Thus, when people emigrate to America, they enter a new world, leaving the nightmare of Europe. They then ascend to the idyllic farming community offered them if they are industrious and honest. If they are unable to sustain themselves in the morally upright communities of farmers, they are forced out into the wilderness, clearly a pattern of descent since people there are little more than carnivorous animals.[7]

While some may fail in America, by and large James is optimistic. In order to demonstrate the almost limitless possibilities of the continent, he provides the example of Andrew the Hebridean: "I therefore present you with the short history of a simple Scotchman, though it contain not a single remarkable event to amaze the reader, no tragical scene to convulse the heart, or pathetic narrative to draw tears from sympathetic eyes. All I wish to delineate is the progressive steps of a poor man, advancing from indigence to ease, from oppression to freedom, from obscurity and contumely to some degree of consequence—not by virtue of any freaks of fortune, but by the gradual operation of sobriety, honesty, and emigration" (84). What James wishes to do here is to make the experience of Andrew's Americanization comprehensible, to order the experiences of Andrew's life so that Mr. F. B. and the reader will apprehend the moral, social, and historical importance of the example. At the same time, Crèvecoeur presents a tale that in many of its outlines exemplifies the structure of romance, and thus the structure of *Letters* as a whole.

James traces Andrew's metaphorical route as he journeys out of the night world into the idyllic world of the middle landscape. If Europe is a figurative lower region for the American yeoman, the bustling cities of America's coast are only the first step up for the newly arrived immigrant. Confused and lost, the European can expect to experience pain, separation, and struggle in his new environment. Nonetheless, James is optimistic, constantly insisting that obstacles can be overcome; the idyll awaits after the trials of the night world, just as it has before, because "these are the struggles through which our forefathers have waded, and they have left us no other records of them but the possession of our farms" (85-86). James himself reaffirms his role as benefactor by aiding the ignorant Scotsman as he earlier helped his bees, on the principle that the wise must always lead the foolish. While Andrew is successful in farming and establishing a community with his neighbors, Crèvecoeur inserts several incidents that appear ironic in view of later letters. For example, Andrew's apparently humorous ineffectiveness in dealing with a band of Indians seems foreboding in light of both the Indian attacks described in Letter 12 and James's projected sojourn among an Indian tribe, especially because James will be almost as inexperienced on the frontier as Andrew was in his first encounter with "savages." Furthermore, while Andrew manages to become a member of his community, and thus to integrate himself and his family into the life of America, James will seek to avoid overly close contacts with his Indian neighbors. After all, the frontier is still a demonic world for James.

Despite these shadows, though, the story of Andrew the Hebridean basically involves a movement from the demonic worlds of Europe through Philadelphia to an idyllic farming community like James's own home. Andrew's history is really the story of James's father, the founder of James's fortune who rose above the negative elements of life on the frontier to become a morally and materially successful man.

It is at this point that James spends five letters (4-8) describing Martha's Vineyard and Nantucket. Why does Crèvecoeur spend so much time discussing the islands when he is really only restating virtues that he presented in Letters 1-3? He does so in order to establish the potential of the idyllic world as strongly as possible, to prevent its being completely vitiated by the less-satisfying aspects of life in America. He must do this since the next letter, Letter 9, introduces a society in which virtually all the earlier values of the colonies are denied. This abrupt shift from episode to episode is, of course, characteristic of the romance, enabling the author to order the experiences presented into a coherent moral pattern, and Crèvecoeur's moral position is made amply clear in a variety of ways. For example, he introduces a style of living that is utterly antithetical to earlier moderation:

> Charles Town is, in the north, what Lima is in the south; both are capitals of the richest provinces of their respective hemispheres; you may therefore conjecture that both cities must exhibit the appearances necessarily resulting from riches. . . . The inhabitants are the gayest in America; it is called the centre of our beau monde and is always filled with the richest planters in the province, who resort hither in quest of health and pleasure. . . . The climate renders excesses of all kinds very dangerous, particularly those of the table; and yet, insensible or fearless of danger, they live on and enjoy a short and a merry life. The rays of their sun seem to urge them irresistibly to dissipation and pleasure. . . .
>
> (160-61)

Charles Town's inhabitants are completely self-indulgent: in a climate in which excess is dangerous, they persist in excesses of all kinds, and they needlessly die young. Such attitudes mean that in James's view Charles Town is very close to Europe. Even his vocabulary reflects this idea when he writes of Charles Town as "the centre of our beau monde" and claims that the inhabitants "have reached the *ne plus ultra* of worldly felicity" (161). The farmer never resorted to French when describing Pennsylvania or Nantucket, and his constant stress on "riches," "luxury," "dissipation," and "pleasure" reinforces his criticism. Thus, Thomas Philbrick is correct when he writes that "Insofar as Letter IX contributes to the depiction of American experience, it functions to establish a foil to the sturdy and humane life of the farmers and fishermen of the North" (48).[8]

This connection between Charles Town and Europe is, of course, crucial to the romance structure of *Letters* as a whole since the city is yet another night world into which the unwary American may descend. James's language, then, suggests that Charles Town is a center of urban decadence, a moral wilderness that is every bit as dangerous as the physical wilderness examined in Letter 3. Indeed, James's constant comments on the "dissipation" and "pleasure" of the inhabitants of Charles Town should recall his earlier comments on the barbarous frontiersmen where he focused on *their* "idleness" and "frequent want of economy," as well as other faults, in condemning them: "When discord, want of unity and friendship, when either drunkenness or idleness prevail in such remote districts, contention, inactivity, and wretchedness must ensue" (66). Those who escape such a life do so as Andrew the Hebridean has done, or as James's own father did: "my father himself was one of that class, but he came upon honest principles and was therefore one of the few who held fast; by good conduct and temperance, he transmitted to me his fair inheritance, when not above one in fourteen of his contemporaries had the same good fortune" (67). Those who wish to escape the dangerous style of living in Charles Town must also embrace the principles of "good conduct and temperance" if they wish to pass on a "fair inheritance" to their descendants. In sum, all this suggests that the South, like the frontier, may be atypical of America for Crèvecoeur, but nonetheless it *is* part of the new land. While James's southern experience does not completely negate his earlier praise of America, it certainly qualifies that praise heavily. Letter 9 thus demonstrates in a most forceful manner that it is possible to descend into a demonic world at at least two points in America itself: on the frontier and in the South.

Charles Town is part of the night world not only because its climate is too luxurious, however. Rather, the climate combines with wealth to produce a class of people who build careers upon slavery, and it is slavery that embodies James's distrust of the South. In his eyes, southern slavery is so vicious because the planters are devoid of "kindness and affection" (163). While many northern men, including James himself, hold slaves, he views his blacks as happy inferiors who "participate in many of the benefits of our society without being obliged to bear any of its burthens" (165). While not excusing James's slave holding, the reader recognizes the sincerity of his hope that all slaves will soon be emancipated and is, like him, deeply offended by the unnecessary cruelty that he sees in and around Charles Town.

The result of James's trip to Charles Town is that James believes he has sunk into what is almost literally a nightmare world, and the closing episode of Letter 9, the tale of the caged Negro, clearly confirms this view. As James tells the tale, he is walking through the woods to dine with a planter. In the course of his journey, he encounters a Negro, in a suspended cage, who is almost dead, half-devoured by birds of prey. James fires at the birds and scares them off, only to have the man immediately attacked by insects. It is clear, too, that the birds will soon return to continue their grisly feast. This scene is really the cause of all James's troubled thoughts. As he points out when he begins the anecdote, "The following scene will, I hope, account for these melancholy reflections and apologize for the gloomy thoughts with which I have filled this letter: my mind is, and always has been, oppressed since I became a witness to it" (171). The kinds of imagery used to develop this narrative sequence are crucial. For example, the fact that the Negro is being devoured by birds and insects darkly echoes the episode in Letter 2 in which James destroys a kingbird and liberates some bees. Here James cannot intervene to rescue the Negro: he runs out of ammunition before he can do for a man what he did for lowly honeybees in the North on his farm. His impotence defines the debilitated state in which James finds himself in this demonic world. It is a moral wasteland in which his beliefs and desires are assaulted, thwarted, and finally defeated, and these attacks are a measure of the loss of the

idyll. The fact that the positive values that James spent eight letters developing can be undercut in only one is a mark of the fragility of the idyll.

If Letter 9 destroys much of what has been done prior to this point, does Letter 10 continue the destruction or does it attempt to restore the idyll's power? In fact, just as the Nantucket section of the book expands and illustrates the idyllic world of James's farm, Letter 10, which also takes place there, expands and further proves the existence of the demonic world.[9] The chapter consists of two parts, a discussion of snakes and a discussion of hummingbirds, both of which force the reader to recognize the effect of the South on James's whole outlook. What he now sees are destructive elements in nature which he can no longer control. In Letter 2, for example, James could talk about his role as law giver in his barnyard, and, when the demonic intruded, he could act to defend his idyllic existence, to save his bees. By the time of Letter 10 he can only act as an observer. He can only follow along behind the snake fight; he can only observe the hummingbird: "When it feeds, it appears as if immovable, though continually on the wing; and sometimes, from what motives I know not, it will tear and lacerate flowers into a hundred pieces, for, strange to tell, they are the most irascible of the feathered tribe" (178). This unexpected destruction again stresses his powerlessness before this new nature. In fact, the descriptions of both the snakes and the hummingbird reveal a man who is shattered before the mounting evidence of instability in his life. Just as he responded with exquisite pleasure to his farm in the early letters, he now responds with exquisite pain to the destruction of his dreams.

In an effort to reassure himself, James turns from his own experience of the demonic world and invokes John Bartram, a gentle man, a farmer, a Quaker. Admittedly James does not, perhaps cannot, write the description given in Letter 11 of life on Bartram's farm himself, but the fact that he clings so desperately to the idyll suggests the continuing power of James's earlier vision, despite the trials he has recently undergone. When James presents the letter as the writing of Ivan, a Russian gentleman, he once again allows the reader to see the idyll from the point of view of the man escaping the Old World and entering the New to be redeemed. The proxy visit to Bartram is, however, only an interlude, and the last letter, "Distresses of a Frontier Man," begins with James plunged once more into despair because "the hour is come at last that I must fly from my house and abandon my farm!" (194). The American Revolution is upon James. Once more the kingbirds of Europe assault the democratic bees of America, but here the assault of the demonic world is no longer parable (as it was in Letter 2), but reality, and in his final letter James reveals what happens to him when his world becomes unstable and insecure: "Whichever way I look, nothing but the most frightful precipices present themselves to my view, in which hundreds of my friends and acquaintances have already perished; of all animals that live on the surface of this planet, what is man when no longer connected with society, or when he finds himself surrounded by a convulsed and a half-dissolved one? . . . I feel as if my reason wanted to leave me, as if it would burst its poor weak tenement" (195).

But James's reason does not leave him in the course of *Letters from an American Farmer*; instead, he makes a choice. He decides to move west. James worries that his children may become "savages" rather than husbandmen, but he has chosen to live with a peaceful tribe of Indians, and he will do what he can to take his farm with him. Fearing that "the imperceptible charm of Indian education may seize [his] younger children," James argues that he has "but one remedy to prevent this great evil, and that is to employ them in the labour of the fields as much as I can; I have even resolved to make their daily subsistence depend altogether on it. As long as we keep ourselves busy in tilling the earth, there is no fear of any of us becoming wild; it is the chase and the food it procures that have this strange effect" (213-14). With all hope of remaining on his farm gone, the best James can do is head west and reassert the power of the idyll;[10] in this sense, the hope held out to Ivan in Letter 11, and to Europeans generally in Letters 2 and 3, is reaffirmed by the American farmer himself.

James's success remains in doubt, of course. He can only assert his plans, and he, like the reader, foresees dangers. In some respects, though, it is this very uncertainty that connects *Letters* to the coming tradition of the American romance. As Richard Chase points out on the first page of his study: "The American novel tends to rest in contradictions and among extreme ranges of experience. When it attempts to resolve contradictions, it does so in oblique, morally equivocal ways" (1). The ending of *Letters from an American Farmer* clearly conforms to Chase's generalization, and it does so for several important reasons. Frye points out that "most romances end happily": "This means that most romances exhibit a cyclical movement of descent into a night world and a return to the idyllic, or to some symbol of it like a marriage . . ." (54). More specifically, "the quest romance takes on a spiral form, an open circle where the end is the beginning transformed and renewed by the heroic quest" (174). This means that those values established in *Letters* that are associated with the idyllic world of James's farm, those that constitute the central myth of life in America that the work promulgates and defends, should be celebrated at the work's conclusion. After all, as James is told by his minister in Letter 1 when America is extolled as a place worthy of consideration, "Here everything would inspire the reflecting traveller with the most philanthropic ideas; his imagination, instead of submitting to the painful and useless retrospect of revolutions, desolations, and plagues, would on the contrary, wisely spring forward to the anticipated fields of future cultivation and improvement, to the future extent of those generations which are to replenish and embellish this boundless continent" (37). That is, theoretically America should still be what it was for Crèvecoeur in Letter 1, and what it became for those nineteenth-century romantic his-

torians like George Bancroft and Francis Parkman, a land whose history was clearly "progressive" (Bell 6-8).

By the time of Letter 12, however, Crèvecoeur must confront a contemporary historical dilemma: the revolution and "desolations," which he must take into account, are not "retrospective" but immediate, and he needs to explain what such a war means to the typical American husbandman who cannot fully understand the experience in which he finds himself involved. As James says, "The great moving principles which actuate both parties are much hid from vulgar eyes, like mine; nothing but the plausible and the probable are offered to our contemplation. . . . Great events are not achieved for us, though it is *by* us that they are principally accomplished, by the arms, the sweat, the lives of the people" (198). Thus, while Crèvecoeur's initial impulse leads him to employ some of the same structures his successors would use, he cannot distance himself sufficiently from his materials to see precisely how—or even whether—James's idyllic world will be "transformed and renewed" through the Revolution.

As Stubbs points out, "History gave the nineteenth-century romancer his simplest solution to the problem of artistic distance. A fictional work could be set off from the world of the reader through time. Such a work would have the advantage, over straightforward history, of fictional shaping" (28). Thus he could, as noted earlier, structure his materials in patterns so that the reader could "comprehend" those historical materials, not just as a sequence of discrete events, but as parts of a larger moral pattern that was the real subject of the romancer. Crèvecoeur, however, because of his own historical situation, must confront the Revolution with no mediating perspective, and, as a result, *Letters* can only end with the outcome of James's emigration unresolved, with the larger pattern finally unfinished. James can only convey as much of the experience as he can understand, and he clearly does not understand the Revolution.

The result of this, for Letter 12, is that the book closes with a prayer in which James asks God's mercy so that he and his family may once again find peace and happiness.[11] His prayer here evokes the prayer for the distressed Europeans James recites at the beginning of the anecdote of Andrew the Hebridean (83-84). Now the American farmer is as troubled and as frightened as the newly arrived Europeans. However, in asserting his faith in God, James once again raises the narrative of the book from the demonic to the level of the everyday world. In so doing, he has come to what Sacvan Bercovitch terms a "sense of intermediate identity, . . . an identity in progress, advancing from prophecies performed towards paradise to be regained" (143). That is, the representative American is about to start *Letters from an American Farmer* over again. What he succeeds in doing in Letter 12 is identical to what he did in Letter 1; he reconfirms that America is a fitting subject for consideration. Although the idyll is pushed further west, it is not completely vitiated because James maintains enough faith in it to set out again. Just as the European comes to America to escape the devastation of his home-land, so James sets out for the frontier, extending the path his father followed. At the end of *Letters from an American Farmer,* James is poised in the everyday world of romance, uncertain whether he can ascend to the idyllic world or will instead descend to the demonic.

Letters from an American Farmer leaves the reader poised as well—at the beginning of a developing tradition of American romance. As Crèvecoeur grappled with the ambiguities he saw in American history and culture, he created a series of structures to deal with those materials that are strikingly like those developed by Cooper, Hawthorne, and Melville. Behind what at first appears to be a series of separate treatments of diverse American subjects lies a larger pattern, what Stubbs calls "an ideal truth or an abstract universal pattern beneath the surface of reality" (13). Thus, while Crèvecoeur was not a theoretician of romance as was Hawthorne, he *was,* nevertheless, a conscious craftsman who was led by his American materials to structures that unmistakably anticipate major works of nineteenth-century fiction like *The Pioneers, The House of the Seven Gables,* and *The Confidence-Man.*

As a result, Crèvecoeur occupies a significant position in the development of American literature. One hundred and fifty years earlier, John Winthrop confidently proclaimed that the plantations of New England would "be as a city upon a hill" as long as he and his fellow settlers fulfilled the terms of their covenant with God, and he concluded his sermon with the injunction to move forward, to "choose life, / that we, and our seed, / may live; by obeying His / voice and cleaving to Him, / for He is our life and / our prosperity" (83-84). In 1630, Winthrop could assert what America should be. Almost one hundred and fifty years after the publication of *Letters from an American Farmer,* F. Scott Fitzgerald could see what America had become. Like Nick Carraway, Fitzgerald recognized that the "transitory enchanted moment" was gone, that one could no longer "[hold] his breath in the presence of this continent, compelled into an aesthetic contemplation he neither understood nor desired, face to face for the last time in history with something commensurate to his capacity for wonder." In 1925, Fitzgerald saw not progress, but regress, as his representative Americans "beat on, boats against the current, borne back ceaselessly into the past" (182). In 1782, Crèvecoeur struggled to develop a form through which he could show what America might still be. Like Cooper, Hawthorne, and Melville, Crèvecoeur was a man whose imagination was "shaped by the contradictions and not by the unities and harmonies of [American] culture" (Chase 1). Like his nineteenth-century successors, Crèvecoeur, too, turned to the romance to explore those contradictions, to investigate both the idyllic and the demonic sides of America, and thus to present his version of America's "intermediate identity" through his representative American.

Notes

1. David Robinson, for example, sees in *Letters* "a much greater balance between the dark and the light

side of human experience, even in the concluding letters" since he sees the work "as the story of the education of the narrator James, who is forced to sift out the relative values of 'civilized' or European society, and 'primitive' or American society at the book's close" (552-53). Mary Rucker sees the entire work shaped by "an important tension" between James, "whose humanitarianism is hardly more than self-indulgent sentimentality and whose approach to the natural and social orders is . . . strictly emotional," and Crèvecoeur himself, "a second consciousness, antithetical and corrective, [who] undercuts James's narrative reliability either implicitly through irony or explicitly through displacement" (193). For James Mohr, "the delineation of an ideal community is not Crèvecoeur's end purpose at all, but rather the first step in developing a larger pattern. The larger pattern is almost circular and involves not simply the fulfillment of social ideals but their failure as well. The idyllic image of America which Crèvecoeur develops during the first eight letters of his book becomes the dream against which the intensity of later disillusionment is measured" (355).

2. See also Chase (12-13).

3. Thomas Philbrick argues that "the letter writer functions not only as a reporter . . . but also as a literary character endowed with a particularized and significant sensibility, equipped with a background of past experience, and meaningfully involved in the world that his letters reveal" (75).

4. There has been considerable discussion of the epistolary form of *Letters,* with most critics arguing that the letters are, essentially, separate documents that produce a loose structure for the work as a whole. See Philbrick (75), Rapping (707-18), Plumstead (287), Marx (109), and Nye (35). For an especially full treatment of the relationship of James and Mr. F. B., see Béranger (73-85).

5. Philbrick, too, recognizes the importance of "order and stability" to James (78), and he writes of Letter 2 as a "fable of government" which "anticipates in many ways what we are later to learn of the society and government of America" (98). Joel Kehler, on the other hand, views James's barnyard as important in terms of his discussion of "self-interest" (208-09).

6. Stone also suggests the danger of James's "interven-[ing] like God in the natural order" (210).

7. For another discussion of the "moral geography" of *Letters,* to a different end, see Marx (107-16).

8. Philbrick also points out that "in Charleston, the New World is already grown old" (45). Henderson echoes this, arguing that the end of Letter 9 shows "the ideal of a society 'better' than that of Europe . . . pursued by the Nemesis of History" (6).

9. Other critics see Letter 10 as little more than a "charming interlude after the tense atmosphere of the

description of Charles Town" (Lewisohn xxii); see also Nye (41). Lawrence, on the other hand, sees the letter as "a fine essay, in its primal, dark veracity" (29).

10. Leo Marx, calling James an "exponent of the pastoral theory in America," says that even as the farmer "veers toward the primitive" he "reaffirms the ideal of the middle landscape" (113). Philip Beidler, on the other hand, contends that Ivan's letter is "largely a desperate rhetorical ploy . . . to shore up the impression of confidence created" earlier and that in the final letter, "confronted with the wreckage of his former assumptions, he envisions new possibilities for their enactment in a setting even further at odds with the realities he surveys, thereby committing himself at the last to the specious rigidities of a mind hopelessly trapped within the mythic designs of its own imaginings" (61). For readings of the conclusion as "disillusionment," see Nye (42-43), Mohr (362-63), Philbrick (85-88), and Rapping (714). Rucker argues that "Both Crèvecoeur and his persona end up where they began: James the incorrigible idealist and moral coward sustains the challenge to his assumptions and regains his comic view of the world; Crèvecoeur the pessimistic realist finds confirmation of his lack of faith in the benevolence of nature and in man and his social constructs" (211). Robinson's more charitable conclusion that Letter 12 forces a "refinement" of James's earlier view of the frontier, now "a place of hope rather than threat" (561), is much closer to my own.

11. Elayne Rapping notes that "The narrative ends where it started, then, with a vision of an agrarian democracy. But there is irony in James's renewed faith, for his reassertion of the model's ideals take [*sic*] the form of prayers rather than statements" (714).

Works Cited

Beidler, Philip D. "Franklin's and Crèvecoeur's 'Literary' Americans." *Early American Literature* 13 (1978): 50-63.

Bell, Michael Davitt. *Hawthorne and the Historical Romance of New England.* Princeton: Princeton Univ. Press, 1971.

Béranger, Jean F. "The Desire for Communication: Narrator and Narratee in *Letters from an American Farmer.*" *Early American Literature* 12 (1977): 73-85.

Bercovitch, Sacvan. *The Puritan Origins of the American Self.* New Haven: Yale Univ. Press, 1975.

Chase, Richard. *The American Novel and Its Tradition.* Garden City: Doubleday Anchor, 1957.

Crèvecoeur, Hector St. John de. *Letters from an American Farmer.* New York: The New American Library, 1963.

Fitzgerald, F. Scott. *The Great Gatsby.* New York: Scribners, 1925.

Frye, Northrop. *The Secular Scripture: A Study of the Structure of Romance.* Cambridge: Harvard Univ. Press, 1976.

Henderson, Harry B., III. *Versions of the Past: The Historical Imagination in American Fiction.* New York: Oxford Univ. Press, 1974.

Kehler, Joel R. "Crèvecoeur's Farmer James: A Reappraisal." *Essays in Literature* 3 (1976): 206-13.

Lawrence, D. H. *Studies in Classic American Literature.* New York: Viking, 1964.

Lewisohn, Ludwig. Introduction. *Letters from an American Farmer.* By J. Hector St. John de Crèvecoeur. New York: Fox, Duffield, 1904.

Marx, Leo. *The Machine in the Garden: Technology and the Pastoral Ideal in America.* 1964; rpt. New York: Oxford Univ. Press, 1967.

Mohr, James C. "Calculated Disillusionment: Crèvecoeur's *Letters* Reconsidered." *South Atlantic Quarterly* 69 (1970): [354]-63.

Nye, Russel. "Michel-Guillaume St. Jean de Crèvecoeur: *Letters from an American Farmer.*" *Landmarks of American Writing.* Ed. Henning Cohen. New York: Basic Books, 1969, 32-45.

Philbrick, Thomas. *St. John de Crèvecoeur.* New York: Twayne, 1970.

Plumstead, A. W. "Crèvecoeur: A 'Man of Sorrows' and the American Revolution." *Massachusetts Review* 17 (1976): 286-301.

Rapping, Elayne Antler. "Theory and Experience in Crèvecoeur's America." *American Quarterly* 19 (1967): 707-18.

Robinson, David. "Crèvecoeur's James: The Education of an American Farmer." *Journal of English and Germanic Philology* 80 (1981): 552-70.

Rucker, Mary E. "Crèvecoeur's *Letters* and Enlightenment Doctrine." *Early American Literature* 13 (1978): 193-212.

Smith, Henry Nash. *Virgin Land: The American West as Symbol and Myth.* 1950; rpt. Cambridge: Harvard Univ. Press, 1970.

Stone, Albert, Jr. "Crèvecoeur's *Letters* and the Beginnings of an American Literature." *Emory University Quarterly* 18 (1962): 197-213.

Stubbs, John Caldwell. *The Pursuit of Form: A Study of Hawthorne and the Romance.* Urbana: Univ. of Illinois Press, 1970.

Winthrop, John. "A Model of Christian Charity." In *The American Puritans.* Ed. Perry Miller. Garden City: Doubleday Anchor, 1956, 79-84.

John Hales (essay date 1985)

SOURCE: "The Landscape of Tragedy: Crèvecoeur's 'Susquehanna,'" in *Early American Literature,* Vol. 20, No. 1, Spring, 1985, pp. 39-63.

[*In the following essay, Hales discusses "Susquehanna," a portion of which appeared in* Sketches of Eighteenth-

Century America, *and which describes the destruction of Wyoming, a community in central Pennsylvania.*]

The last chapters of Hector St. John de Crèvecoeur's *Letters from an American Farmer* are characterized by what Moses Coit Tyler called a "note of pain" that, by Letter 12, "rises into something like a wail" (2:356). The rural bliss described in the first letters has been shattered by the violence and division of the American Revolution, and in Letter 12, "Distresses of a Frontier Man," James explains his intention to abandon his farm and find refuge in a wilderness Indian village. This final letter offers an account of his current unhappiness and a fearful anticipation of the dangers of frontier life, the most distressing of which is the possibility that he and his family might follow the pattern of degeneration he had earlier observed in the backwoods settlements. As a sort of ear plug to the siren song of primitivism, James plans to clear a small farm in the wilderness: "As long as we keep ourselves busy in tilling the earth," he reasons, "there is no fear of any of us becoming wild" (226). Most readers of *Letters* see this statement as the wishful thinking it is. Throughout the book, Crèvecoeur argues that geography determines, to a great extent, the nature of "the American, this new man"—"Men are like plants; the goodness and flavour of the fruit proceeds from the peculiar soil and exposition in which they grow" (50)—and he makes it clear that something terrible happens to human beings when they choose to live in wilderness. "By living in or near the woods," Crèvecoeur tells us of these frontier settlers, "their actions are regulated by the wildness of the neighborhood. . . . Is it then surprising to see men thus situated, immersed in great and heavy labours, degenerate a little?" (57-58).

The phenomenon of wilderness degeneration appears in another sketch as much more than an interesting fact of frontier life that becomes frighteningly relevant in the changed circumstances of Letter 12. **"Susquehanna,"** a long sketch that remained unpublished until 1925 and has yet to be published as the single piece Crèvecoeur intended, features wilderness degeneration as the cause of the destruction of an established and thriving American community. A narrative of three visits to Wyoming, a village on the banks of the Susquehanna River in central Pennsylvania, **"Susquehanna"** describes a small but promising settlement of 1774 that grows into a substantial example of American progress by 1776, only to become a burning ruin in the aftermath of the Wyoming Massacre of 1778. In describing the rise and fall of Wyoming, Crèvecoeur charts an American course of empire that anticipates such later treatments of the ubiquitous theory of civilization's cyclical stages as James Fenimore Cooper's *The Crater* and Thomas Cole's *The Course of Empire*. Arguing that the political context for the massacre is finally less responsible for Wyoming's tragic end than the community's geographical setting, Crèvecoeur responds to the American preoccupation with the past empires of Europe and the future empire of America by asserting that one of America's greatest assets—the exploitable wilderness of the North American continent—also represents the greatest threat to

its survival. In **"Susquehanna,"** Crèvecoeur takes the general problem of nature's destructive and degenerating potential that he discusses in *Letters* and applies it to the specific case of Wyoming. In doing so, he describes a bleak and focused possibility for America's future ruin: the sketch concludes with an apocalyptic vision of an American community swallowed and destroyed by a malevolent wilderness and its degenerated human inhabitants.

"Susquehanna" was composed in 1778, sometime between Crèvecoeur's appearance at Wyoming on July 5 of that year and his flight to the British lines in early 1779. The sketch was not included in the first printing of *Letters* in 1782, probably because its specific political commentary placed it with the other Revolutionary War sketches that were considered too hostile to the American cause to satisfy Crèvecoeur's Whig publisher. And although we know little about the process by which his writings were selected for *Letters,* it is reasonable to assume that Crèvecoeur himself wanted to exclude the more blatantly Loyalist letters from his book. By 1782, Crèvecoeur had suffered a year in British imprisonment on Long Island, had spent time in those intellectual circles of Paris that were sympathetic to the American Revolution, and, as a friend of the American cause, had begun correspondence with Benjamin Franklin and Thomas Jefferson. He undoubtedly saw a future in supporting the soon-to-be-victorious American government, and while **"Susquehanna"**—a description of British forces decimating a Patriot community—might not have jeopardized this future, the publication of such rabidly anti-Patriot sketches as "The American Belisarius" (the story of a virtuous Loyalist tormented by his "ignorant" and "prejudiced" neighbors) would have won Crèvecoeur few friends among leaders of the new country.[1] When these war sketches and other unpublished writings were discovered among the Crèvecoeur family archives in 1923, the editors of the 1925 *Sketches of Eighteenth Century America*—Henri L. Bourdin, Ralph H. Gabriel, and Stanley T. Williams—chose to include only the portion of the sketch describing Crèvecoeur's 1778 visit under the title "The Wyoming Massacre." The rest of **"Susquehanna"** was published in the *Yale Review* as "Crèvecoeur on the Susquehanna, 1774-1776" in the same year *Sketches* was published.[2]

This complicated textual history makes it particularly difficult to establish Crèvecoeur's intentions for **"Susquehanna,"** but all available evidence suggests that he wrote the sketch as a unified whole. To be sure, it is a long, somewhat unwieldy piece, but the sketch is unified—as I will show later—by the three visits to Wyoming and by the consistent voice and point of view that runs throughout. Bourdin, Gabriel, and Williams do not claim manuscript evidence for their decision to divide the text, and A. W. Plumstead has examined Bourdin's typescript and found "no break or suggestion of a break" there (225). Although they do not say so, the editors of *Sketches,* in attempting to limit the size of their volume, may have decided to follow the organization of the French version of Crèvecoeur's Susquehanna travels printed in the 1787

Lettres d'un cultivateur américain. In this greatly expanded and almost entirely rewritten version, Crèvecoeur narrates only his 1774 travels in one long chapter, then describes—using a very different voice and a much less narrative form—the Wyoming Massacre in the following chapter.[3]

Whatever the reason for the sketch's exclusion from Crèvecoeur's first book, "Susquehanna"—unlike many of the other sketches discovered in 1923—would be at home with the letters published in 1782. It is, first of all, a letter, written with James's distinctive voice, to the "great European man" to whom *Letters* is addressed. Crèvecoeur's persona in **"Susquehanna"** displays James's engaging quirks—his studied naivete, his self-conscious sentimentality, his eagerness to engage personally with the characters and events he encounters. More important, **"Susquehanna"** is grounded in the same environmental assumptions that pervade *Letters.* Just as the Nantucket letters describe the way in which the island's inhabitants have responded to their harsh surroundings with a complex division of the poor soil and a successful "farming" of the sea, **"Susquehanna"** describes the Wyoming settlers' attempt to build a community in response to the rugged landscape of the Susquehanna drainage.

Indeed, the motivation for Crèvecoeur's study of Wyoming is clearly stated in Letter 1, where James questions his more worldly wise minister concerning what an American farmer could possibly teach an educated European about America. The minister's answer has been echoed again and again by Americans trying to find a worthy place in the letters of Western civilization: Europeans, the minister tells James, study the nature and history of man by examining the "musty ruins of Rome"—"old towers, useless aqueducts, or impending battlements . . . seeking for the origin . . . and for the cause of so great a decay" (16, 18). Thus, Europeans face several disadvantages. They must look back, tracing "the vestiges of a once flourishing people now extinct" through eyes "clouded with the mist of ages" (16-17). Ruins suggest more questions than they can possibly answer, and what is finally discovered will be as fragmentary as the "musty ruins" themselves. Second, James's minister implies that Europe's ruins are less remnants of past greatness than they are emblems of failure—their builders may have been "a once flourishing people," but we dig to discover "the cause of so great a decay." Furthermore, ancient history does not help us understand the problems of today: Europeans "amuse themselves in viewing the ruins of temples and other buildings which have very little affinity with those of the present age, and must therefore impart a knowledge which appears useless and trifling" (16). In Crèvecoeur's view, Europe is the place of past greatness that has become present failure, while America is the place of future greatness and future success, a model more worthy—and more accessible—to study: "methinks there would be much more real satisfaction in observing among us, the humble rudiments and embryos of societies spreading every where, the recent foundation of our towns, and the settlements of so many

rural districts. I am sure that the rapidity of their growth would be more pleasing to behold, than the ruins of old towers, useless aqueducts, or impending battlements" (16). Rather than "submitting to the painful and useless retrospect of revolutions, desolations, and plagues," the observer "would, on the contrary, wisely spring forward to the anticipated fields of future cultivation and improvement, to the future extent of those generations which are to replenish and embellish this boundless continent" (17).

For Crèvecoeur, then, the European course of empire, spectacular as its remnants might appear, represents a dead end. As Henry Nash Smith has pointed out, much American thinking in Crèvecoeur's time was concerned with establishing America's place as the next great empire—succeeding England in the same way Rome succeeded Greece—and most Americans assumed that their new country would prove to be the exception to the "fall" rule of the course of empire pattern. Current thinking had developed a "stages of civilization" theory that, in Smith's words, could be observed first-hand only in America:

> Although in Europe the successive stages of society were naturally thought of as succeeding one another in time, so that primitive conditions could be studied only through historical and archeological research, the situation in America was quite different. When the theory of civilization became current in this country many observers were struck by its applicability to the actual state of affairs in the West. The comment was frequently made that in America one could examine side by side the social stages that were believed to have followed one another in time in the long history of the Old World.
>
> (218-19)

J. A. Leo Lemay argues that Crèvecoeur's *Letters* may represent the first application of the stage theory and the related theory of cultural evolution to the specifics of American geography and westward movement: Crèvecoeur, Lemay writes, "thus creates what came to be the standard interpretation of civilization's progress in America." Lemay points out that *Letters* had an immediate and substantial influence on such early commentators on the American experience as Benjamin Rush, Brissot de Warville, and Thomas Jefferson, and that Crèvecoeur's views have found more recent expression in the historical and literary writings of Frederick Jackson Turner and Robert E. Spiller (211, 215).

Crèvecoeur's study of the stages of civilization takes two different forms, corresponding to the approaches he takes in *Letters* and in **"Susquehanna."** In *Letters,* he takes us from the highly developed civilization of eastern cities—equal in wealth and sophistication to many European cities (although far superior, in Crèvecoeur's view, in that they are free from the "feudal institutions" of Europe)—through the middle settlements, where the "simple cultivation of the earth purifies" the inhabitants, to the frontier, where, surrounded by unordered wilderness, "men are wholly left dependent on their native tempers" and are much less purified than degenerated (51-52). While Letter 3 charts this course of empire from east to west as a phenomenon Crèvecoeur has observed, he describes it only in the abstract. For his more specific examples of American society in *Letters,* Crèvecoeur takes an approach similar to the European perspective, significantly beginning with thriving communities—not, to be sure, musty ruins, but Nantucket and Charlestown are not "embryos"—and tracing them back to their beginnings. He introduces his detailed study of Nantucket, for example, in these terms: "My simple wish is to trace them throughout their progressive steps, from their arrival here to this present hour; to enquire by what means they have raised themselves from the most humble, the most insignificant beginnings . . ." (95).

Crèvecoeur's intention in **"Susquehanna"** is somewhat different, more along the lines of the minister's advice in Letter 1 to study "the humble rudiments and embryos of societies spreading everywhere, the recent foundations of our towns, and the settlements of so many rural districts." The village of Wyoming, only a few years old when he first visits it in 1774, becomes Crèvecoeur's focus for this peculiarly American opportunity to "contemplate the very beginnings and out-lines of human society, which can be traced no where now but in this part of the world" (*Letters* 18).

While the growth of Wyoming provides the focus and touchstone for the sketch, the geography of the community's wilderness surroundings makes up the bulk of the piece—indeed, rather than naming the sketch "Wyoming," Crèvecoeur names it for the river that shapes the region's landscape. He does not take us directly to Wyoming, as he does to Nantucket in *Letters*; instead, we travel with him along the same wilderness rivers and trails the settlers themselves followed. In choosing this kind of narrative structure, Crèvecoeur places us in a historical context—we glimpse, through his eyes, something of the pre-1774 experience of the settlers—and he places us in the wilderness environment in which Wyoming itself is placed. As we move in and out of wilderness, from "hideous ridges" to "smiling fields" to swamps that are a "perfect chaos," we come to understand the role that landscape will play in the final tragedy. This constant movement from wilderness to civilization and back into wilderness enables us to understand that the geography is both promise and threat: the Susquehanna River Valley is defined by river bottoms of "inexhaustible fertility" everywhere bounded by the "hideous ridges" of pure wilderness that constantly threaten to swallow the smaller settlements and, in 1778, overwhelm even the larger and more established village of Wyoming.

The complex relationship between landscape and the fate of the people who live in the landscape is explained in broad terms in the first paragraphs of **"Susquehanna."** Crèvecoeur tells us that the movement of settlers into the continent's interior is more than the result of what land is available: it is a geographically determined imperative. While the tidewater farmland of the southern colonies is constantly "enriched by the manures" provided by the ocean and "by the mud of rivers,"

This is not however the natural state of our fields in the Northern provinces. The fecundity of the earth is greatly diminished; you may in those of Jersey, New York, Connecticut, etc. already perceive a great vegetative decay. The rich coat which was composed of old decayed leaves and other particles preserved for ages by the existence of timber and sheltered from the devouring impulse of the sun by the shades it produced, is long since exhausted and gone. This it was which enriched the first settlers and procured them such abundant crops. All the art of Man can never repair this. . . .

In order to obtain more uniformly fertile soils, deeper loams, inexhaustible farms, which hitherto have wanted no manure, *you must recede from the sea, you must ascend nearer the sources and springheads of those immense rivers everywhere traversing the great continent.*

(s 554, my emphasis)

Crèvecoeur moves from this statement of the geographical necessity for westward movement into a discussion of the political implications this movement holds for settlers. Under the colony's original charter, Connecticut was granted "a continuation of territory even to the South Sea" (s 556), and many New England emigrants registered their land claims under Connecticut law. Other settlers, traveling up the Susquehanna River from the more settled southeastern regions of Pennsylvania, registered their claims in Philadelphia, and these conflicting titles, compounded by the ideological differences between the democratic small-landholding Yankee New Englanders and the aristocratic land-speculating Pennsylvanians, erupted into the Pennamite Wars of 1771. Though he later notes that this smoldering New England/Pennsylvania division is essentially the same Patriot/Loyalist conflict that would consume Wyoming in 1778, Crèvecoeur argues that geography determines the manner and time of settlement of the Susquehanna Valley, and that political division is a consequence of the geographical fact that there are only two practical routes into the area: one accessible to New England, the other accessible to southeastern Pennsylvania—the two ends of the Susquehanna River. "The petty wars they carried on in support of their mutual claims are objects too extensive, too antecedent, and perhaps to you would appear too uninteresting," Crèvecoeur writes to his sophisticated European correspondent. "The part which I want to select for your amusement is a geographical account of this country" (s 555).[4]

Crèvecoeur begins his "geographical account" with a description of the view from "the summit of the Menisink heights," the first mountain range he encounters on his way west in 1774. This first look into the river valleys of the American interior serves an important function in the narrative: it reads as a landscape painting, a pictorial description of the geographical forces at work in **"Susquehanna."** Crèvecoeur is standing on a summit in the Menisink-Shawangunk mountain range, a system of mountains that effectively separates the long-settled farmland of Orange County, New York (the location of Crèvecoeur's Pine Hill), from the rugged hills and valleys of the Delaware and Susquehanna drainages—the continent's interior, the region of future promise. His back to the settled east, Crèvecoeur looks first into the broad valley of the Delaware River, the location of the last "safe" interior settlement:

> No contrast in this country can be greater and afford a more pleasing idea when on the summit of the Menisink heights, you contemplate below fruitful farms, smiling fields, noble orchards, spacious houses and barns, the substantial habitation of wealthy people settled these 120 years on those happy bottoms. Everything around is smooth, smiling and calculated for the use of Man, whilst the surrounding mountains which incompass them on every side, present nothing but huge masses of rocks and marbles, hideous ridges on which nothing hardly grows.

(s 558)

This long-settled territory (what is probably now the area around Port Jervis) represents Crèvecoeur's ideal, what Leo Marx calls the "middle landscape," an agricultural balance between art and nature that avoids the corruption of pure art—the problem represented by the ruins of Europe and the litigious citizenry of Charlestown described in Letter 9—and the degenerating effect of pure nature—the wilderness of the American interior. The landscape Crèvecoeur describes here has thrived these 120 years because it is fertile bottom land, yearly enriched by spring floods, which welcomes the ordering fact of the plow, and the community is neatly separated from the overly complex civilization of the eastern seaboard by the geographical fact of the mountain range on which Crèvecoeur stands.[5]

While this community is well established—the area has weathered the dangerous period of the early years Crèvecoeur documents in Letter 3—there is still something ominous in the landscape: these "smiling fields" are surrounded by mountains "which incompass them on every side," presenting "nothing but huge masses of rocks and marbles, hideous ridges on which nothing hardly grows." Crèvecoeur's tone here betrays an attitude toward landscape that represents more than a farmer's preference for cultivated land over wilderness: it speaks of a deeply personal relationship between the observer and the landscape he observes. To Crèvecoeur, people's ability to order and regulate the land is an important part of the process by which they order and regulate their emotions, and so the farm becomes both a movement against the chaos of unordered nature and a reflection of a regulated, rational mind. In these terms, the process of plowing is both an *external* act that orders the material world, and an *internal* process by which one might realize his or her Enlightenment potential: "as we silently till the ground," Crèvecoeur writes in *Letters,* "and muse along the odoriferous furrows of our low lands, uninterrupted either by stones or stumps; it is there that the salubrious effluvia of the earth animate our spirits and serve to inspire us . . ." (22). Parting the land with the plow both orders the landscape into straight lines and encourages the kind of romantic yet ultimately ratio-

nal thinking that, for Crèvecoeur, defines civilization. Both the observer and the cultivated fields can "smile" because one is the reflection of the other.[6]

For much the same reason, barren ridges seem "hideous" because they encourage the kind of chaotic passion-driven thinking that defines the degenerate frontier settler. Land that resists farming is more than inconvenient—it represents a barrier to human progress on both the individual and societal level. Crèvecoeur idealizes America because there is always new land to be broken and cultivated, unlimited opportunity for settlers like Andrew the Hebridean to clear land, drain swamps, and plow fields, changing the "wild, woody and uncultivated" landscape into a "fine fertile, well regulated district" (*Letters* 45, 53).

The problem in **"Susquehanna,"** then, results from the peculiar geography of the river drainage: the same river that provides the "uniformly fertile soils" and "deeper loams" of the bottom lands has carved a landscape of "hideous ridges" that can never be cultivated, and Crèvecoeur recognizes this ironic relationship between the fertile bottoms and barren hills. "One would imagine," Crèvecoeur writes, trying to make Enlightenment sense of the juxtaposition, "that by some superior art, by some anterior miracle, the ancient vegetative mould has been washed away to form those romantic plats below" (s 558-59). The result of this "anterior miracle" is that the landscape of **"Susquehanna"** consists of relatively small "romantic plats" immediately adjacent to—and forever limited in size and extent by—pure wilderness. Crèvecoeur describes this geographically determined limit on cultivation in terms that imply a frightening, almost violent, movement against the settled: "On the shores . . . are to be seen the most excellent farms, excellent houses; but these are soon terminated by the perpendicular foot of those mountains which entirely overspread this part of the province and forever prevent its aggrandisement on that side" (s 559). Crèvecoeur describes a landscape at war with itself—the best farmland on the American continent is bounded and forever limited by the most intractable wilderness.[7]

Between these mountains, where Crèvecoeur's trip begins, and the settlement of Wyoming, Crèvecoeur travels through a wilderness broken only by an occasional settlement—often a solitary family. Predictably, his time in these "gloomy forests" takes a psychological toll, and his description illuminates the relationship between the perceiver and his wilderness surroundings, hinting at the more profound changes that define wilderness degeneration:

> I must confess ingeniously that at first I was alarmed at every distant sound and could not find myself at ease until I was either informed or I had guessed what it would be. The drumming of partridges, for instance, heard at a distance greatly resembles the discharge of cannon; the roaring of distant falls produces likewise a singular effect strangely modified either by the wind or the situation in which you stand.

(s 560-61)

"'Tis a feast for an unexperienced traveller to see the sun shine on some open'd grounds, to view clear'd fields," Crèvecoeur writes. "You seem to be relieved from that secret uneasiness and involuntary apprehension which is always felt in the woods" (s 560). Crèvecoeur is relieved to spend one night with a family "seemingly happy and unconcerned at their hermit situation" who alone constitute the settlement of Blooming Grove, but all is not well even in this settled clearing. Perhaps thinking of his metaphor "men are like plants," Crèvecoeur writes, "I must confess that I saw nothing here very tempting or blooming" (s 562), and this pessimistic response is at first surprising. Crèvecoeur celebrates the beginnings of another American farmer in **Letters**—Andrew the Hebridean—and one might expect that Crèvecoeur would view the Blooming Grove family in terms of another hopeful beginning. The difference between Blooming Grove and Andrew's farm is a difference in geographical setting. Andrew clears and drains a spot of wilderness in a largely settled area, and the surrounding farms and settlements provide the "power of example, and check of shame" (53) necessary to counter degeneration. At Blooming Grove, Crèvecoeur is uncomfortable with the confining immediacy of a wilderness of raging creeks and steep wooded hillsides, and he expresses this ambivalence in terms that, once again, suggest a violent movement of the wild against the settled: "the low lands inclosed within it have escaped being tore away by the impetuosity of this torrent" (s 562). Crèvecoeur points out that this geography will sustain a dangerous isolation by limiting the area of cultivation. Twenty-two acres is all that can be cultivated—this will be limited forever by an "impetuous torrent" on one side and mountainous wilderness on the other. As Crèvecoeur notes concerning a neighboring settlement, it is "an awful situation for so few people surrounded on each side with the most gloomy forests" (s 561). While Crèvecoeur is impressed by the industry and independence of the frontier family, he notes that their way of life is determined by their environment: "Like all the inhabitants of the forest," Crèvecoeur's host is "a very expert hunter, I saw him with a Lancaster rifle kill a bird at 300 yards distance which I measured myself. He had brought in, the day before I arrived there, a bear which he overtook by chase" (s 563). Crèvecoeur's ideal American, of course, is not a gun-toting, bearchasing frontier man. In **Letters,** he argues that the necessity of hunting for food is a symptom of the general degeneration humans undergo when placed in a wilderness environment: "Thus our bad people are those who are half cultivators and half hunters; and the worst of them are those who have degenerated altogether into the hunting state" (58-59).[8]

In contrast to the smaller settlements Crèvecoeur encounters, Wyoming is all promise. He describes the Wyoming Valley as a long, broad, and flat landscape defined and made fertile by the Susquehanna: "this fair river issuing from the two lakes I have mentioned before, bending itself in an amazing number of curvatures to gather in its course a greater number of creeks and rivulets and to impart mankind a greater degree of benefits. Few rivers in this part of the world exhibit so great a display of the richest and fer-

tilest land the most sanguine wish of man can possibly covet and desire" (s 566). Crèvecoeur goes on to document, in the kind of detail that may have persuaded his twentieth-century editors to exclude the passage from their book, the fecundity of the Wyoming Valley. This is, to Crèvecoeur's mind, an example of ideal American landscape: fertile lands "yearly enriched by the strong healthy slime deposited by the floods" in a valley broad enough to provide cultivable lots from 250 to 1,000 acres (s 567). The taming of the land requires industry and hard work, of course, but the result is the growth of a prosperous American community. Again, Crèvecoeur moves easily from a description of healthy soil to a description of healthy people because good land provides the foundation for his agrarian ideal, in which clearing and ordering the landscape reflects the ordering and controlling of human nature. As with the individual experience of Andrew, the combination of "good land and freedom" here results in a society marked by a degree of happiness "far superior to what is enjoyed by any civilised nation on the globe" (s 571).

Crèvecoeur leaves this happy landscape of "houses rearing up, fields cultivating, that great extent of industry open'd to a bold indefatigable enterprising people" (s 569) to travel overland to visit more settlements on the west branch of the Susquehanna. The dangerous immediacy of the wilderness on the edge of Wyoming's cultivated landscape is underlined when Crèvecoeur promptly gets lost, geographically as well as psychologically, in a very different landscape: "we were all at once suddenly stopt by a huge pine swamp which had been partly consumed by some accidental fire; immense trees burnt at the roots were oversat, one over the other in an infinite variety of directions. . . . In short, there was no penetrating through such a black scene of confusion; it was a perfect chaos" (s 573). This experience serves as a harsh reintroduction to Crèvecoeur's vision of wilderness. Just as the ordered farm reflects a mind in which passion is subservient to reason, the "perfect chaos" of the swamp reflects Crèvecoeur's confusion and panic. In his mind, the swamp represents more than an inconvenience—it becomes a challenge to his eighteenth-century assumptions. He spends the night in the swamp, weakened by hunger and terrorized by howling wolves that surround his camp, and although he does find his way in the morning, this experience seems to color his response to the smaller, more recently established, and less fortunate settlements he visits on the west branch. In describing these settlements, he demonstrates the way in which this divided landscape affects its inhabitants:

> 'Tis very surprising to observe the boldness, the undiffidence with which these new settlers scatter themselves here and there in the bosom of such an extensive country without even a previous path to direct their steps and without being in any number sufficient either to protect or assist one another. I have often met with these isolated families in my travels, and 'tis inconceivable how soon they will lose their European prejudices and embibe those of the natives. Their children born and educated at such a distance from schools and

opportunities of improvement become a new breed of people neither Europeans nor yet Natives. These are not in general the best people of this country.

(s 575)

Crèvecoeur moves from this expression of primitivist theory—the wilderness environment has created "a new breed of people" who "are not in general the best people of this country"—to a description of the conflict between the New England and Pennsylvania settlers. He repeats much of the historical background given at the beginning of the sketch and, more important, he argues again that the geographical nature of the Susquehanna region has made confrontation inevitable. Too, Crèvecoeur implies that isolation in a wilderness environment encourages antipathy to fellow settlers and a readiness to use violence instead of reason in settling disagreements. The settlers on the west branch involved in the Pennamite Wars were, like Crèvecoeur's host at Blooming Grove, forced to hunt in order to survive—a process that denies civilization because it is antisocial, creating tension, not reasonable neighborliness, between frontier people. As Crèvecoeur expresses it in *Letters,* "a hunter wants no neighbour, he rather hates them, because he dreads the competition" (57). Without sufficient land to order, regulate, and grow what is necessary for survival, the darker impulses in all humans are allowed to take command. In describing this view of human nature, Crèvecoeur writes in **"Susquehanna"** that "mankind carries in their bosoms the rudiments of their own misfortunes and unhappiness, place them where you will . . ." (s 578). If placed in Orange County and given sufficient land, humans will be "purified" and, able to transcend these "rudiments," will settle their differences in court. Given land that, however fertile, is limited in size and surrounded by the degenerating influence of wilderness, these settlers ("not in general the best people") will, if prompted by political circumstances, destroy each other in senseless violence.[9]

Crèvecoeur travels to Wyoming in 1776 by a different route, but he discovers the same kind of tension between wilderness chaos and settlement order. This time tracing part of the route followed by the New England settlers, Crèvecoeur canoes up the Delaware River and observes the wilderness: "Bold rough projecting points in various forms and shapes present to the eyes nothing but a series of promontories frightful to behold." In "astonishing contrast when compared to the smiling ones of the Susquehanna," settlements here are placed in "some little bays formed by the winding of the river. A few acres of arable land have been discovered" (s 579). In describing these isolated Delaware River settlements, Crèvecoeur delineates a variation on the theme of frontier degeneration, establishing another way in which the combination of too small but fertile tracts of land and immediate wilderness changes settlers into a "new breed of people":

> The facility of navigation, the ease with which few acres are cultivated, the great field opened for hunting habituates this people to a desultory life, and in a few

years they seem to be neither Europeans as we observe them in our flourishing settlements nor yet natives. This mode of life which sometimes implies a great share of laziness produces a sort of indolence, indifference, which is the consequence of limited industry.

(s 580)

It is less the harshness of this wilderness environment than the relative ease of farming and hunting that leads these settlers, not necessarily "immersed in great and heavy labours," into degeneration. As Crèvecoeur describes the process in *Letters,* land cleared too easily and woods hunted too profitably lead the farmers to "trust to the natural fecundity of the earth, and therefore do little; carelessness in fencing, often exposes what little they sow to destruction . . . in order therefore to make up the deficiency, they go oftener to the woods." "Once hunters," Crèvecoeur tells us, "farewell to the plough" (57). As Leo Marx points out, Robert Beverley discovered a similar phenomenon in the too fertile regions of Virginia, where the settlers, in Beverley's words, "depend altogether upon the Liberality of Nature, without endeavouring to improve its Gifts, by Art or Industry" (85-86).

Crèvecoeur leaves the Delaware River and travels across the divide between the Delaware and Susquehanna drainages, reaching the Susquehanna River in the vicinity of Ouaquaga, a small Indian settlement a few miles north of what is now Windsor, New York. After spending a week there, he floats down the Susquehanna in the company of two Indians, arriving at Wyoming a few days later.

Wyoming is quickly achieving the promise Crèvecoeur predicted two years earlier, and he enthusiastically describes the flourishing settlements of the rapidly developing Wyoming Valley:

> I observed with pleasure that a better conducted plan of industry prevailed throughout, that many of the pristine temporary huts and humble log houses were converted into neater and more substantial habitations. I saw everywhere the strong marks of growing wealth and population. . . . Nothing could be more pleasing than to see the embryo of future hospitality, politeness, and wealth disseminated in a prodigious manner of shapes and situations all along these banks.

(s 583)

This description of a settled and flourishing landscape concludes his 1776 narrative, and the next paragraph begins the "Wyoming Massacre" passage printed in *Sketches,* Crèvecoeur's narrative of the events of 1778. This is the first mention of the massacre in **"Susquehanna"**—indeed, midway through his 1774 description of Wyoming, Crèvecoeur seems blissfully unaware of the outcome of his piece: "It is here [Wyoming] that human nature undebased by servile tenures, horrid dependence, a multiplicity of unrelieved wants as it is in Europa reacquires its former and ancient dignity,—now lost all over the world except with us. May future revolutions never destroy so noble, so useful a prerogative" (s 571). The fact that Crèvecoeur, describing Wyoming as the "embryo of future greatness," seems unaware of the community's fatal end would lead us to believe that **"Susquehanna"** was written in parts over a period of years and not as one piece in 1778, but the appearance of the **"Susquehanna"** manuscript suggests otherwise. Henri Bourdin, who discovered and transcribed it, believes that while Crèvecoeur may have made notes on his earlier visits, the manuscript was clearly written at one time, probably shortly after his last trip to Wyoming.[10] Even if Crèvecoeur simply rewrote earlier sketches, he certainly had ample opportunity to add more direct foreshadowing, as he does in another sketch dealing with one victim of the Wyoming Massacre. In "The History of Mrs. B.," Crèvecoeur alludes early in the narrative to her later tragic experience at Wyoming. Why then did he choose to write **"Susquehanna"** without the dramatic foreshadowing he applies in many of his other sketches?

One answer has to do with the critical argument concerning Crèvecoeur's innocent pose in *Letters from an American Farmer.* It has only recently been argued that Crèvecoeur's book may be more than a simple homage to American life that inexplicably goes wrong in the last chapter. Tyler, while finding the "two distinct notes—one of great peace, another of great pain," still argues that the pain is more anomalous than thematic—"the reader is tempted to infer that, after all, felicity is the permanent fact there, and that suffering is but a temporary incident" (2:351, 357). Warren Barton Blake's essay on *Letters,* written in 1912 and still included in the currently available Dutton edition of the book, argues that these conflicting points of view prove Crèvecoeur's artlessness, and identifies such conflict as evidence that *Letters* has "very little obvious system" (xii).

This view of *Letters* may result from Crèvecoeur's first modern critics' reading what James *tells* us about his book more closely than they read the book itself. Letter I has been too convincing in establishing James as the artless, simple farmer, and readers have read *Letters* with this expectation in mind—forgetting that James is *not* Crèvecoeur, and that Crèvecoeur the author is more in control of his material than these critics have given him credit for. In challenging the "artlessness" of *Letters,* some scholars now argue that the notes of pleasure and pain run side-by-side—not sequentially—throughout *Letters,* and that Crèvecoeur's journey from innocence to experience is a sudden fall for James, but not for the careful reader. James C. Mohr states that life on James's farm in the first letters is *supposed* to be too good to be true: "the idyllic image of America which Crèvecoeur develops during the first eight letters of his book becomes the dream against which the intensity of later disillusionment is measured" (355). Taking a slightly different approach, Thomas Philbrick writes that the real subject of the book is not the American and his life in America, but the slow recognition that both man and the natural world have a basic malevolence that, if not properly contained, can emerge in human and natural violence. With Mohr, Philbrick finds that Crèvecoeur subtly prepares his reader for the fully realized violence

and despair of the last letter: "Crèvecoeur's exploration of the enigma of man is conducted with such indirection in the preceding letters that its presence may go undetected in a casual reading of the book" (66).

"Susquehanna" follows a similar innocence-to-experience pattern,[11] and the suddenness with which we arrive at the scene of the massacre of 1778 is the result of a very similar kind of strategy—the effect Mohr calls "calculated disillusionment." Just as James's farm functions as an ideal against which the American reality of human and natural evil is measured, Crèvecoeur's celebration of Wyoming in 1774 and 1776 functions as a too ideal American community that represents only the illusion of dominance over the wilderness that surrounds it. If Crèvecoeur had spoken early in **"Susquehanna"** of Wyoming's ultimate fate, he might have sacrificed this quality of disillusionment in an ideal of American progress. Instead, Wyoming's ruin is foreshadowed both by Crèvecoeur's description of a malevolent wilderness at Wyoming's doorstep, and by his description of the violence of the Wyoming settlers' frontier neighbors. If we understand Crèvecoeur's message accurately, the Wyoming Massacre is not an anomalous expression of tragedy, but a predictable consequence of the overwhelming power of the community's geographical setting.

Crèvecoeur also arranges the narrative in a way that underlines the inevitability of the conclusion by manipulating his constant movement from wilderness to civilization to wilderness. The sketch is structured chronologically according to the three visits to Wyoming. But there is another organizing pattern at work, one in which Wyoming in 1778 takes the place of the wilderness that earlier contrasted with it. Crèvecoeur travels from the settled "romantic plats" at the beginning of the sketch into the "hideous ridges" and the isolated settlement of Blooming Grove, finally arriving at civilization—Wyoming in 1774. He leaves Wyoming and loses his way in a swamp, and he finds only degenerated settlers on the west branch and, two years later, in the tiny settlements on the upper Delaware River. He returns to civilization finally in his arrival at Wyoming in 1776. Instead of plunging into wilderness once again—as has been the pattern in the sketch so far—Crèvecoeur moves directly to Wyoming in the aftermath of the massacre of 1778. The placement of the massacre description immediately following the celebration of Wyoming in 1776 underlines the fact that Wyoming has been reclaimed by—has, indeed, *become*—wilderness, and the juxtaposition serves to heighten the tragedy of the "suspension of industry, and the total destruction of their noble beginning" (WM 193) that he finds in his last visit.

Crèvecoeur apparently arrived in the Wyoming Valley in July 1778, in time to witness the aftermath of the Wyoming Massacre. In her 1915 biography of Crèvecoeur, Julia Post Mitchell—writing before Bourdin's manuscript discovery—advances a theory explaining his presence at the scene of the massacre in terms of Letter 12, where James explains his intention to move to the frontier with his family. Mitchell surmises that Crèvecoeur was in the area of Wyoming for the purpose of locating a frontier retreat when he witnessed the aftermath of the massacre (49).[12] If so—and there is little doubt that this is when Crèvecoeur was writing his "Distresses of a Frontier Man"—Mitchell suggests a biographical point of reference for Letter 12. James apparently believes that a token half-dozen acres of farmland will immunize him to the degenerating influence of wilderness. If, as Mitchell suggests, Crèvecoeur himself believed that he could find sanctuary in a frontier Indian village and live in "a state approaching nearer to that of nature, unencumbered either with voluminous laws, or contradictory codes . . . and at the same time sufficiently remote from the brutality of unconnected savage nature" (*Letters* 216), Wyoming's fate was evidence to the contrary. If Crèvecoeur *was* in the Wyoming Valley for the purpose of finding a frontier refuge, the Wyoming Massacre may have served as shocking evidence of what he had known all along, a realistic answer to the wishful thinking of Letter 12. It may be that the disillusionment that is "calculated" in **"Susquehanna"** was a tragic reality in Crèvecoeur's own less-calculated life.

In the context of the **"Susquehanna"** whole, the Wyoming Massacre proves to be more than a consequence of political division: the massacre becomes a tragedy of the community's geographical setting. Crèvecoeur alludes to the "intricate mazes of this grand quarrel" (WM 192) in describing the events leading up to the massacre, but he is still less concerned with the political aspects of revolution than with the way the geography of the American interior affects the manner—and the result—of Revolutionary violence. Crèvecoeur explains that the Loyalists were first driven from their homes in Wyoming by neighbors holding the "modern opinions" of independence from England, and that these displaced people were forced to survive in the wilderness surrounding the river communities:

> Many of those who found themselves stripped of their property took refuge among the Indians. Where else could they go? Many others, tired of that perpetual tumult in which the whole settlement was involved, voluntarily took the same course; and I am told that great numbers from the extended frontiers of the middle provinces have taken the same steps,—some reduced to despair, some fearing the incursions with which they were threatened.
>
> (WM 192)

"So strong is the power of Indian education," Crèvecoeur explains, that whites placed in their company inevitably become "a new set of people" (WM 194). The migration from the relatively civilized river communities to Indian camps and settlements deeper in the wilderness, and the tragic consequences of this displacement, could serve as a case study illustrating the theory of wilderness degeneration Crèvecoeur sets down in *Letters,* providing a concrete example of how a specific group of whites forced to live "remote from the power of example, and check of shame" becomes "the most hideous parts of our society": "As old ploughmen and new men of the woods, as Europeans and new made Indians, they contract the vices of both; they

adopt the moroseness and ferocity of a native, without his mildness, or even his industry at home" (53).

Although Indians were popularly blamed for much of the Revolutionary violence on the frontier, Crèvecoeur minimizes the role Indians play in the massacre.[13] There is a sense that Crèvecoeur's Indians are only doing what Indians are expected to do. The greater tragedy, in his mind, is that the displaced Europeans have *themselves* become savages. In the preceding portion of **"Susquehanna,"** Crèvecoeur describes the region as a country of widely scattered settlements inhabited by Indians and by whites who are "half cultivators and half hunters" balanced on that dangerous line between savagery and civilization. The political upheaval of the American Revolution forced numbers of new settlers into the surrounding wilderness, with predictable results: "The Europeans who had taken refuge among the natives united with them in the same scheme which had been anteriorly proposed, and set on foot by the commandant of Niagra; they were, therefore, joined by several English officers and soldiers. The whole body of these assailants seemed animated with the most vindictive passions, a sacrifice to which many innocent families as well as guilty ones were doomed to fall" (WM 196). This displacement results in a mix of Indians, British regulars, and embittered settlers who, no longer restrained by the soothing influence of settlement and community, become "animated" by their passions and join in the atrocities at Wyoming.

Having documented the cause, Crèvecoeur describes in politically objective detail the effect, and he focuses on both the human suffering and the social tragedy of the destruction of the community he had described before as "the embryo of future hospitality, politeness, and wealth." To be sure, Crèvecoeur pays most attention to the victims of the massacre, but he has almost a larger interest in the fate of the community: Wyoming has served for four years as his study of an American community in embryo, promising with each visit to justify his earlier faith that Wyoming was large and established enough to survive its wilderness surroundings. It is in this sense that Wyoming in 1778 acts as the reality against which the earlier Wyoming becomes, in retrospect, too ideal. Crèvecoeur describes the destruction of the community in the same way he traced the building of it, and he does not miss the significance of this process of societal degeneration:

> Thus perished . . . most of the buildings, improvements, mills, bridges, etc., which had been erected there with so much cost and industry. . . . The complete destruction of these extended settlements was now the next achievement which remained to be done, in order to finish their rude triumph, but it could not be the work of a few days. Houses, barns, mills, grain, everything combustible to conflagrate; cattle, horses, and stock of every kind to gather; this work demanded a considerable time. The collective industry of twelve years could not well be supposed, in so great an extent, to require in its destruction less than twelve days.
>
> (WM 201, 204)

Crèvecoeur finds it equally significant that the settlers are forced to retrace the trail they followed in first settling the valley: "This was the very forest they had traversed with so much difficulty a few years before, but how different their circumstances!" (WM 204).

It is in this way that **"Susquehanna"** anticipates later American artistic and literary treatments of the course of empire paradigm: Crèvecoeur traces an example of American civilization from its wilderness beginnings to ruins reclaimed by wilderness. He begins his first visit to Wyoming in a landscape of "hideous ridges" and howling wolves, and he finds in the Wyoming settlement what seems to be a comforting antithesis to the horrible chaos of wilderness. He finds two years later an ideal American community, a kind of garden that promises to grow generations of "the American, this new man." He describes what he finds in 1778 in terms of a landscape painting— "What a scene an eminent painter might have copied from that striking exhibition, if it had been a place where a painter could have calmly sat with the palette in his hands!" (WM 200)[14]—and the scene he describes is remarkably similar to what Thomas Cole, in a prospectus for *The Course of Empire,* would describe in the fourth painting in his series as "a tempest,—a battle, and the burning of the city . . . masses and groups swaying about like stormy waves . . . the scene of destruction" and in his fifth and final painting as "a desolate ruin . . . the funeral knell of departed greatness" (177-78). Cole implies the inevitability of the empire's destruction in his depiction of a piece of wilderness, a rugged cliff face that remains unchanged in the background throughout the series of five paintings, representing, as the one unchanging element, the timeless inevitability of wilderness.[15] Using a similar point of reference, Crèvecoeur paints throughout **"Susquehanna"** an ominous wilderness represented by a series of wild animals, gloomy forests, and "hideous ridges" always threateningly adjacent to his farms and communities. Indeed, the wolves that made Crèvecoeur's "blood run cold" during the night he was lost in the woods in 1774, representing for him the danger inherent in wilderness, may well be the same wolves he describes in the concluding sentence as descending on the ruins of Wyoming as the last refugees depart: "Such was their situation, while the carcasses of their friends were left behind to feed the wolves of that wilderness on which they had so long toiled, and which they had come to improve" (WM 206). Where Cole's paintings depict a classical scene and so imply a more purely theoretical and universal idea, Crèvecoeur's sketch—like Cooper's *The Crater*—is more peculiarly American. The fact that Crèvecoeur's American course of empire ends with a flaming ruin similar to Cole's underlines the tragic irony of Crèvecoeur's vision: he becomes an American version of the European tourist, pondering "the vestiges of a once flourishing people now extinct." Like the "musty ruins" of Rome, Wyoming has become an emblem of failure, not the shining example of American progress he had set out to document.

"Susquehanna" tells us that there are really two answers to Crèvecoeur's famous question, "What, then, is the American, this new man?" because there are two American landscapes, the settled and the wild. The settled land grows the Andrews, the Crèvecoeurs, the "best people" who order themselves in ordering their land; wilderness grows "our worst people," human reflections of disordered wilderness. The tragedy Crèvecoeur relates in "Susquehanna" is the result of a geography that places the settled land in a dangerous wilderness context, threatening always the individual and social degeneration that defines, finally, the Wyoming Massacre.

Notes

1. For information (and speculation) regarding the selection of sketches for the 1782 *Letters,* see Plumstead (218-21, 228-29); Philbrick (27-31); and Plotkin (391). Concerning Crèvecoeur's changing political sympathies, see Mitchell (41-87) and Jehlen (204-22).

2. Concerning the discovery and editing of the Crèvecoeur manuscripts, see Bourdin and Williams (425-32). Much of this information is repeated in the essays provided by Bourdin (14-24), and Bourdin, Williams, and Gabriel (36-38) for Crèvecoeur, *Sketches.* Regarding the editing of *Sketches*—and the decision to delete most of "Susquehanna"—Thomas Philbrick writes: "Since the sequence of the sketches as they appear in the bound volumes of Crèvecoeur's manuscripts conveys no discernible design, the editors devised their own order, apparently modeling the organization of the book on the general pattern of the *Letters.* Like the twelve *Letters,* the twelve chapters of the *Sketches* begin with the depiction of rural life, move toward generalized sociological and political analysis, and end with a vivid account of the agony brought on by the coming of the Revolution." Philbrick notes that the editors did "considerable violence" to "Susquehanna" in editing the sketch to fit within a framework that was, finally, "the work of his editors, not of Crèvecoeur himself" (108). I have reconstructed "Susquehanna" by joining the portion published in the *Yale Review* as "Crèvecoeur on the Susquehanna, 1774-1776" (cited as s in the text) and the portion published in *Sketches* as "The Wyoming Massacre" (cited as WM in the text).

3. There is yet another twist to the textual history of "Susquehanna." Albert E. Stone announced his intention to reassemble the two halves of the sketch in his 1981 Penguin American Library edition of *Letters from an American Farmer and Sketches of Eighteenth Century America* under the title "On the Susquehanna; The Wyoming Massacre." Unfortunately, a printing error led to the inclusion of only the "On the Susquehanna" portion. Professor Stone has written me that the publisher will restore "The Wyoming Massacre" to its proper place in the second printing.

4. Crèvecoeur describes the effect of the Pennamite Wars on a specific frontier family in "The History of Mrs. B." in *Sketches* 207-20.

5. On Crèvecoeur's version of the "middle landscape," see Marx (107-16).

6. See Elayne Rapping's study of the influence of the Enlightenment on Crèvecoeur's thinking.

7. Roger Stein describes similar eighteenth- and nineteenth-century responses to the landscape of the Susquehanna drainage in *Susquehanna: Images of the Settled Landscape.*

8. The French version of "Susquehanna," translated and almost entirely rewritten by Crèvecoeur and included in the 1787 *Letters,* provides a dramatic example of how Crèvecoeur's primitivist theory changed during his years in Paris. In this version, he describes the Blooming Grove settlement in much more positive terms, concluding that the settlers' situation was less "awful" than "*pittoresque.*" He ends his description with a statement that represents a complete reversal of the view he expresses in the English *Letters* and in "Susquehanna": "I believe therefore the state of the part hunter and part farmer to be superior to all the others, seeing that it offers a man a greater portion of liberty, independence, and therefore, dignity and happiness. . . . If, on one hand, the success of the hunt excites him to travel too-great distances into the woods, on the other hand, his wife, his children, and his fields bring him back under his roof. . . . He holds at the same time to the two extremes of the social chain, without having the drawbacks of either . . ." (3:174, my translation).

9. The theory of wilderness degeneration continues to provide an explanation for acts of human violence. A recent magazine article describing increasing reports of assault and vandalism in national parks and forests quotes a psychologist who theorizes that "a primitive outdoor environment can spark aggressive, bullying behavior in a normally under control person" (Telford 29).

10. Bourdin writes: "His narrative of the excursions he made in the Susquehanna Valley was not written until July, 1778, though evidence points out that they had taken place some time before 1774. . . . I am strongly inclined to believe that he wrote it from notes taken while on his journeys" ("The Crèvecoeur Manuscripts" 23-24). See also Bourdin and Williams, "Unpublished Manuscripts of Crèvecoeur" 431.

11. Plumstead calls "Susquehanna" "a mini-*Letters.* A beautiful wilderness and a happy people are invaded by revolutionaries, killed and burned by Indians and whites" (225).

12. Crèvecoeur was widely known to have been an eyewitness to what was to become an infamous event. Thomas Jefferson wrote to M. Soules, a Frenchman writing an account of the massacre, in 1787: "I have had a long conversation with M. Crève-coeur. He knows well that canton. He was in the neighborhood of the place [Wyoming] when it was destroyed, saw great numbers of the fugitives, aided them with his wagons, and had the story from their mouths. He committed notes to writing at the moment, which are now in Normandy, at his father's. . . . He says there will be a great deal to alter in your narration, and that it must assume a different face, more favorable both to the British and Indians. His veracity may be relied on" (quoted in Mitchell 48-49).

13. Roy Harvey Pearce refers in passing to "Susquehanna" as a sketch "in which Crèvecoeur blames whites for encouraging Indian cruelty on the frontier" (141).

14. Philbrick points out that Crèvecoeur makes conscious use here of the conventions of landscape painting in his portrayal of the massacre's aftermath: "the painterly quality of the description is exhibited in the concern for composition" (131).

15. See Donald A. Ringe's discussion of Cole's paintings and their influence on Cooper's *The Crater* (28-30).

Works Cited

Blake, Warren Barton. Introduction. *Letters from an American Farmer.* By J. Hector St. John de Crèvecoeur. 1912; rpt. New York: Dutton, 1957.

Bourdin, Henri L. "The Crèvecoeur Manuscripts." Crèvecoeur, *Sketches,* 14-24.

———, and Stanley T. Williams. "The Unpublished Manuscripts of Crèvecoeur." *Studies in Philology* 22 (1925):425-32.

———, Stanley T. Williams, and Ralph H. Gabriel. "Note on the Text." In Crèvecoeur, *Sketches,* 36-38.

Cole, Thomas. Letter to Luman Reed, 18 Sept. 1833. In Louis L. Noble, *The Course of Empire, Voyage of Life, and Other Pictures of Thomas Cole.* New York: Cornish, Lamport and Co., 1853, 177-78.

Crèvecoeur, J. Hector St. John de. "Crèvecoeur on the Susquehanna, 1774-1776." Ed. H. L. Bourdin and S. T. Williams. *Yale Review* 24 (1925):552-84.

———. *Letters from an American Farmer.* 1782; rpt. Gloucester, Mass.: Peter Smith, 1968.

———. *Lettres d'un cultivateur américain.* 3 vols. Paris: Cuchet, 1787.

———. *Sketches of Eighteenth Century America.* Ed. Henri L. Bourdin, Stanley T. Williams, and Ralph H. Gabriel. New Haven: Yale Univ. Press, 1925.

———. "The Wyoming Massacre." In *Sketches,* 192-206.

Jehlen, Myra. "J. Hector St. John Crèvecoeur: A Monarcho-Anarchist in Revolutionary America." *American Quarterly* 31 (1979):204-22.

Lemay, J. A. Leo. "The Frontiersman from Lout to Hero." *Proceedings of the American Antiquarian Society* 88 (1978):187-223.

Marx, Leo. *The Machine in the Garden: Technology and the Pastoral Ideal in America.* New York: Oxford Univ. Press, 1964.

Mitchell, Julia Post. *St. Jean de Crèvecoeur.* 1915; rpt. New York: AMS Press, 1966.

Mohr, James C. "Calculated Disillusionment: Crèvecoeur's *Letters* Reconsidered." *South Atlantic Quarterly* 69 (1970):354-63.

Pearce, Roy Harvey. *The Savages of America.* Baltimore: Johns Hopkins Univ. Press, 1953.

Philbrick, Thomas. *St. John de Crèvecoeur.* New York: Twayne, 1970.

Plotkin, Norman A. "Saint-John de Crèvecoeur Rediscovered: Critic or Panegyrist?" *French Historical Studies* 3 (1964):390-404.

Plumstead, A. W. "Hector St. John de Crèvecoeur." In *American Literature 1764-1789: The Revolutionary Years.* Ed. Everett Emerson. Madison: Univ. of Wisconsin Press, 1977, 213-31.

Rapping, Elayne. "Theory and Experience in Crèvecoeur's America." *American Quarterly* 19 (1967):707-18.

Ringe, Donald A. "James Fenimore Cooper and Thomas Cole: An Analogous Technique." *American Literature* 30 (1958):26-36.

Smith, Henry Nash. *Virgin Land: The American West as Symbol and Myth.* 1950; rpt. Cambridge: Harvard Univ. Press, 1978.

Stein, Roger. *Susquehanna: Images of the Settled Landscape.* Binghamton, N.Y.: Roberson Center for the Arts and Sciences, 1981.

Telford, Lyn. "Tales From the Forest Primeval." *Utah Holiday* 10, no. 6 (1981):25-31.

Tyler, Moses Coit. *The Literary History of the American Revolution 1763-1783.* 2 vols. 1897; rpt. New York: Facsimile Library, 1941.

David M. Robinson (essay date 1990)

SOURCE: "Community and Utopia in Crèvecoeur's *Sketches*," in *American Literature,* Vol. 62, No. 1, March, 1990, pp. 17-31.

[*In the following essay, Robinson examines* Sketches of Eighteenth-Century America *as a text that illuminates some of the contradictions often cited in* Letters from an American Farmer.]

I

By the end of the eighteenth century, Leo Marx tells us, the idea that "the American continent may be the site of a new golden age could be taken seriously in politics."[1]

Crèvecoeur's *Letters from an American Farmer* is perhaps the best articulation of this utopian impulse, embodying in its third letter an agrarian version of the American dream. There he presents a vision of a society of social and economic equals, made independent through their economic dependence on the land alone yet bound together in a supportive and compassionate community. The agrarian values that James embodies in the book's opening—familial rootedness, reverence for nature, diligent work, economic egalitarianism, and an openness to those in need—are utopian in essence. They project an ideal society, the image of which becomes a stance for social criticism.[2] Although Crèvecoeur's presentation of the dream has only a peripheral relation to historical truth, something of the utopian impulse of the work has survived history, continuing to present a powerful image of what America might have become before it veered into the Industrial Age. The power of Crèvecoeur's book is its utopian thrust, and as historical developments have rendered it more assuredly utopian, they have augmented the very source of its power.

But what call can Crèvecoeur's agrarian utopia legitimately have upon us? This essentially political question has been the unacknowledged subtext of much conflicting literary interpretation of the book. Recent readers of the *Letters* have been divided over the implications of the dramatic change of tone, some seeing the tragic later chapters as intentional deflation of the earlier optimism, and others finding grounds in the book's conclusion to preserve at least some of the values, though perhaps transmuted, of the earlier chapters.[3] Certain textual questions bear directly on these conclusions, principally the fact that *Letters* was a chosen arrangement from a much wider variety of Crèvecoeur's manuscripts.[4] Other of the manuscripts, discovered in France by Henri Bourdin in 1925, were published as *Sketches of Eighteenth-Century America,* a revealing miscellany of commentary on early American society.[5] Thomas Philbrick has rightly called the *Sketches* a "non-book," seeing it as "an anthology of heterogeneous pieces that lacks a controlling form, a coherent point of view, and a coherent theme" (p. 109). Seen in isolation, and as an aesthetic artifact, it is indeed a book of limited value. But as a shadow text to the *Letters,* it has enormous significance. The book's diversity adds to its importance as a barometer of the conflicting ideas and experiences that Crèvecoeur was attempting to work through in its composition. The book highlights the tensions and contradictions that are inherent in the *Letters,* and suggests that the "utopian mentality" embodied in the book is best regarded as a form of social criticism.[6] It thus confirms the core of cultural criticism in Crèvecoeur's work, amplifying our understanding of his struggles with America's utopian possibilities. One of the most crucial of these struggles is the problem of community formation. While the promise of material gain was a significant factor in the settlement of the frontier, the excessive pursuit of wealth posed a serious obstacle to the formation of a genuine community there. Crèvecoeur depicts this obstacle clearly, but his *Sketches* leaves an implied rather than a fully articulated critique of this pervasive and caustic American materialism. His troubled recognition of the new nation's vulnerability to the transformation of economic opportunity into exclusionary greed is thus mapped in the *Sketches.* Since the new economic opportunity was the fuel of his utopian expectations, its perversion was of serious concern to him. His utopian expectations were tragically deferred as the communities of the New World were formed, and his witness to that deferral made him one of our first cultural critics.

II

Despite the continuing and probably irresolvable differences of interpretation of the *Letters,* one consensus seems to be emerging in the recent criticism. Whether one sees the book's ending as intentionally undercutting its earlier optimism or refining its earlier vision, there is a conscious utopian design and serious social criticism implied by the chosen structure of the work. As James's vision moves from the effusive praise of the possibilities of American life to the threatened destruction of those possibilities in the violence of the Revolution, he constructs a lost paradise, leaving us with the faint hope of its recovery as he moves West to live among the Indians. James's future plans have long been controversial, seeming to some like the purest escapist fantasy. This escape to the West, an "earplug to the siren song of primitivism" as John Hales has recently called it, underscores the seriousness of the tragedy that has gone on before.[7] Either Crèvecoeur himself has lost his grip on the truth, or he has depicted his narrator James as having done so to augment the shock of the collapse of James's world. In either case, Crèvecoeur has left us with a vision of a crumbling American dream.[8] Is that in itself a conscious political statement? Those who regard James's plan of escape as "less quixotic than it might appear," as Myra Jehlen put it (p. 209), can also find in it an affirmation of at least some elements of the original agrarian vision that gives Letter Three its strength of appeal. In this view, James's escape represents the persistence of hope and the continuing capacity to enact it historically.[9]

James's escape to the West results from his victimization by political forces beyond his control, but he is not the only political victim in Crèvecoeur's work. Certain parts of the *Sketches* multiply and deepen the images of tragedy that resulted from the political dislocations of the Revolution. What may have seemed to be Crèvecoeur's rather mild Tory sympathies in the *Letters* are shown instead to be a deep suspicion of the motives of the revolutionaries and a despairing and sometimes savage attack on their intolerance for dissenting views. His opposition to the Revolution would later soften, as he established himself in France, but portions of the *Sketches* were written at the height of personal and social turmoil that manifested itself in a blistering critique of the Revolution.[10] Ironically, this pro-loyalist perspective is of a piece with Crèvecoeur's progressive cultural criticism.

James's powerful statement of the injustice of his situation in Letter Twelve transcends its immediate political context in the Revolution and makes him a representative voice of a populace exploited for the gain of those vying for power. He senses that he is being duped into taking part in the conflict in order to serve the unacknowledged interests of those more powerful than he, and finds this a disturbing pattern of the political relations among the classes. "It is for the sake of great leaders on both sides that so much blood must be spilt; that of the people is counted as nothing. Great events are not achieved for us, though it is *by* us that they are principally accomplished, by the arms, the sweat, the lives of the people."[11] Recognizing that he may be doomed no matter which side he chooses, and having little or no stake in the outcome, James adopts the principle of self-preservation in his decision to flee to the West. In one sense it is a decision to opt out of the political, and now military, conflict that has engulfed the colonies. But on another level, it is fundamentally a political decision, in which James embraces what little alternative to the entrenched warring powers remains. It is less a pro-loyalist stance than a statement of agrarian self-determination.

The book offers other corroborating evidence of the hardship that the Revolution visited upon the innocent. "The Man of Sorrows" adds dramatic detail to the context of James's own predicament as described in Letter Twelve. The sketch attempts to personalize the evil of the war and show it "more visible, more affecting" (p. 342) because of its direct harm to ordinary individuals. The unnamed narrator of the piece describes the transformation of the American frontier into a nightmare of instability and violence for those who have settled there. "No imagination can conceive, no tongue can describe their calamities and their dangers. The echoes of their woods repeat no longer the blows of the axe, the crash of the falling trees, the cheerful songs of the ploughman" (p. 345). Whipsawed between revolutionary and loyalist militia and vulnerable to Indian attack, the frontier settlers epitomize the victimization of the lowly by the powerful. Although the frontier had represented to many of them an escape from political turmoil and violence, it has now become the place where violence is most terribly played out.

The sketch focuses on the fate of a farmer victimized by vigilante justice after being accused of harboring a band of loyalists and Indians. He is accosted while he is working in his field, a scene that epitomizes the disruption of the agrarian utopia by political forces. The man is hastily condemned to hang, and in the presence of his family the execution is actually begun before he is given a last-second reprieve. The incident accentuates the absolute powerlessness of an individual confronting larger political events and reinforces James's argument in the *Letters* about the victimization of the innocent and the powerless. While in this case the revolutionaries are more clearly the target of Crèvecoeur's attack, and the sketch therefore has a more definite loyalist orientation than the *Letters,* both texts share a populist sense of betrayal by larger political forces. There is no escape to the West for this farmer, and it is one of several instances in which the *Sketches* paints a much bleaker picture of frontier conditions and leaves much less room for hope than the *Letters.* But the comparison of this sketch with Letter Twelve underscores that James's plan to flee to the West is a form of political defiance.

James's planned escape raises one serious question that goes to the heart of the agrarian values that are the book's utopian center. James and his family go to the West alone. Certainly this restricts the political significance of his act and suggests one of the key limitations of Crèvecoeur's political vision, its extreme individualism. "Because personal worth for him was measured by autonomy," Jehlen notes, "any area of mutual definition amounted to a sort of entail on the self" (p. 207). Crèvecoeur's depictions of innocent individuals persecuted by large groups or institutions suggest that he regarded social relations as inevitably restrictive of personal freedom. But it should be remembered that these are images of individual autonomy that, again and again, is shown to fail. In this sense, they are less an affirmation of individualism than an implied critique of the myth of individual autonomy. His portrayal of the individual gripped by social violence is best regarded as a nascent attempt to refine the image of agrarian autonomy by showing that it can never be absolute.

Crèvecoeur's ambivalent presentation of the relation of the individual to the larger community is therefore evidence of his groping toward a critique of a failing or destructive individualism. In Letter Twelve, James plans to flee to the West because of the destruction of the community around him. His settlement, a "thinly inhabited" area "inclosed by a chain of mountains," cannot be secured from the marauders who are sheltered by the wilderness, "a door through which they can enter our country whenever they please." The attacks, which "seem determined to destroy the whole chain of frontiers," leave James and his family in continuous fear (pp. 201-02). He does not regard himself as abandoning a community; it has rather collapsed around him. Nor does he see himself launching out entirely on his own; he has aligned himself with a secure and stable new community, an Indian village with which he has had some prior contacts. It is a place of refuge to which James can transport the essential values of his agrarian life.

Similarly, the central figure in "The Man of Sorrows" is the victim of a community which has gone awry, victimized by its own uncontrollable emotions. When the vigilantes hear the accusation that the farmer has lodged potential enemies, they are "suddenly inflamed . . . with the most violent resentment and rage" (p. 346). As they proceed to question and torture the man, they are nearly persuaded to show him compassion until they are reminded of their own past losses. "But all of a sudden one of the company arose, more vindictive than the rest. He painted to them their conflagrated houses and barns, the murder of their relations and friends. The sudden recollection of these dreadful images wrought them up to a pitch of fury fiercer than before." This is an image of violence begetting

violence and of the dangerous emotions that can be unleashed when a community breaks down. The mob is a group working in concert but not a community, and the sketch emphasizes the extent to which a wholesome autonomy is ultimately dependent on a stable community and social order.[12] Crèvecoeur does not suggest that the individual can exist outside any community but rather that the health of the community is vital to the health of the individual.

Ambivalence about the relation of the individual to the community is not, needless to say, an unusual dilemma for an American thinker, and in this respect, Crèvecoeur's problem is representative for American culture. Caught between the impulse to affirm autonomy and a felt need for a supportive community, he is driven to present the primal American cultural experience of starting anew as both an individual and a communal act. James's solid network of friends and neighbors, the various forms of support given to the new immigrant Andrew in Letter Three, and the closely knit communities on Nantucket and Martha's Vineyard are all examples of a regeneration of community that parallels the regeneration of the individual. "From nothing to start into being" (p. 83) is James's description of the regenerative effect of American social conditions on the individual, whose past is effectively swept away in the new world. But something of the same process occurs for American communities as well, as they form anew from the network of needs among the new settlers.

III

The possibility of renewed communal values on the frontier, and not the immediate circumstances of the Revolution, posed the gravest question to Crèvecoeur's utopian vision. While he was concerned to report what he felt were the abuses of the Revolution, his subtext is the birth and evolution of communities: could they flourish in America? Two particularly impressive meditations on this question can be found in the *Sketches,* each of which offers a strikingly similar depiction of the failure of community in America. "The American Belisarius" is the story of an individual farmer who settles new land and prospers, and eventually finds a new community growing up around him. "Reflections on the Manners of Americans" is a similar portrait of a successful pioneer farmer who also finds himself gradually enmeshed in community relations. In both cases, the frontier is a testing ground for the development not only of self-reliance but of effective community. The essential work of individual settlement precedes the growth of the community in each case, and the successful farmer is challenged by his relation to the community that has grown up around him and is in some sense dependent on him.

"The American Belisarius" describes the rise and fall of S. K., who embodies the best values of the American immigrant experience. The sketch contains a politically didactic message about the harm done to one individual by the Revolution, but it also ironically affirms the utopian vision of an interdependent community through its depiction of the unravelling of such a community. The community fails, but the failure is less the result of the politics of the Revolution than of greed and competition for material wealth— the real shadow over Crèvecoeur's agrarian ideal.

S. K.'s rise is the archetype of the American regeneration as Crèvecoeur had expounded it in the *Letters.* Having seen unsettled land beyond the frontier on a hunting expedition, he recognized its potential fertility and claimed it, and thus prepared "to begin the world anew in the bosom of this huge wilderness, where there was not even a path to guide him" (p. 409). With a combination of skill and determined hard work, he made a productive farm, and word of his success spread. Crèvecoeur is careful to note that S. K. had recognized and claimed the most fertile parts of the area and that he was a uniquely talented and disciplined farmer. Those who followed him, however, lacked this combination of circumstances and personal qualities. "Soon after these first successful essays, the fame of his happy beginning drew abundance of inferior people to that neighborhood. It was made a county, and in a short time grew populous, principally with poor people, whom some part of this barren soil could not render much richer" (p. 409). Even at the inception of this community, a loose structure of economic classes had been created. S. K. furthers that process by buying the two remaining parcels of fertile land for his brothers-in-law. "They all grew rich very fast," the narrator tells us, in a tone that celebrates the success as a fulfillment of American promise. "This part of the scene is truly pleasing, pastoral, and edifying: three brothers, the founders of three opulent families, the creators of three valuable plantations, the promoters of the succeeding settlements that took place around them." But this agrarian utopia is strictly limited, principally by the availability of land, and Crèvecoeur's sketch describes a benign form of feudalism taking root as a result.[13] For one who had praised America in the *Letters* precisely because it was an escape from such feudalism, this is deeply ironic. While America represented some important differences to the immigrants, there were also strict limitations to the number of possible success stories. S. K.'s rise to prosperity was thus shadowed by numbers of others who did not thrive and who, in the harder seasons, found themselves in extreme difficulties.

S. K. is a figure of benevolence, preventing many of the newcomers from falling into absolute destitution. "In their extreme indigence, in all their unexpected disasters, they repair to this princely farmer." As the community develops, he becomes "a father to the poor of this wilderness" (p. 411), almost single-handedly holding the community together. S. K. is a different version of the American hero and in many respects an important counter to the mythical hero who was by then taking shape in the national ideology. He finds his strength less in acquiring than in sharing, less in autonomy than in community. Of course he is an American hero with a distinctly patrician cast, and the contradiction of Crèvecoeur's sketch is that it presents the rebirth of feudalistic, not democratic, institutions.[14]

S. K.'s story contains elements of fable, as his generosity seems only to increase his wealth. "What he gave did not appear to diminish his stores; it seemed but a mite, and immediately to be replaced by the hand of Providence" (p. 413). But the fable has a dark turn; his generosity and prosperity become the means of his fall. "His brothers-in-law had long envied his great popularity, of which, however, he had never made the least abuse. They began to ridicule his generosity, and, from a contempt of his manner of living, they secretly passed to extreme hatred." The envy seethed impotently for a while, but the Revolution unleashed it. "Fanned by the general impunity of the times, they, in an underhanded manner, endeavoured to represent him as inimical." The last part of the sketch details S. K.'s unjust persecution and fall, in which he is hunted by the militia like an animal, saved only by his thorough knowledge of the countryside. Readers might be inclined to focus on the polemic against the excesses of the Revolution and the motives of many of the revolutionaries, but Crèvecoeur's description of the relation between frontier settlement and community building has more far-reaching implications. S. K. enacts on a grander scale the utopian success that James has expounded in the *Letters,* but his story also suggests the limits to that vision.

IV

"Reflections on the Manners of Americans" has important affinities with "The American Belisarius" in its presentation of a frontier farmer around whom a community develops. But the subject of this sketch is less consciously conceived as a hero. He is rather "an epitome" of an individual's "progress towards the wilderness" (p. 250), one who can explain through his own experience the nature of frontier development. Significantly, Crèvecoeur proposes economic calculation as the basis of his decision to move west. He is "determined to improve his fortune by removing to a new district and resolves to purchase as much land as will afford substantial farms to every one of his children" (p. 254). It should be noted that this economic calculation is not economic necessity in the strictest sense. The protagonist begins his quest from a secure financial position, and the struggle for the frontier is presented less as a battle with nature and the Indians than as a risky capital venture.

In purchasing land, he must protect himself by a thorough knowledge of the land that is available. "What a sagacity must this common farmer have, first to enable him to choose the province, the country, the peculiar tract most agreeable to his fortune; then to resist, to withstand the sophistry of these learned men armed with all the pomp of their city arguments!" The farmer makes a thorough study of the maps and descriptions of available land and then travels into the frontier to inspect it personally, drawing on his extensive woodsmanship and knowledge of farming to make a profitable selection. After further negotiations with the landowner and legal research on other claims to the land, he makes the purchase. The obstacles to this westward movement arise from the marketplace: "This is a land-merchant who, like all other merchants, has no other rule than to get what he can." Even after successfully locating and negotiating for his land, the farmer begins his new enterprise carrying a significant economic burden. "He purchases fifteen hundred acres at three dollars per acre to be paid in three equal yearly payments. He gives his bond for the same, and the whole tract is mortgaged as a security." The primal engagement of the farmer with uncleared land is thus predated by an economic and legal arrangement that will color his entire career on the land.

That life requires an absolute self-reliance, the capacity to become "master of that necessary dexterity which this solitary life inspires." But for Crèvecoeur, this complete self-sufficiency, though necessary and in many ways edifying, is incompatible with social life in its best sense. "Thus this man devoid of society learns more than ever to center every idea within that of his own welfare. To him, all that appears good, just, equitable has a necessary relation to himself and family. He has been so long alone that he has almost forgot the rest of mankind, except it is when he carries his crops on the snow to some distant market" (p. 260). Such social forgetfulness, combined with his experience of economic combat in purchasing his farm, makes him a problematic founder for an emerging community. One suspects that this farmer may have represented a more objective account of the course of American social development than S. K., whose heroic magnanimity has something of the quality of wish-projection. But in a similar pattern, the increase in settlement that overtook S. K. repeats itself, and the new community begins to place demands on him. "His granary is resorted to from all parts by other beginners, who did not come so well prepared." But his reaction to these conditions is tellingly different. "How will he sell his grain to these people who are strangers to him? Shall he deduct the expense of carrying it to a distant mill? This would appear just; but where is the necessity of this justice? His neighbours absolutely want his supply; they can't go to other places. He therefore concludes upon having the full price. He remembers his former difficulties; no one assisted him then. Why should he assist others?" Self-sufficiency shows its other face in this instance and suggests the inherent problem of frontier community-building. In a disturbing reversal, the successful farmer is transformed into a version of his own former adversary, the land merchant. "Perhaps he takes a mortgage on his neighbour's land. But it may happen that it is already encumbered by anterior and more ponderous debts. He knows instinctively the coercive powers of the laws: he impeaches the cattle; he has proper writings drawn; he gets bonds in judgment." This description of the development of a frontier community hardly bears the weight of utopian expectation. Even the proto-feudalistic vision that had surrounded S. K. is denied here; further removed is the utopian conception at the basis of Crèvecoeur's thought, the democratic egalitarianism of a society of yeoman freeholders.

This potential hero of the American frontier thus becomes a troubling anti-hero, enmeshed in the very marketplace that he seemed earlier to have conquered. In a further irony, the marketplace robs him of his identity as a farmer. "He becomes an innholder and a country merchant. This introduces him into all the little mysteries of self-interest, clothed under the general name of profits and emoluments." He is further tarnished by an ethical slackening in his business dealings. "He sells for good that which perhaps he knows to be indifferent because he also knows that the ashes he has collected, the wheat he has taken in may not be so good or so clean as it was asserted. Fearful of fraud in all his dealings and transactions, he arms himself, therefore, with it." There is a striking contrast between this portrait of the successful farmer become unscrupulous businessman and that of S. K. refusing high prices for his grain in order to protect his poorer neighbors. Although Crèvecoeur presents the farmer without explicit moral judgement, he gradually transforms his career into a negative object-lesson, implying that the farmer's transformation was the inevitable result of his social context. The sketch thus delineates the dystopic conditions of the American frontier.

The problematics of Crèvecoeur's agrarian utopia are thus attributed not to the Revolution but to the structure of frontier experience. This deepens the problem of conceiving of the loose community of the frontier in ideal terms. The arrival of the population which transforms a frontier into a civilized settlement and secures each farmer's economic status is also the process by which the agrarian dream is deferred. In "The American Belisarius" the test of S. K.'s success was "economic" in more than one sense. He was able to prosper as a farmer through the right application of his knowledge and diligence under favorable environmental conditions. But he was also economically successful in that he did not allow his economic status to rob him of his essential humanity in a posture of exclusionary greed. This was a moral success, but the essential moral question concerned the acquisition and disposal of wealth. Similarly, S. K.'s downfall was caused by the greed of his brothers-in-law, who were also envious of his popularity with the community. Their resentment arose from their inability to accept his very different sense of the appropriate stewardship of wealth. They "ridicule[d] his generosity" and felt "contempt of his manner of living" (p. 413), for he exposed by contrast their own impoverishment as social beings. Their revenge, a punishment much in the American grain, was to ostracize one who called the motive for profit into question or in any way limited it. The Revolution only gave them a pretext for their persecution. The warning implicit in "Reflections on the Manners of Americans" is similar then to that of "The American Belisarius." This farmer shared S. K.'s economic success but failed principally because he allowed economic ambition to usurp a commitment to community in his scale of values. S. K. was victimized by those who had the same failing. The farmer in "Reflections on the Manners of Americans" has thus become a captive of his economic success. While this may seem to be a moral criticism aimed at the value system of a particular individual, that individual, we must realize, is representative of the larger society and is crucially shaped by it.

V

The cumulative evidence of Crèvecoeur's work suggests that he labored on the edge of a profound critique of the formation of American culture, seeing its course as a failure to realize his utopian projections. An interpretation of the cultural significance of his work must recognize that his projection of agrarian values onto the formative conditions of the nation gave him the standpoint from which these elements of social tragedy could begin to be identified. If the evidence that Crèvecoeur left seems contradictory, it at least strikes us as frank in its incomplete attempt to report on the survival of utopian hopes in America. And certainly, some of the fragmentary nature of the analysis is the direct result of Crèvecoeur's own shattered life during the late 1770s. But despite the frank and even at times dispiriting criticism of American life, there remains a core of hope in Crèvecoeur's writings that accounts for its initial impact on the reader and its continuing claim. How can we account for it?

Crèvecoeur's projection of the ideal condition of the freehold farmer loosely bound to a supportive community of social and economic equals has powerfully rendered to Americans a best image of themselves. It has proved so potent, in fact, that at times it has been taken as a report on what America is, not what it could or ought to be. The real achievement of his agrarian writing is an enduring critical perspective on the development of American society. Thus James's third letter, read in isolation from the book's later qualifications and critiques, has been seen as an articulation of the success of the American egalitarian melting-pot, rather than an incompletely realized projection of social success. Such cultural misreading has made it particularly important to recognize the way in which Crèvecoeur used his utopian model as a stance from which the course of American culture could be criticized. Perhaps he did not realize how durable that stance might be. In describing the agrarian experiment, he formulated a state of mind "incongruous with the state of reality in which it occurs," and thus inimical to that reality.[15]

Notes

1. *The Machine in the Garden: Technology and the Pastoral Ideal in America* (New York: Oxford Univ. Press, 1964), p. 74.

2. See Elayne Antler Rapping, "Theory and Experience in Crèvecoeur's America," *American Quarterly,* 19 (1967), 707-18, who discusses "agrarian democracy" as "an ideal social structure" (p. 707) which Crèvecoeur's *Letters* explores.

3. Thomas Philbrick has argued that the change of tone in the book establishes a criticism of any overly optimistic version of the American myth and portrays James and his family as trying to "survive as para-

sites on the Indian community." See *St. John de Crèvecoeur* (New York: Twayne, 1970), pp. 81-88. Other excellent arguments which stress the importance of the tragic nature of the ending, or distrust the viability of James's escape at the end, are Rapping, "Theory and Experience in Crèvecoeur's America"; James C. Mohr, "Calculated Disillusionment: Crèvecoeur's Letters Reconsidered," *South Atlantic Quarterly,* 69 (1970), 354-63; Richard Slotkin, *Regeneration Through Violence: The Mythology of the American Frontier, 1600-1860* (Middletown, Conn.: Wesleyan Univ. Press, 1973), pp. 263-67; and Annette Kolodny, *The Lay of the Land: Metaphor as Experience and History in American Life and Letters* (Chapel Hill: Univ. of North Carolina Press, 1975), pp. 52-66. For the perspective that sees certain values of the opening chapters preserved even through the change of tone at the end, see Myra Jehlen, "J. Hector St. John Crèvecoeur: A Monarcho-Anarchist in Revolutionary America," *American Quarterly,* 31 (1979), 204-22; and David Robinson, "Crèvecoeur's James: The Education of an American Farmer," *Journal of English and Germanic Philology,* 80 (1981), 552-70.

4. Crèvecoeur's papers have recently been acquired by the Library of Congress, and a new edition of his work by Everett Emerson is in progress.

5. *Sketches of Eighteenth-Century America,* ed. Henri L. Bourdin, Ralph H. Gabriel, and Stanley T. Williams (New Haven: Yale Univ. Press, 1925).

6. See "The Utopian Mentality" in Karl Mannheim, *Ideology and Utopia* (New York: Harcourt Brace—Harvest, 1936), pp. 192-263.

7. "The Landscape of Tragedy: Crèvecoeur's 'Susquehanna,'" *Early American Literature,* 20 (1985), 39. D. H. Lawrence made a persuasive case for this point of view in his *Studies in Classic American Literature* (1923; rpt. New York: Penguin, 1977).

8. For information on the personal difficulties that Crèvecoeur underwent during the Revolution, see Gay Wilson Allen and Roger Asselineau, *St. John de Crèvecoeur: The Life of an American Farmer* (New York: Viking, 1987), pp. 46-68.

9. J. A. Leo Lemay has argued that Crèvecoeur's *Letters* marked a significant turning point in the cultural reconception of the frontiersman. See "The Frontiersman from Lout to Hero: Notes on the Significance of the Comparative Method and the Stage Theory in Early American Literature and Culture," *Proceedings of the American Antiquarian Society,* 88, Part 2 (1978), 187-223.

10. For the details of Crèvecoeur's career in France after the Revolution, see Allen and Asselineau, pp. 68-101. "The American Belisarius" and "Landscapes" are the most blistering anti-revolutionary pieces in the *Sketches.*

11. *Letters from an American Farmer* and *Sketches of Eighteenth-Century America,* ed. Albert E. Stone (New York: Penguin, 1986), p. 204. Further quotations from the *Letters* and the *Sketches* will be cited parenthetically.

12. Jehlen also notes that Crèvecoeur's individualism is dependent on a stable and secure social order, which the British government in the colonies had represented.

13. See Kolodny's discussion of this sketch in *The Lay of the Land,* in which she notes that the initial representation of the success of the community was tied to a conception of the landscape as feminine (pp. 55-56).

14. For a different perspective on the question of feudalism, see Jehlen, who argues that S. K.'s generosity is an extension of the role of family patriarch to the community as a whole. He represented a "democratic familialism, whose enobling patriarchism had neither the source nor the purpose of the feudal aristocratic variety" (p. 215).

15. Mannheim, p. 192. I would like to acknowledge the support of a National Endowment for the Humanities Summer Stipend in completing this essay.

Stephen Carl Arch (essay date 1990)

SOURCE: "The 'Progressive Steps' of the Narrator in Crèvecoeur's *Letters from an American Farmer,*" in *Studies in American Fiction,* Vol. 18, No. 2, Autumn, 1990, pp. 145-58.

[*In the following essay, Arch challenges the common critical assessment of* Letters *as an American romance, suggesting instead that it is a work of fiction designed to expose the dangers of revolution.*]

Throughout J. Hector St. John de Crèvecoeur's **Letters From An American Farmer,** James, the narrator, is interested in the concept of "progress," especially the "progressive" acculturation of Europeans who have immigrated to America. "All I wish to delineate," he says concerning his short "History of Andrew, the Hebridean," in Letter III, "is the progressive steps of a poor man, advancing from indigence to ease, from oppression to freedom, from obscurity and contumely to some degree of consequence."[1] James' fascination with progress is ironic, since he begins his correspondence with Mr. F. B. as a curiously static personality leading a pleasant but static existence. Letter II reveals that James' farm was left to him by his father, that he has done nothing to improve it, and that, having once considered selling it, he immediately retreated from such a potential alteration in lifestyle, fearing that in a "world so wide . . . there would be no room for [him]" (p. 52). James himself ingenuously admits that his life is an imitation of his father's: "I have but to tread his paths to be happy and a good man like him" (p. 53). Willingly constrained by this narrow life, James initially presents a striking contrast to Andrew the Hebridean, whose history is a record of his progression from oppressed European to free American.[2]

However, James, too, undergoes a "great metamorphosis" in *Letters* and is dislodged from his "narrow circles" (p. 65). His progress is closely linked to the epistolary form and dialogic structure of *Letters.* Many critics have argued that the letters and the dialogue are simply rhetorical devices that have no relevance to the work as a whole; they have argued that the letters are essentially separate documents that produce a loose structure for the whole[3] or that, perhaps, the tenor and subject matter of each letter simply reveal the extent to which Crèvecoeur's own hand can be seen "pointing to the importance of some moral issue by manipulating his protagonist."[4] Thomas Philbrick has gone a bit further, arguing that the "epistolary form . . . is far more than a stratagem by which Crèvecoeur excuses his violations of logical organization; by serving as the vehicle of characterization and narration, it spins its own strands of coherence."[5] In other words, due to its epistolary form, *Letters* might even be considered a "prototypical" or "germinal" American romance.[6] However, these critics take away as much as they mean to give; they praise Crèvecoeur's work as much for what comes later (the "real" American romance) as for what it did, or what it tried to do, in 1782. In fact, the epistolary form and dialogic structure of *Letters* are much more than mere ornament. *Letters* is not a romance that simply and inconclusively juxtaposes opposing sets of terms (the idyllic and the demonic,[7] idealism and realism,[8] romanticism and skepticism), it is a philosophical work of fiction that comments on the dangers of revolution and on the inadequacies of man's fictions about himself.[9]

Letters begins with James, his wife, and his minister discussing Mr. F. B.'s request that James become his American correspondent. James is undecided: he is afraid that, with his "limited power of mind" and undeveloped writing skills, he will not make a good correspondent (pp. 39-40). His wife is even more reluctant, fearing both that Mr. F. B. is too sophisticated and that James' own local reputation might suffer from his being called a writer. It is the minister who convinces James to write to Mr. F. B. He points out that Mr. F. B., in his first letter to James, asserted "that writing letters is nothing more than talking on paper" and indicated that he wants "nothing of [James] but what lies within the reach of [his] experience and knowledge" (p. 41). The minister agrees with this dialogic notion of writing: "What we speak out among ourselves we call conversation," he tells James, "and a letter is only conversation put down in black and white" (p. 44). This argument convinces James to go ahead with the project, and the record of this debate becomes Letter I. James closes with a final admonition to Mr. F. B. not to forget his limitations: "Remember, you are to give me my subjects, and on no other shall I write, lest you should blame me for an injudicious choice. . . . [And I will record] the spontaneous impressions which each subject may inspire" (pp. 49-50).

The first subject provided by Mr. F. B. is American husbandry, a subject on which he has apparently "conversed" at some length in his second letter to James, comparing American farming methods to those practiced in England, Russia, and Hungary. In Letter II James responds to this subject by recounting some of the "spontaneous impressions" he has experienced while working in his fields. True to his insistence that he is "neither a philosopher, politician, divine, or naturalist" (p. 49), James does not overtly discuss politics, science, or other "public" matters. Letter II is a short autobiography revealing that James owns a well-developed farm (inherited from his father), has an excellent wife and healthy children, possesses faithful and industrious Negroes, and is not troubled by unfriendly Indians. James describes an idyllic if static existence on his Pennsylvania farm.

Yet the idyllic scenes of Letter II are not quite apolitical. James links them to current issues at several points. Where, he asks rhetorically, "is that station which can confer a more substantial system of felicity than that of an American farmer possessing freedom of action, freedom of thoughts, ruled by a mode of government which requires but little from us?" (p. 52). His pleasant farm, he remarks a little later, "has established all our [i.e. his family's] rights . . . our rank, our freedom, our power as citizens. . . . This is what may be called the true and the only philosophy of an American farmer" (p. 54). The incursion of such talk into the midst of these "spontaneous impressions" could, of course, be explained by the loose organization of *Letters*; if the individual letters possess no necessary internal relationship to one another, a comment in Letter I need not be consistent with the method in Letter II. However, perfectly consistent with the fictional realism established in Letter I, with the psychology of a rustic such as James writing to someone he perceives as his superior, Crèvecoeur has James try to impress Mr. F. B. in this second letter. James' self-conscious asides about his own inferiority support this reading.[10] So do his political views, for it seems clear that he is merely parroting the minister's arguments, indeed, the minister's vision of America, as the minister expressed them during the debate in Letter I. Here in America, the minister had told James that "'[we] are strangers to those feudal institutions which have enslaved so many. . . . Misguided religion, tyranny, and absurd laws everywhere depress and afflict mankind. Here we have in some measure regained the ancient dignity of our species: our laws are simple and just . . .'" (pp. 42-43). James is unlearned and unlettered; in trying to shoot at something beyond his "limited abilities" in Letter II, he falls back on attitudes and ideas he has heard before. At this point, James' vision of the American dream is as much the minister's as his own.

The imagery James develops in Letter II emphasizes his unquestioning acceptance of the minister's attitudes, specifically his dichotomy between old world oppression and new world freedom. Responding to Mr. F. B.'s description of the "good and evil . . . to be found in all societies" (p. 51), James tells of a selfish wren that fearlessly stole the nest of a larger swallow on James' porch. The wren possesses a "spirit of injustice" that seems almost human; the swallow calls up the image of a "passive Quaker." It seems that all of nature, including man, is in constant conflict. But not on James' farm. A peaceful and benevolent despot, James carries the wren's box to another part of the house to prevent the incident from happening again. Similarly, James describes a swarm of bees that attacks a malicious king-bird; when they quit "their military array," the bees are snapped up one by one and eaten by the impudent bird. It is a bird-eat-bee world out there, James suggests, except that he, whose "indulgence had been carried too far," kills the king-bird, opens his craw, and watches in surprise as many of the bees return to life (p. 56). The existence of a "Russian boor or an Hungarian peasant" may be wretched, and men around the world may be warring (as Mr. F. B.'s second letter apparently argued), but the American farmer as described by James in Letter II lives in peace and harmony in his own "narrow circles," a lawgiver above and beyond the reach of any authority but his own. And here in America, James observes with satisfaction, "the law is to us precisely what I am in my barnyard, a bridle and check to prevent the strong and greedy from oppressing the timid and weak" (p. 57). James' world (and, by extension, his America) may not exactly be one in which the lion lies down with the lamb, but it is one in which "a curious republic of industrious hornets" can live peaceably with James' family, catching flies "even on the eyelids of [his] children" (p. 63). As described by James in Letter II, it is a buzzing garden.

In Letter III James again responds to a subject provided by Mr. F. B.'s ruminations. James' famous question, "What, then, is the American, this new man?" (p. 69), suggests that Mr. F. B. has asked him to expand upon his observations in Letter II concerning the "substantial system of felicity" enjoyed by Americans. In response, James first theorizes about the "new man," then narrates the history of one. Theoretically, the American is a man psychologically and morally remade by his exposure to a new and expansive land. Freed from the religious, political, and spatial constraints of the old world, he is "resurrected"; he undergoes a "great metamorphosis . . . [that] extinguishes all his European prejudices [and allows him to forget] that mechanism of subordination, that servility of disposition which poverty had taught him" (p. 83). The American is a "regenerated" human being.

In Letter II James' "spontaneous impressions" led him to recount his personal history; in Letter III James' response to Mr. F. B. leads him beyond "impressions" (and vague politicizing) to reflection. His theory of the "new man" in America leads him, for example, to group Americans into three "separate and distinct" classes (pp. 71-73). He has gone beyond mere "feelings" to assumptions, reasons, and facts. Just so, his "History of Andrew, the Hebridean," represents another, more extensive act of reflection: he assumes the historian's task of collecting, digesting, and arranging the events of the past. After first protesting the commonplace nature of his history, James defines his methodology: "All I wish to delineate is the progressive steps of a poor man, advancing from indigence to ease, from oppression to freedom, from obscurity and contumely to some degree of consequence . . . by the gradual operation of sobriety, honesty, and emigration" (p. 90). James' history of Andrew is rosy: the merchants who deal with Andrew are honest and faithful; the Indians are kind, though slightly mischievous; the neighbors display warmth and friendship; Andrew's lands and possessions prove to be fertile and flourishing. Andrew is a perfect example of the new man in America, his history a perfect "epitome" (p. 86) of the "progressive" transformation that results in that man. For the first time, James rests content with his effort in a letter, concluding that he is more content with his history of Andrew than is the "historiographer of some great prince or general [who has brought] his hero victorious to the end of a successful campaign" (p. 104). Moving from loose autobiography in Letter II to methodologically-defined biography in Letter III, James "discovers" a world outside his own narrow circles, discovers a prospect that is more "entertaining and instructive" (p. 91) than his own in its view of America and the new American man. It is still highly optimistic.

In the next five letters James, though still responding to Mr. F. B.'s earlier query concerning the precise nature of the "American," takes it upon himself to frame the subject matter of the "conversation." "Sensible how unable I am to lead you through so vast a maze [as America]," he writes, "let us look attentively for some small unnoticed corner" (p. 107), Nantucket Island, which can be analyzed in depth. James has come a long way from the simple farmer afraid of choosing an "injudicious" subject in Letter I. He begins his narrative of Nantucket Island with a comment on his historiographic method:

> You have, no doubt, read several histories of this continent, yet there are a thousand facts, a thousand explanations, overlooked. Authors will certainly convey to you a geographical knowledge of this country; they will acquaint you with the eras of the several settlements, the foundations of our towns, the spirit of our different characters, etc., yet they do not sufficiently disclose the genius of the people. . . . I want not to record the annals of the island of Nantucket; its inhabitants have no annals, for they are not a race of warriors. My simple wish is to trace them throughout their progressive steps from their arrival here to this present hour; to inquire by what means they have raised themselves from the most humble, the most insignificant beginnings, to the ease and the wealth they now possess . . .

(pp. 107-08)

James asserts that he is a historian of America, operating not by "epitome" (as in Andrew's history) but by synecdoche. Nantucket is merely a type of America; "numberless settlements," James says, "each distinguished by some peculiarities, present themselves [to the historian] on every side; all . . . realize the most sanguine wishes that a good man could form for the happiness of his race" (p. 107).

Here, too, James conceives history to be the "delineation" of the "progressive steps" from poverty to wealth. But in this movement from biographer to national historian, James displays a new awareness of his task and, hence, his abilities. He has learned, quite clearly, that history can be written according to any number of methods; he has chosen, in his attempt to "disclose [America's] genius," to examine one small area of the larger whole. This purpose explains why James devotes five letters to Nantucket Island and Martha's Vineyard, and it reflects the growing role that James' powers of reasoning play in his "conversation" with Mr. F. B.

James finds Nantucket a "happy settlement." The Islanders enjoy "a system of rational laws founded on perfect freedom" (p. 109); their society is free from "idleness and poverty, the causes of so many crimes" elsewhere (p. 125); many people enjoy great prosperity, all "an easy subsistence" (p. 143); and slavery is not tolerated. Nantucket, it seems, is a restored Eden, a rocky island made into a garden by the "genius" and "industry" of its settlers; and, James insists, "what has happened here has and will happen everywhere else" in America (p. 110). It is, after all, only one singular scene of happiness amid the great "diffusive scene of happiness reaching from the sea-shores to the last settlements on the borders of the wilderness" (p. 154).

James' account of Nantucket Island and its inhabitants is not completely optimistic, however. Darker elements intrude. James admits that the happiness of Americans might not be as unspoiled as he had thought. It is interrupted by individual folly and by "our spirit of litigiousness" (p. 154). He also finds that the history of Nantucket and, since Nantucket functions as synecdoche, of America is tainted by the corruption which European settlers brought to the Indians in the form of smallpox and rum. Even as he writes, James points out, the descendants of those abused Indians are being annihilated. Finally, James' analysis of the history of Nantucket leads to his discovery that some of the Islanders had recently moved inland to establish a community in North Carolina named, hopefully, New Garden. But, though it is located in a much more fertile region than Nantucket, New Garden does not create the new, regenerated man of America: "It does not breed men equally hardy [to Nantucket Islanders]. . . . It leads too much to idleness and effeminacy" (p. 147). In his peripheral vision, James can see reasons for refuting the romantic vision of America he expressed so confidently in Letter III. He quickly tries to turn away from them.

Essentially, the five Nantucket letters comprise one unit of letters, an integrated history in which, by digging straight down into the history of one region of America instead of "cheerfully . . . skipping from bush to bush" along the ground (p. 90), James is made to confront realities gilded by the rhetoric of his and the minister's romantic notions. In Letter IX, then, James chooses his own subject for the first time, a sign that he has achieved a certain independence of mind. Charles Town, North Carolina, he writes to

Mr. F. B., is one great scene of "joy, festivity and happiness" (p. 168). Now, however, James finds it impossible to ignore the evils that lurk behind that facade of happiness: the climate, which "renders excesses of all kinds very dangerous"; the lawyers, who slowly rob the people of their patrimony; and, crucially, the institution of slavery.

James' subject matter in Letter IX is generated, ironically, by a "spontaneous impression": on his way to visit a planter, he comes upon a black slave suspended in a cage and left to expire of thirst, of pain, or at the beaks of birds of prey. The slave had killed the overseer of the plantation, James learns, and had been tortured and left to die by what the planter refers to as "the laws of self-preservation" (p. 179), that is, as an example to the other slaves. This scene, James somberly tells Mr. F. B., accounts for my "melancholy reflections and . . . for the gloomy thoughts with which I [fill] this letter" (p. 177). The scene accounts, too, for the tremendous leap James makes from the history of Nantucket in Letters IV-VIII to the "history of the earth" (p. 173) that he begins to analyze in Letter IX. Elaborating the intimations of evil he felt upon seeing the slave, James insists that the history of the world, including America, presents nothing "but crimes of the most heinous nature, committed from one end of the world to the other" (p. 173). "What, then, is man?" (p. 170), James asks, echoing his earlier, more famous question. Having moved from a history of the self, to a history of an other, to a history of a people, and now to the history of mankind, James' expanding consciousness arrives at a more basic question. Its answer is not "goodness." Human nature is perverse (p. 174), and God has abandoned it "to all the errors, the follies, and the miseries, which [man's] most frantic rage and [his] most dangerous vices and passions can produce" (p. 173).

This letter, which James calls a "general review of human nature" (p. 177), moves from his discussion of the institution of slavery to his recognition that man is by nature wretched, his principles "poisoned in their most essential parts" (pp. 173-74). James concludes by asking whether he, having realized the true nature of man, should prefer a "primitive" life in the woods to a "civilized" life in society. The question at first seems moot: "Evil preponderates in both" states. But evil, James argues, is "more scarce, more supportable, and less enormous" in the woods than it is in "advanced" society. So, clearly, man should be happier, or less unhappy, in the pastoral state. Yet this "fact" is complicated by man's innate desire and need to people the earth. The dilemma and, more significantly, James' ambivalence are indicative of his state of mind in Letter IX as he approaches the "gloomy" scene at the end. It is as if his realization of the "true" nature of mankind, though the gradual product of his dialogue with Mr. F. B., were still too sudden and too shocking to allow any answers, any firm statements about reality. The ground has shifted beneath him.

It is not by chance, then, that Mr. F. B. initiates the discussion in Letter X, asking James to say something about snakes. Though Mr. F. B.'s choice of subject matter is more than slightly ironic, James certainly *needs* direction. And his recognition of the snake's presence in the new world is a painful but necessary extension of Letter IX. Shocked by his conclusions there, James wishes to turn his face away from the sight of evil: "Why would you prescribe this task?" (p. 180), he asks. James soon finds that the rattlesnake, though "perfectly inoffensive" if not touched and capable even of being tamed, is more likely to kill than not to offend. He narrates the story of a father and son who were killed by pulling on a boot that had two rattlesnake fangs lodged in it. Evil, though not seen, not suspected, preponderates. Once he first notices evil, James finds it everywhere. Retreating to a "simple grove" to watch the humming-bird, "the most beautiful of [birds]," James notes that

> sometimes, from what motive I know about, it will tear and lacerate flowers into a hundred pieces, for, strange to tell, they are the most irascible of the feathered tribe. Where do passions find room in so diminutive a body? They often fight with the fury of lions until one of the combatants falls a sacrifice and dies. . . . [The hummingbird] is a miniature work of our Great Parent . . .
>
> (p. 184)

Evil "preponderates" in man, in Nature, in every work of God, from His most "miniature work" to His most complex.

This second incident marks James' development. In Letter II he had displayed his conviction of the all-powerful nature of man by moving the box of the greedy wren to another part of the house and by shooting the rapacious kingbird that destroyed his bee population. Now, however, a bird provides the very image of passions run amok; James' "grove" is tainted by evil, and he has no power over that evil. His state of mind following this realization is imaged by an "uncommon and beautiful" battle between a black snake and a water snake described at the end of Letter X. James is puzzled by the battle, for the "vindictive rage" expressed by each combatant appears to be unfounded. "Strange was this to behold," he writes. Like the evil he has come to recognize in these later letters versus his own natural good feelings expressed in the early letters, the black snake (the "aggressor") and the water snake struggle, the former solely out of hate, the latter in an attempt to reach "its natural element" (p. 185). The black snake gains control at the end:

> . . . The black snake seemed to retain its wonted superiority, for its head was exactly fixed above that of the other, which it incessantly pressed down under the water, until it was stifled and sunk. The victor no sooner perceived its enemy incapable of further resistance than, abandoning it to the current, it returned on shore and disappeared.
>
> (p. 186)

The exit of the black snake is a metaphor for James' disappearance in Letter XI; he, too, is "stifled and sunk." Letter XI is written by a European traveller named Iw-n Al-z who describes a visit he made to John Bartram, the famous botanist. Iw-n echoes the optimism of James' early letters: "Examine [Pennsylvania] in whatever light you will," Iw-n begins the letter that James sends on to Mr. F. B., "the eyes as well as the mind . . . are equally delighted because a diffusive happiness appears in every part, happiness which is established on the broadest basis" (p. 187). Iw-n's words recall James' statement that America is "one diffusive scene of happiness"; Iw-n's optimism, however, is justified by what he finds at Bartram's farm. Emancipating their slaves, who become "new . . . beings" (thus fulfilling the definition of the American in Letter III), and living peacefully and peaceably themselves, Bartram and his Quaker neighbors follow the "doctrines of Jesus Christ in that simplicity with which they were delivered; a happier system could not have been devised for the use of mankind" (p. 199). Here is a "New Garden." And its juxtaposition with James' gloomy view of the world in Letters IX and X indicates that, for Crèvecoeur, the American "dream" of Letter III *is* possible. He insists, however, that a just and happy society like the one Bartram has created is not an automatic effect of man's arrival on the American continent: the "new man" can more easily become a slave-owning man than he can an Adam.

James, however, continues to retreat in fear from his new perception of evil in the world. Letter I and Letter XI are dominated by voices other than James': the minister and James' wife in Letter I, Iw-n Al-z and John Bartram in Letter XI. Each is followed by a letter in which James' feelings erupt. In Letter II those passionate "feelings" (p. 53) were the result of James' memory of the fear he had experienced when he considered selling his father's farm. Afraid of his own insignificance, James rejected the larger world of experience and remained on his father's farm. Lacking experience, James' letters could only retreat to feelings and impressions, responses conditioned by the thoughts and language of the people James respected: his father, the minister, Mr. F. B. In Letter XII James again retreats to feelings: "Distresses of a Frontier Man." Plagued by the "remembrance of dreadful scenes," not simply the tortured slave, but the battles of the Revolution, James again faces and retreats from his own smallness: "What can an insignificant man do in the midst of these jarring contradictory parties, equally hostile to persons situated as I am?" (p. 205). The ability to reason, which he has discovered in the course of *Letters,* provides no answers, only more questions. "What, then, is life?" he asks, rewriting his most famous question once again. At bottom, he decides, it is "self-preservation" (p. 210). James retreats west, fleeing a world that has lost its senses.

James moves from innocence to experience, from a naive acceptance of the way of life inherited from his father and taught by his minister to a critical awareness of his own need to think, to act, and to create his own future. His progression through the literary genres of autobiography, biography, local history, national history, and epic history is merely an analogue of his intellectual and moral growth.

His final step in this progression toward self-knowledge is a painful one, for what he learns to do late in his conversation with Mr. F. B. is to defictionalize his world, to dismantle the many claims colonial and revolutionary America made on behalf of rational, "objective" truth. Letters II and III reveal James' unquestioning acceptance of his father's life and of the minister's romantic version of the American dream. By the time he ends Letter IV, James makes note of the fact that the success of the Nantucket Islanders is due in part to their simplicity: "I saw neither governors nor any pageantry of state, neither ostentatious magistrates nor any individuals clothed with useless dignity: no artificial phantoms subsist here, either civil or religious" (p. 125). Those who bring their "luxurious" manners to Nantucket, James observes with satisfaction, "could not exist a month; they would be obliged to emigrate" (p. 125). Nantucket Island, in other words, like America itself, had done away with the "artificial phantoms" that oppressed man in Europe. The "false" had been discarded in favor of the "true," the "real."

This first suspicion of the "artificiality" of religion and government is not all-inclusive, of course. James merely extends the minister's romantic condemnation of the old world (pp. 42-44) to include its manners, government, and religion; he praises Nantucket for reducing class distinctions (pp. 125-26), establishing a government "which demands but little for its protection" (p. 109), and practicing a religion "disencumbered . . . from useless ceremonies and trifling forms" (p. 153). One can find a similar sort of rhetoric in many works after 1765 in America. John Adams, for one, argued that, ideally, "government [is] a plain, simple, intelligible thing, founded in nature and reason, and quite comprehensible by common sense." America, Adams went on to say, had thrown off the "arbitrary," artificial tyranny of the old world's canon and feudal law.[11] James, however, soon begins to sense that Nantucket, though it may have simplified life in some ways, has merely replaced one fiction for another. The women of the island, for example, take a dose of opium every morning: "It is hard to conceive how a people always happy and healthy . . . [and] never oppressed with the vapours of idleness, yet should want the fictitious effects of opium to preserve that cheerfulness to which their temperance, their climate, their happy situation, so justly entitle them" (p. 160). Even in this simplified society, mankind willingly chooses fictions, chooses oppressions. In addition, James notices that the law, which he earlier trumpeted as "a bridle and check to prevent the strong and greedy from oppressing the timid and weak" (p. 57), is actually an instrument of oppression. In Nantucket lawyers are an "oppressive burthen under which we groan" (p. 152). The situation is even worse in Charles Town. There, society has become "slaves" to the society of lawyers. James sees that mankind will have its fictions, be its situation never so simple, free, and happy.

James' first question—"What, then, is the American, this new man?"—is followed by his realization that the American is not so different from the old man. Both are oppressed; both create fictions which complicate an otherwise natural existence. Thus his next question—"What, then, is man?"—collapses the new world-old world dichotomy. There is no "American," no "European"; there is man. Traditionally, of course, man had been defined as a fallen creature, capable of regeneration only by the saving grace of Christ. Crèvecoeur plays with the notion of regeneration in *Letters*: the black slave in the cage is a Christ-figure, covered as he is by a swarm of insects "eager to feed on his mangled flesh and to drink his blood" (p. 178); the "old man" (the European) is "regenerated" (p. 68) and "resurrected" (p. 82), reborn as a "new man" (the American); the Nantucket Islanders found a settlement they name "New Garden." But as James is exposed to the horror and the enormity of evil, he comes to realize that any notion of man's goodness is false. Man is not good. "The history of the earth!" James exclaims. "doth it present anything but crimes of the most heinous nature, committed from one end of the world to the other?" (p. 193) Men "are always at war" (p. 174); human nature is perverse; existence is but so "many errors . . . crimes . . . diseases, wants, and sufferings" (p. 177). The myths of Eden and of man's regeneration are not true: man could never have been, nor can he be, good.

James' third question—"What, then, is life?"—indicates that he has continued to strip away layers of enlightenment and romantic belief, rejecting the primacy of human culture and of man in favor of a more elemental subject, experience shorn of its fictions, its appearances. His immediate answer to the question is pessimistic, almost nihilistic: "Life appears to be a mere accident, and of the worst kind: we are born to be victims of diseases and passions, of mischance and death; better not to be than to be miserable" (p. 210). James no longer has faith in his culture and his culture's fictions. The "centre is tumbled down" (p. 211), he says in reference to his beliefs. Unable to believe in "the fictitious society in which [he] lives" (p. 214), James spends most of Letter XII justifying his decision to emigrate to an Indian village somewhere west of Pennsylvania. "Self-preservation," he concludes, "is above all political precepts and rules, and even superior to the dearest opinions of our minds" (p. 210).

One wonders at the phrasing here: "self-preservation." That is the phrase the slave-owner used to defend his murder of the slave in Letter IX (p. 179): language has become malleable and fluid in James' world; it does not signify. Nor, in the end, does James' romantic vision of Indian society. Though he begins to describe it in the same idealistic manner he had described America in Letter III (pp. 213-14), James steps back from that vision with an abrupt realization that he is creating a fiction: "Perhaps my imagination gilds too strongly this distant prospect . . ." (p. 225). There is no answer to his third question, except in the actual act of his choosing to be left, at the end, where so many later American heroes, also stripped of their illusions, of their naive fictions concerning the world around them, will be left: in a liminal space out of which they may, perhaps, project themselves anew in some extra-novelistic future.[12]

James' crisis at the end is Crèvecoeur's imaginative projection of the very real crisis experienced by many Americans during the Revolution. Donald Weber has convincingly shown, for example, how Revolutionary ministers, responding to the bewildering events of the 1760s and 1770s, attempted "to arrest [their] metaphysical fall into interpretive contingency, the hermeneutic void of utter disconnectedness," by articulating a sermon rhetoric that was at first fragmented, disjointed, anti-narrative. "Language itself," Weber writes, "became unmoored from traditional contexts, referents, and canons of style and form" during the Revolution.[13] Myths, of course, are stories a culture invents to confer identity, to achieve and maintain consensus; and they are, as Richard Slotkin has shown, stories in which "the logic of myth" literally flows from "the logic of . . . [its] narrative."[14] In moments of ideological crisis, such as the American Revolution, those myths are challenged, disrupted, and overturned. They do not adequately explain. "New stories are required when the old no longer resonate with explanatory power."[15] The ministers Weber discusses eventually managed to accommodate "their pulpits to the secular American world of the 1790s,"[16] and to invent a rhetoric and accompanying myth that accounted for changed cultural values and their own relation to those values. Their sermons became coherent and dependent on narrative once again.

Like those ministers, James experiences a "metaphysical fall into interpretive contingency." He awakens from his unquestioning acceptance of the world of his fathers into a world in which meanings, values, and language itself are "unmoored from [their] traditional contexts." "I had never before these calamitous times formed any such ideas" about America, about mankind, about life itself, James mourns; "I lived on, laboured and prospered, without having ever studied on what the security of my life and the foundation of my prosperity were established; I perceived them just as they left me" (p. 201). James' predicament is that, having rejected society's fictions, he has none to replace them; having descended into uncertainty, he cannot find solid ground. He has only fragments that cannot cohere into meaning, fragments from which no consensus could possibly be achieved. Seen this way, *Letters* provides a glimpse into that moment at which America stood poised in cultural uncertainty, having severed its ties with the old world and opted for a future the founding fathers, no more than anyone else, could yet imagine. It was that uncertainty, Robert Ferguson has written, "the possibility of collapse through internal dissension, [which] continue[d] to haunt both political considerations and the literary imagination for generations."[17] James' story itself epitomizes the "haunting" which marked American literature in the years subsequent to 1776.

It is as much a distortion of *Letters* to read it as a disjointed series of sketches as it is to read it as a myth of national creation or even a plea for consensus. James is no Rip Van Winkle who awakens to find consensus both in the world around him (Washington's picture as it is painted over King George's) and in his own story (which every "man, woman, [and] child in the neighborhood . . . knew . . . by heart"). He is that still-dazed Rip whose "senses [are] overpowered"[18] not by liquor but by a world gone mad and by his own internalization of that madness through his recognition of the inadequacies of man's fictions about himself. And James' creator, a conservative in politics as well as in morals, is a critic of the psychological, social, and imaginative dangers of revolution, not the exuberant expansiveness of the American dream.

Notes

1. Hector St. John de Crèvecoeur, *Letters From An American Farmer and Sketches of Eighteenth-Century America* (New York: Penguin American Library, 1981), p. 90. Subsequent page references are given parenthetically in the text. For other references to "progress," see p. 76 (on the regression of farmers into hunters), p. 108 (on James' desire to "to trace [the Nantucket Islanders] throughout their progressive steps from their arrival here to this present hour"), p. 130 (on "the progress of [the Nantucket Islanders'] maritime schemes"), and p. 196 (on the Quakers' gradual realization that black slaves are human beings).

2. On James' conservatism and his physical and psychic isolation, see A. W. Plumstead, "Hector St. John de Crèvecoeur," in *American Literature 1764-1789; The Revolutionary Years,* ed. Everett Emerson (Madison: Univ. of Wisconsin Press, 1977), pp. 216-17; Mary E. Rucker, "Crèvecoeur's *Letters* and Enlightenment Doctrine," *EAL* [*Early American Literature*], 13 (1978), 193-96; and Robert P. Winston, "'Strange Order of Things!': The Journey to Chaos in *Letters From An American Farmer,*" *EAL,* 19 (1985), 249-54.

3. See, for example, Leo Marx, *The Machine in the Garden: Technology and the Pastoral Ideal in America* (New York: Oxford Univ. Press, 1964), p. 108; Russell Nye, "Michel-Guillaume St. Jean de Crèvecoeur: *Letters From An American Farmer,*" in *Landmarks of American Writing,* ed. Hennig Cohen (New York: Basic Books, 1969), p. 35; and Plumstead, "Hector St. John de Crèvecoeur," pp. 214-15.

4. See Winston, p. 251.

5. Thomas Philbrick, *St. John de Crèvecoeur* (New York: Twayne Publishers, 1970), p. 75.

6. See Albert Stone, "Introduction," in *Letters From An American Farmer and Sketches of Eighteenth-Century America* (New York: Penguin American Library, 1981), p. 18; Winston, p. 249; and Philbrick, p. 74.

7. See Winston.

8. See Rucker.

9. Jean Beranger discusses the concept of dialogue sensitively in "The Desire of Communication: Narrator and Narratee in *Letters From An American Farmer,*" *EAL,* 12 (1977), 73-85. I agree with him that *Letters* "has a structure and is more coherent than appears at first sight" (p. 85), and that it is dialogue which provides that coherence; but my emphasis is less on the "internal" dialogue (the "desire" to communicate which manifests itself in each character's conversations) than on the narrator's progress as he engages in the primary "conversation," the letters to and from Mr. F. B.

10. See, for example, p. 64: "These [observations] may appear insignificant trifles to a person who has travelled through Europe and America. . . ."

11. John Adams, "A Dissertation on the Canon and Feudal Law," in *The Life and Works of John Adams,* ed. Charles Francis Adams (Boston: Little Brown and Co., 1856), III, 454-55.

12. I think here of Huck Finn, Lambert Strether, Nick Carraway, Professor St. Peter, and Tyrone Slothrop, all of whom experience a "de-fictionalizing" of their world. They are left, at the end, in symbolically liminal spaces—the Mississippi, the Atlantic Ocean, the Midwest, the Professor's study, the Zone—that might represent either pure potentiality or death.

13. Donald Weber, *Rhetoric and History in Revolutionary New England* (New York: Oxford Univ. Press, 1988), pp. 152, 154; cf. Robert Ferguson, "'We Hold These Truths': Strategies of Control in the Literature of the Founders," in *Reconstructing American Literary History,* ed. Sacvan Bercovitch (Cambridge: Harvard Univ. Press, 1986), pp. 1-6.

14. Quoted in Weber, p. 6.

15. Weber, p. 154.

16. Weber, p. 135.

17. Ferguson, p. 4.

18. Washington Irving, *The Sketch Book of Geoffrey Crayon, Gent.,* ed. Haskell Springer (Boston: Twayne Publishers, 1978), pp. 41, 35.

Norman S. Grabo (essay date 1991)

SOURCE: "Crèvecoeur's American: Beginning the World Anew," in *William and Mary Quarterly,* Vol. 48, No. 2, April, 1991, pp. 159-72.

[*In the following essay, Grabo suggests that* Letters, *taken as a whole, not only celebrates America's seemingly endless possibilities, but also expresses the disillusionment accompanying the failure of those possibilities to be realized.*]

In 1779, Mr. James Hector St. John—a French-born New York farmer of loyalist sympathies, but suspected of being a Revolutionary spy—lay sick, hungry, impoverished, and terrified in the New York City prison. Born in Caen, Normandy, in 1735, the forty-four-year-old St. John found himself thrust by circumstances into one of the many bizarre corners of his remarkable career. Educated at the fine Jesuit Collège du Mont, he had spent a year or so with relatives in Salisbury, England, before emigrating to Canada in 1755. There he served with the French army until wounded at Quebec in 1759. Oddly, he cast his lot with the British Americans later that year and, after several years of traveling the frontier as a surveyor and trader (during which period he was formally adopted into the Oneida), married an American woman and purchased 120 acres of farmland in Orange County, New York. The farm—called Pine Hill—thrived, as did his family of three children.

But as hostilities between Revolutionaries and loyalists intensified, St. John, perhaps fearing for his continued control over his American property, decided to return to France to lay good legal claim to his patrimony there (not least for the sake of ensuring that his Normandy properties would pass to his elder son). In New York, awaiting passage, he suddenly found himself a victim of the times, separated from his family, and enjoying only sporadic control over the trunkload of essays and sketches he had been scribbling at over the years.[1]

More than thirty essays—some only a few pages in length, others more fully developed—brilliantly bespoke a new and arresting voice in American letters. While the young Yale poet Joel Barlow was reasoning himself carefully beyond a provincial American literary nationality, St. John leaped boldly into an international republic of enlightened letters for which the world of real politics was not quite ready. St. John's sketches distribute themselves according to two thematic emphases: first, the confident celebration of Arcadian possibilities under a political system that was essentially mild and enabling; second, the horror that accompanied the irrational repudiation of that system. Put somewhat differently, St. John's sketches depicted both the American dream and its brutal subversive nightmare.

Numerous echoes resound through these essays, both European and American—British poets Thomson and Cowper, the ancients Hesiod and Virgil, the French Du Bartas, and colonials Anne Bradstreet's "Quaternions" and Edward Johnson's *Wonder-Working Providence*. But their prose is mainly that of the newspaper essayists of the time—the many hermits, travelers, friends, and the like who by living apart from settled communities could comment wisely upon social matters. St. John assumes the same kind of dignity in his prose, an almost foreign formality of grammar and diction—long sentences, highly subordinated, heavily Latinate. It is the voice of a complacent, successful, and thankful man of means, a simple farmer, yes, but deeply read in and articulate about the book of nature on which his good feelings depend. He is not an abstruse philosopher, and his opinions on government or religion pretend a closeness to what a thoughtful farmer might generate from his very work.

Twenty years of hard traveling throughout the colonies, from the Carolinas to Maine and from Nova Scotia to the Great Lakes, and nine years of developing his New York farm had taught this farmer the pleasures of property. They were not pleasures gained without cost. Living directly off nature was precarious. Natural forces moving with majestic seasonal rhythms drove any sensible person into feverish activity. The sketch of "A Snow-storm as It Affects the American Farmer" opens on that note:

> No man of the least degree of sensibility can journey through any number of years in whatever climate without often being compelled to make many useful observations on the different phenomena of Nature which surround him and without involuntarily being struck either with awe or admiration in beholding some of the elementary conflicts in the midst of which he lives. A great thunder-storm, an extensive flood, a desolating hurricane, a sudden and intense frost, an overwhelming snow-storm, a sultry day—each of these different scenes exhibits regular beauties even in spite of the damage they cause. Often whilst the heart laments the loss to the citizen, the enlightened mind, seeking for the natural causes, and astonished at the effects, awakes itself to surprise and wonder.
>
> [p. 231]

In this sketch of the first blizzard of winter, the farmer needs more than astonishment and surprise. Indeed, surprise is a luxury he cannot afford. Animal pens have to have been prepared and fodder laid down for the stock, firewood made ready and brought in, food preserved, warm clothing and bedding readied. Then let Nature bring down her snows. All that is left is to gather the children from school and the stock from the fields.

The farmer of feelings also looks out for his neighbors when Nature shows its force, for nothing can be accomplished entirely by one's own efforts. In a new land everything requires mutual dependence—the farmer on his "amiable spouse," farm laborers and even slaves upon the farmer's agreeable conditions. People work and play together hard because all see that groups are necessary not only for frolics, songs, and merriment ("Thoughts of an American Farmer on Various Rural Subjects," p. 282), but also for barn raisings, swamp drainings, and rock and stump removal. Mutual interest generates both hard work and good feelings. In "On the Susquehanna: The Wyoming Massacre," St. John wonders at the capacity of tiny communities—sometimes single families—to flourish happily in extreme isolation and in the constant danger of "fire, sickness or enemy" (pp. 360-361).

But against the dangers of Nature and isolation the American farmer who is prudent, observant, tolerant, sagacious, diligent, and industrious can, with a little help from his friends, prevail. No Tintern Abbey ruins thrilled St. John, but neat fields burgeoning with grain, grass, and orchards did. Fatted stock would stick to one's ribs all winter; dried apples came back to luscious life with a little water; the cider warmed one's bones against the blasts. There was constant cost—having to do everything yourself, having to be a *bricoleur* or ingenious jack-of-all-trades, having to attend to differences of soil and the plant life it would support, having to avoid killing the land. American farming in the eighteenth century was different from European, for in Europe land was limited, had been cleared for centuries, was strictly regulated, and worked by peasants ruled over by tyrannical overseers. In America the farmer had to fight rough and overgrown terrain, swamps, frosts that threw his fences over every spring, and hosts of insects, particularly mosquitoes. Labor was expensive and demanding, and quite willing to go elsewhere if treated without dignity. The land was there, but to buy it required going deeply in debt; an economy based entirely on futures was necessarily unstable; failure, a driving threat. The American farmer, St. John was fond of saying, paid his taxes in sweat and worry ("Thoughts," pp. 266-316).

But when he succeeds—not least because of a mild British government and easy credit, as well as by unending industry—the American farmer does what seems to St. John to be natural. He builds a new house out of solid stone to manifest his rock-hard solidity, turning his original crude dwelling into a general store or tavern. Knowing that everyone else is out to mind the main chance and look out for himself, he cheats a little. "He sells for good that which perhaps he knows to be indifferent because he also knows that the ashes he has collected, the wheat he has taken in may not be so good or so clean as it was asserted. Fearful of fraud in all his dealings and transactions, he arms himself, therefore, with it. Strict integrity is not much wanted, as each is on his guard in his daily intercourse; and this mode of thinking and acting becomes habitual" ("Reflections on the Manners of the Americans," p. 262). Believing that religious tolerance in America had bred a religious apathy that made moral and ethical corner cutting acceptable social behavior, St. John says that American farmers put their trust instead in the legal system and litigation: "The law, therefore, and its plain meaning are the only forcible standards which strike and guide their senses and become their rule of action" (p. 262). This judgment is put with neither scorn nor satire. And whatever one may think of the implied Snopesism or Babbittry of St. John's depiction, this is the class of men "who in future will replenish this huge continent, even to its utmost unknown limits, and render this new-found part of the world by far the happiest, the most potent as well as the most populous of any. Happy people! May the poor, the wretched of Europe, animated by our example, invited by our laws, avoid the fetters of their country and come in shoals to partake of our toils as well as of our happiness" ("A Snow-storm," p. 238).

In a world of natural pests—insects, birds, lightning, serpents, mosquitoes, town rats and barn mice, grasshoppers, and who knows how many others we see not—St. John's "Man is a huge monster who devours everything and will suffer nothing to live in peace in his neighborhood" ("Thoughts," p. 294). Nature, if not quite red in tooth and claw, is nonetheless an economy of evil, providing nothing

for nothing: "Thus one species of evil is balanced by another; thus the fury of one element is repressed by the power of the other. In the midst of this great, this astonishing equipoise, Man struggles and lives" ("Thoughts," p. 297). It seems then that the self-interest that turns the American farmer into a litigious opportunist is often in St. John's thought merely an instinctual expression driven by interlocking chains of natural parasitism. If this is Jeffersonian agrarianism, it is hardly an attractive image of either natural or social life, but it is one upon which St. John gazes open-eyed.

Throughout the sketches, man does not control or master Nature; at best he rides its capricious powers, coaxing it like the sap of maples or the swarming of bees into honeyed nurture. The most he can do is divert its evils: tarns can be drained, provision in moments of plenty can outwait the exigencies of want, and men of genius like Benjamin Franklin can devise lightning rods to drain off the vicious excesses of natural disaster:

> Corn-cribs are indispensable because this grain is preserved there longer than anywhere else. You well remember their peculiar structure. Some people are, and all should be, furnished with electrical rods. The best way to place them, in order to save expense, is on a high cedar mast situated between the house and the barn. Its power will attract the lightning sufficiently to save both. Mine is so. I once saw its happy effects and blessed the inventor. My barn was then completely full. I valued it at about seven hundred pounds. What should I have done, had not the good Benjamin Franklin thought of this astonishing invention?
>
> ["Thoughts," p. 314]

There are moments, however, when the successful farmer, aided by devices like Franklin's, comes to feel that he is in charge, is actually managing Nature by appearing to manage his farm. Crops and livestock, slaves, servants, children, and wife become his, all of Nature becomes his, and man is what but a god in little?[2]

Lulled into complacent security by his material opulence, St. John's farmer is not ready for social and political upheaval. Crops can be stolen, houses and barns burned to the ground, families rousted from their beds in the middle of the night and terrorized by thugs, homes looted of all valuables, and entire farms confiscated in the name of a new self-declared revolutionary government. At least eight essays and sketches, including one lengthy play, among those in the trunk seized by the British in New York, recorded St. John's recoil in horror and confusion from the scenes of warfare. All were presumably composed between 1774 and 1779: "The English and the French Before the Revolution" adverts back to his Canadian experiences in the 1750s; "The Man of Sorrows" portrays the torture and terrorism of an innocent farmer by a gang of angry Sons of Freedom; "On the Susquehanna: The Wyoming Massacre" places the sudden, vicious destruction of that community at Wilkes-Barre against the long series of hardships by which it had been wrested from the wilderness; "History of Mrs. B.," a short report rather like a captivity narrative, describes the consequences for a family turned from happy farmers to displaced war refugees; "The Frontier Woman" lives a nightmare of disguises, terror, distress, and barbarity; "The American Belisarius" traces the fall from prosperity of a sensible farmer at the hands of greedy, ignorant, hypocritical, and self-important patriots; "The Grotto" describes the desperate attempts of loyalist landowners to hide from the Revolutionaries; the play, **"Landscapes,"** shows six episodes of the frustration, humiliation, shame, and insult added to the injury of property loss; and "Distresses of a Frontier Man" abstracts the main features of the preceding sketches.

St. John's clear tory sympathies at least kept both the sketches and their author intact in British New York. His own estate was not confiscated, although the house would be lost to fire during the war. He seems to have been a man of no very deep political convictions or principles. He had apparently signed an oath of allegiance to the Revolutionary government, while at the same time he imagined himself (in "The Grotto") bellowing out "Rule Britan[n]ia" from the bowels of a buried hideout in the forests.[3] He might be considered what the satirists of the period called a "trimmer," one who cut his politics to fit whichever party ruled at the moment.[4] But he also seems indifferent to power, which he frequently condemns as a social motive (e.g., **"Landscapes,"** pp. 452, 473). If property conferred education, leisure, acceptance by learned men of means such as his friend Cadwallader Colden, the student of Iroquois culture and sometime lieutenant governor of New York, if it meant handsome meals and fine wines, well it did, and they were his right. He had earned them, and he failed to imagine how others might resent his superior station and manners.

His images of outrage, although cast in terms of sentimental stereotypes—brutalized innocence, lamenting women, terrified children, the homeless and hungry, petty and ignorant officialdom, thoughtless mobs of vigilantes, and venal greedy hypocrites who justified their inhuman seizures by false patriotic slogans and sentiments—are therefore tainted by his political naiveté. Property and the law by which it is secured—that law on which the shrewd farmer had relied—were both more malleable and even transferrable than St. John had appreciated. In **"Landscapes,"** a prominent farmer named Marston has been driven into hiding by suspicion of his British sympathies. Because he has fled his home, it is confiscated by the newly constituted local committee under the authority of militiaman Col. Templeman. Mrs. Marston, with no alternative but to accept her bitter loss, challenges the colonel's humanity and honesty. The exchange, clearly favoring Mrs. Marston's fiery prose, is very telling:

> COLONEL: . . . Where the crime lies, the lawful revenge should take place. Your husband from the beginning has been a supporter of the oppressive acts of Parliament, that venal body which wants freedom at home and loves to spread tyranny abroad. They have not to deal with the inhabitants of Bengal, I promise you. Mr.

Marston has been, in short, exceedingly inimical and a bad man in the true sense of the word.

> MRS. MARSTON: You have so subverted the course and order of things that no one knows what is a bad man in your new political sense; but in spite of modern definition the true meaning of that word stands yet on its old foundation. A bad man is he, sir, who tears up the bowels of his native country; who subverts its best laws; who makes tyranny, informing, injustice, oppression of every kind, the cause of God; who arrests people without cause; imprisons them for whole months and seasons without hearing or inquiries; and leaves them to languish under the accumulated weight of want, despair, and disease. A bad man, sir, is he who when he had it in his power to prevent it, suffered an innocent young man to perish in a suffocating gaol, panting for breath, burnt and scorched by the most excessive fever; and yet would not release him . . .

[pp. 466-467]

Because each side sees the other in the wrong, each sees the other as perverting, and since both use the same language, no reconciliation between the sides seems possible. If St. John gives the nod to the impassioned rhetoric of the distraught woman, he also allows the colonel his pride of resistance to what he sees as injustice.

Indeed, what one sees from the loose collection of sketches is a writer alert to the merits of too many contrary kinds of human beings and principles for his own political good. Finally released from prison, St. John underwent several fairytalelike transformations while sailing from New York to Dublin, thence to London and, after almost a year, to France. In London he contracted with Davies and Davis for publication of a selection of his sketches, which appeared early in 1782 to immediate acclaim. J. Hector St. John had fled America in a large convoy carrying thousands of other war refugees, an ignominious and destitute scribbling farmer. Two years later, in France, he resumed his original patronymic, "de Crèvecoeur," and under that name emerged as full-fledged author of the much read and widely esteemed *Letters from an American Farmer.* He had left a British-American and was now again a Frenchman at war with the British. The once American farmer was now a French knight, honored at many intellectual salons, and introduced to the leading French intellectuals of his time as the foremost authority on American life lived as Rousseau might have imagined it, and indeed enjoying the patronage and friendship of Rousseau's former mistress, Madame d'Houdetot. By 1782 Crèvecoeur was a celebrity.

He was immediately identified with his creation, the mythic American farmer, despite his strong efforts to distance himself from his narrator. If we suppose that St. John worked with his publishers on the concept of his book, several observations leap to attention. The first is that the farmer as distressed frontiersman was fully in St. John's head, written out in other sketches if not quite in the form given in Letter XII. Second, St. John knew where the trajectory of the American Farmer's career would end—in ruin, desolation, and misery. Third, that would mean that the optimism and good feelings of the first three letters were purposely enhanced—even their naiveté made especially beguiling—in the knowledge that they would be undermined or subverted by the end of the book. Letter I, especially, presumably was composed after the material of Letter XII had been thoroughly worked out and after the device of arranging the sketches as a series of epistles to a sophisticated English reader had been decided upon.

Perhaps more than any other, that first letter illustrates St. John's artistic abilities—three near-caricatures (the happy and sentimental farmer of feelings, his rustic timidity overcome by a flattering invitation; his wife the gentle scold, cynical and sharp without shrewishness; and the somewhat pompous Yale-trained minister) engage in mildly satiric dialogue that slips from narrative to dramatic presentation almost imperceptibly—all incorporated within the fiction of a letter. Comparison with his earlier play **"Landscapes"** illustrates at once the greater complexity of his dramatic technique in Letter I. Between the wife's warnings and the minister's judicious flattery, simple-minded Farmer James accepts the invitation to explain America to England. The debate is delicately and mildly comic, masking its own ominous foreshadowings.

What Mistress James tries to do is to keep her husband from playing the fool, putting on airs, rising above his station, trying to appear better than he is, better than their neighbors are (pp. 47-49): "Some would imagine that thee wantest to become either an assemblyman or a magistrate, which God forbid, and that thee art telling the king's men abundance of things. Instead of being well looked upon as now, and living in peace with all the world, our neighbours would be making strange surmises. . . . [L]et it be as great a secret as if it was some heinous crime" (p. 48). Goody James's gentle teasing seems innocent, even though it treats writing as a form of disturbing the peace. But as the letters take on an increasingly somber and melancholy tinge, the notion of scribbling as disturbing the peace deepens. In Letter XI the concept expands from writing to any kind of intellectual activity. When the simple plowman John Bertram discovered his calling as a botanist by contemplating a daisy, he generated a similar alarm in his wife: "I mentioned it to my wife, who greatly discouraged me from prosecuting my new scheme [to study plants systematically], as she called it; I was not opulent enough, she said, to dedicate much of my time to studies and labours which might rob me of that portion of it which is the only wealth of the American farmer. However, her prudent caution did not discourage me . . ." (p. 195). When in the apocalyptic Letter XII the American Farmer's dream is shredded by distrust and suspicion, we see the ambiguous justness of St. John's early planting.

St. John's design for **Letters from an American Farmer** is thus the most complex and ambiguous since William Bradford's *Of Plymouth Plantation,* a resemblance that has not escaped notice.[5] The minister reminds Farmer James that they are on the edge of a vast wilderness with an equally vast sea behind them (p. 44). James also echoes Bradford's amused astonishment at "how quick men will learn when they work for themselves" (pp. 102-103). And when the war drives him to seek refuge in a foreign society, one of his chief worries is how to keep his family together and his children from losing their English ways and manners (pp. 211, 219). But primarily it is the parallel action of watching all one's earthly hopes crumble before new political forces that pulls these books together, along with their disjunctive form.

Letters from an American Farmer is an example of the American tradition of book-as-anthology and authorship-as-editing. As in Bradford's rhapsody, the medley of subjects masks an underlying coherence. That is part of St. John's fiction, of course: Farmer James will not presume to undertake a systematic treatise on America; he will not soar to a grand overview like a majestic eagle. No, he says, "I, a feebler bird, cheerfully content myself with skipping from bush to bush and living on insignificant insects" (p. 90). The book's casual character and superficial disconnections—even the presentation of the sketches as discontinuous letters—go to justify its formal discontinuities. This rhapsodic character achieves another level of justification more consciously than it had with previous writers. That is, in describing the new American, Farmer James emphasizes diversity and variety—different things coming together not in a total blend but in an aggregate like a mosaic. Thus, he maintains, talking about frontier religion, "in a few years this mixed neighbourhood will exhibit a strange religious medley that will be neither pure Catholicism nor pure Calvinism" (p. 75). Languages will likewise mix, as will nationalities and cultures—a veritable hodgepodge of differences. So, too, is the book selected and arranged—a purposeful mosaic, not a smooth and continuous surface.

The ostensible subsurface of St. John's design seems clear enough: the happy farmer resolves to take up the task of describing his life in the New World (Letter I), he describes how it feels to be a successful freeholder (Letter II) and proceeds to generalize about "the true American freeholder" as a class (Letter III). That class could with simple industry and unadorned manners be happily productive farming stone or even plowing the ocean, as the Quakers of Nantucket prove (Letters IV-VIII). These stand in startling contrast to the southern planters near Charleston, who enjoy "all that life affords most bewitching and pleasurable, without labour, without fatigue, hardly subjected to the trouble of wishing" (p. 168). But one sees even in the fierce beauty of hummingbirds or the mortal battle of snakes Nature's lesson that appearances mislead in the struggle for survival (Letter X). The ideal plowman is—like the Quaker botanist John Bertram—he who keeps the simple virtues, continues to clear and bank his swamps, but also achieves a scientific and intellectual grasp of the Nature he cultivates, harvesting the world's respect and admiration (Letter XI). All the work and benevolence and hope, however, can explode into horror and distress in an instant, leaving the farmer in ruin and confusion (Letter XII).

Deeper still is another level of coherence that explains why the dream must turn to horror. That is St. John's underlying conviction of the universal presence of evil. The action of the *Letters* is at that level Farmer James's growth in consciousness of the fundamental ugliness of human existence and the falsity of any system of values and principles that pretends otherwise. This conviction wells up in one of the book's most powerful passages in Letter IX, the wrenching acknowledgment of the pellucid fragility of any human happiness. But it is coyly exposed throughout the earlier letters, which are studded with curiously wrong notes.

Take, for example, Farmer James's story of screwing a seat to his plow so that he can carry his baby son with him as he works—"its motion and that of the horses please him; he is perfectly happy and begins to chat" (p. 54). How Emersonian or Wordsworthian that pleasant image, but what educated reader would not recognize Odysseus plowing with his infant Telemachus and its ancillary associations: Odysseus's refusal to fight against Troy, his feigning madness to escape conscription by plowing with an ox and a horse, his deep ambivalence toward the Achaean campaign? These associations were age-old proverbs by the eighteenth century. And behind them, at least for more learned readers, reverberates Odysseus's descent from Sisyphus, a relationship not without pertinence to St. John's deepest purpose. Other signals of a negative side to Farmer James's insistently beamish portrayal include the havoc wreaked among the republics of bees (pp. 58-60) and massive flights of pigeons (pp. 60-61), in both of which man gains by inducing lower orders of being to betray themselves. Vermillion dye attracts the bees but stains them, allowing the observant Farmer to trace them to their honey; the birds are lured to destruction by a stool pigeon casually blinded and "fastened to a long string." We remember Mrs. Marston's inclusion of informing among the sins of Revolutionary politics. When Fenimore Cooper replicated St. John's pigeon hunting in *The Pioneers,* he left no doubt about its wanton and wasteful character and the sheer blood lust it inspired. Farmer James sees merely prudence, ingenuity, and good fortune. In addition to the ominous images of the backwoods hunter in Letter III there is again a kind of thoughtless or careless disregard in the act of killing the great owl so as to send its talons with candle holders mounted on them to Mr. F. B. "Pray keep them on the table of your study for my sake" (p. 93), he writes of this bit of frontier kitsch, the sort of object that would decorate the Grangerfords' parlor.

More troubling in this set of subverting gestures is the treatment of the Nantucketers. The Quaker simplicity and industry that make the desolate island flourish delight Farmer James. Theirs is a life stripped bare of ornament and adornment—in their clothing, their food, their homes, their worship, and even their unaffected speech. The appearance of natural gaiety and good feeling won in the thundering shudders of the constant surf looks entirely admirable to James, especially as he himself experiences a sharp psychological disorientation in the presence of such

constant, indefinite, and powerful force (pp. 163-164). Letter VIII somewhat undercuts this "diffusive scene of happiness":

> A singular custom prevails here among the women, at which I was greatly surprised and am really at a loss how to account for the original cause that has introduced in this primitive society so remarkable a fashion, or rather so extraordinary a want. They have adopted these many years the Asiatic custom of taking a dose of opium every morning, and so deeply rooted is it that they would be at a loss how to live without this indulgence; they would rather be deprived of any necessary than forego their favourite luxury. This is much more prevailing among the women than the men, few of the latter having caught the contagion, though the sheriff, whom I may call the first person in the island, who is an eminent physician beside and whom I had the pleasure of being well acquainted with, has for many years submitted to this custom. He takes three grains of it every day after breakfast, without the effects of which, he often told me, he was not able to transact any business.

[p. 160]

Letter IX drops the pretense almost completely—"almost," because Farmer James views it even more as an outsider than he is in Nantucket and Martha's Vineyard. Despite Charleston's Frenchified elegance and what one supposes would have been its natural and ethnic attraction to St. John, Farmer James treats it as an exotic and sinister place. None of the values celebrated among the Quakers—health, labor, strenuous activity (p. 148)—matters. The Carolinas call into question all that Farmer James has been maintaining. Charleston is the new land with all the constraints of natural hardship removed. The ease with which opulence becomes luxury is astonishing. Where Nantucket was an extreme of natural deprivation, Carolina is an extreme of natural surplusage. Fecundity and fertility do not corrupt man; they merely provide the occasion for his inherently corrupt nature to manifest itself. At heart, St. John's man is as keenly dark as Joseph Conrad's Kurtz. Remove any need for self-restraint in a condition where there are as well no external constraints and the outcome is predictable—an unquenchable aspiration for power and an attendant social misery.

Profusion is ever the mother of wretchedness, as the history of mankind shows. Provoked by the bitter evidence of black slavery in the south, St. John writes as if he were Jonathan Edwards expounding Original Sin, a deeply embarrassed Gulliver trying to explain to common horse sense why human beings behave as badly as they do, a satanic Philip Traum sick and disgusted with human nature (pp. 173-174). But if J. Hector St. John pushes this conception of an inherent perverseness in human nature beyond even what the Jesuits taught him in Caen, if fertility is inevitably the source of misery instead of happiness—its chief example, black slavery in general, encapsulated in the emblem of the blinded, caged slave Farmer James accidentally encounters on his Charleston visit—then the ideal American Farmer is trapped in a terrible bind. The more successful he becomes, the more certain his misery.

Inside the doctrine of works St. John allows Farmer James to preach is a grim and inevitable comeuppance, a curse if not a damnation. As we can see in the visionary efforts of Timothy Dwight and Joel Barlow at about the same time, the American dream is temporary and fleeting, a stepping-stone to another and transcending condition.[6] Where Dwight foresees a glorified millennium and Barlow a transnational order, St. John envisions a perpetual return to beginnings. We remember that Farmer James's Minister—like Barlow and Dwight, Yale trained—has announced something like this at the very beginning. Europe is the study of the past; America, the future. The traveler to Europe submits his imagination "to the painful and useless retrospect of revolutions, desolations, and plagues," while in America "he might contemplate the very beginnings and outlines of human society" (p. 43). What could be happier? In a visit to Bertram, however, the Russian traveler intuits an uncomfortable identity between past and future:

> I view the present Americans as the seed of future nations, which will replenish this boundless continent; the Russians may be in some respects compared to you; we likewise are a new people, new, I mean, in knowledge, arts, and improvements. Who knows what revolutions Russia and America may one day bring about; we are perhaps nearer neighbours than we imagine. I view with peculiar attention all your towns. . . . Though their foundations are now so recent and so well remembered, yet their origin will puzzle posterity as much as we are now puzzled to ascertain the beginning of those which time has in some measure destroyed. Your new buildings, your streets, put me in mind of those of the city of Pompeii . . .
>
> [p. 189]

In Letter XII St. John shows us that revolutions are eternal and internal, that going back to beginnings is itself the revolution most painful.

When Farmer James bursts upon that encaged slave, he recoils in horror from himself. "We are machines" (p. 98), he had said earlier, but now he sees directly what it means to be a machine with feelings, the victim of forces within himself as well as without. His first reaction is panic and confusion, followed by paralysis of will.[7] His later personal calamity finds him tied like Gulliver among the Lilliputians, "fastened by numerous strings" (p. 205). The suspense of imagined evils locks him into a fascinated terror the way victim-birds are hypnotized by blacksnakes (pp. 180, 183). Gone are the farm and house, and with them all happiness (p. 200). Fright, horror, and shuddering anxiety alone remain, pushing Farmer James to the edge of madness (pp. 201-203). How can creatures of sentiment and reason so quickly become instruments of brutality and bloodshed (p. 204)? Of course, he has already (in Letter IX) generalized from a comfortable distance upon the monstrous character of mankind. The difference now is that personal experience has brought those generalizations home; under the immediate and personal threat of annihilation and torment he finds his social ideals and his political principles vanish (pp. 205-207).

Under the erasure of terror Farmer James is ready to consider the unthinkable. He will yield to the wild and savage, live with and like the Indians, turn to hunting, acknowledge but resist the lure of the primitive, and hope nonetheless to keep the family intact (pp. 211-214). With only this desperate alternative before him, Farmer James consciously closes his series of letters: "this is . . . the last letter you will receive from me" (p. 216). Had his design ended there we would not be surprised. But it did not.

Unlike his parallel Belisarius (p. 417) or the Frontier Woman (pp. 402-406), Farmer James will be with the Indians but not of them. Like Andrew the Hebridean he will accept the use of Indian lands to sustain his family. But almost at once he imagines himself improving Indian village life by the introduction of mechanical devices, prudent management, an increased emphasis upon agriculture, and regulations of trade (p. 221). One minute feeling like an ancient European ruin—"I resemble, methinks, one of the stones of a ruined arch, still retaining that pristine form which anciently fitted the place I occupied, but the centre is tumbled down" (p. 211)—he is the next undertaking "to begin the world anew" (p. 409) like the swallow driven from its nest by a wren: "The peaceable swallow, like the passive Quaker, meekly sat at a small distance and never offered the least resistance; but no sooner was the plunder carried away than the injured bird went to work with unabated ardour, and in a few days the depredations were repaired" (p. 63). The New American Farmer James can no more resist rebuilding his world than can the swallow.

But again the book's subtle organization hints at eternally renewed disaster. This new grandson of Sisyphus is doomed to ambivalent activity that ends in uncertain hope rather than assurance. When Farmer James announces that he is going to the aborigines "determined industriously to work up among them such a system of happiness as may be adequate to my future situation and may be a sufficient compensation for all my fatigues and for the misfortunes I have borne" (p. 226), we wince with the recognition that he has revealed more about "the moral evil with which we are all oppressed" (p. 227) than he himself can comprehend.[8]

St. John, now de Crèvecoeur, basked in the warmth of French intellectual and social approval. *Letters from an American Farmer* won swift praise, though often for inappropriate reasons, throughout western Europe. He prepared a French translation, which appeared in Paris at the very end of 1784, and began work on a larger French version, *Lettres d'un cultivateur américain,* which appeared in Paris during the summer the Constitutional Convention met in Philadelphia, the year of *The Anarchiad,* whose antidote some readers must have been sure it was. Between 1783 and 1785 Crèvecoeur served energetically and effectively to further French interests in the United States as consul in New York. But when Mathew Carey brought out the first American edition of the *Letters* in Philadelphia in 1793, the year of French Terror and the great yellow fever epidemic, it fell on deaf ears and did not sell.

Notes

Unless otherwise indicated, quotations and references in the text are to the Penguin Classics edition of J. Hector St. John de Crèvecoeur, *Letters from an American Farmer and Sketches of Eighteenth-Century America,* ed. Albert E. Stone (New York, 1986), which supplants all previous editions.

1. The most recent and most complete biography is Gay Wilson Allen and Roger Asselineau, *St. John de Crèvecoeur: The Life of an American Farmer* (New York, 1987). The strongest literary interpretation of the writings is Thomas Philbrick, *St. John de Crèvecoeur* (New York, 1970). One should also see A. W. Plumstead, "Hector St. John de Crèvecoeur," in Everett Emerson, ed., *American Literature, 1764-1789: The Revolutionary Years* (Madison, Wis., 1977), 213-231. D. H. Lawrence's essentially appreciative commentary—a welcome piece of critical history but not one of Lawrence's best essays—is so keen to plow its own furrows that it does not much speak to Crèvecoeur's general achievement; see D. H. Lawrence, "Hector St. John de Crèvecoeur," *The Symbolic Meaning: The Uncollected Versions of Studies in Classic American Literature,* ed. Armin Arnold (London, 1962), 53-70. See also Dennis D. Moore, "More Letters from the American Farmer: An Edition of Unpublished and Uncollected Essays in English by J. Hector St. John de Crèvecoeur" (Ph.D. diss., University of North Carolina, 1990); those sketches are described in Plumstead, "Crèvecoeur," 225-227.

   James C. Mohr anticipated some of my observations in "Calculated Disillusionment: Crèvecoeur's *Letters* Reconsidered," *South Atlantic Quarterly,* LXIX (1970), 354-363, but confines himself to the *Letters* and resists the logic of his own perceptions. That Mohr's view of the critical issue remains unchanged may be seen in J. A. Leo Lemay's introduction to Crèvecoeur in *An Early American Reader* (Washington, D. C., 1989), 116-117, which avoids any challenge to the widely assumed optimism of Crèvecoeur, echoing, just to choose one example, Russel B. Nye, *American Literary History: 1607-1830* (New York, 1970), 154-159. Jack Salzman, William L. Hedges, and Mason I. Lowance likewise share Mohr's discomfort with what Philbrick calls Crèvecoeur's ironic and "bitter pathos" in their remarks in the *Columbia Literary History of the United States,* ed. Emory Elliott et al. (New York, 1988), 549-550, 187-188, 68, 150-151, respectively. None faces what Mohr called "disillusionment" squarely.

2. Perhaps the best example of this is the Farmer's Swiftian stance, towering above an entire Virginia republic in the sketch "Ant-Hill Town," particularly pp. 246-249.

3. H. L. Bourdin and S. T. Williams, eds., "Crèvecoeur the Loyalist: The Grotto: An Unpublished Letter from an American Farmer," *Nation,* CXXI (Sept. 23, 1925), 330.

4. See, for example, Bruce Ingham Granger, *Political Satire in the American Revolution, 1763-1783* (Ithaca, N. Y., 1960), particularly the section on "Trimmers and Traitors," pp. 250-269, and the fate of Benjamin Towne, pp. 262-263.

5. Philbrick, *St. John de Crèvecoeur,* 88; Plumstead, "Crèvecoeur," 227.

6. Dwight, "The Conquest of Canaan," Book X, in *The Major Poems of Timothy Dwight,* ed. William J. McTaggart and William K. Bottorff (Gainesville, Fla., 1969), 259-270; Barlow, "The Vision of Columbus," Book IX, in *The Works of Joel Barlow,* vol. 2, ed. William K. Bottorff and Arthur L. Ford (Gainesville, Fla., 1970), 339-358. Benjamin Franklin had talked in similar terms as early as 1731, when he projected "an united Party for Virtue, by forming . . . the Virtuous and good Men of all Nations into a regular Body"; *The Autobiography of Benjamin Franklin: A Genetic Text,* ed. J. A. Leo Lemay and P. M. Zall (Knoxville, Tenn., 1981), 91-92.

7. Philbrick, *St. John de Crèvecoeur,* 79.

8. In his belated review of Nathaniel Hawthorne's *Mosses from an Old Manse,* Herman Melville found this "power of blackness" the driving force of literary art that joined Hawthorne to Shakespeare, implying that high art is only possible if built upon an acknowledgment of evil in the world. Melville, "Hawthorne and His Mosses," in Jay Leyda, ed., *The Portable Melville* (New York, 1952), 406-408. This dismal side of the American Farmer finds a counterpart in the "dark Thoreau" described by Richard M. Bridgman in *Dark Thoreau* (Lincoln, Neb., 1982). Its tradition is traced brilliantly in Michael Kammen, *People of Paradox: An Inquiry Concerning the Origins of American Civilization* (New York, 1972).

Nathaniel Philbrick (essay date 1991)

SOURCE: "The Nantucket Sequence in Crèvecoeur's *Letters from an American Farmer,*" in *New England Quarterly,* Vol. 64, No. 3, September, 1991, pp. 414-32.

[In the following essay, Philbrick claims that the usual assessment of Letters *as an epistolary novel may prove useful in explaining the beginning and ending of the text, but such a reading ignores the middle sequence of letters dealing with Nantucket Island.]*

In the last twenty years, critics have tended to approach J. Hector St. John de Crèvecoeur's ***Letters from an American Farmer*** (1782) as an embryonic epistolary novel. When read in this way, what had earlier been considered a travelogue of isolated set-pieces has been shown to have a "rudimentary plot" that traces the banishment of the ***Letters'*** fictional narrator, James the Farmer, from the pre-Revolutionary Eden of his farm in Pennsylvania. While this approach has provided a convincing means of reconciling the utopian fantasy world of the book's first three letters with the equally fantastic nightmare vision that dominates the last four letters, it has proven less useful in accounting for the book's middle third: five apparently "objective" letters that describe what might seem to be an unlikely subject for an "American Farmer"—Nantucket Island (and, to a limited extent, Martha's Vineyard), cradle of the colonies' whaling fishery.[1]

The same critics who have done so much to broaden our awareness of the symbolic and decidedly literary richness of the *Letters'* beginning and end seem slightly puzzled, even bored, by its factual middle. Thomas Philbrick, in his pioneering study of Crèvecoeur, comments that the island community is "only tangentially related to [James's] own experience."[2] When critics do direct their attention to the Nantucket sequence, they have invariably related it to the utopian claims of the first three letters; given this perspective, the Nantucket sequence does little to move the "plot" of the *Letters* forward. Attention to shifts in narrative voice, however, reveals evidence that James's attitude to the Nantucket "utopia" is anything but static; rather, it modulates from an initial enthusiasm to an ever increasing awareness that island life may not be so ideal after all. In this way, the Nantucket sequence subtly and then directly challenges the optimistic vision of the book's beginning and contributes significantly to Crèvecoeur's gradually unfolding tale of disillusionment.

I

Within the Nantucket sequence, a second narrative voice emerges to compete with and, in large measure, to replace the often passionate and effusive utterances of James, the self-described "farmer of feelings."[3] The new voice proceeds from a more distanced, less emotionally involved observer, who for purposes of clarity I shall refer to as the Farmer. Whereas James typically provides personal glimpses into life on his farm, the Farmer approaches Nantucket Island as if it were a kind of sociological experiment, a society constructed "to prove what mankind can do when happily governed" (p. 107), and he publicizes his findings in a form Philbrick has equated with "the discursive exposition of the local historian and the detailed reports of the touring observer" as he applauds the Nantucketers' dedication to the Quaker values of "sobriety, honesty and industry."[4]

While the Farmer has relatively little trouble convincing his readers that the Nantucketers have carved out a life of enviable industry and frugality on the island, he is less successful when describing the heart of that paradise: the not-so-idyllic business of whaling. Part of the problem stems from James's earlier condemnation of the "degenerated" hunters of the frontier in Letter 3, where he proclaims that "hunting is but a licentious idle life . . . [which] stimulates that propensity to rapacity and injustice" (p. 78). Critic Michael Gilmore is quite right when he says that "the whalemen themselves, pursuing and slaughtering their giant prey, are not unlike the frontiersmen who struggle for survival with the wilderness,"[5] but what Gilmore fails to mention are the great lengths to which the Farmer goes to avoid just that comparison.

In an effort to keep his description of a Quaker whaling community philosophically consistent, the Farmer assiduously portrays whaling as a staid, even gentle pursuit that has more in common with agriculture than it does with a wild and frenzied hunt. The Nantucketers, according to the Farmer, "go to whaling with as much pleasure and tranquil indifference, with as strong an expectation of success, as a landsman undertakes to clear a piece of swamp." Although it requires plenty of nerve, whaling is a "settled plan of life" (p. 141); it may require a certain "boldness of speculation," but that quality is more akin to the savvy of a businessman than it is to the ferocity of a dragonslayer.

In his efforts to mask the inherent savagery of whaling, the Farmer's "objective" voice becomes downright clinical as he drains his sentences of their emotional content. At one point he describes a mother whale with her calf as "a favorable circumstance"; since the baby's safety "attracts all the attention of the dam" (p. 135), she is an easier target to harpoon. This from the same author who, in *Sketches of Eighteenth-Century America,* bursts into sympathetic tears when a beaver's home is destroyed (p. 301). Clearly, under the guise of the Farmer, Crèvecoeur is holding in check the most characteristic and essential elements of his sensibility. If it were otherwise, if Crèvecoeur failed to deflect his narrative stance from James's natural tendency to empathize, the portrayal of the Nantucket whalemen as peaceful and nonviolent would be undermined.

The Farmer's attempts to domesticate the inherent violence of the Nantucketers' livelihood reach an almost absurd climax at the end of Letter 7, when he compares whaling to skimming cream from a milk pail:

> While we are clearing forests, making the face of Nature smile, draining marshes, cultivating wheat . . . , they yearly skim from the surface of the sea riches equally necessary. . . . May the citizens of Nantucket dwell long here in uninterrupted peace, undisturbed either by the waves of the surrounding element or the political commotions which sometimes agitate our continent.
>
> [P. 154]

While this passage has the ring of concluding the sequence, Letter 8, "Peculiar Customs at Nantucket," still remains, and in that letter, Crèvecoeur reintroduces us to the more emotionally truthful voice of James, from whom we have previously heard only briefly.

In Letter 4, the first of the sequence, the Farmer's factual, third-person description of the Nantucket waterfront, in which he offers evidence to back up his claims of Quaker simplicity and hard work, is interrupted by a sudden switch to the first person, in which the voice of James blurts out an observation that does not fit easily with what has preceded it:

At my first landing, I was much surprised at the disagreeable smell which struck me in many parts of the town; it is caused by the whale oil and is unavoidable; the neatness peculiar to these people can neither remove or prevent it.

[P. 111]

This detail about the odor of the waterfront might be just an odd, almost amusing aside from any other observer, but from James it is highly significant. Throughout Letters 1-3, he remarks on the purity and health of the air, both on his farm in particular and in America in general, and that natural feature becomes a metaphor for the fresh potential the colonies have to offer. The European "no sooner breathes our air than he forms schemes . . . he never would have thought of in his own country" (p. 82), we are told. James claims that while he and his American brethren plow their fields, "the salubrious effluvia of the earth animate our spirits and serve to inspire us" (p. 47). In the first letter, the minister assures James that even if his letters "be not elegant, they will smell of the woods" (p. 41), a refreshing contrast to the decadence of Europe, where "the half-ruined amphitheatres and the putrid fevers of the Campania must fill the mind with the most melancholy reflections" (p. 43).

It is no wonder, then, that James is disturbed when he discovers the wharves of Nantucket soaked in a "disagreeable smell," for he has come to expect the smell of a place to reflect its moral essence. Although the Farmer's more impersonal voice quickly resumes the narrative, this brief moment of revelation initiates a disparity between expectation and reality that will provide the underlying tension of the next four letters of the sequence, a tension that only comes to the forefront of the narrative in Letter 8.

In evaluating this interaction of voices in the Nantucket letters, critic M. M. Bakhtin's explanation of the "dialogic" method is particularly useful:

[T]his dialogic tension between two languages and two belief systems, permits authorial intentions to be realized in such a way that we can acutely sense their presence at every point in the work. . . . [T]he author utilizes now one language, now another, in order to avoid giving himself up wholly to either of them; he makes use of this verbal give-and-take, this dialogue of languages at every point in his work, in order that he himself might remain as it were neutral with regard to language, a third party in a quarrel between two people.[6]

I would suggest that the "quarrel" intrinsic to the Nantucket sequence, as well as to the *Letters* as a whole, is that between James's emotionally open approach to life and the Farmer's more intellectual need to organize his observations around a pre-determined thesis. What unites these differing approaches is the similarity of their aims: to claim a utopia that will serve as a refuge from both the injustices of European monarchies and the dangers of the American wilderness. In Letter 8, however, posing James's voice against the Farmer's, Crèvecoeur implements the

dialogic method in what I take to be a fascinating reassessment of the four letters that precede it.

II

After two anecdotal paragraphs about the island's single-horse carts and the universal habit of whittling, the Farmer ungracefully segues, without so much as a paragraph break, into a new subject:

As the sea excursions are often very long, their [the whalemen's] wives in their absence are necessarily obliged to transact business, to settle accounts, and in short, to rule and provide for their families. . . . The absence of so many of them [the husbands] at particular seasons leaves the town quite desolate; and this mournful situation disposes the women to go to each other's house much oftener than when their husbands are at home: hence the custom of incessant visiting has infected every one.

[P. 157]

This scene of a town emptied of men is especially "mournful" and "desolate" when we compare it to the scenes of familial togetherness on James's farm, where even his plow is equipped with a babyseat. From a very personal standpoint, James—who at one point comments that his family is so precious to him that "whenever I go abroad, it is always involuntary" (p. 54)—would certainly find this aspect of Nantucket life very troubling, even unnatural.

Indeed, James's startled voice—the presence of which is signaled by the personal pronoun—intrudes to reveal an unusual aspect of life on Nantucket.

A singular custom prevails here among the women, at which I was greatly surprised and am really at a loss how to account for the original cause that has introduced in this primitive society so remarkable a fashion, or rather so extraordinary a want. They have adopted these many years the Asiatic custom of taking a dose of opium every morning, and so deeply rooted is it that they would be at a loss how to live without this indulgence; they would rather be deprived of any necessary than forego their favourite luxury.

[P. 160]

Opium, rather than Valium, was the "Mother's Helper" of choice on Nantucket two hundred years ago, and the parallel between Nantucket and a twentieth-century commuting town emptied of men gone off to bring home the bacon (or blubber) is eerily close. The Nantucket women may uncomplainingly carry on the duties of raising a family without their husbands, but the evidence of stress is undeniable—a stress symptomatic of a society that must tear itself in half (into the two worlds of work and family) if it is to sustain itself economically.

Although the "mournful situation" of the town provides ample evidence for the addiction James observes, the Farmer, just like James, claims to be completely baffled by the habit:

It is hard to conceive how a people always happy and healthy, in consequence of the exercise and labour they undergo, never oppressed with the vapours of idleness, yet should want the fictitious effects of opium to preserve that cheerfulness to which their temperance, their climate, their happy situation, so justly entitle them.

[P. 160]

Here the Farmer sounds like Gulliver describing the Houyhnhnms; he is unwilling to draw appropriate conclusions from the evidence arrayed before him. Whereas the Farmer ignores the implications of James's observations, James struggles to come to terms with them. At first he had characterized Nantucketers' opium use as a "favourite luxury" which they would choose over any "necessary." Later, James's unflagging empathy leads him to redefine the very nature of luxury and necessity as he relates a conversation with a Nantucket official,

who is an eminent physician beside and whom I had the pleasure of being well acquainted with. . . . He takes three grains of it [opium] every day after breakfast, without the effects of which, he often told me, he was not able to transact any business.

[P. 160]

No judgments are forthcoming. The doctor simply does what he has to do to enhance the performance of his duties.

Albert Stone speaks of "Crèvecoeur's use of James as an innocent mouthpiece . . . [which] sets up the kind of ironic interplay between naïve actor and knowing narrator that . . . is characteristic of many American novels and autobiographies."[7] Certainly James fulfills that function in this passage. Because James's views are posed against those of the Farmer, however, Crèvecoeur's artistic accomplishment in Letter 8 is rather more complex than Stone has allowed. The dialogic interplay of the narrative's two voices (the Farmer versus James) shifts attention from their views—stated and implied—to the beliefs of Crèvecoeur, which are embodied within the form of the whole.

The tension Crèvecoeur creates with his narrative shifts casts doubt on the authority of the Farmer's utopian view of Nantucket. James's observations do not fit comfortably into the categories developed by the Farmer, who has taken great satisfaction in advertising Nantucket as a community both happy and successful because its people enjoy "perfect freedom" and share an inherent belief in honesty and hard work. James, however, "feels" some of the problems pulsing beneath the surface calm. From the mix of scholarly, detached observation and emotional involvement emerges a rich and detailed picture of life on Nantucket, a life which is at once laudable and fraught with the usual cares of humanity.

James has broken out of his shell with the revelation of opium use; soon he steps completely out of the Farmer's role to become what Wayne Booth has termed a "narrator

agent."[8] By taking a local Quaker girl to a "house of entertainment" in the Polpis area of the island, James wreaks havoc with the pat, often stereotypical attitudes of the Farmer's doctrinaire utopianism:

I . . . had the satisfaction of conducting thither one of the many beauties of that island (for it abounds with handsome women), dressed in all the bewitching attire of the most charming simplicity; like the rest of the company, she was cheerful without loud laughs, and smiling without affectation. . . . We returned as happy as we went; and the brightness of the moon kindly lengthened a day which had passed, like other agreeable ones, with singular rapidity.

[P. 162]

The "beauty" described here has a vibrant physical presence that does not correspond to the usual notion of a Quaker as a drab, polite wraith; she is more an ingenuous siren, tempting the Farmer out of his role as objective observer into a rare instance of personal participation in Nantucket life, a direct involvement that inspires a longing and lyrical look at the moon.[9]

As this little passage indicates, not all of James's personal experiences in the Nantucket sequence are dark and despairing. What his revelations do hold in common, however, is a fealty to emotional truth that inevitably works to subvert the glib assurances with which the Nantucket sequence begins. Because of this truthfulness, the most powerful passages of the sequence offer descriptions of a life that is too unmanageable, too threatening, too alluring to let us rest in the belief that the Nantucketers (or anyone else for that matter) have laid to rest all the problems of the world.

In the next and penultimate paragraph of Letter 8, James, now a full-blown narrator agent, takes us on a journey to Siasconset, the easternmost part of the island. Here he discovers a house overlooking an empty beach and the ocean beyond: "I had never before seen a spot better calculated to cherish contemplative ideas, perfectly unconnected with the great world, and far removed from its perturbations" (p. 163). Although James may be initially attracted to the house as a refuge from the world's confusions (a seaside version of the quiet little arbor on his farm), its view of the ocean requires, instead, that he confront the "perturbations" he has come here to escape:

[M]y eyes were involuntarily directed to the horizontal line of that watery surface, which is ever in motion and ever threatening destruction to these shores. My ears were stunned with the roar of its waves rolling one over the other, as if impelled by a superior force to overwhelm the spot on which I stood. . . . [W]ho is the landman that can behold without affright so singular an element?

[P. 163]

Finally we see firsthand the vast and raging "frontier" of the whalemen's hunt, site of "extensive desolations" the

Farmer blithely wished would never be visited upon Nantucket in his conclusion to Letter 7. Most important, this passage provides the sequence with a metaphor of what Bakhtin has called "the brute heteroglossia of the real world"[10] and foreshadows James's ultimate confrontation with the darkness that will force him to abandon his farm.

Certainly, this ocean of unmitigated reality hardly seems like a "field" suitable for passive "cultivation." On the contrary, James now sees the sea for what it is—perilous and terrifying—not so much for the whalers who go to battle with all of the studied nonchalance of fighter pilots with the "right stuff" but for the mothers and wives who must wait and watch from their widows' walks. They are the ones at the mercy of the ocean's hypnotic and spiritually unhealthful "force," which infects them with the babble and addictions of denial as they dart from house to house, breathing in the stench of whale oil. James's recognition that the Atlantic represents a frontier as wild and dangerous as the inland frontier he describes in Letter 3 creates as intermediate closure in the narrative which will be finalized at the end of the book. The supposed paradises of his farm and Nantucket Island are now seen as hemmed in on either side by the forces of chaos and destruction. A claustrophobic panic builds through the letters that follow as these forces march progressively closer to James's farm.

In the next paragraph the Farmer ends the Nantucket sequence by once again resorting to a farming metaphor in an attempt to domesticate the tumultuous sea: "Here . . . human industry has acquired a boundless field to exert itself in—a field which will not be fully cultivated in many ages!" (p. 165). That this statement (as well as its rather desperate exclamation mark) flies in the face of what James experiences on the Siasconset beach goes without saying; but in signaling the end of the Nantucket sequence, it also marks the end of the Farmer's ability to contain the volatility of James's observations. In Letter 9, which carries the action down the coast to South Carolina, the personal vision with which James confronts the sea again gains ascendancy.

This time the violence and unpredictability of the ocean are given a mutilated human face of horrifying immediacy when James describes a slave left to die in a cage. "I found myself suddenly arrested by the power of affright and terror," he reports, "my nerves were convulsed; I trembled; I stood motionless, involuntarily contemplating the fate of this Negro in all its dismal latitude" (p. 178). In both this and the Siasconset beach scene, James's urgent, emotionally charged voice verges on hysteria. All intellectual attempts to explain away the experience are doomed to failure. A greater "truth" has been achieved at the expense of the Farmer's objectivity, but that truth is not liberating.

The interplay of narrative voices in the letters of the Nantucket sequence is indicative of James's internal struggle throughout the book—a struggle between his tendency to live emotionally in the world and his more intellectual need to distance himself from that world. The tragedy of the *Letters* is that James is never able to reconcile these two halves of his sensibility; his all-or-nothing emotional life constrains his intellect to provide a retreat from the world's problems rather than a means of confronting them. Little wonder, then, that when these rickety utopias get kicked asunder by the brutish "real world," James is left intellectually rudderless.

In the final letter, the outbreak of the Revolution renders James virtually incapable of rational thought. As he laments his losses and enumerates his dreads, he admits, "I am convulsed . . . [;] I fly from one erratic thought to another" (pp. 209-10). But in the end he at least realizes that his previous trust in the ability of a well-run microcosm (be it his farm or Nantucket) to achieve its own independent happiness has disregarded the basic fact of man's dependence on other men:

> He cannot live in solitude; he must belong to some community bound by some ties, however imperfect. . . . I had never before these calamitous times formed any such ideas; I lived on, laboured and prospered, without having ever studied on what the security of my life and the foundation of my prosperity were established; I perceived them just as they left me.
>
> [P. 201]

Had he but followed his own instincts on Siasconset beach, James would have acknowledged what he fully comprehends only in the book's last letter: that man is ultimately subservient to forces outside his control and finds his only solace in community.

III

HISTORICAL AFTERWORD

As Bernard Chevignard has demonstrated, the "country seat" of John and Keziah Coffin, which is mentioned in Letter 8 of *Letters from an American Farmer* (p. 159), was not completed until September 1777, indicating that Crèvecoeur either visited Nantucket for a second time or, a more likely alternative, received updated information about the island after the outbreak of the Revolution. Although Chevignard offers this evidence in support of his view that Crèvecoeur may have "recast and enlarged" his original letters "at a time when he had become 'a very different man'—an uprooted and confused 'farmer of feelings,' who was vainly striving in hostile surroundings to ward off depersonalization, destruction, and death,"—Chevignard does not apply this insight to the Nantucket letters themselves; instead, he sees Siasconset beach as providing a "retreat" from "the evils of slavery and of war" that take over the final third of the book.[11]

I would suggest that Crèvecoeur did indeed "recast" his original writings about Nantucket in or after 1777, most thoroughly in the last letter in the sequence, "Peculiar Customs at Nantucket." As I have attempted to demonstrate, the letter previous to it, which ends with a benediction that "the citizens of Nantucket dwell long here in uninterrupted peace, undisturbed . . . by . . . the political commotions which sometimes agitate our continent" (p. 154), seems to conclude the sequence as a whole. This, I would argue, is in fact the original ending of the sequence, which could have been written only before Nantucket began to experience the devastating effects of the Revolution.

As the historian Edward Byers has pointed out, Nantucket's response to the outbreak of hostilities was very similar to Crèvecoeur's:

> Like Crèvecoeur himself, Nantucket sought neutrality. Prospering under the benevolent protection of a distant king, Nantucketers saw no reason to revolt. They hoped only to be left alone. But the Revolution confronted the islanders with the harsh realities of provincial and international politics they had for so long avoided. Their fellow colonists, and the British who dominated the surrounding seas, demanded that Nantucket choose sides.[12]

As they were for Crèvecoeur, the results were disastrous for Nantucket. As early as 1775, the General Court, then in residence at Watertown, grew suspicious that many of the islanders were assisting the British and passed resolves initially cutting off and then severely limiting exports to Nantucket. It was not long before the active port Crèvecoeur depicts in the first letter of the Nantucket sequence experienced a complete and disturbing turnaround. According to Edouard Stackpole in *Nantucket in the American Revolution,* "Whaleships lay idle alongside the wharves, many stripped of sails and rigging; the sloops that regularly carried supplies and provisions to and from Sherborne [on Nantucket] lay idle."[13]

By the fall of 1777, both Continental and British interference had greatly impaired the Nantucketers' ability to carry on their whaling fishery. Inevitably, the Quaker whaling society Crèvecoeur had so applauded for its gentleness and virtue was wracked by the same conflicts that characterized the community surrounding his farm. As Stackpole has shown, the island became increasingly divided in its loyalties, with many influential merchants on the island (such as John and Keziah Coffin) clinging to their royal connections (financial and otherwise) while the lower and middle classes became more and more sympathetic to the Continental cause as increasing numbers of Nantucket sailors were imprisoned in the British prison hulks in New York.[14] It is my contention that under these circumstances, Crèvecoeur could not help but reassess his earlier view of Nantucket as an "undisturbed" and "happy settlement." The final letter in the sequence offers a tortured and heartfelt chronicle of that reluctant reassessment while also demonstrating Crèvecoeur's conscious artistry in adapting the Nantucket material to the developing thematic concerns of the book as a whole.

The preliminary findings of Everett and Katherine Emerson, editors of a forthcoming edition of *Letters from an American Farmer* based on Crèvecoeur's holograph manuscript at the Library of Congress, shed a new and intriguing light on many of these issues. While determining that Crèvecoeur "had the concept, emphases, and limitations of the [Nantucket] series formed in his mind and at least partly on paper by 1770-72," the Emersons have identified several additional post-1772 references of the kind Chevignard described in 1984. Significantly, these later references are not included as insertions in the manuscript "but are in normal position within the lines, on the proper pages and in handwriting indistinguishable from that used through this copy of the Nantucket sequence." Indeed, the neatness of the Nantucket manuscript distinguishes it from that of the other letters. According to the Emersons, the Nantucket letters are "written or copied as a single continuous document" with relatively few changes while "[i]n most or all the other *Letters,* changes in the ms. are so extensive and so radical that they suggest the extant ms. pages began as first or very early drafts and ended up, with all subsequent revisions written on the same paper, as the final drafts." This leads the Emersons to conclude that the Nantucket manuscript "superseded an earlier one, apparently no longer extant."[15]

Acknowledging that "Crèvecoeur could hardly have learned of the Coffins' happenings of 1777 without learning also of the decline of the whaling-based economy," the Emersons rightly ask, "why did he write of Nantucket's prosperity in the present tense rather than update his discussion by at least referring to the current misfortunes?" The Emersons note that "[t]o discuss the depression that later hit the island would emphatically undercut what [Crèvecoeur had already] written, and very likely he did not have enough information to describe a Nantucket in depression, had he wished to attempt it." He therefore inserted post-1772 details into "a document already conceived and substantially composed."[16]

If the rewriting process simply involved the insertion of stray post-1772 details, however, it might have easily been accomplished through the practice of same-page revisions Crèvecoeur used elsewhere in the *Letters.* I would take the existence of a late, fully re-copied Nantucket manuscript as an indication that Crèvecoeur heavily revised his original Nantucket writings, if not in the initial letters, most certainly in the final letter of the sequence, in which the comforting peacetime benediction that ends Letter 7 is exchanged for the raging, war-like image of surf on the Siasconset beach. While the Emersons state that the ending of Letter 7 and other hopeful references in the sequence may date from the earlier draft, they also mention the possibility that Crèvecoeur first wrote these segments "with tongue in cheek" in the later draft, knowing full well that Nantucket was being "convulsed" by just the sorts of misfortunes the narrator wishes the island might avoid.[17] Whether or not it was originally written ironically, the sentiment expressed at the end of Letter 7 is certainly at odds with not only the historical reality of Nantucket in 1777 but the emotional "truth" of the letter that follows it.

Although it is for its literary impact that we most value **Letters from an American Farmer,** its historical authenticity has also been assumed by and well served such scholars as Edward Byers, author of an excellent history of the island. One of the strongest indicators that the book's episodes, although conveyed in fictional form, are based on fact is a first edition of the **Letters** now housed in the Nantucket Atheneum. Owned at one time by George R. Young and containing marginalia written in the nineteenth century by prominent Nantucketer F. C. Sanford (which he identified with his initials), as well as several other unidentified islanders, this copy offers what is in effect a colloquy of elders commenting on the **Letters.** Throughout the marginalia, Sanford and the others clearly accept the account as coming from a person who has been to the island. Even when they disagree with his claims, as they do to the reference to opium use, they find fault with Crèvecoeur's sources on the island rather than accuse him of excessive fictionalizing. "A lie. Without a shadow of foundation," writes one about drug use. Sanford chimes in, "It was only an old man's whim—Dr. Tucker and none other upon the Island," while yet another corrects, "Dr. Tupper—*not Tucker* told the author that this custom prevailed, which was false."

Although a 1905 article in the *Nantucket Historical Association Proceedings* asserts that on the basis of these reactions, we must discredit Crèvecoeur's claims about opium use,[18] I am less inclined to take Sanford and company's righteous indignation at face value. Certainly, the tendency of Nantucketers to close ranks against off-island or "coof" criticism is legendary. In a May 1847 journal entry, in which he records his impressions after a two-week stay on the island, Emerson says that the Nantucketers are "[v]ery sensitive to every thing that dishonours the island because it hurts the value of stock till the company are poorer."[19] And, more to the point, during recent sewer work in downtown Nantucket, many small glass opium bottles, part of the debris buried after the Great Fire of 1846, were unearthed.[20] Although these remains are from a different era, they make one suspect that Crèvecoeur may not have been so misguided after all. Instead, he may well have probed more deeply into the island's secret self than most local residents considered acceptable, and the denials in the margins of the Atheneum's first edition stand as an ultimate tribute to the powers of Crèvecoeur's empathetic (and James-like) insight.

Along the same lines, the Farmer's unwillingness to recognize whaling as a violent hunt almost assuredly accords with the view Nantucketers wanted to project of themselves. Indeed, it was not until Owen Chase's 1821 account of a whale sinking the *Essex* and the horrifying acts of cannibalism to which the survivors of the wreck were reduced, that the public imagination began to come to grips with the essential barbarity of whaling.[21] It would be left to Melville to apply the full truth of this disturbing insight to the Quaker whalemen of Nantucket.

Notes

1. Thomas Philbrick, *St. John de Crèvecoeur* (New York: Twayne, 1970), p. 79. Other critics who are in basic agreement with Philbrick's arguments for the thematic unity of the *Letters* include Albert Stone, introduction to Crèvecoeur's *Letters* (New York: Penguin, 1981); Michael Gilmore, introduction, *Letters* (London: Dent, 1971); and A. W. Plumstead, "Hector St. John de Crèvecoeur," *American Literature, 1774-1789,* ed. Everett Emerson (Madison: University of Wisconsin Press, 1977).

2. Philbrick, *Crèvecoeur,* pp. 80-81; Stone, intro. to *Letters,* p. 16.

3. Crèvecoeur, "*Letters from an American Farmer*" and "*Sketches of Eighteenth-Century America*" (New York: Penguin, 1981), p. 53. Further references are provided in the text.

4. Philbrick, *Crèvecoeur,* p. 44. Other critics who have commented on the change of voice in the Nantucket sequence include, among others, Russel Nye in "Michel-Guillaume St. Jean de Crèvecoeur: *Letters from an American Farmer,*" *Landmarks of American Writing,* ed. Henning Cohen (New York: Basic Books, 1969), p. 39, who speaks of the "change to a less emotional mood"; and David Larson, in "The Expansive Sensibility of Michel-Guillaume Jean de Crèvecoeur," *Exploration* 2 (1974): 40, who claims that "James has dwindled to a ghostly presence" by the time he arrives on Nantucket.

5. Gilmore, intro. to *Letters,* p. ix.

6. M. M. Bakhtin, *The Dialogic Imagination,* ed. Michael Holquist, trans. Caryl Emerson and Michael Holquist (Austin: University of Texas Press, 1981), p. 314.

7. Stone, intro. to *Letters,* pp. 18-19.

8. Wayne Booth, *The Rhetoric of Fiction* (Chicago: University of Chicago Press, 1961), p. 153.

9. In the French *Lettres,* the description of the Quaker girl is even longer and, if anything, heightens her sensuality (a translation appears in Everett Crosby's *Nantucket in Print* [Nantucket: Tetaukimo Press, 1946], p. 85), with detailed references to the "brightness of her complexion," her dark and "beautiful hair," her "charming" waist, and her "grey silk dress."

10. Bakhtin, *The Dialogic Imagination,* p. 385.

11. Bernard Chevignard, "St. John de Crèvecoeur in the Looking Glass: *Letters from an American Farmer* and the Making of a Man of Letters," *Early American Literature* 19 (1984): 183. However, Chevignard was not the first to note that the Nantucket sequence contains several wartime references. Emil F. Guba, in *Nantucket Odyssey,* rev. ed. (Lexington: Lexington Press, 1965), p. 139, determined that the *Letters* "de-

scribe circumstances which were non-existent in 1772. Crèvecoeur became aware of these later events presumably from a second visit to the island prior to his year's imprisonment beginning July 1779 in New York."

12. Edward Byers, *The Nation of Nantucket: Society and Politics in an Early American Commercial Center, 1660-1820* (Boston: Northeastern University Press, 1987), p. 201.

13. Edouard Stackpole, *Nantucket in the American Revolution* (Nantucket: Nantucket Historical Association, 1976), p. 25.

14. Stackpole, *Nantucket in the American Revolution,* p. 47.

15. Everett and Katherine Emerson, "Dating the Nantucket Letters: Summary of Considerations 5/15/91," 9-page memorandum made available to the author, pp. 1-2.

16. Emersons, "Dating the Nantucket Letters," pp. 4-5.

17. Emersons, "Dating the Nantucket Letters," pp. 7-8.

18. "An American Farmer's Letters from Nantucket," *Nantucket Historical Association Proceedings* 11 (1905): 43.

19. Ralph Waldo Emerson, *Journals and Miscellaneous Notebooks,* vol. 10, 1847-48, ed. Merton Sealts, Jr. (Cambridge: Harvard University Press, 1973), p. 63.

20. Told to the author by Edward Dougan, an interpreter for the Nantucket Historical Association, who witnessed some of the excavation.

21. The text of Owen Chase's *Narrative* appears in Thomas Farel Heffernan's *Stove by a Whale* (Middletown: Wesleyan University Press, 1981).

Jeffrey H. Richards (essay date 1998)

SOURCE: "Revolution, Domestic Life, and the End of 'Common Mercy' in Crèvecoeur's 'Landscapes,'" in *William and Mary Quarterly,* Vol. 55, No. 2, April, 1998, pp. 281-96.

[*In the following essay, Richards explores the contrast between the idyllic image of American life in Letter III of* Letters from an American Farmer *and the nightmare of Revolutionary cruelty depicted in "Landscapes."*]

Few Revolutionary-era writers defy categorization as resolutely as Michel Guillaume Jean-de-Crèvecoeur. Best known for his book **Letters from an American Farmer** (1782),[1] Crèvecoeur wrote several essays, sketches, and other short works in English that remained in manuscript until 1925 or, in a few cases, until 1995. One of those fugitive pieces, a collection of dramatic scenes entitled **"Landscapes"** (1776 or 1777), is a bitter, deeply ironic

denunciation of the Revolution that raises critical questions about the idealized America depicted in the famous Letter III, "What Is an American?"[2] Although there is very little scholarship on **"Landscapes"**—indeed, on most of the originally unpublished short works—the play engages a number of significant themes raised in different contexts by **Letters**.[3] For Crèvecoeur, the Revolution proved, at least in its early stages, to be a deeply disappointing, even horrifying event. In **"Landscapes"** the collapse of whig ideals, the perversion of local control over public affairs, and most especially, the dangers for domestic life in a world torn by political tumult reflect darkly the more buoyant depiction of American life in the first half of **Letters**.

In Letter III, Farmer James, the politically neutral narrator of **Letters,** seeks or promotes conditions that ensure the happiness of the individual family.[4] **"Landscapes,"** by contrast, shows a world where whig cruelty destroys the hopes of neutrals and loyalists to recreate anything like home again. Privacy, domestic tranquility, individual religious liberty, freedom of political opinion, even master-slave relations all become casualties of a revolution that in Crèvecoeur's drama has no moral purpose. In the end, the play casts serious doubt on the ability or desire of a new republican regime to continue the policy of prosperity and tolerance to which Farmer James pays eloquent homage in **Letters**.

The basic narrative of **"Landscapes"** features as main character the chairman of a patriot committee of safety, Deacon Beatus, who oversees the wartime interrogation of suspected tories and the confiscation of their properties. Other characters include Beatus's wife, Eltha; Potter, a tavern keeper, who is being put out of business by the strife; various citizens and partisans; two slaves; and loyalist victims of the purge. The play contains an introduction; some stage directions; six interconnected scenes, each a numbered "landscape"; and a description at the end of four "plates" (not pictured in the manuscript) that may have been intended to serve as illustrations for the scenes. Although not unique among his works in having dialogue, **"Landscapes"** is the only piece Crèvecoeur constructed entirely as a drama.

The introduction, written in a mode of address similar to that of Farmer James, argues that the Revolution is "unnatural," that citizens have been "allured" by "poisons and subtle sophisms" to cast off every "ancient prejudice" or allegiance.[5] The narrator proposes to show scenes that are "genuine copies of originals" he has witnessed, and he asks to be judged by their fidelity to truth (pp. 426, 427). In the first landscape, the Deacon, his wife, and their son Eliphalet discuss the previous night's harassment of local tories by another son, Anthony.[6] The family is suddenly visited by Squire Rearman, a suspected loyalist who has just been released from prison. Rearman complains of his treatment, his separation from his family, and the general terror instituted by the committee of safety. After Rearman leaves, Eltha announces that, despite the Sabbath, she and her husband will visit the condemned estate of a loyalist fugitive (Francis Marston) to get an early look at the household goods to be auctioned. Of Mrs. Marston, Eltha remarks, "I want to see how the woman looks with all her little Tory bastards about her" (p. 438). The next, brief scene shows Eltha and Beatus on the road as they converse with a militia officer who has tried unsuccessfully to catch Marston.

The third and fourth landscapes take place in a tavern owned by Potter, a "landlord." The chairman and "chairwoman" have stopped on their way to Marston's and try to convince Potter that life is better under the whigs. The landlord speaks of his obedience to the new regime while indicating that his sentiments lie with the monarchical governance and Anglican worship that he associates with the region's onetime prosperity. After the couple leave, others arrive in the long fourth scene to debate the issues of the day. Some, like Colonel Tempelman and Aaron Blue-Skin (whose surname is slang for a rigid Calvinist), are warm patriots; others, like Ecclestone and the foreigner, Iwan, cast doubts on the nobility of the whig cause. The climactic moment occurs when Captain Shoreditch, a committee militia officer, brings in three Quakers as enemies of the people. That such peaceable folk have become anathema provides Crèvecoeur with a powerful illustration of the reversal of order that is the unnatural dimension of the Revolution.

Scenes five and six show martyred loyalists. In five, Beatus and Eltha examine Mrs. Marston on the whereabouts of her husband, while she takes a principled stand against the destruction of her family and civil order. In six, the committee officers meet "the woman in despair," Martha Corwin, on the road. With her child dead and herself homeless, this victim of patriot justice gives a final voice to the suffering caused by what she sees as committee persecutions.

"**Landscapes**" rarely refers to the military conflict or, in any serious philosophical way, the ideological struggles of the 1770s. Rather, it focuses almost entirely on the consequences of a hostile invasion of the private domain by an anarchic instrument of terror, the committee of safety. The play's power derives from the contrast of the woeful present with the idyllic past, which Crèvecoeur had framed in *Letters* as a vision of "felicity" (p. 52). This type of happiness depends on the skill of the farmer's hands, the richness of his soil, and the silken bands of a "mild government" (p. 67) whose chief purpose, it appears, is to protect the intimate space of individual families from intrusion. This happiness is grounded in domesticity. The metamorphosis of the European peasant into the American farmer culminates at the happy hearth; the chief emblem of this classic transformation is the picture in Letter II of the farmer at home:

> When I contemplate my wife, by my fireside, while she either spins, knits, darns, or suckles our child, I cannot describe the various emotions of love, of gratitude, of conscious pride, which thrill in my heart and often overflow in involuntary tears. I feel the necessity, the

sweet pleasure, of acting my part, the part of an husband and father, with an attention and propriety which may entitle me to my good fortune.

(p. 53)

Thus the end of the American experiment is the farmer's tender contemplation of the domestic scene that is the result of his material success—and his leisure, won by agricultural labor, to write about it.[7]

The paean to domestic felicity comes at the beginning of Crèvecoeur's originally published text. Later letters raise disturbing issues connected to slavery (IX) and to the outbreak of wartime violence in the agricultural district (XII). The future of the happy domestic life is left in doubt when, at the end of the last letter, Farmer James thinks about retreating with his family from the chaos of revolution and living in the wilderness among the natives. Even then, however, James believes it possible to reconstitute the pre-Revolutionary family, albeit in diminished circumstances.

By and large, the prose pieces left unpublished in 1782—including "**Landscapes**"—are a far darker set of writings even than the last chapters of *Letters*. While a few, such as "Various Rural Subjects" and "Snow Storm," continue the lighter epistolary mode made familiar in the early part of *Letters,* combining detailed observation of American natural and social life with commentary on the relative merits of America vis-à-vis Europe, several—"The English and the French," "The Man of Sorrows," "The Wyoming Massacre," "The History of Mrs. B.," "The American Belisarius," and "The Frontier Woman" among them—record the savagery of war, largely from the standpoint of a tory sympathizer. For its part, "**Landscapes**" skewers patriot laws, heroes, and politics with an irony that rivals Jonathan Swift's in intensity and loyalist propagandists' such as Jonathan Sewall in antagonism to a popular regime. It is a long distance from the elegiac yet qualifiedly hopeful tone of Letter XII to the enmity for the Revolution and the satiric vitriol contained in "**Landscapes.**"[8]

As one of the last pieces written by Crèvecoeur before he fled to New York City, "**Landscapes**" reveals the wider implications of the vision of America that precedes it.[9] Gone is any overt reference to the process of personal transformation that Farmer James describes in Letter III: "the progressive steps of a poor man, advancing from indigence to ease, from oppression to freedom" through good habits and "emigration" (p. 90) to English America.[10] Instead, we have episodes of hypocrisy, cruelty, and shocking violence in the farmer's home region, the likes of which are matched in *Letters* only by the horrific image of the slave dying in the cage.

Letters offers a picture of the good life, grounded in liberty and individual autonomy, where personal and familial independence are maintained by honest labor, property ownership, civil rights, mutual respect, peace, and the institution of marriage. Farmer James equates this American package of English liberties with domestic tranquility, rendered as home and polity, yet he refuses to engage in any partisan political rendering of the life he depicts. In **"Land-scapes,"** each of the interlocking components of civil and personal felicity is blasted by the Revolution. The enemies are not outsiders but neighbors—the very whigs whose political doctrine embraces the liberties that James undogmatically affirms. For Crèvecoeur, whig practices defeat whig principles. In the name of peace, the partisans conduct terror; for domestic bliss, the patriots substitute political success. No invader could more resolutely destroy whig principles than the whigs themselves. Letter XII shows a world tilted; **"Landscapes"** pictures that world upside down.

The depiction of committee terror in **"Landscapes"** shows this reversal immediately. Beatus (no last name is given), variously called "Deacon," "Mr. Chairman," and "Colonel," is presented as a Presbyterian hypocrite whose intrusive execution of laws enacted by the Continental Congress ruins the lives of the innocent. Victims of Beatus's intimidation—Squire Rearman, Landlord Potter, and Mrs. Marston—decry the loss of property that gave them some measure of happiness in the past. If there is to be politics at all, Crèvecoeur suggests, then government ought to maintain the rights of citizens to live without intrusion in domestic tranquility. The true commonwealth is in the home. Unfortunately, the relative absence of government in America makes domesticity the first target when local authority steps into the vacuum left by a doctrine of personal autonomy.

The nature of authority, particularly in the application of domestic models to the political sphere, is complexly rendered in **"Landscapes."** In the introduction, Crèvecoeur's narrator invokes analogies to painting to describe what he is about to portray in dramatic terms. Crèvecoeur is known to have sketched his own farm in 1778; he probably had some awareness of European art traditions.[11] The scene that shows Farmer James gazing contentedly on his wife and infant by the fire is cast in a pose reminiscent of the French rural domestic scenes painted by Jean-Baptiste Greuze, Jean-Baptiste-Siméon Chardin, and others that fix, in the manner of a stage tableau, an intensely sentimentalized bond among the family members depicted.[12] The narrator calls his readers' attention to subjects and textures that would escape those who would gaze on "the pompous, the captious, the popular, the ostensible, the brilliant part of these American affairs" (p. 424). In a revealing shift of metaphor, the narrator remarks, "'Tis not the soaring eagle, rivaling the clouds in height and swiftness, I mean to show you; 'tis only the insignificant egg from which it is hatched" (p. 424). It is not the magnificent bird, also the symbol of the patriots, that he wishes to limn, but the egg and, as he adds later, "the nest in which it was hatched" (p. 425)—that is to say, the originating domicile.

But painting may not be adequate as a medium to portray all the shades of contrast between eagle and egg. To capture the desired landscape—a word that can mean "faint or

shadowy representation" or "the depiction or description of something in words" as well as scenic picture—the narrator turns to drama. Reflecting the analogies drawn by Diderot in the 1750s between art and the theater and anticipating the general thrust of stage entertainments in the nineteenth century, the prospective painter becomes distressed dramatist, who turns to a genre more fully suited to represent the scenes he claims to have witnessed.[13] In his own Letters II and III, as in French paintings of humble interiors, the domestic scene is rendered as a sentimental moment, a congeries of emotions, satisfactions, even wonders that, in Michael Fried's term, leads to a powerful "absorption"—in the case of Farmer James, the result of contemplating his own home-centered bliss. Crèvecoeur's earlier writing anticipates the predominating doctrine that motivates the French origination of melodrama: the establishment of a cohesive set of values rooted in home and hearth whose potential or actual disruption creates highly charged images of the ruin of virtue.[14]

The implications of this choice can be seen in the way Crèvecoeur represents domestic life. Where *Letters* focuses largely on the farmer himself as proud husband and father, **"Landscapes"** makes much of women as emblems for the presence or absence of home-centered virtue. As Dennis Moore rightly affirms, the primary female figures in **"Landscapes"** are "among Crèvecoeur's most vivid creations."[15] In fact, unlike Farmer James's wife, a woman usually seen through the filtering gaze of the farmer himself, the women in the scenes speak in their own voices, offering themselves as subjects. Yet the author was certainly aware that the depiction of the female in popular art of the time—notably the political cartoon—amounted frequently to iconographic transferral: the body of the woman was the body of the state—and thus too a symbol of the domestic sphere or, as Judith Sargent Murray called the family, "a well regulated Commonwealth." Because women are focal for the drama, their characterization especially reflects Crèvecoeur's conception of domestic values in the farming region.[16]

The principal female character is Eltha, the wife of the chairman and a prototype of the vindictive Jacobin woman most memorably rendered in the figure of Charles Dickens's Madame de Farge. Eltha behaves consistently throughout the scenes; she is venal, political, calculating, and finally ruthless.[17] As a woman without feeling, she implies the defeat of order in the world. Without a compassionating center—figured in the later ideology of Republican motherhood as the woman of both reason and feeling—the family becomes a dangerous force whose unrestrained desires find power in the politically destabilized world outside the home. While the chairman falsely claims to be above the cupidity of the arch-partisans, Eltha makes no such assertions and no apologies for her persecutions of loyalists.

For Crèvecoeur, whiggish republicanism destroys the home and robs its inhabitants of private life. With the sentimental centrality of the female as an icon for domestic tranquility, any alteration in the image of a woman carries symbolic weight. The woman who, through a vacuum created by the expulsion of the benevolent squirearchy, abandons attachment to home for Machiavellian maneuvering comes to represent dramatically the perversion of Lockean authority in a landscape of revolution. Unlike the loyalist women figured later in the play, Eltha appears as a perversion of female power under the old system; she trades her normal sphere, the care of those in her household, for another, the careless reordering of others' homes. Her character is not so much the cause of the Revolutionary attack on privacy as a reflection of it.

In the first landscape, Eltha, Beatus, and one son, Eliphalet, are introduced as they gather for Sunday morning prayer. When Beatus asks after another son, Anthony, Eltha excuses him by claiming, "He was all night a-Tory-hunting and did not get home till 'most break of day" (p. 428). Eltha seems to play a sentimental role, as excuser of children's lapses to the punishing father, yet because the son has been busy abusing the innocent, his mother's advocacy reveals the decay of familial values in the radical whig home. Shortly after this exchange, Squire Rearman enters, freed from a patriot jail through the protective intervention of an unnamed citizen. When Rearman criticizes the arbitrary power of the committees, Eltha urges him to court popularity by relinquishing such protection. Should the protector himself become a political liability, Rearman would be more exposed to arbitrary justice: "The chairman, to be sure, has got power, but he can't always do as he pleases. I'd have you, good sir, take notice of that. My husband is too good, and were he to follow my advice, some people would not have to reproach him, as they do, with tenderness of heart" (p. 433). Thus, even if Beatus were to show tenderness—not likely in Crèvecoeur's satire—he would find no approval for it from the mother of his children. Again, as with her son, she plays what seems to be a mediating role: defending her husband against criticism from the outside world. Nevertheless, she insists that whatever indulgence he grants his son for hunting tories not be turned toward the enemies of the state. In Crèvecoeur's vision of a whig world gone mad, domestic tenderness has no place in political relations.

In a later scene, Eltha confronts the woman whose wealthy husband, hounded by the whigs, has escaped into British-controlled territory. As a victim of the charges against her husband, Mrs. Marston is to lose her lands and home. Eltha does not sympathize with a woman who defends her husband's honor and her children's interests—what she herself has done in the first landscape—but beats her down with argument after argument, all the while picking out choice Marston family belongings for herself. Where the ideal whig, in the Stoic language of Revolutionary rhetoric, sacrifices self-interest to providential cause, Eltha inverts the formula to suggest that self-interest and cause are one and the same. When a mother gives in to an appetite for personal wealth, her inability to identify with the interests of others represents how far domestic tranquility has been perverted. Eltha's claims to represent her own fami-

ly's interests become, instead, a source for fresh brutality—ironically, against the domestic world of the other—not the rightful desires of an American household.

In wartime, only the example of the widowed or violently estranged woman trying desperately to protect her brood has the possibility—such as it is—of sparking the humanity that once flourished in the countryside.[18] This situation likewise prefigures the supplicating woman of nineteenth-century melodrama who evokes feeling from blunt male characters but is unable herself to right wrongs. The heroic widow here is Mrs. Marston. Eltha attacks her for being "too high" (p. 472), that is, arrogant and unrepentant before the committee. Mrs. Marston replies,

> Oppression rather inflates me; misfortunes animate me. How else should I bear their weight? What precaution have I need to take? You have insulted and treated my husband worse than a slave these six months. You have hired myrmidons to hunt him, to kill him if possible; if not, to threaten setting fire to his house that he might fly to save it; and that, by flying, his extensive estate might become a sweet offering to the rulers of this county. Now you are going to strip me and his children of all we possessed, and pray, what can you do more?

> (p. 472)

Mrs. Marston has heretofore regulated her home to the benefit of all, under the benign authority of her husband and, more distantly, the king. Eltha, by contrast, has not run her home with the same care, but in fact, if the actions of her sons be the proof, has shown herself to be arbitrary in use of authority. When misused domestic power spreads into the political vacuum created with the loss of the monarch, tyranny results.

Domestic life suffers further in revolution when black servants and slaves find themselves with corrupt white masters. In **"Landscapes,"** Crèvecoeur shows some daring as one of the first American writers to include African-American characters in a play.[19] We know already from *Letters* that race is problematic in Crèvecoeur's rural space. As Doreen Alvarez Saar notes, in *Letters* both Africans and Native Americans "have been covertly excluded from the process of Americanization: they remain outside the melting pot process open to the English and the Europeans."[20] In the early pieces, Farmer James, in both his own voice and that of his wife, comments on his fat, happy slaves. In Letter IX, James cries out against the cruelties of southern slavery, which he lays at the feet of the planter class, who parade their wealth among the *beau monde* of the corrupt urban landscape. Most notable is the end of that letter, when James, visiting friends in South Carolina, comes across a black man caged as a punishment for wrongdoing. The man's eyes are pecked out by birds, and he is desperately thirsty; after getting water from James, he asks, in dialect, that he be poisoned and put out of his pain. James cannot oblige that last desire; instead, he must go to dinner with the slave's abusers. Symbolically, the exile and treatment of the slave can be traced in part to moral rot at the domestic core of the white household.[21]

In **"Landscapes,"** black people appear as characters or in references on several occasions but always in connection with a white household. Crèvecoeur complicates the issue of black loyalty by showing what happens to a domestically stable slave system under a whig regime.[22] The first African character who enters is Tom, slave to the Deacon's family.[23] At the end of the first landscape, Eltha charges Tom to ready the horses for the ride she and Beatus will take to interrogate tories. Her way of encouraging his execution of the task is to offer him whiskey on Sunday morning, to which he replies, "Tanke you, Missy. Wisky is good these cold weather for Negro" (p. 439). Not only does this add to the picture of Eltha as a religious hypocrite, but it also shows that black loyalty to patriot families must be bought through the corruption of the slave's otherwise loyal and good nature. Proper management of blacks comes from the property owner who makes it his duty to care for benighted slaves. Eltha's offering Tom alcohol shows she does not have the moral authority, grounded in her role as sentimental center of the household, to gain his natural compliance.

By contrast, Nero, the slave of Mrs. Marston, remains at his post for better reasons than Tom. Eltha asks Nero if he would come live with her son, the tory-hunting Anthony: "They say you are a good fellow, only a little Toryfied, like most of your colour" (p. 472). Nero rejects the bribe: "No, Missy, me stay and help Massa children. What do here without Nero, you been by, take all meat, all bread, all clothes?" When Eltha counters that he must be sold and might as well live with Anthony as anyone, Nero again refuses on moral grounds; "me never live with a white man who shot my master." Responds Eltha, "You are a liar, you black dog, and I'll soon make [you] sing a new song" (p. 472). Crèvecoeur's awareness of color as a sign can be seen later. Mrs. Marston, in a long speech denouncing the overthrow of all previously revered order, remarks, "Everything is strangely perverted; black is become white, and white is become black" (pp. 478-79). For her, black means the loyal servant who contributes to the happiness of the white squire and family; for Eltha, black is nothing more than an extension of white vice, venal and corrupt.

This linkage of black characters with loyalty, in its several senses, is maintained even at the very end, after all the black characters have departed from the scene. Eltha blisters Martha Corwin for her charges against whigs: "These Tories are just like the Negroes; give them an inch, they will take an ell" (pp. 487-88). Thus the final marginalization of tories is to think of them in racial terms: the alliance between blacks and tories is one of apparent natural loyalty (and natural class distinction) and must be suppressed through the destruction of the loyalist home. Crèvecoeur's patriots here see elimination of "natural" forms of relationships, including loyal black slave to "kind" master, as key to the success of their rebellion.[24]

Slaves may have suffered greatly from whig attitudes, but they were not alone. Certainly, the play details cruelties that are intended to make its readers revile the perpetrators. The most pathetic victims are those who have children and the children themselves. Like melodramatists a half century later, Crèvecoeur maximizes the distress created by violence against the family by surrounding the moaning adults with suffering innocents. In the sixth landscape, the Deacon and Eltha come upon Martha Corwin, the widow of a man hanged by Lord Sterling, the patriot commander. She is mad, or so the others interpret her raving speech, but she has clearly been driven to distraction by the loss of her husband and her world. She reproves the hypocrites, as she calls them, for persecuting the defenseless and allowing her child to die, while it now lies unburied. Her last speech, the penultimate one in the play, serves as a remonstrance against the rapine spawned from seeking violent change: "Great God, give me strength and patience to wait with resignation for that day when the restoration of government shall restore to us some degree of peace and security" (p. 488). This heartrending cry resonates with Crèvecoeur's position on government: only distant and established authority, not local and upstart power, can ensure the tranquility necessary for families to live in peace.

Behind the violence that leaves the innocent dead is another casualty of war, religious toleration. Crèvecoeur, whose farmer all along has been suspicious of state religion, seeing America as that place where one is free not only to profess but also from profession, identifies his villains as Presbyterians with a marked taste for George Whitefield's sermons. Although Whitefield was an Anglican with Methodist leanings, the play voices the fear, grounded in a generic distrust of New Light enthusiasm, that an ideologically rigid Calvinism will be imposed as a state doctrine and thus intrude on the private choices made by the family. The object of his satire is clear from the first scene. After the Deacon's sons have returned home from tory hunting and Eliphalet has regaled the family with Anthony's adventures in persecution, Beatus offers up thanks:

> (*Here he fetches a deep sigh, and with a quivering voice,* [thus] *goes on.*) Gracious God, pour Thy blessings on Thy favourite people. Make [us thy] chosen race to increase and prosper by the influence of Thy heavenly showers——.
>
> (p. 429)[25]

The play identifies the American Calvinist rhetoric of the chosen people as a source of revolutionary violence, for it justifies acts against helpless and innocent civilians. As Squire Rearman declares, in a speech that might serve as a motto for all of Crèvecoeur's wartime essays, "Common mercy is departed (p. 431).

Crèvecoeur privileges no sect, although he clearly excoriates the Presbyterians. Rather, religion serves society only insofar as it encourages a form of social interaction that relies on mercy and tolerance. The Deacon cannot recognize that, as the squire chides him, "Tories are men as well as yourself" (p. 432); at the same time, judicial proceedings conducted under the Deacon's authority as chairman of the committee of safety are without "the least show of humanity or even reason" (p. 433). Beatus and Eltha play right into those charges in a following scene, when Eltha prophesies the new Jerusalem and the Deacon claims, "God is good; God is great; His mercy is immense. If we serve Him faithfully, I am sure, He tells my heart, that He will reward us with the spoil of our enemies" (p. 441). These "pretended saints, veteran Puritans" (p. 451), as another character, Ecclestone, calls them, are in fact inadequate interpreters of truth. Acting from passion and not from reason, ill-educated religious fanatics force a narrow Calvinism on society, destroying, in the name of God's mercy, the sustaining doctrine of family life—common mercy.[26]

The hypocrisy of the Revolutionaries and their self-justifying faith appears most tellingly in the long fourth landscape at the tavern. Although colonial inns sometimes had reputations for disorder, the tavern in **"Landscapes"** makes another house, a refuge whose internal order has been violated by the imposition of arbitrary laws of condemnation and confiscation. Once the symbol of a rightly ordered society—a place of tolerance for a variety of backgrounds and beliefs—Landlord Potter's establishment now becomes an emblem, the gathering point, for clashing voices and irreconcilable attitudes. One visitor, committee of safety member Aaron Blue-Skin, enters to denounce tories and praise God. After he leaves, Iwan, a foreign visitor, takes his measure:

> This is a curious fellow, admirably well-fitted for the time. No wonder he stands so high in the estimation of the people. Profligate yet apparently religious, conceited and stubborn, he can do mischief with all the placidity of a good man and carefully avoid the ostensible parts of the sinner.
>
> (p. 459)

Another example of social division occurs in the tavern scene at the entrance of Captain Shoreditch, his militiamen, and three Quakers, the latter tied up and under arrest for noncompliance with the laws of military support and service. Their peaceable manners and courtesy contrast with the patriot Colonel Tempelman's hotheaded denunciations of their creed; Tempelman, like the Deacon and his wife and like Aaron Blue-Skin, speaks a policy of political-sectarian cleansing. We will have an orderly society, he says, as soon as these "Toryfied gentry" (p. 467) and "pernicious" (p. 466) Quakers are expelled. Set up "New Pennsylvania" (p. 466)—a social experiment based on peace and tolerance—on the moon, says the colonel.

While the bound Quakers argue for something like Farmer James's earlier ideal of a polity in which all sects are encouraged—perhaps as checks to each other—"under the benign shadow of a just and upright government" (p. 464), the text promises affliction for the advocates of peace. The upshot of a world in which religiously inspired violence is

sanctioned by law and directed primarily against the family is a choice between death or exile. The very differences between neighbors celebrated in Letters II and III as elements of a peaceful society based on mutual respect now become intolerable forms of persecution. Landlord Potter, whose establishment has mimicked the domestic in accommodating those harmless little quarrels that occur in all households, can only give away his wares and look to expulsion from his own tavern. Public spaces, once mirrors of the domestic situation of the American farmer, now become sites of the counter-domestic in which loyalty is political, not familial, and tolerance a sign of weakness, not the precondition to human metamorphosis. Given a Quaker-like refusal to join in intolerance, characters are left with flight or death as the last principled option for those who believe in common mercy. It is not much of a choice.

Throughout **"Landscapes,"** the language of exile makes itself felt. Mrs. Marston reminds the committee leaders that her husband has done what he can to protect his family and home, but with whig patrols out hunting and threatening to kill him, he has no choice but to flee. Perhaps laying the groundwork for his own flight from spouse and farm, Crèvecoeur portrays Francis Marston as a man of deep suffering, who must abandon those he loves to give them any chance at peace. Yet the whole effort proves futile. Mrs. Marston argues with Beatus and Eltha that forcing her husband to decide among hateful alternatives makes a mockery of his supposed free will:

> They sent word that if he did not quit in three hours, the whole should be in flames. He roused himself up once more and with streaming eyes and a bleeding heart he bade me farewell. Yet this is the man you proclaim a traitor. He would have been a traitor to himself had he stayed any longer. 'Tis for my sake and that of his children, 'tis to preserve these buildings and what they contain, that he quitted. Can you in the face of that pure sun, can you say he went away out of choice?
>
> (p. 480)

Mrs. Marston's cry reflects Crèvecoeur's locus philosophy, delineated in such sunny fashion only a few years before. Where once voluntary flight from Europe led the wanderer to the welcoming American landscape—that asylum, as Farmer James calls it—now that ground is itself spoiled, and those who remain risk treachery to themselves to stay. The domestic refuge cannot survive in a corrupted world.

In **Letters,** James ends by planning to flee his farm for the frontier. Although in Letter III he criticizes frontiersmen as depraved, by Letter IX he declares that, in terms of comparative corruption, cities are worse than the backwoods. Thus in Letter XII, "Distresses of a Frontier Man," he imagines taking his family to live with the Indians, not without regret, but as a measure that will allow him some freedom to hold the hearts and minds of his children to some part of civility, even in the heart of the forest. No such possibility exists in **"Landscapes."** By the time he writes the play, Crèvecoeur knows that the backwoods are full of renegade tories and Indians—the very people who attack his own home when he flees to New York City. For the exiles in the drama, wandering is all that is left.

This fate is most ruefully depicted in the sixth and final landscape, which features Martha Corwin. Her husband hanged, a child recently dead and unburied, Martha wanders the roads, a person whose sufferings ought to spur the conscience of any feeling human being. In prophetic language, Crèvecoeur puts in her mouth the most powerful accusations of the play. Responding to the cruelty of Beatus and Eltha, she cries, "Gracious God, why dost Thou suffer these rulers to plunder the widows and their children and call their rags their country's inheritance—a miserable one, which, to feed and pamper a few, leaves hundreds desolate, a prey to death and despair? And you are the chairman!" The Deacon's only response is to deny her authority: "You are mad" (p. 486).

But madness is relative. When Eltha later repeats the charge of "mad" against Martha, the victim regales her antagonist with the crux of Crèvecoeur's complaint against the Revolution, the despoliation of the domestic realm. In an ironic reversal of Letter II, which shows Farmer James admiring his wife as she nurses their child, Martha cries out to her calumniators that her milk has gone, "and my poor baby, by still suckling the dregs, fed awhile on the dregs of sorrow." She turns on Eltha, who, in a world where domestic bliss feeds on the cozy sentiments of the heart, should be sympathetic to a suffering woman:

> Aye, ma'am, that's spoken like yourself. Mingle religion with obduracy of heart, softness of speech with that unfeeling disposition which fits you so well for a chairman's wife. Despise the poor; reject the complaints of the oppressed; crush those whom your husband oversets; and our gazettes shall resound with your praise. Mad woman! Yes, I am mad to see ingratitude and hypocrisy on horseback, virtue and honesty low in the dirt.
>
> (pp. 486-87)

Once political power hardens the heart, children may be starved, widows condemned, and all justice overturned. It is a bleak ending, promising not a good thrashing of the whigs, as an earlier anonymous pro-British play, *The Battle of Brooklyn*, does, but only foreseeing a long continuation of conflict, bigotry, and the destruction of domestic peace in the middle ground. In its anticipation of the melodramatic situation—the threat to domestic expressions of sentiment by implacable enemies to feeling—"**Landscapes**" serves as forerunner of the plays that would hold American dramatic audiences until nearly the twentieth century. Yet unlike those plays—such Anglo-American vehicles of middle-class domestic value as Douglass Jerrold's *Black-Ey'd Susan* or George Aiken's version of *Uncle Tom's Cabin* or Augustin Daly's *Under the Gaslight*—where salvation comes at the last minute, Crèvecoeur's play offers little hope that threats to hearth and home will, by a timely entrance, be overcome in favor of middling manners.[27]

Crèvecoeur cannot resist one parting shot. After the last scene, he adds four numbered paragraphs, three of which augment or repeat what has been described in the landscapes. The first paragraph describes a "copper plate" (p. 488) that shows two chained men on horseback, falling after being shot, perhaps suggesting the kind of violence perpetrated by the Deacon's son Anthony. The second illustrates the persecution of the tied Quakers by Captain Shoreditch and the militiamen. The third portrays Martha Corwin leaning against a tree, talking with Eltha and Beatus. The fourth, which may have been intended for an unwritten scene,[28] reads: "A stallion rushing from the woods and covering the mare on which Eltha rides; she stoops on the neck; her husband [behind whipping] the horse, but in vain" (p. 489).[29] This symbolic rape of Eltha by the backwoods stallion is the only indication of some kind of justice in the play; as such, it is crude and perplexing. The narrator's vengeance on the Revolution is to imagine the bestial humiliation of the woman, Eltha, whose corruption personifies the destruction of domestic stability. As with cartoons that displayed Britannia or America being raped or abused by leering representatives of contending countries, Crèvecoeur here makes the rape of the female emblematic of historical retribution. Omitting the scene as part of his dramatic text, he renders it at the last as a landscape of perverse violence. In this form, Crèvecoeur offers a picture of the anti-Columbia. Inverting the rape-mutilation cartoons, this final picture leaves a reader with no sympathy for the victim—and no hope for the restoration of the domestic ideal short of the violent return of the old order.

Crèvecoeur is not, at the end of his American essay-sketch-play-writing career, Farmer James. If he is to be identified with any one of his characters, it is Francis Marston, the escaping tory, who abandons his home in a futile attempt to save it. Shortly after writing his protest play against the Revolution, the author himself fled to New York, leaving family behind, perhaps hoping that his absence would increase the likelihood of mild treatment for the rest. Yet unlike *Letters*, in which Farmer James posits at least the possibility of a reconstructed domestic sphere among the denizens of the frontier, the voice of "**Landscapes**" offers a pessimistic rejection of the idea that a system of independent, well-regulated households can ensure an ordered society. In its protest, the play reveals the fundamental error behind a vision of society that relies on domestic tranquility as the end of political life. The lesson of "**Landscapes**," then, is this: No society constructed on the belief that venality will be tempered by a commodious farm and fertile soil can resist the implacable surge of human passions. In other words, prosperity alone cannot combat the appeal to power fostered by revolutions. The man who gave Americans for many generations the picture of themselves they most wanted to see—the tolerant, prosperous, landholding, peaceable, and domestic people outlined in Letter III—also gave them in "**Landscapes**" the image of its opposite, a nightmare of popular cruelty and personal despair. And that landscape, in Crèvecoeur's time and for many years, could not be shown on any literal American stage.

Notes

1. Originally published under his adopted American name, J. Hector St. John, *Letters from an American Farmer* (London, 1782; 2d ed., 1783). Most modern editions are based on the 1783 edition, which includes largely nonsubstantive corrections whose authority is difficult to identify. Editions in French, published as *Letters d'un Cultivateur Américain* (Paris, 1784; 1787), include material not in the 1783 English edition, but in some cases the French essays differ from the equivalent pieces in the long unpublished manuscripts in English. An authoritative edition of *Letters,* based on the Crèvecoeur manuscripts now owned by the Library of Congress, is being prepared by Everett Emerson and Katherine Emerson.

2. "Landscapes" first appeared in *Sketches of Eighteenth Century America: More "Letters from an American Farmer" by St. John de Crèvecoeur,* ed. Henri Bourdin, Ralph Gabriel, and Stanley Williams (New Haven, 1925). Albert E. Stone, ed., *Letters from an American Farmer and Sketches of Eighteenth-Century America* (New York, 1981), 424-89, reprints the 1925 version and for purposes of readability is the source of all quotations from Crèvecoeur cited parenthetically in this article. Dennis D. Moore, ed., "Landskapes," *More Letters from the American Farmer: An Edition of the Essays in English Left Unpublished by Crèvecoeur* (Athens, Ga., 1995), 230-93, reproduces the literal text of the manuscript in modern typography. Moore includes a more complete version of Crèvecoeur's introduction to the play and prints a few other prose pieces (separate from "Landskapes") not found in the 1925 or 1981 versions. All passages from Stone have been checked against the text established by Moore, and significant differences are so noted.

3. One of the first critics to take the *Sketches* seriously was John Brooks Moore in "The Rehabilitation of Crèvecoeur," *Sewanee Review,* 35 (1927), 216-30, but few others have followed up. See, however, Emerson, "Hector St. John de Crèvecoeur and the Promise of America," *Forms and Functions of History in American Literature: Essays in Honor of Ursula Brumm,* ed. Winfried Fluck, Jürgen Peper, and Willi Paul Adams (Berlin, 1981), 44-55; John Hales, "The Landscape of Tragedy: Crèvecoeur's 'Susquehanna,'" *Early American Literature,* 20 (1985), 39-63; and David M. Robinson, "Community and Utopia in Crèvecoeur's Sketches," *American Literature,* 62 (1990), 17-31.

   "Landscapes" is discussed in the context of other works by Crèvecoeur in Thomas Philbrick, *St. John de Crèvecoeur* (New York, 1970), 126-28; Manfred Putz, "Dramatic Elements and the Problem of Literary Mediation in the Works of Hector St. John de Crèvecoeur," *REAL: The Yearbook of Research in English and American Literature,* 3 (1985), 111-30; Norman S. Grabo, "Crèvecoeur's American: Beginning the World Anew," *William and Mary Quarterly,*

3d Ser., 48 (1991), 164-65; and Moore, ed., *More Letters from the American Farmer,* xviii, xxi, xxii, xxiv, xxv, xxvii, xxxvii, xxxviii, xl, xlii-xlvii. There is almost nothing on "Landscapes" in studies of American drama. Two recent histories of early drama, including one that covers the 18th century quite comprehensively, ignore it entirely. See, for example, the appropriate period study in Walter J. Meserve, *An Emerging Entertainment: The Drama of the American People to 1828* (Bloomington, Ind., 1977), 60-91.

4. The use of familial language in the works of other writers has been documented by Edwin G. Burrows and Michael Wallace, "The American Revolution: The Ideology and Psychology of National Liberation," *Perspectives in American History,* 6 (1972), 167-306; and Jay Fliegelman, *Prodigals and Pilgrims: The American Revolution against Patriarchal Authority, 1750-1800* (Cambridge, 1982). For Crèvecoeur, the literal family's fortunes become symbolic of the national fate.

5. The matter of voice in Crèvecoeur is complex and not easily resolved. Philbrick thinks the voice of "Landscapes" is "inappropriate" for Farmer James in *St. John de Crèvecoeur,* 120. Moore implicitly distinguishes the "narrator" of "Landskapes" from Farmer James in *More Letters from the American Farmer,* xli. However, the very format of a play makes determination of a voice in a deliberately multivocal performance problematic. Crèvecoeur includes an introduction to the play that, as will be noted, casts a grim look at the American scene. While this voice is not entirely consistent with the more naive-sounding James of *Letters,* a theme of declension pervades both *Letters* and the play. On his portrayal of a declining world in the former see Grantland S. Rice, "Crèvecoeur and the Politics of Authorship in Republican America," *EAL,* [*Early American Literature*] 28 (1993), 91-119.

6. As Moore's edition of the manuscript shows, Crèvecoeur inconsistently labels each part as either a "landskape" or a "scene." Stone's edition, following the 1925 transcription, labels each part a "landscape."

7. For an intriguing discussion of the act of writing letters and the consequent tensions between public and private see Elizabeth Heckendorn Cook, *Epistolary Bodies: Gender and Genre in the Eighteenth-Century Republic of Letters* (Stanford, 1996), chap. 5.

8. The tendency in Crèvecoeur criticism has been to see him as a hopeful, if not utopian, writer on America. This view has been promoted by decades of anthologizing Letter III, but even among scholars who see darker elements in his 1782 collection, the consensus is that there is some hope in the vision of an agrarian paradise. See, for example, Russel B. Nye, "Aristocrat in the Forest," in *American Literary History, 1607-1830* (New York, 1970), 154-59; James C. Mohr, "Calculated Disillusionment: Crèvecoeur's

Letters Reconsidered," *South Atlantic Quarterly,* 69 (1970), 354-63; Emerson, "Hector St. John de Crève-coeur"; Grabo, "Crèvecoeur's American"; and Joseph Fichtelberg, "Utopic Distresses: Crèvecoeur's Letters and Revolution," *Studies in the Literary Imagination,* 27 (1994), 85-101. The problem of anthologizing Crèvecoeur is succinctly analyzed by Cathy Davidson, *Revolution and the Word: The Rise of the Novel in America* (New York, 1986), 257.

9. Biographical information on Crèvecoeur drawn from Stone, Introduction, *Letters,* 7-25; Gay Wilson Allen and Roger Asselineau, *St. John de Crèvecoeur: The Life of an American Farmer* (New York, 1987); and Everett Emerson and Katherine Emerson, private correspondence, citing their manuscript article on Crèvecoeur for the forthcoming *American National Biography.*

10. Scholars have recently tended to read *Letters* as an epistolary novel in order to reconcile contradictions in the text. Stephen Carl Arch, for example, makes use of the quoted passage to indicate the wholeness of *Letters* in "The 'Progressive Steps' of the Narrator in Crèvecoeur's *Letters from an American Farmer,*" *Studies in American Fiction,* 18 (1990), 145-58. By reading "Landscapes" and other pieces that were not included in *Letters,* however, one can see that the attempts to find unity do not fully account for Crève-coeur's thoughts on Revolutionary America.

11. Allen and Asselineau, *St. John de Crèvecoeur,* 21-22, 35. In addition to his knowledge of French and other European painting, Crèvecoeur may also have seen engravings of works by the American Benjamin West, who had set up in London. See Dorinda Evans, *Benjamin West and His American Students* (Washington, D. C., 1980), and James Thomas Flexner, *American Painting: First Flowers of Our Wilderness* (Cambridge, Mass., 1947), 194-243. The painted landscape of Pine Hill is reproduced in the frontispiece of Howard Rice, *Le Cultivateur Américain: Etude sur l'oeuvre de Saint John de Crèvecoeur* (Paris, 1933).

12. The relation between painting and theater for these works is discussed fully in Michael Fried, *Absorption and Theatricality: Painting and Beholder in the Age of Diderot* (Berkeley, 1980).

13. Definitions 4d, 4g, *OED.* Although the staging of plays during the middle 18th century was uncommon in America, writers during the Revolution often turned to drama as a genre suited to political topics. See Jeffrey H. Richards, *Theater Enough: American Culture and the Metaphor of the World Stage, 1607-1789* (Durham, N. C., 1991), 247-91; Jared Brown, *The Theatre in America during the Revolution* (Cambridge, 1995); and Ginger Strand, "The Many Deaths of Montgomery: Audiences and Pamphlet Plays of the Revolution," *American Literary History,* 9 (1997), 1-20.

14. Fried, *Absorption and Theatricality,* esp. 7-70; Peter Brooks, *The Melodramatic Imagination: Balzac, Henry James, Melodrama, and the Mode of Excess* (New Haven, 1995; orig. pub. 1976), 82-93.

15. Moore, ed., *More Letters from the American Farmer,* xlv. On the matter of Farmer James's wife in view of other comments by Crèvecoeur, literal and metaphorical, on women see Anna Carew-Miller, "The Language of Domesticity in Crèvecoeur's *Letters from an American Farmer,*" *EAL,* 28 (1993), 248-51. D. H. Lawrence typified James's wife as the "Amiable Spouse" in his *Studies in Classic American Literature* (New York, 1964; orig. pub. 1923), 24.

16. Murray, "On the Domestic Education of Children" (1790), *Heath Anthology of American Literature,* ed. Paul Lauter et al. (Lexington, Mass., 1990), 1:1030. A number of works have looked at the iconographic representation of females in the Revolutionary era, among them Linda K. Kerber, *Women of the Republic: Intellect and Ideology in Revolutionary America* (Chapel Hill, 1980), and Lester C. Olson, *Emblems of American Community in the Revolutionary Era: A Study in Rhetorical Iconology* (Washington, D. C., 1991). A recent formulation that identifies the domestic implications of the use of the abused, mutilated, violated, and fetishized body in late 18th-century images is Shirley Samuels, *Romances of the Republic: Women, the Family, and Violence in the Literature of the Early American Nation* (New York, 1996), 3-22.

17. Eltha does not fit the characterization of "Crève-coeur's women [as] stereotypes of domestic enterprise but frailty under stress" maintained by A. W. Plumstead, "Hector St. John de Crèvecoeur," in *American Literature, 1764-1789: The Revolutionary Years,* ed. Emerson (Madison, 1977), 223.

18. In another Crèvecoeur sketch, "The History of Mrs. B.," a tory fighter recounts to the narrator the haunting story of a patriot woman with two nursing children whose heroic acceptance of her fate causes him some pangs. More famously, the image of the butchered domestic woman coalesced in the story of Jane McCrea some months after Crèvecoeur wrote "Landscapes." See June Namias, *White Captives: Gender and Ethnicity on the American Frontier* (Chapel Hill, 1993), 117-44.

19. Two earlier contenders for the honor of first do not hold up under scrutiny. Both Thomas Forrest, *The Disappointment* (1767), and Robert Munford, *The Candidates* (1770 or 1771), have characters who are referred to in the literature as black but are likely not. See David Mays, Introduction, *The Disappointment; or, The Force of Credulity* by Thomas Forrest (Gainesville, 1976), and Rodney M. Baine, *Robert Munford: America's First Comic Dramatist* (Athens, Ga., 1967), 64-65. A better candidate for first is John Leacock, *The Fall of British Tyranny: Or, American Liberty Triumphant* (Philadelphia, 1776).

20. Saar, "The Heritage of American Ethnicity in Crève-coeur's *Letters from an American Farmer,*" in *A Mixed Race: Ethnicity in Early America,* ed. Frank Shuffelton (New York, 1993), 245.

21. *Letters,* 49, 53. In Letter XI, 188-89, 195-97, Farmer James quotes a traveler, Iwan, who listens with approval as the botanist John "Bertram [Bartram]" describes how he has freed slaves and admitted them to his table as freemen. Thus Crèvecoeur dodges the question of equality by reincorporating former slaves into the domestic space ruled over by a benevolent, home-centered landholder. Since he uses an Iwan in "Landscapes," Crèvecoeur may also be saying that this foreign visitor can see the problems of race in America more clearly than an Anglo-American.

22. In Leacock's play, the blacks in Virginia identify their interests as allied to Lord Dunmore's forces and thus are seen in the whig politics of *The Fall of British Tyranny* as enemies of American "freedom." This use of the slave issue to attack patriot interests can be seen in another episode from 1776. In Westmoreland County, Va., Henry Glass's complaint to the local committee of safety that patriots' slaves were "ill used" led to his "Censure." See Richard Barksdale Harwell, ed., *The Committees of Safety of Westmoreland and Fincastle: Proceedings of the County Committees, 1774-1776* (Richmond, 1956), 52-53.

23. The precise status of blacks in the play, as servants or slaves, is not entirely clear. In *Letters,* blacks routinely appear as slaves unless Crèvecoeur is trying to make a point, as in the account of John Bartram's farm. Without evidence to the contrary, I assume that Tom and Nero are slaves.

24. Crèvecoeur's attitudes toward blacks in the letters and sketches have not yet been adequately explained. Despite his impassioned plea through Farmer James in Letter IX for the humanity of blacks, Crèvecoeur nowhere else asserts the picture of independent African-American lives that are the equivalent of whites. Blacks become part of the white domestic identity; he grants them human nature but sees them only as reflections of white treatment. Sentimentalized victims of extreme wealth in South Carolina, an easily bought drunk in "Landscapes," utterly loyal slaves turned servants in the portrait of Bartram in Letter XI—the overall picture of black people in Crèvecoeur emphasizes control of their subjectivity through benevolent-seeming white patronage in the home. See, however, Cook, *Epistolary Bodies,* 164-67.

25. Words in brackets indicate the actual words, if not spelling, of Crèvecoeur's original, replacing incorrect transcription from 1925 text. See Moore, ed., *More Letters from the American Farmer,* 236.

26. Crèvecoeur's narrator also inveighs against the disruptive and, finally, antidomestic ardor of true believers in "Liberty of Worship," one of the essays omitted in 1782.

27. *The Battle of Brooklyn. A Farce . . .* (New York, 1776); Jerrold, *Black-Ey'd Susan; or, "All in the Downs." A Nautical and Domestic Drama . . .* (1829), in *Nineteenth-Century Plays,* ed. George Rowell (London, 1953), 1-43; Aiken, *Uncle Toms's Cabin; or, Life among the Lowly, a Domestic Drama . . .* (1852), in *Early American Drama,* ed. Richards (New York, 1997), 373-443; Daly, *Under the Gaslight; or, Life and Love in These Times* (1867), in *American Melodrama,* ed. Daniel C. Gerould (New York, 1983), 135-81.

28. Because he only refers to violence in speeches, never showing it on stage, I do not think Crèvecoeur really intended to write the rape into the play itself. But see Moore's note to this passage in *More Letters from the American Farmer,* 375.

29. For other slight variants from the Penguin edition compare ibid., 293.

FURTHER READING

Biographies

Mitchell, Julia Post. *St. John de Crèvecoeur.* New York: Columbia U.P., 1916, 362 p.
> A seminal work on the life and writings of Crèvecoeur, written before the discovery of *Sketches* in 1925.

Philbrick, Thomas. *St. John de Crèvecoeur.* New York: Twayne, 1970, 178 p.
> Considered a cornerstone of the study of Crèvecoeur, this work examines the influences and motifs found in the author's limited canon.

Criticism

Beidler, Philip D. "Franklin's and Crèvecoeur's 'Literary' Americans." *Early American Literature* 13, No. 1 (Spring 1978): 50-63.
> Suggests that Crèvecoeur reshaped contemporary literary conventions and produced a work of fiction that anticipated the nineteenth-century novel.

Carew-Miller, Anna. "The Language of Domesticity in Crèvecoeur's *Letters from an American Farmer.*" *Early American Literature* 28, No. 3 (1993): 242-54.
> Examines the domestic scene described in the Nantucket letters and suggests that the contradictions apparent throughout the letters are indicative of Crèvecoeur's uneasiness with changing gender roles in America.

Chevignard, Bernard. "St. John de Crèvecoeur in the Looking Glass: *Letters from an American Farmer* and the Making of a Man of Letters." *Early American Literature* 19, No. 2, (Fall 1984): 173-90.

Discusses connections between incidents in Crève-coeur's life and incidents described in *Letters from an American Farmer.*

Fichtelberg, Joseph. "Utopic Distresses: Crèvecoeur's *Letters* and Revolution." *Studies in the Literary Imagination* 27, No. 1 (Spring 1994): 85-101.
    Challenges the role of *Letters* as a faithful rendering of republican ideology in pre-Revolutionary America.

Holbo, Christine. "Imagination, Commerce, and the Politics of Associationism in Crèvecoeur's *Letters from an American Farmer.*" *Early American Literature* 32, Vol. 1 (1997): 20-65.
    Analyzes *Letters from an American Farmer* within the context of the eighteenth-century narrative model associated with the language of sensibility and imagination.

Hurst, Richard M. "Snakelore Motifs in the Writings of J. Hector St. John de Crèvecoeur and Other Colonial Writers." *New York Folklore* 9, No. 3-4 (Winter 1983): 55-97.
    Claims that Crèvecoeur made extensive use of colonial folklore in his writings.

Philbrick, Thomas. "Crèvecoeur as New Yorker." *Early American Literature* 11, No. 1 (Spring 1976): 22-30.
    Argues that Crèvecoeur's years as a resident of New York gave him the unique perspective of both insider and outsider to the colonial American experience, and that this dual perspective is reflected in his writing.

Putz, Manfred. "Dramatic Elements and the Problem of Literary Mediation in the Works of Hector St. John de Crèvecoeur." *Yearbook of Research in English and American Literature* 3 (1985): 111-30.
    Explores Crèvecoeur's work in terms of its dramatic elements.

Rice, Grantland S. "Crèvecoeur and the Politics of Authorship in Republican America." *Early American Literature* 28, No. 2 (1993): 91-119.
    Claims that *Letters from an American Farmer* is best understood if analyzed as an early novel.

Saar, Doreen Alvarez. "Crèvecoeur's 'Thoughts on Slavery': *Letters from an American Farmer* and Whig Rhetoric." *Early American Literature* 22, No. 2 (Fall 1987): 192-203.
    Maintains that Crèvecoeur's letter on the evils of slavery was meant to be understood both literally and symbolically since slavery as a symbol of the relationship between Britain and her colonies in America was part of well-established Whig rhetorical conventions.

Werge, Thomas. "Thomas Shepard and Crèvecoeur: Two Uses of the Image of the Bosom Serpent before Hawthorne." *Nathaniel Hawthorne Journal* (1974): 236-39.
    Discusses serpent imagery in Crèvecoeur's writing.

Additional coverage of Crèvecoeur's life and career is contained in the following source published by the Gale Group: *Dictionary of Literary Biography,* **Vol. 37.**

Our Mutual Friend

Charles Dickens

The following entry presents criticism of Dickens's novel *Our Mutual Friend* (1864-65). For information on Dickens's complete career, see *NCLC*, Volumes 3, 8, 18, and 26; for discussion of Dickens's novels *Oliver Twist, Hard Times,* and *A Tale of Two Cities,* see *NCLC,* Volumes 37, 50, and 86 respectively.

INTRODUCTION

The last of Dickens's novels to be issued as a twenty-part monthly serial, *Our Mutual Friend* has long been considered one of the author's darkest works, the product of his declining years when exhaustion and disillusionment were taking over his life and his writing. The novel was not terribly successful at the time of its publication and was unfavorably compared to his earlier, more optimistic works. In addition, the popularity of serialized novels had peaked some twenty years earlier and the form was being replaced by less expensive monthly magazines. Critics today, for the most part, consider the novel in a more favorable light, appreciating the complexity of its numerous characters and multiple plot lines, and praising its unified presentation of the themes of money and predation.

BIOGRAPHICAL INFORMATION

Charles Dickens was born in 1812 in Portsmouth, Hampshire, England, to John and Elizabeth Barrow Dickens. The second of eight children, Dickens spent his childhood on the southern coast of England, where he attended a good school until the age of eleven. The family then moved to London and shortly thereafter his father was sent to debtor's prison. Young Charles went to work in a blacking warehouse and was forced to live on his own in cheap lodgings in a state of near starvation. Although he was soon rescued by his father and sent to school in London, the brief period of abandonment and uncertainty affected his life and his writings for years to come. Dickens did not attend college but was admitted as a reader to the library of the British Museum, where he immersed himself in the study of great literature, particularly Shakespeare. He worked for some time as a clerk, as a shorthand reporter, and eventually as a news reporter for the *Morning Chronicle,* a position which required him to travel all over the country.

Dickens's first success, both critical and popular, was *Sketches by Boz* (1836), a series of short pieces on life in London. His first novel, *Posthumous Papers of the Pickwick Club* (1837), was published, as were all of his novels, in serial form, and by the time the fourth monthly installment was issued, Dickens was the most popular author in England. Over the next thirty years, he continued to publish successful novels, among them: *Oliver Twist* (1838), *A Christmas Carol In Prose* (1843), *The Personal History of David Copperfield* (1850), *Bleak House* (1853), *Hard Times for These Hard Times* (1854), *A Tale of Two Cities* (1859), and *Great Expectations* (1861). His writing, once full of hope and optimism, grew increasingly pessimistic as he aged, with images of decay and corruption dominating the later works. *Our Mutual Friend* was his last completed novel; with its images of dustheaps and death, it is widely considered one of the author's darkest visions. In 1870, while working on *The Mystery of Edwin Drood,* Dickens suffered an aneurysm in the brain and died the next day. He was buried in the Poet's Corner of Westminster Abbey.

PLOT AND MAJOR CHARACTERS

There are numerous plots and subplots in *Our Mutual Friend,* the main one involving a young man, John Harmon, who returns to England after an absence of many years. Before his death, his wealthy father had made his son's inheritance contingent upon his marriage to Bella Wilfer, a beautiful but mercenary young woman. Shortly after leaving the ship that brought him back to England, Harmon is supposedly murdered; a body found in the Thames is identified as his and he does nothing to correct the error. Assuming first the name of Julius Handford, and then John Rokesmith, Harmon takes a position as secretary to Mr. Boffin—a former employee and now heir of the elder Harmon's estate—in order to assess the character of his bride-to-be while in disguise. Uneasy with their newly-acquired wealth, the Boffins have taken Bella into their home in order to give her the advantages she would have had if she had married Harmon. As Rokesmith, Harmon professes his love for Bella, but believing she is capable of making a far better match, she refuses him and Mr. Boffin discharges him for impudence.

During this time, Boffin has changed from a kindly generous man to a materialistic miser as part of an elaborate charade to teach Bella a lesson about the hazards of greed. The young woman becomes so disturbed by the changes in her benefactor, she returns to her father's house, giving up the material advantages of life with the Boffins. Bella sees the error of her ways and determines to marry for love. When Rokesmith reappears, she agrees to marry him, and their marriage is happy despite their modest means. Eventually the mystery surrounding Rokesmith's true identity is unraveled and his fortune restored, making Bella the wealthy wife she had once dreamed of being.

The other major narrative involves Lizzie Hexam, the daughter of a river scavenger, Gaffer Hexam, the very man who discovered the body thought to be Harmon's. At the inquest, Lizzie is noticed by Eugene Wrayburn, a bored, upper-class lawyer. Lizzie's brother, a churlish youth, hates Wrayburn and tries to steer his sister's affections away from the lawyer and towards Bradley Headstone, a severe schoolmaster whose repressed anger surfaces when Lizzie rejects his proposal. Lizzie escapes the attentions of both men by retreating to a small country village. Returning from a visit to Lizzie, Wrayburn is attacked and thrown into the river by Headstone. Lizzie rescues him, and he is slowly nursed back to life with the help of Jenny Wren, a dolls' dressmaker with whom Lizzie had lived in London. Jenny determines that Wrayburn's wish is to marry Lizzie; she brings a clergyman from London and arranges a bed-side ceremony for the pair.

Subplots include the attempted blackmail of Mr. Boffin by his employee Silas Wegg, who has been hired to read to the illiterate Boffins. Wegg had taken possession of the Boffin house and dustheap when the Boffins departed for more luxurious quarters. When Wegg finds another of the elder Harmon's wills, this one leaving the fortune to the state, he tries, with the aid of a taxidermist named Mr. Venus, to coerce his employer into sharing the estate. The plot is foiled by Venus's offer to testify against Wegg.

A second case of attempted blackmail involves Rogue Riderhood, a river scavenger who witnesses the attack on Wrayburn and tries to extract money from Headstone in exchange for his silence. As the two argue and struggle, they both fall into the river and drown.

The upper classes make up what Dickens called "the so-cial chorus," a group whose only apparent function is to represent society's views on the events of the main narra-tives as they unfold. Their lives are empty and their activi-ties are limited to gossiping about the Harmons, the Bof-fins, and the other characters who lead more active lives. The main members of the social chorus are the Veneer-ings, a newly-rich couple who hold dinner parties in an at-tempt to ingratiate themselves with the more established members of London society; the Podsnaps, who are rich, self-satisfied, and rigid; and the Lammles, who married each other for money only to discover that each had been trying to deceive the other and they were both penniless.

At the opposite end of the economic spectrum is Betty Higden, a poor woman hounded by her fear of dying in the poorhouse. She would prefer to starve than to suffer the cruelties and indignities associated with the almshouse, and that's exactly what she does, dying in a field as Lizzie Hexam tries to comfort her.

MAJOR THEMES

The major theme of *Our Mutual Friend* is money and the hazards associated with its misuse. The well-to-do charac-ters, almost without exception, are negatively portrayed, and the Harmon fortune makes it necessary for its heir to hide his identity in order to assess the character of the Bo-ffins and Bella Wilfer with any accuracy, the implication being that a rich man can never determine who his true friends are. A related theme is predation—several chapter headings refer to birds of prey—wherein the possibility of extracting wealth from another by less than honorable means proves too tempting for such characters as Silas Wegg, Rogue Riderhood, and others. The very opening scene of the novel involves Gaffer Hexam, bent over the edge of his boat like a vulture, looking for bodies in the river—bodies that he then robs before turning them over to the authorities.

Many critics have pointed out the emphasis on surfaces and depths throughout the novel. Hexam and Riderhood plumb the depths of the Thames searching for bodies and whatever other treasures they can find, while the Veneer-ings are all glossy surface with no depth at all. Masks, dis-guises, and cases of mistaken identity occur repeatedly within the narrative. John Harmon is taken for dead be-cause a man who resembles him has been murdered by mistake. Harmon then assumes a new identity and lives as John Rokesmith, allowing the community to believe the error. Mr. Boffin pretends to be a miser in order to instruct Bella Wilfer on the perils of materialism and greed. Brad-ley Headstone disguises himself as Rogue Riderhood so that the attack on Wrayburn will be blamed on the water-man. Both the river and the dustheaps, which forms the basis of the Harmon fortune, are recurring motifs in the work and both are associated with death and decay but, at the same time, they provide a livelihood for some. As critic Richard A. Lanham puts it, "if the river is the liquid sewer of London, the dust-heap is the dry one, and the two together provide food and drink for the majority of the characters in the novel."

Reading and literacy are also prominent features of *Our Mutual Friend*. The Boffins' illiteracy provides an employ-ment opportunity for Weggs, who pretends to be an expert in literary matters. Gaffer Hexam's illiteracy means he must memorize the posters and pamphlets of missing per-sons who have possibly met their deaths in the river. His daughter Lizzie's illiteracy provides the excuse for Wray-burn's involvement with her, as the lawyer offers to pro-vide reading lessons for both Lizzie and Jenny Wren.

Overall, the tone of the narrative is grim and bleak; the cumulative effect of the numerous references to corrup-tion, decay, and death is a darkness that becomes oppres-sive. Although there are humorous instances throughout the novel, most especially those associated with the Ve-neerings and the Podsnaps, they are satiric in nature rather than comic.

CRITICAL RECEPTION

Critical response to *Our Mutual Friend* was long shaped by Henry James's famous 1865 review in the *Nation*. James called it "the poorest of Mr Dickens's works," claiming that the novel was "poor with the poverty not of momentary embarrassment, but of permanent exhaustion." Most scholars agreed with this assessment and termed the work incoherent and implausible. The reading public, meanwhile, was put off by the novel's relentless pessimism; subscriptions fell off monthly as installments were published. Most modern critics, though, tend to recognize the complexity of the work and to appreciate the multiple plot lines and numerous characters. Some of these characters, such as Gaffer Hexam and Betty Higden, were possibly inspired by real Londoners who had been interviewed by Henry Mayhew for his nonfiction work *London Labour and the London Poor*. Harland S. Nelson has examined these possible connections by comparing the two texts. Other possible sources of inspiration have been suggested by Lewis Horne, who believes that Homer's hero Odysseus was the model for three of Dickens's characters; and Howard W. Fulweiler, who suggests that Darwin's theories informed Dickens's later fiction, particularly *Our Mutual Friend*.

Concentrating too completely on characters and the weaknesses in their representation has led, according to Philip Hobsbaum, to many negative assessments of *Our Mutual Friend*. Critics would be better served, he claims, by concentrating on the novel's central images, particularly dust and the river. Other critics claim the novel is unified by the motifs of reading and literacy, among them Stanley Friedman, who believes that these recurring elements provide character definition and aid in plot development. Michael Greenstein, meanwhile, has studied the many unifying themes and motifs that focus on mutuality. As a whole, late twentieth-century scholars have dismissed the early negative appraisals of *Our Mutual Friend* and now urge a new appreciation of this complicated novel.

PRINCIPAL WORKS

Sketches by Boz, Illustrative of Every-Day Life and Every-Day People [as Boz] (sketches and short stories) 1836

*Posthumous Papers of the Pickwick Club [as Boz] (novel) 1837

*Oliver Twist (novel) 1838

*The Life and Adventures of Nicholas Nickleby (novel) 1839

*Barnaby Rudge (novel) 1841

*The Old Curiosity Shop (novel) 1841

American Notes for General Circulation (travel essay) 1842

A Christmas Carol in Prose (short story) 1843

The Chimes (short story) 1844

*The Life and Adventures of Martin Chuzzlewit (novel) 1844

The Cricket on the Hearth (short story) 1845

Pictures from Italy (travel essay) 1846

*Dealings with the Firm of Dombey and Son (novel) 1848

The Haunted Man, and The Ghost's Bargain (short stories) 1848

*The Personal History of David Copperfield (novel) 1850

*Bleak House (novel) 1853

*Hard Times for These Times (novel) 1854

*Little Dorrit (novel) 1857

*A Tale of Two Cities (novel) 1859

*Great Expectations (novel) 1861

The Uncommercial Traveller (sketches and short stories) 1861

*Our Mutual Friend (novel) 1865

No Thoroughfare [with Wilkie Collins] (drama) 1867

The Mystery of Edwin Drood (unfinished novel) 1870

*All of Dickens's novels were originally published serially in magazines, usually over periods of from one to two years.

CRITICISM

Henry James (essay date 1865)

SOURCE: Review of *Our Mutual Friend*, in *Nation*, 21 December, 1865, reprinted in *Dickens: Hard Times, Great Expectations, and Our Mutual Friend*, ed. by Norman Page, Macmillan Press, 1979, pp. 152-56.

[*In the following review, James asserts that* Our Mutual Friend *is uninspired and disappointing, filled with implausibly eccentric characters.*]

Our Mutual Friend is, to our perception, the poorest of Mr Dickens's works. And it is poor with the poverty not of momentary embarrassment, but of permanent exhaustion. It is wanting in inspiration. For the last ten years it has seemed to us that Mr Dickens has been unmistakably forcing himself. **Bleak House** was forced; **Little Dorrit** was labored; the present work is dug out as with a spade and pickaxe. Of course—to anticipate the usual argument—who but Dickens could have written it? Who, indeed? Who else would have established a lady in business in a novel on the admirably solid basis of her always putting on gloves and tieing a handkerchief round her head in moments of grief, and of her habitually addressing her family with 'Peace! hold!' It is needless to say that Mrs Reginald Wilfer is first and last the occasion of considerable true humor. When, after conducting her daughter to Mrs Boffin's carriage, in sight of all the envious neighbors, she is described as enjoying her triumph during the next quarter of an hour by airing herself on the door-step 'in a kind of splendidly serene trance,' we laugh with as uncritical a laugh as could be desired of us. We pay the same tribute to her assertions, as she narrates the glories of the society she enjoyed at her father's table, that she has known as many as three copper-plate engravers exchanging the most exquisite sallies and retorts there at one time. But when to these we have added a dozen more happy examples of the humor which was exhaled from every line of Mr Dickens's earlier writings, we shall have closed the list of the merits of the work before us. To say that the conduct of the story, with all its complications, betrays a long-practised hand, is to pay no compliment worthy the author. If this were, indeed, a compliment, we should be inclined to carry it further, and congratulate him on his success in what we should call the manufacture of fiction; for in so doing we should express a feeling that has attended us throughout the book. Seldom, we reflected, had we read a book so intensely *written*, so little seen, known, or felt.

In all Mr Dickens's works the fantastic has been his great resource; and while his fancy was lively and vigorous it accomplished great things. But the fantastic, when the fancy is dead, is a very poor business. The movement of Mr Dickens's fancy in Mrs Wilfer and Mr Boffin and Lady Tippins, and the Lammles and Miss Wren, and even in Eugene Wrayburn, is, to our mind, a movement lifeless, forced, mechanical. It is the letter of his old humor without the spirit. It is hardly too much to say that every character here put before us is a mere bundle of eccentricities, animated by no principle of nature whatever. In former days there reigned in Mr Dickens's extravagances a comparative consistency; they were exaggerated statements of types that really existed. We had, perhaps, never known a Newman Noggs, nor a Pecksniff, nor a Micawber; but we had known persons of whom these figures were but the strictly logical consummation. But among the grotesque creatures who occupy the pages before us, there is not one whom we can refer to as an existing type. In all Mr Dickens's stories, indeed, the reader has been called upon, and has willingly consented, to accept a certain number of figures or creatures of pure fancy, for this was the author's poetry. He was, moreover, always repaid for his concession by a peculiar beauty or power in these exceptional characters. But he is now expected to make the same concession with a very inadequate reward. What do we get in return for accepting Miss Jenny Wren as a possible person? This young lady is the type of a certain class of characters of which Mr Dickens has made a speciality, and with which he has been accustomed to draw alternate smiles and tears, according as he pressed one spring or another. But this is very cheap merriment and very cheap pathos. Miss Jenny Wren is a poor little dwarf, afflicted, as she constantly reiterates, with a 'bad back' and 'queer legs,' who makes dolls' dresses, and is for ever pricking at those with whom she converses, in the air, with her needle, and assuring them that she knows their 'tricks and their manners.' Like all Mr Dickens's pathetic characters, she is a little monster; she is deformed, unhealthy, unnatural; she belongs to the troop of hunchbacks, imbeciles, and precocious children who have carried on the sentimental business in all Mr Dickens's novels; the little Nells, the Smikes, the Paul Dombeys.

Mr Dickens goes as far out of the way for his wicked people as he does for his good ones. Rogue Riderhood, indeed, in the present story, is villanous with a sufficiently natural villany; he belongs to that quarter of society in which the author is most at his ease. But was there ever such wickedness as that of the Lammles and Mr Fledgeby? Not that people have not been as mischievous as they; but was any one ever mischievous in that singular fashion? Did a couple of elegant swindlers ever take such particular pains to be aggressively inhuman?—for we can find no other word for the gratuitous distortions to which they are subjected. The word *humanity* strikes us as strangely discordant, in the midst of these pages; for, let us boldly declare it, there is no humanity here. Humanity is nearer home than the Boffins, and the Lammles, and the Wilfers, and the Veneerings. It is in what men have in common with each other, and not in what they have in distinction. The people just named have nothing in common with each other, except the fact that they have nothing in common with mankind at large. What a world were this world if the world of ***Our Mutual Friend*** were an honest reflection of it! But a community of eccentrics is impossible. Rules alone are consistent with each other; exceptions are inconsistent. Society is maintained by natural sense and natural feeling. We cannot conceive a society in which these principles are not in some manner represented. Where in these pages are the depositaries of that intelligence without which the movement of life would cease? Who represents nature? Accepting half of Mr Dickens's persons as intentionally grotesque, where are those exemplars of sound humanity who should afford us the proper measure of their companions' variations? We ought not, in justice to the author, to seek them among his weaker—that is, his mere conventional—characters; in John Harmon, Lizzie Hexam, or Mortimer Lightwood; but we assuredly cannot find them among his stronger—that is, his artificial creations. Suppose we take Eugene Wrayburn and Bradley Headstone. They occupy a half-way position between the habitual probable of nature and the habitual impossible of Mr Dickens. A large portion of the story rests upon the enmity borne by Headstone to Wrayburn, both being in love with the same woman. Wrayburn is a gentleman, and Headstone is one of the people. Wrayburn is well-bred, careless, elegant, sceptical, and idle: Headstone is a high-tempered, hard-working, ambitious young schoolmaster. There lay in the opposition of these two characters a very good story. But the prime requisite was that they should *be* characters: Mr Dickens, according to his usual plan, has made them simply figures, and between them the story that was to be, the story that should have been, has evaporated. Wrayburn lounges about with his hands in his pockets, smoking a cigar, and talking nonsense. Headstone strides about, clenching his fists and biting his lips and grasping his stick. There is one scene in which Wrayburn chaffs the schoolmaster with easy insolence, while the latter writhes impotently under his well-bred sarcasm. This scene is very clever, but it is very insufficient. If the majority of readers were not so very timid in the use of words we should call it vulgar. By this we do not mean to indicate the conventional impropriety of two gentlemen exchanging lively personalities; we mean to emphasise the essentially small character of these personalities. In other words, the moment, dramatically, is great, while the author's conception is weak. The friction of two *men,* of two characters, of two passions, produces stronger sparks than Wrayburn's boyish repartees and Headstone's melodramatic commonplaces. Such scenes as this are useful in fixing the limits of Mr Dickens's insight. Insight is, perhaps, too strong a word; for we are convinced that it is one of the chief conditions of his genius not to see beneath the surface of things. If we might hazard a definition of his literary character, we should, accordingly, call him the greatest of superficial novelists. We are aware that this definition confines him to an inferior rank in the department of letters which he adorns; but we accept this consequence of our proposition. It were, in our opinion, an offence against humanity to place Mr Dickens among the greatest novelists. For, to repeat what we have already intimated, he has created nothing but figure. He has added nothing to our understanding of human character. He is master of but two alternatives: he reconciles us to what is commonplace, and he reconciles us to what is odd. The value of the former service is questionable; and the manner in which Mr Dickens performs it sometimes conveys a certain impression of charlatanism. The value of the latter service is incontestable, and here Mr Dickens is an honest, an admirable artist. But what is the condition of the truly great novelist? For him there are no alternatives, for him there are no oddities, for him there is nothing outside of humanity. He cannot shirk it; it imposes itself upon him. For him alone, therefore, there is a true and a false; for him alone it is possible to be right, because it is possible to be wrong. Mr Dickens is a great observer and a great humorist, but he is nothing of a philosopher. Some people may hereupon say, so much the better; we say, so much the worse. For a novelist very soon has need of a little philosophy. In treating of Micawber, and Boffin, and Pickwick, *et hoc genus omne,* he can, indeed, dispense with it, for this—we say it with all deference—is not serious writing. But when he comes to tell the story of a passion, a story like that of Headstone and Wrayburn, he becomes a moralist as well as an artist. He must know *man* as well as *men,* and to know man is to be a philosopher. The writer who knows men alone, if he have Mr Dickens's humor and fancy, will give us figures and pictures for which we cannot be too grateful, for he will enlarge our knowledge of the world. But when he introduces men and women whose interest is preconceived to lie not in the poverty, the weakness, the drollery of their natures, but in their complete and unconscious subjection to ordinary and healthy human emotions, all his humor, all his fancy, will avail him nothing, if, out of the fulness of his sympathy, he is unable to prosecute those generalisations in which alone consists the real greatness of a work of art. This may sound like very subtle talk about a very simple matter; it is rather very simple talk about a very subtle matter. A story based upon those elementary passions in which alone we seek the true and final manifesta-

tion of character must be told in a spirit of intellectual superiority to those passions. That is, the author must understand what he is talking about. The perusal of a story so told is one of the most elevating experiences within the reach of the human mind. The perusal of a story which is not so told is infinitely depressing and unprofitable.

Philip Hobsbaum (essay date 1963)

SOURCE: "The Critics and *Our Mutual Friend,*" in *Essays in Criticism,* Vol. 13, No. 3, July, 1963, pp. 231-40.

[*In the following essay, Hobsbaum examines common misreadings of* Our Mutual Friend *and suggests that they are caused by an overemphasis on character, whereas a study of the novel's central images would yield a greater understanding and appreciation of the work.*]

Even the greatest novel can lend itself to misreading if there is some uncertainty in its execution. The misreading may, however, be considerably in excess of the uncertainty.

For example, the young Henry James came out decisively against *Our Mutual Friend* when it first appeared. He regarded it as an unsuccessful attempt on Dickens's part to carry on his earlier, comic, vein. The view of Dickens as an instinctive eccentric was one characteristically found among Victorian highbrows, as George H. Ford has demonstrated in his valuable study of Dickens's early readers. How mistaken it is was shown recently by Professor Butt and Mrs. Tillotson in their study of Dickens's working methods.

But it is a view which, with less excuse, has its counterpart in serious critics of our own time. Santayana's slighting ascription of the great entertainer has been given a fresh currency in our own time in the strictures of Dr. Leavis. Another *Scrutiny* critic, R. C. Churchill, suggests that the characters in the book would be more amusing if they had not already occurred, far better done, in earlier works.

This preoccupation with character is a major cause of critical deflection in the reading of Dickens. Tracing parallels between his various personae may, as William de Morgan suggested in his preface to the Waverley Edition, blind us to the effect of these personae in their dramatic context. It may also prevent our comprehending the total effect of the novel.

Hence, perhaps, the remarkable range of valuation of *Our Mutual Friend,* even in modern times: all the way from K. J. Fielding, who finds it incoherent, to Jack Lindsay, who regards it as one of the greatest prose works ever written.

Much, no doubt, depends on the expectations with which a reader approaches the book. Henry James particularly objects to Dickens's handling of the fine gentleman's pursuit of the boatman's daughter. He says that this gentleman, Wrayburn, is no more than a stock cigar-smoking type. And if Dr. Fielding is more conscious that Wrayburn is a new departure, for him it is only one which anticipates the dandies of Oscar Wilde.

Yet other critics have seen more in Wrayburn than this. Although, like James, George Orwell regarded *Our Mutual Friend* as an extension of Dickens's earlier manner, he concedes that the episode of Wrayburn and Lizzie is treated very realistically. Wrayburn has too much decency to attempt seducing Lizzie, but not enough to jettison his family by marrying her. G. K. Chesterton goes so far as to say that, in Wrayburn's pursuit of Lizzie, Dickens 'has marvellously realised the singularly empty obstinacy that drives the whims and pleasures of a leisured class'.

Even if one plays the game of comparing Wrayburn with earlier creations of Dickens, he will be seen to be more than an imitation. Edmund Wilson finds him more sympathetic than Harthouse or Gowan; Humphry House, more interesting than Steerforth. Monroe Engel, in a recent study, has said that, with this character, Dickens added a new dimension to the consideration of class in English fiction: Wrayburn is too careless even to protect himself.

This state of mind has been ably analysed by another recent critic, J. Hillis Miller. 'The character feels that life is altogether ridiculous because every move in it has been decided beforehand.'

But the realistic presentation of ennui would hardly in itself be impressive if it was not part of a developing moral pattern. Edmund Wilson, among others, has shown how this is so. The conjunction of the upper with the lower class is, in his view, a criticism of the middle-class society satirised elsewhere in the book—this has become dissociated from everything that is admirable in English life. Edgar Johnson has suggested that Wrayburn's scepticism of received values made him an effective instrument for Dickens's criticism of society. And, in his final denial of society, Wrayburn has learned affirmation; in deserving Lizzie's love, 'he has achieved purpose and respect'.

Both Monroe Engel and Hillis Miller emphasize the importance of the river in this regeneration. Wrayburn's disfigurement and immersion render it possible for him to cast off his old life and begin anew. The enactment may be seen to take place on several planes. For, as Jack Lindsay points out, Dickens never loses hold of the social aspects of this marriage. It transcends the bonds of the society in which Wrayburn has been imprisoned.

This is an example of the way in which a consideration of a Dickens 'character' will often prove to be far more than that. Here, it is a way into the symbolic drama of the book.

But there is always some reason for a divergence of opinion. James's strictures on Wrayburn as an original charac-

ter and on the book's norm of conduct are not without foundation. Wrayburn's moral position may seem equivocal if only because Lizzie, the character with whom he is most closely associated, is (as James said) a conventional figure. Few critics have come to her defence. Edmund Wilson and Jack Lindsay may have accurately diagnosed a social intention on Dickens's part when he took his heroine from the lowest and most illiterate classes. But they do not seem to see that the moral would have more point if her behaviour and accent were less resolutely that of a middle-class heroine. 'Think of me as belonging to another station and quite cut off from you in honour . . . if you feel towards me, in one particular, as you might if I was a lady, give me the full claim of a lady upon your generous behaviour.' (IV, vi.)

Lizzie's moral position is also rather equivocal. Chesterton found her too romantic to be pathetic. Humphry House charged her with being coy—enhancing her attractiveness as well as her virtue by running away. Messrs. Engel and Miller do well to stress that part Lizzie plays in the regeneration of Wrayburn, but both note how powerfully this is reinforced by the river as a motivating symbol.

It is true that the scheme of *Our Mutual Friend* does not depend for its success on the realism of an individual character. In this way, the book may be said to carry Lizzie. Nevertheless, she cannot be termed a satisfactory dramatic creation. And her social and moral indeterminacy may well, for some readers, put Wrayburn, with whom she is so closely associated, in an equivocal light. This does not justify James's opinion that Wrayburn is a character out of stock. But it may go far towards explaining it.

Preconceptions similar to those which led James to identify the eccentric characters of *Our Mutual Friend* with earlier efforts in a purely comic vein led him also to the judgement that even so central a character as the dustman, Boffin, is 'lifeless, forced, mechanical . . . the letter of his old humour without the spirit. . . . Humanity is nearer home than the Boffins.'

Once more, we may deduce that 'character' is being considered in isolation. James gives something of his case away by recognizing that a distinction, if only of value, must be made between Boffin and other 'comic' characters. George Orwell draws no such distinction. For him, Boffin is just the same as other 'good rich men' such as the Cheerybles in *Nicholas Nickleby.* This can, fortunately, be shown to be a misreading not only of the intention of the book but of the effect that it is likely to have on readers who come to it without these preoccupations.

For, on inheriting his mounds of dust, Boffin deteriorates into a miser. Dr. Fielding has called this 'a fantastic pretence' but, as Gissing pointed out, in fact the presentation of Boffin's miserdom is convincing. '"What!" said Mr. Boffin, gathering himself together in his most suspicious attitude, and wrinkling his face into a very map of curves and corners, "Don't I know what grabs are made at a man with money? If I didn't keep my eyes open and my pockets buttoned, shouldn't I be in the work-house before I knew where I was?'" (III, xv).

Hillis Miller has pointed out that this is no sudden change. We find the Boffins early on in the book planning to leave their Bower and take a new mansion. 'Our old selves weren't people of fortune; our new selves are', says Mr. Boffin in explanation of his changed way of life. His predecessor as custodian of the Mounds was Harmon, also proprietor of 'Harmony' Gaol: 'a tremendous old rascal who . . . grew rich as a Dust Contractor, and lived in a hollow in a hilly country entirely composed of Dust'. (I, ii.) It seems that Boffin inherits something of Harmon's temperament along with his Mounds. Jack Lindsay says that fortune perverts Boffin's whole character. Humphry House relates, as one should, this degeneration in Boffin to the development of the action—'everything is corrupted and distorted by money'.

James and Orwell may have been misled by the benevolent aspect Boffin wears in the earlier part of the book. Yet there is more than a hint of criticism in the author's presentation of this. He is shown to be a very odd-looking fellow altogether. 'Morning, sir! Morning! Morning! Morning, Morning, morning, morning!' (I, v.) Almost insistently odd, we may feel. He is revealed as being sentimental and tough at the same time in I, viii; snobbish in I, ix; and, in I, xv, the beginnings of real miserdom come. He makes the 'secretary' Rokesmith work hard to get him into his new house just for the sake of making him work hard. '"Well, it ain't that I'm in a mortal hurry," said Mr. Boffin, "only when you *do* pay people for looking alive, it's as well to know that they are looking alive."'

This is not the benevolence of the characters in the earlier Dickens. However, since Boffin eventually reverts to something like his initial aspect, and the action is, correspondingly, not worked out to its logical conclusion, James and Orwell may have some reason for their belief that Boffin is little more than a lesser Cheeryble; though this, again, need not justify their opinion.

A number of critics—Gissing, Chesterton and House among them—believe that Dickens changed his plot in mid-novel. After nine-tenths of an action showing the corrupting influence of wealth—symbolized by the mounds of dust—the good people of the beginning of the novel end up rich as well.

There have been attempts to justify this change in the action. Mr. Miller, for instance, suggests that, in acting the rôle of a miser, Boffin was defining himself as the refusal to be his situation and appearance. This seems rather far-fetched. Mr. Lindsay has a better point when he says that we fail to believe Boffin's miserdom is assumed. There is, indeed, little playacting in the savage attack on Rokesmith—'I know this young lady, and we all three know that it's Money she makes a stand for—money, money, money—and that you and your affections and hearts are a Lie, sir!' (III, xv.)

The scene is at once consonant with the general pattern of the book and, in itself, a powerful projection of greed and suspicion. The fact that Boffin turns out to be a faithful custodian after all does not remove the impression it leaves. And it certainly does not make the book an imitation *Nicholas Nickleby* or Boffin another Cheeryble. What we most clearly remember in *Our Mutual Friend* is not the universal panacea of individual kindliness but the corruption of Boffin and the relentless struggle for possession of the mounds of dust.

This symbol in action is a moral condemnation. It attracts to itself the anti-social attitudes criticized in the book. This is why it is not germane to say, as Dr. Fielding does, that the symbol is used ambiguously. The only deduction he draws from the Mounds is 'that there is no objection to inheriting wealth without working for it, and that it is only wrong for a man like Harmon to build it up by providing an honest service to the community'. Even as a political point, this is highly arguable. In any case, it is contradicted by Dr. Fielding's own account of the plot: he says that it is the 'golden-hearted' Boffin who has built the Mounds up.

Yet it cannot be denied that the ending of the book permits such misreading. Dickens was not the thoroughgoing socialist that Jack Lindsay, for example, would have us believe. Orwell makes a good point about his liberal idealism. 'It was beyond him to grasp that, given the existing form of society, certain evils cannot be remedied.' Dickens's criticism of society was, of course, a moral one. He attacks, not the existence of private property, but some of the uses to which it is put.

However, this very idealism saves the end of the book from being the failure it might have been. Hillis Miller has called this a fable. 'When one has recognized that gold is dust, one can go on to make gold of dust.' Bella's rejection of her old self and of Boffin's miserdom makes the Harmon gold, in Dickens's own words, 'turn bright again after a long long rust in the dark'. (IV, v.) This is not the stern resolution that might have been desired, but neither is it a gross inconsistency.

Neither is it true to say that the dust-heaps themselves are inconclusive as a symbol. Yet one can see how such a judgement could come about. The position of Dickens with regard to criticism has been very similar to that of Shakespeare before the work of Wilson Knight. Many of Dickens's earlier critics have abstracted the characters from the total pattern of the book. There is a poetic application of symbolism in Dickens's greatest novels which would do very much to explain the currency he has had in spite of the very incomplete attempts to explicate his work. Explication is not the same as appreciation. It may be that critics have lacked tools with which to approach the problems raised by a reading of Dickens. All the same, it is more than a coincidence that the critics who have a low opinion of *Our Mutual Friend*—James, Orwell, Chesterton, Gissing—do not seem to be aware of it offering anything more to a reader than the plot-and-character appeal with which the minor Victorian novel has so familiarized us. It was in these terms that G. H. Lewes attacked Dickens and in these same terms that Gissing replied to him. Naturally the reply was inadequate. George H. Ford, comparing the two, said 'The effort of nineteenth century critics to set up criteria which would consistently differentiate the novel from poetry was a necessary effort, but one which has now spent its force.'

It is not impertinent to say that by such criteria many of these adverse critics were judging Dickens's work. And with them one may link Dr. Fielding, who has attempted to hold their position against the more radical interpretation of Dickens initiated by Edmund Wilson and carried on largely by American critics. We can point to no such landmark of Dickens criticism as Wilson Knight's discussion of *Measure for Measure* which began a new phase in the reading of Shakespeare. Nevertheless, a good deal can be shown to be going on in *Our Mutual Friend* which was not accounted for in the aesthetic of Henry James, or even of George Orwell. And it can be done through a consideration of the striking consensus of views among critics who regard the book as a dramatic poem.

One of the points Edmund Wilson made was about the predominance of the dust in *Our Mutual Friend*—it blows through the book, in Dickens's own phrase, like some mysterious currency. Humphry House has shown how the dust collected from the streets came to have great value. The dust-heaps may be filth but, as Mr. Engel says, they are nevertheless money. And from this recognition it is a short step to the working out of a metaphor in which dust and money are equated. Money, the ascription of nominal value to what has no value in itself is, as Hillis Miller says, the central symbol in *Our Mutual Friend* of the successful humanization of the world.

Professor Johnson has shown how society in relation to Boffin is compared with the buzzing and creeping creatures attracted by a dung-hill. Mr. Lindsay, too, links the image with political values: the dust-heap is the one great prize for which everyone is fighting.

The Mounds are also the débris of history. In Mr. Miller's sense of the ruins of an ancient city, certainly, but also in the sense of the past. John Rokesmith in his sleepless nights buries his old identity deeper and deeper beneath imaginary piles of dust.

The objects are dead, but still have power to dominate the lives that are lived in their midst. So says Mr. Miller, and, indeed, the struggle for the dust shows that they do.

The action of the Mounds is to decay and to corrupt. Mr. Engel has shown how Harmon is the ruined victim of his own money, and how it begins to corrupt Boffin and his ward, Bella. In other words, the symbolism is integral to the action of the book, and can no more be effectively separated from it than can the characters. Thus, the weight of matter in the world of the Podsnaps and the Veneerings is related to the Mounds. Mr. Miller reminds us of the scene where the heavy articles of Podsnap's table are weighed and assessed, like so much scrap. (I, xi.)

In the discussion of the dust symbolism there is, as we have seen, a remarkable consensus of opinion among the critics, although there have been some notable absences from the discussion. Clearly, something of the same experience has been shared by a number of different readers. It may be that a critical explication of the book would be best managed through a consideration of its central images. As Mr. Miller has pointed out, the drama of the novel derives from the central opposition between the death that is represented by the Harmon Mounds and death by water.

The river cannot, any more than the Mounds, be equated with a simple property. If it could, there would be little point in using it as a symbol at all. It includes far more than any one summary of its effect can convey. One needs to aggregate the accounts critics have given to suggest its complexity. The river regenerates the good and drags down those who are evil (Edmund Wilson). Immersion can be drowning but also spiritual rebirth (Edmund Wilson, Edgar Johnson) and the reaffirmation of life (J. Hillis Miller). The river is an agent of retribution in the deaths of Radfoot, Hexam, Riderhood and Headstone, and of regeneration for Harmon, Wrayburn and Lizzie (Monroe Engel). It cuts through social distinctions (Monroe Engel) and is the great stream of life (Jack Lindsay) as well as the waters of suffering (Edgar Johnson). It is the otherness of nature, the movement of life, a more intense reality (J. Hillis Miller, Monroe Engel).

It would be easy to demonstrate the variation in these accounts, taken individually. But they do not contradict each other. Each fills in a necessary aspect of the whole. And each can be related to the text and found relevant to it. Drowned corpses, struggling bodies, float through the book. The symbolism is the action, not a convenient summary of it. 'Thus, like the tides on which it had been borne to the knowledge of men, the Harmon Murder—as it came to be popularly called—went up and down, and ebbed and flowed, now in the town, now in the country, now among palaces, now among hovels, now among lords and ladies and gentlefolks, now among labourers and hammerers and ballast-heavers, until at last, after a long interval of slack water, it got out to sea and drifted away.' (I, iii.)

Enough has been said to indicate that *Our Mutual Friend* will yield little to a reader who sees it only as the sum of its disparate characters. It is true that the novel has not the formal perfection of, say, *Emma* or *Victory*. Its weaknesses may give rise to misunderstanding: the eccentricities of Wegg, the wanderings of Betty Higden, the indeterminate dialect of Lizzie, the rather too liberal conclusion. Around such weaknesses all of the basic divergences of opinion have occurred. It is a pity that they have led to such diverse valuations of the novel in the past.

However, since the publication of Edmund Wilson's pioneer essay, there has been an increasing recognition of the novel's strength. The exceptions have been K. J. Fielding, who is an anologist for Dickens, and the *Scrutiny* critics, who are not. That the latter should give so severe an account of Dickens is a matter for some surprise. For to them we owe the critical concept of the Novel as Dramatic Poem. And, more than any other work in the language, except perhaps *Moby Dick, Wuthering Heights* and *Women in Love,* does **Our Mutual Friend** live up to and justify this concept.

Works Cited

Henry James, *Our Mutual Friend* (1865), reprinted in *The House of Fiction* (ed. Edel), 1957.

G. H. Lewes, *Dickens in Relation to Criticism, Fortnightly Review,* XVII, 1872.

George Gissing, *Charles Dickens: A Critical Study* (1898).

G. K. Chesterton, *Charles Dickens* (1906).

G. B. Shaw, *Introduction to Hard Times* (Waverley Edition, 1912).

George Santayana, *Charles Dickens* (1921), rep. *Soliloquies in England* (1922).

George Orwell, *Charles Dickens* (1939), rep. *Critical Essays* (1954).

Edmund Wilson, *Dickens: The Two Scrooges* (1939), rep. *The Wound and the Bow* (1941).

Humphry House, *The Dickens World* (1941).

F. R. Leavis, *The Great Tradition,* Chapter 1 (1948).

R. C. Churchill, *Dickens, Drama and Tradition, Scrutiny,* Vol. X no. 4, revised for the *Pelican Guide to Literature,* Vol. VI.

Jack Lindsay, *Charles Dickens* (1950).

Edgar Johnson, *Charles Dickens, His Tragedy and Triumph* (1953).

George H. Ford, *Dickens and his Readers* (1955).

John Butt and Kathleen Tillotson, *Dickens at Work* (1957).

K. J. Fielding, *Charles Dickens: A Critical Introduction* (1958).

J. Hillis Miller, *Charles Dickens, The World of his Novels* (1958).

Monroe Engel, *The Maturity of Dickens* (1959).

Richard A. Lanham (essay date 1963)

SOURCE: "*Our Mutual Friend*: The Birds of Prey," in *Victorian Newsletter,* Vol. 24, Fall, 1963, pp. 6-12.

[*In the following essay, Lanham claims that the theme of* Our Mutual Friend *is predation rather than money.*]

Our Mutual Friend's reputation began in the cellar with Henry James' famous review, and climbed steadily in critical esteem until Edmund Wilson's reappraisal established it at the top of the house. The two opinions make a startling contrast. James had begun his review, "**Our Mutual Friend** is, to our perception, the poorest of Mr. Dickens's works. And it is poor with the poverty not of momentary embarrassment, but of permanent exhaustion. It is wanting in inspiration."[1] Dickens was certainly a hard- (if self-) driven man while he was working on the novel, as anyone reviewing the period in Johnson or in the *Letters* will quickly recall. But the pressures of his readings and of his personal life can hardly have been fatal to his writing, to judge from Wilson's verdict on this, his last complete novel: "Dickens has here distilled the mood of his later years, dramatized the tragic discrepancies of his characters, delivered his final judgment on the whole Victorian exploit, in a fashion so impressive that we realize how little the distractions of this period had the power to direct him from the prime purpose of his life: the serious exercise of his art."[2] One could scarcely find a comparable gulf in esteem for one of the earlier mature novels, **Bleak House** for example. Why for **Our Mutual Friend**? James was put off, to be sure, by the unrelieved grimness of the novel, by a spectrum of characters who seem never to break out of the shades of grey. His principal objection, though, was more comprehensive; the adverse verdict of a realist against a form of the novel which diverged markedly and persistently from the canons of realism: "What a world were this world if the world of '**Our Mutual Friend**' were an honest reflection of it!" "Who," he asks later in the same review, "represents nature?" Wilson, more sympathetic perhaps with Dickens' social views, certainly less doctrinaire critically, was willing to credit **Our Mutual Friend** for its successes, rather than reproaching it for a failure in what it hardly even aims at—the recreation of everyday reality. These two positions can stand as the two polar positions taken on the novel in our own time. On the one hand, discussion has centered on the artistic quality of the novel: Had Dickens written himself out? Had he soured the well-springs of joy which transformed the equally forbidding urban landscape of his earlier years into the joyous "world," as it is now called, of the first novels? Is the large cast of minor characters like so many mutilated frogs, as George Henry Lewes charged about the Dickensian characters generally, each capable of but a single response to all stimuli? Is credibility destroyed by Boffin's temporary change of character? And so on. The second locus of debate has been the nature and accuracy of Dickens' social statement: Do we actually learn anything of practical value about the afflictions and evils of the full Victorian prosperity? Or is the novel simply an elaborate emotional, even sentimental, outburst which tells us little more than that something is dreadfully wrong? The later charge has persisted. Walter Bagehot made it of the earlier novels, in fact, even before *Our Mutual Friend* was written (in the essay on Dickens in Volume II of *Literary Studies*). It has been elaborated from Lewes down to Orwell. Dickens, Orwell writes, seems always to "reach out for an idealised version of the existing thing,"[3] rather than analyzing the structure of society in any mature way. The Marxist critics have maintained precisely the opposite. The novel is a brilliant damnation of the capitalist experiment. Reaching down to those levels of primitive myth and symbol available to all, Dickens has laid before us with his unforgettable vivid particulars the ugly surface and worse than ugly heart of an acquisitive society.

What Dickens has tried to do, then, and how well he has done it have been asked of *Our Mutual Friend* more often than the perhaps simpler question: *how* does Dickens embody his social criticism? None of the three can be considered separately, of course. Each problem constantly modifies our assessment of the other two. But to the extent that any one can be singled out, perhaps it should be method. The shortest path to Dickens' method seems to me to be through theme.

Money, it seems generally agreed, is the central theme of *Our Mutual Friend.* As Robert Morse wrote several years ago: "Each novel, then, is *about* something, and furthermore about something serious . . . *Our Mutual Friend* deals with Money. . . ."[4] Money is embodied in the Dust Heap which is the hub of plot as well as theme. The dead hand which reaches out from the grave to set the novel in motion is the force of money. The minor characters all seek money. It is Bella Wilfer's most compelling goal until she is dissolved in sentimentality at the end of the novel. It is the catalyst in Boffin's fake chemical change from Daddy Warbucks to Simon Legree. It is everywhere and in everything. But what, one is entitled to ask, does it represent? Is it intrinsically bad? Hardly. The upper-middle-class, *rentier* life which Orwell so perceptively isolated as Dickens' version of earthly paradise demands it in quantity. It is the chief force behind the sentimental happy ending in most of the later novels. No, money itself as a central theme would lead to a fundamental inconsistency.

Yet the central theme must be related to money integrally, for its omnipresence in the novel is undeniable. I would like to suggest that money was, for Dickens, symptom rather than disease: the disease, and the real theme, is predation. The thematically typical incident of the novel seems to me that of one man's preying on another. The opening scene of the novel, one few will forget, shows us Gaffer Hexam at his loathsome job of fishing, not for souls, but for bodies. In the Marcus Stone illustration—the first in the novel—we see the Gaffer bent forward in the stern of his dory, watching his taut grappling line like a vulture. He and his daughter are doing something, Dickens remarks bitterly, "that they often did, and were seeking what they often sought. Half savage as the man showed, with

no covering on his matted head, with his brown arms bare . . . still there was business-like [a phrase the reader should remember when he meets the respectable business world of Podsnap and Veneering] usage in his steady gaze. So with every lithe action of the girl, with every turn of her wrist, perhaps most of all with her look of dread or horror; they were things of usage."[5] Not simply the preying upon one's fellow man, but the *habit* of it repels us. This ghastly habit is not, however, the final horror for the reader. The Gaffer's attitude toward his work provides that. Lizzie's shudder of disgust at the faint red outline left in the bottom of the boat by a previous corpse, elicits this single-minded reply from a Gaffer intent on his work: "'What ails you?' . . . 'I see nothing afloat.'" (p. 2) When the corpse is finally hooked and gaffed (surely the pun, in a novel where word-play is so frequent, is intentional), Lizzie blanches at the prospect of sitting next to it. "'As if it wasn't your living! As if it wasn't meat and drink to you!'" (p. 3) And with this delightfully apt metaphor (which the Gaffer goes on to amplify) the pattern of predation with which Dickens chose to begin the novel comes clearly into focus. Lizzie is not alone in her predicament, the debt her flesh and blood owes to the grisly "business" we have just witnessed. For if the river is the liquid sewer of London, the dust-heap is the dry one, and the two together provide food and drink for the majority of the characters in the novel.

Gaffer's character is not complete as yet. He must encounter a fellow scavenger (Rogue Riderhood) envious of the Gaffer's "luck." The irony here needs emphasis if not elucidation; in this novel "luck" for someone always implies ill-luck for someone else. Every crust of bread consumed must be snatched from another's mouth. Here at the beginning, by describing the "lucky" catch of a sodden corpse, Dickens burns this inescapable pattern of predation into the reader's mind. The scene closes with the Gaffer's indignation at Rogue's calling him "pardner." Rogue, we learn, has been caught robbing a *live* man; he is not fit to associate with respectable folk of the Hexams' ilk, who prey off the dead. The blindness here, so ridiculous as almost but not quite to fall over into humor, is widespread in the world of *Our Mutual Friend.* Perfectly respectable "luck" is cherished on more than one level of society. As for Gaffer's explanation:

> Has a dead man any use for money? Is it possible for a dead man to have money? What world does a dead man belong to? T'other world. What world does money belong to? This world. How can money be a corpse's? Can a corpse own it, want it, spend it, claim it, miss it? Don't try to go confounding the rights and wrongs of things in that way.
>
> (pp. 4-5)

The ripples of irony spread out in ever-larger circles through the novel's plot, a plot about the will of a dead man toward another supposedly "dead" man. Gaffer is speaking of money. But his horrible moral blindness, not the money which occasions it, is what we are meant to attend.

"Gaffer," Dickens tells us, "was no neophyte and had no fancies." (p. 5) When we turn the page we plunge into a world which is nothing but the fancies of neophytes: "Mr. and Mrs. Veneering were bran-new people in a bran-new house in a bran-new quarter of London." (p. 6) And off Dickens goes for another *tour de force* paragraph. The comparison implied by the juxtaposition is clear. The world of Podsnappery and Veneering is scarcely more than a polite form of the predatory behavior we have just left behind. The Veneerings, if we may speak symbolically, have come up from somewhere in the vicinity of the river. As with Gaffer, it is not money, but attitude toward one's fellow-man—cold and mechanical—which is significant. It is the money, though, which attracts that sympathetic and impoverished professional dinner guest, Twemlow. In his own way Twemlow is a "bird of prey," too. Ludicrous and inoffensive aristocratic furniture that he is, still he lives off the bounty of others.

To follow this pattern of predation out in the minor characters is to establish its centrality beyond doubt. Consider the fetching pair of lovers Alfred Lammle and Sophronia Akersham. Each lives on the fringes of the middle-class world watching, like a pike in a pond, for a fat victim, until with fine poetic justice the two pikes fasten on one another. They wake up, willy-nilly, as a team, and immediately turn on the weakest fish in sight, Georgiana Podsnap. That they should choose to feed her to that young-in-years but old-in-guile whiskerless shark, Fledgby, seems, in the world which Dickens builds up, almost inevitable.

James to the contrary notwithstanding, Eugene Wrayburn and Mortimer Lightwood are two of Dickens' more engaging minor characters. They display a sophistication, are drawn with lightness of touch, in which he did not often indulge himself. Though they are present at the Veneerings' first surrealistic feast, we really meet them in the coach riding home:

> 'I hate,' said Eugene, putting his legs up on the opposite seat, 'I hate my profession.'
>
> 'Shall I incommode you if I put mine up too?' returned Mortimer. 'Thank you. I hate mine.'
>
> (pp. 19-20)

In a novel so intimately bound up with "getting ahead," "getting rich," these two are anomalies. The contrast with young Hexam, pushed by Lizzie a step or two up learning's impoverished ladder of respectability, could be deliberate. The contrast with Headstone is intended beyond doubt. The two lawyers contrast too, though in a different way, with Podsnap and Veneering: failure and success. The men of law are Gentlemen, of course, as the other two are not, but all four live in the same world of scrambling acquisitiveness:

> 'Then idiots talk,' said Eugene, leaning back, folding his arms, smoking with his eyes shut, and speaking slightly through his nose, 'of Energy. If there is a word in the dictionary under any letter from A to Z that I

abominate, it is energy. It is such a conventional superstition, such parrot gabble! What the deuce! Am I to rush out into the street, collar the first man of a wealthy appearance that I meet, shake him, and say, "Go to law upon the spot, you dog, and retain me, or I'll be the death of you?" Yet that would be energy.'

(p. 20)

Though Dickens may simply be drawing two callow young men too lazy even to be wild, such portraits hardly seem adequate motive for their creation. They are, in fact, walking repudiations of that vulgar aggressiveness which has propelled Podsnap and Veneering to wealth and honor in the city. They are against work. Look, for example, at Eugene's rejoinder, when Boffin holds up the bees as a model of pertinacious industry:

> 'And how do *you* like the law?'
>
> 'A———not particularly,' returned Eugene.
>
> 'Too dry for you, eh? Well, I suppose it wants some years of sticking to, before you master it. But there's nothing like work. Look at the bees.'
>
> 'I beg your pardon,' returned Eugene, with a reluctant smile, 'but will you excuse my mentioning that I always protest against being referred to the bees?'
>
> 'Do you!' said Mr. Boffin.
>
> 'I object on principle,' said Eugene, 'as a biped———'
>
> 'As a what?' asked Mr. Boffin.
>
> 'As a two-footed creature;—I object, on principle, as a two-footed creature, to being constantly referred to insects and four-footed creatures. I object to being required to model my proceedings according to the proceedings of the bee, or the dog, or the spider, or the camel. . . . I am not clear, Mr. Boffin, but that the hive may be satirical.'
>
> 'At all events, they work,' said Mr. Boffin.
>
> 'Ye-es,' returned Eugene, disparagingly, 'they work; but don't you think they overdo it? They work so much more than they need—they make so much more than they can eat—they are so incessantly boring and buzzing at their one idea till Death comes upon them—that don't you think they overdo it?'
>
> (pp. 93-4)

A curious passage from Dickens, obsessed by work as he was, and still odder in a novel supposedly devoted, as the Marxists would have us believe, to class-hatred. Whom are we to hate? If anyone, surely those who live as unproductive drones on the hive of dutiful proletarian workers. Yet we don't hate Eugene and Mortimer; they are civilization itself compared to that model of energetic work, Bradley Headstone, or even to Podsnap or Veneering. Why? Because they have contracted out of the business of the world. This is admirable, for the business of the world is simply preying on one's fellow man. They are against work. *Ergo,* they are not predators. The Protestant gospel of work, Dickens seems to be saying through them, is simply apotheosized greed and anyone who has the wit to see it and resign from the rat-race deserves one's admiration, whatever his social class.

If Dickens had been as blinded by the class-struggle as his later Marxist readers, he would hardly have given us Headstone and young Hexam. Of Headstone it is perhaps not fair to speak, since his true place is not in a social class at all but rather among the Dickens gallery of psychological grotesques drawn for their own sakes. But what of young Hexam? He is the stuff young Socialist workers are made of; young, ambitious, earnest. But he is also progressively more unkind, grasping, selfish and insensitive. He ultimately turns on Headstone, his benefactor and teacher, an apostasy which may offend the reader even more than his abuse of his sister, when she refuses to marry Headstone. No, though a proletarian, he is caught up in the same pernicious ethic of "success" which has forced the young solicitor and barrister into their hatred professions, and which allows Rogue Riderhood, and Gaffer himself, to look upon that latter scavenger as, given his calling and opportunities, a "success."

Even down to the least important characters, the pattern of predation is traced. Hard, cold, joyless Silas Wegg, for example. He attaches himself to Boffin like a leach. While still at the old stall, he "speculates," he "invests" a bow in Boffin. It pays off. He spends the rest of the novel in alternate scheming to rob Boffin and comic self-praise for his own virtue and industry in so doing. He replies to Mr. Venus' query about Rokesmith's honesty, after the secretary had stopped by the "Bower" one evening, with: "'Something against him'? repeats Wegg. 'Something? What would the relief be to my feelings—as a fellow-man—if I wasn't the slave of truth, and didn't feel myself compelled to answer, Everything!'" (p. 306) It is a comic repetition, at a lower level, of Podsnap's blind, self-righteous indignation at all which might bring a blush to the cheek of a young person. Still more nightmarish a predator, though he is finally redeemed by authorial fiat, is Wegg's co-conspirator, Mr. Venus. That enemy of the fertility his name implies (he is also, one remembers, an unsuccessful lover) keeps a shop which retails the bones of the dead. In the panorama of birds of prey which Dickens gives us, he makes an honest living by keeping the charnel house. Wegg initially finds his way to Venus' shop because Venus had bought the bone of the leg which Wegg had lost in a hospital amputation. Wegg now wishes to buy the bone back, to retrieve it for a keepsake from the tray of "human various" where it lives in Venus' shop:

'You're casting your eye round the shop, Mr. Wegg. Let me show you a light. My working bench. My young man's bench. A Wice. Tools. Bones, warious. Skulls, warious. Preserved Indian baby. African ditto. Bottled preparations, warious. Everything within reach of your hand, in good preservation. The mouldy ones a-top. What's in those hampers over them again, I don't quite remember. Say, human warious. Cats. Articulated English baby. Dogs. Ducks. Glass eyes, warious. Mum-

mied bird. Dried cuticle, warious. Oh dear me! That's the general panoramic view.'

(p. 81)

Comic and bizarre as the pair are, their illustration of the general "predation" theme is unmistakable. Venus' shop, like the dust-heap and the river, preys on and purveys a particular variety of human waste.

From the orphan-selling business to the sweat of Rogue Riderhood's brow, the world of *Our Mutual Friend* is full of predators, each trying to live at the expense of the others. Sometimes the earnestness of effort is comic wholly, as with Mortimer Lightwood's clerk, Young Blight. Blight one remembers is driven by his own zeal and his employer's sloath (he has the energy Mortimer and Eugene lack) to invent a whole file of imaginary clients to labor for. Sometimes the moral blindness is as pathetic as repugnant, as with Gaffer Hexam. But in every case, Dickens' verdict is clear: society is so arranged that its members, if they are to survive, must prey off one another. As Mortimer Lightwood says flippantly to Lady Tippins a few pages from the end of the novel:

'Say, how did you leave the savages?' asks Lady Tippins.

'They were becoming civilized when I left Juan Fernandez,' says Lightwood. 'At least they were eating one another, which looked like it.'

(p. 816)

The reader is free to make what he wishes of this kaleidoscopic pattern of predators. He can interpret it as a gasp of horror at the Victorian conception of a flourishing society. He can infer that Dickens felt a change of heart rather than a change of economic system was in order. Or, the novel can be construed as a savage attack on Industrial Capitalism, as a system which converts a presumably benign state of natural society into a jungle. The real core of the Capitalistic malaise, an economy run for private profit, is singled out clearly enough to support such an interpretation. Or, still more grandly, he can credit Dickens with that breadth of philosophic wisdom needful to see that society itself, at all times and places, has been a pike-pond; that mankind is tragically condemned to prey one on the other. Not capitalism, not Victorian vulgarity as a subspecies of it, but drives far older and more difficult to cope with, may be the final theme of the novel.

Dickens forces not one of these constructions on the reader. He presents us with a concrete series of human encounters which together form an abstract pattern of predation. We are free, as we are in life itself, to make of it what we choose. I myself would opt for the last conjecture. Dickens has not, it seems to me, stayed very long or convincingly within the boundaries of topical satire. Victorian England, like the money which most directly represents it, was not the cause of evil but only one of its manifestations. This is but to say that *Our Mutual Friend* is satire, and that satire always uses current abuses as a platform from which to inveigh against eternal evils. Satire owes to society, properly speaking, no explicit rebuilding duties at all. Implicit in its criticism, of course, must be the values society needs to recreate itself in a more pleasing image. But satire is under no constraint to say, "You must tear down slums! You must open homes for unwed mothers!" The satirist is not obliged to be a social worker; still more importantly the social worker's solutions are bound to damage the strength and blur the focus of the satire. Surely this is Dickens' mistake here, indeed in all the satirical novels; he is too explicit. Special abuses, special laws are touted up in passing; not used as building blocks for a larger pattern of indictments but introduced to impel the mass of his readers to specific action. Thus those embarrassing, maudlin passages we should all like to forget: the turgid, inflated rhetorical expostulations to the political powers about Jo, the half-wit crossing sweeper in **Bleak House**; the shouts of pathetic rage at the poor laws which accompany the unforgivable sentimental slaughter of Betty Higden. When Dickens is specific in his social criticism, he commits the satirist's fatal error. He bores us.

What satirist, after all, has ever made really valuable, forward-looking criticisms of the transformations which the Industrial Revolution has brought about? These transformations have been clearly the real subject of satire in England and America since Pope's time. The satirists from Pope onward have all been wrong, backward, blinded. From the beginning they have regarded industrialization as a wild horse which must be beaten but will never be tamed. They have celebrated none of its promises. They have been conservative because it is their business as satirists to conserve. However progressive the satirist may be when he takes up the pen on other occasions, when he sits down as satirist he becomes a partisan of the *status quo ante*. His job is to point out the values in the old scheme of things which are in danger of being lost. However good life may become, however pregnant with hope for all, he is forced to be a prophet of doom. If we are not willing to grant this constraint of the form, satire has been largely a blind alley for the last two and a half centuries. Fielding is, I suppose, the consummate prose satirist of the 18th century, as well as the one most comparable to Dickens (*Jonathan Wild* is clearly an ancestor of **Our Mutual Friend**). Fielding's diagnosis of society's ills was sound, but his remedies were worthless. Wordsworth could point out precisely how the world was too much with us, but his proposals for disengaging us and it were infantile. So with Dickens. Orwell is perfectly right: Dickens wanted not to abolish bosses, but to make them kind. Not to alter society but to make it get along. This advice is not much help to a social planner. The charge that Dickens the social critic is inept, not a thinker but a feeler, has been persuasively stated, from Bagehot to Lewes and Orwell. T. S. Eliot will stand as the social critic of our 20th-century poets, yet he is subject to the same strictures. His social remedies begin as repulsive and finish as irrelevant. But this does not really detract from the value of his diagnosis of what is wrong with our society. This diagnosis will remain perti-

nent, just as Dickens' will, because it is not tied to the particular circumstances which gave it birth.

The fundamental irrelevance of the Orwellian criticism of Dickens' satiric novels can be illustrated from one of Orwell's own satires, *Coming Up for Air.* This is a longish, rather entertaining narrative by a middling-successful English insurance salesman speaking in 1938. He is nostalgic over the relaxed life-style which prevailed before the War, and which the War partially destroyed and the coming Second War will finish off. What is wrong? What has changed? One doesn't know. The pace of life, the struggle for a phantom "success," the drummed-up competition of capitalism, the obsession with money, all are suggested. They are the same problems which concerned Dickens in **Our Mutual Friend,** in fact. Orwell's protagonist Bowler by name, is really a feeler not a thinker. He knows that something is very wrong, but cannot quite make out what. He is like Gaffer Hexam when he becomes a suspect character among the "honest" waterfront birds of pray: "'Have we got a pest in the house? Is there summ'at deadly sticking to my clothes? What's let loose upon us? Who loosed it?'" (p. 76) Isn't this the satirist's perennial, unavoidable question?

We cannot expect Dickens to prescribe the needed changes. This is foolish. No one knows even now what they should be. The most we can legitimately expect is that Dickens will answer Gaffer's question, tell us what has been loosed upon us. The central thesis of the novel does precisely this. What has been loosed is man's natural rapacity, and not only loosed but institutionalized and applauded. To support this central theme, subsidiary ones have been introduced. Here, as elsewhere, critics of Dickens have been tempted to take the symptom for the disease. Robert Morse, for example, points to a sub-theme of "Doubleness."[6] But this is only an indication of the real problem: loss of identity. The plot turns on mistaken identity, of course. But the theme goes deeper. The Veneering-Podsnap world, all the new arrivals in **Our Mutual Friend,** really are plagued with the doubt of, or with a plain absence of, real identity. The instances of this are nearly endless in the novel: Podsnap and Veneering have trouble in identifying one another in the first of the grisly banquet scenes; the divine Tippins double character—the shrivelled hag and the adolescent mask; the self-doubts that beset Harmon-Hanford-Rokesmith during the course of his deception; the change of identity that Boffin (and, in a different direction, Bella Wilfer) go through. The fear of losing identity, traced often now to a change in social class, is a commonplace in contemporary fiction. Its presence in **Our Mutual Friend** indicates powers of analysis only grudgingly accorded its author.

What of the theme of money? This is scarcely new. But look at the aspects of it Dickens chooses to emphasize: not the traditional hollow rewards of greed, but rather the mechanization of personality and of personal relations. The anonymity of money, its depersonalizing pressures, have been widely discussed in our own time by social scientists and by occasional literary critics, Ian Watt for example. As this novel proves, those pressures Dickens saw clearly. In any society organized primarily for private profit, money is bound to be part of most daily encounters. In Dickens' world, it becomes the primary agent of contact between man and man. People have but two roles to play: buyer and seller. All other human attributes are squeezed out. Human personality becomes a plain matter of poor or rich. The spontaneity which for Dickens constituted essential humanity simply dries up. People tend to become indistinguishable from things, and *vice versa*. The novel is full of imagery making precisely this point. The grisly humor of Twemlow as a table, in the early pages of the novel, is a good illustration:

> There was an innocent piece of dinner-furniture that went upon easy castors and was kept over a livery stable-yard in Duke Street, Saint James's, when not in use, to whom the Veneerings were a source of blind confusion. The name of this article was Twemlow . . . Mr. and Mrs. Veneering . . . arranging a dinner, habitually started with Twemlow, and then put leaves in him, or added guests to him. Sometimes, the table consisted of Twemlow and half-a-dozen leaves; sometimes, of Twemlow and a dozen leaves; sometimes Twemlow was pulled out to his utmost extent of twenty leaves.
>
> (p. 6)

Bradley Headstone has learned his job purely by rote:

> He had acquired mechanically a great store of teacher's knowledge. He could do mental arithmetic mechanically, sing at sight mechanically, blow various wind instruments mechanically, even play the great church organ mechanically. From his early childhood up, his mind had been a place of mechanical stowage. The arrangement of his wholesale warehouse, so that it might be always ready to meet the demands of retail dealers. . . .
>
> (p. 217)

In metaphor as in character, human personality and potentiality is sacrificed to the demands of commerce. From here, of course, it is but a step to Dickens' persistent theme that society warps and perverts innate—and benign—human capacity. And but a step further to the general mechanization of the spirit which has been a literary theme since the Industrial Revolution began.

The themes could be discussed at great length but the discussion would add little to the point to be proved. Dickens' satire was not brilliantly original, but it aimed at the same targets English satire had shot at for two centuries and more. It hit them as well as most. But it hit them as it were with a new weapon. Dickens' satiric method differed markedly from that of his predecessors. To gain what Kenneth Burke has called a "perspective by incongruity," look for a moment at a novel mentioned earlier in this essay, Fielding's *Jonathan Wild*. The similarities between the two are unexpected, especially if one remembers G. H. Lewes' remark that, "Compared with Fielding or Thackeray . . . [Dickens] was merely an animal intelligence."[7] Both nov-

els are studies in predatory behavior. The psychology of the pike pond dominates both. In both, all human relations, with the exception of those between the good but put-upon characters who support the sentimental plot, are reduced to terms of gain or loss. The sentimental characters, with nothing to offer more formidable than love and sincerity, are constantly defeated—until the author steps in to set all straight in the end. Both novels use money as a prominent symbol and impetus to plot-development. Especially strong in the two is the awareness that money, because it is anonymous and tells no tales, will be a fundamental agent in the dissolution of the traditional bonds holding society together. Implicit in both novels is the assumption that a civilization knowing no effective principles of regulation higher than dog-eat-dog has really ceased to be a civilization at all. For all the noticeable difference between the two in this respect, the great age of Capitalist economic theory might never have taken place.

Both novels are sentimental, but the sentiment is much less important in Fielding's. The last-page reward is so patent that it hardly affects the preceding several hundred pages' grim and sustained irony. The path of the heart is plainly a chancy solution—though it may be the only one—and Fielding knows it. Only a thoroughgoing overhaul, a radical revision of society will do any lasting good. And of course Fielding had such a revision in mind; a return to the old ideal agrarian, church-centered, stratified society which had served Christendom for a thousand years. For Fielding, the traditional cosmology still lived and he could present it in his satire as a norm against which to measure the conduct of his "great men." Such a background, still implicitly accepted by most of his readers, enabled him to create a unified, consistent and sustained ironic framework which Dickens could not support. It is the lack of this implicit background, finally, which coarsens so much of Dickens' irony, makes it seem sometimes blunt and abusive. Dickens' characters, like Lightwood and Wrayburn when they do have the sensitivity and intelligence to resign from the rat-race society tries to force upon them, have no place to go. Their traditional roles, whatever they might have been, have evaporated. So Dickens substituted the passive tranquility of the Victorian gentleman of independent means:

> His heroes, once they had come into money, and "settled down," would not only do no work; they would not even ride, hunt, shoot, fight duels, elope with actresses or lose money at the races. They would simply live at home, in feather-bed respectability, and preferably next door to a blood-relation living exactly the same life.[8]

It is even more inadequate than that quiet life in the country which was the 18th-century's most common last-page reward. Like the older pastoral dream from which it derives, it is frankly impossible. It is clear from *Jonathan Wild* that Fielding knew this, but not clear from **Our Mutual Friend** that Dickens did. Yet any less passive solution would put a character right back in the ambitious struggle Dickens wished him to escape. In the Dickens world, certainly in the world of *Our Mutual Friend,* there is no room for significant, for effective action. There is the good Reverend Frank Milvey to be sure, but like even the sympathetic do-gooders in Dickens' novels, he is ineffective. Dickens was, in fact, too far on the road to our modern world to turn back, though all his instincts told him he should. His satiric posture was weakened by having no informing world vision behind it. As has been said often enough before, there is no God in any meaningful sense in Dickens' novels—sentimental kindness takes His place, but cannot fill it. Kindness brings no specific social order with it.

The most striking difference between Fielding's view of an acquisitive society and Dickens' is in scope and vividness. Though Dickens' intellectual framework is narrower and thinner, his panorama of character is vast by the side of Fielding's, and infinitely more vivid. Fielding concentrates on a single group of characters, Dickens on a large array: "There is no central protagonist in *Our Mutual Friend.* Far more even than *Bleak House,* it is multi-plotted novel."[9] This technique, a spectrum of characters, is one answer to the charge brought by James and others, that the minor characters of *Our Mutual Friend* are flat and incredible. They were meant to be flat, to present but a single facet of the grim predatory world of the novel. Jenny Wren, a cripple trapped by a drunken father who depends upon her like a child, is but one example of the pressure of society on the defenseless in it. Of herself she is not of great importance. As one variation of a pattern repeated again and again, she is highly indicative. Realistically construed, of course, she is incredible. But the novel is not a realistic novel. If she had been credible she would have taken up too large a share of the reader's attention.

Our Mutual Friend has far more in common with allegory than with realism. Dickens hardly even pretends to keep up the realistic mask. The dialogue is frankly incredible most of the time. Riah, for instance, replies to Eugene Wrayburn's rude importunities that he leave the deserted Lizzie Hexam to his care, ". . . Christian gentleman . . . I will hear only one voice to-night desiring me to leave this damsel. . . ." (405-6) Allegorically, "damsel" is perfect. Or pick at random any line of Mrs. Wilfer's: it is impossible to believe anyone ever said it. But as the representation not of a person but of an attitude toward wealth and position, her speech is unforgettable. Then too, the novel is far and away the most frankly grotesque of the later novels. The Veneerings' banquets are surrealistically drawn and Dickens never pretends they are not. Not realism, but a pattern of abstractions, is the satiric technique of *Our Mutual Friend.* Making the obvious qualifications, one could call it satiric allegory. Allegory is not far to seek in any of the mature novels, but in this one it is closest to the surface. Boffin lives in a Bower; "sailors to be got the better of" are necessary to Pleasant Riderhood's "Eden"; Jenny calls Riah "Fairy Godmother"; Fledgby, when he is to be paid off in lashes, is got up in Turkish trousers like a pagan devil. We should be careful not to press these instances of superficial allegory too far. Dickens is not writ-

ing a thoroughgoing allegory obviously. Yet, in fact, the novel is closer to the *Fairie Queene* than to a novel by Henry James, in the methods it employs to make us believe in it. Character consistency, for example. One of the standard criticisms of *Our Mutual Friend* is the inconsistency of some of its characters. Yet in a novel which is controlled by theme and not by character consistency of character is largely irrelevant. As with the *Faerie Queene,* it is not the consistency of the whole structure but the vivid scene, the dramatic confrontation, which does the work of the novel. The spiritual cousin of Headstone's grief-scene after being rejected by Lizzie is the Cave of Despair. As with allegory in general, it is not the intellectual subtlety of Dickens' vision which strikes us so much as the unforgettable vividness of its crucially symbolic scenes. A pattern of scenes, each an amplification of the general theme of predation, of joy only at the expense of grief, is Dickens' technique of persuasion. The demands of allegorical intensity completely dominate probability. Dickens' characters were doubtless as real in his own mind as Spenser's were in his—real as only the figments of the pure imagination can be—but they can hardly have seemed real, fully three-dimensional, to his readers then or now. No, the effect is made another way. The birds of prey rise clear of everyday reality, of time and place, and become a vision of man everywhere and at all times.

They do not, unfortunately, rise altogether clear of an overlong, offensively sentimental ending. Dickens' weaknesses in this direction have been so thoroughly illuminated that no more light is needed here. But if the charges of excessive gloominess, of unnaturalism, of failing creative powers, cannot be made to stick, that of sentimental falsification of experience can. The tender-hearted way out offends here as nowhere else in the canon. For the symbolism of the first two-thirds of the novel is too strong to allow the reader, caught up and appalled as he must be by the picture Dickens so powerfully draws, to feel anything but offended when this power is systematically sapped by wishful thinking and an eye to the marketplace.

Notes

1. In a review of the novel in *The Nation* of 1865, reprinted in *The Future of the Novel,* ed. Leon Edel (Vintage Books, 1956), pp. 75-80, and elsewhere.

2. "Dickens: The Two Scrooges," in *The Wound and the Bow* (Cambridge, Mass., 1941), p. 75.

3. "Charles Dickens," *Inside the Whale and other essays* (London, 1940), p. 53.

4. *Our Mutual Friend,* reprinted in *The Dickens Critics* ed. George H. Ford and Lauriat Lane, Jr. (Ithaca, N. Y., 1961), pp. 204-05.

5. *Our Mutual Friend* ("The New Oxford Illustrated Dickens"), ed. E. Salter Davies (Oxford University Press, 1952), pp. 1-2. All subsequent citations in the text are to this edition.

6. Morse, pp. 206ff.

7. "Dickens in Relation to Criticism," *Fortnightly Review,* vol. 17 (Feb. 1872), 151. (Reprinted in Ford and Lane.)

8. "Charles Dickens," p. 64.

9. J. Hillis Miller, *Charles Dickens, the World of His Novels* (Cambridge, Mass., 1958), p. 281.

Harland S. Nelson (essay date 1965)

SOURCE: "Dickens's *Our Mutual Friend* and Henry Mayhew's *London Labour and the London Poor,*" in *Nineteenth-Century Fiction,* Vol. 20, No. 3, December, 1965, pp. 207-22.

[*In the following essay, Nelson studies possible sources for the characters Betty Higden and Gaffer Hexam in* Our Mutual Friend *from among the poor Londoners interviewed by Henry Mayhew for his nonfiction work.*]

Betty Higden (the character in **Our Mutual Friend** who would rather die than go to the poorhouse, and does) offended some of Dickens's readers, the same ones, no doubt, who felt about Jacob's Island in **Oliver Twist,** and the Yorkshire schools in **Nicholas Nickleby,** and Chancery and foreign missions in **Bleak House,** and the Circumlocution Office in **Little Dorrit,** that things were nowhere near as bad as all that, if indeed anything was really wrong at all. Dickens replied to these defenders of the Establishment as he always had: what he had embodied in fiction was verifiable in fact. To the "Circumlocutional champions disposed to be warm with me on the subject of my view of the Poor Law," he asserted in his "Postscript" to **Our Mutual Friend** that "the records in our newspapers, the late exposure by THE LANCET, and the common sense and senses of common people" bore him out: there really were "deserving Poor who prefer death by slow starvation and bitter weather, to the mercies of some Relieving Officers and some Union Houses. . . ."[1] Betty Higden, in other words, was no piece of whimsy.

Where, specifically, would Dickens have got the idea for such a character? Finding a probable source for something in Dickens is of interest to the finder purely for its own sake; but because it also offers the chance to see Dickens at work, how he shaped his raw materials to his specific fictive aims, it becomes a matter of more general scholarly concern as well. Not, of course, that he absolutely had to have a model for Betty Higden; but even in his most fertile days, Dickens based many characters on people he knew or had read about, and he was not so inventive in his latter days as he once had been. Forster says that while writing **Our Mutual Friend** he drew on the notebook of potentially useful details (names, motifs, scraps of dialogue) that he had begun keeping in January, 1855.[2] There are traces of some characters in **Our Mutual Friend** among these memoranda (including Gaffer Hexam, of whom more later), but Betty Higden is not one of them.

Still, if Dickens turned to his own notebook it is plausible that he looked to other sources as well; and it seems to me more than a chance resemblance that in her ruling passion, her loathing for the poorhouse, Betty Higden is very like an old woman Henry Mayhew wrote of in *London Labour and the London Poor.*

Literary relationships, as everyone knows, are rarely matters of simple one-to-one equivalences, and I do not mean to deny that Dickens got any ideas from the sources he explicitly named in his "Postscript," or from his own observations. His own periodical articles, however, record the hardships of people trying to get into workhouses but not able to, rather than cases of people who prefer dying to going there; and since he certainly did not find Betty in "the late exposure by THE LANCET," I feel reasonably certain that his mention of the newspapers in the same breath as his mention of the British medical journal is also an appeal to corroborative evidence and not identification of a source.[3] But Betty's obsession is Dickensian enough so that to find it elsewhere than in Dickens suggests the parallel is more than coincidence. Further, the relationship with *London Labour and the London Poor* becomes still more plausible on the discovery of two other passages in Mayhew. One contains touches suggesting Gaffer Hexam, the dredgerman (river scavenger) in **Our Mutual Friend,** touches that include distinct verbal reminiscences and parallel details. The other is an extensive section on London dustmen and the garbage they collected, matter that (considering the use made of dust and the dust trade in **Our Mutual Friend**) certainly would have caught Dickens's eye, if indeed it was not what drew his attention to the book in the first place. But there is yet another circumstance that argues for the relationship I have suggested between *London Labour and the London Poor* and **Our Mutual Friend.** In a work running to nearly six hundred closely printed pages, the passage about the dredgermen occurs only four pages after the one dealing with the old woman, and only nine pages before the section on dust begins; so that not only a methodical reader, but a browser, or a skimmer, or a novelist looking for material, would be likely to run across all of them. It was while browsing, in fact, that I discovered these passages myself.

But why might Dickens have chosen to look into Mayhew? Assuming that he knew of the book at all, its title alone would have suggested its intrinsic interest for him. Dickens's own acquaintance with lower class life in London, gained in after-dark patrols with the detective police and in those long restless walks that the heat of composition (and later the misery of his marriage) drove him to, was profound and long-enduring; the authenticity of his observation is attested to by the remarkable parallels between the slum scenes and characters in **Oliver Twist** and the findings of Mayhew a dozen years later. Beyond that fundamental affinity, the possible usefulness of *London Labour and the London Poor* in developing one theme of his work in progress, as I have said, could have occurred to Dickens: Johnson's chapter on **Our Mutual Friend** emphasizes how integral dust is to the design of the novel.

Whatever the reason, if Dickens, his imagination at work on his themes in *Our Mutual Friend,* turned over these pages one day, it seems entirely believable to me that his creative instinct would have led him to discern the usefulness to him of Mayhew's old woman and his dredgermen. Given Dickens's lifelong rage at the Poor Law, the old woman (as will be clear from the passage) would have caught his attention willy-nilly; and by reason of another of Dickens's obsessive concerns, so would Mayhew's passage about dredgermen.[4]

All this presumes that Dickens knew Mayhew's lively, immensely detailed study of the ways that London street folk made their livings in the mid-nineteenth century. It is possible that he did not; but it is next to inconceivable.[5] For one thing, he knew Mayhew. Mayhew was a member of the *Punch* circle during its early years—one of the magazine's founders, in fact—and Dickens was intimate enough with them to join them occasionally at "The Table," the regular dinner-business meeting at which the *Punch* staff made a good many of their editorial decisions.[6] More definite evidence of acquaintanceship is provided by the common interest of the Dickens and *Punch* circles in dramatics. Dickens cast some of his acquaintances from *Punch* in the amateur productions that he directed, managed, and acted in; and Henry Mayhew played in the first of these, as old Knowell in Jonson's *Every Man in His Humour,* on September 20, 1845.[7]

Furthermore, Mayhew's interviews with London street folk were well enough known for Dickens to have been aware of them whether he knew Mayhew or not. Mayhew first told well-off readers of the shifts by which the poor of London stayed alive from one day to the next in the *Morning Chronicle* in 1849-1850.[8] The work appeared in a bewildering variety of amended, augmented, edited, and reorganized editions during the next dozen years and more. The publisher's list appended to the third volume of my set calls it a "celebrated work"; and it must indeed have been, for according to the *Dictionary of National Biography* the final version of the work was reprinted in 1864 and again in 1865. Dickens was writing *Our Mutual Friend* in 1864 and 1865; it would be strange if he did not know something at least about material so relevant to his interests, especially if he was having trouble finding enough matter to fill out his story.[9]

That Dickens could have used Mayhew as a source, then, seems to me on external evidence to be hardly disputable. I find the internal evidence just as striking: the passages in *London Labour and the London Poor* that would be likely to catch Dickens's eye, and that suggest characters or bear on matters in *Our Mutual Friend*; the proximity of these passages in Mayhew's book; and the accountability, in the light of Dickens's thematic purposes, of the differences between Dickens's characters and their presumptive originals. There is also, in the case of Gaffer Hexam, some particular evidence (based on Dickens's periodical writings) that indicates Dickens's levy on Mayhew. It is time now to examine the relevant passages of *Our Mutual Friend*

and *London Labour and the London Poor,* and I will turn first to Betty Higden.

The trait that I am concerned with is her ruling passion, her fierce horror of the poorhouse:

> "Kill me sooner than take me there. Throw this pretty child under cart-horses' feet and a loaded waggon, sooner than take him there. Come to us and find us all a-dying, and set a light to us all where we lie, and let us all blaze away with the house into a heap of cinders, sooner than move a corpse of us there! . . .
>
> "Johnny, my pretty," continued old Betty, caressing the child, and rather mourning over it than speaking to it, "your old Granny Betty is nigher fourscore year than threescore and ten. She never begged nor had a penny of the Union money in all her life. She paid scot and she paid lot when she had money to pay; she worked when she could, and she starved when she must. You pray that your Granny may have strength enough left her at the last (she's strong for an old one, Johnny), to get up from her bed and run and hide herself, and swown to death in a hole, sooner than fall into the hands of those Cruel Jacks we read of, that dodge and drive, and worry and weary, and scorn and shame, the decent poor"
>
> (Bk. I, ch. xvi).

This is the note that sounds every time she appears. Her aversion to the charity of the parish becomes her motive for action: it is in order to keep off illness, and to keep from being forced into the poorhouse by the decrepitude of age, that she sets off into the country to make her living as an itinerant pedlar.

The person in *London Labour and the London Poor* who like Betty Higden prefers death out-of-doors to the poorhouse is a sixty-year-old widow, a pure-finder, whom Mayhew found sick and starving in her dismal slum lodgings.

> There's such a dizziness in my head now, I feel as if it didn't belong to me. No, I have earned no money to-day. I have had a piece of dried bread that I steeped in water to eat. I haven't eat anything else to-day; but, pray, sir, don't tell anybody of it. I could never bear the thought of going into the "great house" [workhouse]; I'm so used to the air, that I'd sooner die in the street, as many I know have done. I've known several of our people, who have sat down in the street with their basket alongside them, and died. I knew one not long ago, who took ill just as she was stooping down to gather up the Pure, and fell on her face; she was taken to the London Hospital, and died at three o'clock in the morning. I'd sooner die like them than be deprived of my liberty, and be prevented from going about where I liked. No, I'll never go into the workhouse. . . .[10]

Now it is true that this distaste for public charity is almost the sole point of resemblance between the two. From other parts of her statement we learn that Mayhew's informant has been married and widowed twice; that all her children are dead and she is alone in the world; that pure-finding used to be very much better than it is now; and that most people who gather pure have come to it as a last resort. But except that Betty Higden too is old and has outlived her children, none of these other circumstances match her case. Her health, when we meet her, is good. Her home, though poor, is immaculate. And she is not a pure-finder but a laundress and minder of children for working parents of her own class.

Still these differences are explicable. Mayhew's old pure-finder exists for us in a single scene from what must surely have been the last act of her life; Betty Higden's story extends through some expanse of time, during which she passes from health to infirmity and finally to death, and from precarious to more precarious independence. The other differences are the same sort that usually occur when Dickens works observed life into his art: the life is shaped to support his fictional purpose. One need only recall (besides the instances I mentioned at the very outset) that both Mr. Micawber and William Dorrit are versions of Dickens's father.[11] Dickens is able to discern in the actual world's body the particular tissue he needs and transplant it to his fictional world. Seen in this light, Betty Higden's occupation is not evidence against my contention; for Betty Higden some less repellent activity than pure-finding (something having to do with "purity" in a more conventional sense, perhaps, like laundering?) would be preferable, Podsnappery among Dickens's readers being what it was, and Dickens's purpose being what it was. Dickens, attacking the Poor Law once more, would be careful not to distract readers from his point—that the law made public charity insupportable to the people who most deserved it—by giving Betty such a sensational occupation; something plausible, but commonplace, would be called for here. Nor would he risk making her an object of disgust: the Deserving Poor, to his readers, would have to be not only honest and self-reliant but clean. And finally there is a difference in motivation which is also understandable in the light of Dickens's purpose. What appears to be the pure-finder's mere vagabond hatred of confinement ("I'd sooner die [in the street] than . . . be prevented from going about where I liked") is something more than that in Betty Higden: anger, and outrage, at the violation of personal dignity involved in parish relief under the Poor Law ("[I would rather] swown to death in a hole, sooner than fall into the hands of those Cruel Jacks we read of, that dodge and drive, and worry and weary, and scorn and shame, the decent poor").[12]

Essentially, then, to argue that Mayhew's old pure-finder exists in some way in Dickens's indomitable old laundress is to say that Dickens cut away everything about her irrelevant or damaging to the theme that this strand of his narrative deals with; he remodelled what he could use of the original to make it bear more weightily on his point; and he fitted a static scene into a narrative line. Considering Dickens's characteristic use of his materials, such a metamorphosis is certainly credible. What about the case of Gaffer Hexam?

The use of *London Labour and the London Poor* in Gaffer's case (if it is use) is slightly different; the relationship here is as exposition to narrative. When Gaffer finds the body supposed to be John Harmon's in the river, he searches its pockets and appropriates the money he finds before towing it ashore (I, i). Later, when Mortimer Lightwood and Eugene Wrayburn are called on to identify the body if they can, they see from the handbill printed by the police that only papers were found on the body. "Only papers," echoes Gaffer.

> "No money," pursued Mortimer; "but threepence in one of the skirt-pockets."
>
> "Three. Penny. Pieces," said Gaffer Hexam, in as many sentences.
>
> "The trousers pockets empty, and turned inside out."
>
> Gaffer Hexam nodded. "But that's common. Whether it's the wash of the tide or no, I can't say. Now, here," moving the light to another similar placard, "*his* pockets was found empty, and turned inside out. And here," moving the light to another, "*her* pocket was found empty, and turned inside out. And so was this one's. And so was that one's . . ."
>
> (I, iii).

The particular habit of dredgermen that Dickens embodies in narrative Mayhew reports in his own person:

> The dredgers . . . are the men who find almost all the bodies of persons drowned. If there be a reward offered for the recovery of a body, numbers of the dredgers will at once endeavour to obtain it, while if there be no reward, there is at least the inquest money to be had—beside other chances. What these chances are may be inferred from the well-known fact, that no body recovered by a dredgerman ever happens to have any money about it, when brought to shore. There may, indeed be a watch in the fob or waistcoat pocket, for that article would be likely to be traced. There may, too, be a purse or pocket-book forthcoming, but somehow it is invariably empty
>
> (*LLLP*, II, 167).

Further, Mayhew goes on to say, "The dredgers cannot by any reasoning or argument be made to comprehend that there is anything like dishonesty in emptying the pockets of a dead man. They consider them as their just perquisites." And in chapter i of his novel, Dickens makes Gaffer say much the same; having rifled the supposed John Harmon's pockets, Gaffer defends his action by saying, "Has a dead man any use for money? Is it possible for a dead man to have money? What world does a dead man belong to? T'other world. What world does money belong to? This world. How can money be a corpse's? Can a corpse own it, want it, spend it, claim it, miss it?"

Now it is true that Dickens could have gotten this without recourse to Mayhew; according to Mayhew, the pennilessness of drowned men was a "well-known fact." Perhaps so; but it just may have escaped Dickens's personal observation. He had a preoccupation with the river, and drowning, that came near being an obsession; not to speak of its role in his fiction, it appears in a number of his periodical articles.[13] In one of these, **"Down with the Tide"** (*Household Words,* February 5, 1853; included in *Reprinted Pieces* in collected editions), the subject is handled more lightly than usual, even whimsically. But that article interests me just here for another reason, too. It is one of a series Dickens did on the police, whose work fascinated him and whose expertise drew his admiration. In this one Dickens reports on a river patrol he took with the Thames Police. We get an interview with the toll collector at Waterloo Bridge, full of macabre drollness (the man's cheerful precision about the habits of prospective suicides), and an account of the various sorts of scavengers that the police keep an eye on; and among these, Dickens gives some space to dredgermen. But there is not a word about their work of recovering bodies, or about their peculiar perquisites—omissions doubly odd if Dickens knew about these matters, considering his persistent interest in drownings, and the prominence of suicide by drowning in this particular piece.

But having written about dredgermen himself Dickens would probably notice them the more readily later in the writings of others; and their macabre salvage activity, as reported by Mayhew, would certainly recommend them to his attention. Not that he owes the whole conception to Mayhew. Three items in his book of memoranda went into the Hexam strand of the narrative. Forster mentions two of them, without making clear that he is echoing Dickens's notes: the father and son I referred to earlier (note 11 above), and "the many handbills [Dickens] saw posted up, with dreary descriptions of persons drowned in the river," during his walks along the waterfront (*Life,* IX, v). Dickens's own memoranda are "The uneducated father / or uncle? / in fustian, and the educated boy in spectacles. Whom Leech and I saw at Chatham" (Holograph Memoranda Book, p. 6) and "Found Drowned. The descriptive bill upon the wall, by the waterside" (p. 8). The third item, the one which does not appear in Forster, follows the "Found Drowned" one a few entries down the same page: "A 'long shore' man—woman—child—or family. [something cancelled] qs. [? question] Connect the Found Drowned Bill with this?"

Specific details of Hexam's character and circumstances, however, do *not* appear in these memoranda or in any of the others; and it is certainly remarkable that a number of such details occur together in the short space of Mayhew's passage on dredgermen (II, 165-168). In fact, everything that Mayhew reports about them, except the history of their occupation and his calculations of the total capital invested in the dredging trade, and except for elisions accountable in view of Dickens's purposes, appears in *Our Mutual Friend* in connection with Gaffer Hexam. Mayhew reports that the dredgermen are often at work at two or three in the morning "if the tide answers" (*LLLP,* II, 166); Gaffer's working hours too are governed by the tide (*OMF,* I, xiii). Mayhew says dredgermen are very skilled at estimating where the tides are likely to lodge things that fall into the water, and the dredgerman whose remarks are quoted boasts that he knows "where the holes and furrows is at the bottom of the river, and where things is to be found" (*LLLP,* II, 166-167). Gaffer's eyes sweep the river incessantly; he is looking for places where the suck of the tide is impeded, allowing drifting objects to collect and settle (*OMF,* I, i). Mayhew says further that, unlike others of their class, the dredgermen are of sober and industrious habits, maintaining homes adequately if barely furnished and limiting their relaxations to a pipe and "a pint or two of beer" at a pub (*LLLP,* II, 166). Gaffer has been a patron in good standing at Miss Abby Potterson's Six Jolly Fellowship-Porters, where temperance principles are rigidly enforced (*OMF,* I, vi); and his home, apart from some details that enforce the ominous aura with which Dickens surrounds him, answers to Mayhew's estimate of such homes (*OMF,* I, iii). Almost all the dredgermen are illiterate, Mayhew says (II, 166); and Gaffer, showing the handbills of drowned persons to Mortimer and Eugene, remarks "I can't read, nor I don't want to it, for I know 'em by their places on the wall" (I, iii). The reason for the dredgermen's lack of education, according to Mayhew, is that the boys are taken by their fathers to help with the work as soon as they are able to do anything, and they quickly lose all inclination for education. In *Our Mutual Friend* Charley Hexam goes to school over the opposition of his father, and only at the insistence and with the active management of his sister Lizzie, who urges upon him the absolute necessity of an education if he is to break free from the sinister occupation of his father (I, iii, vi).

There are also some verbal reminiscences and close parallels of detail that strengthen the presumption of a relation between Gaffer Hexam and Meyhew's passage on dredgermen. They appear in the opening chapter of *Our Mutual Friend,* where Dickens introduces Gaffer at work, and in Mayhew's description of a typical dredgerman and his boat (*LLLP,* II, 167). The boat has "always the appearance of labour about [it], like a ship returning after a long voyage, daubed and filthy, and looking sadly in need of a thorough cleansing." Gaffer's boat is "allied to the bottom of the river rather than the surface, by reason of the slime and ooze with which it [is] covered, and its sodden state. . . ." Gaffer himself is dirty and unkempt, with "such dress as he wore seeming to be made out of the mud that begrimed his boat," and with "brown arms bare to between the elbow and the shoulder. . . ." Mayhew's dredgerman has a face "soiled and blackened with perspiration," and he wears "a soiled check shirt, with the sleeves turned up above the elbows, and exhibiting a pair of sunburnt brawny arms. . . ."

Something remains to be said about Gaffer Hexam, but before I go into that I wish to review the whole case thus far. The evidence that Mayhew's *London Labour and the London Poor* contributed significantly to Dickens's development of these two characters in *Our Mutual Friend* seems to me very strong. Besides such specific parallels as those I have just described, there are three distinct kinds of evidence, all of it tending to the same conclusion; and such convergence increases probability geometrically, not arithmetically. There is first the likelihood that these particular passages would catch Dickens's attention (the passage about the old pure-finder because her hatred of the workhouse touched a long-standing preoccupation of Dickens, the one about dredgermen because it touched another). And there is the likelihood that because of their proximity a reader will come across them both at the same sitting (which would reinforce their noteworthiness for Dickens, having special appeal for him as I think they would).

And finally, there is the plausibility not only of the resemblances between these alleged ancestors and their descendants, but considering how Dickens worked, of the disparities between them as well. I have already pointed out how Betty Higden's differences from Mayhew's old pure-finder are accountable in the light of Dickens's purpose in **Our Mutual Friend.** The differences between Gaffer and Mayhew's dredgermen are explicable in the same way: Gaffer is no ordinary dredger, and his presence in the opening chapter provides a way into the novel consistent with Dickens's whole theme. Mayhew's dredgers pick up many things besides bodies (II, 166)—finding a body, which means a fixed fee ("inquest money") and perhaps a reward, is occasional and outside the routine of their regular business—but Dickens's Hexam seems to have little interest in anything else. In fact, Dickens is at pains in his opening to make clear what Gaffer is not: not a fisherman, for he has no net, hook, or line; not a waterman, or a lighterman, or a river-carrier; all the equipment he has is a coil of rope and a rusty boat-hook (which suggests that the reader is expected to remember from his name the verb "to gaff"). Mayhew's dredgerman has grappling irons, rope, and a dredging net, and in his boat there is a clutter of salvage: coals, bones, old rope. But there is nothing in Gaffer's—except the "rotten stain" in the bottom which resembles "the outline of a muffled human form." Mayhew's dredgerman is to be seen "pulling at the sculls, not with the ease and lightness of the waterman, but toiling and tugging away like a galley slave, as he scours the bed of the river with his dredging-net in search of some hoped-for prize." Gaffer's daughter Lizzie can row for him because he tows no heavy dredging-net. He scours the surface of the river only, and only with his eyes, peering especially at those places "wheresoever the strong tide met with an impediment . . . at every mooring chain and rope, at every stationary boat or barge that split the current into a broad-arrow-head, at the offsets from the piers of Southwark Bridge"—anywhere that a body borne down on the tide might lodge.[14]

The grim scene and macabre activity create the sinister ground-tone that underlies the whole novel. But more than mood is involved. The figure of Gaffer Hexam, unlike Mayhew's dredgerman so singular in his industry, is another example of Dickens's most effective technique for social criticism, the symbolism he used consistently in his later novels. Like Betty Higden, Gaffer Hexam embodies a theme; but unlike her, he does not state explicitly in his own person (or provide occasion for the narrator to do so) a criticism of contemporary England. As in the case of the dust mounds that form the basis of wealth, and as in the superficiality and mutability of the new Veneering society, the commentary offered in Gaffer Hexam is implicit: a man afloat on a river; the setting archetypally suggestive at once of life, death, and resurrection, the renewal of life through death—but in this case bringing forth only corpses; the man figuratively living on death; the whole a powerful introduction to the world and civilization of **Our Mutual Friend.**[15]

Notes

1. Wherever I quote Dickens's fiction or periodical articles in this paper, I am using the text of the Gadshill edition. Where I quote from his letters, I am using the Nonesuch edition.

2. John Forster, *The Life of Charles Dickens,* Bk. IX, ch. vii, "Hints for Books Written and Unwritten." Forster quotes nearly all of the entries in the book (though not the ones of interest to me in this paper), pointing out the specific uses Dickens made of some, and arranging some topically. A consequence of this categorization is that the order in which Dickens's memoranda (all of them undated) are set down in the notebook is completely obliterated in Forster. However, since Dickens's Holograph Memoranda Book has been preserved (it is now part of the Henry W. and Albert A. Berg Collection of The New York Public Library), Forster's disarrangement of its contents is a less serious handicap for students of Dickens's craft and art than it would otherwise have been.

I wish to thank Mr. Henry Charles Dickens, and The New York Public Library, for granting me permission to publish three of Dickens's memoranda; and Mr. John D. Gordan, curator of the Berg Collection, who verified my transcriptions.

3. *The Lancet,* Edgar Johnson says in *Charles Dickens: His Tragedy and Triumph* (New York, 1952), had reported "deaths by freezing and slow starvation among the poor who had preferred that to the mercies of Relieving Officers and Union Houses" (p. 1032), but as Johnson's wording suggests, he is merely paraphrasing Dickens's "Postscript." The "Postscript" is dated Sept. 2, 1865. Dickens was referring to a series of reports, which had been appearing in *The Lancet* since July 1, 1865, by The Lancet Sanitary Commission for Investigating the State of the Infirmaries of Workhouses. Betty Higden had appeared in *Our Mutual Friend* nearly a year before that, in the Sept., 1864, number. Further, since that was the fifth number, it may already have been composed when the novel began appearing in May; Dickens told Forster he wanted that many numbers on hand before he began printing (*Life,* IX, v). It was certainly composed within the month, for on June 10, 1864, the sixth number was finished (*The Letters of Charles Dickens,* ed. Walter Dexter [Bloomsbury, 1938], III, 391).

It is clear from the reports of the Lancet Commission why Dickens cites them in connection with Betty

Higden: the infirmaries of metropolitan London parish workhouses were such that patients recovered in spite of their care and treatment there rather than because of it, and sensible persons would stay out of them if they could. The reports continued to appear until Sept. 1, 1866; a new commission reported on rural workhouses during the autumn of 1867 (finding conditions in them even worse). Editorial comment in *The Lancet* during this period on reaction to commission findings suggests that readers who criticized Dickens's propaganda for reform of the Poor Law were just as virulent as he claimed.

The periodical articles of Dickens that I refer to are "Wapping Workhouse" in the collection entitled *The Uncommercial Traveller* (where a loiterer tells the Traveller of a ruse by which prostitutes obtain entrance for a night's lodging) and "A Nightly Scene in London" (*Household Words,* Jan. 26, 1856; in *Miscellaneous Papers* in recent editions), where Dickens tells of having found homeless women crouching outside a workhouse because there was no room inside.

4. The significance of Mayhew's section on dust for the case I want to make is instrumental, not substantial. I see no certain evidence of a debt to Mayhew in Dickens's use of dust (although one of the proposed titles listed in the memoranda book is *The Cinder Heap*; and Mayhew's essay on dust proper [II, 186] begins by pointing out that ashes and cinders predominate in London dust). Perhaps one might argue for such direct borrowing at the opening of I, xii, of *Our Mutual Friend,* where the wind drives dust swirling in choking clouds through the streets (Mayhew remarks, "In some parts of the suburbs on windy days London is a perfect dust-mill" [II, 210], and goes on to specify the health hazard posed by street dust); but anybody who walked London's streets as much as Dickens did would need no Mayhew to tell him that. Besides, there is very little specific detail about dust in *Our Mutual Friend.* It is a presence, meaningful because it is the source of wealth, but it is not much in the focus of the narrative. And whether Dickens might have seized upon the thematic significance of dust from reading Mayhew, or went to Mayhew for detail to furnish out a theme already conceived, it is quite impossible to say.

So far as I am concerned here, the point is that a passage which would have been of interest to Dickens at this time, whether he actually made use of it or not, occurs so near these other passages. Its significance is that it is one of several elements within a few pages of *London Labour and the London Poor* which run parallel to details of *Our Mutual Friend*: the more such elements, the greater the possibility of a relationship.

5. I ought to point out that Johnson does not mention Mayhew's work, nor does Forster; nor do any of the other standard studies of Dickens and his novels.

Humphry House, whose attention to Betty Higden and the Poor Law might well have led him to quote one of the passages from Mayhew that I deal with below, mentions instead an 1862 case of death by starvation that has far less immediate bearing (*The Dickens World,* 2nd ed. [London, 1942], p. 105n). And K. J. Fielding, remarking on Dickens's need in *Our Mutual Friend* to supplement flagging invention by mining his notebooks (see note 9 below), would have done well to cite the same passage from Mayhew. But he does not; in fact, he thinks that Betty Higden is one of the few characters in *Our Mutual Friend* to be developed with Dickens's old inventive power (*Charles Dickens: A Critical Introduction* [London, 1958]. p. 185).

I cannot claim, however, to be the first to suggest in print Dickens's acquaintance with Mayhew's work. Catching up on Dickens studies recently, I found that R. D. McMaster has arrived independently at the same opinion, in "Birds of Prey: A Study of *Our Mutual Friend,*" *Dalhousie Review,* XL (1960), 372-381. McMaster says, "Dickens might have derived Hexam's hatred of learning from Mayhew's description of the defiant ignorance of dredgers" (p. 381, n. 8); but he does not follow up the line of inquiry that his remark suggests.

P. A. W. Collins, in "*Bleak House* and Dickens's *Household Narrative,*" *Nineteenth-Century Fiction,* XIV (March, 1960), 345-349, mentions *London Labour and the London Poor* (p. 348), but only to show that an event reported by *Household Narrative* was of general interest (Mayhew remarked on it too). He does not suggest that Dickens owed anything to Mayhew, either in *Household Narrative* or in *Bleak House.*

6. R. G. G. Price, *A History of Punch* (London, 1957), pp. 31 f., 52; *The Unpublished Letters of Charles Dickens to Mark Lemon,* ed. Walter Dexter (London, 1927), p. 100.

7. On Aug. 27, 1845 Dickens wrote to George Cattermole asking him to take a part (tactfully omitting to mention that George Cruikshank had been offered the part first); "some of the Punch people," he said, were in the cast (*Letters,* I, 699). In his letter to Cruikshank (Aug. 22), Dickens had appended a list of the cast as it then stood, with the name "Mayhew" standing opposite the character "Old Knowell" (*Letters,* I, 697). He could have meant Henry's brother Horace (also a member of the *Punch* circle), or Henry might have been replaced before the play opened. The cast of characters as listed on the printed programs, however, is unambiguous: old Knowell was played by Henry Mayhew. Dickens was Bobadil (S. J. Adair Fitz-Gerald, *Dickens and the Drama* [London, 1910], p. 17, where the date is wrongly given as Sept. 21; *Letters to Mark Lemon,* p. 61, where full casts are also given for productions of July 26, 1847, May 17, 1848, and Nov. 18-20, 1850).

Presumably Mayhew acted the part again when the production was repeated on Nov. 15 and Jan. 3, 1846 (Johnson, *Dickens,* pp. 571 f.). The casts of the later productions given by Dexter in *Letters to Mark Lemon* do not include Mayhew.

8. Kathleen Tillotson says 1848-1849 in *Novels of the Eighteen-Forties* (London, 1956), p. 63, but this is a mistake. There were seventy-six articles in all, the first appearing Oct. 19, 1849 and the last Oct. 31, 1850. Two other series were running concurrently with Mayhew's, dealing with conditions among factory workers in the manufacturing districts of England and agricultural workers in the rural districts. Writers were identified only as the *Chronicle*'s "correspondents"; Mayhew is named as the author of the London series in a news story of Jan. 18, 1850, reporting a meeting of journeymen tailors to consider problems of employment.

The articles were printed in regular rotation, six a week (two in each series), until the end of Jan., 1850. Thereafter the requirements of reporting the debates in Parliament made it necessary to sandwich in the articles whenever space was available. All series appeared less often, and less regularly, while Parliament was in session; Mayhew's articles appeared most often. There is no clue in his final article that no more were forthcoming, but there is one in editorial comment on the same page: Mayhew had a falling-out with his employers, claiming (what the *Chronicle* denied) that articles of his had been censored, and apparently he was fired.

The *Morning Chronicle* undertook these investigations, according to editorial explanation on Oct. 18, 1849, to obtain more comprehensive and detailed information about the condition of the poor than was currently available, in order that intelligent action to improve conditions might be undertaken. The response of press and public, as measured by the *Chronicle*'s printing of letters, editorials from other newspapers, and reports of many meetings of the sort mentioned above, was impressive. The human interest of the personal interviews conducted by the correspondents stirred people as the usual factual studies in this age, painstaking as they often were, could not.

I have not attempted even a sketch of the publishing history of *London Labour and the London Poor.* According to *DNB* [*Dictionary of National Biography*], Mayhew published two volumes of his articles in 1851, "but their circulation was interrupted by litigation in chancery, and was long suspended, but in March 1856 Mayhew announced its resumption, and a continuation of it appeared in serial monthly parts as 'The Great World of London,' which was ultimately completed and published as 'The Criminal Prisons of London' in 1862. The last portion of it was by [John] Binny. 'London Labour and the London Poor' appeared in its final form in 1864, and

again in 1865. . . ." But information from Professor John L. Bradley of Ohio State University (editor of a selection from Mayhew's work forthcoming in the Oxford World's Classics) shows that the *DNB* account is substantially in error. The bibliographical problem involved in *London Labour and the London Poor* is far more complex than *DNB* makes it appear.

I wish to acknowledge here the valuable assistance provided me by Professor Bradley in tracking down and obtaining copies of Mayhew's articles.

9. "The enormous folds of the nineteen-number novel hang loosely over the characters and plot, which are not expansive enough to fill them out. . . . Once again, Dickens felt a need to resort to the same notebook that he had used when writing *Little Dorrit*" (Fielding, *Dickens,* pp. 183 f., 185).

J. H. Stonehouse's *Catalogue of the Library of Charles Dickens from Gadshill* (London, 1935) does not mention Mayhew's *London Labour and the London Poor.* But he does list five other works under the general heading "London," and four other books about London and its environs appear elsewhere in the catalogue. On the face of it, this is evidence against my contention. On the other hand, there is no guarantee that Stonehouse's catalogue (a reprint of the list published by the book dealer who bought Dickens's library) is definitive; Dickens doubtless kept books at the *All the Year Round* office too, especially books as valuable for current information as *London Labour and the London Poor.* And of course a man need not own a book to have read it.

Dickens probably knew Mayhew's work from its earliest appearance. The lively reception the articles received, the interest Dickens took in the press at all times, and his association with Mayhew at about that time make it not unlikely. I have found some evidence suggesting that he did, and that in an oblique way the original articles may have entered into *Our Mutual Friend.* In the novel Fanny Cleaver, who calls herself Jenny Wren, is a precocious sharp-witted child who, though crippled, supports herself and her pathetic drink-enslaved father by making dresses for dolls. There is no doll's dressmaker in my edition of *London Labour and the London Poor.* But there is a maker of dolls' eyes (III, 241); and in the article where that passage originally appeared (Feb. 28, 1850) Mayhew also wrote briefly of a man and wife who knitted cotton dresses, bonnets, muffs, and even parasols for dolls. This article is the third and last in a sequence dealing with toymakers of London. In the first of them, on Feb. 21, Mayhew dwelt at unusual length upon a crippled maker of wooden toys who, bedridden for four years waiting for his thighbone to mend, had carried on his trade with the help of his daughter (fifteen years old at the beginning of the ordeal). She had offered to help with the heavy work, and when with no real hope he let her try, he found that "*she* learnt at once what it had taken [him] *months* to acquire." He saw "the hand of the Almighty in it all." The girl thought, said Mayhew, "it must have been her affection for her poor father that made her take to it so quick. . . ." The attractive pair stand out from the mass of people Mayhew interviewed by their simple cheer in the face of adversity, and by their modest success. Their cottage, as Mayhew describes it, has just the sort of teeming variety that Dickens loved. The devoted daughter is the kind of figure Dickens had a weakness for, and she stands a little in the parent's place as Jenny Wren does entirely. The whole sequence of articles, in fact, is on a subject that Dickens would have found piquant and suggestive in its way of his own craft.

Is this another instance of Dickens making the raw material his own? The doll's eye shop episode in Mayhew's book is bizarre enough to have caught Dickens's attention, and perhaps have sent him looking through the original articles; or perhaps he had an early edition of *London Labour and the London Poor* available to him that contained the texts of the articles as they originally appeared; or it may be a case of unconscious assembly of half-remembered fact, in somewhat the way that a glance at a pile of letters in 1855 set Dickens off in a reverie that he could not account for—until he turned again to the letters and realized that he must have unconsciously recognized the handwriting of one. It was from the sweetheart of his youth, Maria Beadnell, whom he had not seen or heard from for more than twenty years (Johnson, *Dickens,* pp. 830 f.).

10. *London Labour and the London Poor* (1861), II, 161. "Pure" was a euphemism for dog dung, derived from the use of it in tanning, as Mayhew explains: ". . . the pure is rubbed by the hands of the workman into the skin he is dressing. This is done to 'purify' the leather, I was told by an intelligent leather-dresser, and from that term the word 'pure' has originated. The dung has astringent as well as highly alkaline, or, to use the expression of my informant, 'scouring,' qualities" (II, 159).

11. For a detailed treatment of the relation between fact and fiction in *Bleak House,* see Butt and Tillotson's chapter on that novel in *Dickens at Work* (London, 1957), and Butt's article, "The Topicality of *Little Dorrit," University of Toronto Quarterly,* XXIX (1959), 1-10. More immediately relevant perhaps is a remark of Dickens to Forster when he was just beginning to think about *Our Mutual Friend:* "I must use somehow the uneducated father in fustian and the educated boy in spectacles whom Leech and I saw at Chatham" (*Letters,* III, 271 [1861]; this also appears in Dickens's notebook). Forster takes this to be a touch Dickens worked into Gaffer Hexam and his son Charley (*Life,* IX, v). If so, the originals have been abridged and transformed in the same way as I am contending Mayhew's were, with the difference that the resemblance Forster sees follows at a greater distance from the originals than in the instances I am concerned with.

12. Even the difference in age—Betty is nearly eighty and Mayhew's pure-finder about sixty—is explicable in the light of Dickens's propagandizing purpose. If self-reliance at sixty is admirable, it is even more admirable at eighty.

13. Besides the article dealt with in the text, see (in the collection of *All the Year Round* articles entitled *The Uncommercial Traveller*) "Wapping Workhouse," "Travelling Abroad," and "Some Recollections of Mortality." "The Shipwreck," in the same collection, is about the victims of an 1859 sea disaster. And in "On Duty with Inspector Field" (*Household Words,* June 14, 1851; in *Reprinted Pieces*) occurs this paragraph: "I should like to know where Inspector Field was born. In Ratcliffe Highway, I would have answered with confidence, but for his being equally at home wherever we go. *He* does not trouble his head as I do, about the river at night. *He* does not care for its creeping, black and silent, on our right there, rushing through sluice-gates, lapping at piles and posts and iron rings, hiding strange things in its mud, running away with suicides and accidentally drowned bodies faster than midnight funeral should, and acquiring such various experience between its cradle and its grave. It has no mystery for *him.*"

14. Even Gaffer's illiteracy is made to intensify his absorption in his work: he knows the descriptions of the various drowned persons by heart.

15. McMaster ("Birds of Prey," p. 374) quotes Dickens's letter to Forster about this: "I see my opening perfectly, with the one main line on which the story is to turn" (*Letters,* III, 364 [Oct. 1863]). McMaster takes this as a reference to the predator-scavenger-vermin metaphorical complex that he examines in his article. This is unlikely. Dickens's remarks to Forster about his works in progress were always in terms of character and event; he probably meant by the "main line" the subject of Harmon's identity. As to the tonal quality of the opening, of course, McMaster is quite correct.

Ray J. Sherer (essay date 1971)

SOURCE: "Laughter in *Our Mutual Friend,*" in *Texas Studies in Literature and Language,* Vol. 13, No. 3, Fall, 1971, p. 509-21.

[*In the following essay, Sherer examines* Our Mutual Friend *as a prime example of Dickens's ability to create humor while treating serious themes.*]

Dickens' enigmatic *Our Mutual Friend,* the last complete novel he wrote, is an ideal place to examine his mature genius for creating humor. The laughter of the novel is abundant and varied and is related in complex ways to what is unique in Dickens' art. Most characteristic of the work itself is its comprehensiveness. Its innumerable scenes and characters generate a web of themes in which all is ultimately related. At the same time, the structural insularity of its parts provides a variety of situations well suited to manifest a wide tonal range of laughter. A brief look at overall structure shows how this is so.

Two independently developed spheres of intrigue are structurally connected, appropriately, only by the roles of certain mutual friends. The larger segment concerns John Harmon, the Boffins, the Hexams, the Riderhoods, and only slightly more peripherally, the Wilfers, Wegg and Venus, Eugene and Mortimer, Bradley Headstone, Jenny Wren, and others. The second part is dominated by the Podsnaps, the Veneerings and their company, the Lammles, Fledgeby, and other lesser characters. The novel is compartmentalized not only by this structure, but also by abrupt shifts between chapters. As Hillis Miller observes, "The basic structural technique of the novel is the complete transformation of tone and milieu from chapter to chapter."[1] Within this structure Dickens' laughter ranges from the mock battles of Mrs. Wilfer and her irrepressible Lavinia to the diabolical tormenting of Bradley Headstone.

Dickens' late humor is never completely without the depth of feeling and seriousness of theme that distinguish it from the comic. Nevertheless much of the novel's laughter approaches near enough the briskness and innocence of the comic so that the term may be validly applied, especially when the analysis of the laughable demands terms like "comic mechanism," named after the comic but applicable to other material as well.

Close to the heart of much of what is unique in Dickens' laughter is a recurring set of elements broadly definable as decadent. T. S. Eliot refers to "the terribly serious, even savage humor, the humor which spent its last breath in the decadent genius of Dickens."[2] The decadence of Dickens' writing is unlike that of most writers in whom we are used to finding it, probably because decadence tends to inspire poor writers, and Dickens is, as Eliot says, a genius. The decadent writer characteristically writes with little energy, or seems to trap the reader's energy in a sinister way instead of organizing and freeing it, as truly great writing does. In contrast, Dickens writes with enormous energy. The sense in which his writing can be called decadent depends mostly on the way energy is organized in it. The energy of his writing seems to be engaged in a centrifugal flight outward from the human soul and rationality to the grosser functions, then to the limbs of the body, and finally to inanimate matter. This phenomenon has given rise to many critical observations that are by now clichés: that Dickens' characters are like puppets or cardboard figures; that his characters channel great energy through limited, physical means of expression; or that, in Dickens' works, characters seem like things, and things seem human. In short, this diffusion of energy, over which one senses Dickens had only a limited amount of control, approximates the more obvious insidious quality which we spot in a minor decadent. Dickens' diffusing structures of energy, while they operate at a much higher artistic level, share the re-

gressive, ultimately annihilating nature of decadence. This quality of his writing is greatly amplified by the variety of cunning ways in which he induces an almost psychosomatic involvement on the part of the sympathetic reader—a subject which has fascinated many critics.[3]

Mainly for these reasons we find in Dickens a uniquely palpable sense of the sentimental. His sentimentality is basically an indulgence of the movement toward annihilation in a context of tonal assurance that the real or threatened suffering of the "sentimental victim" is fully felt and paid for by someone who witnesses it, and the reader is always one such witness. Our response to the danger of the Dickensian sentimental victim is the opposite of that of a genuinely tragic victim. In one we obtain a perverse pleasure accompanied by something like a draining of our own energy; in the other our unpleasant emotional exhaustion is accompanied by an inner gain of equilibrium. It is not surprising that when Dickens releases his jugular hold on our sentiment in order to mock sentimentality, we laugh especially loudly.

These unpleasantries are, admittedly, anything but humorous. But it is their radically serious nature which provides their essential relationship to the laughable. Freud defines humor specifically in terms of its ability to make acceptable to the ego energy aroused by serious emotions. "Thus," says Freud, "some artists have worked wonders in gaining humor at the expense of fear and disgust."[4] Similarly Bergson, despite his constant assertions that "laughter has no greater foe than emotion," bases his theory of comic mechanism on the same type of fear which is central to Dickens' sensibility: the fear arising from the intuitive realization that what is rigid, inelastic, or mechanical is inimical to the "tension and elasticity" fundamental to human life-response.[5] Emerson, in his brief essay "The Comic," adds a significant contribution to these later and more ostensibly sophisticated theories relating the serious to the laughable. "We have no deeper interest than our own integrity, and that we should be made aware by joke or by stroke of any lie we entertain."[6] In this, Emerson in a sense goes beyond both Freud's and Bergson's statements by revealing our fears about our own integrity, or identity, as central in our response of laughter. The essential structure which evokes our laughter in a wide range of literary material is the sudden realization that our own identity possesses the necessary "tension and elasticity" lacked by the comic character, or conversely, that the character does possess tension and elasticity and that we may feel safe in identifying with him. All in a moment the adequacy of our own life-response is confirmed as superior, underlying fears about specious identity (and ultimately, annihilation) are allayed and made acceptable to the ego, and we laugh.

Much of the laughter of *Our Mutual Friend* works in this way. Identity is in fact one of the main themes of the novel, and the reader's identity often seems threatened by the empathetic seductiveness of Dickens' writing. Moreover, Dickens presents us with an elaborate hierarchy of

characters at whom we laugh because we realize their specious identities or because they alternate between real and
specious identities; in other cases we laugh because threats
to those with whom we identify are revealed as inconse-
quential.

Indisputably at the top of this hierarchy is Podsnap. He is
portrayed precisely in terms of his tenacious hold on his
own identity. Podsnap seldom fails to be funny. Our laughter at him is conditioned by our sense of his enormity—
the fearful extent to which his hideous identity imposes itself on an entire culture. As such, the humor of Podsnap is
closely associated with the central structure of diffusing
energy in the novel. The encompassing piles of ordure and
the dirt blowing through London's streets are a compelling
physical analogue of Podsnap and his all-consuming credo.
Just as the dirt reaches out to embrace all of London, Podsnap's power reaches out to pervert all unstable identity
and freed energy to his cause of unabashed materialism.
Podsnap's credo is certainly among the foremost of Dickens' virtuoso set-pieces:

> Elsewhere, the world got up at eight, shaved close at a
> quarter-past, breakfasted at nine, went to the City at
> ten, came home at half-past five, and dined at seven.
> Mr. Podsnap's notions of the Arts in their integrity
> might have been stated thus. Literature; large print, re-
> spectively descriptive of getting up at eight, shaving
> close at a quarter-past, breakfasting at nine, going to
> the City at ten, coming home at half-past five, and din-
> ing at seven. Painting and sculpture; models and por-
> traits of professors of getting up at eight, shaving close
> at a quarter-past, breakfasting at nine, going to the City
> at ten, coming home at half-past five, and dining at
> seven. Music; a respectable performance without varia-
> tions on stringed and wind instruments, sedately ex-
> pressive of getting up at eight, shaving close at a
> quarter-past, breakfasting at nine, going to the City at
> ten, coming home at half-past five, and dining at seven.
> Nothing else to be permitted to those same vagrants of
> the Arts, on pain of excommunication. Nothing else To
> Be—anywhere!

(Ch. 11)[7]

Here humor is intensified not only by our fearful resentment of Podsnap, but by great precision of verbal form. It
is interesting to note how much of the humor is deleted if,
for example, we simply take out all the "close's" and add
"o'clock's" to the hours named. This destroys the essential
lilt of the passage's rhythm, and the loss of "close" deprives it of a surprising amount of its imagistic force. This
loss might be explained by noting that "shaving close" approaches nearest to concreteness among the images of
Podsnap's refrain, and it is to an extent metaphorical of
the linguistic structure of the whole passage. Podsnap's
language and life are "shaved close" of all that is decently
human. The implied image of wet lather, repulsive face,
and ruthless blade significantly informs our response. It is
meaningful that, among all the notable rogues of *Our Mutual Friend,* Podsnap is the only one at whom Dickens allows us no last laugh.

Like Podsnap (and almost all the characters of the second
group), Mr. and Mrs. Veneering are nearly always funny.

Unlike Podsnap, the Veneerings' hold on aristocratic identity is tenuous. Beneath his veneer of aristocratic prowess,
Veneering is pathetically innocent. Our laughter at him is
likewise innocent, a blend of much scorn and some sympathy. Veneering moves in distracted confusion between
prowess and innocence. His comedy reaches its height in
Chapter 20, "A Piece of Work," one of the three most
purely comic chapters of the book and a showpiece of
comic structuring. Early in the chapter, Dickens enlists our
partial sympathy for Veneering by dramatizing the devastating intimidation he undergoes in getting Podsnap to
"rally round" (Ch. 20). Here Veneering's unreality and
Podsnap's monstrous solidity are directly contrasted. Veneering is further undercut by the cynicism of Lady Tippins, who in a sense plays Black Queen to Podsnap's Black
King. In her "going about" she repeatedly stresses the far-
cicality of Veneering's campaign. Our own scorn of Veneering is effectively channelled through Tippins' diatribe:
"'And who is the dearest friend I have in the world? A
man of the name of Veneering. Not omitting his wife, and
I positively declare I forgot their baby, who is the other.
And we are carrying on this little farce to keep up appearances, and isn't it refreshing! Then, my precious child, the
fun of it is that nobody knows who these Veneerings are.
. . . Curious to see 'em, my dear? Say you'll know 'em.
Come and dine with 'em. They shan't bore you'" (Ch. 20).
The humor of this passage is modified by a technique not
noticeable within the quotation—Dickens' sudden shift to
a combination of third-person narrative and dramatic
monologue. This creates one of the weird distancing effects that, among other things, often gives his writing the
hallucinatory quality of a dream. The immediacy of dramatic monologue superimposed over the distancing effect
of third-person narration puts us in the place of the dreamer
who is at once in and apart from his dream. We become
caught up in the same half-pleasant, half-fearful confusion
of identity which Veneering is made to undergo. Dickens
uses a similar device in Veneering's conversation with
Podsnap. Podsnap's responses are quoted directly, Veneering's indirectly. The effect is a similar superimposing of
reality and hallucinatory dream. Our dreamlike identification with Veneering is set against the abiding realization
that he is in fact a pretentious rascal well worthy of censure. This colors our laughter at him so that it is emotionally akin to the bemused chuckle with which we recall
some mildly threatening dream of a previous night.

The chapter has two comic climaxes—Veneering's trip to
accept the representation of Pocket Breeches and the final
victory banquet at Veneering's home. His trip is wonderfully funny because it is so anticlimactic. Veneering arrives at the sleepy hamlet of Pocket Breeches after the furious helter-skelter of "going about" in London.
Accompanying him are powerful Podsnap and innocent
Twemlow, whose presence undercuts his pretensions from
two directions at once. Veneering mounts to the window
of the town hall "with some onions and bootlaces under
it" and speaks "to the listening earth." Dickens adds an
exquisite crowning touch: "In the moment of his taking
his hat off, Podsnap, as per agreement with Mrs. Veneer-

ing, telegrams to that wife and mother, 'He's up.'" Veneering is further pilloried in the description of his inane speech. It is important to the chapter's comic structure that his entanglements in the "No Thoroughfares of speech" carry over the other ironic spatial metaphors of "rallying round" and "going about." The sense of vigor and bustle in the previous metaphors effectively magnify Veneering's hopeless, isolated bravado. Podsnap and Twemlow stand out front, yelling "H-E-A-R H-E-A-R!" whenever Veneering "can't by any means back himself out of some very unlucky No Thoroughfare" (Ch. 20).

The second and lesser climax, the Veneerings' victory dinner, is an effective bit of parodied sentimentality. Comic tension in the scene is enhanced by the scarcely checked revulsion of Podsnap and the Analytical at Mrs. Veneering's account of the baby's restlessness on the night of the election. The vivid image of Veneering dragging out his over-wrought wife "backwards, with her feet impressively scraping the carpet" ends the chapter in an appropriately spatial way. The image of feet scraping the carpet here typifies another of Dickens' favorite techniques: amplifying ludicrous bodily movements by setting them against concrete visual backdrops. The generally obtrusive presence of setting in Dickens' writing gives almost all his scenes a sense of stagelike confinement, lending actions and even dialogue a muscular grotesqueness effective in reinforcing a wide range of emotions, including laughter.

Fledgeby is much like Veneering in that he is funny because of a dual identity. He is both a capricious, powerful financial manipulator and an ingenuous coward. But whereas Veneering's two identities create comedy by their simultaneous functioning, Fledgeby's tend to operate alternately. He plays his role of innocent coward throughout his first appearance in Chapter 21, "Cupid Prompted." This produces the complete dismay of Lammle, who is apparently acquainted with Fledgeby only in his other role at this point. The laughter of this whole chapter is bountiful and enormously poignant. Like the previous one, it has a carefully manipulated structure, beginning with a strategic marshaling of our sympathies and proceeding to a series of distinct comic climaxes. In this chapter evil lies closer to the surface. The victims are not faceless country people, but Georgiana Podsnap, for whom Dickens creates in us a definite sympathy. The beginning of the chapter describes Mrs. Lammle's revelation to Georgiana that her suitor is at hand:

> "Oh, no, don't! Please don't!" cried Miss Podsnap, putting her fingers in her ears. "I'd rather not."
>
> Mrs. Lammle laughed in her gayest manner and, removing her Georgiana's hands and playfully holding them in her own at arm's length, sometimes near together and sometimes wide apart, went on:
>
> "You must know, you dearly beloved little goose. . . ."
>
> (Ch. 21)

Dickens fuses humor with brutality skillfully in this image. The shrewdly interjected "sometimes near together and sometimes wide apart" amplifies both emotions at once.

A key encounter with Mrs. Lammle also sets up some sympathy for Fledgeby:

> "Warm weather, Mrs. Lammle," said Fascination Fledgeby. Mrs. Lammle thought it scarcely as warm as it had been yesterday.
>
> "Perhaps not," said Fascination Fledgeby, with great quickness of repartee, "but I expect it will be devilish warm tomorrow."
>
> He threw off another little scintillation. "Been out today, Mrs. Lammle?"
>
> Mrs. Lammle answered, for a short drive.
>
> "Some people," said Fascination Fledgeby, "are accustomed to take long drives, but it generally appears to me that if they make 'em too long, they overdo it."
>
> Being in such a feather, he might have surpassed himself in his next sally, had not Miss Podsnap been announced.
>
> (Ch. 21)

In the following scenes, the physical violence of Mr. Lammle's nature is held in check only by his desperate need to maintain decorum in his Cupid's work. Much of our laughter at Fledgeby is applause at his thwarting the Lammles' wicked designs. It is effectively ironic that Fledgeby causes their discomfort by the same means Mrs. Lammle used to make him seem foolish moments earlier. He refuses to talk to Georgiana, and the Lammles are forced into defensive maneuvers in trying to maintain a semblance of conviviality. Our laughter at Fledgeby is conditioned by our sense of his "comic resilience"—our awareness that, within the terms of Dickensian justice, he will come to no severe harm. Fledgeby's role as coward has a fundamental innocence which renders the sins of his other role venial. Thus we can enjoy his evil-doing and relish the gathering storm of Lammle's wrath with a certain abandon. The flippant pranks of Eugene Wrayburn are superficially similar to Fledgeby's, but in fact they are of a vastly more serious nature, as the punishment of the two men suggests.

It can be seen that the characters of the second group account for much of what is overtly funny in *Our Mutual Friend.* Within the main character group, two sets of characters generate laughter of a similar kind: the Wilfers and the Wegg-Venus-Boffin triad.

The Wilfers are funny primarily in terms of the threatened and self-assertive types of identity we have already seen. Mrs. Wilfer has one important thing in common with Podsnap—the desire to impose her identity on everyone around her. She embodies in a literal way the annihilating quality of self-assertive identity. At one point Lavinia feels obliged to rescue George Sampson "from being annihilated" (Ch. 55). Pa Wilfer stands in constant danger of being annihilated. Lavinia stands in absolutely no danger of being annihilated, and her abstracted title of "Irrepressible" connotes that fact.

In the three chapters grouped around Mrs. Wilfer, Dickens evokes laughter by carefully apportioning comic resilience. George Sampson has a kind of resilience because we care little about him, and we know he will survive. He is a mere figment, passively elastic, a pinball caroming around the woman-haunted house of Wilfers. But Pa Wilfer is a fully human character, and Dickens carefully develops our sympathy for him. He has only tenuous comic resilience. The strongly sentimental strain in his character suggests a tragic potential. It is significant that the sentimental in Pa Wilfer is closely bound up with his domesticity, his earnest concern to provide his family with necessities. Throughout Dickens' works, fully realized domestic security is the magnetic center of sentimental emotion. The final securing of spouse, income, and furnished dwelling is the magical bulwark against the fears that pervade the world of his novels. In this way Mrs. Wilfer's annihilating assaults on Pa create the kind of palpable threat that can provide great force for comic retribution. Lavinia is just the one to provide such retribution. Her highly creative savagery directly confronts her mother's, producing brilliant comedy.

Bella's relationship with Pa, another source of frequent laughter, develops these structures of identity in an interesting way. Bella's identity shares the dual, archetypal nature for which Jenny Wren in part becomes a symbol: woman as ambiguous giver and taker of man's life.[8] Throughout the novel we see Bella rescuing Pa from Mrs. Wilfer and other predators. But at the same time, Bella is her mother's daughter, and she constantly senses in herself a latent savagery that threatens to unleash itself against Pa. Hence Pa and Bella carry on constant rituals in which Bella's destructiveness is exorcised in comic terms:

> Arrived at Mr. Boffin's door, she set him with his back against it, tenderly took him by the ears as convenient handles for her purpose, and kissed him until he knocked muffled double-knocks at the door with the back of his head.
>
> (Ch. 26)

Or more explicitly:

> "Did I hurt you much, poor little Pa?" asked Bella, laughing (notwithstanding her repentence), with fantastic pleasure in the picture, "when I beat you with my bonnet?"
>
> "No, my child, wouldn't have hurt a fly."
>
> (Ch. 54)

The description of Bella as a newlywed is one of the comic high points of the novel. Here all the sentimental emotion attached to Dickens' hallowed domestic ideal is channeled through the tension between savagery and love in Bella's new identity as housewife. In this way the full force of sentimental emotion, its grossness purged away by purifying tension and the absence of any victim, can be brought to bear on such comic vignettes as Bella's exasperation with her cookbook.

In the machinations of Wegg, Venus, and Boffin, questions of identity are much less involved as a source of comic tension, and the laughter that these worthies create is (with some notable exceptions) of a correspondingly less anxious kind. Boffin's dual identity is admittedly important, but it functions more as a device of plot than as a formula of our emotional response. In terms of character, the structure of comedy here is that of "the robber robbed"—the Jonsonian situation of reprehensible knaves heaping just deserts on each other. The stuffed frogs dueling in Venus' window are a marvelous icon of this whole subplot. Within the subplot, the tonal range of laughter has representative spatial poles, varying from the macabre of Venus' shop to the lighter scenes of Boffin's Bower.

The dreamlike quality of Dickens' writing is much at work in the shop scenes. As in a dream, there is a "leveling" of tonal affect: the significant and the insignificent seem to impress themselves with equal force on our awareness.[9] The perennially dark shop, seen only through small rings of candlelight, approximates the unpleasant lack of visual control in dreams. Coupled with this is the sensation that the whole place is about to come grotesquely alive, and there is an ambiguous fear of bodily dismemberment. In all, Dickens creates a genuine sense of fright which cannot fail to magnify any bit of comic release that develops in the shop. Chiefly for these reasons, incidents like Venus' mistake in giving the delivery boy two human teeth in change (Ch. 7) and Boffin's hiding behind the alligator (Ch. 47) are very funny.

One example of the comic in Boffin's Bower is particularly illustrative of Dickens' use of rhetoric and the minutiae of situation to evoke laughter. Wegg has just finished administering his first reading from *The Fall of the Roman Empire* to the Boffins: "With the death of this personage, Mr. Wegg terminated his first reading, long before which consummation several total eclipses of Mrs. Boffin's candle behind her black velvet disk would have been very alarming, but for being regularly accompanied by a potent smell of burnt pens when her feathers took fire, which acted as a restorative and woke her" (Ch. 5).

Dickens appropriately picks on the feathers of Mrs. Boffin's "fashionable" hat as a symbol of the Boffins' foolish pretensions to gentility, which are being undercut in the passage. In part, comic structure here is similar to that of Mrs. Veneering's feet scraping on the carpet: the absurdity of bodily motion is intensified when set against a concrete visual backdrop. Moreover, Dickens' techniques are greatly enhanced by his sense of rhythm and timing. It is entirely characteristic of his method to present the ludicrous image of Mrs. Boffin as a kind of flashback. In one quietly delivered sentence we are made to realize an action that has been repeated with incredible regularity of space and time over a period of hours. Thus the several images of Mrs. Boffin repeatedly dozing and waking in front of the candle flash through our minds like a series of quick-cut shots from a Chaplin movie. Comedy is amplified by the tension between credulity and disbelief: we know it could not possibly happen that way, but it happens so fast we scarcely have time to disbelieve it.

Similar devices of comic rhythm occur frequently in Dickens' syntax. His constant misuse of "which" as a combination of pronoun and adjective, his strained use of participles (both exemplified in the passage above), and his superfluous commas are three of the devices that give whole passages a violent bucking rhythm of flashback and forward motion.

Overtly dark laughter is also frequent in *Our Mutual Friend,* and its presence inevitably colors the lighter moments. Not surprisingly, much of this dark laughter centers on Eugene Wrayburn. In Eugene's cruelty to Charley Hexam, Mr. Dolls, and Bradley Headstone, Dickens makes us laugh in spite of ourselves. In an important conversation between Eugene and his friend Mortimer, the nature of this laughter is directly related to the theme of diffusing energy:

> "Precisely my view of the case, Eugene. But show me a good opportunity, show me something really worth being energetic about, and *I'll* show you energy."

> "And so will I," said Eugene.

> And it is likely enough that ten thousand other young men within the limits of the London Post-Office town-delivery made the same hopeful remark in the course of the same evening.

> (Ch. 3)

Just as energy flows outward from soul to surroundings in Dickens' world, so on a larger scale the energy of culture as a whole in *Our Mutual Friend* flows outward into individual characters. This exemplifies a typical pattern of decadent culture. Havelock Ellis, paraphrasing Nietzsche, explains that "we are apt to overlook the fact that the energy which in more primitive times marked the operations of the community as a whole has now simply been transferred to individuals themselves, and this aggrandizement of the individual really produces an even greater amount of energy."[10] Eugene becomes symbolic of the massive, restless energy of a generation of Victorians. The destructiveness of this energy is made clear in the character-doubling of Eugene and Headstone during the chase scenes. They are doubled in their roles as suitors of Lizzie Hexam and as complementary symbols of decadent energy gone awry. Eugene's creative energy seemingly can find release only in tormenting others, and Headstone's dark, Blakean passion for Lizzie has turned inward to become a kind of self-torture. Dickens contrasts love and destructiveness skillfully in this pairing. It is precisely the energy that should effect sexual union and regeneration that, in the persons of Eugene and Headstone, has turned toward death. Never does Eugene experience such satisfying glee as when, leading Headstone on a false trail through London after Lizzie, he doubles back and nonchalantly passes the agonized schoolteacher, who supposes himself following unseen. In Eugene's amusement and the image of Headstone's seemingly bodiless head moving through London we have a paradigm of the laughter of *Our Mutual Friend,* as it moves between poles of love and death.

Comedy and the laughter of despair interpenetrate not only by being placed side by side, but by means of a whole range of nuances in which both are fused. One can open the book almost at random and find, even in the most serious passages, an excessive nervous energy manifested in incipiently humorous rhetorical flourish, circumlocution, and convoluted syntax. In countless turns of phrase and sudden bursts of insight, Dickens reveals "with a relish suggestive of the finest oysters" (Ch. 10) that he knows the depths of our minds where the impermissible festers. Around every second corner of his laughter we seem to risk coming face to face with what is scatological, embarrassing, or personally obscene. By means of either repression or taste Dickens never lets these things materialize. Yet, even in something like his facial caricatures we sometimes feel that human souls are being mangled, and that the musty evil of Venus' bottled babies is near at hand. Here again he provides an appropriate symbol of his own art. The animal howls of Sloppy express the pure visceral horror underlying the laughter of the book.

Psychoanalytic critics have provided one possible explanation for the scatalogical, regressive undertones of much of Dickens' writing. In his preoccupations with dirt and fog, spastic language, loss of bodily control, and breakdown between the living and nonliving they see symptoms of a regression of psychic energy back toward the mental condition of the infant obsessed with its own excretion. There is much to be said for this point of view. Aside from classical psychoanalysis, however, we can look to Dickens' generally worsening state of mind in his last years as a cause of the pessimistic, schizoid, vaguely sexual undertones of his humor. It is well known that he was involved in a traumatic train accident around the time of his writing of *Our Mutual Friend* and that he had become obsessed with acting out the murder scene from *Oliver Twist* before popular audiences. In this novel there is more than a suggestion that his pessimism and obsessiveness have not only crept into his art, but have in part become directed against it. It can be no coincidence that all three artist figures in this novel have highly ambiguous creative-destructive natures. Jenny Wren, an obvious parallel to the novelist, creates a whole world of lifelike dolls, dressed for all occasions. But Jenny, as already mentioned, also has a destructive side to her personality. Similarly, Mr. Venus creates lifelike stuffed figures, but he is a man of very unhealthy temperament, and his mistake of using human teeth for change is a tempting analogue of Dickens' lucrative trade in dissected fictional characters. Silas Wegg is also ambiguous in being both a creator of ballads and a treacherous impostor. One scene is particularly suggestive of Wegg's character as a parody of Dickens' own role as artist. In Boffin's Bower, Wegg is reading biographies of famous misers to Boffin: "On the way to this crisis Mr. Wegg's wooden leg had gradually elevated itself more and more, and he had nudged Mr. Venus with his opposite elbow deeper and deeper, until at length the preservation of his balance became incompatible with the two actions, and he now dropped over sideways upon that gentleman, squeezing him against the settle's edge. Nor did either of the two, for some few seconds, make any effort to recover himself; both remaining in a kind of pecuniary swoon" (Ch. 39).

Here comedy provides a thin veil over darkly suggestive sexual innuendo. A moment later, Wegg pulls himself and Venus up in a "masterly manner." The scene combines thematic threads of the artist-as-deceiver, schizoid character duality, and an onanistic displacement of sexual love by cash nexus. If Dickens does identify in some way with Wegg and Venus, and it seems he inevitably must, this scene is testimony to his growing awareness that his own art is not a product of the high and altruistic social motives he had long prized, but rather a somewhat perverse self-indulgence, originating in mental crisis and directed at financial gain. The sexual metaphor is expressive of both his realization of the deep creative-destructive wellsprings of his art and his suspicion that his work is in a sense mere wasted energy, a deception successful in titillating the minds of an unenlightened public. His suggestion of onanism as a parody of art is thus meaningful in explaining the gratuitousness, the obsessive repetition, the frequent sense of ecstatic preciousness and spent energy, and the somewhat bitter involutedness of laughter of *Our Mutual Friend.*

Notes

1. Joseph Hillis Miller, *Dickens: The World of His Novels* (Cambridge, Mass., 1958), p. 284.

2. "Christopher Marlowe," *Selected Essays* (New York, 1932), p. 105.

3. Hillis Miller stresses the extent to which Dickens' novels create a total milieu in which the reader becomes deeply immersed. In *Dickens: The Dreamer's Stance* (Ithaca, N. Y., 1965) Taylor Stoehr analyzes the frequent hallucinatory, dream-like quality of Dickens' fiction by revealing in it extensive patterns which Freud has shown to be characteristic of the "dream work" or dream-making process of the unconscious. My paper draws on Stoehr's analysis in dealing with Lady Tippins' monologue and Venus' shop.

4. Sigmund Freud, "Wit and Its Relation to the Unconscious," *The Basic Writings of Sigmund Freud,* tr. A. A. Brill (New York, 1938), p. 801.

5. See Henri Bergson, "Laughter," *Comedy,* ed. Wylie Sypher (New York, 1956), p. 72.

6. Ralph Waldo Emerson, "The Comic," *Theories of Comedy,* ed. Paul Lauter (New York, 1964), p. 380.

7. All references to *Our Mutual Friend* correspond to *The Works of Charles Dickens,* Standard Library Edition, ed. Edwin Percy Whipple and others (New York, 1894), vols XXV-XXVI.

8. By turning Riah into a "godmother" she helps to save him; by turning her father into a child she hastens his destruction. Jenny's ambiguity is also reflected by such things as her voodoo-witch gestures with her needle.

9. See Stoehr, pp. 88 ff., for the relationship of this "leveling" effect to Freudian dream theory.

10. Introduction to J. K. Huysman's *Against the Grain,* tr. John Howard (New York, 1922), p. x.

Garrett Stewart (essay date 1973)

SOURCE: "The 'Golden Bower' of *Our Mutual Friend,*" in *ELH,* Vol. 40, No. 1, Spring, 1973, pp. 105-30.

[*In the following essay, Stewart analyzes the character of Jenny Wren; unlike most critics who either ignore or disparage her, Stewart considers the character central to the novel's symbolic meaning.*]

> 'You are talking about Me, good people,' thought Miss Jenny, sitting in her golden bower, warming her feet. 'I can't hear what you say, but *I* know your tricks and your manners!'

Miss Jenny is Fanny Cleaver, alias Jenny Wren, the crippled seamstress in *Our Mutual Friend* who fashions out of rags and refuse her miniature dresses for dolls and who, almost unheralded, moves gradually to the symbolic center of Dickens's last completed novel. Miss Jenny is not only the book's most brilliant idea, she marks the climax of that Dickensian tradition of fitful and harassed refuge in imagination sought by certain characters whom a spoiled world seems increasingly in danger of spoiling. It is a tradition of progressively minor, marginal people airing their fancies at a self-enforced distance from a society scarred everywhere by too unvisionary a dreariness, a line of declining confidence from Sam Weller in *Pickwick Papers* and Dick Swiveller in *The Old Curiosity Shop* through Mrs. Gamp in *Martin Chuzzlewit* to Wemmick in *Great Expectations*—and beyond, with some refurbished affirmation, to Jenny Wren. The tag phrase Dickens uses with formulaic frequency to announce Miss Wren is "the dolls' dressmaker." For Jenny is a maker; she stitches, and binds, and seams, and in so doing tries to repair the chaos of her days. And she sings beautifully, and has had visions. One of the most profoundly moving characters ever brought forth from those inspired Dickensian marriages of gift and craft, Jenny Wren can be seen in her own creative making to act out such a union of vision and device. As in the case of Sam Weller especially, at the other end of the career, the artistic marvel of Jenny's conception is itself a large part of the significance toward which her whole being tends.[1] She is not only created by, she comes in fact to symbolize the Dickensian fancy at its most spacious and versatile.

It is only fair to admit that I am venturing an opinion here that has never been universally received. Jenny herself has been rather ill-received or mistreated by important critics (among the few who have dealt with her at all) from Henry

James, who hated her, to Robert Garis, who, we will find, seems strangely to misjudge her. To see with James only that Jenny is "deformed, unhealthy, and unnatural" and then to dismiss her as a "little monster"[2] is to see next to nothing. Instead, I would like to proceed as if James's initial question about her had not been merely rhetorical. For it is much worth asking, *and answering*: "What do we get in return for accepting Miss Jenny Wren as a possible person?"[3] The rewards appear to me enormous, and our epigraph should give us a start as soon as we give it context.

The metaphor of Jenny's "golden bower" is a far cry from idle analogy. Just before her unvoiced address in the epigraph, Jenny and Riah the Jew have met for the first time Miss Abbey Potterson, who has complimented Jenny on her exquisite blond hair, her "golden bower." "'Why, what lovely hair!' cried Miss Abbey. 'And enough to make wigs for all the dolls in the world'" (III,2).[4] Already it is hinted that the materials of Jenny's artistry can be somehow self-supplied, here in one sense, later in another. "'Call *that* a quantity?' returned Miss Wren. 'Poof! What do you say to the rest of it?' As she spoke, she untied a band, and the golden stream fell over herself and over the chair, and flowed down to the ground." In keeping with the idea that the raw matter of her craft can be furnished directly from her own person, the oddly overspecified "herself" in that last sentence (rather than the more likely "her") underscores the reflexive nature of this self-containing embowerment. Jenny Wren is the Romantic motif of psychic haven *physically bodied forth*. It is a motif repeatedly used by Dickens both in *Our Mutual Friend* and before, but nowhere else is the symbol so intrinsic. Jenny Wren physically incorporates the retreat she has beaten from the world. She has sought a bower apart from "the weariness, the fever, and the fret" of society, and in searching she has *become* that bower. In her own proper person she is the Romantic idea she personifies, what Keats (once again, and in another place) called the "bower quiet for us" that art promises to maintain. Yet there is a caustic, an embittered side of her nature also caught in our brief epigraph, that defensive solipsism which forces upon "me" a capital "M," twists "I" into italics,[5] and thereby underlines Jenny's morbid privatism and paranoia. The war between such neurosis and her visionary access is the struggle I will be tracing through *Our Mutual Friend*. But it is important first to open out even more widely the context of that epigraph and to see the place of Jenny's "golden bower" in the larger development of Dickensian pastoralism.

It is a theme more often than not savagely ironic. Dickens's satire scores repeatedly against such loudly vaunted but fraudulent pastoral sympathies as Mrs. Skewton's "Arcadian" longings in *Dombey and Son* to live "entirely surrounded by cows" (*D.S.,* 21), the bogus and parasitic romanticism of Harold Skimpole in *Bleak House,* who takes an aesthete's delight in the downfall of Richard Carstone, characterized by Skimpole as the "present shepherd, our pastoral Richard" (*B.H.,* 37), or that final ostentation of sensibility in *Little Dorrit* when Mrs. Merdle sings mechanically of a lapsed Arcadia:

'If we were in a more primitive state, if we lived under roofs of leaves, and kept cows and sheep and creatures, instead of banker's accounts (which would be delicious; my dear, I am pastoral to a degree, by nature), well and good. But we don't live under leaves, and keep cows and creatures.'

(*L.D.,*I,33)

Yet it is also in *Little Dorrit* that we meet the only heartily endorsed explicit pastoral in the novels. It is no sentimental idyl but a domestic comedy in one paragraph, describing a "little fiction in which Mrs. Plornish unspeakably rejoiced." Her parlor boasts a painted wall mural representing an exterior view of "a counterfeit cottage" that becomes "a perfect pastoral to Mrs. Plornish, the Golden Age revived" (*L.D.,*II,13). The "little fiction" is here no destructive "counterfeit," no lie, but a delightful game—and that "most wonderful deception" which is art itself.

Two novels later we come to another haven of fancy, a moated world of literally garrisoned imagination at Walworth Castle that is also a pastoral enclave. For Wemmick, in *Great Expectations,* fancy has sheared off from the daily run of his existence into a defensive privacy, an emotional schizophrenia that necessitates his rigorous quarantine of imagination. Only when he is safely within the confines of the Castle, far from Jaggers's London office, is Wemmick's fancy allowed to take root, and it flowers there amidst a thriving natural stronghold: "—At the back, there's a pig, and there are fowls and rabbits; then I knock together my own little frame, you see, and grow cucumbers; and you'll judge at supper what sort of salad I can raise" (*G.E.,*25). The Castle is "in point of provisions" a place of bounty and fruition, staunchly defended against siege by drawbridge and cannon. Wemmick is the sole architect of the miracle, the Prospero of this magic place: "I am my own engineer, and my own carpenter, and my own plumber, and my own gardener, and my own Jack of all Trades. . . . Well, it's a good thing, you know. It brushes the Newgate cobwebs away, and pleases the aged." As this last admission shows, the Castle is not just art for art's sake; by means of it Wemmick has provided a blooming and delightful home for his aged parent, who recognizes it for the "pretty pleasure-ground" it is. The Castle also houses a "museum" that displays "among small specimens of china and glass, various neat trifles made by the proprietor of the museum, and some tobacco-stoppers carved by the Aged." And finally, as we might have expected, this maker and connoisseur has even built in the middle of his pleasure-ground a "bower," and an "ornamental lake, on whose margin the bower was raised."

By the very next novel we have arrived at Boffin's Bower in Jenny Wren's own book. The haven of Mr. and Mrs. Boffin is a domestic compromise between her taste for fashion and his for comfort, so that as Mr. Boffin himself explains, "we have at once, Sociability (I should go melancholy mad without Mrs. Boffin), Fashion, and Comfort" (I,5). Their Bower, of course, is as artificial as Acrasia's in *The Faerie Queene,* but there is no attempt to seduce us, in any sense, with the illusion. Everything is blatantly "art," and the sympathetic imagination is needed in large doses to make of the "flowery carpet" a terrain of lush "vegetation," a "flowery bed" (I,5). Just as in Wemmick's sanctuary, the art here finds compensation in edible provisions, and "while the flowery land displayed such hollow ornamentation as stuffed birds and waxen fruits under glass shades, there were, in the territory where vegetation ceased, compensatory shelves on which the best part of a large pie and likewise of a cold joint were plainly discernible among other solids" (I,5). The novel's next chapter opens on a description of a tavern called the Six Jolly Fellowship-Porters, the bar of which is, once again, just such a fusion of art and natural bounty, containing "cordial-bottles radiant with fictitious grapes in bunches" and all manner of delectables. Dickens tells us in so many words that the tavern is a "haven" of human warmth and enjoyment "divided from the rough world," indeed a place of "enchanting delusion" (I,6). The convivial joys of the tavern come straight from the Pickwickian world, and have had previous incarnations in The Maypole Inn of *Barnaby Rudge* and the Blue Dragon of *Martin Chuzzlewit.* Yet the ideas of refuge and "enchanting delusion" are new, an index to the darkening world outside the tavern. The enchantment of *Pickwick* is now just that, a spell, an illusion, still delightful but less safe and lasting.

It is no accident that Boffin's Bower and the Fellowship-Porters come back to back in *Our Mutual Friend.* They are both havens from an unsympathetic world, and the parallel is worked out in quiet detail. The Bower is itself "fitted and furnished more like a luxurious amateur tap-room than anything else," and when we adjourn to the professional tap-room in the next chapter, here is what we are told:

> The wood forming the chimney-pieces, beams, partitions, floors, and doors, of the Six Jolly Fellowship-Porters, seemed in its old age fraught with confused memories of its youth. In many places it had become gnarled and riven, according to the manner of old trees; knots started out of it; and here and there it seemed to twist itself into some likeness of boughs.

The bar is itself a bower, a natural hideaway.

> Not without reason was it often asserted by the regular frequenters of the Porters, that when the light shone full upon the grain of certain panels, and particularly upon an old corner cupboard of walnut-wood in the bar, you might trace little forests there, and tiny trees like the parent-tree, in full umbrageous leaf.

(I,6)

It is also hardly accidental that these two versions of imaginative haven should come together in this particular novel, for in ways that have never been fully noticed *Our Mutual Friend* is Dickens's finest study of imagination, its outlets and repressions. Finally, it can be no coincidence—but rather a rounding out of Dickens's bower motif by a sort of concentric symbolism—that we have recently left

Jenny Wren in the inner sanctum of this very bar: the lame artist surrounded by the golden bower of her hair within the enchanted bower of the tavern itself. Miss Abbey Potterson is in fact the proprietor of the Six Jolly Fellowship-Porters, and at her first meeting with Jenny she began by offering the child, just before we entered the scene, a draught of that most pastoral-sounding beverage, "shrub" (III,2).

To appreciate the widest import of Jenny's golden embowerment, we must return now to her first scene and follow her troubled passage through the awesome sprawl and mass of this remarkable book. In the deadening constriction of its atmospheres and the symbolic completeness of their delineation, *Our Mutual Friend* is Dickens's most modern novel, *The Waste Land* of his career as Johnson has put it.[6] Dickens has even anticipated Eliot with a specific image in connection with Jenny Wren. The famous symbol in *Prufrock* for the torpor and insensibility of modern life—the evening "spread out against the sky / Like a patient etherised upon a table"—is much like the description of Jenny's neighborhood in London as it is first approached by Charley Hexam and Bradley Headstone. In a world where the escape motive is so widespread, even the personified city seeks release, appearing "with a deadly kind of repose on it, more as though it had taken laudanum than fallen into a natural rest" (II,1). London itself in this bleak sector seems narcotized upon the landscape, and in the very center of such spiritual desolation Jenny must fight off the inertia of her own crippled body and the enervation that attends everything about her—in order simply to live. On the next page, Bradley and Charley arrive at her lodgings and are taken aback by this "child—a dwarf—a girl—a something." Miss Abbey will later ask, "Child, or woman?" and Riah's reply will be, "Child in years, . . . Woman in self-reliance and trial" (III,2).

For her two first visitors the matter is less certain. Before Bradley and Charley even discover her occupation, however, they cannot help realizing her rare skill: "The dexterity of her nimble fingers was remarkable" (II,1). Here I think we are being asked to link Jenny's skill, in the abstract, to that of the other precise craftsman in the novel, Mr. Venus. Silas Wegg is, of course, in his mangled readings from Gibbon and his extemporaneous balladeering, the "literary man" as con-artist, the sham poetizer of *Our Mutual Friend,* a one-legged charlatan of art whose own body is partly artificial. The true imaginative man, the true dreamer and romantic in the novel, the passionate lover and, if not a conventional artist, then a most accomplished artisan, is Mr. Venus. He takes an artist's pride in his work, but his beloved Pleasant Riderhood will have nothing to do with the "exquisite neatness" of his craftmanship, even though he has just sent "a Beauty—a perfect Beauty—to a school of art" (I,7). Venus is no troubadour; he loves like one and pines like one, languishing in true courtly fashion, and he even has the perfect name for one, but he does not articulate exactly like a poet does, piecing and shaping words into an organic whole. Mr. Venus is, rather, an "Articulator of human bones" (I,7). This is what has become in Dickens of the articulating imagination. It is the symbolic decline and fall of poetry, and only Jenny's verbal wit seems to have survived the ruin.

As a parodist rather than a parasite, in contrast to Wegg's mercenary versifying, Jenny breaks into her own "impromptu rhyme" after realizing that Charley and Bradley have come to see Lizzie, not her:

> "You one two three,
> My com-pa-nie,
> And don't mind me. . . ."
>
> (II,1)

And later, accompanied by a "prodigiously knowing" glance at Lizzie when Eugene visits:

> "Who comes here?
> A Grenadier.
> What does he want?
> A pot of beer."

This is satire by irrelevance, and she baits Bradley Headstone with another form of it, a stretch of nonsensical alliterative prose-poetry she calls "a game of forfeits," when he first tries to guess her occupation: "I love my love with a B because she's Beautiful; I hate my love with a B because she is Brazen; I took her to the sign of the Blue Boar, and I treated her with Bonnets; her name's Bouncer, and she lives in Bedlam.—Now, what do I make with my straw?" (II,1). Language like this lives on the edge of its own Bedlam, but under Jenny's control it becomes both the ironist's defense against insanity and a weapon against dullness.

Jenny can tamper playfully with vocables, as in "Lizzie-Mizzie-Wizzie" (II,2), or she can defiantly turn a cliché against its wielder, as when her father whines out "Circumstances over which had no control" and Jenny converts his empty nouns into punitive verbs: "*I*'ll circumstance you and control you too" (II,2). Or there is the time when Eugene tries to extort information about Lizzie's whereabouts, and Jenny retorts with a pun: "And of course it's on the subject of a doll's dress—or *ad*dress—whichever you like" (III,10). But nothing places Jenny more conclusively in the line of Dickens's verbal satirists than her variation on the famous "Wellerism" formula: "Let me see, said the blind man" (II,2). In *Pickwick Papers* Sam Weller often uses such comic asides ("as the man said when . . .") partially to confront, partially to avert and control a grimmer reality, but Jenny's variant also seems to carry her back to a probable source for Sam's own habit, in an expression of that earlier manservant Sancho Panza who was so much admired by Dickens: "So for Heaven's sake, let me have the estate, and then we'll see, as one blind man said to the other" (*Don Quixote*, Part I, Ch. 50). Of necessity, however, Miss Wren's ironies are far more defensive than Sancho's or Sam's. When it works, her sardonic wit curtains her from the world, and an entire career in satiric wariness is summed up when, after a harsh

dismissal of her drunken father, Dickens shows us Jenny "laughing satirically to hide that she had been crying" (III,10).

Like Dickens himself, Jenny Wren is also a tireless coiner of names, ironic and otherwise. Fledgeby becomes "Little Eyes," Riah "Fairy Godmother," and even "Jenny Wren" is her own idea. The girl who identifies herself late in the novel as one of those "Professors who live on our taste and invention" (IV,9) has in fact invented her own name. So we learn soon after meeting her: "Her real name was Fanny Cleaver; but she had long ago chosen to bestow upon herself the appellation of Miss Jenny Wren" (II,2). She thus offers the perfect foil for the lassitude and slack acceptance of Eugene Wrayburn, who, on the very next page of the novel, answers her query, "Mr. Eugene Wrayburn, ain't it?" with "So I am told." *The Oxford Companion to English Literature* leaves much unsaid when it explains its entry "Jenny Wren" simply as the "business name" of Fanny Cleaver. Surely it must deserve space on the roster of allegorical names in Dickens, for she has tried to enroll it there herself. A "jenny" is a female bird in general; the wren is a bird noted for warbling, and we know that Jenny has a lovely voice; the two together, as the *OED* tells us, form the "popular, and especially nursery name for the wren . . . sometimes regarded in nursery lore as the wife, bride, or sweetheart of Robin Redbreast," and we know that Jenny waits patiently for the clumsy sweetheart who will one day come courting. The girl who hates children for the fun they have made of her, and yet who has devoted her life to dressing dolls for children, here borrows from the literature of childhood for her own rechristening. Her art and her imagination, by which she has been baptized anew, seem to elevate her beyond her own sad prejudices. With more application and no less conviction, the dolls' dressmaker might well join nurse Gamp in the neat self-assuring formula: "Jenny Wren is my name, and Jenny Wren my nature." Fanny Cleaver has bestowed upon herself a liberating pseudonym, a *nom de plumage* whose assonant lift is meant to carry her fancy above the sordidness of her cares and labors; it is no "business" matter at all, but for Miss Wren a matter of life instead of death. Gnawed at and severely flawed by experience, deprived, coarsened, Jenny has never been numbed. She has spirit still, and she must go vigilantly in order to levitate it against the fatal drag of a world from which all élan has long since been evacuated.

At the end of Jenny's first chapter, the first in Book II, an odd coincidence comes to light. Lizzie explains that she met the poor girl by "chance at first, as it seemed, Charley. But I think it must have been more than chance." Jenny turns out to be the granddaughter of "the terrible drunken old man" on one of the bills in the old Hexam cottage, those notices of drowned people who became the ghoulish inventory of Gaffer Hexam's trade. We first learn of these obituary posters in the scene where Eugene looks in through the window and sees Lizzie "weeping by the rising and falling of the fire," with the pictures of the drowned men on the walls "starting out and receding by turns" (I,13). As a descendant of one man among these oscillating firelit forms, Jenny seems to have come up from Lizzie's past with all the fanciful powers (and more, as we will see) once associated with the Hexam hearth and with fire-gazing there, the very activity debated by brother and sister later in the chapter where we learn about Jenny's heritage. Like Louisa Gradgrind "reading" her fire in the "Never Wonder" chapter of **Hard Times** (I,8), and pitted also against an insensitive brother, Lizzie Hexam was once able to envision past, present, and future in the dance of her coal blaze. It is typical of Charley that he now wants to cast off the moral and emotional burden of this memory: "'You are such a dreamer,' said the boy, with his former petulance. 'It was all very well when we sat before the fire—when we looked into the hollow down by the flare—but we are looking into the real world now'" (II,1). Later in the chapter he explains to Bradley that "I used to call the fire at home her books, for she was always full of fancies—sometimes quite wise fancies, considering—when she sat looking at it."

With this idea of reading a coal fire as if it were a book, Dickens has returned through ten major novels to his own private archetype for imagination, the furnace fire in **The Old Curiosity Shop**—back, perhaps, even to the Romantic *locus classicus* in Coleridge's "Frost at Midnight," where a mere piece of soot, or "film," lingering after a hearth fire is felt to perform, like the midnight frost, its own "secret ministry":

> . . . the thin blue flame
> Lies on my low-burnt fire, and quivers not;
> Only the film, which fluttered on the grate,
> Still flutters there, the sole unquiet thing.
> Methinks its motion in this hush of nature
> Gives it dim sympathies with me who live,
> Making it a companionable form,
> Whose puny flaps and freaks the idling Spirit
> By its own moods interprets. . . .
>
> (13-21)

Certainly the foundryman who gives Little Nell a warm place to lie down amid the volcanic industrial landscape of **The Old Curiosity Shop** "interprets" the momentous fire he stokes as a "companionable form": "It has been alive as long as I have. . . . We talk and think together all night long" (*O.C.S.,* 44). As the fire is personified, it emerges as a sort of *genius loci* in the center of this industrial hell. Amid the hammering engines whose very power it supplies, the foundryman's fire becomes, so to speak, a *deus inter machinas,* a protean and enduring force, the prime mover and special providence of the furnace-tender's affections and fancies. Here is his astonishing confession of faith:

> 'It's like a book to me,' he said—'the only book I ever learned to read; and many an old story it tells me. It's music, for I should know its voice among a thousand, and there are other voices in the roar. It has pictures too. You don't know how many strange faces and different scenes I trace in the red-hot coals. It's my memory, that fire, and shows me all my life.'
>
> (*O.C.S.,*44)

This fire myth assumes many shapes on the way to **Our Mutual Friend.** Paul Dombey, an "old-fashioned" creature of imagination like Jenny Wren who is often seen "cogitating and looking for explanation in the fire" (*D.S.,*8), treats the fire "like a book" in an almost voodooistic way, "studying Mrs. Pipchin, and the cat, and the fire, night after night, as if they were a book of necromancy, in three volumes" (*D.S.,*8). Characters as different as the idiot Barnaby Rudge (*B.R.,*17) and the novelist David Copperfield (*D.C.,*8,59) are addicted to fire-gazing, but when Charley explains Lizzie's firelight as a "library," the "mechanical" schoolmaster Bradley Headstone is triggered into a brief self-condemning outburst: "I don't like that!" (II,1). The fire motif itself will finally seem to take revenge on Bradley, as Jenny in a way predicts when she compares him, not without demonic overtones, to "a lot of gunpowder among lighted lucifer matches" (II,11). After Bradley's smouldering passions have erupted in criminal violence, alone, on his last night alive, he will find himself locked in a kind of creeping rigor mortis "before the fire, as if it were a charmed flame that was turning him old" (IV,15). It is as if, just before his death, Bradley were himself transformed into a dying fire, his face "turning whiter and whiter as if it were being overspread with ashes." We cannot be surprised that such a man should hate firegazing, nor that Jenny, on the other hand, should be quite enchanted by the custom. Here she is with Lizzie:

> 'Look in the fire, as I like to hear you tell how you used to do when you lived in that dreary old house that had once been a windmill. Look in the—what was its name when you told fortunes with your brother . . . ?'
>
> 'The hollow down by the flare?'
>
> 'Ah! That's the name! . . .'
>
> (II,11)

Miss Wren knows only too well the inevitable fissuring of vision from the daily blankness of routine, and she is instinctively sympathetic to anyone's effort at uniting the real and the ideal. She herself cannot. She must always fluctuate between the remembered beauties of her innocent imagination and the sullied bondage of experience. Yet her energy is so intense that it has brought her a glimpse, for a time only, but sublime, of a departed dream more glorious than any of the fire-conjured "pictures of what is past" in Lizzie's "hollow down by the flare" (I,3). For Jenny Wren has had a revelation.

In this connection, the most interesting comment J. Hillis Miller has made about Dickens he made not in his long and well-known book on the novels,[7] but indirectly, in a lecture on George Eliot to a Comparative Literature Colloquium at Yale on March 4, 1971. He suggested on that occasion how the history of nineteenth-century fiction can be seen in part as the history of its internalization for individual characters of that Romantic experience previously restricted to the extraordinary imagination of the gifted poet. To document such a history for Dickens's novels in particular would surely call for a final chapter on the tran scendental visions of Jenny Wren and their collapse into the narcotic escapism of John Jasper in the next and last novel. At one point soon after her first appearance, revealing by her own imitative drone that ear for phrase which Dickens has shared with her, Jenny asks: "I wonder how it happens that when I am work, work, working here, all alone in the summer-time, I smell flowers" (II,2). (Notice the difference in effect between the comma punctuation of "work, work, working" here and the accelerating hyphenation of the phrase "skip-skip-skipping," used by Jenny in the previous chapter to describe the games of other children.) Eugene Wrayburn "was growing weary of the person of the house" and "suggested languidly" that "As a common-place individual, I should say . . . that you smell flowers because you *do* smell flowers." But Jenny's response makes it clear that hers was not at all a common-place question:

> 'No, I don't . . . this is not a flowery neighborhood. It's anything but that. And yet, as I sit at work, I smell miles of flowers. I smell roses till I think I see the rose-leaves lying in heaps, bushels, on the floor. I smell fallen leaves till I put down my hand—so—and expect to make them rustle. I smell the white and the pink May in the hedges, and all sorts of flowers that I never was among. For I have seen very few flowers indeed, in my life.'

There are no gardens, no "bower," except in her own imagination, as Lizzie realizes. "'Pleasant fancies to have, Jenny dear!' said her friend: with a glance towards Eugene as if she would have asked him whether they were given the child in compensation for her losses." Jenny also tells of the delightful birds she hears at such times: "'Oh!' cried the little creature, holding out her hand and looking upward, 'how they sing!'" And as Jenny continues, her face becomes overspread with a look "quite inspired and beautiful."

Now comes the unfolding of her childhood dream of heaven, the lost but still sponsoring vision to which she seems to owe her recurring pastoral "fancies":

> 'I dare say my birds sing better than other birds, and my flowers smell better than other flowers. For when I was a little child,' in a tone as though it were ages ago, 'the children that I used to see early in the morning were very different from any others that I ever saw. They were not like me: they were not chilled, anxious, ragged, or beaten; they were never in pain. They were not like the children of the neighbours; they never made me tremble all over, by setting up shrill noises, and they never mocked me. Such numbers of them, too! All in white dresses, and with something shining on the borders, and on their heads, that I have never been able to imitate with my work, though I know it so well. They used to come down in long bright slanting rows, and say all together, "Who is this in pain?" When I told them who it was, they answered, "Come and play with us!" When I said, "I never play! I can't play!" they swept about me and took me up, and made me light. Then it was all delicious ease and rest till they laid me down, and said all together, "Have patience,

> and we will come again." Whenever they came back, I used to know they were coming before I saw the long bright rows, by hearing them ask, all together a long way off, "Who is this in pain?" And I used to cry out, "Oh, my blessed children, it's poor me! Have pity on me! Take me up and make me light!"'

(II,2)

In the tread and build of this soliloquy, from the tentative "I dare say" through the transfiguring conjunctive rise of "swept about me and took me up, and made me light" to its plaintive, partial re-sounding at the end, this is magnificent writing, a brilliantly inflected prose whose repetitions are spell-binding and incantatory, with no smirch of sentimentality. So powerfully Blakean, it is a breath-taking Romantic vision that also becomes Dickens's own "Intimations Ode." Jenny is indeed inland far from her immortal sea, but she has tried to keep safe her imagination of angels, and their long bright slanting rows offer a "fountain-light" (to echo Wordsworth once again) by which, in the arid, blackened wastes of London, her desolation is sometimes bathed, her griefs quenched. When Jenny realizes that Lizzie is heading for trouble with Eugene, she even tries to delegate her fancy as a kind of spiritual support: "Oh my blessed children, come back in the long bright slanting rows, and come for her, not me. She wants help more than I, my blessed children!" (II,11).

Real children mocked Jenny with "shrill noises," so her fancy comforted her with the blessed unison of cherubs. The initial glory and the dream have gone, but at times Jenny smells flowers and hears a chorus of songbirds. And she has almost achieved what she has dreamed in her own person, despite the bad back and queer legs, for Jenny Wren has named herself a songbird—developing an eye as "bright and watchful as the bird's whose name she had taken" (II,11)—and has grown herself a bower. Her initial vision was not of the world, or for it; it could not be willed or sustained. It came and went as a blessing, a recompense, but it was a divine and ultimately inaccessible beauty which she has "never been able to imitate" in her dolls' dresses. The vision cannot be accommodated, and her art must always remain a partially unsatisfactory mediation between what is ordinary, even wretched in her life and those surprising splendors of her epiphany.

The latter are short-lived indeed. During her recitation, Jenny's "late ecstatic look returned, and she became quite beautiful" (II,2), yet all too soon, after the return of her drunken father, she reverts to a pitiful and largely pitiless cripple, a victim and yet a victimizer:

> As they went on with their supper, Lizzie tried to bring her round to that prettier and better state. But the charm was broken. The person of the house was the person of a house full of sordid shames and cares, with an upper room in which that abased figure was infecting even innocent sleep with sensual brutality and degradation. The dolls' dressmaker had become a little quaint shrew; of the world, worldly; of the earth, earthy.

(II,2)

This is the recurring tragedy of Jenny's life: that fancy is an unreliable refuge from drudgery, that what is beautiful in her life must inevitably evaporate, the lovely lapsing away into what is mean and demeaning, and that at such times all glory is of the imagination, unimaginable. Robert Garis's uneasiness here is hard to fathom. After quoting the above passage, he objects strenuously that Jenny is "an impressive human being able to choose her own moods and her own expressions."[8] This is just what Dickens has told us she is *not* able to do, her paradisal vision not a matter of choosing, but a descent of grace. Garis insists that "Jenny Wren is not a 'shrew', quaint, little or otherwise; there is no significant perspective in the novel from which her feelings can be accused of being 'worldly' or 'earthly'. . . ." Take her or leave her, Jenny Wren can only be what Dickens tells us about her, and the question-begging circularity of Garis's argument is typical of the backhanded compliments he pays Dickens throughout his book. When he complains that the passage in question is "symptomatic of the whole novel in that it almost knowingly disgraces its possibilities,"[9] he is missing the large point about Jenny Wren that she is her own worst enemy, that her greatest grief is her own knowing disgrace of finer possibilities.

Jenny's "shrewishness" is kept perfectly in character by Dickens because it is always shrewd, and her insistence that she is the one and only "person of the house" is a just retaliation against her father's abdicated humanity. Her relation with Mr. Dolls is indeed a vexing one, but no less so for Jenny than for us. She seems driven by adversity almost beyond guilt. There is no doubt about her callous humiliation of Mr. Dolls, and yet there is no way to decide precedence in his debauchery, the unforgivable on his part or the unforgiving on hers. The "dire reversal of the places of parent and child" (II,2) is simply the given of their lives. Dickens, too, is at least as hard on Mr. Dolls as his daughter is. The old man's drunken approach to insentience is complete at his death, and the balanced repetitions of Dickens's prose fix the terrible parallel for us when we are told that "in the midst of the dolls with no speculation in their eyes, lay Mr. Dolls with no speculation in his" (IV,9). With Mr. Dolls reduced to a state no better than that of his namesakes, those wax effigies of human life, a pattern is completed that began in the previous chapter with an intriguing parallel between Jenny herself and one of her dolls. There we heard Miss Wren "trolling in a small sweet voice a mournful little song, which might have been the song of the doll she was dressing, bemoaning the brittleness and meltability of wax . . ." (IV,8). And we may even recall at this point one of the earliest descriptions of Jenny, in which she seemed to be "articulated" like one of her own dolls: "As if her eyes and her chin worked together on the same wires" (II,1). A less obtrusive balance of syntax and sense in "a small sweet voice a mournful little song" performs a quieter service than in the description of Mr. Dolls. The strange mirroring in this sentence begins mildly when Jenny's song is said to be as "little" as the "small" voice that sings it—and then slides into a curious instance of Dickensian animism enacting

here a kind of ingrown allegory by which art bewails its own perishability. In her dual role as artist, Jenny is both a singer and, as Riah put it earlier with his own symmetrical phrasing, "a little dressmaker for little people" (II,5), and the reciprocal littleness now of singer (or voice) and song is matched here again by a second (if indirect) identification between maker and made. Meaning folds over itself once more as the artifact inherits the natural anxiety of the artist and laments the mutability (or "meltability") of its own medium.

Even before his death, Mr. Dolls was blessed with no more speculation than one of his daughter's lifeless dolls, and yet there is a mysterious side of things in this novel where a doll herself (and I use the personifying pronoun advisedly) can indulge in as much speculation about death and ends as anyone in the book. Through a psychic atmosphere thick with such violent imaginative extremes, between slumps of torpor and the reaches of certain miraculous vitalities, the dolls' dressmaker must steer her fancy, must pilot her life. Small wonder that her "betterness" is constantly imperilled. By her earliest raptures Jenny Wren was literally transported, lifted out of her life, borne free. Later came her birds and miles of flowers. Short of this grace, far below it, with her fancy all but chafed away to a cutting edge in satire, falls her defensive wit; yet her imagination, worn thin and harsh, has still managed to hold on, and even her acidity is tonic. What alone deadens is that final phase of her bitterness when even the "better look" is effaced and forgotten, the cruel victory of the everyday that grounds all memories of her transport and grinds them to a halt, like one of her own dreamed birds struck down.

We have to believe Dickens when he tells us that for Jenny Wren there can be no willed maneuvers of renewal. Yet as the prison house closes about her, she must keep guard against a complete walling-up of the apertures to wonder, and Jenny has been able to stake out a limited opening upon transcendence in her unlikely haven on the roof of Pubsey and Co. There we find Jenny and Lizzie seated reading "against no more romantic object than a blackened chimney-stock" (II,5). There are no magnificent "miles of flowers" now, but only a "few boxes of humble flowers." As Riah and Fledgeby join them, Jenny will become the prophet of her own divine vision, with the unimaginative Fledgeby excommunicate from the fold of true believers. Dickens is implicitly participating here in that scaling and codification of fancy suggested by his eminent fellow Victorian John Ruskin, who saw the "pathetic fallacy" as the result of a temperament "borne away, or over-clouded, or over-dazzled by emotion," and who knew that this "is a more or less noble state, according to the force of the emotion which has induced it."[10] No one could have agreed with Ruskin more completely than did Dickens that "it is no credit to a man that he is not morbid or inaccurate in his perceptions, when he has no strength of feeling to warp them; and it is in general a sign of higher capacity and stand in the ranks of being, that the emotions should be strong enough to vanquish, partly, the intellect, and make it believe what they choose."[11] Fledgeby is a man, as it were, monstrously unwarped, falling at the lower end of Ruskin's fourfold ranking as "the man who perceives rightly, because he does not feel." Jenny Wren is the closest Dickens ever comes to the polar fourth stage. Beyond the first and second orders of poets, Jenny is one of those creatures who "see in a sort untruly, because what they see is inconceivably above them. This last is the usual condition of prophetic inspiration."[12] For this twain in Dickens there is no convergence: Fledgeby is conducted to Jenny's rooftop sanctuary by Riah, "who might have been the leader in some pilgrimage of devotional ascent to a prophet's tomb," but Fledgeby is not at all "troubled by any such weak imagining" (II,5).

Jenny soon explains her latest "pleasant fancy"—how, above the closeness and clamor of the city, "you see the clouds rushing on above the narrow streets, not minding them, and you see the golden arrows pointing at the mountains in the sky from which the wind comes, and you feel as if you were dead." Grammar and definition in the participial phrase "not minding them" are beautifully loosened, as if set free—the normal tethers of reference, both lexical and syntactic, here disengaged. The verb "minding" registers as either (or both) "mindful of" and "troubled by," and, complicated by its ambiguous referent, makes for an unusual tri-valent syntax. What or who is "not minding" what? The clouds pay no attention to the streets; neither, therefore, are they troubled by them. And the claustral streets, of course, pay heaven no mind. "You" too are with the clouds, neither worrying over nor even noticing the despoiled place you have climbed free of. When asked by Fledgeby what it feels like "when you are dead," this is Jenny's reply: "'Oh, so tranquil!' cried the little creature, smiling. 'Oh, so peaceful and so thankful!'" The adjective "thankful" answers in near echo to "tranquil" (as restated by "peaceful") in the way that Jenny's profound sense of gratitude follows upon her achieved and private sanctity, a condition of the spirit which she goes on to explain in a serene conjunctive series: "And you hear the people who are alive, crying, and working, and calling to one another down in the close dark streets, and you seem to pity them so! And such a chain has fallen from you, and such a strange good sorrowful happiness comes upon you!" Our interest, in the last clause, is drawn by an incremental rhythm through the unpunctuated chain of prenominal adjectives to the strange good paradox at its end, that "sorrowful happiness" which marks Jenny's attempt to wrest elation from the slavish levellings of melancholy. We have recently noted how the doubled adjectives in "small sweet voice" and "mournful little song" helped imply the quiet paralled Dickens had in mind, and here again his habit of multiplied adjectives is turned to special account. As always in his style, Dickens refuses to rest easy in the habitual, pressing it constantly for new yields. His fondness for the pre-nominal loading of modifiers can even be impressed, as we are about to see, into imitative service.[13]

To pick up the text where I left off, it is important to realize that the "sorrowful happiness" which Jenny recom-

mends when "you feel as if you were dead," this crucial phase of her escape artistry, is in fact subjunctive, an "as if" hypothesis. This has nothing in common with Little Nell's actual death-wishes in *The Old Curiosity Shop*. Like any romantic, Jenny simply dreams of a finer time, remembered or foreseen. Once again, though, her dreaming seems to approach achievement, for she herself appears to Riah like a vision, "the face of the little creature looking down out of a Glory of her long bright radiant hair, and musically repeating to him, like a vision: 'Come up and be dead! Come up and be dead!'" Here the mimetically elongated phrase "long bright radiant hair," describing what is often her bower, here her Glory, seems to echo—to be "musically repeating"—the adjectival cadence of her divine children's "long bright slanting rows," just as Jenny herself approximates in her own person at such moments, "like a vision," the best she has imagined. Mantled in the radiance of her golden hair, Jenny stands revealed as the type or emblem of the miracle only she has witnessed, and that almost far-fetched conditional metaphor of the "prophet's tomb" (to which Riah "might have been" leading Fledgeby) is now doubly actualized. Jenny's vision is not "prophetic" only; her rooftop vantage does in fact become a kind of "tomb," from which we are invited by Jenny, shrouded in the raiment of her Glory, to "Come up and be dead!" Little Nell never knew anything like this. Closely neighbored by the paradox of "sorrowful happiness," the predication "be dead" is all the more clearly an exonerating oxymoron, reminding us that we are now in the presence not of suicidal surrender but of vivifying transcendence, not of death and non-being, but of rebirth.

Jenny's gift for commuting between life and death in no way blinds her to the final reality of the latter. Justifying to Riah her inability "to hire a lot of stupid undertaker's things" for her father's funeral, she says that it would seem "as if I was trying to smuggle 'em out of this world with him, when of course I must break down in the attempt, and bring 'em all back again. As it is, there'll be nothing to bring back but me, and that's quite consistent, for *I* shan't be brought back some day!" (IV,9). In terms not too distantly cousined to her own transcendental vocabulary, this is the inexorable "consistency" of life's track toward dying: that you can come up and be dead as often as you like, but that one day body will catch up with soul, and then no one, not even yourself, will be able to bring you down and back. Such terms seem deliberately to recur at the book's spiritual nadir, and again they set a terminus. After two false starts and pointless backtrackings, Bradley Headstone, followed by Riderhood, passes onto the wooden bridge in the direction of the locks where the two men will soon be found dead. It is Bradley's last aimless setting-out in the novel, and there is a proleptic irony in Riderhood's "The Weir's there, and you have to come back, you know" (IV,15). Jenny would of course know better; there is a day for all of us when we do not come back. Riderhood has once before "gone down" into the Thames, into death, and his spirit brought nothing back from that descent. It was his last chance. Having already encountered Jenny on the rooftop, Fascination Fledgeby says to her at their second meeting, "Instead of coming up and being dead, let's come out and look alive" (IV,8). By such reminders along the way, it would seem, we are conditioned to hear a final distorted echo of Jenny's invitation in Headstone's death summons to Riderhood. "I'll hold you living, and I'll hold you dead," he promises, and his last words in the novel are "Come down!" (IV,15). Come down and die, he says, for death is our long-sought mutual friend, and for us there will be only death, not the luxury of "being dead." Death cannot be outfaced or deflected. And only by a miracle of imagination like Jenny's can it be understood, unburdened of its terror, returned into the cycle of the living.

Though we see no one at all mourning the joint death of Headstone and Riderhood, Jenny herself is deeply moved by the frightful passing of her father. Her understatement records anything but indifference: "'I must have a very short cry, godmother, before I cheer up for good,' said the little creature, coming in. 'Because after all a child is a child, you know'" (IV,9). That last tautological catch phrase is in fact, by Jenny's own eccentric definition, a poignant ambiguity. She has always referred to her father as her bad "child," and a child is a child, however prodigal. But Jenny is herself a child, and may be admitting here to her own vulnerability: I have tried to put away childish things, like dependency, like tears, but after all a daughter *is* a daughter. In the wake of pain, however, there must be restoration, and Jenny later tells Riah that at the height of her mourning, "while I was weeping at my poor boy's grave," she had the inspiration to model clothes for a doll after the clergyman's surplice. The energies of her own craft have in a sense "brought her back" from the grave this time, reclaimed her spirit, as she turns the ceremony of chill finality into one of warmth and continuity. For her clergyman doll will not be found presiding at funerals, but rather "uniting two of my young friends in matrimony" (IV,9). When dressing herself in mourning, Jenny eased her grief by imagining what her future sweetheart would think if he were there to see her fine clothes, and once more, at graveside, death has been replaced by human union in Miss Wren's fancy. This imaginative conversion takes place one last time in the novel's next chapter, "The Dolls' Dressmaker Discovers a Word." There language moves past mere communication into a sacramental communion, as Jenny manages to understand the one word, "Wife," that may retrieve Eugene from the edge of death where he is muttering it repeatedly. I think Dickens wants us to consider the word "Wife" here as a solitary expression of the ultimate Word, a creative sign that defines one person in terms of another and brings about that true "mutuality" which alone might redeem society. By discovering the "Word," and thus bringing Lizzie and Eugene together, Jenny has once again, through her unique powers, transformed mortality into matrimony, Eugene's deathbed into a marriage altar. And when the wedding service is read, a text "so rarely associated with the shadow of death," it is only fitting that Jenny should be in attendance, and that she should at last freely give way to her feelings: "The dolls' dressmaker, with her hands before her face, wept in her golden bower" (IV,11).

There is still more to notice about her time as Eugene's nurse. After he has been brutally beaten by Headstone, Jenny is called in at his own request to attend Eugene in his feverish coma. She is "all softened compassion now" (IV,10), and she watches over him as tirelessly as she was once to him tiring. It comes about that "through this close watching (if through no secret sympathy or power) the little creature attained an understanding of him that Lightwood did not possess." Here Dickens's strategic parenthesis *is* his thesis. Jenny does have a "secret power" that brings her *once again* into contact with that other world on whose border Eugene is now wandering, "as if she were an interpreter between this sentient world and the insensible man" (IV,10). Her nimbleness and agility, the "natural lightness and delicacy of touch, which had become very refined by practice in her miniature work"— these very skills of her imaginative craft now give her an "absolute certainty of doing right" in dressing wounds, easing ligatures, and adjusting bedclothes. The practical dexterity of Dickens's most visionary character, previously used to approximate those heavenly glimpses in her worldly art, now makes of Jenny Wren the perfect nurse. This is the ministering imagination in its finest hour, and it suggests an important parallel with Lizzie, who was only able to save Eugene from the river four chapters earlier through a skill similarly "refined by practice" in her old life with her father: "A sure touch of her old practised hand, a sure step of her old practised foot, a sure light balance of her body, and she was in the boat" (IV,6). The past itself has been salvaged for good ends, as Jenny had hoped in another context when asking Riah to "Change Is into Was and Was into Is, and keep them so" (III,2). The thrust of Jenny's visionary energy is like a lone cantilever stabbing into the free space of imagination; nothing meets it to complete a span, yet there are converging pressures that brace it at the point of departure, reinforcements that gird it at its human base. The deliberate parallel with Lizzie's saving skills is one of these.

"If there is a word in the dictionary under any letter from A to Z that I abominate, it is energy." Eugene went on record with this statement in the novel's third chapter, but now the dolls' dressmaker, described at one point as "rigid from head to foot with energy" (IV, 9), has helped rehabilitate Eugene, by a kind of psychic osmosis, for a new life of "purpose and energy" (IV, 11). Eugene originally summons Jenny, however, for another and more astounding sort of osmosis, a transference of fancy by which he hopes to bring Jenny's visionary solace into the orbit of his own stricken and fevered brain. When Jenny first arrives, Eugene asks if she has seen "the children," and, puzzled at first, Jenny finally replies with "that better look" upon her, rehearsing for us her visionary history and its gradual domestication into the pastoral:

> 'You mean my long bright slanting rows of children, who used to bring me ease and rest? You mean the children who used to take me up, and make me light?'

Eugene smiled, 'Yes.'

'I have not seen them since I saw you. I never see them now, but I am hardly ever in pain now.'

'It was a pretty fancy,' said Eugene.

'But I have heard my birds sing,' cried the little creature, 'and I have smelt my flowers. Yes, indeed I have! And both were most beautiful and most Divine!'

'Stay and help to nurse me,' said Eugene, quietly. 'I should like you to have the fancy here, before I die.'

(IV,10)

The imagination meets its apotheosis through an act of mercy, in one of the most perfect and moving scenes Dickens ever wrote. It is as if Jenny's "most Divine" visions will help guarantee heaven for Eugene; the limited artist of imagination must now aid in imagining the limitless, and this is her great ministration. Jenny has a doll called Mrs. (not Miss) Truth which she has used with Bradley Headstone as a kind of lie-detector or moral touchstone (II,11), but the highest Truth she has envisioned she has never been able to dress her dolls in, never been able to marry with the world. Only now in her own person, self-lessly and feelingly, can she become that accommodation which she could not willfully achieve in her art. Just as she became herself "like a vision" on the rooftop in singing out her invitation to come up and be dead, so now she is again her transcendent fancies given flesh within the golden bower of her hair, a personification at Eugene's side of her own dream of heaven, the very vision of her vision.

When Mr. Sloppy first meets Miss Wren at the end of the novel, it is an "event, not grand, but deemed in the house a special one" (IV,16). Her luxuriant blond hair accidentally tumbles down about her shoulders, and when Sloppy marvels, Jenny for the first time drops the defensive and often belligerent periphrasis "my back's bad, and my legs are queer" to admit point-blank, "I am lame." But when Sloppy sees her use her crutch-stick and tells her "that you hardly want it at all," Jenny is obviously touched. A rare thing has happened—a spontaneous exchange of friendship has, without recourse to her visions, brought "that better look upon her." When Jenny next explains to Sloppy the supposedly yet unsolved mystery of "Him, Him, Him" who is coming to court her, Sloppy breaks into such uncontrolled, raucous glee that Jenny finds it irresistible: "At the sight of him laughing in that absurd way, the dolls' dressmaker laughed very heartily indeed. So they both laughed, till they were tired." For the first time in *Our Mutual Friend* Jenny Wren laughs out loud in unembittered, uninhibited good spirits, and the result is a good weariness this time, not ennui or exhaustion. I believe we are encouraged to see the advent of Mr. Sloppy as the Coming of Him, and to notice how imaginatively well-matched he and Miss Wren really are. Not only is Sloppy an artisan like herself, an accomplished cabinet-maker who also appreciates the fine arts and will consider himself "better paid with a song than with any money" (IV,16)

for the work he plans to do on Jenny's crutch, but he will also be able to entertain Jenny in return. For Sloppy's imagination has found play in impersonation, one of the comic novelist's own favorite forms of articulation. As Betty Higden told us early in the novel, "You mightn't think it, but Sloppy is a beautiful reader of a newspaper. He do the Police in different voices" (I,11). Abetting one's suspicions about T. S. Eliot's debt to Dickens and his own "Unreal City" in *Our Mutual Friend,* the recently published drafts of *The Waste Land* unveil "He do the Police in Different Voices" as the joint title of the original two-part format.[14] Like Fresca in a canceled portion of "The Fire Sermon" (and here it is of course only I and not Eliot in turn who is alluding), Jenny Wren's "style is quite her own."[15] "Not quite an adult, and still less a child, / By fate misbred," Miss Wren too might have been "in other time or place" a "lazy laughing Jenny." When the happy laughter Sloppy brings to the close of her story begins to re-dress fate's imbalance in genuine emotional terms, we leave *Our Mutual Friend* on the eve of a great victory for the theme of imagination in Dickens.

Betty Higden, who praised Sloppy's newspaper recitations, is of course another figure for this theme in the novel. Although there is "abundant place for gentler fancies . . . in her untutored mind" (III,8), when faced with the vastness of the river Betty hears only a suicidal beckoning, "the tender river whispering to many like herself, 'Come to me, come to me! . . . death in my arms is peacefuller than among the pauper-wards. Come to me!'" (III,8). This is death, and it is very different from the transcendence of Jenny's invitation to "Come up and be dead!" Betty finds peace in Lizzie Hexam's arms in the famous death scene at the end of the chapter from which I have been quoting, but Jenny's imagination is much stronger than Betty's "gentler fancies," and she does not have to die. To borrow Dickens's last words about Betty Higden, Jenny's paradisal visions alone "lifted her as high as heaven." When we first met Jenny, she taunted Bradley Headstone with that "game of forfeits." Life for her has been such a game, but she has managed by imagination to cheat destiny, to forfeit as little as possible and to keep much intact. Through the help of her intermittent refuge in fancy, those therapeutic visions for her crippled days, she has, by the time of Sloppy's arrival, almost won the game. The honest, the authentic imagination in Dickens suffices and fulfills. After all the waverings, the prevarications, the foul violations of experience, some remarkable "pleasant fancies" have seen Jenny Wren through, safe within her "golden bower," to a relief and a leniency.

Notes

1. In Steven Marcus's recent return to *Pickwick Papers* there is no retraction whatever about Sam as a "great poet and impressario of the language," indeed "one brilliantly split off, deflected, and reorganized segment" of Dickens himself. See "Language into Structure: Pickwick Revisited," *Daedalus,* 101 (Winter, 1972), 183. This new essay by Marcus is a distinguished homecoming and succeeds in going one bet-

ter his own pioneering study of the novel in *Dickens: From Pickwick to Dombey* (New York: Basic Books, 1965).

2. James's review of *Our Mutual Friend* in *The Nation,* 21 December 1865; rpt. in *Dickens: The Critical Heritage,* ed. Philip Collins (New York: Barnes & Noble, 1971), p. 471.

3. James, p. 470.

4. All quotations are from the *New Oxford Illustrated Dickens* (London: Oxford Univ. Press, 1948-1958), but references in parentheses follow standard practice with Dickens by pointing simply to chapter and, where applicable, to book, in order to make location easier in the many widely available editions. The following abbreviations are used for novels cited other than *Our Mutual Friend*: O.C.S. for *The Old Curiosity Shop,* B.R. for *Barnaby Rudge,* D.S. for *Dombey and Son,* D.C. for *David Copperfield,* B.H. for *Bleak House,* L.D. for *Little Dorrit,* and G.E. for *Great Expectations.*

5. To adapt to the present case a pocket of latter-day Dickensian word play from Vladimir Nabokov's *Transparent Things* (New York: McGraw-Hill, 1972), one might say that the italicized "characters" here (both Jenny herself and the pronoun that proclaims her, as Nabokov distinguishes between "personae" and "signs") are protectively self-"inclined" (see p. 92).

6. Edgar Johnson, *Charles Dickens: His Tragedy and Triumph,* II (New York: Simon and Schuster, 1952), 1043.

7. Miller, *Charles Dickens: The World of His Novels* (Cambridge, Mass.: Harvard Univ. Press, 1958).

8. Garis, *The Dickens Theatre: A Reassessment of the Novels* (Oxford: Clarendon Press, 1965), p. 252.

9. *Ibid.*

10. Ruskin, "The Pathetic Fallacy" from *Modern Painters,* III (1856); rpt. in *The Literary Criticism of John Ruskin,* ed. Harold Bloom (New York: Anchor Books, 1965), pp. 65-66.

11. Ruskin, p. 66.

12. Ruskin, p. 67.

13. The most histrionic use of frontal adjectives in these mimetic jam-ups certainly comes in the thudding bravura of Lady Tippins's description, with her "immense obtuse drab oblong face, like a face in a tablespoon" (I,2).

14. T. S. Eliot. *The Waste Land: A Facsimile and Transcript of the Original Drafts Including the Annotations of Ezra Pound,* ed. Valerie Eliot (New York: Harcourt Brace Jovanovich, 1971). Calling her father a "swipey old child," Jenny says at one point that he is "fit for nothing but to be preserved in the liquor

that destroys him" (III,10), conjuring up an image of the preserved and bottled "children" in Mr. Venus's shop, those "hydrocephalic" babies (III,14). To die by "water on the brain" is no inapplicable end in a symbolic drama many of whose cast, from the title character John Harmon on down, are threatened with or succumb to "Death by Water," including Gaffer Hexam, Rogue Riderhood, Bradley Headstone, and Eugene Wrayburn. Surely the section of Eliot's poem bearing this title does not resist such associations, and there is that especially curious mention of an "infant hydrocephalous" in a passage Eliot himself subsequently struck from the "Death by Water" manuscript (p. 75).

15. Eliot, p. 27. All the brief quotations here are from this page of the manuscript.

Stanley Friedman (essay date 1973)

SOURCE: "The Motif of Reading in *Our Mutual Friend*," in *Nineteenth-Century Fiction,* Vol. 28, No. 1, June, 1973, pp. 38-61.

[*In the following essay, Friedman explores the way the motifs of reading and literacy serves not only to reinforce the themes of* Our Mutual Friend, *but also to help move the plot forward and to define characters.*]

Two-thirds of the way through Dickens' *Our Mutual Friend,* Eugene Wrayburn responds to his friend's criticism:

> "You charm me, Mortimer, with your reading of my weaknesses. (By-the-bye, that very word, Reading, in its critical use, always charms me. An actress's Reading of a chambermaid, a dancer's Reading of a hornpipe, a singer's Reading of a song, a marine painter's Reading of the sea, the kettle-drum's Reading of an instrumental passage, are phrases ever youthful and delightful.)"[1]

Eugene's casual digression, a leisurely "by-the-bye" meandering from an extremely serious discussion, reflects his insouciance and languor. But this wordplay, with its reference to various arts, fulfills another purpose, that of directing our attention to the subject of *reading* as a leitmotif of some significance in *Our Mutual Friend*'s thematic development. Although Eugene is here concerned with figurative uses of the word, there are throughout the novel many references to the actual process of reading—the interpretation of written or printed symbols: characters often engage in reading and respond to it, while the narrator and others in the story frequently comment on the concept of literacy. Indeed, the motif of reading serves not only to reinforce the novel's theme, but also to advance the plot and to illuminate the personalities of various characters.

Critics studying *Our Mutual Friend* have cited a number of themes and images that Dickens employs as unifying devices to bind more closely his two principal stories, the John Harmon-Bella Wilfer and Lizzie Hexam-Eugene Wrayburn matches. Money, the dust-heaps, and the river have been seen as the main symbols, features that help develop such themes as avarice, predation, death and rebirth, the quest for identity, and pride.[2] To these images and ideas, we may add what Monroe Engel calls the "social themes of *Our Mutual Friend*—having to do with money-dust, and relatedly with the treatment of the poor, education, representative government, even the inheritance laws."[3] The motif that I intend to examine closely—reading, or literacy—is, of course, related to education, but Engel and other scholars who have discussed Dickens' interest in education have been chiefly concerned with methods of formal classroom instruction.[4] The primary goal of this paper is to isolate the many references to literacy and illiteracy, to books in general, and to the reading of specific books by characters in *Our Mutual Friend,* and to interpret the artistic usefulness of such references in illuminating the novel's meaning.

The two most extensive uses of the motif of reading in *Our Mutual Friend* appear in the scenes in which Noddy Boffin hears Wegg's renditions of Gibbon's *The Decline and Fall of the Roman Empire* and, afterwards, listens to various accounts of notorious misers. Moreover, these reading sessions, even though only a few are described, are understood by us to continue for most of the time period included in the narrative.

When Boffin is initially introduced (Bk. 1, ch. 5), he enlists Wegg as a retainer who can open the gates of print for him. It is Noddy's interest in reading, therefore, that brings the balladmonger into one of the narrative's main plots, and the one-legged scoundrel then serves as a villain and comic butt, playing a part in the moral education of Bella and the testing of Mr. Venus. Wegg's employment allows the Golden Dustman to adopt, as part of his feigned degeneration, a pretended bibliomania for books about misers, the reading of which is instrumental in accomplishing the frustration of the avaricious Wegg, since the accounts of misers tempt and mislead him.

Although Boffin confesses to illiteracy, he nevertheless shows remarkable enthusiasm for literature, repeatedly expressing joy once he has arranged to have Wegg read: "Print is now opening ahead of me. This night, a literary man—*with* a wooden leg . . . will begin to lead me a new life" (I.v.55-56). Noddy considers literacy a great benefit, even though his work for the elder Harmon evidently did not require it.

In discussing the proposed employment, Wegg refers to print as a horse or some kind of animal antagonist: "I believe you couldn't show me the piece of English print, that I wouldn't be equal to collaring and throwing" (I.v.52). His metaphor suggests that for him reading is a struggle,[5] and, indeed, Boffin himself apparently views it as a demanding physical task—an attitude which explains his awe at Wegg's ability to read despite his wooden leg.

Such feelings increase Noddy's discomfort at his own insufficiency: "Here am I, a man without a wooden leg, and yet all print is shut to me" (I.v.52). Referring to his neglected education, Boffin adds that he can recognize the "B" beginning his last name, but implies that this letter is the only one he knows.[6] He exclaims, "Now, it's too late for me to begin shovelling and sifting at alphabeds and grammar-books" (I.v.53), another expression that links reading with strenuous physical labor and facetiously suggests that Boffin sees it in terms of his previous work with dust-mounds.

Later in the novel, however, we learn that Noddy is not so illiterate as he at first seems. On one occasion he is seen in "severe literary difficulties," his nose and forehead besmeared with ink: "Many disordered papers were before him. . . . He had been engaged in some attempts to make notes of these papers" (I.xv.184-85). Despite Boffin's frustration, his having tried to sort and abstract bills suggests that he can, at least to some extent, read and write. When we are subsequently told of his receiving Mr. Venus' card proposing a secret meeting, no mention is made of Boffin's requiring anyone to read the note to him (III.xiv.596). Moreover, when Wegg later threatens to report his discovery of another Harmon will, Noddy requests "to see the document" (IV.iii.680). In Venus' shop, Wegg holds Boffin's arms after telling Venus, "If you'll open it [the will] and hold it well up in one hand, sir, and a candle in the other, he can read it charming." The narrator then reports, "Venus . . . produced the document, and Mr. Boffin slowly spelt it out. . . ." (IV.iii.681-82).

But Boffin, although he may be partly literate, is hardly proficient, becoming evasive when queried by Rokesmith about the spelling of "Harmon's" (I.viii.103). Unless we consider Dickens inconsistent on this point, we may assume that Boffin can read, but only with great difficulty.[7]

According to their original agreement, Wegg was to read to Boffin for two hours a night, six nights a week (I.v.53). After the move from the Bower to a fashionable mansion, the hours are changed and perhaps increased, a reflection of the Golden Dustman's unabated appetite for reading (II.vii.308). But the initial talk with Wegg also reveals other details about Boffin's attitude toward books. Even before hiring the peddler, Noddy has purchased an eight-volume set of Gibbon's *Decline and Fall,* a choice evidently based on the volumes' physical features, since Boffin is "slightly disappointed" when, after describing the books' appearance, he is asked by Wegg, "The book's name, sir?" (I.v.55). The mistake in the reply—"Decline-and-Fall-Off-The-Rooshan-Empire"—may safely be ascribed to Boffin rather than the bookseller and may humorously reflect continuing Russophobia in England after the recently concluded Crimean War.[8]

During their first reading session, the unsophisticated Noddy experiences a stronger response than his "literary man" does: "Mr. Wegg having read on by rote and attached as few ideas as possible to the text, came out of the encounter fresh; but, Mr. Boffin, who had soon laid down his unfinished pipe, and had ever since sat intently staring with his eyes and mind at the confounding enormities of the Romans, was so severely punished that he could hardly wish his literary friend Good-night. . . ." (I.v.62). Afterwards, Boffin reflects upon the events he has heard related: "Wegg takes it easy, but upon-my-soul to a old bird like myself these are scarers" (I.v.63). Boffin is both excited and frightened by ancient Rome's violence and turmoil, while for Wegg the words he has been reading have produced little effect.

Nevertheless, Noddy's thoughts after this first reading session hint that his understanding of Gibbon is limited:

> "Commodious fights in that wild-beast-show, seven hundred and thirty-five times, in one character only! As if that wasn't stunning enough, a hundred lions is turned into the same wild-beast-show all at once! As if that wasn't stunning enough, Commodious, in another character, kills 'em all off in a hundred goes!"
>
> (I.v.63)

These recollections suggest Boffin's failure to realize that when Commodus competed "seven hundred and thirty-five times, in one character" (that of the *Secutor,* a gladiator armed with helmet, sword, and buckler, who was matched against the *Retiarius,* equipped with trident and net), the Emperor was fighting human beings. Moreover, Noddy either disregards or jumbles chronology, since in Gibbon's account Commodus' killing of one hundred lions precedes his appearances as a gladiator. For Gibbon (in chapter 4 of the *Decline and Fall*), Commodus' feats in the arena are ignoble, cruel, and contemptible, but Boffin seems awed rather than outraged. In noting the limitations of Noddy's response, however, we should remain aware that Gibbon's prose is often extremely difficult to follow when auditory rather than visual perception is used, and we should also remember Wegg's obvious inadequacy as a reader.

The primary significance of the sessions in which Wegg reads Gibbon may seem unclear. E. D. H. Johnson suggests, "Boffin and his wife are Dickens' agents for ridiculing respectively the snobbish aspiration for culture and the love of fashionable display which accompany newly gained riches."[9] But the first part of this assertion appears unwarranted, since Noddy does not seek to parade his interest in Gibbon before others. Northrop Frye offers another explanation: "Dickens's view of the liberalizing quality of the Victorian Classical training is perhaps symbolized by the grotesque scenes of Silas Wegg stumbling through Gibbon's *Decline and Fall* to the admiration of the illiterate Boffins: an unskillful performance which nobody understands."[10] But Frye's point, too, seems questionable, for Wegg clearly has not received "the Victorian Classical training" and therefore does not represent one of its products.

Dickens himself, in a note in the Memorandum Book he kept from about 1855 to 1865, gives one clue about his intentions: "Gibbons's Decline and Fall. The two characters.

One reporting to the other as he reads. Both getting confused as to whether it is not all going on now."[11] In the novel, a comment by the narrator, when Boffin asks Wegg to resume the account of the affairs of Belisarius, seems partly intended to develop this idea: "Which [affairs], indeed, had been left overnight in a very unpromising posture, and for whose impending expedition against the Persians the weather had been by no means favourable all day" (I.xv.196). The remark reminds us that time in a narrative remains suspended while the reader is away from his book (or awaiting the next installment of a serial publication) and also suggests that Boffin's great interest virtually makes Belisarius a contemporary. Except for this passage, however, Dickens apparently modified his original plan, leading John Forster to comment, before presenting the note from the Memorandum Book, "The studies of Silas Wegg and his patron as they exist in *Our Mutual Friend,* are hardly such good comedy as in the form which the first notion seems to have intended."[12]

Dickens' note also implies a parallel between Victorian England and ancient Rome, and various critics have seen the novelist's reference to Gibbon as an effort to foretell the decline and fall of Great Britain, another empire distinguished by greed and corruption.[13] But this idea, too, is not really developed in the text, for no specific parallels are advanced. If, as several commentators suggest, Dickens knew the *Decline and Fall* well,[14] we may wonder why he did not call attention to an incident like Didius Julianus' purchase of the throne (in Gibbon's chapter v), especially since this event occurs right after the death of Pertinax, referred to in *Our Mutual Friend* (I.viii.90). The purchase parallels on a grand scale Veneering's successful attempt to buy a seat in Parliament. Furthermore, when we examine the pages that mention the reading of Gibbon (I.v.61-63; I.viii.90; II.vii.308; III.vi.495), we may also wonder why Dickens makes reference to so few other details from the *Decline and Fall*.

Although Wegg reads up to the death of Commodus, nearly four chapters of the *Decline and Fall,* at the first session (I.v.62), his pace later seems to slacken greatly. Despite the fact that he presumably reads six times a week and completes approximately three percent of the text on the first evening, Wegg takes over a year to finish; the Lammles get married and celebrate their first anniversary in the period between Wegg's initial reading and his conclusion of the work (III.vi.495), Dickens having virtually ignored these continuing reading sessions for almost fifteen chapters. At the beginning of the eighth monthly installment, we are told that the Romans "were by this time on their last legs" (II.vii.308), but not until the middle of the twelfth monthly number does the narrator mention the Romans again, to tell us that the Empire had "worked out its destruction" (III.vi. 495).

At one time, however, Dickens apparently intended to give the reading of Gibbon more prominence. Ernest Boll, in "The Plotting of *Our Mutual Friend,*"[15] offers a transcript of the working notes for the novel and includes the following lines:

Lead up to Boffin's Bower

and to "declining and falling off the Rooshan Empire." Mrs Boffin a High-Flyer at Fashion. In a hat and feathers. *This to go through the Work.*

From "Mrs. Boffin" through "the Work" appears on one line in Boll. But Boll, in transcribing Dickens' handwriting into print, has made some misleading changes. The . . . remark, "This to go through the Work," should appear directly under the . . . comment, "and to 'declining and falling off the Rooshan Empire'" (the single underlining being continued to the end of the line), while the phrase "In a hat and feathers" should be placed directly under "Mrs Boffin a High-Flyer at Fashion," with both comments about Mrs. Boffin placed at the left and separated from the other notes by three straight lines, forming (with the margin) an irregular box. In other words, the comment "This to go through the Work" clearly applies to the "declining and falling off," not to Mrs. Boffin's interest in fashion. But in the novel itself the relative infrequency of references to Gibbon would seem to indicate a change in plans. Perhaps Dickens realized that unless he summarized or quoted extensively from Gibbon, relatively few readers of **Our Mutual Friend** would be sufficiently familiar with the *Decline and Fall* to appreciate parallels to the story, while lengthy quotation or paraphrase from Gibbon might disrupt the flow of the narrative.

After the reading of Gibbon has been completed, Boffin tries Charles Rollin's *Ancient History,* Josephus' *Wars of the Jews,* and Plutarch's *Lives,* but only the last of these seems to interest him. Dickens, in mentioning these new reading ventures, provides virtually no details, presenting merely the names of authors and titles of the texts with a few general remarks on their contents. And, before long, Noddy abandons his concern with ancient history and arrives one evening at the Bower with books about misers. Unlike Wegg, we are not surprised, since we have seen Boffin developing an apparent bibliomania for such narratives (III.v.486). This bibliomania and the subsequent sessions with Wegg provide the most important use of the motif of reading to be found in **Our Mutual Friend.** As we learn later, Boffin feigns an interest in misers in order to offer a monitory example to Bella and to test and punish Wegg. Assessing the morality of Noddy's ruse, Humphry House remarks, "Even apart from his pretended miserhood he [Boffin] behaves to Silas Wegg rather like mistresses who leave half-crowns in corners hoping the servants will steal them. . . ."[16] But Wegg evokes little sympathy, especially since his "friendly move" antedates Boffin's pretense and is a poor compensation for the Golden Dustman's generosity.

In the scene in which Wegg reads accounts of specific misers (III.vi.498-505), we find lengthy quotations from the texts, instead of the extremely brief reports given of the readings from the *Decline and Fall.* The books brought to the Bower by Boffin actually exist, and were among the volumes found in Dickens' library at the time of his death: the *Annual Register,* James Caulfield's *Characters,* R. S.

Kirby's *Wonderful Museum,* Frederick Somner Merryweather's *Lives and Anecdotes of Misers,* and Henry Wilson's *Characters.*[17] Moreover, in creating Wegg's readings, Dickens makes extraordinarily close use of source material found in two of these texts, those by Merryweather and Kirby.

Wegg, "turning to the table of contents and slowly fluttering the leaves" of Merryweather's book, reads out the names of seven misers: John Overs, John Little, Dick Jarrel, John Elwes, the Rev. Mr. Jones of Blewbury, Vulture Hopkins, and Daniel Dancer (III.vi.500). Since Merryweather's table of contents does not contain the full forms for two of these names, and since the table lists Dancer's name prior to that of Elwes, perhaps Wegg—and Dickens—first took from the table of contents the names of Overs, Little, Jarret (mistakenly called "Jarrel"), and Elwes, and then leafed through the actual text to get the names of "the Reverend Mr. Jones of Blewbury" (mentioned in the table of contents only as "the reverend Miser of Blewbury") and Vulture Hopkins (whose surname alone appears in the table of contents), before settling on the chapter describing Dancer.[18]

Wegg calls out the correct page number, "a hundred and nine," and then actually reads the contents description at the head of Merryweather's eighth chapter: Dickens quotes exactly, except for some changes in capitalization and punctuation. Next, Wegg offers a brief summary of this chapter's first eighteen pages, one detail (the reference to Dancer's "warming his dinner by sitting on it") evidently remembered by Dickens from another source, since Merryweather, although he refers to this incident in the chapter's list of contents ("A substitute for a Fire"), omits it.[19] Then, Wegg reads out nearly verbatim the final two paragraphs from Merryweather's chapter, Dickens' only variations being slight changes in punctuation or spelling, a few very minor alternations in wording, and the omission of two clauses and one long sentence.

The next story mentioned, the account of Elwes, appears after that of Dancer in Merryweather's book, and the subsequent details about female misers and a French miser can also be found in this text. Continuing with Wegg's reading, we find that the lengthy description of the Jardines is another direct quotation, the only changes being trivial except for the omission of four sentences within the passage Wegg is reading and two sentences at the end. Dickens therefore copied nearly verbatim (1) the description of contents preceding Merryweather's chapter on Dancer, (2) a long passage about Dancer, and (3) most of a long paragraph about the Jardines—these three segments containing, respectively, about 70, 265, and 190 words.[20]

The novelist then has Wegg present a lengthy passage, about 230 words, taken almost exactly from Kirby's book, the account describing the "most extraordinary case" of the will left by Roger Baldwin. Indeed, the only changes in this passage, except for punctuation, are extremely minor, consisting of a few omissions, several slight verbal changes, and the fusing of two sentences.[21] In addition, we find that Boffin gives the correct volume number for this narrative, and that the three stories Wegg thumbs through before finding this one—"Remarkable petrifaction," "Memoirs of General John Reid, commonly called The Walking Rushlight," and "Remarkable case of a person who swallowed a crown-piece"—are all found in Kirby's text, the order of their appearance being identical with the sequence followed by Wegg.[22]

We probably cannot determine whether Dickens believed such close use of sources would be noticed by his public. Having found these passages, he evidently considered them perfect for his purposes and proceeded to incorporate them skillfully into the chapter.

In the various scenes of pretended miserliness, Boffin shows great histrionic ability, at one point seeming to contradict his once high valuation of reading. Speaking to Rokesmith in the presence of Bella, Boffin asserts, ". . . it ain't that I want to occupy your whole time; you can take up a book for a minute or two when you've nothing better to do, though I think you'll almost always find something useful to do" (III.v.482). This disparagement of the utility of reading fits in with Boffin's pose and resembles the remark previously made to Jenny Wren by Fledgeby, the truly avaricious man (II.v.291).

Besides feigning bibliomania for books about misers, Boffin also pretends to be guided by these accounts. Bella notices "that, as he pursued the acquisition of those dismal records with the ardour of Don Quixote for his books of chivalry, he began to spend his money with a more sparing hand" (III.v.487). So seriously does the Golden Dustman follow his studies that Wegg thinks Boffin sees an "evident parallel" between the behavior described in the passages read and that of old Harmon (III.vii.517). Afterwards, in talking to Rokesmith and then to Bella, Boffin seems to identify with some of these misers whom he has come to know through books (III.xv.611, 615). And later, when Wegg is asked by Noddy not to tell Mrs. Boffin about the extortion which is to take much of their wealth, the "literary man" replies, "I suspect, Boffin . . . that you've found out some account of some old chap, supposed to be a Miser, who got himself the credit of having much more money than he had" (IV.iii.683). Apparently, Wegg believes that Noddy's behavior is being influenced by the stories.

Various critics have questioned whether Boffin's degeneration was always planned by Dickens to be mere pretense, especially since the narrator, after Boffin has left Wegg and Venus at the latter's shop and is walking home alone, comments on Noddy's doubt concerning the taxidermist: "It was a cunning and suspicious idea, quite in the way of his school of Misers, and he looked very cunning and suspicious as he went jogging through the streets" (III.xiv.606).[23] But F. X. Shea, examining the holograph manuscript now in the Pierpont Morgan Library, has found, both in the working notes and in various passages Dickens

cancelled because of space limitations, convincing evidence that the novelist apparently never intended Boffin to become actually corrupted.[24] Moreover, Mrs. Boffin's obviously constrained behavior during her husband's attack on Rokesmith (III.xv.619, 621) seems to confirm Noddy's later assertion that his wife was disturbed by the pretense (IV.xiii.800). One other explanation of the convincing nature of Boffin's pose is offered by Masao Miyoshi:

> Boffin's miserliness was originally put on in the interests of Rokesmith and Bella, but it served Boffin himself as well, as a way of obviating an unpleasant new self that could very well have emerged from his sudden condition of wealth.[25]

By pretending to be a Don Quixote of avarice, Boffin helps Bella to reject the mercenary values of Victorian society, but, as he later tells her, the books about misers were also obtained "partly for the punishment of . . . Wegg, by leading him on . . ." (IV.xiii.800). And Wegg responds to the stories in an entirely predictable way: he is tempted to indulge his own avarice. Having been led to assume that Boffin is emulating famous misers, Wegg begins searching for hidden wills and treasure, since the readings his employer selects include stories of money left in a teapot and a will hidden in a desk (III.vi.502, 505). Significantly, Wegg's reaction differs from that of Venus, whom Boffin is also testing. A moral man who has been induced to join Wegg because of disappointment in love, Venus, although initially fascinated by the descriptions of misers, later decides to warn Boffin. Whether the continued reading of tales of avarice has caused the taxidermist to react against Wegg's greed is uncertain, but, whatever the reasons, Venus does repent.

There is, of course, a paradox in Boffin's pretense that the literature about misers reinforces his own newly developed tendencies to avarice, for virtually all tales about misers present them as negative exemplars, people who experience great unhappiness as a result of their greed. Indeed, Rokesmith, when asked if he knows about the misers John Elwes and Daniel Dancer, gives the conventional moral: "They lived and died very miserably" (III.v.493). After Wegg's exposure, his claim that these tales have corrupted him is therefore self-condemnatory. Moreover, our awareness that he began plotting the "friendly move" well before Boffin started the pretense (II.vii.315) makes the following excuse absurd: ". . . it's not easy to say how far the tone of my mind may have been lowered by unwholesome reading on the subject of Misers, when you was leading me and others on to think you one yourself, sir" (IV.xiv.814). Although Wegg here seeks to blame reading for his moral failings, we have seen that his treatment of the Romans showed extreme insensitivity to print. He responded excitedly to the stories of misers simply because his own avaricious tendencies led him to believe that these accounts contained clues about Boffin's behavior (III.vii.517).

Wegg, a villain whose limited literacy makes comic his role as a "literary man," pretentiously seeks to mask his ignorance: ". . . know him? Old familiar declining and falling off the Rooshan? Rather, sir!" (I.v.55). His absurd mispronunciations of Roman names—"Polly Beeious" for Polybius, "Commodious" for Commodus, "Vittle-us" for Vitellius, "Bully Sawyers" for Belisarius (I.v.62-63; I.xv.193)—and his ludicrous offerings of doggerel verse, together with his assertion that reciting poetry places a "strain upon the intellect" (I.v.54), make him a comic butt, vastly inferior both in morality and literacy to Mr. Venus, who corrects his renditions (III.xiv.595-96). Like Riderhood, Wegg is a lazy, envious, and deceitful scoundrel who attempts extortion. A mock schoolmaster, he serves as the main villain of the Bella-John story, just as Headstone is the principal antagonist in the Lizzie-Eugene plot, Headstone's passionate violence contrasting with Wegg's crafty threatening.

Bella apparently is exposed to the literature about misers only during visits to booksellers, since Boffin, although he makes a point of taking her on his shopping expeditions, later keeps the books hidden (III.v.485-86). These books are therefore primarily important in tormenting Wegg, while the major effort to teach Bella her true nature is made in the scenes in which Boffin berates and ridicules Rokesmith. The feigned bibliomania seems intended to enhance the credibility of Boffin's behavior in these scenes, by serving as an added symptom and also, perhaps, as a supposed contributory cause.

Boffin's illiteracy, besides bringing Wegg into the story, also facilitates the task of John Harmon, disguised as Rokesmith, in gaining a position as Noddy's secretary. Subsequently, this appointment enables John to gain a closer acquaintance with Bella, to become recognized by the Boffins, and to receive their help, through the pretended degeneration of Noddy, in reforming Bella—or, at least, in leading her to discover and reveal her true self.

In addition, the motif of reading, or literacy, serves very important purposes in the other major strand of Dickens' narrative, the story of Lizzie and Eugene. Since Gaffer Hexam is opposed to literacy, Lizzie sends her brother, Charley, away to acquire his education. The boy's isolation and ability lead to his becoming the protégé of Bradley Headstone, who then enters the Lizzie-Eugene story as the primary villain.

Lizzie's illiteracy helps to increase Wrayburn's involvement with her, since he offers to arrange for lessons for both Lizzie and Jenny Wren. Subsequently, the educational pursuits of these two young women lead them to closer acquaintance with Mr. Riah, who invites them to study their books in the garden he has planted on the roof of Fledgeby's Pubsey and Co. (II.v.290-91). Later, Lizzie, having learned to read and write, can comprehend Betty Higden's letter of identification and can send a note to the Boffins, Rokesmith, and Bella; this communication in turn leads to the friendship between the heroines that is one of the devices Dickens uses to connect the two plots (III.viii.533-34).

The motif of reading, moreover, is also linked with Betty Higden in another way, since her flight is largely attributable to fear caused by her reading of newspaper reports describing the Poor House (I.xvi.206). For Betty, although she has difficulty understanding handwriting, can comprehend "most print" and also enjoys listening to Sloppy's reading of the police news, a pastime that has led him to develop a talent for using different voices (I.xvi.204-5).[26]

Dickens uses the motif of literacy not only to assist developments in his narrative, but also to reveal character, such disclosure frequently being made through the attitudes various figures express towards reading. Lizzie Hexam, whose illiterate father, Gaffer, wishes to keep his children uneducated, remarks, "I can't so much as read a book, because, if I had learned, father would have thought I was deserting him. . . ." (I.iii.30).[27] Even though Gaffer is willing to use Charley's furtively acquired literacy in summoning Lightwood, the bird of prey is pleased when his son pretends to be writing in a slow, slovenly manner (I.iii.28). Nevertheless, Gaffer himself employs a substitute for reading, a strong memory, evidently developed as a compensation for illiteracy. Indeed, this antiliterate man, ironically, is interested in print, for he memorizes handbills announcing drownings and keeps these as souvenirs adorning his walls (I.iii.23).

In this novel, however, literacy is not a moral gauge. For Gaffer, despite his occupation, is not presented as an evil figure, his kindness to Lizzie contrasting with Rogue Riderhood's treatment of Pleasant. While Hexam may be seen, in part, as a victim, a man whose lack of education debases him, Riderhood emerges as so extreme a villain that we may wonder whether schooling would have made him more adept in wrongdoing. His illiteracy is emphasized when Betty Higden faints near Plashwater Weir Mill Lock, where he is Deputy Lock-keeper. Had Riderhood been able to comprehend Betty's letter of identification, he might perhaps have devised plans for extorting money from her friends: "The Deputy Lock opened the letter with a grave face, which underwent no change as he eyed its contents. But it might have done, if he could have read them" (III.viii.530). Later, Riderhood's illiteracy is again stressed when he invades Headstone's classroom, asks the schoolmaster to write his name on the blackboard, and then requests that the class read the name: "I ain't a learned character myself . . . but I do admire learning in others. I should dearly like to hear these here young folks read that there name off, from the writing" (IV.xv.818). Of course, his interest is purely practical, as when he previously had Pleasant write a letter for him requesting various favors of Lightwood (III.xi.568, 570). Before Riderhood's visit to the school, Headstone, apprehensive about being revealed as Eugene's assailant, had hoped not to be found; knowing Riderhood "to be a very ignorant man who could not write, he [Headstone] began to doubt whether he was to be feared at all. . . ." (IV.xv.816-17). But Riderhood, the illiterate, proves in some ways more shrewd than the schoolmaster.

Indeed, Headstone, although educated, is not intelligent, his face revealing "a naturally slow or inattentive intellect that had toiled hard to get what it had won . . ." (II.i.225). Literacy has enabled him to rise from his origins as "a pauper lad" (II.i.226), just as literacy will help Charley Hexam to rise. Charley, however, while not guilty of a crime like Headstome's assault on Eugene, is in some ways even less appealing than the schoolmaster. For the latter, despite his villainy, commands some sympathy because of his intense suffering and his capacity for kindness, as indicated by the bequest of his watch to Miss Peecher (IV.xv.820). Unlike the passion-driven Headstone, Charley is coolly rational, an entirely selfish boy who ungratefully denounces Lizzie after her refusal of the schoolmaster (II.xv.419) and then spurns both benefactors. When we first meet Charley, in the Veneering library, the narrator comments: "There was a curious mixture in the boy, of uncompleted savagery, and uncompleted civilisation . . . he glanced at the backs of the books, with an awakened curiosity that went below the binding. No one who can read, ever looks at a book, even unopened on the shelf, like one who cannot" (I.iii.19). Charley's literary interest is shown by his ready comparison of the drowned body to "Pharoah's multitude, that were drowned in the Red Sea," and his reference to Lazarus (I.iii.19). But he immediately incurs Eugene's anger by a slighting reference to Lizzie, whom Wrayburn has not yet met: "She ain't half bad . . . but if she knows her letters it's the most she does—and them I learned her" (I.iii.20).

Lizzie differs in many ways from her brother. An extremely sensitive girl, she strongly regrets her illiteracy: "I should be very glad to be able to read real books. I feel my want of learning very much, Charley" (I.iii.31). Just before this, her brother has remarked, in one of his few tender moments, "You said you couldn't read a book, Lizzie. Your library of books is the hollow down by the flare, I think" (I.iii.31). Lizzie has developed a substitute for reading, the ability to see pictures in the fire.[28] Just as Gaffer's memory compensates to an extent for his illiteracy, so Lizzie uses her imagination to visualize scenes from the past and express hopes for the future. Even after she has actually learned to read print, her reading in the fire still provides encouragement and inspiration. In the village where Betty Higden has died, Lizzie gazes at the fire to describe her intuitions about Bella's true self: "A heart well worth winning, and well won" (III.ix.549); later, after marrying Rokesmith, Bella writes to tell Lizzie "how right she was when she pretended to read in the live coals" (IV.v.709).

During the course of the novel, Bella herself is frequently seen reading, her motives and tastes varying. At one point early in the narrative, Rokesmith observes her engrossed in a book and asks whether the volume is a love story. She replies, "Oh dear no, or I shouldn't be reading it. It's more about money than anything else" (I.xvi.212). Although this remark indicates that Bella is at the time obsessed with money, her subsequent comment, ". . . I forget what it says, but you can find out for yourself. . . . I don't want it any more" (I.xvi.212), suggests a frivolous, capricious attitude. Later, when the narrator, mentioning Bella, refers at times to "her book," but gives no further details, we may

infer that she is merely reading for recreation (II.xiii.389, 393; III.v.480, 482). Occasionally, Bella pretends to be absorbed in reading so that Boffin or Rokesmith will not notice how intently she is listening (III.v.482, 484, 491).

After her marriage to Rokesmith, Bella's literary inclinations become extremely practical. She frequently goes "for advice and support to a sage volume entitled The Complete British Family Housewife" (IV.v.705), a book she finds so difficult that she is forced to read with an "expression of profound research" (IV.v.705).[29] In addition, she devotes herself to "the mastering of the newspaper, so that she might be close up with John on general topics when John came home" (IV.v.705). Marriage evidently has made Bella more serious, a transformation reflected by the change in her reading habits and also, perhaps, by the fact that John gives her a book as a birthday present (IV.xii.784).

Rokesmith himself is, of course, thoroughly literate. He wins a position as a secretary, before the Boffins recognize him, by his ability to prepare abstracts of some business papers he has quickly read through (I.xv.186). In this same chapter, we learn from the Boffins that the young child John Harmon was frequently found "sitting with his little book" (I.xv.191). And when Bella inspects the room that John is renting from her parents, she sees "shelves and stands of books, English, French, and Italian" (III.iv.469). Earlier, in reply to a question by Wilfer, John reveals that he has read several travel books about Africa (II.xiv.395); in his extended soliloquy, he refers to his reading "in narratives of escape from prison" (II.xiii.380); and, in a conversation with Boffin, he indicates familiarity with stories about two famous misers, John Elwes and Daniel Dancer (III.v.492-93)—although, of course, Boffin may have prepared John for questions, since the latter knew beforehand of the plot to pretend miserliness (IV.xiii.797). Certainly, however, Dickens wants us to see Rokesmith as an educated, well-read man. Moreover, although the novel's other hero, Eugene Wrayburn, does not seem much given to reading, the barrister is obviously literate and is eager to arrange for Lizzie's education.

As we might anticipate, two of the satiric butts in the novel, Podsnap and Veneering, appear insensitive to reading. The latter, the "bran-new" man, owns "a library of bran-new books, in bran-new bindings liberally gilded" (I.iii.18), a collection designed for display, while Podsnap's idea of literature is simple and routine: "large print, respectively descriptive of getting up at eight, shaving close at a quarter-past, breakfasting at nine, going to the City at ten, coming home at half-past five, and dining at seven" (I.xi.133-34). In general, the appetite for reading shown by many of the novel's admirable figures is lacking in the less attractive characters.

In *Our Mutual Friend,* the numerous references to books and reading, besides being useful in advancing the plot and developing characterization, also reflect the Victorians' great dedication to print. Dickens' characters often remind us that, for English men and women in the mid-nineteenth century, reading was a primary source of recreation as well as an indispensable instrument in many matters of government and business.[30]

The section of the novel in which the motif of reading is most fully developed presents Wegg's rendition of the lives of actual misers. These historical figures paradoxically make Dickens' fictional characters seem more real, for the major figures in *Our Mutual Friend* are more fully depicted than misers like the Jardines. And when Dickens shows his characters reading, they seem more vivid than the figures they are reading about, an effect comparable to that often achieved by the play-within-the-play device or by interpolated stories.[31] When Mortimer Lightwood refers, in general terms, to novels (I.ii.15-16), he suggests that he himself is not simply a character in a novel. And, at another point, the narrator comments, "it was not gentle spring ethereally mild, as in Thomson's Seasons, but nipping spring with an easterly wind, as in Johnson's, Jackson's, Dickson's, Smith's, and Jones's Seasons" (I.xii.149), a remark implying that the world of Dickens' novel is more real than that described in "literature." Moreover, Boffin's pretense at miserliness offers another variety of the "play"-within-the-novel device. When the deception has been explained to Bella, she tells the Golden Dustman that she understands his wish to become "a glaring instance kept before her" (IV.xiii.799), implying that a living negative example is more convincing than a negative example in a book, be the book fictional or historical. And she also intimates to us that the fictional Boffin is a "living" example, especially when she compares him, this time to his advantage, with the misers he has had Wegg read about (IV.xiii.798).

The Victorian interest in literacy was certainly shared by Dickens, even though his personal reading is generally thought to have been neither systematic nor scholarly.[32] Moreover, although *Our Mutual Friend* seems the novel by Dickens in which the idea of reading is most recurrent, this motif does occasionally appear in his other works—for example, in the references to childhood reading by Scrooge in *A Christmas Carol* ("Stave Two: The First of the Three Spirits") and by David Copperfield (ch. 4); the disclosure in *Bleak House* of Krook's effort to teach himself to read and write, since he trusts no other instructor (ch. 14); the mention in *Hard Times* of the fanciful tales Sissy Jupe formerly read to her father (Bk. 1, ch. 7) and of Mr. Gradgrind's concern about the Coketown library (Bk. 1, ch. 8); Arthur Clennam's recollection in *Little Dorrit* of his mother's gloomy Bible reading on Sundays (Bk. 1, ch. 3); the references in *Great Expectations* to Mr. Wopsle's readings (chs. 15, 18), to Herbert Pocket's mother's constant devotion to a book about aristocratic titles (chs. 22, 23), to Pip's study with Herbert's father (ch. 25), to Pip's later reading to satisfy his own inclinations (ch. 39), and to his reading in foreign languages to please Magwitch (ch. 40); and the description in *Edwin Drood* of Miss Twinkleton's censored readings to Rosa (ch. 22).

Nevertheless, the extent to which Dickens' use of the motif of reading in *Our Mutual Friend* was deliberate is difficult to determine. His Memorandum Book contains the note: "The uneducated father (or uncle?) in fustian, and the educated boy in spectacles. Whom Leech and I saw at Chatham." Forster, suggesting that Dickens sent him a letter including a similar comment, asserts that this observation led to Gaffer and Charley Hexam.[33] The Memorandum Book, as we have previously remarked, also contains a note on the reading of Gibbon, while some of the working notes bound in with the holograph manuscript of the novel stress the importance of the feigned bibliomania and the scene in which Wegg reads the accounts of misers: "Work in *The Misers*—to bring out his pretended love of money," and "More books, and the misers, and about hidden wills / *relieve by making Wegg as comic as possible.*"[34] Then, too, Eugene's digression on the word "reading," quoted at the beginning of this essay, offers a clue, for this comment would seem to direct our attention to a motif that is frequently introduced but relatively unnoticed, possibly because of its commonplace nature.

In referring to the actress, the dancer, the singer, the painter, and the drummer, Eugene uses "reading" in its figurative senses of acting and interpreting. Like the actress, Boffin "reads" a part, while Wegg, young John Harmon, and Sloppy play other roles. As the dancer, the singer, the painter, and the drummer give "readings," so Boffin and John "read" Bella and Wegg, while the latter "misreads" Boffin. But Eugene's banter also reminds us of the literal meaning of "reading" and helps us to recognize the significance in this novel of the image and the idea of literacy. For Dickens' use of the motif of reading makes more credible Boffin's feigned degeneration, helps to test Mr. Venus and punish Wegg, and brings Lizzie closer to the patron of her literacy, Eugene. Although most of the virtuous characters seem to appreciate reading, relative illiteracy does not prevent Boffin from being an admirable man, nor does difficulty in reading handwritten script (I.xvi.204 and II.x.346-47) limit the merits of Mrs. Boffin and Mrs. Higden. On the other hand, mere literacy does not improve the moral natures of Wegg, Charley Hexam, Fledgeby, Podsnap, Veneering, and Headstone. Nevertheless, any tendency to romanticize ignorance is countered by the examples of Riderhood and Gaffer. Philip Collins may be justified in noting Dickens' suspicion of "educated and urban man," but he would seem to overextend that suspicion when he remarks, referring to all of Dickens' novels, ". . . none of his characters who have received much education, whether or not it has been shown in the book, enjoy a richer quality of life as a result."[35] If this comment is considered in relation to *Our Mutual Friend,* we may reply that admirable characters like Rokesmith and Lightwood reveal an alertness implicitly attributable to education, the virtuous Lizzie values learning, and worthy figures like Boffin and Mrs. Higden regret their lack of schooling (I.v.52; II.xiv.400) and attract the reader's sympathy with that regret. Moreover, for Lizzie education becomes a way of reducing class barriers and making more feasible her marriage with a barrister.

In dealing with literacy, Dickens avoids easy generalizations but certainly sees its worth. Inability to read is recognized as both a social stigma and an intellectual barrier, even though Dickens invariably considers heart more important than mind. Furthermore, implicit in **Our Mutual Friend** and in Dickens' other novels is the belief that, through reading, men's hearts as well as their minds may be reached and strengthened. In such betterment rests the reward for both the novelist and his public.

Notes

1. *Our Mutual Friend,* introd. Monroe Engel (New York: Modern Library, 1960), Bk. 3, ch. 10, p. 562. Citations in the text are to this edition and indicate book, chapter, and page.

2. For examples of illuminating discussions of money, dust, and the river, see Robert Morse, *"Our Mutual Friend"* in *The Dickens Critics,* ed. George H. Ford and Lauriat Lane, Jr. (Ithaca, N.Y.: Cornell Univ. Press, 1963), pp. 197-213 (reprint of essay originally published in *Partisan Review,* 16 [1949], 277-89); Edgar Johnson, *Charles Dickens: His Tragedy and Triumph,* 2 vols. (New York: Simon and Schuster, 1952), II, 1028-31, 1043-44; and J. Hillis Miller, *Charles Dickens: The World of His Novels* (Cambridge, Mass.: Harvard Univ. Press, 1958), pp. 294, 312. R. D. McMaster in "Birds of Prey: A Study of *Our Mutual Friend,"* *Dalhousie Review,* 40 (1960), 372-81, and Richard A. Lanham in *"Our Mutual Friend*: The Birds of Prey," *VN [Victorian Newsletter],* No. 24 (Fall 1963), pp. 6-12, stress predation, while Masao Miyoshi in "Resolution of Identity in *Our Mutual Friend,"* *VN,* No. 26 (Fall 1964), pp. 5-9, emphasizes crises of identity.

3. "A Note to *Our Mutual Friend,"* introduction to Engel's edition, p. xii. See also Montoe Engel's *The Maturity of Dickens* (Cambridge, Mass.: Harvard Univ. Press. 1959), pp. 135-37, and his "The Novel of Reality: An Illustrative Study of the Genesis, Method, and Intent of *Our Mutual Friend,"* Diss. Princeton University 1954, pp. 109-10, reproduced by University Microfilms.

4. See, besides Engel, John Manning, *Dickens on Education* (Toronto: Univ. of Toronto Press, 1959); Philip Collins, *Dickens and Education* (New York: St. Martin's Press. 1963); and Arnold Kettle, *"Our Mutual Friend"* in *Dickens and the Twentieth Century,* ed. John Gross and Gabriel Pearson (London: Routledge and Kegan Paul, 1962), pp. 216-17.

5. Later in the novel, in a variation of a metaphor that traditionally refers to a struggling writer rather than reader, the narrator remarks, "The adverse destinies ordained that one evening Mr. Wegg's labouring bark became beset by polysyllables, and embarrassed among a perfect archipelago of hard words" (III.xiv.596). Wegg himself subsequently compares his reading to waiting "like a set of skittles, to be set up and knocked over . . . by whatever balls—or

books—he [Boffin] chose to bring against me" (III.xiv.602) and later remarks that he has had to bear "the Roman yoke" (IV.iii.678), a metaphor associating his role with that of a beast of labor and the book (Gibbon's *Decline and Fall*) with a plow or cart to be pulled.

6. In *Great Expectations,* Joe Gargery takes pride in his ability to read the letters *J* and *O* (ch. 7).

7. T. W. Hill, "Notes to *Our Mutual Friend,"* *Dickensian,* 43 (1947), 85-90, 142-49, 206-12, who is, I believe, the only previous commentator to question Noddy's illiteracy, writes, "Mr. Boffin may have been uneducated but he must have been able to read to choose the books he later brought home for Wegg to read aloud; and it remains a puzzle how he could have known so much about the misers. . . ." (p. 88). But Boffin reveals that "the bookseller read . . . out of" one volume (III.vi.504), and we may perhaps assume that the bookseller also provided the rest of Boffin's information.

8. Edgar Johnson, II, 825, 827, cites two letters in which Dickens expresses Russophobia. See *The Letters of Charles Dickens,* ed. Walter Dexter, 3 vols. (Bloomsbury [London]: The Nonesuch Press, 1938), II, 615, 603, for these statements, written in 1855 and 1854; in subsequent notes I use *Letters* for Dexter's edition. Ada Nisbet, however, in her preface to *Dickens Centennial Essays* (Berkeley: Univ. of California Press, 1971), p. vii. quotes the novelist's angry assertion that "every miserable redtapist" is using the Crimean War as an excuse to ignore the need for "domestic reforms." Indeed, the war, because of its mismanagement by the English bureaucracy, served as a stimulus for *Little Dorrit,* as Dickens' preface to the 1857 edition of that novel indicates.

9. *Charles Dickens: An Introduction to His Novels* (New York: Random House, 1969), p. 38.

10. "Dickens and the Comedy of Humors," in *Experience in the Novel,* Selected Papers from the English Institute, ed. Roy Harvey Pearce (New York: Columbia Univ. Press, 1968), p. 64.

11. See *Letters,* III, 787. Dexter includes an appendix, "Dickens's Memorandum Book," in III, 785-96, but his transcript is incomplete and rearranged, as are those offered earlier by John Forster in *The Life of Charles Dickens* (Bk. 9, ch. 7: "Hints for Books Written and Unwritten, 1855-65"), II, 298-311, in the edition by A. J. Hoppé (London: Dent, 1966), and by Mrs. J. Comyns Carr in *Reminiscences,* ed. Eve Adam, 2nd ed. (London: Hutchinson, 1926), pp. 280-95 (ch. 21, "The Dickens Note-Book"). For one helpful description of these three transcripts, see Felix Aylmer, "John Forster and Dickens's Book of Memoranda," *Dickensian,* 51 (1954), 19-23; Ada Nisbet notes additional descriptions in *Victorian Fiction: A Guide to Research,* ed. Lionel Stevenson (Cambridge, Mass.: Harvard Univ. Press, 1964), p.

47, n. 4. The passage about the reading of Gibbon appears on p. 21 of the Memorandum Book, now in the New York Public Library's Berg Collection, to which I am indebted for permission to examine various entries. (Subsequent references to Forster are to Hoppé's edition.) Forster is responsible for considerable confusion, for, as Madeline House and Graham Storey point out in the preface to Volume I of the Pilgrim edition of *The Letters of Charles Dickens* (Oxford: Clarendon Press, 1965), p. xv, he "introduced, once more as if quoting letters to himself, early ideas for *Our Mutual Friend* and *Edwin Drood* which Dickens had noted down in his 'Book of Memoranda.'" The edition of the Memorandum Book now being prepared by K. J. Fielding will probably be the first reliable published version.

12. Forster, II, 301.

13. See Miller, p. 296; Engel, *The Maturity of Dickens*, p. 137; McMaster, p. 374; Earle Davis, *The Flint and the Flame: The Artistry of Charles Dickens* (Columbia: Univ. of Missouri Press, 1963), p. 273; and Kenneth Muir, "Image and Structure in *Our Mutual Friend*" in *Essays and Studies Collected for the English Association*, N.S., 19 (1966), 92-105 (see p. 101). Doris B. Kelly, "A Check List of Nineteenth-Century English Fiction about the Decline of Rome," *BNYPL*, [72 (1968), 400-413, states that many nineteenth-century novels "make use of the decline and fall for their historical background," partly because this setting "gave writers opportunities to draw parallels between ancient Rome and modern England" (p. 400).

14. T. W. Hill, "Books That Dickens Read," *Dickensian*, 45 (1949), 81-90, 201-7, makes such a claim (p. 86), as does Edgar Johnson, II, 1131. Dickens did own a copy of the *Decline and Fall,* in eight volumes, the size of the edition purchased by Boffin (I.v.54). See J. H. Stonehouse, ed., *Catalogues of the Libraries of Charles Dickens and W. M. Thackeray* (London: Piccadilly Fountain Press, 1935), p. 50.

15. *MP* [*Modern Philology*], 42 (1944), 96-122. See esp. p. 103. I am indebted to the Pierpont Morgan Library, which now owns the holograph manuscript of *Our Mutual Friend,* for permission to verify Boll's transcript of the working notes bound in with that manuscript.

16. *The Dickens World,* 2nd ed. (London: Oxford Univ. Press, 1965), p. 169.

17. See Stonehouse, pp. 7, 19, 68, 80, and 118. The actual title of Caulfield's work is *Portraits, Memoirs, and Characters, of Remarkable Persons,* 4 vols. (London: T. H. Whitely, 1819-20); of Henry Wilson's, *Wonderful Characters,* 3 vols. (London: Albion Press, 1821). Dickens owned 104 volumes of the *Annual Register,* evidently the complete set of the original series, running from 1758 through 1862 (not from 1748 through 1860, the dates in the cata-

logue Stonehouse reprints), with volume 27 covering two years (1784-85). Boffin and Bella carry home only about forty-eight volumes, even though Noddy supposedly purchases "a whole set" (III.v.486), and even though *Our Mutual Friend* is placed in the 1860's—in "these times of ours" (I.i.2). Hill, in "Books That Dickens Read," p. 201, maintains that all of the texts used by Wegg and Boffin were in Dickens' library, but although three of the books read before the accounts of misers (the works by Gibbon, Plutarch, and Charles Rollin) are listed by Stonehouse (pp. 50, 93, 98), Josephus' *Wars of the Jews* is not. For descriptions of the books used by Boffin, see Hill, "Notes to *Our Mutual Friend,*" pp. 147-49. The titles listed by the narrator (III.v.486), "Lives of eccentric personages," "Anecdotes of strange characters," "Records of remarkable individuals," seem generic rather than specific and apparently refer to works like *The Lives of Eminent & Remarkable Characters, Born or Long Resident in the Counties of Essex, Suffolk, & Norfolk* (London, 1820); although the latter is not listed by Stonehouse, Dickens was, of course, not confined to the volumes he owned. Moreover, the catalogue reprinted by Stonehouse includes only books found in Dickens' library after his death.

18. See F. Somner Merryweather, *Lives and Anecdotes of Misers* (London, 1850), pp. 8-10, 89, 105, and 109. Another possibility is that Wegg glanced at the chapter titles and headlines on p. 52 or 53 (Overs), 71 (Little), and 86 (Jarret), then skipped to p. 129 or 133 (Elwes), and then went back to pp. 90-91 ("The Rev. Mr. Jones, / The Miser of Blewbury"), 105 (Vulture Hopkins), and 109 or 110 (Dancer).

19. Dickens may have read of Dancer's food-warming technique in Wilson's *Wonderful Characters,* II, 49. The novelist previously showed interest in Dancer and Elwes in *Bleak House* (ch. 39).

20. See Merryweather, pp. 109-28, 129-41, 145-48, 154-55, and 165-66, esp. pp. 109, 127-28, and 165-66. Merryweather's sources may have included the *Annual Register*—see, e.g., the accounts of Elizabeth Wilcocks and the Jardine brothers, found, respectively, in volume 11, . . . *For the Year 1768* (London, 1768), p. 118 in the "Chronicle" section, and volume 10, . . . *For the Year 1767* (London, 1768), pp. 100-101 in the "Chronicle" section. Hill, "Notes to *Our Mutual Friend,*" pp. 148-49, is, I believe, the only commentator to call attention to the fact that Dickens owned the various works concerning misers and quoted extensively from Merryweather and Kirby. McMaster, p. 381, n. 11, observes that Dickens owned the text by Merryweather, but offers no further comment.

21. See R. S. Kirby, *Kirby's Wonderful and Eccentric Museum; or, Magazine of Remarkable Characters* . . . (London: R. S. Kirby, 1820), IV, 99-100.

22. Ibid., IV, 29-37, 97-99.

23. See E. Salter Davies' introduction to the edition of *Our Mutual Friend* in the New Oxford Illustrated Dickens (London: Oxford Univ. Press, 1963), p. viii.

24. See "No Change of Intention in *Our Mutual Friend*," *Dickensian*, 63 (1967), 37-40.

25. Miyoshi, p. 8.

26. This talent and also Sloppy's ability to sleep standing are later used in frustrating Wegg (IV.xiv.809). Cf. Lizzie's rescue of Eugene by the use of skills acquired in earlier days (IV.vi.723-24). T. S. Eliot's manuscript of *The Waste Land,* only recently discovered, reveals that Mrs. Higden's remark about Sloppy, "He do the Police in different voices," served as the working title for that poem. See Donald Gallup, "The 'Lost' Manuscripts of T. S. Eliot," *BNYPL,* 72 (1968), 641-52, a revision of an article appearing in *TLS* [*Times Literary Supplement*], 7 Nov. 1968, pp. 1238-40. For comments on the significance intended by Eliot and on Sloppy's intelligence, see the correspondence in *TLS* by Thomas and Brian Kelly (9 Jan. 1969, p. 38, and 6 Mar. 1969, p. 242), Douglas Hewitt (23 Jan. 1969, p. 86; 13 Feb. 1969, p. 158; and 20 Mar. 1969, p. 299), and D. A. N. Jones (30 Jan. 1969, p. 110).

27. McMaster, p. 381, n. 8, refers to Henry Mayhew's *London Labour and the London Poor,* 4 vols. (London: Griffin, Bohn, 1861-62), II, 147-50, and suggests "Dickens might have derived Hexam's hatred of learning from Henry Mayhew's description of the defiant ignorance of dredgers." Harland S. Nelson in "Dickens's *Our Mutual Friend* and Henry Mayhew's *London Labour and the London Poor,*" *NCF* [*Nineteenth-Century Literature*], 20 (1965), 207-22, observes, p. 211, n. 5, that he had independently reached the same view. For an interesting comparison, see Joseph H. Gardner's "Gaffer Hexam and Pap Finn," *MP,* 66 (1968), 155-56.

28. Cf. Louisa Gradgrind, another devoted sister, who also looks at the fire and tries to envision the future (*Hard Times,* Bk. 1, chs. 8, 14; Bk. 3, ch. 9).

29. Hill, "Notes to *Our Mutual Friend,*" p. 210, suggests that the volume used by Bella may be *The British Housewife* (London, 1790) or *The British Housekeeper* (London, 1843), but the former is a very short work (72 pages), while the latter, more accurately called *The British Housekeeper's Statement of Cash* (compiled by "J. K."), seems mainly concerned with domestic economy. Dickens was perhaps thinking of some lengthy work, real or imaginary, like E. Smith's 400-page *The Complete Housewife* (London, 1773) or *The Book of Household Management,* ed. Isabella Mary Beeton (London: S. O. Beeton, 1861), a very popular 1,112-page guide, recently reissued in a facsimile edition (New York: Farrar, Straus, and Giroux, 1969).

30. For material on the Victorians' attitudes towards literacy and their intense responses to private and public reading, see such standard works as Amy Cruse, *The Victorians and Their Books* (London: Allen and Unwin, 1935); Richard Altick, *The English Common Reader: A Social History of the Mass Reading Public, 1800-1900* (Chicago: Univ. of Chicago Press, 1957); R. K. Webb, "The Victorian Reading Public" in *From Dickens to Hardy,* vol. 6 in *The Pelican Guide to English Literature,* ed. Boris Ford (Baltimore, Md.: Penguin Books, 1958); and Louis James, *Fiction for the Working Man, 1830-1850* (London/New York: Oxford Univ. Press, 1963). A useful warning about the difficulty of assessing Victorian literacy appears in G. S. R. Kitson Clark's *An Expanding Society: Britain, 1830-1900* (London/New York: Cambridge Univ. Press, 1967), pp. 88-90. See, too, Guinevere L. Griest, *Mudie's Circulating Library and the Victorian Novel* (Bloomington: Indiana Univ. Press, 1970).

31. J. Hillis Miller, "Three Problems of Fictional Form: First-Person Narration in *David Copperfield* and *Huckleberry Finn*" in *Experience in the Novel,* suggests, p. 30, that stories-within-stories and multiple narrators may produce an effect that "parallels the effect of the play within the play in Renaissance drama." But see, too, Maynard Mack's "Engagement and Detachment in Shakespeare's plays." in *Essays on Shakespeare and Elizabethan Drama in Honor of Hardin Craig,* ed. Richard Hosley (Columbia: Univ. of Missouri Press, 1962), pp. 275-96, for the idea that a play-within-a-play both increases realism and, paradoxically, reminds us that the work is fictive, "an artful composition" (p. 281).

32. Steven Marcus. *Dickens: From Pickwick to Dombey* (New York: Basic Books, 1965), pp. 20-22, cogently rejects the view, largely attributable to George Henry Lewes, that Dickens lacked real interest in literature. For various other opinions on Dickens' reading, see Kathleen Tillotson, "Writers and Readers in 1851" in Geoffrey and Kathleen Tillotson, *Mid-Victorian Studies* (London: Athlone Press, 1965), p. 309; Sylvère Monod's "Dickens' Culture" in *Dickens the Novelist* (Norman: Univ. of Oklahoma Press, 1968), pp. 30-46; Philip Collins, "Dickens's Reading," *Dickensian,* 60 (1964), 136-51; and Hill, "Books That Dickens Read."

33. See Mrs. J. Comyns Carr, p. 290, quoting from p. 6 of the Memorandum Book, and Forster, II, 291 (see n. 11 above for a warning about Forster's reliability).

34. See Boll, p. 113. After examining Dickens' original notes, I have emended Boll's reading from "hidden wiles" to "hidden wills."

35. Collins, *Dickens and Education,* pp. 193-94.

Jennifer Gribble (essay date 1975)

SOURCE "Depth and Surface in *Our Mutual Friend*," in *Essays in Criticism,* Vol. 25, No. 2, April, 1975, pp. 197-214.

[*In the following essay, Gribble suggests that the character of Eugene Wrayburn represents Dickens's interest in the conflict between individual identity and the social persona required by a repressive Victorian society.*]

A note from Dickens to Forster in 1861 suggests the genesis of *Our Mutual Friend*:

> —a man, young and perhaps eccentric, feigning to be dead, and *being* dead to all intents and purposes external to himself, and for years retaining the singular view of life and character so imparted, would be a good leading incident for a story.[1]

Readers of the story have generally agreed that the incident of John Harmon's feigned death is little more than a mechanical plot device. But the note to Forster points as well to what, in the completed novel, becomes its greatest strength. In the curious uncongenial figure of Eugene Wrayburn, also a young man 'feigning to be dead, and *being* dead to all intents and purposes external to himself', Dickens explores more compellingly than ever before something that continued to fascinate him. In the imaginative world of *Our Mutual Friend,* Eugene experiences most fully its central problem: a social identity at odds with deeper promptings.[2] The quality of the novel's engagement with this impasse is such as to directly challenge the view that for Dickens 'identity was behaviour'[3] and invariably remained so.

Of course the preoccupation of *Our Mutual Friend* with identity is not consistently impressive. At its most notional, it is the source of the novel's obvious weaknesses. Mr. Boffin's 'change of heart' is as sentimental as John Harmon's change of identity is diagrammatic; Dickens cannot embody in Lizzie Hexam a sufficiently convincing source of Eugene Wrayburn's change of heart (hence the evasive retreat to the simplest operation of the novel's symbolism, which confers on him a watery regeneration); while the sentimentality that gathers around such things as Bella's change of heart, the Boffins' good heartedness, and the struggles of Betty Higden, gestures feebly and often embarrassingly towards Dickens's feeling for what is noble in human nature.

Nor do I want to discount the novel's oppressive atmosphere, which suffuses Dickens's habitual comic delight with the sardonic and the grotesque, and which is unrelieved by the kind of humane consciousness that is characteristic of other Dickens novels. Eugene represents a very different kind of humanity from David Copperfield or Arthur Clennam, and there is certainly no Little Dorrit. The extremity of Eugene's condition, and the radical experiment John Harmon undertakes, indicate a world more than usually hostile to all that is spontaneous, genuine, and creative in the self. People are variously compelled (with varying degrees of artistic success) to act out dissembling roles, ranging from Boffin's impersonation of the miser and the too long-suffering Riah's acceptance of the manipulating Fledgeby's identity, to the Lammles' grimly comic pretence of a happy and prosperous marriage, Bradley Headstone's sheltering in the disguise of Rogue Riderhood, and Charlie Hexam's drive to create a 'self' that answers to his ideals of social respectability. Human lives are transformed by dust and drowning or veneered into highly polished objects. Furthermore, the labours and the arts by which the self is expressed and known are felt to be the antithesis of all that is creative. Mr. Boffin, caretaker of the mounds of dust, Miss Pleasant at her 'leavings' trade, Jenny the doll's dressmaker, lovingly recreating the preenings of 'society', Riderhood and Hexam, fishing for human bodies, Mr. Venus, articulating new bodies out of old, act out the process imaged in the mounds of dust, of a society living off its own waste.

Such distortions help to explain why *Our Mutual Friend* has been dismissed as the work of an exhausted Dickens.[4] But if the weariness, even cynicism, of the novel's vision makes for strained and flat writing, it takes on a very different quality in the study of Eugene. There, the exploration of weariness and cynicism is paradoxically energetic, and a clear sign of Dickens's extended interest in those depths of the personality suppressed by Victorian civilization. Eugene has in him something of both Arthur Clennam and Henry Gowan, those contrasting studies in *Little Dorrit,* where significance lies almost as much in likeness as in dissimilarity. In Eugene, the impulse towards Clennam's type of self-questioning about the purpose of his life is continually countered by Gowan's self-assured defensiveness—the manner of the bored dilettante, too confirmed in cynicism to question anything: 'You know what I am, my dear Mortimer. You know how dreadfully susceptible I am to boredom. You know that when I become enough of a man to find myself an embodied conundrum, I bored myself to the last degree by trying to find out what I meant.' (II. 6) (p. 338-9). Eugene's dilemma, and its origins, are here rendered in the effete cadences of an engaging and empty gentility circumscribing every impulse towards openness. In bringing Eugene to confront a self he can't acknowledge, Dickens responds to a challenge much stronger than that suggested by the rather mechanically plotted connections between John Harmon's drowned self and his assumed identity.

Dickens's previous novels show a recurring interest in the alter ego: Sidney Carton sacrifices his own life to preserve in Charles Darnay the embodiment of a more worthy self, and even the redeemed Pip seems to have been 'paid for' by the puzzling Orlick.[5] *Great Expectations* suggests Dickens's growing awareness of the costs of that muted gentility he liked to give his heroes. And yet, in the case of both Pip, and Arthur Clennam in *Little Dorrit,* the movement towards an acceptable and settled place in society seems to tame deeper, more anarchic impulses merely hinted at. *Our Mutual Friend,* however, starts from the recognition that 'Society' suppresses spontaneous assertion of the self. No alter ego siphons off Eugene Wrayburn's upsurges of ruthlessness and passion. They are felt as manifestations of an intransigent if 'buried self' within him.

Dickens's insight into Eugene's social identity is acute. Eugene is apparently as dead as he feigns to be, 'buried alive in the back of his armchair' at the start of the novel. No figure of comparable interest in all Dickens develops so remarkably out of the caricaturing mode in which Dickens normally celebrates artistically what he regards as morally unregenerate states of being. Like the other diners at the Veneering table, Eugene is very much at home in a setting where existence is simply a matter of endlessly reflecting highly polished surfaces. Even when he talks intimately with his friend Mortimer about the purposelessness of their lives and their uselessness as lawyers, a certain ritualized quality in the conversation suggests postures of boredom and disaffection that are mutually sustained and acquiescent. Their accepting the ready-made social identity handed out by the Veneerings or by their own families, entails a degree of self-caricature but no very profound self-questioning. On the contrary, Eugene performs himself before poor innocent Mr. Boffin in a way that appears to reaffirm that self. Boffin ventures to enquire how Eugene likes the law:

> 'A—not particularly', returned Eugene.

> 'Too dry for you, eh? Well, I suppose it wants some years of sticking to, before you master it. But there's nothing like work. Look at the bees.'

> 'I beg your pardon', returned Eugene, with a reluctant smile, 'but will you excuse my mentioning that I always protest against being referred to the bees? . . . Conceding for a moment that there is any analogy between a bee and a man in a shirt and pantaloons (which I deny), and that it is settled that the man is to learn from the bee (which I also deny), the question still remains, what is he to learn? To imitate? Or to avoid? When your friends the bees worry themselves to that highly fluttered extent about their sovereign, and become perfectly distracted touching the slightest monarchical movement, are we men to learn the greatness of Tuft-hunting, or the littleness of the Court Circular? I am not clear, Mr. Boffin, but that the hive may be satirical.'

> 'At all events, they work,' said Mr. Boffin.

> 'Ye—es,' returned Eugene, disparagingly, 'they work; but don't you think they overdo it? They work so much more than they need—they make so much more than they can eat—they are so incessantly boring and buzzing at their one idea till Death comes upon them—that don't you think they overdo it? And are human labourers to have no holidays, because of the bees? And am I never to have change of air, because the bees don't? Mr. Boffin, I think honey excellent at breakfast; but regarded in the light of my conventional schoolmaster and moralist, I protest against the tyrannical humbug of your friend the bee . . .'.

(I. 9) (p. 138-9)

Eugene's accelerating rhetoric shows that Dickens, too, is warming to his theme. Garis rightly emphasizes Dickens's love of a performance (he enjoyed the performance of lawyers from **Pickwick** on) and here he clearly enjoys tilting at social darwinism and mocking Boffin's simple unquestioning industry. However, the performance is offered not just as a performance but as an insight. Stung out of his moral inertia, Eugene can be an engaging presence. He can even be bothered to defend himself: here, defensiveness rapidly moves through irritation to that devastating, self-protective politeness. But while he enjoys that movement, Dickens also has an ear for something brittle in the wit, for something in the energies released that is in excess of the object. Eugene's quickness and imagination can find no more adequate fulfilment than putting down his intellectual and social inferiors. His training in the legal profession simply gives him the fluency to throw off easy burlesques of that or any other kind of work.

Dickens here raises, with striking ease and tact, important questions about the possibilities this society offers for genuine self-definition and growth. If Boffin is in the end too simple a target for Eugene's cynicism, Bradley Headstone is a more formidable spokesman for honest industry. Headstone and his pupil Charlie Hexam establish the novel's serious interest in the sort of social thinking that Eugene parodies. Headstone presents himself to Eugene as one who is raising himself 'in the scale of society' by his own efforts, and he prompts in Eugene a far more deadly, cool, and compulsive display of class superiority:

> 'You think me of no more value than the dirt under your feet,' said Bradley to Eugene, speaking in a carefully weighed and measured tone, or he could not have spoken at all.

> 'I assure you, Schoolmaster,' replied Eugene, 'I don't think about you.'

> 'That's not true,' returned the other; 'you know better.'

> 'That's coarse,' Eugene retorted; 'but you *don't* know better.'

> 'Mr. Wrayburn, at least I know very well that it would be idle to set myself against you in insolent words or overbearing manners. That lad who has just gone out could put you to shame in half-a-dozen branches of knowledge in half an hour, but you can throw him aside like an inferior. You can do as much by me, I have no doubt, beforehand.'

> 'Possibly,' remarked Eugene.

> 'But I am more than a lad,' said Bradley, with his clutching hand, 'and I *WILL* be heard sir.'

> 'As a schoolmaster,' said Eugene, 'you are always being heard. That ought to content you.'

> 'But it does not content me,' replied the other, white with passion. 'Do you suppose that a man, in forming himself for the duties I discharge, and in watching and repressing himself daily to discharge them well, dismisses a man's nature?'

'I suppose you,' said Eugene, 'judging from what I see as I look at you, to be rather too passionate for a good schoolmaster.' As he spoke, he tossed away the end of his cigar.

'Passionate with you, sir, I admit I am. Passionate with you, sir, I respect myself for being. But I have not Devils for my pupils.'

'For your Teachers, I should rather say,' replied Eugene.

'Mr. Wrayburn.'

'Schoolmaster.'

'Sir, my name is Bradley Headstone.'

'As you firstly said, my good sir, your name cannot concern me. Now, what more?'

'This more. Oh, what a misfortune is mine,' cried Bradley, breaking off to wipe the starting perspiration from his face as he shook from head to foot, 'that I cannot so control myself as to appear a stronger creature that this, when a man who has not felt in all his life what I have felt in a day can so command himself!' He said it in a very agony, and even followed it with an errant motion of his hands as if he could have torn himself.

Eugene Wrayburn looked on at him, as if he found him beginning to be rather an entertaining study.

(II. 6) (p. 344-5)

The effects of the given social identity—'schoolmaster', 'lawyer'—are sharply registered. Bradley Headstone's efforts towards social respectability, 'watching and repressing himself daily', have dammed up all that breaks loose here, in the clutching hands. Eugene's goading, performed with a self-command that we feel to be hateful, instantly penetrates the rigorous habits of command that Bradley Headstone has won in the classroom. But the self-assured lawyer's logic and upper-class superiority are as much signs of Eugene's deep malaise as they are the evidence of his coolness—'a man who has not felt in all his life what I have felt in a day'. Our sympathies ebb and flow until the final irony makes itself felt: just such an astutely deployed social identity has been Bradley Headstone's goal, as it is the goal of Society at large in *Our Mutual Friend*. Bradley's ambitions are exactly like those of Eugene's father, who produces not sons and brothers, but 'heir', 'pillar of the church', 'barrister', 'circumnavigator' and 'mechanical genius' (I. 12) (p. 193-4) in that order.

The bitter hostility between Eugene and Headstone begins to take on the aspect of a strange kinship: 'there was some secret, sure perception between them, which set them against one another in all ways' (II. 6) (p. 341). Locked together in enmity, each draws from the other feelings and forces that neither of them has ever before recognized. 'No man knows till the time comes what depths are within him', Headstone says (II. 15) (p. 454). It is one of the most striking insights of the novel that Lizzie Hexam, ostensible cause of the men's rivalry, should fade into insignificance as the bizarre relationship between her two lov-

ers develops. Although the novel clearly wishes to suggest that, for Eugene, the feelings brought alive in him by Lizzie at last create a more worthwhile self, it also strongly and more interestingly implies that such feelings, since they are usually ignored or suppressed, take on anarchic and perverted forms. Neither of the lovers feels his passion for Lizzie as a spontaneous or freely developing thing, but as something wrung out of him, and violently destructive:

'You draw me to you. If I were shut up in a strong prison, you would draw me out. I should break through the wall to come to you.'

(II. 15) (p. 454)

Such bareness of speech expressing such intensity of feeling is rare in the nineteenth-century novel, and certainly rare in Dickens. Headstone's intensity here comes in part from frustrated energies: the need to share with Lizzie his hard-won respectability is baffled by a feeling for her that robs his respectability of its meaning, annihilating all that he has made himself. Eugene's compulsive feeling for Lizzie does make him speak with a new directness and humility:

'You don't know how you haunt me and bewilder me. You don't know how the cursed carelessness that is over-officious in helping me at every other turning of my life, won't help me here.'

(IV. 6) (p. 760)

But like his rival, he experiences that passion as something baffling and uncreative: he can neither approve, nor disregard the social assumptions that make marriage to 'a waterman's daughter' impossible.

It isn't just that the feelings are denied their appropriate fulfilment. They are confused and perverted in their very origin and the form in which they actually find expression suggests neurotic complicity. The rival lovers begin to play out their mutual tormenting in a strange nocturnal chase. Night after night, Bradley Headstone and Eugene Wrayburn pursue each other through a clandestine London, dark and labyrinthine, quite dissociated from the daytime life of social surface and activity. Bradley Headstone, 'tied up all day with his disciplined show upon him . . . he broke loose at night like an ill-tamed wild animal', is engaged in 'a kind of perverse pleasure akin to that which a sick man sometimes has in irritating a wound upon his body' (III. 11) (p. 609). For Eugene, too, 'the pleasures of the chase' are diabolical. Mortimer's questions about the state of his feelings and his intentions have been met with the usual poses—'I have no design whatever, I am incapable of designs. If I conceived a design I should speedily abandon it, exhausted by the operation' (III. 10) (p. 348). Incapable of meaningful action or decision, Eugene has to live off Bradley Headstone's wild energies. He describes to Mortimer how he goads the schoolmaster to madness:

'I make the schoolmaster so ridiculous, and so aware of being made ridiculous, that I see him chafe and fret at every pore when we cross one another. The amiable occupation has been the solace of my life, since I was baulked in the manner unnecessary to recall. I have derived inexpressible comfort from it. I do it thus: I stroll out after dark, stroll a little way, look in at a window and furtively look out for the schoolmaster. Sooner or later I perceive the schoolmaster on the watch; sometimes accompanied by his hopeful pupil; oftener pupilless. Having made sure of his watching me, I tempt him on, all over London. One night I go east, another night north, in a few nights I go all round the compass. Sometimes, I walk; sometimes, I proceed in cabs, draining the pocket of the schoolmaster, who then follows in cabs. I study and get up abstruse No Thoroughfares in the course of the day. With Venetian mystery I seek those No Thoroughfares at night, glide into them by means of dark courts, tempt the schoolmaster to follow, turn suddenly, and catch him before he can retreat. Then we face one another, and I pass him as unaware of his existence, and he undergoes grinding torments. Similarly, I walk at a great pace down a short street, rapidly turn the corner, and, getting out of his view, as rapidly turn back. I catch him coming on post, again pass him as unaware of his existence, and again he undergoes grinding torments. Night after night his disappointment is acute, but hope springs eternal in the scholastic breast, and he follows me again tomorrow. . . .'

'This is an extraordinary story,' observed Lightwood, who heard it out with serious attention. 'I don't like it.'

(III. 10) (p. 605)

What interests Dickens is the way in which this performance reveals the detached self as unable to sustain its disengagement. The blasé tone can't conceal a rising excitement that makes Eugene as much prey as he is hunter. Indeed the antagonists seem to become more and more, each for the other, a substitute for the desired but thwarting mistress. Eugene can be fully articulate about what he does, and its calculated effects; but he is unable to reckon with those involuntary promptings that the writing evokes—sadistic, foolhardy, suicidal—nor to see in his 'object' what we see:

Looking like the hunted, but not the hunter: baffled, worn, with the exhaustion of deferred hope and consuming hate and anger in his face, white-lipped, wild-eyed, draggle-haired, seamed with jealousy and anger, and torturing himself with the conviction that he showed it all and they exalted in it, he went by them in the dark like a haggard head suspended in the air: so completely did the force of his expression cancel his figure.

(III. 10) (p. 608)

In this context, the culmination of Bradley's murderous passion in the attack on Eugene has its inevitable rightness. But it also has the effect of blurring what Dickens wants to show in Eugene, the discovery of a self that is not façade, but which seeks expression in direct speech and honest feelings. Just before the climactic attack, Dickens attempts, in Eugene's conversation with Lizzie, and the self-catechism that follows it (IV. 6) (pp. 759-766),

what Garis supposes to be 'the norm for serious art . . . the dramatization of moral choice in the inner life of the individual human consciousness'.[6] But the degree of stiffness in Eugene's 'thinking aloud' betrays Dickens's lack of confidence and interest in that mode of revelation. And the outcome is that Eugene's 'choice' is made for him by the turn of events.

Nevertheless, the study of Eugene Wrayburn, and the revelation of the 'inner life' his social surface glosses over is certainly 'serious art'. The depths are made to illumine the surface: the poise with which Dickens confronts what is obnoxious in Eugene comes from an understanding of the depths of his nature and how it has been formed by the superficial 'Society' in which he lives.

Since in the world which Eugene inhabits the depths are hidden, people become unnaturally watchful, uneasily conspiratorial. The strained, alert watchfulness of the Hexams in the opening chapter recurs again and again: Silas Wegg's sly vigilance, Bella's earnest studying of Mr. Boffin's changing face, Eugene's detached contemplation of the drunken Mr. Dolls crossing a road, the Lammles' appraising looks, all evoke a world in which people present themselves to each other as objects of scrutiny. In the second chapter, Dickens's scrutiny of social surface is as quickly glancing as it is comic. The diners at the Veneering table are as dead as the corpses for which the Hexams peer into the river. But the gaze that surveys the reflections thrown out by the Veneering mirror is as lively and relevant in its notations as its subjects are fixed and dead: 'Reflects charming old Lady Tippins on Veneering's right; with an immense obtuse drab oblong face, like a face in a tablespoon, and a dyed Long Walk up to the top of her head, as a convenient public approach to the bunch of false hair behind . . .' (I. 2) (p. 53). Society has conspired with the *nouveau-riche* Veneerings to accept them as its centre—Lady Tippins is to go campaigning for Veneering's seat in Parliament; 'the fun of it is that nobody knows who these Veneerings are, and that they know nobody, and that they have a house out of the Tales of the Genii, and give dinners out of the Arabian Nights' (I. 3) (p. 301). Further, Society agrees to be the Veneerings' 'dearest friends', to the puzzlement of honest Twemlow, uncertain whether he is Veneering's oldest friend or newest friend.

With Lady Tippins, the Podsnaps, the Veneerings, the comic liveliness comes from Dickens's characteristic ear for the gross insincerities of 'the language of society' and his eye for the magical transforming power of material possessions. But this veneering is not just observed—it is dramatized as a process, dynamic and self-perpetuating. The sustained comedy of Book I, Chapter 10, 'A Marriage Comedy', celebrates the great social *coup* of the Veneerings in bringing together in marriage 'the mature young lady' and 'the mature young gentleman' of the opening dinner party. The wedding ceremony is a lavish display of *nouveau-richesse* masquerading as 'a family affair', in which the worthy Twemlow, in the presence of other oldest and dearest friends and a hoard of 'pokey unknowns', gives away the bride. The 'contract' simply ratifies the Veneering game of conferring identity and relationships. (It has its obvious connections with the marriage plans made for Eugene by his father, in which Eugene, labelled "'ELIGIBLE, ON VIEW'", is to court an unknown young lady, similarly labelled.) (I. 12) (p. 194). The mature young couple, mutually-deceiving fortune hunters, are themselves willing conspirators. The contract is seen through by sharp Lady Tippins on the one hand, who privately notes 'Bride, five-and-forty if a day, thirty shillings a yard, veil fifteen pound, pocket-handkerchief a present' (I. 10) (p. 163), and on the other by Twemlow, who can recall social relationships based on genuine feeling, and who is assailed by tremors of tenderness for 'the adorable bridesmaid'. As the jollification reaches its climax, the indispensable things said and done, Lady Tippins declining into insensibility, the brass bands and spectators assembled to send the couple on their nuptual journey, the melancholy Analytical falls victim to a heavy shoe, cast after the couple by a Buffer in the hall, 'as an auspicious omen' (I. 10) (p. 167).

The acceleration of sham and humbug into a bathetic comeuppance is familiar enough in Dickens. But in the subsequent progress of the Lammles, Dickens's imaginative touches are of a striking and less predictable kind. The couple, honeymooning on the Isle of Wight, are viewed first not in mutual recrimination, but as superficial impressions on the very sand:

> Mr. and Lammle have walked for some time on the Shanklin sands, and one may see by their footprints that they have not walked arm in arm, and that they have not walked in a straight track; and that they have walked in a moody humour; for, the lady has prodded little spirting holes in the damp sand before her with her parasol, and the gentleman has trailed his stick after him. As if he were of the Mephistopheles family indeed, and had walked with a drooping tail.
>
> (I. 10) (p. 168)

We're made to take the Lammles on their own terms: reduced to scrutinizing the surface they present to the world, but prevented from accepting it by the intimations of the little spirting holes and the drooping tail. Wryness deepens into a more sardonic awareness of what the surface hides:

> There was a mirror on the wall before them, and her eyes just caught him smirking in it. She gave the reflected image a look of the deepest disdain, and the image received it in the glass. Next moment they quietly eyed each other, as if they, the principals, had had no part in that expressive transaction.
>
> (II. 4) (p. 312)

This deftly catches their habit of giving and receiving a reflected self—a habit traced out in the juxtaposition of their public and private conversations—and touches on the recurring habit of watchfulness in the novel as a whole.

The Lammles rapidly discover the true meaning of their contract. It makes them keep up the identity they have offered to each other and the world. As 'young people' of property, charmingly in love, they are initiated into the procedures by which Society is kept up, which entail their deceiving others as they themselves have been deceived— 'always looking at palatial residences in the best situations and always very nearly taking or buying one', and scheming to marry off Fascination Fledgeby, 'of an excellent family and rich' to Georgiana Podsnap, now Mrs. Lammles' 'dearest friend'. Chapter 4 of Book II, 'Cupid Prompted', describes their efforts with the lovers, and relates them to their efforts with each other. The high point is a visit to the Opera:

> They sat in this order: Mrs. Lammle, Fascination Fledgeby, Georgiana, Mr. Lammle. Mrs. Lammle made leading remarks to Fledgeby, only requiring monosyllabic replies. Mr. Lammle did the like with Georgiana. At times Mrs. Lammle would lean forward to address Mr. Lammle to this purpose. 'Alfred, my dear, Mr. Fledgeby very justly says, apropos of the last scene, that true constancy would not require any such stimulant as the stage deems necessary.' To which Mr. Lammle would reply, 'Ay, Sophronia, my love, but as Georgiana has observed to me, the lady had no sufficient reason to know the state of the gentleman's affections'. To which Mrs. Lammle would rejoin, 'Very true, Alfred; but Mr. Fledgeby points out,' this. To which Alfred would demur: 'Undoubtedly, Sophronia, but Georgiana acutely remarks,' that. Through this device the two young people conversed at great length and committed themselves to a variety of delicate sentiments, without having once opened their lips, save to say yes or no, and even that not to one another.

> Fledgeby took his leave of Miss Podsnap at the carriage door, and the Lammles dropped her at her own home, and on the way Mrs. Lammle archly rallied her, in her fond and protecting manner, by saying at intervals, 'Oh little Georgiana, little Georgiana!' Which was not much; but the tone added, 'You have enslaved your Fledgeby'.

> And thus the Lammles got home at last, and the lady sat down moody and weary, looking at her dark lord engaged in a deed of violence with a bottle of soda-water as though he were wringing the neck of some unlucky creature and pouring its blood down his throat. As he wiped his dripping whiskers in an ogreish way, he met her eyes, and pausing, said, with no very gentle voice:

> 'Well?'

> 'Was such an absolute Booby necessary to the purpose?'

> 'I know what I am doing. He is no such dolt as you suppose.'

> 'A genius, perhaps?'

> 'You sneer, perhaps; and you take a lofty air upon yourself, perhaps! But I tell you this:—when that young fellow's interest is concerned, he holds as tight as a horse-leech. When money is in question with that young fellow, he is a match for the Devil.'

> 'Is he a match for you?'

'He is. Almost as good a one as you thought me for you. He has no quality of youth in him, but such as you have seen to-day. Touch him upon money, and you touch no booby then. He really is a dolt, I suppose, in other things; but it answers his one purpose very well.'

'Has she money in her own right in any case?'

'Ay! she has money in her own right in any case. You have done so well to-day, Sophronia, that I answer the question, though you know I object to any such questions. You have done so well to-day, Sophronia, that you must be tired. Get to bed.'

(II. 4) (pp. 318-9)

This chapter begins by noting that 'to use the cold language of the world, Mrs. Alfred Lammle rapidly improved the acquaintance of Miss Podsnap. To use the warm language of Mrs. Lammle, she and her sweet Georgiana soon became one: in heart, in mind, in sentiment, in soul' (p. 306). There is a difference, but no real distinction, between these two forms of Society's language (as Lady Tippins's conversations remind us), the formal and the effusive being alternative ways of covering up any real feelings. Here, the passage is quoted in full because it shows how flexibly the Lammles deploy the language of Society, whether cold or warm, while making us aware of feelings the language doesn't take account of. The Lammles' formal, public conversation, artfully masquerading as the more intimate exchange between the unfortunate 'lovers', indicates in fact their own private complicity; the innuendoes of Sophronia's private exchange with Georgiana craftily hint at a public announcement and a formal commitment, yet the too-gushing warmth isn't entirely inconsistent with the concern for Georgiana that emerges in Sophronia's conversation with Alfred. A great deal of direct communication takes place, and yet the most naked feelings—Sophronia's kindness, her fear and loathing of her husband, and Alfred's sadistic cruelty—are held in check by a practised formality of utterance. The scene penetrates one by one the layers of social surface, resting for a moment in this confrontation between the Lammles, before the brisk opening of the next chapter gives us yet another perspective:

Fledgeby deserved Mr. Alfred Lammle's eulogium. He was the meanest cur existing, with a single pair of legs. And instinct (a word we all clearly understand) going largely on four legs, and reason always on two, meanness on four legs never attains the perfection of meanness on two.

(II. 5) (p. 320)

That crisp tone is characteristic of the novel's transitions at their best—lively, unobtrusively witty. There is little trace in this novel of the old stylistic stand-bys of the Inimitable. Nevertheless, it is an aspect of the novel's strength that we should be aware of a narrator whose penetration of sham and artificiality is not only lively, but tactful. Fledgeby is here seen for what, beyond his entanglements with the Lammles, he finally is—less a person than a phenomenon. In him, animal and human vicious-ness unite so remarkably that he can only be regarded with a kind of detached wit. With the Lammles, in the preceding scene, the writing appropriately registers a deeper involvement. The unflagging good humour of the public performance at the Opera, contrasting with the virulence of their scene at home, arouses in Dickens and in us something close to admiration for the astonishing efficiency and energy with which the Lammles keep up appearances. The Lammles are people who demand to be dwelt on and understood.

In the Lammles, then, *Our Mutual Friend* studies Veneering as a process. Marriage is indeed the pillar by which Society is upheld, and the Podsnaps, Veneerings and Lammles each make their tribute to its solidity. In the present scene, the Lammles return, vicariously, to their own courtship, in which the young couple, chaperoned out of any real contact with each other, are propelled into setting up an establishment. If the got-up 'conversation' between Fledgeby and Georgiana seems crude, it is a crudity that answers to their debilitated social presences. They offer themselves for the depersonalizing process comically enacted here, as the Lammles did before them, suppressing themselves into a state of dumbness that can only be taken as acquiescence.

By stressing the things that I find especially strong in the novel I don't want to imply that the context Dickens gives them is feeble. On the contrary the 'background' is extraordinarily diverse and varied, extraordinarily ambitious in its rendering and evaluating of a whole society in terms of precisely-noted actualities—things like manners, 'language', institutions, attitudes, myths, taste. Well before William Morris, and with a keener imagination, Dickens is aware of the inter-related aesthetic and moral implications of Victorian taste. In *Our Mutual Friend,* Dickens recreates a distinctively Victorian pride in proprietorship, illustrated variously by the Podsnap drawing room, where that ponderous respect for appearances so readily translates itself into Podsnappery in speech and action, by Boffin's bower, with its acknowledgement of the masculine and feminine tastes, its provisions generously displayed next to the waxen fruits under glass shades and the stuffed birds. Mr. Venus is more than a grotesque parody of such pride: he supplies those cases of stuffed animals, preserved family pets, and bizarre museum pieces through which perverted feelings manifest themselves in possession and display. An atmosphere of secrecy surrounds those who earn their living from scavenging among the sewerage, or stuffing corpses, or fishing for them, and decent people like Lizzie Hexam and Miss Pleasant Riderhood are shamed by the livelihoods of their nearest and dearest. But the novel perceives that Victorian society, while keeping up the pretence that such activities are obscene, in fact domesticates them, its taste for pleasing surface going together with a prurient fascination with the *outré* and the sordid. Such a fascination links the audience of Mortimer's story of 'The Man from Nowhere' with the consumers of Silas Wegg's ballads, and the readers of 'The Treasures of a Dunghill'.

Although in *Our Mutual Friend* lives are formed by a common condition, they do not act on each other as they do, for instance, in *Middlemarch*. The dynamism in Dickens's novel comes from his own probing interest in the relationship between individual depth and social surface. Henry James's phrase about Dickens being 'the greatest of superficial novelists'[7] thus has an irony that, for once, its author did not intend.

Notes

1. *The Life of Charles Dickens* (London, 1966), p. 291.

2. Stephen Gill, from whose Penguin edition of *Our Mutual Friend* (1971) all quotations will be made, draws attention to Dickens's fascination with the problem of identity (p. 22). However, he regards the story of Wrayburn as largely independent of the rest of the novel (p. 21).

3. Garis, Robert: *The Dickens Theatre* (Oxford, 1965), p. 243.

4. See Henry James's review of 1865: 'poor with the poverty not of momentary embarrassment, but of permanent exhaustion', in *The House of Fiction* (London, 1957), p. 253. For a useful survey of the diverse valuations of the novel, see Philip Hobsbaum, 'The Critics and *Our Mutual Friend*' in E[ssays] in C[riticism], Vol. XIII, No. 3, p. 231.

5. This case is argued by Julian Moynahan in *E in C*, Vol. X, No. 1, p. 60.

6. Garis, *op. cit.,* p. 254.

7. *Loc. cit.,* p. 256.

Barry V. Qualls (essay date 1978)

SOURCE: "Savages in a 'Bran-New' World: Carlyle and *Our Mutual Friend*," in *Studies in the Novel,* Vol. 10, No. 2, Summer, 1978, pp. 199-217.

[*In the following essay, Qualls suggests that Thomas Carlyle's vocabulary, stock characters, and social concerns strongly influenced Dickens's writing of* Our Mutual Friend.]

Though Dickens, a few months before beginning *Our Mutual Friend,* wrote to Carlyle of "always reading you faithfully and trying to go your way,"[1] no close attention has been given to any role Carlyle's work might play in that novel.[2] Yet in essential ways Carlyle's presence is as strong and significant in Dickens's last completed work as in the more "obviously" Carlylean *Hard Times* and *Tale of Two Cities.* Many of its themes had of course been in the air for decades, and to say "Dickens is using Carlyle here and here and here" is a dangerous and even silly business. Concern with Mechanism in 1864 was hardly a fresh concern. But *Our Mutual Friend* is Carlylean because ideas long associated with Carlyle—the challenge hurled at

Benthamite radicalism in the Age of Machinery, the assertion that men must not be Cains though we all have the Cain-like in us, the stress on the drugged state seeking after Mammon and respectability induces—are cast in an undeniably Carlylean framework. We find here not only his vocabulary but his stock characters: the dilettante, the respectable mammonite, the varnisher, the logic-chopping soul-denying rationalist, the poor woman who cannot prove her sisterhood in a bargain-and-sale world, the biped-of-prey. Dickens's creative use of this stock company and of the ideas which they had illustrated recalls Arnold's belief that great literary works come from a mind "happily inspired by a certain intellectual and spiritual atmosphere, by a certain order of ideas, when it finds itself in them." The statement precisely places Carlyle's function in *Our Mutual Friend.*[3]

I

From *Sartor Resartus* and *The French Revolution* onward Carlyle warned his countrymen about the "Aristocracy of the Moneybag" (*FR*: III, 314) and what it signified. Money's "enchantment" led, finally, to the subversion of man's moral sense (*PP*: 194), to the vanquishing of any real Gospel of Brotherhood and a substituting in its place of the Brotherhood of Cain. The end result: cannibalism (*FR*: II, 70). In the 1843 *Past and Present* he could still find hope: "When Mammon-worshippers here and there begin to be God-worshippers, and bipeds-of-prey become men, and there is a Soul felt once more in the huge-pulsing elephantine mechanic Animalism of this Earth, it will be again a blessed Earth" (*PP*: 291). But by 1850 Carlyle saw this "dusky potent insatiable *animalism*" (*LDP* [*Latter-Day Pamphlets*] : 53) stalking everywhere. Because "the chief end of man" is now "to make money and spend it" (*LDP*: 18), "British industrial existence seems fast becoming one huge poison-swamp of reeking pestilence physical and moral; a hideous *living* Golgotha of souls and bodies buried alive" (*LDP*: 27), "a continent of fetid ooze" and "wreck of deadmen's bones" (*LDP*: 313). And "enchanted" man is happy to find himself amongst fellow "doleful creatures"; he is "no longer a man, but a greedy, blind two-footed animal, 'without soul, except what saves him the expense of salt and keeps his body with its appetites from putrefying'; . . . nothing now but a human money-bag and meat trough" (*LDP*: 258). The world is, simply, "an enormous Life-in-Death" (*LDP*: 320).

This image of man as a money-hungry feeding animal wallowing in filth and ooze dominates *Our Mutual Friend.* "[T]hese times of ours" introduced on its first page are marked by the "huge torrents of extinct exuviae, dung and rubbish" (*LDP*: 164) which Carlyle saw as choking the soul out of England and which loom over London in the form of those dust mounds that are the greatest source of real wealth. A foreigner even thinks that Mr Podsnap means to include horse-dung as one of the "Tokens . . . Marks . . . Signs, you know" of "our British Constitution in the Streets" (pp. 178-79).[4] Members of Society are certainly not put off by filth when money is involved. When the Boffins set up in their mansion, Society swarms to the "Dismal Swamp": "behold all manner of crawling, creeping, fluttering, and buzzing creatures, attracted by the gold dust of the Golden Dustman" (p. 257). Though these people may think their dinners "worthy of the Golden Age" (p. 478), those heaps of dust indicate, as Carlyle noted, not "the new Golden Age," but "a long *Scavenger Age*" (*LDP*: 329). Such a Hell-on-Earth needs an "Articulator of Human Bones" and a shop devoted to such activity; it needs scavengers and scavengers' carts dashing about its streets; and it needs, perhaps less, books extolling "The Treasures of a Dunghill" (p. 543). Old Silas Wegg, falling into "a kind of pecuniary swoon" (p. 545) as he reads of the money and wonders of dunghills to the Golden Dustman, is given a proper adieu when he is unmasked for the biped-of-prey he is: he is hurled into "a scavenger's cart" (p. 862).[5]

Indeed, this chase after the Dustman's lucre transforms almost everyone into animals. Fascination Fledgeby becomes simply the "meanest cur existing, with a single pair of legs," when money is the issue (pp. 319-20). His parallel among the "amphibious human-creatures" (p. 118) along the river is Rogue Riderhood, who is sheer stalking animalism ("Shaking himself as he got up like the surly brute he was, he gave his growl"—p. 695); even his hat has absorbed something of his nature as well as more than a bit of the world about him: "an old sodden fur cap . . . that looked like a furry animal . . . drowned and decaying" (p. 195). Appropriately, the chapter (Book II, ch. 12) presenting Riderhood and his daughter at home is called "More Birds of Prey." That is his only business: preying—on the living (Hexam), on the dying (Betty Higden), and on the dead. This cannibal is even trying to collect damages on his own "death," an act of preying that suggests the incredible moral disorder of this world.

High and low do the same thing. The first character we meet is Gaffer Hexam, a "bird of prey" (p. 45) hunting amidst the "slime and ooze" (p. 43) for dead bodies with coin on them. And Dickens parallels this activity to the goings-on in Society's dining rooms. There the "aquiline-nosed and fingered" (p. 52) Mrs Veneering operates precisely as the "hook-nosed" Hexam does: she has often "dived" into the gossipy streams of the Harmon murder, and she and her husband have "prospered exceedingly" upon this death (pp. 180-81), news of which sets them up socially quite as much as the coin Hexam finds on the body of the supposed Harmon fuels him.

"Soul, take thy ease, it is all *well* that thou art a vulture-soul"—this is the prayer Carlyle ascribed to Mammon-worshippers "during hours of mastication and rumination, which they call hours of meditation" (*PP*: 189). It is the constantly iterated "prayer" of almost everyone in *Our Mutual Friend,* as any Veneering or Podsnap dinner amply illustrates. Dinners amongst this Society are precisely what they were in *The French Revolution*: "the *ultimate* act of communion," with the element of cannibalism thrown in of course; English society has become that

"Atreus' Palace" (*FR*: II, 5) that Carlyle saw France to be. "If man's *Soul* is indeed . . . a kind of *Stomach*," Teufelsdröckh discovered, "what else is the true meaning of Spiritual Union but an Eating together?" (*SR* [*Sartor Resartus*] : 116-17).[6] "So it came to pass that Mr and Mrs Podsnap requested the honour of the company of seventeen friends of their souls at dinner; and that they substituted other friends of their souls . . ." (p. 176). And at dinner Mr Podsnap, extolling the glories of Providentially-blessed Britain (pp. 178-79), will refuse to hear such a "disagreeable" topic as starvation because, after all, "Providence has declared that you shall have the poor always with you . . . it is not for me to impugn the workings of Providence" (pp. 187-88). As Carlyle wrote, "O sumptuous Merchant-Prince, illustrious game-preserving Duke, is there no way of 'killing' thy brother but Cain's rude way!" (*PP*: 149).

Evidently not. For Society's Cains, "realities" are not people and starvation but talk of "poverty and wealth" (p. 376). And inextricably connected to this is the sense of man as nothing more than a digesting machine. Sophronia Lammle defines that "money-speculation" (p. 476) which is her marriage as a "scheming together for to-day's dinner and tomorrow's breakfast—till death divorces us" (p. 689). As Teufelsdröckh feared, the individual has become "a mere Work-Machine, for whom the divine gift of Thought were no other than the terrestrial gift of Steam is to the Steam-engine; a power whereby cotton might be spun, and money and money's worth realised" (*SR*: 259). Thus, if someone saves another's life, the question of remuneration is easily handled, according to the "Voice of Society" (here a Contractor, speaking of Lizzie Hexam):

> "You speak of that annuity in pounds sterling, but it is in reality so many pounds of beefsteaks and so many pints of porter. . . . Those beefsteaks and that porter are the fuel to that young woman's engine. She derives therefrom a certain amount of power to row the boat; that power will produce so much money . . ."
>
> (p. 890).

As Carlyle's Cain says, "'Am I my brother's keeper?' Did I not pay my brother *his* wages, the thing he has merited from me?" (*PP*: 149).

These people are, quite simply, living "a perpetual life-in-death," crying—with Podsnap leading the "social chorus"—"'peace and peace where there is no peace'" (*PP*: 245). In this world only death, as the Doll's Dressmaker says, is "peaceful" (p. 334). Everyone, "every day of our lives when we wake, . . . is instinctively unwilling to be restored to the consciousness of this existence" (p. 505), indeed would prefer death or something resembling it. It is not surprising that the Veneerings have bought control in a drughouse (p. 76); this is the only business guaranteed to induce some "Lethean sleep" and soul's ease.

The context of Dickens's presentation of these Mammonites and their drugged state is assertively Carlylean. In "Characteristics" he had noted that "The Whole Life of

Society must now be carried on by drugs" (C: XXVIII, 20), so much had men ceased to have any "moral communion" with each other as money more and more severed human ties. In the *Pamphlets* money-intoxication has grown so immense that "your poor life and all its manifold activities [are] stunned into frenzy and comatose sleep by it" (*LDP*: 206). Besides "their purse and their abdominal department," "Semblances" are the only thing real (*LDP*: 74).

This is the structure and these are the terms of Dickens's presentation. In *Our Mutual Friend* "working and rallying round . . . to keep up appearances" (p. 301) and to keep reality from consciousness is the chief occupation, finally. "These times of ours" require no Mrs General instructing in the art of Varnish. In Podsnap the thing is done, and in the Veneerings it is proceeding apace. These people come together for dinners because they must "work" to sustain their life-in-death; indeed, this collaboration is the only tie binding this drugged crowd together. Like Carlyle's Bull, they wander aimlessly "in an extinct world of wearisome, oppressive and expensive shadows" (*LDP*: 285); Podsnap's dinner guests move about his "heavy" rooms "like a revolving funeral" (p. 185); or else remain in that state of "suspended-animation" (*OMF*: 181, *LDP*: 157) that Carlyle ascribed to people who deny reality with such determination. Outside the atmosphere cooperates. Over London there hangs an "air of death" (p. 450), and the fog and filthy air throw "animate London" into "blinking, wheezing, and choking" (p. 479). Even the streets of the city seem drugged: "there was a deadly kind of repose on it, more as though it had taken laudanum than fallen into a natural rest" (p. 271).

In such a shadow-world, where life and death are so confused, there is none the less frantic activity to avoid Hell. But it is the Hell Carlyle described in *Past and Present*, which is dominated by the "terror of 'Not succeeding'; of not making money, fame, or some figure in the world,—chiefly of not making money" (*PP*: 148).

> They were all feverish, boastful, and indefinably loose.
> . . . They all spoke of sums of money, and only mentioned the sums and left the money to be understood.
> . . . They were always in a hurry, and yet seemed to have nothing tangible to do; except a few of them (these, mostly asthmatic and thick-lipped) who were for ever demonstrating . . . how money was to be made
>
> (p. 313).

This is not a working Mammonism. The present time is the Scrip-Age, with "Scrip-Church" and "Fathers" to expound its doctrines (p. 690). As Humphry House pointed out, "the Podsnaps, Veneerings, and Lammles live in a world in which investment has taken the place of work."[7] And has become, indeed, one of the chief opiates.

> O mighty Shares! To set those blaring images so high, and to cause us smaller vermin, as under the influence of *henbane* or *opium*, to cry out, night and day, "Relieve us of our money, scatter it for us, buy us and sell

us, ruin us, only we beseech ye take rank among the powers of the earth, and *fatten on us*"!

> (p. 160, my italics).

The Veneerings and Podsnaps and Lammles and Fledgeby are about the same business as Wegg and Riderhood, that of getting money—and finding some victual in the process—without working. Idle Mammonism is here in that "somnambulist state" Carlyle ascribed to Dilettantism (*PP*: 175). "*Praying . . . by Working*"? (*PP*: 230). Well, yes: "Soul, take thy ease, it is all *well* that thou art a vulture-soul."

II

In his portrayal of "money, money, money, and what money can make of life" (p. 521), Dickens uses one of the most often repeated items in Carlyle's lexicon. From his earliest essays Carlyle had damned the man who would sell his soul for "Respectability," who would never cease "cobbling together two Inconsistencies"—good and evil—to attain his goals (C: XXVIII, 254). And money has a central place in this pursuit. In *The French Revolution* Carlyle noted that "Moneybag of Mammon" is "what the respectable Republic for the Middle Classes will signify" (*FR*: III, 115). Dickens had long before *Our Mutual Friend* explored this connection between money and respectability. The term first appears in *Bleak House,* where the "very respectable Mr Vholes" is drawn as a "vampire" cannibalizing the young, all for those three daughters and his father in the Vale of Taunton. There Dickens underlined his use of Carlyle by noting how Vholes, cobbling together opposites, happily defined "immoral" as "unlawful" (ch. 60), and by showing him driving a "gig" (ch. 37), the symbol Carlyle made notorious as an emblem of the respectable man. *Our Mutual Friend* lacks a gig, but it has the other elements of Carlyle's attack, and they form the central focus of the novel. Indeed, the reason for this society's money-intoxication is finally its desperation to be thought respectable. And to achieve this status necessarily involves a refusal to recognize the mutual claims of one man on another.

The "so eminently respectable" Mr Podsnap (p. 175) is the touchstone of the respectable world. He is Society's law-giver, and its chief proponent of the Age of Machinery. Means and ends are to him the same, and no irregularity—no pulse of life—is allowed to interrupt the routine of his day, or his notions of others' days. But Dickens's examination of respectability is not centered on this hollow man and other "elders of tribes." Lizzie Hexam and her brother are his chief means of exploring the idea's implications and its interrelationship with money and with the "Gospel of Enlightened Selfishness" that Podsnap preaches and to which so many subscribe.

Lizzie Hexam represents in *Our Mutual Friend* the attributes which Dr Leavis sees in Sissy Jupe in *Hard Times,* and represents them more profoundly, I think. Sissy comes from a circus-haven, Lizzie from the slime and ooze of

London low life. She preserves her inner life only through her imagination, through her intuitive sense (inspired by the fire-induced "fancies") that there *must* be some world elsewhere better than that her father inhabits. Thus (to use Leavis's words about Sissy) Lizzie "stands for vitality as well as goodness—they are seen, in fact, as one; she is generous, impulsive life, finding self-fulfilment in self-forgetfulness—all that is the antithesis of calculating self-interest."[8] Wrayburn's first glimpse of her suggests the rich and instinctive life, undefiled by her origins amongst the slime and ooze: "A deep rich piece of colour, with the brown flush of her cheek and the shining lustre of her hair, though sad and solitary, weeping by the rising and the falling of the fire" (p. 211). But Lizzie's "life" is hemmed in, smothered by all about her. Not only the Podsnap crowd, but the conventionally good and decent people Lizzie encounters show souls deadened and drugged when it comes to questions of their fellow man—and for the same reason: respectability. Miss Abbey Potterson, proprietor of the Six Jolly Fellowship Porters tavern, has very definite notions of those whom she will allow into her "fellowship." And they do not include men who *look* like Cains.

> "Lizzie Hexam, Lizzie Hexam," then began Miss Potterson "how often have I held out to you the opportunity of getting clear of your father, and *doing well*? . . . Leave him. You needn't break with him altogether, but leave him. Do well away from him; . . . be persuaded into being *respectable* and happy"
>
> (pp. 111, 113, my italics).

Podsnap would feel quite easy with this idea of fellowship. Miss Potterson's setting of Hexam apart from the rest of society is, as Lizzie instinctively realizes, to put the mark of Cain upon him. Her brother, entering the mainstream of Victorian society through education, happily denies his family and assumes the real mark of Cain, but it is a "stigma" which society applauds for its very "respectability."

The first scene between Lizzie and Charley provides an interchange that, in its quiet statement, is one of the most psychologically telling in the novel.

> "Then as I sit a-looking at the fire, I seem to see in the burning coal—like where that glow is now—"
>
> "That's gas, that is," said the boy. . . .
>
> "Don't disturb it, Charley, or it'll be all in a blaze. . . . When I look at it of an evening, it comes like pictures to me, Charley"
>
> (pp. 70-71).

"That's gas": before we ever get to the chapter on Charley's education, Dickens shows it factual emphasis and intimates the antiwonder, finally antihuman system that Charley will give his allegiance to. Paradoxically, education in this society is fundamentally destructive of all natural relationships; like the appearance of possessing money, it is a way to respectability. Lizzie instinctively feels this; she refuses to learn because "want of learning" is the "tie be-

tween me and father," the "stay" that keeps him from going "wild and bad" (pp. 72-73). Terrifyingly, she sees that education can destroy the human in man. Yet ironically, it is Lizzie, trying "to cut" Charley away from his environment in order to give him "a new and good beginning" (p. 73), who starts him on his "respectable" career.

Hexam's education is like that of his teacher Bradley Headstone—and eminently more successful. Neither approves Lizzie's fire-induced fancies. For Charley, "It was all very well" to dream before the fire, "but we are looking into the real world, now" (p. 278). And the real world does not bother itself with the past and making amends for wrongs committed by one's father. Lizzie's plea that some necessity compels her to live by the river receives from her brother the contemptuous sneer "Dreaming again!" (p. 278). Charley has no time for such dreaming, and because he fears the weight of the past he all the more energetically tries to sweep it away with Podsnapian self-will. He sees Lizzie's refusal of Headstone's marriage offer as a refusal to "rise" and abandon that unrespectable past; and he determines to take action to cancel her from his life.

> "Upon my soul," exclaimed the boy, "you are a nice picture of a sister! . . . And so all my endeavours to cancel the past and to raise myself in the world, and to raise you with me, are to be beaten down by *your* low whims. . . . I am determined that after I have climbed out of the mire, you shall not pull me down. You can't disgrace me if I have nothing to do with you, and I *will* have nothing to do with you for the future"
>
> (pp. 459,481).

That it was Lizzie who got him out of the mire does not matter. "He threw up his ungrateful and ungracious hand as if it set up a barrier between them, and flung himself upon his heel and left her" (p. 462). It is a gesture from Podsnappery, and one given a second airing when Charley confronts his "best friend" Headstone after the attempted murder of Wrayburn, in a chapter titled "Better to Be Abel than Cain."

> "Mr Headstone, you are in all your passions so selfish, and so concentrated upon yourself, that you have not bestowed one proper thought upon me. . . . It is . . . an extraordinary circumstance attendant on my life, that every effort I make towards perfect respectability, is impeded by somebody else through no fault of mine! . . . I have done with my sister as well as with you"
>
> (pp. 780-81).

Charley's speeches to Headstone and to his sister are straight out of Podsnap's missal, "interchangeable" in "tone and language," as Arnold Kettle has pointed out, with Podsnap's own final judgment on Lizzie and her marriage: "'Then all *I* have to say is,' returns Podsnap, putting the thing away with his right arm, 'that my gorge rises against such a marriage . . . !'" (p. 889).[9]

This union of respectability and selfishness is a Carlylean insight, an idea he had been urging since the 1830s. In

"The Diamond Necklace" he had noted how "Self . . . comes on us . . . as Vanity, and the shadow of an imaginary Hunger for Applause; under the name of what we call 'Respectability'" (C: XXVIII, 326). It is this belief in Respectability that gradually winnows away men's souls (Ibid., p. 327). Charley Hexam's education has shown him the way he should go if he is to secure the world's good opinion, and it has in the process totally negated his sister's influence, leaving him with a "hollow empty heart" (p. 780). For Charley, Podsnappery is the Gospel, and its main commandment is submission to the "force of public opinion," a force requiring only that "a 'God-created Man' all but abnegat[e] the character of Man; [and] . . . exist, automatised, mummy-wise (scarcely in rare moments audible or visible from amid his wrappages and cerements), as a Gentleman or Gigman" (C: XXVIII, 324-35). And, as Carlyle had first asserted in "Signs of the Times," this hollow life is another reason for society's drugged state, for the "nightmare sleep" which comes when Mechanism "encumbers the whole movements of our mind" (C: XXVII, 78-80).

In the world of Carlyle and Dickens, the voice of respectability, whether that of a Podsnap or Hexam or other Gigman, is finally the voice of Cain. Dickens underlines this Carlylean presentation with the story of Betty Higden. She is his last Irish Widow figure, "not a logically-reasoning woman" (p. 246) and thus cut off utterly from a world where felicific calculus governs all. That the last creature she meets in her flight toward death is Riderhood—"the Samaritan in his latest accredited form" (p. 573)—and that he takes her money form a damning indictment of this society. Riderhood's attitude is not different from Podsnap's or that of any other representative man; it is just less fastidious. "Am I my brother's keeper?" Respectability gives the same answer as Cain.

III

There are those living in this murky world who are not vultures hungry for respectability, who share some of Teufelsdröckh's intuition that "Soul is *not* synonymous with Stomach" (*SR*: 159). In these people, in Rokesmith-Harmon and Bella Wilfer, in Mortimer Lightwood and Eugene Wrayburn, in Bradley Headstone and Lizzie Hexam, Dickens investigates once again the incredible efforts required of those who would preserve some inner reality in this society; and he also explores, in Headstone, the psychic damage done to those who are, finally, unwilling or unable to make the effort. In suggesting the immensity of the task, he returns to the ideas he had used in *Hard Times* and *Little Dorrit,* Carlyle's ideas about mechanism and about the influence of the past on the present.

Our Mutual Friend is a novel where time is at once man's "seed-field" and the element "wherein man's soul here below lives imprisoned" (C: XXVIII, 79). Whereas Teufelsdröckh had seen the present growing out of the past naturally, for those in Dickens's world the present is utterly "trammelled with the Past" (*SR*: 47), which hovers over it

like a vampire, draining out all reality and energy, and making the future seem, in Teufelsdröckh's words, "wholly a Stygian Darkness, spectre-bearing" (*SR*: 150). People here are the "victims" of their parents or financial benefactors, who "pre-arrange" all from the hour of birth (the quoted words are Wrayburn's, p. 193). Lightwood, like Wrayburn, feels that his small income has been "an effective Something, in the way of preventing me from turning to at Anything" (p. 885). Lizzie Hexam, confronted by her brother's demand that she leave the riverside in order to obliterate the past, replies: "I can't get away from it. . . . It's no purpose of mine that I live by it still"; it is impossible, she feels, not "to try to make some amends" for wrongs done by her father (p. 278). Old Twemlow, that rare Dickensian "gentleman" who has some worth, is a parasitic hanger-on to Lord Snigsworth, who has denied him the opportunity, as if by fiat, "to do something, or be something, in life" (p. 467).

But the pressure of the past on the inner life, which Carlyle saw as the "iron, ignoble circle of Necessity [that] embraces all things [and] binds the youth of these times into a *sluggish thrall*" (C: XXVIII, 30, my italics) is most fully illustrated in Harmon and Wrayburn. Harmon is the "living-dead man" (p. 430) who must ask himself if he should "come to life," so morally timid has he been rendered by his Mammon-worshipping father. Those dust mounds he inherits are for him and those about him a constant reminder of what Hillis Miller calls "the great inescapable weight of history" in this world.[10] It is not until Harmon is recognized by the Boffins, those who gave him love as a child, that the "shadow" of the past begins to lift, that he discovers a way to test Bella and free her of her money-lust, that he, finally, feels free to become again John Harmon. Appropriately, Dickens has Harmon and Bella take up their new house "on the very day when the last waggon-load of the last Mound was driven out at the gates of Boffin's Bower" (p. 849). They are at last free of the past's shackles.

Harmon's recall to life and Bella's liberation from money-lust seem, in this life-in-death Golgotha, to have come with very little sacrifice. She learns that "she must not sell her sense of what was right and what was wrong" for money and respectability (p. 672); she sees how morally ugly a "bargain and sale" (p. 244) world can be; and she has her original desires for wealth satisfied too, plus the gift of a jewel casket. The victory—the word is really too strong—is rather tawdry (and that jewel case is vulgar). The Harmons and their "doll's house" are as unsatisfactory as Esther and her flower-encircled Bleak House, and they diminish the novel's complexity. Lizzie Hexam, Wrayburn, and Headstone, however, do not. They rank with the Dorrits and Louisa Gradgrind as Dickens's most significant and profound dramatization of the difficulty of keeping an inner self alive in a mechanical age.

Eugene Wrayburn is, on the "surface," a character straight out of Carlyle's description of the Dilettante who languishes his life away.[11] Pungent, witty, idle, he satirizes all who work, even using the slogan of the Peterloo workers in one of his "ridiculous humours": "A fair day's wages for a fair day's work is ever my partner's motto" (p. 213). Carlyle had made this slogan one of the main motifs of *Past and Present* (p. 203), and he would have damned such levity to Gehenna-fires. Yet Dickens refuses to draw Wrayburn as he did Harthouse in *Hard Times,* as the "One monster . . . in the World" Carlyle proclaimed the idle man to be (*PP*: 203). Wrayburn is not one of the Lammles or Veneerings or Fledgebys. He and Lightwood attend Society's cookery affairs with disdainful "weariness," despising their "unlimited monotony." Like Lady Dedlock, these men feel their ennui, and that becomes a saving grace.

Wrayburn's weariness is the first sign of life beneath that dull surface. The second is his refusal to participate in his father's marriage arrangements for him, a "No" which marks his resistance to the "bargain and sale" bazaar of this Vanity Fair world. The final and telling proof that he is more than a mere clothes screen is his reaction to Lizzie Hexam, whom he glimpses amidst the slime and ooze of the river bank. It marks the turning point of his life; the chance to break into freedom is offered him, the chance to become "earnest" (the word is used again and again) about something. Meeting Lizzie at once gives Wrayburn the opportunity "to be of use to somebody" (p. 286) and forces him, in Carlyle's words, to look into his "inner man, and see if there be any traces of a *soul* there" (*PP*: 31). Lizzie understands his needs and recognizes that his failings "have grown up through his being like one cast away, for the want of something to trust in, and care for, and think well of" (p. 405).

The process of Wrayburn's discovery of his better self brings him face to face with death and its agent Bradley Headstone. Their scenes comprise Dickens's most subtle attack on the profit-and-loss mechanists who denied value to feeling, to any dynamic element within the human personality. Both Wrayburn and Headstone, as John Lucas has remarked, have identities "which are fixed for them by the social process" and which thus imprison them.[12] The one sees himself as a born idler, the other works earnestly to become a "respectable" man of the middle class. Wrayburn's easy self-possession offers a telling psychic contrast to Headstone's "stiffness," and makes the teacher feel that his respectability is a veneer, put on like those "decent" clothes which never seem completely adapted to him (p. 266). Yet Headstone would have been vastly superior to the idle man had he, a pauper's child, not been the product of a Benthamite education; or had he, like Teufelsdröckh, had influences that negated the disastrous effects of such an education.[13]

> He had acquired mechanically a great store of teacher's knowledge. He could do mental arithmetic mechanically, sing at sight mechanically, blow various wind instruments mechanically, even play the great church organ mechanically. From his early childhood up, his mind had been a place of mechanical storage.
>
> (p. 266)

"By repeating 'mechanical,'" Harvey Sucksmith points out, "Dickens draws attention to the way the instinctive man in Bradley Headstone has been repressed beneath a difficulty acquired veneer of culture."[14] Carlyle's attack in *Sartor* is phrased in much the same language: Teufelsdröckh's "Greek and Latin were 'mechanically' taught; Hebrew scarce even mechanically." His teacher, "an inanimate, mechanical Gerund grinder," had no notion that a mind was developed by "Thought kindling itself at the fire of living Thought" (*SR*: 104-5). And Teufelsdröckh himself notes the effect of such an education on the moral side of man. "Wonder . . . is the basis of Worship: the reign of wonder is perennial, indestructible in Man; only at certain stages (as the present), it is, for some short season, a reign *in partibus infidelium.*" His Editor adds: "That progress of Science, which is to destroy Wonder, and in its stead substitute Mensuration and Numeration, finds small favor with Teufelsdröckh" (*SR*: 67-68).

A sense of wonder, of feeling, has been completely obliterated by Headstone's education: "I don't know what I feel; some of us are obliged habitually to keep it down. To keep it down" (p. 400). The quietest utterance he makes in the novel comes after Charley Hexam has described Lizzie's "education" (and Charley's disapproving "too much" should not be overlooked):

> "Lizzie has as much thought as the best, Mr Headstone. Too much, perhaps, without teaching. I used to call the fire at home, her books, for she was always full of fancies—sometimes quite wise fancies, considering—when she sat looking at it."
>
> "I don't like that," said Bradley Headstone.
>
> (p. 281)

"I don't like that": the scene is one more forceful dramatization of the suffocating effect the Benthamite-mechanical ideas had on life. "Undue cultivation of the outward," Carlyle asserted, though "for the time productive of many palpable benefits, must, in the long-run, by destroying Moral Force, which is the parent of all other Force, prove . . . pernicious" (C: XXVII, 73).[15] The benefits of Headstone's education, of rising to a "respectable" position as schoolteacher, finally come to nothing; wonder, "living Thought," has been a will-o'-the'wisp to him. And because it has, the "truly vital" in him has been suppressed and perverted, and with that gone nothing is left but the satanic demon-empire: "what was animal and . . . what was fiery (though smouldering)" can no longer be imprisoned beneath that veneer of educated respectability (p. 267).

The light and animal images that Dickens uses to portray the eruption of Headstone's nether self after Lizzie rejects him (he has been attracted to her in spite of all "reason") are identical to those Carlyle uses to show Teufelsdröckh's aimless wandering before the God-born in his nature asserts control and frees him for creative work and for love of his fellows. In *Sartor* Carlyle had written that in everyone there lies "a whole world of internal Madness, an authentic Demon-Empire" (*SR*: 260). Before Teufelsdröckh emerges from the Everlasting No, the balance seems tipped toward that demon-empire. With "a hot fever of anarchy and misery raging within" (*SR*: 158), he walks "in the temper of ancient Cain" (p. 156), and finds the Universe "one huge, dead, immeasurable Steam-engine" (p. 164).

Similarly, Headstone, "[t]ied up all day with his disciplined show upon him, subdued to the performance of his routine of educational tricks, . . . broke loose at night like an ill-tamed wild animal" (p. 609). Following Wrayburn in order to glimpse him with Lizzie, he becomes a seething Cain indeed. During these murderous wanderings, he meets Riderhood, that stalking animal who resembles him and whose clothes he will copy. Riderhood is, of course, Headstone's *Doppelgänger,* the concrete embodiment of the demonic energy so suppressed and perverted by his mechanical education. The preying-animal images associated with Riderhood transfer to Headstone; "the passion-wasted nightbird with respectable feathers" becomes "the worst nightbird of all" (p. 618). Then, with the sun down and "the landscape . . . dyed red" (p. 701), Headstone appears at the Plashwater Weir Mill wearing clothes like Riderhood's, and strikes Wrayburn.

This wilderness attack comes at the very moment of Wrayburn's "inquiry into his own nature," an inquiry pitting that part of him which believes in Lizzie, in "her beauty and her worth," against the "Brute Beast" in him which would seduce her (p. 765). Indeed, the meeting of these two men is essentially Wrayburn's confrontation with his own brutal selfishness. Just before the blow falls, there is in him a psychomachia between the "God-born" and "devil's-dung" aspects of his self that Carlyle, especially in *Sartor,* emphasized as comprising man's nature, his "whole Me" (*SR*: 167).

> "Temptations in the Wilderness!" exclaims Teufelsdröckh: "Have we not all to be tried with such? Not so easily can the Old Adam, lodged in us by birth, be dispossessed. Our Life is compassed round with Necessity; yet is the meaning of Life itself no other than Freedom, than Voluntary Force: thus have we a warfare; in the beginning, especially a hard-fought battle. . . . Name it as we choose: with or without visible Devil, whether in the natural Desert of rocks and sands, or in the populous moral Desert of selfishness and baseness,—to such Temptation are we all called."
>
> (*SR*: 183-84)

Wrayburn is tempted, the dual parts of his personality pitted in battle, and the good triumphs: "I am wearily out of sorts with one Wrayburn who cuts a sorry figure" (pp. 764-65), he says. And when his battle with this "Brute Beast" is at its most intense, Headstone strikes him: "In an instant, with a dreadful crash, the reflected night turned crooked, flames shot jaggedly across the air, and the moon and stars came bursting from the sky. Was he struck by lightning?" (pp. 766-67). The imagery parallels remarkably Carlyle's description of Teufelsdröckh's internal battle. Dickens uses elements of that Wanderer's helpless despair to suggest Headstone's nature, and elements of his fire baptism to suggest Wrayburn's rebirth into freedom.

> "And as I so thought, there rushed like a stream of fire over my whole soul; and I shook base Fear away from me forever. . . . The Everlasting No had said: 'Behold, thou art fatherless, outcast, and the Universe is mine (the Devil's)'; to which my whole Me now made answer: '*I* am not thine, but Free, and forever hate thee!' It is from this hour that I incline to date my Spiritual Newbirth, or Baphometic Fire-baptism; perhaps I directly thereupon began to be a Man."
>
> (*SR*: 167-68)

Teufelsdröckh's Temptation in the Wilderness results, finally, in his awakening "to a new Heaven and a new Earth" (p. 186). He is even tempted to name Nature God, for he has discovered that the "Universe is not dead and demoniacal, a charnel-house with spectres, but godlike, and my Father's" (p. 188). These same ideas and images, albeit reduced, accompany Wrayburn and Headstone after their encounter. The one requests some "fancy" of nature: "Ask [Jenny Wren] if she has smelt the flowers" (p. 806); the other finds that the "earth looked spectral" (p. 770). Wrayburn's encounter with Headstone is his recognition of the Cain-like selfishness in himself, and he has conquered it. But that the image he awakens to is one of imagined flowers and singing birds rather than the real things (Amy Dorrit had brought flowers to Clennam) suggests how singular and tenuous is his—or anyone's—hold on the "godlike"; in this charnel-house world, fancies of nature are as close as one comes to the "godlike" in it, except as other human beings may embody it.

For Headstone the spectral earth becomes a "Penal Tartarus" indeed (Carlyle's name for the murderer's world—*FR*: III, 25). And his descent into the devil's-dung of the Everlasting No is underlined in the chapter following the murder attempt, "Better to Be Abel than Cain." He may discard the Riderhood clothes for his own "decent" ones, but he cannot elude "the pursuing shadow" of his deed. His existence has become terrifying, particularly after Hexam's denial of him. "A desolate air of utter and complete loneliness fell upon him like a visible shade . . . he drooped his devoted head when the boy was gone, and shrank together on the floor, and grovelled there, with the palms of his hands tight-clasping his hot temples, in unutterable misery, and unrelieved by a single tear" (pp. 779, 781-82). His spiritual state is, again, Teufelsdröckh's *before* the God-born in him takes dominion; as he noted, "Invisible yet impenetrable walls, as of Enchantment, divided me from all living. . . . The heart within me, unvisited by any heavenly dewdrop was smouldering in sulphurous, slow-consuming fire. Almost since earliest memory I had shed no tear" (*SR*: 163, 165).[16]

Headstone's death is inevitable now. Cut off from the one man for whom he can feel an emotional attachment, the animal nature that he has so long stifled comes to the fore, and he kills it when he kills Riderhood. Their encounter in the classroom, with Riderhood giving a lesson, is grimly comic, and a telling illustration of the horrors of an unbalanced psyche in a Carlylean sense. Bradley Headstone pays the price of denying whatever is dynamic and vital, of perverting moral force to a calculation. And in the process he loses all power to act creatively or constructively. It is inevitable that his end be Riderhood's: "lying under the ooze and scum" (p. 874).[17]

Wrayburn, on the other hand, gains in winning Lizzie some sense of freedom and moral worth. But their victory is not at all comparable to Amy Dorrit and Arthur Clennam's; there is not even a hint of social significance in their marriage, of some small society—where "two or three are gathered together" (*SR*: 214)—preserving what is good.[18] Their marriage does, however, suggest the continuance, somewhere on this "continent of fetid ooze," of "all that is the antithesis of calculating self-interest," in Dr Leavis's words on *Hard Times*.[19] In marrying, they have flouted that voice of public opinion which governs with Argus eyes in an Age of Machinery ("Signs," C: XXVII, 78-79). It is the novel's one *significant* personal victory, a victory for the God-born in man.

Of course the "Voice of Society" does not acknowledge this. In the last chapter Lightwood has a conversation with Lady Tippins about Lizzie and her friends which indicates how topsy-turvy this world is, and how hopeless is any spiritual renewal:

> "Long banished Robinson Crusoe," says the charmer, exchanging salutations, "how did you leave the Island?"
>
> "Thank you," says Lightwood. "It made no complaint of being in pain anywhere."
>
> "Say, how did you leave the savages?" asks Lady Tippins.
>
> "They were becoming civilized when I left Juan Fernandez," says Lightwood. "At least they were eating one another, which looked like it."
>
> (p. 888)

"Savages," "civilized," "eating one another": the words resonate through every part of the novel. To civilize savages is, "*in partibus infidelium*," to teach them to prey on their fellow human beings. We remember that Charley Hexam is first described as a "curious mixture . . . of uncompleted savagery, and uncompleted civilization" (p. 60). His education, his ascension into respectability, certainly and completely civilizes him—and in the way Podsnap defines the word. As for Lizzie and Wrayburn and genuine feeling, "such a ridiculous affair is condemned by the voice of Society" (p. 888). Its way is cannibalism or leave-it-alone. The Podsnap crowd needs the Veneering drug-house desperately in order to preserve its Lethean sleep, quite as Charley needs his Political-Economy. Anything to keep reality out of mind.[20]

"Surely" Carlyle wrote at the end of *Latter-Day Pamphlets*, "surely this ignoble sluggishness, sceptical torpor, indifference to all that does not bear on Mammon and his interests is not the natural state of human creatures; and is not doomed to be their final one!" (p. 335). His own presentation of their state in the eight pamphlets and Dickens's in *Our Mutual Friend* suggest that their "civilized" state is the final one. In his novel Dickens has even ceased his insistence that man recognize his interdependence with all men. And significantly, he gives no rounding-off to this story, no tying together of plot strands as he had in *Little Dorrit* and the other novels. Instead, *Our Mutual Friend* closes with Podsnap and his hangers-on babbling away. It is a tableau much like Carlyle's "Apes by the Dead Sea" in his last pamphlet. They are, as he prophesied in *Past and Present*, "the *enchanted* Dilettanti" (p. 170), "with heads full of mere extraneous noises, with eyes wide-open but visionless,—for the most part, in the somnambulist state!" (*PP*: 175). "Our poor friends 'the Apes by the Dead Sea' have now no Heaven either; they look into this Universe now, and find it tragically grown to *be* the Humbug they insisted on its being" (*LDP*: 334). Only Twemlow, weak parasite though he is, challenges Society on a principle; he insists that any man can be a gentleman by nature, that the quality of feeling is what tells. In *Our Mutual Friend* it is a significantly life-affirming statement.

. . . . .

Our Mutual Friend is, then, a recapitulation of Dickens's Carlylean emphases: the fog and filthy air of all the post-1850 novels and of the *Latter-Day Pamphlets* are there; the fear of Benthamites and their "Gospel of 'Enlightened Selfishness'" is a central concern of the Hexam-Headstone plot line; and the ennui which attacks the monied class when "external varnish" becomes—as Carlyle noted in the *Pamphlets*—"the chief duty of man" (*LDP*: 289) pervades the Veneering-Podsnap sections. *Our Mutual Friend* is at once Dickens's final attack on the Age of Machinery and his last affirmation of Carlyle's importance to his work. The word "influence" is not too strong: the extensive similarities, ranging from matters of minute detail to essential and preoccupying concerns, testify, as by converging probabilities, to Dickens's deep indebtedness to Carlyle's "way."

And yet, with these verbal and thematic borrowings and similarities explored, something more needs saying. George Levine, Frank Kermode, and René Girard, analyzing the basic structures of the novel, have suggested that its movement is through Apocalypse to Paradise Regained.[21] Dickens's novels and Carlyle's "*non*-fictions" (his emphasis more than ours) affirm this—and yet illustrate the breakdown of those patterns which men had used to make sense of otherwise chaotic experience. Dickens's novels until this last had been structured around pilgrims journeying toward "light": Miss Flite's prophecies were fulfilled, plots became sensible, a wedding rewarded the suffering with community. At *Sartor*'s end, the editor and reader await the rebirth of England foreshadowed in Teufelsdröckh's fire-baptism. *Past and Present*'s editor envisions a "green flowery world." But the *Pamphlets* end in devil's-dung, even as *Our Mutual Friend* stops amongst "civilized" savages. And Carlyle's 1867 "Shooting Niagara" announces that if "the unclassed Aristocracy by Nature" also fails, "then indeed it is all ended" (C: XXX, 16, 21). Carlyle's and Dickens's final "vision" is of a "brannew" world of nightmarish "life."

Notes

1. 13 April 1863. *Letters of Charles Dickens,* ed. Walter Dexter (Bloomsbury: Nonesuch, 1938), III, 348.

2. In neither of the book-length studies of Carlyle and Dickens—Michael Goldberg, *Carlyle and Dickens* (Athens: Univ. of Georgia Press, 1972), and William Oddie, *Dickens and Carlyle* (London: Centenary Press, 1972)—is Carlyle's place in *Our Mutual Friend* considered at any length. And Oddie, pp. 149-50, sees in the last three novels no "compelling reason why Carlyle's influence should be invoked as a significant part of their ideological background." Both studies show conclusively how thoroughly familiar Dickens was with Carlyle's writings, and how often he referred to them throughout his writing career.

3. The following abbreviations to Carlyle's works are used with page numbers parenthetically throughout the text: *Works,* ed. H. D. Traill (New York: Charles Scribner's Sons, 1896-1901), followed by volume number and page number; *FR*: I, II, III: *French Revolution,* Vols. II, III, and IV of *Works*; *LDP*: *Latter-Day Pamphlets,* Vol. XX of *Works*; *SR*: *Sartor Resartus,* ed. C. F. Harrold (New York: Odyssey, 1937); *PP*: *Past and Present,* ed. Richard D. Altick (Boston: Houghton Mifflin, 1965).

4. All quotations are from the Penguin edition of *Our Mutual Friend,* ed. Stephen Gill (Baltimore, 1971).

5. One of the novel's marginal pamphlet-sermons on this "dust" problem offers a striking example of the ease with which Dickens could fall into Carlyle's mannerisms:

   > My lords and gentlemen and honourable boards, when you in the course of your dust-shovelling and cinder-raking have piled up a mountain of pretentious failure, you must off with your honourable coats for the removal of it, . . . or it will come rushing down and bury us alive. . . . It may not be so written in the Gospel according to Podsnappery; you may not "find these words" for the text of a sermon, in the Returns of the Board of Trade; but they have been the truth since the foundations of the universe were laid, and they will be the truth until the foundations of the universe are shaken by the Builder.

   > (pp. 565-66)

   The phrasing and images, the references to the universe and its Builder, the apocalyptic warnings, the humor—all are characteristic Carlylese, as any *Pamphlet* will illustrate.

6. Barbara Hardy, *The Moral Art of Dickens* (London: Athlone, 1972), pp. 139-40, offers a healthy corrective to the tendency of critics to see the feasts in Dickens as signs of communion. She notes that throughout his work "the same moral values are attached to meals—to the giving, receiving, eating, and serving of food. These values might be summed up as good appetite without greed, hospitality without show, and ceremony without pride or condescension." The "cannibalism" in *Our Mutual Friend* is, finally, not much different from that practiced by Vholes or Chadband or Scrooge, only—in the case of Society—more refined.

7. *The Dickens World,* 2nd ed. (1942; rpt. London: Oxford, 1960), pp. 167-68. Carlyle, in the Hudson *Pamphlet,* makes great sport of the Scrip-Age and its "English Vishnu" (pp. 255-56).

8. *Dickens the Novelist* (London: Chatto and Windus, 1970), p. 191.

9. "*Our Mutual Friend,*" in *Dickens and the Twentieth Century,* ed. John Gross and Gabriel Pearson (Toronto: Univ. of Toronto Press, 1962), p. 217.

10. *Charles Dickens: The World of His Novels* (1958; rpt. Bloomington: Indiana Univ. Press, 1969), p. 295.

11. Oddie, though he notes that Wrayburn conforms to Carlyle's definition of the Dilettante, dismisses him as lacking "any strictly Carlylean overtones" (p. 90).

12. *The Melancholy Man* (London: Methuen, 1970), p. 328.

13. Ross H. Dabney, *Love and Property in the Novels of Dickens* (Berkeley: Univ. of California Press, 1967), p. 170, notes that, "in terms of the Carlylean values of work and earnestness which Dickens usually asserts," Headstone is "incomparably the better man."

14. *The Narrative Art of Charles Dickens* (Oxford: Clarendon, 1970), p. 64.

15. Dickens stresses that Headstone's moral nature has been developed at a school which taught "that you were to do good, not because it *was* good, but because you were to make a good thing of it" (p. 264). "Virtue," Carlyle wrote in "Signs," has become "a calculation of the Profitable" (C: XXVII, 74).

16. It is Wrayburn who is finally able to shed tears of purgation as Lizzie pledges her love (pp. 823-24).

17. Grahme Smith, *Dickens, Money, and Society* (Berkeley: Univ. of California Press, 1968), p. 185, states that "In their confrontation, Bradley comes face to face with the objectified form of his own truest nature and can do nothing but destroy it." For an illuminating analysis of their meeting in Headstone's classroom, see Barbara Hardy, "The Community of Dickens," in *Dickens 1970,* ed. Michael Slater (New York: Stein and Day, 1970), pp. 32-33.

18. Smith, p. 188, notes the "utter isolation" of Eugene and Lizzie at the novel's end, and thus offers a salutary corrective to the imaginative creations of Robert Garis who, in *The Dickens Theatre* (Oxford: Clarendon, 1965), p. 230, discerns "social prophecy" in the

marriage, an intimation that "the condition of England can be saved only by a new and deep amalgamation of the classes."

19. See p. 191.

20. Carlyle's discussion of the present tense in *The French Revolution* illuminates Dickens's use of it throughout the Podsnap-Veneering sections of *Our Mutual Friend* (as well as in *Bleak House* and *A Tale of Two Cities*): "For indeed it is a most lying thing that same Past Tense always. . . . Not *there* does Fear dwell, nor Uncertainty, nor Anxiety; but it dwells *here*; haunting us, tracking us; running like an accursed ground-discord through all the music-tones of our Existence;—making the Tense a mere Present one!" (*FR*: III, 81). Dickens noted, in the summer before he began writing *Bleak House,* that he was reading *The French Revolution.* "for the 500th time" (*Letters,* II, 335).

21. Levine, *The Boundaries of Fiction* (Princeton: Princeton Univ. Press, 1968), p. 15; Kermode, *The Sense of an Ending* (London: Oxford, 1966), p. 58; Girard, *Deceit, Desire, and the Novel,* trans. Yvonne Freccero (Baltimore: Johns Hopkins, 1965), pp. 290-98.

Rosemary Mundhenk (essay date 1979)

SOURCE: "The Education of the Reader in *Our Mutual Friend*," in *Nineteenth-Century Fiction,* Vol. 34, No. 1, June, 1979, pp. 41-58.

[In the following essay, Mundhenk maintains that some of the confusing plot elements in Our Mutual Friend *are caused by the author's deliberate attempts to manipulate and deceive his readers and thus to educate them about the limitations of individual perception.]*

The narrator of *Our Mutual Friend* describes Twemlow as a creature "condemned to a passage through the world by such narrow little dimly-lighted ways, and picking up so few specks or spots on the road."[1] Vexed by the "insoluble question whether he was Veneering's oldest friend, or newest friend" (I, 2), fooled by Fascination Fledgeby into thinking that Riah is the villain who controls his debts, the Knight of the Simple Heart is confused by appearances in the world of the novel. Although Twemlow's crisis of perception and knowledge is both more comic and greater in degree than those of the other characters, everyone in the novel must meander for a while through "dimly-lighted ways" only to be confused by lack of knowledge or misled by a few "specks or spots on the road." The reader too cannot escape temporary confusion. Like many characters, he is deceived by the appearances of things. Like many characters, he is confronted periodically with his own limited knowledge.

In particular, Dickens's narration of Noddy Boffin's stint as miser forces the reader to be misled and to fall into er-

Charles Dickens, 1812–1870.

ror about Boffin's real self and intentions. Dickens limits the reader's perception of Boffin during those chapters in which Boffin plays the miser so that the reader is compelled to share Bella Wilfer's belief that Boffin has changed. In fact, Boffin's performance is so persuasive that it has led many critics to question Dickens's intention and judgment. Jack Lindsay argues that "the picture of the perversion through wealth has been too true, too effectively done. In point of fact we feel two Boffins."[2] Similarly, A. O. J. Cockshut finds Boffin's confession unconvincing because Boffin's acting was so convincing: "There can be no doubt that in the miserly passages, especially as Boffin listens to the grotesque stories of misers past, a very deep excitement spreads into the writing."[3] Boffin's piece of acting led G. K. Chesterton to suspect that Dickens originally intended Boffin's avarice to be real, but changed his mind at the last minute.[4] Chesterton's mistaken assumption has been corrected by F. X. Shea's investigation of the holograph manuscript, which proves that Dickens early planned the plot between Rokesmith and Boffin, a plot which included Boffin's posing as miser.[5] Although Shea has resolved the question of intention, Dickens's manipulation of the Boffin plot remains unsettling to many readers and critics. I suggest that Dickens deliberately makes the Boffin masquerade unsettling for the benefit of the reader, in an attempt to shock the reader with his own misjudgment, thereby to educate him. Dickens does for the reader what Boffin does for Bella. The reader is forced to learn that his perception has been limited and his knowledge partial.

The narration of Boffin's supposed change is handled very differently from that of John Harmon's disguise, the other "pious fraud" in *Our Mutual Friend.* Unlike the other disguises in the novel, such as Bradley Headstone's donning a Rogue Riderhood costume and Wegg's pretending to be a literary man, Harmon's and Boffin's pretenses are undertaken for the best of reasons: John Harmon wishes to save both Bella and himself from a maliciously arranged marriage, and Noddy Boffin wishes to educate Bella and to save her from her own greed. Yet the narrative is structured so that the reader learns of the truth behind these two disguises in very different ways. The narrator allows the reader to recognize early that Julius Hanford and John Rokesmith are John Harmon, but the reader must wait with Bella for Noddy's revelation. Dickens's choice of contrasting methods of narration indicates that he intended them to have contrasting effects on the reader.

In the Postscript to *Our Mutual Friend,* Dickens stated his intention to suggest that Harmon is alive and has assumed new identities: "When I devised this story, I foresaw the likelihood that a class of readers and commentators would suppose that I was at great pains to conceal exactly what I was at great pains to suggest: namely, that Mr. John Harmon was not slain, and that Mr. John Rokesmith was he." Clearly, his plan was not to tell but to suggest that Rokesmith is Harmon. He wanted the reader to draw the obvious conclusion for himself and perhaps to suppose that the author is attempting to conceal Rokesmith's identity. Dickens's intention is borne out by the novel. The figure of John Harmon, dead or alive, ties together the otherwise unconnected first five chapters and is prominent in the mind of the reader from the outset. Although the narrator does not confirm the identity of Harmon-Rokesmith until the pivotal chapter "A Solo and a Duett," late in Book II, the earlier clues are too numerous and too important to ignore: the mysterious, agitated manner of Julius Hanford at Hexam's and at the police station; Rokesmith's "constrained" and "troubled" manner at his first meeting with Bella (I, 4); his lack of references; the coincidence of his securing a room at the Wilfer home and employment at Boffin's; his seemingly maniacal avoidance of Mortimer Lightwood. Dickens leads the reader to conclude for himself that Hanford and Rokesmith are Harmon.

On the other hand, whereas Dickens was at great pains to suggest Harmon's identity, he was at great pains to conceal from the reader that Boffin is only playing the miser. The final notes for the novel indicate that Boffin's "pious fraud" was meant to deceive the reader as well as Bella. The reader's perception of Boffin's avarice is to be tied carefully to Bella's point of view; in the plans for Book III, chapter 4, Dickens writes:

> Work up to *Bella's account* of the change in Mr. Boffin—*broken to the reader through her*—

> Mercenary Bella, Money, Money, money *Lay the ground very carefully all through*

Dickens's . . . [emphasis] suggests his care in limiting the reader's knowledge to what Bella knows. Similarly, the notes for chapter 5 indicate Dickens's plan to keep both Bella and the reader unaware:

> Mr Boffin and Rokesmith and Mrs Boffin, having, unknown to reader, arranged their plan, now strike in with it

> She always touched and hurt by even the pretended change in her husband. Can't bear Bella to see him so.

> Work in The Misers—to bring out his pretended love of money

> *Lay the ground for Mrs Lammle*

> *Bella at war with herself*[6]

> Keep Bella watching, and never suspecting

Adhering to these plans, Dickens first indicates the change in Boffin in a conversation between Bella and Mr. Wilfer at the end of Book III, chapter 4: "But Mr. Boffin is being spoilt by prosperity, and is changing every day." Because the reader has not seen Boffin for some six chapters, Bella's sudden revelation is plausible. Then, in chapter 5, Bella's suspicions are dramatized for the reader. In the opening scene, Bella and the reader witness Boffin setting Rokesmith's salary, announcing that he intends to "buy *him* out and out," and proposing that Bella and the Boffins join together "to hold our own now, against everybody (for everybody's hand is stretched out to be dipped into our pockets), and we have got to recollect that money makes money, as well as makes everything else." Although Bella's perception of Boffin's behavior is verified by the narrator's mention of Mrs. Boffin's unease, the scene is dominated by Bella's point of view. Bella's consciousness frames the scene. The chapter opens with Bella's entering Mr. Boffin's room in the midst of a discussion between Boffin and Rokesmith: "On that very night of her return from the Happy Return, something chanced which Bella closely followed with her eyes and ears. . . . Mr. and Mrs. Boffin were reported sitting in this room [Boffin's], when Bella got back. Entering it, she found the Secretary there too." The scene closes with Bella's private reaction to what she has just witnessed: "What he said was very sensible, I am sure, and very true, I am sure. It is only what I often say to myself. Don't I like it then? No, I don't like it, and, though he is my liberal benefactor, I disparage him for it." Spatially and temporally, the scene is presented from Bella's point of view. The reader, like Bella, has no access to the conversation that took place before Bella's arrival.[7]

Although the conversation itself is presented dramatically by an external narrator, the scene is punctuated by brief descriptions of Bella's observing and reacting to Boffin's display of greed. Bella barely speaks, and yet the narrator emphasizes her presence as an observer. At Rokesmith's exit, "Bella's eyes followed him to the door, lighted on

Mr. Boffin complacently thrown back in his easy-chair, and drooped over her book." While Boffin lectures, Bella "ventured for a moment to look stealthily towards him under her eyelashes, and she saw a dark cloud of suspicion, covetousness, and conceit, overshadowing the once open face." Of the four characters in the room, Bella is the only one whose thoughts are described or implied by the narrator: she "felt that Mrs. Boffin was not comfortable"; she is a "deceiving Bella . . . to look at him with that pensively abstracted air, as if her mind were full of her book, and she had not heard a single word" (III, 5). The reader's perception of the scene thus is closely allied with Bella's. Both Bella and the reader suffer the same lack of knowledge, and both are deceived by Boffin's performance. Granted, the reader is ironically distanced from Bella in that he, more than Bella, recognizes its aptness and perhaps its potential lesson for the mercenary Bella. Nevertheless, Dickens manipulates point of view in order to place Bella and the reader in similar states of unknowing.

Dickens uses the same technique in the other scenes in which Noddy performs for Bella. At the end of this chapter Boffin lectures Rokesmith for spending too much money. Again, Bella's consciousness—her studious watching of Boffin—frames the scene, and throughout the scene her presence as an observer is emphasized. When Boffin's treatment of his secretary later forces Bella to defend Rokesmith and to leave the Boffin home, the climactic scene is framed by Bella's perspective. Within the scene itself, the narrator departs from his objective reporting of externals only when he discloses Bella's state of mind; for instance, Bella "involuntarily" raises her eyes, and she begins "to understand what she had done" (III, 15). The account of Boffin's visits to bookstores in search of biographies of misers is limited even more explicitly to Bella's perceptions (III, 5). In this case, the narration is dominated by the limited, third-person point of view.

Although the reader's knowledge of the change in Boffin is determined for the most part by Bella's knowledge—the reader sees what Bella sees—the narrator allows the reader to witness Boffin's performances in another context, Boffin's scenes with Wegg and Venus. In Book III, chapter 6, Boffin brings his volumes on misers to the Bower for a reading. Although the scene is narrated objectively by an external narrator, the reader sees Boffin exactly as Wegg and Venus see him. Before Boffin arrives, the friendly movers discuss their plot against him. Subsequently, the reader's perception of Boffin's miserly obsession is influenced by his knowledge of Wegg's plot, just as Wegg and Venus have in mind their friendly move as they watch Boffin. Like the reader, Wegg and Venus are clearly observers, suspiciously eyeing Boffin. Furthermore, in describing their watchfulness, the narrator implies their reactions:

> Mr. Wegg and Mr. Venus looked at one another wonderingly: and Mr. Wegg, in fitting on his spectacles, opened his eyes wide over their rims, and tapped the side of his nose: as an admonition to Venus to keep himself generally wide awake.

And again:

Venus complying with the invitation while it was yet being given, Silas pegged at him with his wooden leg to call his particular attention to Mr. Boffin standing musing before the fire, in the space between the two settles.

By aligning the reader's observations with those of Wegg and Venus, Dickens clearly intends that this scene substantiate the reader's earlier acceptance (with Bella) of Boffin's avarice. In the plans for this chapter, Dickens directed himself to *relieve by making Wegg as comic as possible.*[8] There would be no need for comic relief if the reader were not expected to take Boffin's behavior seriously and to regard Boffin as another in the long list of characters dehumanized by greed. Furthermore, the care which Dickens takes in describing Boffin's library suggests his intention to convince the reader that Boffin is indeed a miser. As Stanley Friedman argues, the "feigned bibliomania seems intended to enhance the credibility of Boffin's behavior in these scenes, by serving as an added symptom and also, perhaps, as a supposed contributory cause."[9]

Until Boffin's pretense is revealed, Dickens continues to limit the reader's perception of Boffin to the perceptions of the gulled characters in one of three ways: by narrating a scene from the implied point of view of the gull, as in Wegg's and Venus's observation of Boffin's touring the Mounds (III, 6); by externally and objectively narrating a scene but limiting the facts to those perceived by one or more of the gulled characters, as in Boffin's visit to Venus's shop (III, 14) and Wegg's coming to terms with Boffin (IV, 3); or by punctuating an otherwise externally narrated scene with the point of view of the gulled characters, as in Boffin's meeting with the Lammles (IV, 2).

Only once does Dickens depart from this technique to offer the reader a glimpse of Boffin performing without witnesses. Near the end of Book III, chapter 14, as Boffin leaves Venus, the narrator allows the reader to witness the inner Boffin, seemingly engrossed in his miser's role and performing for no audience at all:

> "Now, I wonder," he meditated as he went along, nursing his stick, "whether it can be, that Venus is setting himself to get the better of Wegg? Whether it can be, that he means, when I have bought Wegg out, to have me all to himself and to pick me clean to the bones?"
>
> It was a cunning and suspicious idea, quite in the way of his school of Misers, and he looked very cunning and suspicious as he went jogging through the streets. More than once or twice, more than twice or thrice, say half-a-dozen times, he took his stick from the arm on which he nursed it, and hit a straight sharp rap at the air with its head. Possibly the wooden countenance of Mr. Silas Wegg was incorporeally before him at those moments, for he hit with intense satisfaction.

E. Salter Davies has pointed out the problem created by this passage: "Was Boffin the sort of man who would keep up his miserly pretence when there was no one to observe him?" Davies' defense of the passage, that Boffin "showed considerable ability as an actor in his long-drawn-out struggle with Silas Wegg,"[10] is plausible but somehow doesn't satisfy. If we bear in mind Dickens's careful manipulation of the reader throughout the Boffin plot, Boffin's performance in this passage seems intended to deceive the reader and the reader alone.[11] The passage is deliberately ambiguous. The narrator's use of the seemingly pejorative words "cunning" and "suspicious" leads the reader to conclude that Boffin is totally avaricious and self-absorbed. While it is possible that the conditional nature of Boffin's speech and the suppositional nature of the narrator's description ("looked very cunning" and "Possibly") indicate that the scene may not be a performance at all but the real Boffin's reaction to what he has just witnessed, Dickens nevertheless forces the reader to arrive at the wrong conclusion. Having absorbed the reactions of Bella, Wegg, and Venus, the reader now interprets this passage as a confirmation of Boffin's depravity.

Unlike Dickens's handling of the Harmon plot, the plotting of Boffin's disguise is planned and executed so that the reader—like Bella, Wegg, and Venus—is deceived. Boffin's pretense serves more than the "double purpose" that Arnold Kettle suggests: "Bella is tested and changed by her experiences . . . and at the same time the possibilities of corruption inherent in the Boffin-situation are triumphantly revealed."[12] The possibilities of corruption would not be so triumphantly revealed if the reader were not forced to believe in the possibility of Boffin's greed. Another purpose, suggested by Masao Miyoshi, is that Boffin's "role-playing" can be seen as his "way of obviating an unpleasant new self that could very well have emerged from his sudden condition of wealth."[13] Both theories are substantiated by the text. From the beginning, Boffin is uneasy with and suspicious of his newly acquired riches. After a session in which he is advised by Lightwood of his inheritance and teased by Wrayburn, Boffin emerges convinced that money is "a great lot to take care of." Shortly thereafter, confronted by a job-seeking Rokesmith, Boffin wonders "How much? . . . It must be coming to money" (I, 8). Well before the pretense, Boffin is dismayed by the "dismal swamp" of sycophants attracted by his money: "He could not but feel that, like an eminently aristocratic family cheese, it was much too large for his wants, and bred an infinite amount of parasites; but he was content to regard this drawback on his property as a sort of perpetual Legacy Duty" (II, 8).

Dickens's careful narration of Boffin's life as miser has still another purpose and another effect: the reader's education. Boffin fulfills the docetic function of the satirist, as Sylvia Manning notes, by "doing in life, with himself as material, what the satirist at least claims to do in art: presenting the ugly, without disguise and possibly even exaggerated in its ugliness, so that we will be able to recognize it for what it is."[14] The reader's lesson differs from Bella's. While she learns of the dehumanizing effects of greed and materialism and of the truth of her own nature, the reader learns of the error of easy judgments. Whereas Bella recognizes that she has misjudged her own nature, the reader finds that he too readily has judged the character of Noddy Boffin. Dickens manipulates the reader into misapprehending the essential Boffin on the basis of external, superficial behavior and limited perceptions of the gulled characters. Like Bella, the reader faces an awakening (primarily an aesthetic and cognitive one, whereas Bella's awakening is moral): the awareness of his limited vision.[15] As John M. Robson argues in his rhetorical analysis of the first number of the novel, "At the very least, Dickens may be seen as attempting, like a rhetor, to change his audience's attitudes and behavior."[16] Realizing his error, the reader also recognizes his exaggerated pride in his ability to perceive and to judge.

The juxtaposition of the soon-transparent Harmon disguise with the Boffin disguise further complicates both the reader's error in judgment and his lesson. By allowing the reader to guess early and correctly that Rokesmith is Harmon, Dickens inflates the reader's confidence in his powers of detection and judgment. Had Dickens's narrator simply *told* the reader of Harmon's identity, the reader would not be so convinced of his own ability to discover the truth behind appearances. There is a certain gamesmanship in Dickens's handling of this narration, as indicated in the Postscript's comment that some readers "would suppose that I was at great pains to conceal exactly what I was at great pains to suggest." Having recognized Harmon, the reader assumes that he knows what Dickens's narrator is about: the narrator has offered more clues to Harmon's identity to the reader than to the other characters and probably will continue to allow the reader more knowledge than the individual characters. The narrator, it seems, shares more of his omniscience with the reader than with any character, except perhaps Harmon.[17] The narrator, however, manipulates Boffin's disguise so that the reader knows less than some characters (Harmon, Mrs. Boffin, Mr. Boffin) and only as much as the gulled characters (Bella, Wegg, Venus). Thus, when Boffin reveals his disguise, the reader's inflated belief in his role as detective and in his powers to perceive and to judge is deflated.

By learning of his limited powers of perceiving and knowing, the reader becomes engaged actively in the thematic concerns of the novel. The world of ***Our Mutual Friend*** is one of surfaces and veneers which often belie essences. Each character searches for knowledge or truth in an environment of fog and dimmed light: "It was a foggy day in London, and the fog was heavy and dark. Animate London, with smarting eyes and irritated lungs, was blinking, wheezing, and choking; inanimate London was a sooty spectre, divided in purpose between being visible and invisible, and so being wholly neither" (III, 1). Like Mr. Venus's shop of "objects, vaguely resembling pieces of leather and dry stick, but among which nothing is resolvable into anything distinct" (I, 7), the world of the novel is not entirely obscure, but, more cruelly, only partially obscure, tantalizing the perceiver with half-truths. Twemlow is confused by the appearance of friendship and entirely deceived by Fledgeby's false humility. At her death, Betty Higden takes Lizzie to be "the boofer lady," Bella. Georgiana Podsnap, reared in the shade, seeing life mainly in the reflections of her father's boots and in "the walnut and rosewood tables of the dim drawing-room" (I, 11), naïvely accepts the Lammles' interest in her as genuine. Sophronia and Alfred Lammle mistake the appearance of wealth for wealth, realize their error only after marriage, and resolve to use appearances to prey upon others. Bradley Headstone devotes his life to the appearance of respectability and, in so caging his own nature, teases the beast within him.

In such a world of limited knowledge and confused perception, the ability to understand and to judge is flawed. Bella misjudges herself by thinking that wealth is all that she values. Limited information leads Miss Potterson to believe Riderhood and to condemn Hexam, and Jenny Wren to misjudge Riah. Like the reader who misapprehends Boffin, these characters err innocently because they do not know all there is to know. At the other extreme is Podsnap, proud in his ignorance, dismissing with a flourish of his right arm the facts which do not conform to his preconceptions: "I don't want to know about it; I don't choose to discuss it; I don't admit it!" (I, 11).

Throughout the novel, only John Harmon has both the inclination and the position to acquire sufficient knowledge before judging and acting. The initial reason for his return to London in disguise is his desire to know Bella before acceding to his father's wishes. Later, his supposed death allows him the flexibility to prove Bella, to seek the truth behind the charges against Hexam, to "repair a wrong" against Lizzie (II, 13), and to resolve his questions about his own identity. Yet even Harmon's power to know and to set things right with his knowledge is limited. There are areas, as James A. Davies notes, "where his efforts have no effect, the Headstone/Wrayburn sequence being the main example. His effectiveness is pessimistically qualified by our sense of a world of dark and uncontrollable emotion and violence, unsusceptible to order or to virtuous influence."[18]

The narrator of *Our Mutual Friend* does not free the reader from the limitations on knowledge which plague the characters but immerses him in the crowded world of appearances and entanglements. Only occasionally does the narrator immediately share his omniscience and invite the reader to judge with him. This happens primarily in the heavily satiric passages: the descriptions of Society, the Veneerings, the Podsnaps, and Mrs. Wilfer. For much of the novel, however, the reader is forced to discover for himself, as in his gradual perception of the Harmon disguise, and in the case of Boffin, to learn from the error of his discoveries.

The equation of reading with a process of learning and discovery has been described by Wolfgang Iser in his study of the development of the author-reader relationship from Bunyan to Beckett: "The reader discovers the meaning of the text, taking negation as his starting-point; he discovers a new reality through a fiction which, at least in part, is different from the world he himself is used to; and he discovers the deficiencies inherent in prevalent norms and in his own restricted behavior." The nineteenth-century novel, according to Iser, makes a transition between the form of the eighteenth-century novel, which "gives the reader the impression that he and the author are partners in discovering the reality of human experience," and the twentieth-century novel, which forces the reader "to strive for himself to unravel the mysteries of a sometimes strikingly obscure composition."[19] The relationship between the author and the reader in *Our Mutual Friend* clearly falls between these two poles and, if one accepts Iser's notion of development, can be seen as a transition between the eighteenth-century and twentieth-century forms. On the one hand, the satiric and morally righteous voices of Dickens's narrator create a partnership between reader and author, so that when the narrator judges, the reader shares his moral sympathies; even when the reader is misjudging Boffin, he is allied with the narrator in condemning greed. On the other hand, the reader of *Our Mutual Friend* is not always *told,* but often offered clues which lead him to unravel for himself the complexities of plot and character and, in the case of Boffin's pretense, to misapprehend reality.

The manipulation of the reader's knowledge in the Boffin case is only one instance of Dickens's confusing the reader in order to force him into a more active role of discovery. The first chapter of the novel offers examples of two stratagems which Dickens continues to use throughout the novel. First, in the opening paragraphs, the narrator seems tentative or even unsure about the Thames scene he describes:

> The figures in this boat were those of a strong man with ragged grizzled hair and a sun-browned face, and a dark girl of nineteen or twenty, sufficiently like him to be recognisable as his daughter. The girl rowed, pulling a pair of sculls very easily; the man, with the rudder-lines slack in his hands, and his hands loose in his waistband, kept an eager lookout. He had no net, hook, or line, and he could not be a fisherman; his boat had no cushion for a sitter, no paint, no inscription, no appliance beyond a rusty boat-hook and a coil of rope, and he could not be a waterman; his boat was too crazy and too small to take in a cargo for delivery, and he could not be a lighterman or river-carrier; there was no clue to what he looked for, but he looked for something, with a most intent and searching gaze. The tide, which had turned an hour before, was running down, and his eyes watched every little race and eddy in its broad sweep, as the boat made slight headway against it, or drove stern foremost before it, according as he directed his daughter by a movement of his head. She watched his face as earnestly as she watched the river. But, in the intensity of her look there was a touch of dread or horror.
>
> (I, 1)

As he reads this passage, the reader's role is not unlike that of the detective searching for the clue which will bring the scene into focus and make sense of what he sees. Much of the description proceeds by negatives: "He had no net, hook, or line, and he could not be a fisherman; his boat had no cushion for a sitter, no paint, no inscription, no appliance beyond a rusty boat-hook and a coil of rope, and he could not be a waterman." The mystery and tentativeness are compounded by the narrator's repetition of the words "something" and "thing" throughout the first chapter. In the girl's look there is "a touch of dread or horror," not "dread *and* horror" but "dread *or* horror," as if the narrator is guessing; similarly, her age is "nineteen or twenty." Secondly, in this initial description, the narrator withholds significant facts and thus offers the reader only partial knowledge. The "something" that the "strong man with ragged grizzled hair" searches for is later revealed to be a corpse. The "something" that he washes in the river (I, 1) turns out to be money. Dickens continues to use these two stratagems, description by negation and withholding of information, to engage the reader in the themes of the novel and to force upon him a limited perspective.

By far Dickens's most effective way of limiting the reader's knowledge in *Our Mutual Friend* is the narrator's shifting point of view, particularly his adoption of limited, third-person points of view. Throughout the novel the narrator manipulates point of view, as we have already seen him doing in the Boffin plot. Either he limits the reader's point of view to the perspective of one character, or he includes the internal perspective of one character in an otherwise objective narration. Furthermore, the character whose perceptions are most accessible to the reader is often confused by what he witnesses, misled by his perceptions, or ill-prepared to understand thoroughly what he perceives. For instance, Bradley Headstone's mysterious pursuit of Eugene Wrayburn through the Plashwater Weir Mill Lock is presented from the point of view of a rather sleepy Riderhood, who only gradually recognizes his visitor and still cannot account for Headstone's "honest man's dress":

> When Riderhood had run to his second windlass and turned it, and while he leaned against the lever of that gate to help it to swing open presently, he noticed, lying to rest under the green hedge by the towing-path astern of the Lock, a Bargeman.
>
> The water rose and rose as the sluice poured in, dispersing the scum which had formed behind the lumbering gates, and sending the boat up, so that the sculler gradually rose like an apparition against the light from the bargeman's point of view. Riderhood observed that the bargeman rose too, leaning on his arm, and seemed to have his eyes fastened on the rising figure.
>
> (IV, 1)

Headstone's subsequent attack on Wrayburn is narrated entirely from Wrayburn's point of view, but Wrayburn is emotionally torn by the crisis in his relationship with Lizzie and unable to recognize the disguised Headstone in the darkness:

> He had sauntered far enough. Before turning to retrace his steps, he stopped upon the margin, to look down at the reflected night. In an instant, with a dreadful crash, the reflected night turned crooked, flames shot jaggedly across the air, and the moon and stars came bursting from the sky.
>
> Was he struck by lightning? With some incoherent halfformed thought to that effect, he turned under the blows that were blinding him and mashing his life, and closed with a murderer, whom he caught by a red neckerchief—unless the raining down of his own blood gave it that hue.
>
> Eugene was light, active, and expert; but his arms were broken, or he was paralysed, and could do no more than hang on to the man with his head swung back, so that he could see nothing but the heaving sky. After dragging at the assailant, he fell on the bank with him, and then there was another great crash, and then a splash, and all was done.
>
> (IV, 6)

Similarly, the reader's perception of the first meeting between Rokesmith and Boffin (I, 8) is limited almost entirely to the point of view of Boffin, who is uncomfortable with his new wealth and who has just been confused by Wrayburn's teasing. Although the reader maintains some ironic distance from Boffin, he perceives Rokesmith much as Boffin does and is given access to only Boffin's thoughts. Later when Harmon visits Pleasant Riderhood (II, 12), the reader is given Pleasant's perspective; of the two characters, she has the lesser ability to understand the meeting.

As Fred W. Boege has argued in his important article on Dickens's use of point of view, our image of Dickens as "primarily an objective novelist who uses the loosely omniscient point of view" is "incomplete."[20] Although Dickens's narratives hardly anticipate the consistent and studied use of the limited point of view in the fiction of James or Conrad, Dickens was clearly aware of the effect on the reader. Richard Stang also notes Dickens's use of the technique in *Our Mutual Friend* and argues that Dickens "saw it as a valuable means of rendering the inner life of his characters."[21] Certainly John Harmon's long monologue (II, 13) and Bella's debates with herself are designed to render the inner life. Yet Dickens's frequent choice of the perspective of exceptionally minor characters indicates that he uses the limited point of view not only to give his characters psychological depth, but also to limit the reader's perspective and thereby engage him in the blurred and shadowy world of the novel. Thus, to describe the Harmon wedding, the narrator creates Gruff and Glum and renders the scene from the perspective of the old pensioner who plays no other role in the novel (IV, 4).[22] Or the narrator will invent only an undelineated presence, limited in space and time, like the "Whosoever" of the following passage:

> Whosoever had gone out of Fleet Street into the Temple at the date of this history, and had wandered disconsolate about the Temple until he stumbled on a dismal churchyard, and had looked up at the dismal windows commanding that churchyard until at the most dismal window of them all he saw a dismal boy, would in him

have beheld, at one grand comprehensive swoop of the eye, the managing clerk, junior clerk, common-law clerk, conveyancing clerk, chancery clerk, every refinement and department of clerk, of Mr. Mortimer Lightwood, erewhile called in the newspapers eminent solicitor.

(I, 8)

The frequent shifting of what Uspensky calls the temporal and spatial planes, from the omniscient, objective voice of the narrator to the third-person, limited points of view of numerous characters, shatters the reader's expectation of a controlled, unified world in the novel. At the very least, the accessibility of whatever unity there is has been limited.

By frequently limiting the reader to the impaired perspective of confused or gulled characters, by deliberately suspending knowledge or obscuring what the reader wants to know, the narrator thus creates a structure characterized by "the juxtaposition of incompatible fragments in a pattern of disharmony or mutual contradiction," as J. Hillis Miller argues.[23] Although given clues, the reader must often form his own pattern of the fragments, resolve for himself the contradictions and participate actively in the process of discovery that he shares with the characters. In this process of discovery, the reader is led by the narrator's clues into confusion and error.

Dickens's active engagement of the reader in the world of **Our Mutual Friend** should not surprise us. Dickens is always the rhetorical artist, fashioning from the matter of his world structures and narrations designed to affect his reader. From Dickens's handling of character and plot to his manipulation of point of view, all the techniques of his craft work to affect the reader: to arouse him to sympathy or anger, to confuse him, to instruct him.[24] In a letter to Forster, Dickens spoke of "that particular relation . . . which subsists between me and the public."[25] Indeed, that relation was very "particular" because, as a nineteenth-century writer, he enjoyed an audience for whom the popular novel and the serious novel had not become antithetical forms and because he, more than any other nineteenth-century novelist, emotionally and aesthetically depended upon the reactions of his readers. The public readings, which he pursued so feverishly that they hastened his death, were to him "like writing a book in company."[26] Similarly, periodical publication was suited to that relationship between Dickens and his public, for it offered him the knowledge of his readers' reactions to a novel before it was completed and the luxury of responding to those reactions.[27] Furthermore, as editor of *Household Words* and *All the Year Round,* he insisted that his contributors not underestimate the intelligence of the audience, "that, though their essays must be clear, they should not write down to their audience."[28] This advice he himself took seriously, particularly in the later novels in which he increasingly told the reader less and led him to discover more. Thus in **Our Mutual Friend** "that particular relation" assumes a very active form. In his last completed novel, Dickens

limits the reader's perspective and knowledge and leads him through error to discovery.

Notes

1. *Our Mutual Friend,* introd. E. Salter Davies, New Oxford Illustrated Dickens (London: Oxford Univ. Press, 1952), Bk. III, ch. 13. Subsequent references are to this text and indicate book and chapter.

2. *Charles Dickens* (New York: Philosophical Library, 1950), p. 382.

3. *The Imagination of Charles Dickens* (New York: New York Univ. Press, 1962), p. 181.

4. Introd., *Our Mutual Friend,* Everyman's Library ed. (New York: Dutton; London: Dent, 1907), p. xii.

5. "No Change of Intention in *Our Mutual Friend,*" *Dickensian,* 63 (1967), 37-40.

6. Ernest Boll, "The Plotting of *Our Mutual Friend,*" *Modern Philology,* 42 (1944), 113. Boll's article includes a transcript of Dickens's notes for the novel. The manuscript may be found at the Pierpont Morgan Library in New York.

7. Boris Uspensky, *A Poetics of Composition,* trans. Valentina Zavarin and Susan Wittig (Berkeley and Los Angeles: Univ. of California Press, 1973), pp. 57-80, discusses point of view on several planes: the ideological plane, the phraseological plane, the spatial and temporal plane, and the psychological plane. He defines the spatial and temporal plane as follows: "The author accompanies the character but does not merge with him; then the authorial description is not limited to the subjective view of the character but is 'suprapersonal.' In such cases the positions of the author and character correspond on the spatial plane, but diverge on the planes of ideology, phraseology, and so forth" (p. 58). Similarly, the narrator "may count time and order the chronological events from the position of one of the characters" (pp. 65-66).

8. Boll, p. 113.

9. "The Motif of Reading in *Our Mutual Friend,*" NCF [*Nineteenth-Century Literature*], 28 (1973), 52. See pp. 38-61 for a thorough account of the sources and thematic implications of Boffin's reading.

10. Introd., *Our Mutual Friend,* p. viii.

11. Mrs. Lammle shows up soon after, but there is no indication that she witnesses Boffin's performance and none that he was aware of her watching.

12. "*Our Mutual Friend,*" *Dickens and the Twentieth Century,* ed. John Gross and Gabriel Pearson (Toronto: Univ. of Toronto Press, 1962), p. 215.

13. "Resolution of Identity in *Our Mutual Friend,*" *Victorian Newsletter,* No. 26 (Fall 1964), p. 8.

14. *Dickens as Satirist* (New Haven: Yale Univ. Press, 1971), p. 225.

15. This argument, of course, does not account for the reader's emotional reaction, his sense of being "tricked." There is a serious problem in the rather simple psychology of the "pious fraud": having been shown his error, one is supposed to reform or convert. The strategy works with Bella, but it may not be so effective with a sophisticated reader. Furthermore, the problem is augmented by the modern reader's difficulty in accepting Bella's effusive gratitude after Boffin confesses.

16. "*Our Mutual Friend*: A Rhetorical Approach to the First Number," *Dickens Studies Annual,* ed. Robert B. Partlow, Jr., III (Carbondale: Southern Illinois Univ. Press, 1974), 198.

17. The narrator gives the reader a sense of omniscience by allowing him geographical and temporal freedom; the reader witnesses more scenes than any one character. Yet, in many scenes, the reader's knowledge is limited to the perspective of one or two characters.

18. "Boffin's Secretary," *Dickensian,* 72 (1976), 156. See pp. 148-57 for a discussion of the relationship between Harmon's position as Secretary and his increasing power and knowledge.

19. *The Implied Reader* (Baltimore: Johns Hopkins Univ. Press, 1974), pp. xiii, 102. Iser uses *Vanity Fair* to illustrate that the realistic novel is the halfway point in the development. Although he sees traces of the modern relationship between author and reader in Dickens's fiction, he cites primarily the early novels and is more interested in the narrator who is less identified with the implied author and more apt to become a character within the novel (like the narrator of *Vanity Fair*).

20. "Point of View in Dickens," *PMLA* [*Publications of the Modern Language Association*], 65 (1950), 91.

21. *The Theory of the Novel in England, 1850-1870* (New York: Columbia Univ. Press, 1959), p. 103.

22. J. Hillis Miller cites Gruff and Glum as an indication of the narrator's need to see the world from the perspective of persons engaged in it and as an example of the fragmented world of the novel. See *Charles Dickens: The World of His Novels* (Cambridge, Mass.: Harvard Univ. Press, 1958), p. 292.

23. Miller, p. 284.

24. See Harvey P. Sucksmith, *The Narrative Art of Charles Dickens* (Oxford: Clarendon Press, 1970), for the fullest treatment of Dickens's fiction as rhetorical art.

25. John Forster, *The Life of Charles Dickens,* ed. J. W. T. Ley (New York: Doubleday Doran, 1928), p. 646.

26. *The Letters of Charles Dickens,* ed. Walter Dexter, The Nonesuch Dickens, 3 vols. (London [Bloombury]: Nonesuch Press, 1938), II, 825.

27. George H. Ford, *Dickens and His Readers* (1955; rpt. New York: Gordian Press, 1974), p. 23, aptly

compares the reciprocity offered by periodical publication to the dynamic relationship between a stage actor and his audience.

28. Stang, p. 99.

Jerome Meckier (essay date 1981)

SOURCE: "Boffin and Podsnap in Utopia," in *The Dickensian,* Vol. 77, No. 3, Autumn, 1981, pp. 154-61.

[*In the following essay, Meckier discusses the use of the characters Podsnap and Boffin in Aldous Huxley's* Brave New World *and William Morris's* News from Nowhere, *respectively.*]

During the lecture-tour at the commencement of *Brave New World,* the Director of the Central London Hatchery and Conditioning Centre boasts about Bokanovsky's Process: from a 'bokanovskified egg', he gloats, as many as ninety-six embryos will grow, each eventually yielding a mentally retarded but 'full-sized adult.'[1] One can staff an entire plant with a work force of 'identical twins', docile products of a single, super-energized egg (*BNW,* 5). The sole drawback to applying Henry Ford's best-known idea, the principle of mass production, to biology is that, under normal conditions, it still takes thirty years for prospective workers from each hyperactivated egg to reach physical maturity. To prevent such inefficiency, the Director explains, brave new worlders have implemented 'Podsnap's Technique' (*BNW,* 7). Thanks to a new method of accelerating the ripening process of egg and embryo, the scientific violation of human development now requires two years instead of three decades.

At first, this reference to ***Our Mutual Friend*** in A.F. 632 seems inexplicable. Since no one decanted in the brave new world wastes time reading, the Director probably knows less about Podsnap than Benito Hoover and Bernard Marx do about their namesakes. Dickens's towering Philistine, his supreme snob, would eschew the technicalities of mass procreation as a touchy subject certain to crimson the cheek of Miss Podsnap. The joke, then, is largely Huxley's. 'Podsnap's Technique' is apparently a high-powered 'forcing apparatus' more insidious than the strategies employed at Dr Blimber's Academy.[2] It speeds up the maturation process but is actually hostile to genuine growth, for the object is to ensure greater conformity among the general population in the shortest time possible. 'So satisfied' with the status quo that he cannot understand anyone feeling differently,[3] Podsnap gives his name to a marvellous procedure for making sure that, in the London of the future, contentment with existing conditions is universal: 'Everybody's happy now' (*BNW,* 88). Regimentation of a mindlessly loyal work force is an ideal the Gospel of Podsnappery would certainly sanction.

In the successful purveyor of marine assurance Huxley recognized a literary prototype of the modern behaviourist.

Podsnap's congenital sympathy for the life-style of an au-tomaton identifies him as a tailor-made caricature of the dedicated Pavlovian.[4] A worshipper of unquestioned rou-tine, Podsnap devises for himself—and eagerly imposes on others—a repressive daily regimen: 'Getting up at eight, shaving close at quarter past, breakfasting at nine, going to the City at ten, coming home at half-past five, and dining at seven' (*OMF*, 174-5). As he performs his diurnal rounds, this expert on self-conditioning is as programmed as Epsi-lon Semi-Morons in the brave new world or dehumanized workers endlessly executing the same task on Ford's as-sembly line. Podsnap's 'Hideous solidity' (*OMF*, 177), the hallmark of the bourgeois Victorian, is analogous to the predictability cherished by the behaviourist mentality, so Huxley named a solution to one of the difficulties in the brave new world after Dickens's Mr Podsnap.

Actually, it is Mustapha Mond who perfects the technique for which Podsnap is best remembered. He uses Mr Pod-snap's 'favourite right-arm flourish' (*OMF*, 180) to illus-trate an 'inspired saying of Our Ford's':

'History', he repeated slowly, 'is bunk'.

He waved his hand; and it was as though, with an in-visible feather whisk, he had brushed away a little dust, and the dust was Harappa, was Ur of the Chaldees; some spider-webs, and they were Thebes and Babylon and Cnossos and Mycenae, Whisk, whisk—and where was Odysseus, where was Job, where Jupiter and Gotama and Jesus? Whisk—and those specks of an-tique dirt called Athens and Rome, Jerusalem and the Middle Kingdom—all were gone. Whisk—the place where Italy had been was empty. Whisk the cathedrals; whisk, whisk, King Lear and the Thoughts of Pascal. Whisk, Passion; whisk, Requiem; whisk Symphony; whisk . . .

(*BNW*, 38-39)[5]

The brave new world is founded on Ford's outrageous as-sumption and Podsnap's dismissive gesticulation. Hux-ley's recollection of ***Our Mutual Friend*** is responsible for Mond's obliterating hand motion. Allusion to Dickens also explains the pervasive sense of past civilizations and their heroes as 'dust' and 'dirt' ready to be swept away by Henry Ford, history's Golden Dustman.

Huxley uses Podsnap to undercut Mond's egotistic belief in the modern Age of Science as the pinnacle for the life process. He links Ford's disdain for the past with the short-sighted, insular complacency of Mr Podsnap, who regards other countries as 'a mistake'. It is customary for Podsnap to clear the world 'of its most difficult problems by sweep-ing them behind him' (*OMF*, 174), a move which, on one occasion, puts Europe, 'the whole of Asia, Africa, and America nowhere' (*OMF*, 180). Our Ford's complete con-fidence in breaking with the past ceases to be courageous and innovative; instead, it becomes a monstrous expres-sion of reactionary Podsnappery. Mustapha Mond, Henry Ford, and Mr Podsnap are birds of a feather. The pseudo-Messianic premise that history began all over again with the limited flowering of Ford's technological genius is placed in proper perspective as a modern variation of Pod-snap's view of himself as a spokesman for Providence.[6]

With a flawless method for 'getting rid of disagreeables' (*OMF*, 174), Podsnap behaves in Dickens's novel as dicta-torially as a World Controller. He occasions the death of the arts by insisting that Literature, Painting, Sculpture, and Music celebrate nothing but his own business-like regularity. Similarly, Mond abolishes further adventures in science and art. He censors 'A New Theory of Biology' because it dares to explain life in terms of 'some enlarge-ment of knowledge' instead of reaffirming a narrow-minded hedonism as the 'Sovereign Good' (*BNW*, 208-209). If Podsnap has his way as society's lawgiver, rising, shaving, breakfasting, and doing business will be the ex-tent of human activity: 'Nothing else to be permitted . . . Nothing else To Be—anywhere!' (*OMF*, 174-175).

Mond keeps brave new worlders childlike by refusing to tolerate ideas that might stimulate their minds.[7] Podsnap behaves analogously when he invokes as his constrictive ideal the naive mind and juvenile morals of 'the young person' (*OMF*, 175). Censoriously, he demands that 'ev-erything in the universe . . . be filed down and fitted to' this standard. A militant Procrustean with a hatred for life's multiplicities, Podsnap confines thinking and behav-ing to a few basic procedures, just as Pavlovians account for man in terms of stimuli and response. The perfect Lon-don for Podsnap would be commercial and strait-laced, whereas Mond's is a paradise for consumer and the pleasure-oriented. Yet both places are repressive and es-sentially puritanical. Above all, both are soulless. Huxley's borrowings seem thoroughly legitimate because they un-derscore the truth in Dickens's observation that the world of Mr Podsnap 'was not a very large world, morally' (*OMF*, 174). Neither is Mond's, which has no past and, since it forbids change, no future.

Using Podsnap as one of his models for Mustapha Mond enabled Huxley to divulge the reality beneath the mores of the superficially liberated brave new world. This sexually permissive, *soma*-drugged society is as conformist and spiritually repressed as mid-Victorian England, the citadel of Podsnappery. Mond and Henry Ford are not reputable futurists but outdated conservatives as pompous as Pod-snap. Reciprocally, this personage is not merely the 'offen-sive ass' (*OMF*, 51) Twemlow considers him. Huxley's al-lusions to ***Our Mutual Friend*** reveal that Podsnap is also a misguided perfectibilitarian who confuses England in the 1860s with the millenium.

The use of Podsnap in *Brave New World*, however, is not as startling as Mr Boffin's appearance in *News from No-where*. Bob and Dick are entertaining William Guest, who is newly arrived in the future via a dream-vision, when they are interrupted by a Dickensian apparition. Like Guest, the modern reader is immediately reminded 'of many pleasant hours passed in reading Dickens.'[8] He re-members Silas Wegg's first glimpse of Nicodemus Boffin as a broad, round-shouldered, one-sided old fellow in mourning, coming comically ambling toward the corner, dressed in a pea over-coat, and carrying a large stick. He wore thick shoes, and thick leather gaiters, and thick gloves like a hedger's. Both as to his dress and to himself, he was of an overlapping rhinoceros build, with folds in his cheeks, and his forehead, and his eyelids, and his lips, and his ears; grey eyes, under his ragged eyebrows, and broad-brimmed hat. A very odd-looking old fellow altogether.

(*OMF*, 90).

But in Morris's utopia the 'minion of fortune and the worm of the hour,' as Wegg enviously dubs Boffin (*OMF*, 361), has become a magnificient butterfly. 'I looked over my shoulder,' says Guest,

and saw something flash and gleam in the sunlight that lay across the hall; so I turned round, and at my ease saw a splendid figure slowly sauntering over the pavement; a man whose surcoat was embroidered most copiously as well as elegantly, so that the sun flashed back from him as if he had been clad in golden armour. The man himself was tall, dark-haired, and exceedingly handsome, and though his face was no less kindly in expression than that of the others, he moved with that somewhat haughty mien which great beauty is apt to give to both men and women.

(*NfN* [*News from Nowhere*], 28-29)

Guest wrongly assumes that such a glamorous Boffin must be at least a senator, yet he is just a man named Henry Johnson. Dick explains that Johnson is called Boffin 'as a joke,' 'partly because he is a dustman, and partly because' he dresses 'so showily,' wearing as much gold 'as a baron of the Middle Ages' (*NfN*, 30). Like Huxley's joke in *Brave New World*, Morris's seems very much in earnest: his notion for an ideal future asserts its excellence by making Dickens's ironic description of Boffin as 'the Golden Dustman' come true literally. In Morris's reincarnation of the mediaeval world, life has become so aesthetically satisfying that dustmen are indeed gilded.

Boffin's requests for a lengthy interview with Guest are firmly discouraged, and the story quickly leaves him behind. His manifestation nevertheless provides the key to Morris's intentions as an utopist. It occurs in the Guest House during the first chapter in which the narrator fully realises that he has entered the future. Morris's refulgent Boffin is the opposite of Dickens's quaint, grotesquely attired old gentleman. At the same time, the pastoral, arts-and-crafts world of *News from Nowhere* is supposedly the reverse of the society Dickens anatomized in *Our Mutual Friend*.

Unlike the Director in *Brave New World*, Dick is thoroughly familiar with Dickens's novel. When Boffin appears, Dick expects the reader, along with Guest, to 'take the allusion' (*NfN*, 30). Morris's book is crammed full of references to Dickens's last completed novel for a very good reason. A communist society that redresses the pervasive deficiencies Dickens underlined in 1864-65, Morris

seems to be arguing, deserves to be called utopian. Morris maintains the implication that *News from Nowhere* is on the other side of the coin from *Our Mutual Friend.* He ingratiates himself with the reader by suggesting that the community he portrays is what Dickens secretly really wanted or should have proposed had he faced the consequences of his satire. In turn, a utopia that earns its name by reversing the social failing in *Our Mutual Friend* reveals that Dickens, in Morris's opinion, was describing England as dystopia.

To transform 'Dusty Boffin,' Morris merely imagines the converse, and Mr Boffin's outward appearance becomes as attractive as his heart and soul were in Dickens. To create a model society, Morris inverts the dystopian aspects of life in London that Dickens recounted twenty-five years earlier. For example, Dickens assails a society obsessed with 'money, money, money, and what money can make of life!' (*OMF*, 521) In Morris's finest comic scene Guest tries to purchase a pipe in a society that uses no currency (*NfN*, 49). Dickens's ironic title acquires literal validity in Morris's ideal society: friendship is universal. Readers of *Our Mutual Friend* are exhorted to ignore character, cultivation, and ideas but to 'have Shares' (159-160). Morris removes the satire from this directive by envisioning a non-materialistic society in which everyone is an equal partner when it comes to sharing power and pleasure.

Old Hammond depresses Guest when he brands the nineteenth century 'The Degradation,' a time when people were 'living in dung' (*NfN*, 198, 117). This sentiment originates in a recollection of *Our Mutual Friend*. Morris's socialism in *News from Nowhere* comes as much from his reading of Dickens as it does from a personal sense of society's ills. Dickens downgrades Parliament by having Veneering elected to it, the satire by association working against both parties. As their carriage jogs past the Houses of Parliament, Dick informs Guest that these relics from an unenlightened age have been preserved as 'a storage place for manure' (*NfN*, 43). Dickens inspires an excremental approach to Victorian politics when he accuses 'My Lords and gentlemen and honourable boards' of doing 'dust-shovelling' and 'cinder raking' until they 'have piled up a mountain of pretentious failure' (*OMF*, 565).

Dickens reproves the Victorian world in *Our Mutual Friend* for its burdensome but ineffectual government apparatus, its rigid class system, and its degenerating natural environment. Morris meticulously eliminates these shortcomings. As Hammond tells Guest, there are no politics and no professional politicians. Important decisions are made by an informed majority in commune, parish, or ward. Although genuinely democratic, government in *News from Nowhere* remains informal, personal, and virtually invisible. Social barriers have also disappeared. A dustman outfitted as a mediaeval baron supplies ample proof of this. Morris peers into the future and permits Hammond to describe approvingly the revolution of downtrodden workers that Dickens, like Carlyle, forecasted and feared. Class upheaval turns out to have reverse effects from the anarchy Dickens anticipated. It results in an orderly society that has no cream and no dregs, no Podsnap and Tippins atop the social pyramid and no outraged Hexam, Riderhood, or Headstone at its base. Instead, one finds what Hammond calls 'a system of life founded on equality and Communism' (*NfN*, 158).

Such a system was not the ideal Dickens had in mind. Huxley takes from *Our Mutual Friend* less ambitiously than Morris but more honestly and successfully. He can be said to make use of Dickens, whereas Morris and socialist criticism in general tend to abuse him. The manner in which *News from Nowhere* borrows from *Our Mutual Friend* explains how thinkers like Morris could see Dickens as a fellow socialist. If the satire in *Our Mutual Friend* gives a negative vision to which Morris believes he is furnishing the implied opposite, Dickens becomes the darling of the Marxists in spite of himself. Morris's procedures rest upon controversial assumptions, such as his apparent belief that satirists favour the opposite of systems they attack and his conviction that the mediaevel society of *News from Nowhere* is the only imaginable obverse of Dickens's England. Students of satire and Dickensians familiar with Dickens's contempt for the benighted past are unlikely to countenance either of these presuppositions.

The alternative vision Morris offers, since it is certainly not Dickens's, reminds one that the greatest Victorian novelist was radical in his complaints but traditionalist in his solutions. It could be that Morris's blueprint for the future originates from an aggrieved awareness of this discrepancy, as well as from appreciation of Dickens as a social critic. Dickens's outlook is frequently bleak enough to attract modern dystopians, but his recommendations rarely exceed the secularised Christian ethic he shared with the majority of his readers. Effectively satirical without any counter-balancing utopian impulses, the later Dickens had a frame of mind the thoroughly sceptical Huxley found congenial when designing his brave new world. Presumably, Dickens's attitude annoyed Morris and gave him an opportunity to do what he felt Dickens ought to have done on his own.

Throughout *Our Mutual Friend* darkness and dirt predominate. An environmental catastrophe, London is singularly lacking in such restoratives as sunlight and fresh air. To make conditions more intolerable, Dickens employs the pathetic fallacy satirically: shrubs wring their hands, trees are unhappy, and sparrows, fooled by a false spring, repent having married too early. Wrapped in fog, the city and its inhabitants blend together as one disease: with 'smarting eyes and irritated lungs . . . blinking, wheezing, and choking . . . the whole metropolis was a heap of vapours . . . enfolding a gigantic catarrh' (*OMF*, 479). In *News from Nowhere,* by contrast, all England, not just the Boffin domicile, can be called a bower. Morris repairs the parodic pastorals that Dickens used to comment on the ugliness of city life in an industrial age.

Morris's utopian mediaevalists comprehend the relationship between happiness and pleasant surroundings. They have reversed the deterioration of the human and natural environment so evident in Dickens. Waking for the first time in the communist future, Guest notices the freshness of the air. He swims in the Thames and marvels at the clarity of the water; for the pollution process has been arrested, and the river is packed with salmon. Now that heavy industry is banished from its banks, the Thames flows past a London that resembles an unsullied country town. Where Dickens complained that 'the national dread of colour' gave London 'an air of mourning' (*OMF*, 450), Morris's extravagantly dressed utopians 'make the bright day and the flowers feel ashamed of themselves' (*NfN*, 175).

Our Mutual Friend and *News from Nowhere* are novels of the river. The limited success of Morris's implicit claim to have conceived the only suitable answer to Dickens's dystopian satire relies heavily on this realisation. Morris establishes the worth of his political system by making a river of life out of Dickens's floating graveyard. Dickens undoubtedly would have embraced the results but denied the philosophy that allegedly can produce them. In Dickens the Thames claims Gaffer Hexam, Riderhood, and Headstone; Betty Higden dies along its banks after briefly finding, as Lizzie also does, one of the few towns near its source where 'the young river' flows 'unpolluted by the defilements that lie in wait for it on its course' (*OMF*, 567). Accompanied by Clara and Dick, Guest spends his last days in utopia sculling up a redeemed river toward an aesthetically satisfying past of guilds and communal harvesting. When Eugene Wrayburn sculls upstream in search of Lizzie, he is ambushed, assaulted, and violently disfigured by an incensed Bradley Headstone.[9] By contrast, Guest's Lizzie is the beautiful Ellen. She rows him up the river of time, and he grows younger with every mile. Morris creates utopia by reversing Dickens's environmental nightmare, by translating a river of darkness into an idyllic waterway. Insistently and quite successfuly, the idea of a reformed river is used to symbolize the virtues of Morris's new dispensation.

Allusions to *Our Mutual Friend* in *Brave New World* and *News from Nowhere* make the essence of each of these three novels clearer. The ostensibly amoral brave new world is surprisingly Podsnappian. It requires conformity from its hedonists. Evasive and prudish, it has merely evolved a new set of taboos. With Morris's help, Dickens's London can be recognised as a Victorian conception of dystopia. When Guest dreams of its alleged opposite, the earthly paradise of *News from Nowhere* springs into existence. Morris may have written to refute Bellamy's industrial utopia,[10] but the point of the rejection seems to be that the ideas the American socialist expressed in *Looking Backward* are not a major departure from the system Dickens decries. *Our Mutual Friend* has been called Dickens's most powerful statement about the difficulty of maintaining an independent inner self in a mechanical age.[11] It inspires Huxley and Morris as they wrestle with the same problem. It also provides fresh evidence of Dickens's continuing hold on the modern futurist imagination. *Our Mu-*

tual Friend, like *Hard Times,* deserves to be grouped with *Brave New World, 1984,* and the industrial wasteland in *Lady Chatterley's Lover:* it helps to start a movement in which utopia, formerly perfect but far-removed or hypothetical, becomes negative and imminent.[12]

Boffin and Podsnap are opposite poles in Dickens's novel: one collects dust, the other is full of it. Morris and Huxley present future worlds in which a Dickens character enters what is asserted to be his rightful kingdom. Each of these utopians discovers in a Dickens character a symbol for the type of personality he believes will control the future. Huxley cannot imagine anything worse than a future administered by a totalitarian regime of Podsnappian conformists. Although Morris renders the new with less skill than Dickens dissected the old, he pays the Victorian social critic a tremendous compliment: he can think of nothing better than a society that has solved the major problems Dickens identified in *Our Mutual Friend.* Key aspects of the brave new world are a logical extension of Dickens's nightmare, while the nostalgic, old-fashioned *News from Nowhere,* a less compelling novel of ideas than Huxley's, is a solution Dickens would not have welcomed as a plausible reversal of his negative visions. Indeed, the idea of reversal seems contrary to the momentum toward anti-utopia that *Our Mutual Friend* generates. It seems likely, therefore, that Podsnap will arrive in utopia before Boffin.

Notes

1. Aldous Huxley, *Brave New World* (London: Chatto & Windus, 1932), p. 5. Subsequent references are by page numbers with the abbreviation *BNW.*

2. Charles Dickens, *Dombey and Son* (New York: Dell, 1963), p. 174.

3. Charles Dickens, *Our Mutual Friend* (Baltimore: Penguin Books, 1971), p. 174. Subsequent references appear in the text by page number after the abbreviation *OMF.*

4. Pavlov was only fifteen in 1864-65 and did not study conditioning until past fifty, so Podsnap, as a natural behaviourist, is ahead of his times.

5. Mond's quotation from Ford was initially followed by an explanation: 'We have now given practical effect to what was, when Our Ford first uttered it, a counsel of perfection. The Past, the stupid unnecessary Past, has been abolished.' After deleting this passage during revision, Huxley remembered Mr Podsnap and added the specific names and places that are whisked away by Fordian maxim. See Donald Watt, 'The Manuscript Revisions of *Brave New World,' Journal of English and Germanic Philology,* 77 (July, 1978), 372.

6. With Ford as deity, time is told in years A.F. (After Ford). Dates are not needed for the period prior to his birth since nothing of consequence happened until then.

7. The model usually suggested for Mustapha Mond is Sir Alfred Mond, M.P., Minister of Health, financier, and industrialist. He became prominent in 1926 for the number and importance of enterprises he was connected with and for the scale of amalgamations incorporated in the firm of Imperial Chemical Industries, Ltd. Huxley's Mond is evidently a composite of Ford, Pavlov, Sir Alfred, and Podsnap. Huxley had also read Fulke Greville's *Mustapha* (1609), in which the poet ponders problems of statecraft and human malignity. Dickens modelled Podsnap on his friend and literary advisor, John Forster. Ley records the general opinion that Forster was dictatorial. Edgar Johnson confirms that Forster's mannerisms are 'embedded in Podsnap,' especially 'the sweeping gesture of dismissal.' See *The Dickens Circle* (New York: Dutton, 1918), p. 338; *Charles Dickens: His Tragedy and Triumph* (New York: Simon and Schuster, 1952), II, 1053; and James A. Davies, 'The Making of Podsnap,' *The Dickensian,* 70 (September, 1974), 145-158.

8. William Morris, *News from Nowhere* (New York: Monthly Review Press, 1966), p. 30. Subsequent references are included in the text by page number after the abbreviation *NfN.* About Morris J. W. Mackail writes: 'Of Dickens himself his knowledge and appreciation were both complete. It is not without value as an illustration of his curiously compounded personality that in the moods when he was not dreaming of himself as Tristram or Sigurd, he identified himself very closely with two creations of a quite different mould, Joe Gargery and Mr Boffin. Both of these amiable characters he more or less consciously copied, if it be not truer to say more or less naturally resembled, and knew that he resembled'. See the World Classics Edition of *The Life of William Morris* (London: Oxford University Press, 1950), Part I, p. 227.

9. On the second day up the Thames, Dick and Guest learn from Walter of a recent love triangle at Maple-Durham that recalls the imbroglio involving Wrayburn, Lizzie, and Headstone. But in Morris the community gives good advice before and during the crisis. It also takes therapeutic action after the disappointed suitor is killed in an attack upon his successful rival. See pp. 203-205.

10. Philip Henderson, *William Morris: His Life, Work and Friends* (New York: McGraw-Hill, 1967), p. 328.

11. Barry V. Qualls, 'Savages in a 'Bran-New' World: Carlyle and *Our Mutual Friend,' Studies in the Novel,* 10 (Summer, 1978), 209.

12. See Jerome Meckier, 'Dickens and the Dystopian Novel: From *Hard Times* to *Lady Chatterley's Lover',* R. G. Collins, ed., *The Novel and Its Changing Form* (Manitoba: University of Manitoba Press, 1972), pp. 51-58. An earlier version of the present essay was delivered to the Dickens Seminar at the annual meet-

ing of the Dickens Society during the MLA convention in San Francisco (1979).

Lewis Horne (essay date 1982)

SOURCE: "*Our Mutual Friend* and the Test of Worthiness," in *Dalhousie Review,* Vol. 62, No. 2, Summer, 1982, pp. 292-302.

[*In the following essay, Horne suggests that three of the characters in* Our Mutual Friend—*John Harmon, Silas Wegg, and Bradley Headstone—can be compared to Homer's hero Odysseus.*]

Shortly before he reveals his real name to her, John Rokesmith tells his wife Bella, "The time will come . . . when you *will* be tried,"[1] and with his warning articulates one of the central themes of *Our Mutual Friend.* Others are sounded throughout this dark work—themes of greed, money, identity—but the theme of trial, in this case a test of worthiness, provides a distinctive underpinning for the narrative and its events. The test I wish to discuss is self-imposed, directed toward the goal of domestic happiness, and concerns three male figures—John Harmon, Silas Wegg, and Bradley Headstone. In Harmon's case, the goal sets the novel apart from other works with a similar narrative pattern, that in which a central figure withdraws from activities in hopes of learning more about the moral qualities of those with whom he associates. The types range from a figure like Volpone with his malice-tinged roguery to someone like the morally engaged Duke in *Measure for Measure.* But for the three characters of this group, a reader finds a stronger analogue in the hero of Homer's *Odyssey.*

Although many features of the epic are missing from *Our Mutual Friend*—qualities of the central figures' personalities, the risky adventures of Odysseus, the magical apparatus and the appearances of supernatural beings, the proud and rowdy nature of the suitors—certain key elements overlap that make a comparison useful in exploring features of theme and unity in the novel. Dickens presents three Odyssean men, each trying to establish a home based on qualities conducive to Victorian domestic happiness. Each has different views of that happiness, faces different problems in his effort to achieve it. Each, in some manner, is a "disguised" guest. Each succeeds or fails not exclusively but primarily because of his own character and efforts, his efforts, in each case, involving the well-being of others. The Third Priest in *Murder in the Cathedral* says that "the steadfast can manipulate the greed and lust of others, / The feeble is devoured by his own."[2] If we see John Harmon trying to manipulate for the good of others, manipulating others as a loving parent might be construed to "manipulate" his children, then we can see the man as a "steadfast" Odysseus-figure. On the other hand, if we consider the careers of Bradley Headstone and Silas Wegg, we find—in both dramatic (or melodramatic) and comic

terms—the "feeble" Odysseus-figure being devoured by his own "greed and lust." The act of manipulating becomes an act of testing, both others and one's self, and the patterns of action involved find illuminating parallels in part of Homer's epic.

Homer's hero is himself large enough in variety of experience and character to encompass all three of the novel's male figures—John Harmon, the organizer and compassionate doer; Bradley Headstone, the self-destructive, obsessed, and wily man; Silas Wegg, the buffoon and trickster. No one of them combines all of Odysseus' attributes, appears as multi-faceted in achievement as W. B. Stanford finds Homer's hero to be—"the wise king, the loving husband and father, the brave warrior, the eloquent and resourceful *politique,* the courageous wanderer, the goddess-beloved hero, the yearning exile, the deviser of many ruses and disguises, the triumphant avenger, the grandson of Autolycus and the favorite of Athene."[3]

Yet John Harmon shows wiliness, courage, strength, can use the disguises and chicanery of the trickster—shows himself in many ways a Victorian Odysseus returning to his wife and hearth. If the wife is not yet his, she has been promised, and she must be won as Odysseus had again to win Penelope. In Harmon one observes in full nineteenth-century British measure the qualities Athene finds so important in Odysseus as he stands returned to the shore of Ithaka: he is civilized, intelligent, self-possessed.[4]

Michael Seidel has noted that "exiled heroes tend to remain apart from their tainted home until both they and the power they represent are ready to retake it."[5] As does Odysseus, so does John Harmon. He is prepared to leave London should Bella Wilfer fail his test rather than submit either her or himself to marriage without love. His identity held secret, he is known variously as the stranger, as Julius Handford, as the "man from Jamaica" (p. 54), the "man from Somewhere" (p. 55), "the man . . . whose name is Harmon" (p. 55). Noddy Boffin thinks of him momentarily as a piece of furniture. He is Lizzie Hexam's "unknown friend" (p. 587). Of himself, Harmon says, "I am nobody" (p. 140), and "I come . . . from many countries" (p. 141). His own comments and situation echo Odysseus, whether he claims to be "nobody" or "no man" to Polyphemus or whether he returns to Ithaka as a beggar, disguised, one so socially negligible in the eyes of nearly all the suitors that he is next to being "nobody."

Harmon makes of himself the disguised guest, Odysseus to Bella Wilfer's Penelope. One might see Bella's vanity and desire for money—her "lust and greed"—as allegorical versions of the suitors that Odysseus/Harmon must vanquish in order to discover the loyal Penelope/Bella. With the help of Noddy Boffin, the two men "manipulate" conditions when they carry out their scheme to have Boffin act out Bella's own greed. But such allegorical labelling is only partly apt, since most of the decent forces reside within the girl anyway and need only be strengthened, brought to the front. Her affection for her father, her awareness of her own faults, her admiration for Rokesmith, though that admiration she herself fails to recognize for a time—these are redeeming features susceptible to Noddy Boffin's charade. They are expressed most revealingly in her talk with Lizzie Hexam after Betsy Higgins' funeral and in the effect that Lizzie's quiet strength has on her. She describes the latter to Rokesmith, telling him that

> ". . . I feel as if whole years had passed since I went into Lizzie Hexam's cottage[.]"
>
> "We have crowded a good deal into the day," he returned, "and you were much affected in the churchyard. You are over-tired."
>
> "No, I am not at all tired. I have not quite expressed what I mean. I don't mean that I feel as if a great space of time had gone by, but that I feel as if much had happened—to myself, you know."
>
> "For good, I hope?"
>
> "I hope so," said Bella.
>
> (p. 593)

Not long after, Bella sees "The Golden Dustman At His Worst," leaves the Boffins for her own home, and marries Rokesmith in "A Runaway Match." The forces of her conceit and greed have been conquered by the forces of goodness she has held within for too long and also by the manipulations of Harmon/Rokesmith, those manipulations designed to test personal worthiness.

But other characters are not the only ones tested—in Ithaka or London. George deF. Lord has pointed out the importance of Odysseus' disguise to the hero himself, describing its significance as "inexhaustible":

> It enables him to test the charity of the suitors, and charity is one of the essential virtues in the world of the *Odyssey*. It suggests the fundamental weakness of all men and their dependence on their brothers. It dramatizes divine immanence in human affairs in accordance with the idea that the gods often take upon themselves the basest and poorest human shapes. It is a further demonstration that human worth is not graded according to rank or position or power. It represents the theme that all men are beggars, outcasts, and wanderers in some sense at one time or another, a theme that is traced through the fugitive Theoclymenus and such displaced persons as Eurycleia and Eumaeus. It is, finally, a test of Odysseus' own inner strength—his patience and self-restraint.[6]

If Harmon does not himself appear so severely tested as Odysseus, it is because we do not follow him through his period of tribulation but observe him at the end of that period, his lessons learned. Odysseus, as many critics have noted, is moving from the world in which the old heroic virtues, as characterized in the *Iliad,* are held as ideal, to a world in which domestic values are more significant.[7] The change he must undergo requires a dramatic shift from what was. Most of John Harmon's lessons of "patience and self-restraint" have already been learned. As Mortimer

Lightwood tells the story, Harmon has shown strength in standing against his unjust father on behalf of his sister's marriage plans, is so "shocked and terrified" at the older man's response, so unable to "manipulate" the man's "greed and lust," as it were, that he "takes flight, seeks his fortune" and wins it to some degree as a "small proprietor, farmer, grower—whatever you like to call it" (p. 57)—in "the country where they make the Cape Wine" (p. 55). He survives not only calamity on his return but a crisis of identity as well. Attacked, robbed, left for dead, he can wonder, so strong is the impression of having lost his self, his being, about "the scene of my death" (p. 422). He feels as though he must rediscover himself. "It is a sensation not experienced by many mortals," he thinks, "to be looking into a churchyard on a wild windy night, and feel that I no more hold a place among the living than these dead do, and even to know that I lie buried somewhere else, as they lie buried here. Nothing uses me to it. A spirit that was once a man could hardly feel stranger or lonelier, going unrecognized among mankind, than I feel" (p. 422).

Harmon begins a long monologue in Chapter 13 of *Book the Second* with a statement suggesting the quality in himself that he must—through steadfastness—conquer. He came back to England "mistrustful," he tells himself.

> '. . . I came back, shrinking from my father's money, shrinking from my father's memory, mistrustful of being forced on a mercenary wife, mistrustful of my father's intention in thrusting that marriage on me, mistrustful that I was already growing avaricious, mistrustful that I was slackening in gratitude to the two dear noble honest friends who had made the only sunlight in my childish life or that of my heartbroken sister."
>
> (p. 423)

More than that, he thinks, "I came back, timid, divided in my mind, afraid of myself and everybody here . . ." (p. 423).

As a result of his mistrust, his timidity, he had formulated his plan of disguising himself with the treacherous George Radfoot, so he could "form some judgment of my allotted wife . . . [and] try Mrs. Boffin and give her a glad surprise" (p. 424). Radfoot killed, identities confused, Harmon is pronounced dead. Should he return from the grave? That is the question Harmon faces. The answer depends mainly on Bella—on Bella's love of the man, not the name; on whether or not she would be better off to continue living as she is with the Boffins where she is already improving in character and charity, redeeming herself from the faults intensified in her by the older Harmon's will. By acknowledging the value of his own demise, Harmon wins a part of his own trial. He tests patience and trust, risks disappointment in Bella. He tests his own capacity for greed in his willingness to give up his inheritance to the Boffins. He tests his ability to *harmon*ize his environment, reversing the impulse of his father to *harm one*. He wins Bella through his own deeds and merit and not through his father's *fiat*.

The harmony is of the kind Odysseus achieved, the harmony of reconciliation. Love wins over lust and greed. And the reconciliation is presented, however much a modern reader might squirm at the sentimentality of its presentation, through the triumph of domestic bliss—the family with its infant Telemakhos.

Harmon succeeds much as a Victorian Odysseus might. He even has his own Eurykleia, Mrs. Boffin, to affirm that he is not Nobody but indeed the man who will fulfill the destiny only he can. Turning to Silas Wegg, however, we find a figure who pretends to the worth of Odysseus and his destiny. Wegg is parody. He is a rogue marked with villainish features, though Dickens' comic treatment keeps him at some distance from becoming the criminal character that Rogue Riderhood approaches. He is a grand illustration of that Affectation Fielding sees as a source of the comic, a man who should wish to think of himself as acting "like a genteel person," who has "a prospect of getting on in life" (p. 127)—both of which aims would be commendable if they were not grounded so fully in fraud.

A related feature of the man is his belief in his own cause, his own self-delusion. So much has he come to look on the house that the Boffins buy as "Our House" that he can and does view its new owners as interlopers, can and does claim "to be in its [the house's] confidence" (p. 88). So strong is his sense in the rightness of his cause that he can scarcely look on Noddy Boffin.

> "Every time I see him putting his hand in his pocket, I
> see him putting it into my pocket. Every time I hear
> him jingling his money, I hear him taking liberties with
> my money. Flesh and blood can't bear it."
>
> (p. 645)
>
> . . . . .
>
> ". . . Was it outside the house at present ockypied, to
> its disgrace, by the minion of fortune and worm of the
> house . . . that I, Silas Wegg, five hundred times the
> man he ever was, sat in all weathers, waiting for a er-
> rand or a customer? Was it outside that very house as I
> first set eyes upon him, rolling in the lap of luxury,
> when I was selling halfpenny ballads there for a living?
> And am I to grovel in the dust for *him* to walk over?
> No!"
>
> (p. 646)

Like Odysseus, Wegg waits for his moment. But one of the "feeble," he is "devoured by his own" greed and lust. Where Harmon has taken on the role of Nobody, of another, in order to verify the merits of others and, indirectly, of himself before becoming the Somebody that he truly is, Silas Wegg tries to become Somebody he is not, to take on a role that is not his. With his missing leg, with his stall, he is the mendicant. He sees himself as "an orphan" deserving aid from the Boffins, an orphan who has given up in the Boffins' cause "Miss Elizabeth, Master George, Aunt Jane, and Uncle Parker" (p. 386). Noddy Boffin, he fumes, is "the Usurper" (p. 554). Noddy Boffin—and his wife with him—is the suitor who must be

driven out of the home of his imagined family so he can take what he construes his rightful place to be. But when he tries the bow, as it were, when he tries to assert his claim through the device of the will he has discovered, he learns how far his greed has overextended itself, especially set alongside the love and generosity of the Boffins.

As he does in other novels, Dickens doubles some of his characters. Through this device, we find emphasized how fully Wegg fails his test and the Boffins pass theirs. As Wegg's double, Noddy Boffin shows us the loyal family retainer Wegg likes to think he is, one who holds the position of trust in the family that Wegg claims with Miss Elizabeth and company, one with the sensitivity Wegg would profess to have. Boffin has the humility and charity Wegg lacks: he hopes to increase his knowledge; he tries to assist others. These are features a reader notices. But in Wegg's eyes, Mr. Boffin embodies qualities Wegg fails to see in himself—greed, guile, blindness to moral direction. Rather than establish harmony, Wegg wants to disrupt it. Rather than own the right of his claim, he pretends to it. A reader could feel anxious about the danger he poses for the Boffins, but Dickens treats the man comically, makes him a parody of John Harmon, so that the reader does not squirm with apprehension as he goes about his crooked business but smiles with amusement.

The case of Bradley Headstone is more complex. In terms of his personality, he is driven by two desires—his love of Lizzie Hexam, his determination to advance himself. In terms of his presentation, his character has two reflectors—Rogue Riderhood, who shows in an extreme and debased form what social position Headstone wants to escape, and Eugene Wrayburn, who stands higher socially than Headstone can ever hope to stand and, partly by his position, partly by his manner, partly by his being Headstone's rival for Lizzie's love, taunts the schoolmaster, sometimes by cruel verbal jibes, sometimes by being simply who he is—and what Headstone would like to be. Yet Headstone, too, plays the Odyssean role, its parts more fragmented but still clear—Lizzie mirroring Penelope, Charlie Hexam Telemakhos, and Eugene Wrayburn the most insolent of the suitors. He is guest on the threshold of a world he cannot win, sometimes the proper and stiffly dressed schoolmaster, sometimes the rudely dressed workman. Which suit of clothes—or disguise—is more apt? Dickens raises the question, places Rogue Riderhood to suggest one possibility, Eugene Wrayburn another, but he does not provide an answer. If finally, Headstone fails, he fails not because Penelope fails the test but because he himself does. Though one might call him "steadfast" in his pursuit, that quality of character is flawed with a feebleness, moral and mental, that makes the man finally pathetic. He lacks the grandeur in his failure to evoke admiration but not the pathos to call forth pity.[8]

In Headstone, steadfastness becomes self-destructive obsession; prudence and reason give way to rashness and passion. The man's tormented awareness of Wrayburn's social position stiffens what is already a deforming restraint. Dickens provides telling details of his manner—emphasizing the word "decent" in describing the man's coat and waistcoat, shirt, tie, pantaloons, watch, and hair-guard for the watch; observing that "there was a certain stiffness in his manner of wearing this [kind of dress], as if there were a want of adaptation between him and it"; indicating the way in which Headstone has stored up a great deal of knowledge "mechanically," bearing it all with "a constrained manner, over and above." That "there was enough of what was animal, and of what was fiery (though smouldering) still visible in him" is amply borne out in certain gestures the man uses (pp. 266-7).

Two of the most important that indicate his deterioration have to do with hands and blood. They connect clearly with Headstone's attempted murder of Wrayburn and with the death of Rogue Riderhood and Headstone himself, but earlier descriptions of them provide dramatic preliminaries. Headstone's hands show his feelings, whether he clasps young Charlie Hexam's arm on first hearing of Wrayburn's interest in Lizzie or whether "the respectable right-hand clutching the respectable hair-guard of the respectable watch" shows that under Wrayburn's taunting Headstone "could have wound it round his throat and strangled him with it" (p. 342). His hands gesture dangerously whenever Wrayburn is part of the conversation. Talking to Jenny Wren about Lizzie, knowing he is the weaker rival, he wrenches "at the seat of his chair with one hand, as if he would have wrenched the chair to pieces" (p. 401). Later, Lizzie herself starts "at the passionate sound of the last words [he spoke to her], and at the passionate action of his hands, with which they were accompanied" (p. 452)—an action "which was like flinging his heart's blood down before her in drops upon the pavement-stones" (p. 453). Finally, with the despairing cry that "I hope I may never kill [Wrayburn]," he strikes a stone "with a force that laid the knuckles raw and bleeding" (p. 456).

In addition to these violent gestures, many of them associated with blood and all of them called forth by thoughts of Wrayburn, is the evidence of surging blood in his body, the flushed and perspiring face, the quivering lips, the way "his face turned from burning red to white, and from white back to burning red, and so for the time to lasting deadly white" (p. 400)—this while he talked to Jenny Wren. Later, the effect is striking, but not surprising to the reader, when "a great spirt of blood burst from his nose" (p. 704) as he conspires with Rogue Riderhood.

He is driven further in his madness because his disguise signifies more than it conceals. While Harmon, like Odysseus, can be Nobody, knowing who he is without shame, and while Wegg lacks the self-knowledge to know that he is Nobody or to know anything but what, rightly or wrongly, he thinks himself to be, Headstone is trying desperately to escape being Nobody. When he balks angrily at giving Wrayburn his name, the latter capitalizes on the fumble and calls him Schoolmaster, refusing to acknowledge him with more explicit identification. When Headstone pursues him in the London streets, Wrayburn leads him down a No Thoroughfare, turns to retrace his steps and in so doing "pass[es] him as unaware of his existence" (p. 606), as though he were Nobody. How many readers can forget the description of Headstone at that moment—"the exhaustion of deferred hope and consuming hate and anger in his face, white-lipped, wild-eyed, draggle-haired, seamed with jealousy and anger, and torturing himself with the conviction that he showed it all"—but more telling still the way in which the Schoolmaster passed his tormentor "like a haggard head suspended in the air" (p. 608)? How vividly Nobody this man has become!

With Rogue Riderhood, he does attempt a disguise, masking the Schoolmaster as a criminal. In the process the Schoolmaster is lost. After Headstone's failed attempt to murder Wrayburn, Riderhood enters the classroom, and, wanting to learn his name, asks Headstone to write it on the blackboard. Stirred by Riderhood, the schoolchildren twice read it out. Then Riderhood shows the bundle of clothes with which Headstone had disguised himself and afterward flung into the river.

> ". . . I drawed this here bundle out of a river! It's a Bargeman's suit of clothes. You see, it had been sunk there by the man as wore it, and I got it up."
>
> "How did you know it was sunk by the man who wore it?" asked Bradley.
>
> "Cause I see him do it," said Riderhood.
>
> They looked at each other. Bradley, slowly withdrawing his eyes, turned his face to the black board and slowly wiped his name out.
>
> (p. 867)

The implications of Headstone's simple act are strong. The Schoolmaster is no more. Even if he were to destroy Riderhood, Headstone the Schoolmaster could never be as he was. What he is now is the man Rogue Riderhood knows, the bargeman that in his madness and through disguise he had tried to become—that through his death and Riderhood's he finally succeeded in becoming. As Bradley Headstone, Odysseus never freed himself of his beggar's weeds.

Each of the three men has endeavored, as it were, *to enter.* What it is they try to get into is what sets them apart from others in the novel and gives them their kinship with Odysseus: their objective and the associated concern with identity. Many in the novel want to achieve the "center" of some kind—of power, political or financial; of social standing—but what Harmon, Wegg, and Headstone want, each in his own way, is the center of the family and home: "the place of Peace," as John Ruskin describes it in *Sesame and Lilies,* "the shelter, not only from all injury, but from all terror, doubt, and division . . . , a sacred place, a vestal temple, a temple of the hearth watched over by Household Gods.'"[9] For Harmon, the sacred place is touched by memories of childhood, both hopeful and despairing but finally at the novel's conclusion hopeful—and blissful. Wegg's is imaginary, the "Miss Elizabeth, Master George,

Aunt Jane, and Uncle Parker" of his fancy given a kind of obsessive reality that supports his greed. Headstone's hopeless passion for Lizzie is a Tristan-like fixation, but shading and coloring it are hints of domesticity—whether in the strange half-brotherly, half-fatherly concern Headstone shows for young Charlie or in Miss Peachum's doll-house environment placed so close to Headstone's self-concern that a reader sees not only what the Schoolmaster rejects but also what he seeks albeit through a different tenant.

Central to this idea of domestic happiness are the Boffins. Though childless, they have kept a family together, provided the basic grounding for the harmony to be found in Harmony Jail, have helped to transform the implications of the name. Through his treatment of the Boffins, Dickens presents one more test, it might be construed—this one for the reader. A reader feels cheated at what looks like trickery on Dickens' part in keeping Noddy Boffin's testing of Bella and Wegg a secret from the reader, not letting a hint of his motives and real feelings slip through.[10] But perhaps the trickery is of another sort. Perhaps in hindsight we catch the narrator sitting back and winking. *Were you deceived? Could you really think Noddy Boffin would lapse so?* And going further: *Where is your faith in humanity? If Noddy could fail—well, what hope have we?* With the Boffins, home and happiness is possible, Dickens would seem to say.

The Odysseus-figure with which we are concerned is not the exile or the adventurer but the homecomer. As Penelope's returned husband is not Odysseus, her pre-Trojan husband, but rather an amalgam of the warrior, the wanderer, the beggar, so is John Harmon not the John Harmon decreed to marry Bella but rather an amalgam of the Caribbean planter, the nearly drowned man, the disguised sailor, Julius Handford, John Rokesmith. The test he passes is aptly posed by P. J. M. Scott: "can the younger man avoid being implicated in the ethics of the world all around him, in the morality of which his parent's career was so unrelenting an embodiment?"[11] Of which, one can continue, Silas Wegg is colorful and comic embodiment, one of the "feeble" forcefully drawn. Unlike Harmon, the self-effacing and melancholy man who becomes the very model of a Victorian gentleman, Wegg is unchanging, shows no moral growth. His shabby activities repeat themselves. In contrast, Headstone, so desperate to change, is driven by his own deep passion from the entrance of the circle he worked so hard to approach. Harmon lives within narrow moral limits. Driven, Headstone breaks destructively through them and in so doing annihilates any hope for the home that was his goal.

In this novel, the wicked come apart, but the center holds, in the domesticity not only of Bella and John Harmon but also of Lizzie and Eugene Wrayburn, Jenny Wren and Sloppy—all of those who are bonded through a love that survives trial and transcends self.

Notes

1. Charles Dickens, *Our Mutual Friend,* ed. Stephen Gill (New York: Penguin Books, 1971), p. 815. All other citations in the text refer to this edition of the novel.

2. T. S. Eliot, *The Complete Poems and Plays* (New York: Harcourt, Brace and Company, 1950), p. 177.

3. *The Ulysses Theme,* 2nd ed. (1963; Ann Arbor: The University of Michigan Press, 1968), p. 211.

4. See Stanford's discussion in Chapter 3, "The Favorite of Athene," in *The Ulysses Theme.* The translation he uses of the passage in question is E. V. Rieu's: Odysseus has "civilized gentleness, intuitive intelligence, and firm self-possession" (p. 65).

5. "Crusoe in Exile," *PMLA,* [*Publications of the Modern Language Association*], 96 (May 1981), 364.

6. "The *Odyssey* and the Western World," *The Sewanee Review,* 62 (Summer, 1954), 425.

7. See deF. Lord, p. 420.

8. Some critics see Headstone's "decent" clothes as something false to him rather than as something alien or uncomfortable, suggesting that his efforts to rise in society, to improve in education, are negative features. For example, in "The Intelligibility of Madness in *Our Mutual Friend* and *The Mystery of Edwin Drood*," *Dickens Studies Annual,* 5 (1976), Lawrence Frank suggests that the man's death frees him from "his respectable suit of clothes and his respectable life" (pp. 192-3). But such a view ignores the tremendous drive and will that it must have taken Headstone to achieve what he has. Indeed, such a view tends to deny achievement. To deny that achievement is to wish Headstone to remain what he was—at best a Charley Hexam, at worst a Rogue Riderhood.

9. *The Works of John Ruskin,* Vol. 18, ed. E. T. Cook and Alexander Wedderburn (London: George Allen, 1905), p. 122.

10. Joseph Gold maintains that "Dickens never fooled us for a minute. We know him and Boffin too well for that. . . ." (*Charles Dickens: Radical Novelist* [Minneapolis: University of Minnesota Press, 1972], p. 272). Among other defenses of Dickens' treatment of Boffins, one might note Rosemary Mundhenk, 'The Education of the Reader in *Our Mutual Friend,*" *Nineteenth-Century Fiction,* 34 (June 1979), 41-58, and Robert Newson, "'To Scatter Dust': Fancy and Authenticity in *Our Mutual Friend,*" *Dickens Studies Annual,* 8 (1980), 39-60.

11. *Reality and Comic Confidence in Charles Dickens* (London: The Macmillan Press, Ltd., 1979), p. 16.

Angus P. Collins (essay date 1985)

SOURCE: "Dickens and *Our Mutual Friend*: Fancy as Self-Preservation," in *Etudes Anglaises,* Vol. 38, No. 3, July-September, 1985, pp. 257-65.

[*In the following essay, Collins examines the therapeutic quality of Dickens's use of fancy and imagination in* Our Mutual Friend, *and suggests that this is reflective of the author's preoccupation with his own dwindling creative powers.*]

For J. Hillis Miller Dickens's attention to the "otherness of elemental matter" in *Our Mutual Friend* (1864-65) functions as a kind of anti-transcendental vision: "the river, the dust, the wind, and the fire are what they are: mere matter." They "are not symbols, if that means expressions of some reality which transcends them, and for which they stand."[1] Yet transcendence and renewal, as Miller well realises, are part of the very fabric of *Our Mutual Friend,* their presence inseparable from the novel's concern with a world of remorseless physical disintegration. Inseparable from this same "Gestalt," as I hope to show, is the novel's ubiquitous emphasis on the idea of the fancy. For one reason why the fancy looms so large in the novel is because in writing it Dickens had been made to confront as never before the possible exhaustion of his own creative gift.[2] Nevertheless Dickens's belief in the fancy, from the time of his first crucial contacts with the contents of his father's library, had long depended on his own experience of the therapeutic potential of fanciful activity at a time of personal crisis. So now, amid the creative vicissitudes of *Our Mutual Friend,* the fancy continued to make itself available as an instrument of adjustment. It did so, however, not by providing any blessed release from professional or domestic care (for such consolations were all but extinct), but by allowing him to use his vocation to deflect the now unmistakable signs of his own mortality. Thus Hillis Miller is quite right to stress the degree of Dickens's concern in *Our Mutual Friend* with the problem of "how to assume death into life—without simply and literally dying."[3] But what he does not explore are the connections between his insight and the actual circumstances of composition. The purpose of this essay is to complement Miller's analysis (and more recent work by Andrew Sanders and Albert Hutter) by showing how in *Our Mutual Friend* Dickens's preoccupation with the terms of his art is rooted in his personal and creative situation, and testifies in particular to his longing for some form of human permanence.[4]

Dickens in *Our Mutual Friend* is acutely aware of the idea of futurity. Such an emphasis is implicit in some occasional yet very direct tributes to vocational goodness which occur throughout the book, and which contrast so markedly with the more general tone of acerbic disenchantment. Old Harmon, for example, has attempted to tamper with the lives of others from the grave itself.[5] He has also directed himself to be buried "with certain eccentric ceremonies and precautions against his coming to life."[6] Yet even his nature could not remain indifferent to

"the moral straightness" of the Boffins, and the recognition brings from Dickens a remarkable statement of affirmation: "In its own despite, in a constant conflict with itself and them, it had done so. And this is the eternal law. For, Evil often stops short at itself and dies with the doer of it! but Good never" (p. 101).

Dickens can rarely have expressed himself so quixotically, yet in a late passage of obvious personal relevance, especially when we consider that he was soon to embark on the calculated conventionalities of his novel's resolution, he again delivers himself of another highly conspicuous tribute, this time to the merits of that "good Christian pair," the Milveys. The Milveys, he tells us, are representative "of hundreds of other good Christian pairs as conscientious and as useful, who merge the smallness of their work in its greatness, and feel in no danger of losing dignity when they adapt themselves to incomprehensible humbugs" (p. 748). Present here perhaps is a certain amount of professional constraint, suggestive of Dickens's possible impatience as he prepared once more to confront the demands of popular taste in his denouement. Yet the regard for professional dedication is so striking (House notes that the Milveys are "almost alone" in the novels in showing the workings of a well run parish),[7] that it is by no means impaired by the final shift of tone.

The Milveys then, and the Boffins, Betty Higden, and Lizzie Hexam also, reflect the Dickensian ideal of practical benevolence with particular clarity. "'No one is useless in this world,'" remarks John Harmon to Bella, "'who lightens the burden of it for anyone else'" (p. 520). The emphasis is familiar yet at the same time novel, for Dickens in *Our Mutual Friend* would seem to be writing with an awareness new to him that the life of the work might well outlast his own. Knowing full well that evil, just as much as good, was by no means compelled "to die with the doer of it," Dickens confronts in this novel all his considerable powers of posthumous influence. Dickens however seems always to wish to hold in check the more destructive possibilities of his own increasing years, and he indulges in none of Old Harmon's attempts to subvert the possibility of life after death. Rather it seems he is concerned (albeit unconsciously) to promote that very thing, and I would submit that with the possible exception of his public readings his most conspicuous instrument in that strategy resides in his work itself. From this perspective the painful yet supremely dedicated composition of *Our Mutual Friend* is both a *memento mori* and a means of coping with that same recognition: death is defeated (in a strategy both classic and intensely local) by means of a defiant act of will and an accommodatory insistence on the power of the word.

Such a contention finds support in one of the novel's most intriguing motifs, that concerned with the preservation or possible cancellation of the name. Thus one of the reasons John Harmon adduces for continuing to live as Rokesmith is that "dead," he has been able to enjoy the spectacle of the Boffins "'making my memory an incentive to good actions done in my name'" (p. 372). And the Boffins have indeed insisted that his own name, and that of his sister, written as children on the walls of Harmony Jail, shall be preserved: "'We must take care of the names, old lady,' said Mr. Boffin. 'We must take care of the names. They shan't be rubbed out in our time, nor yet, if we can help it, in the time after us'" (p. 184). Part of Bradley Headstone's tragedy, of course, is that he has created an identity which makes such remembrance impossible. When Charley Hexam rejects him he is totally friendless, and when in the schoolroom scene with Riderhood he erases his name from his own blackboard the image is one with the immense and self-reflexive power of the scene as a whole. For Bradley, in his commitment to earth, merely ensures the triumph of earth. Dickens, in his flawed contending commitment to spirit, seems to envisage the triumph of his own spirit, his memory too preserved as "an incentive to good actions done in my name." In this way that elemental dissolving otherness of which he seems so conscious, the vision not just of social and moral collapse but of literal, physical disintegration, can be confronted and contained. Thus if Dickens at the time of *Our Mutual Friend* was burdened by the threat of decline both physical and creative, the *idea* of imagination continued to be available to him as a resource and defence. Springing as it does from a situation of unparalleled compositional difficulty, but also from Dickens's need to contain the evidence of apparent dissolution, the theme of the fancy in *Our Mutual Friend* is present in ways that are unprecedented in Dickens's previous work.

The roots of Dickens's theory of fancy are essentially private: fancy functions morally, is a source of private and public redemption, because Dickens had himself known its efficacy, its utility as a means of personal comfort and accommodation. In ways that have by no means been exhausted by previous criticism the supreme exponent of Dickensian fancy in *Our Mutual Friend* is Jenny Wren.[8] However, before proceeding to an examination of Jenny's role in the novel, and in particular to the connections between that role and Dickens's own situation, I should like to look briefly at one other character, Mortimer Lightwood's solitary clerk, Blight, who also employs the imagination as a strategy of containment.

Early in the novel Mortimer expresses his doubts about the impact on Blight's moral sense of his confinement, "'high up an awful staircase commanding a burial ground,'" at which he has nothing to do all day but look. "'What he will turn out when arrived at maturity,'" Mortimer cannot conceive. "'Whether, in that shabby rook's nest, he is always plotting wisdom, or plotting murder; whether he will grow up, after so much solitary brooding, to enlighten his fellow creatures, or to poison them; is the only speck of interest that presents itself to my professional view'" (p. 20). Mortimer's question is quintessentially Dickensian, yet Blight does come through, saved by imaginative activity that not only allows him to cope with his predicament, but prevents him from committing the mayhem Mortimer fears because of it. "'Wearing in his

solitary confinement no fetters that he could polish, and being provided with no drinking cup that he could carve,'" Blight has fallen on the device of "ringing alphabetical changes" in Mortimer's Appointments and Callers' Books. "Without this fiction of an occupation" his mind would since have been "shattered to pieces" (p. 87).

Blight's rote permutations of Aggs, Baggs, Caggs, Daggs and so on may seem not at all like the inventions of a particularly active imagination, and they (and his name) may well contain something of Dickens's compositional difficulty. Yet his activities are most certainly therapeutic, and they allow him not only to preserve his sanity but to deflect the pressures of the graveyard with considerable success. For Blight is Dickens's comic and distancing projection both of his own compositional exigencies and of his continuing need to believe in the imagination's accommodatory power. Thus if Blight's "eyrie" is a dusty one (p. 86), he is decidedly not a bird of prey. His real allegiance is to air rather than earth and in this he participates in that central cluster of images that is so important in defining the significance of Jenny Wren. Only in Jenny Wren however does Dickens reveal the full strain to which he was now exposed by the decline of his health and talent.

For Richard A. Lanham, "*Our Mutual Friend* has far more in common with allegory than with realism,"[9] and of no scenes in the book is this more true than of those in which Jenny participates. Jenny reveals what Dickens has always seemed to wish to provide for his contemporary audience, the fancy as a means of accommodation and imaginative compensation. She also embodies Dickens's empirical belief in the imagination as moral instrument: her visions come to her not just as an apparent "compensation for her losses" (p. 239), or as a blessed release from her labours, but are invariably associated with her "prettier and better state." The great difference between Jenny and her creator, however, was that Dickens was now increasingly denied the imaginative release that Jenny enjoys so thoroughly. This difference becomes particularly clear if we consider the most important scenes which involve Jenny Wren, those which take place on the rooftop of Pubsey and Co., for no scenes in the novel embody Dickens's condition more graphically.

Here our understanding increases immeasurably if we consider the actual context of composition. For the chapter in question belongs to number seven in the original parts publication, the number which Dickens began immediately after receiving news of the five thousand drop in circulation that occurred between the first and second number. "This leaves me," he wrote to Forster (10 June 1864), "going round and round like a carrier pigeon before swooping on number seven."[10] His choice of verb implies confidence perhaps, yet his letters of July and August contain some of his most anxious statements about his failing health and powers. "This week," he wrote on 29 July, "I have been very unwell, am still out of sorts, and, as I know from two days slow experience, have a very mountain to climb before I shall see the open country of my work."[11] The novel was obviously proving an immense burden for him, and as sales continued to fall he turned to the Christmas story of that year as a kind of liberation, even though it was adding to his labours. So on 1 October he wrote to W. H. Wills: "Mrs. Lirriper is again in hand. I have flown off from the finish of No. IX of Our Mutual, to perch upon her cap."[12] But since October marked the appearance of number six of the novel, it is clear that between June, when he was very close to being on schedule, and October, Dickens had indeed lost one number of his original four number advance. Some of the most memorable and intimate scenes in all of Dickens stem from the onset of this period of intense private and creative stress.

Crucially, therefore, the sole reason Jenny and Lizzie are on the rooftop is that it is a holiday: "'Busy early and late . . . early and late . . . in bye-times, as on this holiday,'" Jenny and Lizzie "'go to book-learning'" (p. 280). And they do so up in the air, in a rooftop garden amidst an "encompassing wilderness of dowager old chimneys" looking on "in a state of airy surprise" (p. 279). Clearly present here is what Garrett Stewart has described as Dickens's version of the myth of romantic haven,[13] but so also is that pole of Dickens's romantic dialectic which Stewart tends to underplay. The rooftop partakes not just of the pastoral bower but of the schoolroom: it is "a relief and a leniency"[14] certainly, but also a shaping, a strategical retreat which makes possible a moral strengthening. The scene describes a conscious moment apart that is also a preparation for return, a return that is clearly perceived and accepted in the knowledge that it can now be borne more easily.

Above all, however, the rooftop sequence is a lyric epitome of Dickens's view of his own function while at the same time it springs from deep within his personal situation. For if Jenny Wren's visions are unquestionably therapeutic, propounding a mode of transcendence necessary for everyone who labours, this was a condition which Dickens knew all too rarely as he toiled over a work which so often failed to take flight. So at the heart of Jenny's remarks is the sense of a world of work and deprivation, of the needs of all those "'who are alive, crying, and working, and calling to one another in the close dark streets'" (p. 281). They too need to be taken up and made light: their needs are Dickens's needs as Jenny's speech embodies the possibilities of imagination not just in a new dark age but in a time of private darkness.[15] "'Come up and be dead,'" says Jenny, "'come up and be dead.'" Dead, that is, to the world, to the self, to its burdens, and its otherwise intolerable loneliness. Dead, that is, in order to be reborn, reborn through fancy, so as to be able to re-enter the world and shoulder its burdens afresh. Dickens by contrast had to shoulder the burden of physical and mental decay without that sense of creative release with which he had been long familiar, and from which his theory of fancy ultimately derives. The rooftop scenes are replete with all of Dickens's nostalgia for a form of therapy that he now found increasingly unavailable, but which out of the pressures of his own situation he continued to wish to make available to others.

Thus in *Our Mutual Friend* we have the spectacle of a novelist who suspects himself to have reached the decline of his powers but who nonetheless contrives to find in imagination the means of his own salvation. For if Dickens at this time was increasingly deprived of those moments of imaginative release that had formerly helped buttress his creative commitment, so was he impelled as never before by the need to use imagination to contain his own mortality. Dickens's need to complete the novel was therefore enormous. At the same time, however, his desire for an end to the pressures of composition appears to have been intense. So, in a letter written about this time to the book's eventual dedicatee, Sir James Emerson Tennent, Dickens resorts to the same revealing imagery of imprisonment he had used for Blight and Jenny Wren. "After receiving your kind note," he writes (26 August 1864), "I resolved to make another trial. But the hot weather and a few other drawbacks did not mend the matter, for I have dropped astern this month instead of going ahead. So I have seen Forster and shown him my chains, and am reduced to taking exercise in them like Baron Trench."[16]

Blight and Jenny Wren on their respective rooftops knew what it was to lose such chains. "'And such a chain has fallen from you,'" says Jenny, "'and such a strange good sorrowful happiness comes upon you'" (p. 281). Debarred almost entirely from joining them there, Dickens, only a few months later came to indite his remarkable comments on the half-drowned Riderhood: "And yet, like us all, when we swoon—like us all, every day of our lives when we wake—he is instinctively unwilling to be restored to the consciousness of this existence, and would be left dormant, if he could" (p. 444-45). The pressure of personal statement is visible here to an extraordinary extent, for the passage's intrusive insistence is matched by the fact that for many in the book's original audience it must have seemed seriously lacking in application. Again, however, the actual context of composition proves illuminating. For the passage comes from the second chapter ("A Respected Friend in a New Aspect") of number eleven. If we remember that number nine was complete by October 1, it seems clear that Dickens should have been at work on number eleven some time in November. Yet in this same month he again wrote to Forster complaining that he had not done his number, and on this occasion ascribing his difficulties to the death of his friend Leech.[17]

Leech's death on October 29 was the latest in a long series of bereavements that Dickens had experienced since the beginning of the decade: Dickens's mother, his son Walter, the novelist Thackeray (with whom Dickens had only recently been reconciled), and a variety of other members of Dickens's family and circle of friends had all died during the period of the novel's gestation and composition.[18] Death for Dickens in these years is all-pervasive, and clearly there were times when he was not indifferent to it as a solution to his difficulties. Death, however, may not only seduce but inspire, and inspire by suggesting the strategies of its own defeat. For if Jenny Wren sings (as in part she does) of the sweetness of oblivion with all the compassionate restful inclusiveness for which Dickens longs, Dickens, in creating her, resists her nightingale-like song, and finds, with Keats, his true "high requiem" in the work itself. Death in those famous scenes on the rooftop most certainly announces a movement back into life, not simply as a general existential emphasis such as Miller describes, but immediately, specifically, into the life of the work as it will outlast and preserve the man.

Notes

1. "Afterword," *Our Mutual Friend* (New York: New American Library, 1964), p. 910.

2. For a still important early survey of the concept of fancy in Dickens, see P. A. W. Collins, "'Queen Mab's Chariot among the Steam Engines': Dickens and 'Fancy,'" *ES* [*English Studies: A Journal of English Language and Literature*], 42 (1961), 78-90.

3. *Charles Dickens: The World of His Novels* (Cambridge, Mass.: Harvard University Press, 1958), p. 316.

4. See Andrew Sanders, *Charles Dickens: Resurrectionist* (London: Macmillan, 1982), and two essays by Albert D. Hutter, "Dismemberment and Articulation in *Our Mutual Friend*," *Dickens Studies Annual*, 11 (1983), 135-75, and "The Novelist as Resurrectionist: Dickens and the Dilemma of Death," *Dickens Studies Annual*, 12 (1983), 1-39.

5. This, of course, was a power with which Dickens was himself familiar, and changes in one of his own wills date from 1861, the year in which the novel's title was conceived. See Edgar Johnson, *Charles Dickens: His Tragedy and Triumph* (New York: Simon and Schuster, 1952), II, 1110-111, and xcv, note 23a.

6. New Oxford Illustrated Edition (London: Oxford University Press, 1952), p. 15. All subsequent page references are to this edition.

7. *The Dickens World*, 2nd ed. (1941; London: Oxford University Press, 1942), p. 110.

8. See in particular Garrett Stewart, "The Golden Bower of *Our Mutual Friend*," in *Dickens and the Trials of Imagination* (Cambridge, Mass.: Harvard University Press, 1974), pp. 198-221.

9. "*Our Mutual Friend*: The Birds of Prey," *Victorian Newsletter*, 24 (1963), 11.

10. John Forster, *The Life of Charles Dickens*, ed. A. J. Hoppé (London: J. M. Dent, 1966), II, 293. Robert L. Patten indicates an initial printing of 40,000 copies (of which 35,000 were stitched), this declining by the time of the sixth number in October to 28,000 copies (24,000 stitched), and to 25,000 (19,000 stitched) by the time of the final double number in November 1865. See Robert L. Patten, *Charles Dickens and His Publishers* (Oxford: Clarendon Press, 1978), p. 446.

11. Forster, II, 293.

12. *The Letters of Charles Dickens*, ed. Walter Dexter (Bloomsbury: The Nonesuch Press, 1938), III, 399.

13. *Dickens and the Trials of Imagination*, p. 199 ff.

14. Ibid., p. 221.

15. Compare Dickens's famous rebuttal of the criticism of Hippolyte Taine that his work suffered from an imaginative excess akin to madness: see Forster, *The Life of Charles Dickens*, II, 279.

16. *Letters*, III, 396.

17. *Letters*, III, 404.

18. For a full account of Dickens's losses in these years, see Edgar Johnson, *Charles Dickens: His Tragedy and Triumph*, II, 970, 997-1017. See also Andrew Sanders's chapter, "This Tremendous Sickle . . .," in *Charles Dickens: Resurrectionist*, pp. 37-63.

Bruce Beiderwell (essay date 1985)

SOURCE: "The Coherence of *Our Mutual Friend*," in *Journal of Narrative Technique*, Vol. 15, No. 3, Fall, 1985, pp. 234-43.

[*In the following essay, Beiderwell explores the distinct writing styles Dickens uses to describe the two different social worlds represented in* Our Mutual Friend.]

The first two chapters of ***Our Mutual Friend*** introduce two apparently distinct social worlds. The novel opens in the dark, primitive, and dangerous world of Gaffer Hexam. The second chapter introduces the unbearably bright, new, and insular world of the Veneerings. Dickens allows the two chapters to stand with no explicit connection until the last sentence of the second chapter. Mortimer receives a message which allows him to close his story of the man from somewhere: "Man's drowned!"[1] But even this link to Gaffer's hunt serves to emphasize the separateness of these two worlds. The corpse in chapter one is an actuality. For Gaffer or Riderhood it is an unfanciful item to grasp, hold, search, and (in a sense) sell. And for Lizzie the body is a horrifying "it." In chapter two the corpse is experienced as a second-hand curiosity. The Veneering circle perceives the corpse as a titillating and satisfying close to a moderately entertaining story.

These characters, their perceptions, the settings in which they act, and the actions they take are rendered in appropriately distinct styles. The first chapter opens in a rather slow, patient manner, befitting the patient hunt it describes. The second chapter begins with a series of static repetitive equations which reduce people to properties. Dickens multiplies this strategy of contrast throughout the novel. The various social groups carry with them their own histories and their own styles. ***Our Mutual Friend*** is both a multi-plotted novel and a multi-styled novel. The effects can be both dazzling and distracting. J. Hillis Miller likens *Our Mutual Friend* to a cubist collage:

> The basic structural technique of the novel is the complete transformation of tone and milieu from chapter to chapter. . . . The novel seems to be a large group of impenetrable milieus with characters buried untouchably at their centers. These milieus exist side by side, but do not organize themselves into a large whole.[2]

Certainly the characters of the novel cannot perceive or organize a "large whole," but Dickens is not so limited. He manages to portray the fragmentation within his fictional world and, at the same time, offer a more subtle and connected vision than his characters are capable of achieving. If the novel lacks a clear narrative center, it does not lack thematic coherence. Mr. Podsnap is more a part of the larger world than he realizes. The language of the opening chapters of this novel signal more than differences.[3] Despite the radical shifts in tone and style, Dickens begins to establish—through the recurrence of certain words and phrases—a network of associations that project a coherent sense of a decaying world which deals in death and is losing its human dimension. A study of specific grammatical and lexical features in the first two chapters clarifies Dickens' strategy of opposition and repetition. And a look beyond those chapters reveals Dickens' continued play upon this strategy as he coheres the narrative threads of this vast work.

The novel's first sentence (a one sentence paragraph) suggests an impersonal sense of mystery through its structure. It leaves us with a few questions, some uneasy conjectures, and little specific knowledge:

> In these times of ours, though concerning the exact year there is no need to be precise, a boat of dirty and disreputable appearance, with two figures in it, floated on the Thames, between Southwark Bridge which is of iron, and London Bridge which is of stone, as an autumn evening was closing in.
>
> (1)

The opening prepositional phrase serves as an adverb. But before we get to the verb there is a fairly long parenthetical element which generalizes the already general adverb before it. The subject and its modifiers follow, including a prepositional phrase which functions as an adjective and contains the only human element in the sentence: "with two figures in it." We then have the verb and prepositional phrases which tell us where the boat floated. Finally, we return to the temporal dimension with a subordinate clause which modifies the main verb.

It is particularly striking that Lizzie and her father are introduced as unnamed "figures" buried passively in the middle of the sentence and thereby locked in the time and place of the action. The time frame, for example, comprises nearly half of this rather lengthy sentence (twenty-four words out of fifty-four). The sheer number of words establishing the time serves to enclose and deemphasize

the "figures" in the boat. Yet no specific time is created. The figures are first placed in a very general background of time which moves inexorably to death and darkness by the sentence's end. All takes place "as an autumn evening was closing in." This essential vagueness subverts the sense of linear or narrative time and suggests an atemporal condition with which the novel will deal.[4]

Dickens withholds, and continues to withhold for several paragraphs, the exact nature of the action. (In fact, Dickens never names what Gaffer finds in the river, but as the action progresses, the omission serves to emphasize a known horror, not anticipate an unknown one.) The initial delay increases our sense of uncertainty and fear. In the second paragraph the mystery and horror are heightened by a series of negative descriptions: we are told what the unnamed figure cannot be doing. The man with "ragged grizzled hair" is not a fisherman, not a waterman, not a river carrier. We know enough to be uneasy and fearful, but we do not know enough to explain or dispel the pervasive sense of horror that hangs about the scene.

Dickens does, however, let us on to some important points. The girl who rows the boat is the man's daughter and is not new to her work on the river: she pulls the sculls "very easily." But although she is not new to her work, she is not accustomed to it either. At the end of the paragraph, Dickens draws the first clear distinction between the character of the man and his daughter. Our sympathies are wholly aligned with the latter. Gaffer looks on the river with a "most intent and searching gaze." But Lizzie's attention is given as much to her father as it is to the river, and "in the intensity of her look there was a touch of dread or horror" (p. 1).

The first sentence of the third paragraph begins to group this sense of dread, the mysterious search, and the absence of human control in terms that recur throughout the novel:

> Allied to the bottom of the river rather than the surface, by reason of the slime and ooze with which it was covered, and its sodden state, this boat and the two figures in it obviously were doing something that they often did, and were seeking what they often sought.
>
> (p. 1)

The lengthy absolute construction establishes an important contrast which will reappear in the much different context of the second chapter. *Our Mutual Friend* is largely about surfaces and depths—both of which are identified with death. Gaffer is identified with the bottom; he cannot rise from the depths he touches. Like his boat, Gaffer is in a "sodden state." He has no fancies and no friends, other than the river itself. In the second chapter, the Veneerings are presented as all surface; they cannot touch the real or the human through the fake and the material. Like their furniture, they are shiny and new. And everyone is at once their oldest and their newest "friend." The confusion between (or fusion of) the human and the material in the Veneering chapter is also anticipated by this sentence from the third paragraph of the first chapter. The boat is given as active a role in the search as the figures in it. Grammatically they function together: all are allied to the bottom rather than the surface; all take part in the same hunt; all have worked together often.

But Dickens is careful not to make the identity too complete. Lizzie (still unnamed at this point) is a part of the hunt, but she is not given over to the deathly world she must act in. Her father goes about his work with a look of "business-like usage." But Lizzie, despite the dismal experiences of her life, retains youth and the capacity to feel the horror of her situation: "So with every lithe action of the girl, with every turn of her wrist, perhaps most of all with her look of dread and horror; they were things of usage" (p. 2). Dickens maintains the contrast between Lizzie and her father throughout the hunt scene. Lizzie's attention continually shifts from Gaffer's face to the river and back. Her look betrays horror or pain. Gaffer's attention is always focused on the river. His gaze betrays not the slightest feeling or concern for anything but his business.

Gaffer's business remains a mystery, but its connections with death become more clear:

> So the girl eyed him. But, it happened now, that a slant of light from the setting sun glanced into the bottom of the boat, and, touching a rotten stain there which bore some resemblance to the outline of a muffled human form, coloured it as though with diluted blood. This caught the girl's eye, and she shivered.
>
> (p. 2)

The "setting sun" recalls the sense of time which encloses the two figures in the first sentence of the novel. Also the dying light glances into the "bottom" of the boat to reveal the human shaped, blood-colored, "rotten stain." But the most important thing here is Lizzie's awareness. Her eye moves from her father to the stain and she shivers. She anticipates the connection we are being led to make between Gaffer and the world of the dead.[5]

Gaffer's own cold and limited response is again set off against Lizzie's awareness. The opposition helps to identify, order, and interpret the symbolic pattern of the novel. Jonathan Culler's discussion of the symbolic code clarifies this process. Antithesis is the device that governs the logic of symbols. An antithesis:

> sets in motion an experiment in extrapolation in which the reader correlates this opposition with thematic oppositions that it might manifest. . . . The reader can pass from one opposition to another, trying them out, even inverting them, and determining which are pertinent to larger thematic structures which encompass other antitheses presented in the text.[6]

Culler goes on to maintain that these extrapolated thematic oppositions must meet the "demands of symbolic force." In other words, the reader pushes toward the most basic level of meaning that the general paradigm will allow (Culler, pp. 226-28).

The paradigm in *Our Mutual Friend* encourages one to press toward the most basic level of all—life and death. Lizzie is young; Gaffer is old. Lizzie is painfully sensitive; Gaffer is unfeeling. After Gaffer finds a body and secures it to his boat, he offers to trade places with Lizzie, but Lizzie will not move closer to that body. She maintains both a literal and a symbolic distance from the dead:

> "Here! and give me hold of the sculls. I'll take the rest of the spell."
>
> "No, no, father! No! I can't indeed. Father!—I cannot sit so near it!"
>
> He was moving towards her to change places, but her terrified expostulation stopped him and he resumed his seat.
>
> (p. 3)

Gaffer then holds both a literal and symbolic closeness to the dead. The end of the chapter emphasizes that dangerous closeness and foreshadows Gaffer's eventual death by drowning: "What he had in tow, lunged itself at him sometimes in an awful manner when the boat was checked, and sometimes seemed to try to wrench itself away, though for the most part it followed submissively" (p. 5).

Defining Gaffer's symbolic role through his opposition to Lizzie also helps us to interpret and link other foregrounded elements. For example, Gaffer's "business-like" gaze stands out in its context of the mysterious and horrifying atmosphere which dominates the opening pages of the book. His lack of imagination is similarly emphasized. Looking back upon the corpse he has in tow: "A neophyte might have fancied that the ripples passing over it were dreadfully like faint changes of expression on a sightless face; but Gaffer was no neophyte and had no fancies" (p. 5). In addition, images of hunger, feeding, and prey occur several times and only in reference to Gaffer. Gaffer feeds off death for a "living." Gaffer's eyes dart a "hungry look" (p. 2). He bears a striking likeness to a "roused bird of prey" (p. 3). And Rogue Riderhood thinks Gaffer, like the "wultures," scents out the dead (p. 4). Again the antithesis to Lizzie is made clear. Gaffer charges Lizzie with ingratitude to the river:

> "As if it wasn't your living! As if it wasn't meat and drink to you!"
>
> At these latter words the girl shivered again, and for a moment paused in her rowing, seeming to turn deadly faint. It escaped his attention, for he was glancing over the stern at something the boat had in tow.
>
> (p. 3)

Significantly, although Lizzie cooks for her father and her brother, she eats only with poor Jenny Wren, the doll's dressmaker. And a "wren" is no bird of prey.[7]

Dickens' style marks the shift to a seemingly (or superficially) different environment in chapter two. The Veneerings are introduced in a series of short, repetitive clauses which define them as reflections of their possessions—all "new" possessions. This introduction denies the Veneerings any personal history and denies them any existence independent of the things they possess:

> Mr. and Mrs. Veneering were bran-new people in a bran-new house in a bran-new quarter of London. Everything about the Veneerings was spick and span new. All their furniture was new, all their friends were new, all their servants were new, their plate was new, their carriage was new, their harness was new, their horses were new, their pictures were new, they themselves were new, they were as newly married as was lawfully compatible with their having a bran-new baby, and if they had set up a great-grandfather, he would have come home in matting from the Pantechnicon, without a scratch upon him, French polished to the crown of his head.
>
> (p. 6)

The absence of any internal punctuation in the first sentence rushes people and things together. The pace is much faster than the slow opening of the first chapter. And the repetitive phrasing throughout the paragraph makes it impossible to determine any sense of priorities. The linking verbs do just that; they link the Veneerings and their many things to newness without any hint that there may be differences among the various equations.

This newness is also represented stylistically by a shift to the present tense in the sixth paragraph of the chapter. The Veneerings act only in the present. They have no past. The hypothetical great-grandfather of the first paragraph would be bran-new "if" he did exist. And they have no future. Their place in the social world is as tenuous as the financial basis for the "friendships" they cultivate. If the Veneerings could not maintain a new carriage, could they maintain a new friend?

The second chapter is further distinguished from the first by the quick summary judgments it contains. Gaffer and Lizzie are introduced slowly in chapter one. And the play of light and shade gives physical objects and movements an uncertain, shifting quality. In chapter two the essence of things and people is captured more easily. There is no confusing play of light and shadow in the Veneering house. Things can be described and dismissed. People can be tagged with tags that sum up their entire existence: the "bran-new" Veneerings have to dinner "the Member, the Engineer, the Payer-off of the National Debt, the Poem on Shakespeare, the Grievance, and the Public Office" (p. 7). And although the Veneering world is a very busy world, only poor, muddled Tremlow finds it an unfathomable one.

Tremlow mistakenly looks for a solidity that does not exist in the Veneering world. He puzzles over the question "whether he was Veneering's oldest friend, or newest friend" (p. 7). He does not realize that for Veneering "oldest" is an empty word. The present surface is all there is of Veneering. One cannot know him (or his circle) below that surface. Dickens describes the entire Veneering dinner party by describing their reflections in a mirror:

> Reflects Veneering; forty, wavy-haired, dark, tending to corpulence, sly, mysterious, filmy—a kind of sufficiently well looking veiled-prophet, not prophesying. Reflects Mrs. Veneering; fair, aquiline nosed and fingered. . . . Reflects mature young lady; raven locks, and complexion that lights up well when well powdered—as it is—carrying on considerably in the captivation of mature young gentleman; with too much nose in his face, too much ginger in his whiskers, too much torso in his waistcoat, too much sparkle in his studs, his eyes, his buttons, his talk, and his teeth.
>
> (p. 10)

The deletion of the subject (the mirror) in these sentences give the passage a quickly moving, impressionistic effect. The repetition of the present tense verb "reflects" adds to this effect and again emphasizes the Veneering newness and shallowness. An immaterial, one-dimensional reflection sufficiently represents the Veneering world. The deletion of the article in the last reflection further denies any particular human identity to the objects of the verb: "mature young lady" . . . "in the captivation of mature young gentleman."[8]

Clearly, there is little at either the sentence or the narrative level to link chapter two to chapter one, but these chapters are marked by a shared lexis. Words relating in some way to surface and bottom, food, prey, and business take on a special resonance in chapter two. Gaffer's boat ("allied to the bottom") describes Gaffer. The Veneering's furniture ("in a state of bright varnish and polish") describes the Veneerings: "What was observable in the furniture, was observable in the Veneerings—the surface smelt a little too much of the workshop and was a trifle sticky" (p. 6). Tremlow, however, finds these surfaces open to great depths. He is used to being treated as an item of social value: "this he was used to, and could take soundings of" (p. 6). But the question whether he is the oldest or the newest friend of the Veneerings seems insoluble—an "abyss to which he could find no bottom" (p. 7). Images of feeding also link these two worlds. A meal is nearly as unappetizing at the Veneerings' as it is on Gaffer's river search. The apparent thoughts of one gloomy servant provide a running commentary on the Veneering dinner. This "Analytical Chemist" seems to announce guests with the pronouncement: "Here is another wretched creature come to dinner; such is life" (p. 7). He seems to offer Chablis with a whispered, "you wouldn't if you knew what it's made of" (p. 10). And he says "Dinner is on the table!" as if he were saying, "Come down and be poisoned, ye unhappy children of men" (p. 9). The mood is more appropriate to a funeral than to a feast.

In chapter one, Lizzie senses the awful connection between her "meat and drink" and its source. Other than perhaps the Analytical Chemist, the characters in chapter two do not fully understand the nature of their feeding; or, if they do, they are entirely insensitive to its moral implications. Tremlow is old and confused. Lady Tippins sleeps and becomes insensible. Mortimer (note *mort*) is half-asleep. Eugene is "buried alive" (p. 11). The sleepy characters of the Veneering world feed off each other just as Gaffer feeds off the dead. The Veneerings feed off Tremlow's kinship to Lord Snigsworth. Tremlow becomes merely a dining-table in its normal state: "Mr. and Mrs. Veneering, for example, arranging a dinner, habitually started with Tremlow, and then put leaves in him, or added guests to him" (p. 6). In turn, Tremlow, an impoverished gentleman, takes sustenance from the Veneerings' new wealth. Finally, the mirror reflects Podsnap "prosperously feeding." The hair on each side of his otherwise bald head looks like "wiry wings" (p. 10). The word "prosperously" and the image of a bird feeding make Podsnap one of the novel's most successful birds of prey. Such verbal associations help us to place Podsnap in strange company. The bottom, feeding, business, prey, and lack of imagination are all associated with Gaffer. The surface, feeding, business, prey, and lack of imagination are all associated with Podsnap. The verbal links force us to seek the qualities which underlie these two seemingly separate characters. Such links also remind us (if we need reminding) that money is very much a part of the whole of this vast, deathly, and dusty world of surfaces and depths.

This verbal connectedness functions throughout *Our Mutual Friend.* Its importance seems plain enough to us when we consider the sheer length of the novel. Certainly its first readers needed some help in cohering such a vast, diverse work over its nineteen months of serial publication.[9] The links established in the first two chapters can be followed to the very end. The events of one world inevitably comment upon the events of another. Gaffer thinks that money clearly belongs to the living: "What world does a dead man belong to? T'other world. What world does money belong to? This world" (p. 4). But Gaffer's confidence in such a neat distinction is obviously misplaced. We would expect such confidence from the Veneering world as well. Gaffer takes money from the pockets of the dead man, washes a coin in the river, and spits upon it once "for luck" (p. 3). Soon after, Rogue Riderhood appears out of a "dark place" and asks: "In luck again, Gaffer? . . . I knowed you was in luck again by your wake as you come down" (p. 3). The "luck" he refers to is a body. In the short first chapter some form of the word "luck" occurs six times. The first (Gaffer's spitting on the coin) ties "luck" to money. The next three uses of the word refer to Riderhood. Riderhood believes himself to be "out-of-luck." But Gaffer believes Riderhood should "think himself lucky" for getting away with robbing a "live" man.

The next conspicuous occurrence of the word "luck" comes at the end of book one, chapter thirteen. Riderhood leads Mr. Inspector, Eugene, and Mortimer on a hunt after his former "pardner." He catches a glimpse of a corpse tied behind Gaffer's boat: "he's in luck again, by George if he ain't!" (p. 169). In the next chapter, the transitional or precarious state between life and death is emphasized by the twilight images, the flickering fire, and the unsteady boat. We are also reminded of the connection between death and money: the letters upon wharves and warehouses look to Eugene "like inscriptions over the graves of dead businesses" (p. 171).

In this atmosphere of death and within the space of a page the word "luck" occurs another five times: "in luck" becomes "his luck" and finally "the luck." The expression becomes a thing: Gaffer's luck becomes Gaffer himself. The dead have pulled him into the water with them: "The object he had expected to take in tow floats by, and his boat tows him dead to where we found him, all entangled in his own line" (p. 175). In death, Gaffer holds on to the coins he had sought; "t'other world" claims him through the lure of what he supposed was this one.

Luck, money, and death come together again in a line from the eleventh chapter of book three. Bradley Headstone gives Rogue Riderhood two coins and forms with him a vague compact against their mutual enemy, Eugene Wrayburn. Riderhood suggests they close their understanding with a drink: "no luck never come yet of a dry acquaintance. Let's wet it in a mouthful of rum and milk, T'otherest Governor" (p. 554). The money and the word "luck" should touch us with a chill foreboding by this point in the novel. "Dry" and "wet" anticipate the doubles' eventual death by drowning. And Riderhood's tags for Eugene and Headstone—"T'other Governor" and "T'otherest Governor"—recall Gaffer's distinction between "t'other world" and this one. At this point, both Eugene and Headstone may be taken as touching the "t'other world"; Headstone is appropriately the "t'otherest."

If we return to Riderhood's first words we may follow other suggestive lines in the extraordinarily dense verbal network Dickens creates: "I knowed you was in luck again by your wake as you come down." "Come down" or "come up" recur several times in the novel and play upon the sense of moving to or away from the depths (or death) that the main characters touch. The Analytical Chemist seems to announce: "Come down and be poisoned, ye unhappy children of men." Mr. Inspector tugs at Gaffer's lifeless body and coaxes it from the water: "You *must* come up. I mean to have you" (p. 173). Jenny Wren calls Riah away from the confusion of the city streets: "Come up and be dead! Come up and be dead! (p. 282). And Bradley Headstone's final words before he falls into the weir grasping his dark double Riderhood are "I'll hold you living, and I'll hold you dead. Come down!" (p. 802).

Dickens has given us a great deal to work with in this novel. In a postscript to *Our Mutual Friend,* Dickens suggested that, as an artist, he might "be trusted to know what he is about in his vocation" (p. 821). He was referring to his plotting of the story; we should extend that trust to his language as well, for his language in this case is as much the story as his management of dramatic incident or the fate of his characters.

Notes

1. Charles Dickens, *Our Mutual Friend* (Oxford: Oxford University Press, 1952), p. 17. All further references to this work appear in the text.

2. J. Hillis Miller, *Charles Dickens: The World of His Novels* (Cambridge: Harvard University Press, 1958), p. 316.

3. Victor Brombert discusses openings of several nineteenth-century novels in his "Opening Signals in Narrative," *New Literary History,* 11 (1980), 489-502. Brombert maintains that openings constitute both "incantation" and "initiation"; the thematic whole may be implicit in the first sentences. Edwin M. Eigner argues that Dickens subordinates his narrative to an *a priori* thematic concern. The whole is in essence conceived before the opening sentence. Incidents may be added as the narrative progresses, but not because the narrative itself demands it. See Eigner, *The Metaphysical Novel in England and America: Dickens, Bulwer, Hawthorne, Melville* (Berkeley: University of California Press, 1978), pp. 28-38.

4. Frank Kermode suggests that Henry Fielding would have been "surprised though not confounded by the opening of *Our Mutual Friend,*" but he would have been baffled by the opening of a late James novel. Yet, as Kermode notes, if Dickens does not consciously invite multiple readings in his opening sentences, he hardly lays down a simple sequence of relevant facts as does Trollope in *Doctor Thorne.* See "Novels: Recognition and Deception," *Critical Inquiry,* 1 (1974), 104. Also see J. Hillis Miller, *Fiction and Repetition: Seven English Novels* (Cambridge: Harvard University Press, 1982), pp. 1-21. Miller concentrates on the ways in which repetition works against definitive readings which depend upon the linear sequence of the narrative.

5. Lizzie's relationship to death is developed by her role in the scene of Betty Higden's death and by her rescue of the nearly dead Wrayburn. See Alexander Welsh, *The City of Dickens* (London: Oxford University Press, 1971), pp. 204-05.

6. Jonathan Culler, *Structuralist Poetics* (Ithaca: Cornell University Press), pp. 225-26. Further references will appear in the text.

7. But a wren is apparently a rather saucy bird. Jenny's name alludes to the traditional story of the wren who rejects the robin who had nursed her back to health. See Iona Opie and Peter Opie, eds., *The Oxford Dictionary of Nursery Rhymes* (London: Oxford University Press, 1951), pp. 242-43. Jenny's real name—Fanny Cleaver—further complicates her moral position, although Dickens' affection for her is clear.

8. J. Hillis Miller provides a detailed and fascinating reading of the mirror passage in his *The Form of Victorian Fiction* (Notre Dame: University of Notre Dame Press, 1968), pp. 36-48.

9. Michael Lund argues that teaching Victorian serial novels in parts better approximates the reading experience of the initial audience. He focuses primarily on how our responses to characters are enriched by the extended involvement in time that serial publication requires. Such a teaching strategy might profit from attention to repeated words, phrases, images.

One could note how quickly and how accurately serial readers school themselves in the signs that overlap the parts and cohere those parts. See Lund, "Teaching Long Victorian Novels in Parts," *Victorian Newsletter,* No. 58 (1980), pp. 29-32.

J. Fisher Solomon (essay date 1988)

SOURCE: "Realism, Rhetoric, and Reification: Or the Case of the Missing Detective in *Our Mutual Friend,*" in *Modern Philology,* Vol. 86, No. 1, August, 1988, pp. 34-45.

[*In the following essay, Solomon discusses the critical controversy surrounding two confusing plot lines within* Our Mutual Friend: *the one involving John Harmon's "death" and the one involving Noddy Boffin's feigned change of character.*]

> But more extraordinary than any chapter is the preface, or postscript, or apology, for we don't know what to call it, which closes the work. It is divided into five sections, and each section contains a separate fallacy, except one, which contains two. In the first, Mr. Dickens lays down the proposition "that an artist (of whatever denomination) may, perhaps, be trusted to know what he is about in his vocation." Mr. Dickens's later works are the best refutation of his own words.
>
> [J. R. Wise, from a review of ***Our Mutual Friend***][1]

"When I devised this story," Charles Dickens declares rather testily in the "postscript" to his last completed novel, "I foresaw the likelihood that a class of readers and commentators would suppose that I was at great pains to conceal exactly what I was at great pains to suggest: namely, that Mr. John Harmon was not slain, and that Mr. John Rokesmith was he."[2] Just how the reader of ***Our Mutual Friend*** is to receive this "explanation," however, is not very clear. Our choice, at any rate, is not very attractive, for Dickens appears to confess here either that he had known all along that the Harmon plot of the novel had been badly handled or that he had deliberately written it, as J. Hillis Miller remarks of ***Bleak House,*** "in a way calculated to make the reader a bad detective."[3] Either way, it appears, the reader loses, which may explain why the Harmon plot has so dissatisfied those generations of readers who, like J. R. Wise in *Westminster Review,* have experienced a sudden feeling of aesthetic betrayal when, in the thirteenth chapter of the second book of the novel, John Harmon abruptly gives away the secret to his "murder" with fully one half of the story to go. Why, we ask, has Dickens given us so few clues heretofore, only to spring his trap suddenly without allowing us sufficient time to guess the truth for ourselves? Why has Dickens tantalized us with a mystery only to sweep it away in a single revelatory stroke? Has Dickens simply written a bad plot, or is it possible that he has indeed deliberately planned to make both his audience and the characters in his story bad readers as well as bad detectives? And if so, why?

    OUR MUTUAL FRIEND

To be fair to Dickens, it is true that there is some evidence supporting his claim to the "pains" that he had taken to suggest "that Mr. John Harmon was not slain, and that Mr. John Rokesmith was he." Rokesmith's rather clumsy attempt (at least in hindsight) to deflect any suspicion on Boffin's part that he might have some previous acquaintance with the name of "Harmon"—"Harmoon's . . . Harmarn's. How do you spell it?" Rokesmith stammers—(p. 143) is certainly a clue of some sort. And it is also true that in the notes to the chapter in which the doubly disguised Rokesmith confronts Rogue Riderhood ("More Birds of Prey"), Dickens reminds himself to "work on to possessing the reader with the fact that he [John Rokesmith] is John Harmon."[4] The trouble with this latter set of clues, however, is that Rokesmith's confrontation with Riderhood only occurs in the chapter immediately preceding the one in which the mystery is suddenly given away. We simply are given too little preparation for this revelation too late, and with so much of the story remaining to be told the reader might well be forgiven for feeling that he has been needlessly tempted into a maze. At any rate, a good deal of wind is taken from the sails of the Harmon plot, making it difficult not to sympathize with Stephen Gill's conclusion that "the Harmon plot is the albatross about Dickens's neck. The interest of what is revealed about Bella is out of all proportion to the fantastic technical problems presented in the disguise story, which has, in itself, no interest at all. The result is that Dickens is forced to employ desperate measures to keep the plot moving intelligibly at all. Book II, Chapter 13 is a confession of breakdown."[5]

Other critics have remained equally unimpressed. "At a half way point even the dullest reader has the mystery solved for him through Harmon's confessional monologue," writes Andrew Sanders; while Philip Collins remarks that the Harmon plot constitutes "a silly and trivial mystery, but fortunately Dickens could feel that he had thus done his duty in providing the obligatory 'mystery' element for this novel."[6] In defense of Dickens, H. M. Daleski argues that the Harmon disguise plot dramatizes London society's "absence of true identity," so supporting the novel's thematic search for a "true identity, one that will sustain life in the city of death.'"[7] And to a certain extent, Gill concurs. Dickens, he writes, "does draw good things from this plot" since he "has always been fascinated by the problem of identity, of the difference between people's real selves and their social selves." Still Gill concludes, Dickens's success here "hardly compensates for the clumsiness."[8]

In the midst of such criticism it is possible to conclude that Dickens himself simply lost interest in the Harmon mystery halfway through the novel and decided to concentrate his energies on the development of the Headstone-Wrayburn rivalry, which, in Gill's judgment, constitutes "the commanding success of the novel."[9] Having anticipated his readers' dissatisfaction with this abandonment, such an argument might run, Dickens accordingly penned his "postscript" hoping to fend off his critics while implic-

itly acknowledging the legitimacy of their complaints. Closer scrutiny of the offending chapter indeed seems to confirm our suspicions of authorial indifference here, for in John Harmon's soliloquy we find not only the abrupt solution to *his* mystery but also the appearance of a brand new mystery that Dickens never even begins to pursue. Why are we tantalized with the prospect of a continuing mystery if it is not to be developed? Why did Dickens fail to exploit his own story's possibilities? If "indifference" is *not* the explanation (and I do not suggest that it is), then how else can we account for this "failure"? To answer such questions we might look more closely at what Harmon does tell us in "A Solo and a Duett," searching both for the "mystery" that never quite gets off the ground and for possible reasons for its sudden grounding.

Significantly, there is as much mystification in Harmon's monologue as there is revelation. All that we discover for certain from it is the apparent fact that Harmon was shanghaied by George Radfoot and that both men were thrown into the Thames. But as many questions are raised by this plot revelation as are answered. Who, we might well ask, threw Harmon and Radfoot into the river? Rogue Riderhood? For his part, Harmon has his suspicions of Riderhood's complicity in the affair, and we can be fairly certain that Riderhood provided the near-fatal drug, but even Harmon is "far from sure" about this (pp. 424-25), and there are still many more unanswered questions surrounding the case. Who, for instance, is the "black man" in steward's dress who serves Harmon the doctored coffee, and had he any active role in the matter? Who are the men who struggle over Harmon's valise as he lies insensate on the floor? Was Riderhood among them? Again, Harmon has his suspicions, but in his confrontation with the Rogue we find what appears to be genuine surprise on Riderhood's part when he learns of Radfoot's death. "Now then!" Riderhood exclaims in his confrontation with the disguised Harmon, "I want to know how George Radfoot come by his death, and how you come by his kit?" (p. 417). These are not bad questions, and the reader might want to ask at least one of them too, but Harmon only replies, to Riderhood and to us as well, that "if you ever do know, you won't know now" (p. 417).

The reader, as it turns out, will never be much more enlightened about the affair than will Riderhood, for Harmon explicitly determines not to pursue the case any further, refusing to "enlighten human Justice concerning the offence of one far beyond it who may have a living mother" or to "enlighten it with the lights of a stone passage, a flight of stairs, a brown window-curtain, and a black man" (p. 429). Thus, while in all of these clues we have the ingredients for a fully revived mystery plot, the fact remains that Dickens makes no attempt to revive it. The excuse that Harmon himself gives for this neglect—that is, his fear of the effect on the Boffins and on Bella Wilfer of his "coming to life again"—is not convincing, however, both because Harmon *does* come back to life for the Boffins in the hidden action of the very next chapter (though the reader is given no hint of this) and because Dickens could very easily have reactivated his "Night Inspector" in order to solve the case after all. Instead, the Night Inspector effectively vanishes from the story, only to return late in the going with the wry narrative suggestion that while he was "once meditatively active in this chronicle" (p. 830), he now appears merely as a foil for Harmon's final revelations. In other words, nothing within the story itself prevented Dickens from continuing the already introduced detective element in his novel. All the ingredients are there for the kind of developed "mystery" that Dickens's readers apparently demanded (if we may believe Collins). So the question remains, then, why does Dickens abandon both his mystery and his detective at the risk of disappointing his readers? Is it simply to provide more space for the testing of Bella Wilfer and for the development of the Wrayburn-Headstone rivalry?

Certainly it might be argued that Dickens indeed deliberately submerged the explicit Harmon mystery in order to make room for his notoriously well-concealed Boffin plot, but then we have to ask just why Dickens kept *this* new development so completely in the dark. Might he not have provided the kind of clues into Boffin's true intentions that an astute "mystery" reader would appreciate (as he does in the "testing" of Esther Summerson in the concluding chapters of **Bleak House**), thus making the final revelation of the scheme less of a shock? Dickens's failure to provide such clues, his failure even to tempt us into decoding Boffin's behavior, certainly appears to justify Gill's complaint that, in comparison with the Harmon mystery, the "story of Boffin's feigned degradation is not just clumsy, it is a major tactical error. Paradoxically, it is so damaging just because Dickens's art is so good, because he (and Mr. Boffin) deceive the reader so completely."[10] In short, because Boffin's apparent slide into miserliness fits in so nicely with the novel's condemnation of money worship, it "is a shock to the reader to find that all this is deceit, that open, friendly Noddy Boffin has never changed at all. It is a shock, however, not just because we resent being kept in the dark, but because the development of Mr. Boffin has seemed so completely natural, so in keeping with the rest of the novel's social analysis."[11] Thus, not only does the Boffin plot constitute a bad (because too well-concealed) "mystery element" in **Our Mutual Friend,** but it appears to undermine the larger themes of the novel as well.

But it is not my purpose here to condemn the Harmon-Boffin plot as an aesthetic failure. Rather, what I wish to examine here is the possible significance of the fact that the "mystery element" in the Harmon-Boffin plot does fail so badly. I do not believe that we can attribute this failure to mere authorial incompetence. After all, the creator of Inspector Bucket still had in him an **Edwin Drood** to conclude his career, so we can hardly question either Dickens's ability to write a good tale of crime and detection or his continuing interest in the genre. But why, then, is the "mystery element" in the novel so unsatisfactory? Is it really only a sop to Dickens's readers, and thus better left out to begin with if it is not to be pursued effectively? Or

can we see the very failure of the "mystery element" in **Our Mutual Friend** as a *positive* component in the novel's overall thematic design, that is to say, as a calculated aesthetic strategy in Dickens's social criticism?

To answer such questions we might compare the world of **Our Mutual Friend** to the **Bleak House** world as it has been rather programmatically interpreted by Hillis Miller. "**Bleak House** is a document about the interpretation of documents," a dramatization of the moral effects of "the act of interpretation itself, the naming which assimilates the particular into a system, giving it a definition and a value, incorporating it into a whole."[12] The world Dickens dramatizes might be seen accordingly to correspond to the "modern times" that Mathew Arnold apprehends in his essay on "Heinrich Heine," times that "find themselves with an immense system of institutions, established facts, accredited dogmas, customs, rules, which have come to them from times not modern. In this system their life has to be carried forward; yet they have a sense that this system is not of their own creation, that it by no means corresponds exactly with the wants of their actual life, that, for them, it is customary, not rational."[13] Thus inscribed within an already accomplished institutional system governed by such objectively impersonal documents as constitutions, legal codes, and, significantly, Wills, modern man has suffered a diminution of subjective vitality. As Georg Simmel has put it, the "development of modern culture is characterized by the preponderance of . . . the 'objective spirit' over the 'subjective spirit.'" This preponderance, Simmel continues, is reflected in the domination of modern life by "that organ which is least sensitive and quite remote from the depth of the personality," that is, by the calculating "head" rather than by the sympathetic "heart."[14] Subjective, sympathetic human activity, Simmel suggests, has been replaced by the reifying forces of a capitalist economy—and a "capital," of course, is first of all a "head."

The *literary* repercussions of urban capitalism, Georg Lukács has argued, have been reflected in a historical division between aesthetic realism and aesthetic naturalism. "The truly great realists," Lukács explains, "present social institutions as human relationships," while in the naturalistic novel "man and his surroundings are always sharply divided."[15] That is, where the realistic novel represents a dialectical relationship between subjective free will and the will of the social group, the naturalistic novel represents the breakdown of this dialectical equilibrium, leading to a breakdown of subjective freedom itself as all subjects come to be determinately constrained by their objective environments. "I would classify as naturalistic," Philip Rahv writes accordingly, "that type of realism in which the individual is portrayed not merely as subordinate to his background but as wholly determined by it—that type of realism, in other words, in which the environment displaces its inhabitants in the role of hero."[16]

Consider, for example, the rooftop world of Pubsey and Company as Dickens describes it in **Our Mutual Friend,** a world in which the paradoxical vitality of an "encompassing wilderness of dowager old chimneys" that "[twirl] their cowls and [flutter] their smoke" (p. 332) seems to overwhelm the lives of the human characters who enter it both as a haven from the harsh realities of urban London and as a place to be "dead." Is it any accident that the imaginative mistress of this scene is a cripple in the "employ" of wealthy dolls whose own prestige and privilege have reified the subjective worth of their dressmaker? Indeed, with her peculiarly dwarfed appearance and the mechanical chop of her jaw, Jenny Wren is almost indistinguishable from the dolls that she serves.

Death itself in *Our Mutual Friend* can be a force for capitalistic reification, as victims of the Thames become commodities in Gaffer Hexam's grisly trade, while skeletal and embryonic remains are routinely commodified in the dark recesses of Venus's shop. It is no anachronism here to blame finance capitalism for these reifications in Dickens's novel, for it is the cash economy of mid-century London that provides the dominant metaphor for the story. Money, like "dust," is wholly impersonal and objective. As Simmel puts it, it "is concerned only with what is common to all: it asks for the exchange value, it reduces all quality and individuality to the question: How much?"[17]

Dickens's caustic response to the reifying effect of a capitalist economy, to the ways in which it transforms all things, subjects as well as objects, into a system of exchangeable commodities, is inscribed in the often comic rhetoric of his novel. The reductions of Twemlow to the status of a dining table, of the Veneering baby to an "article" for sentimental exhibition, and of Bradley Headstone's mind to a "warehouse" for economically saleable knowledge are pointed examples. Such "characters" as "Boots and Brewer," the "Member," the "Payer-off of the National Debt," and the "Poem on Shakespeare" similarly have all been metonymically reduced from what they subjectively *are* to what they objectively *do,* with the broad implication that they *are* nothing at all. Thus the Veneerings themselves, though ostensibly presented with a proper name, are simply rhetorical caricatures: filmy, vacuous, parvenu, the clan fairly reeks of the scent of freshly painted lacquer. As figures for London's capitalists, money-people connected to a world founded on nothing more solid than a stock exchange, the Veneering circle thus appears to us in a play of rhetorical signs that signify nothing more substantial than the repeated exchange of monetary signifiers, or "shares," that "grounds" it. Neither share nor shareholder, in other words, has an axiological grounding in any substantially motivated value system. In effect, the shareholding class thus becomes indistinguishable from what it holds: both shareholder and share are tropes, impersonal substitutes for a world of value that is forever deferred. In such a world, Dickens laments, the best strategy indeed is to have "no antecedents, no established character, no cultivation, no ideas, no manners; have Shares" (pp. 159-60).

But it should be stressed that these are the novel's (comic) villains, and Dickens so presents them to ridicule them,

not to represent them as the necessary essence of urban character. Dickens's portrait of a society based on an ungrounded play of monetary signs, in other words, does not represent his conviction that tropological substitution is simply in the nature of things or that the "only escape from the circle of signs would be the end of the world or death."[18] Miller's interpretation of the Dickens world thus only pertains to a particular segment of it. For *Our Mutual Friend,* as I shall argue, does present us with a way of escape, a way allegorized by John Harmon's refusal to submit to the system that oppresses him by his building of a new family untainted by the "evil" that Miller, paradoxically enough, finds in "any social organization based on membership in a family."[19]

In order to grasp the precise nature of Harmon's escape, we must first investigate the logical connection between the urban experience as such and the genre of detective fiction in which *Our Mutual Friend* so notably fails, because Harmon's scheme, as we shall see, is precisely an attempt to subvert the very logic of the detective novel. This connection can be found in the semiotic quality both of urban life in general and of detective work in particular. For as the city fills up with objects—that is, with reified subjects and depersonalized (as well as depersonalizing) things and institutions—it ceases to appear to us as a construct designed for human purposes by human wills and begins to appear more as a mysterious sequence of mere signs, of objective signifiers with no apparent signified meanings. The sheer multiplication of objects in the city drains each object of meaning even as it teases us into interpreting it. And so, Geoffrey Hartman observes, with our very environment reduced to a mysterious play of signs, even the art that represents this environment comes to feel "itself to be *écriture,* signs of signs."[20] Thus, as the representation of a man who "reads" his environment successfully where the rest of us fail, giving meaning to the apparently meaningless signs of our experience, the detective novel proper comes to perfectly reflect urban consciousness. As Hartman puts it, "the detective novel . . . suggests at once the desire and the difficulty of giving to daily existence that 'seriousness' which Erich Auerbach saw emerging in the great realistic novels of the nineteenth century. For the hopeful and productive aspects of industrialization are being replaced by a purely semiotic and indifferent urbanization. 'We are surrounded by emptiness,' Lefebvre sighs, 'but it is an emptiness filled with signs! Metalanguage replaces the missing city.'" And from this space of unlimited signification, Hartman concludes, there emerges "the ghostly sensationalism of detective fiction, in which every detail, howsoever small, is potentially a telltale sign of human purposes, even if it disappoints an imagination it excites into voyeurism."[21]

Is *Our Mutual Friend,* then, a naturalistic novel by such criteria or a realistic one? Is it a tale of urban reification and semiotic emptiness, or does it reflect "the hopeful and productive aspects of [nineteenth-century] industrialization?" I suggest that it is something of both, with its rhetorical texture functioning pessimistically (or naturalistically) and its plot functioning hopefully (or realistically). John Harmon's struggle to subvert the Harmon Will can be interpreted as a kind of "realistic" allegory of subjective resistance to the naturalistic determination of signs because the Harmon Will comes down to the living characters of the story much as the institutions come from the past that Arnold sees as failing to correspond "exactly with the wants of . . . [modern] life." The Will, accordingly, can either be surrendered to with a kind of naturalistic shrug or ignored on behalf of more subjective values. The novel's characters, in other words, have a choice in the face of the Will. They can either bow to its dictates or rebel against it. Bella Wilfer, before her testing, simply bows and appears ridiculous for it, draping herself in mourning for a "husband" she has neither met nor married. Silas Wegg, in a different spirit, still serves the Will by trying to make it serve him, seeking, like the Smallweeds of *Bleak House,* "to find out the hidden place of another in the system" in order "to be able to manipulate him, to dominate him, and of course to make money out of him."[22] But howsoever "clumsy" it may appear as a plot device, the Harmon-Boffin disguise plot represents the contrary choice, dramatizing a deliberate rebellion by a group of people who refuse to be manipulated by their world. No one can manipulate Harmon because no one (excepting the Boffins) can guess his secret before Harmon himself reveals it. In short, Harmon's scheme subverts the naturalistic (and semiotic) dictates of the past (as represented by the Will) on behalf of a subjective plan to take control of his own life. And the fact that Harmon so rebels against a world dominated by coldly objective signs can at least partly explain why the mystery, or detective, element in Dicken's story must fail.

To see this we might review the fundamental nature of a typical detective story. As Hartman suggests, a detective is a reader of signs. He decodes clues presented to him from an already completed past, giving meaning to his world, so to speak, retroactively. For this reason, the detective's work, while certainly active and ingenious, is profoundly uncreative. Nothing new can emerge from his interpretations except either judgment or revenge (and not always that, as we can see from such morally futile tales as Poe's "Murders in the Rue Morgue"). Because the detective story points to no future events, its proper narrative tense, in Robert Champigny's words, is thus properly the "what will have happened" rather than the "what will happen" or "what should happen."[23] In a sense, then, the detective is essentially amoral. He is not concerned with values as such, only with interpretation.

It is accordingly of some interest to us to note the kind of treatment that the "detectives" in *Our Mutual Friend* receive. The Night Inspector, of course, is a conventional figure from the genre of detective fiction. There is no question that we are made to sympathize with "Mr. Inspector" in the novel, but as Jerry Palmer has suggested, the motives for Dickens's portrayal here were more political than aesthetic. Palmer attributes the sympathetic representations of Dickens's detectives to a desire to redeem the London police force from its general unpopularity.[24] In other words, Dickens can be said to be doing a little public relations here, and the fact that the Night Inspector virtually vanishes from the pages of *Our Mutual Friend* following the discovery of Gaffer Hexam's drowning does suggest a certain ironic coolness toward the figure of the detective in this novel.

The figurative detectives of *Our Mutual Friend* receive even worse treatment. Silas Wegg, for example, is one such "detective." Not only does he follow Noddy Boffin around like a bloodhound, but his entire connection with the Boffins is as a reader of signs, both as a hired "literary man" and as a reader of the Will with which he seeks to control his employer. Like Krook in *Bleak House* (who, of course, is literally illiterate), Silas Wegg is a believer in the power of signs (Charley Hexam's arrogant pride in his literacy offers another example of this), and this is why he is so greatly thwarted by the Harmon-Boffin scheme, for he is unable to imagine that anyone might have the capacity to rebel against the sign, against the written Will that Boffin so blithely ignores apparently in detriment of his own material interests. Boffin is more concerned with what he believes to be right than with the decodeable dictates of a dead man's Will, and it is on this quiet subversion of the testamentary institutions of nineteenth-century England that the Harmon plot stands.

There are at least two more "detectives" in *Our Mutual Friend* with which we are certainly not intended to sympathize. Rogue Riderhood is one such "detective," for this man who places such faith in the inscribed power of an "Alfred David" is very good at decoding other people's intentions through the reading of their actions. For example, Riderhood is able to sniff out Bradley Headstone's attempt to incriminate him by the simple act of correctly interpreting Headstone's strategy of dressing exactly like him. Riderhood's decoding of Headstone's red bandana is worthy of a more conventional detective, and his bloodhound-like tracking of Headstone ironically resembles good police work rather than a blackmailer's plot.

But, of course, Riderhood is unredeemable, and it is significant that he perishes in the murderous embrace of Bradley Headstone, who is himself a kind of detective. For Headstone's careful reading of the Eugene Wrayburn-Lizzie Hexam affair, too, turns upon his decoding of external signs, and his constant tracking of Wrayburn through the streets of London and beyond into the countryside again resembles the work of a competent policeman. In an oddly parallel fashion, Eugene Wrayburn's own guilt feelings after playing the detective in the stakeout for Gaffer Hexam constitute yet another example of the sinister appearance of detective work in *Our Mutual Friend.* The detective's work, that is to say, appears to be more criminal than heroic in this novel. And indeed, it is John Harmon, alias Julius Handford, the chief suspect in the Harmon "murder," who turns out to be the true hero of the tale, not the detective who searches for him.

Thus, it is the suspect, not the policeman, who emerges at the center of the novel. And it is significant that John Harmon, even in his own underworld operations, never plays the detective; because as the center of his own mystery, Harmon already knows everything that there is to know about his "murder." When he does perform what looks like a little detective work in his pressuring of Rogue Riderhood, he simply acts on what he already knows and, as we have already seen, more or less ignores what he does not know. That is, Harmon could easily seek to illuminate the remaining mysteries in his story, but he does not pursue the "case." His only reason for approaching Riderhood at all is to remove the cloud from Lizzie Hexam's name. Rather than attempting to read the signs from his past in order to resolve that past, Harmon is only interested in the future moral effects of his actions. Realizing that his disguise plot has injured an innocent woman, Harmon acts to undo the injury. Otherwise he is apparently uninterested in the unanswered questions as to his own "mystery," refusing to play the detective in spite of the great temptations he has for doing so.

When Harmon and the Boffins finally do reveal their machinations to Bella, the scene had all the appearance of a detective story's typical denouement—but in reverse. That is, at the conclusion of a conventional detective tale, our interest is focused not on what will happen next to the characters but on the clever deductive process by which the detective has solved a crime that has been completed *before* the deductive action, and the visible story itself, can begin. Poirot makes his little speech and everything becomes clear. But what Harmon reveals to Bella is how he himself plotted to bring out her "true" identity, an identity that is projected forward to the moment when it is completed at the very instant of Harmon's revelation. In other words, Bella's testing is not really over until she hears all of the details of the "plot" upon her and approves of them. She could, after all, resent the whole thing and walk out (as she has walked out before), but she does not. Bella's learning of the plot is thus *a part of the plot*; it is not simply a device for telling the reader "who did what and when" because nothing has been fully accomplished yet: it is only *being accomplished* in the course of a dynamic narrative.

To put this another way, Harmon is less Poirot than Jeeves, for just as Wodehouse's valet cleverly plots to produce certain social results *within* the course of the action, so too does Harmon direct his actions towards the achievement of as yet unactualized goals. Both Jeeves and Harmon, then, as reverse detectives, read the present in order to produce potential future results. And what such figures can reveal at the end is not how they have decoded someone else's already accomplished deeds, but how they themselves have interpreted the dynamic potentialities of the present (e.g., the moral potential of Bella Wilfer) in order to produce the actual circumstances that obtain at the end of their stories (Bella's moral redemption). It is a case not of the detective's "what will have happened" but rather, of the "what has been made to happen."

Harmon's inversion of the standard mystery story, his creation of a kind of antidetective tale, can be seen, then, to

be part of *Our Mutual Friend*'s general thematic attack on urban reification. For rather than serving the signs of the past (the Will), Harmon subjectively constructs his own social present, answerable to his own needs. In essence, he does escape from the circle of signs without dying precisely *by* building a family. In this sense, then, the novel can be seen as a product of realism, in spite of its naturalizing rhetoric, because its solution is achieved through the working out of human social relations undaunted by naturalistic, or objectifying, forces.

If we return now to the chapter that has offended so many readers with its bald declaration of the Harmon "mystery," we may discern yet another instance of the "realistic" allegory at work here: the allegory, that is, of a subjective rebellion against the city's reifying effects. So let us look more closely at the precise words by which Harmon describes his state just preceding his ejection into the river. The passage is worth quoting at some length:

> I heard a noise of blows, and thought it was a woodcutter cutting down a tree. I could not have said that my name was John Harmon—I could not have thought it—but when I heard the blows, I thought of the woodcutter and his axe, and had some dead idea that I was lying in a forest.
>
> This is still correct? Still correct, with the exception that I cannot possibly express it to myself without using the word I. But it was not I. There was no such thing as I, without my knowledge.
>
> [P. 426]

Harmon's temporary loss of subjective identity under the influence of the drug can be seen as a kind of allegory of a life lived in the face of reifying forces ever prepared to convert the living "I" into an objectified "it" for the sake of a quick profit. Such indeed is the literal fate of those Londoners who, having fallen into the Thames, become "property" of the rivermen, of the Gaffer Hexams to whom they are no longer subjects capable of holding their own property but objects to be cashed in for some reward. And it is also the figural fate for any Londoner "drowned," so to speak, by life in the urban crowd, a drowning whose significance has been more starkly represented in T. S. Eliot's own symbolic depiction of the Thames as a sterile stream dominated by the figures of the drowned sailor and the fisher king. Dickens's nineteenth-century sailor thus seems to anticipate Eliot's twentieth-century one. But there is, of course, a difference between John Harmon and Phlebas the Phoenician.

Harmon survives, rising both from the water and from the metaphoric objectivity of the forest floor, and the course of his actions taken after his escape dramatizes his subjective rebellion against the objectifying forces around him—a rebellion that succeeds precisely because everyone thinks that he is dead. For the Harmon Will still lingers over the son's life, the living man trapped in the inscribed web of a dead man's desire. And so, Harmon himself is content to be "dead" for a while, playing his own sexton by interring the name of Harmon fathoms deep beneath "alp" upon alp of burial clay. In thus disguising himself, Harmon voluntarily enters into his own semiotic play, passing from Harmon to Handford to Rokesmith, and even, for a short time, becoming a "Secretary" in both senses of the term, confused by Noddy Boffin for the article of furniture that "secretary" also names (pp. 141-43). But Harmon consents to this sort of semiotic displacement, or rhetorical figuration, in order to defeat the designs of the written Will and the money-worship (itself a form of sign worship) that have poisoned his world.

"The physical world," Raymond Williams has written, "is never in Dickens unconnected with man. It is of his making, his manufacture, his interpretation. That is why it matters so much what shape he has given it."[25] But this is precisely the problem with the London of *Our Mutual Friend*: it has ceased to be designed by living wills and is simply dictated to by lifeless Wills from the past and dominated by a political economy founded on nothing more solid than impersonal contracts and monetary scrip: representations of representations. Such a society relates to its members as language does to a parrot, and the city it builds is a city of furnished rooms. And so Harmon builds his own world by creating a new family, one that includes the creatively imaginative members of London, the Lizzie Hexams and Jenny Wrens, rather than the readers of dead signs (we do not see Charley Hexam reunited with his sister). Symbolized by the Harmony Mansion, Harmon's refashioned society is thus subjectively constructed on the defeat of the past, as "Uncle Parker's" townhouse (so often employed by Wegg to condemn the creative freedom of his "enemies") is redesigned to accommodate a new family. It is as if the old city of the furnished room and of the dead man's inscribed desire has been invaded by a living host of interior decorators. For the house here is no mere sign, no evanescent facade before the inherent emptiness of the city. In its restoration from its ironic and destructive entrapment in the "Harmony Jail," the name of Harmon reachieves its true value in the creative (and procreative) "Harmony Mansion." The building of the house parallels the building of a family, just as the hoarding of a dust mound once accompanied the destruction of one.

Still, Dickens faces what is perhaps an insuperable difficulty in the end that can threaten to undermine his entire program. That is, the denouement of the Harmon plot is not only sentimental; it also cannot escape the fact that it is indeed only an allegory. Nothing in the London that is outside the novel has been changed by Harmon's scheme, and that is the London with which Dickens is most concerned. What is more, the allegory of the Harmon plot must itself be read—decoded by the literary detective, so to speak. Is there any way that we can move from the semiotic activity of reading to the moral activity of social action? I believe that there is, but in order to make the move from the allegorical text to a nonallegorical reality we must first be convinced by that text's rhetoric, by which I mean the rhetoric of *persuasion* rather than that of figu-

ration. And here, perhaps, is where *Our Mutual Friend* most sorely fails, for its failure to "keep contract" with its readers in its development of the Harmon mystery plot simply distracts us from the message behind the medium. We expect a detective story (the medium) and, missing it, miss the message as well. Still, if in spite of this rhetorical failure we may see Harmon's refusal to play the detective, to serve the signs that the city has already written for him, as a symbol for a general rebellion against the very world that produces a desire for detective stories, then perhaps we may be persuaded in spite of all to make the kind of moral commitments that the Harmon plot allegorizes and, by so doing, break out of the circle of signs. Allegories, after all, *are* didactic, and while there is no necessary connection between the allegorical text and what it may persuade us to do, there is a potential connection because, as in Brecht's theater, there is nothing to prevent us from acting on its message. In other words, while *Our Mutual Friend,* like *Bleak House,* may indeed locate the causes of social decay "in the ineradicable human tendency to take the sign for the substance,"[26] it denies that this *tendency,* or disposition, is "ineradicable." Rather, like John Harmon, we may exercise our potential not simply to make and interpret more signs but to refashion our world around solid human relationships. In the end, what the city and its society have wrought is not so important in *Our Mutual Friend* as what *we* might yet bring to pass. The hero of the novel, and, by extension, of the extranovelistic world, is not the reader of signs, not the Silas Weggs nor the Night Inspectors or even the passive reader of its tale: it is the active reader, the reader who in reading the story resolves to create a better world.

Notes

1. J. R. Wise, "Belles Lettres," in the *Westminster Review,* N.S. 29 (April 1866): 584.

2. Charles Dickens, *Our Mutual Friend,* ed. Stephen Gill (New York, 1971), p. 893. All subsequent page references will be given in the text.

3. J. Hillis Miller, introduction to Charles Dickens, *Bleak House* (New York, 1971), p. 20.

4. See Ernest Boll's "The Plotting of *Our Mutual Friend,*" *Modern Philology* 42 (November 1944): 96-122.

5. Stephen Gill, introduction to *Our Mutual Friend* (New York, 1971), p. 22.

6. Andrew Sanders, "'Come Back and Be Alive': Living and Dying in *Our Mutual Friend,*" *The Dickensian* 74 (September 1978): 140. As cited in H. M. Daleski's *Dickens and the Art of Analogy* (London, 1970), pp. 274-75.

7. Daleski, p. 275.

8. Gill, p. 22.

9. Ibid., p. 25.

10. Ibid., p. 23.

11. Ibid., pp. 23-24.

12. Miller, pp. 11, 21-22.

13. Matthew Arnold, "Heinrich Heine," in his *Essays in Criticism* (Boston, 1866), p. 143.

14. Georg Simmel, "The Metropolis and Mental Life," in his *On Individuality and Social Forms* (Chicago, 1971), p. 337.

15. Georg Lukács, *Studies in European Realism,* trans. Edith Bone (London, 1950), pp. 92-93.

16. Philip Rahv, "Notes on the Decline of Naturalism," in his *Image and Idea* (New York, 1949), pp. 132-33.

17. Simmel, p. 326.

18. Miller (n. 3 above), p. 28.

19. Ibid., p. 27.

20. Geoffrey Hartman, *Easy Pieces* (New York, 1985), p. 19.

21. Ibid., pp. 106-7.

22. Miller, p. 19.

23. See Robert Champigny, *What Will Have Happened* (Bloomington, Ind., 1977), passim.

24. Jerry Palmer, *Thrillers* (London, 1978), pp. 134-35.

25. Raymond Williams, *The Country and the City* (New York, 1973), p. 161.

26. Miller (n. 3 above), p. 33.

Wilfred P. Dvorak (essay date 1990)

SOURCE: "Dickens and Popular Culture: Silas Wegg's Ballads in *Our Mutual Friend*," in *The Dickensian,* Vol. 86, No. 3, Autumn, 1990, pp. 142-57.

[*In the following essay, Dvorak examines Dickens's use of Victorian popular ballads to illuminate the character of Silas Wegg and to reinforce the themes of* Our Mutual Friend.]

Recently (in *The Dickensian,* 1972), Lillian Ruff reminded us that 'Dickens's novels are a rich source of information about popular vocal music in the first half of the nineteenth century', and she noted more than 200 songs 'of social and historical interest', suggesting that Dickens's original readers would have 'quickly recognized these scraps of song, and mentally heard the tune'.[1] The ballad literature which Dickens has Silas Wegg distort in *Our Mutual Friend* is a particularly good case in point in this regard: the fifteen ballads from which Wegg quotes were very familiar to both Dickens and his readers (middle class and lower class alike) and represent a rich and diverse popular culture which they shared.[2] But in using these ballads Dickens seems to have had much more in mind than just

to add 'charm and quaintness' to Wegg's dialogue or to merely provide comedy or humour in his novel. Rather, more importantly, Dickens uses the ballads to reveal and refine the nature of Wegg's character and thereby develop (or at least reinforce) his major themes in *Our Mutual Friend.* Moreover, it is an indication of Dickens's particular genius as a popular artist that he is able so clearly to capture the attention and enrich the understanding of his readers by artistically shaping this familiar and popular ballad material into an important thematic statement about his own times: in effect, he manages to 'teach' his readers important moral truths, while engaging them in the delightful parade of many of his and their favourite musical tunes.

In the amount of space Dickens gives to him, Silas Wegg is one of the most important minor characters in *Our Mutual Friend,* appearing as a leading figure in nine chapters of the novel, and effectively embodying Dickens's central concern about the pursuit of money as a false goal (involving such additional themes as avarice, predation, search for identity, pride, education, and moral reformation).[3] When we first meet Wegg in Bk. I, Ch. 5, he combines traits of the Victorian ballad-monger and those of the incipient miser. His stall, with its 'choice collection of half-penny ballads', is typical of that of other ballad-hawkers of the 1860's described by Mayhew and others (including Dickens's contributors to *All the Year Round*);[4] and his placard is itself his own most-loved ballad:

> Errands gone
> On with fi
> Delity By
> Ladies and Gentleman
> I remain
> Your humble Serv[t]:
> Silas Wegg

Wegg's placard suggests that he most likely has learned to read and write from a love of popular ballads. And it is really a similar hunger for learning and literature which motivates Noddy Boffin to approach Wegg for the first time in this chapter to ask him to become his 'literary man'. For Boffin has earlier heard Wegg sing his ballads to the butcher-boy and been very much taken with admiration for the songs themselves and for Wegg's felicity in singing them. Ironically, however, it is precisely Boffin's request of Wegg, leading as it does to Wegg's self-congratulatory self-deception about the importance of his role as Boffin's reader, that initiates the process of his corruption by avarice. I do not think that Dickens is implying at this point that ballad-sellers are necessarily ridiculous, exploitative, or self-deceptive, but he is revealing his ambivalence about Victorian ballad culture. Evidently he feels sympathy for Boffin's aspirations and sees ballads as one way for him to satisfy them. But, at the same time, he recognizes that the aspirations of the illiterate are often exploited by unscrupulous ballad-sellers like Wegg who crave only money. And this then is the theme he develops in the subsequent dialogue (still Bk. I, Ch. 5) between Boffin and Wegg about poetry, which eventually leads Wegg to quote for the first time from a popular ballad.

As Wegg explains to Boffin in their conversation, poetry 'would come dearer' because 'he should expect to be paid for its weakening effect on his mind', and by the time he is done with Boffin, who had hoped poetry would be a gift from a friend genuinely moved by feeling, Wegg has tricked the honest Dustman into agreeing to pay 'double the money' for his quoting poetry (p. 95). Not surprisingly, the immediate result is Wegg 'drops' into poetry to pretend a long familiarity with the 'Decline-And-Fall-Off-The-Rooshan Empire' (the first book he has consented to read for Boffin):[5]

> 'But know him? Old familiar declining and falling off the Rooshan? Rather, sir! Ever since I was not so high as your stick. Ever since my eldest brother left our cottage to enlist into the army. On which occasion, as the ballad that was made about it describes:
>
>> Beside that cottage door, Mr Boffin,
>>   A girl was on her knees;
>> She held aloft a snowy scarf, Sir,
>>   Which (my eldest brother noticed) fluttered in the breeze.
>> She breathed a prayer for him, Mr Boffin;
>>   A prayer he could not hear.
>> And my eldest brother lean'd upon his sword, Mr Boffin,
>>   And wiped away a tear.'
>
> (p. 96)

Noddy Boffin is 'much impressed' by Wegg's 'family circumstance' and his 'friendly disposition' in quoting verse, but Dickens's readers, who would have recognized immediately that Wegg was distorting the second stanza of Thomas Bayly's 'The Soldier's Tear,' instead would have been amused and instructed by Wegg's actions. Bayly's ballad was one of the most popular sentimental parlour songs of the nineteenth century, celebrating the English soldier's courage and genuine feeling for his country and its people (thus his 'tear'). In using the poem, Dickens makes it quite clear that in attempting to solidify his hold on Boffin, Wegg is expressing his mercenary designs, for he has transformed a song affirming values supportive of the stability of the social community into a verse validating his own greed, which is indeed a genuine threat to any moral community.

Essentially the same pattern continues throughout *Our Mutual Friend* whenever Dickens uses the popular ballads to develop or refine Wegg's character. Thus on the next four occasions during which Wegg sings ballads he does so to continue his 'friendly gesture' to gain as much money from the Boffins as he can, all the while revealing to the reader his progressive corruption by avarice. For example, when we next hear Wegg quoting poetry it is in Bk. I, Ch. 15, when he is reported complimenting Mrs Boffin on her coming into possession of 'his' house (the one in front of which he kept his stall) with the lines

> 'The gay, the gay and festive scene,
> The halls, the halls of dazzling light.'
>
> (p. 230)

And Wegg adds on this occasion that he 'would be willing to put himself out of the way' in order to cheer up Mrs Boffin should she become depressed, when he goes on to play on the lines

> 'I'll tell thee how the maiden wept, Mrs Boffin,
> When her true love was slain, ma'am,
> And how her broken spirit slept, Mrs Boffin,
> And never woke again, ma'am.
> I'll tell thee (if agreeable to Mr Boffin) how the steed
>   drew nigh,
> And left his lord afar;
> And if my tale (which I hope Mr Boffin might excuse)
>   should make you sigh,
> I'll strike the light guitar.'
>
> (p. 230)

The poem Wegg is appropriating for his own purposes is H. S. Van Dyke's well-known 'The Light Guitar', a parlour song of melancholy love and death, and implied seduction. Wegg's use of the ballad (especially his interjections) is wonderfully comic, but more importantly it is also another indication of his intensifying mercenariness, for so eager has he become to gain money from the Boffins that he has taken a poem totally inappropriate to celebrate a house-buying or to overcome depression and tried to transform it into a festive song. Though he succeeds in duping the Boffins, who are highly pleased, he also reveals to the aware reader that he neither respects the Boffins integrity nor that of the poetry he so crassly distorts, and he suggests as well that he will seek to 'seduce by poetry' both Mr and Mrs Boffin in his pursuit of their wealth.

However, the full extent of Wegg's mercenary designs on the Boffins is not yet clear at this point in *Our Mutual Friend,* either to Wegg himself or to the reader (the Boffins remain ignorant altogether still). But these designs are pretty much clarified when Wegg next appears at Boffin's Bower (still Bk. I. Ch. 15), to once again drop into poetry, no less than three times in succession. The circumstances are telling. Boffin has decided to hire Rokesmith as his secretary and he is concerned that Wegg will be 'liable to jealousy' (p. 234). For, as the narrator explains, 'The man of low cunning had, of course, acquired a mastery over the man of high simplicity. The mean man had, of course, got the better of the generous man' (p. 234). Consequently, when Wegg appears at the Bower, Boffin is prepared to offer him the job as its resident caretaker to keep him content:

> 'What do you think,' said Mr Boffin, 'of not keeping a stall, Wegg?'
>
> 'I think, sir,' replied Wegg, 'that I should like to be shown the gentleman prepared to make it worth my while!'

'Here he is,' said Mr Boffing.

Mr Wegg was going to say, My Benefactor, and had said My Bene, when a grandiloquent change came over him.

'No, Mr Boffin, not you, sir. Anybody but you. Do not fear, Mr Boffin, that I shall contaminate the premises which your gold has bought, with *my* lowly pursuits. I am aware, sir, that it would not become me to carry on my little traffic under the windows of your mansion. I have already thought of that, and taken my measures. No need to be bought out, sir. Would Stepney Fields be considered intrusive? If not remote enough, I can go remoter. In the words of the poet's song, which I do not quite remember:

"Thrown on the wide world, doom'd to wander and roam,
Bereft of my parents, bereft of a home,
A stranger to something and what's his name joy.
Behold Little Edmund, the poor Peasant Boy."

—And equally,' said Mr Wegg, repairing the want of direct application in the last line, 'behold myself on a similar footing!'

(p. 235-36)

This dialogue, with Wegg attempting ineffectually to quote from John Parry's immensely popular 'The Peasant Boy', finally makes clear Wegg's motive in trying to get the Boffins to buy 'his' mansion: he believed that if they did he himself would be in a position to be 'bought off'. And, in this context, Parry's ballad provides a nice irony against Wegg, which Dickens's readers must have caught, for the song celebrates a poor peasant boy who, unlike Wegg, is 'willing' to 'labour' and 'toil' but *cannot* find work and so must wander and roam without a home, truly 'a stranger to pleasure, comfort and joy' (the line which Wegg cannot remember).

Boffin, however, is taken in by Wegg's resort to poetry, noting that Wegg is 'too sensitive'. As their conversation continues, Wegg attempts to exploit Boffin's feelings about his sensitivity hoping that he will indeed be pensioned-off, but ironically the honest Dustman fools him with emphasizing that Wegg will have to work 'to deserve' money. Significantly, Wegg's response to Boffin's assertion is to again turn to poetry:

'That, sir,' replied Mr Wegg, cheering up bravely, 'is quite another pair of shoes. Now, my independence as a man is again elevated. Now, I no longer

"Weep for the hour,
When to Boffines bower,
The Lord of the valley with offers came;
Neither does the moon hide her light
From the heavens to-night.
And weep behind her clouds o'er any individual in the present Company's shame."

—Please to proceed, Mr Boffin.'

(p. 236)

From one point of view, Wegg's recovery from his disappointment by exploiting lines from Tom Moore's popular seduction ballad 'Evelyn's Bower' is ingenious: Wegg does dupe Boffin again, even eliciting from him a 'Thank'ee' for his confidence and dropping into poetry (p. 236). But, ironically, Dickens has also provided his readers with another telling sign: Boffin is hardly Moore's 'Lord of the Valley' seeking with 'false vows' to seduce Wegg; but Wegg *is* trying to seduce Boffin, by an appeal to poetry. Wegg's avariciousness has indeed intensified to a deplorable degree.

Nevertheless, Wegg is not yet finished with poetry on this occasion. Having finally been offered the job of keeper of the Bower—with assurances that he will thereby gain additional moneys—Wegg makes a poetical acceptance:

'Mr Boffin, consider it done. Say no more, sir, not a word more. My stall and I are for ever parted. The collection of ballads will in future be reserved for private study, with the object of making poetry tributary . . . Tributary, to friendship, Mr Boffin, don't allow yourself to be made uncomfortable by the pang it gives me to part from my stock and stall. Similar emotion was undergone by my own father when promoted for his merits from his occupation as a waterman to a situation under Government. His Christian name was Thomas. His words at that time (I was then an infant, but so deep was their impression on me, that I committed them to memory) were:

"Then farewell, my trim-built wherry,
Oars and coat and badge farewell!
Never more at Chelsea Ferry
Shall your Thomas take a spell!"

—My father got over it, Mr Boffin, and so shall I.'

(p. 237)

So much for Wegg's fidelity to his poetical stock and stall! But at least Wegg's direct quote from Charles Dibdin's famous 'Poor Tom!' does help to convince Boffin that he has successfully worked out an arrangement with Wegg and need have no further concern. However, Dickens's aware readers would have known better, for Dibdin's song is richly ironic in this context. In the opera *The Waterman*, 'Poor Tom!' represents a bogus melodramatic threat by the hero Tom Hugg against the heroine Wilelmina that if she continues to be indecisive about her suit he will join a man-of-war to pursue death and thereby cause her grief. But, unlike Tom Tugg, Silas Wegg is dishonest in his protestations: he has no genuine feeling for Boffin, nor does he desire to be Boffin's friend; in fact, his ballad represents a declaration of war against Boffin's wealth, for it is becoming clear in *Our Mutual Friend* that his avariciousness is one thing Wegg will never get over.

When we next encounter Wegg (Bk. II, Ch. 7), he has become firmly entrenched in the Bower; and we discover that Boffin's fear that Wegg would become jealous over Rokesmith becoming secretary has been realized. But, though Wegg complains that he has been 'banished' to the

Bower, he also takes advantage of his presence there to search the Dustmounds for hidden wealth. And in this regard Wegg again turns to poetry (he cannot help himself), as he discovers that he needs the assistance of Venus to perpetrate his 'friendly move' on Boffin. For example, when he tries to convince Venus to help him scavenge through the dust mounds to ferret out old Harmon's treasure, including any wills or codicils that Boffin may have hidden, Wegg breaks into song:

> 'As one that the poet might have had his eye on, in writing the national naval words:
>
> "Helm a-weather, now lay her close,
>   Yard arm and yard arm she lies;
> Again, cried I, Mr Venus, give her t'other dose,
>   Man shrouds and grapple, sir, or she flies!"'
>
> (p. 355-56)

On this occasion, Wegg is creating his own version of 'The Tar for All Weathers', Charles Dibdin's very popular idealized celebration of the English sailor—the man of courage, duty, and perseverance who nobly and philosophically accepts his work in life—in order to flatter Venus into believing that their plan to rob Boffin is indeed noble and right. Of course the ironic contrast between Dibdin's admirable sailor and the mercenary Wegg, to Wegg's discredit, would not have been missed by Dickens's readers.

For the moment, however, Wegg does succeed in entrapping Venus in his schemes, and he assures him, again echoing Dibdin, that in their 'friendly move' against Boffin 'you will have a glorious object to rouse you', in 'secrecy, fidelity, and perseverance' (p. 357-58). Nevertheless, by the next time we see Wegg and Venus in *Our Mutual Friend* (Bk. III, Ch. 6), Venus is beginning to have serious doubts about Wegg and their 'friendly move'. And this time even Wegg's three efforts at poetry do not pacify Venus. Wegg tries poetry immediately on this occasion, since Venus greets him coldly:

> 'Walk in brother,' said Silas, clapping him on the shoulder, and take your seat in my chimley corner; for what says the ballad?
>
> "No malice to dread, sir,
> And no falsehood to fear,
> But truth to delight me, Mr Venus,
> And I forget what to cheer.
> Li toddle de om dee.
> And something to guide,
> My ain fireside, sir,
> My ain fireside."
>
> (p. 538)

Wegg is trying to quote from Elizabeth Hamilton's popular 'My Ain Fireside', and his distortions and memory lapses, which Dickens's readers would have caught, reveal that by this time in *Our Mutual Friend* he has become so single-minded that all he can think of *is* the falsehood and malice he actually intends toward Venus. That is the 'truth'

which delights him, of course, and consequently he cannot remember that in the ballad it is friendship which is supposed to cheer him, with the 'fireside' standing as a metaphor for the happiness and peace of mind which come from living free of the very pursuit of wealth which he so craves, with all of the 'flattery' and 'boastings' which go with such a false pursuit.

Apparently Venus himself senses that in his poetry Wegg is being less than honest and friendly on this occasion, moreover, for he is not moved by the attempted flattery. But Wegg, not daunted, tries verse a second time:

> 'We'll devote the evening, brother,' exclaimed Wegg, 'to prosecute our friendly move. And afterwards, crushing a flowing wine-cup—which I allude to brewing rum and water—we'll pledge one another. For what says the Poet?
>
> "And you needn't Mr Venus be your black bottle,
> For surely I'll be mine,
> And we'll take a glass with a slice of lemon in it to
>   which your're partial,
> For auld lang syne."'
>
> (p. 539)

Of course the lines with which Wegg is trying to win Venus this time are from Robert Burns's wildly famous 'Auld Lang Syne'; and in his attempt to quote Burns's last stanza (while evidently thinking of the rest of the poem as well) again Wegg signals that he simply cannot understand what real friendship is: ironically, as Dickens's readers would have known, Burns's 'cup o' kindness' pledged between *trusting*, loving friends has become a comic 'glass with a slice of lemon in it'. Though Wegg's 'flow of quotation' may not be very good poetry, once again it exposes perfectly his exploitative, mercenary attitude toward Venus.

Still, for all of his poetic efforts, Wegg has not allayed Venus's doubts about the wisdom of digging in the Harmon dust mounds; in fact, Venus has about decided to give up. So, predictably, Wegg's response is a third try at poetry:

> 'Charge, Chester, charge
> On, Mr Venus, on!'
>
> (p. 539)

As a last resort, Wegg is trying out Scott's *Marmion* on Venus. The lines are from Canto VI, Stanza 23, celebrating Marmion's selfless devotion to country and liberty to the very end of his life. As Dickens's readers would have seen at once (for even schoolboys knew the lines), Wegg's use of Scott is ludicrous, though a quite understandable reflection of his mercenary character: ironically, by this time in *Our Mutual Friend*, Wegg perceives himself as an heroic figure like Marmion locked in a noble battle to the death, pursuing the only object which *he* values—money—and he sees Venus as a fellow soldier who needs buoying up, by poetical means.

Not surprisingly, however, once again Wegg fails to excite Venus, whose resolution to extricate himself from the 'friendly move' is strengthened when Boffin arrives at the Bower and Wegg reads about the misers from Merryweather's *Lives and Anecdotes* and Kirby's *Wonderful Museum* (Bk. III, Ch. 6). For, though Wegg learns nothing from these stories about the misers' despicable behaviour, Venus does—that Wegg himself is an avaricious miser who cannot be trusted—and this lesson is reinforced when, after the reading, Wegg entertains murderous thoughts about Boffin, finally admitting to Venus that he has in fact already discovered a Harmon will which he has concealed from him, even while he was trying to convince him through poetry to continue searching the dust mounds. Clearly, at this point in the novel, Venus (and the reader) must suspect that Wegg's avarice has driven him to such a 'pitch of insatiable appetite' (p. 552) that he has become mentally unbalanced. Yet, rather quickly, Wegg regains the appearance of sanity (in Bk. III, Ch. 7), again taking up the 'disguise' as Venus's 'brother'. Of course, from his point of view, Wegg now has a serious problem: he must regain control over Venus by somehow concealing the full extent of his duplicity. And, not surprisingly, once again Wegg's method is to try to overwhelm Venus with more verse, as in this description of how he found the Harmon will:

> 'On a certain day, sir, I happened to be walking in the yard—taking my lonely round—for, in the words of a friend of my own family, the author of All's Well arranged as a duet:
>
> > 'Deserted, as you will remember Mr Venus, by the waning moon,
> > When starts, it will occur to you before I mention it, proclaim night's cheerless noon,
> > On tower, fort, or tented ground,
> > The sentry walks his lonely round,
> > The sentry walks!"
>
> —under those circumstances, sir, I happened to be walking in the yard early one afternoon, and happened to have an iron rod in my hand, with which I have been sometimes accustomed to beguile the monotony of a literary life, when I struck it against an object not necessary to trouble you by naming—'
>
> (p. 555)

Wegg is stalling, trying to avoid revealing to Venus the contents of the will by quoting from the popular 'All's Well' which appeared in Thomas Dibdin's often performed *The English Fleet*. Like so many of Charles Dibdin's ballads, Thomas Dibdin's duet is a tribute to the English sailor, summarizing the play's main theme: that 'The post of watchman with a British captain is one too full of honour to decline; and, while English sailors are at hand to assist us, there's little to fear that the word will be "All's well."'[6] As Dickens's readers could not have missed, ironically, once again the crafty Wegg has tried to present himself as a noble, heroic figure, while in fact he remains a scavenger trying to foist his corrupt value system upon Venus—and England.

Nevertheless, Wegg's attempt to put off Venus does not work: slowly but surely Venus forces the fact about the Harmon will from Wegg, then the will itself, which he reads and takes into safe-keeping. To be sure, Wegg is not happy with the turn of events, Venus has become determined to resist him, even when Wegg makes one last attempt at winning him over with still more flattering poetry:

> 'There you sit, sir, in the midst of your works, looking as if you'd been called upon for Home, Sweet Home, and was obleeging the company!
>
> "A exile from home splendour dazzles in vain,
> O give you your lovely Preparations again,
> The birds stuffed so sweetly that can't be expected to come at your call,
> Give you these with the peace of mind dearer than all.
> Home, Home, Home, sweet Home!"
>
> —Be it ever', added Mr Wegg, in prose as he glanced about the shop, 'ever so ghastly, all things considered there's no place like it.'
>
> (p. 562)

By referring to John Howard Payne's immensely popular 'Home, Sweet Home', Wegg is trying to find out about Venus's relationship with Pleasant Riderhood, evidently in the hope that this knowledge will allow him to regain some power over Venus. As usual, Wegg reshapes Payne's ballad rather creatively, as Dickens's readers would have noted, for clearly he is confused and upset, straining to *almost* offer genuine sympathy to Venus. Finally, however, for Wegg the virtues of the home and hearth which 'Home, Sweet Home' celebrates are insufficient and he remains dazzled by the very 'splendour' of riches which the poem seeks to expose as false. Thus Venus and his home must remain to Wegg 'ever so ghastly', 'worthless for his purpose'; and 'casting about for ways and means of dissolving the connexion without loss of money, reproaching himself for having been betrayed into an avowal of his secret, and complimenting himself beyond measure on his purely accidental good luck' (that Venus still seems to want money, in part), Wegg sets out from Venus's shop to go to Boffin's house where he hovers 'in the superior character of its Evil Genius' (p. 563-64). For, by this point in *Our Mutual Friend,* Wegg has succumbed entirely to his greed, and what he misperceives in Boffin has become only too true of himself: 'he's GROWN TOO FOND OF MONEY' (p. 565).

So far we have seen Wegg trying to manipulate by means of poetry both Boffin and Venus in his efforts to acquire money. In the remaining chapters of *Our Mutual Friend* in which he appears, Wegg's desire for money intensifies into a lust for power, which, when particularly inflamed, he indulges in by dropping into poetry. For Wegg has now set about preparing 'a grindstone for Mr Boffin's nose' (Bk. III, Ch. 14). The first time we see Wegg in his new role is when he pays a visit to Venus's shop (with Boffin hidden behind the alligator observing) to see the will, the thought of which is enough to cause him to break into verse (still Bk. III, Ch. 14):

'If you please, partner,' said Wegg, rubbing his hands. 'I wish to see it jintly with yourself. Or, in similar words to some that was set to music some time back:

> "I wish you to see it with your eyes,
> And I will pledge with mine."'

(p. 644)

In his enthusiasm, Wegg is appropriating lines from Ben Jonson's popular 'Drink to Me Only with Thine Eyes', which Dickens's readers would have known as a beautiful pledge of unselfish love, contrasting sharply with Wegg's pledge of avaricious lust, reflected also in a speech he makes to Venus (and the hidden Boffin) right after quoting from Jonson's ballad:

> 'I tell you what, Mr Venus; it comes to this; I must be overbearing with Boffin, or I shall fly into several pieces. I can't contain myself when I look at him. Every time I see him putting his hand in his pocket, I see him putting it into my pocket. Every time I hear him jingling his money, I hear him taking liberties with my money. Flesh and blood can't bear it!'

(p. 645)

Sadly, in his lust for the power which he believes Boffin's money can bring him, Wegg has mentally appropriated Boffin's wealth. Yet Wegg is still not at his 'worst': that state in which he desires an insolent 'revenge' on Boffin for making him, Silas Wegg, actually work for money. And, significantly, just as Wegg begins to reach his worst state, he tries to draw back from total vileness, through poetry:

> '. . . your speaking countenance remarks, Mr Venus, that I'm duller and savager than usual. Perhaps I *have* allowed myself to brood too much. Begone, dull Care! 'Tis gone, sir. I've looked in upon you, and empire resumes her sway. For, as the song says—subject to your correction, sir—
>
> "When the heart of a man is depressed with cares,
> The mist is dispelled if Venus appears.
> Like the notes of a fiddle, you sweetly, sir, sweetly,
> Raises our spirits and charms our ears."
>
> Good-night, sir."'

(p. 647)

Wegg is adapting lines from 'Would You Have a Young Virgin?', a famous song which appears in John Gay's *The Beggar's Opera*, Act III, Scene 3, sung by the opera's hero, Macheath. Ironically, as Dickens's readers would have caught immediately, instead of signalling that Wegg is coming out of his avaricious spell the song confirms how much entranced he remains, for the ballad actually expresses Macheath's insatiable lust for women in the context of the moral: 'And a Man who loves Money, might as well be contented with one Guinea, as I with one Woman.'[7] Evidently poor Wegg is so obsessed with money by this time that even when he *tries* to take his mind away from it he can't.

It remains in *Our Mutual Friend* for Wegg to confront Boffin directly to try to take his insolent revenge; and this he begins to do in the next chapter in which he appears (Bk. IV, Ch. 3), not surprisingly, in the process again turning to poetry. In fact, Wegg's greeting to Boffin when he arrives (with Venus) at the Bower on this occasion is poetical:

> 'Step in, sir.
>
> "If you'll come to the Bower I've shaded for you,
> Your bed shan't be roses all spangled with doo;
> Will you, will you, will you, will you, come to the Bower?
> Oh, won't you, won't you, won't you, won't you, come to the Bower?"'

(p. 719)

As the narrator observes, 'an unholy glare of contradiction and offence' shine in Wegg's eyes as he greets Boffin, for he is taking lines from Tom Moore's famous 'Will You Come to the Bower?' And it is obvious, or at least it would have been to Dickens's readers, that Wegg has something in mind for Boffin which is even worse than the 'gentle' seduction which is the subject of Moore's poem. Moreover, significantly, for the first time in *Our Mutual Friend*, Wegg's poetic lines instead of trying to conceal his intention from his victim largely gave it away openly: not at his worst, Wegg is about to try to take his revenge.

Wegg's notion of getting revenge on Boffin involves getting paid for doing nothing, which, ironically, he imagines as freeing himself from 'the Roman yoke' and pandering to Boffin's 'depraved appetite for miserly characters' (p. 721). Yet, most of all, Wegg wants the power of money over Boffin so that he can humiliate him; he wants Boffin to 'ask to be allowed as a favour to come to terms' because 'I'm as good a man as you, and better' (p. 722). Indeed, so grossly exaggerated is Wegg's sense of importance by this time, because he really believes that Boffin's money *belongs* to him, that for one last time he exults in poetry:

> 'I've got him under inspection, and I'll inspect him.
>
> "Along the line the signal ran,
> England expects as this present man
> Will keep Boffin to his duty."'

(p. 727)

Dickens has chosen well, for he has Wegg appropriate one of the most well-known poetical refrains of the nineteenth century, from S. J. Arnold's 'The Death of Nelson'. Of course, as virtually every Victorian knew, Arnold's ballad celebrates Lord Nelson's devotion to duty, his pursuit of honour throughout his life, 'for England, home and beauty'. And Wegg's misapplication of the poem nicely concludes the ironical movement of Wegg's balladry by showing him at the height of his self-deception in *Our Mutual Friend*: indeed, Wegg has gone so far as to imagine himself as the immortal Lord Nelson, pursuing Honour and saving England, while he is actually relishing his dishonourable avariciousness and thereby suggesting a mode of behavior which clearly in Dickens's view threatens England's very survival.

Wegg appears only one more time in *Our Mutual Friend* (Bk. IV, Ch. 4), when the 'friendly move' against Boffin receives its checkmate. On this occasion, not surprisingly, Wegg does not quote verse, though he remains as mercenary and self-deceptive as ever, including about his ballads. As Wegg explains, in 'avaricious humiliation', after Boffin indicates a willingness to set him up in another stall, 'when I first had the honour of making your acquaintance, I had got together a collection of ballads which was, I may say, above price' (p. 860). And Wegg does not stop with complaining about the loss of his ballads but goes on to list his other losses as well, ironically, even to complain about a 'lowering' of the tone of his mind by the 'unwholesome reading on the subject of Misers' when Boffin was in his disguise. Of course Wegg is right in complaining that it is difficult to 'put a price upon his mind' (p. 862), but even in making this statement he is trying to negotiate a price. For, unfortunately, Silas Wegg has learned nothing from his experiences with Boffin, and he will not accept responsibility for his own actions. Valuing only money to the end, it is appropriate that Wegg is seized by Sloppy at this point in *Our Mutual Friend* and exits deposited in a dust-cart.

Overall, Dickens has Silas Wegg quote poetry at least once in all but two of the chapters in which he appears in *Our Mutual Friend*; and, in the two chapters in which Wegg does not quote verse, Dickens makes it clear that Wegg refrains because he sees nothing to gain monetarily by doing so (in Bk. I. Ch. 7, when Wegg first makes arrangements with Venus to purchase his amputated leg; and in Bk. IV, Ch. 14, when Wegg's 'friendly move' is finally thwarted). Of course Dickens's comic presentation of Wegg is so rich in authorial commentary, incidents, and dialogues that it is quite possible for a reader to get some sense of Wegg's character even if he does not notice Wegg's propensity to quote from ballads, or does not know the ballads from which Wegg quotes. But certainly one of the important ways in which Dickens *intends* Wegg to be understood is in terms of his ballads—as a man who very much thinks in ballad lines and who, as he becomes increasingly mercenary, naturally expresses his growing avariciousness in the way he sings tunes. Thus, in the end, Wegg's misquotations of the ballads which he appropriates do reveal nicely his progressive corruption by avarice. First, in his initial greed, Wegg sings ballads as a 'friendly gesture' to try to gain as much money as he can from the Boffins as their 'literary man' (Bayly's 'The Soldier's Tear', in Bk. I, Ch. 5; and Van Dyke's 'The Light Guitar', Parry's 'The Peasant Boy', Moore's 'Evelyn's Bower', and Charles Dibdin's 'Poor Tom!', in Bk. I, Ch. 15). Then, secondly, as his greed becomes a compulsive disease, Wegg sings ballads to try to enlist and to keep the aid of Venus in his 'friendly move' against Boffin though his discovery of the Harmon will (Charles Dibdin's 'The Tar for

All Weathers', in Bk. II, Ch. 7; Hamilton's 'My Ain Fireside', Burns' 'Auld Lang Syne', and Scott's *Marmion,* in Bk. III, Ch. 6; and Thomas Dibdin's 'All's Well' and Payne's 'Home, Sweet Home', in Bk. III, Ch. 7). And, finally, when his avariciousness has resulted in derangement, Wegg sings ballads to celebrate the power he thinks he has over Boffin in trying to gain his insolent revenge (Jonson's 'Drink to Me Only with Thine Eyes' and Gay's 'Would You Have a Young Virgin?' in Bk. III, Ch. 14; and Moore's 'Will You Come to the Bower?' and Arnold's 'The Death of Nelson', in Bk. IV, Ch 3.). All in all, Wegg's performance, as orchestrated by Dickens, is indeed a revealing tragi-comic one.

As James Kincaid has rightly pointed out, Silas Wegg illustrates 'most of the main themes of Podsnappery'.[8] Most importantly, Wegg is one of Dickens's most important illustrations of the complex theme of money in *Our Mutual Friend,* for he turns out to be a genuine miser, a man who has been driven insane by avarice, and as such he stands as a foil to the characters in the novel who do not succumb to avarice: for example, John Harmon, Bella Wilfer, Eugene Wrayburn, Lizzie Hexam, Betty Higden, Noddy Boffin, and Venus. Indeed, in comic parody, Wegg's pursuit of money *is* his quest for identity. If John Harmon, Bella Wilfer, Eugene Wrayburn, and Lizzie Hexam, the novel's successful major characters, learn to take pride in their identities as loved and loving human beings free of any mercenary desires, Wegg learns how to sacrifice all genuine feelings for money; he identifies himself finally as a predatory creature of the dust-cart, the primordial slime, a 'literary man' whose art is dissimulation, the use of words, including poetical ones, to mislead and to conceal truth from himself and others. Of course the only thing that could save Wegg and Podsnappery would be a transformation of consciousness, the kind of death and rebirth Eugene Wrayburn undergoes; but such a transformation is evidently impossible, in Dickens's view, for either Wegg or Podsnappery: in the end, neither realizes that they *need* to experience a transformation because each believes the avaricious pursuit of wealth is the only value system worth treasuring. Consequently, as Dickens makes clear when Wegg's 'friendly move' is finally thwarted, even a good law—say about wills—is not protection from a man like Wegg who is determined to use it for evil purposes. In fact, in *Our Mutual Friend* the only thing that does preserve goodness is a hardmindedness—like that of John Harmon, Boffin, and Venus—which acts forcefully on the conviction that generosity and love are the only virtues that can bring genuine happiness to the self and others and so must be fought for and protected continuously.

It is no exaggeration to say that one of the most effective ways by which Dickens expresses these complex themes about money and morality to his contemporary readers in his novel is through the use he makes of the Victorian popular ballads. As we have seen, the fifteen ballads from which Wegg quotes are an integral part of his nature. And, no matter how sentimental or insipid we in the twentieth century may find them, free of the distortions which Wegg provides, these songs do represent a value system which is much more moral and attractive than the one Wegg creates from them. Though it is probably impossible to know whether Dickens himself believed completely or even in part in the value system expressed by these ballads, he deliberately used that value system to provide a telling ironic contrast by which his readers could evaluate the mercenary ethic of the nineteenth century which Silas Wegg embodies. That Dickens makes these ballads such a revealing part of Wegg's psychology and behaviour is part of his genius as a popular artist: in effect, by comic means, Dickens is able to expose one of the most serious evils of the 1860s by making his readers see clearly how Wegg's avariciousness leads him to pervert one of the things which they themselves hold most dear—the popular ballads.

Notes

1. Lillian M. Ruff, 'How Musical was Charles Dickens?', *The Dickensian*, 68 (1972), 40-41. See also Charles Haywood, 'Charles Dickens and Shakespeare; or The Irish Moor of Venice, *O'Thello*, with Music', *The Dickensian*, 73 (1977), 67-88, James T. Lightwood, *Charles Dickens and Music* (London: Kelly, 1912), Percy A. Scholes, 'Dickens and Music', in *Everyman and His Music* (London: Kegan Paul, 1917), pp. 114-17, Arthur L. Hayward, *The Days of Dickens* (London: Routledge, 1926), Charles Cudworth, 'Dickens and Music', *The Musical Times*, 3 (1969), 588-90, and the series of articles by J. W. T. Ley in *The Dickensian* between 1930-33 (Vols. 26-28), especially 'The Songs of Silas Wegg', 26 (1930), 111-17, as well as T. W. Hill, 'Note to *Our Mutual Friend*', *The Dickensian*, 43 (1947), 85-90, 142-49, 206-12.

2. For the most relevant discussion of Victorian balladry, see J. S. Bratton, *The Victorian Popular Ballad* (London, 1975); see also Martha Vicinus, *The Industrial Muse* (New York, 1974) and 'The Study of Victorian Popular Culture', *Victorian Studies*, 18 (1975), 473-83; Robert Collison, *The Story of Street Literature* (Santa Barbara, California, 1973), W. Henderson, *Victorian Street Ballads* (London, 1937), Leslie Shepard, *The History of Street Literature* (Newton Abbot, 1973), and Maurice Wilson Disher, *Victorian Song: From Dive to Drawing Room* (London, 1955).

Victorian popular ballads are often quite unlike both the earlier orally-transmitted rural ballads collected by Child (*The English and Scottish Popular Ballad*, 5 vols., Boston, 1882-98) and the sophisticated literary forms developed by the Romantic poets. Rather, they are the popular songs of the great urban communities of the nineteenth century, which had an audience of tens of thousands, in theatres, concert rooms, village halls, and in the streets of London and the newly emerging industrial centres of northern England. For example, all of the Ballads Wegg quotes were immensely popular, even in the 1860's. Five of the ballads first appeared as songs in English operas:

Arnold's 'The Death of Nelson' in *The Americans* (1811), Thomas Dibdin's 'All's Well' in *The English Fleet* (1905), Charles Dibdin's 'Poor Tom?' in *The Waterman* (1774), Payne's 'Home, Sweet Home' in *Clari* (1823), and Gay's 'Would You Have a Young Virgin?' in *The Beggar's Opera* (1728). And the remaining ten ballads achieved a great popularity into the '60s primarily as a result of being frequently sung at musical entertainments: Jonson's 'Drink to Me Only with Thine Eyes' and Burns's 'Auld Lang Syne' were especially popular in public and private drawing rooms; 'The Soldier's Tear', Party's 'Peasant Boy', Van Dyke's 'The Light Guitar', Hamilton's 'My Ain Fireside', Charles Dibdin's 'The Tar for All Weathers', and Moore's 'Evelyn's Bower' and 'Will You Come to the Bower?' were favourite 'parlour' ballads; and, of course, Scott's lines describing the death of Marmion were sung everywhere, including by schoolboys. Moreover, all of the songs were also commonly being reprinted throughout the 1860s in song-books, ballad collections, and on broadsides printed in Seven Dials, so that they would have been well known by members of all classes. For a sampling of what remains extant, see especially Thomas Crampton, ed., *Collection of Broadside Ballads Printed in London*, 7 vols. (London, 1860-70?), which includes sheets of ballads printed in Seven Dials. See also Sabine Baring-Gould, ed., *Broadside Collection*, 9 vols. (London, 1800-70), in the British Museum, and the many song-books there as well, especially *Comic, Sentimental Songster* (London, 1858) and *The Popular Songster* (London, 1890).

Together, the fifteen popular ballads which Dickens uses for *Our Mutual Friend* give a good indication of the most common ballad themes celebrated in Victorian England: the home and the hearth, brotherhood and friendship, sentimental, melancholic, and unrequited love, the dangers of seduction, sympathy for the plight of the deserving poor, and the idealization of the bravery of the soldiers and sailors who are on guard to preserve England's liberty. Moreover, these ballads seem also to have been among Dickens's special favourites. For example, he owned copies of and often sang the songs by Gay, Jonson, Burns, Scott, Charles Dibdin, and Moore, as well as alluded to these songs and others by their authors in his novels. In addition, he also loved to sing the other seven songs, especially 'Home, Sweet Home', on long trips away from London, and 'All's Well', as a bedtime lullaby for his children. No wonder these ballads came to mind when he turned to popular Victorian songs to help create and develop the character of that delicious rascal, Silas Wegg! (Dickens's love of the ballads which Wegg distorts, and his relationship with their authors, is detailed by Lightwood and Ley, cited in note 1; see also the letters, especially in the Pilgrim Edition.)

3. All references in the text are to the Penguin edition of *Our Mutual Friend* (Harmondsworth, 1971). Useful discussions of money and related themes include my own 'Charles Dickens's *Our Mutual Friend* and Frederick Somner Merryweather's *Lives and Anecdotes of Misers*', *Dickens Studies Annual*, 9 (1981), 117-41, Jack Lindsay, *Charles Dickens* (New York, 1950), pp. 380-85, J. Hillis Miller, '*Our Mutual Friend*', in *Dickens*, ed. Martin Price (Englewood Cliffs, N.J., 1967), pp. 169-77, Angus Wilson, *The World of Charles Dickens* (New York, 1972), pp. 278-83, Richard A. Lanham, *Our Mutual Friend*: The Birds of Prey', *VN* [*Victorian Newsletter*], 26 (1964), 6-12, and Masao Miyoshi, 'Resolution of Identity in *Our Mutual Friend*', *VN*, 26 (1964), 5-9.

4. See Henry Mayhew, *London Labour and the London Poor* (New York, 1968 [1862-62], Vol. I, pp. 220-51. Other interesting contemporaneous accounts include 'Street Ballads', *National Review*, 13 (1861), 397-419, M. T. Bass, *Street Music* (London, 1864, 'The Poetry of Seven Dials', *Quarterly Review*, 122 (1867), 382-496, Dickens's own 'Seven Dials', in *Sketches by Boz* (London: Oxford University Press, 1959 [1836], pp. 69-73, and the numerous descriptions in *All the Year Round*, especially 'Manager and Music Halls', 4 (Mar. 23, 1861), 558-61, 'An Unreported Speech', 6 (Nov. 16, 1861), 179-81, Andrew Halliday, 'The Battle of the Barrels', 11 (June 11, 1864), 421-24, and Henry Morley, 'Old, New, and No Music', 12 (Oct. 22, 1854), 260-64.

5. The motifs of reading, language, deception, and education have received much analysis of late. See especially Stanley Friedman, 'The Motif of Reading in *Our Mutual Friend*', *Nineteenth Century Fiction*, 28 (1973), 38-61, G. W. Kennedy, 'Naming and Language in *Our Mutual Friend*', *Nineteenth Century Fiction*, 28 (1973), 165-78, Robert S. Baker, 'Imagination and Literacy in Dickens's *Our Mutual Friend*, *Criticism*, 18 (1976), 57-72, and Rosemary Mundhenk, 'The Education of the Reader in *Our Mutual Friend*', *Nineteenth Century Fiction*, (1979), 59-72.

6. Thomas Dibden, *The English Fleet* (Cumberland's British Theatre, 1834), Vol. 32, p. 39.

7. John Gay, *The Beggar's Opera* (London, 1749), 6th ed., p. 27. This is the edition Dickens had in his library.

8. James R. Kincaid, *Dickens and the Rhetoric of Laughter* (London, 1971), p. 248.

Richard T. Gaughan (essay date 1990)

SOURCE: "Prospecting for Meaning in *Our Mutual Friend*," in *Dickens Studies Annual*, Vol. 19, 1990, pp. 231-46.

[*In the following essay, Gaughan explores the various characters in* Our Mutual Friend *and the different strategies they employ to negotiate their way around the roles each has been assigned by a rigid social system.*]

So many of Dickens' characters in *Our Mutual Friend* are so entrapped and mutilated by the roles they are forced to play and by the rules and values of their society that meaningful action seems all but impossible. Characters like Lizzie Hexam and John Harmon are forced to live stories they did not author and cannot rewrite. Jenny Wren, the attenuated and battered symbol of imagination in the novel and a parody of childhood and all that childhood means to Dickens, is a reminder of the irreversible damage the social world has already done to the hopes of any escape from that world through innocence or imagination. The only characters who seem to have any freedom at all are those who, like Fascination Fledgby and Lammle, manipulate and dominate others through the secret exercise of their will behind the mask of social propriety. But, even this freedom is illusory. Lammle and Fledgeby are so bound to each other and so completely defined by the version of the social game that they play that their schemes amount to little more than the rearrangement of players in a closed and zero-sum game.

The reason meaningful action seems impossible in this novel is because the narrative world is so closed and self-sufficient that it is, or pretends to be, a complete and impenetrable reality independent of the characters who comprise it. All the apparent divisions within the social world, like the division between the world of Podsnap and the world of the waterfront, are only superficial. The waterfront community's values, its tolerance of the robbing of dead men but intolerance of even the hint of scandal, perfectly parallel Podsnap's tolerance of political corruption and his peremptory dismissal of everything that does not conform to his narrow morality. Gaffer Hexam disinherits his son as impetuously as old man Harmon disinherits his and tries to impose his own ideas on his family as rigorously as "My Respectable Father" does on Eugene Wrayburn. There are, ultimately, only the values and rules of the social world endlessly repeated, sometimes unintentionally parodied, but almost always embraced even by those characters, like Charley Hexam and Bradley Headstone, who are partly or wholly excluded from respectable society. The apparent social mobility of characters, though it may seem vertical—a climbing or descending the social ladder—is always lateral and cyclical. There is no up or down in this world,[1] no winners or losers, only the relentless repetition of a fixed set of social roles. Movement and change are only the occasional exchange of roles by actors who are individually dispensable.

There seems to be no alternative to the dehumanized world presented in the novel except the alternative of what Adorno calls negation. Adorno claims that art and thought realize themselves most fully not in what they can assert as positive and systematic but in what is discovered through the negation and decomposition of what can be positively thought or systematically expressed.[2] Whatever is positive and can be formalized is, by virtue of that fact alone, antithetical to the critical dialectic of thought and is, to some extent, oppressive and dehumanizing. Similarly, in *Our Mutual Friend* Dickens presents a social world that is both positive and dehumanized and must enact the decomposition of thematic and formal coherence to find in negation what is denied or perverted by both the social and narrative systems.

Since the triumph of the human will, especially the will to subdue everything to a coherent order, seems to be at the root of the problem[3] (hence the elaborate pun on Harmon's will), Dickens uses passivity in the character most centrally involved in the novel's plots, John Harmon, to find in the negation of will the human qualities that have been lost in its exercise. The suspension of Harmon's will frees him from his narrowly defined social identity so that he can create an identity based on his relationship with others. This is not to say that Harmon is free to create an identity *sui generis*. The identity he can create will be social but in a broader sense than the identity prescribed by the closed system of social conventions and values. This identity will be social in the sense that it is based on the relationships Harmon can establish with other characters, but these relationships must develop outside socially prescribed roles. To establish these relationships, Harmon uses temporary and symbolic versions of himself—his disguises—to test the responsiveness of others.

Harmon's use of symbolic versions of himself to discover his identity, however, is perilously close to society's use of masks to manipulate and dominate others and, in particular, to Bradley Headstone's use of disguise to stalk Lizzie Hexam and Eugene Wrayburn. The only difference between Harmon's and Headstone's use and understanding of symbolic disguises is the fine but significant distinction between using symbolic forms as a way of responding to and understanding a world that is not defined entirely by the social will and imposing symbolic forms as realities in and of themselves. As slight as this distinction may seem, it is one that frees Harmon to search for an authentic identity and condemns Headstone to live out to the death the spiritual sterility of the society whose values he has so completely embraced.

The way John Harmon escapes from the tyranny of social conventions and the fatal repetition of his family's history sets the pattern for how the novel will proceed. Harmon's presumed death places him outside the social world and the influence of his father's will, but he is not free of the effects of the values that control the social world. He can create and sustain a new identity only through deception and duplicity—the very methods society thrives on. John Harmon cannot successfully escape the tyranny of the past unless he conceals the fact that he is still alive and finds a way back into the world that is not already controlled by social values. This forced concealment and Harmon's need to find out the truth about his world make him act in ways that are reminiscent of the way society functions. There is, however, a difference in purpose. Like Jenny Wren, Harmon is aware that his deceptions and disguises are a self-conscious means of protecting himself in a hostile world. His disguises are at once decoys to draw off the predators, or even the predator in any given character, and a filter through which he can clarify possible relations between himself and others. They are questions he asks of others so that he can define himself in terms of a response and not a fixed social role. By using his disguises to sift through his world to find something authentic, Harmon reverses and redeems his father's greedy sifting through the mounds of dust for lost and discarded valuables.

Although both Harmon's disguises and the conventions and values of society are artificial and self-conscious, there is an important difference in the way each is self-conscious. Harmon's disguises are self-conscious not only because he is aware that he is not, or is not entirely, the person he pretends to be, but also because he is aware that these symbolic versions of himself alter the way others can be seen as well as the way others see him. In his disguise as John Rokesmith, Harmon gives up the social power he could have by laying claim to his father's legacy so that he can learn how others will act towards him in the position of relative powerlessness. Only by circumventing the power relationships on which society thrives in ways such as this can Harmon make his relationships to others authentic.

The self-consciousness of social values and conventions, on the other hand, is little more than the awareness of the arbitrariness of those values and conventions—the awareness, in other words, of the need to exclude everything that is not defined by the closed system of those values and conventions. Paradoxically, because social roles and identities are understood as arbitrary they must be imposed on others as absolutely true to conceal their arbitrariness. The only trick is making others recognize and accept any given social persona: the outward appearance of wealth, success, or power. Since there is no provision in the collective mind of society for the possibility that the ways society orders and understands the world might not be entirely true, surface appearances that conform to social values must be accepted as true. This is why masks and social positions are exchanged and circulated with the same rapidity and ease as currency and with the same uncritical belief in an assumed and usually inflated value. Nevertheless, as Lammle and Fledgby understand, the complacency and self-satisfaction of the guardians of society in their splendid and shining structure is neither the whole of the social reality nor even its most crucial part.

The self-reflective nature of conventionalized social life, in fact, indicates the troubling leap of faith made by society to conceal the grave discrepancy between its elaborate displays of power and luxury and the precarious resources on which those displays rest. Implied in self-reflection is a sense of limited resources which must be expanded through increasingly elaborate interpretive structures. The more elaborately resources are circulated, the longer it takes for the exhausted system to crash. Because Harmon's use of disguise eventually produces something new—an identity that is based on relationships that are outside the system—it is a resource for establishing a relationship to the world and not, as are social masks, a shell game to protect dangerously depleted resources.[4]

Although Harmon's disguises do help keep him safe from society, he must also somehow use the advantage of disguise to reenter that world. This advantage, the ability to change identities, however, is based on his own lack of identity. After Harmon, in disguise, revisits the scene of his betrayal, he quite literally becomes the Man from Nowhere (an ironic fulfillment of the role assigned him by Mortimer Lightwood during his narration of the Veneerings) but only once his disguise is off:

> "It is a sensation not experienced by many mortals," said he, "to be looking into a churchyard on a wild windy night, and to feel that I no more hold a place among the living than these dead do, and even to know that I lie buried somewhere else, as they lie buried here. Nothing uses me to it. A spirit that was once a man could hardly feel stranger or lonelier, going unrecognized among mankind, than I feel."[5]

Immediately after this reflection Harmon admits, "'But this is the fanciful side of the situation. It has a real side, so difficult that, though I think of it every day, I never thoroughly think it out'" (422). Harmon's recollection of his drugging and near death, the events which have made him the man from nowhere, leads him to an even more radical confusion of identity and more total alienation from the world:

> "I could not have said that my name was John Harmon—I could not have thought it—I didn't know it—but when I heard the blows, I thought of the woodcutter and his axe, and had some dead idea that I was lying in a forest.
>
> "This is still correct? Still correct, with the exception that I cannot possibly express it to myself without using the word I. But it was not I. There was no such thing as I, within my knowledge."
>
> (426)

Disguise serves many purposes, but, because it is self-conscious, it cannot alleviate Harmon's alienation from the world. He must use disguises to rediscover his "I" and not as substitutes for that identity. Harmon needs to find a way to reintegrate himself among the living without submitting to his father's legacy. This is the "real" side of his dilemma, the side which involves losing the security and power of disguise. The only way available to him is to accept a suspended or interrupted identity, to be a stranger even to himself, so that his identity can be a process of responding to the world and not a submission to predetermined social roles.

A version of this necessary passivity in the face of a predetermined social world is the phenomenon of near-death. Miller has commented on the baptismal character of the river and the rebirth signified by near-death (Miller, *Our Mutual Friend,* p. 177). Near-death, however, is also the suspension of the human will. It is the state in which human life itself exists only as pure potential. As such, it escapes the tyranny of social conventions and any definition as simply materiality. A conscious desire to live in the world does not have much to do with this suspension of life or its subsequent recovery, as this description of Riderhood suggests:

> Now he is struggling harder to get back. And yet—like us all, when we swoon—like us all, every day of our lives when we wake—he is instinctively unwilling to be restored to the consciousness of this existence, and would be left dormant, if he could.
>
> (505)

It is the suspension itself that is important because it undermines the assumption that things have to be the way they are. Even in the case of the incorrigible Riderhood, the witnesses, to his revival instinctively hope that he will return from his state of suspended animation a changed and better man. The very fact that he has fallen between the cracks of the ordinary conceptual categories that both he and his society use to order and define the world means that those categories might not entirely define the way things are and that a radical change in the way the world is imagined is possible.

To bring about such change, however, whether through near-death or disguise, requires not only the relinquishing of power over others but also the surrender of certainty about personal identity. For Riderhood to have a new life means he must surrender his old habit of thinking solely in terms of calculated self-interest. He must, as Harmon does, accept an identity that is open and responsive to others. When this opportunity to relinquish certainty about identity is refused, as it is in the case of Riderhood, the values of society, especially the power relations that underlie society, take over as the source of personal identity. This is what happens to the unfortunate Bradley Headstone whose refusal to be responsive to the reality of himself and others perverts the depths of his character and turns the respectable schoolmaster into a psychotic killer.

In many important respects Bradley Headstone is the character who best personifies the thematic forces at work in the novel. Like Lizzie and Charley Hexam, Headstone comes from a socially disreputable class. He aspires to and attains a measure of respectability by accepting respectability as an end in itself and by repressing himself into the appropriate shape for his role in respectable society. When he meets Lizzie, however, the mechanisms of this repression fail him and he is forced to come to terms with that part of himself which exceeds the conventions of respectability, and he must do this without the aid of those conventions and his veneer of respectability.

This division in Bradley Headstone is more than just a conflict between good and evil or between the emotional and the rational (Wilson, p. 82). Headstone embodies the conflict that pervades the novel between what is real and what is accepted as real. His passion for Lizzie alienates him from the conventionalized social world and forces him to find a new relationship to himself and his world that can better accommodate that part of him that cannot be reduced to respectability. For this reason, Headstone is a genuinely tragic character. He is forced to confront, on an isolated and intensely personal level, a conflict of values which is characteristic of the world in which he lives. All that is admitted by society as real and all that is not converge in Bradley Headstone when he has lost the safety of his respectable life. He is the logical consequence of the values of the world in *Our Mutual Friend* and must face the consequences of these values in a way no other character does. The novel is, in many ways, the story of Bradley Headstone writ large.

The tragedy of Bradley Heastone is so powerful that it threatens to dominate the novel and overshadow Harmon's redemptive mission. Headstone's tragedy, however, is compromised by his unwillingness to forego the values dictated by society. Even in the midst of his suffering Headstone never surrenders his subservience to the idea of respectability. He refuses to see Lizzie in any way other than as a lower class woman who can be recuperated to respectability under his tutelage. In spite of his passion, Headstone never acknowledges Lizzie's reality as an independent character. Lizzie is, at first, a symbol of his repressed past (perhaps even a symbol of his mother), and later, she becomes a symbol of the passions he can no longer repress for the sake of respectability.

Headstone's use of Lizzie as a symbol betrays the relationship between symbol and reality. Symbolic apprehension of reality, as it is practiced by Jenny Wren and Harmon, attempts to interpret possible relationships between self and world without pretending to appropriate the world in the symbol.[6] Jenny and Harmon try to build a relationship between themselves and the world that can then be adjusted and that is responsive to others. Headstone's passion for Lizzie, too, can put him in a new and more adequate relation to the reality of his own feelings but he forfeits this opportunity by turning Lizzie into an object to be possessed.

Just as society mediates everything through its conventions, Bradley Headstone, ultimately, mediates his love for Lizzie through his personal mythology. Similarly, he makes Wrayburn and Rogue Riderhood into symbolic characters in his private psychodrama. Wrayburn comes to represent the easy respectability that must always elude Headstone because of his class origins and Riderhood comes to represent the class that Headstone has left but from which he can never escape. By forcing these characters into symbolic roles which are themselves defined by society's values, Headstone translates the depths of his inner self into terms commensurate with the values and conventions of society. Instead of apprehending his own inner reality and the reality of others outside the conventions of society, Headstone turns himself into a character in a conventional and fairly trite social and literary melodrama and becomes a victim and villain rather than a tragic figure.

Headstone's inability to free himself from the values of society makes his use of disguises a way to impose his will, that is, the will of society, on others. Harmon's disguises, on the other hand, are intended as ways to allow a relationship between himself and others to develop. Harmon's identity depends entirely on the way others respond to him not on what he can make others do by concealing himself. Headstone's identity depends on denying relationships to others and on restraining and concealing himself. Headstone, in other words, fails to use his disguises symbolically, as the medium of an encounter with the world. As a result, Headstone repeats Harmon's experience of lost identity with a chillingly ironic twist. Headstone becomes literally and permanently the Man from Nowhere: he loses his personal identity entirely, because he clings so tenaciously to the phantom identity assigned him by society. Not surprisingly, then, it is Headstone, and not Harmon, who loses all control over his disguises. By the end of the novel it is virtually impossible to say whether the role of schoolmaster fits Headstone any better than the role of bargeman.

Because Headstone stakes so much on his disguise, because he identifies symbol and reality, any frustration of his will locks him into a spiraling need for more fictions, all of which serve to justify the image of respectability. Even when he is frustrated in his pursuit of respectability, he erects perverse justifications for his frustration:

> The state of the man was murderous, and he knew it. More; he irritated it, with a kind of perverse pleasure akin to that which a sick man sometimes has in irritating a wound upon his body.
>
> (609)

Headstone imposes a contrived and self-serving structure on events which then becomes his only reality. However perverse Headstone's behavior, he is consistent in seeking to support the *image* he has of himself and is forced constantly to substitute one fictitious version of himself after another once his passion for Lizzie obliterates his fiction of respectability and leaves him with nothing but his conflicting desires.

Like the society of Lady Tippins, the Veneerings, and Podsnap, Headstone gets lost among his own constructs. From the start society is immersed in mutually supporting fictions, but Bradley Headstone shows that the origins of such self-enclosed and self-generating systems lie in the choices an individual makes in the attempt to define a self and a world. Headstone, stripped of his veneer of respectability, is the embodiment of the conflict between the conventional and all that exceeds the conventional and can, like John Harmon, defy society by making this conflict the basis of his identity. Instead, he denies this conflict, thereby effectively denying himself, and locks Wrayburn, Riderhood, Lizzie, and himself in a personal and nightmarish version of society's more dressed-up dance of death. His selection of the bargeman's disguise only reflects his loss of himself and completes his regression into fixed social and conventional patterns that have long since splintered his character and condemned him to destruction.

This is the darker and more individual relationship to the personal and social values that are the origin of the larger self-enclosed and self-generating social systems. In Headstone's decision to force his deeper nature into the confines of the conventional are the origins of Chancery, the Circumlocution Office, and Podsnappery. Bradley Headstone is a Pip whose expectations are exposed more savagely and more honestly. If Bradley Headstone is an evil character, he is evil for very specific and very familiar reasons. He is evil because he chooses to make his life into a fiction and because he denies anything outside that fiction. He refuses to establish a relationship between himself and his own inner reality and the reality of others. Instead, he chooses the grim struggle for power that has always lurked just beneath the surface of respectable restraint.

When Headstone drowns Riderhood in a fatal embrace, he is doing more than killing a past he has worked so hard to deny. He is killing that part of himself that rejected a more authentic approach to the depths of himself and the complexities of his world. The man who rejects a new life and the man who rejects a new sense of what is real fall into the lock, the mechanism designed to alter and control the water's natural flow, and die in the stagnant slime of their refusals.

As important as the contrast between Harmon and Headstone is for the thematic concerns of the novel, it is even more important as a clue about a conflict in formal tendencies and values that Dickens uses to develop an identity for his novel that is independent of the constraints of the world depicted by the novel. Harmon and Headstone are not only characters who represent or embody thematic categories (for example, good and evil, passivity and will, etc.), they are also characters who represent or embody the more purely symbolic and narrative problems in the novel that produce and are reflected by the thematic conflicts. Taken as contraries in Blake's sense, they represent the two tendencies that define the novel as a symbolic form: its tendency to impose formal coherence and its capacity to express multiple and often incongruous perspectives on experience. These more purely narrative concerns are not, like the values of society, arranged in a static and self-reflecting order. Instead, they are set into direct and creative conflict with each other.

Each of these tendencies, through the character who embodies it, asserts itself as preeminent—as a definitive description of the novel as a symbolic form. But, each assertion also calls forth its contrary assertion, in effect, its own negation. The demands of formal coherence, for example, cannot be asserted without exposing the need for a contrary: the multiple and heterogeneous ways the novel symbolically represents and explores the world. There is no resolving the conflict between these contraries since the contraries continually change how each can be understood at any given moment in the novel. As a result, Dickens is not exorcising any artistic, let alone moral, demons in the conflict between Headstone and Harmon but is displaying and using self-consciously the novel as a symbolic form

so that a relationship to the world that is obscured by the self-reflecting symbolic systems of the social world on the thematic level can be recaptured on this symbolic and more purely narrative level. These contraries and the ways they define each other become a kind of purely symbolic story about narrative concerns that parallels and, in some ways, redeems the thematic story.

In this narrative about narrative, the novel at times is represented by Bradley Headstone. In many ways, the novel shares Headstone's Pygmalion fantasy and sets about to shape its thematic content into its own chosen coherent image. This is a necessary part of what the novel does and what the novel is, and though it is not the only or, given the values criticized, the most savory part, the novel is always at least a little like Bradley Headstone and can, unless there is a balancing contrary, share his fate. The novel also shares John Harmon's search for a responsive relationship to the world it depicts. It is a symbolic form through which new and inclusive relations to experience can be imagined. To the extent that it is like this, however, the novel, like Harmon, cannot be presented by Dickens as nothing more than a self-sufficient coherent reality. It must be open—a pattern of reciprocally related imaginative responses to experience rather than a coherent system in which symbols and truth are hastily equated. The novel must have, like Harmon, a suspended identity.

That Dickens features both Harmon and Headstone so prominently in the novel is one important way Dickens can escape repeating in his exploration of the novel's symbolic and narrative identity not only Headstone's self-destructive identification with his fictions but also the sterile coherence of the social world. What is at issue here is not just the moral ambiguity of Dickens making symbolic forms that are every bit as tyrannous as the social world that is depicted, it is that the novel as a symbolic form is inherently and formally ambiguous and that Dickens deliberately uses this ambiguity as an alternative to the dehumanizing certainties of the social world.[7]

Nor are Harmon and Headstone the only characters who represent such purely narrative concerns about the novel. Silas Wegg, for example, expresses, in comic form, his society's values and parodies the stories of other characters. Wegg's extortion scheme and his prospecting for treasure are a pointed parody of Harmon's relationship to Bella and Headstone's relationship to Lizzie and a less direct parody of both the narrator's and Harmon's attempts to sift and pan the social world for authenticity. But, because he knows, or thinks he knows, what he is looking for he simply repeats the errors of the social world and, like Headstone, ends up chasing a phantom of his own making.

Wegg's habit of chasing his own phantoms also serves another important purpose in the novel. Wegg, together with Venus, represents the potential failure of the novel to achieve a balance between responsiveness to the world and the demands of coherence. Wegg, who mimics the values of the social world, and Venus, who articulates creatures out of their remains, represent what the novel would be if it limited itself simply to reproducing the values of the social world. For this reason, Wegg and Venus haunt the novel like a comic bad conscience. That Venus is eventually saved may have less to do with any redeeming moral qualities he may have than with the fact that he never fully believes in Wegg's schemes. This gives Venus the self-consciousness he needs to save himself, a self-consciousness that resembles in its saving purpose Harmon's self-consciousness. Wegg, on the other hand, is adept at creating fictions, like the one about "Our House," which he then accepts as true. This disastrous habit of believing in his own fictions not only parodies society's and Headstone's belief in their own fictions, it serves as a constant reminder of what the novel must not do.

If Wegg and Venus illustrate some traps the novel must avoid, Jenny Wren illustrates the kind of complex relationship the novel can establish to its world. As the dolls' dressmaker, Jenny, like Dickens, reproduces in miniature the world of the glamorous and captures it in its most characteristic costumes. But, this reproduction of the social world, like the novel's own, only serves to highlight the terrible price that society exacts for the sake of its carefully controlled show. That Jenny is physically crippled and emotionally hurt by the very world she reproduces so faithfully indicates the very real effects the narrow and self-serving symbol system of society has on those it excludes and ignores.

Jenny responds to this oppressive world with a sadly precocious cynicism that makes what should be her fairytale dreams of romance into fantasies of defensive and retaliatory violence. But Jenny also acts in a way that is directly contrary to the values of the world that has hurt her. She uses her hands and her quick observation not only to reproduce the world of the glamorous but to find and make contact with her own world. Unlike the hands that grasp for power and money or the clenched fist Bradley Headstone slams down on the burial-ground enclosure, Jenny's hands search for a responsive contact with those she loves and trusts. This kind of touching implies a relationship to another who has not been already appropriated and digested by the demands of a system, either personal or social. The touch is the only real alternative on the thematic level to a social system that thrives on sameness and dominance. It is a moment of contact between characters who regard each other as independent fellow creatures, not as objects to be possessed or controlled. Even the most extreme version of touching, violent blows, is a way Harmon and Wrayburn are freed from their imprisoning social roles and are able to reconstitute their relationship to the world.

For Dickens to reenact on the symbolic level of the novel Jenny's touching of others on the thematic level, he must minimize the violent imposition of symbolic forms that produces moral and physical deformity, transform this violence into a form of human response to the world and not simply an act of aggression against it, and delineate the way the social world is made by those who seem to be

nothing more than its mirrors. He needs to attack that world at its core, and this core is its certainty about its wholeness. To mount such an attack, Dickens decomposes the social world into the many symbolic perspectives and assertions that go into its making, thereby making the apparently complete social whole a multiform set of assertions about the world that then creates the need for other assertions, no one of which predominates over any other.

The many characters who make these symbolic assertions together form what Bakhtin calls a dialogue about the novel and its relationship to its world.[8] The characters wrangle with each other over how and what their world means and in so doing wrangle with each other over how and what the novel itself means. Such a dynamic arrangement is decidedly contrary to the neat arrangement of the representatives of society around the Veneerings' dining-room table where the characters act like so many Leibnizian monads, each reflecting, from his own particular angle, the totality of the social world. This static arrangement of monads, however, is an ideological sleight-of-hand used to conceal the underlying struggle for power.[9] Once this illusion is exposed and dispelled and the characters are understood as incarnations of symbolic assertions about the world, their arrangement becomes something more akin to the structure of an atom. The characters are related as symbolic force fields which determine and shape each other through their energy and momentary configuration rather than through their reflective powers. The coherence they have is the result of these momentary configurations and not of a settled system mirroring itself in all its details. By operating on both levels simultaneously, Dickens can decompose into a search for meaning, on the narrative and symbolic level, the story he is composing into a coherent system of meaning on the thematic level.

On this level of decomposed form, the story about how the novel means, Dickens works out his alternative to the otherwise monolithic social world he creates. For it is on this symbolic level that Dickens can do what the social world he depicts cannot: make not only explicit symbolic assertions about the world but also show the way each assertion, once made, changes the world it seeks to define, thereby changing what the assertion itself can mean. The social world, like its representative, Podsnap, flourishes away whatever does not conform or cannot be reduced to its norms. Characters like Riah and Betty Higden who, because of religion or class, do not fit the mold are relegated to the margins of the social world. Such characters, of course, cannot escape and are not freed from the effects of the society that neglects and ostracizes them. Riah must play the odious role of the Jewish usurer to protect his respectable Christian master and Betty Higden is hounded by the specter of the poor house up until her death. But, such characters are effectively excluded from the way society conceives of itself, from the identity the society develops for itself.

Dickens, on the other hand, not only includes characters like these in his story, he makes the marginalized world they inhabit, a world of symbolic values that is created by the dominance of the social world but that is also a response to all that is ignored by it, an integral part of the novel's identity as a narrative and symbolic form. The novel, in other words, unlike the social world, is about not only what it can assert directly and explicitly about its world and about itself, but also about the effects of all assertions on what the world can mean and, therefore, on how the world is. The world the novel represents, then, is not some truer and fully developed world that has been buried or submerged by society and can be excavated. It is the world that has been obscured by certainty but that is always being revealed through the conflict among the characters' various attempts to define and live in it. This is one reason why the characters never seem to find what they are looking for or find only what they don't expect. The treasure they are looking for is never what it seems because, by searching for the treasure, the characters have changed everything, including the role they play and what the treasure is.

Similarly, for Dickens, the meaning of his novel cannot be simply a nugget sifted out from meaningless dirt. What happens to the dirt and the change that takes place in the landscape and in the prospector, are as important as any nugget that might be found. Like his many failed prospectors but with more foresight and skill, Dickens sets out to sift and pan this curious and dead world to find out what, if anything, is still alive. But, as certainty and system fail, as meaning slips, like so much dirt, through the fingers grasping for power or money, Dickens makes it increasingly clear that the search for meaning itself, the act of sifting and panning, and not any fixed center of meaning, is the only real treasure to be found.

Notes

1. The only real exception to the moral geometry of the novel is Jenny Wren's invitation to Riah to "Come up and be dead!" (335). The paradoxical nature of this invitation already suggests that the formal coherence characteristic of the novel's world will not give the characters the authenticity they seek.

2. Theodor Adorno, *Minima Moralia,* trans. E. F. N. Jephcott (London: Veso, 1974), 126-127, 144, 227.

3. J. Hillis Miller says of the world in *Our Mutual Friend*: "Man has absorbed the world into himself, and the transformed world has absorbed him into itself, in an endless multiplication of nothing by nothing." *Charles Dickens: The World of his Novels* (Cambridge: Harvard UP, 1959), 298. Here, Miller extends the discussion of the ambiguity of will in Dickens, especially the tendency of will, however well motivated, to become just one more form of aggression, to the collective human determination to subdue the world to definite human ends. The results, though entirely human in one sense, are also entirely dehumanizing.

4. I have in mind here Ruskin's idea that labor is an act of creation, similar to the labor of birth, and that profit is based on the production or discovery of something new. In contrast to Ruskin's ideas about labor is Marx's idea that labor is the basis of value in a closed economic system and that profit is the surplus value derived from unpaid labor. The social world of *Our Mutual Friend* seems to operate according to Marx's ideas, especially the idea of deriving profit from deprivation, while Harmon and, I believe, the novel as a whole operate according to Ruskin's. See John Ruskin, *Unto This Last and Other Writings,* ed. Clive Wilmer (New York: Penguin Books, 1985), 213, 217 and Karl Marx, *Wages, Price and Profits* (Peking: Foreign Languages Press, 1975) 48-49, 54.

5. Charles Dickens, *Our Mutual Friend* (New York: Penguin Books, 1971) 422. All future quotations will be from this edition and will be cited in parentheses.

6. The conception of symbolism I am using here is based on Cassirer's ideas. Cassirer claims that symbols, especially language and art, are not mental creations affixed to the world or separate realities derived from or imposed on the world but are ways of objectifying knowledge of and responses to it and therefore are instruments of discovery, rather than simple definitions. See Ernst Cassirer, "Language and Art I," in *Symbol, Myth, and Culture: Essays and Lectures of Ernst Cassirer 1935-1945,* ed. Donald Philip Verene (New Haven: Yale UP, 1979) 148, and *An Essay on Man* (New Haven: Yale UP, 1944) 143. I take Cassirer's use of the term objective to mean shared knowledge or perception rather than the more usual meaning of a reification of the living world.

7. My ideas about the formal conflicts that go into the identity of the novel are based in part on Adorno's ideas about the dialectical nature of art. Adorno conceives of autonomous art, art freed from serving any purpose other than its own self-defined purposes (for example, religious art), as locked in a struggle, perhaps a losing struggle, with its own contradictions. Foremost among these contradictions is form's relationship to content. Content is assimilated to and integrated with the internal demands of form, but, since content comes from the world outside the art work, this assimilation and integration must always be incomplete. Form, then, at least according to its own laws of integration, must fail if it is to succeed at all. If it were to succeed completely, it would fail even more seriously since it would then produce a kind of art completely divorced from the human world or a kind of art completely divorced from the human world or a kind of art that is fundamentally dishonest. Theodor Adorno, *Aesthetic Theory,* trans, C. Lenhardt, eds. Gretel Adorno and Rolf Tiedermann (London: Routledge & Kegan Paul, 1984). Adorno's ideas about the dialectical nature of art, both in relation to its autonomous concerns and in relation to the world art seems to withdraw from, are scattered

throughout the work, but pages 6-11, 201, 207, 255, and 266-267 seem to be fairly representative.

8. M. M. Bakhtin, "Discourse in the Novel," in *The Dialogic Imagination: Four Essays,* trans, Caryl Emerson and Michael Holquist, ed. Michael Holquist (Austin: U of Texas P, 1981) 259-422. Bakhtin makes this comment that seems directly applicable to *Our Mutual Friend*:

> Languages of heteroglossia, like mirrors that face each other, each reflecting in its own way a piece, a tiny corner of the world, force us to guess at and grasp for a world behind their mutually reflecting aspects that is broader, more multileveled, containing more and varied horizons than would be available to a single language or a single mirror.

(414-415)

See also "The Problem of Speech Genres," in *Speech Genres & Other Late Essays,* trans, Vern W. McGee, eds., Caryl Emerson and Michael Holquist (Austin: U. of Texas P, 1986) for a more general treatment of the way language necessarily becomes a dialogue about the world.

9. Miller, *Charles Dickens: The World of his Novels,* p. 291. Here Miller says:

> The proper model of the universe of *Our Mutual Friend* is not that of a non-Euclidean space filled with incommensurate local monads entirely isolated from one another. It is rather that of a large number of interlocking perspectives on the world, each what Whitehead would call a special *prehension* of the same totality. But Dickens can never present the totality as it is in itself. Indeed, there is no such thing as the world in itself.

I would agree that the model of isolated monads is inadequate and that Dickens cannot present the totality directly and explicitly, but I believe that the totality is always changed by the characters' attempts to define it and that Dickens does present the totality indirectly on the symbolic level of the novel as the open totality of all the attempts to define and live in the world.

Works Cited

Adorno, Theodor. *Aesthetic Theory.* Trans. C. Lenhardt. Eds. Gretel Adorno and Rolf Tiedermann (London: Routledge & Kegan Paul, 1984).

———. *Minima Moralia.* Trans. E. F. N. Jephcott (London: Veso, 1974).

Bakhtin, M. M. "Discourse in the Novel." In *The Dialogic Imagination: Four Essays.* Trans. Caryl Emerson and Michael Holquist. Ed. Michael Holquist (Austin: U. of Texas P, 1981).

———. "The Problem of Speech Genres." In *Speech Genres & Other Late Essays.* Trans. Vern W. McGee. Eds. Caryl Emerson and Michael Holquist (Austin: U. of Texas P, 1986).

Cassirer, Ernst, *An Essay on Man* (New Haven: Yale UP, 1944).

———. "Language and Art I," in *Symbol, Myth, and Culture: Essays and Lectures of Ernst Cassirer 1935-1945.* Ed. Donald Philip Verene (New Haven: Yale UP, 1979).

Dickens, Charles. *Our Mutual Friend* (New York: Penguin Books, 1971).

Marx, Karl. *Wages, Price and Profits* (Peking: Foreign Languages Press, 1975).

Miller, J. Hillis. *Charles Dickens: The World of His Novels* (Cambridge: Harvard UP, 1959).

———. "*Our Mutual Friend,*" in *Dickens: A Collection of Critical Essays.* Ed. Martin Price (Englewood Cliffs: Prentice-Hall, Inc., 1967).

Ruskin, John. *Unto This Last and Other Writings.* Ed. Clive Wilmer (New York: Penguin Books, 1985).

Wilson, Edmund. "Dickens: The Two Scrooges." In *The Wound and the Bow.* (New York: Farrar, Straus, Giroux, 1970).

Patrick O'Donnell (essay date 1990)

SOURCE: "'A Speeches of Chaff': Ventriloquy and Expression in *Our Mutual Friend,*" in *Dickens Studies Annual,* Vol. 19, 1990, pp. 247-79.

[*In the following essay, O'Donnell examines issues of ventriloquy and representation of narrative voice in* Our Mutual Friend, *suggesting that identity and relationships are called into question continuously throughout the novel.*]

In an age of public spectacle for which P. T. Barnum serves as the ultimate exemplar, Dickens' novels provide a succession of forays into the spectacular. The spectacle can be viewed as a displacement of "private" anxieties and fantasies onto the public stage. The authorial dream of omnipotence, for example, is represented in spectacle via the guise of the master of entertainments or the entrepreneur. This dream is countered by the illusory heterogeneity of the entertainment itself which, fractured into the diversionary activities of clowns, mimes, freaks, and the vertiginous confusion of the "three-ring" circus or sequential "sideshows," threatens to slip out of the ringmaster's control. As the carnivalesque accoutrements of the spectacle indicate, it is transgressive, often blurring the line between "public" and "private," or "outside" and "inside." In this way, the authority which ordains a fictive world and fills it with "identities" is questioned by the very spectacle that theatricalizes authorial projections and ordinations.

In Dickens' novels, the spectacle or story unfolds as a profusion of voices; the author is at odds to maintain control over this cacophony for the sake of his identity as the origin *of this work.* As Alexander Welsh's recent reconstruction of Dickens' biography argues, commencing with the writing of **Martin Chuzzlewit,** Dickens became markedly, at times, obsessively, concerned with issues of copyright and control over his work—and, by extension, with the nature of his authorial identity as a form of writing (cf. especially 104-22). Dickens, no doubt, delighted himself and his readers with the early discovery that he was capable of ventriloquizing a capacious assortment of "typical voices." Even more, he found that he was able to create such convincing new characters as to provide a readership with a growing body of work that was more recognizably "Dickensian" with each new installment of "the Dickens world." Yet the incorporation of this world carries with it a price in the form of an authorial self-recognition. Founded upon the very "stuff" of Dickens' art—his ability to consume and recast fictions, plots, characters and voices, representing them as part of a spectacle—the whole production, made public and jettisoned from the authorial self, has the capacity to alter radically the consistency and homogeneity of authorial identity in its separation from its "source." The "publication" of identity which, paradoxically, necessitates a questioning of the origins of identity as other than itself, might be said to characterize the crucial project of Dickens' major novels.[1]

To focus upon the specific representation of identity that I wish to discuss in this essay, particularly in the later fictions (but observable throughout his work), Dickens "throws" or scripts the tumultuous voices of his many characters with an increasing sense that, the more successful or spectacular the act of ventriloquy, the more self-questioned is the singular identity who is the source of those voices. The problematic endings of such novels as **Bleak House, Great Expectations,** and **Our Mutual Friend** are symptomatic of what might be termed Dickens' "modernization," where, increasingly, the constraints of plot become more self-consciously artificial in the effort, if not to control, then at least to remark ironically upon the relation between the created "world" and the authoring identity which serves as the foundation of that world. The "double-voiced" discourse of **Bleak House,** wherein Esther and a parodic echo of the classic omniscient narrator alternate chapters, the doubled-back commentary on narrative identity formulated by **Great Expectations**'s skeptical revision of **David Copperfield,** the sheer lack of vocal singularity in any aspect of **Our Mutual Friend**—all speak to Dickens' growing sense that identity is a linguistic effect or a figure of speech, a represented form of indeterminacy that reveals its foundations in the "unrepresentable."

In Dickens' last-completed novel, identity has become (to use Bakhtin's terminology) "pluralized" to the extent that Dickens' most successful ventriloquistic spectacle is a most public abandonment of the private, coherent "self," though the novel retains skeletal traces of the attempt to preserve an older, more masterful version of identity.[2] In **Our Mutual Friend,** Dickens is compelled to give up for good the "private" self—that idealized and narcissistic embodiment of knowledge, control, and desire—for a version of the "public" self, split up or spread amongst the novel's characters. These garner representation as a multitude of fragmentary voices whose origin is an "overhearing," a recapitulation and reformation of acculturated linguistic expressions that bear the marks of passage from privacy to "publication." In the most characteristic expression of the novel, Sloppy, that paragon of disorder, "do the Police," those paragons of order and authority, "in many voices" as he reads to Betty Higden from a newspaper. The phrase neatly summarizes the master trope of the novel—that of ventriloquy. Throughout **Our Mutual Friend** ventriloquy serves as a figure for Dickens' historic revision of the power and uses of voice in a novel which reflects the anxious recognition that the representation of "voice," in reading and writing, signifies the conversion of identity into a public spectacle. It is what this spectacle both represses and reflects—even as it formulates a commentary on this double movement—that is the subject of my analysis.

One of Dickens' lesser-known contemporaries, an historian of ventriloquy and a publicist who "spoke for" a popular impersonator, provides some interesting conceptions of the figure of ventriloquy that illuminate the dramatization of voice in **Our Mutual Friend.** Dickens may not have read George Smith's *Programme of the Entertainment: Preceded by Memoirs of Mr. Love, the Dramatic Polyphanist* upon its publication in 1856, but he may well have had occasion to view Mr. Love's act during one of the impersonator's two thousand performances in the City of London between 1836 and 1856.[3] The Dickens fascinated by the glossolalia experienced by the subjects of mesmeric trances, the stage performer who "did" the voices of his own characters to the point of exhaustion in public (and before his daughter and a mirror in private) would surely have found the activities of the "polyphanist" pertinent to his own attempts at ordaining and controlling the vocalizations of his novels.[4] Smith's pamphlet describes Mr. Love as, literally, a man of many parts: not only are his programs largely comprised of dramatic sketches in which he plays all the roles and throws all the voices, but they also occasionally include the performer's lecture on "The Difference Between True and Spurious Ventriloquy" or, perhaps, "A Zoological Concert, Consisting of Imitations and the Voices and Cries of Animated Nature" (32; 35).[5] Such characters as "Mr. Sparkle" and "Mr. Multiple" fill Love's programs and offer interesting, if coincidental prefigurations of the glittering Veneerings, the "Sparkler" of **Little Dorrit,** or the multiple Harmon-Handford-Rokesmith of Dickens most ventriloquistic narrative. Smith argues that the genuine ventriloquist (i.e., anyone who projects different voices and breathes life into either an impersonated character or a dummy) "can summon up innumerable spirits" and must possess "a natural flexibility of features, so as to be able to destroy, to all outward appearance, his own identity, and to assume instantaneously any expression of countenance which the character to be sustained . . . may require" (20-21). For Smith, as I will argue, for Dickens, ventriloquy and impersonation are conflated activities which create the illusion of simultaneity between the actor and the personality he assumes (or the ventriloquist and the dummy he manipulates). At the same time, in the act of ventriloquy the illusion of simultaneity is shown up for its pretense as the erasure of an identity which is really imposed upon the simulated "other," even as it is disguised *as* "other." The success of the spectacle depends entirely upon the controlled suppression of the authorial "self" and an equally controlled sublimation or multiplication of the self as "characters."

The ventriloquist speaks *for* another *through* the impersonated other. In the illusory abolition of his own identity, he generates the fiction that he is merely standing in for the other who is controlling the disclosure while, all the while, the impresario dictates what is said.[6] For the spectacle to work, its metonymical underpinnings must be disguised by the author and "suspended" by the third party in the act, the audience, who knows that the "spontaneous" dialogue between the dummy and the ventriloquist is a pre-scripted monologue. Similarly, in the case of the "polyphanist," who Smith describes as speaking in several languages and "throwing his voice" into the various characters he impersonates, the audience must be willing to ignore the fact that one person is playing all of the roles even while it delights in the virtuosity of the single performer. Smith quotes an unidentified "modern writer" in suggesting that control over distance is the crucial factor in successfully creating this proper, contradictory relation with the audience:

> It would seem to follow, that the closer the person to be deceived is to the ventriloquist, the illusion must be more complete, seeing that the sound imitated, is the sound that strikes the performer's own ear, which it is obvious may not suit the variously arranged auditors in a larger theater. As the sound which reaches our ears must necessarily vary with the distance it has come— and as each variation is a specific imitable sound—so the ventriloquist has only (but assuredly it requires exquisite skill and ingenuity to do this artistically and effectively) to vary his imitation progressively, in either direction, to give a perfect illusion of advance and retreat.
>
> (14)

In this example, the distance between the ventriloquist and the audience is measured and closed, while it is exactly this distance (similar to the "concavity" that Hollander notes must be present, literally and figuratively, for an echo to occur [1-2]) that allows for the successful completion of the illusion. The fictions of ventriloquy and impersonation operate by means of several paradoxical effects that must be accepted, then ignored by the audience. These include maintaining control over the gaps between the performer and the spectators which must be disguised to simulate identification and proximity; establishing the singular omniscience of the ventriloquist or impersonator who must be pluralized, as voice is "thrown," into multiple roles; and concealing the identity of the ventriloquist who must go under the guise of the public "other" to the absconded author of these illusions.

So stand the conditions of Smith's ventriloquistic aesthetic, and they are illuminating for the discussion of "voice" in a novel made of simulated voices—mediatory and authorial, silent and domineering, spontaneous and prescribed. Sloppy may "do the Police in different voices" (243), but he is hardly an exceptional "polyphanist" in *Our Mutual Friend.* If the ventriloquist or impersonator is viewed as one who dominates the discourse while disguising that domination as an impersonation, then the Lammles, Fledgeby, Boffin, Podsnap, Jenny Wren, and even John Harmon are all ventriloquists pursuing various ends. Dickens' impersonation of his own characters in public and private "impersonates" the doubled, ventriloquistic relations between author and characters in the novels, especially in the case of those who, like Podsnap, see themselves as officially dispersed in others: "it was a trait in Mr. Podsnap's character . . . that he could not endure a hint of disparagement of any friend or acquaintance of his. 'How dare you,' he would seem to say, in such a case. 'What do you mean? I have licensed this person. This person has taken out *my* certificate. Through this person you strike at me, Podsnap the Great'" (307). As Dickens licenses Podsnap to say these things (significantly, in the mode of indirect discourse), so Podsnap certifies or prohibits the voices and actions, indeed the very being, of others—he speaks through them; they are his agents. Podsnap's gestures are authoritative and orchestral as he waves pieces of unpleasant reality out of existence; he dominates the mind of his daughter as an author might feel the necessity of "speaking for" a particularly passive, "weak" character.

Though he is admonished in the novel, Podsnap bears some faint resemblances to his maker who, in George Henry Lewes's recollection, "once declared to me that every word said by his characters was distinctly *heard* by him; I was at first not a little puzzled to account for the fact that he could hear language so utterly unlike the language of real feeling, and not be aware of its preposterousness; but the surprise vanished when I thought of the phenomena of hallucination" (101-2). Lewes notes that while evidence of "the phenomena of hallucination" (that is, speaking or hearing in different voices) is a sign of insanity in most instances, for the artist it is a mark of creativity. For Lewes, the difference between the schizophrenic and the sane artist is a matter of belief: "The characteristic point in the hallucinations of the insane, that which distinguishes them from hallucinations equally vivid in the same, is the coercion of the image in *suppressing comparison* and all control of the experience. Belief always accompanies a vivid image, for a time; but in the sane this belief will not persist against rational control" (95-96). Thus, Lewes would say Dickens is sane and brilliant (despite some artistic faults such as lack of true ideas) because he had mastery over the voices he hears, does not ultimately believe in their reality, and can successfully channel them into the rationally patterned work of art. Unlike Sloppy who merely reads the voices he imitates, and who, with his "polysyllabic bellow" (250) can barely manage his own apparel ("he stood . . . a perfect Argus in the way of buttons" [390]; his hat is a patchwork conglomeration "from which the imagination shrunk discomfited and the reason revolted" [391]), Lewes's Dickens originates and orchestrates the voices he overhears. More like Podsnap effectually, if not intentionally, this version of Dickens is that of the successful impersonator: he not only "does the Police" but, as an artist who employs and contains the dichotomies of reason and the imagination, he polices well the momentary illusion of being overwhelmed by the public projections of his own voice. For Lewes, as for Smith, the maintenance of distance within the illusion of similitude is the crucial factor in determining the successful projection of voice. In Lewes's rationalization of "hallucination," and in an exhibition of authorial domination that becomes fascistic under the iron hand of Podsnappery, Dickens is both "medium" and "control," author and impersonated character, keeping his own lips buttoned while intonating and harmonizing the voices of the spectacle's assembled cast.

Lewes hints at the possibility, however momentary, of an "insane" Dickens gone out of control, unable to transform the many voices he projects into the designs of art because he has forgotten whose singular identity originates those voices. To control the discourse, in this sense, is to remember who (like "Podsnap the Great") lies behind authored expressions, and "who" is their point of reference. Yet, in *Our Mutual Friend,* the portrayal of unsuccessful attempts to control speech and thought, paired with interwoven cases of mistaken or forgotten identity, create an "authorial crisis" of such magnitude that Dickens must ironically cast the conclusion of the novel in the form of a precocious magical realism complete with an Edenic arbor, a golden bower, and even a floating infant bearing the maker's mark ("By a master stroke of secret arrangement, the inexhautible baby here appeared at the door, suspended in mid-air by invisible agency" [841]). The harmonic, fairy-tale ending of the novel has called for a good many causal readings. As a conclusion that evidently configures a new society founded upon charity rather than greed, or rather, a beneficent rather than stingy patrimony, it closes off one of Dickens' most resolute plots. Still, there survives the sense, represented by the ceaseless wails of "the inexhaustible," that the raised voices and spirits of *Our Mutual Friend,* while abruptly silenced by the contingencies of plot and closure, have hardly been brought under control.[7] Indeed, what might be called the theatricalizations of voice in the novel—the cries of the infant, the unstilled babble of the Veneerings and "The Voice of Society," the pastoral echoes of the Upper Thames which commemorate the death of Betty Higden—variously serve as ironic commentary upon the inefficacy of plot and its containments when countered by the noisy, "sloppy," unharmonious supplements of voice and impression.

Henry James's famous complaint in his negative review of *Our Mutual Friend* was just this: that Dickens had lost control over his artistry, that he had failed to administer his own fancies properly, and that, as an author, he was "exhausted."[8] Yet we may regard this exhaustion as a recognition that there is something in "voice" that floods the confines of narrative architecture, a residue that can not be wholly contained, or only represented as a sign of that which precedes and escapes "narration." This vocal residue may be seen as a kind of negativity marking the distance (that element of ventriloquy which, again according to Smith, *must* remain under the artist's control) between voice as projected, or written down, and its origins. Such distance is an absence that both contravenes and necessitates the fiction of an authorial "presence" behind the voice, just as there must be distance between the ventriloquist and his dummy so that a voice can be thrown, or concavity so that echo can be heard. The conception of voice which, Michael Beaujour suggests, links sounds and presence within the Judeo-Christian tradition is challenged by the increasingly conflicted recognitions of impersonation in Dickens' novels:

> Indeed, until very recently, voice implied presence, a spatial and temporal coincidence between a speaker and at least one hearer. . . . In the context of myth and poetry, in . . . certain heightened mutual states, people would hearken to the voices of deities, angels, saints, and spirits of the dead. Even animals and inanimate things would be expected to speak under the proper circumstances. Although "hearing voices" remained an uncanny experience, it was not exclusively a pathological one. Witness Abraham, or Moses. "God called unto him out of the midst of a bush, and said: 'Moses, Moses.' And he said: 'Here I am.'" Such a call could lead to a *vocation.* . . . A person might also feel *possessed* by a supernatural being, who would substitute its own voice for that of its human *medium.* Voice manifested presence. A voice-event was an epiphany. Even simulation, the actor's, for instance, or that of the rhapsodist and the ventriloquist, indicated that someone was sufficiently present to confer presence upon a fictitious, alien voice.

(273)

Lewes wanted to portray Dickens ordaining and "overhearing" the voices of his own characters—the author playing both God and Moses—as a vocational, rather than a pathological event, but for Dickens himself, the distinction may not have been so easy to make. This is particularly so in *Our Mutual Friend* where "alien voices" seem to possess their originator and threaten, rather than ensure the self-sustaining epiphanic moment. As Beaujour argues, the simulation and mimicry of other voices for which Dickens is so well known suggests the presence of the author behind the roles. But in *Our Mutual Friend,* the fragmentation of the complex relation between represented speech (the only way voice may be "thrown" in writing) and authorial presence posits a crucial revision of "voice" as the public expression of the self which undermines what that expression formerly guaranteed: the locating and representing of identity ("Here I am") and its authoritative sources.[9] In short, the novel portrays a crisis of representation; it is most self-revelatory when, beneath its harmonies, the residual, parasitical "noise" of speech is heard.[10]

In the most general sense, acts of ventriloquy or impersonation constitute an attempt to create a fictive "other," then to control the other's speech while representing it as issuing forth from the "individual." If the illusion is successfully conveyed, the "author" has accomplished the double task of making himself and his "characters" present at once. Such acts abound in *Our Mutual Friend*: they run the gamut from instances where one, simply, speaks for another to the employment of catechisms, highly artificial frames of reference, dictated speeches, and soliloquies disguised as "duets," all imposed upon potentially dialogic situations for the purpose of mastering the discourse. Acts of ventriloquy are employed by villains, like the Lammles, or heroes, like Boffin and Harmon; their apparent success in the novel varies with the manifest moral worth of the scheme the impersonator perpetrates.

Yet, especially in the most successful ventriloquizations, such as the one where the Boffins and Harmon co-author the script of Bella's transformation from greedy rags to beneficent riches, the "act" seems excessive, the threat of failure ever-present, and the balance between good intentions and domineering method tenuously maintained. In cases of failed ventriloquy, of course, the moral point is strongly made ("one should not try to control the speech and actions of others *if* the ends are self-serving"). In these instances, wrongdoers, like the Lammles, are exiled from Eden to the hell of "the Continent," or like Fledgeby, meted out a physical punishment fitting the crime. But decidedly in those acts of ventriloquy supposedly motivated by good intentions, after the rewards have been distributed, there still remains the sense that the crucial distance between origin and medium has broken down, and that the "ventriloquist" is made to wear the emperor's new clothes—a sense that may help explain the response, continuous since the novel was first published, that the Golden Dustman's conversion into philanthropist from miser is unconvincing and fraudulent. Somehow, the transference of identity has been *too* successful, and the "polyphanist" playing the part of the miser begins to receive dictation from the persona he has created and directed:

> "Never thought of it afore the moment, my dear!" Boffin observed to Bella. "When John said, if he had been so happy as to win your affections and possess your heart, it comes into my head to turn around upon him with 'Win her affections and possess her heart! Mew says the cat, Quack quack says the duck, and Bow-wow-wow says the dog.' I couldn't tell you how it came into my head or where from, but it had so much the sound of a rasper that I astonished myself. I was awful nigh bursting out a laughing though, when it made John stare!"
>
> (848)

In this scene of comic recognition, Boffin's "rasper" seems harmless enough, but recalling the moment itself, he admits loss of control over the origins of his speech as he sinks to an animalistic level in an imitation of the cat's meow and the dog's bark. The comic framing of this admission allows the narrator and the reader to pass it all off as part of the good design—perhaps, even, the coup de grâce—that will bring Bella into harmony with the mind of Harmon. But in this condoned speech act there is some

interference, a rasping that surpasses design and intention while revealing the anxiety that accompanies all speech acts in *Our Mutual Friend* as they negotiate the extremes of failure and overdetermination.

To focus on Boffin's "rasper" or any of the many other instances where expression is excessive or noisy in *Our Mutual Friend* is to notice a slippage in the connection between "voice" and "identity" which the presence of voice naturally assumes, and which the figures of ventriloquy and impersonation serve to complicate. The artificiality of the connection is most notable when those who have tenuous identities attempt to speak. George Sampson, the pale, wan suitor of Bella, then her sister, Lavinia, is thoroughly dominated by the many-voiced Mrs. Wilfer (herself a compilation of roles) to the extent that even when he is full of feeling, he cannot speak: "The friend of the family was in that stage of tender passion which bound him to regard everybody else as the foe of the family. He put the round head of his cane in his mouth, like a stopper, when he sat down. As if he felt himself full to the throat with affronting sentiments" (155). Lady Tippins, whose identity is composed of fictions about non-existent lovers, is known "by a certain yellow play in her throat, like the legs of scratching poultry" (54). Rogue Riderhood, who plays Lightwood to Headstone's Wrayburn, can be heard to "throw his words . . . for his voice was as if the head of his boat's mop were down his throat" (109). Headstone himself, when he plays the role of teacher, is a master of language, but when he is confronted by the object of passion whom he wishes to teach, his voice becomes a parodic representation of repressed desire: "'I should like to ask you,' said Bradley Headstone, grinding his words slowly out, as though they came from a rusty mill: 'I should like to ask you, if I may without offence, whether you would have objected—no; rather, I should like to say, if I may without offence, that I wish I had the opportunity of coming here with your brother and devoting my poor abilities and experience to your service'" (401). To a cab driver, Old Harmon is "a speeches of chaff" (98), as if voice conveyed the husk of personality rather than any internal presence of being. Rokesmith's voice is "agreeable in tone, albeit constrained" (141); Jenny Wren's voice crazily alternates between the angelic and the demonic as she speaks of visiting seraphim one moment, then talks of the punishment she would confer upon a fictive husband ("Him") should he turn out to be, like her father, a drunkard: "'When he was asleep, I'd make a spoon red hot, and I'd have some boiling liquor bubbling in the saucepan, and I'd take it out hissing, and I'd open his mouth with the other hand—or perhaps he'd sleep with his mouth ready open—and I'd pour it down his throat, and blister and choke him'" (294). This seems a particularly fitting punishment for a potential wastrel in a novel where "voice" is often the conveyance of will, and "harmoney" a kind of moral reward.

Figuratively, the intensity of these examples resides less with the content of the communication and more with the faulty instruments of mouths and throats often envisioned as stopped up, unhinged, or in some way mutilated. Speech is often *disfigured* in **Our Mutual Friend**: what we "hear" in each of these cases is the noisy interference of the linguistic medium itself. Something stands between the "self" who wishes to speak and what gets said; this "something" signifies a partial loss of control over the speech act both for those who act as ventriloquists or impersonators as they attempt to script the discourse (like Boffin), and those who are the subjects of ventriloquy (like Bella or Georgiana Podsnap). These are instances of parasitical speech in Michael Serres's sense of the "parasite" as the element in communication that generates static, feeding off the relation between speaker and hearer, both complicating and, paradoxically, nurturing that relation (3-47; 94-97; see also Wilden 395-412). The "speech defects" of the novel thus work to question the efficacy and origins of speech in the individual speaker, and the ability of the speaker to transmit "self-presence" to another.

More revealing examples of such "interference" occur when a certain kind of speech act, intended to promote and control discourse going under the illusion of "communication," actually thwarts that effort—a failed ventriloquy in the literal sense. When the Lammles attempt to open up lines of communication between an uncooperative Fledgeby and Georgiana Podsnap, or when they try to convince the Boffins to take them as stand-ins for Rokesmith and Bella, they assume the role of ventriloquists who cannot get the dummy to speak. In the former instance, the "conversation" begins with Alfred Lammle trying to force Fledgeby to pay Georgiana a false compliment:

> "Georgiana," said Mr. Lammle, low and smiling, sparkling all over, like a harlequin; "you are not in your usual spirits. Why are you not in your usual spirits, Georgiana?"
>
> Georgiana faltered that she was much the same as she was in general; she was not aware of being difficult.
>
> "Not aware of being different!" retorted Mr. Alfred Lammle. "You, my dear Georgiana! who are always so natural and unconstrained with us? who are such a relief from the crowd that are all alike! who are the embodiment of gentleness, simplicity, and reality!"
>
> Miss Podsnap looked at the door, as if she entertained confused thoughts of taking refuge from these compliments in flight.
>
> "Now I will be judged," said Mr. Lammle, raising his voice a little, "by my friend Fledgeby."
>
> "OH DON'T!" Miss Podsnap fairly ejaculated: when Mrs. Lammle took the prompt-book.
>
> "I beg your pardon, Alfred, my dear, but I cannot part with Mr. Fledgeby quite yet; you must wait for him a moment. Mr. Fledgeby and I are engaged in a personal discussion."
>
> Fledgeby must have conducted it on his side with immense art, for no appearance of uttering one syllable had escaped him.
>
> (315)

The painful discussion goes on in this vein for several pages, with the Lammles taking both their own parts and those of Fledgeby and Georgiana, who remain nearly silent throughout. The Lammles' attempts to "raise the spirits" of their guests are fruitless, but their purpose—which is merely to produce speech between two silent parties and, thus, initiate a deeper relation—is clearly frustrated in the ventriloquistic effort to originate and dominate the substance of speech. Instead, the silent parties inadvertently control the speech of the sparkling "harlequin" and his wife by virtue of their refusal to talk: each new task in the discussion becomes increasingly predictable and more easily subverted by those who wish to avoid communication. Eventually, the Lammles' discourse, with its false starts, repetitions, and clichés appears to be scripted by those playing the dummy hand. The failure of these parasites is both communicative and economic: they succeed in generating only noise where they would create a relation between dominated identities; appropriately, in the end, they are exiled from the master's table where they sought to feed. Their scheming begins on a honeymoon when the celebration of their own new relation is revealed to be a case of reciprocal mistaken identity; since they cannot leech off each other, they attempt to construct a system of communication that will allow them to "parasite" others. Here, the inability to articulate a social identity—the harlequinade as airy as the illusory perfect house which the Lammles have never seen and will never buy, but which all their friends are convinced is "made for them"—is projected as vain speech.

The Lammles, of course, are castigated, and the Boffins and Harmons elevated according to the worth of their intentions, but as I have suggested, the means by which all achieve these ends are similar. Just as the Lammles try to "script" Georgiana and Fledgeby, so is Bella scripted by her husband and adopted parents. The novel authorizes the latter activity through the concordances of plot, but in both cases, there is a contamination of expression—whether a "rasping" or the furious intonations of a frustrated harlequin—which interferes with the "clarity" of a speech act portending the desire for the creation of "proper" relations. Indeed, contamination, mutilation, and disarticulation of expressions, bodies, voices, and rivers abound to such an extent in **Our Mutual Friend** that, to take one of these elements alone, the disfigured vocal embodiments of problematic identities threaten to drown out any celestial strains issuing forth from the golden bower of the Harmons' domestic paradise. Before he dies, Gaffer Hexam fearfully asks Lizzie, "'Have we got a pest in the house? Is summ'at deadly sticking to my clothes? What's let loose upon us? Who loosed it?'" (121). His questions express a general anxiety regarding the pest that contaminates the house of this novel, typified by all of the parasites who live off the waste and death of others. Venus's decomposed skeletons, Jenny Wren's mutilated dolls, and Boffin's dust heaps may be seen as physical analogues to the disfigurations and "waste" of speech in the novel, from Wrayburn's pointless riddles to Wegg's mutilation of the classics. The incremental effect of the novel's literal and figural parasitical relations suggests that the "world" of *Our Mutual Friend*, while highly organized, is also entropic, and that such a world sustains its orders and hierarchies at the expense, and in fear of, that within it—death, alterity, heterogeneity—which it would silence. The systems of communication which authorize this suppression are, thus, inherently ironic, in that the suppression, like the attempts to ventriloquize speech, actually *produces* the interferences of the novel.

So fragile and tenuously maintained are the communicative systems of *Our Mutual Friend* that many of its speakers feel compelled to create unnecessary fictions in order to frame speech, as if it needed to be, literally, shored up. Similarly, the speakers of the novel often talk too much, as if the generation of a linguistic excess ensures the continuance of a speech act verging on insignificance even as it is more elaborately framed and compounded. Between Mary Ann and Miss Peecher there must be the fiction of a catechetical "exam" in order to enable a discussion about Headstone's relationship to Lizzie; between the Inspector, Lightwood, and Wrayburn there emerges the sheer linguistic waste of an elaborate fiction about lime barges and lime salesmen which outruns its initial use as a cover for their investigation of Gaffer's disappearance long before the talk of lime is ended. Perhaps the most egregious example of this kind of linguistic excess is devised within a scene apparently concerned with the portrayal of an act of clerical benevolence, but an act that almost disastrously interferes with the progress of the novel at a climactic point. Near the end, Lightwood, the Milveys, and Jenny Wren are hurrying to Eugene, who is close to death. The Milveys are delayed from a timely arrival at the train station by one Mrs. Sprodgkin, an annoying parishioner who inevitably demands their attention at moments when they can least afford to return it. Mrs. Sprodgkin is portrayed as having "an infection of absurdity about her, that communicated itself to everything with which, and everybody with whom, she came into contact" (817). Mrs. Milvey refers to this parasite as "'such a marplot,'" a fair and accurate label considering that Mrs. Sprodgkin threatens to bring the advancement of the climax to a screeching halt by keeping the Milveys from their appointed time and place in the text. A more visible pest like Silas Wegg is simply a Mrs. Sprodgkin writ large, for the only useful purpose the wrecker of ballads and syntax serves is to foul up Boffin's schemes for restricting Harmons' identity and reuniting him with his pre-destined bride; like Mrs. Sprodgkin, Wegg is all noise and marplot. To be sure, the Milveys get to the station on time, just as the dust heaps and Wegg are carted away in the conclusion of the novel: the contamination of the discourse is partially absolved through the highly contrived concordance of plot. But in between the initiation of the mystery of mistaken identity and its resolution, Dickens has generated a good many plots and characters who resemble the "no thoroughfare" down which Wrayburn leads Headstone. These, figuratively, are blind alleys where the only "self-discovery" comes in the form of mirroring or doubling that reflects an "identity" borne of the excesses and repetitions of desire, either unsuccessfully re-

pressed or allowed expression in the excesses of language: thus, after a nightlong chase, Wrayburn faces his alter ego while speaking casual nonsense to Lightwood. From the old pensioner who appears at Bella's wedding (and who, with two wooden legs, doubles Wegg) to Old Riah, whose lengthy complicity with Fledgeby simply *interferes* with all attempts to see him as the good Jew counterpart to Fagin, Dickens "contaminates" his own novel with apparent and real parasites, and with parasitical plots and relations that unnecessarily complicate the narrative communications and exchanges of *Our Mutual Friend.*

In a large sense, such contaminations are what fiction is made of: fiction can be viewed as a conglomeration of voices, or entanglements, or unnecessary complications that separate beginning from end, intention from act.[11] But this conception of fiction is countered by that ventriloquistic desire which comes under the name of "authorial intention." To recall Smith's discourse on ventriloquy, the successful polyphanist must control the distance between the real and apparent origins of voice so that the audience can indulge in the paradoxical illusion that the actor simultaneously is and is not the voice he projects, or that the dummy is a separate identity containing the displaced "presence" of the ventriloquist. The contaminations of speech in *Our Mutual Friend* undermine the assumed or intended connections between voice and presence and dispel the illusion of simultaneity between speaker, medium, and represented speech. In its very constitution, the act of ventriloquy puts its own illusory processes into question as it theatricalizes the re-presentation of identity. In similar ways, *Our Mutual Friend* stages the disarticulation and reconstitution of the "I" who speaks, but within this process it necessarily produces something else—a supplement or noise—that precedes the formation of any articulated identity.

. . . . .

John Harmon's story originates in the tale of "The Man from Somewhere," told by the laconic Mortimer Lightwood within view of "the great looking-glass above the sideboard" of Veneering's table. In this scene, J. Hillis Miller remarks, "Veneering gradually manifests himself like an ectoplasmic vision at a seance, hovering in the space behind the mirror, a space which is both the imaginary space of the novel and the inner space of the reader's mind" (*Form*, 41). While Dickens summons forth Veneering's substanceless spirit at the novel's inception, he cancels Harmon and displaces his identity onto, successively, Julius Handford and John Rokesmith. The "original" Harmon is reconstituted in the end not as an "ectoplasm," but as the reincarnation of the "real" John Harmon nicely juxtaposed to the vanquished Veneerings.

But Dickens does not stop there. In the "Postscript, in Lieu of a Preface" to the novel, he recounts the salvation of his own text from the Staplehurst railway accident of 1865. Of his own potential conversion into an ectoplasm, Dickens writes: "I remember with devout thankfulness that I can never be much nearer parting company with my readers for ever, than I was then, until there be written against my life the two words with which I have this day closed this book—THE END" (894). In sealing his narrative with the temporary deliverance of his own identity, Dickens openly declares one of the conscious purposes of his writing: to establish a "company" of "kept" readers. This readerly company is analogous to the new community assembled in the Golden Bower at the novel's redemptive conclusion—a resurrected society established in direct contrast to the "Society" of noisy Veneerings and Podsnaps, who are reduced to so much hot air in the end.

Thus, the plot of this novel of mistaken and found identities appears to fulfill the discovered intentions of the postface, save that Dickens brings up the "writing against life" which presently closes the novel and will serve as the monumental inscription marking the passing of the author. In this retrospective supplement to the novel (which displaces a non-existent "preface," or a more proper introduction, and which can also be seen as an instance of the author stepping from behind the mask to "face" the audience) Dickens offers a revealing commentary upon those artifices of *Our Mutual Friend*—especially the constraints of plot—which he has contrived in order to establish an ironic "authority" over the novel's unruly spirits. Here, Dickens both commemorates the saving of the self and the text while foreshadowing the disappearances of the authorial self as something recorded *by* a text, a "writing against life." In so doing, he reforges the conception of identity as "the subject in process," a continuous evolving of the "self" in language as both the expression and repression of what comes "outside" language—what Julia Kristeva calls "the chora" or "the modality of significance in which the linguistic sign is not yet articulated as the absence of an object" (28). For Kristeva, the "semiotic" is that aspect of language which cuts across its "symbolic," formalistic, syntactically "correct," "logical" dimensions. The semiotic ruptures of discourse—its "noise," lyric and prosaic excesses, rhythmic resonances, and play—faintly echo what she conceives to be the "preface" of discourse, society, and identity, which is the absence of these as separable from the negated subject, the maternal body, *become* an object in the realm of the symbolic. In the "Postface," Dickens appears to turn away from the negated subject of Ellen Ternan. She accompanied him on the journey and was rescued by the author, but her presence on the scene was unrecorded for fear that her being identified as Dickens' fellow traveller would result in bad publicity—he, thus, records her absence in the epitaph.[12] In bringing up, as it were, both the death of the author and the negation of the subject, the "Postface" reflects back on the novel proper to suggest that the disfigurations of voice and body in *Our Mutual Friend* counterbalance its postings of identity even as the fiction of identity attempts to frame, silence, or symbolize the linguistic traces of "the absent object" which precedes it. In scrutinizing the novel's "semiotic" dimension, those places where the representations of speech, like the bodies which speak, are partial, cut up, discontinuous, we can shadow that absent object of *Our Mutual Friend,* which is, indeed, its hidden subject—

what stands behind its author and the profusion of characters and voices he projects.

I have previously suggested how ventriloquy can stand as a figure for the complex process of identity formation Kristeva describes, and what that process reveals and represses. Surrounded by those who would make her speak words she cannot say and who cut her short when she begins to voice her own desires, Georgiana Podsnap typifies all of the novel's subjects who are silenced or whose voices and fates seem to be pre-scripted by the dominating, authorial discourse of fathers, avuncular stand-ins, would-be husbands, domineering hostesses, shrewish wives. To a lesser extent, Bella, Lizzie Hexam, Twemlow, Mr. Wilfer, even Jenny Wren (who is a ventriloquist herself) find themselves the subjects of attempted acts of ventriloquy which would confer upon the ventriloquized subject an identity, but one that is not his or her "own." Perhaps the most comic portrayal of this state of affairs can be seen in the case of Pleasant Riderhood, who is pressed by the articulator of bodies, Mr. Venus, to say the right word to his proposal of marriage, but who successfully refuses the subjection to him in declaring that she "will not be seen in that bony light." In *Our Mutual Friend,* while the Georgianas and the Lizzies may often stay silent before the onslaught of a louder, more domineering voice, the speaking subject—because it is plural, multivocal—cannot be so easily disposed of. With its huge cast of characters, each with his or her own idom and idiosyncrasy, the novel pursues the notion of a "collective subject" which in its more disruptive moments speaks against the vacuous "voice of Society" and the sentimentalized homogeneity of the charmed circle of the Golden Bower. In this way, the idea of a single voice, an authorized speaker, a ventriloquistic presence, is challenged by the sheer "partiality" of voice and character in the novel. Indeed, even in those speakers who most effectively seek to ventriloquize others, there is a civil war between "authorized" or "articulated" speech and those rebellious intonations which exceed or refuse the rigidities of official discourse: an hysterical tone can be heard in Harmon's midnight soliloquies as well as Headstone's passionate outbursts; Boffin can complete with Wegg or the Lammles or Podsnap in the art of double-talk, though, of course, he is "just playing."

Eruptions of what Kristeva refers to as the "semiotic" into speech acts occur, of course, in all of Dickens' novels, but they are often located within the confines of the habitual speech patterns of particular (usually eccentric) characters such as a Sam Weller, or a Sarah Gamp, or a Flora Finching. As a counterweight to these, there is the controlling voice of authority—that of the omniscient narrator of many early novels; or the older, world-weary self reflecting back on youth in *Great Expectations*; or the dry, jaded voice of the quasi-omniscient narrator of *Bleak House* acting as an ironic corrective to Esther's presumed sentimentality and egotism. *Our Mutual Friend* might be seen as the result of the intensification of the semiotic in Dickens' corpus; here, there is no normative "center" of speech, not even that of the furtive narrator who, when he speaks, does so in the voice of the mock-parliamentarian or mock-historian. The type of "speech defect" exhibited in the more concentrated medium of Flora Finching in *Little Dorrit* becomes, in *Our Mutual Friend,* what might be termed a "communication disorder" to be observed in many aspects of the novel. Flora introduces herself to Mr. Dorrit, who does not know her, in this manner:

> "I beg Mr. Dorrit to offer a thousand apologies and indeed they would be far too few for such an intrusion which I know must appear extremely bold in a lady and alone too, but I thought it best upon the whole however difficult and even apparently improper though Mr. F.'s aunt would have willingly accompanied me and as a character of great force and spirit would probably have struck one possessed of such a knowledge of life as no doubt with so many changes must have been acquired, for Mr. F. himself said frequently that although well educated in the neighbourhood of Blackheath at as high as eighty guineas which is a good deal for parents and the plate kept back too on going away but that is more a meanness than its value that he had learnt more in his first years as a commercial traveller with a large commission on the sale of an article that nobody would hear of much less buy which preceded the wine trade a long time than in the whole six years in that academy conducted by a college Bachelor, though why a Bachelor more clever than a married man I do not see and never did but pray excuse me that is not the point"

(680).

Naturally, Mr. Dorrit is speechless before this onslaught, the subject of which is deferred beyond the point of logic and reason. Even if one were to regard Flora's speech as having the potential to "make sense," working back through it in order to determine its original point of reference would involve laborious and improbable speculations whose yield, in terms of knowledge of "what she is talking about," would be small. Flora's speech is both rhapsodic and dissociative, and it functions as a kind of jamming device in *Little Dorrit.* Such speech undermines "relationality" in several senses; within it, syntactical chains are broken, patterns of significance are skewed, and information is converted into pure sound as Flora's narcissistic relation to the world of persons and objects around her is rendered as a linguistic meandering, all echo and repetition. This severing of language from a referential ground signifies the intrusion of the semiotic into the discourse of Dickens' novels.

Linguistic disorders of this kind are dispersed throughout *Our Mutual Friend.* Eugene, for example, interrupts the Veneerings' dinner-table conversation with this piece of nonsense about "the man from Tobago," the introduction to the story of "the man from Somewhere," John Harmon: "'Except . . . our friend who long lived on rice-pudding and isinglass, till at length to his something or other, his physician said something else, and a leg of mutton somehow ended in daygo'" (54). Eugene's statement is a parody of reference, a riddle which confounds the relation be-

tween answers and clues while providing a groundless "context" for Harmon's story. Later in the novel, Eugene will mystify Boffin by confusing the literal and metaphorical implications of the parable of the bees, as he will madden Headstone by taking pieces of his figurative speech literally, out of context, in order to drive the schoolmaster from the room. After Headstone has gone, Eugene remarks to Mortimer that "one would think the schoolmaster had left behind him a catechizing infection" (348), though whether the communicative breakdown has begun in Headstone's strained questions or Eugene's punning answers is unclear—this "infection," analogous to Mrs. Sprodgkin's spreading "contamination" of speech, defines the "no thoroughfare" of their relation to each other.

In his own realm of influence, Headstone participates in an education system where "the adult pupils were taught to read (if they could learn) out of the New Testament; and by dint of stumbling over the syllables and keeping their bewildered eyes on the particular syllables coming round to their turn, were absolutely ignorant of the sublime history, as if they had never heard of it" (264). Here and elsewhere, in the fragmentation of discourse, the distance between linguistic sign and point of reference is so great that elaborate fictions of reference and cohesion (like that of the lime salesman) must be produced so that the threatened loss of connection between sign and signified can be reconstituted and sustained. Frequently, the difference between the literal and figurative levels of language are collapsed in an effort to articulate and embody "selfhood" amidst the "disarticulation" of the novel. A "non-reader" like Rogue Riderhood believes nothing exists until it is "took" down and "spelled out," that is, until his oral lies are converted into inscribed truths by "the binding powers of pen and ink" (196), never mind that the unreadable syllables of inscription bear no relation to the reality they supposedly describe. For Wegg, every far-fetched rhyme can be transformed into occasional verse; for Podsnap, a single "no" and a gesture can sweep away whole worlds and their contexts; for Mrs. Wilfer, every stray piece of conversation is transformed into a reference concerning her undeserved fate as Mrs. Wilfer. Even Harmon (in the role of Rokesmith) both "figures" and disfigures language as he vows to bury "John Harmon additional fathoms deep" and to heap "mounds and mounds of earth over John Harmon's grave" (425), as if he could sever his relation to the past merely through the employment of a figure of speech which metaphorically entombs its speaker while bearing literal reference to the most tangible element of his past, his inheritance of the dust mounds.

As is the case with those instances where ventriloquy fails in its efforts to control speech, these forced connections, while intended to reforge syntactic relations and to represent identity, actually work to undermine them. The collapsing of the distance between, for example, the literal and figurative senses of a phrase inevitably result in a parody of sense, just as Eugene's nonsense, or Jenny Wren's demonic rhapsodies, or the fragmented remembrances of Headstone's pupils abjure the cohesion of "normal" speech. These relational breakdowns are, again, evidence of the semiotic, which is "articulated by flow and marks: facilitation, energy transfers, the cutting up of the corporeal and social continuum as well as that of the signifying material" (40). In Kristeva's view, this form of "articulation" is in counterpoint to "the realm of signification . . . a realm of *positions*" and of the "*identification* of the subject" (43). In a novel of mistaken identity, it is "identity" seen as a linguistic positioning or form of signification that is questioned in the disfigurations of language, even as identities, represented as characters, are contained by the form of plot. Analogously, as Kristeva suggests, the "social continuum" and the "corporal" are "cut up" in the novel, and in the representation of bodies in *Our Mutual Friend,* Dickens gives fullest expression to the semiotic "origins" of identity in the inarticulate.

The "social continuum" can be defined as a network of class and kinship relations which contribute to the formation of the "self" as a body and being related to others through economic and linguistic systems of exchange. In Lévi-Strauss's classic formulation, the objects or signs of these exchanges are women, and the subjects, men, both of whose social identities depend upon the continuance of a totemic, partriarchal economic system.[13] In *Our Mutual Friend,* the skewing of familial and genealogical relations occurs alongside the exploding of linguistic relations, and in these disfigurations, the connection between "the semiotic" and "the social" is forged. Bella, Jenny, and Lizzie are all daughters of non-existent or spurious mothers: with the exception of Betty Higden, a Mother Hubbard figure who disappears, significantly, into the pastoral landscape of the novel less than half-way through, the "proper" maternal bodies of the novel are absent. As if to compensate, the relations of the three major female characters to their fathers are defined in terms of a mother to her child. Metaphorically, Bella, Lizzie, and Jenny are orphans (like Harmon) biologically born of their parents, but in fact, socially responsible for mothering their own fathers in an overdetermined manner: as Roger Henkle argues, the portrayal of Jenny and her relation to her father is a parody of all those Dickensian "little women" in whom the good mother and the "daughterly" woman are combined.[14] Women are, thus, "positioned" in their nominative common roles as mothers, but the social continuum which depends on their acceptance of these positions is made vulnerable to a collapse of the relational differences which "normally" exist between fathers and daughters when the daughters become mothers or wives. When this takes place in a novel where the collapsing of the distance between the literal and figural levels of language is a common occurrence, then the "incest threat" takes on a doubled, and more than faintly symbolic quality. These displaced manifestations of the maternal body in the relations between fathers and daughters in *Our Mutual Friend* signify disruptions of "the normal order," as if to say that what lies behind the order for Kristeva—the mother, the female subject—*will* exhibit herself. But within the dominant masculine order that Dickens represents as assuming control with "the happy ending" of the novel, the representation of the female subject must appear as hysterical (Jenny), cloyingly sentimental and, paradoxically, greedy (Bella), or rhapsodic (Lizzie).

One, indeed, senses an irreparable breakdown of the social continuum when analogous reversals of father-daughter relations are seen to extend elsewhere to other gender and class relations. In *Our Mutual Friend,* where fathers become infants, an heir to a fabulous fortune becomes a secretary (for the purpose of seeing how a poor girl will do if *she* crosses class lines) while his servants become his masters. Heterosexual relations are thoroughly skewed when one regards the broken affair between Venus and Pleasant Riderhood as a disagreement over stuffed parrots, or the promised intimacy between Sloppy and Jenny Wren an the culmination of a fiction about "the coming of Him" in a striking deflation of Lizzie's salvatory relation to Wrayburn. A poor Jew is made to play the role of a rich usurer, and poor Twemlow is continually at odds to explain the difference between acquaintance and friendship. In short, relations and identities of all kinds are in a constant state of flux and crisis in the novel; this is most evident in the rivalries between symbolic brothers or "partners" (Headstone/Wrayburn, Riderhood/Gaffer, Harmon/Handford/Rokesmith). Everything, of course, appears to be set right at last, but the positioning of characters into "proper" relations in the novel's conclusion requires a kind of authorial force that explodes into violence (the sadism of Fledgeby's beating, the "well-deserved" junking of Wegg, Wrayburn's drowning, Headstone's and Riderhood's double-murder) all expended for the sole purpose, in terms of plot, of getting Bella and Harmon and Lizzie and Wrayburn together. In a sense, the "victory" is Pyrrhic, and the damage has been done. Despite Twemlow's admirable, but impotent rejoinders, not only is the vacuous "Voice of Society" the last chord struck in the novel, not only does Dickens feel it necessary to tack on a postface which connects his authorship with acts of textual and corporeal redemption while repressing the female subject, but even with the closing act—Harmon's accession to fortune and the death and rebirth of Eugene Wrayburn—there is the sense that the "reward," the confirmation and renewal of identity, is a socially capricious act of providence undertaken by an ironic author through the vehicles of Lizzie and the Boffins.[15] As the language and vocalizations of the novel are fragmented, so its social fabric is still torn even after authorial recuperation. The attempt to mend it, beyond the level of plot, results in a self-referential, authorial "salvation" that leaves its marks upon the text, as well as upon the bodies of its characters.

Eugene Wrayburn is a crucial representation in *Our Mutual Friend* of what Kristeva refers to as "the corporeal," and he is one of Dickens' most complex creations: much like Charles Freeman of John Fowles's *The French Lieutenant's Woman,* he can be viewed as either the last Victorian or the first Modern.[16] Wrayburn has all the symptoms of a peculiarly modern disease—urban anomie—yet he also stands as Dickens' satiric comment on the leisurely Victorian gentleman: well-educated and bored, typically in pursuit of a lower-class woman whom he is willing to bed but whom he will not marry against a paternal injunction. If Henry James thought that *Our Mutual Friend* bore the strain of authorial exhaustion, then surely that malady is most readily located in Wrayburn. Through much of the first half of the novel, Wrayburn possesses no "self" in the usual senses of the word: he has no work, no project, no relationships save his thoroughly laconic friendship with Mortimer and his distanced, parasitical relation with his father. Up to a point, his one legitimate function in the novel seems to be that of the *eiron,* a voice who mocks the pretensions of those of his own class. Then he meets Lizzie and Headstone, and the pursuit of both not only gives him something to do, but confers upon him a personality and a body—those of the lover and the revenger.

Eugene thereby becomes the focal point of one of the novel's double plots, and upon his living or dying (as the elaborate passages describing his "rising and "sinking" would lead us to believe) hinges much of the general pathetic effect of the novel. The resurrection of his body from the waters above Henley bears enormous symbolic weight, for it seems it would not have been enough just to "save" Bella alone: that salvation is "spiritual," a change of heart about the importance of money. Wrayburn's revival, on the other hand, gives "body" to the salvatory scheme of the novel, as if there is the necessity of a physical exchange for the corpse (George Radfoot's) which floats up out of the Thames at the beginning of the novel. Wrayburn's rising body potentially "redeems" all the dead who have sunk, unnoticed, into the river and who have floated up to the surface again, their identities erased by the work of time and nature, their bodies resurrected in pieces as contributions to the likes of Venus's miscellanies. Risen and reborn, Eugene is the anti-parasite, a metaphorical response to the overwhelming social "world" of the novel where life is a matter of feeding off the wastes or riches of another. Like Bella, Wrayburn undergoes a personality change in the end, but this is only the final result of the ordeal his body endures after it has been beaten and drowned, and after this distended recovery where he resembles a corpse lacking speech. His body, like Esther Summerson's, is permanently mutilated by what has happened to it: "Sadly wan and worn was the once gallant Eugene, and walked resting on his wife's arm, and leaning heavily upon a stick. But, he was daily growing stronger and better, and it was declared by the medical attendants that he might not be much disfigured by-and-by" (883). While the disclaimer (like the one stating that true love can ignore Esther's scars in *Bleak House*) is recuperative, Eugene's body, salvaged from the river, is his old body; it bears the marks, as a figure for the body of the text, of what has passed; it is disfigured, though "not much," by symbolic orderings of plot.

Eugene's body is one of the tropes for the semiotic in *Our Mutual Friend,* one of the places where signification— here, the representation of corporeal identity—is "cut up." His voice is low and serious, robbed of its ironic gaiety, and now conveying the diminished presence of a sober,

fully-initiated Wrayburn; but his face, which impassively has stared down an enraged Headstone in an alley, is a kind of slate upon which is written the partially erased marks recalling the passionate violence he has suffered. Even his name suggests this paradox: "Eugene" comes from the Greek, meaning "well-born," but "Wrayburn" suggests one who has been scarred by the sun. Fathers, whether biological (Eugene refers to his father as M.R.F. or My Reverend Father) and authorial have not been kind to Eugene, and their distance from him is scored as an intimacy of relation in other ways, whether it is in M.R.F.'s attempt to control genealogy by dictating who his wife will be, or Dickens' need to mark Wrayburn, as he does Esther with the "summer son," with the signs of passage. Eugene eventually gets his way with his father, who will accept his marriage to Lizzie, a "will" which is part of the larger incorporation of his salvaged and renewed identity into the redemptive social scheme of the novel: he vows to Mortimer that he will work at his vocation and proudly parade Lizzie about town as his wife in defiance of the older, unregenerate, "Society" of the novel. In so doing, he has joined that smaller, utopian society which includes the Harmons, the Boffins, Lizzie, Sloppy, Jenny Wren, and by extension, Twemlow.

Eugene's identity has been formed and his "voice" socialized, but his body, like the other disarticulations and disfigurations of *Our Mutual Friend,* reminds us that the presence bearing the nominative language of the well-born has been preceded by *and is founded upon* separation, non-identity, the "sinking" of the speaking subject before it rises to speech and the whispered word that will convert the "other" (Lizzie) into an object ("wife"). Eugene's scars heal over what Kristeva calls "the scissions of matter" (160) that mark the return in language of what has been rejected, or re-thrown (like voice) by the subject in the process of transformation into an identity proper. What has been rejected in *Our Mutual Friend* may be viewed as the form of self-negation represented in the character of Headstone, Wrayburn's rival and double, whose erotic energies are translated into the suicidal impulses that result in his embracing of a muddy grave with Rogue Riderhood. Eugene's body registers this rejected negation, as surely as it retains it. Similarly, Jenny Wren's dolls stand in for that rejected part of her make-up, her befuddled father ("Mr. Dolls") and her own crippled body, which she would transcend: even as she speaks through her dolls, they act as displacements and retentions of her own dwarfish corporeality, as well as representing the "high lady" she is not.

This form of negation is pervasive, and it seems that the characters of the novel are either in the process of succumbing to it or "controlling" and displacing it through acts of impersonation and ventriloquy. Thus, Podsnap "negates" a daughter and, in so doing, represses the threat to his own identity as father and author of this child—a threat temporarily embodied in the ambivalent positions of other daughters-cum-mothers in the novel before they are reincorporated back into the masterful familial harmony of the plot. Thus, in "The Feast of the Three Hobgoblins," where

Mr. Wilfer is "revived" with the news that Bella and John are engaged, Bella is soon to engage in a series of "mysterious disappearances" as she is enfolded in Harmon's arms: "'Well,'" replied "the cherub" (Mr. Wilfer), "'when you—when you come back from retirement, my love, and reappear on the surface, I think it will be time to lock up and go'" (674). Here, Bella's identity—her *will,* which has been represented throughout the novel as motivated by greed—is doubly-sunk, almost as if to parody Eugene's "surfacing" from the Thames as an identity with a will at last. Before her father, who has, here, resumed his authoritative role (he will "lock up" shop at this point, his daughter now properly disposed of), Bella "sinks into" the breast of her husband, a "disappearing" which is the sign of romantic love and the final vanquishing of her old willful, acquisitive "self." These disappearances are the parodic echoes and final suppressions of the foundations of "identity" in *Our Mutual Friend* represented as, precisely, a negation ("sinking") which precedes its formation.

In a larger sense, corporeality, the visible sign of this negation, is what is "abjected" in the novel, to use the term Kristeva develops in *Power of Horror.* For Kristeva, the abject is everything that the body casts off from itself (excrement, filth, skin, food) in the continuous reformation of a "clean," "proper" identity; this process, and the abjected material itself, signifies a recollection of sorts: "Abjection preserves what existed in the archaism of pre-objectal relationship, in the immemorial violence with which a body becomes separated from another body in order to be" (10). That "other body" is, as I mentioned earlier, the maternal body, which for Kristeva is *not* the biological mother but the name for the subject *before* it becomes a subject—an authorized, singular, sexual and social being in submission to the paternal laws and orders of existence. So great is the fear wrought by the recognition that all of these orders rest on their own negation—for by definition, "order" is the maintenance of a hierarchy of differences, whether syntactic, sexual, or social—that all traces of the pre-subjectival "past," the heterogeneous "before" of identity's nonfiguration under the rules of signification, must be repressed, though these traces are retained in the semiotic representations of the body, politic and corporeal. What is "abjected" or thrown off, then, and what reappears piecemeal as the semiotic in *Our Mutual Friend* is the noise, subjective displacements, linguistic and bodily contaminations and disarticulations, excremental waste of the dust heaps and muddy flats of the river, drowned bodies and skeletons, and drowned out, disfigured voices that fill the novel. These signify the "horror" of the maternal body "viewed as an engendering, hollow and vaginated, expelling and rejected boy" (*Revolution,* 153). This cast-off body is a form of absence, but it is also the "place" where identity begins, just as echo, the repetition of sound, "begins" in a hollow. Physical and textual bodies, always on the verge of disarticulation and abjecting their "wastes" even as they retain traces of their origin, serve as commemorations of identity and its foundations in the absent maternal body—an "identity" which

voice and body make "present" in the form of a meditation between origins and ends.

Derrida suggests that speech is a kind of theft, an expulsion of breath and voice "spirited away" from the body that recalls to the "speaking subject . . . his irreducible secondarity, his origin that is . . . eluded; for the origin is always . . . eluded on the basis of an organized field of speech in which the speaking subject vainly seeks a place that is always missing" ("La parole soufflée" 175; 178). As I have been suggesting, Dickens constructs the "organized field of speech" in *Our Mutual Friend* nostalgically, through the concordances of plot and voices at the end of the novel, or parodically, through the "Voice of Society" heard in the conversations at Veneering's dinner table. But what "eludes" the organization of the novel, the semiotic element, remains as that which has been "thrown" or abjected. The anxiety aroused by the recognition of the abject which implicates the abysmal foundation of all signifying orders and proffers "the horror" of non-identity represented in Western culture as the maternal, the feminine, the contaminated, is to some extent "managed" in the novel by the appropriations of voice and plot, most often in those instances where daughters are spoken for by fathers and husbands. But the controlling act, as the figure of ventriloquy suggests, resurrects this *anagnorisis* even as it seeks to suppress it. The throwing of voice, Dickens' multiplication of identity into a heterogeneous assortment of "many voices," recalls the abject, that which escapes objectification, just as the recasting of Eugene's identity recalls, fadingly, his immersion into the maternal, excremental element of the river as the climactic event in the deadly rivalry with his brother/double, Headstone.

For the author who seeks to order the identities of his many characters into being, to give them inimitable forms of speech and personality, then to plot their destinies, such recognitions necessarily must be as disturbing as they are unavoidable. *Our Mutual Friend* is "about" this recognition and its discontents. Dickens' "intention" in this regard is a complicated matter, for on the one hand, as Lewes's testimony, the Postface, and the figure of ventriloquy all suggest, he viewed himself as "the inimitable" origin of all his characters and voices, and their savior. Identity, in this authorial view, is not a matter of social, historical, or biological relations, but a gift benevolently conferred by the maker of his stand-ins. Bella's sense that new identities (babies) come floating down the Thames when they will (like the corpses with which the novel beings its fluctuations), compounded with Eugene's death and rebirth by water, confirm the notion that the articulation of selfhood within this authorial vision is symbolic and transcendental. Finding one's true self in this equation would be equivalent to finding one's true voice (that is, the "one" which is determined to be true by the author): thus, Eugene whispers the magic word to Jenny ("Wife") that initiates recovery; Harmon and Boffin speak in their "own" sincere voices to Bella in the recognition scene, while Mrs. Boffin, silenced throughout the third and fourth books because her voice would give her away, can speak again at last. Accordingly, the novel, in its symbolic aspect, reflects a strong sense of identity as having its origins in a providential author; this symbolic order is sustained by the renewed society of the novel's ending, and by the laws of marriage and the redistribution of wealth—as Boffin "gives back" Harmon his own inheritance—amongst men.

On the other hand, countering this sense of authorship, is what must be seen as the novel's center of gravity: its disfigurations and multiple voices, its rhapsodies and hysterical outbursts, its labyrinths, doublings, and dead ends. Focusing as we have on the semiotic aspects of the novel, we can see a different version of authorship and identity emerging—one which Dickens "recognized" even as he suppressed it, and even then, ironically, if one regards the artificialities of closure in this novel as parodic. Here, Dickens countering "intention" may be seen as an irrepressible consciousness of the limitations of his power as an authorial identity who wholly originates and controls all that he has conjured up. For if, as the novel seems to tell us in so many ways, "identity" can be seen as a "voice" constituted by the fictions of law, genealogy, and paternal economy, but ever-recalling (abjecting) its "dissolute," maternal origins, then the identity of the author, brought under question as "the identity of identities," is subject to the same paradoxical definition. In this view, the author is the "origin" of the characters and voices he creates, but if that origin is *represented* in writing as a form of negation, then "who" is Charles Dickens, and what is his vocation? The intensity with which both questions about authorship and identity are implicitly asked in the novel suggests the modernity of Dickens' vision in which his own sense of identity is clearly conflicted and unresolved.

Perhaps Henry James was right, after all, that the author had been exhausted by his "labors" (the maternal body, again, resurfaces), but the exhaustion suggests less a lack of inspiration than a revelation that writing cannot fully contain or figure forth the authorial inspiration of character with life and speech. Notably, the attempts to "write down" identity in the novel are nearly always portrayed parodically, from Riderhood's swearing "himself" in the form of an "Alfred David," to Eugene's thought that he can "organize himself" with the purchase of a "secretary" containing a pigeon-hole for every letter of the alphabet, to Harmon's notion that he can hide his former self and be reborn in the form of a secretary who takes dictation from Boffin. The inscription of identity into nominative and narrative orders becomes, in these examples, a form of deciphering that simply repeats the arbitrary signs of the name imposed upon a body and the nominal subject. As an author who generates names and identities by the hundreds, Dickens both creates and loses his subject in this novel, which is the recovery and reformation of one's "own" identity. Like Shakespeare's "farewell to the stage," *Our Mutual Friend* might be seen as a work in which authorial identity is at stake—most crucially, in Dickens' case, in terms of its gender, as the authoring father recalls and "throws" off the non-identical origins of identity in the voices of his characters and the scenes of his spectacle. As in *The Tem-*

pest, the crisis of authority in *Our Mutual Friend* may be partially resolved by "magic," but it is hardly expunged by the resolution. And while, unlike Prospero, Dickens does not give up his art in this novel, he does discover that what founds the making of novels and the projection of voice into character is quite different from any version of intention or identity he could possibly authorize. In *Our Mutual Friend,* Dickens discovers that to throw one's voice is a kind of suicide—as Derrida suggests, a separation of the spirit from the body, and more specifically, an unsettling abnegation of the (male) authorial self. He finds that to be an author—a father of identities—is to confront the facelessness of one's own identity, or to face one's own "maternal" aspect, and to acknowledge identity's groundless origins even as writing it down marks its entrance into the world.

Notes

1. The discussion of self-construction and identity in Dickens' fiction has a long history, beginning with Miller's analysis in *Charles Dickens* where he develops the theme of identity as a representation of "intersubjectivity" always threatened by "bad communication"; in *The Form of Victorian Fiction,* Miller goes on to relate the "theme" of intersubjectivity to the form of the novel itself. My divergence from these early readings of Miller's resides in a more complex notion of the relation between "voice" and "subject." Useful thematic discussions of self-construction in *Our Mutual Friend* are offered by Stewart and Knopflemacher; more recently, compelling discussions of identity in Dickens besides Miller's are those of Weinstein and Welsh (*From Copyright to Copperfield*). Weinstein's readings of *David Copperfield* and *Little Dorrit* are concerned to establish the relation between character and desire as the psychological projection of identity against its social confinement; Welsh is concerned to thematize the relation between writing and identity. In contrast, my reading of *Our Mutual Friend* stresses "identity" as resulting from a semiotic process that is thoroughly "social" and that, in narrative terms, fractures the conventions of theme, character, and figure. My ideas about identity coincide to a large degree with those of van Boheemen, whose insightful work on genre, gender, and identity appeared as I was composing my own views of subjectivity in Dickens. In her Lacanian feminist analysis, van Boheemen writes that "[t]he novel as a family romance, reductively personifying the complexity of experience as the contrastive pair of father and mother, is both the intensified reflection of the implication of gender in signification and the prime object for studying its history and functioning, especially with regard to the constitution of the subject" (30). This succinct formulation leads van Boheemen to conclude that the "plot" of the novel is its exclusion of the "other," or mother, and it will be seen to what extent "she" is the *partially* excluded middle of *Our Mutual Friend,* or rather, how that exclusion can be characterized as

the unsuccessfully repressed partial object(s), of the maternal body. But in her reading of *Bleak House,* van Boheeman, in my view, totalizes this plot, thus re-repressing the semiotic element which I claim "survives" such totalization, as well as founding it: the story of the novel can be seen equally as a history of the semiotic rupturing of discourse and as a history of the patriarchal plot of "the family romance."

2. My use of the Bakhtinian vocabulary in this essay suggests the basis of my argument in his understanding of "heteroglossia" in the novel as induced by generic and historical circumstances; however, I also intend to modify the sense of "heteroglossia" by my reading of subjectivity in Dickens. See *The Dialogic Imagination,* 84-259, 262-63, for the development of this concept. Bakhtinian readings of *Our Mutual Friend* include Garrett (89-94), who is primarily concerned with the relation between form and rhetoric, and who unproblematically accepts Bakhtih's "totalization" of the novel, and Larson (281-312), who interestingly discusses the relation between verbal fragmentation, allusion, and indeterminacy in the novel but who still insists upon the sporadic orchestration of multiple voices in Dickens which serves, occasionally, to "stabilize" the discourse. Prow uses Bakhtin to discuss "register" in *Little Dorrit,* i.e., the presence of different ideologically grounded linguistic modes by which "the reality-effects and fiction-effects of the literary text are generated" (269).

3. The full title of George Smith's *Programme* is *Programme of the Entertainment: Preceded by Memoirs of Mr. Love, the Dramatic Polyphonist; Remarks on Single-Handed Entertainments, Anecdotes of Eminent By-Gone Professors; An Explanation of the Phenomena of Polyphony, & c.; Being Mr. Love's Improvement in Point of Distance, Power, Number of Voices, and Variety of Expression, on the Art of the Ventriloquist; in Which the Errors of Writers on the Subject, and the Impositions Practised on the Public by Pretended Teachers and Lecturers on the Talent, are Clearly Pointed Out.* Smith writes that Mr. Love "has been enabled to appear with almost uninterrupted success, for more than TWO THOUSAND NIGHTS in the metropolis; a circumstance entirely without parallel in the history of public amusements really, or professedly, sustained by individual talent" (29). The Pilgrim Edition of the *Letters of Charles Dickens* indicates a letter from Dickens of 10 March 1843 addressed to a Mr. Love: the letter itself, mentioned in the *Samuel T. Freeman & Co. Catalogue* of April, 1917 is not reprinted in the Pilgrim Edition (III, 461). The editors of the *Letters* note that Mr. Love is "unidentified"; the Mr. Love of George Smith's pamphlet had many London engagements in 1843, so it seems likely that Dickens wrote the ventriloquist, perhaps to express appreciation for one of his performances.

4. See Kaplan for a description of John Elliotson's Svengaliesque mesmerizing of the O'kee sisters during 1838: the sisters often passed into "a state of harmless but vocal delirium" under Elliotson's influence, or spoke in many tongues (41). Kapian meticulously details Dickens' longstanding involvement with Elliotson and the pseudoscience of mesmerism beginning in the late 1830s. Mamie Dickens' oft-noted description of her father acting out his characters before a mirror occurs in her *My Father As I Recall Him,* quoted in Page (144).

5. Lambert briefly discusses the practice of the "monopolylogue" in the Victorian popular arts which featured a single actor taking on several different roles (91). For Lambert, the "monopolylogist" can stand as a figure for Dickens' authorship, particularly in his early novels where, Lambert argues, he is particularly concerned to represent and impose his authorial singularity through his several characters. Quite problematically, in my view, Lambert declares that Dickens' later fiction (because it contains, statistically, fewer "suspended quotations") shows Dickens' waning anxiety concerning authorial control and self-reference in his mature work, particularly because he could gain the adulation and attention he sought in increasingly numerous public performances. Control and the maintenance of authorial identity, I will argue, remain problems for Dickens in *Our Mutual Friend,* and their figurations cannot be reduced merely to matters of syntax. Strictly speaking, however, Mr. Love is a "monopolylogist" or "polyphanist" rather than a ventriloquist proper, though the relations between the actor and the character he throws himself into, and the ventriloquist and his dummy, are clearly analogous "speech acts"; or, rather, the latter is a heightened parody of the former. Smith argues that any act of throwing one's voice, or casting oneself in the voice of another, is ventriloquistic, and distinct from acts of "imitation" or mimicry involving animal sounds, miming of idiolects, etc.

6. Interestingly, Smith insists that the "entertainment" of the good ventriloquist must be carefully constructed and written down. The "natural" imitator who fails to adhere to the discipline of the dramatic principles which arise when the act is "written down" and when its forms of delivery are prescribed will both bore the audience and antiquate himself: "The mere ventriloquist who appears before his auditors, without having previously provided himself with a set entertainment, or, having done so, without knowing how to deliver it, necessarily finds himself under the awkward necessity of uttering what comes uppermost in his mind, or nearly so; and is a character belonging to a by-gone age; one whose stock in trade bears about the same proportion to the effects belonging to a successful modern piece within this department, as the street fiddler to a Paganini, a street-post painter to a Landseer, the tragedian of the booth in a village fair, to an Edmund Kean, or a Macready; or the dismal lamps and ill-made ways of mud, char-

acteristic of olden time, to the brilliant lights and well-constructed iron-roads of the present day" (24). Thus, the sequence of "proper" impersonation for Smith would be, first, authoring the script, then, erasing the identity of the author/impersonator as the voice is "thrown" into another character or a dummy whose identity is, thereby, created in the act. Smith seems to have misunderstood the implications of his pedagogy here when, earlier in the tract, he scolds false ventriloquists for plagiarizing Mr. Love's material!

7. The most interesting explanations of closure in *Our Mutual Friend* are offered by Knopflemacher and Stewart, who argue for the work of the redemptive imagination in the novel's ending, by Hutter, who suggests the novel is balanced between fragmentation and threatening or beneficent forms of "articulation," and by Simpson and Arac, who suggest in quite different ways that the novel negotiates between the tropes of synecdoche and metaphor, with the novel's ending reinforcing metaphor as the figure of social or personal integration.

8. James further notes that in *Our Mutual Friend* Dickens falls to properly "represent" society: "What a World were this world if the world of *Our Mutual Friend* were an honest reflection of it! But a community of eccentrics is impossible. Rules alone are consistent with each other; exceptions are inconsistent. Society is maintained by a natural sense and natural feeling. We cannot conceive a society in which these principles are not in some manner represented" (471). Again, James seems to recognize that *Our Mutual Friend* works against "representation," but this is exactly the nature of the young novelist's complaint. Carroll's discussion of James is revealing in this regard: he describes the Jamesian conception of the subject as centered, framed, and thus represented by the artist (55), though he points out that the relation between the author and the subject or "central consciousness" is made especially problematic in the Prefaces.

9. See Derrida, *Speech and Phenomena* 48-59; 70-87 for the critique of the assumed, semiotic relation between "voice" and "presence." My discussion of voice in *Our Mutual Friend* is indebted to Derrida's understanding of the history of that relation.

10. In his reading of Dickens through Georges Bataille, Kucich describes as "excess" the particular forms of erotic energy which defy representation in language and which motor identity as a kind of negative transcendence. Kucich's work is illuminating in this regard, and my sense of "residue" bears some resemblance to his concept of "excess," but I part company with him when "excess" is coupled with a mystified sense of authorial self-abandonment, contrasted to evidences of Dickensian "self-restraint" in his closed forms and stylistic repressions. My understanding of the problematic of identity in *Our Mutual Friend* relies more upon conceiving identity as a construct of repetition founded upon the negation of its own origins and presencing in voice; it is acculturated and, as something represented in language (the discontents of this representation being part of the problematic), inescapable. See Kucich, *Excess and Restraint* and "Dickens and Fantastic Rhetoric."

11. Different views of "entanglement" as the substance of fiction are offered by Miller, *Fiction and Repetition*, and Brooks, who formulates a psychoanalytic view of repetition and complexity in narrative as forestallments of the "death" or end of the text. Luckacher reads the "no thoroughfares" of *Our Mutual Friend* as blockages by which Dickens both remembers and represses the "primal scene" which lies at the source of his fiction.

12. The biographical details of the Staplehurst railway accident and Dickens' heroic efforts there can be found in Johnson, 1018-21.

13. See Lévi-Strauss, 75-108; see also Rubin for commentary on the contents of Lévi-Strauss's structural anthropology and "the traffic in women."

14. See Kosofsky Sedgwick and Sadoff for divergent views of sexual and familial relations in *Our Mutual Friend*. Zwinger offers the most illuminating discussion I know of father-daughter relations in Dickens' fiction.

15. Welsh (*City*) comments at length on the possible connections between "Dickens" and Providence.

16. In addition to Kristeva, I am indebted to Cameron and Scarry for my understanding of "corporeality" in Dickens.

Works Cited

Arac, Jonathan. *Commissioned Spirits: The Shaping of Social Motion in Dickens, Carlyle, Melville, and Hawthorne.* New Brunswick: Rutgers UP, 1979.

Bakhtin, M. H. *The Dialogic Imagination: Four Essays.* Ed. Michael Holquist. Trans. Caryl Emerson and Michael Holquist. Austin: U of Texas P, 1981.

Beaujour, Michael. "Phonograms and Delivery: The Poetics of Voice," in *Notebooks for Cultural Analysis, Vol. 3: 'Voice'*. Ed. Norman F. Cantor and Nathalia King. Durham: Duke UP, 1986: 266-79.

Brooks, Peter. "Freud's Masterplot: Questions of Narrative." *Yale French Studies,* 55/56 (1977): 280-300.

Cameron, Sharon. *The Corporeal Self: Allegories of the Body in Melville and Hawthorne.* Baltimore: Johns Hopkins UP, 1981.

Carroll, David. *The Subject in Question: The Languages of Theory and the Strategies of Fiction.* Chicago: U of Chicago P, 1982.

Derrida, Jacques. "La parole soufflée." In *Writing and Difference*. Trans. Alan Bass. Chicago: U of Chicago P, 1978: 169-95.

————. *Speech and Phenomena and Other Essays on Husserl's Theory of Signs*. Trans. David B. Allison. Evanston: Northwestern UP, 1973.

Dickens, Charles. The Pilgrim Edition of *The Letters of Charles Dickens, Volume III: 1842-43*. Ed. Madeline House, Graham Storey, and Kathleen Tillotson. Oxford: Clarendon, 1974.

————. *Little Dorrit,*. 1857. Rpt. New York: Penguin, 1967.

————. *Our Mutual Friend*. 1865. Rpt. New York: Penguin, 1971.

Frow, John. "Voice and Register in *Little Dorrit*." *Comparative Literature*, 33 (1981): 258-70.

Garrett, Peter K. *The Victorian Multiplot Novel: Studies in Dialogical Form*. New Haven: Yale UP, 1980.

Henkle, Roger B. *Comedy and Culture: England 1820-1900*. Princeton: Princeton UP, 1980.

Hollander, John. *The Figure of Echo: A Mode of Allusion in Milton and After*. Berkeley: U of California P, 1981.

Hutter, Albert D. "Dismemberment and Articulation in *Our Mutual Friend*." *Dickens Studies Annual*, 11 (1983): 135-75.

James, Henry. "Review" of *Our Mutual Friend*. *The Nation*, 21 December 1865. Rpt. *Dickens: The Critical Heritage*. Ed. Philip Collins. New York: Barnes & Noble, 1971.

Edgar Johnson. *Charles Dickens: His Tragedy and Triumph*. New York: Simon and Schuster, 1952.

Kaplan, Fred. *Dickens and Mesmerism: The Hidden Springs of Fiction*. Princeton: Princeton UP, 1975.

Knoepflmacher, U. C. *Laughter and Despair: Readings in Ten Novels of the Victorian Era*. Berkeley: U of California P, 1971.

Kristeva, Julia. *Powers of Horror: An Essay on Abjection*. Trans. Leon S. Roudiez. New York: Columbia UP, 1981.

————. *Revolution in Poetic Language*. Trans. Margaret Waller. New York: Columbia UP, 1984.

Kucich, John. "Dickens' Fantastic Rhetoric: The Semiotics of Reality and Unreality in *Our Mutual Friend*." *Dickens Studies Annual*, 14 (1985): 167-89.

————. *Excess and Restraint in the Novels of Charles Dickens*. Athens: U of Georgia P, 1981.

Lambert, Mark. *Dickens and the Suspended Quotation*. New Haven: Yale UP, 1981.

Larson, Janet L. *Dickens and the Broken Scripture*. Athens: U of Georgia P, 1985.

Lévi Strauss, Claude. *The Savage Mind*. Chicago: U of Chicago P, 1966.

Lewes, George Henry. "Dickens in Relation to Criticism," in *Literary Criticism of George Henry Lewes*. Ed. Alice Kaminsky. Lincoln: U of Nebraska P, 1964: 94-105.

Lukacher, Ned. *Primal Scenes: Literature, Philosophy, Psychoanalysis*. Ithaca: Cornell UP, 1986.

Miller, J. Hillis. *Charles Dickens: The World of His Novels*. Cambridge: Harvard UP, 1958.

————. *Fiction and Repetition: Seven English Novels*. Cambridge: Harvard UP, 1982.

————. *The Form of Victorian Fiction*. Notre Dame: U of Notre Dame P, 1968.

Page, Norman. *Speech in the English Novel*. London: Longmans, 1973.

Rubin, Gayle. "The Traffic in Women," in *Toward an Anthropology of Women*. Ed. Rayna R. Roiter. New York: Monthly Review P, 1975: 157-210.

Sadoff, Diane. *Monsters of Affection: Dickens, Eliot, and Brontë on Fatherhood*. Baltimore: Johns Hopkins UP, 1982.

Scarry, Elaine. *The Body in Pain: The Making and Unmaking of the World*. New York: Oxford UP, 1985.

Sedgwick, Eve Kosofsky. "Homophobia, Misogyny, and Capital: The Example of *Our Mutual Friend*." *Raritan*, 2 (1983); 126-51.

Serres, Michel. *The Parasite*. Trans. Lawrence R. Schehr. Baltimore: Johns Hopkins UP, 1982.

Smith, George. *Programme of the Entertainment: Preceded by Memoirs of Mr. Love, the Dramatic Polyphonist*. London: W. Kenneth, 1856.

Stewart, Garrett. *Dickens and the Trials of the Imagination*. Cambridge: Harvard UP, 1974.

van Boheeman, Christine. *The Novel as Family Romance: Language, Gender, and Authority from Fielding to Joyce*. Ithaca: Cornell UP, 1987.

Weinstein, Phillip. *The Semantics of Desire: Changing Models of Identity from Dickens to Joyce*. Princeton: Princeton UP, 1984.

Welsh, Alexander. *The City of Dickens*. New York: Oxford UP, 1971.

————. *From Copyright to Copperfield: The Identity of Dickens*. Cambridge: Harvard UP, 1987.

Wilden, Anthony. *System and Structure: Essays on Communication and Exchange*. 2nd Ed. London: Tavistock, 1980.

Zwinger, Lynda. "The Fear of the Father: Dombey and Daughter." *Nineteenth Century Fiction*, 30 (1985): 420-40.

Michael Greenstein (essay date 1991)

SOURCE: "Mutuality in *Our Mutual Friend*," in *Dickens Quarterly*, Vol. 8, No. 3, September, 1991, pp. 127-34

[*In the following essay, Greenstein examines the many unifying themes and motifs highlighting mutuality in* Our Mutual Friend.]

J. Hillis Miller has argued that the milieus of *Our Mutual Friend* exist side by side without organizing themselves into a larger whole: the novel's "structure is formed by the juxtaposition of incompatible fragments in a pattern of disharmony or mutual contradiction" (Miller, 284). While most critics have accepted Miller's view, others like Masao Miyoshi have contested it in favor of a resolution of identity where "the two marriages are the inevitable outcome of the characters' final reconciliation of their own warring selves" (Miyoshi, 8). The pendulum swings again in John Kucich's analysis of Dickens's fantastic rhetoric: "it becomes impossible to say in any single way what Dickens means by concluding *Our Mutual Friend* in the way he does. . . . We are left instead with a feeling of excessive, non-economic resolution, without that resolution being fully named" (Kucich, 184). While the issue of "mutuality" is central to Dickens's last complete novel, its meaning is highly ambiguous; like the coins tested by dredgers along the Thames, the concept of mutuality must be examined from its opposite sides.

The clichéd title of Dickens's penultimate novel underscores the author's need to rejuvenate his language and imagination, a symptom first identified by Henry James. From the first-person plural pronoun to the adjective and noun in the title, the phrase itself contains a certain redundancy, and it is this excessive mutuality that pervades the novel. Structurally the four books' unity reinforces the theme of reciprocal relationship found in plot, character, setting, and imagery. If the first proverb—"There is many a slip between the cup and the lip"—suggests a gap in an otherwise metonymic relationship of conviviality between object and person, the second proverb—"Birds of a feather flock together"—restores a semblance of mutuality through another cliché. Books three and four share a proverb—"It is a long lane that has no turning"—while the final book "A Turning" reveals another aspect of mutuality, namely mutation, transmutation, or mutability—the various turnings within the novel.

Just as the books' titles hint at mutuality, so do many of the titles of chapters. "The Man from Somewhere" and "Another Man," "Mr. Boffin in Consultation" and "Mr. and Mrs. Boffin in Consultation," and "Tracking the Bird of Prey" and "The Bird of Prey Brought Down" overlap, while "A Marriage Contract," "Two New Servants," and "Minders and Re-Minders" reinforce a dialogic structure. This kind of balance runs through every part of *Our Mutual Friend.* As Boffin says to the Lammles at the conclusion of a matter of business: "'it's a very good thing to think well of another person, and it's a very good thing to be thought well of *by* another person'" (716; bk. 4, ch. 2).

"On the Look Out" introduces the importance of visual perspective while the working plans—"Open between the bridges"—result in the first paragraph's "between Southwark Bridge which is of iron, and London Bridge which is of stone" (43; bk. 1, ch. 1). Marcus Stone's cover of the monthly parts of *Our Mutual Friend* depicts one of these arched bridges at the top, for if the Thames serves as a central symbol, then bridges serve to span the banks in a kind of topographic mutuality. Twilight adds to this Turneresque atmosphere of "in betweenness" framed by two bridges and two river banks, while the murky depths create a third dimension: "Allied to the bottom of the river rather than the surface." Dickens pursues this alliance between depths and surfaces in the rest of the novel.

Mutuality first appears in the exchanged gazing of Gaffer and Lizzie Hexam, father and daughter, but the appearance of Rogue Riderhood disturbs this relationship to be replaced by another claim—the claim of partnership. Riderhood repeatedly addresses Hexam with a possessive "pardner" but Hexam refuses to be in league with him. "'I have been swallowing too much of that word, pardner. I am no pardner of yours'" (47; bk. 1, ch. 1). Neither partner not pardoner, Hexam rejects Rogue for having robbed from the living while he justifies his own actions of robbing from the dead who belong to another world. Gaffer's "high morality" distinguishes between the living and the dead, while his chinking of a coin and Riderhood's robbing prepare for various forms of capitalist exchange or mercenary mutuality in the rest of the novel. The final paragraph of the first chapter picks up Dickens's plan of "Taking the body in <tow> tow"—a typographical linkage that accords well with Gaffer's name (Cotsell, 19).

"Gaffer was no neophyte and had no fancies." These concluding words in the first chapter prepare for the Veneering neophyte in Chapter 2 and contrast with Lizzie who reads fancies in the fire. Where Hexam's boat is allied to the slime and ooze of the river's bottom, the Veneerings' "surface smelt a little too much of the workshop and was a trifle stickey" (48; bk. 1, ch. 2). What should be noted in this world of Veneerings, aside from superficiality and brand-newness, is the function of wood from table to Twemlow. Dickens insists on the metonymic relationship or mutuality between Twemlow and table, with the addition of leaves from trees to pages of writing. The addition or subtraction of leaves is not the source of Twemlow's confusion; rather, the abyss to which he can find no bottom is the insoluble question as to whether he is Veneering's oldest or newest friend. The bond of union proves hollow without any established order, but this transfer between furniture and personality reappears when Boffin confuses Rokesmith's meaning of "secretary."

Any recurrent image, such as birds of prey, river, or dust, unifies the novel and reinforces the theme of mutuality. Wood imagery serves the same function. Gaffer's shining eyes dart out a hungry look at "floating logs of timber lashed together" (44; bk. 1, ch. 1). Not only Hexam's visual apparatus assimilates the wooden world, but the rest of him relies on it also as he explains to Lizzie: "'The very fire that warmed you when you were a babby, was picked out of the river alongside the coal barges. The very basket that you slept in, the tide washed ashore. The very rockers that I put it upon to make a cradle of it, I cut out of a piece of wood that drifted from some ship or another'" (45-6; bk. 1, ch. 1). From cradle to coffin, wood floats on the Thames and may come ashore as dust: "Coal-dust . . . bone-dust . . . rough dust and sifted dust,—all manner of Dust" (56; bk. 1, ch. 2). This oxymoronic quality of wood participating in life and death appears in the name of Mortimer Lightwood who floats while Bradley Headstone is weighted down, or in the proximity of Boffin's Bower and Harmon's Heap. Like floating wood riding the tides, the story of the Harmon Murder "went up and down, and ebbed and flowed, . . . until at last, after a long interval of slack water it got out to sea and drifted away" (74; bk. 1, ch. 3).

Silas Wegg, "a man with a wooden leg," introduces "Boffin's Bower": "All weathers saw the man at the post. This is to be accepted in a double sense" (87; bk. 1, ch. 5), for mutual relationships in Dickens always carry a double sense. Wegg "was so wooden a man that he seemed to have taken his wooden leg naturally, and rather suggested to the fanciful observer, that he might be expected . . . to be completely set up with a pair of wooden legs in about six months" (89; bk. 1, ch. 5). The fanciful observer notes that two wooden legs do appear in the person of Gruff and Glum, an old pensioner who witnesses the marriage between Bella and Rokesmith. Gruff and Glum's "timber toes" (731; bk. 4, ch. 4) are therefore related to Wegg's "timber fiction" (357; bk. 2, ch. 7) in a double sense of mutuality. Even Rokesmith, like Wegg, is a "haunting Secretary, stump-stump-stumping overhead in the dark" (257; bk. 1, ch. 17), while Wrayburn displays his "secrétaire" and "abstruse set of solid mahogany pigeon-holes" (337; bk. 2, ch. 6).

With its double sense of "board" *Our Mutual Friend* is a timber fiction. Hexam's house resembles a mill with its rotten wart of wood upon its forehead, its wooden bunk and wooden stair or ladder. Lizzie, who finds refuge in another mill where paper is made (the stuff of timber fiction), reads pictures in the fire to her brother: "'That's gas, that is . . . coming out of a bit of forest that's been under the mud that was under the water in the days of Noah's Ark'" (71; bk. 1, ch. 3). To unearth that first wooden vessel is to invoke mutuality within an archetype where pairs are saved. Lizzie's fanciful energy allied with the fire contrasts with Wrayburn's indolence and abomination of the word, Energy. Indeed, until the establishment of mutuality in marriage Eugene cannot live up to his name: Lizzie transfers her energy so that the ray will henceforth burn.

The Six Jolly Fellowship Porters with its lopsided wooden jumble of corpulent windows is, as its name implies, a haven of mutuality. "The wood . . . seemed in its old age fraught with confused memories of its youth. In many places it had become gnarled and riven, according to the manner of old trees; knots started out of it; and here and there it seemed to twist itself into some likeness of boughs. In this state of second childhood, it had an air of being in its own way garrulous about its early life" (105; bk. 1, ch. 6). Dickensian personification lends mutual friendship to this eccentric tavern whose history comments on the quest of characters and author for a reconsidered childhood. In this family tree of mutuality "you might trace little forests there, and tiny trees like the parent tree, in full umbrageous leaf" (105; bk. 1, ch. 6). The wood bears witness to all the reversed relationships between parents and children seeking their second childhoods. A half-door and a glass partition form the particular locus of exchange in the Six Jolly Fellowship Porters where Identification is finally confirmed.

J. Hillis Miller draws attention to the intermediate zone between Mr. and Mrs. Boffin as an example of the separate spheres of individual characters, but this "region of sand and sawdust" is arranged by "mutual consent" between the Boffins (100; bk. 1, ch. 5). When intermediate zones of sand and sawdust go outdoors, they assume a universal status: "The grating wind sawed rather than blew; and as it sawed, the sawdust whirled about the sawpit. Every street was a sawpit, and there were no top-sawyers; every passenger was an under-sawyer, with the sawdust blinding him and choking him" (191; bk. 1, ch. 12). And when Harmon is drugged and beaten, he "thought of the wood-cutter and his axe, and had some dead idea" (426; bk. 2, ch. 13) that he was lying in a forest. The Harmon Murder does indeed form part of Dickens's timber fiction.

Many of the characters in the novel rely on sticks of one kind or another. Sloppy offers to turn a rare handle for Jenny Wren's crutch-stick (882; bk. 4, ch. 16), Eugene Wrayburn leans heavily upon a stick after being felled by a broken oar, in a comic retribution Lammle beats Fledgeby with three pieces of stick, the Hexams depend on sculls and rudder, Riderhood sits on the blunt wooden levers of his lock-gates. When he first meets Wegg, Boffin carries a knotted stick as if it were a baby that he hugs. In their exchange concerning education and money—two forms of mutuality—Boffin taps Wegg on the breast with the head of his thick stick.

Another sense of "stick" incorporates mutuality. Jenny questions Fledgeby about his interceding: "'Sticking to him is the word'" (784; bk. 4, ch. 8). In contrast to this parasitic form of mutuality, a symbiotic relationship develops in Mrs. Boffin's telling Bella the "story": "'stick to me'" (842; bk. 4, ch. 13) she repeats during the laying on of hands with her husband, John, and Bella. Described as a pile and a heap, this laying on of hands displaces the earlier mounds, and the denouement of mutuality proceeds apace until Mortimer and Twemlow shake hands at the very end of the novel. Where Sloppy gives Jenny both of his hands, Bradley grabs Riderhood with his "iron ring, and the rivets of the iron ring held tight" (874; bk. 4, ch. 15).

Commerce is another form of mutuality in *Our Mutual Friend* from the drug-house of Chicksey, Veneering, and Stobbles to Wegg's stock in trade at "Our House" near Cavendish Square to traffic in Shares (159; bk. 1, ch. 10). Eugene Wrayburn relates his business experience to Jenny: "'Much as people's breaking promises and contracts and bargains of all sorts makes good for *my* trade'" (289; bk.

2, ch. 2). Such may be the case for Fledgeby's transactions "in the merry greenwood of Jobbery Forest, lying on the outskirts of the Share-Market and the Stock Exchange" (324; bk. 2, ch. 5). Dickens exposes the false mutuality of shares and exchanges in market capitalism and in the counting-house of Pubsey and Co. Rogue Riderhood's Limehouse Hole doubles as a Leaving Shop (pawning mutuality) and a Boarding-House, and to reinforce this doubling, the narrator puns on the function of synedoche: "A part of the Hole, indeed, contained so much public spirit and private virtue that not even this strong leverage could move it to good fellowship with a tainted accuser" (406; bk. 2, ch. 12). In these surroundings Pleasant Riderhood discourses on fair trade, but her father, another bird of prey, considers her habit of speaking to be nothing more than "Poll Parroting." Just as Fledgeby's visual habits at the counting-house are duplicitous—"with his small eyes just peering over the top of Pubsey and Co.'s blind. As a blind in more senses than one" (628; bk. 3, ch. 13)—so activity at Limehouse Hole proceeds in a double sense of sinister mutuality: "these creature discomforts serving as a blind to the main business of the Leaving Shop—was displayed the inscription SEAMAN'S BOARDING-HOUSE" (408; bk. 2, ch. 12). These places of business contrast with Rumty's Perch at the counting-house of Chicksey, Veneering, and Stobbles in Mincing Lane.

Venus comments on the nature of commerce with respect to the dust heaps when he questions being "'called upon to exchange my human warious for mere coal-ashes warious, and nothing comes of it'" (539; bk. 3, ch. 6). The double exchange hinges on the phonetic shift from "v" to "w" (double "u") indicating that Venus is indeed wary of these changes. (In a similar light, villainy is seen as Weggery.) Like rogue Riderhood who insists on "pardnership," villainous Wegg tries to establish the strongest bonds with Venus: "brother in arms" (another pun), "harmonizer" (in Harmony's Jail), "comrade," "fellow-man," and "partner in a friendly move" are his terms of mutuality. Mixing drinks and pipes, Wegg tells Venus that "'there's no gold without its alloy'" and exclaims, "'Twin in opinion equally with feeling! Mix a little more!'" Wegg offers his opinion of Rokesmith: "'A double look, you mean, sir,' rejoins Wegg, playing bitterly upon the word. 'That's *his* look. Any amount of singular look for me, but not a double look!'" (360; bk. 2, ch. 7). For one who never bargains, Wegg accepts Boffin's offer at double the money since his poetic licence allows him the linguistic freedom of *doubles entendres*.

Dredging, dust-heaps, counting-houses, and leaving-houses provide a commentary on commercial mutuality. Education in **Our Mutual Friend** reveals another form of exchange. Twemlow still needs to be educated for he never comes to any conclusion. Charley Hexam, a mixture of uncompleted savagery and uncompleted civilization, glances at the backs of books with an awakened curiosity that goes below the binding. "No one who can read, ever looks at a book, even unopened on a shelf, like one who cannot" (61; bk. 1, ch. 3). Dickensian self-reflexiveness

focuses on his characters' literacy. Indeed, pens mark the educational process throughout the novel. Young Blight, Lightwood's clerk, takes up a pen, sucks it, dips it, and runs over previous alphabetical entries before actually writing. The narrator describes Blight's activity of ringing alphabetical changes as "fiction," while an illiterate Boffin studies Lightwood's office in mutual admiration. "Then Mr. Boffin, with his stick at his ear, like a Familiar Spirit explaining the office to him, sat staring at a little bookcase of Law Practice and Law Reports, and at a window, and at an empty blue bag, and at a stick of sealing-wax, and a pen, and a box of wafers, and an apple, and a writing-pad—all very dusty—and at a number of inky smears and blots . . . and at an iron box labelled HARMON ESTATE" (132; bk. 1, ch. 8). Like the narrator, the personified stick whispers in Boffin's ear what has been denied to his eyes. Dust covers everything from a stick of sealing-wax to a stick near ear wax, from a pen to inky smears that mystify the relationship between words and their referents. Education should demystify the mutuality between signifiers and their signified, but higher mysteries often elude even the most literate.

Pen and ink integrate education and the process of writing. In Boffin's case ink is a cheap article that goes far without inscribing a line on the paper before him. Sloppy reads well but Betty Higden does not, the Hexam children strive for education in opposition to their father. Mutuality carried to an extreme, as in the case of Hexam's Preparatory School, becomes "Jumble," an educational system gone awry. Yet Miss Peecher tries to unscramble this jumble for her star pupil Mary Anne in a grammar lesson on the difference between "he says" and "they say." The phrasing concerns Miss Peecher's rival, Lizzie Hexam, and the grammar lesson tries to sort out the relationship between language and mutual feelings. On Miss Peecher's confidential slate and sympathetic paper, she inscribes in invisible ink B's and H's for Bradley Headstone. In "Still Educational," Jenny Wren, manufacturer of pen-wipers, instructs Eugene Wrayburn on the industrious use of pen-wipers for mending his legal trade of broken contracts. And Eugene shows Mortimer his secrétaire with its solid mahogany pigeon-holes, one for every letter of the alphabet, if not for flocking together every bird of prey. Eugene tells Mortimer to "'Observe the dyer's hand, assimilating itself to what it works in'" (604; bk. 3, ch. 1), for like the dyer's the writer's inky hand assimilates its material for fiction. Before beginning her "curtained lecture" to her husband, Bella finishes a letter to Lizzie, wipes her pen and middle finger, and comments that believing is "'like verbs in an exercise'" (755; bk. 4, ch. 5). When Riderhood shows up at Headstone's school, the Jumble organizes itself on the blackboard and in the pupils' "shrill chorus" in preparation for the concluding "Voice of Society" and in response to "A Social Chorus" at the end of Book III.

In the case of Bradley Headstone, mutual friendship is denied from both a pedagogical and matrimonial perspective. Like Old Harmon, the teacher leads a solitary life. The origin of the oxymoronic Harmony Jail explains Dickens's stance with regard to mutuality. It was a jail because of Harmon's solitary confinement, but "Harmony" is more circuitous: "'On accounts of his never agreeing with nobody. Like a speeches of chaff. Harmon's Jail; Harmony Jail. Working it round like'" (98; bk. 1, ch. 5). The cicerone to Boffin's Bower (a hoarse gentleman with his donkey Edward) provides a clue to Dickens's imagination which works around language and ideas, playing with species and speeches. The speciousness and solecism of the guide's double negatives, and the discarding of chaff to dust heaps eventually lead to harmony. Wegg's comic introduction to Boffin's Bower may be contrasted with the "boofer" lady's departure from Boffin. She closes the door of her own room, peeps in at Rokesmith's door, and "Softly opening the great hall door, and softly closing it upon herself, she turned and kissed it on the outside— insensible old combination of wood and iron that it was!" (666; bk. 3, ch. 17). This combination of wood and iron and the numerous thresholds in the novel highlight the mutuality of *Our Mutual Friend.*

Certainly Bella's departure from Boffin's grand abode exemplifies Bakhtin's chronotope of the threshold: highly charged with emotion and value, "it can be combined with the motif of encounter, but its most fundamental instance is as the chronotope of *crisis* and *break* in a life" (Bakhtin 248). Certainly Dickens's dialogic imagination focuses on these thresholds not only as loci of rupture, but as meeting-places of mutuality and turning-points of metamorphosis. Eugene watches his pursuers from his window, business and fellowship transpire at the half-door of Miss Abbey's bar, the board across Betty Higden's doorway acts as a trap, Jenny Wren reciprocates through keyholes, the gate at Boffin's Bower figures prominently, Pleasant Riderhood winds her hair at the threshold of her boarding-leaving-house. Riah, the perpetual outsider, sits down on Fledge-by's threshold: "It was characteristic of his habitual submission, that he sat down on the raw dark staircase, as many of his ancestors had probably sat down in dungeons, taking what befell him as it might befall" (480; bk. 3, ch. 1). Riah eventually reaches a conclusion about individual and collective identity, the mutuality between himself and all Jews.

One of Jenny Wren's rhymes aptly summarizes mutuality:

> You one two three,
> My com-pa-nie,
> And don't mind me.

> (275; bk. 2, ch. 1)

And Mrs. Lammle comments to Twemlow "'how like men are to one another in some things, though their characters are as different as can be'" (688; bk. 3, ch. 17). Like his dolls' dressmaker, Dickens mentally cuts out characters and bastes them mutually from surfaces to depths. Returning from her father's funeral, Jenny creates a doll clergyman, not for purposes of mourning, but to unite two of her friends in matrimony. These well-wrought transformations of matrimony and harmony make up *Our Mutual Friend.*

Works Cited

Bakhtin, M. M. *The Dialogic Imagination: Four Essays.* Trans. Caryl Emerson and Michael Holquist. Austin: U. of Texas, 1981.

Cotsell, Michael. *The Companion to Our Mutual Friend.* London: Allen & Unwin, 1986.

Dickens, Charles. *Our Mutual Friend.* Harmondsworth: Penguin, 1985.

Kucich, John. "Dickens' Fantastic Rhetoric: The Semantics of Reality and Unreality in *Our Mutual Friend,*" *Dickens Studies Annual* 14 (1985): 167-89.

Miller, J. Hillis. *Charles Dickens: The World of His Novels.* Bloomington: Indiana UP, 1969.

Miyoshi, Masao. "Resolution of Identity in *Our Mutual Friend.*" *Victorian Newsletter* 26 (1964): 5-9.

Howard W. Fulweiler (essay date 1994)

SOURCE:: "'A Dismal Swamp': Darwin, Design, and Evolution in *Our Mutual Friend,*" in *Nineteenth-Century Literature,* Vol. 49, No. 1, June, 1994, pp. 51-74.

[*In the following essay, Fulweiler explores the connections between Darwin's theories and Dickens's fiction, particularly* Our Mutual Friend; *both offer worlds of interconnected individuals competing for advantage with no hint of a transcendental master plan for the world.*]

> Let it be borne in mind how infinitely complex and close-fitting are the mutual relations of all organic beings to each other and to their physical conditions of life.

> *The Origin of Species*

A fresh reading of Darwin's *The Origin of Species* (1859) reveals once more the Victorian gentleman-scientist's comprehensive vision of the mutual relationship of organic beings to each other and to their environment. One sees not only Darwin's recognition of the connectedness of things but also his delight in this aspect of the natural world. J. W. Burrow remarks that "this enthusiasm, an almost childlike sense of wonder at the amazing contrivances and interrelations of the natural world . . . is one of the charms of *The Origin* and is a feature of it which is unduly neglected by the many who have found in it merely a brutally materialistic account of a bleak and soulless nature."[1]

Despite Darwin's pleasure in nature, "the many" who have been dismayed at his "materialistic account of a bleak and soulless nature" have had reason for their alarm. For Darwin, of course, there was no intelligent master plan for the natural world, but only a blind struggle for existence. Evolution itself had no goal; it was the result of chance variations coupled with wholesale extinctions. The Darwinian account is an intricate pattern of mutual relationships conducted in a chaotic environment by individuals seeking their own advantage and acting without either a superintending intelligence or a common end.

It is an interesting circumstance that Dickens's last completed novel, *Our Mutual Friend* (1865), published just six years after *The Origin,* closely follows this Darwinian pattern. As its title hints, the novel is an account of the mutual—though hidden—relations between its characters. As usual, Dickens shows his enthusiasm and wonder at the "amazing contrivances and interrelations" of his characters, but offers nonetheless a fictional world of individuals fiercely seeking their own advantage, under the shadow of death and with no sense of transcendent meaning—a "dismal swamp" of "crawling, creeping, fluttering, and buzzing creatures," as Dickens puts it at the beginning of chapter 17.[2]

The relationship between the two works is not one of chance. *Our Mutual Friend* is the last of a series of Dickensian attacks on mid-Victorian political economy and its laissez-faire foundation. Such works as *Oliver Twist, Dombey and Son, Hard Times, Little Dorrit,* and even *A Christmas Carol* are memorable examples of this series. That Dickens should introduce Darwinian thought into his fictional critique after 1859 seems surprising in the light of the laissez-faire origin of *The Origin.* The distinguished biologist Stephen Jay Gould has attributed Darwin's fundamental ideas to late-eighteenth- and early-nineteenth-century capitalist theory as follows:

> First, Darwin argues that evolution has no purpose. Individuals struggle to increase the representation of their genes in future generations, and that is all. If the world displays any harmony and order, it arises only as an incidental result of individuals seeking their own advantage—the economy of Adam Smith transferred to nature.[3]

Smith's "invisible hand" is the economic equivalent of natural selection. In their important recent biography of Darwin, Adrian Desmond and James Moore insist that "Darwin's new way of viewing nature" was very much in sympathy with "the competitive, capitalist, Malthusian dynamics of a poor-law society."[4] Darwin was a convinced Whig "in an age when the Whig government was building the workhouses and the poor were burning them down". Personally Darwin was connected to Malthus through his Wedgwood relatives and to the new political economy through the formidable Harriet Martineau, his brother's intimate friend. Desmond and Moore assert flatly that Darwin's "notebooks make plain that competition, free trade, imperialism, racial extermination, and sexual inequality were written into the equation from the start".

Despite all this, Dickens, the implacable enemy of political economy, had in his library copies of *The Origin* and of Lyell's *Principles of Geology* (1830-33). Peter Ackroyd observes that as some have "suggested that Darwin's own scientific narratives owe much to his reading of Dickens's novels," so "Dickens's own understanding of the symbolic forces of the world is charged with the same group of perceptions defined by contemporary scientists and geologists."[5] Other recent writers on the relation of Victorian fiction to Victorian science have noted mutual influence between Dickens and science. George Levine, in his discussion of Dickens's use of science in *Bleak House* (1852-53), points out how geology forms "part of Dickens's materials for imagining the world."[6] On the other hand, Gillian Beer remarks that "the organisation of *The Origin of Species* seems to owe a good deal to the example of one of Darwin's most frequently read authors, Charles Dickens."[7]

The connection between Dickens and Darwin was not simply one of analogy, however, or "something in the air," but was in fact quite direct. Not only was there a general climate of interest in natural philosophy at mid-century, but this general interest was specifically reflected in Dickens's own periodical, *All the Year Round.* Not only did nonscientific articles find their way into *Our Mutual Friend*—e.g., "The Schoolmaster All Abroad," detailing the pedantry of contemporary schoolmasters, and "The Good Caliph of Baghdad," a feature story on a doll's wardrobe shop[8]—but there were a large number of articles on scientific topics. A review of *The Origin* itself appeared in *All the Year Round* in July 1860. The reviewer remarked on Darwin's speculation that natural selection might give grouse colors to help them against "birds of prey," anticipating in this phrase the controlling metaphor of the opening chapter of *Our Mutual Friend.* He recognized immediately the laissez-faire implications of the struggle for life: "It is Malthus's doctrine applied to the whole animal and vegetable kingdoms, with increased force."[9]

In 1861 an article appeared on "Transmutation of Species," which discussed De Maillet, Lamarck, Chambers, Darwin, and Owen.[10] In 1859 "Mac," an article on a rag and bottle merchant, seems to anticipate the miserly dustman, old John Harmon, as a Darwinian philosopher: "A sombre genius was that which said to its angry stomach, 'Lay out the dead and eat!'" The writer tells us of old Mac, who boiled down dead horses for their grease in his junkyard and remarked that "life was all a chance—it must go as it growed."[11] The feature writer is sure that, despite appearances, old Mac (in analogy to both old Harmon and Noddy Boffin) is not poor.

In 1863 appeared a review of Lyell's *The Geological Evidences of the Antiquity of Man.* The reviewer focuses on the evidence from Danish islands: "heaps of waste oyster-shells, cockle-shells, and waste of other edible shell-fish, mixed with bones of divers eatable beasts and birds and fishes. . . . The Danes call these mounds—which are from three to ten feet high, and some of them a thousand feet long by two hundred wide—kitchen-middens."[12] These "refuse heaps," mixed with instruments and fragments of pottery, are an interesting analogue to the dustheap, the central symbol of *Our Mutual Friend.*

Although Dickens's vision of human society in *Our Mutual Friend* is analogous to Darwin's vision of the natural world in *The Origin of Species,* the purpose of the former is quite different from that of the latter: it is to demonstrate how human values should be made to triumph over the "dismal swamp." The subtitle of Darwin's great work is The Preservation of Favoured Races in the Struggle for Life. Its possible interpretation as a description of laissez-faire economics in an unjust society—recognized immediately by the reviewer in *All the Year Round*—directs our attention to that point at which Dickens, for all his sympathy with science, must part company with the Darwinian vision, at least as it is applicable to human nature. *Our Mutual Friend* shows how mutual relationships may work either for hidden harm, as in the greedy machinations of Silas Wegg or Fascination Fledgeby, or for hidden good, as in the moral altruism of Noddy Boffin or young John Harmon, "our mutual friend."

Earlier criticism of the novel has dealt with these issues from a purely economic point of view. Arnold Kettle's Marxist reading of *Our Mutual Friend* points to the Harmon/Rokesmith "mutual friend" as Dickens's way of breaking down class barriers, "bridging and, in a sense, loosening up the class relationships of the whole world of the novel. For not merely does Harmon/Rokesmith connect the Boffins with the Wilfers, but he is also the unwitting means of introducing Eugene Wrayburn to Lizzie Hexham."[13] Dickens, in Kettle's view, intended to show how wealth could be made to flow to all areas of society through "mutuality."[14] Ruskin, of course, had a similar intention in *Unto this Last,* a work published just five years earlier than *Our Mutual Friend.* In a related reading, Richard A. Lanham suggests "that money was, for Dickens, symptom rather than disease: the disease, and the real theme, is predation."[15] Although Lanham treats the novel as an allegory about "predation," it is remarkable that he never mentions Darwin.

The object of the present essay is to show how Dickens revealed the pattern of mutual relations in his novel not only in the terms of "political economy" but especially in the newly emerging conceptual frame of evolutionary biology. For Dickens in 1865, however, "evolution" was not synonymous with Darwin's explanation of it—as it was not for Tennyson, another imaginative writer deeply absorbed in science.[16] There were many possibilities. Richard Owen, Darwin's bitter antagonist of later years who nonetheless had made a major effort in classifying Darwin's specimens from *The Beagle,* theorized on "the continuous operation of the ordained becoming of living things" (Desmond and Moore, p. 490). Darwin's co-discoverer, Alfred Russel Wallace, ultimately came to believe that evolution worked toward realizing "the ideal of perfect man" (Desmond and Moore, p. 468). *Our Mutual Friend* is saturated with the motifs of Darwinian biology in order to display, ultimately, their inadequacy. Although Dickens made use of the explanatory powers of both natural selection and laissez-faire economics and although he remained sympathetic to science, as his selection of articles in *All the Year Round* demonstrates, finally the novel transcends and opposes both the Malthusian and the Darwinian con-

structs in order to project a teleological and designed evolution in the human world toward a moral community of responsible men and women.

In *Hard Times* (1854), his most vehement and schematic attack on the mixture of utilitarianism and laissez-faire economics that characterized the creed of the industrial midlands, Dickens had presented his theme in a "keynote" chapter, a heavily symbolic description of Coketown, with its coiling serpentine smoke, its "elephant in a state of melancholy madness," and its face of "unnatural red and black like the painted face of a savage."[17] Similarly, Dickens sets the keynote of *Our Mutual Friend* in its very first chapter, which is devoted to the "birds of prey," Gaffer Hexam and Rogue Riderhood, as they search the Thames for dead bodies to scavenge. That life supports itself from death is, of course, the central insight of *The Origin of Species*:

> We behold the face of nature bright with gladness, we often see superabundance of food; we do not see, or we forget, that the birds which are idly singing round us mostly live on insects or seeds, and are thus constantly destroying life; or we forget how largely these songsters, or their eggs, or their nestlings, are destroyed by birds and beasts of prey.

> (*Origin,* p. 116)

When Gaffer's daughter, Lizzie, remarks that she does not like the work, her father is outraged: "As if it wasn't your living! As if it wasn't meat and drink to you!". Levine has pointed out how this famous Darwinian picture of the bright face of nature hiding a sinister underside parallels dozens of similar pictures in nineteenth-century writing: Ruskin's "pathetic fallacy" and George Eliot's idyllic countryside in *Adam Bede,* to name only two.[18]

When Riderhood sees his former partner with a corpse in tow, he further sets the predatory Darwinian ambiance of the scene: "In luck again, Gaffer?. . . . I a'most think you're like the wulturs, pardner, and scent 'em out". The opening of the novel, then, deals with "birds of prey" who live upon the victims luck sends them. They profit from the deaths of others, and their success is determined by random chance, the key signature of the Darwinian view of the world. The role of chance in Darwin's theory of natural selection has been the subject of considerable dispute: so astute a Victorian scientist as Sir John Herschel dismissed natural selection as "the law of higgledy-piggledy" (Beer, p. 9). It is true that Darwin sometimes claimed to be describing a law of nature in opposition to "mere chance." It is equally true that his theorizing is always paradoxical. In writing to Hooker in 1856 he says that "the formation of a strong variety or species I look at as almost wholly due to the selection of what may be incorrectly called chance variations or variability."[19] It is not altogether clear why Darwin thought the term incorrect, since he used it several times. In any case, there can be no doubt at all that the very essence of natural selection was random change—"chance variation"—in opposition to design or preconceived direction.

The intricate interrelations of human predators form the continuing substance of Dickens's novel. The anatomy of human society as a whole reveals a hidden battlefield. In *The Origin* Darwin had emphasized the truth of the simile in which all creation is portrayed as a great tree: "At each period of growth all the growing twigs have tried to branch out on all sides, and to overtop and kill the surrounding twigs and branches, in the same manner as species and groups of species have tried to overmaster other species in the great battle for life". As *Our Mutual Friend* opens with furtive river scavengers, supporting themselves from the dead, so it continues with an ever-enlarging vision of predation as the foundation of life. The plot of the novel turns on the inheritance of old John Harmon, an avaricious garbage contractor who grows rich on the refuse of the city but rejects his own family in a monomaniacal obsession with self-interest. Silas Wegg is a calculating villain whose *idee fixe* is to acquire the wealth of the Harmon dustheaps by betraying his benefactor, Noddy Boffin. "There are no fish of the shark tribe in the Bower waters?" Dickens's narrator asks:

> Perhaps not. Still, Wegg is established there, and would seem, judged by his secret proceedings, to cherish a notion of making a discovery. For, when a man with a wooden leg lies prone on his stomach to peep under bedsteads; and hops up ladders, like some extinct bird, to survey the tops of presses and cupboards; and provides himself an iron rod which he is always poking and prodding into dust-mounds; the probability is that he expects to find something.

As Dickens trains his microscope on the class hierarchy of the Victorian chain of being in its plenitude, more predators continue to come into focus. Alfred and Sophronia Lammle are a pair of adventurers who seek Georgiana Podsnap and the Boffins as prey. Most revealing is their conversation upon realizing that they have been mutually duped into marriage in the belief that the other one was wealthy:

> "Mrs Lammle, we have both been deceiving, and we have both been deceived. We have both been biting, and we have both been bitten. In a nut-shell, there's the state of the case."

Fascination Fledgeby, whose name suggests a young bird of prey, not only conspires with the Lammles to marry the money of Georgiana but supports himself as a secret usurer, pretending that his cruel extortions from poor little Mr. Twemlow and others are caused by his employee, Mr. Riah, an elderly Jew. Fledgeby, Dickens tells us, is "the meanest cur existing, with a single pair of legs". Jenny Wren is deceived for a time by Fledgeby's lies about Mr. Riah and rejects her friend as the archetypal predator, "the Wolf in the Forest, the wicked Wolf!"

At another level are the Veneerings, who are situated at the center of both society and government. These "bran-new people in a bran-new house in a bran-new quarter of London" are motivated by an automatic instinct toward self-interest, and, despite their centrality to the mutual re-lationships of their world, they have no real friends in society, no principles in politics, and no moral values in any sphere. Their continual dinner parties, at which the guests, greeted by them as their "oldest friends," are nearly strangers, serve as the jungle in which predators such as the Lammles may stalk their prey and in which Mr. Podsnap may express the smug, laissez-faire philosophy of the ruling classes.

Among Mr. Podsnap's laughable haut bourgeois foibles so pilloried by Dickens in the chapter entitled "Podsnappery" is his use of "Providence." When one of his guests mentions, almost apologetically, the fact that a number of people have died of starvation in the streets and "that there must be something appallingly wrong somewhere", Mr. Podsnap angrily rejects any notion of interference in this process of death as "Centralization" and as interfering with the decrees of Providence:

> "And you know; at least I hope you know;" said Mr Podsnap, with severity, "that Providence has declared that you shall have the poor always with you?"
>
> The meek man also hoped he knew that.
>
> "I am glad to hear it," said Mr Podsnap with a portentous air. "I am glad to hear it. It will render you cautious how you fly in the face of Providence."

There is an apparent resonance between Podsnap's laissez-faire version of Providence and Darwin's religious awe in the face of natural selection:

> We have seen that man by selection can certainly produce great results, and can adapt organic beings to his own uses, through the accumulation of slight but useful variations, given to him by the hand of Nature. But Natural Selection, as we shall hereafter see, is a power incessantly ready for action, and is as immeasurably superior to man's feeble efforts, as the works of Nature are to those of Art.
>
> (*Origin*, p. 115)

Darwin concludes this discussion of natural selection to suggest that the struggle that seems so brutal on the surface is in fact beneficial, even providential

> When we reflect on this struggle, we may console ourselves with the full belief, that the war of nature is not incessant, that no fear is felt, that death is generally prompt, and that the vigorous, the healthy, and the happy survive and multiply.

It may be remarked that Darwin's own feelings about the sad death of his favorite daughter, Annie, in 1851 had not been so cheerful. He had been devastated. Annie's death destroyed his "tatters of belief in a moral, just universe" and "chimed the final death-knell for his Christianity" (Desmond and Moore, p. 387).

Even the characters who are finally redeemed in *Our Mutual Friend* are deeply involved in the self-seeking world of individual advantage. Bella devotes herself to money until she recognizes the inhuman madness the acquisitive impulse seems to introduce into Noddy Boffin's life. Boffin himself is a grotesque parody of the mechanical search for a competitive edge:

> "We've got to hold our own now, against everybody (for everybody's hand is stretched out to be dipped into our pockets), and we have got to recollect that money makes money, as well as makes everything else. . . .
>
> "I have found out that you must either scrunch them, or let them scrunch you."

Mr. Venus, who finally exposes the evil scheme of Silas Wegg, supports himself by collecting bones and body parts for reassembly, and John Harmon, the mutual friend of the novel, is the victim of attempted murder as he returns to London to deal with his inheritance of giant refuse heaps.

The evolutionary origin of human predation from the ancient reptilian world revealed in Darwinian theory sums up the doctrine of "scrunch or be scrunched" in Silas Wegg's plotting to destroy Noddy Boffin. Wegg is observed in Venus's shop by the stuffed alligator whose "yard or two of smile . . . might have been invested with the meaning, 'All about this was quite familiar knowledge down in the depths of the slime, ages ago'".

The general theme of a competitive environment in which voracious predators struggle against one another—sometimes to the death—in a shadowy world of mechanical self-seeking is a Darwinian theme, but a theme not altogether unknown to Dickens before 1859. The dark animal rapacity of Fagin, the glistening teeth of Carker, the exploitative cruelty of the raven, Tulkinghorne, come to mind. *Our Mutual Friend,* however, offers a setting that reinforces the theme in its particularly Darwinian aspect to an extraordinary degree. The central symbol of the mounds gives the literary geologist the opportunity to uncover endless strata of meaning.

To begin with, the garbage heap itself, possibly related to the *All the Year Round* review of Lyell and his Danish "kitchen-middens," bears an obvious analogy to the chief insight of *The Origin of Species*: that "the accumulation of innumerable slight variations" is the fundamental condition from which natural selection brings about change (*Origin,* p. 435). Like the geological record, the mounds are composed of old bones as well as other disparate objects whose position and value in the mounds have no plan. Instead, they simply accumulate. All of society contributes to the pile, and the dustheap accumulates slowly by chance and random selection. The relation of the mounds to scientific theory is made explicit by Mortimer Lightwood in chapter 2 when their existence is described as the livelihood of the dead Mr. Harmon: "the growling old vagabond threw up his own mountain range, like an old volcano, and its geological formation was Dust. Coal-dust, vegetable-dust, bone-dust, crockery dust, rough dust and sifted dust,—all manner of Dust". The dustheaps are not only a monument to accumulation and random selec-

tion but are also the site of a struggle for existence, as scavengers compete for their malodorous treasures.

The digging in the mounds by Silas Wegg and others leads naturally to an analogy in paleontology. The digging is a search through the fossil record of Victorian London. It is here that a central concern of the Victorian novel comes together with the chief goal of Victorian science: uncovering the secret of inheritance. The endless searching is for a will. The secret of inheritance, it will be remembered, is the goal of paleontology and, further, the riddle that Darwin claimed to have solved in *The Origin of Species*. It is in the solution to the question of inheritance, considered not only in its Darwinian biological aspect but in a larger, human way, that **Our Mutual Friend** will arrive at its ultimate meaning.

The image of the great dustheap gradually accumulating its disparate pieces leads naturally to one of Dickens's more wildly improbable yet finally appropriate characters, Mr. Venus, the bone articulator, conducting his bizarre trade in body parts and pickled babies. His card reads: "Preserver of Animals and Birds" and "Articulator of human bones". The shop, in its random confusion, reflects both the Harmon dustheap that has contributed to it and the geological record itself:

> "A Wice. Tools. Bones, warious. Skulls, warious. Preserved Indian baby. African ditto. Bottled preparations, warious. Everything within reach of your hand, in good preservation. The mouldy ones a-top. What's in those hampers over them again, I don't quite remember. Say, human warious. Cats. Articulated English baby. Dogs. Ducks. Glass eyes, warious. Mummied bird. Dried cuticle, warious. Oh, dear me! That's the general panoramic view."

Mr. Venus tells Wegg, who is hoping to retrieve his leg bone, that the bone will not fit into a "miscellaneous" skeleton, although he often constructs such products: "I have just sent home a Beauty—a perfect Beauty—to a school of art. One leg Belgian, one leg English, and the pickings of eight other people in it". In fact, Mr. Venus's skill in all sorts of anatomy is a matter of intense pride to him: "I've gone on improving myself in my knowledge of Anatomy, till both by sight and by name I'm perfect. Mr Wegg, if you was brought here loose in a bag to be articulated, I'd name your smallest bones blindfold equally with your largest, as fast as I could pick 'em out, and I'd sort 'em all, and sort your wertebrae, in a manner that would equally surprise and charm you". The miscellaneous shop of Mr. Venus, with its odd assortment of parallel bone structures, is a comic analogue to Darwin's description of bone patterns among widely varied mammals:

> The framework of bones being the same in the hand of a man, wing of a bat, fin of the porpoise, and leg of the horse,—the same number of vertebrae forming the neck of the giraffe and the elephant,—and innumerable other such facts, at once explain themselves on the theory of descent with slow and slight successive modifications.
>
> (*Origin,* p. 451)

It is equally possible that Dickens had Darwin's antagonist Richard Owen in mind. Owen was widely recognized as the greatest anatomist of the day. The proceedings of the British Association of 1846 are described as being "dominated by Owen's numbingly technical paper comparing the homologous bones in fish, reptiles, and mammals" (Desmond and Moore, p. 336).

An especially interesting detail is the continuing motif of a skeletal "French gentleman" whom Mr. Venus is assembling and who presides over the entire establishment. In "Earliest Man," an 1861 article in *All the Year Round,* the writer had referred to human fossils that the "Scientific World" refused to acknowledge, "when a very troublesome French gentleman—M. Boucher de Perthes—Wanted it to believe that certain remains of man were to be found in the gravel." The writer continues with jokes about the doubts of "Professor Oolite" and "Sir Protogin Felspar," quoting with approval the discoveries of Owen and Lyell in opposition to the rest of the benighted "Scientific World."[20] One wonders if "the troublesome French gentleman" who insisted on the existence of certain human fossils has somehow been transformed through the alchemy of Dickens's creative imagination into the human skeleton under construction that presides over the jumble of bones in Mr. Venus's shop.

Readers of *The Origin of Species* are meant to be struck by Darwin's created persona, the careful and patient scientist who takes a lifetime to collect and piece together innumerable small bits of evidence, the painstaking investigator who is finally forced in 1859 to publish an "Abstract" of his evidence, only the tip of a gigantic iceberg.[21] Silas Wegg describes in similar terms the qualifications of Mr. Venus for a search for the hidden will:

> He expatiates on Mr Venus's patient habits and delicate manipulation; on his skill in piecing little things together; on his knowledge of various tissues and textures; on the likelihood of small indications leading him on to the discovery of great concealments.

Harriet Martineau described Darwin succinctly as "simple, childlike, painstaking, effective."[22] It is significant, of course, for the final meaning of *Our Mutual Friend* that Mr. Venus transcends the predatory world of Wegg, symbolized by the grinning, stuffed alligator in his shop, to turn to the human world of moral responsibility and that—in keeping with his name—he is rewarded by the love of Pleasant Riderhood, who at his first advances had refused "to regard myself, nor yet to be regarded in that boney light".

As observed earlier, it is a commonplace that one of the great subjects of nineteenth-century fiction is the role of wills and inheritance—from *Pride and Prejudice,* to *Vanity Fair,* to *Middlemarch.* The thematic centrality of inheritance is even more obvious in Dickens: Oliver Twist must learn his identity and recover his father's name; David Copperfield begins his career in a probate court, Doctors Commons; *Bleak House* turns on the settling of the Jarndyce will in Chancery. In *Great Expectations* Pip must reconcile himself to a convict father-figure who has made him his heir. *Our Mutual Friend* is no exception. It is about the strange series of wills of an unhappy miser, John Harmon. The search for the valid will poses symbolically a human question larger than the material one: Will the self-seeking character traits of the miser, as well as his money, be inherited through his will? Will Bella Wilfer sell herself for money? Will Noddy Boffin? Silas Wegg? Mr. Venus? These questions are posed against a background of related characters being similarly tested and within a consciously created Darwinian world: the survival of the fittest. John Harmon's son, who had so narrowly missed extinction in the dog-eat-dog environment of the waterfront, removes himself from sight, a "mutual friend" who will watch the testing and interpret its meaning.

It is a wonderfully apt irony that the moral test set for Bella and for Silas Wegg by Noddy Boffin should involve his pretended mania on the subject of misers, their miserable deaths, and their wills. Wegg's reading for an avid Noddy Boffin is both extravagant Dickensian caricature and also an emblem of the theme: "'The Miser's Mansion. The finding of a treasure. . . . The Miser dies without a Shirt. The Treasures of a Dunghill—'". Wegg continues with the story of Dancer, pursuing "the biography of that eminent man through its various phases of avarice and dirt, through Miss Dancer's death on a sick regimen of cold dumpling, and through Mr Dancer's keeping his rags together with a hayband, and warming his dinner by sitting upon it, down to the consolatory incident of his dying naked in a sack". Wegg goes on to describe the inheritance of Dancer's miserable house and, after reading of various other misers, concludes with an unfinished account of the hidden wills of "Robert Baldwin" and his father, acrimonious instances of inheritance and disinheritance caused by the competitive quarrels of fathers and sons. This last story, of course, is a parallel to the various hidden wills of John Harmon. When Noddy Boffin stops the reading in the middle of the tale, the still-unanswered question of *Our Mutual Friend* emerges clearly: What is worthy to be inherited? How can the legacy of the past evolve into the present and future?

This central question of the novel, as it is the central question of Samuel Butler's Lamarckian novel *The Way of All Flesh* (1903), is parallel to the biological question Darwin attempted to answer, as have all evolutionary theories: How is the past being transformed into the future? The laissez-faire answer to the question, of which Darwinian theory is a variety, is given by Noddy Boffin in his representation of himself as a miser, the natural heir of old Mr. Harmon. Whene young Harmon/Rokesmith expresses his intent to win Bella's love rather than her material inheritance, Boffin gives an answer—repeated several times in the novel—that summarizes life as simply animal competition:

> "Win her affections," retorted Mr Boffin, with ineffable contempt, "and possess her heart! Mew says the cat, Quack-quack says the duck, Bow-wow-wow says the

dog! Win her affections and possess her heart! Mew, Quack-quack, Bow-wow!"

The question of inheritance is related to the question of accumulation. Accumulation is the foundation of success in the laissez-faire world of Adam Smith and Victorian political economy. The miser is the extreme example of the accumulator; he has become the obsessed image of his theory in the flesh. He is the pathetic "Dancer" of *Our Mutual Friend* just as he is the unhappy Ebenezer Scrooge of *A Christmas Carol.* The miser shares some character traits with the Victorian scientist, a patient and careful collector of bits of evidence, in the comic fictional version of Mr. Venus or in the actual life of the author of *The Origin of Species* himself. As the "golden dustman" demonstrates his new role with an obsessive "Mew, Quack-quack, Bow-wow!" we remember that the doctrine of accumulation is the foundation of natural selection as well as of capitalism. A central lesson Darwin's theory teaches "is that in the position previously assigned to a deity there actually functions a means dependent on random variation. Where God was, accumulating variation is."[23] Both capitalism and natural selection are imaged in the mounds, partially composed of fossils that are at the same time saleable garbage—filthy lucre. Both the economic and biological theories contain a similar paradox. On the one hand both depend upon mutuality: as all living beings are mutually related as to their success in life, so all economic units are interdependent. On the other hand both doctrines insist upon an automatic environment in which each unit or being blindly follows its own self-interest in a fragmented world of individuals. There is no plan. There is much mutuality, but little cooperation.

It is striking how this paradoxical state of affairs corresponds to the plot and characters of *Our Mutual Friend.* All of the characters are divided—either against themselves or separated in some way from society or humanity at large—and thus often mysterious. Veneeering is an MP and a leader of society but does not know his constituents or his guests. Almost all the characters in the novel lead double lives—some actually in disguise. Noddy Boffin pretends to be a miser; Silas Wegg, with his wooden leg, pretends to be a loyal retainer; Jenny Wren is mother to her father; Mr. Riah pretends to be a grasping loan shark, while his employer, Fascination Fledgeby, is the shark; Rumty Wilfer pretends to be an obsequious husband but leads a hidden life with his daughter; Eugene Wrayburn is a dilettante who becomes obsessed with a working-class woman; the Lammles appear to be wealthy young socialites, whereas in fact they are destitute; Bradley Headstone is a dull but respectable schoolteacher who is nonetheless driven by frustration, hatred, and sexual aggression and who finally attempts murder; Bella Wilfer is divided between her spontaneous nature of cheerful and unselfish affection and the lure of the Harmon will to self-seeking materialism. John Harmon finally establishes a kind of harmony, but it must not be forgotten that he is an orphan, has been separated from society because of his supposed death, and leads a life of disguise throughout most of the novel.

The denouement of the narrative takes place against the background of laissez-faire and natural selection but is a denial of both. The accumulated traits of avarice and selfishness will not be transmitted to the heirs of old Harmon. Those who seek their own advantage will not succeed, will not be the fittest for successful human life. All comes together in an extraordinary moment of thematic revelation in chapter 13 of Book 4, "Showing How the Golden Dustman Helped to Scatter Dust."

In an epiphanic tableau, Mr. and Mrs. Boffin, John Harmon, and Bella all join bands over the new baby on Bella's lap, in a symbol not only of hidden mutuality but of overt cooperation. Rather than inheriting self-seeking greed with the mounds, all four adults have chosen charity and generosity, thus changing the course of evolution. Their success is evidenced in the baby, the result of love rather than cunning. The Boffins, instead of operating automatically on the basis of self-interest, had wept for joy on losing their material inheritance but receiving instead a returned child. "These two," Harmon tells Bella, "whom I come to life to disappoint and dispossess, cry for joy!".

Not only do the Boffins reject laissez-faire doctrine, but they have devised a test for Bella to prove to her lover that she too would reject it for human moral values:

> "What will content you? If she was to stand up for you when you was slighted, if she was to show herself of a generous mind when you was oppressed, if she was to be truest to you when you was poorest and friendliest, and all this against her own seeming interest, how would that do?"

Bella, of course, passes the test in rejecting Boffin in his disguise as a selfish miser. As always is the case with Dickens, the material goods of this world are never the problem. One may inherit money without harm, but inheriting the trait of seeking only one's own advantage is a lethal flaw that does not in the long run produce an appropriate evolution.

The final will in the Dutch bottle gave everything to Mr. Boffin, who had hidden it lest a slur be cast on the names of the Harmon children. His selfless act now brings about the good results of the novel: the Lammles are dismissed, and Silas Wegg is thrown out—symbolically—on a scavenger's cart. Although—as often in Dickens—the "good father" of the novel is a man with no biological children, Boffin's legacy of human decency is the "fittest" trait to be inherited for an appropriate human evolution. John Harmon states this theme explicitly: "I owe everything I possess, solely to the disinterestedness, uprightness, tenderness, goodness . . . of Mr and Mrs Boffin".

Our Mutual Friend is filled not only with predators but with characters who demonstrate moral responsibility, human affection, and charity: not only the Boffins, but the Rev. and Mrs. Frank Milvey, Mr. Riah, Jenny Wren, Betty Higden, and Sloppy. The brutality of Boffin's pretended materialism—"Mew, Quack-quack, Bow-wow!"—is countered brilliantly by a powerfully symbolic image that draws together the previous Darwinian motifs and reverses them in a scene of charity and generosity. In the children's hospital the dying orphan child, Johnny, is given a toy Noah's Ark, an emblem of the animal world very different from the Darwinian model:

> This was no less than the appearance on his own little platform in pairs, of All Creation, on its way into his own particular ark: the elephant leading, and the fly, with a different sense of his size, politely bringing up the rear. A very little brother lying in the next bed with a broken leg, was so enchanted by this spectacle that his delight exalted its enthralling interest.

The dying child expresses Dickens's view of the generosity of spirit that should inform the human world and should be the basis for making wills and the proper inheritance to pass on to the future:

> "Him!" said the little fellow. "Those!"
>
> The doctor was quick to understand children, and, taking the horse, the ark, the yellow bird, and the man in the Guards, from Johnny's bed, softly placed them on that of his next neighbour, the mite with the broken leg. . . .
>
> Having now bequeathed all he had to dispose of, and arranged his affairs in this world, Johnny, thus speaking, left it.

Although Johnny's "Creation" is the toy of a dying orphan, its suggestion of a chain of being organized around generosity of spirit is Dickens's answer to the economic world of Adam Smith and David Ricardo and to the biological world of Charles Darwin.

The fact that **Our Mutual Friend** upholds the traditional human virtues of generosity and love against the new mechanical world of science does not mean that Dickens's characters escape injury. There is a war in nature: Little Johnny dies, as does Betty Higden; Jenny Wren is crippled; her alcoholic father is dehumanized. All the characters are in some way distorted by their environment. Dickens does not simply reject the vision of *The Origin of Species* any more than he rejected capitalism altogether. **Hard Times** had been dedicated, after all, to Carlyle and had anticipated appropriate captains of industry who could make humanly acceptable connections between mill workers, educators, and capitalists. Mr. Rouncewell, the industrialist in **Bleak House,** had appeared to embody hope for the future.

Similarly, it is clear that Dickens was familiar with Darwin and used specific details from *The Origin* with which to structure his fiction. Underlying Darwin's theory of natural selection and Malthus's theory of population, for instance, is the powerful agency of death. "We already see," Darwin writes, "how it (natural selection) entails extinction; and how largely extinction has acted in the world's history, geology plainly declares" (*Origin,* p. 170). The ubiquity of death is the most striking aspect of **Our**

Mutual Friend—from the search for corpses floating in the river, to the supposed death of John Harmon, to the death struggle of Rogue Riderhood with the death-directed schoolmaster, so aptly named Bradley Headstone.

The struggle between life and death in the novel, as in Darwin's picture of evolutionary processes, is closely linked to the relation of the sexes. Sexual selection is a central feature of **Our Mutual Friend,** almost as much as it is in the more self-consciously Darwinian Wessex fiction of Hardy at the end of the century. The central pair are Bella and John Harmon, who mate and reproduce successfully. Similarly, Mr. Venus leaves the "paths of Weggery" and wins the hand of Pleasant Riderhood. Mr. Twemlow, however, is the offshoot of a large aristocratic family that—sadly—will not reproduce. Although Bradley Headstone struggles to the death with Rogue Riderhood, his most significant battle is the sexually based conflict with Eugene Wrayburn for Lizzie Hexam. Little Miss Peecher, the schoolmistress who loves Headstone, lacks the power to attract him. Lizzie, however, awakens life in the drifting Wrayburn and activates his struggle with death in the symbolic mating competition with the fey Headstone, who rushes blindly toward extinction as thanatos overwhelms eros.

It is important to remember that both Dickens and Darwin were popular authors, well known to the reading public. Some twenty years previous to the publication of *The Origin,* they both had been elected to the Athenaeum Club on the same day, 21 June 1838.[24] Not only was **Our Mutual Friend** a popular work, but so also, on a lesser scale, was *The Origin of Species.* As Burrow notes in his introduction, after initial hesitation on the part of its publisher, "1,250 copies were printed, which sold out on the first day. A second edition was rushed out and appeared in January 1860". Both works were in tune with the popular educated mind and, as we have seen, resonated with each other. Both attempted to construct a coherent picture of a complex pattern of phenomena.

The two books can he interpreted as being part of a general nineteenth-century impulse to see the meaning behind the dessicated classifications of eighteenth-century science, itself based on a moribund natural theology. James Paradis has pointed to Coleridge's belief that the work of pre-Darwinian taxonomists like Linnaeus, for instance, was "part of a blind mnemonic impulse that . . . would destroy language itself" and "gave little insight into the deeper structure and reality of things."[25]

Dickens, of course, shared Coleridge's feelings about empty scientific classifications. His most memorable expression of his opinions on the subject is Bitzer's definition of a horse in the Gradgrind School in **Hard Times.** The topic appears again, with even greater force, in the characterization of Bradley Headstone, the murderous schoolmaster of **Our Mutual Friend:**

> From his early childhood up, his mind had been a place of mechanical stowage. The arrangement of his whole-

sale warehouse, so that it might be always ready to meet the demands of retail dealers—history here, geography there, astronomy to the right, political economy to the left—natural history, the physical sciences, figures, music, the lower mathematics, and what not, all in their several places—this care had imparted to his countenance a look of care. . . . There was a kind of settled trouble in the face.

The emptiness of rote scientific classifications is shown at its worst in the more sinister parody delivered by Rogue Riderhood as he torments the guilty Headstone in the presence of his pupils:

"Wot's the diwisions of water, my lambs? Wot sorts of water is there on the land?"

Shrill chorus: "Seas, rivers, lakes, and ponds."

"Seas, rivers, lakes, and ponds," said Riderhood. "They've got all the lot, Master!"

Many students of Victorian England have pointed to the intellectual intercourse between its eminent scientists, artists, politicians, and intellectuals, the common effort to deal with common problems, often with intellectual frameworks and vocabularies that seem quite similar. The fact that Victorian artists and scientists dealt with the same problems with similar language did not, however, ensure that they would reach the same conclusions. The scientists themselves often disagreed. Darwin's battle with Owen was a continuing reminder of the divisions among able Victorian scientists. Even more telling was Lyell's refusal, to Darwin's great chagrin, ever to endorse evolution by natural selection, even in *The Antiquity of Man*.[26] Darwin was hurt by Herschel's description of natural selection as "the law of higgledy-piggledy," as Gillian Beer has pointed out. This phrase, she remarks, "exactly expresses the dismay many Victorians felt at the apparently random—and so, according to their lights, trivialised—energy that Darwin perceived in the natural world" (*Darwin's Plots,* p. 9).

It is unlikely that Dickens disapproved of natural selection on the philosophic and scientific grounds of Herschel or Owen, but it is clear that the picture of the world presented in **Our Mutual Friend,** despite its many affinities with *The Origin,* and despite the fact that it occupies considerable common ground, diverges from it sharply. Since **Oliver Twist,** the complex of social ideas associated with laissez-faire economics had been a chief object of Dickens's moral indignation. Although the evidence of *The Origin of Species* may have come from the voyage of *The Beagle,* the theory itself came from Adam Smith and Thomas Malthus.

Related to Dickens's lifelong political and moral position is his understanding of himself as an artist. George Levine points out how a storyteller like Dickens, working in a theatrical and literary tradition like that of the nineteenth century, may use "chance" frequently, as Darwin does, but must make it "part of a larger moral design" (*Darwin and the Novelists,* p. 138). It is true of **Our Mutual Friend,** as

it is of all of Dickens's novels, that design and teleology are at the core of its fictional intent and thus diametrically opposed to the special vision of Darwin. This fact does not render Dickens an obscurantist opponent of "evolution": the panoply of articles on the subject in *All the Year Round* deny such an interpretation. It is not necessary to accept Darwin's theory of evolution as the only or finally complete one. In the 1840s, for instance, evolutionary ideas had been associated not only with the enemies of the Anglican Church establishment, but with working-class revolution against all established repression, including that of capitalism. It would be quite in character for Dickens to approve evolution as a progressive idea but to reject Darwin's Malthusian explanation. Both Dickens and Tennyson, the two most prominent artists of their age, were intensely interested in science and both were evolutionists, but neither were "Darwinians" in a philosophical sense. If natural selection is the sole explanation of evolution, it is an odd paradox, as Levine has said, that natural selection "is an oxymoron" invented as an analogy to human breeding practices: "it implies the activity of design and a designer, and yet denies it". For all their sympathy with scientific issues in general and evolution in particular, neither the author of *In Memoriam* nor the author of **Our Mutual Friend** could accept as the scientific explanation of nature an ultimate appeal to the irrationality of chance, joined in marriage to the mechanical economic theories of late-eighteenth- and early-nineteenth-century capitalism.

The beautiful conclusion of *The Origin of Species,* with its lyric contemplation of "an entangled bank" and its invocation of natural laws such as "Growth with Reproduction," "Inheritance," "Variability, "a Struggle for Life," and "Natural Selection", is closely related to the entangled bank of **Our Mutual Friend,** with its emphasis on inheritance, variety, a struggle for life, and natural selection. The issues are the same. The solutions are very different. For Dickens, as for Richard Owen or Adam Sedgwick, it was the teleological tradition of natural theology—even if accepted only unconsciously—that touched his imagination and led to a deeper reality behind the multitudinous array of phenomena. Although the suggestion that he was heir to the assumptions of medieval scholasticism might have evoked outraged denial in Dickens, the medieval tradition of "Natural Law," defined by Thomas Aquinas as the intelligible relation of a rational being to its creator, was more palatable to the author of **Our Mutual Friend** than was a natural design with no designer.

Notes

1. Introduction to Charles Darwin, *The Origin of Species by Means of Natural Selection; or, The Preservation of Favoured Races in the Struggle for Life,* ed. Burrow (Harmondsworth: Penguin Books, 1968), p. 13.

2. *Our Mutual Friend,* ed. Stephen Gill (Harmondsworth: Penguin Books, 1971), p. 257.

3. *Ever Since Darwin: Reflections in Natural History* (New York: W. W. Norton, 1977), p. 12.

4. *Darwin* (New York: Warner, 1991), pp. 275-76.

5. *Dickens* (New York: HarperCollins, 1990), p. 663.

6. *Darwin and the Novelists: Patterns of Science in Victorian Fiction* (Cambridge, Mass.: Harvard Univ. Press, 1988), p. 122.

7. *Darwin's Plots: Evolutionary Narrative in Darwin, George Eliot, and Nineteenth-Century Fiction* (London: Routledge and Kegan Paul, 1983), p. 8.

8. See *All the Year Round*, 2 (1860), 315-17; and 3 (1860), 32-36.

9. "Natural Selection" (review of *The Origin of Species*), *All the Year Round*, 3 (1860), 297. See *Origin*, pp. 133-34; and Burrow's introduction, p. 68.

10. See *All the Year Round*, 4 (1861), 519-21.

11. *All the Year Round*, 1 (1859), 515, 517.

12. "How Old Are We?" (review of *The Antiquity of Man*), *All the Year Round*, 9 (1863), 33.

13. Kettle, "*Our Mutual Friend*," in *Dickens and the Twentieth Century*, ed. John Gross and Gabriel Pearson (London: Routledge and Kegan Paul, 1962), p. 215.

14. Wilfred Paul Dvorak writes that Kettle believes Dickens's "thematic aim is to show how the 'area of wealth'—the Podsnaps, the Veneerings, old Harmon, the Boffins—is connected with the 'area of poverty'—Wegg, the Wilfers, old Betty Higden, Jenny Wren—by developing the idea of 'mutuality' as involving more than personal relationships of individual characters" (*Dickens and Money: Our Mutual Friend in the Context of Victorian Monetary Attitudes and All the Year Round*, diss., Indiana University, 1972, p. 13).

15. "*Our Mutual Friend*: The Birds of Prey," *Victorian Newsletter*, no. 24 (1963), 7.

16. See my "Tennyson's *In Memoriam* and the Scientific Imagination," *Thought: A Review of Culture and Idea*, 59 (1984), 296-318.

17. *Hard Times*, ed. George Ford and Sylvere Monod (New York: W. W. Norton, 1966), p. 17.

18. See *Darwin and the Novelists*, p. 104

19. Letter to J. D. Hooker, 23 November 1856, in *The Life and Letters of Charles Darwin,* Including an Autobiographical Chapter, ed. Frances Darwin, 2 vols. (New York: D. Appleton, 1896), I, 445.

20. *All the Year Round*, 4 (1861), 366.

21. *Origin*, p. 65. Richard Stanley Grove offers an interesting analysis of Darwin's creation of a literary persona in "A Re-Examination of Darwin's Argument in *On the Origin of Species*," diss., Univ. of Missouri, 1969, pp. 26ff.

22. Quoted in Desmond and Moore, p. 206.

23. Phillip Barrish, "Accumulating Variation: Darwin's *On the Origin of Species* and Contemporary Literary and Cultural Theory," *Victorian Studies*, 34 (1991), 440.

24. See Desmond and Moore, p. 253.

25. James Paradis, "Darwin and Landscape," in *Victorian Science and Victorian Values: Literary Perspectives*, ed. Paradis and Thomas Postlewait (New York: New York Academy of Sciences, 1981), p. 91.

26. See Desmond and Moore, p. 515.

Cathy Shuman (essay date 1995)

SOURCE: "Invigilating *Our Mutual Friend*: Gender and the Legitimation of Professional Authority," in *Novel*, Vol. 28, No. 2, Winter, 1995, pp. 154-72.

[*In the following essay, Shuman posits that* Our Mutual Friend *demystifies the Victorian domestic sphere at the same time it legitimates the professionalism of the intellectual worker.*]

Examining the contradictions of nineteenth-century professional authorship and the gendered separation of public and private in *David Copperfield*, Mary Poovey argues that "stabilizing and mobilizing a particular image of woman, the domestic sphere, and woman's work were critical" to the fixing of "the English writer's social role" and "the legitimation and depoliticization of capitalist market and class relations" (89). Since Poovey, it has become a truism to assert that professional Victorian intellectuals rely on the extraeconomic authority granted the domestic woman by the doctrine of separate spheres in order to resolve the contradictions of their place in capitalist relations of production: they may then depict themselves as policing the line between the public and private spheres rather than challenging it.[1] At the end of *David Copperfield*, David and Agnes preside together over a Copperfield household full of children named for the novel's characters. In the following pages, I will argue that in *Our Mutual Friend* (1864-65), however, the relationship between professional and domestic authority is not nearly so collaborative.

Instead, the novel provides a model of professional expertise, as valuable yet invaluable as domestic power, yet freed from its fragility. If we trace the plots that lead to the emergence of the novel's two normative intellectual workers—John Harmon and Eugene Wrayburn—we find that the novel's *demystification* of domestic ideology plays a key role in mystifying and legitimating the professional's place in the Victorian economic system. It does so by replacing domesticity's doctrine of separate spheres with a new version of that doctrine, one that makes a surprisingly unDickensian use of the growing Victorian state and its institutions. *Our Mutual Friend* appropriates the paradigmatic form of interaction between the state and the intellectual worker—the examination—as the paradigmatic form of interaction between its characters. Invigilating at the examinations of *Our Mutual Friend,* scrutinizing its many test takers (and givers), we find gender reemerging as crucial, not in the Victorian home, but in the strategies of the Victorian schoolroom.

I.

One of the novel's first examinations takes place when Noddy Boffin interviews Silas Wegg for the job of reader early in *Our Mutual Friend.* Part of the comedy of their interchange arises from Boffin's uncertainty about what sort of object the objectified knowledge of the professional intellectual laborer is and what form of exchange can procure it:

> Now, it's too late for me to begin shovelling and sifting at alphabeds and grammar-books. . . . But I want some reading—some fine bold reading, some splendid book in a gorging Lord-Mayor's-Show of wollumes" (probably meaning gorgeous, but misled by association of ideas); "as'll reach right down your pint of view, and take time to go by you. How can I get that reading, Wegg? By . . . paying a man truly qualified to do it, so much an hour (say twopence) to come and do it.

(94)

Boffin begins by depicting learning to read as a version of his own former job ("shovelling and sifting") and ends by assuming that, like that job, reading itself fits neatly into a conventional capitalist/worker relationship. The "profit" he expects from this relationship, however, cannot be characterized as the capitalist's surplus value. Part of a realm of luxury and leisure, intellectual labor may not be labor at all. Sandwiched between his market-based analogy is an association of the act of reading with consumption rather than production, reminding us of the problematic distinction, for intellectual laborer, between employer and customer. Boffin's "Lord Mayor's Show" hints, however, not so much at the power of a Victorian consumer as at the anachronistic glamour of Renaissance display, implying that intellectual attainments might not be something that nineteenth-century money can buy. At the same time, the narrator's knowingly literate parenthetical remark in the midst of Boffin's comic ignorance suggests that, while Wegg is hardly the "man truly qualified," such qualifications do exist. An authentic professional authority, inaccessible to characters like Boffin (at this stage of the novel, anyway) and Wegg, hovers over these confusions. However complex the valuing of intellectual labor may prove, it has value nonetheless.

The valuing of intellectual work in the context of mid-nineteenth-century capitalism was a crucial task for the emerging British professional at the time of the writing of *Our Mutual Friend.*[2] Magali Sarfatti Larson shows that, while "the constitution of professional markets which began in the nineteenth century inaugurated a new form of

structured inequality . . . different . . . from the model of social inequality based on property and identified with capitalist entrepreneurship," the commodification of expertise was still crucial to professionalization (xiv, 40). Nineteenth-century authorship, for example, was "conceptualized simultaneously as superior to the capitalist economy and as hopelessly embroiled within it" (Poovey 106). This contradiction is a necessary one for intellectual laborers, who are particularly liable to damage by being placed either in or outside the capitalist marketplace. While bargain and sale threaten to devalue their intangible products, placement beyond the market threatens to deny them access to consumers of these products.[3]

For the Victorians, the distinction between the economic and the extraeconomic is inevitably tied to the gendered division of labor. *Our Mutual Friend* begins to loosen this link as Boffin and Wegg complete their agreement, emphasizing a division between the public, masculine genre of history (in the suitably impressive form of Edward Gibbon's *The Decline and Fall of the Roman Empire*) and the intimate, feminine genre of "poetry" (in the less-canonical form of Wegg's stock of penny ballads, most of which feature domestic settings):

> "Was you thinking at all of poetry?" Mr Wegg inquired, musing. . . .
>
> "To tell you the truth Wegg," said Boffin, "I wasn't thinking of poetry, except in so fur as this:—If you was to happen now and then to feel yourself in the mind to tip me and Mrs Boffin one of your ballads, why then we should drop into poetry."
>
> "I follow you, sir," said Wegg. "But not being a regular musical professional, I should be loath to engage myself for that; and therefore when I dropped into poetry, I should ask to be considered so fur, in the light of a friend."

(95)

In other words, Wegg and Boffin classify intellectual work as both production and consumption, capitalist and precapitalist, valuable and invaluable, by invoking the doctrine of separate spheres: one masculine, public, market-dominated (the historical reading Wegg does for Boffin at an hourly wage), one feminine, domestic, devoted to leisure (Wegg "dropping into poetry" for "me and Mrs Boffin," not as an employee, but as a friend). Together, these separate spheres make a whole which fixes the relation between the money value produced in the marketplace and the moral values produced at home. The implication is that intellectual labor, rather than challenging this relation, reproduces it within itself.

But the problems posed by intellectual labor's relation to capitalist market relations cannot here be solved by recourse, "in the last instance," to Ruskinian domesticity. Wegg, after all, is no gentlemanly protagonist whose personal as well as professional identity form the problematic center of the novel, but a humorous grotesque whose legitimating use of the domestic sphere is continually exposed as incompetence and greed. Although the "poetry" Wegg frequently drops into usually depicts domestic scenes of a sentimentally imagined past, he uses it, with often ludicrous results, to express his own thoroughly prosaic, market-dominated concerns. Whereas the Victorian writer's feminized authority places him above the dangers of the marketplace, Wegg's parody of such authority, as Frances Armstrong notes, makes even the marketplace look good (140-41).

When he arrives at Boffin's Bower, Wegg provides a textbook example of professional authority's simultaneous reliance on and exclusion of the private sphere when he corrects his employer's mistitling of *The Decline and Fall*:

> *"I think you said Rooshan Empire, sir?"*
>
> *"It is Rooshan; ain't it, Wegg?"*
>
> *"No, sir. Roman. Roman."*
>
> *"What's the difference, Wegg?"*
>
> *"The difference, sir?" Mr Wegg was faltering and in danger of breaking down, when a bright thought flashed upon him. "The difference, sir? There you place me in a difficulty, Mr Boffin. Suffice it to observe, that the difference is best postponed to some other occasion when Mrs Boffin does not honour us with her company. In Mrs Boffin's presence, sir, we had better drop it."*
>
> (103)

To save his status as "literary man," Wegg must mark out history as an area from which proper ladies must be excluded. At the same time, he transforms a joke about Britain's imperial competitor[4] into a lesson in the proper way of conducting middle-class gender relations. Boffin, newly risen from the working class, takes the lesson to heart, feeling that "he had committed himself in a very painful manner" (103). But as Wegg begins to read, the Boffins' interpretations of the public and political activities of the Roman Empire challenge Wegg's reliance on the complementarity of public and private by taking unintentional advantage of his incompetence: "Then, Mr Wegg . . . entered on his task . . . stumbling at Polybius (pronounced Polly Beeious, and supposed by Mr Boffin to be a Roman virgin, and by Mrs Boffin to be responsible for that necessity of dropping it) . . ." (103). The combined work of Wegg, Mr Boffin, and Mrs Boffin transforms the ancient historian (one of Gibbon's sources for the *Decline and Fall*) and progenitor of cultural capital into a woman whose offspring we can only imagine as literal, domestic, and illegitimate. In the figure of Silas Wegg, we see the androgynous intellectual's "manly delicacy" (103) subverting the very task it sets out to accomplish.

It should come as no surprise, then, that the doctrine of separate spheres, the last resort of intellectual pretenders like Silas Wegg, receives a sustained attack in *Our Mutual Friend*. When Eugene Wrayburn and Mortimer Lightwood set up house together, Eugene has one room "very completely and neatly fitted as a kitchen," joking that its "moral influence . . . in forming the domestic virtues,

may have an immense influence upon me" (337). Despite the disapproval we are expected to feel towards Eugene at this stage, this literalizing parody of the benefits of domestic influence would seem to be echoed by the novel itself. The novel's well-known condemnation of capitalist exchange is not balanced by a celebration of the home as an enclave shielded from market forces; instead, the domestic woman's special influence is depicted as illusory or futile. Family happiness and the maintenance of separate spheres seem unrelated: the novel makes no meaningful division between couples who work together in either sphere and those whose work is divided between them.[5] Bella Wilfer and Lizzie Hexam do provide their eventual husbands with certification as the novel's normative voices—but *not* by embodying domestic power. In fact, the counterfeit secretary John Rokesmith/Harmon and the reluctant barrister Eugene Wrayburn—the men who will turn out to be "truly qualified" at novel's end—gain their qualifications through the demystification of domestic power and its replacement by pedagogic authority.[6]

There is scarcely a Dickens novel without a portrait of some kind of school, but not even in *Hard Times* is a preoccupation with the methods and effects of pedagogy so marked as in *Our Mutual Friend*. Narrative itself appears structured by pedagogy when we compare the static presentation and thwarted projects of the "Social Chorus" characters to the novel's two main plots: the River plot features a struggle over who will teach Lizzie and the Dust Heap plot Bella's testing in disinterestedness and loyalty. When Mortimer questions Eugene about his intentions towards Lizzie after Bradley and Charley visit their chambers, Eugene complains that "one would think the schoolmaster had left behind him a catechizing infection" (348). This "infection" pervades *Our Mutual Friend*. The novel's well-known obsession with reading and writing is filtered through a continual barrage of quizzes and qualifying examinations, often comic (Wegg's job interview, Bella's quizzing of her infantilized "schoolboy" father, Miss Peecher's self-interested questioning of her favorite pupil, Mary Anne), but also chilling (Rogue Riderhood's "inspection" of Bradley's class, Gaffer's scholarly display of his "Body Found" posters), thought-provoking (Jenny's questioning of Lizzie about her feelings for Eugene, John's "cross-examin[ation]" during his first proposal to Bella [433]), and melodramatic (the final test of Bella's loyalty during the near-arrest of her husband, Jenny's discovery of Eugene's sickbed desire to marry Lizzie). If, as J. Hillis Miller claims, "the true mode of existence in *Our Mutual Friend* is intersubjectivity" (288), the true mode of intersubjectivity in the novel is the examination.

Twentieth-century readers tend to be disappointed by the transformation of the independent Bella into "the doll in the doll's house" at Blackheath (746), doing scholarly research into cookery books and living in true wifely ignorance of her husband's City job. But this process is also one in which middle-class domesticity itself is first parodied, then shown to be artificially constructed, and finally rendered irrelevant. When Mr Inspector arrives at the cottage to arrest Bella's husband, he plays on the distinction between "matters of business" and those "of a strictly domestic character" in order to avoid doing so in front of her:

> [L]adies are apt to take alarm at matters of business—being of that fragile sex that they're not accustomed to them when not of a strictly domestic character—and I do generally make it a rule to propose retirement from the presence of ladies, before entering upon business topics.
>
> (830-31)

The inspector's intervention, of course, will result in no rough masculine business from which Bella must be shielded. Rather, it will reveal that Bella's contented isolation at Blackheath is not the novel's happy ending, but merely a test of her loyalty and lack of avarice, the passing of which will lead her out of that isolation. In fact, the novel's actual happy ending demands the dissolution of the division between matters of "business" and of "a strictly domestic character." Once Bella is installed in her West End mansion, she will be too rich to need to read cookbooks, and her husband's City job will be exposed as a mere fiction. Bella accomplishes her husband's triumph not through her adaptation of domesticity, but through the placing of that domesticity in a pedagogical framework, not by becoming a good bourgeois wife, but by *passing a test* as a good bourgeois wife.

The rewriting of domesticity as examination entails the rewriting of the supervisory authority of the domestic woman (see N. Armstrong) as that of the masculine invigilator (an authority Wegg seeks—but never attains—in his blackmailing surveillance of Boffin). From the early days of the deception, Bella is always accompanied by John's "semi-omniscient" surveillance (Jaffe, *Vanishing* 14-15). When she and John leave Betty Higdon's funeral, narrator, reader, and even the train they take are asked to share in John's eroticized view of her:

> O boofer lady, fascinating boofer lady! If I were but legally executor of Johnny's will [where he leaves "a kiss for the boofer lady"]! If I had but the right to pay your legacy and to take your receipt!—Something to this purpose surely mingled with the blast of the train as it cleared the stations, all knowingly shutting up their green eyes and opening their red ones when they prepared to let the boofer lady pass.
>
> (594)

In other words, although we do not "see" him, as the ruse progresses, John's perspective melts into that of a suddenly arch and personified narrator, always present to supervise and judge Bella's progress in her scholarly attempts at domesticity:

> [A]bove all such severe study! For Mrs J.R., who had never been wont to do too much at home as Miss B.W., was under the constant necessity of referring for advice and support to a sage volume entitled *The Complete British Family Housewife*, which she would sit consult-

ing, with her elbows on the table and her temples on her hands. . . .

(749)

There need be no division between professional life and domestic life; it is replaced by the division between teacher and student.

When we first meet that most domestically angelic of heroines, Lizzie Hexam, she plans a future with her father, "keeping him as straight as I can, watching for more influence than I have" (73). But as she seems to suspect, Lizzie exudes womanly influence to singularly little effect. Not only does she fail to reform Gaffer, but the brother she raises with such perfect womanly self-sacrifice grows up selfish and cruel. Her would-be seducer, Eugene, changes his ways not because of her virtuous pleading but because of Bradley's more masculine chastisement. When Lizzie does wield domestic power effectively, she does so against her own will, and destructively. Bradley claims that Lizzie "could draw me to any good," but this seems an afterthought to his main point, which is that "[Y]ou could draw me to any exposure and disgrace. This and the confusion of my thoughts, so that I am fit for nothing, is what I mean by your being the ruin of me" (455). When he discovers her hiding place, Eugene makes use of the concept of womanly influence to suggest that Lizzie's power be blamed for her own potential ruin as well: "I don't complain that you design to keep me here. But you do it, you do it" (759).

Eugene's pursuit of Lizzie is nevertheless synonymous, as Eve Kosofsky Sedgwick shows, with his transformation from aristocratic to professional gentleman. It is not, however, as an angelic influence that Lizzie makes Eugene into a good lawyer, but as the contested site of pedagogic action. Coaxing her to accept his gift of lessons, he claims that

> "Your false pride does wrong to yourself and does wrong to your dead father."
>
> "How to my father, Mr Wrayburn?" she asked, with an anxious face.
>
> "How to your father? Can you ask! By perpetuating the consequences of his ignorant and blind obstinacy. By resolving not to set right the wrong he did you. By determining that the deprivation to which he condemned you, and which he forced upon you, shall always rest upon his head."
>
> It chanced to be a subtle string to sound, in her who had so spoken to her brother within the hour. It sounded far more forcibly, because of the change in the speaker for the moment; the passing appearance of earnestness, complete conviction, injured resentment of suspicion, generous and unselfish interest.
>
> (286)

His claim to be the "idlest and least of lawyers" (287) is hardly convincing: expert at arguing a shaky case, and at convincing the jury of his belief in his client's innocence,

Eugene demonstrates in his pursuit of Lizzie-as-pupil the makings of an excellent barrister.

The novel's replacement of the domestic angel with the schoolgirl raises two questions. First, why *school*? Why does the novel turn from the domestic haven to the figurative classroom as a site for the legitimation of professional authority? Second, why *girl*? How can the masculine intellectual laborer make use of a femininity robbed of domestic authority? In Part II, I will suggest that the school functions as the paradigmatic state-run institution in a novel where institutions are depicted in a strangely un-Dickensian manner. The novel becomes a vast examination room, denigrating masculine modes of transmitting knowledge and granting women a special capability for blocking such transmissions. Femininity can then serve masculine professional authority by producing and containing a reified knowledge immune from the risks of exchange.

II.

Despite the failure of domesticity in the novel, privileged anticapitalist enclaves do exist in *Our Mutual Friend*. If the novel's homes fail to provide an effective setting for domestic power, professional power is cozily at home in the novel's state institutions. The authority of such figures as the doctors in the Children's Hospital, the police inspector, and the schoolmistresslike Abbey Potterson goes unchallenged within their walls. When the inspector orders "You *must* come up. I mean to have you," even Gaffer's hidden corpse responds, becoming untangled from the rope it is caught in (220-21). An "inveterate visitor of institutions" (Collins 3), Dickens was also a famously inveterate critic of schools, prisons, courts, workhouses, and government offices in his fiction. In *Our Mutual Friend*, however, while Betty Higdon's story condemns the Victorian workhouse, it is hinted that keeping little Johnny in her charming cottage leads to his death. At the Children's Hospital where he goes to die, the doctor comments, "This should have been days ago. Too late!" (383). Once arrived at the hospital, however, the former rather sulky infant becomes "one of a little family, all in little quiet beds," guarded by "a coloured picture . . . representing as it were another Johnny seated on the knee of some Angel surely who loved little children" (384). Throughout the novel, institutions are havens of peace, order, nourishment, and tenderness (F. Armstrong 148). The violence and disorder of the riverside neighborhood are excluded when Mortimer and Eugene go to view Gaffer Hexam's find at "the wicket-gate and bright light of a Police Station; where they found the Night-Inspector, with a pen and ink, and ruler, posting up his books in a whitewashed office, as studiously as if he were in a monastery on top of a mountain . . ." (66). Positive depictions of private businesses in the novel depend on their mimicking, not families, but public institutions: Miss Abbey Potterson, landlady of the Six Jolly Fellowship Porters (one of Dickens's most inviting pubs), has "more of the air of a schoolmistress than mistress of" her pub, and Riderhood approaches her "as if he were one of her pupils in disgrace" (107).

Our Mutual Friend is sometimes called Dickens's "modernist" novel, questioning the Victorian certainties of his earlier works. Jonathan Arac argues that the lack of a typical Dickensian overview in the novel is related to contemporary advances in centralization and institutionalization (181-82). Certainly, in resolving the contradictions of nineteenth-century intellectual labor, the novel gives the state-run institution a new role. In fact, *Our Mutual Friend* replaces the division between the economic and the domestic with a new "public/private" split: that between a "private" sphere of personal and economic relations and a "public" sphere composed of the state and its institutions.[7] The new "public" institutions in the novel provide the same cozy shelter from the painful and disorderly "private" world of economic and domestic relations that the old "private" domesticity provided from the old "public" marketplace.

The familial havens provided by institutions were seen by Victorians as a way of remaking working-class culture in bourgeois culture's image. Schools, for example, should replace family for working-class children, who "should not take their parents for their example" (Digby and Searby 127). The professional—doctor, teacher, social-worker—was to play the same role for the working class as the domestic woman plays for the middle class, an angel in this state-rum "house." Given the view of domesticity provided in *Our Mutual Friend*, however, this figuring of institutionalized professional power suggests that it might share the isolation and fragility of domestic angels.

Arac argues that institutionalization influenced *Our Mutual Friend* by taking the novelist's job: "What had once been the novelist's prophetic task [overview] is now safely in the hands of the constituted authorities . . . the novelist steps away from complicity with the establishment by abandoning the position of overview" (187). By 1865, centralized institutions provided the glue of Victorian society, so the novelist could abandon centralizing omniscience for "the inner view" (Arac 187). But the actual institutions depicted in *Our Mutual Friend* represent its least-connected entities. Enclaves of comfort and order, they are nevertheless threatened enclaves, fragile, tiny, and, like Lizzie's womanly influence, ultimately ineffectual. Despite the power of professional expertise within their borders, it cannot transcend them. Little Johnny can be comforted by the cleanliness and company at the hospital, but he dies nonetheless. The inspector proceeds with his monklike task only by ignoring the "howling fury of a drunken woman . . . banging herself against a cell-door in the back-yard at his elbow" (66), and he never does apprehend George Radfoot's murderer. Like the novel's other institutions, the rather sterile schools run by Bradley Headstone and Miss Peecher are placed by their opening description in the realm of fantasy, fairy tales, and childhood:

> *The schools were newly built, and there were so many like them all over the country, that one might have thought the whole were but one restless edifice with the locomotive gift of Aladdin's palace. They were in a neighbourhood which looked like a toy neighbourhood*

*taken in blocks out of a box by a child of particularly
incoherent mind. . . .*

(267-68)

This very placement, however, emphasizes the extent to
which this realm is also one of dissociation and powerlessness, where the institution's very ubiquity suggests not
plenitude, but a "restless" scarcity.

In *Reproduction in Education, Society, and Culture,* Pierre
Bourdieu and Jean-Claude Passeron provide a valuable
sketch of the actual mechanisms by which Althusser's
School Ideological State Apparatus reproduces the subjects
of capitalism,[8] demonstrating how institutionalized education can dispense with the mystification that guards the in-
explicit education provided by the family:

> *[T]he ES [Educational System] would lay itself open to
> the question of its right to set up a relation of peda-
> gogic communication and to delimit what deserves to
> be inculcated—were it not that the very fact of institu-
> tionalization gives it the specific means of annihilating
> the possibility of this question.*

(62)

Institutionalization allows the task of the ES—the reproduction of relations of production—to become explicit
without becoming demystified. Because of the gradual,
piecemeal process of its institutionalization in Britain,
however, the disinterestedness of the Educational System
could never be taken for granted in the nineteenth century.
Although famously early in developing capitalist relations
of production, Britain was notoriously late in developing a
state school system.[9] In the years leading up to the Education Act of 1870, a growing number of Victorians advocated compulsory, state-supported education for all, but
this was bitterly opposed by powerful sectarian interests
and equally powerful fears of excessive state interference.
The compromise reached was a system of government
grants for elementary schools run by church and other or-
ganizations. The result of this "uneven development" is
that the school became the focus of conflicts over the relationship between capitalism and the state, before that relationship was finally taken for granted. *Our Mutual Friend*
takes advantage of this moment of ambivalence, relying
on figurative versions of the classroom examination to authenticate an intellectual authority that transcends market
value, but also insisting on the incapacity of the actual
school—"hopelessly embroiled" in a capitalist economy of
"restless" exchange—to do so.

By the 1860s, the examination had become the primary
mechanism for the occupational self-definition of intellectual laborers (Reader 71, 98). At the same time, it began to
play a key role in structuring relations between working-
class students, teachers, and the state. The Revised Code
of 1862 established "the notorious principle of payment by
results. In order to encourage high and regular attendance
and keep a careful fiscal check . . . grants, instead of being of a more general nature, should be based on atten-

dance plus examination" of each student in reading, writing, and arithmetic by state inspectors (Midwinter 37).
Controversial from its inception, the Code fostered an emphasis on basic skills, rote learning, and memorization.
Robert Lowe, the code's originator, defended his creation
by making explicit the link between payment by results
and high-capitalist economic principles: "Hitherto we have
been living under a system of bounties and protection.
Now we propose to have a little free trade" (qtd. in Midwinter 38). In this model, the infant public sphere of state-
funded education is metaphorically privatized: the state
wields the ultimate authority in the same way that the customer, in an open market, is always right. Schools were to
compete for this customer by producing the best commodities, or students who could pass the Inspector's test.
Because the school was granted a specific amount for each
passing grade, schoolteachers' jobs depended on their students' answers. During the yearly inspection of the Tysoe
village school in Warwickshire,

> *The master hovered round, calling children out as they
> were needed. The children could see him start with
> vexation as a good pupil stuck at a word in the reading-
> book he had been using all the year. . . . The master's
> anxiety was deep, for his earnings depended on the
> children's work. One year the atmosphere of anxiety so
> affected the lower standards that, one after another as
> they were brought to the Inspector, the boys howled
> and the girls whimpered.*

(qtd. in Digby and Searby 9)

One mistress collapsed in front of her class under the
strain of such an examination.

In *Our Mutual Friend,* free-trade education finds its most
dramatic comeuppance in the career of the self-made
schoolteacher turned homicidal maniac, Bradley Headstone. Bradley's "wholesale warehouse" of a brain is firmly
associated with the market economy so savagely critiqued
throughout the novel (David 57). The instructor's dependence on the answers of his students in the state examinations and the way in which the inspections undermined his
authority by causing him to display his anxiety are taken
one step further during Riderhood's blackmailing inspection, "in the way of school," after the attack on Eugene:

> *"Master, might I, afore I go, ask a question of these
> here young lambs of yourn?"*
>
> *"If it is in the way of school," said Bradley, always
> sustaining his dark look at the other, and speaking in
> his suppressed voice, "you may."*
>
> *"Oh! It's in the way of school!" cried Riderhood. "I'll
> pound it, Master, to be in the way of school. Wot's the
> diwisions of water, my lambs? Wot sorts of water is
> there on the land?"*
>
> *Shrill chorus: "Seas, rivers, lakes, and ponds."*
>
> *"Seas, rivers, lakes, and ponds," said Riderhood.
> "They've got all the lot, Master! Blowed if I shouldn't
> have left out lakes, never having clapped eyes upon*

one, to my knowledge. Seas, rivers, lakes, and ponds. Wot is it, lambs, as they ketches in seas, rivers, lakes, and ponds?"

Shrill chorus (with some contempt for the ease of the question): "Fish!"

"Good a-gin!" said Riderhood. "But wot else is it, my lambs, as they sometimes ketches in rivers?"

Chorus at a loss. One shrill voice: "Weed!"

"Good agin!" cried Riderhood. "But it ain't weed neither. You'll never guess, my dears. Wot is it, besides fish, as they sometimes ketches in rivers? Well! I'll tell you. It's suits o' clothes."

Bradley's face changed.

"Leastways, lambs," said Riderhood, observing him out of the corner of his eyes, "that's wot I my own self sometimes ketches in rivers. For strike me blind, my lambs, if I didn't ketch in a river the wery bundle under my arm!"

The class looked at the master, as if appealing from the irregular entrapment of this mode of examination. The master looked at the examiner, as if he would have torn him to pieces.

(866-67)

Although payment-by-results inspections were conducted child by child, and never on such advanced subjects as "the diwisions of water," this passage nevertheless bears a striking resemblance to the Tysoe school inspection and others like it. Riderhood's blackmailing threat fits with startling ease into the inspection scenario set up by the Revised Code.

Riderhood's examination translates knowledge into money even more directly than actual payment-by-results inspections, as he threatens to clear out Bradley's literal, as well as his scholastic, bank account:

"You can't get blood out of a stone, Riderhood."

"I can get money out of a schoolmaster though."

(871)

It would seem that the institution's fragility in *Our Mutual Friend* stems, paradoxically, from its not being institutional enough. To return to Bourdieu and Passeron's terms, when the "cultural arbitrary" inculcated by "pedagogic action" is insufficiently backed by the culture, it becomes merely—and all too visibly—arbitrary.[10] Riderhood's exam raises the possibility that Lowe's "free trade" renders "pedagogic authority" a little *too* free. Because of its emphasis on authorized versions, the Revised Code would seem to be the perfect way to distinguish legitimate from illegitimate knowledge. Indeed, Riderhood establishes his right to question Bradley's students with his pedagogically-phrased question about "diwisions of water." By the time his lesson becomes less conventional, it is too late. Although the class notes and objects to the unorthodoxy of the answer "suits o' clothes," their only ap-

peal is to the already-conquered Bradley. Despite its constant policing of the boundaries of knowledge, free-trade education lets them slip here with fatal ease: the classification of bodies of water slides into the discovery of the clue to an attempted murder, failing to mark the distinction between the things children should know and the things they should be shielded from. Riderhood can cause this slippage, replacing the "highly certificated" (265) Bradley and destroying the latter's authority over his students, merely by "pounding" his threat "to be in the way of school."

Part of the horror in Riderhood's examination is that, while vanquishing Bradley, he also serves as his double—dramatizing (and demonizing) the class displacement Bradley himself represents. Like many Victorian advocates of increased state support for education, Dickens saw the education of the working class as a deterrent to crime (Collins 6). In Riderhood's inspection of Bradley's class, however, the ability of education to replace crime seems to be figured in a nightmare reversal: the ability of crime to replace education and of educational methods to represent the crime of blackmail. The use of market imagery to figure educational processes thus subjects education to the endless and arbitrary replacement of any commodity with any other. In fact, the novel draws many comparisons between Bradley's market-determined methods of learning and his methods of committing murder. He uses the same strategies of production and exchange when he attempts to implicate Riderhood by copying his clothing ("he must have committed [Riderhood's clothing] to memory, and slowly got it by heart" [697]) as he has used to fill his warehouse-brain with knowledge:

He had acquired mechanically a great store of teacher's knowledge. . . . The arrangement of his wholesale warehouse, so that it might be always ready to meet the demands of retail dealers—history here, geography there, astronomy to the right, political economy to the left . . . this care had imparted to his countenance a look of care. . . .

(266-67)

There is even a hint that Bradley is an ineffective murderer for the same reasons that he is an ineffective teacher. In both activities, he is a slow, plodding, inflexible thinker (776).

Our Mutual Friend thus enacts a profound uneasiness about institutionalized free-trade education and the ease with which it can be perverted to private—indeed to criminal—ends. Bradley's market-classroom provides no protection against unauthorized systems of knowledge, because, in Bourdieu and Passeron's terms, it is unable to "resolve by its very existence the questions raised by its existence" (62). As fragile as the novel's other institutional enclaves, the school fails because it is too easily identified as imposing a "cultural arbitrary." The novel instead invites us to invigilate at a series of examinations that take place outside the literal classroom, and that thus authorize legitimate agents of pedagogic action without displaying the arbitrariness of their authority.

These examinations institute a distinction between "masculine" and "feminine" pedagogical methods, one that continues to haunt discussions on gender and pedagogy. In the 1986 *Women's Ways of Knowing,* for example, Mary Field Belenky, Blythe McVicker Clinchy, Nancy Rule Goldberger, and Jill Mattuck Tarule use Paulo Freire's description of the "banking concept" of education in order to develop a gendered contrast between "objectivist" and "subjectivist" (Stone, "Toward" 122-23) models of education:

> *Midwife-teachers are the opposite of banker-teachers. While the bankers deposit knowledge in the learner's head, the midwives draw it out. They assist the students in giving birth to their own ideas, in making their own tacit knowledge explicit and elaborating it.*
>
> (Belenky et al. 217)

Later feminist theorists of pedagogy have been rightly suspicious of the banker/midwife couple (Ellsworth; Stone, "Toward"). Like the couples subject/object, consumption/production, and gender/class, midwife/banker mystifies the mutually constitutive class and gender relations that structure both nineteenth- and twentieth-century Western culture. By placing it in a competitive relationship with the "masculine" banking model, the proponents of the midwife model allow us to forget where babies come from: the "tacit knowledge" midwife-teachers deliver is always the result of insemination by ideology. Bourdieu and Passeron critique

> *the spontaneist Utopia which accords the individual the power to find within himself the principle of his own "fulfillment". . . . The idea of a "culturally free" PA, exempt from arbitrariness in both the content and the manner of its imposition, presupposes a misrecognition of the objective truth of PA in which there is still expressed the objective truth of a violence whose specificity lies in the fact that it generates the illusion that it is not violence.*
>
> (16-17)

All pedagogic action inculcates a cultural arbitrary. But some pedagogies may hide this fact better than others, and thus prove more effective.

In *Our Mutual Friend,* as in *Women's Ways of Knowing,* the bringing forth of preexisting ideas in female pupils is strongly valued over the depositing of information in male heads: while the latter is associated with the illicit climb to professional status of working-class men like Bradley, Wegg, and Charley Hexam, the former is associated with the happy rise to haute-bourgeois wifehood of Bella Wilfer and Lizzie Hexam. Invigilating the novel's male and female test takers, we can catch the banking-teacher's promiscuous transmission of knowledge being countered by a midwife-pedagogy where no transmission of knowledge takes place. Bourdieu and Passeron point out that the

power relations maintained by pedagogic communication remain intact "even when the information transmitted tends towards zero" (21). In *Our Mutual Friend,* the maintenance of these relations actually depends on the transmission of zero information; education escapes the fragility of institutional enclaves only when it does not involve the transference of knowledge from one person to another.

As feminist narrative theory demonstrates, bourgeois narratives of female education are traditionally paradoxical. Subject at once to the demands of the *bildung* and the retention of a marriageable inexperience, girls must become self-conscious producers of unconscious naturalness and accomplished scholars in ignorance (Abel et al., Johnson). Ruth Bernard Yeazell argues that Georgiana Podsnap's truncated story in *Our Mutual Friend* represents Dickens's recognition of the cultural contradiction generated by the relationship between feminine innocence and novelistic plot, while Bella and Lizzie, successfully negotiating the "vast interval" between maiden consciousness and secure middle-class marriage, suggest his retreat from that recognition. The important role played by the "teaching of ignorance" (Johnson) in their stories, however, implies that the distinction may be one of degree rather than kind. For example, Lizzie's virtue seems inseparable from her unconscious resistance to the most innocent transferred knowledge. As she and Jenny pursue their studies in Riah's rooftop garden, "they both pored over one book; both with attentive faces; Jenny with the sharper; Lizzie with the more perplexed" (332). Despite her conscious desire for it, Lizzie has no real need for booklearning. She is already amply supplied with her own form of untransferable expertise, one put to the test as she literally catches a middle-class husband by showing how little her subsequent education has affected her original skill as a waterwoman.[11] Bradley comments to Charley Hexam that

> "[Y]our sister—scarcely looks or speaks like an ignorant person."
>
> "Lizzie has as much thought as the best, Mr Headstone. Too much, perhaps, without teaching. I used to call the fire at home, her books, for she was always full of fancies—sometimes quite wise fancies, considering—when she sat looking at it."
>
> "I don't like that," said Bradley Headstone.
>
> (281)

Many observers besides Bradley have noticed that, indeed, Lizzie "scarcely . . . speaks like an ignorant person" (Morris 130). But here the novel codes her middle-class diction not as the result of class-bound classroom training but as an inherent virtue. It comes as no surprise that Bradley, exemplar of free-trade education, should have objections to such a relation to knowledge. Lizzie will not provide her more successful suitor Eugene with a return on an investment of transferable knowledge (sexual favors for the lessons he pays for), but with the gift of her intrinsic worth.

Before her test in disinterested loyalty, Bella frequently proclaims her greediness for money, but most often as a joke in the quasi-flirtation the "lovely woman" carries on with her father, and "she is always shown as partly affecting her mercenariness" (Hardy 49). Rather than learning goodness, the novel suggests, Bella simply needs to unlearn the surface knowledge that interferes with what she already knows. Bella's final triumph, for example, is throughout a triumph of ignorance. Whirled down to the Fellowship Porters for the identification and vindication of her husband, she is

> *perfectly unable to account for her being there, perfectly unable to forecast what would happen next, or whither she was going, or why; certain of nothing in the immediate present, but that she confided in John, and that John seemed somehow to be getting more triumphant. But what a certainty was that!*

> (833)

The narrowing of her awareness to this single certainty is what finally convinces John to reveal the ruse and present Bella with her reward.

If Bella is not really mercenary, at least on a metaphorical level her examiners would seem to be. Boffin expresses his faith in Bella's innate unselfishness and love for John: "She may be a leetle spoilt, and nat'rally spoilt . . . by circumstances, but that's only the surface, and I lay my life . . . that she's the true golden gold at heart" (843). The "Golden Dustman's" choice of metaphor here draws attention to the central contradiction of Bella's education. Bella *is* the "true golden gold," rather than wishing to possess the Golden Dustman's—with which she will be rewarded for her preciousness (Barbour 65-66). Boffin and Harmon wish (like Gaffer Hexam as he turns corpses' pockets inside out, like Wegg and Venus as they explore the dust heaps) to displace the spoiled "surface" and uncover the "true golden gold." Bella's "certainty" is thus assigned a value, but one that—like a scavenger's find—cannot easily be subjected to a valuation based on the labor theory of value. Whereas Bradley's knowledge is currency to be passed from hand to hand, Bella's "certainty" is a treasure buried within the heart. The novel's gendered opposition of pedagogies achieves what recourse to the doctrine of separate spheres cannot: the paradoxical figuring of a reified knowledge that nevertheless escapes commodification.

Much of the criticism on **Our Mutual Friend** returns over and over to the question of whether or not—and how—Dickens presents an escape from the imagery of capitalist exchange that dominates the novel.[12] But if, as we have seen, intellectual labor must balance on the line between the market and transcendence, then an economics that blurs that division may be more valuable than transcendence itself. The testing of Bella and Lizzie provides such an economics for John and Eugene, one that supplements the exchange of commodities with the finding and keeping of treasure. It is perhaps appropriate that the novel's most brilliant examiner, Noddy Boffin, is also its "Golden Dustman." The novel's famous crowd of scavengers—dustmen,

corpse-pickpockets, articulators of bones, etc.—serves to illustrate the dangers and benefits of the borderland between the economic and the extraeconomic for those who must also inhabit it, its equally numerous intellectual laborers—lawyers, secretaries, "literary men," and schoolteachers.[13]

Notes

1. On the relationship between Victorian professionalization and gender roles see also Hearn, Sawyer, and Witz.

2. For the relation between Dickens's own professional career and the production and content of his fiction, see Feltes, Welsh (*Copyright*), Poovey, and Duncan. Here, my goal is to connect the intellectual workers of *Our Mutual Friend* to the institutionalization of qualifying practices (i.e. the proliferation of the examination) rather than to the professionalization of authorship.

3. An uneasiness about the role they play in capitalist relations still haunts the self-examination of twentieth-century intellectual laborers. One of the most significant problems in Marxist thought after Marx has been the need to account for the phenomenon of the professionalization of intellectual labor and its disturbance (real or apparent) of nearly all the crucial concepts of historical materialism: the class struggle, the historical succession of modes of production, and the relation between the economic and the extraeconomic (or base and superstructure). See, for example, Gramsci, Ehrenreich and Ehrenreich, and Block and Hirschhorn.

4. Cotsell notes that "despite the relative success of the Crimean War (1854-56), the British continued to mistrust the ambitions of the gigantic and illiberal Russian Empire" (58-59).

5. The bourgeois nuclear family is, of course, rarely celebrated in Dickens, where it is usually the site of disorder, lovelessness, and conflict, and where happy domestic groups are more likely to be formed by chance than blood ties. Welsh reminds us that Dickens's famous snug interiors are most often created by additions to or variations on "the conjugal family" (*City* 151). Ingham notices a pervasive "disturbance of family relationships, which are overwritten by new and more highly valued bonds" (118). In *Our Mutual Friend,* however, this disturbance seems to extend from the family itself to the very idea of domesticity: one need only compare Lizzie Hexam's ineffectiveness to the almost superhuman effectiveness of Dickensian angels like *Hard Times*'s Sissy Jupe or *Little Dorrit*'s Amy Dorrit.

6. Bourdieu and Passeron define "pedagogic action" (PA) as a form of "symbolic violence" that inculcates "cultural arbitraries," or culturally established categories of knowledge, through its command of "pedagogic authority" (PAu), an authority always granted

by a particular political entity (such as a social class). I am arguing here that gender categories play an important role in the process by which pedagogic authority is granted to the Victorian professional in the novel.

7. See Fraser's discussion of both public/private splits, where she critiques Habermas's opposition between the "lifeworld" of familial relationships and the "official economy" (119).

8. According to Althusser, the "educational apparatus" is the dominant Ideological State Apparatus for the reproduction of capitalist relations of production (153-54). In *Our Mutual Friend,* the Victorian school, with its complex and tenuous relation to the Victorian state, is also the paradigmatic state institution.

9. While Britain's first state-run schools were created by the 1870 Education Act, universal, compulsory, free elementary schooling was not implemented until 1891. On the development of the British educational system, see Digby and Searby, and Midwinter.

10. See note 6 for a brief account of Bourdieu and Passeron's use of these terms.

11. David points out that "Lizzie affirms in her words and in her actions a powerful determinant of social situation [the class difference between her and Eugene], and her affirmation leads to its ambiguous transcendence" (57).

12. For example, Miller cites Jenny's famous rooftop cry, "come up and be dead," as the novel's model of transcendence, and David argues that *Our Mutual Friend* both represents and transcends the social reality which is a pervasive determinant of the restlessness and dissatisfaction of its characters" (55). For Gallagher, the novel's "Bioeconomics" provide an escape from commodification for the novel's heroines. Jaffe (*Vanishing*) argues that the novel privileges a different kind of transcendence of reification for a male character, John Harmon, in the disembodied subjectivity of omniscience.

13. This way of signifying the professional's place in capitalism seems to extend beyond Dickens: Jaffe demonstrates that in Mayhew and Conan Doyle, beggars and gentlemen (including financiers and authors) share a participation in an "illegitimate production" of representation rather than products ("Detecting" 109).

Works Cited

Abel, Elizabeth, Marianne Hirsch, and Elizabeth Langland, eds. *The Voyage In: Fictions of Female Development.* Hanover: UP of New England, 1983.

Althusser, Louis. *Lenin and Philosophy and Other Essays.* Trans. Ben Brewster. New York: Monthly Review, 1971.

Arac, Jonathan. *Commissioned Spirits: The Shaping of Social Motion in Dickens, Carlyle, Melville, and Hawthorne.* New Brunswick: Rutgers UP, 1989.

Armstrong, Frances. *Dickens and the Concept of Home.* Ann Arbor: UMI, 1990.

Armstrong, Nancy. *Desire and Domestic Fiction: A Political History of the Novel.* New York: Oxford UP, 1987.

Barbour, Judith. "Euphemism and Paternalism in *Our Mutual Friend.*" *Sydney Studies in English* 7 (1981-82): 55-68.

Belenky, Mary Field, Blythe McVicker Clinchy, Nancy Rule Goldberger, and Jill Mattuck Tarule. *Women's Ways of Knowing: The Development of Self, Voice, and Mind.* New York: Basic, 1986.

Block, Fred, and Larry Hirschhorn. "New Productive Forces and the Contradictions of Contemporary Capitalism." *Theory and Society* 7 (1979): 363-95.

Bourdieu, Pierre, and Jean-Claude Passeron. *Reproduction in Education, Society, and Culture.* Trans. Richard Nice. London: Sage, 1977.

Collins, Philip. *Dickens and Education.* London: Macmillan, 1963.

Costell, Michael. *The Companion to* Our Mutual Friend. London: Allen, 1986.

David, Deirdre. *Fictions of Resolution in Three Victorian Novels*: North and South, Our Mutual Friend, *and* Daniel Deronda. New York: Columbia UP, 1981.

Dickens, Charles. *Our Mutual Friend.* 1864-65. Harmondsworth: Penguin, 1971.

Digby, Anne, and Peter Searby. *Children, School and Society in Nineteenth-Century England.* London: Macmillan, 1981.

Duncan, Ian. *Modern romance and transformations of the novel: The Gothic, Scott, Dickens.* Cambridge: Cambridge UP, 1992.

Ehrenreich, Barbara, and John Ehrenreich. "The Professional-Managerial Class." *Between Labor and Capital.* Ed. Pat Walker. Boston: South End, 1979. 5-45.

Ellsworth, Elizabeth. "Why Doesn't This Feel Empowering? Working Through the Repressive Myths of Critical Pedagogy." Stone, *Education* 300-27.

Feltes, N. N. *Modes of Production of Victorian Novels.* Chicago: U of Chicago P, 1986.

Fraser, Nancy. "What's Critical About Critical Theory? The Case of Habermas and Gender." *Unruly Practices: Power, Discourse and Gender in Contemporary Social Theory.* Minneapolis: U of Minnesota P, 1989. 113-43.

Gallagher, Catherine. "The Bioeconomics of *Our Mutual Friend.*" *Subject to History: Ideology, Class, Gender.* Ed. David Simpson. Ithaca: Cornell UP, 1991. 47-69.

Gramsci, Antonio. *An Antonio Gramsci Reader.* Ed. David Forgacs. Trans. Quintin Hoare and Geoffrey Nowell-Smith. New York: Schocken, 1988.

Hardy, Barbara. *The Moral Art of Dickens.* New York: Oxford UP, 1970.

Hearn, Jeff. "Notes on Patriarchy, Professionalization and the Semi-Professions." *Sociology* 16 (1982): 184-202.

Ingham, Patricia. *Dickens, women and language.* London: Harvester, 1992.

Jaffe, Audrey. "Detecting the Beggar: Arthur Conan Doyle, Henry Mayhew, and 'The Man with the Twisted Lip.'" *Representations* 31 (1990): 96-117.

———. *Vanishing Points: Dickens, Narrative, and the Subject of Omniscience.* Berkeley: U of California P, 1991.

Johnson, Barbara. "Teaching Ignorance: *L'Ecole des Femmes.*" *Yale French Studies* 63 (1982): 165-82.

Larson, Magali Sarfatti. *The Rise of Professionalism: A Sociological Analysis.* Berkeley: U of California P, 1977.

Midwinter, Eric. *Nineteenth-Century Education.* London: Longman, 1970.

Miller, J. Hillis. *Charles Dickens: The World of His Novels.* Cambridge: Harvard UP, 1958.

Morris, Pam. *Dickens's Class Consciousness: A Marginal View.* London: Macmillan, 1991.

Poovey, Mary. *Uneven Developments: The Ideological Work of Gender in Mid-Victorian England.* Chicago: U of Chicago P, 1988.

Reader, W. J. *Professional Men: The Rise of the Professional Classes in Nineteenth-Century England.* New York: Basic, 1966.

Sawyer, Paul. "Ruskin and the Matriarchal Logos." *Victorian Sages and Cultural Discourse: Renegotiating Gender and Power.* Ed. Thais E. Morgan. New Brunswick: Rutgers UP, 1990. 129-41.

Sedgwick, Eve Kosofsky. *Between Men: English Literature and Male Homosocial Desire.* New York: Columbia UP, 1985.

Stone, Lynda, ed. *The Education Feminism Reader.* New York: Routledge, 1994.

Stone, Lynda. "Toward a Transformational Theory of Teaching." Stone, *Education* 221-28.

Welsh, Alexander. *The City of Dickens.* Oxford: Clarendon, 1971.

———. *From Copyright to Copperfield: The Identity of Dickens.* Cambridge: Harvard UP, 1987.

Witz, Anne. *Professions and Patriarchy.* New York: Routledge, 1992.

Yeazell, Ruth Bernard. "Podsnappery, Sexuality, and the English Novel." *Critical Inquiry* 9.2 (1982): 339-57.

Rodney Stenning Edgecombe (essay date 1996)

SOURCE: "'The Ring of Cant': Formulaic Elements in *Our Mutual Friend,*" in *Dickens Studies Annual,* Vol. 24, 1996, pp. 167-84.

[*In the following essay, Edgecombe studies the "cant" often disparaged by critics of* Our Mutual Friend, *and suggests that this was part of a deliberate and highly-controlled strategy to reinforce the primary concerns of the author.*]

At one point of **Our Mutual Friend** Dickens turns to the Podsnaps in his audience and attacks them for their reductive use of language, for the way in which they have blocked sentient human responses with unreal, inhuman formulae. The rebuke to some extent recalls the arraignment of Scrooge by the Spirit of Christmas Present—"Man . . . if man you be in heart, not adamant, forbear that wicked cant until you have discovered What the surplus is, and Where it is" (**Christmas Books,** 47; Stave 3):

> A surprising spirit in this lonely woman after so many years of hard working and hard living, my Lords and Gentlemen and Honourable Boards! What is it that we call it in our grandiose speeches? British independence, rather perverted? Is that, or something like it, the ring of the cant?
>
> (199; I, ch. 16)

"Ring" might at first glance seem to be inappropriate to the tiredness of cant, but Dickens seems to have chosen it for its monetary clink, an oblique pointer to an idea stated and restated ad infinitum throughout the novel—namely, that moral debility results from an obsession with wealth. Moral debility in this and in other instances also brings with it a linguistic debility that Dickens mimics and mocks repeatedly in **Our Mutual Friend.**

This authorially emphasized languor might account for the disfavor with which **Our Mutual Friend** has sometimes been viewed. For example, James's review objected to its putative "exhaustion" and factitiousness: "we should . . . congratulate [Dickens] on his success in what we should call the manufacture of fiction; for in so doing we should express a feeling that has attended us throughout the book. Seldom, we reflected, had we read a book so intensely *written,* so little seen, known, or felt" (32). Of course, James read **Our Mutual Friend** with a polemical purpose, and, trying as he was to open up a new seam in nineteenth-century fiction, he probably felt compelled to announce the exhaustion of Dickens' particular mine. But even if we make allowance for this tendentiousness, it is possible that his dismissal might also have had something to do with the "cant" element in the novel. I shall argue, however, that far from being a defect, this "cant" (and the "exhaustion" it seems to evoke) is wholly controlled and put there to enhance the author's chief concerns.

Early on we find Lightwood using stereotypic phrases to reduce the story of Bella and the Harmon will to a sort of marionettish *commedia dell'arte.* His clichés trivialize and distance its human content, and reduce living persons to functions in a plot:

> ". . . At this stage of the affair the poor girl respectfully intimated that she was secretly engaged to that popular character whom the novelists and versifiers call Another, and that such a marriage would make Dust of

her heart and Dust of her life—in short, would set her up, on a very extensive scale, in her father's business. Immediately, the venerable parent—on a cold winter's night, it is said—anathematised and turned her out."

. . . . .

"The pecuniary resources of Another were, as they usually are, of a very limited nature. I believe I am not using too strong an expression when I say that Another was hard up. However, he married the young lady, and they lived in a humble dwelling, probably possessing a porch ornamented with honeysuckle and woodbine twining, until she died."

(14; I, ch. 2)

Lightwood's offhand manner in telling the story registers above all in phrases so typical and conforming as to have been all but emptied of significance. Popular fiction might indeed characterize its stock patriarchs with the epithet "venerable," but surely the phrase ought not to remain mindlessly in place when he is banishing a child. In the same way, the adverbs of habitude—"as they *usually* are" and "*probably* possessing"—sap the narrative of tension, and since narrative without tension conduces to boredom, boredom finally issues in languor. The clichés also infect and flatten the rhetorical surge of the Harmon girl's avowal. Since it contains *in ovo* parts of Bella's story, and since its metaphor is one that Dickens will orchestrate and augment throughout the novel, it deserves worthier treatment than Lightwood's indifferent paraphrase. Its disengaged, even tone is further secured by the upper case he gives to "Dust," as though it were a stock item on a par with "Another." If the speaker's witty detachment were set in abeyance, the story, even with all its archetypal components in place, could be made to register very differently.

Heinrich Heine's lyric "Ein Jüngling liebt ein Mädchen" dramatizes the way a narrator can, by a sudden shift from mechanical to engaged delivery, convert cliché to divine commonplace. After two stanzas of pat, formulaic delivery—Heine's "And're" is the exact equivalent of Lightwood's "Another"—he breaks open the stock triangle to reveal real suffering beneath the geometry—"dem bricht das Herz entzwei":

> Ein Jüngling liebt ein Mädchen,
> die hat einen Andern erwählt;
> der And're liebt eine And're,
> und hat sich mit dieser vermählt.
>
> Das Mädchen heirathet aus Aerger
> den ersten besten Mann,
> der ihr in den Weg gelaufen;
> der Jüngling ist übel dran.
>
> Est ist eine alte Geschichte,
> doch bleibt sie immer neu;
> und wem sie just passiret,
> dem bricht das Herz entzwei.
>
> [A youth oft loves a maiden,
> Who for another sighs,
> Perchance he loves another,

And weds the blooming prize.

> The maiden thus neglected,
> Weds the first who comes that way,
> Then he who has been rejected,
> To grief doth become a prey.
>
> It is but an olden story,
> And yet it is ever new;
> The last fond youth who suffer'd
> He broke his heart so true.]

(Schumann, 204-05)

Only to the cynical and the world-weary—and Lightwood's stance is not dissimilar to that of the prophet in Ecclesiastes—is there nothing new under the sun. Having no emotional pulse, they cannot feel the recurrent force of the archetype.

A. O. J. Cockshut has remarked that although Lightwood "tells the story . . . as a stock comic melodrama; it is not that he really lacks sympathy; he is simply playing the Veneering game in the approved fashion" (172). That is so, but for the greater part of *Our Mutual Friend,* Dickens gives no hint that Lightwood and Wrayburn, his model, will undergo a conversion from degagé triviality to a life of purpose. They register primarily as characters of a type Dickens all but invented, and which Oscar Wilde later appropriated as his own persona. Because epigrams can be forged only by a cool, detached sensibility, with often prides itself on being above the "vulgarity" of large emotion, as witness the Wildean dictum about a heart of stone and the death of Little Nell. Also, because epigrams often turn on inverting received wisdom and commonplaces, their purveyors have shown a contemptuous and guarded attitude towards ordinary human responses, and, equating ordinariness with cliché, have demonstrated their contempt by inverting it. Thus when Umberto Eco claims fastidiousness as a "note" of post-modernism, he seems to have forgotten a comparable rarefaction in the aesthetics of the Aesthetes: "I think of the postmodern attitude as that of a man who loves a very cultivated woman, and knows he cannot say to her, 'I love you madly,' because he knows—and she knows that he knows—that the words have already been written by Barbara Cartland" (67). In Eco's view such knowledge commits the speaker to an ironic, self-masking kind of declaration not unlike Lightwood's handling of the Harmon story.

This handling, however, while it establishes the dominant ethos of *Our Mutual Friend,* is not without precedent in the work of Dickens. The elder Chester in *Barnaby Rudge* provides a partial prototype for Lightwood and Wrayburn, expressing a dislike for "what are called family affairs, which are only fit for plebeian Christmas days," and evading the language of bereavement simply because—to find a pre-Romantic parallel for Barbara Cartland—Mrs. Radcliffe had already done it to death in *The Mysteries of Udolpho*:

"You have me to thank, Ned, for being of good family; for your mother, charming person as she was, and almost broken-hearted, and so forth, as she left me, when she was prematurely compelled to become immortal—had nothing to boast of in that respect."

(118; ch. 15)

Because of his "witty" indifference to human feeling, the speaker shorthands a husband's grief with a "so forth" and thus reduces it to a tiresome predictability. At the same time, since he is the husband in question, he is manifestly (and impenitently) confessing his own inability to feel intense emotion.

There are many comparable instances of perfunctory dismissal in *Our Mutual Friend,* so many indeed that Lightwood's manner might be said to have provided a paradigm for Dickens' *own* narrative conduct in parts of the novel. J. Hillis Miller has pointed out that the "Veneering dinner parties are an elaborate theatrical ceremony resting on nothing, and the people who come to these parties have been so dehumanized by their submission to money that they exist not as individuals, but as their abstract roles, "Boots," "Brewer," and so on" (171). But even though these sections are written in a way that disengages them from the texture of the novel, they are not wholly *sui generis.* One can easily adduce other analogues for the disengaged, formulaic discourse of Lightwood. For example, Hillis Miller has also noted how the Veneering dinners are often "described in the present tense, in language that is cold and withdrawn, terse, with an elliptical economy new in Dickens. Sometimes verbs and articles are omitted . . ." (175). Much the same, *mutatis mutandis,* could be said of the compliments that Lightwood pays to Mrs. Boffin, though here the ellipticality seems not so much terse as debilitated:

Mr. Lightwood murmured "Equal honour—Mrs. Boffin's head and heart."

. . . . .

Mr. Lightwood murmured "Vigorous Saxon spirit—Mrs. Boffin's ancestors—bowmen—Agincourt and Cressy.

(90; I, ch. 8)

This is a languor too wan to turn up the volume, too tired to bother with conventional syntax, too bored by the predictability of its own formulae. Compare Dickens' own wearied impatience with blood lines at the start of Chapter 4 and the wholly unremarkable quality of their "remarkable facts":

Reginald Wilfer is a name with rather a grand sound, suggesting on first acquaintance brasses in country churches, scrolls in stained-glass windows, and generally the De Wilfers who came over with the Conqueror. For, it is a remarkable fact in genealogy that no De Any ones came over with Anybody else.

(32)

Chapter 4 is a chapter twice removed from the previous Veneering sequence, but some of the Veneering narrative

habits have not been shed. Dickens characterizes William by function rather than by name, and he indifferently throws open the French patronymic to the "Any's," bored by the predictability of snobs as Lightwood had been bored by the predictability of the Harmon saga. The same sort of reader self-help occurs in a jibe at Mrs. Veneering. Having established a stock analogy, Dickens indifferently hands us the reins of the narrative for the moment, and says, "Do as you will": "[she] repeats in a distracted and devoted manner, compounded of Ophelia and any self-immolating female of antiquity you may prefer, 'We must work'" (244; II, ch. 3). Then again, at a moment of climactic "sincerity" in a Veneering speech, nonce words trivialize and open out the options to such an extent that meaning all but drains through the interstices: "for we couldn't think of spending sixpence on it, my love, and can only consent to be brought in by the spontaneous thingummies of the incorruptible whatdoyoucallums" (250; II, ch. 3).

Indifference and ennui also register in other ways, as when Lightwood foregoes the effort of fresh speech, but at the same time apologizes for having offered a cliché instead:

"[. . .] You could put the whole in a cash-box tomorrow morning, and take it with you—say, to the Rocky Mountains. Inasmuch as every man," concluded Mr. Lightwood, with an indolent smile, "appears to be under a fatal spell which obliges him, sooner or later, to mention the Rocky Mountains in a tone of extreme familiarity to some other man, I hope you'll excuse my pressing you into the service of that gigantic range of geographical bores."

(88-89; I, ch. 8)

To some extent this parallels Dickens' habit in *Our Mutual Friend* of invoking outmoded iconographic conventions which he clearly finds absurd, but applies notwithstanding. For example, in rendering Mrs. Wilfer's grotesque formality (comic antimasque to the formality of the Veneering world), he resorts to self-apologetic clichés à la Lightwood:

As that was all the rum and water, too, or, in other words, as R. W. delicately signified that his glass was empty by throwing back his head and standing the glass upside down on his nose and upper lip, it might have been charitable in Mrs. Wilfer to suggest replenishment. But that heroine briefly suggesting "Bedtime" instead, the bottles were put away, and the family retired; she cherubically escorted, like some severe saint in a painting, or merely human matron allegorically treated.

(42; I, ch. 4)

This strategy is not unique to *Our Mutual Friend.* Dickens also resorts to mock history painting in earlier novels, as when Charity Pecksniff stages a domestic tableau for the elder Chuzzlewit:

See the neat maiden, as with pen in hand, and calculating look addressed towards the ceiling, and bunch of keys within a little basket at her side, she checks the housekeeping expenditure! From flat-iron, dish-cover, and warming-pan; from pot and kettle, face of brass footman, and black-leaded stove; bright glances of approbation wink and glow upon her. The very onions dangling from the beam, mantle and shine like cherubs' cheeks.

(333; ch. 20)

Here the comedy is more oblique, for the various properties and postures of hagiographic painting have been *contained* in their domestic equivalents. Charity's eyeline recalls the beatific upward roll of such paintings as Raphael's "St. Catherine of Alexandria" (acquired by the National Gallery in 1839), her pen the emblem of an Evangelist or a martyr's palm, the onion swags the cherubim of sacred art. In the treatment of Mrs. Wilfer, on the other hand, the grandiose conventions engulf and swamp the domestic element altogether. Speaking like a bad translation of Sophocles, she can be said to have earned her formulaic treatment as an allegorization of motherhood—frigid and statuesque and far removed from the cosy images of maternity favored by bourgeois Victorian painters.

Perhaps because he could so effortlessly forge allegory from quotidian materials, Dickens seems to have felt antipathy for more solemn and self-conscious versions of the mode. We see this above all in his repeated mockery of neoclassic art. In *Great Expectations* Pip puts aside pre-Romantic allegory as a childish thing:

> This was always followed by Collins's Ode on the Passions, wherein I particularly venerated Mr. Wopsle as Revenge, throwing his blood-stained sword in thunder down, and taking the War-denouncing trumpet with a withering look. It was not with me then, as in later life, when I fell into the society of the Passions, and compared them with Collins and Wopsle, rather to the disadvantage of both gentlemen.

(40; ch. 7)

In *Our Mutual Friend* Dickens disavows another aspect of neoclassic art—what he seems to conceive as the suave unreality of its loco-descriptive verse. At one point he incorporates a standard Thomsonian adjective-noun-adjective into a sentence as graceless and as gauche as he can make it. Thomson himself loses his poetic selfhood, crushed by a stampede of Cockney men for whom his seasonal idylls have no relevance at all:

> It was not summer yet, but spring; and it was not gentle spring ethereally mild, as in Thomson's Seasons, but nipping spring with an easterly wind, as in Johnson's, Jackson's, Dickson's, Smith's, and Jones's Seasons.

(144; I, ch. 12)

Even the token symmetry of the disyllabic surnames that initially displace "Thomson" gets crushed and disarranged with the advent of Smith and of Jones, the last chosen for a possessive form harsh enough to make the cadence seem more ugly still.

Given this impatience with the "inert" heritage of neoclassic poetry, it is startling to find Silas Wegg surveyed by a

personification that might have stepped from Collins's "Ode to Evening," duly draped in a "gradual dusky veil" (466): "But when night came, and with her veiled eyes beheld him stumping towards Boffin's Bower, he was elated too" (54; I, ch. 5). Dickens seems to have placed it there as a sort of residuum of the Veneering mode, where comparably dated formulae figure in Lady Tippins's rococo pastoral, her cupids and her "rough Cymons" dragged in from Boccaccio. Dickens also personifies Fashion in his account of the Boffin marriage, but because Fashion never figures in history paintings, and because the personification is cobbled from one of Mrs. Boffin's fashion plates, the effect is a touch more energetic: "Fashion, in the form of her black velvet hat and feathers, tried to prevent it; but got deservedly crushed in the endeavour" (56). Dickens nonetheless seems to be mocking the deific formulae and intercessory posture of a Collins ode when he observes that "Mrs. Boffin's Fashion" was a "less inexorable deity than the idol usually worshipped under that name" (57).

Dickens seems deliberately to have laced *Our Mutual Friend* with mock eighteenth-century prosopopoeia—the prosopopeia that Coleridge condemned as being forged from nothing more solid than the upper case. In Book I, Chapter 15, the curtain goes up on a tableau of Mr. and Mrs. Boffin in the Bower. Although there is no syntactic compulsion to use capital letters for "Care and Complication," the author has applied them as a sort of neoclassical cant, as though prosperity had brought a pretentious but exhausted literary mode with it, and forced it on its victims: "Mr. and Mrs. Boffin sat after breakfast, in the Bower, a prey to prosperity. Mr. Boffin's face denoted Care and Complication. Many disordered papers were before him . . ." (178). Bella's use of the uppercase at a later point of the novel also tends to formalize and flag the patness of her bestiary similes, much as Lightwood had common-placed dust with a capital D: "for I am naturally as obstinate as a Pig" (528); "I chatter like a Magpie" (529; III, ch. 8).

Having claimed this sort of reductiveness for upper case nouns, I must point out that they tend to function reductively only when a "domestic" (i.e., cosy) prose texture throws them out as creatures unnative and unendued to their element. When, on the other hand, Dickens is working within his repertoire of universal symbols, or writing prophetically *in propria persona,* his afflatus imps the wing of capitalized abstractions. We can find an instance of this in one of Lizzie's reveries—"As she came beneath the lowering sky, a sense of being involved in a murky shade of Murder dropped upon her; and, as the tidal swell of the river broke at her feet without her seeing how it gathered, so, her thoughts startled her by rushing out of an unseen void and striking at her heart. . . . And as the great black river with its dreary shores was soon lost to her view in the gloom, so, she stood on the river's brink unable to see into the vast blank misery of a life suspected, and fallen away from by good and bad, but knowing that it lay dim before her, stretching away to the great ocean, Death" (70-71; I; ch. 6). Such passages are far removed from the sort of allegory we find in Gray or Collins. There it seems altogether more regulated, marked off into specific visual frames and clarifying tableaux. By contrast, we find nothing so premediated in Dickens' treatment of "Murder" and "Death," and the spatial deixis and placement of neoclassical art (*ut pictura poesis*) bears little relation to his violent dynamism ("rushing") and inconceivable space ("the vast blank misery of a life suspected"). Cant has thus been subsumed by a vigorous imagination, and the languor of cliché galvanized by rampant energy.

We have seen how Dickens uses conventional phrases in his narrative of fashionable life to stress its emotional and moral enfeeblement. At such times he could be said to have followed the Lightwood/Wrayburn solution to cliché—viz., to tweezer it disdainfully. We see this, for example, in his perfunctory application of nuptial topoi to the Lammle marriage. Images once meaningful in the hands of Catullus or Spenser have here been reduced to pasteboard trimming:

> While the Loves and Graces have been preparing this torch for Hymen, which is to be kindled tomorrow, Mr. Twemlow has suffered much in his mind. It would seem that both the mature young lady and the mature young gentleman must indubitably be Veneering's oldest friends. Wards of his, perhaps? Yet that can hardly be, for they are older than himself.
>
> (114; I, ch. 10)

Having discarded these tired pseudo-Spenserian properties with contemptuous despatch, Dickens turns to an alternative tactic for exposing cant—that of interrogating its insincerity from an innocent viewpoint. One can reject a convention as an untenable cliché, crushing it wearily under the weight of such accumulated experience as says there is nothing new under the sun, or one can feign total innocence, and turn it into a ridiculous kenning, as in Dickens's faux-naif account of painterly cherubs:

> So the gridiron was put in requisition, and the good-tempered cherub, who was often as un-cherubically employed in his own family as if he had been in the employment of some of the Old Masters, undertook to grill the fowls. Indeed, except in respect of staring about him (a branch of the public service to which the pictorial cherub is much addicted), this domestic cherub discharged as many odd functions as his prototype; with the difference, say, that he performed with a blacking-brush on the family's boots, instead of performing on enormous wind instruments and double-basses, and that he conducted himself with cheerful alacrity to much useful purpose, instead of foreshortening himself in the air with the vaguest intentions.
>
> (454; III, ch. 4)

Dickens here effects a renovation of cliché by "innocently" confusing utilitarian and aesthetic functions. A cherub which stares and points might in fact have a real purpose in a pictorial design—that of *repoussoir*, say—and a foreshortened *putto* might indeed help to define a perspective line. Only someone wholly ignorant of artistic function would so improbably cross lines.

Yet that is precisely Twemlow's mistake when he tries to root Veneering cant in sincerity and fact. The Veneerings and Podsnaps have founded their lives on phrases which they have severed from fact and emptied of meaning. Twemlow's difficulty centers on an unmeaning use of "oldest friend" and the contradictions that spring from that use:

> The abyss to which he could find no bottom, and from which started forth the engrossing and ever-swelling difficulty of this life, was the insoluble question whether he was Veneering's oldest friend, or newest friend.
>
> (7; I, ch. 2)

The joke recurs again and again as Veneering fits the phrase to each new acquaintance in turn. While such cant might be a leitmotiv of the fashionable world, however, it also figures in its dark social antitype, the world of the watermen. Rogue Riderhood is quite as ready as Veneering to remove the substance of a phrase and traffic with its empty vessel. Dickens stresses its vacancy by rattling it again and again:

> "Lawyer Lightwood," ducking at him with a servile air, "I am a man as gets my living, and as seeks to get my living, by the sweat of my brow. Not to risk being done out of the sweat of my brow, by any chances, I should wish afore going further to be swore in."
>
> (148; I, ch. 12)

Having thus mass-produced the cliché, Dickens even lets Eugene fit it into its predictable sockets. His languor recalls Lightwood's manner of story-telling:

> "Of seaman's pocket," said Mr. Riderhood. "Whereby I was in reality the man's best friend, and tried to take care of him."
>
> "With the sweat of your brow?" asked Eugene.
>
> "Till it poured down like rain," said Roger Riderhood.
>
> (150)

And, as if to signal the start of Mr. Boffin's moral displacement, Dickens has him appropriate a stock element from the ballads that, by way of antimasque to the tired allusions and topoi of fashionable discourse, Silas Wegg is always forcing upon the circumstances of his own life:

> "[. . .] My literary man was so friendly as to drop into a charming piece of poetry on that occasion, in which he complimented Mrs. Boffin on coming into possession of—how did it go, my dear?'
>
> Mrs. Boffin replied:
>
> "'The gay, the gay and festive scene,
> The halls, the halls of dazzling light.'"
>
> . . . . .

"[. . .] To let him feel himself anyways slighted now, would be to be guilty of a meanness, and to act like having one's head turned by the halls of dazzling light. . . ."

(181-2; I; ch. 15)

By interpolating H. S. van Dyke's verse into Mr. Boffin's bluff idiom, Dickens on the one hand conveys his ingenuousness, but at the same time he also seems to hint at a sort of mechanical adaptation of Veneeringspeak, and to hint the imminent quenching of the dustman's spontaneity. It is only to be expected, therefore, that when he needs to modulate into the *un*predictable and *un*precedented intensity of Headstone's passion, he should effect the transition by disavowing the sort of standard commonplace associated with other parts of the novel: "Love at first sight is a trite expression quite sufficiently discussed; enough that in certain smouldering natures like this man's, that passion leaps into a blaze, and makes such head as fire does in a rage of wind, when other passions, but for its mastery, could be held in chains" (341; II, ch. 3). Those chains, reminiscent of the stock topos of the *vinculum amoris,* enact the very ordinariness from which the man's intensity breaks free.

Tired iconography and empty phrases are one means by which Dickens gives a character of listlessness to *Our Mutual Friend,* but there are many additional devices of indifference and lassitude. Repetition is one of them. It goes without saying that repetition is a key feature of Dickens' art, and it is made to serve a multitude of thematic ends. In *Our Mutual Friend,* however, the iterative patterns often seem more pronounced and insistent than usual, helping to image the mechanical impulse behind every effort to conform. It calls to mind the elder Chester's "so forth," that verbal "etc." sign which lets the material generate itself on automatic pilot. The following extract from *Sketches by Boz* provides a foil to its listlessness:

It was a neat, dull little house, on the shady side of the way, with new, narrow floorcloth in the passage, and new, narrow stair-carpets up to the first floor. The paper was new, and the paint was new, and the furniture was new; and all three, paper, paint and furniture, bespoke the limited means of the tenant.

(42; **"Our Parish,"** ch. 7)

Context is everything, of course, and because the accumulated "new's" proceed here with the lively reportorial interest that the young Dickens takes in his environment, the repetitions seem accordingly to bounce instead of dragging. Come *Our Mutual Friend,* however, and the iteration, as if by contact with the deadening conformities of the society it analyses, levels the stylistic landscape for miles on end:

Mr. and Mrs. Veneering were bran-new people in a bran-new house in a bran-new quarter of London. Everything about the Veneerings was spic and span new. All their furniture was new, all their friends were new, all their servants were new, their plate was new, their carriage was new, their harness was new, their horses were new, their pictures were new, they themselves were new, they were as newly married as was lawfully compatible with their having a bran-new baby, and if they had set up a great-grandfather, he would have come home in matting from the Pantechnicon, without a scratch upon him, French-polished to the crown of his head.

(6; I, ch. 7)

In this passage the documentary newness in **"Our Parish"** has been stylized almost out of recognition, not only because Dickens has sustained the *heratio* with a more daring insistence, but also because he applies the epithet mechanically, and makes no attempt to distinguish between animate and inanimate items. The Veneerings develop a bright toy-like surface on the one hand, and on the other, a grandfather clock stands in as a nonce ancestor. Such flat, cumulative structures recall comparable moments in nursery rhymes—"The House that Jack Built," for example—and impart a sort of undifferentiated infantility to the Veneerings. (Part of the novel's distinctive color can be attributed to what John Robson has called its "remarkable series of references to nursery rhymes, games, and tales, songs, ballads, adages and images of childhood"—205). As a further token of this infantility, Wrayburn mentions the man from Tobago (from Marshall's *Anecdotes and Adventures of Fifteen Gentlemen*) at a Veneering dinner party, and makes the allusion doubly trivial by garbling it. (The implication is that it is hardly worth the effort of memory.) His *tibicines* (metrical prop lines) create an effect of indifference similar to the elder Chester's "so forth," and, by mangling both the invalid's diet and the diet of his cure, he makes nonsense of the entire poem:

"Tobago, then."

"Nor yet from Tobago."

"Except." Eugene strikes in: so unexpectedly that the mature young lady, who has forgotten all about him, with a start takes the epaulette out of his way: "except our friend who long ago lived on rice-pudding and isinglass, till at length to his something or other, his physician said something else, and a leg of mutton somehow ended in daygo."

(11; I, ch. 2)

Compare the purposeful "before" and "after" in the original: "There was a sick man of Tobago, / Liv'd long on rice-gruel and sago; / To his bliss / The physician said this / 'To a roast leg of mutton you may go'" (Opie, pl. XIX, opp. 407). Although Lady Tippins rebukes Eugene on this occasion for forgetting his nursery rhymes, she herself makes heavy weather of an equally formulaic allusion to the Dunmow flitch of bacon: "And dear Mrs. Lammle and dear Mr. Lammle, how do you do, and when are you going down to what's-its-name place—Guy, Earl of Warwick, you know—what is it?—Dun Cow—to claim the flitch of bacon?" (409; II, ch. 16). The stock-figure unreality of folklore and nursery rhyme also pervades the treatment of the Podsnaps, one of whose conversations Dickens renders in the manner of Simple Simon's exchange with the Pieman:

> Said Mr. Podsnap to Mrs. Podsnap, "Georgiana is almost eighteen."
> Said Mrs. Podsnap to Mr. Podsnap, assenting, "Almost eighteen."
> Said Mr. Podsnap then to Mrs. Podsnap, "Really I think we should have some people on Georgiana's birthday."
> Said Mrs. Podsnap then to Mr. Podsnap, "Which will enable us to clear off all those people who are due."
>
> (130; I, ch. 11)

Relief is promised to the woodenness of this conversation by the author's adding a variant ("assenting") to the mirrored *verba dicendi*—but that variant, being tautological, cannot offer variety. As G. W. Kennedy has pointed out, there are moments in *Our Mutual Friend* when "language tends to perish almost completely, becoming totally disconnected from any human or physical reality" (169).

Since the whole ethos of Podsnappery centers on conventionality, it is not surprising that Dickens should also use repetition to render the joyless exigence of its forms. He even paraphrases a recreational quadrille chez the Podsnaps as a dance to the Protestant work ethic:

> Then the discreet automaton who had surveyed his ground, played a blossomless tuneless "set," and sixteen disciples of Podsnappery went through the figures of—1, Getting up at eight and shaving close at a quarter-past—2, Breakfasting at nine—3, Going to the City at ten—4, Coming home at half-past five—5, Dining at seven, and the grand chain.
>
> (137-38; I, ch. 11)

Only the final section of the Lancers escapes the paraphrase, but by contagion with the other sections, it has by now acquired the dead weight of a manacle. If life is a lifeless inventory for Podsnap, it is no less so for Bradley Headstone as he aspires to enter the "respectable" world. In this instance, the uniformity of repetition becomes the verbal icon of a literal uniform. What in early Dickens had been a trope of exuberance is recreated here (as in the fog sequence in *Bleak House,* and the "red brick" proem to *Hard Times*) as the vector of ennui and disaffection:

> Bradley Headstone, in his decent black coat and waistcoat, and decent white shirt, and decent formal black tie, and decent pantaloons of pepper and salt, with his decent silver watch in his pocket and its decent hairguard round his neck, looked a thoroughly decent young man of six-and-twenty. . . . He could do mental arithmetic mechanically, sing at sight mechanically, blow various wind instruments mechanically, even play the great church organ mechanically.
>
> (217; II, ch. 1)

Just as Dickens imparts an additional mechanicality to the Podsnap party by cancelling the spontaneity of dance, so

here he gives Headstone a superadded harshness by subsuming the spontaneity of music to mental arithmetic and uniting the disciplines through a mechanical adverb. Peter Sucksmith has also pointed out how, by "repeating 'mechanical', Dickens draws attention to the way the instinctive man in Bradley Headstone has been repressed beneath a difficulty acquired veneer of culture; by repeating 'decent,' the novelist stresses that the professional *persona* of the schoolmaster is overcompensating for his social origin" (64-65).

Few verbal structures could be more mechanical than the rote lessons of Victorian primary schools, with their preformulated responses and preformulated questions. As if further to satirize a lifeless, formulary outlook in *Our Mutual Friend,* Dickens turns several sections into a catechism. He himself uses a question-and-answer antiphony in his satire on shares:

> Where does he come from? Shares. Where is he going to? Shares. What are his tastes? Shares. Has he any principles? Shares. What squeezes him into Parliament? Shares.
>
> (114; I, ch. 10)

In a lighter vein, the improbable exchanges between Miss Peecher and Mary Anne relay gossip about Bradley Headstone and Lizzie via labyrinthine grammatical interrogations:

> "They say she is very handsome."
>
> "Oh, Mary Anne, Mary Anne!" returned Miss Peecher, slightly colouring, and shaking her head, a little out of humour; "how often have I told you not to use that vague expression, not to speak in that general way? When you say *they* say, what do you mean? Part of speech They?"
>
> Mary Anne hooked her right arm behind her in her left hand, as being under examination, and replied:
>
> "Personal pronoun."
>
> (220; II, ch. 1)

Then there also is Riderhood's lesson on river, in which he torments Headstone (who alone knows the right answer) by asking a Sphinxian question of his pupils. Their innocently formulaic minds cannot begin to encompass its horror:

> "[. . .] Wot is it, lambs, as they ketches in seas, rivers, lakes, and ponds?"
>
> Shrill chorus (with some contempt for the ease of the question): "Fish!"
>
> "Good agin!" said Riderhood. "But what else is it, my lambs, as they sometimes ketches in rivers?"
>
> Chorus at a loss. One shrill voice: "Weed!"
>
> (794; IV, ch. 15)

And, finally, there is Podsnap's patronage of his French dinner guest:

"It merely referred," Mr. Podsnap explained, with a sense of meritorious proprietorship, "to Our Constitution, Sir. We Englishmen are Very Proud of our Constitution, Sir. It Was Bestowed Upon Us by Providence. No Other Country is so Favoured as This Country."

"And ozer countries," the foreign gentleman was beginning, when Mr. Podsnap put him right again.

"We do not say Ozer; we say Other; the letters are "T" and "H;" you say Tay and Aish, You Know;" (still with clemency). "The sound is 'th'—'th!'"

(133; I, ch. 11)

At the same time as Dickens uses the uppercase to register the patronizing, schoolmasterly distinctness of Podsnap's articulation, he also uses it to draw a separative line round each element of the lesson. Words no longer have the flexibility and litheness that they would ordinarily bring to human discourse, but lead a lifeless, discrete existence as counters in a formulary world view.

And although his outlook is very different, and his mental process diametrically opposed, Eugene Wrayburn is as guilty as Mr. Podsnap is of using capital letters in a reductive way. By means of the "institutional" uppercase, and by means of a world-weary desire to abbreviate, he devitalizes into frigid capitals the otherwise significant bond of father and son. Because, on Eugene's half-reliable testimony, the father does not himself escape the taint of Podsnappery, there is some justice in the reduction:

"With some money, of course, or he would not have found her. My respected father—let me shorten the dutiful tautology by substituting in future M. R. F., which sounds military, and rather like the Duke of Wellington."

"What an absurd fellow you are, Eugene!"

"Not at all, I assure you. M. R. F. having always in the clearest manner provided (as he calls it) for his children by pre-arranging from the hour of the birth of each, and sometimes from an earlier period, what the devoted little victim's calling and course in life should be. . . ."

(146; I, ch. 12)

Several allusions lie under the languid becalmment of this speech. The Duke of Wellington was, of course, the icon for the reactionary forces that had tried to obstruct social progress in Britain after the defeat of Napoleon, a fact which makes the conformity of militarism seem all the more airless and unprogressive. There is also a fleeting allusion to Gray's "Ode on a Distant Prospect of Eton College"—"Alas, regardless of their doom, / The little victims play!" (59)—bringing with it a whiff of the neo-classicism that Dickens approaches so distrustfully here and elsewhere in his novels. It also brings with it the memory of the final line ("No more; where ignorance is bliss / 'Tis folly to be wise"), a gesture of effacement which Dickens would probably have aligned with Podsnap's.

In taking Lightwood's narrative as point of departure for this article, and in suggesting that it offers a sort of proto-

type for a calculated and subversive languor affected in many parts of his novel, I have really been speaking about levels of engagement, levels which are crucially bound up in the choice of narrative vantage. Just as the elder Wrayburn foreknows the destiny of each of his children, and so figures as a dark Calvinistic deity preordaining the fate of each, so too Lightwood, by his offhand use of the third-person omniscient, turns prompter to a set of squeaking marionettes. A narrator can alienate us from his characters by denying us direct access to their thoughts, omitting *verba dicendi,* and smoothing a once impassioned utterance into an unpersuasive flatness. The terrible anagnorisis of the Lammles' marriage provides a case in point. Their lives henceforth will mask an unrehearsed private hell with a public script. This disparity is caught in the rendering, for the apparent immediacy of the historic present makes the third person mode seem all the more manipulative and remote:

She bursts into tears, declaring herself the wretchedest, the most deceived, the worst-used of women. Then she says that if she had the courage to kill herself, she would do it. Then she calls him a vile impostor. Then she asks him why, in the disappointment of his base speculation, he does not take her life with his own hand, under the present favourable circumstances. Then she cries again. Then she is enraged again, and makes some mention of swindlers.

(125; I, ch. 10)

In that relentless anaphoraic chant of "then's," which stylize living reactions into an inventory of postures, and in that muffled relay of passion where hyperbole, cut off from the power of the speaking voice, must necessarily issue as cliché—in these and in many other features of *Our Mutual Friend,* we hear that characteristic "ring of the cant."

In his pioneering essay on Dickens, George Orwell concluded that what one might term the "narrative face" of the author is

the face of a man who is always fighting against something, but who fights in the open and is not frightened, the face of a man who is *generously angry*—in other words, of a nineteenth-century liberal, a free intelligence, a type hated with equal hatred by all the smelly little orthodoxies which are now contending for our souls.

("Charles Dickens," *Decline of the English Murder and Other Essays,* 140-41)

Some of those "smelly little orthodoxies" were also abroad in the nineteenth century, and they figure as stagnant bywaters in *Our Mutual Friend,* cut off from the energetic momentum of the novel by their formulaic listlessness. Orthodoxies are based on creeds, and creeds, themselves the most summary reduction of imponderables, are shored up by the preformulated antiphons of the catechism, whether cut to the Gospel of Christ or of Marx or of Mao. Writing of one kind of orthodoxy—the political—Orwell also noted that its "language—and with variations this is true of all political parties, from Conservatives to Anarchists—is designed to make lies sound truthful and murder respectable, and to give an appearance of solidity to pure wind" ("Politics and the English Language," *Inside the Whale and Other Essays,* 156). No better epigraph could be adduced for the world of Podsnap and Veneering.

Works Cited

Cockshut, A. O. J. *The Imagination of Charles Dickens.* London: Collins, 1961.

Dickens, Charles. *Barnaby Rudge: A Tale of the Riots of 'Eighty.* Introduced by Kathleen Tillotson. London: Oxford UP, 1954.

———. *Christmas Books.* Introduced by Eleanor Farjeon. London: Oxford UP, 1954.

———. *Great Expectations.* Introduced by F. W. Pailthorpe. London: Oxford UP, 1953.

———. *Martin Chuzzlewit.* Edited by Margaret Cardwell. Oxford: Clarendon, 1982.

———. *Our Mutual Friend.* Introduced by E. Salter Davies. London: Oxford UP, 1952.

———. *Sketches by Boz Illustrative of Every-Day Life and Every-Day People.* Introduced by Thea Holme. London: Oxford UP, 1957.

Eco, Umberto. *Reflections on "The Name of the Rose."* London: Secker and Warburg, 1985.

Gray, Thomas. *The Poems of Gray, Collins and Goldsmith.* Edited by Roger Lonsdale. London: Longman, 1969.

James, Henry. *Selected Literary Criticism.* Edited by Morris Shapira. 1963; Rpt. Harmondsworth: Penguin, 1968.

Kennedy, G. W. "Naming and Language in *Our Mutual Friend,*" *Nineteenth-Century Fiction* 28 (1973): 165-78.

Miller, J. Hillis. "Our Mutual Friend," in *Dickens: A Collection of Critical Essays.* Edited by Martin Price. Englewood Cliffs: Prentice-Hall, 1967.

Opie, Iona and Peter. *The Oxford Dictionary of Nursery Rhymes.* Oxford: Clarendon, 1951.

Orwell, George. *Decline of the English Murder and Other Essays.* Harmondsworth: Penguin, 1965.

———. *Inside the Whale and Other Essays.* Harmondsworth: Penguin, 1957.

Robson, John M. "*Our Mutual Friend*: A Rhetorical Approach," *Dickens Studies Annual* 3 (1974): 198-213.

Schumann, Robert. *Songs by Schumann.* London: Boosey and Company, No Date.

Sucksmith, Harvey Peter. *The Narrative Art of Charles Dickens: The Rhetoric of Sympathy and Irony in his Novels.* Oxford: Clarendon, 1970.

FURTHER READING

Criticism

Baker, Robert S. "Imagination and Literacy in Dickens' *Our Mutual Friend.*" *Criticism* 18, no. 1 (Winter 1976): 57-72.
Examines the connection between literacy and the moral issues Dickens addressed in the novel.

Cotsell, Michael. "Secretary or Sad Clerk? The Problem with John Harmon." *Dickens Quarterly* 1, no. 4 (December 1984): 130-36.
Suggests that Dickens had two contradictory intentions for the character of John Harmon: one as the resourceful, capable man, and the other as the sad, defeated child.

Hutter, Albert D. "Dismemberment and Articulation in *Our Mutual Friend.*" *Dickens Studies Annual* 11 (1983): 135-75.
Studies the Victorian fascination with mutilation and dismemberment and the way they are represented in *Our Mutual Friend.*

Jaffe, Audrey. "Omniscience in *Our Mutual Friend*: On Taking the Reader by Surprise." *Journal of Narrative Technique* 17, no. 1 (Winter 1987): 91-101.
Takes issue with critics who claim that there is no prominent omniscient narrative presence in *Our Mutual Friend.*

Kennedy, G. W. "Naming and Language in *Our Mutual Friend.*" *Nineteenth-Century Fiction* 28, no. 2 (Sept. 1973): 165-78.
Studies the way various characters in *Our Mutual Friend* passively accept the domination of the novel's collective consciousness, as opposed to the small number of characters who assert their individual wills in opposition to it.

Kucich, John. "Dickens' Fantastic Rhetoric: The Semantics of Reality and Unreality in *Our Mutual Friend.*" *Dickens Studies Annual* 14 (1985): 167-89.
Studies the relationship between realism and romance at the semantic level in *Our Mutual Friend.*

MacKay, Carol Hanbery. "The Encapsulated Romantic: John Harmon and the Boundaries of Victorian Soliloquy." *Dickens Studies Annual* 18 (1989): 255-76.

Reviews John Harmon's lengthy soliloquy, often considered problematic by scholars, and suggests that its combination of Victorian and Romantic features is of far more importance than its length and form.

Miller, Michael G. "The Fellowship-Porters and the Veneerings': Setting, Structure and Justice in *Our Mutual Friend*." *The Dickensian* 85 (1989): 64–74.

Examines two of *Our Mutual Friend*'s settings, noting the contrast between the comfortable tavern and the cold, uninviting home of the Veneerings.

Newman, S. J. "Decline and Fall Off? Towards an Appreciation of *Our Mutual Friend*." *The Dickensian* 85, no. 2 (Summer 1989): 99-104.

Claims that the central problem of *Our Mutual Friend* is how seriously its author intended readers to take it.

Palmer, William J. "The Movement of History in *Our Mutual Friend*." *PMLA* [*Publications of the Modern Language Association*] 89, no. 3 (May 1974): 487-95.

Examines the way various characters deal with past history and the many ways they misread its meanings.

Robson, John M. "Crime in *Our Mutual Friend*." In *Rough Justice: Essays on Crime in Literature,* edited by M. L. Friedland, pp. 114-40, Toronto: University of Toronto Press, 1991.

Studies the many and various instances of criminal activity and violent acts in *Our Mutual Friend.*

Shea, F. X. "Mr. Venus Observed: the Plot Change in *Our Mutual Friend*." *Papers on Language and Literature* 4, no. 2 (Spring 1968): 170-181.

Concludes from a study of the manuscript that Dickens changed the plot of the novel while writing it, resulting in an attack on the upper middle class that was much weaker than originally intended.

Smith, Peter. "The Aestheticist Argument of *Our Mutual Friend*." *Cambridge Quarterly* 18, no. 4 (1989): 362-82.

Argues that beauty is the theme of *Our Mutual Friend*, and that all other themes and motifs—from greed and social injustice to the river and the dustheaps—must be considered subordinate to the novel's primary concern.

Yeazell, Ruth Bernard. "Podsnappery, Sexuality, and the English Novel." *Critical Inquiry* 9, no. 2 (December 1982): 339-57.

Explores the illusion of young female innocence which accounts for the elimination of information not only about sexuality, but also about social problems, in the Victorian novel in general, and in *Our Mutual Friend* in particular.

Additional coverage of Dickens's life and career is contained in the following sources published by The Gale Group: *Authors and Artists for Young Adults,* **Vol. 23;** *Concise Dictionary of British Literary Biography 1832-1890;* *DISCovering Authors;* *DISCovering Authors: British;* *DISCovering Authors: Canadian;* *DISCovering Authors Modules: Most Studied Authors* **and** *Novelists;* *DISCovering Authors 3.0;* *Dictionary of Literary Biography,* **Vols. 21, 55, 70, 159, 166;** *Junior DISCovering Authors; Major Authors and Illustrators for Children and Young Adults; Novels for Students,* **Vol. 5;** *Something About the Author,* **Vol. 15;** *Short Story Criticism,* **Vol. 17; and** *World Literature Criticism, 1500-Present.*

Solomon Northup
1808-1863

(Surname also rendered as Northrup and Northrop) American autobiographer.

INTRODUCTION

Northup's only written work is his autobiography, *Twelve Years a Slave. Narrative of Solomon Northup, a Citizen of New-York, Kidnapped in Washington City in 1841, and Rescued in 1853, from a Cotton Plantation Near the Red River, in Louisiana* (1853). Northup's slave narrative, the tale of a free African American man who is kidnapped, sold into slavery, and lives as a slave for twelve years, was a best-seller for its genre and time. *Twelve Years a Slave* is praised for its detailed examination of slavery and plantation society, particularly in its contrast to his previous life as a musician and citizen of New York. Northup's narrative also has been cited as illustrative of slavery's horrors and has been used to support the depictions in Harriet Beecher Stowe's *Uncle Tom's Cabin*. As slave narratives relating such detail are relatively rare, Northup's story is used as an example of the kidnapped slave narrative subgenre. Though considered of value mainly for the accurate description of his experiences, Northup's narrative has come to be recognized as a complex account of slavery that eschews many of the recognized conventions of the slave narrative.

BIOGRAPHICAL INFORMATION

Solomon Northup was born in July, 1808, in Minerva, New York. The son of Mintus Northup, a freed slave who bore his former owners' last name, Northup learned of slavery through his father's experiences but grew up an educated and literate free man. Northup also maintained contact with the white Northup family and particularly with Henry B. Northup, in part because they lived in the same region. In 1829 Northup married Anne Hampton with whom he had three children. Between 1829 and 1841, Northup lived near Lake Champlain and Saratoga Springs, New York. He supported his family through various positions, including that of raftsman, farmer, and hack driver, earning extra money as a musician at social gatherings. In March, 1841, Northup was approached by two strangers who convinced him to accompany them to Washington City by offering him employment as a musician in the circus with which they claimed to be connected. Once they had traveled out of the state of New York, Northup was drugged, stripped of his free papers, shackled, and whipped. He was then delivered to a slave trader and taken to New Orleans where he was sold. Renamed Platt, Northup lived in Louisiana as a slave for twelve years, belonging to several different owners during that time. Despite the fact that Northup kept his real identity secret for fear of repercussion, his previous life as a free man—particularly his education, work experiences, and abilities as a musician—set him apart from other slaves both in terms of perspective and in value to his masters. In 1852 Northup met a white carpenter named Samuel Bass who agreed to help Northup gain his freedom by secretly contacting Northup's New York acquaintances. Upon learning of Northup's situation, Henry B. Northup traveled to Louisiana and secured the legal help of John P. Waddill. Together they found Northup, established his true identity, and secured his liberty. Northup was reunited with his family in New York in January 1853 and the news of his kidnapping, slavery, and release generated considerable attention in the news and in his community. Soon after his return David Wilson, a local lawyer, approached Northup about collaborating on his memoirs, and *Twelve Years a Slave* was published later that year. Northup's narrative led to the trial of his kidnappers, which generated a significant amount of public interest, though the charges were eventually dismissed. Northup did not publish any other writings about his experiences but moved to Glens Falls where he lived out the rest of his life as a carpenter. It is believed that Northup died in 1863, but little information exists on how he spent his final years.

MAJOR WORKS

Although Northup was literate, *Twelve Years a Slave* was written with David Wilson serving as Northup's amanuensis. The prose style of Northup's account is attributed to Wilson, but the narrative is considered to be Northup's own. *Twelve Years a Slave* is unusual in that it is considered to be a well-balanced account of slavery, recounting many of its horrors but also discussing aspects of plantation life that made slavery more tolerable. The narrative is noted most often for its wealth of details, many of which were easily verified by public records and eyewitness accounts. Northup's observations supported his analysis of Southern life and critique of slavery. This balance enabled a public response to the narrative as an anti-slavery document of great historical worth. Because Northup's experiences were both sensational and true, the narrative enjoyed an immediate commercial and critical success. Its initial release and subsequent reprints sold over thirty thousand copies, and the narrative was favorably compared with Harriet Beecher Stowe's *Uncle Tom's Cabin* by critics and reviewers alike. Later reprints of Northup's narrative capitalized on this comparison by including a dedicatory page to Stowe and the novel.

CRITICAL RECEPTION

Northup's slave narrative has been acknowledged as having significant value for many reasons. Northup's contemporaries used his narrative as an illustration of slavery's wrongs or, as Harriet Beecher Stowe's reaction demonstrates, as a validation of their own writings on slavery. Sue Eakin and Joseph Logsdon succinctly expressed the narrative's continuing worth in their introduction to their 1968 edition of *Twelve Years a Slave*. As a historical record, Northup's easily authenticated tale, with its details about slave life, information on the daily operations of plantations, and the depictions of Southern culture provides a complex examination of slavery. Critics also note that Northup's narrative demonstrates his unusual position as an outsider and an insider: Northup was a free, literate African American man from the North whose first-hand knowledge of slavery and the South began as an adult after he was kidnapped and sold. Northup's slave narrative reflects the complexities of both his own situation and the broader cultural context in which slavery existed in the United States. His narrative is considered by many critics to be a unique contribution to the body of slave narratives and it has been used as primary documentation for broad examinations of slavery and the South, including the work of scholars such as Charles H. Nichols and Karen Cole. As literature, however, *Twelve Years a Slave* has been evaluated generally as a slave narrative of secondary importance. Often it is compared unfavorably with other slave narratives, notably that of Frederick Douglass. This is in part due to Northup's less-unified and externally-focused narrative style, as well as his lack of overt self-construction. The narrative's debatable position as a work of literature is also attributed to the recognizable stylistic presence of David Wilson. Thus many critics, including Robert B. Stepto and James Olney, have questioned the status of *Twelve Years a Slave* as an autobiography and even Northup's categorization as an author. More recently, scholars have reasserted that Northup's descriptions and structure of the narrative supersede Wilson's contributions and clearly establish Northup as the author. Sam Worley suggests that Northup's tale, precisely because it breaks with commonly-held conventions for the slave narrative, serves as an example of an important literary and historical document.

PRINCIPAL WORKS

Twelve Years a Slave. Narrative of Solomon Northup, a Citizen of New-York, Kidnapped in Washington City in 1841, and Rescued in 1853, from a Cotton Plantation Near the Red River, in Louisiana. [with David Wilson as amanuensis] (slave narrative) 1853

CRITICISM

Harriet Beecher Stowe (essay date 1853)

SOURCE: "Kidnapping," in *A Key to Uncle Tom's Cabin; Presenting the Original Facts and Documents upon which the Story is Founded. Together with Corroborative Statements Verifying the Truth of the Work,* Kennikat Press, Inc., 1968, pp. 173-74.

[*In the following excerpt from the companion book, originally published in 1853, to* Uncle Tom's Cabin, *Stowe presents an abridged account of Northup's kidnapping, slavery, and liberation as was reported by the* New York Times *in order to support her fictionalized account of slavery.*]

KIDNAPPING

The principle which declares that one human being may lawfully hold another as property leads directly to the trade in human beings; and that trade has, among its other horrible results, the temptation to the crime of kidnapping.

The trader is generally a man of coarse nature and low associations, hard-hearted, and reckless of right or honor. He who is not so is an exception, rather than a specimen. If he has anything good about him when he begins the business, it may well be seen that he is in a fair way to lose it.

Around the trader are continually passing and repassing men and women who would be worth to him thousands of dollars in the way of trade,—who belong to a class whose rights nobody respects, and who, if reduced to slavery, could not easily make their word good against him. The probability is that hundreds of free men and women and children are all the time being precipitated into slavery in this way.

The recent case of *Northrop,* tried in Washington, D. C., throws light on this fearful subject. The following account is abridged from the *New York Times*:

> Solomon Northrop is a free colored citizen of the United States; he was born in Essex county, New York, about the year 1808; became early a resident of Washington county, and married there in 1829. His father and mother resided in the county of Washington about fifty years, till their decease, and were both free. With his wife and children he resided at Saratoga Springs in the winter of 1841, and while there was employed by two gentlemen to drive a team South, at the rate of a dollar a day. In fulfilment of his employment, he proceeded to New York, and, having taken out free papers, to show that he was a citizen, he went on to Washington city, where he arrived the second day of April, the same year, and put up at Gadsby's Hotel. Soon after he arrived he felt unwell, and went to bed.

> While suffering with severe pain, some persons came in, and, seeing the condition he was in, proposed to give him some medicine, and did so. This is the last thing of which he had any recollection, until he found himself chained to the floor of Williams' slave-pen in this city, and handcuffed. In the course of a few hours, James H. Burch, a slave-dealer, came in, and the colored man asked him to take the irons off from him, and wanted to know why they were put on. Burch told him it was none of his business. The colored man said he was free, and told where he was born. Burch called in a man by the name of Ebenezer Rodbury, and they two stripped the man and laid him across a bench, Rodbury holding him down by his wrists. Burch whipped him with a paddle until he broke that, and then with a cat-o'-nine-tails, giving him a hundred lashes; and he swore he would kill him if he ever stated to any one that he was a free man. From that time forward the man says he did not communicate the fact from fear, either that he was a free man, or what his name was, until the last summer. He was kept in the slave-pen about ten days, when he, with others, was taken out of the pen in the night by Burch, handcuffed and shackled, and taken down the river by a steamboat, and then to Richmond, where he, with forty-eight others, was put on board the brig *Orleans.* There Burch left them. The brig sailed for New Orleans, and on arriving there, before she was fastened to the wharf, Theophilus Freeman, another slave-dealer, belonging in the city of New Orleans, and who in 1833 had been a partner with Burch in the slave-trade, came to the wharf, and received the slaves as they were landed, under his direction. This man was immediately taken by Freeman and shut up in his pen in that city. He was taken sick with the small-pox immediately after getting there, and was sent to a hospital, where he lay two or three weeks. When he had sufficiently recovered to leave the hospital, Freeman declined to sell him to any person in that vicinity, and sold him to a Mr. Ford, who resided in Rapides Parish, Louisiana, where he was taken and lived more than a year, and worked as a carpenter, working with Ford at that business.

> Ford became involved, and had to sell him. A Mr. Tibaut became the purchaser. He, in a short time, sold him to Edwin Eppes, in Bayou Beouf, about one hundred and thirty miles from the mouth of Red river, where Eppes has retained him on a cotton plantation since the year 1843.

> To go back a step in the narrative, the man wrote a letter, in June, 1841, to Henry B. Northrop, of the State of New York, dated and post-marked at New Orleans, stating that he had been kidnapped and was on board a vessel, but was unable to state what his destination was; but requesting Mr. N. to aid him in recovering his freedom, if possible. Mr. N. was unable to do anything in his behalf, in consequence of not knowing where he had gone, and not being able to find any trace of him. His place of residence remained unknown until the month of September last, when the following letter was received by his friends:

> *Bayou Beouf, August,* 1852. Mr. William Peny, or Mr. Lewis Parker.

> Gentlemen: It having been a long time since I have seen or heard from you, and not knowing that you are living, it is with uncertainty that I write to you; but the necessity of the case must be my excuse. Having been born free just across the river from you, I am certain you know me; and I am here now a slave. I wish you to obtain free papers for me, and forward them to me at Marksville, Louisiana, Parish of Avovelles, and oblige Yours, Solomon Northrop.

> On receiving the above letter, Mr. N. applied to Governor Hunt, of New York, for such authority as was necessary for him to proceed to Louisiana as an agent to procure the liberation of Solomon. Proof of his freedom was furnished to Governor Hunt by affidavits of several gentlemen, General Clarke among others. Accordingly, in pursuance of the laws of New York, Henry B. Northrop was constituted an agent, to take such steps, by procuring evidence, retaining counsel, &c., as were necessary to secure the freedom of Solomon, and to execute all the duties of his agency.

The result of Mr. Northrop's agency was the establishing of the claim of Solomon Northrop to freedom, and the restoring him to his native land.

It is a singular coincidence that this man was carried to a plantation in the Red river country, that same region where the scene of Tom's captivity was laid; and his account of this plantation, his mode of life there, and some incidents which he describes, form a striking parallel to that history. We extract them from the article of the *Times:*

The condition of this colored man during the nine years that he was in the hands of Eppes was of a character nearly approaching that described by Mrs. Stowe as the condition of "Uncle Tom" while in that region. During that whole period his hut contained neither a floor, nor a chair, nor a bed, nor a mattress, nor anything for him to lie upon, except a board about twelve inches wide, with a block of wood for his pillow, and with a single blanket to cover him, while the walls of his hut did not by any means protect him from the inclemency of the weather. He was sometimes compelled to perform acts revolting to humanity, and outrageous in the highest degree. On one occasion, a colored girl belonging to Eppes, about seventeen years of age, went one Sunday, without the permission of her master, to the nearest plantation, about half a mile distant, to visit another colored girl of her acquaintance. She returned in the course of two or three hours, and for that offence she was called up for punishment, which Solomon was required to inflict. Eppes compelled him to drive four stakes into the ground at such distances that the hands and ankles of the girl might be tied to them, as she lay with her face upon the ground; and, having thus fastened her down, he compelled him, while standing by himself, to inflict one hundred lashes upon her bare flesh, she being stripped naked. Having inflicted the hundred blows, Solomon refused to proceed any further. Eppes tried to compel him to go on, but he absolutely set him at defiance, and refused to murder the girl. Eppes then seized the whip, and applied it until he was too weary to continue it. Blood flowed from her neck to her feet, and in this condition she was compelled the next day to go into the field to work as a field-hand. She bears the marks still upon her body, although the punishment was inflicted four years ago.

When Solomon was about to leave, under the care of Mr. Northrop, this girl came from behind her hut, unseen by her master, and, throwing her arms around the neck of Solomon, congratulated him on his escape from slavery, and his return to his family; at the same time, in language of despair, exclaiming, "But, O God! what will become of me?"

These statements regarding the condition of Solomon while with Eppes, and the punishment and brutal treatment of the colored girls, are taken from Solomon himself. It has been stated that the nearest plantation was distant from that of Eppes a half-mile, and of course there could be no interference on the part of neighbors in any punishment, however cruel, or how ever well disposed to interfere they might be.

Had not Northrop been able to write, as few of the free blacks in the slave states are, his doom might have been sealed for life in this den of misery. . . .

Charles H. Nichols (essay date 1963)

SOURCE: "The Driver's Lash," in *Many Thousands Gone: The Ex-Slaves' Account of Their Bondage and Freedom,* E. J. Brill, 1963, pp. 62-70.

[*In the following excerpt, Nichols analyzes several firsthand accounts of the physical systems of control of slaves, particularly that of punishment.*]

"No more driver's lash for me,
No more, no more,
No more driver's lash for me,
Many thousand gone."

Holidays, gifts, opportunities to work for wages, religious training, the hope of freedom all served to make slaves more contented and controllable. But to a considerable extent the master depended on physical controls: the driver's or overseer's whip, the patrols and the law. To be sure the slaves were not without means of bringing their masters to terms either. They resisted, pretended illness, loafed, petitioned, ran off to the woods (on "strike"), mutilated themselves, or ran away forever. These are, however, aspects of slave behavior which will be discussed in a succeeding chapter. Unpaid labor had to be constantly supervised and forced to work. Nearly all the travellers in the South and especially Lyell and Olmsted noticed the laziness and inefficiency of slave labor. The driver's lash was, there fore, an indispensable aid to the system's functioning. It seemed to Olmsted that Northern agricultural labor worked harder than the slaves, but the latter he, noted, were

constantly and steadily driven up to their work, and the stupid, plodding, machine-like manner in which they labour, is painful to witness. This was especially the case with the hoe gangs . . . I repeatedly rode through the lines at a canter, with other horsemen, often coming upon them suddenly, without producing the smallest change or interruption in the dogged action of the labourers or causing one of them, so far as I could see, to lift an eye from the ground . . . I think it told a more painful story than any I had ever heard of the cruelty of slavery. It was emphasized by a tall and powerful negro who walked to and fro in the rear of the line, frequently cracking his whip, and calling out in the surliest manner, to one and another, 'Shove your hoe, there! Shove your hoe.'[1]

James Williams and Solomon Northup were drivers, and both report that when a driver failed to do his cruel work, he was himself flogged. For eight years Northup was a driver on a Louisiana plantation where (in consideration for his fellow victims) he learned to handle the whip with marvellous dexterity and precision, "throwing the lash within a hair's breadth of the back, the ear, the nose without, however, touching either of them."[2] And when the overseer appeared he would lash vigorously, and "according to arrangement" the slaves would "squirm and screech as if in agony." Such humaneness and fellow feeling were not very common, for the narrators often found themselves under cruel drivers as well as overseers. Any slave who did not do his task or failed to be properly submissive was flogged. Nor were these whippings in any way comparable to the gentle chastisement given to school boys. The instrument employed for the purpose, the "bull whip," is described by John Brown:

First a stock is chosen of a convenient length, the butt end of which is loaded with lead, to give the whip force. The stock is then cleverly split to within a foot or so of the butt, into twelve strips. A piece of tanned leather divided into eight strips, is then drawn on the stock so that the split lengths can be plaited together. This is done very regularly, until the leather tapers down to quite a fine point, the whip being altogether about six feet long, and as limber and lithesome as a snake. The thong does not bruise but cuts; and those who are expert in the use of it, can do so with such dexterity, as to only raise the skin and draw blood or cut clean through to the bone. I have seen a board a quarter of an inch thick cut through it, at one blow . . . It is also employed to whip down savage bulls or unruly cattle. I have seen many a horse cut with it right through the hollow of the flank, and the animal brought quivering to the ground. The way of using it is to whirl it round until the thong acquires a certain forward power, and then to let the end of the thong fall across the back, . . . the arm being drawn back with a kind of sweep. But although it is so formidable an instrument, it is seldom employed on slaves in such a manner as to disable them . . .[3]

All the narrators report that they were whipped at some time during their enslavement, and many displayed their scarred and stripped backs to amazed audiences at abolitionist meetings. At times the victim was tied to a tree, bent over a barrel or staked to the ground and whipped. Other slave were strung up on cross beams with their toes barely touching the ground and whipped in that position. Twenty-five lashes were considered slight correction. A serious infraction of the law of the plantation—stealing, running away, talking back to a white man—might merit the offender as many as three hundred lashes. Both men and women were whipped—usually on the bare back. That the whipping of a recalcitrant Negro might properly subdue the rest, all the slaves were called to witness whippings. Having run away Henry Bibb was seized and chastised. The sound of the overseer's horn brought all the slaves to witness his punishment. His clothing was stripped off and he was compelled to lie down on the ground with his face to the earth. Four stakes were driven in the ground, to which his hands and feet were tied. Then the overseer stood over him with the lash and struck him repeatedly as his master looked on. Fifty lashes were laid on without stopping. He was then lectured about going to prayer meeting without permission and for running away to escape flogging. Cut and bleeding, the victim's wounds were then washed in salt brine to prevent the putrefaction of the flesh.[4] Runaways were also confined in stocks, collared or chained.

Usually on these isolated plantations the overseer was judge, jury, prosecutor and executioner, and he often wielded his power like a medieval monarch. No slave could testify against any white person anywhere in the South so that no brutal act of an overseer could be brought before the courts unless it had been witnessed by a white person. Occasionally a slave might run off and appeal to his master. Other Negroes resisted and sometimes whipped the overseer. But overseers were armed and did not hesitate to kill a slave who was so bold, for the law supported his right to kill a Negro who struck a white man. One overseer told Olmsted, "I wouldn't mind killing a nigger

more than I would a dog."[5] A Negro whom the overseer could not easily handle could be subdued by patrols, who committed him to jail and whipped him soundly. The ex-slaves were very much aware of the patrols, who often trounced a slave found off the plantation without a pass. John Thompson and Austin Steward tell of lively clashes with patrols. Masters in towns or cities might for a small fee have their naughty slaves whipped at the local jail. William Wells Brown was sent to jail with a note and a dollar to be whipped but cleverly sent another Negro in his place.

The following letter written in 1847 by Charles Manigault to his overseer on a Georgia plantation suggests the stealth and subtle reassurance by which he hoped to control a recalcitrant Negro:

> With regard to Jacob (whom you say is the only disorderly one) you had best think carefully respecting him, and always keep in mind the important old plantation maxim—viz: 'never to *threaten* a negro' or *he will run.* But with such a one whenever things get too bad, you should take a certain opportunity, when, for instance, he is with the driver in the provision room, and you at the door, with a string in your pocket—then pull it out and order him tied—for if in such a case a negro succeeds in dodging or running from you, the annoyance is great—but having got him if you wish to make an example of him, take him down to the Savannah jail and give him prison discipline and by all means solitary confinement for 3 weeks, when he will be glad to get home again—but previous to his coming out, let them jog his memory again, mind then and tell him that you and he are quits—that you will never dwell on old quarrels with him—that he now has a clear track before him, and all depends on himself, for he now sees how easy it is to fix a 'bad disposed nigger.' Then give my compliments to him and tell him that you wrote me of his conduct, and I say if he don't change for the better I'll sell him to a slave trader who will send him to New Orleans, where I have already sent several of the gang for their misconduct, or their running away for no cause.[6]

All these punishments—whipping, chaining, selling, shooting—were legal and customary, but laws designed to protect the property of owners and court cases show that the mutilation, burning, smothering and torture alleged by the ex-slaves were not unknown. Many of the narratives contain accounts of such outrages. Moses Roper tells of a slaveholder who put his ill-behaved chattels into a barrel into which nails had been driven and rolled them down a steep hill. Thompson alleges that a neighboring slaveholder once put a slave girl's head under the fence and sat on the fence. Harriet Jacobs claims that a runaway slave was brought back and put between the screws of the cotton gin and crushed to death, while another, a woman, was shot through the head. Ben Simpson tells of his Georgia master who branded his slaves and never took off their chains. "When we work, we drug them chains with us. At night he lock us to a tree to keep us from running off." This same owner took a coffle to Texas and shot a female slave who, exhausted, with raw feet and swollen legs, refused to go on.[7] John Brown was, he says, the guinea pig for a sadistic doctor. Experimenting with the effects of sun and heat stroke, the doctor put Brown into a hot pit and kept him there until he fainted several times; then he tried bleeding the slave, gouging and blistering him to see how deep his black skin went.[8] Olmsted records the burning of a Negro.

Such charges as these may be dismissed as incredible, but surely court cases detailing similar cruelties are reliable. In 1811 a prisoner was indicted for the "malicious stabbing of a slave" in Virginia.[9] In 1827 a master was indicted for "maliciously and inhumanly beating a slave almost to death." The court, however, decided it had no jurisdiction and presumably the defendant was freed although the court "deplored that an offense so odious and revolting as this, should exist to the reproach of humanity."[10] In the case of Souther vs. the Commonwealth (October, 1850) the deposition charged that Souther

> after the tying, whipping, cobbing, striking, stamping, wounding, bruising, lacerating, burning, washing and torturing [the slave] as aforesaid, the prisoner untied the deceased from the tree in such a way as to throw him with violence to the ground; and he then and there did knock, kick, stamp . . . the deceased on the head, temples and various parts of the body. That the prisoner then had the deceased carried into a shed-room of his house, and there he compelled one of his slaves, in his presence, to confine the deceased's feet in the stocks—and to tie a rope about the neck of the deceased and fasten it to a bedpost in the room, thereby strangling, choking, and suffocating the deceased—and he again compelled his two slaves to apply fire to the body of the deceased—and the count charged that from these various modes of punishment and torture the slave Sam then and there died.[11]

In this case the court convicted the master of second degree murder and sentenced him to five years in the penitentiary.

Those who are familiar with lynching in the South know that extralegal punishment upon troublesome Negroes is part of the Southern backwoods tradition.

The *ante bellum* South lived in constant fear of servile rebellion especially after the Turner insurrection of 1831. The Negroes resisted individually and collectively attempts made to punish them. John Thompson, Frederick Douglass and Solomon Northup whipped their overseers. Northup was himself involved in two near-rebellions. The narratives are full of accounts of servile resistance. The patrols and little armies of the slave states were, therefore, everywhere in evidence and apparently needed to protect the slave system. In many states every white man was expected to do patrol duty or furnish a substitute. When an insurrection was feared these men went into action indiscriminately whipping, beating, lynching and terrifying Negroes. About the time of Nat Turner's uprising Harriet Jacobs witnessed proceedings of this kind.

> Every day for a fortnight, if I looked out, I saw horsemen with some poor panting negro tied to their saddles,

and compelled by the lash to keep up with their speed, till they arrived at the jail yard. Those who had been whipped too unmercifully to walk were washed with brine, tossed into a cart and carried to jail.[12]

According to Henry "Box" Brown after Nat Turner's insurrection, great numbers of slaves were loaded with irons; some were "half hung"—that is, suspended from some tree with a rope about their necks, adjusted so as not quite to strangle them—and then pelted by men and boys with rotten eggs.[13] The murdering and maiming of Negroes were so long continued after the uprisings of Vesey in 1822 and of Turner in 1831 that the masters themselves implored the states to put a stop to this indiscriminate slaughter.

The fear of servile rebellion prompted the slave states to make more and more stringent laws in regard to the Negro. Slaves were defined by the laws as "chattels personal" to be disposed of at their master's pleasure, except that for cruel and unusual punishments a master was liable to prosecution under the law. But the laws established the supremacy of the white group as thoroughly as possible. Should a slave refuse

> to submit to and undergo the examination of any white person, it is lawful for such white person to pursue, apprehend, and moderately correct such slave, and if such slave shall assault and strike such white person, such slave may be lawfully killed.[14]

The slave had, of course, no political or civil rights. He could not testify in court except against another slave, nor could he hold property, contract marriage, (or enter into any other contract) or assemble with other slaves where no white person was present. There were laws restraining persons from teaching him to read or write. In short, the law provided that "the slave lives for his master's service. His time, his labor, his comforts are all at his master's disposal."[15]

> The legislation of the Southern States with regard to slaves [wrote de Tocqueville] presents at the present day such unparalleled atrocities as suffice to show that the laws of humanity have been totally perverted, and to betray the desperate position of the community in which that legislation has been promulgated . . . In antiquity precautions were taken to prevent the slave from breaking his chains; at the present day measures are adopted to deprive him *even of the desire for freedom* . . . But the Americans of the South who do not admit that the Negroes can ever be commingled with themselves, have forbidden them under severe penalties to be taught to read or write; and as they will not raise them to their own level, they sink them as nearly as possible to that of the brutes.[16]

Judicial decisions in regard to the Negro sustained this general concept that he was merely a chattel. Such decisions culminated in the well-known pronouncement of Roger Taney in the case of Dred Scott: The Negro had "no rights which the white man was bound to respect."[17]

Olmsted felt that the public guard of Virginia was in direct violation of the constitutional provision forbidding the states to keep troops in time of peace. Yet the slave states were never really at peace, for the Negro population had to be kept in subjection by force.

> In Richmond and Charleston and New Orleans, [he writes] the citizens are as careless and gay as in Boston or London, and their servants a thousand times as child-like and cordial, to all appearance in their relations with them as our servants are with us. But go to the bottom of this security and dependence, and you come to police machinery such as you never find in towns under free government: citadels, sentries, passports, grape-shotted cannon, and daily public whippings for accidental infractions of police ceremonies. I happened myself to see more direct expression of tyranny in a single day and night at Charleston, than at Naples [under Bomba] in a week.[18]

Nor was this tyranny in the Old South confined to the Negro. The white population had its freedom sharply limited by the exigencies of the slave system. The white citizen was compelled to do patrol duty; he was sharply limited in the literature he could read and circulate. Indeed the slaveholders went so far as to open the mails and burn abolitionist or incendiary publications. By 1840 it was clear to many northerners that the South was fastening the shackles of its peculiar institution on the entire nation. The "gag rule" prohibited the discussion of the question of slavery in the House of Representatives; anti-slavery petitions lined the halls of Congress, but it was some time before anyone dared read one in the House. John Quincy Adams, who did yeoman service in breaking the gag rule, was no abolitionist. He was anxious to save some vestige of representative government and did so in the teeth of tremendous opposition. And in 1850 every American citizen was compelled by law to be a slave-catcher.

This elaborate system of control maintained by the slaveholders, indeed the slave system itself, rested on one widely accepted ideological foundation: the notion of Negro inferiority. The idea that the African race was savage, uncivilized and innately incapable of high cultural development obtained all over the land. The editors of the *North American Review* had asserted, "It is not slavery that is the curse of the South; it is Africa." The majority of the American people were deeply sympathetic with the South in its attempts to keep the black population from slaughtering them in their beds. The author of *The Laws of Race* maintained as a first principle that "the white race must of necessity, by reason of its superiority, govern the negro wherever the two live together." Dr. J. H. Van Evrie produced a book, in which he essayed to prove the physical, mental, and moral inferiority of the black race. He insisted that Negroes could not stand erect, that the color of a man's skin was an index to his character, that no Negro could "speak the language of the white man with absolute correctness," that the African was not educable, and was, in short, mercifully held in slavery by a wise creator.[19] John Quincy Adams told Fanny Kemble "with a serious expression of sincere disgust" that all the misfortunes of Desde-

mona were "a very just judgment upon her for having married a 'nigger.'"[20]

Fitzhugh and the fire-eaters, Calhoun and all the apologists had a rationalization made-to-order which most of America accepted without question. The idea of the Negro's inferiority, however, was not propagated only by the self-interest of slaveholders. The degradation of the Negro in America was a realistic, observable fact. The brutish field hand, the degenerate, poverty-stricken Negroes in Northern cities were there for everybody to see. Even the Negroes themselves accepted the idea of their inferiority. A few observers recognized that slavery and caste status had degraded the Negro, but their voices were lost in the general hue and cry.

The slaveholder, however, was not satisfied to use the concept of inferiority as a rationalization. The idea had to be dramatized in the personal etiquette of his servants so that each passing day would reinforce society's awareness of the Negro's subordinate caste, and the Negro himself, his self-esteem shattered, would accept slave status. Redpath, Olmsted, Kemble, Lyell, and Martineau noticed with embarrassment the fawning and obeisance accorded them by Negroes in the South, forgetting that the master class enforced its caste etiquette with the lash. William Grimes was flogged for referring to a slave woman as "Miss." John Brown says of John Glasgow: "His brave look, when spoken to, offended his master, who swore he 'would flog his nigger pride out of him.'"[21] "Ten years," writes Solomon Northup, "I was compelled to address him [the master] with downcast eyes and uncovered head—in the attitude and language of a slave."[22] The whip was the antidote to any infringement of this caste etiquette:

> Does a slave look dissatisfied? It is said he has the devil in him, and it must be whipped out. Does he speak loudly when spoken to by his master? Then he is getting high-minded, and should be taken down a button-hole lower. Does he forget to pull off his hat at the approach of a white person? Then he is wanting in reverence, and should be whipped for it. Does he venture to vindicate his conduct when censured for it? Then he is guilty of impudence,—one of the greatest crimes of which a slave can be guilty. Does he ever venture to suggest a different mode of doing things from that pointed out by his master? He is indeed presumptuous and getting above himself.[23]

The caste etiquette was designed to transform the Negro into a cringing serf. "Every distinction should be created," wrote the memorialists to the South Carolina legislature, "between the whites and the Negroes, calculated to make the latter feel the superiority of the former."[24] The conflicts of personality occasioned by the caste status are difficult to discover, but this is the burden of the next three chapters, the consideration of the mind of the slave.

The "inside view" of slavery may not be the whole view, but it is certainly an indispensable, though almost neglected, phase of the subject. A realistic understanding of the economic and social aspects of slavery—the slave trade, the plantation system, and the controls by which each was maintained—is of vital importance to our knowledge of the socio-economic framework of our country. The extent to which the shadow of slavery falls on present-day America will be shown in a later chapter.

Notes

1. *Cotton Kingdom,* II., p. 202.

2. *Twelve Years a Slave,* pp. 226-227.

3. *Slave Life in Georgia,* p. 131.

4. *Narrative of Henry Bibb,* p. 132.

5. *Cotton Kingdom,* II., p. 203.

6. *Documentary History of American Industrial Society,* II., pp. 31-32.

7. B. A. Botkin, *Lay My Burden Down,* p. 75.

8. *Slave Life in Georgia,* pp. 45-52.

9. *Judicial Cases,* I., p. 122.

10. *Ibid.,* I., pp. 150-151.

11. Quoted by Harriet Beecher Stowe in *Dred,* pp. 347-348.

12. *Incidents in the Life of a Slave Girl,* p. 103.

13. *Narrative of the Life of Henry Box Brown,*

14. *Industrial Resources,* II., p. 285.

15. *Ibid.,* p. 278.

16. *Democracy in America,* I., pp. 379-380.

17. *Judicial Cases,* V., p. 199.

18. *Seaboard Slave States,* I., pp. 22-23.

19. *Negroes and Negro Slavery* (N. Y., 1861).

20. *Journal,* p. 86.

21. *Slave Life in Georgia,* p. 37.

22. *Twelve Years a Slave,* p. 183.

23. *Narrative of Frederick Douglass,* p. 79.

24. *Documentary History of American Industrial Society,* p. 113.

Sue Eakin and Joseph Logsdon (essay date 1968)

SOURCE: Introduction to *Twelve Years a Slave: By Solomon Northup,* Louisiana State University Press, 1968, pp. ix-xxiv.

[*In the following essay, Eakin and Logsdon consider the significance of Northup's narrative and provide an overview of the primary and secondary sources which preceded their edition.*]

The story of Solomon Northup approaches the incredible. "It is a strange history," wrote Frederick Douglass when the book was first published in 1853; "its truth is stranger than fiction." The nineteenth-century title itself evokes disbelief: ***Twelve Years a Slave, Narrative of Solomon Northup, a Citizen of New York, Kidnapped in Washington City in 1841, and Rescued in 1853, from a Cotton Plantation Near the Red River in Louisiana.*** This—the abduction of a free Negro adult from the North and his enslavement in the South—provides a sensational element which cannot be matched in any of the dozens of narratives written by former slaves. Douglass, who had already detailed his own harrowing experiences under slavery, recognized the compounded tragedy in Northup's account: "Think of it: For thirty years a *man,* with all a man's hopes, fears and aspirations—with a wife and children to call him by the endearing names of husband and father— with a home, humble it may be, but still a *home* . . . then for twelve years a *thing,* a chattel personal, classed with mules and horses. . . . Oh! it is horrible. It chills the blood to think that such are."[1]

This sensationalism, which made Northup's narrative a best seller of its genre, might very reasonably call its historical value into question. Although his abduction was certainly not unique,[2] the seizure and sale of free Negroes was not a normal occurrence in antebellum days. Even Harriet Beecher Stowe acknowledged that the known cases of such crimes were rare and, when discovered by Southern authorities, were "generally tried with great fairness and impartiality."[3]

Nevertheless, despite the bizarre and almost unbelievable aspects of Solomon Northup's story, the leading students of American slavery have universally praised its historical value. Kenneth Stampp relied upon it heavily; Stanley Elkins thought it "particularly convincing"; and Ulrich B. Phillips, who questioned the authenticity of slave memoirs as a matter of course, singled out Northup's autobiography as "a vivid account of plantation life from the under side."[4]

The tragic turn in Northup's life gave him a unique set of qualifications for observation and analysis. He entered slavery educated, curious, and fully aware of his former freedom and dignity. Without that prior experience it is doubtful that he would have been able to present so detailed and accurate a description of slave life and plantation society. His thirty-two years in New York had given him a perspective which he could fruitfully apply to the whole Southern scene. There are many other travel accounts of the Old South, but the visitors who wrote about slavery only observed it; they did not endure its hardships. Neither the veil of color nor the barriers of status obscured Northup's vision. He shared the experiences of Southern slaves both as an outside critic and as a fellow Negro chattel. No other commentator on American slavery has those credentials.

No other slave has left such a detailed picture of life in the Gulf South—the dynamic locale of the "peculiar institution" during the three decades before the Civil War.[5] Relatively few slaves ever managed to win their freedom from this region, either by manumission or by escape. Almost all of the slave narrators, therefore, came from the border states or the Atlantic seaboard.[6] Without the legal assistance due him as a citizen of New York, Solomon Northup would surely have died—silent—along the banks of the Red River in Louisiana. Unaided flight, as he himself discovered, was almost beyond possibility, and manumission was quite unlikely. To have freed Northup voluntarily in 1853, his master would have had to win the support of three-fourths of the local police jury and, in addition, post $150 in order to send Northup to Africa—when he could easily have sold him for over $2,000.[7]

Shortly after his rescue from Louisiana, Northup apparently decided to publish his memoirs. Without any fear of recapture, he could tell his full story immediately—unlike other fugitives who either had to use pseudonyms or had to wait until after the Civil War. The appetite of Northerners for such reading had already been amply demonstrated. If Northup was unaware of this readers' market, he soon learned about it. The Washington correspondent for the New York *Times,* who was the first reporter to broadcast Northup's story, quickly pointed to its striking similarity to *Uncle Tom's Cabin,* the novel which was sweeping the Western world.[8] The reporter's long interview with the homeward-bound Northup reappeared in many Northern newspapers, and Harriet Beecher Stowe herself seized upon the article as a "striking parallel" to her novel. Then at work on *The Key to Uncle Tom's Cabin,* she related the facts of Northup's enslavement and noted "the singular coincidence that this man was carried to a plantation in the Red River country, that same region where the scene of Tom's captivity was laid."[9]

Northup's return to his family in Glens Falls, New York, on the evening of January 20, 1853, kept the local community buzzing for some time.[10] The morning after his arrival a large reception was held for him at Sandy Hill (now Hudson Falls). During that reception, or shortly thereafter, a local lawyer named David Wilson arranged to help Northup publish his autobiography. Unlike most of the amanuenses of slave narratives, Wilson was not an abolitionist. Although he was a newly elected member of the state legislature, there is no evidence that he ever tried to reap any political advantage from his association with the book. Like other neighbors and friends of Northup, he merely became intrigued with the tragedy and recognized its publishing potential.

A former superintendent of the area's public schools, Wilson had already written some poetry and local history. None of his writings, however, dealt with slavery; he concentrated almost entirely on matters of local concern. The Democratic newspaper in his hometown indicated his reputation in the community by gracefully accepting his election to the state legislature in 1852: "Mr. Wilson is not only one of the most eloquent orators at the bar, but one of the purest and sweetest poets in northern New York. We are sorry he is a Whig."[11]

There is no evidence that Wilson ever became a convert to antislavery ranks, even after his encounter with Northup. Wilson wrote two other books, but neither of these were concerned with slavery. The first, *The Life of Jane McCrea,* recounted a local Indian massacre during Burgoyne's march to disaster at Saratoga in 1777; the second, *Henrietta Robinson,* detailed the life of an insane murderess whose highly publicized trial took place in Troy, New York, in 1855.[12] Both books, like Northup's narrative, were obvious attempts to capitalize on rather sensational stories of local interest. While they may demonstrate Wilson's interest in quick profits, they do not show any abiding concern in antislavery propaganda. The prose style of the narrative clearly belongs to Wilson. Even a cursory look at his subsequent books of 1853 and 1855 quickly indicates a consistency of phrasing and composition. There is no reason, however, to doubt his statement, in the original preface of the work, that he had dedicated himself to an accurate transcription of Northup's reminiscences.

Wilson and Northup worked rapidly on their joint project. Within three months of Northup's return to New York, they had a revised manuscript ready for publication. By the middle of July, copies of the book were in the hands of the reviewers, who helpfully noted its similarity to *Uncle Tom's Cabin.* The newspaper of Thurlow Weed, Whig party boss of New York, made the narrative the topic of a lead editorial entitled, "Uncle Tom's Cabin—No. 2."[13] When the highly partisan Democratic newspaper in Sandy Hill first heard that the work was in preparation, it sarcastically labeled the project "Uncle Sol."[14] But Wilson and Northup apparently did not mind the comparison; indeed, in an obvious attempt to capitalize on the phenomenal success of her novel, they dedicated their book to Harriet Beecher Stowe.

The narrative was an immediate success; the first printing of eight thousand copies was sold within a month. In subsequent editions the authors added to their dedication page a portion of Mrs. Stowe's reference to Northup in *The Key to Uncle Tom's Cabin,* which had just appeared. The printing of the narrative continued through 1856, and over thirty thousand copies were sold. Although never approaching the million mark of Mrs. Stowe's fictional account, Northup's true life story was one of the most profitable of its kind. Its sales induced the publishers, Derby and Miller, to take on other slave narratives, including an expanded edition of Frederick Douglass' 1845 autobiography.

Despite the obvious pressures to duplicate the fictional images in *Uncle Tom's Cabin,* Northup presents a well-balanced narrative. His recollections include many dreadful episodes, but he presents much more than indiscriminate accusation. He gives a detailed, rather straightforward survey of his life as a slave. At no point does he strain the reader's credulity by relating obvious impossibilities. Reviewers were quick to take note of his apparent lack of bitterness. A more recent critic, John Herbert Nelson, has written: "Northup's performance appears still more remarkable—as nothing short of astounding.

. . . In spite of this horrible ordeal in the South, he still found it possible to recount his misfortunes with fairness and justice—a feat of no small magnitude, and one which few men, certainly few white men, would be capable."[15]

Not that Northup fails to illustrate the cruelties of slavery; he points to them again and again, and he illustrates the psychological impact as well as the physical effects of forced servitude. But he also points out the amenities that made his life endurable. While clearly recognizing the brutalizing effects of slavery on individual men, he insists upon the resilience of the human spirit and the continuing eagerness for freedom among his fellow chattels in one of the worst slave areas in the Deep South. He makes distinctions in the behavior of his various masters and in the outlook of his fellow slaves. He recounts both the sensational and the ordinary aspects of plantation life; his recollections of the brutal detention, transportation, and sale of slaves are as vivid as any that have ever been written. At the same time, his descriptions of cotton and sugar production are recognized classics, and his observations of daily existence constitute one of the most detailed portrayals of the accommodations and routine of slaves in the Gulf South.

In the last analysis, however, Solomon Northup's narrative deserves to be believed not simply because he "seems" to be talking reasonably, not merely because he adorns his tale with compelling and persuasive details. At every point where materials exist for checking his account, it can be verified. The story, in its essentials, had already been told by Northup in his interview with the New York *Times* reporter in Washington—weeks before he met Wilson and arranged the publication of his experiences. At the abortive trial of the slave traders in 1853, witnesses had identified Northup and described his treatment at the hands of the traders. The official records in Louisiana, which have fortunately survived war, climate, and human carelessness, also document Northup's tale. These extant manuscript records verify every sale of Northup, as well as other property transactions of his masters.[16] The descriptions of the Bayou Boeuf are unquestionably accurate in their smallest detail; in fact, the recall of time, distance, and people is almost uncanny. The misspelling of individual names is understandable; even though Northup was literate, as a chattel he seldom saw the written word and therefore had to depend on phonetics in preparing his account. Few autobiographers, however, have matched the precision of his recollection.

No one, in any case, came forward to challenge Northup's memory of things past. The only available reaction in Louisiana newspapers occurred shortly after his rescue. The Marksville *Villager* saw the whole incident as a vindication of Southern legal propriety. In describing the lack of resistance to Northup's rescuers, the editors complained: "What a contrast this presents to the treatment which Southerners receive at the hands of the North, when in pursuit of their fugitive slaves. . . . Well may the South boast of its justice and loyalty."[17]

For Northup's Northern neighbors, his misfortune in the South remained a matter of concern for several years. Although the Democratic newspapers generally ignored the discussion of the autobiography, Whig editors gave it prominent attention. Northup personally distributed copies among his friends in the community. One of them, the editor of the Salem *Press*, was so moved by the tale that he urged his readers: "For the sake of humanity and truth, we bespeak for the work an extensive sale."[18]

Of the thousands who eventually read the book, none was so important for Northup as Thaddeus St. John, a county judge from Fonda, New York. The narrative forced St. John to recall certain incidents of his trip to Washington, D.C. in 1841. In Baltimore, on his way to the Capitol, he had encountered two old friends from New York, Alexander Merrill and Joseph Russell, who were traveling with an unknown Negro companion.

The attitude of his friends, the judge remembered, was very strange. Knowing that Merrill went south frequently on gambling excursions, he blurted out to the younger man: "What are you doing here, Joe?" Merrill, however, rushed up and, motioning to the stranger, urged St. John not to use their real names. Later, in Washington, St. John met the same three men at their hotel on the eve of William Henry Harrison's funeral. He left them drinking there about eight o'clock and did not see them again until he arrived in Baltimore on his return trip to New York.

This time the two white men were alone, and their appearance had been drastically improved. Their long hair was cut and their beards were shaved clean; they wore new clothing and sported ivory canes and gold watches. Surprised by their sudden change of fortune, St. John laughingly accused them of selling their Negro friend or robbing some nabob in Washington. When he jokingly suggested that they must have received $500 for their former companion, Merrill told him to raise the price by $150. When questioned more seriously about where they had obtained this windfall, Russell explained that they had won the money from Southern gamblers.[19] St. John returned home and never took any serious interest in the incident.

Northup's description of his kidnapping, however, was too close to what St. John remembered to be merely coincidental. Suspecting the truth, then, the judge arranged a meeting with Northup in Fonda shortly after he finished reading the narrative. They recognized each other instantly, and, after comparing notes, both became convinced that Russell and Merrill were the infamous kidnappers. With this information Solomon contacted his rescuer, Henry B. Northup, who was equally determined to apprehend the kidnappers.

After additional probing in central New York, the two men tracked down the culprits. They luckily found Merrill visiting his parents for the July Fourth festivities; it was one of his infrequent visits to New York since taking up residence in the South in 1841. A local reporter described the dramatic encounter: "Merrill was arrested this morning at his mother's, at Wood Hollow, and brought here (Gloversville) for examination. Henry B. Northrop [sic.] has spent a great deal of time and money ferreting out the scoundrel, and they have no doubt got the man. Solomon identifies him without a doubt. Merrill has long been regarded as a desperate fellow. They found him asleep, with a heavy bowie knife and a brace of pistols on the floor by his side. The arrest has caused very general excitement."[20]

Within a few days, two police officers picked up Russell, who was then working as a canal boat captain on the Erie. Handcuffed, he was brought for arraignment to Ballston Spa, the seat of Saratoga County, where the kidnappers had first made contact with Northup in 1841. Russell and Merrill were given an immediate hearing. Northup, whose testimony was admissible in a New York court, pointed out the two men; Thaddeus St. John followed and stunned the courtroom with his long and incriminating story; and a third witness, Norman Pringle, who claimed that he had warned Solomon not to leave Saratoga with Merrill and Russell on that fateful day in 1841, added the finishing touches to the conclusive identification. The defendants' lawyer could only plead that the New York statute of limitations barred prosecution after the lapse of three years following the commission of a crime. District Attorney William T. Odell, however, insisted that the prisoners had been continuously committing the offense as long as Northup remained in slavery. The court agreed and indicted the defendants; they were released on bail of $5,000 each, pending trial in the fall.[21]

The trial opened on October 4, 1854, before a crowded and excited courtroom in Ballston Spa. Merrill and Russell had hoped to settle the matter with Solomon Northup out of court, but he refused. The defendants' lawyers therefore requested a postponement in order to obtain testimony from the slave traders in Washington, D.C. The court agreed; it put off the trial until February and, in the meantime, dispatched a deputy to obtain depositions from James H. Birch and Benjamin Shekell.[22]

Birch, although one of the city's most notorious slave traders, was a man of some prominence in Washington; he served as the commander of the Auxiliary Guard which formed part of the Capital's police force. Having been embarrassed once by the Northup incident, he was no doubt anxious to avoid any further complicity in the crime. In his deposition, he once more claimed (as he had during his own trial in 1853) that he innocently purchased Northup from a Georgia planter named Brown. Elaborating this time on his former story, he also insisted that Northup participated voluntarily in the sale, that he "played, at least, an hour" on a borrowed fiddle to prove his worth and plainly said "that he was the property of this man—calling him master—that he was a slave and raised in his family in Georgia, that he knew the reason he wanted to sell him, that his master had been on a frolic and had got into a gambling house and lost all his money and that was the only way he had money to get home." Birch continued with his amazing testimony:

> I told him that if I bought him I should send him to the South. He replied that he would rather go South as he was raised in a Southern country. I asked him who he knew in Georgia. He mentioned a few names which I do not now recollect. In order to find if all was represented, I told him, if I purchased him, I should send him to the cotton fields where he would be severely punished and that I intended to whip him for a sample of what he would get. In answer to which the negro said, "My master has a right to sell me and I must submit". . . . I will further state that after the sale of the negro to me by Brown both appeared to be very much affected at parting—so much so as to shed tears.[23]

Even though the other slave trader, Benjamin Shekell, supported his partner's testimony, the lawyers for Merrill and Russell ignored the absurd depositions when the trial reopened on February 13, 1855. Instead, the defense based its case on legal technicalities. The four-part indictment against the kidnappers had been drawn from two laws passed in the early 1840's during the governorship of William H. Seward. The first law made it illegal to kidnap or entice any Negro out of the state with the intent of selling him into slavery. The second made it a criminal offense to sell any Negro into slavery.[24] The initial charge of the indictment was drawn up on the basis of the first law; the remaining charges on the basis of the second law. The accused pleaded not guilty to the first charge, and their lawyers maintained that the other parts of the indictment should be dismissed, since these were inapplicable. As the crime of selling Northup was committed in Washington, the courts of New York, they argued, had no jurisdiction over that offense.

Since the first law carried a maximum sentence of only ten years imprisonment, the prosecuting attorneys, William Odell and Henry B. Northup, refused to accept the challenge to the indictment. As a result, they were drawn into a legal thicket over the matter of jurisdiction. To settle the difficult question, the presiding judge ruled against the contested parts of the indictment, in order to have the point of law clarified before the state supreme court.[25]

The supreme court considered the matter a few days later but withheld judgment until the next session. In the meantime, local Democratic newspapers opened their first racist attack on Northup, calling for the acquittal of Merrill and Russell. Whig newspapers, in turn, came to Northup's defense.[26] When the supreme court reassembled on July 13—almost a year after the opening of the trial—the justices in a 2 to 1 decision sustained the dismissal of the contested portions of the indictment.[27]

Determined not to back down, the district attorney brought the case on a writ of error before the state court of appeals, the final arbiter of such matters in New York. In June, 1856—almost two years after the apprehension of the kidnappers—this court refused to rule on the indictment. Under New York law, the court of appeals could not rule on any part of an indictment while other parts remained unquestioned. Before deciding on the contested charges, therefore, the lower courts had to try Merrill and Russell on the first part of the indictment, that is, kidnapping or enticing Northup out of the state with the intention of selling him as a slave.[28]

The litigation had dragged on for so long that New York newspapers apparently were tired of it; they ignored this last decision. Even the papers in Northup's own community failed to note the action of the court of appeals. Fully absorbed in the politics of "Bloody Kansas," the citizens of the area seemed to lose interest in their once famous neighbor. The state, for one reason or another, never retried Merrill and Russell; the two apparently went unpunished for the crime.

Justice, therefore, never came to Solomon Northup, either in the South or in the North. He had no choice but to try and pick up his life where he had left it in 1841. He had received only a pathetic recompense for the stolen years—three thousand dollars for selling the copyright of his memoirs. With part of the money, he purchased some property in Glens Falls next to the home of his married daughter, Margaret.[29] With his wife and only son, Alonzo, he lived in the home of his son-in-law for the next several years. Two other Negro families, the Vanpelts and the Vanrankins, were Northup's immediate neighbors; together these households (a total of twenty-two persons) formed a small segregated island in Glens Falls. Solomon took up his old trade of carpentry; his son and son-in-law remained unemployed.[30]

What finally became of Solomon Northup can only be conjectured. Property records of 1863 show that his wife and son-in-law sold their adjoining property that year.[31] Solomon evidently had died, and his family now moved from the area, perhaps to Oswego, where his brother and son once lived. His simple, moving wish at the conclusion of the narrative was never honored; he does not rest in the churchyard where his father sleeps.

Shortly after the Civil War, Northup's narrative was republished by a Philadelphia firm. The editors made no attempt to ascertain the fate of its author. They felt that such an attempt was unnecessary since Northup's story had blended into the larger panorama of the nation's past.

> To take in or to understand the exact status of such a people in all its bearings, we can pursue no better course than to live among them, to become one of them, to fall from a condition of freedom to one of bondage, to feel the scourge, to bear the marks of the brands, and the outrage of manacles. . . . It can be taken for what it is worth—a personal narrative of personal sufferings and keenly felt and strongly resented wrongs; but in our opinion, the individual will be lost or merged in the general interest and the work will be regarded as a history of an institution which our political economy has now happily superseded, but which, however much

its existence may be regretted, should be studied—indeed, must be studied—by everyone whose interest in our country incites him to obtain a correct knowledge of her past existence.[32]

One hundred years later, this still constitutes a valid judgment on the significance of Solomon Northup's life and the importance of his narrative.

Notes

1. *Liberator,* August 26, 1853, quoted from *Frederick Douglass's Newspaper.*

2. For a similar kidnapping case, see Kate E. R. Pickard, *The Kidnapped and the Ransomed, Being the Personal Recollections of Peter Still and His Wife, Vina, After Forty Years of Slavery* (Syracuse, 1856). Still was seized as a child in Philadelphia and sold as a slave in Kentucky. William Houston, a British seaman, was kidnapped in New Orleans; his experiences were recounted in the New Orleans *Daily Delta,* June 1, 1850. Depositions and records of Houston's suit for freedom are available in New Orleans, Fourth District Court, No. 3729.

3. Harriet Beecher Stowe, *The Key to Uncle Tom's Cabin* (London, 1853), 345.

4. Kenneth Stampp, *The Peculiar Institution* (New York, 1956), 60, 74, 90, 162, 287, 323, 359, 380; Stanley Elkins, *Slavery* (Chicago, 1959), 4; Ulrich B. Phillips, *Life and Labor in the Old South* (Boston, 1929), 219. Phillips made a similar judgment of the narrative in his earlier work, *American Negro Slavery* (New York, 1918), 445: "Though the books of this class are generally of dubious value this one has a tone which engages confidence."

5. Neither James B. Sellers in his *Slavery in Alabama* (University, Ala., 1950) nor Charles S. Sydnor in his *Slavery in Mississippi* (New York, 1933) used any slave testimony. Joe Gray Taylor, however, was able to humanize his study with Northup's account. See his *Negro Slavery in Louisiana* (Baton Rouge, 1963), 49, 65, 66, 77, 108, 129, 130, 131, 149, 188, 189, 220.

6. There are more than eighty extant slave narratives; most, unfortunately, can only be found in a few specialized collections in the United States. For the best analysis of these accounts, see Charles H. Nichols, *Many Thousand Gone* (Leiden, Netherlands, 1963). This work is a revision of Nichols' more detailed dissertation, "A Study of the Slave Narrative" (Brown University, 1948). Two other dissertations have been written on the subject: Margaret Y. Jackson, "An Investigation of Biographies and Autobiographies of American Slaves. . . ." (Cornell University, 1954) and Marion W. Starling, "The Slave Narrative: Its Place in American Literary History" (New York University, 1946).

7. Taylor, *Negro Slavery in Louisiana,* 155-57. In St. Mary Parish, where Epps rented Northup during

sugar cane harvests, slave prices in 1853 "were considered exceptionally high and at one judicial sale in the parish a Negro 'in no way remarkable' was sold for $2300." Lynn Delaune (de Grummond), "A Social History of St. Mary Parish, 1845-1860," *Louisiana Historical Quarterly*, XXXII (1949), 36.

8. New York *Times*, January 19, 20, 1853.

9. Stowe, *The Key to Uncle Tom's Cabin*, 342.

10. Saratoga *Whig*, January 21, February 4, 1953; Sandy Hill *Herald*, January 25, 1853; Salem *Press*, January 25, 1853.

11. Whitehall *Democrat*, February n. d., 1852. Quoted in Clarence E. Holden, "Local History Sketches," (MS in the possession of Mrs. John T. Morton, town historian of Whitehall, N.Y.). The editors are indebted to Mrs. Morton for the information which she has collected about David Wilson.

12. David Wilson, *Henrietta Robinson* (Auburn, N.Y., 1855) and *The Life of Jane McCrea, with an Account of Burgoyne's Expedition in 1777* (New York, 1853). The body of Jane McCrea, who was killed by Indians, was exhumed and reburied in 1852. The rekindling of local interest in the event probably led Wilson to write his account of the massacre.

13. Albany *Evening Journal*, July 18, 1853. A collection of reactions to the narrative appeared in the New York *Tribune*, August 19, 1853.

14. Sandy Hill *Herald*, March 8, 1853.

15. John Herbert Nelson, *The Negro Character in American Literature* (Lawrence, Kan., 1926), 62. Nelson unfortunately explained the magnanimity as one of the "virtues peculiar to the race."

16. Property records have survived in two of the parishes in which Northup was sold, Avoyelles and Orleans. The records in Rapides Parish were destroyed by fire.

17. Marksville *Villager*, January 13, 1953, as quoted in the New Orleans *Bee*, January 22, 1853.

18. Salem *Press*, August 16, 1853.

19. The recollection of St. John is taken from his courtroom testimony which was reported in great detail by the Saratoga *Whig*, July 14, 1854.

20. Albany *Evening Journal*, July 9, 1854.

21. Saratoga *Whig*, July 14, 1854.

22. *Ibid.*, October 6, 1854.

23. These depositions, along with other manuscript records of the trial, are in the files of the Clerk of Saratoga County, Box A83.

24. Ironically these laws were passed along with others in 1841—the year of Northup's kidnapping—in order to erase "the last vestiges of slavery from the state." Edgar J. McManus, *A History of Negro Slavery in New York* (Syracuse, 1966), 179.

25. Saratoga *Whig*, February 16, 1855.

26. *Ibid.*, February 23, 1855. An editorial from the Ballston *Democrat* appeared in the issue criticizing the position taken by the Saratoga *Republican* in regard to the trial.

27. Saratoga *Whig*, July 13, 1855. The court's decision and the minority dissent are in the office of the Clerk of Saratoga County, Box A83.

28. *New York. Decisions of the Court of Appeals*, Vol. 414, pp. 5-26.

29. *Warren County Deed Records*, Liber U, 297, Liber S, 379.

30. *New York. Census Records* (MS) Second Election District, Town of Queensbury, Warren County, June 9, 1855, House No. 110, 111, 112.

31. *Warren County Deed Records*, Liber 9, 527, 528.

32. Solomon Northup, *Twelve Years a Slave* (Philadelphia, 1869), xv-xvi.

Robert B. Stepto (essay date 1979)

SOURCE: "I Rose and Found My Voice: Narration, Authentication, and Authorial Control in Four Slave Narratives," in *From Behind the Veil: A Study of Afro-American Narrative*, University of Illinois Press, 1991, pp. 3-16.

[*In the following excerpt, originally published in 1979, Stepto discusses Northup's work as an example of an integrated slave narrative that places documents authenticating the slave experience into the tale.*]

The strident, moral voice of the former slave recounting, exposing, appealing, apostrophizing, and above all *remembering* his ordeal in bondage is the single most impressive feature of a slave narrative. This voice is striking because of what it relates, but even more so because the slave's acquisition of that voice is quite possibly his only permanent achievement once he escapes and casts himself upon a new and larger landscape. In their most elementary form, slave narratives are full of other voices which are frequently just as responsible for articulating a narrative's tale and strategy. These other voices may belong to various "characters" in the "story," but mainly they appear in the appended documents written by slaveholders and abolitionists alike. These documents—and voices—may not always be smoothly integrated with the former slave's tale, but they are nevertheless parts of the narrative. Their primary function is, of course, to authenticate the former slave's account; in doing so, they are at least partially responsible for the narrative's acceptance as historical evidence. However, in literary terms, the documents collectively create something close to a dialogue—of forms as well as voices—which suggests that, in its primal state or first phase, the slave narrative is an *eclectic narrative* form. A "first phase" slave narrative that illustrates these points rather well is Henry Bibb's *Narrative of the Life and Adventures of Henry Bibb, an American Slave* (1849).

When the various forms (letters, prefaces, guarantees, tales) and their accompanying voices become integrated in the slave narrative text, we are presented with another type of basic narrative which I call an *integrated narrative*. This type of narrative represents the second phase of slave narrative narration; it usually yields a more sophisticated text, wherein most of the literary and rhetorical functions previously performed by several texts and voices (the appended prefaces, letters, and documents as well as the tale) are now rendered by a loosely unified single text and voice. In this second phase, the authenticating documents "come alive" in the former slave's tale as speech and even action; and the former slave—often while assuming a deferential posture toward his white friends, editors, and guarantors—carries much of the burden of introducing and authenticating his own tale. In short, as my remarks on Solomon Northup's *Twelve Years a Slave* (1854) will suggest, a "second phase" narrative is a more sophisticated narrative because the former slave's voice is responsible for much more than recounting the tale.

Because an integrated or second-phase narrative is less a collection of texts and more a unified narrative, we may say that, in terms of narration, the integrated narrative is in the process of becoming—irrespective of authorial intent—a generic narrative, by which I mean a narrative of discernible genre such as history, fiction, essay, or autobiography. This process is no simple "gourd vine" activity: an integrated narrative does not become a generic narrative overnight, and indeed, there are no assurances that in becoming a new type of narrative it is transformed automatically into a distinctive generic text. What we discover, then, is a third phase to slave narration wherein two developments may occur: the integrated narrative (phase II) may be dominated either by its tale or by its authenticating strategies. In the first instance, as we see in Frederick Douglass's *Narrative of the Life of Frederick Douglass, an American Slave, Written by Himself* (1845), the narrative and moral energies of the former slave's voice and tale so resolutely dominate the narrative's authenticating machinery (voices, documents, rhetorical strategies) that the narrative becomes, in thrust and purpose, far more metaphorical than rhetorical. When the integrated narrative becomes, in this way, a figurative account of action, landscape, and heroic self-transformation, it is so close generally to history, fiction, and autobiography that I term it a *generic narrative*.

In the second instance, as we see in William Wells Brown's *Narrative of the Life and Escape of William Wells Brown* (1852; appended to his novel, *Clotel, or The President's Daughter*), the authenticating machinery either remains as important as the tale or actually becomes, usually for some

purpose residing outside the text, the dominant and motivating feature of the narrative. Since this is also a sophisticated narrative phase, figurative presentations of action, landscape, and self may also occur; however, such developments are rare and always ancillary to the central thrust of the text. When the authenticating machinery dominates in this fashion, the integrated narrative becomes an *authenticating narrative*.

As these remarks suggest, one reason for investigating the phases of slave narrative narration is to gain a clearer view of how some slave narrative types become generic narratives, and how, in turn, generic narratives—once formed, shaped, and set in motion by certain distinctly Afro-American cultural imperatives—have roots

The Three Phases of Narration

PHASE I: Basic Narrative (a): "Eclectic Narrative"—authenticating documents and strategies (sometimes including one by the author of the tale) are *appended* to the tale

PHASE II: Basic Narrative (b): "Integrated Narrative"—authenticating documents and strategies are *integrated* into the tale and formally become voices and/or characters in the tale

PHASE III: (a) "Generic Narrative"—authenticating documents and strategies are totally *subsumed by the tale*; the slave narrative becomes an identifiable generic text, e.g., autobiography (b) "Authenticating Narrative"—the tale is *subsumed by the authenticating strategy*; the slave narrative becomes an authenticating document for other, usually generic, texts, e.g., novels, histories

In the slave narratives. All this is, of course, central to our discussion of Washington's *Up from Slavery,* Du Bois's *The Souls of Black Folk,* Johnson's *The Autobiography of an Ex-Coloured Man,* Wright's *Black Boy,* and Ellison's *Invisible Man.* Moreover, it bears on our ability to distinguish between narrative modes and forms, and to describe what we see. When a historian or literary critic calls a slave narrative an autobiography, for example, what he or she sees most likely is a first-person narrative that possesses literary features to distinguish it from ordinary documents providing historical and sociological data. But a slave narrative is *not* necessarily an autobiography. We need to observe the finer shades between the more easily discernible categories of narration, and we must discover whether these stops arrange themselves in progressive, contrapuntal, or dialectic fashion—or if they possess any arrangement at all. As the scheme described above (. . .) suggests, I believe there are at least four identifiable modes of narration within the slave narratives, and that all four have a direct bearing on the development of subsequent Afro-American narrative forms.

PHASE I: ECLECTIC NARRATIVE

Henry Bibb's *Narrative of the Life and Adventures of Henry Bibb, an American Slave,* begins with several introductory documents offering, collectively, what may be the most elaborate guarantee of authenticity found in the slave narrative canon. What is most revealing—in terms of eclectic narrative form, authenticating strategy, and race rituals along the color line—is the segregation of Bibb's own "Author's Preface" from the white-authored texts of the "Introduction." Bibb's "Author's Preface" is further removed from the preceding introductory texts by the fact that he does not address or acknowledge what has gone before. There is no exchange, no verbal bond, between the two major units of introductory material; this reflects not only the quality of Bibb's relations with his benefactors, but also his relatively modest degree of control over the text and event of the narrative itself.

The "Introduction" is basically a frame created by Bibb's publisher, Lucius Matlack, for the presentation of guarantees composed mostly by abolitionists in Detroit (where, in freedom, Bibb chose to reside). Yet Matlack, as the publisher, also has his own authenticating duties to perform. He assures the reader that while he did indeed "examine" and "prepare" Bibb's manuscript, "The work of preparation . . . was that of orthography and punctuation merely, an arrangement of the chapters, and a table of contents—little more than falls to the lot of publishers generally." When Matlack tackles the issue of the tale's veracity, he mutes his own voice and offers instead those of various "authentic" documents gathered by the abolitionists. These gentlemen, all members of the Detroit Liberty Association, appear most sympathetic to Bibb, especially since he has spoken before their assemblies and lived an exemplary Christian life in their midst. To aid him—and their cause—they have interrogated Bibb (to which he submitted with "praiseworthy spirit") and have solicited letters from slaveholders, jailors, and Bibb's acquaintances, so that the truth of his tale might be established. No fewer than six of these letters plus the conclusion of the Association's report, all substantiating Bibb's story, appear in the "Introduction"; and, as if to "guarantee the guarantee," a note certifying the "friendly recommendation" of the abolitionists and verifying Bibb's "correct deportment" (composed, quite significantly, by a Detroit *judge*) is appended as well.

The elaborate authenticating strategy contained in Matlack's "Introduction" is typical of those found in the first-phase or eclectic narrative. The publisher or editor, far more than the former slave, assembles and manipulates the authenticating machinery, and seems to act on the premise that there is a direct correlation between the quantity of documents or texts assembled and the readership's acceptance of the narrative as a whole. I would like to suggest that Matlack's "Introduction" also constitutes a literary presentation of race rituals and cultural conditions, and that, as such, it functions as a kind of metaphor in the narrative.

To be sure, Matlack displays typical nineteenth-century American enthusiasm and superficiality when he writes of the literary merits of slave narratives: "Gushing fountains of poetic thought have started from beneath the rod of violence, that will long continue to slake the feverish thirst of humanity outraged, until swelling to a flood it shall rush with wasting violence over the ill-gotten heritage of the oppressor." However, the thrust of his "Introduction" is to guarantee the truth of a tale and, by extension, the *existence* of a man calling himself Henry Bibb. In his own aforementioned remarks regarding the preparation of Bibb's text for publication, Matlack appears to address the issue of the author's—Bibb's—credibility. However, the issue is really the audience's—white America's—credulity: their acceptance not so much of the former slave's escape and newfound freedom, but of his literacy. Many race rituals are enacted here, not the least of which is Matlack's "conversation" with white America across the text and figurative body of a silent former slave. The point we may glean from them all is that, insofar as Bibb must depend on his publisher to be an intermediary between his text and his audience, he relinquishes control of the narrative—which is, after all, the vehicle for the account of how he obtained his voice in freedom.

While we are impressed by the efforts of the Detroit Liberty Association's members to conduct an investigation of Bibb's tale, issue a report, and lend their names to the guarantee, we are still far more overwhelmed by the examples of the cultural disease with which they wrestle than by their desire to find a cure. That disease is, of course, cultural myopia, the badge and sore bestowed upon every nation mindlessly heedful of race ritual instead of morality: Henry Bibb is alive and well in Detroit, but by what miraculous stroke will he, as a man, be able to cast his shadow on this soil? The effort in the narrative's "Introduction" to prove that Bibb exists, and hence has a tale, goes far to explain why a prevailing metaphor in Afro-American letters is, in varying configurations, one of invisibility and translucence. Indirectly, and undoubtedly on a subconscious level, Matlack and the abolitionists confront the issue of Bibb's inability "to cast his shadow." But even in their case we may ask: Are they bolstering a cause, comforting a former slave, or recognizing a man?

The letters from the slaveholders and jailors Bibb knew while in bondage must not be overlooked here, for they help illuminate the history of the disease we are diagnosing. The letter from Silas Gatewood, whose father once owned Bibb, is designed solely to portray Bibb as "a notorious liar . . . and a rogue." Placed within the compendium of documents assembled by the abolitionists, the letter completes, through its nearly hysterical denunciation of Bibb, the "Introduction's" portrait of America at war with itself. The debate over Bibb's character, and, by extension, his right to a personal history bound to that of white Americans, is really nothing less than a literary omen of the Civil War. In this regard, the segregation of Bibb's "Author's Preface" from the introductory compendium of documents is, even more than his silence within the compendium, indicative of how the former slave's voice was kept muted and distant while the nation debated questions of slavery and the Negro's humanity.

Bibb's "Preface" reveals two features to his thinking, each of which helps us see how the former slave approached the task of composing a narrative. In answer to his own rhetorical question as to why he wrote the narrative, he replies, "in no place have I given orally the detail of my narrative; and some of the most interesting events of my life have never reached the public ear." This is not extraordinary except in that it reminds us of the oral techniques and traditions that lay behind most of the written narratives. The former slave's accomplishment of a written narrative should by no means be minimized, but we must also recognize the extent to which the abolitionist lecture circuit, whether in Michigan, Maine, or New York, gave former slaves an opportunity to structure, to embellish, and above all to polish an oral version of their tale—and to do so before the very audiences who would soon purchase hundreds, if not thousands, of copies of the written account. The former slave, not altogether unlike the semi-literate black preacher whose sermons were (and are) masterpieces of oral composition and rhetorical strategy, often had a fairly well developed version of his or her tale either memorized or (more likely) sufficiently *patterned* for effective presentation, even before the question of written composition was entertained. Certainly such was the case for Bibb, and this reminds us not to be too narrow when we call the basic slave narrative an eclectic narrative form. Oral as well as written forms are part of the eclectic whole.

The second revealing feature of Bibb's "Preface" returns us to a point on which his publisher, Matlack, began. Bibb appears extremely aware of the issue of his authorship when he writes:

> The reader will remember that I make no pretension to literature; for I can truly say, that I have been educated in the school of adversity, whips, and chains. Experience and observation have been my principal teachers, with the exception of three weeks schooling which I have had the good fortune to receive since my escape from the "grave yard of the mind," or the dark prison of human bondage.

That Bibb had only three weeks of formal schooling is astonishing; however, I am intrigued even more by the two metaphors for slavery with which he concludes. While both obviously suggest confinement—one of the mind, the other of his body—it seems significant that Bibb did not choose between the two (for reasons of style, if no other). Both images are offered *after* the act of writing his tale, possibly because Bibb is so terribly aware of both. His body is now free, his mind limber, his voice resonant; together they and his tale, if not his narrative, are his own.

On a certain level, we must study Matlack's "Introduction," with all its documents and guarantees, and Bibb's "Author's Preface" as a medley of voices, rather than as a loose conglomerate of discrete and even segregated texts. Together, both in what they do and do not say, these statements reflect the passions, politics, interpersonal relations, race rituals, and uses of language of a cross-section of America in the 1840's. But on another level, we must hold

fast to what we have discovered regarding how Bibb's removal from the primary authenticating documents and strategy (that is, from the "Introduction") weakens his control of the narrative and, in my view, relegates him to a posture of partial literacy. Bibb's tale proves that he has acquired a voice, but his narrative shows that his voice does not yet control the imaginative forms which his personal history assumes in print.

In the Bibb narrative, the various texts within the "Introduction" guarantee Bibb and his tale; Bibb sustains this strategy of guarantee late in his tale by quoting letters and proclamations by many of the same figures who provided documents for the "Introduction." As we will discover in Solomon Northup's narrative, this use of authenticating documents within the text of the tale indicates the direction of more sophisticated slave narrative texts. Indeed, the question of whether the authenticating documents and strategies have been integrated into the central text (usually the tale) of the slave narrative is a major criterion by which we may judge author and narrative alike. The inclusion and manipulation of peripheral documents and voices suggests a remarkable level of literacy and self-assurance on the part of the former slave, and the reduction of many texts and strategies into one reflects a search, irrespective of authorial intent, for a more sophisticated written narrative form. Here, then, is a point of departure from which we may study the development of pregeneric narratives into generic and other sophisticated narrative types.

PHASE II: INTEGRATED NARRATIVE

While I am not prepared to classify Solomon Northup's *Twelve Years a Slave* (1854) as an autobiography, it is certainly a more sophisticated text than Henry Bibb's, principally because its most important authenticating document is integrated into the tale as a voice and character. *Twelve Years a Slave* is, however, an integrated narrative unsure of itself. Ultimately, its authenticating strategy depends as much upon an appended set of authenticating texts as upon integrated documents and voices.

In comparison to the Bibb "Introduction," the Northup introductory materials appear purposely short and undeveloped. Northup's editor and amanuensis, a Mr. David Wilson, offers a one-page "Preface," not a full-blown "Introduction," and Northup's own introductory words are placed in the first chapter of his tale, rather than in a discrete entry written expressly for that purpose. Wilson's "Preface" is, predictably, an authenticating document, formulaically acknowledging whatever "faults of style and of expression" the narrative may contain while assuring the reader that he, the editor and a white man, is convinced of Northup's strict adherence to the truth. Northup's own contributions, like Bibb's, are not so much authenticating as they are reflective of what a slave may have been forced to consider while committing his tale to print.

Northup's first entry is simply and profoundly his signature—his proof of literacy writ large, with a bold, clear hand. It appears beneath a pen-and-ink frontispiece portrait entitled "Solomon in His Plantation Suit." His subsequent entries quite self-consciously place his narrative amid the antislavery literature of the era, in particular, with Harriet Beecher Stowe's *Uncle Tom's Cabin* (1852) and *Key to Uncle Tom's Cabin* (1853). If one wonders why Northup neither establishes his experience among those of other kidnapped and enslaved blacks nor positions his narrative with other narratives, the answer is provided in part by his dedicatory page. There, after quoting a passage from *Key to Uncle Tom's Cabin* which, in effect, verifies his account of slavery because it is said to "form a striking parallel" to Uncle Tom's, Northup respectfully dedicates his narrative to Miss Stowe, remarking that his tale affords "another *Key to Uncle Tom's Cabin.*"

This is no conventional dedication; it tells us much about the requisite act of authentication. While the Bibb narrative is authenticated by documents provided by the Detroit Liberty Association, the Northup narrative begins the process of authentication by assuming kinship with a popular antislavery novel. Audience, and the former slave's relationship to that audience, are the key issues here: authentication is, apparently, a rhetorical strategy designed not only for verification purposes, but also for the task of initiating and insuring a readership. No matter how efficacious it undoubtedly was for Northup (or his editor) to ride Miss Stowe's coattails and share in her immense notoriety, one cannot help wondering about the profound implications involved in authenticating personal history by binding it to historical fiction. In its way, this strategy says as much about a former slave's inability to confirm his existence and "cast his shadow" as does the more conventional strategy observed in the Bibb narrative. Apparently, a novel may authenticate a personal history, especially when the personal history is that of a former slave.

While not expressing the issue in these terms, Northup seems to have thought about the dilemma of authentication and that of slave narratives competing with fictions of both the pro- and antislavery variety. He writes:

> Since my return to liberty, I have not failed to perceive the increasing interest throughout the Northern states, in regard to the subject of Slavery. Works of fiction, professing to portray its features in their more pleasing as well as more repugnant aspects, have been circulated to an extent unprecedented, and, as I understand, have created a fruitful topic of comment and discussion.

> I can speak of Slavery only so far as it came under my own observation—only so far as I have known and experienced it in my own person. My object is, to give a candid and truthful statement of facts: to repeat the story of my life, without exaggeration, leaving it for others to determine, whether even the pages of fiction present a picture of more cruel wrong or a severer bondage.

Clearly, Northup felt that the authenticity of his tale would not be taken for granted, and that, on a certain peculiar but

familiar level enforced by rituals along the color line, his narrative would be viewed as a fiction competing with other fictions. However, in this passage Northup also inaugurates a counter-strategy. His reference to his own observation of slavery may be a just and subtle dig at the "armchair sociologists" of North and South alike, who wrote of the slavery question amid the comforts of their libraries and verandas. But more important, in terms of plot as well as point of view, the remark establishes Northup's authorial posture as a "participant-observer" in the truest and (given his bondage) most regrettable sense of the phrase. In these terms, then, Northup contributes personally to the authentication of *Twelve Years a Slave*: he challenges the authenticity of the popular slavery fictions and their power of authenticating his own personal history by first exploiting the bond between them and his tale and then assuming the posture of an authenticator. One needn't delve far into the annals of American race relations for proof that Northup's rhetorical strategy is but a paradigm for the classic manipulation of the master by the slave.

As the first chapter of *Twelve Years a Slave* unfolds, Northup tells of his family's history and circumstances. His father, Mintus Northup, was a slave in Rhode Island and in Rensselaer County, New York, before gaining his freedom in 1803 upon the death of his master. Mintus quickly amassed property and gained suffrage; he came to expect the freedoms that accompany self-willed mobility and self-initiated employment, and gave his son, Solomon, the extraordinary advantage of being born a free man. As a result, Solomon writes of gaining "an education surpassing that ordinarily bestowed upon children in our condition," and he recollects leisure hours "employed over my books, or playing the violin." Solomon describes employment (such as lumber-rafting on Lake Champlain) that was not only profitable but also, in a way associated with the romance of the frontier, adventurous and even manly. When Solomon Northup married Anne Hampton on Christmas Day of 1829, they did not jump over a broomstick, as was the (reported) lot of most enslaved black Americans; rather, the two were married by a magistrate of the neighborhood, Timothy Eddy, Esq. Furthermore, their first home was neither a hovel nor a hut but the "Fort House," a residence "lately occupied by Captain Lathrop" and used in 1777 by General Burgoyne.

This saga of Solomon's heritage is full of interest, and it has its rhetorical and strategical properties as well. Northup has begun to establish his authorial posture removed from the condition of the black masses in slavery—a move which, as we have indicated, is as integral to the authenticating strategy as to the plot of his tale. In addition to portraying circumstances far more pleasant and fulfilling than those which he suffers in slavery, Northup's family history also yields some indication of his relations with whites in the district, especially the white Northups. Of course, these indications also advance both the plot and the authenticating strategy. One notes, for example, that while Mintus Northup did indeed migrate from the site of his enslavement once he was free, he retained the Northup surname and labored for a relative of his former master. Amid his new prosperity and mobility, Mintus maintained fairly amicable ties with his past; apparently this set the tone for relations between Northups, black and white. One should be wary of depicting New York north of Albany as an ideal or integrated area in the early 1800's, but the black Northups had bonds with whites—perhaps blood ties. To the end Solomon depends on these bonds for his escape from slavery and for the implicit verification of his tale.

In the first chapter of *Twelve Years a Slave,* Henry B. Northup, Esq., is mentioned only briefly as a relative of Mintus Northup's former master; in the context of Solomon's family history, he is but a looming branch of the (white) Northup family tree. However, as the tale concludes, Henry Northup becomes a voice and character in the narrative. He requests various legal documents essential to nullifying Solomon's sale into bondage; he inquires into Solomon's whereabouts in Bayou Boeuf, Louisiana; he presents the facts before lawyers, sheriffs, and Solomon's master, Edwin Epps; he pleads Solomon's case against his abductors before a District of Columbia court of law; and, most important, after the twelve years of assault on Solomon's sense of identity, Henry Northup utters, to Solomon's profound thanksgiving, Solomon's given name—not his slave name. In this way Henry Northup enters the narrative, and whatever linguistic authentication of the tale Solomon inaugurated by assuming the rather objective posture of the participant-observer-authenticator is concluded and confirmed, not by appended letter, but by Henry Northup's presence.

This strategy of authentication functions hand in hand with the narrative's strategy of reform. Like the carpenter, Bass, who jeopardizes his own safety by personally mailing Solomon's appeals for help to New York, Henry Northup embodies the spirit of reform in the narrative. In terms of reform strategy, Henry Northup and Bass—who, as a Canadian, represents a variation on the archetype of deliverance in Canada—are not only saviors but also models whose example might enlist other whites in the reform cause. Certainly abolitionists near and far could identify with these men, and that was important. Slave narratives were often most successful when they were as subtly pro-abolition as they were overtly anti-slavery—a consideration which could only have exacerbated the former slave's already sizeable problems with telling his tale in such a way that he, and not his editors or guarantors, controlled it.

But Henry Northup is a different kind of savior from Bass: he is an American descended from slaveowners, and he shares his surname with the kidnapped Solomon. Furthermore, his posture as a family friend is inextricably bound to his position in the tale as a lawyer. At the end of *Twelve Years a Slave,* Henry Northup appears in Louisiana as an embodiment of the law, as well as of Solomon Northup's past (in all its racial complexity) come to reclaim him. In this way, Solomon's *tale* assumes the properties of an integrated narrative—the authenticating texts (here, the words

and actions of Henry Northup) are integrated into the former slave's tale. But in what follows after the tale, we see that Solomon's *narrative* ultimately retrogresses to the old strategies of a phase-one eclectic narrative. Whereas the Bibb narrative begins with a discrete set of authenticating texts, the Northup narrative ends with such a set—an "Appendix."

The Northup Appendix contains three types of documents. First comes the New York state law, passed May 14, 1840, employed by Henry Northup and others to reclaim Solomon Northup from bondage in Louisiana. There follows a petition to the Governor of New York from Solomon's wife, Ann Northup, replete with legal language that persists in terming her a "memorialist." The remaining documents are letters, mostly from the black Northups' white neighbors, authenticating Solomon's claim that he is a free Negro. Despite our initial disappointment upon finding such an orthodox authenticating strategy appended to what had heretofore been a refreshingly sophisticated slave narrative (the narrative does not need the Appendix to fulfill its form), the Appendix does have its points of interest. Taken as a whole, it portrays the unfolding of a law; the New York law with which it begins precipitates the texts that follow, notably, in chronological order. On one level, then, Northup's Appendix is, far more than Bibb's Introduction, a story in epistolary form that authenticates not only his tale but also those voices within the tale, such as Henry Northup's. On another level, however, the Appendix becomes a further dimension to the reform strategy subsumed within the narrative. Just as Bass and Henry Northup posture as model reformers, the narrative's Appendix functions as a primer, complete with illustrative documents, on how to use the law to retrieve kidnapped free Negroes. Thus, the Appendix, as much as the tale itself, can be seen (quite correctly) as an elaborate rhetorical strategy against the Fugitive Slave Law of 1850.

In the end, the Northup narrative reverts to primitive authenticating techniques, but that does not diminish the sophistication and achievement of the tale within the narrative. We must now ask: To what end does the immersion of authenticating documents and strategies within the texture of Northup's tale occur? Furthermore, is this goal literary or extraliterary? In answering these questions we come a little closer, I think, to an opinion on whether narratives like Northup's may be autobiographies.

Northup's conscious or unconscious integration and subsequent manipulation of authenticating voices advances his tale's plot and most certainly advances his narrative's validation and reform strategies. However, it does little to develop what Albert Stone has called a literary strategy of self-presentation. The narrative renders an extraordinary experience, but not a remarkable self. The two need not be exclusive, as Frederick Douglass's 1845 *Narrative* illustrates, but in the Northup book they appear to be distinct entities, principally because of the eye or "I" shaping and controlling the narration. Northup's eye and "I" are not so much introspective as they are inquisitive; even while in the pit of slavery in Louisiana, Northup takes time to inform us of various farming methods and of how they differ from practices in the North. Of course, this remarkable objective posture results directly from Northup assuming the role of a participant-observer for authentication purposes. But it all has a terrible price. Northup's tale is neither the history nor a metaphor for the history of his life; and because this is so, his tale cannot be called autobiographical. . . .

James Olney (essay date 1984)

SOURCE: "'I Was Born': Slave Narratives, Their Status as Autobiography and as Literature," in *Callaloo,* No. 20, Winter, 1984, pp. 46-60.

[*In the following excerpt, Olney provides a list of slave-narrative conventions and considers the impact of white amanuenses on the construction of slave narratives. Olney also compares the narratives of Frederick Douglass, Henry Box Brown, and Solomon Northup.*]

Anyone who sets about reading a single slave narrative, or even two or three slave narratives, might be forgiven the natural assumption that every such narrative will be, or ought to be, a unique production; for—so would go the unconscious argument—are not slave narratives autobiography, and is not every autobiography the unique tale, uniquely told, of a unique life? If such a reader should proceed to take up another half dozen narratives, however (and there is a great lot of them from which to choose the half dozen), a sense not of uniqueness but of overwhelming *sameness* is almost certain to be the result. And if our reader continues through two or three dozen more slave narratives, still having hardly begun to broach the whole body of material (one estimate puts the number of extant narratives at over six thousand), he is sure to come away dazed by the mere repetitiveness of it all: seldom will he discover anything new or different but only, always more and more of the same. This raises a number of difficult questions both for the student of autobiography and the student of Afro-American literature. Why should the narratives be so cumulative and so invariant, so repetitive and so much alike? Are the slave narratives classifiable under some larger grouping (are they history or literature or autobiography or polemical writing? and what relationship do these larger groupings bear to one another?); or do the narratives represent a mutant development really different in kind from any other mode of writing that might initially seem to relate to them as parent, as sibling, as cousin, or as some other formal relation? What narrative mode, what manner of story-telling, do we find in the slave narratives, and what is the place of memory both in this particular variety of narrative and in autobiography more generally? What is the relationship of the slave narratives to later narrative modes and later thematic complexes of Afro-American writing? The questions are multiple and manifold. I propose to come at them and to offer some tentative

answers by first making some observations about autobiography and its special nature as a memorial, creative act; then outlining some of the common themes and nearly invariable conventions of slave narratives; and finally attempting to determine the place of the slave narrative 1) in the spectrum of autobiographical writing, 2) in the history of American literature, and 3) in the making of an Afro-American literary tradition.

I have argued elsewhere that there are many different ways that we can legitimately understand the word and the act of autobiography; here, however, I want to restrict myself to a fairly conventional and common-sense understanding of autobiography. I will not attempt to define autobiography but merely to describe a certain kind of autobiographical performance—not the only kind by any means but the one that will allow us to reflect most clearly on what goes on in slave narratives. For present purposes, then, autobiography may be understood as a recollective/narrative act in which the writer, from a certain point in his life—the present—, looks back over the events of that life and recounts them in such a way as to show how that past history has led to this present state of being. Exercising memory, in order that he may recollect and narrate, the autobiographer is not a neutral and passive recorder but rather a creative and active shaper. Recollection, or memory, in this way a most creative faculty, goes backward so that narrative, its twin and counterpart, may go forward: memory and narration move along the same line only in reverse directions. Or as in Heraclitus, the way up and the way down, the way back and the way forward, are one and the same. When I say that memory is immensely creative I do not mean that it creates for itself events that never occurred (of course this can happen too, but that is another matter). What I mean instead is that memory creates the *significance* of events in discovering the pattern into which those events fall. And such a pattern, in the kind of autobiography where memory rules, will be a teleological one bringing us, in and through narration, and as it were by an inevitable process, to the end of all past moments which is the present. It is in the interplay of past and present, of present memory reflecting over past experience on its way to becoming present being, that events are lifted out of time to be resituated not in mere chronological sequence but in patterned significance.

Paul Ricoeur, in a paper on "Narrative and Hermeneutics," makes the point in a slightly different way but in a way that allows us to sort out the place of time and memory both in autobiography in general and in the Afro-American slave narrative in particular. "*Poiesis,*" according to Ricoeur's analysis, "both reflects and resolves the paradox of time"; and he continues: "It reflects it to the extent that the act of emplotment combines in various proportions two temporal dimensions, one chronological and the other non-chronological. The first may be called the episodic dimension. It characterizes the story as made out of events. The second is the configurational dimension, thanks to which the plot construes significant wholes out of scattered events."[1] In autobiography it is memory that, in the recollecting and retelling of events, effects "emplotment"; it is memory that, shaping the past according to the configuration of the present, is responsible for "the configurational dimension" that "construes significant wholes out of scattered events." It is for this reason that in a classic of autobiographical literature like Augustine's *Confessions,* for example, memory is not only the mode but becomes the very subject of the writing. I should imagine, however, that any reader of slave narratives is most immediately struck by the almost complete dominance of "the episodic dimension," the nearly total lack of any "configurational dimension," and the virtual absence of any reference to memory or any sense that memory does anything but make the past facts and events of slavery immediately present to the writer and his reader. (Thus one often gets, "I can see even now. . . . I can still hear. . . . ," etc.) There is a very good reason for this, but its being a very good reason does not alter the consequence that the slave narrative, with a very few exceptions, tends to exhibit a highly conventional, rigidly fixed form that bears much the same relationship to autobiography in a full sense as painting by numbers bears to painting as a creative act.

I say there is a good reason for this, and there is: The writer of a slave narrative finds himself in an irresolvably tight bind as a result of the very intention and premise of his narrative, which is to give a picture of "slavery *as it is.*" Thus it is the writer's claim, it *must* be his claim, that he is not emplotting, he is not fictionalizing, and he is not performing any act of *poiesis* (=shaping, making). To give a true picture of slavery as it really is, he must maintain that he exercises a clear-glass, neutral memory that is neither creative nor faulty—indeed, if it were creative it would be *eo ipso* faulty for "creative" would be understood by skeptical readers as a synonym for "lying." Thus the ex-slave narrator is debarred from use of a memory that would make anything of his narrative beyond or other than the purely, merely episodic, and he is denied access, by the very nature and intent of his venture, to the configurational dimension of narrative.

Of the kind of memory central to the act of autobiography as I described it earlier, Ernst Cassirer has written: "Symbolic memory is the process by which man not only repeats his past experience but also reconstructs this experience. Imagination becomes a necessary element of true recollection." In that word "imagination," however, lies the joker for an ex-slave who would write the narrative of his life in slavery. What we find Augustine doing in Book X of the *Confessions*—offering up a disquisition on memory that makes both memory itself and the narrative that it surrounds fully symbolic—would be inconceivable in a slave narrative. Of course ex-slaves do exercise memory in their narratives, but they never talk about it as Augustine does, as Rousseau does, as Wordsworth does, as Thoreau does, as Henry James does, as a hundred other autobiographers (not to say novelists like Proust) do. Ex-slaves *cannot* talk about it because of the premises according to which they write, one of those premises being that there is nothing doubtful or mysterious about memory: on

the contrary, it is assumed to be a clear, unfailing record of events sharp and distinct that need only be transformed into descriptive language to become the sequential narrative of a life in slavery. In the same way, the ex-slave writing his narrative cannot afford to put the present in conjunction with the past (again with very rare but significant exceptions to be mentioned later) for fear that in so doing he will appear, from the present, to be reshaping and so distorting and falsifying the past. As a result, the slave narrative is most often a non-memorial description fitted to a preformed mold, a mold with regular depressions here and equally regular prominences there—virtually obligatory figures, scenes, turns of phrase, observances, and authentications—that carry over from narrative to narrative and give to them as a group the species character that we designate by the phrase "slave narrative."

What is this species character by which we may recognize a slave narrative? The most obvious distinguishing mark is that it is an extremely mixed production typically including any or all of the following: an engraved portrait or photograph of the subject of the narrative; authenticating testimonials, prefixed or postfixed; poetic epigraphs, snatches of poetry in the text, poems appended; illustrations before, in the middle of, or after the narrative itself;[2] interruptions of the narrative proper by way of declamatory addresses to the reader and passages that as to style might well come from an adventure story, a romance, or a novel of sentiment; a bewildering variety of documents—letters to and from the narrator, bills of sale, newspaper clippings, notices of slave auctions and of escaped slaves, certificates of marriage, of manumission, of birth and death, wills, extracts from legal codes—that appear before the text, in the text itself, in footnotes, and in appendices; and sermons and anti-slavery speeches and essays tacked on at the end to demonstrate post-narrative activities of the narrator. In pointing out the extremely mixed nature of slave narratives one immediately has to acknowledge how mixed and impure classic autobiographies are or can be also. The last three books of Augustine's *Confessions,* for example, are in a different mode from the rest of the volume, and Rousseau's *Confessions,* which begins as a novelistic romance and ends in a paranoid shambles, can hardly be considered modally consistent and all of a piece. Or if mention is made of the letters prefatory and appended to slave narratives, then one thinks quickly of the letters at the divide of Franklin's *Autobiography,* which have much the same extra-textual existence as letters at opposite ends of slave narratives. But all this said, we must recognize that the narrative letters or the appended sermons haven't the same intention as the Franklin letters or Augustine's exegesis of Genesis; and further, more important, all the mixed, heterogeneous, hetero*generic* elements in slave narratives come to be so regular, so constant, so indispensable to the mode that they finally establish a set of conventions—a series of observances that become virtually *de riguer*—for slave narratives unto themselves.

The conventions for slave narratives were so early and so firmly established that one can imagine a sort of master outline drawn from the great narratives and guiding the lesser ones. Such an outline would look something like this:

A. An engraved portrait, signed by the narrator.

B. A title page that includes the claim, as an integral part of the title, "Written by Himself" (or some close variant: "Written from a statement of Facts Made by Himself"; or "Written by a Friend, as Related to Him by Brother Jones"; etc.)

C. A handful of testimonials and/or one or more prefaces or introductions written either by a white abolitionist friend of the narrator (William Lloyd Garrison, Wendell Phillips) or by a white amanuensis/editor/author actually responsible for the text (John Greenleaf Whittier, David Wilson, Louis Alexis Chamerovzow), in the course of which preface the reader is told that the narrative is a "plain, unvarnished tale" and that naught "has been set down in malice, nothing exaggerated, nothing drawn from the imagination"—indeed, the tale, it is claimed, understates the horrors of slavery.

D. A poetic epigraph, by preference from William Cowper.

E. The actual narrative:

1. a first sentence beginning, "I was born . . . ," then specifying a place but not a date of birth;

2. a sketchy account of parentage often involving a white father;

3. description of a cruel master, mistress, or overseer, details of first observed whipping and numerous subsequent whippings, with women very frequently the victims;

4. an account of one extraordinarily strong, hardworking slave—often "pure African"—who, because there is no reason for it, refuses to be whipped;

5. record of the barriers raised against slave literacy and the overwhelming difficulties encountered in learning to read and write;

6. description of a "Christian" slaveholder (often of one such dying in terror) and the accompanying claim that "Christian" slaveholders are invariably worse than those professing no religion;

7. description of the amounts and kinds of food and clothing given to slaves, the work required of them, the pattern of a day, a week, a year;

8. account of a slave auction, of families being separated and destroyed, of distraught mothers clinging to their children as they are torn from them, of slave coffles being driven South;

9. description of patrols, of failed attempt(s) to escape, of pursuit by men and dogs;

10. description of successful attempt(s) to escape, lying by during the day, travelling by night guided by the North Star, reception in a free state by Quakers who offer a lavish breakfast and much genial thee/thou conversation;

11. taking of a new last name (frequently one suggested by a white abolitionist) to accord with new social identity as a free man, but retention of first name as a mark of continuity of individual identity;

12. reflections on slavery.

F. An appendix or appendices composed of documentary material—bills of sale, details of purchase from slavery, newspaper items—, further reflections on slavery, sermons, anti-slavery speeches, poems, appeals to the reader for funds and moral support in the battle against slavery.

About this "Master Plan for Slave Narratives" (the irony of the phrasing being neither unintentional nor insignificant) two observations should be made: First, that it not only describes rather loosely a great many lesser narratives but that it also describes quite closely the greatest of them all, *Narrative of the Life of Frederick Douglass, An American Slave, Written by Himself,*[3] which paradoxically transcends the slave narrative mode while being at the same time its fullest, most exact representative; Second, that what is being recounted in the narratives is nearly always the realities of the institution of slavery, almost never the intellectual, emotional, moral growth of the narrator (here, as often, Douglass succeeds in being an exception without ceasing to be the best example: he goes beyond the single intention of describing slavery, but he also describes it more exactly and more convincingly than anyone else). The lives of the narratives are never, or almost never, there for themselves and for their own intrinsic, unique interest but nearly always in their capacity as illustrations of what slavery is really like. Thus in one sense the narrative lives of the ex-slaves were as much possessed and used by the abolitionists as their actual lives had been by slaveholders. This is why John Brown's story is titled *Slave Life in Georgia* and only subtitled "A Narrative of the Life, Sufferings, and Escape of John Brown, A Fugitive Slave," and it is why Charles Ball's story (which reads like historical fiction based on very extensive research) is called *Slavery in the United States,* with the somewhat extended subtitle "A Narrative of the Life and Adventures of Charles Ball, A Black Man, who lived forty years in Maryland, South Carolina and Georgia, as a slave, under various masters, and was one year in the navy with Commodore Barney, during the late war. Containing an account of the manners and usages of the planters and slaveholders of the South—a description of the condition and treatment of the slaves, with observations upon the state of morals amongst the cotton planters, and the perils and sufferings of a fugitive slave, who twice escaped from the cotton country." The central focus of these two, as of nearly all the narratives, is slavery, an institution and an external reality, rather than a particular and individual life as it is known internally and subjectively. This means that unlike autobiography in general the narratives are all trained on one and the same objective reality, they have a coherent and defined audience, they have behind them and guiding them an organized group of "sponsors," and they are possessed of very specific motives, intentions, and uses understood by narrators, sponsors, and audience alike: to reveal the truth of slavery and so to bring about its abolition. How, then, could the narratives be anything but very much like one another?

Several of the conventions of slave-narrative writing established by this triangular relationship of narrator, audience, and sponsors and the logic that dictates development of those conventions will bear and will reward closer scrutiny. The conventions I have in mind are both thematic and formal and they tend to turn up as often in the paraphernalia surrounding the narratives as in the narratives themselves. I have already remarked on the extra-textual letters so commonly associated with slave narratives and have suggested that they have a different logic about them from the logic that allows or impels Franklin to include similarly alien documents in his autobiography; the same is true of the signed engraved portraits or photographs so frequently to be found as frontispieces in slave narratives. The portrait and the signature (which one might well find in other nineteenth-century autobiographical documents but with different motivation), like the prefatory and appended letters, the titular tag "Written by Himself," and the standard opening "I was born," are intended to attest to the real existence of a narrator, the sense being that the status of the narrative will be continually called into doubt, so it cannot even begin, until the narrator's real existence is firmly established. Of course the argument of the slave narratives is that the events narrated are factual and truthful and that they all really happened to the narrator, but this is a second-stage argument; prior to the claim of truthfulness is the simple, existential claim: "I exist." Photographs, portraits, signatures, authenticating letters all make the same claim: "This man exists." Only then can the narrative begin. And how do most of them actually begin? They begin with the existential claim repeated. "I was born" are the first words of Moses Roper's *Narrative,* and they are likewise the first words of the narratives of Henry Bibb and Harriet Jacobs, of Henry Box Brown[4] and William Wells Brown, of Frederick Douglass[5] and John Thompson, of Samuel Ringgold Ward and James W. C. Pennington, of Austin Steward and James Roberts, of William Green and William Grimes, of Levin Tilmon and Peter Randolph, of Louis Hughes and Lewis Clarke, of John Andrew Jackson and Thomas H. Jones, of Lewis Charlton and Noah Davis, of James Williams and William Parker and William and Ellen Craft (where the opening assertion is varied only to the extent of saying, "My wife and myself were born").[6]

We can see the necessity for this first and most basic assertion on the part of the ex-slave in the contrary situation of an autobiographer like Benjamin Franklin. While any reader was free to doubt the motives of Franklin's memoir, no one could doubt his existence, and so Franklin begins not with any claims or proofs that he was born and now really exists but with an explanation of why he has chosen to write such a document as the one in hand. With the ex-slave, however, it was his existence and his identity, not his reasons for writing, that were called into question: if the former could be established the latter would be obvious and the same from one narrative to another. Franklin cites four motives for writing his book (to satisfy descendants' curiosity; to offer an example to others; to provide himself the pleasure of reliving events in the telling; to satisfy his own vanity), and while one can find narratives by ex-slaves that might have in them something of each of these motives—James Mars, for example, displays in part the first of the motives, Douglass in part the second, Josiah Henson in part the third, and Samuel Ringgold Ward in part the fourth—the truth is that behind every slave narrative that is in any way characteristic or representative there is the one same persistent and dominant motivation, which is determined by the interplay of narrator, sponsors, and audience and which itself determines the narrative in theme, content, and form. The theme is the reality of slavery and the necessity of abolishing it; the content is a series of events and descriptions that will make the reader see and feel the realities of slavery; and the form is a chronological, episodic narrative beginning with an assertion of existence and surrounded by various testimonial evidences for that assertion.

In the title and subtitle of John Brown's narrative cited earlier—*Slave Life in Georgia: A Narrative of the Life, Sufferings, and Escape of John Brown, A Fugitive Slave*—we see that the theme promises to be treated on two levels, as it were titular and subtitular: the social or institutional and the personal or individual. What typically happens in the actual narratives, especially the best known and most reliable of them, is that the social theme, the reality of slavery and the necessity of abolishing it, trifurcates on the personal level to become subthemes of literacy, identity, and freedom which, though not obviously and at first sight closely related matters, nevertheless lead into one another in such a way that they end up being altogether interdependent and virtually indistinguishable as thematic strands. Here, as so often, Douglass' *Narrative* is at once the best example, the exceptional case, and the supreme achievement. The full title of Douglass' book is itself classic: *Narrative of the Life of Frederick Douglass, An American Slave, Written by Himself.*[7] There is much more to the phrase "written by himself," of course, than the mere laconic statement of a fact: it is literally a part of the narrative, becoming an important thematic element in the retelling of the life wherein literacy, identity, and a sense of freedom are all acquired simultaneously and without the first, accordingly to Douglass, the latter two would never have been. The dual fact of literacy and identity ("written" and "himself") reflects back on the terrible irony of the phrase in apposition, "An American Slave": How can both of these—"American" and "Slave"—be true?

And this in turn carries us back to the name, "Frederick Douglass," which is written all around the narrative: in the title, on the engraved portrait, and as the last words of the text:

> Sincerely and earnestly hoping that this little book may do something toward throwing light on the American slave system, and hastening the glad day of deliverance to the millions of my brethren in bonds—faithfully relying upon the power of truth, love, and justice, for success in my humble efforts—and solemnly pledging myself anew to the sacred cause,—I subscribe myself,
>
> FREDERICK DOUGLASS

"I subscribe myself"—I write my self down in letters, I underwrite my identity and my very being, as indeed I have done in and all through the foregoing narrative that has brought me to this place, this moment, this state of being.

The ability to utter his name, and more significantly to utter it in the mysterious characters on a page where it will continue to sound in silence so long as readers continue to construe the characters, is what Douglass' *Narrative* is about, for in that lettered utterance is assertion of identity and in identity is freedom—freedom from slavery, freedom from ignorance, freedom from non-being, freedom even from time. When Wendell Phillips, in a standard letter prefatory to Douglass' *Narrative,* says that in the past he has always avoided knowing Douglass' "real name and birthplace" because it is "still dangerous, in Massachusetts, for honest men to tell their names," one understands well enough what he means by "your real name" and the danger of telling it—"Nobody knows my name," James Baldwin says. And yet in a very important way Phillips is profoundly wrong, for Douglass had been saying his "real name" ever since escaping from slavery in the way in which he went about creating and asserting his identity as a free man: *Frederick Douglass.* In the *Narrative* he says his real name not when he reveals that he "was born" Frederick Bailey but when he puts his signature below his portrait before the beginning and subscribes himself again after the end of the narrative. Douglass' name-changes and self-naming are highly revealing at each stage in his progress: "Frederick Augustus Washington Bailey" by the name given him by his mother, he was known as "Frederick Bailey" or simply "Fred" while growing up; he escaped from slavery under the name "Stanley," but when he reached New York took the name "Frederick Johnson." (He was married in New York under that name—and gives a copy of the marriage certificate in the text—by the Rev. J. W. C. Pennington who had himself escaped from slavery some ten years before Douglas and who would produce his own narrative some four years after Douglass.) Finally, in New Bedford, he found too many Johnsons and so gave to his host (one of the too many—Nathan Johnson) the privilege of naming him, "but told him he must not take from me the name of 'Frederick.' I must hold on to that, to preserve a sense of my identity." Thus a new social identity but a continuity of personal identity.

In narrating the events that produced both change and continuity in his life, Douglass regularly reflects back and forth (and here he is very much the exception) from the person written about to the person writing, from a narrative of past events to a present narrator grown out of those events. In one marvellously revealing passage describing the cold he suffered from as a child, Douglass says, "My feet have been so cracked with the frost, that the pen with which I am writing might be laid in the gashes." One might be inclined to forget that it is a vastly different person writing from the person written about, but it is a very significant and immensely effective reminder to refer to the writing instrument as a way of realizing the distance between the literate, articulate writer and the illiterate, inarticulate subject of the writing. Douglass could have said that the cold caused lesions in his feet a quarter of an inch across, but in choosing the writing instrument held at the present moment—"the pen with which I am writing"—by one now known to the world as Frederick Douglass, he dramatizes how far removed he is from the boy once called Fred (and other, worse names, of course) with cracks in his feet and with no more use for a pen than for any of the other signs and appendages of the education that he had been denied and that he would finally acquire only with the greatest difficulty but also with the greatest, most telling success, as we feel in the quality of the narrative now flowing from the literal and symbolic pen he holds in his hand. Here we have literacy, identity, and freedom, the omnipresent thematic trio of the most important slave narratives, all conveyed in a single startling image.[8]

There is, however, only one Frederick Douglass among the ex-slaves who told their stories and the story of slavery in a single narrative, and in even the best known, most highly regarded of the other narratives—those, for example, by William Wells Brown, Charles Ball, Henry Bibb, Josiah Henson, Solomon Northup, J. W. C. Pennington, and Moses Roper[9]—all the conventions are observed—conventions of content, theme, form, and style—but they remain just that: conventions untransformed and unredeemed. The first three of these conventional aspects of the narratives are, as I have already suggested, pretty clearly determined by the relationship between the narrator himself and those I have termed the sponsors (as well as the audience) of the narrative. When the abolitionists invited an ex-slave to tell his story of experience in slavery to an anti-slavery convention, and when they subsequently sponsored the appearance of that story in print,[10] they had certain clear expectations, well understood by themselves and well understood by the ex-slave too, about the proper content to be observed, the proper theme to be developed, and the proper form to be followed. Moreover, content, theme, and form discovered early on an appropriate style and that appropriate style was also the personal style displayed by the sponsoring abolitionists in the letters and introductions they provided so generously for the narratives. It is not strange, of course, that the style of an introduction and the style of a narrative should be one and the same in those cases where introduction and narrative were written by the same person—Charles Stearns writing introduction and narrative of Box Brown, for example, or David Wilson writing preface and narrative of Solomon Northup. What is strange, perhaps, and a good deal more interesting, is the instance in which the style of the abolitionist introducer carries over into a narrative that is certified as "Written by Himself," and this latter instance is not nearly so isolated as one might initially suppose. I want to look somewhat closely at three variations on stylistic interchange that I take to represent more or less adequately the spectrum of possible relationships between prefatory style and narrative style, or more generally between sponsor and narrator: Henry Box Brown, where the preface and narrative are both clearly in the manner of Charles Stearns; Solomon Northup, where the enigmatical preface and narrative, although not so clearly as in the case of Box Brown, are nevertheless both in the manner of David Wilson; and Henry Bibb, where the introduction is signed by Lucius C. Matlack and the author's preface by Henry Bibb, and where the narrative is "Written by Himself"—but where also a single style is in control of introduction, author's preface, and narrative alike.

Henry Box Brown's *Narrative,* we are told on the title-page, was

WRITTEN FROM A
STATEMENT OF FACTS MADE BY HIMSELF.
WITH REMARKS UPON THE REMEDY FOR SLAVERY.
BY CHARLES STEARNS.

Whether it is intentional or not, the order of the elements and the punctuation of this subtitle (with full stops after lines two and three) make it very unclear just what is being claimed about authorship and stylistic responsibility for the narrative. Presumably the "remarks upon the remedy for slavery" are by Charles Stearns (who was also, at 25 Cornhill, Boston, the publisher of the *Narrative*), but this title-page could well leave a reader in doubt about the party responsible for the stylistic manner of the narration. Such doubt will soon be dispelled, however, if the reader proceeds from Charles Stearns' "preface" to Box Brown's "narrative" to Charles Stearns' "remarks upon the remedy for slavery." The preface is a most poetic, most high-flown, most grandiloquent peroration that, once cranked up, carries right over into and through the narrative to issue in the appended remarks which come to an end in a REPRESENTATION OF THE BOX in which Box Brown was transported from Richmond to Philadelphia. Thus from the preface: "Not for the purpose of administering to a prurient desire to 'hear and see some new thing,' nor to gratify any inclination on the part of the hero of the following story to be honored by man, is this simple and touching narrative of the perils of a seeker after the 'boon of liberty,' introduced to the public eye . . . ," etc.—the sentence goes on three times longer than this extract, describing as it proceeds "the horrid sufferings of one as, in a *portable prison,* shut out from the light of heaven, and nearly deprived of its balmy air, he pursued his fearful journey. . . ." As is usual in such prefaces, we are addressed directly by the author: "O reader, as you peruse this heart-

rending tale, let the tear of sympathy roll freely from your eyes, and let the deep fountains of human feeling, which God has implanted in the breast of every son and daughter of Adam, burst forth from their enclosure, until a stream shall flow therefrom on to the surrounding world, of so invigorating and purifying a nature, as to arouse from the 'death of the sin' of slavery, and cleanse from the pollutions thereof, all with whom you may be connected." We may not be overwhelmed by the sense of this sentence but surely we must be by its rich rhetorical manner.

The narrative itself, which is all first person and "the plain narrative of our friend," as the preface says, begins in this manner:

> I am not about to harrow the feelings of my readers by a terrific representation of the untold horrors of that fearful system of oppression, which for thirty-three long years entwined its snaky folds about my soul, as the serpent of South America coils itself around the form of its unfortunate victim. It is not my purpose to descend deeply into the dark and noisome caverns of the hell of slavery, and drag from their frightful abode those lost spirits who haunt the souls of the poor slaves, daily and nightly with their frightful presence, and with the fearful sound of their terrific instruments of torture; for other pens far abler than mine have effectually performed that portion of the labor of an exposer of the enormities of slavery.

Suffice it to say of this piece of fine writing that the pen—than which there were others far abler—was held not by Box Brown but by Charles Stearns and that it could hardly be further removed than it is from the pen held by Frederick Douglass, that pen that could have been laid in the gashes in his feet made by the cold. At one point in his narrative Box Brown is made to say (after describing how his brother was turned away from a stream with the remark "We do not allow niggers to fish"), "Nothing daunted, however, by this rebuff, my brother went to another place, and was quite successful in his undertaking, obtaining a plentiful supply of the finny tribe."[11] It may be that Box Brown's story was told from "a statement of facts made by himself," but after those facts have been dressed up in the exotic rhetorical garments provided by Charles Stearns there is precious little of Box Brown (other than the representation of the box itself) that remains in the narrative. And indeed for every fact there are pages of self-conscious, self-gratifying, self-congratulatory philosophizing by Charles Stearns, so that if there is any life here at all it is the life of that man expressed in his very own overheated and foolish prose.[12]

David Wilson is a good deal more discreet than Charles Stearns, and the relationship of preface to narrative in ***Twelve Years a Slave*** is therefore a great deal more questionable, but also more interesting, than in the *Narrative of Henry Box Brown.* Wilson's preface is a page and a half long; Northup's narrative, with a song at the end and three or four appendices, is three hundred thirty pages long. In the preface Wilson says, "Many of the statements contained in the following pages are corroborated by abundant evidence—others rest entirely upon Solomon's assertion. That he has adhered strictly to the truth, the editor, at least, who has had an opportunity of detecting any contradiction or discrepancy in his statements, is well satisfied. He has invariably repeated the same story without deviating in the slightest particular. . . ."[13] Now Northup's narrative is not only a very long one but is filled with a vast amount of circumstantial detail, and hence it strains a reader's credulity somewhat to be told that he "invariably repeated the same story without deviating in the slightest particular." Moreover, since the style of the narrative (as I shall argue in a moment) is demonstrably not Northup's own, we might well suspect a filling in and fleshing out on the part of—perhaps not the "onlie begetter" but at least—the actual author of the narrative. But this is not the most interesting aspect of Wilson's performance in the preface nor the one that will repay closest examination. That comes with the conclusion of the preface which reads as follows:

> It is believed that the following account of his [Northup's] experience on Bayou Boeuf presents a correct picture of Slavery, in all its lights and shadows, as it now exists in that locality. Unbiased, as he conceives, by any prepossessions or prejudices, the only object of the editor has been to give a faithful history of Solomon Northup's life, as he received it from his lips.

In the accomplishment of that object, he trusts he has succeeded, notwithstanding the numerous faults of style and of expression it may be found to contain.

To sort out, as far as possible, what is being asserted here we would do well to start with the final sentence, which is relatively easy to understand. To acknowledge faults in a publication and to assume responsibility for them is of course a commonplace gesture in prefaces, though why the question of style and expression should be so important in giving "a faithful history" of someone's life "as . . . received . . . from his lips" is not quite clear; presumably the virtues of style and expression are superadded to the faithful history to give it whatever literary merits it may lay claim to, and insofar as these fall short the author feels the need to acknowledge responsibility and apologize. Nevertheless, putting this ambiguity aside, there is no doubt about who is responsible for what in this sentence, which, if I might replace pronouns with names, would read thus: "In the accomplishment of that object, David Wilson trusts that he [David Wilson] has succeeded, notwithstanding the numerous faults of style and of expression [for which David Wilson assumes responsibility] it may be found by the reader to contain." The two preceding sentences, however, are altogether impenetrable both in syntax and in the assertion they are presumably designed to make. Casting the first statement as a passive one ("It is believed . . .") and dangling a participle in the second ("Unbiased . . ."), so that we cannot know in either case to whom the statement should be attached, Wilson succeeds in obscuring entirely the authority being claimed for the narrative.[14] It would take too much space to analyze the syntax, the psychology (one might, how-

ever, glance at the familiar use of Northup's given name), and the sense of these affirmations, but I would challenge anyone to diagram the second sentence ("Unbiased . . .") with any assurance at all.

As to the narrative to which these prefatory sentences refer: When we get a sentence like this one describing Northup's going into a swamp—"My midnight intrusion had awakened the feathered tribes [near relatives of the 'finny tribe' of Box Brown/Charles Stearns], which seemed to throng the morass in hundreds of thousands, and their garrulous throats poured forth such multitudinous sounds—there was such a fluttering of wings—such sullen plunges in the water all around me—that I was affrighted and appalled" (p. 141)—when we get such a sentence we may think it pretty fine writing and awfully literary, but the fine writer is clearly David Wilson rather than Solomon Northup. Perhaps a better instance of the white amanuensis/ sentimental novelist laying his mannered style over the faithful history as received from Northup's lips is to be found in this description of a Christmas celebration where a huge meal was provided by one slaveholder for slaves from surrounding plantations: "They seat themselves at the rustic table—the males on one side, the females on the other. The two between whom there may have been an exchange of tenderness, invariably manage to sit opposite; for the omnipresent Cupid disdains not to hurl his arrows into the simple hearts of slaves" (p. 215). The entire passage should be consulted to get the full effect of Wilson's stylistic extravagances when he pulls the stops out, but any reader should be forgiven who declines to believe that this last clause, with its reference to "the simple hearts of slaves" and its self-conscious, inverted syntax ("disdains not"), was written by someone who had recently been in slavery for twelve years. "Red," we are told by Wilson's Northup, "is decidedly the favorite color among the enslaved damsels of my acquaintance. If a red ribbon does not encircle the neck, you will be certain to find all the hair of their wooly heads tied up with red strings of one sort or another" (p. 214). In the light of passages like these, David Wilson's apology for "numerous faults of style and of expression" takes on all sorts of interesting new meaning. The rustic table, the omnipresent Cupid, the simple hearts of slaves, and the woolly heads of enslaved damsels, like the finny and feathered tribes, might come from any sentimental novel of the nineteenth century— one, say, by Harriet Beecher Stowe; and so it comes as no great surprise to read on the dedication page the following: "To Harriet Beecher Stowe: Whose Name, Throughout the World, Is Identified with the Great Reform: This Narrative, Affording Another Key to Uncle Tom's Cabin, Is Respectfully Dedicated." While not surprising, given the style of the narrative, this dedication does little to clarify the authority that we are asked to discover in and behind the narrative, and the dedication, like the pervasive style, calls into serious question the status of *Twelve Years a Slave* as autobiography and/or literature . . .[15]

Notes

1. Professor Ricoeur has generously given me permission to quote from this unpublished paper.

2. I have in mind such illustrations as the large drawing reproduced as frontispiece to John Andrew Jackson's *Experience of a Slave in South Carolina* (London: Passmore & Alabaster, 1862), described as a "Facsimile of the gimlet which I used to bore a hole in the deck of the vessel"; the engraved drawing of a torture machine reproduced on p. 47 of *A Narrative of the Adventures and Escape of Moses Roper, from American Slavery* (Philadelphia: Merrihew & Gunn, 1838); and the "REPRESENTATION OF THE BOX, 3 feet 1 inch long, 2 feet wide, 2 feet 6 inches high," in which Henry Box Brown travelled by freight from Richmond to Philadelphia, reproduced following the text of the *Narrative of Henry Box Brown, Who Escaped from Slavery Enclosed in a Box 3 Feet Long and 2 Wide. Written from a Statement of Facts Made by Himself. With Remarks upon the Remedy for Slavery. By Charles Stearns.* (Boston: Brown & Stearns, 1849). The very title of Box Brown's *Narrative* demonstrates something of the mixed mode of slave narratives. On the question of the text of Brown's narrative see also notes 4 and 12 below.

3. Douglass' *Narrative* diverges from the master plan on E4 (he was himself the slave who refused to be whipped), E8 (slave auctions happened not to fall within his experience, but he does talk of the separation of mothers and children and the systematic destruction of slave families), and E10 (he refuses to tell how he escaped because to do so would close one escape route to those still in slavery; in the *Life and Times of Frederick Douglass* he reveals that his escape was different from the conventional one). For the purposes of the present essay—and also, I think, in general—the *Narrative* of 1845 is a much more interesting and a better book than Douglass' two later autobiographical texts: *My Bondage and My Freedom* (1855) and *Life and Times of Frederick Douglass* (1881). These latter two are diffuse productions (*Bondage and Freedom* is three to four times longer than *Narrative, Life and Times* five to six times longer) that dissipate the focalized energy of the *Narrative* in lengthy accounts of post-slavery activities—abolitionist speeches, recollections of friends, trips abroad, etc. In interesting ways it seems to me that the relative weakness of these two later books is analogous to a similar weakness in the extended version of Richard Wright's autobiography published as *American Hunger* (originally conceived as part of the same text as *Black Boy*).

4. This is true of the version labelled "first English edition"—*Narrative of the Life of Henry Box Brown, Written by Himself* (Manchester: Lee & Glynn, 1851)—but not of the earlier American edition—*Narrative of Henry Box Brown, Who Escaped from Slavery Enclosed in a Box 3 Feet Long and 2 Wide. Written from a Statement of Facts Made by Himself. With Remarks upon the Remedy for Slavery. By Charles Stearns.* (Boston: Brown & Stearns, 1849). On the beginning of the American edition see the

discussion later in this essay, and on the relationship between the two texts of Brown's narrative see note 12 below.

5. Douglass' *Narrative* begins this way. Neither *Bondage and Freedom* nor *Life and Times* starts with the existential assertion. This is one thing, though by no means the only or the most important one, that removes the latter two books from the category of slave narrative. It is as if by 1855 and even more by 1881 Frederick Douglass' existence and his identity were secure enough and sufficiently well known that he no longer felt the necessity of the first and basic assertion.

6. With the exception of William Parker's "The Freedman's Story" (published in the February and March 1866 issues of *Atlantic Monthly*) all the narratives listed were separate publications. There are many more brief "narratives"—so brief that they hardly warrant the title "narrative": from a single short paragraph to three or four pages in length—that begin with "I was born"; there are, for example, twenty-five or thirty such in the collection of Benjamin Drew published as *The Refugee: A North-Side View of Slavery.* I have not tried to multiply the instances by citing minor examples; those listed in the text include the most important of the narratives—Roper, Bibb, W. W. Brown, Douglass, Thompson, Ward, Pennington, Steward, Clarke, the Crafts—even James Williams, though it is generally agreed that his narrative is a fraud perpetrated on an unwitting amanuensis, John Greenleaf Whittier. In addition to those listed in the text, there are a number of other narratives that begin with only slight variations on the formulaic tag—William Hayden: "The subject of this narrative was born"; Moses Grandy: "My name is Moses Grandy; I was born"; Andrew Jackson: "I, Andrew Jackson, was born"; Elizabeth Keckley: "My life has been an eventful one. I was born"; Thomas L. Johnson: "According to information received from my mother, if the reckoning is correct, I was born. . . ." Perhaps more interesting than these is the variation played by Solomon Northup, who was born a free man in New York State and was kidnapped and sent into slavery for twelve years; thus he commences not with "I was born" but with "Having been born a freeman"—as it were the participial contingency that endows his narrative with a special poignancy and a marked difference from other narratives.

There is a nice and ironic turn on the "I was born" insistence in the rather foolish scene in *Uncle Tom's Cabin* (Chapter XX) when Topsy famously opines that she was not made but just "grow'd." Miss Ophelia catechizes her: "'Where were you born?' 'Never was born!' persisted Topsy." Escaped slaves who hadn't Topsy's peculiar combination of Stowe-ic resignation and manic high spirits in the face of an imposed non-identity, non-existence were impelled to assert over and over, "I *was* born."

7. Douglass' title is classic to the degree that it is virtually repeated by Henry Bibb, changing only the name in the formula and inserting "Adventures," presumably to attract spectacle-loving readers: *Narrative of the Life and Adventures of Henry Bibb, An American Slave, Written by Himself.* Douglass' *Narrative* was published in 1845, Bibb's in 1849. I suspect that Bibb derived his title directly from Douglass. That ex-slaves writing their narratives were aware of earlier productions by fellow ex-slaves (and thus were impelled to sameness in narrative by outright imitation as well as by the conditions of narration adduced in the text above) is made clear in the preface to *The Life of John Thompson. A Fugitive Slave; Containing His History of 25 Years in Bondage, and His Providential Escape. Written by Himself* (Worcester: Published by John Thompson, 1856), p. v: "It was suggested to me about two years since, after relating to many the main facts relative to my bondage and escape to the land of freedom, that it would be a desirable thing to put these facts into permanent form. I first sought to discover what had been said by other partners in bondage once, but in freedom now. . . ." With this forewarning the reader should not be surprised to discover that Thompson's narrative follows the conventions of the form very closely indeed.

8. However much Douglass changed his narrative in successive incarnations—the opening paragraph, for example, underwent considerable transformation—he chose to retain this sentence intact. It occurs on p. 52 of the *Narrative of the Life of Frederick Douglass . . .* , ed. Benjamin Quarles (Cambridge, Mass., 1960); on p. 132 of *My Bondage and My Freedom,* intro. Philip S. Foner (New York, 1969); and on p. 72 of *Life and Times of Frederick Douglass,* intro. Rayford W. Logan (New York, 1962).

9. For convenience I have adopted this list from John F. Bayliss' introduction to *Black Slave Narratives* (New York, 1970), p. 18. As will be apparent, however, I do not agree with the point Bayliss wishes to make with his list. Having quoted from Marion Wilson Starling's unpublished dissertation, "The Black Slave Narrative: Its Place in American Literary History," to the effect that the slave narratives, except those from Equiano and Douglass, are not generally very distinguished as literature, Bayliss continues: "Starling is being unfair here since the narratives do show a diversity of interesting styles. . . . The leading narratives, such as those of Douglass, William Wells Brown, Ball, Bibb, Henson, Northup, Pennington, and Roper deserve to be considered for a place in American literature, a place beyond the merely historical." Since Ball's narrative was written by one "Mr. Fisher" and Northup's by David Wilson, and since Henson's narrative shows a good deal of the charlatanry one might expect from a man who billed himself as "The Original Uncle Tom," it seems at best a strategic error for Bayliss to include them

among those slave narratives said to show the greatest literary distinction. To put it another way, it would be neither surprising nor specially meritorious if Mr. Fisher (a white man), David Wilson (a white man), and Josiah Henson (The Original Uncle Tom) were to display "a diversity of interesting styles" when their narratives are put alongside those by Douglass, W. W. Brown, Bibb, Pennington, and Roper. But the really interesting fact, as I shall argue in the text, is that they do *not* show a diversity of interesting styles.

10. Here we discover another minor but revealing detail of the convention establishing itself. Just as it became conventional to have a signed portrait and authenticating letters/prefaces, so it became at least semi-conventional to have an imprint reading more or less like this: "Boston: Anti-Slavery Office, 25 Cornhill." A Cornhill address is given for, among others, the narratives of Douglass, William Wells Brown, Box Brown, Thomas Jones, Josiah Henson, Moses Grandy, and James Williams. The last of these is especially interesting for, although it seems that his narrative is at least semi-fraudulent, Williams is on this point, as on so many others, altogether representative.

11. *Narrative of Henry Box Brown. . . .* (Boston: Brown & Stearns, 1849), p. 25.

12. The question of the text of Brown's *Narrative* is a good deal more complicated than I have space to show, but that complication rather strengthens than invalidates my argument above. The text I analyze above was published in Boston in 1849. In 1851 a "first English edition" was published in Manchester with the specification "Written by Himself." It would appear that in preparing the American edition Stearns worked from a ms. copy of what would be published two years later as the first English edition—or from some ur-text lying behind both. In any case, Stearns has laid on the True Abolitionist Style very heavily, but there is already, in the version "Written by Himself," a good deal of the abolitionist manner present in diction, syntax, and tone. If the first English edition was really written by Brown this would make his case parallel to the case of Henry Bibb, discussed below, where the abolitionist style insinuates itself into the text and takes over the style of the writing even when that is actually done by an ex-slave. This is not the place for it, but the relationship between the two texts, the variations that occur in them, and the explanation for those variations would provide the subject for an immensely interesting study.

13. *Twelve Years a Slave: Narrative of Solomon Northup, a Citizen of New-York, Kidnapped in Washington City in 1841, and Rescued in 1853, from a Cotton Plantation Near the Red River, in Louisiana* (Auburn: Derby & Miller, 1853), p. xv. References in the text are to this first edition.

14. I am surprised that Robert Stepto, in his excellent analysis of the internal workings of the Wilson/

Northup book, doesn't make more of this question of where to locate the real authority of the book. See *From Behind the Veil: A Study of Afro-American Narrative* (Urbana, Ill., 1979), pp. 11-16.

Whether intentionally or not, Gilbert Osofsky badly misleads readers of the book unfortunately called *Puttin' On Ole Massa* when he fails to include the "Editor's Preface" by David Wilson with his printing of *Twelve Years a Slave: Narrative of Solomon Northup*. There is nothing in Osofsky's text to suggest that David Wilson or anyone else but Northup had anything to do with the narrative—on the contrary: "Northup, Brown, and Bibb, as their autobiographies demonstrate, were men of creativity, wisdom and talent. Each was capable of writing his life story with sophistication" (*Puttin' On Ole Massa* [New York, 1969], p. 44). Northup precisely does *not* write his life story, either with or without sophistication, and Osofsky is guilty of badly obscuring this fact. Osofsky's literary judgement, with two-thirds of which I do not agree, is that "The autobiographies of Frederick Douglass, Henry Bibb, and Solomon Northup fuse imaginative style with keenness of insight. They are penetrating and self-critical, superior autobiography by any standards" (p. 10).

15. To anticipate one possible objection, I would argue that the case is essentially different with *The Autobiography of Malcolm X,* written by Alex Haley. To put it simply, there were many things in common between Haley and Malcolm X; between white amanuenses/editors/authors and ex-slaves, on the other hand, almost nothing was shared. . . .

Sam Worley (essay date 1997)

SOURCE: "Solomon Northup and the Sly Philosophy of the Slave Pen," in *Callaloo,* Vol. 20, No. 1, Winter, 1997, pp. 243-59.

[*In the following essay, Worley argues that Northup's work presents a critical position on slavery, one that favorably compares with the writings of Frederick Douglass. Worley also asserts that Northup's narrative does not depend upon either a rational or providential construction.*]

Several rather sweeping assumptions about 19th-century slave narratives have made it difficult to fully understand or appreciate the significance of Solomon Northup's 1853 autobiography, *Twelve Years a Slave.* One assumption is that slave narratives must, as their formal telos, demonstrate "through a variety of rhetorical means that they regard the *writing* of autobiography as in some ways uniquely self-liberating" (Andrews xi). This romantic model of writing and selfhood, which elegantly conflates self-expression, self-mastery, and self-advancement, typically takes Frederick Douglass' 1845 *Narrative* as the foremost representative of the genre.[1] Another assumption,

to a degree consequent upon the first, is that those narratives which rely on a white amanuensis are inherently less interesting than those which do not. The argument in this latter case is that however honorable his intentions, the amanuensis will inevitably shape the narrative to some extent, thereby undermining its authenticity both as history and autobiography. The only other organizational scheme readers have proven capable of recognizing in slave narratives is the providential: that found in those religiously-driven narratives (and narrative-inspired novels) for which the misfortunes and accidents undergone by the self achieve significance through the unveiling of their spiritual significance or necessity. Unlike the Douglass' paradigm which is developed primarily through temporal figures, the providential mode chiefly utilizes spatial figures. *Twelve Years a Slave* conforms to neither of these models, and its reputation has suffered accordingly.

Northup's narrative, though well known, has often been treated as a narrative of the second rank, albeit one with an unusually exciting and involving story as well as, thanks to the research of its modern editors, Sue Eakin and Joseph Logsdon, one with considerable historical value. However, Northup's reliance on a white amanuensis, David Wilson, as well as the failure of the narrative to fulfill certain formal, generic expectations, has meant that analysis of the narrative patterns and philosophical perspective of the work have been almost entirely neglected. Its value has been seen as one of fact or historical record and not, as in the case of the so-called classic narratives, a matter of imposing meaningful, interpretive form on its subject matter. To the limited extent that the form of *Twelve Years* has been examined, it has been dismissed as a clichéd and none-too-skilled repetition of narrative motifs and figures from a hundred other slave stories. David Wilson, the amanuensis, too, is taken to task for the obtrusiveness of his stale, genteel diction and images.[2]

Now Wilson is, admittedly, a problem. But in his defense let it be said that, in regard to slavery at least, Wilson appears to have had no particular political agenda to whose ends he manipulates the story. A small town lawyer, former school superintendent, and amateur writer, Wilson's only other works include *The Life of Jane McCrea, with an Account of Burgoyne's Expedition in 1777,* an account of an Indian massacre of that year, and *Henrietta Robinson,* an account of a notorious murder in 19th-century New York. There is no record indicating any activity on his part in antislavery. Instead, Wilson seems to have primarily seen Northup's adventures as merely an opportunity to tell and sell a particularly sensationalistic tale.[3] His lack of tendentiousness allows Northup's own nuanced vision of slavery to be articulated within the work without polemical oversimplification. *Twelve Years* is convincingly Northup's tale and no one else's because of its amazing attention to empirical detail and unwillingness to reduce the complexity of Northup's experience to a stark moral allegory. Whereas the firm, confident teleological structure of Douglass' *Narrative* reflects his intention to persuade, the more problematic organization and emphasis of *Twelve Years* can be most usefully seen as reflecting Northup's own difficulty in making sense of his experiences. Even if Northup had possessed Douglass' rhetorical prowess, it seems doubtful that he would have constructed a narrative as assured in its judgments and analysis as Douglass'. *Twelve Years* moves toward an understanding of the ironies of slavery quite unlike that of Douglass or most other antislavery writers of the day.

Of course assigning an independent perspective to a protagonist whom we only see second-hand through the prose of his amanuensis seems a shaky proposition at best and speculating on the narrative he might have written under other circumstances is even more problematic. But even in its present form, *Twelve Years* does in fact display a narrative strategy which is reducible neither to Wilson's good story nor to the shared structures and figures of slave narratives in general. Northup's narrative offers a critical vision of slavery which implicitly rejects two prevailing methods for understanding both the individual slave and the institution as a whole—the rational and the providential and their chief organizational schemes, the temporal and the spatial. Moreover, in offering his critique, Northup displays an understanding of the nature of justice and individual identity unlike almost anything else I have seen in contemporary narratives.

The nature of Northup's originality is evident when seen in comparison to what is probably the best-known slave narrative. The philosophical underpinnings of Northup's narrative couldn't be farther from the rational moral idealism which structures Frederick Douglass' *Narrative*. Criticism of Douglass' first autobiography has repeatedly shown the extent to which it is complicit with individualist bourgeois thought both through its elevation of Douglass as a self-made man as well as its downplaying of the crucial role of the slave community.[4] However, beyond its politically problematic nature, this individualism is equally culpable from the standpoint of its effect on the narrative's moral argument. Parallel to Douglass' representation of himself as independent of community is the narrative's representation of the just or the good as radically unconditioned, independent of any social or historical context. The relative isolation of Douglass as a moral agent denies the work the sort of nuanced and complex moral vision possible only when the self is seen enmeshed in and mediated by an intricate network of social relations and contexts.

Northup's story, by contrast, emphasizes not inherently meaningful form, but its absence. *Twelve Years a Slave* sets out from the beginning to contradict and question the archetypal plot for American autobiography: the Franklinesque rise from humble beginnings to prosperity through hard work and ability. Unlike those narratives such as Douglass' where the subject's vague antecedents both emphasize the cruelty of slavery as well as the subject's absolute self-creation, what Olney calls the "sketchy account of parentage" characteristic of most narratives (153), Northup gives a comparatively extensive account of his forebears. Northup represents his family history as

continuous and free from any violent breaks. Race, normally the source of discontinuity in such histories, is minimized in two different ways. Solomon Northup, black, continues to enjoy friendly relations with Henry Northup, a white man and the descendant of the family which owned Northup's ancestors. Thanks to the "persevering interest" of the latter in Solomon's well-being, Henry Northup will play a crucial role in obtaining Solomon's release and return. Solomon Northup is able to relate with considerable precision the four places in which his father lived and worked after he was set free. Reinforcing this familial continuity, Solomon recounts the various ways in which his father molded the character of his two sons. Solomon tells of his father's industry and integrity, the fact that he always remained a farmer without descending to those more demeaning occupations "which seem to be especially allotted to the children of Africa" (5). He gave his children more of an education than most Black children could expect. He owned sufficient property to entitle him to vote in New York. He taught his children morality and a degree of religion. More importantly in this context, while his father regretted slavery, he continued to express "the warmest emotions of kindness, and even of affection towards the family, in whose house he had been a bondsman" (5). Adding to the softening influence of his father's lack of racial animosity is the racial origin of Solomon's own wife, Anne Hampton, on which he places particular emphasis. He writes that

> She is not able to determine the exact line of her descent, but the blood of three races mingled in her veins. It is difficult to tell whether the red, white, or black predominates. The union of them all, however, in her origin, has given her a singular but pleasing expression, such as is rarely to be seen. Though somewhat resembling, yet she can not properly be styled a quadroon, a class to which, I have omitted to mention, my mother belonged.
>
> (7)

Both the accounts of his father and his wife allow Northup to situate his own early life in an unbroken network of family and society that contrasts dramatically with the chaotic family relations found in most other narratives as well as in the later portion of Northup's own story.

The problem for the most familiar type of slave narrative is that slavery denies the slave the very stuff of which personal narratives are composed—origins, family identity or name, education, and increasing self-determination leading up to the moment at which the narrator becomes capable of writing the narrative itself. In the archetypal slave narrative, these things are problematic. The slave has little sense of his origins, his first name is usually given him by his master, his true family name is unknown, he is denied education, and slavery itself restricts the extent to which the events of his life may be said to result from his own volition. The denial of these narrative building blocks is simply another aspect of the denial of the slave's personhood. Keeping in mind Aristotle's crucial definition in *The Politics* of the slave as one capable of obeying rational commands but, lacking reason himself, incapable of giving them, we can see how to be a slave is on a profound level to be defined as a creature whose life cannot be construed as a narrative, whose days and works are merely submoments of the master's biography and cannot be, according to the ideology of the slaveholder, meaningful or coherent in themselves.

In the dynamic of most slave narratives, the absence of conventional elements of personal narrative is compensated for by making the slave story one of how those various elements had to be created by the subject. Douglass' 1845 narrative offers the most brilliant and conspicuous example of this substitution and shows how, far from being the antithesis of Bildungsroman, this variety of slave narrative is arguably its highest form since the individual slave not only undergoes an education in self-mastery but must create both the education and himself. The act of writing the narrative becomes the ultimate act of self-redemption, for by writing of his own origins the ex-slave can make himself his own author in a sense and displace the onus of having been merely the effect of events and becomes instead the source of all the narrative moments. The act of reflecting upon and representing moments of victimization or subjection allows the author to master them, to make them, at least symbolically, the effects of his own consciousness. Moreover, he can bestow form and meaning upon events which were, because of their relative contingency and unwilled nature, previously without significance or meaning.

Yet here again, Northup's narrative responds differently. *Twelve Years a Slave* opens with a detailed recounting of Northup's early days in New York told with explicit attention to its fulfillment of cultural, usually white, stereotypes of hard work and social advancement. Ironically, the telos of most slave narratives, freedom and economic self-sufficiency, are the conditions from which Northup begins. Consequently, Northup's kidnapping and descent into slavery undermines the stability implicit in both the basic narrative model as well as its slave narrative variant. A narrative like Douglass' assumes that principles of justice are available anywhere, anytime to the rational mind. As a result, his sense of injustice grows in tandem with his developing sense of self. Implicit in this relationship is the idea that his self results from his rational apprehension of injustice. The Aristotelian definition of slave nature is denied through the exercise of reason. Northup's narrative, however, directly challenges this association. Any hope of rational narrative form is shattered by his kidnapping. His descent into slavery brings with it a vision of the world as a place of contingency, illusion, and disorder, neither inherently rational nor irrational. Douglass shows through the exercise of reason, his unsuitability for slavery; Northup shows the irrationality of slavery when he is torn from his rational existence. Douglass works to create his own identity; Northup must be brutally trained to deny his. Each time he fails to remember his new slave name or inadvertently says something that suggests his life before the kidnapping, he is punished with a beating.

Northup's economic collapse similarly violates the narrative pattern characteristic of Douglass, whose first narrative operates to a large extent as a type of Franklinesque (or, to be anachronistic, Algeresque) rise from poverty to prosperity through the exercise of self-discipline, self-improvement, and hard work. Douglass' economic conquest is paralleled by his mastery of linear time: to be a successful free man is to impose the linear narrative time as the shape or form of one's life. Meaning is bestowed on one's life by acting to guarantee that each moment of life contributes to the next advance. The achievement of such form triumphs in the evasion of history and contingency. Effaced in such a narrative is the possibility of further change, the return of history, the possibility that prosperity may be as fragile and temporary as poverty has proven to be. The stakes of such a return are immense since in the Franklinesque narrative form the self's value derives solely from this narrative of economic transcendence just as the narrative is taken as the manifestation or realization of the subject's intrinsic value. The loss of such value threatens to completely undermine the subject's claim to meaning.

The first section of the narrative shows how seemingly stable and complete Northup's prosperity was. His father, a freed slave in Rhode Island, "was a man respected for his industry and integrity" (5). He was an independent farmer and steadfastly refused "those more menial positions, which seem to be especially allotted to the children of Africa." He acquired enough property to enable him to vote in New York, and he educated all of his children to a degree unheard of for a farmer's children. He taught his children the work ethic: religion, morality, and hard work. Solomon, in turn, takes up "a life of industry" (7). He moves into a building which, as he specifically points out, had played a role in the Revolutionary War, thereby further implying his connection to American life and history. Similarly, when he tells us that he worked on the construction of the Champlain Canal, he implies a connection between his personal labor and success and the national prosperity. With these wages he buys a pair of horses and tows rafts of lumber along the canal. He lists in notable detail all of his economic vicissitudes from that time forward: cutting timber, buying a farm and livestock, planting corn and oats, part-time work as a fiddle player, his wife's work in the kitchen of Sherril's Coffee House, his relocation to Saratoga Springs to work as a driver for tourists, and eventually more fiddle playing, this time for the railroad workers. Even his financial setback in Saratoga Springs is put into service as a further example of the truth of the work ethic:

> Though always in comfortable circumstances, we had not prospered. The society and associations at that world-renowned watering place, were not calculated to preserve the simple habits of industry and economy to which I had been accustomed, but, on the contrary, to substitute others in their stead, tending to shiftlessness and extravagance.

(11)

But in one respect this passage deviates significantly from the Franklin narrative model: Northup concedes the disastrous effect of environment upon character; he situates his failure in a specific cultural context rather than using the episode solely as evidence of value or lack of value in character. This is not just incidental; this is a way of thinking about character that will occur again and again in his story. We can only grasp the significance of Northup's detailed accounting of his general economic prosperity when we see it in the context of the book as a whole, for where the narrative of economic transcendence usually ends, Northup begins. His is a catastrophic fall that raises questions not about his intrinsic worth but about the truth of such narratives as Douglass' and the vision of selfhood they imply.

Moving even farther away from this association of selfhood and narrative time, Northup emphasizes how when he is drugged and kidnapped he loses all sense of time: "From that moment I was insensible. How long I remained in that condition—whether only that night, or many days and nights—I do not know" (19). By bringing together the loss of access to the standard narrative of economic progress and freedom, Northup's lost sense of time, and ultimately the loss of his very identity, this passage demonstrates how the collapse of the conventional, teleological narrative destroys at once both conventional subjectivity and controlled, linear time.

Twelve Years is particularly good at showing the irrational and brutal nature of the slavemaster's ostensible rationalization of time.[5] One of the greatest ironies of Northup's account is that while production is rationalized to absurd and frightening lengths, the time of the slave's world is increasingly disjoined from any standard sense of time. We see how the slave is initially beaten to produce the maximum amount of cotton and how that extreme quantity then becomes the standard against which all the slave's subsequent pickings will be judged. Yet alongside such passages, *Twelve Years* also tells of how slaves are made to stay up all night dancing to entertain the master, work around the clock during the cane harvest, and work on the Sabbath. The slave is expected to labor in a rationally quantifiable, predictive manner, but, in his role as a thing or possession himself, he is treated without regard to any sense of time. Emblematic of this contrast between the rationalization of labor and the irrational life of the slave, his double role as a producer of commodities and a commodity himself, is Northup's own work as overseer in which he is both the one who overworks and is himself overworked in the name of production. The absurdities and deceits practiced in the name of reason further dispels any sense of there being an objective order of rationality which can be appealed to in the name of justice. The steady unfolding of narrative time and the conception of an individual life as a matter of imposing meaningful form on that time are both explicitly undermined. Reason, both the formal and philosophical key to Douglass' narrative, appears in *Twelve Years* as merely a mask for selfishness and injustice.

In fact, so thorough is the way in which slavery conflicts with conventional notions of time in *Twelve Years* and so

thorough is the amount of coincidence and flashback and the highly literary way in which the significance of seemingly impertinent details—Northup's trip to Montreal, his ability with rafts, the name of the store where he bought his children's clothes—becomes apparent only as the story reaches its final section that it makes one suspect that the crucial influence is not the linear timeline of Franklin or Douglass but the providential mode of *Uncle Tom's Cabin*.[6]

As is well known, Northup's work exhibits an important awareness of Harriet Beecher Stowe's *Uncle Tom's Cabin*. This is explicit in Northup's dedication "To Harriet Beecher Stowe / Whose Name, / Throughout the World, is Identified with the *Great Reform*; THIS NARRATIVE, AFFORDING ANOTHER KEY TO UNCLE TOM'S CABIN, / Is RESPECTFULLY DEDICATED" and only slightly less explicit in his challenge in the first chapter where he asks "whether even the pages of fiction present a picture of more cruel wrong or a severer bondage" (3).[7] If in Douglass' *Narrative,* the central feature of the plot, escape from slavery, appears as a rational development, in Stowe's work the plot reflects not reason but Providence. The diaspora-like effect in which Stowe's black characters are scattered and at least some are eventually recollected to an extent recurs in Northup as do conspicuous echoes of Stowe's own heavy irony.[8]

Admittedly, in speaking of Stowe's novel we are no longer strictly dealing with slave narratives. Stowe drew on the testimony and narratives of ex-slaves, written and oral, in the creation of both her great novel and her commentary on it in *A Key to Uncle Tom's Cabin*. The important thing in this instance is not the authority of the novel in comparison to slave autobiography, but its representativeness of a certain mode of construing the experience of slavery and escape. That mode is, of course, providential; its cosmology, Christian. In a manner consistent with many other mid-19th century novels, *Uncle Tom's Cabin* offers a dramatic picture of lives scattered then recollected, of virtue thwarted or ignored then vindicated, of relations lost then recovered.[9] Providence displays itself like a parlor trick, the message is written down on a piece of paper, folded neatly, shredded into a thousand pieces or tossed into the fire and then quite suddenly makes its miraculous reappearance whole and intact in the magician's gloved hand. The working of Providence, its plot, proceeds inevitably, if at times mysteriously. In place of the fire or the shredding, Stowe's characters, torn from family and home, live episodically, buffeted by a series of seemingly contingent events. They are regularly frustrated in their efforts to impose form or meaning on their lives—except in one crucial respect. Those characters which maintain a belief in God and assume a providential design at work in their lives are able to maintain some sense of purpose and direction in their lives in spite of their apparent chaos: the meaning or design is present but not visible because unlike secular narratives, here the significance is not a human creation. While it is not a particularly complex concept, the relevance and usefulness of the providential mode to narratives of slave life, fictional or true, is important enough to work out in detail.

Modern or bourgeois subjectivity is, on one crucial level, a narrative phenomenon. The life of an individual consists of a beginning, middle, and an end; the requirements of freedom and rationality are comprised of a series of causal relations between the events of a life. Self-determination is, within certain bounds, ultimately a matter of being able to write your own story. Part of the horror of slave life to the 19th-century imagination arose from the slave's inability to do just this. The absence of such agency was, for an antislavery writer such as Stowe, a result of injustice; for proslavery writers it reflected instead, the slave's imputed lack of reason (and out of this, consequent denials of family feeling, maternal feeling, introspection, a capacity for abstract thought—in short, all the stuff of novelistic character). Those who would try to offer a sympathetic representation of the character of slaves while representing the chaotic circumstances of slave life were faced with the problem of how to show the presence of the very potentiality they were arguing had been repressed: that human dignity normally expressed in the ability to make one's life an expression of one's character. The providential mode characteristically shows the failure of conventional narrative subjectivity and its replacement with a non-secular understanding of identity. Souls are revealed precisely by their resistance or inaccessibility to narrative conventions. The significance of Tom's life, for instance, is all the more dramatic for its triumph not merely over but through his apparent lack of control over his earthly destiny. The ability to work out one's salvation with fear and trembling is not significantly compromised by one's lack of control over one's worldly fate. Paradoxically, slavery is well-suited to the display of Providence precisely because the slave exercises so little control over his own life.

Within providential narratives, slavery appears as a sort of anti-narrative, disrupting continuity and linear progress. Its disruption of human aims and desires helps to shift the emphasis onto religious concerns. Yet however much *Uncle Tom's Cabin* influences **Twelve Years,** Northup's narrative also does much to revise aspects of that novel. Stowe's use of space or geography reflects her desire to tell *Uncle Tom's Cabin* as a religious allegory. It builds on the familiar image of the spiritual journey as a physical one, life as a pilgrimage. Tom's movement southward is a descent into a more and more sinful environment and greater and greater temptations. The rigors of this movement require a belief in providence; the author's ability to miraculously resolve separations corresponds to the anticipated ultimate unveiling of providential design. In short, Stowe's representation of life in spatial terms is religious and allegorical; **Twelve Years** is neither.

Just as we saw Northup raising questions about the distorting effects slavery has over conventional narrative time, the peculiar institution also has peculiar effects on the representation of space. Brown and Hamilton's deception is couched in the language of freedom and pleasure. Northup tells us they are well-dressed circus performers out sightseeing in the north before they return to their troupe in Washington. As tourists, they present an image of absolute freedom as they move about the countryside at will. Crucially, however, this will prove to be merely a front. They invite Northup to come along and play his violin at their performances. He quickly agrees to accompany them both for the money and the chance to see something of the world, to share the absolute freedom they seem to represent. They continue to lure him away with the promise of easy money until finally they have him safely in Washington and the domain of slavery. Then the same surreptitious drugging which made him lose all sense of time, also makes him lose his ability to perceive physical space. Northup's description of this event is remarkably vivid in its emphasis on the way the drugs distort his perceptions:

> I only remember, with any degree of distinctness, that I was told it was necessary to go to a physician and procure medicine, and that pulling on my boots, without coat or hat, I followed them through a long passageway, or alley, into the open street. It ran out at right angles from Pennsylvania Avenue. On the opposite side there was a light burning in a window. My impression is there were then three persons with me, but it is altogether indefinite and vague, and like the memory of a painful dream. Going towards the light, which I imagined proceeded from a physician's office, and which seemed to recede as I advanced, is the last glimmering recollection I can now recall. From that moment I was insensible. How long I remained in that condition— whether only that night, or many days and nights—I do not know; but when consciousness returned, I found myself alone, in utter darkness, and in chains.
>
> (19)

Northup's description of William's slave pen is the first of his painstaking accounts of specific buildings and regions that he passes through. So meticulous are most of these descriptions that one could easily produce a map or architectural drawing from them. What is unique about William's slave pen, however, is its invisibility to outsiders. Both physically and symbolically, Northup emphasizes how the structure defies the understanding both of geographic and ideological space:

> It was like a farmer's barnyard in most respects save it was so constructed that the outside world could never see the human cattle that were herded there . . . Its outside presented only the appearance of a quiet private residence. A stranger looking at it, would never have dreamed of its execrable uses. Strange as it may seem, within plain sight of this same house, looking down from its commanding height upon it, was the Capitol. The voices of patriotic representatives boasting of freedom and equality, and the rattling of the poor slave's chains, almost commingled. A slave pen within the very shadow of the Capitol!
>
> (22-23)

Faced with the lucidity and rationality of the enlightened values which lay behind America's political rhetoric, **Twelve Years** represents American slavery as opaque and well-nigh impossible to map. The association of freedom with individual autonomy as symbolized by the two kid-nappers proves to be a vicious deception. The Capitol, which pretends to be both the symbol of democracy and, as the seat of government, its literal substance, is tainted by slavery, the reality of which is hypocritically hidden behind a seemingly innocent housefront; The Capitol itself becomes a false front for corruption. Society as represented in *Twelve Years* is not composed of autonomous individuals and discrete institutions; rather, all individuals and institutions are contingent upon one another. Slavery, though ideologically invisible, nevertheless invades the space of democracy. The symbolic confusion is reinforced by the funeral pomp of William Henry Harrison's funeral:

> The roar of the cannon and the tolling of the bells filled the air, while many houses were shrouded with crepe, and the streets were black with people. As the day advanced, the procession made its appearance, coming slowly through the Avenue, carriage after carriage, in long succession, while thousands upon thousands followed on foot—all moving to the sound of melancholy music. They were bearing the dead body of Harrison to the grave.
>
> (17)

This daytime street activity foreshadows the evening street activity when Northup and the other slaves are led from the pen to the docks. In both instances, the streets are "black with people." Similarly, the "tolling of bells" anticipates the tolling of the ship's bell as it passes Washington's grave at Mount Vernon carrying its slave cargo on to Norfolk. And the dead body, in the first instance Harrison, is to be the socially-dead Northup carried off down these streets to the grave of slavery. In case there should remain any doubt about the ironic juxtaposition, Northup melodramatically underscores the irony of the slaves slipping out of Washington that night:

> So we passed, hand-cuffed and in silence, through the streets of Washington—through the Capital of a nation, whose theory of government, we were told, rests on the foundation of man's inalienable right to life, LIBERTY, and the pursuit of happiness! Hail! COLUMBIA, happy land, indeed!
>
> (34)

The emphatic references to space and geography continue through the remainder of the narrative. Occasionally they simply amount to detailed descriptions and sometimes they reflect Northup's need to hide or deny his own origins in the North (at one point he is severely beaten for telling a prospective buyer that he is from New York.)[10] More typical are those instances which stress the meaninglessness and mysteriousness of Northup's movements, such as when his first letter back home fails to get him rescued because he has no idea where he is being taken and, consequently, cannot tell his friends where to find him. At the heart of *Twelve Years*'s exploration of spatial metaphors are two puzzles: the effects of all these disruptive movements on his character—typically leading at least one mistress to speculate that he has "seen more of

the world than [he] admitted" (175); and the general inadequacy of spatial figures as a way of gauging or mastering life, specifically Northup's confrontation with "the limitless extent of wickedness" (27).

Related to this questioning of the categories of time and space as structuring elements in narrative is the attention *Twelve Years* pays to the effect of environment on character. Perhaps because of its antecedents in spiritual autobiography, the slave narrative ordinarily emphasizes the ability of character to master environment or the innate superiority and independence of the individual subject to its surroundings. The strange modesty, even skepticism, of Northup's vision here as elsewhere, breaks with the genre. From the early instance in which his determination and work ethic are undermined by the resort atmosphere of Saratoga Springs, Northup repeatedly reflects upon the role in which the self, far from being discrete and self-mastering, is actually subject to innumerable external influences.

Of course, many others, black and white, who wrote about slavery mentioned the deleterious effects it had upon the moral character of whites. Northup certainly repeats these observations, but, more remarkably, he makes us see the moral blindness of slaveholders as itself the result of environment rather than innate evil or irrationality:

> [I]t is but simple justice to him when I say, in my opinion, there never was a more kind, noble, candid, Christian man than William Ford. The influences and associations that had always surrounded him, blinded him to the inherent wrong at the bottom of the system of Slavery. He never doubted the moral right of one man holding another in subjection. Looking through the same medium with his fathers before him, he saw things in the same light. Brought up under other circumstances and other influences, his notions would undoubtedly have been different. . . . Were all men such as he, slavery would be deprived of more than half its bitterness.
>
> (62)

Northup is equally clear, however, about the effect of environment on the character of slavers. Bass, the Canadian laborer who befriends Northup, clearly voices the antislavery view of *Twelve Years* as a whole when he says in his argument with Epps about slavery that

> These riggers are human beings. If they don't know as much as their masters, whose fault is it? They are not *allowed* to know anything. You have books and papers, and can go where you please, and gather intelligence in a thousand ways. But your slaves have no privileges. You'd whip one of them if caught reading a book. They are held in bondage, generation after generation, deprived of mental improvement, and who can expect them to possess much knowledge? If they are not brought down to a level with the brute creation, you slaveholders will never be blamed for it. If they are baboons, or stand no higher in the scale of intelligence than such animals, you and men like you will have to answer for it.
>
> (207)

One particularly strange aspect of Northup's concern for the effects of conditions upon character is that *Twelve Years* frequently includes details about slave management, though perhaps not surprisingly, given that Northup himself served as an overseer for a period during his captivity.

Northup emphasizes that while conventional owners believe that beatings and other severities like constant malnourishment keep the slaves tractable and production up, his own experience suggests the opposite: "those who treated their slaves leniently, were rewarded by the greatest amount of labor" (70). The observation itself is not as remarkable as the manner in which it is made. This, like most of his comments on discipline, is relatively free from overt moralizing.

Reflecting this general insistence on seeing character in context is the comparatively sophisticated way in which *Twelve Years* presents slavery as only one part of a vast set of social and economic arrangements. Northup does not simply describe the experience of picking cotton; he does not present cotton production as a process tangential to slave life. The cycle of cotton production is, instead, shown to shape the very contours of slave life on cotton plantations. Northup gives several pages to cotton production, from the initial preparation of the beds through the actual harvest beginning in August. The description, however, is distinguished by never being reified into a series of impersonal processes: each stage of cotton's development appears as human, specifically slave, labor. Further underlining the inseparability of production and slave life, Northup's fullest discussion of a slave's nourishment appears at the end of the cotton production description ironically sandwiched between comments about the feeding of livestock:

> This [the day's picking] done, the labor of the day is not yet ended, by any means. Each one must then attend to his respective chores. One feeds the mules, another the swine—another cuts the wood, and so forth; besides, the packing if all done by candle light. Finally, at a late hour, they reach the quarters, sleepy and overcome with the long day's toil. Then a fire must be kindled in the cabin, the corn ground in the small handmill, and supper, and dinner for the next day in the field, prepared. All that is allowed them is corn and bacon, which is given out at the corncrib and smokehouse every Sunday morning. Each one receives, as his weekly allowance, three and a half pounds of bacon, and corn enough to make a peck of meal. That is all—no tea, coffee, sugar, and with the exception of a very scanty sprinkling now and then, no salt. I can say, from a ten years' residence with Master Epps, that no slave of his is ever likely to suffer from the gout, superinduced by excessive high living. Master Epps' hogs were fed on *shelled* corn—it was thrown out to his 'riggers' in the ear. The former, he thought, would fatten faster by shelling, and soaking it in the water—the latter, perhaps, if treated in the same manner, might grow too fat to labor. Master Epps was a shrewd calculator, and knew how to manage his own animals, drunk or sober.
>
> (127)

He goes on to describe the procedure by which slaves grind their own corn, the material they are given for bedding, their cabins, the horn that wakes them up a few hours later, and their breakfast of "cold bacon and corn cake" (128). Even the production of the corn for slaves and livestock is described. After the last cotton picking is completed in January, slaves must then turn to harvesting the corn. Northup additionally recounts the rounding-up of hogs from the swamps, hogkilling, preservation, cattle raising, and vegetable gardening. A bit farther on in the narrative, Northup gives an almost equally detailed account of sugar cane production and the form of slave life accompanying it (159-63).

What is important about the full and complex picture of slave labor is the image it gives of slavery as a single practice taking place amidst a multitude of other practices. The same holistic perspective which refused to see individuals apart from their circumstances similarly refuses to see slavery as a discrete practice. This emphasis further distances *Twelve Years* from the theological allegory or the rational self-creation models. Neither *Uncle Tom's Cabin* nor Douglass' *Narrative* pays attention to slave life in relation to slave labor or specific practices of production.

What Northup's representation of slavery suggests is that it exists as a practice related to, though not explicitly determined by, a network of other practices with which it exists. Such a broad perspective might seem to risk leading to a sort of relativism. After all, viewing slavery as only one part of a complementary set of social relations is virtually the very same defense many white southerners offered for the peculiar institution. This sense of the seeming naturalness of slavery when viewed by the customs and standards of the South went hand in hand with the ridicule they heaped upon the sort of absolutism reflected in higher laws or moral idealism.

But it is precisely in regard to this question that *Twelve Years* distinguishes itself from run of the mill antislavery writings. The insight in question is not developed fully, but what there is of it suggests a unique strategy for arguing the injustice of slavery. At three different points in the text, Northup asserts that slavers know slavery to be wrong and know the meaning and value of freedom, but only on the last occasion does he explain why he thinks this:

> It is a mistaken opinion that prevails in some quarters, that the slave does not understand the term—does not comprehend the idea of freedom. Even on the Bayou Boenf, where I conceive slavery exists in its most abject and cruel form—where it exhibits features altogether unknown in more northern States—the most ignorant of them generally know its full meaning. They understand the privileges and exemptions that belong to it—that it would bestow upon them the fruits of their own labors, and that it would secure to them the enjoyment of domestic happiness. They do not fail to observe the difference between their own condition and the meanest white man's, and to realize the injustice of

the laws which place it in his power not only to appropriate the profits of their industry, but to subject them to unmerited, and unprovoked punishment, without remedy, or the right to exist, or to remonstrate.

(200)

Slaves, who were traditionally denied their freedom by virtue of being assigned to a position on the margins or entirely outside the community, demonstrate their membership in society, their contiguity with it, through the very fact that they know what freedom is. Consequently, their knowledge of freedom, precisely because it comes about through their de facto membership in society, proves their right to freedom. The relation of freedom to slavery, an intellectual problem for Douglass, a moral one for Stowe, is here both contingent and determining. Northup uses one undeniable and unavoidable aspect of slavery—its continuity with society—to refute another part of it, its relegation of slaves to a position outside society.[11]

As this example shows, Northup can make an immanent critique of the peculiar institution because of his grasp of the way in which social practices loosely impinge upon one another. Northup represents social practices as contingent and potentially contradictory, and it is these qualities which make immanent critique possible.[12] This is not a philosophical perspective that reduces all social practices to a master code of, say, economics, and it is, as noted before, decidedly not one that calls the practice into judgment with a transcendent code of reason or religion. His picture of slavery as related to other agricultural and social practices, his destabilizing of those linear, rationalistic systems of space and time which conventionally structure individual lives, his narration of the chaotic, often disrupted, picaresque structure of his bondage instead of the focused, single-minded plot of most other slave lives, are all ultimately aspects of this uncommon perspective on society and slavery. All of these characteristics, which seem at first to undermine the narrative's ability to offer sustained moral critique, are, in fact, essential to the type of critique it offers.

But abandonment of transcendent principles in moral justification is one thing and actually knowing how to live in a world in which right conduct must be interpreted, moral guidelines created and recreated, is another. Slave narrators who rely upon rational self-initiative and those who construct their experience in religious terms have a consistent basis for moral judgment and, consequently, a basis for a morally consistent identity. But while *Twelve Years* does have its own method of moral argument, the absence of an unchanging foundation for right action requires a different model for behavior. The fluid nature of experience results in a world in which moral judgment must be made on a case by case basis; the unavailability of absolute standards outside the flux of history means that the ethical life must be constantly recreated or improvised. As William James writes in describing such a pragmatic ethics,

Abstract rules can indeed help; but they help the less in proportion as out intuitions are more piercing, and our

vocation is the stronger for the moral life. For every real dilemma is in literal strictness a unique situation; and our exact combination of ideals realized and ideals dissipated which each decision creates is always a universe without precedent, and for which no adequate previous role exists.

(209)

Arguably, the awareness of such an open universe is the central fact of Northup's character. Northup's identity consists not of his allegiance to a fixed transcendent order but in his creative powers, his ability to search out and even author a new moral stance in each changing situation. Again, comparison with our other two models will help. The characteristic actions in Douglass are reading and writing, specifically learning to represent or express himself. In *Uncle Tom's Cabin,* the characteristic actions are listening and speaking, primarily the chain of evangelization and conversion, in order to turn one's own life into a sort of representation of Christ's life. But the action that epitomizes Northup's relation to the world is not representative at all: his violin playing. His ability to play triggers the ruse by which he is at first kidnapped and later is the means by which he augments his own value and gains a degree of mobility when he is permitted to play for dances at neighboring plantations. When he is called upon by the slavetrader to play in the slave pen for the other slaves, it foreshadows what is perhaps the best known moment in the narrative, when Northup, as slave overseer, must himself whip another slave. Northup specifically contrasts his compliance with the forbearance Uncle Tom shows in a similar situation:

> At Huff Power, when I first came to Epps', Tom, one of Roberts' negroes, was driver. He was a burly fellow, and severe in the extreme. After Epps' removal to Bayou Boeuf, that distinguished honor was conferred upon myself. Up to the time of my departure I had to wear a whip about my neck in the field. If Epps was present, I dared not show any lenity, not having the Christian fortitude of a certain well-known Uncle Tom sufficiently to brave his wrath, by refusing to perform the office. In that way, only, I escaped the immediate martyrdom he suffered, and, withal, saved my companions much suffering, as it proved in the end. . . . 'Practice makes perfect,' truly; and during my eight years' experience as a driver I learned to handle my whip with marvelous dexterity and precision, throwing the lash within a hair's breadth of the back, the ear, the nose, without, however, touching either of them. If Epps was observed at a distance, or we had reason to apprehend he was sneaking somewhere in the vicinity, I would commence plying the lash vigorously, when, according to arrangement, they would squirm and screech as if in agony, although not one of them had in fact been even grazed. Patsey would take occasion, if he made his appearance presently, to mumble in his hearing some complaints that Platt was lashing them the whole time, and Uncle Abram, with an appearance of honesty peculiar to himself, would declare roundly I had just whipped them worse than General Jackson whipped the enemy at New Orleans.

(172-73)[13]

Ultimately, Northup's heroism, if that is not too grand a word for it, consists of his adaptability, quick wittedness, and ingenuity. Whether trying to foresee the probable outcome of serving as overseer or cooperating with his captors or simply manufacturing ink from white maple bark and pilfering a sheet of paper, Northup exemplifies a practical and creative heroism that acts without the reassurance of foundations.

The open nature of Northup's representation of experience is the chief cause of **Twelve Years**'s seeming lack of rhetorical or aesthetic control. The rambling nature of the narrative, which lacks the framing and condensation of classic slave narratives, merely expresses the unusual but deeply reflective perspective Northup brings to his experience of race and slavery. In other words, the very characteristics that have kept **Twelve Years** from receiving the attention given to better-known narratives are, in fact, signs of its greatest distinction.

Notes

1. William Andrews, on the other hand, finds the second of Douglass' autobiographies, *My Bondage and My Freedom* (1855), the finest, due largely to its broader scope and greater complexity (218-19).

2. Valerie Smith writes that "the presence of an intermediary renders the majority of the narratives not artistic constructions of personal experience but illustrations of someone else's view of slavery" (9). James Olney is perhaps the most extreme in his criticism of Northup's narrative, questioning its status "as autobiography and/or literature," largely on the grounds of what he sees as Wilson's intrusive and unhelpful presence (Davis and Gates 163). Olney insists that aside from the "great one by Frederick Douglass," all slave narratives are too conventionalized and cliché-ridden to be considered seriously as literature (168). Stepto, though less harsh in his judgments overall, similarly dismisses *Twelve Years* as autobiography: "Northup's eye and 'I' are not so much introspective as they are inquisitive . . . Northup's tale is neither the history nor a metaphor for the history of his life; and because this is so, his tale cannot be called autobiographical" (Davis and Gates 237).

3. Eakin and Logsdon are similarly persuaded that Wilson was drawn primarily to the story's "publishing potential" (xiii).

4. Valerie Smith, for example, writes that "the plot of the narrative offers a profound endorsement of the fundamental American plot, the myth of the self-made man. His broad-based indictments notwithstanding, by telling the story of one man's rise from slavery to the status of esteemed orator, writer, and statesman, he confirms the myth shared by generations of American men that inner resources alone can lead to success" (27).

5. For the effect of the capitalist rationalization of time on slave life, see Genovese 285-94.

6. Stowe, of course, is well aware of the double nature of the slave as the title on one of her chapters suggests: "The Man Who Was a Thing."

7. Andrews sees *Twelve Years* as an example of "a new discursive contract" that emerges in post-Uncle Tom narratives in which "the further the new autobiographer placed himself or herself outside the conventions of the standard discourse on slavery, the more truthful this autobiographer claimed to be" (183). Andrews also discusses the relationship of *Twelve Years, Uncle Tom's Cabin,* and Stowe's *A Key to Uncle Tom's Cabin* (181-83). Robert Stepto also discusses the role of Stowe's novel as an "authenticating document" for Northup's story (232).

8. I am thinking in particular of the description of the slave trader Theophilus Freeman at the opening of chapter six or the bitterly ironic descriptions of the sadistic Epps in chapter twelve.

9. Only think of the 19th-century board game that came out in an effort to capitalize on the Uncle Tom craze. Players moved their pieces around the board through various hazards in an effort to reunite their slave family. See Gossett (164). This motif of the family providentially reunited recurs throughout post-emancipation fiction as well. Consider the almost comic opera series of improbable recognitions and reunions that occur in the postwar scenes of novels like Harper's otherwise splendid *Iola Leroy.*

10. Another interesting reversal of the slave narrative paradigm is that where so many tell of a narrator who discards a false, white-imposed name and engages in a crucial act of self-naming, Northup starts out with a name, has it taken from him, and marks his return to freedom by, in part, reclaiming his original name. On the importance of names and self-naming in the narratives, see Sidonie Smith (19-22).

11. On the various ways in which slaves become aware of the nature of freedom in other narratives, see Foster (116-17).

12. My own understanding of immanent social criticism stems largely from Michael Walzer's set of lectures published as *Interpretation and Social Criticism.* Walzer contrasts immanent criticism (which endeavors to interpret or model our existing morality with all its multiple and often contradictory demands) with the path of discovery (the search for and articulation of some sort of transcendent foundation for morality) and the path of invention (the attempt to create a new moral scheme without reference to the pre-existing one). See especially the first of the lectures, "Three Paths in Moral Philosophy" (3-32).

13. Northup's own ambiguous position in this equation, both as the man who attempts to work the master's will and, as much as he can, to look out for the well-being of Patsey compares interestingly with Deborah McDowell's remarks in "Making Frederick Douglass

and the Afro-American Narrative Tradition" concerning the sexual bias encoded in most slave narratives' representations of female slaves being whipped.

Works Cited

Andrews, William L. *To Tell a Free Story: The First Century of Afro-American Autobiography, 1760-1865.* Urbana: University of Illinois Press, 1986.

Davis, Charles T., and Henry Louis Gates, Jr., eds. *The Slave's Narrative.* New York: Oxford University Press, 1985.

Foster, Francis Smith. *Witnessing Slavery: The Development of Ante-Bellum Slave Narratives.* Westport, CT: Greenwood Press, 1979.

Genovese, Eugene. *Roll Jordan Roll: The World the Slaves Made.* New York: Random House, 1974.

Gossett, Thomas. *Uncle Tom's Cabin and American Culture.* Dallas: Southern Methodist University Press, 1985.

James, William. "The Moral Philosopher and the Moral Life." *'The Will to Believe' and Other Essays in Popular Philosophy.* New York: Dover Books, 1956. 184-215.

McDowell, Deborah. "Making Frederick Douglass and the Afro-American Narrative Tradition." *African-American Autobiography: A Collection of Critical Essays.* Ed. William Andrews. Englewood Cliffs, NJ: Prentice Hall, 1993. 36-58.

Northup, Solomon. *Twelve Years a Slave.* Ed. Sue Eakin and Joseph Logsdon. Baton Rouge: Louisiana State University Press, 1968.

Olney, James, ed. *Studies in Autobiography.* New York: Oxford University Press, 1988.

Smith, Sidonie. *Where I'm Bound: Patterns of Slavery and Freedom in Black American Autobiography.* Westport, CT: Greenwood Press, 1974.

Smith, Valerie. *Self-Discovery and Authority in Afro-American Narrative.* Cambridge: Harvard University Press, 1987.

Walzer, Michael. *Interpretation and Social Criticism.* Cambridge: Harvard University Press, 1987.

FURTHER READING

Biography

Knight, Michael, adapter. *In Chains to Louisiana: Solomon Northup's Story.* New York: Dutton, 1971, 123 p.

Northup's narrative as adapted for juvenile readership.

Criticism

Blassingame, John W. "Using the Testimony of Ex-Slaves: Approaches and Problems." In *The Slave's Narrative* edited by Charles T. Davis and Henry Louis Gates, Jr., pp. 78-98. Oxford: Oxford University Press, 1985.

Considers the difficulties in studying black testimonies, including revisions by white editors, using Northup's narrative as an example.

Cole, Karen. "A Message from the Pine Woods of Central Louisiana: The Garden in Northup, Chopin, and Dormon." In *Louisiana Literature: A Review of Literature and the Humanities* 14, No. 11 (Spring 1997): 64–74.

Considers how the garden as portrayed in Northup's narrative represents a negotiation between wilderness and civilization and reveals the costs of human labor in that negotiation.

Diedrich, Maria. "The Characterization of Native Americans in the Antebellum Slave Narrative." In *CLA College Language Association] Journal,* 31, No. 4 (June 1988): 412-35.

Examines depictions of Indians in several slave narratives, including those of Solomon Northup, Henry Bibb, Josiah Henson, and Austin Steward.

Southern, Eileen. "Antebellum Rural Life." In *The Music of Black Americans: A History,* pp. 151-204. New York: Norton, 1997.

Provides a survey of Black American music in the South, including several references to Northup's use of music in his slave narrative.

Stampp, Kenneth M. "From Day Clean to First Dark." In *The Peculiar Institution: Slavery in the Ante-Bellum South,* pp. 34-85. New York: Knopf, 1968.

Examines slavery as the South's labor system by integrating and analyzing information from, among other things, slave narratives.

Starling, Marion Wilson. "The Slave Narrative After 1836." In *The Slave Narrative: Its Place in American History,* pp. 106-220. Washington, D. C.: Howard University Press, 1988.

Provides overview of slave narratives concurrent with Northup and a contextualization of his experience.

How to Use This Index

The main references

Calvino, Italo
1923-1985 .... CLC 5, 8, 11, 22, 33, 39,
73; SSC 3

list all author entries in the following Gale Literary Criticism series:

BLC = *Black Literature Criticism*
CLC = *Contemporary Literary Criticism*
CLR = *Children's Literature Review*
CMLC = *Classical and Medieval Literature Criticism*
DA = *DISCovering Authors*
DAB = *DISCovering Authors: British*
DAC = *DISCovering Authors: Canadian*
DAM = *DISCovering Authors: Modules*
      DRAM: *Dramatists Module;* *MST:* *Most-Studied Authors Module;*
      MULT: *Multicultural Authors Module;* *NOV:* *Novelists Module;*
      POET: *Poets Module;* *POP:* *Popular Fiction and Genre Authors Module*
DC = *Drama Criticism*
HLC = *Hispanic Literature Criticism*
LC = *Literature Criticism from 1400 to 1800*
NCLC = *Nineteenth-Century Literature Criticism*
NNAL = *Native North American Literature*
PC = *Poetry Criticism*
SSC = *Short Story Criticism*
TCLC = *Twentieth-Century Literary Criticism*
WLC = *World Literature Criticism, 1500 to the Present*

The cross-references

See also CANR 23; CA 85-88;
obituary CA116

list all author entries in the following Gale biographical and literary sources:

AAYA = *Authors & Artists for Young Adults*
AITN = *Authors in the News*
BEST = *Bestsellers*
BW = *Black Writers*
CA = *Contemporary Authors*
CAAS = *Contemporary Authors Autobiography Series*
CABS = *Contemporary Authors Bibliographical Series*
CANR = *Contemporary Authors New Revision Series*
CAP = *Contemporary Authors Permanent Series*
CDALB = *Concise Dictionary of American Literary Biography*
CDBLB = *Concise Dictionary of British Literary Biography*
DLB = *Dictionary of Literary Biography*
DLBD = *Dictionary of Literary Biography Documentary Series*
DLBY = *Dictionary of Literary Biography Yearbook*
HW = *Hispanic Writers*
JRDA = *Junior DISCovering Authors*
MAICYA = *Major Authors and Illustrators for Children and Young Adults*
MTCW = *Major 20th-Century Writers*
SAAS = *Something about the Author Autobiography Series*
SATA = *Something about the Author*
YABC = *Yesterday's Authors of Books for Children*

Literary Criticism Series
Cumulative Author Index

Aurobindo, Sri
See Ghose, Aurabinda

Austen, Jane 1775-1817 ...... **NCLC 1, 13, 19, 33, 51, 81, 95; DA; DAB; DAC; DAM MST, NOV; WLC**
See also AAYA 19; BYA 3; CDBLB 1789-1832; DA3; DLB 116; EXPN; LAIT 2; NFS 1; WLIT 3; WYAS 1

Auster, Paul 1947- .... **CLC 47, 131**
See also CA 69-72; CANR 23, 52, 75; CMW; CN; DA3; DLB 227; MTCW 1

Austin, Frank
See Faust, Frederick (Schiller)
See also TCWW 2

Austin, Mary (Hunter) 1868-1934 . **TCLC 25**
See also Stairs, Gordon
See also ANW; CA 109; 178; DLB 9, 78, 206, 221; FW; TCWW 2

Averroes 1126-1198 .... **CMLC 7**
See also DLB 115

Avicenna 980-1037 .... **CMLC 16**
See also DLB 115

Avison, Margaret 1918- .... **CLC 2, 4, 97; DAC; DAM POET**
See also CA 17-20R; CP; DLB 53; MTCW 1

Axton, David
See Koontz, Dean R(ay)

Ayckbourn, Alan 1939- ...... **CLC 5, 8, 18, 33, 74; DAB; DAM DRAM; DC 13**
See also BRWS 5; CA 21-24R; CANR 31, 59; CBD; CD; DFS 7; DLB 13; MTCW 1, 2

Aydy, Catherine
See Tennant, Emma (Christina)

Ayme, Marcel (Andre) 1902-1967 ... **CLC 11; SSC 41**
See also CA 89-92; CANR 67; CLR 25; DLB 72; EW; GFL 1789 to the Present; RGSF; RGWL; SATA 91

Ayrton, Michael 1921-1975 .... **CLC 7**
See also CA 5-8R; 61-64; CANR 9, 21

Azorin .... **CLC 11**
See also Martinez Ruiz, Jose

Azuela, Mariano 1873-1952 . **TCLC 3; DAM MULT; HLC 1**
See also CA 104; 131; CANR 81; HW 1, 2; MTCW 1, 2

Baastad, Babbis Friis
See Friis-Baastad, Babbis Ellinor

Bab
See Gilbert, W(illiam) S(chwenck)

Babbis, Eleanor
See Friis-Baastad, Babbis Ellinor

Babel, Isaac
See Babel, Isaak (Emmanuilovich)
See also SSFS 10

Babel, Isaak (Emmanuilovich)
1894-1941(?) .... **TCLC 2, 13; SSC 16**
See also Babel, Isaac
See also CA 104; 155; MTCW 1; RGSF; RGWL

Babits, Mihaly 1883-1941 .... **TCLC 14**
See also CA 114

Babur 1483-1530 .... **LC 18**

Babylas 1898-1962
See Ghelderode, Michel de

Baca, Jimmy Santiago 1952-
See also CA 131; CANR 81, 90; CP; DAM MULT; DLB 122; HLC 1; HW 1, 2

Bacchelli, Riccardo 1891-1985 .... **CLC 19**
See also CA 29-32R; 117

Bach, Richard (David) 1936- .... **CLC 14; DAM NOV, POP**
See also AITN 1; BEST 89:2; BPFB 1; BYA 5; CA 9-12R; CANR 18, 93; CPW; FANT; MTCW 1; SATA 13

Bachman, Richard
See King, Stephen (Edwin)

Bachmann, Ingeborg 1926-1973 .... **CLC 69**
See also CA 93-96; 45-48; CANR 69; DLB 85; RGWL

Bacon, Francis 1561-1626 .... **LC 18, 32**
See also CDBLB Before 1660; DLB 151, 236; RGEL

Bacon, Roger 1214(?)-1294 .... **CMLC 14**
See also DLB 115

Bacovia, George 1881-1957 .... **TCLC 24**
See also Bacovia, G.; Vasiliu, Gheorghe
See also DLB 220

Badanes, Jerome 1937- .... **CLC 59**

Bagehot, Walter 1826-1877 .... **NCLC 10**
See also DLB 55

Bagnold, Enid 1889-1981 ...... **CLC 25; DAM DRAM**
See also BYA 2; CA 5-8R; 103; CANR 5, 40; CBD; CWD; CWRI; DLB 13, 160, 191; FW; MAICYA; RGEL; SATA 1, 25

Bagritsky, Eduard 1895-1934 .... **TCLC 60**

Bagrjana, Elisaveta
See Belcheva, Elisaveta

Bagryana, Elisaveta .... **CLC 10**
See also Belcheva, Elisaveta
See also CA 178; DLB 147

Bailey, Paul 1937- .... **CLC 45**
See also CA 21-24R; CANR 16, 62; CN; DLB 14; GLL 2

Baillie, Joanna 1762-1851 .... **NCLC 71**
See also DLB 93; RGEL

Bainbridge, Beryl (Margaret) 1934- . **CLC 4, 5, 8, 10, 14, 18, 22, 62, 130; DAM NOV**
See also BRWS 6; CA 21-24R; CANR 24, 55, 75, 88; CN; DLB 14, 231; MTCW 1, 2

Baker, Elliott 1922- .... **CLC 8**
See also CA 45-48; CANR 2, 63; CN

Baker, Jean H. .... **TCLC 3, 10**
See also Russell, George William

Baker, Nicholson 1957- .... **CLC 61; DAM POP**
See also CA 135; CANR 63; CN; CPW; DA3; DLB 227

Baker, Ray Stannard 1870-1946 .... **TCLC 47**
See also CA 118

Baker, Russell (Wayne) 1925- .... **CLC 31**
See also BEST 89:4; CA 57-60; CANR 11, 41, 59; MTCW 1, 2

Bakhtin, M.
See Bakhtin, Mikhail Mikhailovich

Bakhtin, M. M.
See Bakhtin, Mikhail Mikhailovich

Bakhtin, Mikhail
See Bakhtin, Mikhail Mikhailovich

Bakhtin, Mikhail Mikhailovich
1895-1975 .... **CLC 83**
See also CA 128; 113; DLB 242

Bakshi, Ralph 1938(?)- .... **CLC 26**
See also CA 112; 138; IDFW 3

Bakunin, Mikhail (Alexandrovich)
1814-1876 .... **NCLC 25, 58**

Baldwin, James (Arthur) 1924-1987 . **CLC 1, 2, 3, 4, 5, 8, 13, 15, 17, 42, 50, 67, 90, 127; BLC 1; DA; DAB; DAC; DAM MST, MULT, NOV, POP; DC 1; SSC 10, 33; WLC**
See also AAYA 4, 34; AFAW 1, 2; AMWS 1; BW 1; CA 1-4R; 124; CABS 1; CAD; CANR 3, 24; CDALB 1941-1968; CPW; DA3; DFS 11; DLB 2, 7, 33; DLBY 87; EXPS; LAIT 5; MTCW 1, 2; NFS 4; RGAL; RGSF; SATA 9; SATA-Obit 54; SSFS 2

Bale, John 1495-1563 .... **LC 62**
See also DLB 132; RGEL

Ball, Hugo 1886-1927 .... **TCLC 104**

Ballard, J(ames) G(raham) 1930- . **CLC 3, 6, 14, 36, 137; DAM NOV, POP; SSC 1**
See also AAYA 3; CA 5-8R; CANR 15, 39, 65; CN; DA3; DLB 14, 207; HGG; MTCW 1, 2; NFS 8; RGEL; RGSF; SATA 93; SFW

Balmont, Konstantin (Dmitriyevich)
1867-1943 .... **TCLC 11**
See also CA 109; 155

Baltausis, Vincas 1847-1910
See Mikszath, Kalman

Balzac, Honore de 1799-1850 ... **NCLC 5, 35, 53; DA; DAB; DAC; DAM MST, NOV; SSC 5; WLC**
See also DA3; DLB 119; GFL 1789 to the Present; RGSF; RGWL; SSFS 10

Bambara, Toni Cade 1939-1995 ...... **CLC 19, 88; BLC 1; DA; DAC; DAM MST, MULT; SSC 35; WLCS**
See also AAYA 5; AFAW 2; BW 2, 3; BYA 12; CA 29-32R; 150; CANR 24, 49, 81; CDALBS; DA3; DLB 38; EXPS; MTCW 1, 2; RGAL; RGSF; SATA 112; SSFS 4, 7, 12

Bamdad, A.
See Shamlu, Ahmad

Banat, D. R.
See Bradbury, Ray (Douglas)

Bancroft, Laura
See Baum, L(yman) Frank

Banim, John 1798-1842 .... **NCLC 13**
See also DLB 116, 158, 159; RGEL

Banim, Michael 1796-1874 .... **NCLC 13**
See also DLB 158, 159

Banjo, The
See Paterson, A(ndrew) B(arton)

Banks, Iain
See Banks, Iain M(enzies)

Banks, Iain M(enzies) 1954- .... **CLC 34**
See also CA 123; 128; CANR 61; DLB 194; HGG; INT 128; SFW

Banks, Lynne Reid .... **CLC 23**
See also Reid Banks, Lynne
See also AAYA 6; BYA 7

Banks, Russell 1940- .... **CLC 37, 72; SSC 42**
See also AMWS 5; CA 65-68; CAAS 15; CANR 19, 52, 73; CN; DLB 130

Banville, John 1945- .... **CLC 46, 118**
See also CA 117; 128; CN; DLB 14; INT 128

Banville, Theodore (Faullain) de
1832-1891 .... **NCLC 9**
See also GFL 1789 to the Present

Baraka, Amiri 1934- . **CLC 1, 2, 3, 5, 10, 14, 33, 115; BLC 1; DA; DAC; DAM MST, MULT, POET, POP; DC 6; PC 4; WLCS**
See also Jones, LeRoi
See also AFAW 1, 2; AMWS 2; BW 2, 3; CA 21-24R; CABS 3; CAD; CANR 27, 38, 61; CD; CDALB 1941-1968; CP; CPW; DA3; DFS 3, 11; DLB 5, 7, 16, 38; DLBD 8; MTCW 1, 2; PFS 9; RGAL; WP

Baratynsky, Evgenii Abramovich
1800-1844 .... **NCLC 103**
See also DLB 205

Barbauld, Anna Laetitia
1743-1825 .... **NCLC 50**
See also DLB 107, 109, 142, 158; RGEL

Barbellion, W. N. P. .... **TCLC 24**
See also Cummings, Bruce F(rederick)

Barber, Benjamin R. 1939- .... **CLC 141**
See also CA 29-32R; CANR 12, 32, 64

Barbera, Jack (Vincent) 1945- .... **CLC 44**
See also CA 110; CANR 45

Barbey d'Aurevilly, Jules-Amedee
1808-1889 .... **NCLC 1; SSC 17**
See also DLB 119; GFL 1789 to the Present

Beauvoir, Simone (Lucie Ernestine Marie
  Bertrand) de 1908-1986 .... **CLC 1, 2, 4,**
  8, 14, 31, 44, 50, 71, 124; DA; DAB;
  DAC; DAM MST, NOV; SSC 35; WLC
  See also BPFB 1; CA 9-12R; 118; CANR
  28, 61; DA3; DLB 72; DLBY 86; EW;
  FW; GFL 1789 to the Present; MTCW 1,
  2; RGSF; RGWL

Becker, Carl (Lotus) 1873-1945 ..... **TCLC 63**
  See also CA 157; DLB 17

Becker, Jurek 1937-1997 .... **CLC 7, 19**
  See also CA 85-88; 157; CANR 60; CWW
  2; DLB 75

Becker, Walter 1950- .... **CLC 26**

Beckett, Samuel (Barclay)
  1906-1989 .. **CLC 1, 2, 3, 4, 6, 9, 10, 11,**
  14, 18, 29, 57, 59, 83; DA; DAB; DAC;
  DAM DRAM, MST, NOV; SSC 16;
  WLC
  See also BRWS 1; CA 5-8R; 130; CANR
  33, 61; CBD; CDBLB 1945-1960; DA3;
  DFS 2, 7; DLB 13, 15, 233; DLBY 90;
  GFL 1789 to the Present; MTCW 1, 2;
  RGSF; RGWL; WLIT 4

Beckford, William 1760-1844 .... **NCLC 16**
  See also BRW; DLB 39,213; HGG; SUFW

Beckman, Gunnel 1910- .... **CLC 26**
  See also CA 33-36R; CANR 15; CLR 25;
  MAICYA; SAAS 9; SATA 6

Becque, Henri 1837-1899 .... **NCLC 3**
  See also DLB 192; GFL 1789 to the Present

Becquer, Gustavo Adolfo 1836-1870
  See also DAM MULT; HLCS 1

Beddoes, Thomas Lovell
  1803-1849 .... **NCLC 3; DC 15**
  See also DLB 96

Bede c. 673-735 .... **CMLC 20**
  See also DLB 146

Bedford, Donald F.
  See Fearing, Kenneth (Flexner)

Beecher, Catharine Esther
  1800-1878 .... **NCLC 30**
  See also DLB 1

Beecher, John 1904-1980 .... **CLC 6**
  See also AITN 1; CA 5-8R; 105; CANR 8

Beer, Johann 1655-1700 .... **LC 5**
  See also DLB 168

Beer, Patricia 1924- .... **CLC 58**
  See also CA 61-64; 183; CANR 13, 46; CP;
  CWP; DLB 40; FW

Beerbohm, Max
  See Beerbohm, (Henry) Max(imilian)
  See also BRWS 2; FANT

Beerbohm, (Henry) Max(imilian)
  1872-1956 .... **TCLC 1, 24**
  See also CA 104; 154; CANR 79; DLB 34,
  100

Beer-Hofmann, Richard
  1866-1945 .... **TCLC 60**
  See also CA 160; DLB 81

Beg, Shemus
  See Stephens, James

Begiebing, Robert J(ohn) 1946- ...... **CLC 70**
  See also CA 122; CANR 40, 88

Behan, Brendan 1923-1964 ...... **CLC 1, 8, 11,**
  15, 79; DAM DRAM
  See also BRWS 2; CA 73-76; CANR 33;
  CBD; CDBLB 1945-1960; DFS 7; DLB
  13, 233; MTCW 1, 2

Behn, Aphra 1640(?)-1689 .... **LC 1, 30, 42;**
  DA; DAB; DAC; DAM DRAM, MST,
  NOV, POET; DC 4; PC 13; WLC
  See also BRWS 3; DA3; DLB 39, 80, 131;
  FW; WLIT 3

Behrman, S(amuel) N(athaniel)
  1893-1973 .... **CLC 40**
  See also CA 13-16; 45-48; CAD; CAP 1;
  DLB 7, 44; IDFW 3; RGAL

Belasco, David 1853-1931 .... **TCLC 3**
  See also CA 104; 168; DLB 7; RGAL

Belcheva, Elisaveta 1893-1991 .... **CLC 10**
  See also Bagryana, Elisaveta

Beldone, Phil "Cheech"
  See Ellison, Harlan (Jay)

Beleno
  See Azuela, Mariano

Belinski, Vissarion Grigoryevich
  1811-1848 .... **NCLC 5**
  See also DLB 198

Belitt, Ben 1911- .... **CLC 22**
  See also CA 13-16R; CAAS 4; CANR 7,
  77; CP; DLB 5

Bell, Gertrude (Margaret Lowthian)
  1868-1926 .... **TCLC 67**
  See also CA 167; DLB 174

Bell, J. Freeman
  See Zangwill, Israel

Bell, James Madison 1826-1902 ... **TCLC 43;**
  BLC 1; DAM MULT
  See also BW 1; CA 122; 124; DLB 50

Bell, Madison Smartt 1957- ...... **CLC 41, 102**
  See also BPFB 1; CA 111, 183; CAAE 183;
  CANR 28, 54, 73; CN; CSW; MTCW 1

Bell, Marvin (Hartley) 1937- ...... **CLC 8, 31;**
  DAM POET
  See also CA 21-24R; CAAS 14; CANR 59;
  CP; DLB 5; MTCW 1

Bell, W. L. D.
  See Mencken, H(enry) L(ouis)

Bellamy, Atwood C.
  See Mencken, H(enry) L(ouis)

Bellamy, Edward 1850-1898 ...... **NCLC 4, 86**
  See also DLB 12; RGAL; SFW

Belli, Gioconda 1949-
  See also CA 152; CWW 2; HLCS 1

Bellin, Edward J.
  See Kuttner, Henry

Belloc, (Joseph) Hilaire (Pierre Sebastien
  Rene Swanton) 1870-1953 ...... **TCLC 7,**
  18; DAM POET; PC 24
  See also CA 106; 152; CWRI; DLB 19, 100,
  141, 174; MTCW 1; SATA 112; WCH;
  YABC 1

Belloc, Joseph Peter Rene Hilaire
  See Belloc, (Joseph) Hilaire (Pierre Sebastien Rene Swanton)

Belloc, Joseph Pierre Hilaire
  See Belloc, (Joseph) Hilaire (Pierre Sebastien Rene Swanton)

Belloc, M. A.
  See Lowndes, Marie Adelaide (Belloc)

Bellow, Saul 1915- . **CLC 1, 2, 3, 6, 8, 10, 13,**
  15, 25, 33, 34, 63, 79; DA; DAB; DAC;
  DAM MST, NOV, POP; SSC 14; WLC
  See also AITN 2; AMW; BEST 89:3; BPFB
  1; CA 5-8R; CABS 1; CANR 29, 53, 95;
  CDALB 1941-1968; CN; DA3; DLB 2,
  28; DLBD 3; DLBY 82; MTCW 1, 2;
  NFS 4; RGAL; RGSF; SSFS 12

Belser, Reimond Karel Maria de 1929-
  See Ruyslinck, Ward
  See also CA 152

Bely, Andrey **TCLC 7; PC 11**
  See also Bugayev, Boris Nikolayevich
  See also MTCW 1

Belyi, Andrei
  See Bugayev, Boris Nikolayevich
  See also RGWL

Benary, Margot
  See Benary-Isbert, Margot

Benary-Isbert, Margot 1889-1979 .... **CLC 12**
  See also CA 5-8R; 89-92; CANR 4, 72;
  CLR 12; MAICYA; SATA 2; SATA-Obit
  21

Benavente (y Martinez), Jacinto
  1866-1954 .... **TCLC 3; DAM DRAM,**
  MULT; HLCS 1
  See also CA 106; 131; CANR 81; GLL 2;
  HW 1, 2; MTCW 1, 2

Benchley, Peter (Bradford) 1940- . **CLC 4, 8;**
  DAM NOV, POP
  See also AAYA 14; AITN 2; BPFB 1; CA
  17-20R; CANR 12, 35, 66; CPW; HGG;
  MTCW 1, 2; SATA 3, 89

Benchley, Robert (Charles)
  1889-1945 .... **TCLC 1, 55**
  See also CA 105; 153; DLB 11; RGAL

Benda, Julien 1867-1956 .... **TCLC 60**
  See also CA 120; 154; GFL 1789 to the
  Present

Benedict, Saint c. 480-c. 547 .... **CMLC 29**

Benedict, Ruth (Fulton)
  1887-1948 .... **TCLC 60**
  See also CA 158

Benedikt, Michael 1935- .... **CLC 4, 14**
  See also CA 13-16R; CANR 7; CP; DLB 5

Benet, Juan 1927-1993 .... **CLC 28**
  See also CA 143

Benet, Stephen Vincent 1898-1943 . **TCLC 7;**
  DAM POET; SSC 10
  See also CA 104; 152; DA3; DLB 4, 48,
  102; DLBY 97; HGG; MTCW 1; RGAL;
  RGSF; WP; YABC 1

Benet, William Rose 1886-1950 .... **TCLC 28;**
  DAM POET
  See also CA 118; 152; DLB 45; RGAL

Benford, Gregory (Albert) 1941- ..... **CLC 52**
  See also BPFB 1; CA 69-72; 175; CAAE
  175; CAAS 27; CANR 12, 24, 49, 95;
  CSW; DLBY 82; SCFW 2; SFW

Bengtsson, Frans (Gunnar)
  1894-1954 .... **TCLC 48**
  See also CA 170

Benjamin, David
  See Slavitt, David R(ytman)

Benjamin, Lois
  See Gould, Lois

Benjamin, Walter 1892-1940 .... **TCLC 39**
  See also CA 164; DLB 242

Benn, Gottfried 1886-1956 .. **TCLC 3; PC 35**
  See also CA 106; 153; DLB 56; RGWL

Bennett, Alan 1934- .... **CLC 45, 77; DAB;**
  DAM MST
  See also CA 103; CANR 35, 55; CBD; CD;
  MTCW 1, 2

Bennett, (Enoch) Arnold
  1867-1931 .... **TCLC 5, 20**
  See also BRW; CA 106; 155; CDBLB 1890-
  1914; DLB 10, 34, 98, 135; MTCW 2

Bennett, Elizabeth
  See Mitchell, Margaret (Munnerlyn)

Bennett, George Harold 1930-
  See Bennett, Hal
  See also BW 1; CA 97-100; CANR 87

Bennett, Hal **CLC 5**
  See also Bennett, George Harold
  See also DLB 33

Bennett, Jay 1912- .... **CLC 35**
  See also AAYA 10; CA 69-72; CANR 11,
  42, 79; JRDA; SAAS 4; SATA 41, 87;
  SATA-Brief 27; YAW

Bennett, Louise (Simone) 1919- ...... **CLC 28;**
  BLC 1; DAM MULT
  See also BW 2, 3; CA 151; DLB 117

Benson, E(dward) F(rederic)
  1867-1940 .... **TCLC 27**
  See also CA 114; 157; DLB 135, 153;
  HGG; SUFW

Benson, Jackson J. 1930- .... **CLC 34**
  See also CA 25-28R; DLB 111

Benson, Sally 1900-1972 .... **CLC 17**
  See also CA 19-20; 37-40R; CAP 1; SATA
  1, 35; SATA-Obit 27

Blacklin, Malcolm
See Chambers, Aidan
Blackmore, R(ichard) D(oddridge)
1825-1900 .... **TCLC 27**
See also CA 120; DLB 18; RGEL
Blackmur, R(ichard) P(almer)
1904-1965 .... **CLC 2, 24**
See also AMWS 2; CA 11-12; 25-28R;
CANR 71; CAP 1; DLB 63
Black Tarantula
See Acker, Kathy
Blackwood, Algernon (Henry)
1869-1951 .... **TCLC 5**
See also CA 105; 150; DLB 153, 156, 178;
HGG; SUFW
Blackwood, Caroline 1931-1996 .... **CLC 6, 9,
100**
See also CA 85-88; 151; CANR 32, 61, 65;
CN; DLB 14, 207; HGG; MTCW 1
Blade, Alexander
See Hamilton, Edmond; Silverberg, Robert
Blaga, Lucian 1895-1961 .... **CLC 75**
See also CA 157; DLB 220
Blair, Eric (Arthur) 1903-1950
See Orwell, George
See also CA 104; 132; DA; DA3; DAB;
DAC; DAM MST, NOV; MTCW 1, 2;
SATA 29
Blair, Hugh 1718-1800 .... **NCLC 75**
Blais, Marie-Claire 1939- .... **CLC 2, 4, 6, 13,
22; DAC; DAM MST**
See also CA 21-24R; CAAS 4; CANR 38,
75, 93; DLB 53; FW; MTCW 1, 2
Blaise, Clark 1940- .... **CLC 29**
See also AITN 2; CA 53-56; CAAS 3;
CANR 5, 66; CN; DLB 53; RGSF
Blake, Fairley
See De Voto, Bernard (Augustine)
Blake, Nicholas
See Day Lewis, C(ecil)
See also DLB 77
Blake, William 1757-1827 .... **NCLC 13, 37,
57; DA; DAB; DAC; DAM MST,
POET; PC 12; WLC**
See also CDBLB 1789-1832; CLR 52;
DA3; DLB 93, 163; EXPP; MAICYA;
PAB; PFS 2; 12; SATA 30; WLIT 3; WP
Blanchot, Maurice 1907- .... **CLC 135**
See also CA 117; 144; DLB 72
Blasco Ibanez, Vicente
1867-1928 .... **TCLC 12; DAM NOV**
See also BPFB 1; CA 110; 131; CANR 81;
DA3; EW; HW 1; MTCW 1
Blatty, William Peter 1928- .... **CLC 2; DAM
POP**
See also CA 5-8R; CANR 9; HGG
Bleeck, Oliver
See Thomas, Ross (Elmore)
Blessing, Lee 1949- .... **CLC 54**
See also CAD; CD
Blight, Rose
See Greer, Germaine
Blish, James (Benjamin) 1921-1975 . **CLC 14**
See also BPFB 1; CA 1-4R; 57-60; CANR
3; DLB 8; MTCW 1; SATA 66; SCFW 2;
SFW
Bliss, Reginald
See Wells, H(erbert) G(eorge)
Blixen, Karen (Christentze Dinesen)
1885-1962
See Dinesen, Isak
See also CA 25-28; CANR 22, 50; CAP 2;
DA3; MTCW 1, 2; NCFS 2; SATA 44
Bloch, Robert (Albert) 1917-1994 .... **CLC 33**
See also AAYA 29; CA 5-8R, 179; 146;
CAAE 179; CAAS 20; CANR 5, 78;
DA3; DLB 44; HGG; INT CANR-5;
MTCW 1; SATA 12; SATA-Obit 82; SFW;
SUFW

Blok, Alexander (Alexandrovich)
1880-1921 .... **TCLC 5; PC 21**
See also CA 104; 183; EW; RGWL
Blom, Jan
See Breytenbach, Breyten
Bloom, Harold 1930- .... **CLC 24, 103**
See also CA 13-16R; CANR 39, 75, 92;
DLB 67; MTCW 1; RGAL
Bloomfield, Aurelius
See Bourne, Randolph S(illiman)
Blount, Roy (Alton), Jr. 1941- .... **CLC 38**
See also CA 53-56; CANR 10, 28, 61;
CSW; INT CANR-28; MTCW 1, 2
Bloy, Leon 1846-1917 .... **TCLC 22**
See also CA 121; 183; DLB 123; GFL 1789
to the Present
Blume, Judy (Sussman) 1938- .. **CLC 12, 30;
DAM NOV, POP**
See also AAYA 3, 26; BYA 1; CA 29-32R;
CANR 13, 37, 66; CLR 2, 15, 69; CPW;
DA3; DLB 52; JRDA; MAICYA; MAIC-
YAS; MTCW 1, 2; SATA 2, 31, 79; WYA;
YAW
Blunden, Edmund (Charles)
1896-1974 .... **CLC 2, 56**
See also CA 17-18; 45-48; CANR 54; CAP
2; DLB 20, 100, 155; MTCW 1; PAB
Bly, Robert (Elwood) 1926- .... **CLC 1, 2, 5,
10, 15, 38, 128; DAM POET**
See also AMWS 4; CA 5-8R; CANR 41,
73; CP; DA3; DLB 5; MTCW 1, 2; RGAL
Boas, Franz 1858-1942 .... **TCLC 56**
See also CA 115; 181
Bobette
See Simenon, Georges (Jacques Christian)
Boccaccio, Giovanni 1313-1375 ... **CMLC 13;
SSC 10**
See also RGSF; RGWL
Bochco, Steven 1943- .... **CLC 35**
See also AAYA 11; CA 124; 138
Bodel, Jean 1167(?)-1210 .... **CMLC 28**
Bodenheim, Maxwell 1892-1954 .... **TCLC 44**
See also CA 110; 187; DLB 9, 45; RGAL
Bodker, Cecil 1927- .... **CLC 21**
See also CA 73-76; CANR 13, 44; CLR 23;
MAICYA; SATA 14
Boell, Heinrich (Theodor)
1917-1985 ... **CLC 2, 3, 6, 9, 11, 15, 27,
32, 72; DA; DAB; DAC; DAM MST,
NOV; SSC 23; WLC**
See also Boll, Heinrich
See also CA 21-24R; 116; CANR 24; DA3;
DLB 69; DLBY 85; EW; MTCW 1, 2
Boerne, Alfred
See Doeblin, Alfred
Boethius c. 480-c. 524 .... **CMLC 15**
See also DLB 115; RGWL
Boff, Leonardo (Genezio Darci)
1938- .... **CLC 70; DAM MULT; HLC 1**
See also CA 150; HW 2
Bogan, Louise 1897-1970 .... **CLC 4, 39, 46,
93; DAM POET; PC 12**
See also AMWS 3; CA 73-76; 25-28R;
CANR 33, 82; DLB 45, 169; MTCW 1,
2; RGAL
Bogarde, Dirk
See Van Den Bogarde, Derek Jules Gaspard
Ulric Niven
Bogosian, Eric 1953- .... **CLC 45, 141**
See also CA 138; CAD; CD
Bograd, Larry 1953- .... **CLC 35**
See also CA 93-96; CANR 57; SAAS 21;
SATA 33, 89
Boiardo, Matteo Maria 1441-1494 .... **LC 6**
Boileau-Despreaux, Nicolas 1636-1711 . **LC 3**
See also GFL Beginnings to 1789; RGWL
Bojer, Johan 1872-1959 .... **TCLC 64**
See also CA 189

Bok, Edward W. 1863-1930 .... **TCLC 101**
See also DLB 91; DLBD 16
Boland, Eavan (Aisling) 1944- .. **CLC 40, 67,
113; DAM POET**
See also BRWS 5; CA 143; CANR 61; CP;
CWP; DLB 40; FW; MTCW 2; PFS 12
Boll, Heinrich
See Boell, Heinrich (Theodor)
See also BPFB 1; RGSF; RGWL
Bolt, Lee
See Faust, Frederick (Schiller)
Bolt, Robert (Oxton) 1924-1995 ...... **CLC 14;
DAM DRAM**
See also CA 17-20R; 147; CANR 35, 67;
CBD; DFS 2; DLB 13, 233; LAIT 1;
MTCW 1
Bombal, Maria Luisa 1910-1980 ...... **SSC 37;
HLCS 1**
See also CA 127; CANR 72; HW 1; RGSF
Bombet, Louis-Alexandre-Cesar
See Stendhal
Bomkauf
See Kaufman, Bob (Garnell)
Bonaventura **NCLC 35**
See also DLB 90
Bond, Edward 1934- .... **CLC 4, 6, 13, 23;
DAM DRAM**
See also BRWS 1; CA 25-28R; CANR 38,
67; CBD; CD; DFS 3,8; DLB 13; MTCW
1
Bonham, Frank 1914-1989 .... **CLC 12**
See also AAYA 1; BYA 1; CA 9-12R;
CANR 4, 36; JRDA; MAICYA; SAAS 3;
SATA 1, 49; SATA-Obit 62; TCWW 2;
YAW
Bonnefoy, Yves 1923- .. **CLC 9, 15, 58; DAM
MST, POET**
See also CA 85-88; CANR 33, 75, 97;
CWW 2; GFL 1789 to the Present; MTCW
1, 2
Bontemps, Arna(ud Wendell)
1902-1973 ..... **CLC 1, 18; BLC 1; DAM
MULT, NOV, POET**
See also BW 1; CA 1-4R; 41-44R; CANR
4, 35; CLR 6; CWRI; DA3; DLB 48, 51;
JRDA; MAICYA; MTCW 1, 2; SATA 2,
44; SATA-Obit 24; WCH; WP
Booth, Martin 1944- .... **CLC 13**
See also CA 93-96; CAAE 188; CAAS 2;
CANR 92
Booth, Philip 1925- .... **CLC 23**
See also CA 5-8R; CANR 5, 88; CP; DLBY
82
Booth, Wayne C(layson) 1921- .... **CLC 24**
See also CA 1-4R; CAAS 5; CANR 3, 43;
DLB 67
Borchert, Wolfgang 1921-1947 .... **TCLC 5**
See also CA 104; 188; DLB 69, 124
Borel, Petrus 1809-1859 .... **NCLC 41**
See also GFL 1789 to the Present
Borges, Jorge Luis 1899-1986 ... **CLC 1, 2, 3,
4, 6, 8, 9, 10, 13, 19, 44, 48, 83; DA;
DAB; DAC; DAM MST, MULT; HLC
1; PC 22, 32; SSC 4, 41; WLC**
See also AAYA 26; BPFB 1; CA 21-24R;
CANR 19, 33, 75; DA3; DLB 113; DLBY
86; DNFS; HW 1, 2; MTCW 1, 2; RGSF;
RGWL; SFW; SSFS 4,9; TCLC 109;
WLIT 1
Borowski, Tadeusz 1922-1951 .... **TCLC 9**
See also CA 106; 154; RGSF
Borrow, George (Henry)
1803-1881 .... **NCLC 9**
See also DLB 21, 55, 166
Bosch (Gavino), Juan 1909-
See also CA 151; DAM MST, MULT; DLB
145; HLCS 1; HW 1, 2

Brunner, John (Kilian Houston)
1934-1995 .... **CLC 8, 10; DAM POP**
See also CA 1-4R; 149; CAAS 8; CANR 2,
37; CPW; MTCW 1, 2; SCFW 2; SFW

Bruno, Giordano 1548-1600 .... **LC 27**
See also RGWL

Brutus, Dennis 1924- .... **CLC 43; BLC 1;
DAM MULT, POET; PC 24**
See also BW 2, 3; CA 49-52; CAAS 14;
CANR 2, 27, 42, 81; CP; DLB 117, 225

Bryan, C(ourtlandt) D(ixon) B(arnes)
1936- .... **CLC 29**
See also CA 73-76; CANR 13, 68; DLB
185; INT CANR-13

Bryan, Michael
See Moore, Brian
See also CCA 1

Bryan, William Jennings
1860-1925 .... **TCLC 99**

Bryant, William Cullen 1794-1878 . **NCLC 6,
46; DA; DAB; DAC; DAM MST,
POET; PC 20**
See also AMWS 1; CDALB 1640-1865;
DLB 3, 43, 59, 189; EXPP; PAB; RGAL

Bryusov, Valery Yakovlevich
1873-1924 .... **TCLC 10**
See also CA 107; 155; SFW

Buchan, John 1875-1940 .... **TCLC 41; DAB;
DAM POP**
See also CA 108; 145; CMW; DLB 34, 70,
156; HGG; MTCW 1; RGEL; RHW;
YABC 2

Buchanan, George 1506-1582 .... **LC 4**
See also DLB 152

Buchanan, Robert 1841-1901 .... **TCLC 107**
See also CA 179; DLB 18, 35

Buchheim, Lothar-Guenther 1918- .... **CLC 6**
See also CA 85-88

Buchner, (Karl) Georg 1813-1837 . **NCLC 26**
See also EW; RGSF; RGWL

Buchwald, Art(hur) 1925- .... **CLC 33**
See also AITN 1; CA 5-8R; CANR 21, 67;
MTCW 1, 2; SATA 10

Buck, Pearl S(ydenstricker)
1892-1973 .... **CLC 7, 11, 18, 127; DA;
DAB; DAC; DAM MST, NOV**
See also AITN 1; AMWS 2; BPFB 1; CA
1-4R; 41-44R; CANR 1, 34; CDALBS;
DA3; DLB 9, 102; LAIT 3; MTCW 1, 2;
RGAL; RHW; SATA 1, 25

Buckler, Ernest 1908-1984 .... **CLC 13; DAC;
DAM MST**
See also CA 11-12; 114; CAP 1; CCA 1;
DLB 68; SATA 47

Buckley, Vincent (Thomas)
1925-1988 .... **CLC 57**
See also CA 101

Buckley, William F(rank), Jr. 1925- . **CLC 7,
18, 37; DAM POP**
See also AITN 1; BPFB 1; CA 1-4R; CANR
1, 24, 53, 93; CMW; CPW; DA3; DLB
137; DLBY 80; INT CANR-24; MTCW
1, 2; TUS

Buechner, (Carl) Frederick 1926- . **CLC 2, 4,
6, 9; DAM NOV**
See also BPFB 1; CA 13-16R; CANR 11,
39, 64; CN; DLBY 80; INT CANR-11;
MTCW 1, 2

Buell, John (Edward) 1927- .... **CLC 10**
See also CA 1-4R; CANR 71; DLB 53

Buero Vallejo, Antonio 1916-2000 ... **CLC 15,
46, 139**
See also CA 106; 189; CANR 24, 49, 75;
DFS 11; HW 1; MTCW 1, 2

Bufalino, Gesualdo 1920(?)-1990 ...... **CLC 74**
See also CWW 2; DLB 196

Bugayev, Boris Nikolayevich
1880-1934 .... **TCLC 7; PC 11**
See also Bely, Andrey; Belyi, Andrei
See also CA 104; 165; MTCW 1

Bukowski, Charles 1920-1994 ... **CLC 2, 5, 9,
41, 82, 108; DAM NOV, POET; PC 18;
SSC 45**
See also CA 17-20R; 144; CANR 40, 62;
CPW; DA3; DLB 5, 130, 169; MTCW 1,
2

Bulgakov, Mikhail (Afanas'evich)
1891-1940 . **TCLC 2, 16; DAM DRAM,
NOV; SSC 18**
See also BPFB 1; CA 105; 152; NFS 8;
RGSF; RGWL; SFW

Bulgya, Alexander Alexandrovich
1901-1956 .... **TCLC 53**
See also Fadeyev, Alexander
See also CA 117; 181

Bullins, Ed 1935- .... **CLC 1, 5, 7; BLC 1;
DAM DRAM, MULT; DC 6**
See also BW 2, 3; CA 49-52; CAAS 16;
CAD; CANR 24, 46, 73; CD; DLB 7, 38;
MTCW 1, 2; RGAL

**Bulwer-Lytton, Edward (George Earle
Lytton)** 1803-1873 .... **NCLC 1, 45**
See also DLB 21; RGEL; SFW; SUFW

Bunin, Ivan Alexeyevich
1870-1953 .... **TCLC 6; SSC 5**
See also CA 104; RGSF; RGWL

Bunting, Basil 1900-1985 ..... **CLC 10, 39, 47;
DAM POET**
See also BRWS 7; CA 53-56; 115; CANR
7; DLB 20; RGEL

Bunuel, Luis 1900-1983 .. **CLC 16, 80; DAM
MULT; HLC 1**
See also CA 101; 110; CANR 32, 77; HW
1

Bunyan, John 1628-1688 .... **LC 4, 69; DA;
DAB; DAC; DAM MST; WLC**
See also BRW 2; BYA 5; CDBLB 1660-
1789; DLB 39; RGEL; WLIT 3

Buravsky, Alexandr .... **CLC 59**

Burckhardt, Jacob (Christoph)
1818-1897 .... **NCLC 49**
See also EW

Burford, Eleanor
See Hibbert, Eleanor Alice Burford

Burgess, Anthony ..... **CLC 1, 2, 4, 5, 8, 10, 13,
15, 22, 40, 62, 81, 94; DAB**
See also Wilson, John (Anthony) Burgess
See also AAYA 25; AITN 1; BRWS 1; CD-
BLB 1960 to Present; DLB 14, 194;
DLBY 98; MTCW 1; RGEL; RHW; SFW;
YAW

Burke, Edmund 1729(?)-1797 .... **LC 7, 36;
DA; DAB; DAC; DAM MST; WLC**
See also DA3; DLB 104; RGEL

Burke, Kenneth (Duva) 1897-1993 ... **CLC 2,
24**
See also AMW; CA 5-8R; 143; CANR 39,
74; DLB 45, 63; MTCW 1, 2; RGAL

Burke, Leda
See Garnett, David

Burke, Ralph
See Silverberg, Robert

Burke, Thomas 1886-1945 .... **TCLC 63**
See also CA 113; 155; CMW; DLB 197

Burney, Fanny 1752-1840 .... **NCLC 12, 54**
See also BRWS 3; DLB 39; RGEL

Burney, Frances
See Burney, Fanny

Burns, Robert 1759-1796 . **LC 3, 29, 40; DA;
DAB; DAC; DAM MST, POET; PC 6;
WLC**
See also CDBLB 1789-1832; DA3; DLB
109; EXPP; PAB; RGEL; WP

Burns, Tex
See L'Amour, Louis (Dearborn)
See also TCWW 2

Burnshaw, Stanley 1906- .... **CLC 3, 13, 44**
See also CA 9-12R; CP; DLB 48; DLBY
97

Burr, Anne 1937- .... **CLC 6**
See also CA 25-28R

Burroughs, Edgar Rice 1875-1950 . **TCLC 2,
32; DAM NOV**
See also AAYA 11; BPFB 1; BYA 4; CA
104; 132; DA3; DLB 8; FANT; MTCW
1, 2; RGAL; SATA 41; SFW; YAW

Burroughs, William S(eward)
1914-1997 .. **CLC 1, 2, 5, 15, 22, 42, 75,
109; DA; DAB; DAC; DAM MST,
NOV, POP; WLC**
See also Lee, William; Lee, Willy
See also AITN 2; AMWS 3; BPFB 1; CA
9-12R; 160; CANR 20, 52; CN; CPW;
DA3; DLB 2, 8, 16, 152, 237; DLBY 81,
97; HGG; MTCW 1, 2; RGAL; SFW

Burton, Sir Richard F(rancis)
1821-1890 .... **NCLC 42**
See also DLB 55, 166, 184

Busch, Frederick 1941- .... **CLC 7, 10, 18, 47**
See also CA 33-36R; CAAS 1; CANR 45,
73, 92; CN; DLB 6

Bush, Ronald 1946- .... **CLC 34**
See also CA 136

Bustos, F(rancisco)
See Borges, Jorge Luis

Bustos Domecq, H(onorio)
See Bioy Casares, Adolfo; Borges, Jorge
Luis

Butler, Octavia E(stelle) 1947- .... **CLC 38,
121; BLCS; DAM MULT, POP**
See also AAYA 18; AFAW 2; BPFB 1; BW
2, 3; CA 73-76; CANR 12, 24, 38, 73;
CLR 65; CPW; DA3; DLB 33; MTCW 1,
2; NFS 8; SATA 84; SFW; SSFS 6; YAW

Butler, Robert Olen, (Jr.) 1945- ...... **CLC 81;
DAM POP**
See also BPFB 1; CA 112; CANR 66; CSW;
DLB 173; INT CA-112; MTCW 1; SSFS
11

Butler, Samuel 1612-1680 .... **LC 16, 43**
See also DLB 101, 126; RGEL

Butler, Samuel 1835-1902 . **TCLC 1, 33; DA;
DAB; DAC; DAM MST, NOV; WLC**
See also BRWS 2; CA 143; CDBLB 1890-
1914; DA3; DLB 18, 57, 174; RGEL;
SFW; TEA

Butler, Walter C.
See Faust, Frederick (Schiller)

Butor, Michel (Marie Francois)
1926- .... **CLC 1, 3, 8, 11, 15**
See also CA 9-12R; CANR 33, 66; DLB
83; EW; GFL 1789 to the Present; MTCW
1, 2

Butts, Mary 1890(?)-1937 .... **TCLC 77**
See also CA 148; DLB 240

Buxton, Ralph
See Silverstein, Alvin; Silverstein, Virginia
B(arbara Opshelor)

Buzo, Alexander (John) 1944- .... **CLC 61**
See also CA 97-100; CANR 17, 39, 69; CD

Buzzati, Dino 1906-1972 .... **CLC 36**
See also CA 160; 33-36R; DLB 177;
RGWL; SFW

Byars, Betsy (Cromer) 1928- .... **CLC 35**
See also AAYA 19; BYA 3; CA 33-36R,
183; CAAE 183; CANR 18, 36, 57; CLR
1, 16, 72; DLB 52; INT CANR-18; JRDA;
MAICYA; MAICYAS; MTCW 1; SAAS
1; SATA 4, 46, 80; SATA-Essay 108;
WYA; YAW

Byatt, A(ntonia) S(usan Drabble)
1936- ...... **CLC 19, 65, 136; DAM NOV, POP**
See also BPFB 1; BRWS 4; CA 13-16R; CANR 13, 33, 50, 75, 96; DA3; DLB 14, 194; MTCW 1, 2; RGSF; RHW

Byrne, David 1952- .... **CLC 26**
See also CA 127

Byrne, John Keyes 1926-
See Leonard, Hugh
See also CA 102; CANR 78; CD; DFS 13; INT 102

Byron, George Gordon (Noel)
1788-1824 ...... **NCLC 2, 12; DA; DAB; DAC; DAM MST, POET; PC 16; WLC**
See also Lord Byron
See also BRW; CDBLB 1789-1832; DA3; DLB 96, 110; EXPP; PFS 1; RGEL; WLIT 3

Byron, Robert 1905-1941 .... **TCLC 67**
See also CA 160; DLB 195

C. 3. 3.
See Wilde, Oscar (Fingal O'Flahertie Wills)

Caballero, Fernan 1796-1877 .... **NCLC 10**

Cabell, Branch
See Cabell, James Branch

Cabell, James Branch 1879-1958 .... **TCLC 6**
See also CA 105; 152; DLB 9, 78; FANT; MTCW 1; RGAL

Cabeza de Vaca, Alvar Nunez
1490-1557(?) .... **LC 61**

Cable, George Washington
1844-1925 .... **TCLC 4; SSC 4**
See also CA 104; 155; DLB 12, 74; DLBD 13; RGAL

Cabral de Melo Neto, Joao
1920-1999 .... **CLC 76; DAM MULT**
See also CA 151; LAW

Cabrera Infante, G(uillermo) 1929- . **CLC 5, 25, 45, 120; DAM MULT; HLC 1; SSC 39**
See also CA 85-88; CANR 29, 65; DA3; DLB 113; HW 1, 2; LAW; MTCW 1, 2; RGSF; WLIT 1

Cade, Toni
See Bambara, Toni Cade

Cadmus and Harmonia
See Buchan, John

Caedmon fl. 658-680 .... **CMLC 7**
See also DLB 146

Caeiro, Alberto
See Pessoa, Fernando (Antonio Nogueira)

Caesar, Julius **CMLC 47**
See also Julius Caesar
See also RGWL

Cage, John (Milton, Jr.) 1912-1992 . **CLC 41**
See also CA 13-16R; 169; CANR 9, 78; DLB 193; INT CANR-9

Cahan, Abraham 1860-1951 .... **TCLC 71**
See also CA 108; 154; DLB 9, 25, 28; RGAL

Cain, G.
See Cabrera Infante, G(uillermo)

Cain, Guillermo
See Cabrera Infante, G(uillermo)

Cain, James M(allahan) 1892-1977 .. **CLC 3, 11, 28**
See also AITN 1; BPFB 1; CA 17-20R; 73-76; CANR 8, 34, 61; CMW; DLB 226; MTCW 1; RGAL

Caine, Hall 1853-1931 .... **TCLC 97**
See also RHW

Caine, Mark
See Raphael, Frederic (Michael)

Calasso, Roberto 1941- .... **CLC 81**
See also CA 143; CANR 89

Calderon de la Barca, Pedro
1600-1681 .... **LC 23; DC 3; HLCS 1**
See also RGWL

Caldwell, Erskine (Preston)
1903-1987 .. **CLC 1, 8, 14, 50, 60; DAM NOV; SSC 19**
See also AITN 1; AMW; BPFB 1; CA 1-4R; 121; CAAS 1; CANR 2, 33; DA3; DLB 9, 86; MTCW 1, 2; RGAL; RGSF

Caldwell, (Janet Miriam) Taylor (Holland)
1900-1985 .. **CLC 2, 28, 39; DAM NOV, POP**
See also BPFB 1; CA 5-8R; 116; CANR 5; DA3; DLBD 17; RHW

Calhoun, John Caldwell
1782-1850 .... **NCLC 15**
See also DLB 3

Calisher, Hortense 1911- ..... **CLC 2, 4, 8, 38, 134; DAM NOV; SSC 15**
See also CA 1-4R; CANR 1, 22, 67; CN; DA3; DLB 2; INT CANR-22; MTCW 1, 2; RGAL; RGSF

Callaghan, Morley Edward
1903-1990 ...... **CLC 3, 14, 41, 65; DAC; DAM MST**
See also CA 9-12R; 132; CANR 33, 73; DLB 68; MTCW 1, 2; RGEL; RGSF

Callimachus c. 305B.C.-c.
240B.C. .... **CMLC 18**
See also DLB 176; RGWL

Calvin, Jean
See Calvin, John
See also GFL Beginnings to 1789

Calvin, John 1509-1564 .... **LC 37**
See also Calvin, Jean

Calvino, Italo 1923-1985 .... **CLC 5, 8, 11, 22, 33, 39, 73; DAM NOV; SSC 3**
See also CA 85-88; 116; CANR 23, 61; DLB 196; MTCW 1, 2; RGSF; RGWL; SFW; SSFS 12

Cameron, Carey 1952- .... **CLC 59**
See also CA 135

Cameron, Peter 1959- .... **CLC 44**
See also CA 125; CANR 50; DLB 234; GLL 2

Camoens, Luis Vaz de 1524(?)-1580
See also EW; HLCS 1

Camoes, Luis de 1524(?)-1580 .... **LC 62; HLCS 1; PC 31**
See also RGWL

Campana, Dino 1885-1932 .... **TCLC 20**
See also CA 117; DLB 114

Campanella, Tommaso 1568-1639 .... **LC 32**
See also RGWL

Campbell, John W(ood, Jr.)
1910-1971 .... **CLC 32**
See also CA 21-22; 29-32R; CANR 34; CAP 2; DLB 8; MTCW 1; SFW

Campbell, Joseph 1904-1987 .... **CLC 69**
See also AAYA 3; BEST 89:2; CA 1-4R; 124; CANR 3, 28, 61; DA3; MTCW 1, 2

Campbell, Maria 1940- .... **CLC 85; DAC**
See also CA 102; CANR 54; CCA 1; NNAL

Campbell, (John) Ramsey 1946- ..... **CLC 42; SSC 19**
See also CA 57-60; CANR 7; HGG; INT CANR-7; SUFW

Campbell, (Ignatius) Roy (Dunnachie)
1901-1957 .... **TCLC 5**
See also AFW; CA 104; 155; DLB 20, 225; MTCW 2

Campbell, Thomas 1777-1844 .... **NCLC 19**
See also DLB 93; 144; RGEL

Campbell, Wilfred **TCLC 9**
See also Campbell, William

Campbell, William 1858(?)-1918
See Campbell, Wilfred
See also CA 106; DLB 92

Campion, Jane **CLC 95**
See also AAYA 33; CA 138; CANR 87

Camus, Albert 1913-1960 ...... **CLC 1, 2, 4, 9, 11, 14, 32, 63, 69, 124; DA; DAB; DAC; DAM DRAM, MST, NOV; DC 2; SSC 9; WLC**
See also AAYA 36; BPFB 1; CA 89-92; DA3; DLB 72; EXPN; EXPS; GFL 1789 to the Present; MTCW 1, 2; NFS 6; RGSF; RGWL; SSFS 4

Canby, Vincent 1924-2000 .... **CLC 13**
See also CA 81-84; 191

Cancale
See Desnos, Robert

Canetti, Elias 1905-1994 .. **CLC 3, 14, 25, 75, 86**
See also CA 21-24R; 146; CANR 23, 61, 79; CWW 2; DA3; DLB 85, 124; MTCW 1, 2; RGWL

Canfield, Dorothea F.
See Fisher, Dorothy (Frances) Canfield

Canfield, Dorothea Frances
See Fisher, Dorothy (Frances) Canfield

Canfield, Dorothy
See Fisher, Dorothy (Frances) Canfield

Canin, Ethan 1960- .... **CLC 55**
See also CA 131; 135

Cankar, Ivan 1876-1918 .... **TCLC 105**
See also DLB 147

Cannon, Curt
See Hunter, Evan

Cao, Lan 1961- .... **CLC 109**
See also CA 165

Cape, Judith
See Page, P(atricia) K(athleen)
See also CCA 1

Capek, Karel 1890-1938 ... **TCLC 6, 37; DA; DAB; DAC; DAM DRAM, MST, NOV; DC 1; SSC 36; WLC**
See also CA 104; 140; DA3; DFS 7, 11 !**; MTCW 1; RGSF; RGWL; SCFW 2; SFW

Capote, Truman 1924-1984 . **CLC 1, 3, 8, 13, 19, 34, 38, 58; DA; DAB; DAC; DAM MST, NOV, POP; SSC 2, 47; WLC**
See also AMWS 3; BPFB 1; CA 5-8R; 113; CANR 18, 62; CDALB 1941-1968; CPW; DA3; DLB 2, 185, 227; DLBY 80, 84; EXPS; GLL 1; LAIT 3; MTCW 1, 2; NCFS 2; RGAL; RGSF; SATA 91; SSFS 2

Capra, Frank 1897-1991 .... **CLC 16**
See also CA 61-64; 135

Caputo, Philip 1941- .... **CLC 32**
See also CA 73-76; CANR 40; YAW

Caragiale, Ion Luca 1852-1912 ...... **TCLC 76**
See also CA 157

Card, Orson Scott 1951- ..... **CLC 44, 47, 50; DAM POP**
See also AAYA 11; BPFB 1; BYA 5; CA 102; CANR 27, 47, 73; CPW; DA3; FANT; INT CANR-27; MTCW 1, 2; NFS 5; SATA 83; SFW; YAW

Cardenal, Ernesto 1925- .... **CLC 31; DAM MULT, POET; HLC 1; PC 22**
See also CA 49-52; CANR 2, 32, 66; CWW 2; HW 1, 2; MTCW 1, 2; RGWL

Cardozo, Benjamin N(athan)
1870-1938 .... **TCLC 65**
See also CA 117; 164

Carducci, Giosue (Alessandro Giuseppe)
1835-1907 .... **TCLC 32**
See also CA 163; EW; RGWL

Carew, Thomas 1595(?)-1640 . **LC 13; PC 29**
See also BRW 2; DLB 126; PAB; RGEL

Carey, Ernestine Gilbreth 1908- ...... **CLC 17**
See also CA 5-8R; CANR 71; SATA 2

Carey, Peter 1943- .... **CLC 40, 55, 96**
See also CA 123; 127; CANR 53, 76; CN; INT 127; MTCW 1, 2; RGSF; SATA 94

Carleton, William 1794-1869 .... **NCLC 3**
See also DLB 159; RGEL; RGSF

Cervantes (Saavedra), Miguel de
1547-1616 .. LC 6, 23; DA; DAB; DAC;
DAM MST, NOV; HLCS; SSC 12;
WLC
See also BYA 1; EW; LAIT 1; NFS 8;
RGSF; RGWL

Cesaire, Aime (Fernand) 1913- . CLC 19, 32,
112; BLC 1; DAM MULT, POET; PC
25
See also BW 2, 3; CA 65-68; CANR 24,
43, 81; DA3; GFL 1789 to the Present;
MTCW 1, 2; WP

Chabon, Michael 1963- .... CLC 55, 149
See also CA 139; CANR 57, 96

Chabrol, Claude 1930- .... CLC 16
See also CA 110

Challans, Mary 1905-1983
See Renault, Mary
See also CA 81-84; 111; CANR 74; DA3;
MTCW 2; SATA 23; SATA-Obit 36

Challis, George
See Faust, Frederick (Schiller)
See also TCWW 2

Chambers, Aidan 1934- .... CLC 35
See also AAYA 27; CA 25-28R; CANR 12,
31, 58; JRDA; MAICYA; SAAS 12;
SATA 1, 69, 108; YAW

Chambers, James 1948-
See Cliff, Jimmy
See also CA 124

Chambers, Jessie
See Lawrence, D(avid) H(erbert Richards)
See also GLL 1

Chambers, Robert W(illiam)
1865-1933 .... TCLC 41
See also CA 165; DLB 202; HGG; SATA
107; SUFW

Chamisso, Adelbert von
1781-1838 .... NCLC 82
See also DLB 90; RGWL

Chandler, Raymond (Thornton)
1888-1959 .... TCLC 1, 7; SSC 23
See also AAYA 25; AMWS 4; BPFB 1; CA
104; 129; CANR 60; CDALB 1929-1941;
CMW; DA3; DLB 226; DLBD 6; MSW;
MTCW 1, 2; RGAL

Chang, Eileen 1921-1995 .... SSC 28
See also CA 166; CWW 2

Chang, Jung 1952- .... CLC 71
See also CA 142

Chang Ai-Ling
See Chang, Eileen

Channing, William Ellery
1780-1842 .... NCLC 17
See also DLB 1, 59, 235; RGAL

Chao, Patricia 1955- .... CLC 119
See also CA 163

Chaplin, Charles Spencer
1889-1977 .... CLC 16
See also Chaplin, Charlie
See also CA 81-84; 73-76

Chaplin, Charlie
See Chaplin, Charles Spencer
See also DLB 44

Chapman, George 1559(?)-1634 .... LC 22;
DAM DRAM
See also BRW 1; DLB 62, 121; RGEL

Chapman, Graham 1941-1989 .... CLC 21
See also Monty Python
See also CA 116; 129; CANR 35, 95

Chapman, John Jay 1862-1933 .... TCLC 7
See also CA 104; 191

Chapman, Lee
See Bradley, Marion Zimmer
See also GLL 1

Chapman, Walker
See Silverberg, Robert

Chappell, Fred (Davis) 1936- ..... CLC 40, 78
See also CA 5-8R; CAAS 4; CANR 8, 33,
67; CN; CP; CSW; DLB 6, 105; HGG

Char, Rene(-Emile) 1907-1988 .... CLC 9, 11,
14, 55; DAM POET
See also CA 13-16R; 124; CANR 32; GFL
1789 to the Present; MTCW 1, 2; RGWL

Charby, Jay
See Ellison, Harlan (Jay)

Chardin, Pierre Teilhard de
See Teilhard de Chardin, (Marie Joseph)
Pierre

Charlemagne 742-814 .... CMLC 37

Charles I 1600-1649 .... LC 13

Charriere, Isabelle de 1740-1805 .. NCLC 66

Chartier, Emile-Auguste
See Alain

Charyn, Jerome 1937- .... CLC 5, 8, 18
See also CA 5-8R; CAAS 1; CANR 7, 61,
101; CMW; CN; DLBY 83; MTCW 1

Chase, Adam
See Marlowe, Stephen

Chase, Mary (Coyle) 1907-1981 .... DC 1
See also CA 77-80; 105; CAD; CWD; DFS
11; DLB 228; SATA 17; SATA-Obit 29

Chase, Mary Ellen 1887-1973 .... CLC 2
See also CA 13-16; 41-44R; CAP 1; SATA
10

Chase, Nicholas
See Hyde, Anthony
See also CCA 1

Chateaubriand, Francois Rene de
1768-1848 .... NCLC 3
See also DLB 119; EW; GFL 1789 to the
Present; RGWL

Chatterje, Sarat Chandra 1876-1936(?)
See Chatterji, Saratchandra
See also CA 109

Chatterji, Bankim Chandra
1838-1894 .... NCLC 19

Chatterji, Saratchandra TCLC 13
See also Chatterje, Sarat Chandra
See also CA 186

Chatterton, Thomas 1752-1770 ..... LC 3, 54;
DAM POET
See also DLB 109; RGEL

Chatwin, (Charles) Bruce
1940-1989 . CLC 28, 57, 59; DAM POP
See also AAYA 4; BEST 90:1; BRWS 4;
CA 85-88; 127; CPW; DLB 194, 204

Chaucer, Daniel
See Ford, Ford Madox
See also RHW

Chaucer, Geoffrey 1340(?)-1400 .. LC 17, 56;
DA; DAB; DAC; DAM MST, POET;
PC 19; WLCS
See also BRW 1; CDBLB Before 1660;
DA3; DLB 146; LAIT 1; PAB; RGEL;
WLIT 3; WP

Chavez, Denise (Elia) 1948-
See also CA 131; CANR 56, 81; DAM
MULT; DLB 122; FW; HLC 1; HW 1, 2;
MTCW 2

Chaviaras, Strates 1935-
See Haviaras, Stratis
See also CA 105

Chayefsky, Paddy CLC 23
See also Chayefsky, Sidney
See also CAD; DLB 7, 44; DLBY 81;
RGAL

Chayefsky, Sidney 1923-1981
See Chayefsky, Paddy
See also CA 9-12R; 104; CANR 18; DAM
DRAM

Chedid, Andree 1920- .... CLC 47
See also CA 145; CANR 95

Cheever, John 1912-1982 ..... CLC 3, 7, 8, 11,
15, 25, 64; DA; DAB; DAC; DAM
MST, NOV, POP; SSC 1, 38; WLC
See also AMWS 1; BPFB 1; CA 5-8R; 106;
CABS 1; CANR 5, 27, 76; CDALB 1941-
1968; CPW; DA3; DLB 2, 102, 227;
DLBY 80, 82; EXPS; INT CANR-5;
MTCW 1, 2; RGAL; RGSF; SSFS 2

Cheever, Susan 1943- .... CLC 18, 48
See also CA 103; CANR 27, 51, 92; DLBY
82; INT CANR-27

Chekhonte, Antosha
See Chekhov, Anton (Pavlovich)

Chekhov, Anton (Pavlovich)
1860-1904 .... TCLC 3, 10, 31, 55, 96;
DA; DAB; DAC; DAM DRAM, MST;
DC 9; SSC 2, 28, 41; WLC
See also CA 104; 124; DA3; DFS 1, 5, 10,
12; EW; EXPS; LAIT 3; RGSF; RGWL;
SATA 90; SSFS 5

Cheney, Lynne V. 1941- .... CLC 70
See also CA 89-92; CANR 58

Chernyshevsky, Nikolai Gavrilovich
See Chernyshevsky, Nikolay Gavrilovich

Chernyshevsky, Nikolay Gavrilovich
1828-1889 .... NCLC 1
See also DLB 238

Cherry, Carolyn Janice 1942-
See Cherryh, C. J.
See also CA 65-68; CANR 10; FANT; SFW;
YAW

Cherryh, C. J. CLC 35
See also Cherry, Carolyn Janice
See also AAYA 24; BPFB 1; DLBY 80;
SATA 93

Chesnutt, Charles W(addell)
1858-1932 .. TCLC 5, 39; BLC 1; DAM
MULT; SSC 7
See also AFAW 1, 2; BW 1, 3; CA 106;
125; CANR 76; DLB 12, 50, 78; MTCW
1, 2; RGAL; RGSF; SSFS 11

Chester, Alfred 1929(?)-1971 .... CLC 49
See also CA 33-36R; DLB 130

Chesterton, G(ilbert) K(eith)
1874-1936 . TCLC 1, 6, 64; DAM NOV,
POET; PC 28; SSC 1, 46
See also BRW; CA 104; 132; CANR 73;
CDBLB 1914-1945; CMW; DLB 10, 19,
34, 70, 98, 149, 178; FANT; MTCW 1, 2;
RGEL; RGSF; SATA 27; SUFW

Chiang, Pin-chin 1904-1986
See Ding Ling
See also CA 118

Ch'ien Chung-shu 1910- .... CLC 22
See also CA 130; CANR 73; MTCW 1, 2

Chikamatsu Monzaemon 1653-1724 ... LC 66
See also RGWL

Child, L. Maria
See Child, Lydia Maria

Child, Lydia Maria 1802-1880 .. NCLC 6, 73
See also DLB 1, 74; RGAL; SATA 67

Child, Mrs.
See Child, Lydia Maria

Child, Philip 1898-1978 .... CLC 19, 68
See also CA 13-14; CAP 1; RHW; SATA
47

Childers, (Robert) Erskine
1870-1922 .... TCLC 65
See also CA 113; 153; DLB 70

Childress, Alice 1920-1994 .. CLC 12, 15, 86,
96; BLC 1; DAM DRAM, MULT,
NOV; DC 4
See also AAYA 8; BW 2, 3; BYA 2; CA 45-
48; 146; CAD; CANR 3, 27, 50, 74; CLR
14; CWD; DA3; DFS 2,8; DLB 7, 38;
JRDA; LAIT 5; MAICYA; MTCW 1, 2;
RGAL; SATA 7, 48, 81; YAW

Cooke, M. E.
   See Creasey, John
Cooke, Margaret
   See Creasey, John
Cook-Lynn, Elizabeth 1930- . CLC 93; DAM
   MULT
   See also CA 133; DLB 175; NNAL
Cooney, Ray CLC 62
   See also CBD
Cooper, Douglas 1960- .... CLC 86
Cooper, Henry St. John
   See Creasey, John
Cooper, J(oan) California (?)- .... CLC 56;
   DAM MULT
   See also AAYA 12; BW 1; CA 125; CANR
   55; DLB 212
Cooper, James Fenimore
   1789-1851 .... NCLC 1, 27, 54
   See also AAYA 22; AMW; BPFB 1;
   CDALB 1640-1865; DA3; DLB 3; LAIT
   1; NFS 9; RGAL; SATA 19
Coover, Robert (Lowell) 1932- ...... CLC 3, 7,
   15, 32, 46, 87; DAM NOV; SSC 15
   See also AMWS 5; BPFB 1; CA 45-48;
   CANR 3, 37, 58; CN; DLB 2, 227; DLBY
   81; MTCW 1, 2; RGAL; RGSF
Copeland, Stewart (Armstrong)
   1952- .... CLC 26
Copernicus, Nicolaus 1473-1543 .... LC 45
Coppard, A(lfred) E(dgar)
   1878-1957 .... TCLC 5; SSC 21
   See also CA 114; 167; DLB 162; HGG;
   RGEL; RGSF; SUFW; YABC 1
Coppee, Francois 1842-1908 .... TCLC 25
   See also CA 170
Coppola, Francis Ford 1939- ... CLC 16, 126
   See also AAYA 39; CA 77-80; CANR 40,
   78; DLB 44
Corbiere, Tristan 1845-1875 .... NCLC 43
   See also GFL 1789 to the Present
Corcoran, Barbara (Asenath)
   1911- .... CLC 17
   See also AAYA 14; CA 21-24R; CAAE 191;
   CAAS 2; CANR 11, 28, 48; CLR 50;
   DLB 52; JRDA; RHW; SAAS 20; SATA
   3, 77, 125
Cordelier, Maurice
   See Giraudoux, Jean(-Hippolyte)
Corelli, Marie TCLC 51
   See also Mackay, Mary
   See also DLB 34, 156; RGEL
Corman, Cid CLC 9
   See also Corman, Sidney
   See also CAAS 2; DLB 5, 193
Corman, Sidney 1924-
   See Corman, Cid
   See also CA 85-88; CANR 44; CP; DAM
   POET
Cormier, Robert (Edmund)
   1925-2000 .... CLC 12, 30; DA; DAB;
   DAC; DAM MST, NOV
   See also AAYA 3, 19; BYA 1; CA 1-4R;
   CANR 5, 23, 76, 93; CDALB 1968-1988;
   CLR 12, 55; DLB 52; EXPN; INT CANR-
   23; JRDA; LAIT 5; MAICYA; MTCW 1,
   2; NFS 2; SATA 10, 45, 83; SATA-Obit
   122; WYA; YAW
Corn, Alfred (DeWitt III) 1943- .... CLC 33
   See also CA 179; CAAE 179; CAAS 25;
   CANR 44; CP; CSW; DLB 120; DLBY
   80
Corneille, Pierre 1606-1684 ..... LC 28; DAB;
   DAM MST
   See also GFL Beginnings to 1789; RGWL
Cornwell, David (John Moore)
   1931- .... CLC 9, 15; DAM POP
   See also le Carre, John
   See also CA 5-8R; CANR 13, 33, 59; DA3;
   MTCW 1, 2

Corso, (Nunzio) Gregory 1930-2001 . CLC 1,
   11; PC 33
   See also CA 5-8R; 193; CANR 41, 76; CP;
   DA3; DLB 5, 16, 237; MTCW 1, 2; WP
Cortazar, Julio 1914-1984 ... CLC 2, 3, 5, 10,
   13, 15, 33, 34, 92; DAM MULT, NOV;
   HLC 1; SSC 7
   See also BPFB 1; CA 21-24R; CANR 12,
   32, 81; DA3; DLB 113; EXPS; HW 1, 2;
   MTCW 1, 2; RGSF; RGWL; SSFS 3;
   WLIT 1
Cortes, Hernan 1485-1547 .... LC 31
Corvinus, Jakob
   See Raabe, Wilhelm (Karl)
Corvo, Baron
   See Rolfe, Frederick (William Serafino Aus-
   tin Lewis Mary)
   See also GLL 1; RGEL
Corwin, Cecil
   See Kornbluth, C(yril) M.
Cosic, Dobrica 1921- .... CLC 14
   See also CA 122; 138; CWW 2; DLB 181
Costain, Thomas B(ertram)
   1885-1965 .... CLC 30
   See also BYA 3; CA 5-8R; 25-28R; DLB 9;
   RHW
Costantini, Humberto 1924(?)-1987 . CLC 49
   See also CA 131; 122; HW 1
Costello, Elvis 1955- .... CLC 21
Costenoble, Philostene 1898-1962
   See Ghelderode, Michel de
Costenoble, Philostene 1898-1962
   See Ghelderode, Michel de
Cotes, Cecil V.
   See Duncan, Sara Jeannette
Cotter, Joseph Seamon Sr.
   1861-1949 ...... TCLC 28; BLC 1; DAM
   MULT
   See also BW 1; CA 124; DLB 50
Couch, Arthur Thomas Quiller
   See Quiller-Couch, Sir Arthur (Thomas)
Coulton, James
   See Hansen, Joseph
Couperus, Louis (Marie Anne)
   1863-1923 .... TCLC 15
   See also CA 115; RGWL
Coupland, Douglas 1961- .... CLC 85, 133;
   DAC; DAM POP
   See also AAYA 34; CA 142; CANR 57, 90;
   CCA 1; CPW
Court, Wesli
   See Turco, Lewis (Putnam)
Courtenay, Bryce 1933- .... CLC 59
   See also CA 138; CPW
Courtney, Robert
   See Ellison, Harlan (Jay)
Cousteau, Jacques-Yves 1910-1997 .. CLC 30
   See also CA 65-68; 159; CANR 15, 67;
   MTCW 1; SATA 38, 98
Coventry, Francis 1725-1754 .... LC 46
Cowan, Peter (Walkinshaw) 1914- .... SSC 28
   See also CA 21-24R; CANR 9, 25, 50, 83;
   CN; RGSF
Coward, Noel (Peirce) 1899-1973 . CLC 1, 9,
   29, 51; DAM DRAM
   See also AITN 1; BRWS 2; CA 17-18; 41-
   44R; CANR 35; CAP 2; CDBLB 1914-
   1945; DA3; DFS 3, 6; DLB 10; IDFW 3,
   4; MTCW 1, 2; RGEL
Cowley, Abraham 1618-1667 .... LC 43
   See also BRW 2; DLB 131, 151; PAB;
   RGEL
Cowley, Malcolm 1898-1989 .... CLC 39
   See also AMWS 2; CA 5-8R; 128; CANR
   3, 55; DLB 4, 48; DLBY 81, 89; MTCW
   1, 2
Cowper, William 1731-1800 ..... NCLC 8, 94;
   DAM POET
   See also DA3; DLB 104, 109; RGEL

Cox, William Trevor 1928- ... CLC 9, 14, 71;
   DAM NOV
   See also Trevor, William
   See also CA 9-12R; CANR 4, 37, 55, 76;
   CD; CN; DLB 14; INT CANR-37;
   MTCW 1, 2
Coyne, P. J.
   See Masters, Hilary
Cozzens, James Gould 1903-1978 . CLC 1, 4,
   11, 92
   See also AMW; BPFB 1; CA 9-12R; 81-84;
   CANR 19; CDALB 1941-1968; DLB 9;
   DLBD 2; DLBY 84, 97; MTCW 1, 2;
   RGAL
Crabbe, George 1754-1832 .... NCLC 26
   See also DLB 93; RGEL
Craddock, Charles Egbert
   See Murfree, Mary Noailles
Craig, A. A.
   See Anderson, Poul (William)
Craik, Mrs.
   See Craik, Dinah Maria (Mulock)
   See also RGEL
Craik, Dinah Maria (Mulock)
   1826-1887 .... NCLC 38
   See also Craik, Mrs.; Mulock, Dinah Maria
   See also DLB 35, 163; MAICYA; SATA 34
Cram, Ralph Adams 1863-1942 ..... TCLC 45
   See also CA 160
Crane, (Harold) Hart 1899-1932 .... TCLC 2,
   5, 80; DA; DAB; DAC; DAM MST,
   POET; PC 3; WLC
   See also AMW; CA 104; 127; CDALB
   1917-1929; DA3; DLB 4, 48; MTCW 1,
   2; RGAL
Crane, R(onald) S(almon)
   1886-1967 .... CLC 27
   See also CA 85-88; DLB 63
Crane, Stephen (Townley)
   1871-1900 .... TCLC 11, 17, 32; DA;
   DAB; DAC; DAM MST, NOV, POET;
   SSC 7; WLC
   See also AAYA 21; AMW; BPFB 1; BYA 3;
   CA 109; 140; CANR 84; CDALB 1865-
   1917; DA3; DLB 12, 54, 78; EXPN;
   EXPS; LAIT 2; NFS 4; PFS 9; RGAL;
   RGSF; SSFS 4; WYA; YABC 2
Cranshaw, Stanley
   See Fisher, Dorothy (Frances) Canfield
Crase, Douglas 1944- .... CLC 58
   See also CA 106
Crashaw, Richard 1612(?)-1649 .... LC 24
   See also BRW 2; DLB 126; PAB; RGEL
Craven, Margaret 1901-1980 .... CLC 17;
   DAC
   See also BYA 2; CA 103; CCA 1; LAIT 5
Crawford, F(rancis) Marion
   1854-1909 .... TCLC 10
   See also CA 107; 168; DLB 71; HGG;
   RGAL; SUFW
Crawford, Isabella Valancy
   1850-1887 .... NCLC 12
   See also DLB 92; RGEL
Crayon, Geoffrey
   See Irving, Washington
Creasey, John 1908-1973 .... CLC 11
   See also CA 5-8R; 41-44R; CANR 8, 59;
   CMW; DLB 77; MTCW 1
Crebillon, Claude Prosper Jolyot de (fils)
   1707-1777 .... LC 1, 28
   See also GFL Beginnings to 1789
Credo
   See Creasey, John
Credo, Alvaro J. de
   See Prado (Calvo), Pedro

DeLillo, Don 1936- ..... **CLC 8, 10, 13, 27, 39, 54, 76, 143; DAM NOV, POP**
See also AMWS 6; BEST 89:1; BPFB 1; CA 81-84; CANR 21, 76, 92; CN; CPW; DA3; DLB 6, 173; MTCW 1, 2; RGAL

de Lisser, H. G.
See De Lisser, H(erbert) G(eorge)
See also DLB 117

De Lisser, H(erbert) G(eorge) 1878-1944 .... **TCLC 12**
See also de Lisser, H. G.
See also BW 2; CA 109; 152

Deloire, Pierre
See Peguy, Charles (Pierre)

Deloney, Thomas 1543(?)-1600 .... **LC 41**
See also DLB 167; RGEL

Deloria, Vine (Victor), Jr. 1933- ...... **CLC 21, 122; DAM MULT**
See also CA 53-56; CANR 5, 20, 48, 98; DLB 175; MTCW 1; NNAL; SATA 21

Del Vecchio, John M(ichael) 1947- .. **CLC 29**
See also CA 110; DLBD 9

de Man, Paul (Adolph Michel) 1919-1983 .... **CLC 55**
See also CA 128; 111; CANR 61; DLB 67; MTCW 1, 2

DeMarinis, Rick 1934- .... **CLC 54**
See also CA 57-60, 184; CAAE 184; CAAS 24; CANR 9, 25, 50

Dembry, R. Emmet
See Murfree, Mary Noailles

Demby, William 1922- .... **CLC 53; BLC 1; DAM MULT**
See also BW 1, 3; CA 81-84; CANR 81; DLB 33

de Menton, Francisco
See Chin, Frank (Chew, Jr.)

Demetrius of Phalerum c. 307B.C.- .... **CMLC 34**

Demijohn, Thom
See Disch, Thomas M(ichael)

Deming, Richard 1915-1983
See Queen, Ellery
See also CA 9-12R; CANR 3, 94; SATA 24

Democritus c. 460B.C.-c. 370B.C. . **CMLC 47**

de Montherlant, Henry (Milon)
See Montherlant, Henry (Milon) de

Demosthenes 384B.C.-322B.C. ...... **CMLC 13**
See also DLB 176; RGWL

de Natale, Francine
See Malzberg, Barry N(athaniel)

de Navarre, Marguerite 1492-1549 ..... **LC 61**
See also Marguerite de Navarre
See also EW

Denby, Edwin (Orr) 1903-1983 .... **CLC 48**
See also CA 138; 110

Denis, Julio
See Cortazar, Julio

Denmark, Harrison
See Zelazny, Roger (Joseph)

Dennis, John 1658-1734 .... **LC 11**
See also DLB 101; RGEL

Dennis, Nigel (Forbes) 1912-1989 ...... **CLC 8**
See also CA 25-28R; 129; DLB 13, 15, 233; MTCW 1

Dent, Lester 1904(?)-1959 .... **TCLC 72**
See also CA 112; 161; CMW; SFW

De Palma, Brian (Russell) 1940- ...... **CLC 20**
See also CA 109

De Quincey, Thomas 1785-1859 ..... **NCLC 4, 87**
See also CDBLB 1789-1832; DLB 110, 144; RGEL

Deren, Eleanora 1908(?)-1961
See Deren, Maya
See also CA 192; 111

Deren, Maya CLC 16, 102
See also Deren, Eleanora

Derleth, August (William) 1909-1971 .... **CLC 31**
See also BPFB 1; BYA 9; CA 1-4R; 29-32R; CANR 4; CMW; DLB 9; DLBD 17; HGG; SATA 5; SUFW

Der Nister 1884-1950 .... **TCLC 56**

de Routisie, Albert
See Aragon, Louis

Derrida, Jacques 1930- .... **CLC 24, 87**
See also CA 124; 127; CANR 76, 98; DLB 242; MTCW 1

Derry Down Derry
See Lear, Edward

Dersonnes, Jacques
See Simenon, Georges (Jacques Christian)

Desai, Anita 1937- ..... **CLC 19, 37, 97; DAB; DAM NOV**
See also BRWS 5; CA 81-84; CANR 33, 53, 95; CN; CWRI; DA3; DNFS; FW; MTCW 1, 2; SATA 63

Desai, Kiran 1971- .... **CLC 119**
See also CA 171

de Saint-Luc, Jean
See Glassco, John

de Saint Roman, Arnaud
See Aragon, Louis

Desbordes-Valmore, Marceline 1786-1859 .... **NCLC 97**
See also DLB 217

Descartes, Rene 1596-1650 .... **LC 20, 35**
See also GFL Beginnings to 1789

De Sica, Vittorio 1901(?)-1974 .... **CLC 20**
See also CA 117

Desnos, Robert 1900-1945 .... **TCLC 22**
See also CA 121; 151

Destouches, Louis-Ferdinand 1894-1961 .... **CLC 9, 15**
See also Celine, Louis-Ferdinand
See also CA 85-88; CANR 28; MTCW 1

de Tolignac, Gaston
See Griffith, D(avid Lewelyn) W(ark)

Deutsch, Babette 1895-1982 .... **CLC 18**
See also BYA 3; CA 1-4R; 108; CANR 4, 79; DLB 45; SATA 1; SATA-Obit 33

Devenant, William 1606-1649 .... **LC 13**

Devkota, Laxmiprasad 1909-1959 . **TCLC 23**
See also CA 123

De Voto, Bernard (Augustine) 1897-1955 .... **TCLC 29**
See also CA 113; 160; DLB 9

De Vries, Peter 1910-1993 ..... **CLC 1, 2, 3, 7, 10, 28, 46; DAM NOV**
See also CA 17-20R; 142; CANR 41; DLB 6; DLBY 82; MTCW 1, 2

Dewey, John 1859-1952 .... **TCLC 95**
See also CA 114; 170; RGAL

Dexter, John
See Bradley, Marion Zimmer
See also GLL 1

Dexter, Martin
See Faust, Frederick (Schiller)
See also TCWW 2

Dexter, Pete 1943- .. **CLC 34, 55; DAM POP**
See also BEST 89:2; CA 127; 131; CPW; INT 131; MTCW 1

Diamano, Silmang
See Senghor, Leopold Sedar

Diamond, Neil 1941- .... **CLC 30**
See also CA 108

Diaz del Castillo, Bernal 1496-1584 .. **LC 31; HLCS 1**

di Bassetto, Corno
See Shaw, George Bernard

Dick, Philip K(indred) 1928-1982 ... **CLC 10, 30, 72; DAM NOV, POP**
See also AAYA 24; BPFB 1; BYA 11; CA 49-52; 106; CANR 2, 16; CPW; DA3; DLB 8; MTCW 1, 2; NFS 5; SCFW; SFW

Dickens, Charles (John Huffam) 1812-1870 .... **NCLC 3, 8, 18, 26, 37, 50, 86, 105; DA; DAB; DAC; DAM MST, NOV; SSC 17; WLC**
See also AAYA 23; BRW; BYA 1; CDBLB 1832-1890; CMW; DA3; DLB 21, 55, 70, 159, 166; EXPN; HGG; JRDA; LAIT 1, 2; MAICYA; NFS 4, 5, 10; RGEL; RGSF; SATA 15; SUFW; WCH; WLIT 4; WYA

Dickey, James (Lafayette) 1923-1997 .... **CLC 1, 2, 4, 7, 10, 15, 47, 109; DAM NOV, POET, POP**
See also AITN 1, 2; AMWS 4; BPFB 1; CA 9-12R; 156; CABS 2; CANR 10, 48, 61; CDALB 1968-1988; CP; CPW; CSW; DA3; DLB 5, 193; DLBD 7; DLBY 82, 93, 96, 97, 98; INT CANR-10; MTCW 1, 2; NFS 9; PFS 6, 11; RGAL

Dickey, William 1928-1994 .... **CLC 3, 28**
See also CA 9-12R; 145; CANR 24, 79; DLB 5

Dickinson, Charles 1951- .... **CLC 49**
See also CA 128

Dickinson, Emily (Elizabeth) 1830-1886 ..... **NCLC 21, 77; DA; DAB; DAC; DAM MST, POET; PC 1; WLC**
See also AAYA 22; AMW; AMWR; CDALB 1865-1917; DA3; DLB 1; EXPP; MAWW; PAB; PFS 1, 2, 3, 4, 5, 6, 8, 10, 11; RGAL; SATA 29; WP; WYA

Dickinson, Mrs.Herbert Ward
See Phelps, Elizabeth Stuart

Dickinson, Peter (Malcolm) 1927- .. **CLC 12, 35**
See also AAYA 9; BYA 5; CA 41-44R; CANR 31, 58, 88; CLR 29; CMW; DLB 87, 161; JRDA; MAICYA; SATA 5, 62, 95; SFW; WYA; YAW

Dickson, Carr
See Carr, John Dickson

Dickson, Carter
See Carr, John Dickson

Diderot, Denis 1713-1784 .... **LC 26**
See also GFL Beginnings to 1789; RGWL

Didion, Joan 1934- .... **CLC 1, 3, 8, 14, 32, 129; DAM NOV**
See also AITN 1; AMWS 4; CA 5-8R; CANR 14, 52, 76; CDALB 1968-1988; CN; DA3; DLB 2, 173, 185; DLBY 81, 86; MTCW 1, 2; NFS 3; RGAL; TCWW 2

Dietrich, Robert
See Hunt, E(verette) Howard, (Jr.)

Difusa, Pati
See Almodovar, Pedro

Dillard, Annie 1945- .. **CLC 9, 60, 115; DAM NOV**
See also AAYA 6; AMWS 6; CA 49-52; CANR 3, 43, 62, 90; DA3; DLBY 80; LAIT 5; MTCW 1, 2; NCFS 1; RGAL; SATA 10

Dillard, R(ichard) H(enry) W(ilde) 1937- .... **CLC 5**
See also CA 21-24R; CAAS 7; CANR 10; CP; CSW; DLB 5

Dillon, Eilis 1920-1994 .... **CLC 17**
See also CA 9-12R, 182; 147; CAAE 182; CAAS 3; CANR 4, 38, 78; CLR 26; MAICYA; SATA 2, 74; SATA-Essay 105; SATA-Obit 83; YAW

Dimont, Penelope
See Mortimer, Penelope (Ruth)

Dinesen, Isak CLC 10, 29, 95; SSC 7
See also Blixen, Karen (Christentze Dinesen)
See also EXPS; FW; HGG; LAIT 3; MTCW 1; NFS 9; RGSF; RGWL; SSFS 6; WLIT 2

Ding Ling CLC 68
See also Chiang, Pin-chin

Drabble, Margaret 1939- ...... **CLC 2, 3, 5, 8, 10, 22, 53, 129; DAB; DAC; DAM MST, NOV, POP**
See also BRWS 4; CA 13-16R; CANR 18, 35, 63; CDBLB 1960 to Present; CN; CPW; DA3; DLB 14, 155, 231; FW; MTCW 1, 2; RGEL; SATA 48

Drapier, M. B.
See Swift, Jonathan

Drayham, James
See Mencken, H(enry) L(ouis)

Drayton, Michael 1563-1631 ..... **LC 8; DAM POET**
See also DLB 121; RGEL

Dreadstone, Carl
See Campbell, (John) Ramsey

Dreiser, Theodore (Herman Albert) 1871-1945 .... **TCLC 10, 18, 35, 83; DA; DAC; DAM MST, NOV; SSC 30; WLC**
See also AMW; CA 106; 132; CDALB 1865-1917; DA3; DLB 9, 12, 102, 137; DLBD 1; LAIT 2; MTCW 1, 2; NFS 8; RGAL

Drexler, Rosalyn 1926- .... **CLC 2, 6**
See also CA 81-84; CAD; CANR 68; CD; CWD

Dreyer, Carl Theodor 1889-1968 ...... **CLC 16**
See also CA 116

Drieu la Rochelle, Pierre(-Eugene) 1893-1945 .... **TCLC 21**
See also CA 117; DLB 72; GFL 1789 to the Present

Drinkwater, John 1882-1937 .... **TCLC 57**
See also CA 109; 149; DLB 10, 19, 149; RGEL

Drop Shot
See Cable, George Washington

Droste-Hulshoff, Annette Freiin von 1797-1848 .... **NCLC 3**
See also DLB 133; RGSF; RGWL

Drummond, Walter
See Silverberg, Robert

Drummond, William Henry 1854-1907 .... **TCLC 25**
See also CA 160; DLB 92

Drummond de Andrade, Carlos 1902-1987 .... **CLC 18**
See also Andrade, Carlos Drummond de
See also CA 132; 123

Drury, Allen (Stuart) 1918-1998 .... **CLC 37**
See also CA 57-60; 170; CANR 18, 52; CN; INT CANR-18

Dryden, John 1631-1700 .... **LC 3, 21; DA; DAB; DAC; DAM DRAM, MST, POET; DC 3; PC 25; WLC**
See also BRW 2; CDBLB 1660-1789; DLB 80, 101, 131; EXPP; IDTP; RGEL; TEA; WLIT 3

Duberman, Martin (Bauml) 1930- ..... **CLC 8**
See also CA 1-4R; CAD; CANR 2, 63; CD

Dubie, Norman (Evans) 1945- .... **CLC 36**
See also CA 69-72; CANR 12; CP; DLB 120; PFS 12

Du Bois, W(illiam) E(dward) B(urghardt) 1868-1963 ... **CLC 1, 2, 13, 64, 96; BLC 1; DA; DAC; DAM MST, MULT, NOV; WLC**
See also AAYA 40; AFAW 1, 2; AMWS 2; BW 1, 3; CA 85-88; CANR 34, 82; CDALB 1865-1917; DA3; DLB 47, 50, 91; EXPP; LAIT 2; MTCW 1, 2; NCFS 1; RGAL; SATA 42

Dubus, Andre 1936-1999 ..... **CLC 13, 36, 97; SSC 15**
See also AMWS 7; CA 21-24R; 177; CANR 17; CN; CSW; DLB 130; INT CANR-17; RGAL; SSFS 10

Duca Minimo
See D'Annunzio, Gabriele

Ducharme, Rejean 1941- .... **CLC 74**
See also CA 165; DLB 60

Duchen, Claire CLC 65

Duclos, Charles Pinot- 1704-1772 .... **LC 1**
See also GFL Beginnings to 1789

Dudek, Louis 1918- .... **CLC 11, 19**
See also CA 45-48; CAAS 14; CANR 1; CP; DLB 88

Duerrenmatt, Friedrich 1921-1990 ... **CLC 1, 4, 8, 11, 15, 43, 102; DAM DRAM**
See also Durrenmatt, Friedrich
See also CA 17-20R; CANR 33; DLB 69, 124; EW; MTCW 1, 2

Duffy, Bruce 1953(?)- .... **CLC 50**
See also CA 172

Duffy, Maureen 1933- .... **CLC 37**
See also CA 25-28R; CANR 33, 68; CBD; CN; CP; CWD; CWP; DLB 14; FW; MTCW 1

Du Fu
See Tu Fu
See also RGWL

Dugan, Alan 1923- .... **CLC 2, 6**
See also CA 81-84; CP; DLB 5; PFS 10

du Gard, Roger Martin
See Martin du Gard, Roger

Duhamel, Georges 1884-1966 .... **CLC 8**
See also CA 81-84; 25-28R; CANR 35; DLB 65; GFL 1789 to the Present; MTCW 1

Dujardin, Edouard (Emile Louis) 1861-1949 .... **TCLC 13**
See also CA 109; DLB 123

Dulles, John Foster 1888-1959 .... **TCLC 72**
See also CA 115; 149

Dumas, Alexandre (pere) 1802-1870 ...... **NCLC 11, 71; DA; DAB; DAC; DAM MST, NOV; WLC**
See also AAYA 22; BYA 3; DA3; DLB 119, 192; EW; GFL 1789 to the Present; LAIT 1, 2; RGWL; SATA 18; WCH

Dumas, Alexandre (fils) 1824-1895 .... **NCLC 9; DC 1**
See also DLB 192; GFL 1789 to the Present; RGWL

Dumas, Claudine
See Malzberg, Barry N(athaniel)

Dumas, Henry L. 1934-1968 .... **CLC 6, 62**
See also BW 1; CA 85-88; DLB 41; RGAL

du Maurier, Daphne 1907-1989 .. **CLC 6, 11, 59; DAB; DAC; DAM MST, POP; SSC 18**
See also AAYA 37; BPFB 1; BRWS 3; CA 5-8R; 128; CANR 6, 55; CMW; CPW; DA3; DLB 191; HGG; LAIT 3; MTCW 1, 2; NFS 12; RGEL; RGSF; RHW; SATA 27; SATA-Obit 60

Du Maurier, George 1834-1896 ..... **NCLC 86**
See also DLB 153, 178; RGEL

Dunbar, Paul Laurence 1872-1906 . **TCLC 2, 12; BLC 1; DA; DAC; DAM MST, MULT, POET; PC 5; SSC 8; WLC**
See also AFAW 1, 2; AMWS 2; BW 1, 3; CA 104; 124; CANR 79; CDALB 1865-1917; DA3; DLB 50, 54, 78; EXPP; RGAL; SATA 34

Dunbar, William 1460(?)-1520(?) .... **LC 20**
See also DLB 132, 146; RGEL

Duncan, Dora Angela
See Duncan, Isadora

Duncan, Isadora 1877(?)-1927 .... **TCLC 68**
See also CA 118; 149

Duncan, Lois 1934- .... **CLC 26**
See also AAYA 4, 34; BYA 6; CA 1-4R; CANR 2, 23, 36; CLR 29; JRDA; MAI-CYA; SAAS 2; SATA 1, 36, 75; YAW

Duncan, Robert (Edward) 1919-1988 .... **CLC 1, 2, 4, 7, 15, 41, 55; DAM POET; PC 2**
See also CA 9-12R; 124; CANR 28, 62; DLB 5, 16, 193; MTCW 1, 2; RGAL; WP

Duncan, Sara Jeannette 1861-1922 .... **TCLC 60**
See also CA 157; DLB 92

Dunlap, William 1766-1839 .... **NCLC 2**
See also DLB 30, 37, 59; RGAL

Dunn, Douglas (Eaglesham) 1942- .... **CLC 6, 40**
See also CA 45-48; CANR 2, 33; CP; DLB 40; MTCW 1

Dunn, Katherine (Karen) 1945- .... **CLC 71**
See also CA 33-36R; CANR 72; HGG; MTCW 1

Dunn, Stephen 1939- .... **CLC 36**
See also CA 33-36R; CANR 12, 48, 53; CP; DLB 105

Dunne, Finley Peter 1867-1936 ...... **TCLC 28**
See also CA 108; 178; DLB 11, 23; RGAL

Dunne, John Gregory 1932- .... **CLC 28**
See also CA 25-28R; CANR 14, 50; CN; DLBY 80

Dunsany, Edward John Moreton Drax Plunkett 1878-1957
See Dunsany, Lord
See also CA 104; 148; DLB 10; MTCW 1; SFW

Dunsany, Lord TCLC 2, 59
See also Dunsany, Edward John Moreton Drax Plunkett
See also DLB 77, 153, 156; FANT; RGEL

du Perry, Jean
See Simenon, Georges (Jacques Christian)

Durang, Christopher (Ferdinand) 1949- .... **CLC 27, 38**
See also CA 105; CAD; CANR 50, 76; CD; MTCW 1

Duras, Marguerite 1914-1996 . **CLC 3, 6, 11, 20, 34, 40, 68, 100; SSC 40**
See also BPFB 1; CA 25-28R; 151; CANR 50; CWW 2; DLB 83; GFL 1789 to the Present; IDFW 4; MTCW 1, 2; RGWL

Durban, (Rosa) Pam 1947- .... **CLC 39**
See also CA 123; CANR 98; CSW

Durcan, Paul 1944- .... **CLC 43, 70; DAM POET**
See also CA 134; CP

Durkheim, Emile 1858-1917 .... **TCLC 55**

Durrell, Lawrence (George) 1912-1990 .... **CLC 1, 4, 6, 8, 13, 27, 41; DAM NOV**
See also BPFB 1; BRWS 1; CA 9-12R; 132; CANR 40, 77; CDBLB 1945-1960; DLB 15, 27, 204; DLBY 90; MTCW 1, 2; RGEL; SFW

Durrenmatt, Friedrich
See Duerrenmatt, Friedrich
See also RGWL

Dutt, Toru 1856-1877 .... **NCLC 29**
See also DLB 240

Dwight, Timothy 1752-1817 .... **NCLC 13**
See also DLB 37; RGAL

Dworkin, Andrea 1946- .... **CLC 43, 123**
See also CA 77-80; CAAS 21; CANR 16, 39, 76, 96; FW; GLL 1; INT CANR-16; MTCW 1, 2

Dwyer, Deanna
See Koontz, Dean R(ay)

Dwyer, K. R.
See Koontz, Dean R(ay)

Dwyer, Thomas A. 1923- .... **CLC 114**
See also CA 115

Dybek, Stuart 1942- .... **CLC 114**
See also CA 97-100; CANR 39; DLB 130

Dye, Richard
See De Voto, Bernard (Augustine)

Dyer, Geoff 1958- .... **CLC 149**
   See also CA 125; CANR 88
Dylan, Bob 1941- .... **CLC 3, 4, 6, 12, 77**
   See also CA 41-44R; CP; DLB 16
Dyson, John 1943- .... **CLC 70**
   See also CA 144
E. V. L.
   See Lucas, E(dward) V(errall)
Eagleton, Terence (Francis) 1943- .. **CLC 63,**
   132
   See also CA 57-60; CANR 7, 23, 68; DLB
   242; MTCW 1, 2
Eagleton, Terry
   See Eagleton, Terence (Francis)
Early, Jack
   See Scoppettone, Sandra
   See also GLL 1
East, Michael
   See West, Morris L(anglo)
Eastaway, Edward
   See Thomas, (Philip) Edward
Eastlake, William (Derry)
   1917-1997 .... **CLC 8**
   See also CA 5-8R; 158; CAAS 1; CANR 5,
   63; CN; DLB 6, 206; INT CANR-5;
   TCWW 2
Eastman, Charles A(lexander)
   1858-1939 .... **TCLC 55; DAM MULT**
   See also CA 179; CANR 91; DLB 175;
   NNAL; YABC 1
Eberhart, Richard (Ghormley)
   1904- .. **CLC 3, 11, 19, 56; DAM POET**
   See also AMW; CA 1-4R; CANR 2;
   CDALB 1941-1968; CP; DLB 48; MTCW
   1; RGAL
Eberstadt, Fernanda 1960- .... **CLC 39**
   See also CA 136; CANR 69
Echegaray (y Eizaguirre), Jose (Maria
   Waldo) 1832-1916 .... **TCLC 4; HLCS 1**
   See also CA 104; CANR 32; HW 1; MTCW
   1
Echeverria, (Jose) Esteban (Antonino)
   1805-1851 .... **NCLC 18**
   See also LAW
Echo
   See Proust, (Valentin-Louis-George-Eugene-
)Marcel
Eckert, Allan W. 1931- .... **CLC 17**
   See also AAYA 18; BYA 2; CA 13-16R;
   CANR 14, 45; INT CANR-14; SAAS 21;
   SATA 29, 91; SATA-Brief 27
Eckhart, Meister 1260(?)-1327(?) ... **CMLC 9**
   See also DLB 115
Eckmar, F. R.
   See de Hartog, Jan
Eco, Umberto 1932- .... **CLC 28, 60, 142;**
   DAM NOV, POP
   See also BEST 90:1; BPFB 1; CA 77-80;
   CANR 12, 33, 55; CPW; CWW 2; DA3;
   DLB 196, 242; MTCW 1, 2
Eddison, E(ric) R(ucker)
   1882-1945 .... **TCLC 15**
   See also CA 109; 156; FANT; SFW; SUFW
Eddy, Mary (Ann Morse) Baker
   1821-1910 .... **TCLC 71**
   See also CA 113; 174
Edel, (Joseph) Leon 1907-1997 .. **CLC 29, 34**
   See also CA 1-4R; 161; CANR 1, 22; DLB
   103; INT CANR-22
Eden, Emily 1797-1869 .... **NCLC 10**
Edgar, David 1948- .. **CLC 42; DAM DRAM**
   See also CA 57-60; CANR 12, 61; CBD;
   CD; DLB 13, 233; MTCW 1
Edgerton, Clyde (Carlyle) 1944- ...... **CLC 39**
   See also AAYA 17; CA 118; 134; CANR
   64; CSW; INT 134; YAW
Edgeworth, Maria 1768-1849 .... **NCLC 1, 51**
   See also BRWS 3; DLB 116, 159, 163; FW;
   RGEL; SATA 21; WLIT 3

Edmonds, Paul
   See Kuttner, Henry
Edmonds, Walter D(umaux)
   1903-1998 .... **CLC 35**
   See also BYA 2; CA 5-8R; CANR 2; CWRI;
   DLB 9; LAIT 1; MAICYA; RHW; SAAS
   4; SATA 1, 27; SATA-Obit 99
Edmondson, Wallace
   See Ellison, Harlan (Jay)
Edson, Russell CLC 13
   See also CA 33-36R; WP
Edwards, Bronwen Elizabeth
   See Rose, Wendy
Edwards, G(erald) B(asil)
   1899-1976 .... **CLC 25**
   See also CA 110
Edwards, Gus 1939- .... **CLC 43**
   See also CA 108; INT 108
Edwards, Jonathan 1703-1758 .... **LC 7, 54;**
   DA; DAC; DAM MST
   See also AMW; DLB 24; RGAL
Efron, Marina Ivanovna Tsvetaeva
   See Tsvetaeva (Efron), Marina (Ivanovna)
Ehle, John (Marsden, Jr.) 1925- ...... **CLC 27**
   See also CA 9-12R; CSW
Ehrenbourg, Ilya (Grigoryevich)
   See Ehrenburg, Ilya (Grigoryevich)
Ehrenburg, Ilya (Grigoryevich)
   1891-1967 .... **CLC 18, 34, 62**
   See also CA 102; 25-28R
Ehrenburg, Ilyo (Grigoryevich)
   See Ehrenburg, Ilya (Grigoryevich)
Ehrenreich, Barbara 1941- .... **CLC 110**
   See also BEST 90:4; CA 73-76; CANR 16,
   37, 62; FW; MTCW 1, 2
Eich, Guenter 1907-1972 .... **CLC 15**
   See also Eich, Gunter
   See also CA 111; 93-96; DLB 69, 124
Eich, Gunter
   See Eich, Guenter
   See also RGWL
Eichendorff, Joseph 1788-1857 .... **NCLC 8**
   See also DLB 90; RGWL
Eigner, Larry CLC 9
   See also Eigner, Laurence (Joel)
   See also CAAS 23; DLB 5; WP
Eigner, Laurence (Joel) 1927-1996
   See Eigner, Larry
   See also CA 9-12R; 151; CANR 6, 84; CP;
   DLB 193
Einstein, Albert 1879-1955 .... **TCLC 65**
   See also CA 121; 133; MTCW 1, 2
Eiseley, Loren Corey 1907-1977 .... **CLC 7**
   See also AAYA 5; ANW; CA 1-4R; 73-76;
   CANR 6; DLBD 17
Eisenstadt, Jill 1963- .... **CLC 50**
   See also CA 140
Eisenstein, Sergei (Mikhailovich)
   1898-1948 .... **TCLC 57**
   See also CA 114; 149
Eisner, Simon
   See Kornbluth, C(yril) M.
Ekeloef, (Bengt) Gunnar
   1907-1968 ... **CLC 27; DAM POET; PC**
   23
   See also CA 123; 25-28R; EW
Ekelof, (Bengt) Gunnar
   See Ekeloef, (Bengt) Gunnar
Ekelund, Vilhelm 1880-1949 .... **TCLC 75**
   See also CA 189
Ekwensi, C. O. D.
   See Ekwensi, Cyprian (Odiatu Duaka)
Ekwensi, Cyprian (Odiatu Duaka)
   1921- ...... **CLC 4; BLC 1; DAM MULT**
   See also AFW; BW 2, 3; CA 29-32R;
   CANR 18, 42, 74; CN; CWRI; DLB 117;
   MTCW 1, 2; RGEL; SATA 66; WLIT 2

Elaine TCLC 18
   See also Leverson, Ada
El Crummo
   See Crumb, R(obert)
Elder, Lonne III 1931-1996 .... **DC 8**
   See also BLC 1; BW 1, 3; CA 81-84; 152;
   CAD; CANR 25; DAM MULT; DLB 7,
   38, 44
Eleanor of Aquitaine 1122-1204 ... **CMLC 39**
Elia
   See Lamb, Charles
Eliade, Mircea 1907-1986 .... **CLC 19**
   See also CA 65-68; 119; CANR 30, 62;
   DLB 220; MTCW 1; SFW
Eliot, A. D.
   See Jewett, (Theodora) Sarah Orne
Eliot, Alice
   See Jewett, (Theodora) Sarah Orne
Eliot, Dan
   See Silverberg, Robert
Eliot, George 1819-1880 ...... **NCLC 4, 13, 23,**
   41, 49, 89; DA; DAB; DAC; DAM
   MST, NOV; PC 20; WLC
   See also CDBLB 1832-1890; CN; CPW;
   DA3; DLB 21, 35, 55; RGEL; RGSF;
   SSFS 8; WLIT 3
Eliot, John 1604-1690 .... **LC 5**
   See also DLB 24
Eliot, T(homas) S(tearns)
   1888-1965 ...... **CLC 1, 2, 3, 6, 9, 10, 13,**
   15, 24, 34, 41, 55, 57, 113; DA; DAB;
   DAC; DAM DRAM, MST, POET; PC
   5, 31; WLC
   See also AAYA 28; AMW; AMWR; BRW;
   CA 5-8R; 25-28R; CANR 41; CDALB
   1929-1941; DA3; DFS 4, 13; DLB 7, 10,
   45, 63; DLBY 88; EXPP; LAIT 3; MTCW
   1, 2; PAB; PFS 1, 7; RGAL; RGEL;
   WLIT 4; WP
Elizabeth 1866-1941 .... **TCLC 41**
Elkin, Stanley L(awrence)
   1930-1995 .. **CLC 4, 6, 9, 14, 27, 51, 91;**
   DAM NOV, POP; SSC 12
   See also AMWS 6; BPFB 1; CA 9-12R;
   148; CANR 8, 46; CN; CPW; DLB 2, 28;
   DLBY 80; INT CANR-8; MTCW 1, 2;
   RGAL
Elledge, Scott CLC 34
Elliot, Don
   See Silverberg, Robert
Elliott, Don
   See Silverberg, Robert
Elliott, George P(aul) 1918-1980 .... **CLC 2**
   See also CA 1-4R; 97-100; CANR 2
Elliott, Janice 1931-1995 .... **CLC 47**
   See also CA 13-16R; CANR 8, 29, 84; CN;
   DLB 14; SATA 119
Elliott, Sumner Locke 1917-1991 ..... **CLC 38**
   See also CA 5-8R; 134; CANR 2, 21
Elliott, William
   See Bradbury, Ray (Douglas)
Ellis, A. E. CLC 7
Ellis, Alice Thomas CLC 40
   See also Haycraft, Anna (Margaret)
   See also DLB 194; MTCW 1
Ellis, Bret Easton 1964- ..... **CLC 39, 71, 117;**
   DAM POP
   See also AAYA 2; CA 118; 123; CANR 51,
   74; CN; CPW; DA3; HGG; INT 123;
   MTCW 1; NFS 11
Ellis, (Henry) Havelock
   1859-1939 .... **TCLC 14**
   See also CA 109; 169; DLB 190
Ellis, Landon
   See Ellison, Harlan (Jay)
Ellis, Trey 1962- .... **CLC 55**
   See also CA 146; CANR 92

Fairman, Paul W. 1916-1977
See Queen, Ellery
See also CA 114; SFW

Falco, Gian
See Papini, Giovanni

Falconer, James
See Kirkup, James

Falconer, Kenneth
See Kornbluth, C(yril) M.

Falkland, Samuel
See Heijermans, Herman

Fallaci, Oriana 1930- .... **CLC 11, 110**
See also CA 77-80; CANR 15, 58; FW;
MTCW 1

Faludi, Susan 1959- .... **CLC 140**
See also CA 138; FW; MTCW 1

Faludy, George 1913- .... **CLC 42**
See also CA 21-24R

Faludy, Gyoergy
See Faludy, George

Fanon, Frantz 1925-1961 ... **CLC 74; BLC 2;**
DAM MULT
See also BW 1; CA 116; 89-92; WLIT 2

Fanshawe, Ann 1625-1680 .... **LC 11**

Fante, John (Thomas) 1911-1983 ..... **CLC 60**
See also CA 69-72; 109; CANR 23; DLB
130; DLBY 83

Farah, Nuruddin 1945- .. **CLC 53, 137; BLC**
2; DAM MULT
See also BW 2, 3; CA 106; CANR 81; CN;
DLB 125; WLIT 2

Fargue, Leon-Paul 1876(?)-1947 .... **TCLC 11**
See also CA 109

Farigoule, Louis
See Romains, Jules

Farina, Richard 1936(?)-1966 .... **CLC 9**
See also CA 81-84; 25-28R

Farley, Walter (Lorimer)
1915-1989 .... **CLC 17**
See also CA 17-20R; CANR 8, 29, 84; DLB
22; JRDA; MAICYA; SATA 2, 43; YAW

Farmer, Philip Jose 1918- .... **CLC 1, 19**
See also AAYA 28; BPFB 1; CA 1-4R;
CANR 4, 35; DLB 8; MTCW 1; SATA
93; SFW

Farquhar, George 1677-1707 ... **LC 21; DAM**
DRAM
See also BRW 2; DLB 84; RGEL

Farrell, J(ames) G(ordon)
1935-1979 .... **CLC 6**
See also CA 73-76; 89-92; CANR 36; DLB
14; MTCW 1; RGEL; RHW; WLIT 4

Farrell, James T(homas) 1904-1979 . **CLC 1,**
4, 8, 11, 66; SSC 28
See also AMW; BPFB 1; CA 5-8R; 89-92;
CANR 9, 61; DLB 4, 9, 86; DLBD 2;
MTCW 1, 2; RGAL

Farrell, Warren (Thomas) 1943- ...... **CLC 70**
See also CA 146

Farren, Richard J.
See Betjeman, John

Farren, Richard M.
See Betjeman, John

Fassbinder, Rainer Werner
1946-1982 .... **CLC 20**
See also CA 93-96; 106; CANR 31

Fast, Howard (Melvin) 1914- .. **CLC 23, 131;**
DAM NOV
See also AAYA 16; BPFB 1; CA 1-4R, 181;
CAAE 181; CAAS 18; CANR 1, 33, 54,
75, 98; CMW; CN; CPW; DLB 9; INT
CANR-33; MTCW 1; RHW; SATA 7;
SATA-Essay 107; TCWW 2; YAW

Faulcon, Robert
See Holdstock, Robert P.

Faulkner, William (Cuthbert)
1897-1962 .... **CLC 1, 3, 6, 8, 9, 11, 14,**
18, 28, 52, 68; DA; DAB; DAC; DAM
MST, NOV; SSC 1, 35, 42; WLC
See also AAYA 7; AMW; AMWR; BPFB 1;
BYA 5; CA 81-84; CANR 33; CDALB
1929-1941; DA3; DLB 9, 11, 44, 102;
DLBD 2; DLBY 86, 97; EXPN; EXPS;
LAIT 2; MTCW 1, 2; NFS 4, 8; RGAL;
RGSF; SSFS 2, 5, 6, 12

Fauset, Jessie Redmon
1882(?)-1961 .... **CLC 19, 54; BLC 2;**
DAM MULT
See also AFAW 2; BW 1; CA 109; CANR
83; DLB 51; FW; MAWW

Faust, Frederick (Schiller)
1892-1944(?) .... **TCLC 49; DAM POP**
See also Austin, Frank; Brand, Max; Challis, George; Dawson, Peter; Dexter, Martin; Evans, Evan; Frederick, John; Frost,
Frederick; Manning, David; Silver, Nicholas
See also CA 108; 152

Faust, Irvin 1924- .... **CLC 8**
See also CA 33-36R; CANR 28, 67; CN;
DLB 2, 28; DLBY 80

Fawkes, Guy
See Benchley, Robert (Charles)

Fearing, Kenneth (Flexner)
1902-1961 .... **CLC 51**
See also CA 93-96; CANR 59; CMW; DLB
9; RGAL

Fecamps, Elise
See Creasey, John

Federman, Raymond 1928- .... **CLC 6, 47**
See also CA 17-20R; CAAS 8; CANR 10,
43, 83; CN; DLBY 80

Federspiel, J(uerg) F. 1931- .... **CLC 42**
See also CA 146

Feiffer, Jules (Ralph) 1929- ..... **CLC 2, 8, 64;**
DAM DRAM
See also AAYA 3; CA 17-20R; CAD; CANR
30, 59; CD; DLB 7, 44; INT CANR-30;
MTCW 1; SATA 8, 61, 111

Feige, Hermann Albert Otto Maximilian
See Traven, B.

Feinberg, David B. 1956-1994 .... **CLC 59**
See also CA 135; 147

Feinstein, Elaine 1930- .... **CLC 36**
See also CA 69-72; CAAS 1; CANR 31,
68; CN; CP; CWP; DLB 14, 40; MTCW
1

Feke, Gilbert David CLC 65

Feldman, Irving (Mordecai) 1928- ..... **CLC 7**
See also CA 1-4R; CANR 1; CP; DLB 169

Felix-Tchicaya, Gerald
See Tchicaya, Gerald Felix

Fellini, Federico 1920-1993 .... **CLC 16, 85**
See also CA 65-68; 143; CANR 33

Felsen, Henry Gregor 1916-1995 ..... **CLC 17**
See also CA 1-4R; 180; CANR 1; SAAS 2;
SATA 1

Felski, Rita CLC 65

Fenno, Jack
See Calisher, Hortense

Fenollosa, Ernest (Francisco)
1853-1908 .... **TCLC 91**

Fenton, James Martin 1949- .... **CLC 32**
See also CA 102; CP; DLB 40; PFS 11

Ferber, Edna 1887-1968 .... **CLC 18, 93**
See also AITN 1; CA 5-8R; 25-28R; CANR
68; DLB 9, 28, 86; MTCW 1, 2; RGAL;
RHW; SATA 7; TCWW 2

Ferdowsi, Abu'l Qasem 940-1020 . **CMLC 43**
See also RGWL

Ferguson, Helen
See Kavan, Anna

Ferguson, Niall 1964- .... **CLC 134**
See also CA 190

Ferguson, Samuel 1810-1886 .... **NCLC 33**
See also DLB 32; RGEL

Fergusson, Robert 1750-1774 .... **LC 29**
See also DLB 109; RGEL

Ferling, Lawrence
See Ferlinghetti, Lawrence (Monsanto)

Ferlinghetti, Lawrence (Monsanto)
1919(?)- .... **CLC 2, 6, 10, 27, 111; DAM**
POET; PC 1
See also CA 5-8R; CANR 3, 41, 73;
CDALB 1941-1968; CP; DA3; DLB 5,
16; MTCW 1, 2; RGAL; WP

Fern, Fanny
See Parton, Sara Payson Willis

Fernandez, Vicente Garcia Huidobro
See Huidobro Fernandez, Vicente Garcia

Fernandez-Armesto, Felipe CLC 70

Fernandez de Lizardi, Jose Joaquin
See Lizardi, Jose Joaquin Fernandez de

Ferre, Rosario 1942- ...... **CLC 139; HLCS 1;**
SSC 36
See also CA 131; CANR 55, 81; CWW 2;
DLB 145; HW 1, 2; MTCW 1; WLIT 1

Ferrer, Gabriel (Francisco Victor) Miro
See Miro (Ferrer), Gabriel (Francisco
Victor)

Ferrier, Susan (Edmonstone)
1782-1854 .... **NCLC 8**
See also DLB 116; RGEL

Ferrigno, Robert 1948(?)- .... **CLC 65**
See also CA 140

Ferron, Jacques 1921-1985 .... **CLC 94; DAC**
See also CA 117; 129; CCA 1; DLB 60

Feuchtwanger, Lion 1884-1958 .... **TCLC 3**
See also CA 104; 187; DLB 66

Feuillet, Octave 1821-1890 .... **NCLC 45**
See also DLB 192

Feydeau, Georges (Leon Jules Marie)
1862-1921 .... **TCLC 22; DAM DRAM**
See also CA 113; 152; CANR 84; DLB 192;
EW; GFL 1789 to the Present; RGWL

Fichte, Johann Gottlieb
1762-1814 .... **NCLC 62**
See also DLB 90

Ficino, Marsilio 1433-1499 .... **LC 12**

Fiedeler, Hans
See Doeblin, Alfred

Fiedler, Leslie A(aron) 1917- .. **CLC 4, 13, 24**
See also CA 9-12R; CANR 7, 63; CN; DLB
28, 67; MTCW 1, 2; RGAL

Field, Andrew 1938- .... **CLC 44**
See also CA 97-100; CANR 25

Field, Eugene 1850-1895 .... **NCLC 3**
See also DLB 23, 42, 140; DLBD 13; MAI-
CYA; RGAL; SATA 16

Field, Gans T.
See Wellman, Manly Wade

Field, Michael 1915-1971 .... **TCLC 43**
See also CA 29-32R

Field, Peter
See Hobson, Laura Z(ametkin)
See also TCWW 2

Fielding, Helen 1959(?)- .... **CLC 146**
See also CA 172; DLB 231

Fielding, Henry 1707-1754 ..... **LC 1, 46; DA;**
DAB; DAC; DAM DRAM, MST, NOV;
WLC
See also CDBLB 1660-1789; DA3; DLB
39, 84, 101; RGEL; WLIT 3

Fielding, Sarah 1710-1768 .... **LC 1, 44**
See also DLB 39; RGEL

Fields, W. C. 1880-1946 .... **TCLC 80**
See also DLB 44

Fierstein, Harvey (Forbes) 1954- .... **CLC 33;**
DAM DRAM, POP
See also CA 123; 129; CAD; CD; CPW;
DA3; DFS 6; GLL

Figes, Eva 1932- .... **CLC 31**
See also CA 53-56; CANR 4, 44, 83; CN;
DLB 14; FW
Finch, Anne 1661-1720 .... **LC 3; PC 21**
See also DLB 95
Finch, Robert (Duer Claydon)
1900- .... **CLC 18**
See also CA 57-60; CANR 9, 24, 49; CP;
DLB 88
Findley, Timothy 1930- . **CLC 27, 102; DAC;
DAM MST**
See also CA 25-28R; CANR 12, 42, 69;
CCA 1; CN; DLB 53; FANT; RHW
Fink, William
See Mencken, H(enry) L(ouis)
Firbank, Louis 1942-
See Reed, Lou
See also CA 117
Firbank, (Arthur Annesley) Ronald
1886-1926 .... **TCLC 1**
See also BRWS 2; CA 104; 177; DLB 36;
RGEL
Fish, Stanley
See Fish, Stanley Eugene
Fish, Stanley E.
See Fish, Stanley Eugene
Fish, Stanley Eugene 1938- .... **CLC 142**
See also CA 112; 132; CANR 90; DLB 67
Fisher, Dorothy (Frances) Canfield
1879-1958 .... **TCLC 87**
See also CA 114; 136; CANR 80; CLR 71,;
CWRI; DLB 9, 102; MAICYA; YABC 1
Fisher, M(ary) F(rances) K(ennedy)
1908-1992 .... **CLC 76, 87**
See also CA 77-80; 138; CANR 44; MTCW
1
Fisher, Roy 1930- .... **CLC 25**
See also CA 81-84; CAAS 10; CANR 16;
CP; DLB 40
Fisher, Rudolph 1897-1934 .. **TCLC 11; BLC
2; DAM MULT; SSC 25**
See also BW 1, 3; CA 107; 124; CANR 80;
DLB 51, 102
Fisher, Vardis (Alvero) 1895-1968 ...... **CLC 7**
See also CA 5-8R; 25-28R; CANR 68; DLB
9, 206; RGAL; TCWW 2
Fiske, Tarleton
See Bloch, Robert (Albert)
Fitch, Clarke
See Sinclair, Upton (Beall)
Fitch, John IV
See Cormier, Robert (Edmund)
Fitzgerald, Captain Hugh
See Baum, L(yman) Frank
FitzGerald, Edward 1809-1883 .... **NCLC 9**
See also DLB 32; RGEL
Fitzgerald, F(rancis) Scott (Key)
1896-1940 .. **TCLC 1, 6, 14, 28, 55; DA;
DAB; DAC; DAM MST, NOV; SSC 6,
31; WLC**
See also AAYA 24; AITN 1; AMW; AMWR;
BPFB 1; CA 110; 123; CDALB 1917-
1929; DA3; DLB 4, 9, 86; DLBD 1, 15,
16; DLBY 81, 96; EXPN; EXPS; LAIT 3;
MTCW 1, 2; NFS 2; RGAL; RGSF; SSFS
4
Fitzgerald, Penelope 1916-2000 . **CLC 19, 51,
61, 143**
See also BRWS 5; CA 85-88; 190; CAAS
10; CANR 56, 86; CN; DLB 14, 194;
MTCW 2
Fitzgerald, Robert (Stuart)
1910-1985 .... **CLC 39**
See also CA 1-4R; 114; CANR 1; DLBY
80
FitzGerald, Robert D(avid)
1902-1987 .... **CLC 19**
See also CA 17-20R; RGEL

Fitzgerald, Zelda (Sayre)
1900-1948 .... **TCLC 52**
See also CA 117; 126; DLBY 84
Flanagan, Thomas (James Bonner)
1923- .... **CLC 25, 52**
See also CA 108; CANR 55; CN; DLBY
80; INT 108; MTCW 1; RHW
Flaubert, Gustave 1821-1880 .... **NCLC 2, 10,
19, 62, 66; DA; DAB; DAC; DAM
MST, NOV; SSC 11; WLC**
See also DA3; DLB 119; EXPS; GFL 1789
to the Present; LAIT 2; RGSF; RGWL;
SSFS 6
Flavius Josephus
See Josephus, Flavius
Flecker, Herman Elroy
See Flecker, (Herman) James Elroy
Flecker, (Herman) James Elroy
1884-1915 .... **TCLC 43**
See also CA 109; 150; DLB 10, 19; RGEL
Fleming, Ian (Lancaster) 1908-1964 . **CLC 3,
30; DAM POP**
See also AAYA 26; BPFB 1; CA 5-8R;
CANR 59; CDBLB 1945-1960; CMW;
CPW; DA3; DLB 87, 201; MSW; MTCW
1, 2; RGEL; SATA 9; YAW
Fleming, Thomas (James) 1927- ...... **CLC 37**
See also CA 5-8R; CANR 10; INT CANR-
10; SATA 8
Fletcher, John 1579-1625 .... **LC 33; DC 6**
See also BRW 2; CDBLB Before 1660;
DLB 58; RGEL
Fletcher, John Gould 1886-1950 .... **TCLC 35**
See also CA 107; 167; DLB 4, 45; RGAL
Fleur, Paul
See Pohl, Frederik
Flooglebuckle, Al
See Spiegelman, Art
Flora, Fletcher 1914-1969
See Queen, Ellery
See also CA 1-4R; CANR 3, 85
Flying Officer X
See Bates, H(erbert) E(rnest)
Fo, Dario 1926- .... **CLC 32, 109; DAM
DRAM; DC 10**
See also CA 116; 128; CANR 68; CWW 2;
DA3; DLBY 97; MTCW 1, 2
Fogarty, Jonathan Titulescu Esq.
See Farrell, James T(homas)
Follett, Ken(neth Martin) 1949- ..... **CLC 18;
DAM NOV, POP**
See also AAYA 6; BEST 89:4; BPFB 1; CA
81-84; CANR 13, 33, 54; CMW; CPW;
DA3; DLB 87; DLBY 81; INT CANR-
33; MTCW 1
Fontane, Theodor 1819-1898 .... **NCLC 26**
See also DLB 129; RGWL
Fontenot, Chester CLC 65
Foote, Horton 1916- .... **CLC 51, 91; DAM
DRAM**
See also CA 73-76; CAD; CANR 34, 51;
CD; CSW; DA3; DLB 26; INT CANR-34
Foote, Mary Hallock 1847-1938 .. **TCLC 108**
See also DLB 186, 188, 202, 221
Foote, Shelby 1916- ..... **CLC 75; DAM NOV,
POP**
See also AAYA 40; CA 5-8R; CANR 3, 45,
74; CN; CPW; CSW; DA3; DLB 2, 17;
MTCW 2; RHW
Forbes, Esther 1891-1967 .... **CLC 12**
See also AAYA 17; BYA 2; CA 13-14; 25-
28R; CAP 1; CLR 27; DLB 22; JRDA;
MAICYA; RHW; SATA 2, 100; YAW
Forche, Carolyn (Louise) 1950- ...... **CLC 25,
83, 86; DAM POET; PC 10**
See also CA 109; 117; CANR 50, 74; CP;
CWP; DA3; DLB 5, 193; INT CA-117;
MTCW 1; RGAL

Ford, Elbur
See Hibbert, Eleanor Alice Burford
Ford, Ford Madox 1873-1939 ... **TCLC 1, 15,
39, 57; DAM NOV**
See also Chaucer, Daniel
See also CA 104; 132; CANR 74; CDBLB
1914-1945; DA3; DLB 162; MTCW 1, 2;
RGEL
Ford, Henry 1863-1947 .... **TCLC 73**
See also CA 115; 148
Ford, John 1586-1639 .... **LC 68; DAM
DRAM; DC 8**
See also BRW 2; CDBLB Before 1660;
DA3; DFS 7; DLB 58; IDTP; RGEL
Ford, John 1895-1973 .... **CLC 16**
See also CA 187; 45-48
Ford, Richard 1944- .... **CLC 46, 99**
See also AMWS 5; CA 69-72; CANR 11,
47, 86; CN; CSW; DLB 227; MTCW 1;
RGAL; RGSF
Ford, Webster
See Masters, Edgar Lee
Foreman, Richard 1937- .... **CLC 50**
See also CA 65-68; CAD; CANR 32, 63;
CD
Forester, C(ecil) S(cott) 1899-1966 ... **CLC 35**
See also CA 73-76; 25-28R; CANR 83;
DLB 191; RGEL; RHW; SATA 13
Forez
See Mauriac, Francois (Charles)
Forman, James Douglas 1932- .... **CLC 21**
See also AAYA 17; CA 9-12R; CANR 4,
19, 42; JRDA; MAICYA; SATA 8, 70;
YAW
Fornes, Maria Irene 1930- . **CLC 39, 61; DC
10; HLCS 1**
See also CA 25-28R; CAD; CANR 28, 81;
CD; CWD; DLB 7; HW 1, 2; INT CANR-
28; MTCW 1; RGAL
Forrest, Leon (Richard) 1937-1997 .. **CLC 4;
BLCS**
See also AFAW 2; BW 2; CA 89-92; 162;
CAAS 7; CANR 25, 52, 87; CN; DLB 33
Forster, E(dward) M(organ)
1879-1970 ...... **CLC 1, 2, 3, 4, 9, 10, 13,
15, 22, 45, 77; DA; DAB; DAC; DAM
MST, NOV; SSC 27; WLC**
See also AAYA 2, 37; BRW; CA 13-14; 25-
28R; CANR 45; CAP 1; CDBLB 1914-
1945; DA3; DLB 34, 98, 162, 178, 195;
DLBD 10; EXPN; LAIT 3; MTCW 1, 2;
NCFS 1; NFS 3, 10, 11; RGEL; RGSF;
SATA 57; SUFW; WLIT 4
Forster, John 1812-1876 .... **NCLC 11**
See also DLB 144, 184
Forster, Margaret 1938- .... **CLC 149**
See also CA 133; CANR 62; CN; DLB 155
Forsyth, Frederick 1938- .... **CLC 2, 5, 36;
DAM NOV, POP**
See also BEST 89:4; CA 85-88; CANR 38,
62; CMW; CN; CPW; DLB 87; MTCW
1, 2
Forten, Charlotte L. 1837-1914 .... **TCLC 16;
BLC 2**
See also Grimke, Charlotte L(ottie) Forten
See also DLB 50, 239
Foscolo, Ugo 1778-1827 .... **NCLC 8, 97**
Fosse, Bob CLC 20
See also Fosse, Robert Louis
Fosse, Robert Louis 1927-1987
See Fosse, Bob
See also CA 110; 123
Foster, Hannah Webster
1758-1840 .... **NCLC 99**
See also DLB 37, 200; RGAL
Foster, Stephen Collins
1826-1864 .... **NCLC 26**
See also RGAL

Fuller, Margaret 1810-1850
See Ossoli, Sarah Margaret (Fuller)
See also AMWS 2; DLB 239

Fuller, Roy (Broadbent) 1912-1991 ... **CLC 4, 28**
See also BRWS 7; CA 5-8R; 135; CAAS 10; CANR 53, 83; CWRI; DLB 15, 20; RGEL; SATA 87

Fuller, Sarah Margaret
See Ossoli, Sarah Margaret (Fuller)

Fulton, Alice 1952- .... **CLC 52**
See also CA 116; CANR 57, 88; CP; CWP; DLB 193

Furphy, Joseph 1843-1912 .... **TCLC 25**
See also CA 163; DLB 230; RGEL

Fuson, Robert H(enderson) 1927- .... **CLC 70**
See also CA 89-92

Fussell, Paul 1924- .... **CLC 74**
See also BEST 90:1; CA 17-20R; CANR 8, 21, 35, 69; INT CANR-21; MTCW 1, 2

Futabatei, Shimei 1864-1909 .... **TCLC 44**
See also CA 162; DLB 180; MJW

Futrelle, Jacques 1875-1912 .... **TCLC 19**
See also CA 113; 155; CMW

Gaboriau, Emile 1835-1873 .... **NCLC 14**
See also CMW

Gadda, Carlo Emilio 1893-1973 .... **CLC 11**
See also CA 89-92; DLB 177

Gaddis, William 1922-1998 ... **CLC 1, 3, 6, 8, 10, 19, 43, 86**
See also AMWS 4; BPFB 1; CA 17-20R; 172; CANR 21, 48; CN; DLB 2; MTCW 1, 2; RGAL

Gaelique, Moruen le
See Jacob, (Cyprien-)Max

Gage, Walter
See Inge, William (Motter)

Gaines, Ernest J(ames) 1933- ...... **CLC 3, 11, 18, 86; BLC 2; DAM MULT**
See also AAYA 18; AFAW 1; AITN 1; BPFB 2; BW 2, 3; BYA 6; CA 9-12R; CANR 6, 24, 42, 75; CDALB 1968-1988; CLR 62; CN; CSW; DA3; DLB 2, 33, 152; DLBY 80; EXPN; LAIT 5; MTCW 1, 2; NFS 5, 7; RGAL; RGSF; RHW; SATA 86; SSFS 5; YAW

Gaitskill, Mary 1954- .... **CLC 69**
See also CA 128; CANR 61

Galdos, Benito Perez
See Perez Galdos, Benito

Gale, Zona 1874-1938 .... **TCLC 7; DAM DRAM**
See also CA 105; 153; CANR 84; DLB 9, 78, 228; RGAL

Galeano, Eduardo (Hughes) 1940- . **CLC 72; HLCS 1**
See also CA 29-32R; CANR 13, 32, 100; HW 1

Galiano, Juan Valera y Alcala
See Valera y Alcala-Galiano, Juan

Galilei, Galileo 1564-1642 .... **LC 45**

Gallagher, Tess 1943- ...... **CLC 18, 63; DAM POET; PC 9**
See also CA 106; CP; CWP; DLB 212

Gallant, Mavis 1922- .. **CLC 7, 18, 38; DAC; DAM MST; SSC 5**
See also CA 69-72; CANR 29, 69; CCA 1; CN; DLB 53; MTCW 1, 2; RGEL; RGSF

Gallant, Roy A(rthur) 1924- .... **CLC 17**
See also CA 5-8R; CANR 4, 29, 54; CLR 30; MAICYA; SATA 4, 68, 110

Gallico, Paul (William) 1897-1976 ..... **CLC 2**
See also AITN 1; CA 5-8R; 69-72; CANR 23; DLB 9, 171; FANT; MAICYA; SATA 13

Gallo, Max Louis 1932- .... **CLC 95**
See also CA 85-88

Gallois, Lucien
See Desnos, Robert

Gallup, Ralph
See Whitemore, Hugh (John)

Galsworthy, John 1867-1933 .... **TCLC 1, 45; DA; DAB; DAC; DAM DRAM, MST, NOV; SSC 22; WLC**
See also CA 104; 141; CANR 75; CDBLB 1890-1914; DA3; DLB 10, 34, 98, 162; DLBD 16; MTCW 1; RGEL; SSFS 3

Galt, John 1779-1839 .... **NCLC 1**
See also DLB 99, 116, 159; RGEL; RGSF

Galvin, James 1951- .... **CLC 38**
See also CA 108; CANR 26

Gamboa, Federico 1864-1939 .... **TCLC 36**
See also CA 167; HW 2

Gandhi, M. K.
See Gandhi, Mohandas Karamchand

Gandhi, Mahatma
See Gandhi, Mohandas Karamchand

Gandhi, Mohandas Karamchand 1869-1948 .... **TCLC 59; DAM MULT**
See also CA 121; 132; DA3; MTCW 1, 2

Gann, Ernest Kellogg 1910-1991 ..... **CLC 23**
See also AITN 1; BPFB 2; CA 1-4R; 136; CANR 1, 83; RHW

Garber, Eric 1943(?)-
See Holleran, Andrew
See also CANR 89

Garcia, Cristina 1958- .... **CLC 76**
See also CA 141; CANR 73; DNFS; HW 2

Garcia Lorca, Federico 1898-1936 . **TCLC 1, 7, 49; DA; DAB; DAC; DAM DRAM, MST, MULT, POET; DC 2; HLC 2; PC 3; WLC**
See also CA 104; 131; CANR 81; DA3; DFS 10; DLB 108; HW 1, 2; MTCW 1, 2

Garcia Marquez, Gabriel (Jose) 1928- .... **CLC 2, 3, 8, 10, 15, 27, 47, 55, 68; DA; DAB; DAC; DAM MST, MULT, NOV, POP; HLC 1; SSC 8; WLC**
See also AAYA 3, 33; BEST 89:1, 90:4; BPFB 2; BYA 12; CA 33-36R; CANR 10, 28, 50, 75, 82; CPW; DA3; DLB 113; DNFS; EXPN; EXPS; HW 1, 2; LAIT 2; LAW; MTCW 1, 2; NFS 1, 5, 10; RGSF; RGWL; SSFS 1, 6; WLIT 1

Garcilaso de la Vega, El Inca 1503-1536
See also HLCS 1

Gard, Janice
See Latham, Jean Lee

Gard, Roger Martin du
See Martin du Gard, Roger

Gardam, Jane 1928- .... **CLC 43**
See also CA 49-52; CANR 2, 18, 33, 54; CLR 12; DLB 14, 161, 231; MAICYA; MTCW 1; SAAS 9; SATA 39, 76; SATA-Brief 28; YAW

Gardner, Herb(ert) 1934- .... **CLC 44**
See also CA 149; CAD; CD

Gardner, John (Champlin), Jr. 1933-1982 ...... **CLC 2, 3, 5, 7, 8, 10, 18, 28, 34; DAM NOV, POP; SSC 7**
See also AITN 1; AMWS 5; BPFB 2; CA 65-68; 107; CANR 33, 73; CDALBS; CPW; DA3; DLB 2; DLBY 82; FANT; MTCW 1; NFS 3; RGAL; RGSF; SATA 40; SATA-Obit 31; SSFS 8

Gardner, John (Edmund) 1926- ...... **CLC 30; DAM POP**
See also CA 103; CANR 15, 69; CMW; CPW; MTCW 1

Gardner, Miriam
See Bradley, Marion Zimmer
See also GLL 1

Gardner, Noel
See Kuttner, Henry

Gardons, S. S.
See Snodgrass, W(illiam) D(e Witt)

Garfield, Leon 1921-1996 .... **CLC 12**
See also AAYA 8; BYA 1; CA 17-20R; 152; CANR 38, 41, 78; CLR 21; DLB 161; JRDA; MAICYA; SATA 1, 32, 76; SATA-Obit 90; YAW

Garland, (Hannibal) Hamlin 1860-1940 .... **TCLC 3; SSC 18**
See also CA 104; DLB 12, 71, 78, 186; RGAL; RGSF; TCWW 2

Garneau, (Hector de) Saint-Denys 1912-1943 .... **TCLC 13**
See also CA 111; DLB 88

Garner, Alan 1934- ..... **CLC 17; DAB; DAM POP**
See also AAYA 18; BYA 3; CA 73-76, 178; CAAE 178; CANR 15, 64; CLR 20; CPW; DLB 161; FANT; MAICYA; MTCW 1, 2; SATA 18, 69; SATA-Essay 108; YAW

Garner, Hugh 1913-1979 .... **CLC 13**
See also Warwick, Jarvis
See also CA 69-72; CANR 31; CCA 1; DLB 68

Garnett, David 1892-1981 .... **CLC 3**
See also CA 5-8R; 103; CANR 17, 79; DLB 34; FANT; MTCW 2; RGEL; SFW

Garos, Stephanie
See Katz, Steve

Garrett, George (Palmer) 1929- .. **CLC 3, 11, 51; SSC 30**
See also AMWS 7; BPFB 2; CA 1-4R; CAAS 5; CANR 1, 42, 67; CN; CP; CSW; DLB 2, 5, 130, 152; DLBY 83

Garrick, David 1717-1779 .... **LC 15; DAM DRAM**
See also DLB 84; RGEL

Garrigue, Jean 1914-1972 .... **CLC 2, 8**
See also CA 5-8R; 37-40R; CANR 20

Garrison, Frederick
See Sinclair, Upton (Beall)

Garro, Elena 1920(?)-1998
See also CA 131; 169; CWW 2; DLB 145; HLCS 1; HW 1; WLIT 1

Garth, Will
See Hamilton, Edmond; Kuttner, Henry

Garvey, Marcus (Moziah, Jr.) 1887-1940 ...... **TCLC 41; BLC 2; DAM MULT**
See also BW 1; CA 120; 124; CANR 79

Gary, Romain CLC 25
See also Kacew, Romain
See also DLB 83

Gascar, Pierre CLC 11
See also Fournier, Pierre

Gascoyne, David (Emery) 1916- .... **CLC 45**
See also CA 65-68; CANR 10, 28, 54; CP; DLB 20; MTCW 1; RGEL

Gaskell, Elizabeth Cleghorn 1810-1865 ...... **NCLC 5, 70, 97; DAB; DAM MST; SSC 25**
See also BRW; CDBLB 1832-1890; DLB 21, 144, 159; RGEL; RGSF

Gass, William H(oward) 1924- . **CLC 1, 2, 8, 11, 15, 39, 132; SSC 12**
See also AMWS 6; CA 17-20R; CANR 30, 71, 100; CN; DLB 2, 227; MTCW 1, 2; RGAL

Gassendi, Pierre 1592-1655 .... **LC 54**
See also GFL Beginnings to 1789

Gasset, Jose Ortega y
See Ortega y Gasset, Jose

Gates, Henry Louis, Jr. 1950- .... **CLC 65; BLCS; DAM MULT**
See also BW 2, 3; CA 109; CANR 25, 53, 75; CSW; DA3; DLB 67; MTCW 1; RGAL

Gautier, Theophile 1811-1872 .. NCLC 1, 59;
    DAM POET; PC 18; SSC 20
    See also DLB 119; GFL 1789 to the Present;
    RGWL
Gawsworth, John
    See Bates, H(erbert) E(rnest)
Gay, John 1685-1732 .. LC 49; DAM DRAM
    See also DLB 84, 95; RGEL; WLIT 3
Gay, Oliver
    See Gogarty, Oliver St. John
Gaye, Marvin (Pentz, Jr.)
    1939-1984 .... CLC 26
    See also CA 112
Gebler, Carlo (Ernest) 1954- .... CLC 39
    See also CA 119; 133; CANR 96
Gee, Maggie (Mary) 1948- .... CLC 57
    See also CA 130; CN; DLB 207
Gee, Maurice (Gough) 1931- .... CLC 29
    See also CA 97-100; CANR 67; CLR 56;
    CN; CWRI; RGSF; SATA 46, 101
Gelbart, Larry (Simon) 1928- .... CLC 21, 61
    See also Gelbart, Larry
    See also CA 73-76; CANR 45, 94
Gelbart, Larry 1928-
    See Gelbart, Larry (Simon)
    See also CAD; CD
Gelber, Jack 1932- .... CLC 1, 6, 14, 79
    See also CA 1-4R; CAD; CANR 2; DLB 7,
    228
Gellhorn, Martha (Ellis)
    1908-1998 .... CLC 14, 60
    See also CA 77-80; 164; CANR 44; CN;
    DLBY 82, 98
Genet, Jean 1910-1986 .. CLC 1, 2, 5, 10, 14,
    44, 46; DAM DRAM
    See also CA 13-16R; CANR 18; DA3; DFS
    10; DLB 72; DLBY 86; GFL 1789 to the
    Present; GLL 1; MTCW 1, 2; RGWL
Gent, Peter 1942- .... CLC 29
    See also AITN 1; CA 89-92; DLBY 82
Gentile, Giovanni 1875-1944 .... TCLC 96
    See also CA 119
Gentlewoman in New England, A
    See Bradstreet, Anne
Gentlewoman in Those Parts, A
    See Bradstreet, Anne
Geoffrey of Monmouth c.
    1100-1155 .... CMLC 44
    See also DLB 146
George, Jean
    See George, Jean Craighead
George, Jean Craighead 1919- .... CLC 35
    See also AAYA 8; BYA 2; CA 5-8R; CANR
    25; CLR 1; DLB 52; JRDA; MAICYA;
    SATA 2, 68, 124; YAW
George, Stefan (Anton) 1868-1933 . TCLC 2,
    14
    See also CA 104; 193; EW
Georges, Georges Martin
    See Simenon, Georges (Jacques Christian)
Gerhardi, William Alexander
    See Gerhardie, William Alexander
Gerhardie, William Alexander
    1895-1977 .... CLC 5
    See also CA 25-28R; 73-76; CANR 18;
    DLB 36; RGEL
Gerstler, Amy 1956- .... CLC 70
    See also CA 146; CANR 99
Gertler, T. CLC 134
    See also CA 116; 121
Ghalib NCLC 39, 78
    See also Ghalib, Asadullah Khan
Ghalib, Asadullah Khan 1797-1869
    See Ghalib
    See also DAM POET; RGWL
Ghelderode, Michel de 1898-1962 ..... CLC 6,
    11; DAM DRAM; DC 15
    See also CA 85-88; CANR 40, 77

Ghiselin, Brewster 1903- .... CLC 23
    See also CA 13-16R; CAAS 10; CANR 13;
    CP
Ghose, Aurabinda 1872-1950 .... TCLC 63
    See also CA 163
Ghose, Zulfikar 1935- .... CLC 42
    See also CA 65-68; CANR 67; CN; CP
Ghosh, Amitav 1956- .... CLC 44
    See also CA 147; CANR 80; CN
Giacosa, Giuseppe 1847-1906 .... TCLC 7
    See also CA 104
Gibb, Lee
    See Waterhouse, Keith (Spencer)
Gibbon, Lewis Grassic TCLC 4
    See also Mitchell, James Leslie
    See also RGEL
Gibbons, Kaye 1960- .... CLC 50, 88, 145;
    DAM POP
    See also AAYA 34; CA 151; CANR 75;
    CSW; DA3; MTCW 1; NFS 3; RGAL;
    SATA 117
Gibran, Kahlil 1883-1931 .... TCLC 1, 9;
    DAM POET, POP; PC 9
    See also CA 104; 150; DA3; MTCW 2
Gibran, Khalil
    See Gibran, Kahlil
Gibson, William 1914- .. CLC 23; DA; DAB;
    DAC; DAM DRAM, MST
    See also CA 9-12R; CAD 2; CANR 9, 42,
    75; CD; DFS 2; DLB 7; LAIT 2; MTCW
    2; SATA 66; YAW
Gibson, William (Ford) 1948- ... CLC 39, 63;
    DAM POP
    See also AAYA 12; BPFB 2; CA 126; 133;
    CANR 52, 90; CN; CPW; DA3; MTCW
    2; SCFW 2; SFW
Gide, Andre (Paul Guillaume)
    1869-1951 . TCLC 5, 12, 36; DA; DAB;
    DAC; DAM MST, NOV; SSC 13; WLC
    See also CA 104; 124; DA3; DLB 65; EW;
    GFL 1789 to the Present; MTCW 1, 2;
    RGSF; RGWL
Gifford, Barry (Colby) 1946- .... CLC 34
    See also CA 65-68; CANR 9, 30, 40, 90
Gilbert, Frank
    See De Voto, Bernard (Augustine)
Gilbert, W(illiam) S(chwenck)
    1836-1911 .... TCLC 3; DAM DRAM,
    POET
    See also CA 104; 173; RGEL; SATA 36
Gilbreth, Frank B(unker), Jr.
    1911-2001 .... CLC 17
    See also CA 9-12R; SATA 2
Gilchrist, Ellen (Louise) 1935- .. CLC 34, 48,
    143; DAM POP; SSC 14
    See also BPFB 2; CA 113; 116; CANR 41,
    61; CN; CPW; CSW; DLB 130; EXPS;
    MTCW 1, 2; RGAL; RGSF; SSFS 9
Giles, Molly 1942- .... CLC 39
    See also CA 126; CANR 98
Gill, Eric 1882-1940 .... TCLC 85
Gill, Patrick
    See Creasey, John
Gillette, Douglas CLC 70
Gilliam, Terry (Vance) 1940- .... CLC 21, 141
    See also Monty Python
    See also AAYA 19; CA 108; 113; CANR
    35; INT 113
Gillian, Jerry
    See Gilliam, Terry (Vance)
Gilliatt, Penelope (Ann Douglass)
    1932-1993 .... CLC 2, 10, 13, 53
    See also AITN 2; CA 13-16R; 141; CANR
    49; DLB 14
Gilman, Charlotte (Anna) Perkins (Stetson)
    1860-1935 .... TCLC 9, 37; SSC 13
    See also BYA 11; CA 106; 150; DLB 221;
    EXPS; FW; HGG; LAIT 2; MAWW;
    MTCW 1; RGAL; RGSF; SFW; SSFS 1

Gilmour, David 1949- .... CLC 35
    See also CA 138, 147
Gilpin, William 1724-1804 .... NCLC 30
Gilray, J. D.
    See Mencken, H(enry) L(ouis)
Gilroy, Frank D(aniel) 1925- .... CLC 2
    See also CA 81-84; CAD; CANR 32, 64,
    86; CD; DLB 7
Gilstrap, John 1957(?)- .... CLC 99
    See also CA 160; CANR 101
Ginsberg, Allen 1926-1997 .... CLC 1, 2, 3, 4,
    6, 13, 36, 69, 109; DA; DAB; DAC;
    DAM MST, POET; PC 4; WLC
    See also AAYA 33; AITN 1; AMWS 2; CA
    1-4R; 157; CANR 2, 41, 63, 95; CDALB
    1941-1968; CP; DA3; DLB 5, 16, 169,
    237; GLL 1; MTCW 1, 2; PAB; PFS 5;
    RGAL; WP
Ginzburg, Eugenia CLC 59
Ginzburg, Natalia 1916-1991 .... CLC 5, 11,
    54, 70
    See also CA 85-88; 135; CANR 33; DLB
    177; MTCW 1, 2; RGWL
Giono, Jean 1895-1970 .... CLC 4, 11
    See also CA 45-48; 29-32R; CANR 2, 35;
    DLB 72; GFL 1789 to the Present; MTCW
    1; RGWL
Giovanni, Nikki 1943- .... CLC 2, 4, 19, 64,
    117; BLC 2; DA; DAB; DAC; DAM
    MST, MULT, POET; PC 19; WLCS
    See also AAYA 22; AITN 1; BW 2, 3; CA
    29-32R; CAAS 6; CANR 18, 41, 60, 91;
    CDALBS; CLR 6, 73; CP; CSW; CWP;
    CWRI; DA3; DLB 5, 41; EXPP; INT
    CANR-18; MAICYA; MTCW 1, 2;
    RGAL; SATA 24, 107; YAW
Giovene, Andrea 1904- .... CLC 7
    See also CA 85-88
Gippius, Zinaida (Nikolayevna) 1869-1945
    See Hippius, Zinaida
    See also CA 106
Giraudoux, Jean(-Hippolyte)
    1882-1944 ... TCLC 2, 7; DAM DRAM
    See also CA 104; DLB 65; EW; GFL 1789
    to the Present; RGWL
Gironella, Jose Maria 1917-1991 ..... CLC 11
    See also CA 101; RGWL
Gissing, George (Robert)
    1857-1903 .... TCLC 3, 24, 47; SSC 37
    See also BRW; CA 105; 167; DLB 18, 135,
    184; RGEL
Giurlani, Aldo
    See Palazzeschi, Aldo
Gladkov, Fyodor (Vasilyevich)
    1883-1958 .... TCLC 27
    See also CA 170
Glanville, Brian (Lester) 1931- .... CLC 6
    See also CA 5-8R; CAAS 9; CANR 3, 70;
    CN; DLB 15, 139; SATA 42
Glasgow, Ellen (Anderson Gholson)
    1873-1945 .... TCLC 2, 7; SSC 34
    See also AMW; CA 104; 164; DLB 9, 12;
    MAWW; MTCW 2; RGAL; RHW; SSFS
    9
Glaspell, Susan 1882(?)-1948 . TCLC 55; DC
    10; SSC 41
    See also AMWS 3; CA 110; 154; DFS 8;
    DLB 7, 9, 78, 228; RGAL; SSFS 3;
    TCWW 2; YABC 2
Glassco, John 1909-1981 .... CLC 9
    See also CA 13-16R; 102; CANR 15; DLB
    68
Glasscock, Amnesia
    See Steinbeck, John (Ernst)
Glasser, Ronald J. 1940(?)- .... CLC 37
Glassman, Joyce
    See Johnson, Joyce

Harson, Sley
See Ellison, Harlan (Jay)

Hart, Ellis
See Ellison, Harlan (Jay)

Hart, Josephine 1942(?)- .... **CLC 70; DAM POP**
See also CA 138; CANR 70; CPW

Hart, Moss 1904-1961 .... **CLC 66; DAM DRAM**
See also CA 109; 89-92; CANR 84; DFS 1; DLB 7; RGAL

Harte, (Francis) Bret(t)
1836(?)-1902 ... **TCLC 1, 25; DA; DAC; DAM MST; SSC 8; WLC**
See also AMWS 2; CA 104; 140; CANR 80; CDALB 1865-1917; DA3; DLB 12, 64, 74, 79, 186; EXPS; LAIT 2; RGAL; RGSF; SATA 26; SSFS 3

Hartley, L(eslie) P(oles) 1895-1972 ... **CLC 2, 22**
See also BRWS 7; CA 45-48; 37-40R; CANR 33; DLB 15, 139; HGG; MTCW 1, 2; RGEL; RGSF; SUFW

Hartman, Geoffrey H. 1929- .... **CLC 27**
See also CA 117; 125; CANR 79; DLB 67

Hartmann, Sadakichi 1869-1944 ... **TCLC 73**
See also CA 157; DLB 54

Hartmann von Aue c. 1170-c.
1210 .... **CMLC 15**
See also DLB 138; RGWL

Haruf, Kent 1943- .... **CLC 34**
See also CA 149; CANR 91

Harwood, Ronald 1934- .... **CLC 32; DAM DRAM, MST**
See also CA 1-4R; CANR 4, 55; CBD; CD; DLB 13

Hasegawa Tatsunosuke
See Futabatei, Shimei

Hasek, Jaroslav (Matej Frantisek)
1883-1923 .... **TCLC 4**
See also CA 104; 129; EW; MTCW 1, 2; RGSF; RGWL

Hass, Robert 1941- ... **CLC 18, 39, 99; PC 16**
See also AMWS 6; CA 111; CANR 30, 50, 71; CP; DLB 105, 206; RGAL; SATA 94

Hastings, Hudson
See Kuttner, Henry

Hastings, Selina CLC 44

Hathorne, John 1641-1717 .... **LC 38**

Hatteras, Amelia
See Mencken, H(enry) L(ouis)

Hatteras, Owen TCLC 18
See also Mencken, H(enry) L(ouis); Nathan, George Jean

Hauptmann, Gerhart (Johann Robert)
1862-1946 .... **TCLC 4; DAM DRAM; SSC 37**
See also CA 104; 153; DLB 66, 118; EW; RGSF; RGWL

Havel, Vaclav 1936- ..... **CLC 25, 58, 65, 123; DAM DRAM; DC 6**
See also CA 104; CANR 36, 63; CWW 2; DA3; DFS 10; DLB 232; MTCW 1, 2

Haviaras, Stratis CLC 33
See also Chaviaras, Strates

Hawes, Stephen 1475(?)-1529(?) .... **LC 17**
See also DLB 132; RGEL

Hawkes, John (Clendennin Burne, Jr.)
1925-1998 .. **CLC 1, 2, 3, 4, 7, 9, 14, 15, 27, 49**
See also BPFB 2; CA 1-4R; 167; CANR 2, 47, 64; CN; DLB 2, 7, 227; DLBY 80, 98; MTCW 1, 2; RGAL

Hawking, S. W.
See Hawking, Stephen W(illiam)

Hawking, Stephen W(illiam) 1942- . **CLC 63, 105**
See also AAYA 13; BEST 89:1; CA 126; 129; CANR 48; CPW; DA3; MTCW 2

Hawkins, Anthony Hope
See Hope, Anthony

Hawthorne, Julian 1846-1934 .... **TCLC 25**
See also CA 165; HGG

Hawthorne, Nathaniel 1804-1864 ... **NCLC 2, 10, 17, 23, 39, 79, 95; DA; DAB; DAC; DAM MST, NOV; SSC 3, 29, 39; WLC**
See also AAYA 18; AMW; BPFB 2; BYA 3; CDALB 1640-1865; DA3; DLB 1, 74, 223; EXPN; EXPS; HGG; LAIT 1; NFS 1; RGAL; RGSF; SSFS 1, 7, 11; YABC 2

Haxton, Josephine Ayres 1921-
See Douglas, Ellen
See also CA 115; CANR 41, 83

Hayaseca y Eizaguirre, Jorge
See Echegaray (y Eizaguirre), Jose (Maria Waldo)

Hayashi, Fumiko 1904-1951 .... **TCLC 27**
See also CA 161; DLB 180

Haycraft, Anna (Margaret) 1932-
See Ellis, Alice Thomas
See also CA 122; CANR 85, 90; MTCW 2

Hayden, Robert E(arl) 1913-1980 . **CLC 5, 9, 14, 37; BLC 2; DA; DAC; DAM MST, MULT, POET; PC 6**
See also AFAW 1, 2; AMWS 2; BW 1, 3; CA 69-72; 97-100; CABS 2; CANR 24, 75, 82; CDALB 1941-1968; DLB 5, 76; EXPP; MTCW 1, 2; PFS 1; RGAL; SATA 19; SATA-Obit 26; WP

Hayek, F(riedrich) A(ugust von)
1899-1992 .... **TCLC 109**
See also CA 93-96; 137; CANR 20; MTCW 1, 2

Hayford, J(oseph) E(phraim) Casely
See Casely-Hayford, J(oseph) E(phraim)

Hayman, Ronald 1932- .... **CLC 44**
See also CA 25-28R; CANR 18, 50, 88; CD; DLB 155

Hayne, Paul Hamilton 1830-1886 . **NCLC 94**
See also DLB 3, 64, 79; RGAL

Haywood, Eliza (Fowler)
1693(?)-1756 .... **LC 1, 44**
See also DLB 39; RGEL

Hazlitt, William 1778-1830 ...... **NCLC 29, 82**
See also DLB 110, 158; RGEL

Hazzard, Shirley 1931- .... **CLC 18**
See also CA 9-12R; CANR 4, 70; CN; DLBY 82; MTCW 1

Head, Bessie 1937-1986 .... **CLC 25, 67; BLC 2; DAM MULT**
See also BW 2, 3; CA 29-32R; 119; CANR 25, 82; DA3; DLB 117, 225; EXPS; FW; MTCW 1, 2; RGSF; SSFS 5; WLIT 2

Headon, (Nicky) Topper 1956(?)- ..... **CLC 30**

Heaney, Seamus (Justin) 1939- .... **CLC 5, 7, 14, 25, 37, 74, 91; DAB; DAM POET; PC 18; WLCS**
See also BRWS 2; CA 85-88; CANR 25, 48, 75, 91; CDBLB 1960 to Present; CP; DA3; DLB 40; DLBY 95; EXPP; MTCW 1, 2; PAB; PFS 2, 5, 8; RGEL; WLIT 4

Hearn, (Patricio) Lafcadio (Tessima Carlos)
1850-1904 .... **TCLC 9**
See also CA 105; 166; DLB 12, 78, 189; HGG; RGAL

Hearne, Vicki 1946- .... **CLC 56**
See also CA 139

Hearon, Shelby 1931- .... **CLC 63**
See also AITN 2; AMWS 8; CA 25-28R; CANR 18, 48; CSW

Heat-Moon, William Least CLC 29
See also Trogdon, William (Lewis)
See also AAYA 9

Hebbel, Friedrich 1813-1863 .... **NCLC 43; DAM DRAM**
See also DLB 129; RGWL

Hebert, Anne 1916-2000 .... **CLC 4, 13, 29; DAC; DAM MST, POET**
See also CA 85-88; 187; CANR 69; CCA 1; CWP; CWW 2; DA3; DLB 68; GFL 1789 to the Present; MTCW 1, 2

Hecht, Anthony (Evan) 1923- ...... **CLC 8, 13, 19; DAM POET**
See also CA 9-12R; CANR 6; CP; DLB 5, 169; PFS 6; WP

Hecht, Ben 1894-1964 .... **CLC 8**
See also CA 85-88; DFS 9; DLB 7, 9, 25, 26, 28, 86; FANT; IDFW 3, 4; RGAL; TCLC 101

Hedayat, Sadeq 1903-1951 .... **TCLC 21**
See also CA 120; RGSF

Hegel, Georg Wilhelm Friedrich
1770-1831 .... **NCLC 46**
See also DLB 90

Heidegger, Martin 1889-1976 .... **CLC 24**
See also CA 81-84; 65-68; CANR 34; MTCW 1, 2

Heidenstam, (Carl Gustaf) Verner von
1859-1940 .... **TCLC 5**
See also CA 104

Heifner, Jack 1946- .... **CLC 11**
See also CA 105; CANR 47

Heijermans, Herman 1864-1924 .... **TCLC 24**
See also CA 123

Heilbrun, Carolyn G(old) 1926- .... **CLC 25**
See also Cross, Amanda
See also CA 45-48; CANR 1, 28, 58, 94; CMW; CPW; FW

Heine, Heinrich 1797-1856 .... **NCLC 4, 54; PC 25**
See also DLB 90; RGWL

Heinemann, Larry (Curtiss) 1944- .. **CLC 50**
See also CA 110; CAAS 21; CANR 31, 81; DLBD 9; INT CANR-31

Heiney, Donald (William) 1921-1993
See Harris, MacDonald
See also CA 1-4R; 142; CANR 3, 58; FANT

Heinlein, Robert A(nson) 1907-1988 . **CLC 1, 3, 8, 14, 26, 55; DAM POP**
See also AAYA 17; BPFB 2; BYA 4; CA 1-4R; 125; CANR 1, 20, 53; CPW; DA3; DLB 8; EXPS; JRDA; LAIT 5; MAICYA; MTCW 1, 2; RGAL; SATA 9, 69; SATA-Obit 56; SCFW; SFW; SSFS 7; YAW

Helforth, John
See Doolittle, Hilda

Hellenhofferu, Vojtech Kapristian z
See Hasek, Jaroslav (Matej Frantisek)

Heller, Joseph 1923-1999 . **CLC 1, 3, 5, 8, 11, 36, 63; DA; DAB; DAC; DAM MST, NOV; POP; WLC**
See also AAYA 24; AITN 1; AMWS 4; BPFB 2; BYA 1; CA 5-8R; 187; CABS 1; CANR 8, 42, 66; CN; CPW; DA3; DLB 2, 28, 227; DLBY 80; EXPN; INT CANR-8; LAIT 4; MTCW 1, 2; NFS 1; RGAL; YAW

Hellman, Lillian (Florence)
1906-1984 .. **CLC 2, 4, 8, 14, 18, 34, 44, 52; DAM DRAM; DC 1**
See also AITN 1, 2; AMWS 1; CA 13-16R; 112; CAD; CANR 33; CWD; DA3; DFS 1, 3; DLB 7, 228; DLBY 84; FW; LAIT 3; MAWW; MTCW 1, 2; RGAL

Helprin, Mark 1947- .... **CLC 7, 10, 22, 32; DAM NOV, POP**
See also CA 81-84; CANR 47, 64; CDALBS; CPW; DA3; DLBY 85; FANT; MTCW 1, 2

Helvetius, Claude-Adrien 1715-1771 .. **LC 26**

Helyar, Jane Penelope Josephine 1933-
See Poole, Josephine
See also CA 21-24R; CANR 10, 26; SATA 82

Himes, Chester (Bomar) 1909-1984 .. **CLC 2, 4, 7, 18, 58, 108; BLC 2; DAM MULT**
See also AFAW 2; BPFB 2; BW 2; CA 25-28R; 114; CANR 22, 89; CMW; DLB 2, 76, 143, 226; MTCW 1, 2; RGAL

Hinde, Thomas CLC 6, 11
See also Chitty, Thomas Willes

Hine, (William) Daryl 1936- .... **CLC 15**
See also CA 1-4R; CAAS 15; CANR 1, 20; CP; DLB 60

Hinkson, Katharine Tynan
See Tynan, Katharine

Hinojosa(-Smith), Rolando (R.) 1929-
See also CA 131; CAAS 16; CANR 62; DAM MULT; DLB 82; HLC 1; HW 1, 2; MTCW 2; RGAL

Hinton, S(usan) E(loise) 1950- .... **CLC 30, 111; DA; DAB; DAC; DAM MST, NOV**
See also AAYA 2, 33; BPFB 2; CA 81-84; CANR 32, 62, 92; CDALBS; CLR 3, 23; CPW; DA3; JRDA; LAIT 5; MAICYA; MTCW 1, 2; NFS 5, 9; SATA 19, 58, 115; WYA; YAW

Hippius, Zinaida TCLC 9
See also Gippius, Zinaida (Nikolayevna)

Hiraoka, Kimitake 1925-1970
See Mishima, Yukio
See also CA 97-100; 29-32R; DA3; DAM DRAM; MTCW 1, 2; SSFS 12

Hirsch, E(ric) D(onald), Jr. 1928- .... **CLC 79**
See also CA 25-28R; CANR 27, 51; DLB 67; INT CANR-27; MTCW 1

Hirsch, Edward 1950- .... **CLC 31, 50**
See also CA 104; CANR 20, 42; CP; DLB 120

Hitchcock, Alfred (Joseph)
1899-1980 .... **CLC 16**
See also AAYA 22; CA 159; 97-100; SATA 27; SATA-Obit 24

Hitler, Adolf 1889-1945 .... **TCLC 53**
See also CA 117; 147

Hoagland, Edward 1932- .... **CLC 28**
See also CA 1-4R; CANR 2, 31, 57; CN; DLB 6; SATA 51; TCWW 2

Hoban, Russell (Conwell) 1925- . **CLC 7, 25; DAM NOV**
See also BPFB 2; CA 5-8R; CANR 23, 37, 66; CLR 3, 69; CN; CWRI; DLB 52; FANT; MAICYA; MTCW 1, 2; SATA 1, 40, 78; SFW

Hobbes, Thomas 1588-1679 .... **LC 36**
See also DLB 151; RGEL

Hobbs, Perry
See Blackmur, R(ichard) P(almer)

Hobson, Laura Z(ametkin)
1900-1986 .... **CLC 7, 25**
See also Field, Peter
See also BPFB 2; CA 17-20R; 118; CANR 55; DLB 28; SATA 52

Hoch, Edward D(entinger) 1930-
See Queen, Ellery
See also CA 29-32R; CANR 11, 27, 51, 97; CMW; SFW

Hochhuth, Rolf 1931- .. **CLC 4, 11, 18; DAM DRAM**
See also CA 5-8R; CANR 33, 75; CWW 2; DLB 124; MTCW 1, 2

Hochman, Sandra 1936- .... **CLC 3, 8**
See also CA 5-8R; DLB 5

Hochwaelder, Fritz 1911-1986 .... **CLC 36; DAM DRAM**
See also Hochwalder, Fritz
See also CA 29-32R; 120; CANR 42; MTCW 1

Hochwalder, Fritz
See Hochwaelder, Fritz
See also RGWL

Hocking, Mary (Eunice) 1921- .... **CLC 13**
See also CA 101; CANR 18, 40

Hodgins, Jack 1938- .... **CLC 23**
See also CA 93-96; CN; DLB 60

Hodgson, William Hope
1877(?)-1918 .... **TCLC 13**
See also CA 111; 164; CMW; DLB 70, 153, 156, 178; HGG; MTCW 2; SFW

Hoeg, Peter 1957- .... **CLC 95**
See also CA 151; CANR 75; CMW; DA3; MTCW 2

Hoffman, Alice 1952- ... **CLC 51; DAM NOV**
See also AAYA 37; CA 77-80; CANR 34, 66, 100; CN; CPW; MTCW 1, 2

Hoffman, Daniel (Gerard) 1923- . **CLC 6, 13, 23**
See also CA 1-4R; CANR 4; CP; DLB 5

Hoffman, Stanley 1944- .... **CLC 5**
See also CA 77-80

Hoffman, William 1925- .... **CLC 141**
See also CA 21-24R; CANR 9; CSW; DLB 234

Hoffman, William M(oses) 1939- ..... **CLC 40**
See also CA 57-60; CANR 11, 71

Hoffmann, E(rnst) T(heodor) A(madeus)
1776-1822 .... **NCLC 2; SSC 13**
See also DLB 90; EW; RGSF; RGWL; SATA 27; SUFW; WCH

Hofmann, Gert 1931- .... **CLC 54**
See also CA 128

Hofmannsthal, Hugo von
1874-1929 ...... **TCLC 11; DAM DRAM; DC 4**
See also von Hofmannsthal, Hugo
See also CA 106; 153; DFS 12; DLB 81, 118; RGWL

Hogan, Linda 1947- . **CLC 73; DAM MULT; PC 35**
See also AMWS 4; BYA 12; CA 120; CANR 45, 73; CWP; DLB 175; NNAL; TCWW 2

Hogarth, Charles
See Creasey, John

Hogarth, Emmett
See Polonsky, Abraham (Lincoln)

Hogg, James 1770-1835 .... **NCLC 4**
See also DLB 93, 116, 159; HGG; RGEL

Holbach, Paul Henri Thiry Baron
1723-1789 .... **LC 14**

Holberg, Ludvig 1684-1754 .... **LC 6**
See also RGWL

Holcroft, Thomas 1745-1809 .... **NCLC 85**
See also DLB 39, 89, 158; RGEL

Holden, Ursula 1921- .... **CLC 18**
See also CA 101; CAAS 8; CANR 22

Holderlin, (Johann Christian) Friedrich
1770-1843 .... **NCLC 16; PC 4**
See also EW; RGWL

Holdstock, Robert
See Holdstock, Robert P.

Holdstock, Robert P. 1948- .... **CLC 39**
See also CA 131; CANR 81; FANT; HGG; SFW

Holinshed, Raphael fl. 1580- .... **LC 69**
See also DLB 167; RGEL

Holland, Isabelle 1920- .... **CLC 21**
See also AAYA 11; CA 21-24R; 181; CAAE 181; CANR 10, 25, 47; CLR 57; CWRI; JRDA; LAIT 4; MAICYA; SATA 8, 70; SATA-Essay 103

Holland, Marcus
See Caldwell, (Janet Miriam) Taylor (Holland)

Hollander, John 1929- .... **CLC 2, 5, 8, 14**
See also CA 1-4R; CANR 1, 52; CP; DLB 5; SATA 13

Hollander, Paul
See Silverberg, Robert

Holleran, Andrew 1943(?)- .... **CLC 38**
See also Garber, Eric
See also CA 144; GLL 1

Holley, Marietta 1836(?)-1926 .... **TCLC 99**
See also CA 118; DLB 11

Hollinghurst, Alan 1954- .... **CLC 55, 91**
See also CA 114; CN; DLB 207; GLL 1

Hollis, Jim
See Summers, Hollis (Spurgeon, Jr.)

Holly, Buddy 1936-1959 .... **TCLC 65**

Holmes, Gordon
See Shiel, M(atthew) P(hipps)

Holmes, John
See Souster, (Holmes) Raymond

Holmes, John Clellon 1926-1988 ...... **CLC 56**
See also CA 9-12R; 125; CANR 4; DLB 16, 237

Holmes, Oliver Wendell, Jr.
1841-1935 .... **TCLC 77**
See also CA 114; 186

Holmes, Oliver Wendell
1809-1894 .... **NCLC 14, 81**
See also AMWS 1; CDALB 1640-1865; DLB 1, 189, 235; EXPP; RGAL; SATA 34

Holmes, Raymond
See Souster, (Holmes) Raymond

Holt, Victoria
See Hibbert, Eleanor Alice Burford
See also BPFB 2

Holub, Miroslav 1923-1998 .... **CLC 4**
See also CA 21-24R; 169; CANR 10; CWW 2; DLB 232

Homer c. 8th cent. B.C.- .. **CMLC 1, 16; DA; DAB; DAC; DAM MST, POET; PC 23; WLCS**
See also DA3; DLB 176; EFS 1; LAIT 1; RGWL; WP

Hongo, Garrett Kaoru 1951- .... **PC 23**
See also CA 133; CAAS 22; CP; DLB 120; EXPP; RGAL

Honig, Edwin 1919- .... **CLC 33**
See also CA 5-8R; CAAS 8; CANR 4, 45; CP; DLB 5

Hood, Hugh (John Blagdon) 1928- . **CLC 15, 28; SSC 42**
See also CA 49-52; CAAS 17; CANR 1, 33, 87; CN; DLB 53; RGSF

Hood, Thomas 1799-1845 .... **NCLC 16**
See also DLB 96; RGEL

Hooker, (Peter) Jeremy 1941- .... **CLC 43**
See also CA 77-80; CANR 22; CP; DLB 40

hooks, bell CLC 94; BLCS
See also Watkins, Gloria Jean
See also FW; MTCW 2

Hope, A(lec) D(erwent) 1907-2000 .... **CLC 3, 51**
See also BRWS 7; CA 21-24R; 188; CANR 33, 74; MTCW 1, 2; PFS 8; RGEL

Hope, Anthony 1863-1933 .... **TCLC 83**
See also CA 157; DLB 153, 156; RGEL; RHW

Hope, Brian
See Creasey, John

Hope, Christopher (David Tully)
1944- .... **CLC 52**
See also AFW; CA 106; CANR 47, 101; CN; DLB 225; SATA 62

Hopkins, Gerard Manley
1844-1889 .... **NCLC 17; DA; DAB; DAC; DAM MST, POET; PC 15; WLC**
See also CDBLB 1890-1914; DA3; DLB 35, 57; EXPP; PAB; RGEL; WP

Hopkins, John (Richard) 1931-1998 .. **CLC 4**
See also CA 85-88; 169; CBD; CD

Hopkins, Pauline Elizabeth
1859-1930 ...... **TCLC 28; BLC 2; DAM**
MULT
See also AFAW 2; BW 2, 3; CA 141; CANR
82; DLB 50

Hopkinson, Francis 1737-1791 .... **LC 25**
See also DLB 31; RGAL

Hopley-Woolrich, Cornell George 1903-1968
See Woolrich, Cornell
See also CA 13-14; CANR 58; CAP 1;
CMW; DLB 226; MTCW 2

Horace 65B.C.-8B.C. .... **CMLC 39**
See also DLB 211; RGWL

Horatio
See Proust, (Valentin-Louis-George-Eugene-
)Marcel

Horgan, Paul (George Vincent
O'Shaughnessy) 1903-1995 . **CLC 9, 53;**
DAM NOV
See also BPFB 2; CA 13-16R; 147; CANR
9, 35; DLB 212; DLBY 85; INT CANR-9;
MTCW 1, 2; SATA 13; SATA-Obit 84;
TCWW 2

Horn, Peter
See Kuttner, Henry

Hornem, Horace Esq.
See Byron, George Gordon (Noel)

Horney, Karen (Clementine Theodore
Danielsen) 1885-1952 .... **TCLC 71**
See also CA 114; 165; FW

Hornung, E(rnest) W(illiam)
1866-1921 .... **TCLC 59**
See also CA 108; 160; CMW; DLB 70

Horovitz, Israel (Arthur) 1939- ...... **CLC 56;**
DAM DRAM
See also CA 33-36R; CAD; CANR 46, 59;
CD; DLB 7

Horton, George Moses
1797(?)-1883(?) .... **NCLC 87**
See also DLB 50

Horvath, Odon von
See Horvath, Oedoen von
See also DLB 85, 124; RGWL

Horvath, Oedoen von 1901-1938 ... **TCLC 45**
See also Horvath, Odon von; von Horvath,
Oedoen
See also CA 118

Horwitz, Julius 1920-1986 .... **CLC 14**
See also CA 9-12R; 119; CANR 12

Hospital, Janette Turner 1942- .... **CLC 42,**
145
See also CA 108; CANR 48; CN; RGSF

Hostos, E. M. de
See Hostos (y Bonilla), Eugenio Maria de

Hostos, Eugenio M. de
See Hostos (y Bonilla), Eugenio Maria de

Hostos, Eugenio Maria
See Hostos (y Bonilla), Eugenio Maria de

Hostos (y Bonilla), Eugenio Maria de
1839-1903 .... **TCLC 24**
See also CA 123; 131; HW 1

Houdini
See Lovecraft, H(oward) P(hillips)

Hougan, Carolyn 1943- .... **CLC 34**
See also CA 139

Household, Geoffrey (Edward West)
1900-1988 .... **CLC 11**
See also CA 77-80; 126; CANR 58; CMW;
DLB 87; SATA 14; SATA-Obit 59

Housman, A(lfred) E(dward)
1859-1936 .... **TCLC 1, 10; DA; DAB;**
DAC; DAM MST, POET; PC 2;
WLCS
See also BRW; CA 104; 125; DA3; DLB
19; EXPP; MTCW 1, 2; PAB; PFS 4, 7;
RGEL; WP

Housman, Laurence 1865-1959 .... **TCLC 7**
See also CA 106; 155; DLB 10; FANT;
RGEL; SATA 25

Howard, Elizabeth Jane 1923- ..... **CLC 7, 29**
See also CA 5-8R; CANR 8, 62; CN

Howard, Maureen 1930- .... **CLC 5, 14, 46**
See also CA 53-56; CANR 31, 75; CN;
DLBY 83; INT CANR-31; MTCW 1, 2

Howard, Richard 1929- .... **CLC 7, 10, 47**
See also AITN 1; CA 85-88; CANR 25, 80;
CP; DLB 5; INT CANR-25

Howard, Robert E(rvin)
1906-1936 .... **TCLC 8**
See also BPFB 2; BYA 5; CA 105; 157;
FANT; SUFW

Howard, Warren F.
See Pohl, Frederik

Howe, Fanny (Quincy) 1940- .... **CLC 47**
See also CA 117; CAAE 187; CAAS 27;
CANR 70; CP; CWP; SATA-Brief 52

Howe, Irving 1920-1993 .... **CLC 85**
See also AMWS 6; CA 9-12R; 141; CANR
21, 50; DLB 67; MTCW 1, 2

Howe, Julia Ward 1819-1910 .... **TCLC 21**
See also CA 117; 191; DLB 1, 189, 235;
FW

Howe, Susan 1937- .... **CLC 72**
See also AMWS 4; CA 160; CP; CWP;
DLB 120; FW; RGAL

Howe, Tina 1937- .... **CLC 48**
See also CA 109; CAD; CD; CWD

Howell, James 1594(?)-1666 .... **LC 13**
See also DLB 151

Howells, W. D.
See Howells, William Dean

Howells, William D.
See Howells, William Dean

Howells, William Dean 1837-1920 .. **TCLC 7,**
17, 41; SSC 36
See also AMW; CA 104; 134; CDALB
1865-1917; DLB 12, 64, 74, 79, 189;
MTCW 2; RGAL

Howes, Barbara 1914-1996 .... **CLC 15**
See also CA 9-12R; 151; CAAS 3; CANR
53; CP; SATA 5

Hrabal, Bohumil 1914-1997 .... **CLC 13, 67**
See also CA 106; 156; CAAS 12; CANR
57; CWW 2; DLB 232; RGSF

Hroswitha of Gandersheim c. 935-c.
1000 .... **CMLC 29**
See also DLB 148

Hsi, Chu 1130-1200 .... **CMLC 42**

Hsun, Lu
See Lu Hsun

Hubbard, L(afayette) Ron(ald)
1911-1986 .... **CLC 43; DAM POP**
See also CA 77-80; 118; CANR 52; CPW;
DA3; FANT; MTCW 2; SFW

Huch, Ricarda (Octavia)
1864-1947 .... **TCLC 13**
See also CA 111; 189; DLB 66

Huddle, David 1942- .... **CLC 49**
See also CA 57-60; CAAS 20; CANR 89;
DLB 130

Hudson, Jeffrey
See Crichton, (John) Michael

Hudson, W(illiam) H(enry)
1841-1922 .... **TCLC 29**
See also CA 115; 190; DLB 98, 153, 174;
RGEL; SATA 35

Hueffer, Ford Madox
See Ford, Ford Madox

Hughart, Barry 1934- .... **CLC 39**
See also CA 137; FANT; SFW

Hughes, Colin
See Creasey, John

Hughes, David (John) 1930- .... **CLC 48**
See also CA 116; 129; CN; DLB 14

Hughes, Edward James
See Hughes, Ted
See also DA3; DAM MST, POET

Hughes, (James) Langston
1902-1967 .... **CLC 1, 5, 10, 15, 35, 44,**
108; BLC 2; DA; DAB; DAC; DAM
DRAM, MST, MULT, POET; DC 3;
PC 1; SSC 6; WLC
See also AAYA 12; AFAW 1, 2; AMWR;
AMWS 1; BW 1, 3; CA 1-4R; 25-28R;
CANR 1, 34, 82; CDALB 1929-1941;
CLR 17; DA3; DLB 4, 7, 48, 51, 86, 228;
EXPP 1, X; EXPS; JRDA; LAIT 3; MAI-
CYA; MTCW 1, 2; PAB; PFS 1, 3, 6, 10;
RGAL; RGSF; SATA 4, 33; SSFS 4, 7;
WCH; WP; YAW

Hughes, Richard (Arthur Warren)
1900-1976 .... **CLC 1, 11; DAM NOV**
See also CA 5-8R; 65-68; CANR 4; DLB
15, 161; MTCW 1; RGEL; SATA 8;
SATA-Obit 25

Hughes, Ted 1930-1998 . **CLC 2, 4, 9, 14, 37,**
119; DAB; DAC; PC 7
See also Hughes, Edward James
See also BRWS 1; CA 1-4R; 171; CANR 1,
33, 66; CLR 3; CP; DLB 40, 161; EXPP;
MAICYA; MTCW 1, 2; PAB; PFS 4;
RGEL; SATA 49; SATA-Brief 27; SATA-
Obit 107; YAW

Hugo, Richard F(ranklin)
1923-1982 .... **CLC 6, 18, 32; DAM**
POET
See also CA 49-52; 108; CANR 3; DLB 5,
206

Hugo, Victor (Marie) 1802-1885 .... **NCLC 3,**
10, 21; DA; DAB; DAC; DAM DRAM,
MST, NOV, POET; PC 17; WLC
See also AAYA 28; DA3; DLB 119, 192;
EFS 2; EW; EXPN; GFL 1789 to the
Present; LAIT 1, 2; NFS 5; RGWL; SATA
47

Huidobro, Vicente
See Huidobro Fernandez, Vicente Garcia

Huidobro Fernandez, Vicente Garcia
1893-1948 .... **TCLC 31**
See also CA 131; HW 1

Hulme, Keri 1947- .... **CLC 39, 130**
See also CA 125; CANR 69; CN; CP; CWP;
FW; INT 125

Hulme, T(homas) E(rnest)
1883-1917 .... **TCLC 21**
See also BRWS 6; CA 117; DLB 19

Hume, David 1711-1776 .... **LC 7, 56**
See also BRWS 3; DLB 104

Humphrey, William 1924-1997 .... **CLC 45**
See also CA 77-80; 160; CANR 68; CN;
CSW; DLB 212; TCWW 2

Humphreys, Emyr Owen 1919- .... **CLC 47**
See also CA 5-8R; CANR 3, 24; CN; DLB
15

Humphreys, Josephine 1945- ..... **CLC 34, 57**
See also CA 121; 127; CANR 97; CSW;
INT 127

Huneker, James Gibbons
1860-1921 .... **TCLC 65**
See also CA 193; DLB 71; RGAL

Hungerford, Pixie
See Brinsmead, H(esba) F(ay)

Hunt, E(verette) Howard, (Jr.)
1918- .... **CLC 3**
See also AITN 1; CA 45-48; CANR 2, 47;
CMW

Hunt, Francesca
See Holland, Isabelle

Hunt, Howard
See Hunt, E(verette) Howard, (Jr.)

Hunt, Kyle
See Creasey, John

Hunt, (James Henry) Leigh
1784-1859 .... **NCLC 1, 70; DAM POET**
See also DLB 96, 110, 144; RGEL; TEA

Hunt, Marsha 1946- .... **CLC 70**
See also BW 2, 3; CA 143; CANR 79

Hunt, Violet 1866(?)-1942 .... TCLC 53
   See also CA 184; DLB 162, 197
Hunter, E. Waldo
   See Sturgeon, Theodore (Hamilton)
Hunter, Evan 1926- .... CLC 11, 31; DAM
   POP
   See also AAYA 39; BPFB 2; CA 5-8R;
   CANR 5, 38, 62, 97; CMW; CN; CPW;
   DLBY 82; INT CANR-5; MTCW 1;
   SATA 25; SFW
Hunter, Kristin (Eggleston) 1931- .... CLC 35
   See also AITN 1; BW 1; BYA 3; CA 13-
   16R; CANR 13; CLR 3; CN; DLB 33;
   INT CANR-13; MAICYA; SAAS 10;
   SATA 12; YAW
Hunter, Mary
   See Austin, Mary (Hunter)
Hunter, Mollie 1922- .... CLC 21
   See also McIlwraith, Maureen Mollie
   Hunter
   See also AAYA 13; BYA 6; CANR 37, 78;
   CLR 25; DLB 161; JRDA; MAICYA;
   SAAS 7; SATA 54, 106; YAW
Hunter, Robert (?)-1734 .... LC 7
Hurston, Zora Neale 1891-1960 .. CLC 7, 30,
   61; BLC 2; DA; DAC; DAM MST,
   MULT, NOV; DC 12; SSC 4; WLCS
   See also AAYA 15; AFAW 1, 2; BW 1, 3;
   BYA 12; CA 85-88; CANR 61; CDALBS;
   DA3; DFS 6; DLB 51, 86; EXPS; EXPN;
   FW; LAIT 3; MTCW 1, 2; NFS 3; RGAL;
   RGSF; SSFS 1, 6, 11; YAW
Husserl, E. G.
   See Husserl, Edmund (Gustav Albrecht)
Husserl, Edmund (Gustav Albrecht)
   1859-1938 .... TCLC 100
   See also CA 116; 133
Huston, John (Marcellus)
   1906-1987 .... CLC 20
   See also CA 73-76; 123; CANR 34; DLB
   26
Hustvedt, Siri 1955- .... CLC 76
   See also CA 137
Hutten, Ulrich von 1488-1523 .... LC 16
   See also DLB 179
Huxley, Aldous (Leonard)
   1894-1963 .... CLC 1, 3, 4, 5, 8, 11, 18,
   35, 79; DA; DAB; DAC; DAM MST,
   NOV; SSC 39; WLC
   See also AAYA 11; BPFB 2; BRW; CA 85-
   88; CANR 44, 99; CDBLB 1914-1945;
   DA3; DLB 36, 100, 162, 195; EXPN;
   LAIT 5; MTCW 1, 2; NFS 6; RGEL;
   SATA 63; SCFW 2; SFW; YAW
Huxley, T(homas) H(enry)
   1825-1895 .... NCLC 67
   See also DLB 57
Huysmans, Joris-Karl 1848-1907 ... TCLC 7,
   69
   See also CA 104; 165; DLB 123; EW; GFL
   1789 to the Present; RGWL
Hwang, David Henry 1957- .. CLC 55; DAM
   DRAM; DC 4
   See also CA 127; 132; CAD; CANR 76;
   CD; DA3; DFS 11; DLB 212; INT 132;
   MTCW 2; RGAL
Hyde, Anthony 1946- .... CLC 42
   See also Chase, Nicholas
   See also CA 136; CCA 1
Hyde, Margaret O(ldroyd) 1917- ..... CLC 21
   See also CA 1-4R; CANR 1, 36; CLR 23;
   JRDA; MAICYA; SAAS 8; SATA 1, 42,
   76
Hynes, James 1956(?)- .... CLC 65
   See also CA 164
Hypatia c. 370-415 .... CMLC 35
Ian, Janis 1951- .... CLC 21
   See also CA 105; 187

Ibanez, Vicente Blasco
   See Blasco Ibanez, Vicente
Ibarbourou, Juana de 1895-1979
   See also HLCS 2; HW 1
Ibarguengoitia, Jorge 1928-1983 ...... CLC 37
   See also CA 124; 113; HW 1
Ibsen, Henrik (Johan) 1828-1906 ... TCLC 2,
   8, 16, 37, 52; DA; DAB; DAC; DAM
   DRAM, MST; DC 2; WLC
   See also CA 104; 141; DA3; DFS 1, 6, 8,
   10, 11; EW; LAIT 2; RGWL
Ibuse, Masuji 1898-1993 .... CLC 22
   See also CA 127; 141; DLB 180
Ichikawa, Kon 1915- .... CLC 20
   See also CA 121
Ichiyo, Higuchi 1872-1896 .... NCLC 49
   See also MJW
Idle, Eric 1943-2000 .... CLC 21
   See also Monty Python
   See also CA 116; CANR 35, 91
Ignatow, David 1914-1997 .... CLC 4, 7, 14,
   40; PC 34
   See also CA 9-12R; 162; CAAS 3; CANR
   31, 57, 96; CP; DLB 5
Ignotus
   See Strachey, (Giles) Lytton
Ihimaera, Witi 1944- .... CLC 46
   See also CA 77-80; CN; RGSF
Ilf, Ilya TCLC 21
   See also Fainzilberg, Ilya Arnoldovich
Illyes, Gyula 1902-1983 .... PC 16
   See also CA 114; 109; DLB 215; RGWL
Immermann, Karl (Lebrecht)
   1796-1840 .... NCLC 4, 49
   See also DLB 133
Ince, Thomas H. 1882-1924 .... TCLC 89
   See also IDFW 3, 4
Inchbald, Elizabeth 1753-1821 ...... NCLC 62
   See also DLB 39, 89; RGEL
Inclan, Ramon (Maria) del Valle
   See Valle-Inclan, Ramon (Maria) del
Infante, G(uillermo) Cabrera
   See Cabrera Infante, G(uillermo)
Ingalls, Rachel (Holmes) 1940- .... CLC 42
   See also CA 123; 127
Ingamells, Reginald Charles
   See Ingamells, Rex
Ingamells, Rex 1913-1955 .... TCLC 35
   See also CA 167
Inge, William (Motter) 1913-1973 ..... CLC 1,
   8, 19; DAM DRAM
   See also CA 9-12R; CDALB 1941-1968;
   DA3; DFS 1, 5, 8; DLB 7; MTCW 1, 2;
   RGAL
Ingelow, Jean 1820-1897 .... NCLC 39
   See also DLB 35, 163; FANT; SATA 33
Ingram, Willis J.
   See Harris, Mark
Innaurato, Albert (F.) 1948(?)- ... CLC 21, 60
   See also CA 115; 122; CAD; CANR 78;
   CD; INT CA-122
Innes, Michael
   See Stewart, J(ohn) I(nnes) M(ackintosh)
Innis, Harold Adams 1894-1952 .... TCLC 77
   See also CA 181; DLB 88
Ionesco, Eugene 1912-1994 ... CLC 1, 4, 6, 9,
   11, 15, 41, 86; DA; DAB; DAC; DAM
   DRAM, MST; DC 12; WLC
   See also CA 9-12R; 144; CANR 55; CWW
   2; DA3; DFS 4, 9; GFL 1789 to the
   Present; MTCW 1, 2; RGWL; SATA 7;
   SATA-Obit 79
Iqbal, Muhammad 1877-1938 .... TCLC 28
Ireland, Patrick
   See O'Doherty, Brian
Irenaeus St. 130- .... CMLC 42
Iron, Ralph
   See Schreiner, Olive (Emilie Albertina)

Irving, John (Winslow) 1942- ... CLC 13, 23,
   38, 112; DAM NOV, POP
   See also AAYA 8; AMWS 6; BEST 89:3;
   BPFB 2; CA 25-28R; CANR 28, 73; CN;
   CPW; DA3; DLB 6; DLBY 82; MTCW
   1, 2; NFS 12; RGAL
Irving, Washington 1783-1859 . NCLC 2, 19,
   95; DA; DAB; DAC; DAM MST; SSC
   2, 37; WLC
   See also AMW; CDALB 1640-1865; DA3;
   DLB 3, 11, 30, 59, 73, 74, 186; EXPS;
   LAIT 1; RGAL; RGSF; SSFS 1, 8; YABC
   2
Irwin, P. K.
   See Page, P(atricia) K(athleen)
Isaacs, Jorge Ricardo 1837-1895 ... NCLC 70
   See also LAW
Isaacs, Susan 1943- .... CLC 32; DAM POP
   See also BEST 89:1; BPFB 2; CA 89-92;
   CANR 20, 41, 65; CPW; DA3; INT
   CANR-20; MTCW 1, 2
Isherwood, Christopher (William Bradshaw)
   1904-1986 .. CLC 1, 9, 11, 14, 44; DAM
   DRAM, NOV
   See also BRW; CA 13-16R; 117; CANR 35,
   97; DA3; DLB 15, 195; DLBY 86;
   MTCW 1, 2; RGAL; RGEL; WLIT 4
Ishiguro, Kazuo 1954- . CLC 27, 56, 59, 110;
   DAM NOV
   See also BEST 90:2; BPFB 2; BRWS 4;
   CA 120; CANR 49, 95; CN; DA3; DLB
   194; MTCW 1, 2; WLIT 4
Ishikawa, Hakuhin
   See Ishikawa, Takuboku
Ishikawa, Takuboku
   1886(?)-1912 ... TCLC 15; DAM POET;
   PC 10
   See also CA 113; 153
Iskander, Fazil 1929- .... CLC 47
   See also CA 102
Isler, Alan (David) 1934- .... CLC 91
   See also CA 156
Ivan IV 1530-1584 .... LC 17
Ivanov, Vyacheslav Ivanovich
   1866-1949 .... TCLC 33
   See also CA 122
Ivask, Ivar Vidrik 1927-1992 .... CLC 14
   See also CA 37-40R; 139; CANR 24
Ives, Morgan
   See Bradley, Marion Zimmer
   See also GLL 1
Izumi Shikibu c. 973-c. 1034 .... CMLC 33
J CLC 10, 36, 86; DAM NOV; SSC 20
   See also CA 97-100; CANR 36, 50, 74;
   DA3; DLB 182; DLBY 94; MTCW 1, 2
J. R. S.
   See Gogarty, Oliver St. John
Jabran, Kahlil
   See Gibran, Kahlil
Jabran, Khalil
   See Gibran, Kahlil
Jackson, Daniel
   See Wingrove, David (John)
Jackson, Helen Hunt 1830-1885 .... NCLC 90
   See also DLB 42, 47, 186, 189; RGAL
Jackson, Jesse 1908-1983 .... CLC 12
   See also BW 1; CA 25-28R; 109; CANR
   27; CLR 28; CWRI; MAICYA; SATA 2,
   29; SATA-Obit 48
Jackson, Laura (Riding) 1901-1991
   See Riding, Laura
   See also CA 65-68; 135; CANR 28, 89;
   DLB 48
Jackson, Sam
   See Trumbo, Dalton
Jackson, Sara
   See Wingrove, David (John)

Jackson, Shirley 1919-1965 . CLC 11, 60, 87;
DA; DAC; DAM MST; SSC 9, 39;
WLC
See also AAYA 9; BPFB 2; CA 1-4R; 25-
28R; CANR 4, 52; CDALB 1941-1968;
DA3; DLB 6, 234; EXPS; HGG; LAIT 4;
MTCW 2; RGAL; RGSF; SATA 2; SSFS
1

Jacob, (Cyprien-)Max 1876-1944 .... TCLC 6
See also CA 104; 193; GFL 1789 to the
Present; GLL 2; RGWL

Jacobs, Harriet A(nn)
1813(?)-1897 .... NCLC 67
See also AFAW 1; DLB 239; FW; LAIT 2;
RGAL

Jacobs, Jim 1942- .... CLC 12
See also CA 97-100; INT 97-100

Jacobs, W(illiam) W(ymark)
1863-1943 .... TCLC 22
See also CA 121; 167; DLB 135; EXPS;
HGG; RGEL; RGSF; SSFS 2; SUFW

Jacobsen, Jens Peter 1847-1885 .... NCLC 34

Jacobsen, Josephine 1908- .... CLC 48, 102
See also CA 33-36R; CAAS 18; CANR 23,
48; CCA 1; CP

Jacobson, Dan 1929- .... CLC 4, 14
See also CA 1-4R; CANR 2, 25, 66; CN;
DLB 14, 207, 225; MTCW 1; RGSF

Jacqueline
See Carpentier (y Valmont), Alejo

Jagger, Mick 1944- .... CLC 17

Jahiz, al- c. 780-c. 869 .... CMLC 25

Jakes, John (William) 1932- . CLC 29; DAM
NOV, POP
See also AAYA 32; BEST 89:4; BPFB 2;
CA 57-60; CANR 10, 43, 66; CPW; CSW;
DA3; DLBY 83; FANT; INT CANR-10;
MTCW 1, 2; RHW; SATA 62; SFW;
TCWW 2

James I 1394-1437 .... LC 20
See also RGEL

James, Andrew
See Kirkup, James

James, C(yril) L(ionel) R(obert)
1901-1989 .... CLC 33; BLCS
See also BW 2; CA 117; 125; 128; CANR
62; DLB 125; MTCW 1

James, Daniel (Lewis) 1911-1988
See Santiago, Danny
See also CA 174; 125

James, Dynely
See Mayne, William (James Carter)

James, Henry Sr. 1811-1882 .... NCLC 53

James, Henry 1843-1916 ..... TCLC 2, 11, 24,
40, 47, 64; DA; DAB; DAC; DAM
MST, NOV; SSC 8, 32, 47; WLC
See also AMW; BPFB 2; CA 104; 132;
CDALB 1865-1917; DA3; DLB 12, 71,
74, 189; DLBD 13; EXPS; HGG; LAIT
2; MTCW 1, 2; NFS 12; RGAL; RGEL;
RGSF; SSFS 9

James, M. R.
See James, Montague (Rhodes)
See also DLB 156

James, Montague (Rhodes)
1862-1936 .... TCLC 6; SSC 16
See also CA 104; DLB 201; HGG; RGEL;
RGSF; SUFW

James, P. D. CLC 18, 46, 122
See also White, Phyllis Dorothy James
See also BEST 90:2; BPFB 2; BRWS 4;
CDBLB 1960 to Present; DLB 87; DLBD
17

James, Philip
See Moorcock, Michael (John)

James, Samuel
See Stephens, James

James, Seumas
See Stephens, James

James, Stephen
See Stephens, James

James, William 1842-1910 .... TCLC 15, 32
See also AMW; CA 109; 193; RGAL

Jameson, Anna 1794-1860 .... NCLC 43
See also DLB 99, 166

Jameson, Fredric 1934- .... CLC 142
See also DLB 67

Jami, Nur al-Din 'Abd al-Rahman
1414-1492 .... LC 9

Jammes, Francis 1868-1938 .... TCLC 75
See also GFL 1789 to the Present

Jandl, Ernst 1925-2000 .... CLC 34

Janowitz, Tama 1957- ... CLC 43, 145; DAM
POP
See also CA 106; CANR 52, 89; CN; CPW

Japrisot, Sebastien 1931- .... CLC 90
See also CMW

Jarrell, Randall 1914-1965 .... CLC 1, 2, 6, 9,
13, 49; DAM POET
See also AMW; BYA 5; CA 5-8R; 25-28R;
CABS 2; CANR 6, 34; CDALB 1941-
1968; CLR 6; CWRI; DLB 48, 52; EXPP;
MAICYA; MTCW 1, 2; PAB; PFS 2;
RGAL; SATA 7

Jarry, Alfred 1873-1907 . TCLC 2, 14; DAM
DRAM; SSC 20
See also CA 104; 153; DA3; DFS 8; DLB
192; GFL 1789 to the Present; RGWL

Jawien, Andrzej
See John Paul II, Pope

Jaynes, Roderick
See Coen, Ethan

Jeake, Samuel, Jr.
See Aiken, Conrad (Potter)

Jean Paul 1763-1825 .... NCLC 7

Jefferies, (John) Richard
1848-1887 .... NCLC 47
See also DLB 98, 141; RGEL; SATA 16;
SFW

Jeffers, (John) Robinson 1887-1962 .. CLC 2,
3, 11, 15, 54; DA; DAC; DAM MST,
POET; PC 17; WLC
See also AMWS 2; CA 85-88; CANR 35;
CDALB 1917-1929; DLB 45, 212;
MTCW 1, 2; PAB; PFS 3, 4; RGAL

Jefferson, Janet
See Mencken, H(enry) L(ouis)

Jefferson, Thomas 1743-1826 . NCLC 11, 103
See also CDALB 1640-1865; DA3; DLB
31; LAIT 1; RGAL

Jeffrey, Francis 1773-1850 .... NCLC 33
See also DLB 107

Jelakowitch, Ivan
See Heijermans, Herman

Jellicoe, (Patricia) Ann 1927- .... CLC 27
See also CA 85-88; CBD; CD; CWD;
CWRI; DLB 13, 233; FW

Jemyma
See Holley, Marietta

Jen, Gish CLC 70
See also Jen, Lillian

Jen, Lillian 1956(?)-
See Jen, Gish
See also CA 135; CANR 89

Jenkins, (John) Robin 1912- .... CLC 52
See also CA 1-4R; CANR 1; CN; DLB 14

Jennings, Elizabeth (Joan) 1926- ...... CLC 5,
14, 131
See also BRWS 5; CA 61-64; CAAS 5;
CANR 8, 39, 66; CP; CWP; DLB 27;
MTCW 1; SATA 66

Jennings, Waylon 1937- .... CLC 21

Jensen, Johannes V. 1873-1950 ...... TCLC 41
See also CA 170; DLB 214

Jensen, Laura (Linnea) 1948- .... CLC 37
See also CA 103

Jerome, Saint 345-420 .... CMLC 30
See also RGWL

Jerome, Jerome K(lapka)
1859-1927 .... TCLC 23
See also CA 119; 177; DLB 10, 34, 135;
RGEL

Jerrold, Douglas William
1803-1857 .... NCLC 2
See also DLB 158, 159; RGEL

Jewett, (Theodora) Sarah Orne
1849-1909 .... TCLC 1, 22; SSC 6, 44
See also AMW; CA 108; 127; CANR 71;
DLB 12, 74, 221; EXPS; FW; MAWW;
RGAL; RGSF; SATA 15; SSFS 4

Jewsbury, Geraldine (Endsor)
1812-1880 .... NCLC 22
See also DLB 21

Jhabvala, Ruth Prawer 1927- . CLC 4, 8, 29,
94, 138; DAB; DAM NOV
See also CA 1-4R; CANR 2, 29, 51, 74, 91;
CN; DLB 139, 194; IDFW 3, 4; INT
CANR-29; MTCW 1, 2; RGSF; RGWL;
RHW

Jibran, Kahlil
See Gibran, Kahlil

Jibran, Khalil
See Gibran, Kahlil

Jiles, Paulette 1943- .... CLC 13, 58
See also CA 101; CANR 70; CWP

Jimenez (Mantecon), Juan Ramon
1881-1958 .... TCLC 4; DAM MULT,
POET; HLC 1; PC 7
See also CA 104; 131; CANR 74; DLB 134;
EW; HW 1; MTCW 1, 2; RGWL

Jimenez, Ramon
See Jimenez (Mantecon), Juan Ramon

Jimenez Mantecon, Juan
See Jimenez (Mantecon), Juan Ramon

Jin, Ha
See Jin, Xuefei

Jin, Xuefei 1956- .... CLC 109
See also CA 152; CANR 91

Joel, Billy CLC 26
See also Joel, William Martin

Joel, William Martin 1949-
See Joel, Billy
See also CA 108

John, Saint 107th cent. -100 .... CMLC 27

John of the Cross, St. 1542-1591 .... LC 18
See also RGWL

John Paul II, Pope 1920- .... CLC 128
See also CA 106; 133

Johnson, B(ryan) S(tanley William)
1933-1973 .... CLC 6, 9
See also CA 9-12R; 53-56; CANR 9; DLB
14, 40; RGEL

Johnson, Benj. F. of Boo
See Riley, James Whitcomb

Johnson, Benjamin F. of Boo
See Riley, James Whitcomb

Johnson, Charles (Richard) 1948- .... CLC 7,
51, 65; BLC 2; DAM MULT
See also AFAW 2; AMWS 6; BW 2, 3; CA
116; CAAS 18; CANR 42, 66, 82; CN 7;
DLB 33; MTCW 2; RGAL

Johnson, Denis 1949- .... CLC 52
See also CA 117; 121; CANR 71, 99; CN;
DLB 120

Johnson, Diane 1934- .... CLC 5, 13, 48
See also BPFB 2; CA 41-44R; CANR 17,
40, 62, 95; CN; DLBY 80; INT CANR-
17; MTCW 1

Johnson, Eyvind (Olof Verner)
1900-1976 .... CLC 14
See also CA 73-76; 69-72; CANR 34, 101;
EW

Johnson, J. R.
See James, C(yril) L(ionel) R(obert)

Johnson, James Weldon
1871-1938 .. **TCLC 3, 19; BLC 2; DAM MULT, POET; PC 24**
See also AFAW 1, 2; BW 1, 3; CA 104; 125; CANR 82; CDALB 1917-1929; CLR 32; DA3; DLB 51; EXPP; MTCW 1, 2; PFS 1; RGAL; SATA 31

Johnson, Joyce 1935- .... **CLC 58**
See also CA 125; 129

Johnson, Judith (Emlyn) 1936- .... **CLC 7, 15**
See Sherwin, Judith Johnson
See also CA 25-28R, 153; CANR 34

Johnson, Lionel (Pigot)
1867-1902 .... **TCLC 19**
See also CA 117; DLB 19; RGEL

Johnson, Marguerite (Annie)
See Angelou, Maya

Johnson, Mel
See Malzberg, Barry N(athaniel)

Johnson, Pamela Hansford
1912-1981 .... **CLC 1, 7, 27**
See also CA 1-4R; 104; CANR 2, 28; DLB 15; MTCW 1, 2; RGEL

Johnson, Paul (Bede) 1928- .... **CLC 147**
See also BEST 89:4; CA 17-20R; CANR 34, 62, 100

Johnson, Robert CLC 70

Johnson, Robert 1911(?)-1938 .... **TCLC 69**
See also BW 3; CA 174

Johnson, Samuel 1709-1784 . **LC 15, 52; DA; DAB; DAC; DAM MST; WLC**
See also BRW; CDBLB 1660-1789; DLB 39, 95, 104, 142; RGEL; TEA

Johnson, Uwe 1934-1984 .. **CLC 5, 10, 15, 40**
See also CA 1-4R; 112; CANR 1, 39; DLB 75; MTCW 1; RGWL

Johnston, George (Benson) 1913- .... **CLC 51**
See also CA 1-4R; CANR 5, 20; CP; DLB 88

Johnston, Jennifer (Prudence)
1930- .... **CLC 7, 150**
See also CA 85-88; CANR 92; CN; DLB 14

Joinville, Jean de 1224(?)-1317 ..... **CMLC 38**

Jolley, (Monica) Elizabeth 1923- ..... **CLC 46; SSC 19**
See also CA 127; CAAS 13; CANR 59; CN; RGSF

Jones, Arthur Llewellyn 1863-1947
See Machen, Arthur
See also CA 104; 179; HGG

Jones, D(ouglas) G(ordon) 1929- ..... **CLC 10**
See also CA 29-32R; CANR 13, 90; CP; DLB 53

Jones, David (Michael) 1895-1974 .... **CLC 2, 4, 7, 13, 42**
See also BRW; BRWS 7; CA 9-12R; 53-56; CANR 28; CDBLB 1945-1960; DLB 20, 100; MTCW 1; PAB; RGEL

Jones, David Robert 1947-
See Bowie, David
See also CA 103

Jones, Diana Wynne 1934- .... **CLC 26**
See also AAYA 12; BYA 6; CA 49-52; CANR 4, 26, 56; CLR 23; DLB 161; FANT; JRDA; MAICYA; SAAS 7; SATA 9, 70, 108; SFW; YAW

Jones, Edward P. 1950- .... **CLC 76**
See also BW 2, 3; CA 142; CANR 79; CSW

Jones, Gayl 1949- ..... **CLC 6, 9, 131; BLC 2; DAM MULT**
See also AFAW 1, 2; BW 2, 3; CA 77-80; CANR 27, 66; CN; CSW; DA3; DLB 33; MTCW 1, 2; RGAL

Jones, James 1931-1978 ...... **CLC 1, 3, 10, 39**
See also AITN 1, 2; BPFB 2; CA 1-4R; 69-72; CANR 6; DLB 2, 143; DLBD 17; DLBY 98; MTCW 1; RGAL

Jones, John J.
See Lovecraft, H(oward) P(hillips)

Jones, LeRoi CLC 1, 2, 3, 5, 10, 14
See also Baraka, Amiri
See also MTCW 2

Jones, Louis B. 1953- .... **CLC 65**
See also CA 141; CANR 73

Jones, Madison (Percy, Jr.) 1925- ...... **CLC 4**
See also CA 13-16R; CAAS 11; CANR 7, 54, 83; CN; CSW; DLB 152

Jones, Mervyn 1922- .... **CLC 10, 52**
See also CA 45-48; CAAS 5; CANR 1, 91; CN; MTCW 1

Jones, Mick 1956(?)- .... **CLC 30**

Jones, Nettie (Pearl) 1941- .... **CLC 34**
See also BW 2; CA 137; CAAS 20; CANR 88

Jones, Preston 1936-1979 .... **CLC 10**
See also CA 73-76; 89-92; DLB 7

Jones, Robert F(rancis) 1934- .... **CLC 7**
See also CA 49-52; CANR 2, 61

Jones, Rod 1953- .... **CLC 50**
See also CA 128

Jones, Terence Graham Parry
1942- .... **CLC 21**
See also Jones, Terry; Monty Python
See also CA 112; 116; CANR 35, 93; INT 116

Jones, Terry
See Jones, Terence Graham Parry
See also SATA 67; SATA-Brief 51

Jones, Thom (Douglas) 1945(?)- .... **CLC 81**
See also CA 157; CANR 88

Jong, Erica 1942- .... **CLC 4, 6, 8, 18, 83; DAM NOV, POP**
See also AITN 1; AMWS 5; BEST 90:2; BPFB 2; CA 73-76; CANR 26, 52, 75; CN; CP; CPW; DA3; DLB 2, 5, 28, 152; FW; INT CANR-26; MTCW 1, 2

Jonson, Ben(jamin) 1572(?)-1637 .. **LC 6, 33; DA; DAB; DAC; DAM DRAM, MST, POET; DC 4; PC 17; WLC**
See also BRW 1; CDBLB Before 1660; DFS 4, 10; DLB 62, 121; RGEL; WLIT 3

Jordan, June 1936- .... **CLC 5, 11, 23, 114; BLCS; DAM MULT, POET**
See also Meyer, June
See also AAYA 2; AFAW 1, 2; BW 2, 3; CA 33-36R; CANR 25, 70; CLR 10; CP; CWP; DLB 38; GLL 2; LAIT 5; MAICYA; MTCW 1; SATA 4; YAW

Jordan, Neil (Patrick) 1950- .... **CLC 110**
See also CA 124; 130; CANR 54; CN; GLL 2; INT 130

Jordan, Pat(rick M.) 1941- .... **CLC 37**
See also CA 33-36R

Jorgensen, Ivar
See Ellison, Harlan (Jay)

Jorgenson, Ivar
See Silverberg, Robert

Joseph, George Ghevarughese CLC 70

Josephus, Flavius c. 37-100 .... **CMLC 13**
See also AW; DLB 176

Josiah Allen's Wife
See Holley, Marietta

Josipovici, Gabriel (David) 1940- ...... **CLC 6, 43**
See also CA 37-40R; CAAS 8; CANR 47, 84; CN; DLB 14

Joubert, Joseph 1754-1824 .... **NCLC 9**

Jouve, Pierre Jean 1887-1976 .... **CLC 47**
See also CA 65-68

Jovine, Francesco 1902-1950 .... **TCLC 79**

Joyce, James (Augustine Aloysius)
1882-1941 .. **TCLC 3, 8, 16, 35, 52; DA; DAB; DAC; DAM MST, NOV, POET; PC 22; SSC 3, 26, 44; WLC**
See also BRW; BYA 11; CA 104; 126; CD-BLB 1914-1945; DA3; DLB 10, 19, 36,
162; EXPN; EXPS; LAIT 3; MTCW 1, 2; NFS 7; RGSF; SSFS 1; WLIT 4

Jozsef, Attila 1905-1937 .... **TCLC 22**
See also CA 116

Juana Ines de la Cruz, Sor
1651(?)-1695 ...... **LC 5; HLCS 1; PC 24**
See also FW; LAW; RGWL; WLIT 1

Juana Inez de La Cruz, Sor
See Juana Ines de la Cruz, Sor

Judd, Cyril
See Kornbluth, C(yril) M.; Pohl, Frederik

Juenger, Ernst 1895-1998 .... **CLC 125**
See also Junger, Ernst
See also CA 101; 167; CANR 21, 47; DLB 56

Julian of Norwich 1342(?)-1416(?) . **LC 6, 52**
See also DLB 146

Julius Caesar 100B.C.-44B.C.
See Caesar, Julius
See also AW; DLB 211

Junger, Ernst
See Juenger, Ernst
See also RGWL

Junger, Sebastian 1962- .... **CLC 109**
See also AAYA 28; CA 165

Juniper, Alex
See Hospital, Janette Turner

Junius
See Luxemburg, Rosa

Just, Ward (Swift) 1935- .... **CLC 4, 27**
See also CA 25-28R; CANR 32, 87; CN; INT CANR-32

Justice, Donald (Rodney) 1925- .. **CLC 6, 19, 102; DAM POET**
See also AMWS 7; CA 5-8R; CANR 26, 54, 74; CP; CSW; DLBY 83; INT CANR-26; MTCW 2

Juvenal c. 60-c. 130 .... **CMLC 8**
See also Persius and Juvenal
See also AW; DLB 211; RGWL

Juvenis
See Bourne, Randolph S(illiman)

Kabakov, Sasha CLC 59

Kacew, Romain 1914-1980
See Gary, Romain
See also CA 108; 102

Kadare, Ismail 1936- .... **CLC 52**
See also CA 161

Kadohata, Cynthia CLC 59, 122
See also CA 140

Kafka, Franz 1883-1924 . **TCLC 2, 6, 13, 29, 47, 53, 112; DA; DAB; DAC; DAM MST, NOV; SSC 5, 29, 35; WLC**
See also AAYA 31; BPFB 2; CA 105; 126; DA3; DLB 81; EXPS; MTCW 1, 2; NFS 7; RGSF; RGWL; SFW; SSFS 3, 7, 12

Kahanovitsch, Pinkhes
See Der Nister

Kahn, Roger 1927- .... **CLC 30**
See also CA 25-28R; CANR 44, 69; DLB 171; SATA 37

Kain, Saul
See Sassoon, Siegfried (Lorraine)

Kaiser, Georg 1878-1945 .... **TCLC 9**
See also CA 106; 190; DLB 124; RGWL

Kaledin, Sergei CLC 59

Kaletski, Alexander 1946- .... **CLC 39**
See also CA 118; 143

Kalidasa fl. c. 400-455 .... **CMLC 9; PC 22**
See also RGWL

Kallman, Chester (Simon)
1921-1975 .... **CLC 2**
See also CA 45-48; 53-56; CANR 3

Kaminsky, Melvin 1926-
See Brooks, Mel
See also CA 65-68; CANR 16

Kesselring, Joseph (Otto)
1902-1967 .... **CLC 45; DAM DRAM, MST**
See also CA 150

Kessler, Jascha (Frederick) 1929- ...... **CLC 4**
See also CA 17-20R; CANR 8, 48

Kettelkamp, Larry (Dale) 1933- .... **CLC 12**
See also CA 29-32R; CANR 16; SAAS 3; SATA 2

Key, Ellen (Karolina Sofia)
1849-1926 .... **TCLC 65**

Keyber, Conny
See Fielding, Henry

Keyes, Daniel 1927- ...... **CLC 80; DA; DAC; DAM MST, NOV**
See also AAYA 23; BYA 11; CA 17-20R, 181; CAAE 181; CANR 10, 26, 54, 74; DA3; EXPN; LAIT 4; MTCW 2; NFS 2; SATA 37; SFW

Keynes, John Maynard
1883-1946 .... **TCLC 64**
See also CA 114; 162, 163; DLBD 10; MTCW 2

Khanshendel, Chiron
See Rose, Wendy

Khayyam, Omar 1048-1131 .... **CMLC 11; DAM POET; PC 8**
See also Omar Khayyam
See also DA3

Kherdian, David 1931- .... **CLC 6, 9**
See also CA 21-24R; CAAE 192; CAAS 2; CANR 39, 78; CLR 24; JRDA; LAIT 3; MAICYA; SATA 16, 74; SATA-Essay 125

Khlebnikov, Velimir TCLC 20
See also Khlebnikov, Viktor Vladimirovich
See also RGWL

Khlebnikov, Viktor Vladimirovich 1885-1922
See Khlebnikov, Velimir
See also CA 117

Khodasevich, Vladislav (Felitsianovich)
1886-1939 .... **TCLC 15**
See also CA 115

Kielland, Alexander Lange
1849-1906 .... **TCLC 5**
See also CA 104

Kiely, Benedict 1919- .... **CLC 23, 43**
See also CA 1-4R; CANR 2, 84; CN; DLB 15

Kienzle, William X(avier) 1928- ..... **CLC 25; DAM POP**
See also CA 93-96; CAAS 1; CANR 9, 31, 59; CMW; DA3; INT CANR-31; MTCW 1, 2

Kierkegaard, Soren 1813-1855 ..... **NCLC 34, 78**

Kieslowski, Krzysztof 1941-1996 .... **CLC 120**
See also CA 147; 151

Killens, John Oliver 1916-1987 .... **CLC 10**
See also BW 2; CA 77-80; 123; CAAS 2; CANR 26; DLB 33

Killigrew, Anne 1660-1685 .... **LC 4**
See also DLB 131

Killigrew, Thomas 1612-1683 .... **LC 57**
See also DLB 58; RGEL

Kim
See Simenon, Georges (Jacques Christian)

Kincaid, Jamaica 1949- ..... **CLC 43, 68, 137; BLC 2; DAM MULT, NOV**
See also AAYA 13; AFAW 2; AMWS 7; BRWS 7; BW 2, 3; CA 125; CANR 47, 59, 95; CDALBS; CLR 63; CN; DA3; DLB 157, 227; DNFS; EXPS; FW; MTCW 2; NCFS 1; NFS 3; SSFS 5, 7; YAW

King, Francis (Henry) 1923- .... **CLC 8, 53, 145; DAM NOV**
See also CA 1-4R; CANR 1, 33, 86; CN; DLB 15, 139; MTCW 1

King, Kennedy
See Brown, George Douglas

King, Martin Luther, Jr.
1929-1968 .... **CLC 83; BLC 2; DA; DAB; DAC; DAM MST, MULT; WLCS**
See also BW 2, 3; CA 25-28; CANR 27, 44; CAP 2; DA3; LAIT 5; MTCW 1, 2; SATA 14

King, Stephen (Edwin) 1947- .... **CLC 12, 26, 37, 61, 113; DAM NOV, POP; SSC 17**
See also AAYA 1, 17; AMWS 5; BEST 90:1; BPFB 2; CA 61-64; CANR 1, 30, 52, 76; CPW; DA3; DLB 143; DLBY 80; HGG; JRDA; LAIT 5; MTCW 1, 2; RGAL; SATA 9, 55; SUFW; WYAS 1; YAW

King, Steve
See King, Stephen (Edwin)

King, Thomas 1943- ... **CLC 89; DAC; DAM MULT**
See also CA 144; CANR 95; CCA 1; CN; DLB 175; NNAL; SATA 96

Kingman, Lee CLC 17
See also Natti, (Mary) Lee
See also SAAS 3; SATA 1, 67

Kingsley, Charles 1819-1875 .... **NCLC 35**
See also DLB 21, 32, 163, 190; FANT; RGEL; YABC 2

Kingsley, Sidney 1906-1995 .... **CLC 44**
See also CA 85-88; 147; CAD; DLB 7; RGAL

Kingsolver, Barbara 1955- .... **CLC 55, 81, 130; DAM POP**
See also AAYA 15; AMWS 7; CA 129; 134; CANR 60, 96; CDALBS; CPW; CSW; DA3; DLB 206; INT CA-134; LAIT 5; MTCW 2; NFS 5, 10, 12; RGAL

Kingston, Maxine (Ting Ting) Hong
1940- .... **CLC 12, 19, 58, 121; AAL; DAM MULT, NOV; WLCS**
See also AAYA 8; BPFB 2; CA 69-72; CANR 13, 38, 74, 87; CDALBS; CN; DA3; DLB 173, 212; DLBY 80; FW; INT CANR-13; LAIT 5; MAWW; MTCW 1, 2; NFS 6; RGAL; SATA 53; SSFS 3

Kinnell, Galway 1927- ..... **CLC 1, 2, 3, 5, 13, 29, 129; PC 26**
See also AMWS 3; CA 9-12R; CANR 10, 34, 66; CP; DLB 5; DLBY 87; INT CANR-34; MTCW 1, 2; PAB; PFS 9; RGAL; WP

Kinsella, Thomas 1928- .... **CLC 4, 19, 138**
See also BRWS 5; CA 17-20R; CANR 15; CP; DLB 27; MTCW 1, 2; RGEL

Kinsella, W(illiam) P(atrick) 1935- . **CLC 27, 43; DAC; DAM NOV, POP**
See also AAYA 7; BPFB 2; CA 97-100; CAAS 7; CANR 21, 35, 66, 75; CN; CPW; FANT; INT CANR-21; LAIT 5; MTCW 1, 2; RGSF

Kinsey, Alfred C(harles)
1894-1956 .... **TCLC 91**
See also CA 115; 170; MTCW 2

Kipling, (Joseph) Rudyard
1865-1936 .... **TCLC 8, 17; DA; DAB; DAC; DAM MST, POET; PC 3; SSC 5; WLC**
See also AAYA 32; BRW; BYA 4; CA 105; 120; CANR 33; CDBLB 1890-1914; CLR 39, 65; CWRI; DA3; DLB 19, 34, 141, 156; EXPS; FANT; LAIT 3; MAICYA; MTCW 1, 2; RGEL; RGSF; SATA 100; SFW; SSFS 8; SUFW; WCH; WLIT 4; YABC 2

Kirkland, Caroline M. 1801-1864 . **NCLC 85**
See also DLB 3, 73, 74; DLBD 13

Kirkup, James 1918- .... **CLC 1**
See also CA 1-4R; CAAS 4; CANR 2; DLB 27; SATA 12

Kirkwood, James 1930(?)-1989 .... **CLC 9**
See also AITN 2; CA 1-4R; 128; CANR 6, 40; GLL 2

Kirshner, Sidney
See Kingsley, Sidney

Kis, Danilo 1935-1989 .... **CLC 57**
See also CA 109; 118; 129; CANR 61; DLB 181; MTCW 1; RGSF; RGWL

Kissinger, Henry A(lfred) 1923- ..... **CLC 137**
See also CA 1-4R; CANR 2, 33, 66; MTCW 1

Kivi, Aleksis 1834-1872 .... **NCLC 30**

Kizer, Carolyn (Ashley) 1925- ... **CLC 15, 39, 80; DAM POET**
See also CA 65-68; CAAS 5; CANR 24, 70; CP; CWP; DLB 5, 169; MTCW 2

Klabund 1890-1928 .... **TCLC 44**
See also CA 162; DLB 66

Klappert, Peter 1942- .... **CLC 57**
See also CA 33-36R; CSW; DLB 5

Klein, A(braham) M(oses)
1909-1972 . **CLC 19; DAB; DAC; DAM MST**
See also CA 101; 37-40R; DLB 68; RGEL

Klein, Norma 1938-1989 .... **CLC 30**
See also AAYA 2, 35; BPFB 2; BYA 6; CA 41-44R; 128; CANR 15, 37; CLR 2, 19; INT CANR-15; JRDA; MAICYA; SAAS 1; SATA 7, 57; YAW

Klein, T(heodore) E(ibon) D(onald)
1947- .... **CLC 34**
See also CA 119; CANR 44, 75; HGG

Kleist, Heinrich von 1777-1811 ...... **NCLC 2, 37; DAM DRAM; SSC 22**
See also DLB 90; RGSF; RGWL

Klima, Ivan 1931- .... **CLC 56; DAM NOV**
See also CA 25-28R; CANR 17, 50, 91; CWW 2; DLB 232

Klimentov, Andrei Platonovich
1899-1951 .... **TCLC 14; SSC 42**
See also CA 108

Klinger, Friedrich Maximilian von
1752-1831 .... **NCLC 1**
See also DLB 94

Klingsor the Magician
See Hartmann, Sadakichi

Klopstock, Friedrich Gottlieb
1724-1803 .... **NCLC 11**
See also DLB 97; RGWL

Knapp, Caroline 1959- .... **CLC 99**
See also CA 154

Knebel, Fletcher 1911-1993 .... **CLC 14**
See also AITN 1; CA 1-4R; 140; CAAS 3; CANR 1, 36; SATA 36; SATA-Obit 75

Knickerbocker, Diedrich
See Irving, Washington

Knight, Etheridge 1931-1991 . **CLC 40; BLC 2; DAM POET; PC 14**
See also BW 1, 3; CA 21-24R; 133; CANR 23, 82; DLB 41; MTCW 2; RGAL

Knight, Sarah Kemble 1666-1727 .... **LC 7**
See also DLB 24, 200

Knister, Raymond 1899-1932 .... **TCLC 56**
See also CA 186; DLB 68; RGEL

Knowles, John 1926- . **CLC 1, 4, 10, 26; DA; DAC; DAM MST, NOV**
See also AAYA 10; BPFB 2; BYA 3; CA 17-20R; CANR 40, 74, 76; CDALB 1968-1988; CN; DLB 6; EXPN; MTCW 1, 2; NFS 2; RGAL; SATA 8, 89; YAW

Knox, Calvin M.
See Silverberg, Robert

Knox, John c. 1505-1572 .... **LC 37**
See also DLB 132

Knye, Cassandra
See Disch, Thomas M(ichael)

Koch, C(hristopher) J(ohn) 1932- .... **CLC 42**
See also CA 127; CANR 84; CN

La Fayette, Marie-(Madelaine Pioche de la Vergne) 1634-1693 .... **LC 2**
See also GFL Beginnings to 1789; RGWL

Lafayette, Rene
See Hubbard, L(afayette) Ron(ald)

La Fontaine, Jean de 1621-1695 .... **LC 50**
See also GFL Beginnings to 1789; MAI-CYA; RGWL; SATA 18

Laforgue, Jules 1860-1887 . **NCLC 5, 53; PC 14; SSC 20**
See also GFL 1789 to the Present; RGWL

Lagerkvist, Paer (Fabian) 1891-1974 ...... **CLC 7, 10, 13, 54; DAM DRAM, NOV**
See also Lagerkvist, Par
See also CA 85-88; 49-52; DA3; EW; MTCW 1, 2

Lagerkvist, Par SSC 12
See also Lagerkvist, Paer (Fabian)
See also MTCW 2; RGSF; RGWL

Lagerloef, Selma (Ottiliana Lovisa) 1858-1940 .... **TCLC 4, 36**
See also Lagerlof, Selma (Ottiliana Lovisa)
See also CA 108; MTCW 2; SATA 15

Lagerlof, Selma (Ottiliana Lovisa)
See Lagerloef, Selma (Ottiliana Lovisa)
See also CLR 7; SATA 15

La Guma, (Justin) Alex(ander) 1925-1985 .... **CLC 19; BLCS; DAM NOV**
See also AFW; BW 1, 3; CA 49-52; 118; CANR 25, 81; DLB 117, 225; MTCW 1, 2; WLIT 2

Laidlaw, A. K.
See Grieve, C(hristopher) M(urray)

Lainez, Manuel Mujica
See Mujica Lainez, Manuel
See also HW 1

Laing, R(onald) D(avid) 1927-1989 . **CLC 95**
See also CA 107; 129; CANR 34; MTCW 1

Lamartine, Alphonse (Marie Louis Prat) de 1790-1869 . **NCLC 11; DAM POET; PC 16**
See also GFL 1789 to the Present; RGWL

Lamb, Charles 1775-1834 ..... **NCLC 10; DA; DAB; DAC; DAM MST; WLC**
See also CDBLB 1789-1832; DLB 93, 107, 163; RGEL; SATA 17

Lamb, Lady Caroline 1785-1828 ... **NCLC 38**
See also DLB 116

Lamming, George (William) 1927- ... **CLC 2, 4, 66, 144; BLC 2; DAM MULT**
See also BW 2, 3; CA 85-88; CANR 26, 76; DLB 125; MTCW 1, 2

L'Amour, Louis (Dearborn) 1908-1988 ...... **CLC 25, 55; DAM NOV, POP**
See also Burns, Tex; Mayo, Jim
See also AAYA 16; AITN 2; BEST 89:2; BPFB 2; CA 1-4R; 125; CANR 3, 25, 40; CPW; DA3; DLB 206; DLBY 80; MTCW 1, 2; RGAL

Lampedusa, Giuseppe (Tomasi) di TCLC 13
See also Tomasi di Lampedusa, Giuseppe
See also CA 164; DLB 177; EW; MTCW 2; RGWL

Lampman, Archibald 1861-1899 ... **NCLC 25**
See also DLB 92; RGEL

Lancaster, Bruce 1896-1963 .... **CLC 36**
See also CA 9-10; CANR 70; CAP 1; SATA 9

Lanchester, John CLC 99

Landau, Mark Alexandrovich
See Aldanov, Mark (Alexandrovich)

Landau-Aldanov, Mark Alexandrovich
See Aldanov, Mark (Alexandrovich)

Landis, Jerry
See Simon, Paul (Frederick)

Landis, John 1950- .... **CLC 26**
See also CA 112; 122

Landolfi, Tommaso 1908-1979 .... **CLC 11, 49**
See also CA 127; 117; DLB 177

Landon, Letitia Elizabeth 1802-1838 .... **NCLC 15**
See also DLB 96

Landor, Walter Savage 1775-1864 .... **NCLC 14**
See also DLB 93, 107; RGEL

Landwirth, Heinz 1927-
See Lind, Jakov
See also CA 9-12R; CANR 7

Lane, Patrick 1939- ... **CLC 25; DAM POET**
See also CA 97-100; CANR 54; CP; DLB 53; INT 97-100

Lang, Andrew 1844-1912 .... **TCLC 16**
See also CA 114; 137; CANR 85; DLB 98, 141, 184; FANT; MAICYA; RGEL; SATA 16

Lang, Fritz 1890-1976 .... **CLC 20, 103**
See also CA 77-80; 69-72; CANR 30

Lange, John
See Crichton, (John) Michael

Langer, Elinor 1939- .... **CLC 34**
See also CA 121

Langland, William 1332(?)-1400(?) ... **LC 19; DA; DAB; DAC; DAM MST, POET**
See also BRW 1; DLB 146; RGEL; WLIT 3

Langstaff, Launcelot
See Irving, Washington

Lanier, Sidney 1842-1881 ..... **NCLC 6; DAM POET**
See also AMWS 1; DLB 64; DLBD 13; EXPP; MAICYA; RGAL; SATA 18

Lanyer, Aemilia 1569-1645 .... **LC 10, 30**
See also DLB 121

Lao-Tzu
See Lao Tzu

Lao Tzu c. 6th cent. B.C.-3rd cent. B.C. .... **CMLC 7**

Lapine, James (Elliot) 1949- .... **CLC 39**
See also CA 123; 130; CANR 54; INT 130

Larbaud, Valery (Nicolas) 1881-1957 .... **TCLC 9**
See also CA 106; 152; GFL 1789 to the Present

Lardner, Ring
See Lardner, Ring(gold) W(ilmer)
See also BPFB 2; RGAL; RGSF

Lardner, Ring W., Jr.
See Lardner, Ring(gold) W(ilmer)

Lardner, Ring(gold) W(ilmer) 1885-1933 .... **TCLC 2, 14; SSC 32**
See also Lardner, Ring
See also AMW; CA 104; 131; CDALB 1917-1929; DLB 11, 25, 86, 171; DLBD 16; MTCW 1, 2

Laredo, Betty
See Codrescu, Andrei

Larkin, Maia
See Wojciechowska, Maia (Teresa)

Larkin, Philip (Arthur) 1922-1985 ... **CLC 3, 5, 8, 9, 13, 18, 33, 39, 64; DAB; DAM MST, POET; PC 21**
See also BRWS 1; CA 5-8R; 117; CANR 24, 62; CDBLB 1960 to Present; DA3; DLB 27; MTCW 1, 2; PFS 3, 4, 12; RGEL

Larra (y Sanchez de Castro), Mariano Jose de 1809-1837 .... **NCLC 17**

Larsen, Eric 1941- .... **CLC 55**
See also CA 132

Larsen, Nella 1893-1963 .... **CLC 37; BLC 2; DAM MULT**
See also AFAW 1, 2; BW 1; CA 125; CANR 83; DLB 51; FW

Larson, Charles R(aymond) 1938- ... **CLC 31**
See also CA 53-56; CANR 4

Larson, Jonathan 1961-1996 .... **CLC 99**
See also AAYA 28; CA 156

Las Casas, Bartolome de 1474-1566 ... **LC 31**

Lasch, Christopher 1932-1994 .... **CLC 102**
See also CA 73-76; 144; CANR 25; MTCW 1, 2

Lasker-Schueler, Else 1869-1945 ... **TCLC 57**
See also CA 183; DLB 66, 124

Laski, Harold J(oseph) 1893-1950 . **TCLC 79**
See also CA 188

Latham, Jean Lee 1902-1995 .... **CLC 12**
See also AITN 1; BYA 1; CA 5-8R; CANR 7, 84; CLR 50; MAICYA; SATA 2, 68; YAW

Latham, Mavis
See Clark, Mavis Thorpe

Lathen, Emma CLC 2
See also Hennissart, Martha; Latsis, Mary J(ane)
See also BPFB 2; CMW

Lathrop, Francis
See Leiber, Fritz (Reuter, Jr.)

Latsis, Mary J(ane) 1927(?)-1997
See Lathen, Emma
See also CA 85-88; 162; CMW

Lattimore, Richmond (Alexander) 1906-1984 .... **CLC 3**
See also CA 1-4R; 112; CANR 1

Laughlin, James 1914-1997 .... **CLC 49**
See also CA 21-24R; 162; CAAS 22; CANR 9, 47; CP; DLB 48; DLBY 96, 97

Laurence, (Jean) Margaret (Wemyss) 1926-1987 . **CLC 3, 6, 13, 50, 62; DAC; DAM MST; SSC 7**
See also BYA 13; CA 5-8R; 121; CANR 33; DLB 53; FW; MTCW 1, 2; NFS 11; RGEL; RGSF; SATA-Obit 50; TCWW 2

Laurent, Antoine 1952- .... **CLC 50**

Lauscher, Hermann
See Hesse, Hermann

Lautreamont 1846-1870 .. **NCLC 12; SSC 14**
See also GFL 1789 to the Present; RGWL

Laverty, Donald
See Blish, James (Benjamin)

Lavin, Mary 1912-1996 . **CLC 4, 18, 99; SSC 4**
See also CA 9-12R; 151; CANR 33; CN; DLB 15; FW; MTCW 1; RGEL; RGSF

Lavond, Paul Dennis
See Kornbluth, C(yril) M.; Pohl, Frederik

Lawler, Raymond Evenor 1922- .... **CLC 58**
See also CA 103; CD; RGEL

Lawrence, D(avid) H(erbert Richards) 1885-1930 .... **TCLC 2, 9, 16, 33, 48, 61, 93; DA; DAB; DAC; DAM MST, NOV, POET; SSC 4, 19; WLC**
See also Chambers, Jessie
See also BPFB 2; BRW; CA 104; 121; CD-BLB 1914-1945; DA3; DLB 10, 19, 36, 98, 162, 195; EXPP; EXPS; LAIT 2, 3; MTCW 1, 2; PFS 6; RGEL; RGSF; SSFS 2, 6; WLIT 4; WP

Lawrence, T(homas) E(dward) 1888-1935 .... **TCLC 18**
See also Dale, Colin
See also BRWS 1; CA 115; 167; DLB 195

Lawrence of Arabia
See Lawrence, T(homas) E(dward)

Lawson, Henry (Archibald Hertzberg) 1867-1922 .... **TCLC 27; SSC 18**
See also CA 120; 181; DLB 230; RGEL; RGSF

Lawton, Dennis
See Faust, Frederick (Schiller)

Laxness, Halldor CLC 25
See also Gudjonsson, Halldor Kiljan
See also RGWL

Leonard, Elmore (John, Jr.) 1925- . **CLC 28, 34, 71, 120; DAM POP**
See also AAYA 22; AITN 1; BEST 89:1, 90:4; BPFB 2; CA 81-84; CANR 12, 28, 53, 76, 96; CMW; CN; CPW; DA3; DLB 173, 226; INT CANR-28; MSW; MTCW 1, 2; RGAL; TCWW 2

Leonard, Hugh CLC 19
See also Byrne, John Keyes
See also CBD; DLB 13

Leonov, Leonid (Maximovich)
1899-1994 .... **CLC 92; DAM NOV**
See also CA 129; CANR 74, 76; MTCW 1, 2

Leopardi, Giacomo 1798-1837 .... **NCLC 22**
See also EW; RGWL; WP

Le Reveler
See Artaud, Antonin (Marie Joseph)

Lerman, Eleanor 1952- .... **CLC 9**
See also CA 85-88; CANR 69

Lerman, Rhoda 1936- .... **CLC 56**
See also CA 49-52; CANR 70

Lermontov, Mikhail Yuryevich
1814-1841 .... **NCLC 5, 47; PC 18**
See also DLB 205; EW; RGWL

Leroux, Gaston 1868-1927 .... **TCLC 25**
See also CA 108; 136; CANR 69; CMW; SATA 65

Lesage, Alain-Rene 1668-1747 .... **LC 2, 28**
See also GFL Beginnings to 1789; RGWL

Leskov, N(ikolai) S(emenovich) 1831-1895
See Leskov, Nikolai (Semyonovich)

Leskov, Nikolai (Semyonovich)
1831-1895 .... **NCLC 25; SSC 34**
See also Leskov, N(ikolai) S(emenovich)
See also DLB 238

Leskov, Nikolai Semenovich
See Leskov, Nikolai (Semyonovich)

Lesser, Milton
See Marlowe, Stephen

Lessing, Doris (May) 1919- ... **CLC 1, 2, 3, 6, 10, 15, 22, 40, 94; DA; DAB; DAC; DAM MST, NOV; SSC 6; WLCS**
See also AFW; BRWS 1; CA 9-12R; CAAS 14; CANR 33, 54, 76; CD; CDBLB 1960 to Present; CN; DA3; DLB 15, 139; DLBY 85; EXPS; FW; LAIT 4; MTCW 1, 2; RGEL; RGSF; SFW; SSFS 1, 12; WLIT 2, 4

Lessing, Gotthold Ephraim 1729-1781 . **LC 8**
See also DLB 97; RGWL

Lester, Richard 1932- .... **CLC 20**

Levenson, Jay CLC 70

Lever, Charles (James)
1806-1872 .... **NCLC 23**
See also DLB 21; RGEL

Leverson, Ada 1865(?)-1936(?) .... **TCLC 18**
See also Elaine
See also CA 117; DLB 153; RGEL

Levertov, Denise 1923-1997 .. **CLC 1, 2, 3, 5, 8, 15, 28, 66; DAM POET; PC 11**
See also AMWS 3; CA 1-4R, 178; 163; CAAE 178; CAAS 19; CANR 3, 29, 50; CDALBS; CP; CWP; DLB 5, 165; EXPP; FW; INT CANR-29; MTCW 1, 2; PAB; PFS 7; RGAL; WP

Levi, Jonathan CLC 76

Levi, Peter (Chad Tigar)
1931-2000 .... **CLC 41**
See also CA 5-8R; 187; CANR 34, 80; CP; DLB 40

Levi, Primo 1919-1987 . **CLC 37, 50; SSC 12**
See also CA 13-16R; 122; CANR 12, 33, 61, 70; DLB 177; MTCW 1, 2; RGWL; TCLC 109

Levin, Ira 1929- .... **CLC 3, 6; DAM POP**
See also CA 21-24R; CANR 17, 44, 74; CMW; CN; CPW; DA3; HGG; MTCW 1, 2; SATA 66; SFW

Levin, Meyer 1905-1981 .... **CLC 7; DAM POP**
See also AITN 1; CA 9-12R; 104; CANR 15; DLB 9, 28; DLBY 81; SATA 21; SATA-Obit 27

Levine, Norman 1924- .... **CLC 54**
See also CA 73-76; CAAS 23; CANR 14, 70; DLB 88

Levine, Philip 1928- .. **CLC 2, 4, 5, 9, 14, 33, 118; DAM POET; PC 22**
See also AMWS 5; CA 9-12R; CANR 9, 37, 52; CP; DLB 5; PFS 8

Levinson, Deirdre 1931- .... **CLC 49**
See also CA 73-76; CANR 70

Levi-Strauss, Claude 1908- .... **CLC 38**
See also CA 1-4R; CANR 6, 32, 57; DLB 242; GFL 1789 to the Present; MTCW 1, 2

Levitin, Sonia (Wolff) 1934- .... **CLC 17**
See also AAYA 13; CA 29-32R; CANR 14, 32, 79; CLR 53; JRDA; MAICYA; SAAS 2; SATA 4, 68, 119; YAW

Levon, O. U.
See Kesey, Ken (Elton)

Levy, Amy 1861-1889 .... **NCLC 59**
See also DLB 156, 240

Lewes, George Henry 1817-1878 ... **NCLC 25**
See also DLB 55, 144

Lewis, Alun 1915-1944 .... **TCLC 3; SSC 40**
See also CA 104; 188; DLB 20, 162; PAB; RGEL

Lewis, C. Day
See Day Lewis, C(ecil)

Lewis, C(live) S(taples) 1898-1963 .... **CLC 1, 3, 6, 14, 27, 124; DA; DAB; DAC; DAM MST, NOV, POP; WLC**
See also AAYA 3, 39; BPFB 2; BRWS 3; CA 81-84; CANR 33, 71; CDBLB 1945-1960; CLR 3, 27; CWRI; DA3; DLB 15, 100, 160; FANT; JRDA; MAICYA; MTCW 1, 2; RGEL; SATA 13, 100; SCFW; SFW; SUFW; WCH; WYA; YAW

Lewis, Cecil Day
See Day Lewis, C(ecil)

Lewis, Janet 1899-1998 .... **CLC 41**
See also Winters, Janet Lewis
See also CA 9-12R; 172; CANR 29, 63; CAP 1; CN; DLBY 87; RHW; TCWW 2

Lewis, Matthew Gregory
1775-1818 .... **NCLC 11, 62**
See also DLB 39, 158, 178; HGG; RGEL; SUFW

Lewis, (Harry) Sinclair 1885-1951 . **TCLC 4, 13, 23, 39; DA; DAB; DAC; DAM MST, NOV; WLC**
See also AMW; BPFB 2; CA 104; 133; CDALB 1917-1929; DA3; DLB 9, 102; DLBD 1; LAIT 3; MTCW 1, 2; RGAL

Lewis, (Percy) Wyndham
1884(?)-1957 .. **TCLC 2, 9, 104; SSC 34**
See also BRW; CA 104; 157; DLB 15; FANT; MTCW 2; RGEL

Lewisohn, Ludwig 1883-1955 .... **TCLC 19**
See also CA 107; DLB 4, 9, 28, 102

Lewton, Val 1904-1951 .... **TCLC 76**
See also IDFW 3, 4

Leyner, Mark 1956- .... **CLC 92**
See also CA 110; CANR 28, 53; DA3; MTCW 2

Lezama Lima, Jose 1910-1976 .... **CLC 4, 10, 101; DAM MULT; HLCS 2**
See also CA 77-80; CANR 71; DLB 113; HW 1, 2; RGWL

L'Heureux, John (Clarke) 1934- ...... **CLC 52**
See also CA 13-16R; CANR 23, 45, 88

Liddell, C. H.
See Kuttner, Henry

Lie, Jonas (Lauritz Idemil)
1833-1908(?) .... **TCLC 5**
See also CA 115

Lieber, Joel 1937-1971 .... **CLC 6**
See also CA 73-76; 29-32R

Lieber, Stanley Martin
See Lee, Stan

Lieberman, Laurence (James)
1935- .... **CLC 4, 36**
See also CA 17-20R; CANR 8, 36, 89; CP

Lieh Tzu fl. 7th cent. B.C.-5th cent. B.C. .... **CMLC 27**

Lieksman, Anders
See Haavikko, Paavo Juhani

Li Fei-kan 1904-
See Pa Chin
See also CA 105

Lifton, Robert Jay 1926- .... **CLC 67**
See also CA 17-20R; CANR 27, 78; INT CANR-27; SATA 66

Lightfoot, Gordon 1938- .... **CLC 26**
See also CA 109

Lightman, Alan P(aige) 1948- .... **CLC 81**
See also CA 141; CANR 63

Ligotti, Thomas (Robert) 1953- ...... **CLC 44; SSC 16**
See also CA 123; CANR 49; HGG

Li Ho 791-817 .... **PC 13**

Liliencron, (Friedrich Adolf Axel) Detlev von 1844-1909 .... **TCLC 18**
See also CA 117

Lilly, William 1602-1681 .... **LC 27**

Lima, Jose Lezama
See Lezama Lima, Jose

Lima Barreto, Afonso Henrique de
1881-1922 .... **TCLC 23**
See also CA 117; 181; LAW

Lima Barreto, Afonso Henriques de
See Lima Barreto, Afonso Henrique de

Limonov, Edward 1944- .... **CLC 67**
See also CA 137

Lin, Frank
See Atherton, Gertrude (Franklin Horn)

Lincoln, Abraham 1809-1865 .... **NCLC 18**
See also LAIT 2

Lind, Jakov CLC 1, 2, 4, 27, 82
See also Landwirth, Heinz
See also CAAS 4

Lindbergh, Anne (Spencer) Morrow
1906-2001 .... **CLC 82; DAM NOV**
See also BPFB 2; CA 17-20R; 193; CANR 16, 73; MTCW 1, 2; SATA 33; SATA-Obit 125

Lindsay, David 1878(?)-1945 .... **TCLC 15**
See also CA 113; 187; FANT; SFW

Lindsay, (Nicholas) Vachel
1879-1931 . **TCLC 17; DA; DAC; DAM MST, POET; PC 23; WLC**
See also AMWS 1; CA 114; 135; CANR 79; CDALB 1865-1917; DA3; DLB 54; EXPP; RGAL; SATA 40; WP

Linke-Poot
See Doeblin, Alfred

Linney, Romulus 1930- .... **CLC 51**
See also CA 1-4R; CAD; CANR 40, 44, 79; CD; CSW; RGAL

Linton, Eliza Lynn 1822-1898 .... **NCLC 41**
See also DLB 18

Li Po 701-763 .... **CMLC 2; PC 29**
See also WP

Lipsius, Justus 1547-1606 .... **LC 16**

Lipsyte, Robert (Michael) 1938- ..... **CLC 21; DA; DAC; DAM MST, NOV**
See also AAYA 7; CA 17-20R; CANR 8, 57; CLR 23; JRDA; LAIT 5; MAICYA; SATA 5, 68, 113; WYA; YAW

Lucas, George 1944- .... **CLC 16**
See also AAYA 1, 23; CA 77-80; CANR 30; SATA 56

Lucas, Hans
See Godard, Jean-Luc

Lucas, Victoria
See Plath, Sylvia

Lucian c. 125-c. 180 .... **CMLC 32**
See also DLB 176; RGWL

Ludlam, Charles 1943-1987 .... **CLC 46, 50**
See also CA 85-88; 122; CAD; CANR 72, 86

Ludlum, Robert 1927-2001 .... **CLC 22, 43; DAM NOV, POP**
See also AAYA 10; BEST 89:1, 90:3; BPFB 2; CA 33-36R; CANR 25, 41, 68; CMW; CPW; DA3; DLBY 82; MTCW 1, 2

Ludwig, Ken **CLC 60**
See also CAD

Ludwig, Otto 1813-1865 .... **NCLC 4**
See also DLB 129

Lugones, Leopoldo 1874-1938 ...... **TCLC 15; HLCS 2**
See also CA 116; 131; HW 1

Lu Hsun **TCLC 3; SSC 20**
See also Shu-Jen, Chou

Lukacs, George **CLC 24**
See also Lukacs, Gyorgy (Szegeny von)

Lukacs, Gyorgy (Szegeny von) 1885-1971
See Lukacs, George
See also CA 101; 29-32R; CANR 62; DLB 242; EW; MTCW 2

Luke, Peter (Ambrose Cyprian) 1919-1995 .... **CLC 38**
See also CA 81-84; 147; CANR 72; CBD; CD; DLB 13

Lunar, Dennis
See Mungo, Raymond

Lurie, Alison 1926- .... **CLC 4, 5, 18, 39**
See also BPFB 2; CA 1-4R; CANR 2, 17, 50, 88; CN; DLB 2; MTCW 1; SATA 46, 112

Lustig, Arnost 1926- .... **CLC 56**
See also AAYA 3; CA 69-72; CANR 47; CWW 2; DLB 232; SATA 56

Luther, Martin 1483-1546 .... **LC 9, 37**
See also DLB 179; RGWL

Luxemburg, Rosa 1870(?)-1919 ..... **TCLC 63**
See also CA 118

Luzi, Mario 1914- .... **CLC 13**
See also CA 61-64; CANR 9, 70; CWW 2; DLB 128

L'vov, Arkady **CLC 59**

Lyly, John 1554(?)-1606 .... **LC 41; DAM DRAM; DC 7**
See also BRW 1; DLB 62, 167; RGEL

L'Ymagier
See Gourmont, Remy(-Marie-Charles) de

Lynch, David (K.) 1946- .... **CLC 66**
See also CA 124; 129

Lynch, James
See Andreyev, Leonid (Nikolaevich)

Lyndsay, Sir David 1485-1555 .... **LC 20**
See also RGEL

Lynn, Kenneth S(chuyler) 1923-2001 .... **CLC 50**
See also CA 1-4R; CANR 3, 27, 65

Lynx
See West, Rebecca

Lyons, Marcus
See Blish, James (Benjamin)

Lyotard, Jean-Francois 1924-1998 .... **TCLC 103**
See also DLB 242

Lyre, Pinchbeck
See Sassoon, Siegfried (Lorraine)

Lytle, Andrew (Nelson) 1902-1995 ... **CLC 22**
See also CA 9-12R; 150; CANR 70; CN; CSW; DLB 6; DLBY 95; RGAL; RHW

Lyttelton, George 1709-1773 .... **LC 10**
See also RGEL

Lytton of Knebworth
See Bulwer-Lytton, Edward (George Earle Lytton)

Maas, Peter 1929-2001 .... **CLC 29**
See also CA 93-96; INT CA-93-96; MTCW 2

Macaulay, Catherine 1731-1791 .... **LC 64**
See also DLB 104

Macaulay, (Emilie) Rose 1881(?)-1958 .... **TCLC 7, 44**
See also CA 104; DLB 36; RGEL; RHW

Macaulay, Thomas Babington 1800-1859 .... **NCLC 42**
See also CDBLB 1832-1890; DLB 32, 55; RGEL

MacBeth, George (Mann) 1932-1992 .... **CLC 2, 5, 9**
See also CA 25-28R; 136; CANR 61, 66; DLB 40; MTCW 1; PFS 8; SATA 4; SATA-Obit 70

MacCaig, Norman (Alexander) 1910-1996 .... **CLC 36; DAB; DAM POET**
See also BRWS 6; CA 9-12R; CANR 3, 34; CP; DLB 27; RGEL

MacCarthy, Sir (Charles Otto) Desmond 1877-1952 .... **TCLC 36**
See also CA 167

MacDiarmid, Hugh **CLC 2, 4, 11, 19, 63; PC 9**
See also Grieve, C(hristopher) M(urray)
See also CDBLB 1945-1960; DLB 20; RGEL

MacDonald, Anson
See Heinlein, Robert A(nson)

Macdonald, Cynthia 1928- .... **CLC 13, 19**
See also CA 49-52; CANR 4, 44; DLB 105

MacDonald, George 1824-1905 .... **TCLC 9, 113**
See also BYA 5; CA 106; 137; CANR 80; CLR 67; DLB 18, 163, 178; FANT; MAI-CYA; RGEL; SATA 33, 100; SFW

Macdonald, John
See Millar, Kenneth

MacDonald, John D(ann) 1916-1986 .. **CLC 3, 27, 44; DAM NOV, POP**
See also BPFB 2; CA 1-4R; 121; CANR 1, 19, 60; CMW; CPW; DLB 8; DLBY 86; MTCW 1, 2; SFW

Macdonald, John Ross
See Millar, Kenneth

Macdonald, Ross **CLC 1, 2, 3, 14, 34, 41**
See also Millar, Kenneth
See also AMWS 4; BPFB 2; DLBD 6; RGAL

MacDougal, John
See Blish, James (Benjamin)

MacDougal, John
See Blish, James (Benjamin)

MacDowell, John
See Parks, Tim(othy Harold)

MacEwen, Gwendolyn (Margaret) 1941-1987 .... **CLC 13, 55**
See also CA 9-12R; 124; CANR 7, 22; DLB 53; SATA 50; SATA-Obit 55

Macha, Karel Hynek 1810-1846 .... **NCLC 46**

Machado (y Ruiz), Antonio 1875-1939 .... **TCLC 3**
See also CA 104; 174; DLB 108; EW; HW 2; RGWL

Machado de Assis, Joaquim Maria 1839-1908 ..... **TCLC 10; BLC 2; HLCS 2; SSC 24**
See also CA 107; 153; CANR 91; RGSF; RGWL; WLIT 1

Machen, Arthur **TCLC 4; SSC 20**
See also Jones, Arthur Llewellyn
See also CA 179; DLB 36, 156, 178; RGEL

Machiavelli, Niccolo 1469-1527 ..... **LC 8, 36; DA; DAB; DAC; DAM MST; WLCS**
See also EW; LAIT 1; NFS 9; RGWL

MacInnes, Colin 1914-1976 .... **CLC 4, 23**
See also CA 69-72; 65-68; CANR 21; DLB 14; MTCW 1, 2; RGEL; RHW

MacInnes, Helen (Clark) 1907-1985 .... **CLC 27, 39; DAM POP**
See also BPFB 2; CA 1-4R; 117; CANR 1, 28, 58; CMW; CPW; DLB 87; MSW; MTCW 1, 2; SATA 22; SATA-Obit 44

Mackenzie, Compton (Edward Montague) 1883-1972 .... **CLC 18**
See also CA 21-22; 37-40R; CAP 2; DLB 34, 100; RGEL

Mackenzie, Henry 1745-1831 .... **NCLC 41**
See also DLB 39; RGEL

Mackintosh, Elizabeth 1896(?)-1952
See Tey, Josephine
See also CA 110; CMW

MacLaren, James
See Grieve, C(hristopher) M(urray)

Mac Laverty, Bernard 1942- .... **CLC 31**
See also CA 116; 118; CANR 43, 88; CN; INT CA-118; RGSF

MacLean, Alistair (Stuart) 1922(?)-1987 .. **CLC 3, 13, 50, 63; DAM POP**
See also CA 57-60; 121; CANR 28, 61; CMW; CPW; MTCW 1; SATA 23; SATA-Obit 50; TCWW 2

Maclean, Norman (Fitzroy) 1902-1990 .... **CLC 78; DAM POP; SSC 13**
See also ANW; CA 102; 132; CANR 49; CPW; DLB 206; TCWW 2

MacLeish, Archibald 1892-1982 ... **CLC 3, 8, 14, 68; DAM POET**
See also AMW; CA 9-12R; 106; CAD; CANR 33, 63; CDALBS; DLB 4, 7, 45; DLBY 82; EXPP; MTCW 1, 2; PAB; PFS 5; RGAL

MacLennan, (John) Hugh 1907-1990 . **CLC 2, 14, 92; DAC; DAM MST**
See also CA 5-8R; 142; CANR 33; DLB 68; MTCW 1, 2; RGEL

MacLeod, Alistair 1936- .... **CLC 56; DAC; DAM MST**
See also CA 123; CCA 1; DLB 60; MTCW 2; RGSF

Macleod, Fiona
See Sharp, William
See also RGEL

MacNeice, (Frederick) Louis 1907-1963 .... **CLC 1, 4, 10, 53; DAB; DAM POET**
See also BRW; CA 85-88; CANR 61; DLB 10, 20; MTCW 1, 2; RGEL

MacNeill, Dand
See Fraser, George MacDonald

Macpherson, James 1736-1796 .... **LC 29**
See also Ossian
See also DLB 109; RGEL

Macpherson, (Jean) Jay 1931- .... **CLC 14**
See also CA 5-8R; CANR 90; CP; CWP; DLB 53

MacShane, Frank 1927-1999 .... **CLC 39**
See also CA 9-12R; 186; CANR 3, 33; DLB 111

Marcus Aurelius
See Antoninus, Marcus Aurelius

Marguerite
See de Navarre, Marguerite

Marguerite de Navarre
See de Navarre, Marguerite
See also RGWL

Margulies, Donald CLC **76**
See also DFS 13; DLB 228

Marie de France c. 12th cent. - ..... CMLC **8;**
PC 22
See also DLB 208; FW; RGWL

Marie de l'Incarnation 1599-1672 ...... LC **10**

Marier, Captain Victor
See Griffith, D(avid Lewelyn) W(ark)

Mariner, Scott
See Pohl, Frederik

Marinetti, Filippo Tommaso
1876-1944 .... TCLC **10**
See also CA 107; DLB 114

Marivaux, Pierre Carlet de Chamblain de
1688-1763 .... LC **4; DC 7**
See also GFL Beginnings to 1789; RGWL

Markandaya, Kamala CLC **8, 38**
See also Taylor, Kamala (Purnaiya)
See also BYA 13

Markfield, Wallace 1926- .... CLC **8**
See also CA 69-72; CAAS 3; CN; DLB 2,
28

Markham, Edwin 1852-1940 .... TCLC **47**
See also CA 160; DLB 54, 186; RGAL

Markham, Robert
See Amis, Kingsley (William)

Marks, J
See Highwater, Jamake (Mamake)

Marks-Highwater, J
See Highwater, Jamake (Mamake)

Markson, David M(errill) 1927- .... CLC **67**
See also CA 49-52; CANR 1, 91; CN

Marley, Bob CLC **17**
See also Marley, Robert Nesta

Marley, Robert Nesta 1945-1981
See Marley, Bob
See also CA 107; 103

Marlowe, Christopher 1564-1593 ...... LC **22,**
47; DA; DAB; DAC; DAM DRAM,
MST; DC 1; WLC
See also BRW 1; CDBLB Before 1660;
DA3; DFS 1, 5, 13; DLB 62; EXPP;
RGEL; WLIT 3

Marlowe, Stephen 1928- .... CLC **70**
See also Queen, Ellery
See also CA 13-16R; CANR 6, 55; CMW;
SFW

Marmontel, Jean-Francois 1723-1799 .. LC **2**

Marquand, John P(hillips)
1893-1960 .... CLC **2, 10**
See also AMW; BPFB 2; CA 85-88; CANR
73; CMW; DLB 9, 102; MTCW 2; RGAL

Marques, Rene 1919-1979 ..... CLC **96; DAM**
MULT; HLC 2
See also CA 97-100; 85-88; CANR 78;
DLB 113; HW 1, 2; RGSF

Marquez, Gabriel (Jose) Garcia
See Garcia Marquez, Gabriel (Jose)

Marquis, Don(ald Robert Perry)
1878-1937 .... TCLC **7**
See also CA 104; 166; DLB 11, 25; RGAL

Marric, J. J.
See Creasey, John

Marryat, Frederick 1792-1848 .... NCLC **3**
See also DLB 21, 163; RGEL

Marsden, James
See Creasey, John

Marsh, Edward 1872-1953 .... TCLC **99**

Marsh, (Edith) Ngaio 1899-1982 .... CLC **7,**
53; DAM POP
See also CA 9-12R; CANR 6, 58; CMW;
CPW; DLB 77; MTCW 1, 2; RGEL

Marshall, Garry 1934- .... CLC **17**
See also AAYA 3; CA 111; SATA 60

Marshall, Paule 1929- .. CLC **27, 72; BLC 3;**
DAM MULT; SSC 3
See also AFAW 1, 2; BPFB 2; BW 2, 3;
CA 77-80; CANR 25, 73; CN; DA3; DLB
33, 157, 227; MTCW 1, 2; RGAL

Marshallik
See Zangwill, Israel

Marsten, Richard
See Hunter, Evan

Marston, John 1576-1634 .... LC **33; DAM**
DRAM
See also BRW 2; DLB 58, 172; RGEL

Martha, Henry
See Harris, Mark

Marti (y Perez), Jose (Julian)
1853-1895 ...... NCLC **63; DAM MULT;**
HLC 2
See also HW 2; LAW; RGWL; WLIT 1

Martial c. 40-c. 104 .... CMLC **35; PC 10**
See also DLB 211; RGWL

Martin, Ken
See Hubbard, L(afayette) Ron(ald)

Martin, Richard
See Creasey, John

Martin, Steve 1945- .... CLC **30**
See also CA 97-100; CANR 30, 100;
MTCW 1

Martin, Valerie 1948- .... CLC **89**
See also BEST 90:2; CA 85-88; CANR 49,
89

Martin, Violet Florence
1862-1915 .... TCLC **51**

Martin, Webber
See Silverberg, Robert

Martindale, Patrick Victor
See White, Patrick (Victor Martindale)

Martin du Gard, Roger
1881-1958 .... TCLC **24**
See also CA 118; CANR 94; DLB 65; GFL
1789 to the Present; RGWL

Martineau, Harriet 1802-1876 .... NCLC **26**
See also DLB 21, 55, 159, 163, 166, 190;
FW; RGEL; YABC 2

Martines, Julia
See O'Faolain, Julia

Martinez, Enrique Gonzalez
See Gonzalez Martinez, Enrique

Martinez, Jacinto Benavente y
See Benavente (y Martinez), Jacinto

Martinez de la Rosa, Francisco de Paula
1787-1862 .... NCLC **102**

Martinez Ruiz, Jose 1873-1967
See Azorin; Ruiz, Jose Martinez
See also CA 93-96; HW 1

Martinez Sierra, Gregorio
1881-1947 .... TCLC **6**
See also CA 115

Martinez Sierra, Maria (de la O'LeJarraga)
1874-1974 .... TCLC **6**
See also CA 115

Martinsen, Martin
See Follett, Ken(neth Martin)

Martinson, Harry (Edmund)
1904-1978 .... CLC **14**
See also CA 77-80; CANR 34

Marut, Ret
See Traven, B.

Marut, Robert
See Traven, B.

Marvell, Andrew 1621-1678 .. LC **4, 43; DA;**
DAB; DAC; DAM MST, POET; PC
10; WLC
See also BRW 2; CDBLB 1660-1789; DLB
131; EXPP; PFS 5; RGEL; WP

Marx, Karl (Heinrich) 1818-1883 . NCLC **17**
See also DLB 129

Masaoka, Shiki TCLC **18**
See also Masaoka, Tsunenori

Masaoka, Tsunenori 1867-1902
See Masaoka, Shiki
See also CA 117; 191

Masefield, John (Edward)
1878-1967 ..... CLC **11, 47; DAM POET**
See also CA 19-20; 25-28R; CANR 33;
CAP 2; CDBLB 1890-1914; DLB 10, 19,
153, 160; EXPP; FANT; MTCW 1, 2; PFS
5; RGEL; SATA 19

Maso, Carole 19(?)- .... CLC **44**
See also CA 170; GLL 2; RGAL

Mason, Bobbie Ann 1940- ... CLC **28, 43, 82;**
SSC 4
See also AAYA 5; AMWS 8; BPFB 2; CA
53-56; CANR 11, 31, 58, 83; CDALBS;
CN; CSW; DA3; DLB 173; DLBY 87;
EXPS; INT CANR-31; MTCW 1, 2; NFS
4; RGAL; RGSF; SSFS 3,8; YAW

Mason, Ernst
See Pohl, Frederik

Mason, Hunni B.
See Sternheim, (William Adolf) Carl

Mason, Lee W.
See Malzberg, Barry N(athaniel)

Mason, Nick 1945- .... CLC **35**

Mason, Tally
See Derleth, August (William)

Mass, Anna CLC **59**

Mass, William
See Gibson, William

Massinger, Philip 1583-1640 .... LC **70**
See also DLB 58; RGEL

Master Lao
See Lao Tzu

Masters, Edgar Lee 1868-1950 .... TCLC **2,**
25; DA; DAC; DAM MST, POET; PC
1, 36; WLCS
See also AMWS 1; CA 104; 133; CDALB
1865-1917; DLB 54; EXPP; MTCW 1, 2;
RGAL; WP

Masters, Hilary 1928- .... CLC **48**
See also CA 25-28R; CANR 13, 47, 97; CN

Mastrosimone, William 19(?)- .... CLC **36**
See also CA 186; CAD; CD

Mathe, Albert
See Camus, Albert

Mather, Cotton 1663-1728 .... LC **38**
See also AMWS 2; CDALB 1640-1865;
DLB 24, 30, 140; RGAL

Mather, Increase 1639-1723 .... LC **38**
See also DLB 24

Matheson, Richard (Burton) 1926- .. CLC **37**
See also AAYA 31; CA 97-100; CANR 88,
99; DLB 8, 44; HGG; INT 97-100; SCFW
2; SFW

Mathews, Harry 1930- .... CLC **6, 52**
See also CA 21-24R; CAAS 6; CANR 18,
40, 98; CN

Mathews, John Joseph 1894-1979 .. CLC **84;**
DAM MULT
See also CA 19-20; 142; CANR 45; CAP 2;
DLB 175; NNAL

Mathias, Roland (Glyn) 1915- .... CLC **45**
See also CA 97-100; CANR 19, 41; CP;
DLB 27

Matsuo Basho 1644-1694 .... LC **62; DAM**
POET; PC 3
See also Basho, Matsuo
See also PFS 2, 7

Mattheson, Rodney
　　See Creasey, John
Matthews, (James) Brander
　　1852-1929 .... **TCLC 95**
　　See also DLB 71, 78; DLBD 13
Matthews, Greg 1949- .... **CLC 45**
　　See also CA 135
Matthews, William (Procter, III)
　　1942-1997 .... **CLC 40**
　　See also CA 29-32R; 162; CAAS 18; CANR
　　12, 57; CP; DLB 5
Matthias, John (Edward) 1941- .... **CLC 9**
　　See also CA 33-36R; CANR 56; CP
Matthiessen, F(rancis) O(tto)
　　1902-1950 .... **TCLC 100**
　　See also CA 185; DLB 63
Matthiessen, Peter 1927- ... **CLC 5, 7, 11, 32,**
　　64; DAM NOV
　　See also AAYA 6, 40; AMWS 5; BEST
　　90:4; BPFB 2; CA 9-12R; CANR 21, 50,
　　73, 100; CN; DA3; DLB 6, 173; MTCW
　　1, 2; SATA 27
Maturin, Charles Robert
　　1780(?)-1824 .... **NCLC 6**
　　See also DLB 178; HGG; RGEL
Matute (Ausejo), Ana Maria 1925- .. **CLC 11**
　　See also CA 89-92; MTCW 1; RGSF
Maugham, W. S.
　　See Maugham, W(illiam) Somerset
Maugham, W(illiam) Somerset
　　1874-1965 ... **CLC 1, 11, 15, 67, 93; DA;**
　　DAB; DAC; DAM DRAM, MST, NOV;
　　SSC 8; WLC
　　See also BPFB 2; BRW; CA 5-8R; 25-28R;
　　CANR 40; CDBLB 1914-1945; CMW;
　　DA3; DLB 10, 36, 77, 100, 162, 195;
　　LAIT 3; MTCW 1, 2; RGEL; RGSF;
　　SATA 54
Maugham, William Somerset
　　See Maugham, W(illiam) Somerset
Maupassant, (Henri Rene Albert) Guy de
　　1850-1893 . **NCLC 1, 42, 83; DA; DAB;**
　　DAC; DAM MST; SSC 1; WLC
　　See also DA3; DLB 123; EW; EXPS; GFL
　　1789 to the Present; LAIT 2; RGSF;
　　RGWL; SSFS 4; SUFW; TWA
Maupin, Armistead (Jones, Jr.)
　　1944- .... **CLC 95; DAM POP**
　　See also CA 125; 130; CANR 58, 101;
　　CPW; DA3; GLL 1; INT 130; MTCW 2
Maurhut, Richard
　　See Traven, B.
Mauriac, Claude 1914-1996 .... **CLC 9**
　　See also CA 89-92; 152; CWW 2; DLB 83;
　　GFL 1789 to the Present
Mauriac, Francois (Charles)
　　1885-1970 .... **CLC 4, 9, 56; SSC 24**
　　See also CA 25-28; CAP 2; DLB 65; EW;
　　GFL 1789 to the Present; MTCW 1, 2;
　　RGWL
Mavor, Osborne Henry 1888-1951
　　See Bridie, James
　　See also CA 104
Maxwell, William (Keepers, Jr.)
　　1908-2000 .... **CLC 19**
　　See also CA 93-96; 189; CANR 54, 95; CN;
　　DLBY 80; INT 93-96
May, Elaine 1932- .... **CLC 16**
　　See also CA 124; 142; CAD; CWD; DLB
　　44
Mayakovski, Vladimir (Vladimirovich)
　　1893-1930 .... **TCLC 4, 18**
　　See also Maiakovskii, Vladimir; Mayak-
　　ovsky, Vladimir
　　See also CA 104; 158; EW; MTCW 2; SFW
Mayakovsky, Vladimir
　　See Mayakovski, Vladimir (Vladimirovich)
　　See also WP

Mayhew, Henry 1812-1887 .... **NCLC 31**
　　See also DLB 18, 55, 190
Mayle, Peter 1939(?)- .... **CLC 89**
　　See also CA 139; CANR 64
Maynard, Joyce 1953- .... **CLC 23**
　　See also CA 111; 129; CANR 64
Mayne, William (James Carter)
　　1928- .... **CLC 12**
　　See also AAYA 20; CA 9-12R; CANR 37,
　　80, 100; CLR 25; FANT; JRDA; MAI-
　　CYA; SAAS 11; SATA 6, 68, 122; YAW
Mayo, Jim
　　See L'Amour, Louis (Dearborn)
　　See also TCWW 2
Maysles, Albert 1926- .... **CLC 16**
　　See also CA 29-32R
Maysles, David 1932-1987 .... **CLC 16**
　　See also CA 191
Mazer, Norma Fox 1931- .... **CLC 26**
　　See also AAYA 5, 36; BYA 1; CA 69-72;
　　CANR 12, 32, 66; CLR 23; JRDA; MAI-
　　CYA; SAAS 1; SATA 24, 67, 105; YAW
Mazzini, Guiseppe 1805-1872 .... **NCLC 34**
McAlmon, Robert (Menzies)
　　1895-1956 .... **TCLC 97**
　　See also CA 107; 168; DLB 4, 45; DLBD
　　15; GLL 1
McAuley, James Phillip 1917-1976 .. **CLC 45**
　　See also CA 97-100; RGEL
McBain, Ed
　　See Hunter, Evan
McBrien, William (Augustine)
　　1930- .... **CLC 44**
　　See also CA 107; CANR 90
McCabe, Patrick 1955- .... **CLC 133**
　　See also CA 130; CANR 50, 90; CN; DLB
　　194
McCaffrey, Anne (Inez) 1926- .... **CLC 17;**
　　DAM NOV, POP
　　See also AAYA 6, 34; AITN 2; BEST 89:2;
　　BPFB 2; BYA 5; CA 25-28R; CANR 15,
　　35, 55, 96; CLR 49; CPW; DA3; DLB 8;
　　JRDA; MAICYA; MTCW 1, 2; SAAS 11;
　　SATA 8, 70, 116; SFW; WYA; YAW
McCall, Nathan 1955(?)- .... **CLC 86**
　　See also BW 3; CA 146; CANR 88
McCann, Arthur
　　See Campbell, John W(ood, Jr.)
McCann, Edson
　　See Pohl, Frederik
McCarthy, Charles, Jr. 1933-
　　See McCarthy, Cormac
　　See also CANR 42, 69, 101; CN; CPW;
　　CSW; DA3; DAM POP; MTCW 2
McCarthy, Cormac **CLC 4, 57, 59, 101**
　　See also McCarthy, Charles, Jr.
　　See also AMWS 8; BPFB 2; CA 13-16R;
　　CANR 10; DLB 6, 143; MTCW 2;
　　TCWW 2
McCarthy, Mary (Therese)
　　1912-1989 .. **CLC 1, 3, 5, 14, 24, 39, 59;**
　　SSC 24
　　See also AMW; BPFB 2; CA 5-8R; 129;
　　CANR 16, 50, 64; DA3; DLB 2; DLBY
　　81; FW; INT CANR-16; MAWW; MTCW
　　1, 2; RGAL
McCartney, (James) Paul 1942- . **CLC 12, 35**
　　See also CA 146
McCauley, Stephen (D.) 1955- .... **CLC 50**
　　See also CA 141
McClaren, Peter **CLC 70**
McClure, Michael (Thomas) 1932- ... **CLC 6,**
　　10
　　See also CA 21-24R; CAD; CANR 17, 46,
　　77; CD; CP; DLB 16; WP
McCorkle, Jill (Collins) 1958- .... **CLC 51**
　　See also CA 121; CSW; DLB 234; DLBY
　　87

McCourt, Frank 1930- .... **CLC 109**
　　See also CA 157; CANR 97; NCFS 1
McCourt, James 1941- .... **CLC 5**
　　See also CA 57-60; CANR 98
McCourt, Malachy 1932- .... **CLC 119**
McCoy, Horace (Stanley)
　　1897-1955 .... **TCLC 28**
　　See also CA 108; 155; CMW; DLB 9
McCrae, John 1872-1918 .... **TCLC 12**
　　See also CA 109; DLB 92; PFS 5
McCreigh, James
　　See Pohl, Frederik
McCullers, (Lula) Carson (Smith)
　　1917-1967 .... **CLC 1, 4, 10, 12, 48, 100;**
　　DA; DAB; DAC; DAM MST, NOV;
　　SSC 9, 24; WLC
　　See also AAYA 21; AMW; BPFB 2; CA
　　5-8R; 25-28R; CABS 1, 3; CANR 18;
　　CDALB 1941-1968; DA3; DFS 5; DLB
　　2, 7, 173, 228; EXPS; FW; GLL 1; LAIT
　　3, 4; MAWW; MTCW 1, 2; NFS 6;
　　RGAL; RGSF; SATA 27; SSFS 5; YAW
McCulloch, John Tyler
　　See Burroughs, Edgar Rice
McCullough, Colleen 1938(?)- .... **CLC 27,**
　　107; DAM NOV, POP
　　See also AAYA 36; BPFB 2; CA 81-84;
　　CANR 17, 46, 67, 98; CPW; DA3;
　　MTCW 1, 2; RHW
McDermott, Alice 1953- .... **CLC 90**
　　See also CA 109; CANR 40, 90
McElroy, Joseph 1930- .... **CLC 5, 47**
　　See also CA 17-20R; CN
McEwan, Ian (Russell) 1948- .... **CLC 13, 66;**
　　DAM NOV
　　See also BEST 90:4; BRWS 4; CA 61-64;
　　CANR 14, 41, 69, 87; CN; DLB 14, 194;
　　HGG; MTCW 1, 2; RGSF
McFadden, David 1940- .... **CLC 48**
　　See also CA 104; CP; DLB 60; INT 104
McFarland, Dennis 1950- .... **CLC 65**
　　See also CA 165
McGahern, John 1934- ... **CLC 5, 9, 48; SSC**
　　17
　　See also CA 17-20R; CANR 29, 68; CN;
　　DLB 14, 231; MTCW 1
McGinley, Patrick (Anthony) 1937- . **CLC 41**
　　See also CA 120; 127; CANR 56; INT 127
McGinley, Phyllis 1905-1978 .... **CLC 14**
　　See also CA 9-12R; 77-80; CANR 19;
　　CWRI; DLB 11, 48; PFS 9; SATA 2, 44;
　　SATA-Obit 24
McGinniss, Joe 1942- .... **CLC 32**
　　See also AITN 2; BEST 89:2; CA 25-28R;
　　CANR 26, 70; CPW; DLB 185; INT
　　CANR-26
McGivern, Maureen Daly
　　See Daly, Maureen
McGrath, Patrick 1950- .... **CLC 55**
　　See also CA 136; CANR 65; CN; DLB 231;
　　HGG
McGrath, Thomas (Matthew)
　　1916-1990 ..... **CLC 28, 59; DAM POET**
　　See also CA 9-12R; 132; CANR 6, 33, 95;
　　MTCW 1; SATA 41; SATA-Obit 66
McGuane, Thomas (Francis III)
　　1939- .... **CLC 3, 7, 18, 45, 127**
　　See also AITN 2; BPFB 2; CA 49-52;
　　CANR 5, 24, 49, 94; CN; DLB 2, 212;
　　DLBY 80; INT CANR-24; MTCW 1;
　　TCWW 2
McGuckian, Medbh 1950- .... **CLC 48; DAM**
　　POET; PC 27
　　See also BRWS 5; CA 143; CP; CWP; DLB
　　40
McHale, Tom 1942(?)-1982 .... **CLC 3, 5**
　　See also AITN 1; CA 77-80; 106

McIlvanney, William 1936- .... **CLC 42**
  See also CA 25-28R; CANR 61; CMW;
  DLB 14, 207

McIlwraith, Maureen Mollie Hunter
  See Hunter, Mollie
  See also SATA 2

McInerney, Jay 1955- .... **CLC 34, 112; DAM
  POP**
  See also AAYA 18; BPFB 2; CA 116; 123;
  CANR 45, 68; CN; CPW; DA3; INT 123;
  MTCW 2

McIntyre, Vonda N(eel) 1948- .... **CLC 18**
  See also CA 81-84; CANR 17, 34, 69;
  MTCW 1; SFW; YAW

McKay, Claude **TCLC 7, 41; BLC 3; DAB;
  PC 2**
  See also McKay, Festus Claudius
  See also AFAW 1, 2; DLB 4, 45, 51, 117;
  EXPP; GLL 2; LAIT 3; PAB; PFS 4;
  RGAL; WP

McKay, Festus Claudius 1889-1948
  See McKay, Claude
  See also BW 1, 3; CA 104; 124; CANR 73;
  DA; DAC; DAM MST, MULT, NOV,
  POET; MTCW 1, 2; WLC

McKuen, Rod 1933- .... **CLC 1, 3**
  See also AITN 1; CA 41-44R; CANR 40

McLoughlin, R. B.
  See Mencken, H(enry) L(ouis)

McLuhan, (Herbert) Marshall
  1911-1980 .... **CLC 37, 83**
  See also CA 9-12R; 102; CANR 12, 34, 61;
  DLB 88; INT CANR-12; MTCW 1, 2

McMillan, Terry (L.) 1951- ...... **CLC 50, 61,
  112; BLCS; DAM MULT, NOV, POP**
  See also AAYA 21; BPFB 2; BW 2, 3; CA
  140; CANR 60; CPW; DA3; MTCW 2;
  RGAL; YAW

McMurtry, Larry (Jeff) 1936- .. **CLC 2, 3, 7,
  11, 27, 44, 127; DAM NOV, POP**
  See also AAYA 15; AITN 2; AMWS 5;
  BEST 89:2; BPFB 2; CA 5-8R; CANR
  19, 43, 64; CDALB 1968-1988; CN;
  CPW; CSW; DA3; DLB 2, 143; DLBY
  80, 87; MTCW 1, 2; RGAL; TCWW 2

McNally, T. M. 1961- .... **CLC 82**

McNally, Terrence 1939- ... **CLC 4, 7, 41, 91;
  DAM DRAM**
  See also CA 45-48; CAD; CANR 2, 56; CD;
  DA3; DLB 7; GLL 1; MTCW 2

McNamer, Deirdre 1950- .... **CLC 70**

McNeal, Tom **CLC 119**

McNeile, Herman Cyril 1888-1937
  See Sapper
  See also CA 184; CMW; DLB 77

McNickle, (William) D'Arcy
  1904-1977 .... **CLC 89; DAM MULT**
  See also CA 9-12R; 85-88; CANR 5, 45;
  DLB 175, 212; NNAL; RGAL; SATA-
  Obit 22

McPhee, John (Angus) 1931- .... **CLC 36**
  See also AMWS 3; ANW; BEST 90:1; CA
  65-68; CANR 20, 46, 64, 69; CPW; DLB
  185; MTCW 1, 2

McPherson, James Alan 1943- .. **CLC 19, 77;
  BLCS**
  See also BW 1, 3; CA 25-28R; CAAS 17;
  CANR 24, 74; CN; CSW; DLB 38;
  MTCW 1, 2; RGAL; RGSF

McPherson, William (Alexander)
  1933- .... **CLC 34**
  See also CA 69-72; CANR 28; INT
  CANR-28

McTaggart, J. McT. Ellis
  See McTaggart, John McTaggart Ellis

McTaggart, John McTaggart Ellis
  1866-1925 .... **TCLC 105**
  See also CA 120

Mead, George Herbert 1873-1958 . **TCLC 89**

Mead, Margaret 1901-1978 .... **CLC 37**
  See also AITN 1; CA 1-4R; 81-84; CANR
  4; DA3; FW; MTCW 1, 2; SATA-Obit 20

Meaker, Marijane (Agnes) 1927-
  See Kerr, M. E.
  See also CA 107; CANR 37, 63; INT 107;
  JRDA; MAICYA; MTCW 1; SATA 20,
  61, 99; SATA-Essay 111; YAW

Medoff, Mark (Howard) 1940- ... **CLC 6, 23;
  DAM DRAM**
  See also AITN 1; CA 53-56; CAD; CANR
  5; CD; DFS 4; DLB 7; INT CANR-5

Medvedev, P. N.
  See Bakhtin, Mikhail Mikhailovich

Meged, Aharon
  See Megged, Aharon

Meged, Aron
  See Megged, Aharon

Megged, Aharon 1920- .... **CLC 9**
  See also CA 49-52; CAAS 13; CANR 1

Mehta, Ved (Parkash) 1934- .... **CLC 37**
  See also CA 1-4R; CANR 2, 23, 69; MTCW
  1

Melanter
  See Blackmore, R(ichard) D(oddridge)

Melies, Georges 1861-1938 .... **TCLC 81**

Melikow, Loris
  See Hofmannsthal, Hugo von

Melmoth, Sebastian
  See Wilde, Oscar (Fingal O'Flahertie Wills)

Meltzer, Milton 1915- .... **CLC 26**
  See also AAYA 8; BYA 2; CA 13-16R;
  CANR 38, 92; CLR 13; DLB 61; JRDA;
  MAICYA; SAAS 1; SATA 1, 50, 80;
  SATA-Essay 124; YAW

Melville, Herman 1819-1891 ..... **NCLC 3, 12,
  29, 45, 49, 91, 93; DA; DAB; DAC;
  DAM MST, NOV; SSC 1, 17, 46; WLC**
  See also AAYA 25; AMW; CDALB 1640-
  1865; DA3; DLB 3, 74; EXPN; EXPS;
  LAIT 1, 2; NFS 7, 9; RGAL; RGSF;
  SATA 59; SSFS 3

Membreno, Alejandro **CLC 59**

Menander c. 342B.C.-c. 293B.C. ... **CMLC 9;
  DAM DRAM; DC 3**
  See also DLB 176; RGWL

Menchu, Rigoberta 1959-
  See also CA 175; DNFS; HLCS 2; WLIT 1

Mencken, H(enry) L(ouis)
  1880-1956 .... **TCLC 13**
  See also AMW; CA 105; 125; CDALB
  1917-1929; DLB 11, 29, 63, 137, 222;
  MTCW 1, 2; RGAL

Mendelsohn, Jane 1965- .... **CLC 99**
  See also CA 154; CANR 94

Mercer, David 1928-1980 .... **CLC 5; DAM
  DRAM**
  See also CA 9-12R; 102; CANR 23; CBD;
  DLB 13; MTCW 1; RGEL

Merchant, Paul
  See Ellison, Harlan (Jay)

Meredith, George 1828-1909 .. **TCLC 17, 43;
  DAM POET**
  See also CA 117; 153; CANR 80; CDBLB
  1832-1890; DLB 18, 35, 57, 159; RGEL

Meredith, William (Morris) 1919- ... **CLC 4,
  13, 22, 55; DAM POET; PC 28**
  See also CA 9-12R; CAAS 14; CANR 6,
  40; CP; DLB 5

Merezhkovsky, Dmitry Sergeyevich
  1865-1941 .... **TCLC 29**
  See also CA 169

Merimee, Prosper 1803-1870 ... **NCLC 6, 65;
  SSC 7**
  See also DLB 119, 192; EXPS; GFL 1789
  to the Present; RGSF; RGWL; SSFS 8

Merkin, Daphne 1954- .... **CLC 44**
  See also CA 123

Merlin, Arthur
  See Blish, James (Benjamin)

Merrill, James (Ingram) 1926-1995 .. **CLC 2,
  3, 6, 8, 13, 18, 34, 91; DAM POET; PC
  28**
  See also AMWS 3; CA 13-16R; 147; CANR
  10, 49, 63; DA3; DLB 5, 165; DLBY 85;
  INT CANR-10; MTCW 1, 2; PAB; RGAL

Merriman, Alex
  See Silverberg, Robert

Merriman, Brian 1747-1805 .... **NCLC 70**

Merritt, E. B.
  See Waddington, Miriam

Merton, Thomas 1915-1968 ..... **CLC 1, 3, 11,
  34, 83; PC 10**
  See also AMWS 8; CA 5-8R; 25-28R;
  CANR 22, 53; DA3; DLB 48; DLBY 81;
  MTCW 1, 2

Merwin, W(illiam) S(tanley) 1927- ... **CLC 1,
  2, 3, 5, 8, 13, 18, 45, 88; DAM POET**
  See also AMWS 3; CA 13-16R; CANR 15,
  51; CP; DA3; DLB 5, 169; INT CANR-
  15; MTCW 1, 2; PAB; PFS 5; RGAL

Metcalf, John 1938- .... **CLC 37; SSC 43**
  See also CA 113; CN; DLB 60; RGSF

Metcalf, Suzanne
  See Baum, L(yman) Frank

Mew, Charlotte (Mary) 1870-1928 .. **TCLC 8**
  See also CA 105; 189; DLB 19, 135; RGEL

Mewshaw, Michael 1943- .... **CLC 9**
  See also CA 53-56; CANR 7, 47; DLBY 80

Meyer, Conrad Ferdinand
  1825-1905 .... **NCLC 81**
  See also DLB 129; RGWL

Meyer, Gustav 1868-1932
  See Meyrink, Gustav
  See also CA 117; 190

Meyer, June
  See Jordan, June
  See also GLL 2

Meyer, Lynn
  See Slavitt, David R(ytman)

Meyers, Jeffrey 1939- .... **CLC 39**
  See also CA 73-76; CAAE 186; CANR 54;
  DLB 111

**Meynell, Alice (Christina Gertrude
  Thompson)** 1847-1922 .... **TCLC 6**
  See also CA 104; 177; DLB 19, 98; RGEL

Meyrink, Gustav **TCLC 21**
  See also Meyer, Gustav
  See also DLB 81

Michaels, Leonard 1933- .... **CLC 6, 25; SSC
  16**
  See also CA 61-64; CANR 21, 62; CN;
  DLB 130; MTCW 1

Michaux, Henri 1899-1984 .... **CLC 8, 19**
  See also CA 85-88; 114; GFL 1789 to the
  Present; RGWL

Micheaux, Oscar (Devereaux)
  1884-1951 .... **TCLC 76**
  See also BW 3; CA 174; DLB 50; TCWW
  2

Michelangelo 1475-1564 .... **LC 12**

Michelet, Jules 1798-1874 .... **NCLC 31**
  See also GFL 1789 to the Present

Michels, Robert 1876-1936 .... **TCLC 88**

Michener, James A(lbert)
  1907(?)-1997 .... **CLC 1, 5, 11, 29, 60,
  109; DAM NOV, POP**
  See also AAYA 27; AITN 1; BEST 90:1;
  BPFB 2; CA 5-8R; 161; CANR 21, 45,
  68; CN; CPW; DA3; DLB 6; MTCW 1,
  2; RHW

Mickiewicz, Adam 1798-1855 .. **NCLC 3, 101**
  See also RGWL

Middleton, Christopher 1926- .... **CLC 13**
  See also CA 13-16R; CANR 29, 54; DLB
  40

Monroe, Lyle
See Heinlein, Robert A(nson)
Montagu, Elizabeth 1720-1800 .... **NCLC 7**
See also FW
Montagu, Mary (Pierrepont) Wortley
1689-1762 .... **LC 9, 57; PC 16**
See also DLB 95, 101; RGEL
Montagu, W. H.
See Coleridge, Samuel Taylor
Montague, John (Patrick) 1929- ..... **CLC 13, 46**
See also CA 9-12R; CANR 9, 69; CP; DLB
40; MTCW 1; PFS 12; RGEL
Montaigne, Michel (Eyquem) de
1533-1592 .... **LC 8; DA; DAB; DAC;
DAM MST; WLC**
See also EW; GFL Beginnings to 1789;
RGWL
Montale, Eugenio 1896-1981 ... **CLC 7, 9, 18;
PC 13**
See also CA 17-20R; 104; CANR 30; DLB
114; MTCW 1; RGWL
Montesquieu, Charles-Louis de Secondat
1689-1755 .... **LC 7, 69**
See also GFL Beginnings to 1789
Montessori, Maria 1870-1952 ...... **TCLC 103**
See also CA 115; 147
Montgomery, (Robert) Bruce 1921(?)-1978
See Crispin, Edmund
See also CA 179; 104; CMW
Montgomery, L(ucy) M(aud)
1874-1942 .... **TCLC 51; DAC; DAM
MST**
See also AAYA 12; BYA 1; CA 108; 137;
CLR 8; DA3; DLB 92; DLBD 14; JRDA;
MAICYA; MTCW 2; RGEL; SATA 100;
WYA; YABC 1
Montgomery, Marion H., Jr. 1925- .... **CLC 7**
See also AITN 1; CA 1-4R; CANR 3, 48;
CSW; DLB 6
Montgomery, Max
See Davenport, Guy (Mattison, Jr.)
Montherlant, Henry (Milon) de
1896-1972 ..... **CLC 8, 19; DAM DRAM**
See also CA 85-88; 37-40R; DLB 72; EW;
GFL 1789 to the Present; MTCW 1
Monty Python
See Chapman, Graham; Cleese, John
(Marwood); Gilliam, Terry (Vance); Idle,
Eric; Jones, Terence Graham Parry; Palin,
Michael (Edward)
See also AAYA 7
Moodie, Susanna (Strickland)
1803-1885 .... **NCLC 14**
See also DLB 99
Moody, Hiram F. III 1961-
See Moody, Rick
See also CA 138; CANR 64
Moody, Rick CLC 147
See also Moody, Hiram F. III
Moody, William Vaughan
1869-1910 .... **TCLC 105**
See also CA 110; 178; DLB 7, 54; RGAL
Mooney, Edward 1951-
See Mooney, Ted
See also CA 130
Mooney, Ted CLC 25
See also Mooney, Edward
Moorcock, Michael (John) 1939- ...... **CLC 5,
27, 58**
See also Bradbury, Edward P.
See also AAYA 26; CA 45-48; CAAS 5;
CANR 2, 17, 38, 64; CN; DLB 14, 231;
FANT; MTCW 1, 2; SATA 93; SFW;
SUFW

Moore, Brian 1921-1999 ... **CLC 1, 3, 5, 7, 8,
19, 32, 90; DAB; DAC; DAM MST**
See also Bryan, Michael
See also CA 1-4R; 174; CANR 1, 25, 42,
63; CCA 1; CN; FANT; MTCW 1, 2;
RGEL
Moore, Edward
See Muir, Edwin
See also RGEL
Moore, G. E. 1873-1958 .... **TCLC 89**
Moore, George Augustus
1852-1933 .... **TCLC 7; SSC 19**
See also BRW; CA 104; 177; DLB 10, 18,
57, 135; RGEL; RGSF
Moore, Lorrie CLC 39, 45, 68
See also Moore, Marie Lorena
See also DLB 234
Moore, Marianne (Craig)
1887-1972 .... **CLC 1, 2, 4, 8, 10, 13, 19,
47; DA; DAB; DAC; DAM MST,
POET; PC 4; WLCS**
See also AMW; CA 1-4R; 33-36R; CANR
3, 61; CDALB 1929-1941; DA3; DLB 45;
DLBD 7; EXPP; MAWW; MTCW 1, 2;
PAB; RGAL; SATA 20; WP
Moore, Marie Lorena 1957-
See Moore, Lorrie
See also CA 116; CANR 39, 83; CN; DLB
234
Moore, Thomas 1779-1852 .... **NCLC 6**
See also DLB 96, 144; RGEL
Moorhouse, Frank 1938- .... **SSC 40**
See also CA 118; CANR 92; CN; RGSF
Mora, Pat(ricia) 1942-
See also CA 129; CANR 57, 81; CLR 58;
DAM MULT; DLB 209; HLC 2; HW 1,
2; SATA 92
Moraga, Cherrie 1952- .... **CLC 126; DAM
MULT**
See also CA 131; CANR 66; DLB 82; FW;
GLL 1; HW 1, 2
Morand, Paul 1888-1976 .... **CLC 41; SSC 22**
See also CA 184; 69-72; DLB 65
Morante, Elsa 1918-1985 .... **CLC 8, 47**
See also CA 85-88; 117; CANR 35; DLB
177; MTCW 1, 2; RGWL
**Moravia, Alberto CLC 2, 7, 11, 27, 46; SSC
26**
See also Pincherle, Alberto
See also DLB 177; MTCW 2; RGSF;
RGWL
More, Hannah 1745-1833 .... **NCLC 27**
See also DLB 107, 109, 116, 158; RGEL
More, Henry 1614-1687 .... **LC 9**
See also DLB 126
More, Sir Thomas 1478-1535 .... **LC 10, 32**
See also BRWS 7; RGEL
Moreas, Jean TCLC 18
See also Papadiamantopoulos, Johannes
See also GFL 1789 to the Present
Morgan, Berry 1919- .... **CLC 6**
See also CA 49-52; DLB 6
Morgan, Claire
See Highsmith, (Mary) Patricia
See also GLL 1
Morgan, Edwin (George) 1920- .... **CLC 31**
See also CA 5-8R; CANR 3, 43, 90; CP;
DLB 27
Morgan, (George) Frederick 1922- .. **CLC 23**
See also CA 17-20R; CANR 21; CP
Morgan, Harriet
See Mencken, H(enry) L(ouis)
Morgan, Jane
See Cooper, James Fenimore
Morgan, Janet 1945- .... **CLC 39**
See also CA 65-68
Morgan, Lady 1776(?)-1859 .... **NCLC 29**
See also DLB 116, 158; RGEL

Morgan, Robin (Evonne) 1941- .... **CLC 2**
See also CA 69-72; CANR 29, 68; FW;
GLL 2; MTCW 1; SATA 80
Morgan, Scott
See Kuttner, Henry
Morgan, Seth 1949(?)-1990 .... **CLC 65**
See also CA 185; 132
**Morgenstern, Christian (Otto Josef
Wolfgang)** 1871-1914 .... **TCLC 8**
See also CA 105; 191
Morgenstern, S.
See Goldman, William (W.)
Mori, Rintaro
See Mori Ogai
See also CA 110
Moricz, Zsigmond 1879-1942 .... **TCLC 33**
See also CA 165
Morike, Eduard (Friedrich)
1804-1875 .... **NCLC 10**
See also DLB 133; RGWL
Mori Ogai 1862-1922 .... **TCLC 14**
See also CA 164; DLB 180; TWA
Moritz, Karl Philipp 1756-1793 .... **LC 2**
See also DLB 94
Morland, Peter Henry
See Faust, Frederick (Schiller)
Morley, Christopher (Darlington)
1890-1957 .... **TCLC 87**
See also CA 112; DLB 9; RGAL
Morren, Theophil
See Hofmannsthal, Hugo von
Morris, Bill 1952- .... **CLC 76**
Morris, Julian
See West, Morris L(anglo)
Morris, Steveland Judkins 1950(?)-
See Wonder, Stevie
See also CA 111
Morris, William 1834-1896 .... **NCLC 4**
See also BRW; CDBLB 1832-1890; DLB
18, 35, 57, 156, 178, 184; FANT; RGEL;
SFW; SUFW
Morris, Wright 1910-1998 .. **CLC 1, 3, 7, 18,
37**
See also AMW; CA 9-12R; 167; CANR 21,
81; CN; DLB 2, 206; DLBY 81; MTCW
1, 2; RGAL; TCLC 107; TCWW 2
Morrison, Arthur 1863-1945 .... **TCLC 72;
SSC 40**
See also CA 120; 157; CMW; DLB 70, 135,
197; RGEL
Morrison, Chloe Anthony Wofford
See Morrison, Toni
Morrison, James Douglas 1943-1971
See Morrison, Jim
See also CA 73-76; CANR 40
Morrison, Jim CLC 17
See also Morrison, James Douglas
Morrison, Toni 1931- . **CLC 4, 10, 22, 55, 81,
87; BLC 3; DA; DAB; DAC; DAM
MST, MULT, NOV, POP**
See also AAYA 1, 22; AFAW 1, 2; AMWS
3; BPFB 2; BW 2, 3; CA 29-32R; CANR
27, 42, 67; CDALB 1968-1988; CN;
CPW; DA3; DLB 6, 33, 143; DLBY 81;
EXPN; FW; LAIT 4; MTCW 1, 2; NFS
1, 6, 8; RGAL; RHW; SATA 57; SSFS 5;
YAW
Morrison, Van 1945- .... **CLC 21**
See also CA 116; 168
Morrissy, Mary 1958- .... **CLC 99**
Mortimer, John (Clifford) 1923- ..... **CLC 28,
43; DAM DRAM, POP**
See also CA 13-16R; CANR 21, 69; CD;
CDBLB 1960 to Present; CMW; CN;
CPW; DA3; DLB 13; INT CANR-21;
MSW; MTCW 1, 2; RGEL
Mortimer, Penelope (Ruth)
1918-1999 .... **CLC 5**
See also CA 57-60; 187; CANR 45, 88; CN

Nathan, Daniel
  See Dannay, Frederic
Nathan, George Jean 1882-1958 .... **TCLC 18**
  See also Hatteras, Owen
  See also CA 114; 169; DLB 137
Natsume, Kinnosuke 1867-1916
  See Natsume, Soseki
  See also CA 104
Natsume, Soseki TCLC 2, 10
  See also Natsume, Kinnosuke
  See also DLB 180; RGWL
Natti, (Mary) Lee 1919-
  See Kingman, Lee
  See also CA 5-8R; CANR 2
Naylor, Gloria 1950- .... **CLC 28, 52; BLC 3;**
  DA; DAC; DAM MST, MULT, NOV,
  POP; WLCS
  See also AAYA 6, 39; AFAW 1, 2; AMWS
    8; BW 2, 3; CA 107; CANR 27, 51, 74;
    CN; CPW; DA3; DLB 173; FW; MTCW
    1, 2; NFS 4, 7; RGAL
Neff, Debra CLC 59
Neihardt, John Gneisenau
  1881-1973 .... **CLC 32**
  See also CA 13-14; CANR 65; CAP 1; DLB
    9, 54; LAIT 2
Nekrasov, Nikolai Alekseevich
  1821-1878 .... **NCLC 11**
Nelligan, Emile 1879-1941 .... **TCLC 14**
  See also CA 114; DLB 92
Nelson, Willie 1933- .... **CLC 17**
  See also CA 107
Nemerov, Howard (Stanley)
  1920-1991 .... **CLC 2, 6, 9, 36; DAM**
  POET; PC 24
  See also AMW; CA 1-4R; 134; CABS 2;
    CANR 1, 27, 53; DLB 5, 6; DLBY 83;
    INT CANR-27; MTCW 1, 2; PFS 10;
    RGAL
Neruda, Pablo 1904-1973 .. **CLC 1, 2, 5, 7, 9,**
  28, 62; DA; DAB; DAC; DAM MST,
  MULT, POET; HLC 2; PC 4; WLC
  See also CA 19-20; 45-48; CAP 2; DA3;
    DNFS; HW 1; MTCW 1, 2; PFS 11;
    RGWL; WLIT 1; WP
Nerval, Gerard de 1808-1855 ... **NCLC 1, 67;**
  PC 13; SSC 18
  See also GFL 1789 to the Present; RGSF;
    RGWL
Nervo, (Jose) Amado (Ruiz de)
  1870-1919 .... **TCLC 11; HLCS 2**
  See also CA 109; 131; HW 1; LAW
Nessi, Pio Baroja y
  See Baroja (y Nessi), Pio
Nestroy, Johann 1801-1862 .... **NCLC 42**
  See also DLB 133; RGWL
Netterville, Luke
  See O'Grady, Standish (James)
Neufeld, John (Arthur) 1938- .... **CLC 17**
  See also AAYA 11; CA 25-28R; CANR 11,
    37, 56; CLR 52; MAICYA; SAAS 3;
    SATA 6, 81; YAW
Neumann, Alfred 1895-1952 .... **TCLC 100**
  See also CA 183; DLB 56
Neumann, Ferenc
  See Molnar, Ferenc
Neville, Emily Cheney 1919- .... **CLC 12**
  See also BYA 2; CA 5-8R; CANR 3, 37,
    85; JRDA; MAICYA; SAAS 2; SATA 1;
    YAW
Newbound, Bernard Slade 1930-
  See Slade, Bernard
  See also CA 81-84; CANR 49; CD; DAM
    DRAM
Newby, P(ercy) H(oward)
  1918-1997 .... **CLC 2, 13; DAM NOV**
  See also CA 5-8R; 161; CANR 32, 67; CN;
    DLB 15; MTCW 1; RGEL

Newcastle
  See Cavendish, Margaret Lucas
Newlove, Donald 1928- .... **CLC 6**
  See also CA 29-32R; CANR 25
Newlove, John (Herbert) 1938- .... **CLC 14**
  See also CA 21-24R; CANR 9, 25; CP
Newman, Charles 1938- .... **CLC 2, 8**
  See also CA 21-24R; CANR 84; CN
Newman, Edwin (Harold) 1919- ...... **CLC 14**
  See also AITN 1; CA 69-72; CANR 5
Newman, John Henry 1801-1890 . **NCLC 38,**
  99
  See also BRWS 7; DLB 18, 32, 55; RGEL
Newton, (Sir) Isaac 1642-1727 ...... **LC 35, 52**
Newton, Suzanne 1936- .... **CLC 35**
  See also BYA 7; CA 41-44R; CANR 14;
    JRDA; SATA 5, 77
New York Dept. of Ed. CLC 70
Nexo, Martin Andersen
  1869-1954 .... **TCLC 43**
  See also DLB 214
Nezval, Vitezslav 1900-1958 .... **TCLC 44**
  See also CA 123
Ng, Fae Myenne 1957(?)- .... **CLC 81**
  See also CA 146
Ngema, Mbongeni 1955- .... **CLC 57**
  See also BW 2; CA 143; CANR 84; CD
Ngugi, James T(hiong'o) CLC 3, 7, 13
  See also Ngugi wa Thiong'o
Ngugi wa Thiong'o 1938- .. **CLC 36; BLC 3;**
  DAM MULT, NOV
  See also Ngugi, James T(hiong'o)
  See also BW 2; CA 81-84; CANR 27, 58;
    DLB 125; DNFS; MTCW 1, 2; RGEL
Nichol, B(arrie) P(hillip) 1944-1988 . **CLC 18**
  See also CA 53-56; DLB 53; SATA 66
Nichols, John (Treadwell) 1940- ...... **CLC 38**
  See also CA 9-12R; CAAE 190; CAAS 2;
    CANR 6, 70; DLBY 82; TCWW 2
Nichols, Leigh
  See Koontz, Dean R(ay)
Nichols, Peter (Richard) 1927- .... **CLC 5, 36,**
  65
  See also CA 104; CANR 33, 86; CBD; CD;
    DLB 13; MTCW 1
Nicholson, Linda ed. CLC 65
Ni Chuilleanain, Eilean 1942- .... **PC 34**
  See also CA 126; CANR 53, 83; CP; CWP;
    DLB 40
Nicolas, F. R. E.
  See Freeling, Nicolas
Niedecker, Lorine 1903-1970 ..... **CLC 10, 42;**
  DAM POET
  See also CA 25-28; CAP 2; DLB 48
Nietzsche, Friedrich (Wilhelm)
  1844-1900 .... **TCLC 10, 18, 55**
  See also CA 107; 121; DLB 129; EW;
    RGWL
Nievo, Ippolito 1831-1861 .... **NCLC 22**
Nightingale, Anne Redmon 1943-
  See Redmon, Anne
  See also CA 103
Nightingale, Florence 1820-1910 ... **TCLC 85**
  See also CA 188; DLB 166
Nik. T. O.
  See Annensky, Innokenty (Fyodorovich)
Nin, Anais 1903-1977 ..... **CLC 1, 4, 8, 11, 14,**
  60, 127; DAM NOV, POP; SSC 10
  See also AITN 2; BPFB 2; CA 13-16R; 69-
    72; CANR 22, 53; DLB 2, 4, 152; GLL 2;
    MAWW; MTCW 1, 2; RGAL; RGSF
Nishida, Kitaro 1870-1945 .... **TCLC 83**
Nishiwaki, Junzaburo 1894-1982 .... **PC 15**
  See also CA 107; MJW
Nissenson, Hugh 1933- .... **CLC 4, 9**
  See also CA 17-20R; CANR 27; CN; DLB
    28

Niven, Larry CLC 8
  See also Niven, Laurence Van Cott
  See also AAYA 27; BPFB 2; BYA 10; DLB
    8; SCFW 2
Niven, Laurence Van Cott 1938-
  See Niven, Larry
  See also CA 21-24R; CAAS 12; CANR 14,
    44, 66; CPW; DAM POP; MTCW 1, 2;
    SATA 95; SFW
Nixon, Agnes Eckhardt 1927- .... **CLC 21**
  See also CA 110
Nizan, Paul 1905-1940 .... **TCLC 40**
  See also CA 161; DLB 72; GFL 1789 to the
    Present
Nkosi, Lewis 1936- ... **CLC 45; BLC 3; DAM**
  MULT
  See also BW 1, 3; CA 65-68; CANR 27,
    81; CBD; CD; DLB 157, 225
Nodier, (Jean) Charles (Emmanuel)
  1780-1844 .... **NCLC 19**
  See also DLB 119; GFL 1789 to the Present
Noguchi, Yone 1875-1947 .... **TCLC 80**
Nolan, Christopher 1965- .... **CLC 58**
  See also CA 111; CANR 88
Noon, Jeff 1957- .... **CLC 91**
  See also CA 148; CANR 83; SFW
Norden, Charles
  See Durrell, Lawrence (George)
Nordhoff, Charles (Bernard)
  1887-1947 .... **TCLC 23**
  See also CA 108; DLB 9; LAIT 1; RHW 1;
    SATA 23
Norfolk, Lawrence 1963- .... **CLC 76**
  See also CA 144; CANR 85; CN
Norman, Marsha 1947- .... **CLC 28; DAM**
  DRAM; DC 8
  See also CA 105; CABS 3; CAD; CANR
    41; CD; CSW; CWD; DFS 2; DLBY 84;
    FW
Normyx
  See Douglas, (George) Norman
Norris, Frank SSC 28
  See also Norris, (Benjamin) Frank(lin, Jr.)
  See also AMW; BPFB 2; CDALB 1865-
    1917; DLB 12, 71, 186; RGAL; TCWW
    2
Norris, (Benjamin) Frank(lin, Jr.)
  1870-1902 .... **TCLC 24**
  See also Norris, Frank
  See also CA 110; 160; NFS 12; TUS
Norris, Leslie 1921- .... **CLC 14**
  See also CA 11-12; CANR 14; CAP 1; CP;
    DLB 27
North, Andrew
  See Norton, Andre
North, Anthony
  See Koontz, Dean R(ay)
North, Captain George
  See Stevenson, Robert Louis (Balfour)
North, Milou
  See Erdrich, Louise
Northrup, B. A.
  See Hubbard, L(afayette) Ron(ald)
North Staffs
  See Hulme, T(homas) E(rnest)
Norton, Alice Mary
  See Norton, Andre
  See also MAICYA; SATA 1, 43
Norton, Andre 1912- .... **CLC 12**
  See also Norton, Alice Mary
  See also AAYA 14; BPFB 2; BYA 4; CA
    1-4R; CANR 68; CLR 50; DLB 8, 52;
    JRDA; MTCW 1; SATA 91; YAW
Norton, Caroline 1808-1877 .... **NCLC 47**
  See also DLB 21, 159, 199
Norway, Nevil Shute 1899-1960
  See Shute, Nevil
  See also CA 102; 93-96; CANR 85; MTCW
    2; RHW; SFW

Oppen, George 1908-1984 ..... **CLC 7, 13, 34; PC 35**
See also CA 13-16R; 113; CANR 8, 82; DLB 5, 165; TCLC 107

Oppenheim, E(dward) Phillips
1866-1946 .... **TCLC 45**
See also CA 111; CMW; DLB 70

Opuls, Max
See Ophuls, Max

Origen c. 185-c. 254 .... **CMLC 19**

Orlovitz, Gil 1918-1973 .... **CLC 22**
See also CA 77-80; 45-48; DLB 2, 5

Orris
See Ingelow, Jean

Ortega y Gasset, Jose 1883-1955 ... **TCLC 9; DAM MULT; HLC 2**
See also CA 106; 130; HW 1, 2; MTCW 1, 2

Ortese, Anna Maria 1914- .... **CLC 89**
See also DLB 177

Ortiz, Simon J(oseph) 1941- . **CLC 45; DAM MULT, POET; PC 17**
See also AMWS 4; CA 134; CANR 69; CP; DLB 120, 175; EXPP; NNAL; PFS 4; RGAL

Orton, Joe CLC 4, 13, 43; DC 3
See also Orton, John Kingsley
See also BRWS 5; CBD; CDBLB 1960 to Present; DFS 3, 6; DLB 13; GLL 1; MTCW 2; RGEL; WLIT 4

Orton, John Kingsley 1933-1967
See Orton, Joe
See also CA 85-88; CANR 35, 66; DAM DRAM; MTCW 1, 2

Orwell, George TCLC 2, 6, 15, 31, 51; DAB; WLC
See also Blair, Eric (Arthur)
See also BPFB 3; BYA 5; CDBLB 1945-1960; CLR 68; DLB 15, 98, 195; EXPN; LAIT 5; NFS 3, 7; RGEL; SCFW 2; SFW; SSFS 4; WLIT 4; YAW

Osborne, David
See Silverberg, Robert

Osborne, George
See Silverberg, Robert

Osborne, John (James) 1929-1994 .... **CLC 1, 2, 5, 11, 45; DA; DAB; DAC; DAM DRAM, MST; WLC**
See also BRWS 1; CA 13-16R; 147; CANR 21, 56; CDBLB 1945-1960; DFS 4; DLB 13; MTCW 1, 2; RGEL

Osborne, Lawrence 1958- .... **CLC 50**
See also CA 189

Osbourne, Lloyd 1868-1947 .... **TCLC 93**

Oshima, Nagisa 1932- .... **CLC 20**
See also CA 116; 121; CANR 78

Oskison, John Milton 1874-1947 .. **TCLC 35; DAM MULT**
See also CA 144; CANR 84; DLB 175; NNAL

Ossian c. 3rd cent. - .... **CMLC 28**
See also Macpherson, James

Ossoli, Sarah Margaret (Fuller)
1810-1850 .... **NCLC 5, 50**
See also Fuller, Margaret; Fuller, Sarah Margaret
See also CDALB 1640-1865; DLB 1, 59, 73, 183, 223, 239; FW; SATA 25

Ostriker, Alicia (Suskin) 1937- .... **CLC 132**
See also CA 25-28R; CAAS 24; CANR 10, 30, 62, 99; CWP; DLB 120; EXPP

Ostrovsky, Alexander 1823-1886 .. **NCLC 30, 57**

Otero, Blas de 1916-1979 .... **CLC 11**
See also CA 89-92; DLB 134

Otto, Rudolf 1869-1937 .... **TCLC 85**

Otto, Whitney 1955- .... **CLC 70**
See also CA 140

Ouida TCLC 43
See also De La Ramee, (Marie) Louise
See also DLB 18, 156; RGEL

Ouologuem, Yambo 1940- .... **CLC 146**
See also CA 111; 176

Ousmane, Sembene 1923- ... **CLC 66; BLC 3**
See also Sembene, Ousmane
See also BW 1, 3; CA 117; 125; CANR 81; CWW 2; MTCW 1

Ovid 43B.C.-17 . **CMLC 7; DAM POET; PC 2**
See also DA3; DLB 211; RGWL; WP

Owen, Hugh
See Faust, Frederick (Schiller)

Owen, Wilfred (Edward Salter)
1893-1918 .... **TCLC 5, 27; DA; DAB; DAC; DAM MST, POET; PC 19; WLC**
See also CA 104; 141; CDBLB 1914-1945; DLB 20; EXPP; MTCW 2; PFS 10; RGEL; WLIT 4

Owens, Rochelle 1936- .... **CLC 8**
See also CA 17-20R; CAAS 2; CAD; CANR 39; CD; CP; CWD; CWP

Oz, Amos 1939- ...... **CLC 5, 8, 11, 27, 33, 54; DAM NOV**
See also CA 53-56; CANR 27, 47, 65; CWW 2; MTCW 1, 2; RGSF

Ozick, Cynthia 1928- .... **CLC 3, 7, 28, 62; DAM NOV, POP; SSC 15**
See also AMWS 5; BEST 90:1; CA 17-20R; CANR 23, 58; CN; CPW; DA3; DLB 28, 152; DLBY 82; EXPS; INT CANR-23; MTCW 1, 2; RGAL; RGSF; SSFS 3, 12

Ozu, Yasujiro 1903-1963 .... **CLC 16**
See also CA 112

Pacheco, C.
See Pessoa, Fernando (Antonio Nogueira)

Pacheco, Jose Emilio 1939-
See also CA 111; 131; CANR 65; DAM MULT; HLC 2; HW 1, 2; RGSF

Pa Chin CLC 18
See also Li Fei-kan

Pack, Robert 1929- .... **CLC 13**
See also CA 1-4R; CANR 3, 44, 82; CP; DLB 5; SATA 118

Padgett, Lewis
See Kuttner, Henry

Padilla (Lorenzo), Heberto
1932-2000 .... **CLC 38**
See also AITN 1; CA 123; 131; 189; HW 1

Page, Jimmy 1944- .... **CLC 12**

Page, Louise 1955- .... **CLC 40**
See also CA 140; CANR 76; CBD; CD; CWD; DLB 233

Page, P(atricia) K(athleen) 1916- ...... **CLC 7, 18; DAC; DAM MST; PC 12**
See also Cape, Judith
See also CA 53-56; CANR 4, 22, 65; CP; DLB 68; MTCW 1; RGEL

Page, Stanton
See Fuller, Henry Blake

Page, Stanton
See Fuller, Henry Blake

Page, Thomas Nelson 1853-1922 .... **SSC 23**
See also CA 118; 177; DLB 12, 78; DLBD 13; RGAL

Pagels, Elaine Hiesey 1943- .... **CLC 104**
See also CA 45-48; CANR 2, 24, 51; FW

Paget, Violet 1856-1935
See Lee, Vernon
See also CA 104; 166; GLL 1; HGG

Paget-Lowe, Henry
See Lovecraft, H(oward) P(hillips)

Paglia, Camille (Anna) 1947- .... **CLC 68**
See also CA 140; CANR 72; CPW; FW; GLL 2; MTCW 2

Paige, Richard
See Koontz, Dean R(ay)

Paine, Thomas 1737-1809 .... **NCLC 62**
See also AMWS 1; CDALB 1640-1865; DLB 31, 43, 73, 158; LAIT 1; RGAL; RGEL

Pakenham, Antonia
See Fraser, (Lady)Antonia (Pakenham)

Palamas, Kostes 1859-1943 .... **TCLC 5**
See also CA 105; 190; RGWL

Palazzeschi, Aldo 1885-1974 .... **CLC 11**
See also CA 89-92; 53-56; DLB 114

Pales Matos, Luis 1898-1959
See also HLCS 2; HW 1

Paley, Grace 1922- .... **CLC 4, 6, 37, 140; DAM POP; SSC 8**
See also AMWS 6; CA 25-28R; CANR 13, 46, 74; CN; CPW; DA3; DLB 28; EXPS; FW; INT CANR-13; MTCW 1, 2; RGAL; RGSF; SSFS 3

Palin, Michael (Edward) 1943- .... **CLC 21**
See also Monty Python
See also CA 107; CANR 35; SATA 67

Palliser, Charles 1947- .... **CLC 65**
See also CA 136; CANR 76; CN

Palma, Ricardo 1833-1919 .... **TCLC 29**
See also CA 168

Pancake, Breece Dexter 1952-1979
See Pancake, Breece D'J
See also CA 123; 109

Pancake, Breece D'J CLC 29
See also Pancake, Breece Dexter
See also DLB 130

Panchenko, Nikolai CLC 59

Pankhurst, Emmeline (Goulden)
1858-1928 .... **TCLC 100**
See also CA 116; FW

Panko, Rudy
See Gogol, Nikolai (Vasilyevich)

Papadiamantis, Alexandros
1851-1911 .... **TCLC 29**
See also CA 168

Papadiamantopoulos, Johannes 1856-1910
See Moreas, Jean
See also CA 117

Papini, Giovanni 1881-1956 .... **TCLC 22**
See also CA 121; 180

Paracelsus 1493-1541 .... **LC 14**
See also DLB 179

Parasol, Peter
See Stevens, Wallace

Pardo Bazan, Emilia 1851-1921 .... **SSC 30**
See also FW; RGSF; RGWL

Pareto, Vilfredo 1848-1923 .... **TCLC 69**
See also CA 175

Paretsky, Sara 1947- .. **CLC 135; DAM POP**
See also AAYA 30; BEST 90:3; CA 125; 129; CANR 59, 95; CMW; CPW; DA3; INT 129; RGAL

Parfenie, Maria
See Codrescu, Andrei

Parini, Jay (Lee) 1948- .... **CLC 54, 133**
See also CA 97-100; CAAS 16; CANR 32, 87

Park, Jordan
See Kornbluth, C(yril) M.; Pohl, Frederik

Park, Robert E(zra) 1864-1944 ..... **TCLC 73**
See also CA 122; 165

Parker, Bert
See Ellison, Harlan (Jay)

Parker, Dorothy (Rothschild)
1893-1967 .... **CLC 15, 68; DAM POET; PC 28; SSC 2**
See also CA 19-20; 25-28R; CAP 2; DA3; DLB 11, 45, 86; EXPP; MTCW 1, 2

Perez Galdos, Benito 1843-1920 ... **TCLC 27; HLCS 2**
See also CA 125; 153; HW 1; RGWL

Peri Rossi, Cristina 1941-
See also CA 131; CANR 59, 81; DLB 145; HLCS 2; HW 1, 2

Perlata
See Peret, Benjamin

Perloff, Marjorie G(abrielle)
1931- .... **CLC 137**
See also CA 57-60; CANR 7, 22, 49

Perrault, Charles 1628-1703 ... **LC 2, 56; DC 12**
See also BYA 4; GFL Beginnings to 1789; MAICYA; RGWL; SATA 25

Perry, Anne 1938- .... **CLC 126**
See also CA 101; CANR 22, 50, 84; CMW; CN; CPW

Perry, Brighton
See Sherwood, Robert E(mmet)

Perse, St.-John
See Leger, (Marie-Rene Auguste) Alexis Saint-Leger

Perutz, Leo(pold) 1882-1957 .... **TCLC 60**
See also CA 147; DLB 81

Peseenz, Tulio F.
See Lopez y Fuentes, Gregorio

Pesetsky, Bette 1932- .... **CLC 28**
See also CA 133; DLB 130

Peshkov, Alexei Maximovich 1868-1936
See Gorky, Maxim
See also CA 105; 141; CANR 83; DA; DAC; DAM DRAM, MST, NOV; MTCW 2

Pessoa, Fernando (Antonio Nogueira)
1898-1935 .... **TCLC 27; DAM MULT; HLC 2; PC 20**
See also CA 125; 183; EW; RGWL; WP

Peterkin, Julia Mood 1880-1961 ...... **CLC 31**
See also CA 102; DLB 9

Peters, Joan K(aren) 1945- .... **CLC 39**
See also CA 158

Peters, Robert L(ouis) 1924- .... **CLC 7**
See also CA 13-16R; CAAS 8; CP; DLB 105

Petofi, Sandor 1823-1849 .... **NCLC 21**
See also RGWL

Petrakis, Harry Mark 1923- .... **CLC 3**
See also CA 9-12R; CANR 4, 30, 85; CN

Petrarch 1304-1374 .... **CMLC 20; DAM POET; PC 8**
See also DA3; RGWL

Petronius c. 20-66 .... **CMLC 34**
See also DLB 211; EW; RGWL

Petrov, Evgeny TCLC 21
See also Kataev, Evgeny Petrovich

Petry, Ann (Lane) 1908-1997 ... **CLC 1, 7, 18**
See also AFAW 1, 2; BPFB 3; BW 1, 3; BYA 2; CA 5-8R; 157; CAAS 6; CANR 4, 46; CLR 12; CN; DLB 76; JRDA; LAIT 1; MAICYA; MAICYAS; MTCW 1; RGAL; SATA 5; SATA-Obit 94; TCLC 112

Petursson, Halligrimur 1614-1674 .... **LC 8**

Peychinovich
See Vazov, Ivan (Minchov)

Phaedrus c. 15B.C.-c. 50 .... **CMLC 25**
See also DLB 211

Phelps (Ward), Elizabeth Stuart
See Phelps, Elizabeth Stuart
See also FW

Phelps, Elizabeth Stuart
1844-1911 .... **TCLC 113**
See also Dickinson, Mrs.Herbert Ward
See also DLB 74

Philips, Katherine 1632-1664 .... **LC 30**
See also DLB 131; RGEL

Philipson, Morris H. 1926- .... **CLC 53**
See also CA 1-4R; CANR 4

Phillips, Caryl 1958- . **CLC 96; BLCS; DAM MULT**
See also BRWS 5; BW 2; CA 141; CANR 63; CBD; CD; CN; DA3; DLB 157; MTCW 2; WLIT 4

Phillips, David Graham
1867-1911 .... **TCLC 44**
See also CA 108; 176; DLB 9, 12; RGAL

Phillips, Jack
See Sandburg, Carl (August)

Phillips, Jayne Anne 1952- .... **CLC 15, 33, 139; SSC 16**
See also BPFB 3; CA 101; CANR 24, 50, 96; CN; CSW; DLBY 80; INT CANR-24; MTCW 1, 2; RGAL; RGSF; SSFS 4

Phillips, Richard
See Dick, Philip K(indred)

Phillips, Robert (Schaeffer) 1938- .... **CLC 28**
See also CA 17-20R; CAAS 13; CANR 8; DLB 105

Phillips, Ward
See Lovecraft, H(oward) P(hillips)

Piccolo, Lucio 1901-1969 .... **CLC 13**
See also CA 97-100; DLB 114

Pickthall, Marjorie L(owry) C(hristie)
1883-1922 .... **TCLC 21**
See also CA 107; DLB 92

Pico della Mirandola, Giovanni
1463-1494 .... **LC 15**

Piercy, Marge 1936- .... **CLC 3, 6, 14, 18, 27, 62, 128; PC 29**
See also BPFB 3; CA 21-24R; CAAE 187; CAAS 1; CANR 13, 43, 66; CN; CP; CWP; DLB 120, 227; EXPP; FW; MTCW 1, 2; PFS 9; SFW

Piers, Robert
See Anthony, Piers

Pieyre de Mandiargues, Andre 1909-1991
See Mandiargues, Andre Pieyre de
See also CA 103; 136; CANR 22, 82; GFL 1789 to the Present

Pilnyak, Boris TCLC 23
See also Vogau, Boris Andreyevich

Pincherle, Alberto 1907-1990 .... **CLC 11, 18; DAM NOV**
See also Moravia, Alberto
See also CA 25-28R; 132; CANR 33, 63; MTCW 1

Pinckney, Darryl 1953- .... **CLC 76**
See also BW 2, 3; CA 143; CANR 79

Pindar 518(?)B.C.-438(?)B.C. .... **CMLC 12; PC 19**
See also DLB 176; RGWL

Pineda, Cecile 1942- .... **CLC 39**
See also CA 118; DLB 209

Pinero, Arthur Wing 1855-1934 ... **TCLC 32; DAM DRAM**
See also CA 110; 153; DLB 10; RGEL

Pinero, Miguel (Antonio Gomez)
1946-1988 .... **CLC 4, 55**
See also CA 61-64; 125; CAD; CANR 29, 90; HW 1

Pinget, Robert 1919-1997 .... **CLC 7, 13, 37**
See also CA 85-88; 160; CWW 2; DLB 83; GFL 1789 to the Present

Pink Floyd
See Barrett, (Roger) Syd; Gilmour, David; Mason, Nick; Waters, Roger; Wright, Rick

Pinkney, Edward 1802-1828 .... **NCLC 31**

Pinkwater, Daniel Manus 1941- .... **CLC 35**
See also Pinkwater, Manus
See also AAYA 1; BYA 9; CA 29-32R; CANR 12, 38, 89; CLR 4; CSW; FANT; JRDA; MAICYA; SAAS 3; SATA 46, 76, 114; SFW; YAW

Pinkwater, Manus
See Pinkwater, Daniel Manus
See also SATA 8

Pinsky, Robert 1940- .... **CLC 9, 19, 38, 94, 121; DAM POET; PC 27**
See also AMWS 6; CA 29-32R; CAAS 4; CANR 58, 97; CP; DA3; DLBY 82, 98; MTCW 2; RGAL

Pinta, Harold
See Pinter, Harold

Pinter, Harold 1930- .. **CLC 1, 3, 6, 9, 11, 15, 27, 58, 73; DA; DAB; DAC; DAM DRAM, MST; DC 15; WLC**
See also BRWS 1; CA 5-8R; CANR 33, 65; CBD; CD; CDBLB 1960 to Present; DA3; DFS 3, 5, 7; DLB 13; IDFW 3, 4; MTCW 1, 2; RGEL

Piozzi, Hester Lynch (Thrale)
1741-1821 .... **NCLC 57**
See also DLB 104, 142

Pirandello, Luigi 1867-1936 ...... **TCLC 4, 29; DA; DAB; DAC; DAM DRAM, MST; DC 5; SSC 22; WLC**
See also CA 104; 153; DA3; DFS 4, 9; MTCW 2; RGSF; RGWL

Pirsig, Robert M(aynard) 1928- ... **CLC 4, 6, 73; DAM POP**
See also CA 53-56; CANR 42, 74; CPW 1; DA3; MTCW 1, 2; SATA 39

Pisarev, Dmitry Ivanovich
1840-1868 .... **NCLC 25**

Pix, Mary (Griffith) 1666-1709 .... **LC 8**
See also DLB 80

Pixerecourt, (Rene Charles) Guilbert de
1773-1844 .... **NCLC 39**
See also DLB 192; GFL 1789 to the Present

Plaatje, Sol(omon) T(shekisho)
1878-1932 .... **TCLC 73; BLCS**
See also BW 2, 3; CA 141; CANR 79; DLB 225

Plaidy, Jean
See Hibbert, Eleanor Alice Burford

Planche, James Robinson
1796-1880 .... **NCLC 42**
See also RGEL

Plant, Robert 1948- .... **CLC 12**

Plante, David (Robert) 1940- ...... **CLC 7, 23, 38; DAM NOV**
See also CA 37-40R; CANR 12, 36, 58, 82; CN; DLBY 83; INT CANR-12; MTCW 1

Plath, Sylvia 1932-1963 ..... **CLC 1, 2, 3, 5, 9, 11, 14, 17, 50, 51, 62, 111; DA; DAB; DAC; DAM MST, POET; PC 1; WLC**
See also AAYA 13; AMWS 1; BPFB 3; CA 19-20; CANR 34, 101; CAP 2; CDALB 1941-1968; DA3; DLB 5, 6, 152; EXPN; EXPP; FW; LAIT 4; MTCW 1, 2; NFS 1; PAB; PFS 1; RGAL; SATA 96; WP; YAW

Plato c. 428B.C.-347B.C. .... **CMLC 8; DA; DAB; DAC; DAM MST; WLCS**
See also DA3; DLB 176; LAIT 1; RGWL

Platonov, Andrei
See Klimentov, Andrei Platonovich

Platt, Kin 1911- .... **CLC 26**
See also AAYA 11; CA 17-20R; CANR 11; JRDA; SAAS 17; SATA 21, 86

Plautus c. 254B.C.-c. 184B.C. ...... **CMLC 24; DC 6**
See also DLB 211; RGWL

Plick et Plock
See Simenon, Georges (Jacques Christian)

Plieksans, Janis
See Rainis, Janis
See also CA 170; DLB 220

Plimpton, George (Ames) 1927- .... **CLC 36**
See also AITN 1; CA 21-24R; CANR 32, 70; DLB 185, 241; MTCW 1, 2; SATA 10

Pliny the Elder c. 23-79 .... **CMLC 23**
See also DLB 211

Pritchett, V(ictor) S(awdon)
1900-1997 ...... **CLC 5, 13, 15, 41; DAM NOV; SSC 14**
See also BPFB 3; BRWS 3; CA 61-64; 157; CANR 31, 63; CN; DA3; DLB 15, 139; MTCW 1, 2; RGEL; RGSF

Private 19022
See Manning, Frederic

Probst, Mark 1925- .... **CLC 59**
See also CA 130

Prokosch, Frederic 1908-1989 ...... **CLC 4, 48**
See also CA 73-76; 128; CANR 82; DLB 48; MTCW 2

Propertius, Sextus c. 50B.C.-c.
16B.C. .... **CMLC 32**
See also AW; DLB 211; RGWL

Prophet, The
See Dreiser, Theodore (Herman Albert)

Prose, Francine 1947- .... **CLC 45**
See also CA 109; 112; CANR 46, 95; DLB 234; SATA 101

Proudhon
See Cunha, Euclides (Rodrigues Pimenta) da

Proulx, Annie
See Proulx, E(dna) Annie
See also AMWS 7

Proulx, E(dna) Annie 1935- .. **CLC 81; DAM POP**
See also Proulx, Annie
See also BPFB 3; CA 145; CANR 65; CN; CPW 1; DA3; MTCW 2

Proust,
(Valentin-Louis-George-Eugene-)Marcel
1871-1922 . **TCLC 7, 13, 33; DA; DAB; DAC; DAM MST, NOV; WLC**
See also BPFB 3; CA 104; 120; DA3; DLB 65; EW; GFL 1789 to the Present; MTCW 1, 2; RGWL

Prowler, Harley
See Masters, Edgar Lee

Prus, Boleslaw 1845-1912 .... **TCLC 48**
See also RGWL

Pryor, Richard (Franklin Lenox Thomas)
1940- .... **CLC 26**
See also CA 122; 152

Przybyszewski, Stanislaw
1868-1927 .... **TCLC 36**
See also CA 160; DLB 66

Pteleon
See Grieve, C(hristopher) M(urray)
See also DAM POET

Puckett, Lute
See Masters, Edgar Lee

Puig, Manuel 1932-1990 .... **CLC 3, 5, 10, 28, 65, 133; DAM MULT; HLC 2**
See also BPFB 3; CA 45-48; CANR 2, 32, 63; DA3; DLB 113; DNFS; GLL 1; HW 1, 2; MTCW 1, 2; RGWL; WLIT 1

Pulitzer, Joseph 1847-1911 .... **TCLC 76**
See also CA 114; DLB 23

Purchas, Samuel 1577(?)-1626 .... **LC 70**
See also DLB 151

Purdy, A(lfred) W(ellington)
1918-2000 .... **CLC 3, 6, 14, 50; DAC; DAM MST, POET**
See also CA 81-84; 189; CAAS 17; CANR 42, 66; CP; DLB 88; PFS 5; RGEL

Purdy, James (Amos) 1923- .... **CLC 2, 4, 10, 28, 52**
See also AMWS 7; CA 33-36R; CAAS 1; CANR 19, 51; CN; DLB 2; INT CANR-19; MTCW 1; RGAL

Pure, Simon
See Swinnerton, Frank Arthur

Pushkin, Alexander (Sergeyevich)
1799-1837 . **NCLC 3, 27, 83; DA; DAB; DAC; DAM DRAM, MST, POET; PC 10; SSC 27; WLC**
See also DA3; DLB 205; EW; EXPS; RGSF; RGWL; SATA 61; SSFS 9

P'u Sung-ling 1640-1715 .... **LC 49; SSC 31**

Putnam, Arthur Lee
See Alger, Horatio, Jr.

Puzo, Mario 1920-1999 .... **CLC 1, 2, 6, 36, 107; DAM NOV, POP**
See also BPFB 3; CA 65-68; 185; CANR 4, 42, 65, 99; CN; CPW; DA3; DLB 6; MTCW 1, 2; RGAL

Pygge, Edward
See Barnes, Julian (Patrick)

Pyle, Ernest Taylor 1900-1945
See Pyle, Ernie
See also CA 115; 160

Pyle, Ernie TCLC 75
See also Pyle, Ernest Taylor
See also DLB 29; MTCW 2

Pyle, Howard 1853-1911 .... **TCLC 81**
See also BYA 2; CA 109; 137; CLR 22; DLB 42, 188; DLBD 13; LAIT 1; MAI-CYA; SATA 16, 100; YAW

Pym, Barbara (Mary Crampton)
1913-1980 .... **CLC 13, 19, 37, 111**
See also BPFB 3; BRWS 2; CA 13-14; 97-100; CANR 13, 34; CAP 1; DLB 14, 207; DLBY 87; MTCW 1, 2; RGEL

Pynchon, Thomas (Ruggles, Jr.)
1937- ...... **CLC 2, 3, 6, 9, 11, 18, 33, 62, 72, 123; DA; DAB; DAC; DAM MST, NOV, POP; SSC 14; WLC**
See also AMWS 2; BEST 90:2; BPFB 3; CA 17-20R; CANR 22, 46, 73; CN; CPW 1; DA3; DLB 2, 173; MTCW 1, 2; RGAL; SFW; TUS

Pythagoras c. 582B.C.-c. 507B.C. . **CMLC 22**
See also DLB 176

Q
See Quiller-Couch, Sir Arthur (Thomas)

Qian Zhongshu
See Ch'ien Chung-shu

Qroll
See Dagerman, Stig (Halvard)

Quarrington, Paul (Lewis) 1953- ..... **CLC 65**
See also CA 129; CANR 62, 95

Quasimodo, Salvatore 1901-1968 ..... **CLC 10**
See also CA 13-16; 25-28R; CAP 1; DLB 114; MTCW 1; RGWL

Quay, Stephen 1947- .... **CLC 95**
See also CA 189

Quay, Timothy 1947- .... **CLC 95**
See also CA 189

Queen, Ellery CLC 3, 11
See also Dannay, Frederic; Davidson, Avram (James); Deming, Richard; Fairman, Paul W.; Flora, Fletcher; Hoch, Edward D(entinger); Kane, Henry; Lee, Manfred B(ennington); Marlowe, Stephen; Powell, (Oval) Talmage; Sheldon, Walter J(ames); Sturgeon, Theodore (Hamilton); Tracy, Don(ald Fiske); Vance, John Holbrook
See also BPFB 3; CMW; MSW; RGAL

Queen, Ellery, Jr.
See Dannay, Frederic; Lee, Manfred B(ennington)

Queneau, Raymond 1903-1976 ..... **CLC 2, 5, 10, 42**
See also CA 77-80; 69-72; CANR 32; DLB 72; GFL 1789 to the Present; MTCW 1, 2; RGWL

Quevedo, Francisco de 1580-1645 .... **LC 23**

Quiller-Couch, Sir Arthur (Thomas)
1863-1944 .... **TCLC 53**
See also CA 118; 166; DLB 135, 153, 190; HGG; RGEL; SUFW

Quin, Ann (Marie) 1936-1973 .... **CLC 6**
See also CA 9-12R; 45-48; DLB 14, 231

Quinn, Martin
See Smith, Martin Cruz

Quinn, Peter 1947- .... **CLC 91**

Quinn, Simon
See Smith, Martin Cruz

Quintana, Leroy V. 1944- .... **PC 36**
See also CA 131; CANR 65; DAM MULT; DLB 82; HLC 2; HW 1, 2

Quiroga, Horacio (Sylvestre)
1878-1937 .... **TCLC 20; DAM MULT; HLC 2**
See also CA 117; 131; HW 1; LAW; MTCW 1; RGSF; WLIT 1

Quoirez, Francoise 1935- .... **CLC 9**
See also Sagan, Francoise
See also CA 49-52; CANR 6, 39, 73; CWW 2; MTCW 1, 2

Raabe, Wilhelm (Karl) 1831-1910 . **TCLC 45**
See also CA 167; DLB 129

Rabe, David (William) 1940- .. **CLC 4, 8, 33; DAM DRAM**
See also CA 85-88; CABS 3; CAD; CANR 59; CD; DFS 3, 8, 13; DLB 7, 228

Rabelais, Francois 1494-1553 .... **LC 5, 60; DA; DAB; DAC; DAM MST; WLC**
See also EW; GFL Beginnings to 1789; RGWL

Rabinovitch, Sholem 1859-1916
See Aleichem, Sholom
See also CA 104

Rabinyan, Dorit 1972- .... **CLC 119**
See also CA 170

Rachilde
See Vallette, Marguerite Eymery

Racine, Jean 1639-1699 . **LC 28; DAB; DAM MST**
See also DA3; GFL Beginnings to 1789; RGWL

Radcliffe, Ann (Ward) 1764-1823 ... **NCLC 6, 55**
See also DLB 39, 178; HGG; RGEL; SUFW; WLIT 3

Radiguet, Raymond 1903-1923 ...... **TCLC 29**
See also CA 162; DLB 65; GFL 1789 to the Present; RGWL

Radnoti, Miklos 1909-1944 .... **TCLC 16**
See also CA 118; RGWL

Rado, James 1939- .... **CLC 17**
See also CA 105

Radvanyi, Netty 1900-1983
See Seghers, Anna
See also CA 85-88; 110; CANR 82

Rae, Ben
See Griffiths, Trevor

Raeburn, John (Hay) 1941- .... **CLC 34**
See also CA 57-60

Ragni, Gerome 1942-1991 .... **CLC 17**
See also CA 105; 134

Rahv, Philip CLC 24
See also Greenberg, Ivan
See also DLB 137

Raimund, Ferdinand Jakob
1790-1836 .... **NCLC 69**
See also DLB 90

Raine, Craig (Anthony) 1944- .. **CLC 32, 103**
See also CA 108; CANR 29, 51; CP; DLB 40; PFS 7

Raine, Kathleen (Jessie) 1908- ..... **CLC 7, 45**
See also CA 85-88; CANR 46; CP; DLB 20; MTCW 1; RGEL

Rhys, Jean 1894(?)-1979 ...... **CLC 2, 4, 6, 14, 19, 51, 124; DAM NOV; SSC 21**
See also BRWS 2; CA 25-28R; 85-88; CANR 35, 62; CDBLB 1945-1960; DA3; DLB 36, 117, 162; DNFS; MTCW 1, 2; RGEL; RGSF; RHW

Ribeiro, Darcy 1922-1997 .... **CLC 34**
See also CA 33-36R; 156

Ribeiro, Joao Ubaldo (Osorio Pimentel) 1941- .... **CLC 10, 67**
See also CA 81-84

Ribman, Ronald (Burt) 1932- .... **CLC 7**
See also CA 21-24R; CAD; CANR 46, 80; CD

Ricci, Nino 1959- .... **CLC 70**
See also CA 137; CCA 1

Rice, Anne 1941- .. **CLC 41, 128; DAM POP**
See also Rampling, Anne
See also AAYA 9; AMWS 7; BEST 89:2; BPFB 3; CA 65-68; CANR 12, 36, 53, 74, 100; CN; CPW; CSW; DA3; GLL 2; HGG; MTCW 2; YAW

Rice, Elmer (Leopold) 1892-1967 ...... **CLC 7, 49; DAM DRAM**
See also CA 21-22; 25-28R; CAP 2; DFS 12; DLB 4, 7; MTCW 1, 2; RGAL

Rice, Tim(othy Miles Bindon) 1944- .... **CLC 21**
See also CA 103; CANR 46; DFS 7

Rich, Adrienne (Cecile) 1929- ... **CLC 3, 6, 7, 11, 18, 36, 73, 76, 125; DAM POET; PC 5**
See also AMWS 1; CA 9-12R; CANR 20, 53, 74; CDALBS; CP; CSW; CWP; DA3; DLB 5, 67; EXPP; FW; MAWW; MTCW 1, 2; PAB; RGAL; WP

Rich, Barbara
See Graves, Robert (von Ranke)

Rich, Robert
See Trumbo, Dalton

Richard, Keith CLC 17
See also Richards, Keith

Richards, David Adams 1950- .... **CLC 59; DAC**
See also CA 93-96; CANR 60; DLB 53

Richards, I(vor) A(rmstrong) 1893-1979 .... **CLC 14, 24**
See also BRWS 2; CA 41-44R; 89-92; CANR 34, 74; DLB 27; MTCW 2; RGEL

Richards, Keith 1943-
See Richard, Keith
See also CA 107; CANR 77

Richardson, Anne
See Roiphe, Anne (Richardson)

Richardson, Dorothy Miller 1873-1957 .... **TCLC 3**
See also CA 104; 192; DLB 36; FW; RGEL

Richardson (Robertson), Ethel Florence Lindesay 1870-1946
See Richardson, Henry Handel
See also CA 105; 190; DLB 230; RHW

Richardson, Henry Handel TCLC 4
See also Richardson (Robertson), Ethel Florence Lindesay
See also DLB 197; RGEL; RGSF

Richardson, John 1796-1852 .... **NCLC 55; DAC**
See also CCA 1; DLB 99

Richardson, Samuel 1689-1761 ...... **LC 1, 44; DA; DAB; DAC; DAM MST, NOV; WLC**
See also CDBLB 1660-1789; DLB 39; RGEL; WLIT 3

Richler, Mordecai 1931-2001 .... **CLC 3, 5, 9, 13, 18, 46, 70; DAC; DAM MST, NOV**
See also AITN 1; CA 65-68; CANR 31, 62; CCA 1; CLR 17; CWRI; DLB 53; MAICYA; MTCW 1, 2; RGEL; SATA 44, 98; SATA-Brief 27

Richter, Conrad (Michael) 1890-1968 .... **CLC 30**
See also AAYA 21; BYA 2; CA 5-8R; 25-28R; CANR 23; DLB 9, 212; LAIT 1; MTCW 1, 2; RGAL; SATA 3; TCWW 2; YAW

Ricostranza, Tom
See Ellis, Trey

Riddell, Charlotte 1832-1906 .... **TCLC 40**
See also CA 165; DLB 156

Ridge, John Rollin 1827-1867 ...... **NCLC 82; DAM MULT**
See also CA 144; DLB 175; NNAL

Ridgeway, Jason
See Marlowe, Stephen

Ridgway, Keith 1965- .... **CLC 119**
See also CA 172

Riding, Laura CLC 3, 7
See also Jackson, Laura (Riding)
See also RGAL

Riefenstahl, Berta Helene Amalia 1902-
See Riefenstahl, Leni
See also CA 108

Riefenstahl, Leni CLC 16
See also Riefenstahl, Berta Helene Amalia

Riffe, Ernest
See Bergman, (Ernst) Ingmar

Riggs, (Rolla) Lynn 1899-1954 ..... **TCLC 56; DAM MULT**
See also CA 144; DLB 175; NNAL

Riis, Jacob A(ugust) 1849-1914 ..... **TCLC 80**
See also CA 113; 168; DLB 23

Riley, James Whitcomb 1849-1916 .... **TCLC 51; DAM POET**
See also CA 118; 137; MAICYA; RGAL; SATA 17

Riley, Tex
See Creasey, John

Rilke, Rainer Maria 1875-1926 .. **TCLC 1, 6, 19; DAM POET; PC 2**
See also CA 104; 132; CANR 62, 99; DA3; DLB 81; MTCW 1, 2; RGWL; WP

Rimbaud, (Jean Nicolas) Arthur 1854-1891 . **NCLC 4, 35, 82; DA; DAB; DAC; DAM MST, POET; PC 3; WLC**
See also DA3; EW; GFL 1789 to the Present; RGWL; TWA; WP

Rinehart, Mary Roberts 1876-1958 .... **TCLC 52**
See also BPFB 3; CA 108; 166; RGAL; RHW

Ringmaster, The
See Mencken, H(enry) L(ouis)

Ringwood, Gwen(dolyn Margaret) Pharis 1910-1984 .... **CLC 48**
See also CA 148; 112; DLB 88

Rio, Michel 19(?)- .... **CLC 43**

Ritsos, Giannes
See Ritsos, Yannis

Ritsos, Yannis 1909-1990 .... **CLC 6, 13, 31**
See also CA 77-80; 133; CANR 39, 61; MTCW 1; RGWL

Ritter, Erika 1948(?)- .... **CLC 52**
See also CD; CWD

Rivera, Jose Eustasio 1889-1928 ... **TCLC 35**
See also CA 162; HW 1, 2

Rivera, Tomas 1935-1984
See also CA 49-52; CANR 32; DLB 82; HLCS 2; HW 1; RGAL; TCWW 2; WLIT 1

Rivers, Conrad Kent 1933-1968 .... **CLC 1**
See also BW 1; CA 85-88; DLB 41

Rivers, Elfrida
See Bradley, Marion Zimmer
See also GLL 1

Riverside, John
See Heinlein, Robert A(nson)

Rizal, Jose 1861-1896 .... **NCLC 27**

Roa Bastos, Augusto (Antonio) 1917- .... **CLC 45; DAM MULT; HLC 2**
See also CA 131; DLB 113; HW 1; LAW; RGSF; WLIT 1

Robbe-Grillet, Alain 1922- .... **CLC 1, 2, 4, 6, 8, 10, 14, 43, 128**
See also BPFB 3; CA 9-12R; CANR 33, 65; DLB 83; GFL 1789 to the Present; IDFW 3, 4; MTCW 1, 2; RGWL

Robbins, Harold 1916-1997 .... **CLC 5; DAM NOV**
See also BPFB 3; CA 73-76; 162; CANR 26, 54; DA3; MTCW 1, 2

Robbins, Thomas Eugene 1936-
See Robbins, Tom
See also CA 81-84; CANR 29, 59, 95; CN; CPW; CSW; DA3; DAM NOV, POP; MTCW 1, 2

Robbins, Tom CLC 9, 32, 64
See also Robbins, Thomas Eugene
See also AAYA 32; BEST 90:3; BPFB 3; DLBY 80; MTCW 2

Robbins, Trina 1938- .... **CLC 21**
See also CA 128

Roberts, Charles G(eorge) D(ouglas) 1860-1943 .... **TCLC 8**
See also CA 105; 188; CLR 33; CWRI; DLB 92; RGEL; RGSF; SATA 88; SATA-Brief 29

Roberts, Elizabeth Madox 1886-1941 .... **TCLC 68**
See also CA 111; 166; CWRI; DLB 9, 54, 102; RGAL; RHW; SATA 33; SATA-Brief 27

Roberts, Kate 1891-1985 .... **CLC 15**
See also CA 107; 116

Roberts, Keith (John Kingston) 1935-2000 .... **CLC 14**
See also CA 25-28R; CANR 46; SFW

Roberts, Kenneth (Lewis) 1885-1957 .... **TCLC 23**
See also CA 109; DLB 9; RGAL; RHW

Roberts, Michele (Brigitte) 1949- ..... **CLC 48**
See also CA 115; CANR 58; CN; DLB 231; FW

Robertson, Ellis
See Ellison, Harlan (Jay); Silverberg, Robert

Robertson, Thomas William 1829-1871 .... **NCLC 35; DAM DRAM**
See also Robertson, Tom
See also EW

Robertson, Tom
See Robertson, Thomas William
See also RGEL

Robeson, Kenneth
See Dent, Lester

Robinson, Edwin Arlington 1869-1935 ..... **TCLC 5, 101; DA; DAC; DAM MST, POET; PC 1, 35**
See also AMW; CA 104; 133; CDALB 1865-1917; DLB 54; EXPP; MTCW 1, 2; PAB; PFS 4; RGAL; WP

Robinson, Henry Crabb 1775-1867 .... **NCLC 15**
See also DLB 107

Robinson, Jill 1936- .... **CLC 10**
See also CA 102; INT 102

Robinson, Kim Stanley 1952- .... **CLC 34**
See also AAYA 26; CA 126; CN; SATA 109; SFW

Robinson, Lloyd
See Silverberg, Robert

Robinson, Marilynne 1944- .... **CLC 25**
See also CA 116; CANR 80; CN; DLB 206

Robinson, Smokey CLC 21
See also Robinson, William, Jr.

Robinson, William, Jr. 1940-
See Robinson, Smokey
See also CA 116
Robison, Mary 1949- .... **CLC 42, 98**
See also CA 113; 116; CANR 87; CN; DLB
130; INT 116; RGSF
Rod, Edouard 1857-1910 .... **TCLC 52**
Roddenberry, Eugene Wesley 1921-1991
See Roddenberry, Gene
See also CA 110; 135; CANR 37; SATA 45;
SATA-Obit 69
Roddenberry, Gene CLC 17
See also Roddenberry, Eugene Wesley
See also AAYA 5; SATA-Obit 69
Rodgers, Mary 1931- .... **CLC 12**
See also BYA 5; CA 49-52; CANR 8, 55,
90; CLR 20; CWRI; INT CANR-8; JRDA;
MAICYA; SATA 8
Rodgers, W(illiam) R(obert)
1909-1969 .... **CLC 7**
See also CA 85-88; DLB 20; RGEL
Rodman, Eric
See Silverberg, Robert
Rodman, Howard 1920(?)-1985 .... **CLC 65**
See also CA 118
Rodman, Maia
See Wojciechowska, Maia (Teresa)
Rodo, Jose Enrique 1871(?)-1917
See also CA 178; HLCS 2; HW 2
Rodolph, Utto
See Ouologuem, Yambo
Rodriguez, Claudio 1934-1999 .... **CLC 10**
See also CA 188; DLB 134
Rodriguez, Richard 1944-
See also CA 110; CANR 66; DAM MULT;
DLB 82; HLC 2; HW 1, 2; LAIT 5; WLIT
1
Roelvaag, O(le) E(dvart)
1876-1931 .... **TCLC 17**
See also Rolvaag, O(le) E(dvart)
See also CA 117; 171; DLB 9
Roethke, Theodore (Huebner)
1908-1963 .... **CLC 1, 3, 8, 11, 19, 46,
101; DAM POET; PC 15**
See also AMW; CA 81-84; CABS 2;
CDALB 1941-1968; DA3; DLB 5, 206;
EXPP; MTCW 1, 2; PAB; PFS 3; RGAL;
WP
Rogers, Samuel 1763-1855 .... **NCLC 69**
See also DLB 93; RGEL
Rogers, Thomas Hunton 1927- .... **CLC 57**
See also CA 89-92; INT 89-92
Rogers, Will(iam Penn Adair)
1879-1935 ... **TCLC 8, 71; DAM MULT**
See also CA 105; 144; DA3; DLB 11;
MTCW 2; NNAL
Rogin, Gilbert 1929- .... **CLC 18**
See also CA 65-68; CANR 15
Rohan, Koda
See Koda Shigeyuki
Rohlfs, Anna Katharine Green
See Green, Anna Katharine
Rohmer, Eric CLC 16
See also Scherer, Jean-Marie Maurice
Rohmer, Sax TCLC 28
See also Ward, Arthur Henry Sarsfield
See also DLB 70
Roiphe, Anne (Richardson) 1935- .. **CLC 3, 9**
See also CA 89-92; CANR 45, 73; DLBY
80; INT 89-92
Rojas, Fernando de 1475-1541 .... **LC 23;
HLCS 1**
See also RGWL
Rojas, Gonzalo 1917-
See also HLCS 2; HW 2
Rojas, Gonzalo 1917-
See also CA 178; HLCS 2

**Rolfe, Frederick (William Serafino Austin
Lewis Mary)** 1860-1913 .... **TCLC 12**
See also Corvo, Baron
See also CA 107; DLB 34, 156; RGEL
Rolland, Romain 1866-1944 .... **TCLC 23**
See also CA 118; DLB 65; GFL 1789 to the
Present; RGWL
Rolle, Richard c. 1300-c. 1349 ...... **CMLC 21**
See also DLB 146; RGEL
Rolvaag, O(le) E(dvart)
See Roelvaag, O(le) E(dvart)
See also DLB 212; NFS 5; RGAL
Romain Arnaud, Saint
See Aragon, Louis
Romains, Jules 1885-1972 .... **CLC 7**
See also CA 85-88; CANR 34; DLB 65;
GFL 1789 to the Present; MTCW 1
Romero, Jose Ruben 1890-1952 .... **TCLC 14**
See also CA 114; 131; HW 1
Ronsard, Pierre de 1524-1585 . **LC 6, 54; PC
11**
See also GFL Beginnings to 1789; RGWL
Rooke, Leon 1934- . **CLC 25, 34; DAM POP**
See also CA 25-28R; CANR 23, 53; CCA
1; CPW
Roosevelt, Franklin Delano
1882-1945 .... **TCLC 93**
See also CA 116; 173; LAIT 3
Roosevelt, Theodore 1858-1919 ..... **TCLC 69**
See also CA 115; 170; DLB 47, 186
Roper, William 1498-1578 .... **LC 10**
Roquelaure, A. N.
See Rice, Anne
Rosa, Joao Guimaraes 1908-1967 ... **CLC 23;
HLCS 1**
See also CA 89-92; DLB 113; WLIT 1
Rose, Wendy 1948- .. **CLC 85; DAM MULT;
PC 13**
See also CA 53-56; CANR 5, 51; CWP;
DLB 175; NNAL; RGAL; SATA 12
Rosen, R. D.
See Rosen, Richard (Dean)
Rosen, Richard (Dean) 1949- .... **CLC 39**
See also CA 77-80; CANR 62; CMW; INT
CANR-30
Rosenberg, Isaac 1890-1918 .... **TCLC 12**
See also CA 107; 188; DLB 20; PAB;
RGEL
Rosenblatt, Joe CLC 15
See also Rosenblatt, Joseph
Rosenblatt, Joseph 1933-
See Rosenblatt, Joe
See also CA 89-92; CP; INT 89-92
Rosenfeld, Samuel
See Tzara, Tristan
Rosenstock, Sami
See Tzara, Tristan
Rosenstock, Samuel
See Tzara, Tristan
Rosenthal, M(acha) L(ouis)
1917-1996 .... **CLC 28**
See also CA 1-4R; 152; CAAS 6; CANR 4,
51; CP; DLB 5; SATA 59
Ross, Barnaby
See Dannay, Frederic
Ross, Bernard L.
See Follett, Ken(neth Martin)
Ross, J. H.
See Lawrence, T(homas) E(dward)
Ross, John Hume
See Lawrence, T(homas) E(dward)
Ross, Martin 1862-1915
See Martin, Violet Florence
See also DLB 135; GLL 2; RGEL; RGSF
Ross, (James) Sinclair 1908-1996 ... **CLC 13;
DAC; DAM MST; SSC 24**
See also CA 73-76; CANR 81; CN; DLB
88; RGEL; RGSF; TCWW 2

Rossetti, Christina (Georgina)
1830-1894 . **NCLC 2, 50, 66; DA; DAB;
DAC; DAM MST, POET; PC 7; WLC**
See also BRW; BYA 4; DA3; DLB 35, 163,
240; EXPP; MAICYA; PFS 10; RGEL;
SATA 20; WCH
Rossetti, Dante Gabriel 1828-1882 . **NCLC 4,
77; DA; DAB; DAC; DAM MST,
POET; WLC**
See also CDBLB 1832-1890; DLB 35;
EXPP; RGEL
Rossner, Judith (Perelman) 1935- . **CLC 6, 9,
29**
See also AITN 2; BEST 90:3; BPFB 3; CA
17-20R; CANR 18, 51, 73; CN; DLB 6;
INT CANR-18; MTCW 1, 2
Rostand, Edmond (Eugene Alexis)
1868-1918 .... **TCLC 6, 37; DA; DAB;
DAC; DAM DRAM, MST; DC 10**
See also CA 104; 126; DA3; DFS 1; DLB
192; LAIT 1; MTCW 1
Roth, Henry 1906-1995 ..... **CLC 2, 6, 11, 104**
See also CA 11-12; 149; CANR 38, 63;
CAP 1; CN; DA3; DLB 28; MTCW 1, 2;
RGAL
Roth, (Moses) Joseph 1894-1939 ... **TCLC 33**
See also CA 160; DLB 85
Roth, Philip (Milton) 1933- ... **CLC 1, 2, 3, 4,
6, 9, 15, 22, 31, 47, 66, 86, 119; DA;
DAB; DAC; DAM MST, NOV, POP;
SSC 26; WLC**
See also AMWS 3; BEST 90:3; BPFB 3;
CA 1-4R; CANR 1, 22, 36, 55, 89;
CDALB 1968-1988; CN; CPW 1; DA3;
DLB 2, 28, 173; DLBY 82; MTCW 1, 2;
RGAL; RGSF; SSFS 12
Rothenberg, Jerome 1931- .... **CLC 6, 57**
See also CA 45-48; CANR 1; CP; DLB 5,
193
Rotter, Pat ed. CLC 65
Roumain, Jacques (Jean Baptiste)
1907-1944 ...... **TCLC 19; BLC 3; DAM
MULT**
See also BW 1; CA 117; 125
Rourke, Constance (Mayfield)
1885-1941 .... **TCLC 12**
See also CA 107; YABC 1
Rousseau, Jean-Baptiste 1671-1741 ...... **LC 9**
Rousseau, Jean-Jacques 1712-1778 .... **LC 14,
36; DA; DAB; DAC; DAM MST; WLC**
See also DA3; EW; GFL Beginnings to
1789; RGWL
Roussel, Raymond 1877-1933 .... **TCLC 20**
See also CA 117; GFL 1789 to the Present
Rovit, Earl (Herbert) 1927- .... **CLC 7**
See also CA 5-8R; CANR 12
Rowe, Elizabeth Singer 1674-1737 ..... **LC 44**
See also DLB 39, 95
Rowe, Nicholas 1674-1718 .... **LC 8**
See also DLB 84; RGEL
Rowlandson, Mary 1637(?)-1678 .... **LC 66**
See also DLB 24, 200; RGAL
Rowley, Ames Dorrance
See Lovecraft, H(oward) P(hillips)
Rowling, J(oanne) K. 1966(?)- .... **CLC 137**
See also AAYA 34; CA 173; CLR 66; SATA
109
Rowson, Susanna Haswell
1762(?)-1824 .... **NCLC 5, 69**
See also DLB 37, 200; RGAL
Roy, Arundhati 1960(?)- .... **CLC 109**
See also CA 163; CANR 90; DLBY 97
Roy, Gabrielle 1909-1983 .... **CLC 10, 14;
DAB; DAC; DAM MST**
See also CA 53-56; 110; CANR 5, 61; CCA
1; DLB 68; MTCW 1; RGWL; SATA 104
Royko, Mike 1932-1997 .... **CLC 109**
See also CA 89-92; 157; CANR 26; CPW

Rozanov, Vassili 1856-1919 .... **TCLC 104**

Rozewicz, Tadeusz 1921- ..... **CLC 9, 23, 139;**
   DAM POET
   See also CA 108; CANR 36, 66; CWW 2;
   DA3; DLB 232; MTCW 1, 2

Ruark, Gibbons 1941- .... **CLC 3**
   See also CA 33-36R; CAAS 23; CANR 14,
   31, 57; DLB 120

Rubens, Bernice (Ruth) 1923- .... **CLC 19, 31**
   See also CA 25-28R; CANR 33, 65; CN;
   DLB 14, 207; MTCW 1

Rubin, Harold
   See Robbins, Harold

Rudkin, (James) David 1936- .... **CLC 14**
   See also CA 89-92; CBD; CD; DLB 13

Rudnik, Raphael 1933- .... **CLC 7**
   See also CA 29-32R

Ruffian, M.
   See Hasek, Jaroslav (Matej Frantisek)

Ruiz, Jose Martinez CLC 11
   See also Martinez Ruiz, Jose

Rukeyser, Muriel 1913-1980 . **CLC 6, 10, 15,**
   27; DAM POET; PC 12
   See also AMWS 6; CA 5-8R; 93-96; CANR
   26, 60; DA3; DLB 48; FW; GLL 2;
   MTCW 1, 2; PFS 10; RGAL; SATA-Obit
   22

Rule, Jane (Vance) 1931- .... **CLC 27**
   See also CA 25-28R; CAAS 18; CANR 12,
   87; CN; DLB 60; FW

Rulfo, Juan 1918-1986 ...... **CLC 8, 80; DAM**
   MULT; HLC 2; SSC 25
   See also CA 85-88; 118; CANR 26; DLB
   113; HW 1, 2; MTCW 1, 2; RGSF;
   RGWL; WLIT 1

Rumi, Jalal al-Din 1207-1273 .... **CMLC 20**
   See also RGWL; WP

Runeberg, Johan 1804-1877 .... **NCLC 41**

Runyon, (Alfred) Damon
   1884(?)-1946 .... **TCLC 10**
   See also CA 107; 165; DLB 11, 86, 171;
   MTCW 2; RGAL

Rush, Norman 1933- .... **CLC 44**
   See also CA 121; 126; INT 126

Rushdie, (Ahmed) Salman 1947- .... **CLC 23,**
   31, 55, 100; DAB; DAC; DAM MST,
   NOV, POP; WLCS
   See also BEST 89:3; BPFB 3; BRWS 4;
   CA 108; 111; CANR 33, 56; CN; CPW 1;
   DA3; DLB 194; FANT; INT CA-111;
   MTCW 1, 2; RGEL; RGSF; WLIT 4

Rushforth, Peter (Scott) 1945- .... **CLC 19**
   See also CA 101

Ruskin, John 1819-1900 .... **TCLC 63**
   See also BYA 5; CA 114; 129; CDBLB
   1832-1890; DLB 55, 163, 190; RGEL;
   SATA 24

Russ, Joanna 1937- .... **CLC 15**
   See also BPFB 3; CA 5-28R; CANR 11,
   31, 65; CN; DLB 8; FW; GLL 1; MTCW
   1; SCFW 2; SFW

Russell, George William 1867-1935
   See Baker, Jean H.
   See also CA 104; 153; CDBLB 1890-1914;
   DAM POET; RGEL

Russell, Jeffrey Burton 1934- .... **CLC 70**
   See also CA 25-28R; CANR 11, 28, 52

Russell, (Henry) Ken(neth Alfred)
   1927- .... **CLC 16**
   See also CA 105

Russell, William Martin 1947- .... **CLC 60**
   See also CA 164; DLB 233

Rutherford, Mark TCLC 25
   See also White, William Hale
   See also DLB 18; RGEL

Ruyslinck, Ward CLC 14
   See also Belser, Reimond Karel Maria de

Ryan, Cornelius (John) 1920-1974 ..... **CLC 7**
   See also CA 69-72; 53-56; CANR 38

Ryan, Michael 1946- .... **CLC 65**
   See also CA 49-52; DLBY 82

Ryan, Tim
   See Dent, Lester

Rybakov, Anatoli (Naumovich)
   1911-1998 .... **CLC 23, 53**
   See also CA 126; 135; 172; SATA 79;
   SATA-Obit 108

Ryder, Jonathan
   See Ludlum, Robert

Ryga, George 1932-1987 .... **CLC 14; DAC;**
   DAM MST
   See also CA 101; 124; CANR 43, 90; CCA
   1; DLB 60

S. H.
   See Hartmann, Sadakichi

S. S.
   See Sassoon, Siegfried (Lorraine)

Saba, Umberto 1883-1957 .... **TCLC 33**
   See also CA 144; CANR 79; DLB 114;
   RGWL

Sabatini, Rafael 1875-1950 .... **TCLC 47**
   See also BPFB 3; CA 162; RHW

Sabato, Ernesto (R.) 1911- .... **CLC 10, 23;**
   DAM MULT; HLC 2
   See also CA 97-100; CANR 32, 65; DLB
   145; HW 1, 2; LAW; MTCW 1, 2

Sa-Carniero, Mario de 1890-1916 . **TCLC 83**

Sacastru, Martin
   See Bioy Casares, Adolfo

Sacastru, Martin
   See Bioy Casares, Adolfo
   See also CWW 2

Sacher-Masoch, Leopold von
   1836(?)-1895 .... **NCLC 31**

Sachs, Marilyn (Stickle) 1927- .... **CLC 35**
   See also AAYA 2; BYA 6; CA 17-20R;
   CANR 13, 47; CLR 2; JRDA; MAICYA;
   SAAS 2; SATA 3, 68; SATA-Essay 110;
   WYA; YAW

Sachs, Nelly 1891-1970 .... **CLC 14, 98**
   See also CA 17-18; 25-28R; CANR 87;
   CAP 2; MTCW 2; RGWL

Sackler, Howard (Oliver)
   1929-1982 .... **CLC 14**
   See also CA 61-64; 108; CAD; CANR 30;
   DLB 7

Sacks, Oliver (Wolf) 1933- .... **CLC 67**
   See also CA 53-56; CANR 28, 50, 76;
   CPW; DA3; INT CANR-28; MTCW 1, 2

Sadakichi
   See Hartmann, Sadakichi

Sade, Donatien Alphonse Francois
   1740-1814 .... **NCLC 3, 47**
   See also EW; GFL Beginnings to 1789;
   RGWL

Sadoff, Ira 1945- .... **CLC 9**
   See also CA 53-56; CANR 5, 21; DLB 120

Saetone
   See Camus, Albert

Safire, William 1929- .... **CLC 10**
   See also CA 17-20R; CANR 31, 54, 91

Sagan, Carl (Edward) 1934-1996 .... **CLC 30,**
   112
   See also AAYA 2; CA 25-28R; 155; CANR
   11, 36, 74; CPW; DA3; MTCW 1, 2;
   SATA 58; SATA-Obit 94

Sagan, Francoise CLC 3, 6, 9, 17, 36
   See also Quoirez, Francoise
   See also CWW 2; DLB 83; GFL 1789 to
   the Present; MTCW 2

Sahgal, Nayantara (Pandit) 1927- .... **CLC 41**
   See also CA 9-12R; CANR 11, 88; CN

Said, Edward W. 1935- .... **CLC 123**
   See also CA 21-24R; CANR 45, 74; DLB
   67; MTCW 2

Saint, H(arry) F. 1941- .... **CLC 50**
   See also CA 127

St. Aubin de Teran, Lisa 1953-
   See Teran, Lisa St. Aubin de
   See also CA 118; 126; CN; INT 126

Saint Birgitta of Sweden c.
   1303-1373 .... **CMLC 24**

Sainte-Beuve, Charles Augustin
   1804-1869 .... **NCLC 5**
   See also EW; GFL 1789 to the Present

Saint-Exupery, Antoine (Jean Baptiste
   Marie Roger) de 1900-1944 .... **TCLC 2,**
   56; DAM NOV; WLC
   See also BPFB 3; BYA 3; CA 108; 132;
   CLR 10; DA3; DLB 72; EW; GFL 1789
   to the Present; LAIT 3; MAICYA; MTCW
   1, 2; RGWL; SATA 20

St. John, David
   See Hunt, E(verette) Howard, (Jr.)

St. John, J. Hector
   See Crevecoeur, Michel Guillaume Jean de

Saint-John Perse
   See Leger, (Marie-Rene Auguste) Alexis
   Saint-Leger
   See also GFL 1789 to the Present; RGWL

Saintsbury, George (Edward Bateman)
   1845-1933 .... **TCLC 31**
   See also CA 160; DLB 57, 149

Sait Faik TCLC 23
   See also Abasiyanik, Sait Faik

Saki TCLC 3; SSC 12
   See also Munro, H(ector) H(ugh)
   See also BRWS 6; LAIT 2; MTCW 2;
   RGEL; SSFS 1

Sala, George Augustus 1828-1895 . **NCLC 46**

Saladin 1138-1193 .... **CMLC 38**

Salama, Hannu 1936- .... **CLC 18**

Salamanca, J(ack) R(ichard) 1922- .. **CLC 4,**
   15
   See also CA 25-28R; CAAE 193

Salas, Floyd Francis 1931-
   See also CA 119; CAAS 27; CANR 44, 75,
   93; DAM MULT; DLB 82; HLC 2; HW
   1, 2; MTCW 2

Sale, J. Kirkpatrick
   See Sale, Kirkpatrick

Sale, Kirkpatrick 1937- .... **CLC 68**
   See also CA 13-16R; CANR 10

Salinas, Luis Omar 1937- ..... **CLC 90; DAM**
   MULT; HLC 2
   See also CA 131; CANR 81; DLB 82; HW
   1, 2

Salinas (y Serrano), Pedro
   1891(?)-1951 .... **TCLC 17**
   See also CA 117; DLB 134

Salinger, J(erome) D(avid) 1919- .. **CLC 1, 3,**
   8, 12, 55, 56, 138; DA; DAB; DAC;
   DAM MST, NOV, POP; SSC 2, 28;
   WLC
   See also AAYA 2, 36; AMW; BPFB 3; CA
   5-8R; CANR 39; CDALB 1941-1968;
   CLR 18; CN; CPW 1; DA3; DLB 2, 102,
   173; EXPN; LAIT 4; MAICYA; MTCW
   1, 2; NFS 1; RGAL; RGSF; SATA 67;
   WYA; YAW

Salisbury, John
   See Caute, (John) David

Salter, James 1925- .... **CLC 7, 52, 59**
   See also CA 73-76; DLB 130

Saltus, Edgar (Everton) 1855-1921 . **TCLC 8**
   See also CA 105; DLB 202; RGAL

Saltykov, Mikhail Evgrafovich
   1826-1889 .... **NCLC 16**
   See also DLB 238:

Saltykov-Shchedrin, N.
   See Saltykov, Mikhail Evgrafovich

Samarakis, Antonis 1919- .... **CLC 5**
   See also CA 25-28R; CAAS 16; CANR 36

Sanchez, Florencio 1875-1910 .... **TCLC 37**
   See also CA 153; HW 1

Schorer, Mark 1908-1977 .... **CLC 9**
See also CA 5-8R; 73-76; CANR 7; DLB 103

Schrader, Paul (Joseph) 1946- .... **CLC 26**
See also CA 37-40R; CANR 41; DLB 44

Schreiner, Olive (Emilie Albertina) 1855-1920 .... **TCLC 9**
See also AFW; BRWS 2; CA 105; 154; DLB 18, 156, 190, 225; FW; RGEL; WLIT 2

Schulberg, Budd (Wilson) 1914- .. **CLC 7, 48**
See also BPFB 3; CA 25-28R; CANR 19, 87; CN; DLB 6, 26, 28; DLBY 81

Schulz, Bruno 1892-1942 .. **TCLC 5, 51; SSC 13**
See also CA 115; 123; CANR 86; MTCW 2; RGSF; RGWL

Schulz, Charles M(onroe) 1922-2000 .... **CLC 12**
See also AAYA 39; CA 9-12R; 187; CANR 6; INT CANR-6; SATA 10; SATA-Obit 118

Schumacher, E(rnst) F(riedrich) 1911-1977 .... **CLC 80**
See also CA 81-84; 73-76; CANR 34, 85

Schuyler, James Marcus 1923-1991 .. **CLC 5, 23; DAM POET**
See also CA 101; 134; DLB 5, 169; INT 101; WP

Schwartz, Delmore (David) 1913-1966 ... **CLC 2, 4, 10, 45, 87; PC 8**
See also AMWS 2; CA 17-18; 25-28R; CANR 35; CAP 2; DLB 28, 48; MTCW 1, 2; PAB; RGAL

Schwartz, Ernst
See Ozu, Yasujiro

Schwartz, John Burnham 1965- .... **CLC 59**
See also CA 132

Schwartz, Lynne Sharon 1939- .... **CLC 31**
See also CA 103; CANR 44, 89; MTCW 2

Schwartz, Muriel A.
See Eliot, T(homas) S(tearns)

Schwarz-Bart, Andre 1928- .... **CLC 2, 4**
See also CA 89-92

Schwarz-Bart, Simone 1938- . **CLC 7; BLCS**
See also BW 2; CA 97-100

Schwitters, Kurt (Hermann Edward Karl Julius) 1887-1948 .... **TCLC 95**
See also CA 158

Schwob, Marcel (Mayer Andre) 1867-1905 .... **TCLC 20**
See also CA 117; 168; DLB 123; GFL 1789 to the Present

Sciascia, Leonardo 1921-1989 .. **CLC 8, 9, 41**
See also CA 85-88; 130; CANR 35; DLB 177; MTCW 1; RGWL

Scoppettone, Sandra 1936- .... **CLC 26**
See also Early, Jack
See also AAYA 11; BYA 8; CA 5-8R; CANR 41, 73; GLL 1; SATA 9, 92; YAW

Scorsese, Martin 1942- .... **CLC 20, 89**
See also AAYA 38; CA 110; 114; CANR 46, 85

Scotland, Jay
See Jakes, John (William)

Scott, Duncan Campbell 1862-1947 .... **TCLC 6; DAC**
See also CA 104; 153; DLB 92; RGEL

Scott, Evelyn 1893-1963 .... **CLC 43**
See also CA 104; 112; CANR 64; DLB 9, 48; RHW

Scott, F(rancis) R(eginald) 1899-1985 .... **CLC 22**
See also CA 101; 114; CANR 87; DLB 88; INT CA-101; RGEL

Scott, Frank
See Scott, F(rancis) R(eginald)

Scott, Joan CLC 65

Scott, Joanna 1960- .... **CLC 50**
See also CA 126; CANR 53, 92

Scott, Paul (Mark) 1920-1978 ...... **CLC 9, 60**
See also BRWS 1; CA 81-84; 77-80; CANR 33; DLB 14, 207; MTCW 1; RGEL; RHW

Scott, Sarah 1723-1795 .... **LC 44**
See also DLB 39

Scott, Sir Walter 1771-1832 .... **NCLC 15, 69; DA; DAB; DAC; DAM MST, NOV, POET; PC 13; SSC 32; WLC**
See also AAYA 22; BRW; BYA 2; CDBLB 1789-1832; DLB 93, 107, 116, 144, 159; HGG; LAIT 1; RGEL; RGSF; SSFS 10; SUFW; WLIT 3; YABC 2

Scribe, (Augustin) Eugene 1791-1861 ..... **NCLC 16; DAM DRAM; DC 5**
See also DLB 192; EW; GFL 1789 to the Present; RGWL

Scrum, R.
See Crumb, R(obert)

Scudery, Madeleine de 1607-1701 .. **LC 2, 58**
See also GFL Beginnings to 1789

Scum
See Crumb, R(obert)

Scumbag, Little Bobby
See Crumb, R(obert)

Seabrook, John
See Hubbard, L(afayette) Ron(ald)

Sealy, I(rwin) Allan 1951- .... **CLC 55**
See also CA 136; CN

Search, Alexander
See Pessoa, Fernando (Antonio Nogueira)

Sebastian, Lee
See Silverberg, Robert

Sebastian Owl
See Thompson, Hunter S(tockton)

Sebestyen, Ouida 1924- .... **CLC 30**
See also AAYA 8; BYA 7; CA 107; CANR 40; CLR 17; JRDA; MAICYA; SAAS 10; SATA 39; YAW

Secundus, H. Scriblerus
See Fielding, Henry

Sedges, John
See Buck, Pearl S(ydenstricker)

Sedgwick, Catharine Maria 1789-1867 .... **NCLC 19, 98**
See also DLB 1, 74, 239; RGAL

Seelye, John (Douglas) 1931- .... **CLC 7**
See also CA 97-100; CANR 70; INT 97-100; TCWW 2

Seferiades, Giorgos Stylianou 1900-1971
See Seferis, George
See also CA 5-8R; 33-36R; CANR 5, 36; MTCW 1

Seferis, George CLC 5, 11
See also Seferiades, Giorgos Stylianou
See also RGWL

Segal, Erich (Wolf) 1937- . **CLC 3, 10; DAM POP**
See also BEST 89:1; BPFB 3; CA 25-28R; CANR 20, 36, 65; CPW; DLBY 86; INT CANR-20; MTCW 1

Seger, Bob 1945- .... **CLC 35**

Seghers, Anna CLC 7
See also Radvanyi, Netty
See also DLB 69

Seidel, Frederick (Lewis) 1936- .... **CLC 18**
See also CA 13-16R; CANR 8, 99; CP; DLBY 84

Seifert, Jaroslav 1901-1986 .. **CLC 34, 44, 93**
See also CA 127; DLB 215; MTCW 1, 2

Sei Shonagon c. 966-1017(?) .... **CMLC 6**

Sejour, Victor 1817-1874 .... **DC 10**
See also DLB 50

Sejour Marcou et Ferrand, Juan Victor
See Sejour, Victor

Selby, Hubert, Jr. 1928- .... **CLC 1, 2, 4, 8; SSC 20**
See also CA 13-16R; CANR 33, 85; CN; DLB 2, 227

Selzer, Richard 1928- .... **CLC 74**
See also CA 65-68; CANR 14

Sembene, Ousmane
See Ousmane, Sembene
See also AFW; CWW 2; WLIT 2

Senancour, Etienne Pivert de 1770-1846 .... **NCLC 16**
See also DLB 119; GFL 1789 to the Present

Sender, Ramon (Jose) 1902-1982 ...... **CLC 8; DAM MULT; HLC 2**
See also CA 5-8R; 105; CANR 8; HW 1; MTCW 1; RGWL

Seneca, Lucius Annaeus c. 4B.C.-c. 65 .... **CMLC 6; DAM DRAM; DC 5**
See also AW; DLB 211; RGWL

Senghor, Leopold Sedar 1906- .... **CLC 54, 130; BLC 3; DAM MULT, POET; PC 25**
See also BW 2; CA 116; 125; CANR 47, 74; DNFS; GFL 1789 to the Present; MTCW 1, 2

Senna, Danzy 1970- .... **CLC 119**
See also CA 169

Serling, (Edward) Rod(man) 1924-1975 .... **CLC 30**
See also AAYA 14; AITN 1; CA 162; 57-60; DLB 26; SFW

Serna, Ramon Gomez de la
See Gomez de la Serna, Ramon

Serpieres
See Guillevic, (Eugene)

Service, Robert
See Service, Robert W(illiam)
See also BYA 4; DAB; DLB 92

Service, Robert W(illiam) 1874(?)-1958 .... **TCLC 15; DA; DAC; DAM MST, POET; WLC**
See also Service, Robert
See also CA 115; 140; CANR 84; PFS 10; RGEL; SATA 20

Seth, Vikram 1952- .... **CLC 43, 90; DAM MULT**
See also CA 121; 127; CANR 50, 74; CN; CP; DA3; DLB 120; INT 127; MTCW 2

Seton, Cynthia Propper 1926-1982 .. **CLC 27**
See also CA 5-8R; 108; CANR 7

Seton, Ernest (Evan) Thompson 1860-1946 .... **TCLC 31**
See also ANW; BYA 3; CA 109; CLR 59; DLB 92; DLBD 13; JRDA; SATA 18

Seton-Thompson, Ernest
See Seton, Ernest (Evan) Thompson

Settle, Mary Lee 1918- .... **CLC 19, 61**
See also BPFB 3; CA 89-92; CAAS 1; CANR 44, 87; CN; CSW; DLB 6; INT 89-92

Seuphor, Michel
See Arp, Jean

Sevigne, Marie (de Rabutin-Chantal) 1626-1696 .... **LC 11**
See also GFL Beginnings to 1789

Sewall, Samuel 1652-1730 .... **LC 38**
See also DLB 24; RGAL

Sexton, Anne (Harvey) 1928-1974 ..... **CLC 2, 4, 6, 8, 10, 15, 53, 123; DA; DAB; DAC; DAM MST, POET; PC 2; WLC**
See also AMWS 2; CA 1-4R; 53-56; CABS 2; CANR 3, 36; CDALB 1941-1968; DA3; DLB 5, 169; EXPP; FW; MAWW; MTCW 1, 2; PAB; PFS 4; RGAL; SATA 10

Shaara, Jeff 1952- .... **CLC 119**
See also CA 163

Shaara, Michael (Joseph, Jr.) 1929-1988 .... **CLC 15; DAM POP**
See also AITN 1; BPFB 3; CA 102; 125; CANR 52, 85; DLBY 83

Shackleton, C. C.
See Aldiss, Brian W(ilson)

Shacochis, Bob CLC 39
See also Shacochis, Robert G.

Shacochis, Robert G. 1951-
See Shacochis, Bob
See also CA 119; 124; CANR 100; INT 124

Shaffer, Anthony (Joshua) 1926- ..... **CLC 19; DAM DRAM**
See also CA 110; 116; CBD; CD; DFS 13; DLB 13

Shaffer, Peter (Levin) 1926- .. **CLC 5, 14, 18, 37, 60; DAB; DAM DRAM, MST; DC 7**
See also BRWS 1; CA 25-28R; CANR 25, 47, 74; CBD; CD; CDBLB 1960 to Present; DA3; DFS 5, 13; DLB 13, 233; MTCW 1, 2; RGEL

Shakey, Bernard
See Young, Neil

Shalamov, Varlam (Tikhonovich) 1907(?)-1982 .... **CLC 18**
See also CA 129; 105; RGSF

Shamlu, Ahmad 1925-2000 .... **CLC 10**
See also CWW 2

Shammas, Anton 1951- .... **CLC 55**

Shandling, Arline
See Berriault, Gina

Shange, Ntozake 1948- .... **CLC 8, 25, 38, 74, 126; BLC 3; DAM DRAM, MULT; DC 3**
See also AAYA 9; AFAW 1, 2; BW 2; CA 85-88; CABS 3; CAD; CANR 27, 48, 74; CD; CP; CWD; CWP; DA3; DFS 2, 11; DLB 38; FW; LAIT 5; MTCW 1, 2; NFS 11; RGAL; YAW

Shanley, John Patrick 1950- .... **CLC 75**
See also CA 128; 133; CAD; CANR 83; CD

Shapcott, Thomas W(illiam) 1935- .. **CLC 38**
See also CA 69-72; CANR 49, 83; CP

Shapiro, Jane CLC 76

Shapiro, Karl (Jay) 1913-2000 ...... **CLC 4, 8, 15, 53; PC 25**
See also AMWS 2; CA 1-4R; 188; CAAS 6; CANR 1, 36, 66; CP; DLB 48; EXPP; MTCW 1, 2; PFS 3; RGAL

Sharp, William 1855-1905 .... **TCLC 39**
See also Macleod, Fiona
See also CA 160; DLB 156; RGEL

Sharpe, Thomas Ridley 1928-
See Sharpe, Tom
See also CA 114; 122; CANR 85; CN; DLB 231; INT 122

Sharpe, Tom CLC 36
See also Sharpe, Thomas Ridley
See also DLB 14

Shatrov, Mikhail CLC 59

Shaw, Bernard
See Shaw, George Bernard
See also BW 1; MTCW 2

Shaw, G. Bernard
See Shaw, George Bernard

Shaw, George Bernard 1856-1950 .. **TCLC 3, 9, 21, 45; DA; DAB; DAC; DAM DRAM, MST; WLC**
See also Shaw, Bernard
See also CA 104; 128; CDBLB 1914-1945; DA3; DFS 1, 3, 6, 11; DLB 10, 57, 190; LAIT 3; MTCW 1, 2; RGEL; WLIT 4

Shaw, Henry Wheeler 1818-1885 .. **NCLC 15**
See also DLB 11; RGAL

Shaw, Irwin 1913-1984 .... **CLC 7, 23, 34; DAM DRAM, POP**
See also AITN 1; BPFB 3; CA 13-16R; 112; CANR 21; CDALB 1941-1968; CPW; DLB 6, 102; DLBY 84; MTCW 1, 21

Shaw, Robert 1927-1978 .... **CLC 5**
See also AITN 1; CA 1-4R; 81-84; CANR 4; DLB 13, 14

Shaw, T. E.
See Lawrence, T(homas) E(dward)

Shawn, Wallace 1943- .... **CLC 41**
See also CA 112; CAD; CD

Shchedrin, N.
See Saltykov, Mikhail Evgrafovich

Shea, Lisa 1953- .... **CLC 86**
See also CA 147

Sheed, Wilfrid (John Joseph) 1930- . **CLC 2, 4, 10, 53**
See also CA 65-68; CANR 30, 66; CN; DLB 6; MTCW 1, 2

Sheldon, Alice Hastings Bradley 1915(?)-1987
See Tiptree, James, Jr.
See also CA 108; 122; CANR 34; INT 108; MTCW 1

Sheldon, John
See Bloch, Robert (Albert)

Sheldon, Walter J(ames) 1917-1996
See Queen, Ellery
See also AITN 1; CA 25-28R; CANR 10

Shelley, Mary Wollstonecraft (Godwin) 1797-1851 .... **NCLC 14, 59, 103; DA; DAB; DAC; DAM MST, NOV; WLC**
See also AAYA 20; BPFB 3; BRW; BRWS 3; BYA 5; CDBLB 1789-1832; DA3; DLB 110, 116, 159, 178; EXPN; HGG; LAIT 1; NFS 1; RGEL; SATA 29; SCFW; SFW; WLIT 3

Shelley, Percy Bysshe 1792-1822 .. **NCLC 18, 93; DA; DAB; DAC; DAM MST, POET; PC 14; WLC**
See also CDBLB 1789-1832; DA3; DLB 96, 110, 158; EXPP; PAB; PFS 2; RGEL; WLIT 3; WP

Shepard, Jim 1956- .... **CLC 36**
See also CA 137; CANR 59; SATA 90

Shepard, Lucius 1947- .... **CLC 34**
See also CA 128; 141; CANR 81; HGG; SCFW 2; SFW

Shepard, Sam 1943- .... **CLC 4, 6, 17, 34, 41, 44; DAM DRAM; DC 5**
See also AAYA 1; AMWS 3; CA 69-72; CABS 3; CAD; CANR 22; CD; DA3; DFS 3,6,7; DLB 7, 212; IDFW 3, 4; MTCW 1, 2; RGAL

Shepherd, Michael
See Ludlum, Robert

Sherburne, Zoa (Lillian Morin) 1912-1995 .... **CLC 30**
See also AAYA 13; CA 1-4R; 176; CANR 3, 37; MAICYA; SAAS 18; SATA 3; YAW

Sheridan, Frances 1724-1766 .... **LC 7**
See also DLB 39, 84

Sheridan, Richard Brinsley 1751-1816 .... **NCLC 5, 91; DA; DAB; DAC; DAM DRAM, MST; DC 1; WLC**
See also CDBLB 1660-1789; DFS 4; DLB 89; RGEL; WLIT 3

Sherman, Jonathan Marc CLC 55

Sherman, Martin 1941(?)- .... **CLC 19**
See also CA 116; 123; CANR 86

Sherwin, Judith Johnson
See Johnson, Judith (Emlyn)
See also CANR 85; CP; CWP

Sherwood, Frances 1940- .... **CLC 81**
See also CA 146

Sherwood, Robert E(mmet) 1896-1955 .... **TCLC 3; DAM DRAM**
See also CA 104; 153; CANR 86; DFS 11; DLB 7, 26; IDFW 3, 4; RGAL

Shestov, Lev 1866-1938 .... **TCLC 56**

Shevchenko, Taras 1814-1861 .... **NCLC 54**

Shiel, M(atthew) P(hipps) 1865-1947 .... **TCLC 8**
See also Holmes, Gordon
See also CA 106; 160; DLB 153; HGG; MTCW 2; SFW; SUFW

Shields, Carol 1935- .... **CLC 91, 113; DAC**
See also AMWS 7; CA 81-84; CANR 51, 74, 98; CCA 1; CN; CPW; DA3; MTCW 2

Shields, David 1956- .... **CLC 97**
See also CA 124; CANR 48, 99

Shiga, Naoya 1883-1971 ..... **CLC 33; SSC 23**
See also CA 101; 33-36R; DLB 180; MJW

Shilts, Randy 1951-1994 .... **CLC 85**
See also AAYA 19; CA 115; 127; 144; CANR 45; DA3; GLL 1; INT 127; MTCW 2

Shimazaki, Haruki 1872-1943
See Shimazaki Toson
See also CA 105; 134; CANR 84

Shimazaki Toson TCLC 5
See also Shimazaki, Haruki
See also DLB 180

Sholokhov, Mikhail (Aleksandrovich) 1905-1984 .... **CLC 7, 15**
See also CA 101; 112; MTCW 1, 2; RGWL; SATA-Obit 36

Shone, Patric
See Hanley, James

Shreve, Susan Richards 1939- .... **CLC 23**
See also CA 49-52; CAAS 5; CANR 5, 38, 69, 100; MAICYA; SATA 46, 95; SATA-Brief 41

Shue, Larry 1946-1985 .... **CLC 52; DAM DRAM**
See also CA 145; 117; DFS 7

Shu-Jen, Chou 1881-1936
See Lu Hsun
See also CA 104

Shulman, Alix Kates 1932- .... **CLC 2, 10**
See also CA 29-32R; CANR 43; FW; SATA 7

Shuster, Joe 1914-1992 .... **CLC 21**

Shute, Nevil CLC 30
See also Norway, Nevil Shute
See also BPFB 3; MTCW 2; NFS 9

Shuttle, Penelope (Diane) 1947- .... **CLC 7**
See also CA 93-96; CANR 39, 84, 92; CP; CWP; DLB 14, 40

Sidney, Mary 1561-1621 .... **LC 19, 39**

Sidney, Sir Philip 1554-1586 .... **LC 19, 39; DA; DAB; DAC; DAM MST, POET; PC 32**
See also BRW 1; CDBLB Before 1660; DA3; DLB 167; EXPP; PAB; RGEL; TEA; WP

Siegel, Jerome 1914-1996 .... **CLC 21**
See also CA 116; 169; 151

Siegel, Jerry
See Siegel, Jerome

Sienkiewicz, Henryk (Adam Alexander Pius) 1846-1916 .... **TCLC 3**
See also CA 104; 134; CANR 84; RGSF; RGWL

Sierra, Gregorio Martinez
See Martinez Sierra, Gregorio

Sierra, Maria (de la O'LeJarraga) Martinez
See Martinez Sierra, Maria (de la O'LeJarraga)

Sigal, Clancy 1926- .... **CLC 7**
See also CA 1-4R; CANR 85; CN

Sigourney, Lydia Howard (Huntley)
1791-1865 .... NCLC 21, 87
See also DLB 1, 42, 73, 239
Siguenza y Gongora, Carlos de
1645-1700 .... LC 8; HLCS 2
See also LAW
Sigurjonsson, Johann 1880-1919 ... TCLC 27
See also CA 170
Sikelianos, Angelos 1884-1951 ...... TCLC 39;
PC 29
See also RGWL
Silkin, Jon 1930-1997 .... CLC 2, 6, 43
See also CA 5-8R; CAAS 5; CANR 89; CP;
DLB 27
Silko, Leslie (Marmon) 1948- .... CLC 23, 74,
114; DA; DAC; DAM MST, MULT,
POP; SSC 37; WLCS
See also AAYA 14; AMWS 4; ANW; BYA
12; CA 115; 122; CANR 45, 65; CN; CP;
CPW 1; CWP; DA3; DLB 143, 175;
EXPP; EXPS; LAIT 4; MTCW 2; NFS 4;
NNAL; PFS 9; RGAL; RGSF; SSFS 4, 8,
10, 11
Sillanpaa, Frans Eemil 1888-1964 ... CLC 19
See also CA 129; 93-96; MTCW 1
Sillitoe, Alan 1928- .. CLC 1, 3, 6, 10, 19, 57,
148
See also AITN 1; BRWS 5; CA 9-12R;
CAAE 191; CAAS 2; CANR 8, 26, 55;
CDBLB 1960 to Present; CN; DLB 14,
139; MTCW 1, 2; RGEL; RGSF; SATA
61
Silone, Ignazio 1900-1978 .... CLC 4
See also CA 25-28; 81-84; CANR 34; CAP
2; EW; MTCW 1; RGSF; RGWL
Silone, Ignazione
See Silone, Ignazio
Silver, Joan Micklin 1935- .... CLC 20
See also CA 114; 121; INT 121
Silver, Nicholas
See Faust, Frederick (Schiller)
See also TCWW 2
Silverberg, Robert 1935- .... CLC 7, 140;
DAM POP
See also AAYA 24; BPFB 3; BYA 7; CA
1-4R, 186; CAAE 186; CAAS 3; CANR
1, 20, 36, 85; CLR 59; CN; CPW; DLB
8; INT CANR-20; MAICYA; MTCW 1,
2; SATA 13, 91; SATA-Essay 104; SCFW
2; SFW
Silverstein, Alvin 1933- .... CLC 17
See also CA 49-52; CANR 2; CLR 25;
JRDA; MAICYA; SATA 8, 69, 124
Silverstein, Virginia B(arbara Opshelor)
1937- .... CLC 17
See also CA 49-52; CANR 2; CLR 25;
JRDA; MAICYA; SATA 8, 69, 124
Sim, Georges
See Simenon, Georges (Jacques Christian)
Simak, Clifford D(onald) 1904-1988 . CLC 1,
55
See also CA 1-4R; 125; CANR 1, 35; DLB
8; MTCW 1; SATA-Obit 56; SFW
Simenon, Georges (Jacques Christian)
1903-1989 .... CLC 1, 2, 3, 8, 18, 47;
DAM POP
See also BPFB 3; CA 85-88; 129; CANR
35; CMW; DA3; DLB 72; DLBY 89; EW;
GFL 1789 to the Present; MSW; MTCW
1, 2; RGWL
Simic, Charles 1938- .... CLC 6, 9, 22, 49, 68,
130; DAM POET
See also AMWS 8; CA 29-32R; CAAS 4;
CANR 12, 33, 52, 61, 96; CP; DA3; DLB
105; MTCW 2; PFS 7; RGAL; WP
Simmel, Georg 1858-1918 .... TCLC 64
See also CA 157
Simmons, Charles (Paul) 1924- .... CLC 57
See also CA 89-92; INT 89-92

Simmons, Dan 1948- .... CLC 44; DAM POP
See also AAYA 16; CA 138; CANR 53, 81;
CPW; HGG
Simmons, James (Stewart Alexander)
1933- .... CLC 43
See also CA 105; CAAS 21; CP; DLB 40
Simms, William Gilmore
1806-1870 .... NCLC 3
See also DLB 3, 30, 59, 73; RGAL
Simon, Carly 1945- .... CLC 26
See also CA 105
Simon, Claude 1913-1984 . CLC 4, 9, 15, 39;
DAM NOV
See also CA 89-92; CANR 33; DLB 83;
GFL 1789 to the Present; MTCW 1
Simon, (Marvin) Neil 1927- ... CLC 6, 11, 31,
39, 70; DAM DRAM; DC 14
See also AAYA 32; AITN 1; AMWS 4; CA
21-24R; CANR 26, 54, 87; CD; DA3;
DFS 2, 6, 12; DLB 7; MTCW 1; RGAL
Simon, Paul (Frederick) 1941(?)- ..... CLC 17
See also CA 116; 153
Simonon, Paul 1956(?)- .... CLC 30
Simonson, Rick ed. CLC 70
Simpson, Harriette
See Arnow, Harriette (Louisa) Simpson
Simpson, Louis (Aston Marantz)
1923- .... CLC 4, 7, 9, 32, 149; DAM
POET
See also CA 1-4R; CAAS 4; CANR 1, 61;
CP; DLB 5; MTCW 1, 2; PFS 7, 11;
RGAL
Simpson, Mona (Elizabeth) 1957- ... CLC 44,
146
See also CA 122; 135; CANR 68; CN
Simpson, N(orman) F(rederick)
1919- .... CLC 29
See also CA 13-16R; CBD; DLB 13; RGEL
Sinclair, Andrew (Annandale) 1935- . CLC 2,
14
See also CA 9-12R; CAAS 5; CANR 14,
38, 91; CN; DLB 14; FANT; MTCW 1
Sinclair, Emil
See Hesse, Hermann
Sinclair, Iain 1943- .... CLC 76
See also CA 132; CANR 81; CP; HGG
Sinclair, Iain MacGregor
See Sinclair, Iain
Sinclair, Irene
See Griffith, D(avid Lewelyn) W(ark)
Sinclair, Mary Amelia St. Clair 1865(?)-1946
See Sinclair, May
See also CA 104; HGG; RHW
Sinclair, May TCLC 3, 11
See also Sinclair, Mary Amelia St. Clair
See also CA 166; DLB 36, 135; RGEL
Sinclair, Roy
See Griffith, D(avid Lewelyn) W(ark)
Sinclair, Upton (Beall) 1878-1968 ..... CLC 1,
11, 15, 63; DA; DAB; DAC; DAM
MST, NOV; WLC
See also AMWS 5; BPFB 3; BYA 2; CA
5-8R; 25-28R; CANR 7; CDALB 1929-
1941; DA3; DLB 9; INT CANR-7; LAIT
3; MTCW 1, 2; NFS 6; RGAL; SATA 9;
YAW
Singer, Isaac
See Singer, Isaac Bashevis
Singer, Isaac Bashevis 1904-1991 .. CLC 1, 3,
6, 9, 11, 15, 23, 38, 69, 111; DA; DAB;
DAC; DAM MST, NOV; SSC 3; WLC
See also AAYA 32; AITN 1, 2; AMW;
BPFB 3; BYA 1; CA 1-4R; 134; CANR
1, 39; CDALB 1941-1968; CLR 1; CWRI;
DA3; DLB 6, 28, 52; DLBY 91; EXPS;
HGG; JRDA; LAIT 3; MAICYA; MTCW
1, 2; RGAL; RGSF; SATA 3, 27; SATA-
Obit 68; SSFS 2, 12

Singer, Israel Joshua 1893-1944 .... TCLC 33
See also CA 169
Singh, Khushwant 1915- .... CLC 11
See also CA 9-12R; CAAS 9; CANR 6, 84;
CN; RGEL
Singleton, Ann
See Benedict, Ruth (Fulton)
Sinjohn, John
See Galsworthy, John
Sinyavsky, Andrei (Donatevich)
1925-1997 .... CLC 8
See also Tertz, Abram
See also CA 85-88; 159
Sirin, V.
See Nabokov, Vladimir (Vladimirovich)
Sissman, L(ouis) E(dward)
1928-1976 .... CLC 9, 18
See also CA 21-24R; 65-68; CANR 13;
DLB 5
Sisson, C(harles) H(ubert) 1914- .... CLC 8
See also CA 1-4R; CAAS 3; CANR 3, 48,
84; CP; DLB 27
Sitwell, DameEdith 1887-1964 ...... CLC 2, 9,
67; DAM POET; PC 3
See also BRW; CA 9-12R; CANR 35; CD-
BLB 1945-1960; DLB 20; MTCW 1, 2;
RGEL
Siwaarmill, H. P.
See Sharp, William
Sjoewall, Maj 1935- .... CLC 7
See also Sjowall, Maj
See also CA 65-68; CANR 73
Sjowall, Maj
See Sjoewall, Maj
See also BPFB 3; CMW 1
Skelton, John 1460-1529 .... PC 25, LC 71
See also BRW 1; RGEL
Skelton, Robin 1925-1997 .... CLC 13
See also Zuk, Georges
See also AITN 2; CA 5-8R; 160; CAAS 5;
CANR 28, 89; CCA 1; CP; DLB 27, 53
Skolimowski, Jerzy 1938- .... CLC 20
See also CA 128
Skram, Amalie (Bertha)
1847-1905 .... TCLC 25
See also CA 165
Skvorecky, Josef (Vaclav) 1924- ...... CLC 15,
39, 69; DAC; DAM NOV
See also CA 61-64; CAAS 1; CANR 10,
34, 63; DA3; DLB 232; MTCW 1, 2
Slade, Bernard CLC 11, 46
See also Newbound, Bernard Slade
See also CAAS 9; CCA 1; DLB 53
Slaughter, Carolyn 1946- .... CLC 56
See also CA 85-88; CANR 85; CN
Slaughter, Frank G(ill) 1908-2001 ... CLC 29
See also AITN 2; CA 5-8R; CANR 5, 85;
INT CANR-5; RHW
Slavitt, David R(ytman) 1935- ..... CLC 5, 14
See also CA 21-24R; CAAS 3; CANR 41,
83; CP; DLB 5, 6
Slesinger, Tess 1905-1945 .... TCLC 10
See also CA 107; DLB 102
Slessor, Kenneth 1901-1971 .... CLC 14
See also CA 102; 89-92; RGEL
Slowacki, Juliusz 1809-1849 .... NCLC 15
Smart, Christopher 1722-1771 .. LC 3; DAM
POET; PC 13
See also DLB 109; RGEL
Smart, Elizabeth 1913-1986 .... CLC 54
See also CA 81-84; 118; DLB 88
Smiley, Jane (Graves) 1949- ...... CLC 53, 76,
144; DAM POP
See also AMWS 6; BPFB 3; CA 104;
CANR 30, 50, 74, 96; CN; CPW 1; DA3;
DLB 227, 234; INT CANR-30

Stewart, J(ohn) I(nnes) M(ackintosh)
1906-1994 .... **CLC 7, 14, 32**
See also CA 85-88; 147; CAAS 3; CANR
47; CMW; MTCW 1, 2

Stewart, Mary (Florence Elinor)
1916- .... **CLC 7, 35, 117; DAB**
See also AAYA 29; BPFB 3; CA 1-4R;
CANR 1, 59; CMW; CPW; FANT; RHW;
SATA 12; YAW

Stewart, Mary Rainbow
See Stewart, Mary (Florence Elinor)

Stifle, June
See Campbell, Maria

Stifter, Adalbert 1805-1868 .. **NCLC 41; SSC
28**
See also DLB 133; RGSF; RGWL

Still, James 1906-2001 .... **CLC 49**
See also CA 65-68; CAAS 17; CANR 10,
26; CSW; DLB 9; SATA 29

Sting 1951-
See Sumner, Gordon Matthew
See also CA 167

Stirling, Arthur
See Sinclair, Upton (Beall)

Stitt, Milan 1941- .... **CLC 29**
See also CA 69-72

Stockton, Francis Richard 1834-1902
See Stockton, Frank R.
See also CA 108; 137; MAICYA; SATA 44;
SFW

Stockton, Frank R. TCLC 47
See also Stockton, Francis Richard
See also BYA 4; DLB 42, 74; DLBD 13;
EXPS; SATA-Brief 32; SSFS 3

Stoddard, Charles
See Kuttner, Henry

Stoker, Abraham 1847-1912
See Stoker, Bram
See also CA 105; 150; DA; DA3; DAC;
DAM MST, NOV; HGG; SATA 29

Stoker, Bram TCLC 8; DAB; WLC
See also Stoker, Abraham
See also AAYA 23; BPFB 3; BRWS 3; BYA
5; CDBLB 1890-1914; DLB 36, 70, 178;
RGEL; WLIT 4

Stolz, Mary (Slattery) 1920- .... **CLC 12**
See also AAYA 8; AITN 1; CA 5-8R;
CANR 13, 41; JRDA; MAICYA; SAAS
3; SATA 10, 71; YAW

Stone, Irving 1903-1989 . **CLC 7; DAM POP**
See also AITN 1; BPFB 3; CA 1-4R; 129;
CAAS 3; CANR 1, 23; CPW; DA3; INT
CANR-23; MTCW 1, 2; RHW; SATA 3;
SATA-Obit 64

Stone, Oliver (William) 1946- .... **CLC 73**
See also AAYA 15; CA 110; CANR 55

Stone, Robert (Anthony) 1937- ... **CLC 5, 23,
42**
See also AMWS 5; BPFB 3; CA 85-88;
CANR 23, 66, 95; CN; DLB 152; INT
CANR-23; MTCW 1

Stone, Zachary
See Follett, Ken(neth Martin)

Stoppard, Tom 1937- ... **CLC 1, 3, 4, 5, 8, 15,
29, 34, 63, 91; DA; DAB; DAC; DAM
DRAM, MST; DC 6; WLC**
See also BRWS 1; CA 81-84; CANR 39,
67; CBD; CD; CDBLB 1960 to Present;
DA3; DFS 2,5,8,11, 13; DLB 13, 233;
DLBY 85; MTCW 1, 2; RGEL; WLIT 4

Storey, David (Malcolm) 1933- . **CLC 2, 4, 5,
8; DAM DRAM**
See also BRWS 1; CA 81-84; CANR 36;
CBD; CD; CN; DLB 13, 14, 207; MTCW
1; RGEL

Storm, Hyemeyohsts 1935- ..... **CLC 3; DAM
MULT**
See also CA 81-84; CANR 45; NNAL

Storm, Theodor 1817-1888 .... **SSC 27**
See also RGSF; RGWL

Storm, (Hans) Theodor (Woldsen)
1817-1888 .... **NCLC 1; SSC 27**
See also DLB 129

Storni, Alfonsina 1892-1938 . **TCLC 5; DAM
MULT; HLC 2; PC 33**
See also CA 104; 131; HW 1

Stoughton, William 1631-1701 .... **LC 38**
See also DLB 24

Stout, Rex (Todhunter) 1886-1975 ..... **CLC 3**
See also AITN 2; BPFB 3; CA 61-64;
CANR 71; CMW; MSW; RGAL

Stow, (Julian) Randolph 1935- ... **CLC 23, 48**
See also CA 13-16R; CANR 33; CN;
MTCW 1; RGEL

Stowe, Harriet (Elizabeth) Beecher
1811-1896 .... **NCLC 3, 50; DA; DAB;
DAC; DAM MST, NOV; WLC**
See also AMWS 1; CDALB 1865-1917;
DA3; DLB 1, 12, 42, 74, 189, 239; EXPN;
JRDA; LAIT 2; MAICYA; NFS 6; RGAL;
YABC 1

Strabo c. 64B.C.-c. 25 .... **CMLC 37**
See also DLB 176

Strachey, (Giles) Lytton
1880-1932 .... **TCLC 12**
See also BRWS 2; CA 110; 178; DLB 149;
DLBD 10; MTCW 2

Strand, Mark 1934- .... **CLC 6, 18, 41, 71;
DAM POET**
See also AMWS 4; CA 21-24R; CANR 40,
65, 100; CP; DLB 5; PAB; PFS 9; RGAL;
SATA 41

Stratton-Porter, Gene(va Grace) 1863-1924
See Porter, Gene(va Grace) Stratton
See also ANW; CA 137; DLB 221; DLBD
14; MAICYA; SATA 15

Straub, Peter (Francis) 1943- . **CLC 28, 107;
DAM POP**
See also BEST 89:1; BPFB 3; CA 85-88;
CANR 28, 65; CPW; DLBY 84; HGG;
MTCW 1, 2

Strauss, Botho 1944- .... **CLC 22**
See also CA 157; CWW 2; DLB 124

Streatfeild, (Mary) Noel
1897(?)-1986 .... **CLC 21**
See also CA 81-84; 120; CANR 31; CLR
17; CWRI; DLB 160; MAICYA; SATA
20; SATA-Obit 48

Stribling, T(homas) S(igismund)
1881-1965 .... **CLC 23**
See also CA 189; 107; CMW; DLB 9;
RGAL

Strindberg, (Johan) August
1849-1912 .... **TCLC 1, 8, 21, 47; DA;
DAB; DAC; DAM DRAM, MST; WLC**
See also CA 104; 135; DA3; DFS 4, 9; EW;
MTCW 2; RGWL

Stringer, Arthur 1874-1950 .... **TCLC 37**
See also CA 161; DLB 92

Stringer, David
See Roberts, Keith (John Kingston)

Stroheim, Erich von 1885-1957 ..... **TCLC 71**

Strugatskii, Arkadii (Natanovich)
1925-1991 .... **CLC 27**
See also CA 106; 135; SFW

Strugatskii, Boris (Natanovich)
1933- .... **CLC 27**
See also CA 106; SFW

Strummer, Joe 1953(?)- .... **CLC 30**

Strunk, William, Jr. 1869-1946 ...... **TCLC 92**
See also CA 118; 164

Stryk, Lucien 1924- .... **PC 27**
See also CA 13-16R; CANR 10, 28, 55; CP

Stuart, Don A.
See Campbell, John W(ood, Jr.)

Stuart, Ian
See MacLean, Alistair (Stuart)

Stuart, Jesse (Hilton) 1906-1984 ... **CLC 1, 8,
11, 14, 34; SSC 31**
See also CA 5-8R; 112; CANR 31; DLB 9,
48, 102; DLBY 84; SATA 2; SATA-Obit
36

Stubblefield, Sally
See Trumbo, Dalton

Sturgeon, Theodore (Hamilton)
1918-1985 .... **CLC 22, 39**
See also Queen, Ellery
See also BPFB 3; BYA 9; CA 81-84; 116;
CANR 32; DLB 8; DLBY 85; HGG;
MTCW 1, 2; SCFW; SFW; SUFW

Sturges, Preston 1898-1959 .... **TCLC 48**
See also CA 114; 149; DLB 26

Styron, William 1925- .... **CLC 1, 3, 5, 11, 15,
60; DAM NOV, POP; SSC 25**
See also AMW; BEST 90:4; BPFB 3; CA
5-8R; CANR 6, 33, 74; CDALB 1968-
1988; CN; CPW; CSW; DA3; DLB 2,
143; DLBY 80; INT CANR-6; LAIT 2;
MTCW 1, 2; NCFS 1; RGAL; RHW

Su, Chien 1884-1918
See Su Man-shu
See also CA 123

Suarez Lynch, B.
See Bioy Casares, Adolfo; Borges, Jorge
Luis

Suassuna, Ariano Vilar 1927-
See also CA 178; HLCS 1; HW 2

Suckling, Sir John 1609-1642 .... **PC 30**
See also BRW 2; DAM POET; DLB 58,
126; EXPP; PAB; RGEL

Suckow, Ruth 1892-1960 .... **SSC 18**
See also CA 193; 113; DLB 9, 102; RGAL;
TCWW 2

Sudermann, Hermann 1857-1928 .. **TCLC 15**
See also CA 107; DLB 118

Sue, Eugene 1804-1857 .... **NCLC 1**
See also DLB 119

Sueskind, Patrick 1949- .... **CLC 44**
See also Suskind, Patrick

Sukenick, Ronald 1932- .... **CLC 3, 4, 6, 48**
See also CA 25-28R; CAAS 8; CANR 32,
89; CN; DLB 173; DLBY 81

Suknaski, Andrew 1942- .... **CLC 19**
See also CA 101; CP; DLB 53

Sullivan, Vernon
See Vian, Boris

Sully Prudhomme, Rene-Francois-Armand
1839-1907 .... **TCLC 31**
See also GFL 1789 to the Present

Su Man-shu TCLC 24
See also Su, Chien

Summerforest, Ivy B.
See Kirkup, James

Summers, Andrew James 1942- .... **CLC 26**

Summers, Andy
See Summers, Andrew James

Summers, Hollis (Spurgeon, Jr.)
1916- .... **CLC 10**
See also CA 5-8R; CANR 3; DLB 6

**Summers, (Alphonsus Joseph-Mary
Augustus) Montague**
1880-1948 .... **TCLC 16**
See also CA 118; 163

Sumner, Gordon Matthew CLC 26
See also Sting

Surtees, Robert Smith 1805-1864 .. **NCLC 14**
See also DLB 21; RGEL

Susann, Jacqueline 1921-1974 .... **CLC 3**
See also AITN 1; BPFB 3; CA 65-68; 53-
56; MTCW 1, 2

Su Shi
See Su Shih
See also RGWL

Su Shih 1036-1101 .... **CMLC 15**
See also Su Shi

Suskind, Patrick
    See Sueskind, Patrick
    See also BPFB 3; CA 145; CWW 2
Sutcliff, Rosemary 1920-1992 .... **CLC 26; DAB; DAC; DAM MST, POP**
    See also AAYA 10; BYA 1; CA 5-8R; 139; CANR 37; CLR 1, 37; CPW; JRDA; MAICYA; RHW; SATA 6, 44, 78; SATA-Obit 73; YAW
Sutro, Alfred 1863-1933 .... **TCLC 6**
    See also CA 105; 185; DLB 10; RGEL
Sutton, Henry
    See Slavitt, David R(ytman)
Suzuki, D. T.
    See Suzuki, Daisetz Teitaro
Suzuki, Daisetz T.
    See Suzuki, Daisetz Teitaro
Suzuki, Daisetz Teitaro
    1870-1966 .... **TCLC 109**
    See also CA 121; 111; MTCW 1, 2
Suzuki, Teitaro
    See Suzuki, Daisetz Teitaro
Svevo, Italo TCLC 2, 35; SSC 25
    See also Schmitz, Aron Hector
    See also RGWL
Swados, Elizabeth (A.) 1951- .... **CLC 12**
    See also CA 97-100; CANR 49; INT 97-100
Swados, Harvey 1920-1972 .... **CLC 5**
    See also CA 5-8R; 37-40R; CANR 6; DLB 2
Swan, Gladys 1934- .... **CLC 69**
    See also CA 101; CANR 17, 39
Swanson, Logan
    See Matheson, Richard (Burton)
Swarthout, Glendon (Fred)
    1918-1992 .... **CLC 35**
    See also CA 1-4R; 139; CANR 1, 47; LAIT 5; SATA 26; TCWW 2; YAW
Sweet, Sarah C.
    See Jewett, (Theodora) Sarah Orne
Swenson, May 1919-1989 ...... **CLC 4, 14, 61, 106; DA; DAB; DAC; DAM MST, POET; PC 14**
    See also AMWS 4; CA 5-8R; 130; CANR 36, 61; DLB 5; EXPP; GLL 2; MTCW 1, 2; SATA 15; WP
Swift, Augustus
    See Lovecraft, H(oward) P(hillips)
Swift, Graham (Colin) 1949- ...... **CLC 41, 88**
    See also BRWS 5; CA 117; 122; CANR 46, 71; CN; DLB 194; MTCW 2; RGSF
Swift, Jonathan 1667-1745 ..... **LC 1, 42; DA; DAB; DAC; DAM MST, NOV, POET; PC 9; WLC**
    See also BYA 5; CDBLB 1660-1789; CLR 53; DA3; DLB 39, 95, 101; EXPN; LAIT 1; NFS 6; RGEL; SATA 19; WLIT 3
Swinburne, Algernon Charles
    1837-1909 .... **TCLC 8, 36; DA; DAB; DAC; DAM MST, POET; PC 24; WLC**
    See also CA 105; 140; CDBLB 1832-1890; DA3; DLB 35, 57; PAB; RGEL
Swinfen, Ann CLC 34
Swinnerton, Frank Arthur
    1884-1982 .... **CLC 31**
    See also CA 108; DLB 34
Swithen, John
    See King, Stephen (Edwin)
Sylvia
    See Ashton-Warner, Sylvia (Constance)
Symmes, Robert Edward
    See Duncan, Robert (Edward)
Symonds, John Addington
    1840-1893 .... **NCLC 34**
    See also DLB 57, 144
Symons, Arthur 1865-1945 .... **TCLC 11**
    See also CA 107; 189; DLB 19, 57, 149; RGEL

Symons, Julian (Gustave)
    1912-1994 .... **CLC 2, 14, 32**
    See also CA 49-52; 147; CAAS 3; CANR 3, 33, 59; CMW; DLB 87, 155; DLBY 92; MSW; MTCW 1
Synge, (Edmund) J(ohn) M(illington)
    1871-1909 . **TCLC 6, 37; DAM DRAM; DC 2**
    See also BRW; CA 104; 141; CDBLB 1890-1914; DLB 10, 19; RGEL; WLIT 4
Syruc, J.
    See Milosz, Czeslaw
Szirtes, George 1948- .... **CLC 46**
    See also CA 109; CANR 27, 61; CP
Szymborska, Wislawa 1923- .... **CLC 99**
    See also CA 154; CANR 91; CWP; CWW 2; DA3; DLB 232; DLBY 96; MTCW 2
T. O., Nik
    See Annensky, Innokenty (Fyodorovich)
Tabori, George 1914- .... **CLC 19**
    See also CA 49-52; CANR 4, 69; CBD; CD
Tagore, Rabindranath 1861-1941 ... **TCLC 3, 53; DAM DRAM, POET; PC 8**
    See also CA 104; 120; DA3; MTCW 1, 2; RGEL; RGSF; RGWL
Taine, Hippolyte Adolphe
    1828-1893 .... **NCLC 15**
    See also EW; GFL 1789 to the Present
Talese, Gay 1932- .... **CLC 37**
    See also AITN 1; CA 1-4R; CANR 9, 58; DLB 185; INT CANR-9; MTCW 1, 2
Tallent, Elizabeth (Ann) 1954- .... **CLC 45**
    See also CA 117; CANR 72; DLB 130
Tally, Ted 1952- .... **CLC 42**
    See also CA 120; 124; CAD; CD; INT 124
Talvik, Heiti 1904-1947 .... **TCLC 87**
Tamayo y Baus, Manuel
    1829-1898 .... **NCLC 1**
Tammsaare, A(nton) H(ansen)
    1878-1940 .... **TCLC 27**
    See also CA 164; DLB 220
Tam'si, Tchicaya U
    See Tchicaya, Gerald Felix
Tan, Amy (Ruth) 1952- . **CLC 59, 120; AAL; DAM MULT, NOV, POP**
    See also AAYA 9; BEST 89:3; BPFB 3; CA 136; CANR 54; CDALBS; CN; CPW 1; DA3; DLB 173; EXPN; FW; LAIT 5; MTCW 2; NFS 1; RGAL; SATA 75; SSFS 9; YAW
Tandem, Felix
    See Spitteler, Carl (Friedrich Georg)
Tanizaki, Jun'ichiro 1886-1965 ... **CLC 8, 14, 28; SSC 21**
    See also CA 93-96; 25-28R; DLB 180; MJW; MTCW 2; RGSF; RGWL
Tanner, William
    See Amis, Kingsley (William)
Tao Lao
    See Storni, Alfonsina
Tarantino, Quentin (Jerome)
    1963- .... **CLC 125**
    See also CA 171
Tarassoff, Lev
    See Troyat, Henri
Tarbell, Ida M(inerva) 1857-1944 . **TCLC 40**
    See also CA 122; 181; DLB 47
Tarkington, (Newton) Booth
    1869-1946 .... **TCLC 9**
    See also BPFB 3; BYA 3; CA 110; 143; CWRI; DLB 9, 102; MTCW 2; RGAL; SATA 17
Tarkovsky, Andrei (Arsenyevich)
    1932-1986 .... **CLC 75**
    See also CA 127
Tartt, Donna 1964(?)- .... **CLC 76**
    See also CA 142
Tasso, Torquato 1544-1595 .... **LC 5**
    See also EFS 2; RGWL

Tate, (John Orley) Allen 1899-1979 .. **CLC 2, 4, 6, 9, 11, 14, 24**
    See also AMW; CA 5-8R; 85-88; CANR 32; DLB 4, 45, 63; DLBD 17; MTCW 1, 2; RGAL; RHW
Tate, Ellalice
    See Hibbert, Eleanor Alice Burford
Tate, James (Vincent) 1943- ..... **CLC 2, 6, 25**
    See also CA 21-24R; CANR 29, 57; CP; DLB 5, 169; PFS 10; RGAL; WP
Tauler, Johannes c. 1300-1361 ...... **CMLC 37**
    See also DLB 179
Tavel, Ronald 1940- .... **CLC 6**
    See also CA 21-24R; CAD; CANR 33; CD
Taviani, Paolo 1931- .... **CLC 70**
    See also CA 153
Taylor, Bayard 1825-1878 .... **NCLC 89**
    See also DLB 3, 189; RGAL
Taylor, C(ecil) P(hilip) 1929-1981 .... **CLC 27**
    See also CA 25-28R; 105; CANR 47; CBD
Taylor, Edward 1642(?)-1729 ..... **LC 11; DA; DAB; DAC; DAM MST, POET**
    See also AMW; DLB 24; EXPP; RGAL
Taylor, Eleanor Ross 1920- .... **CLC 5**
    See also CA 81-84; CANR 70
Taylor, Elizabeth 1932-1975 ..... **CLC 2, 4, 29**
    See also CA 13-16R; CANR 9, 70; DLB 139; MTCW 1; RGEL; SATA 13
Taylor, Frederick Winslow
    1856-1915 .... **TCLC 76**
    See also CA 188
Taylor, Henry (Splawn) 1942- .... **CLC 44**
    See also CA 33-36R; CAAS 7; CANR 31; CP; DLB 5; PFS 10
Taylor, Kamala (Purnaiya) 1924-
    See Markandaya, Kamala
    See also CA 77-80; CN
Taylor, Mildred D(elois) 1943- .... **CLC 21**
    See also AAYA 10; BW 1; BYA 3; CA 85-88; CANR 25; CLR 9, 59; CSW; DLB 52; JRDA; LAIT 3; MAICYA; SAAS 5; SATA 15, 70; WYA; YAW
Taylor, Peter (Hillsman) 1917-1994 .. **CLC 1, 4, 18, 37, 44, 50, 71; SSC 10**
    See also AMWS 5; BPFB 3; CA 13-16R; 147; CANR 9, 50; CSW; DLBY 81, 94; EXPS; INT CANR-9; MTCW 1, 2; RGSF; SSFS 9
Taylor, Robert Lewis 1912-1998 .... **CLC 14**
    See also CA 1-4R; 170; CANR 3, 64; SATA 10
Tchekhov, Anton
    See Chekhov, Anton (Pavlovich)
Tchicaya, Gerald Felix 1931-1988 .. **CLC 101**
    See also CA 129; 125; CANR 81
Tchicaya U Tam'si
    See Tchicaya, Gerald Felix
Teasdale, Sara 1884-1933 .... **TCLC 4; PC 31**
    See also CA 104; 163; DLB 45; GLL 1; RGAL; SATA 32
Tegner, Esaias 1782-1846 .... **NCLC 2**
Teilhard de Chardin, (Marie Joseph) Pierre
    1881-1955 .... **TCLC 9**
    See also CA 105; GFL 1789 to the Present
Temple, Ann
    See Mortimer, Penelope (Ruth)
Tennant, Emma (Christina) 1937- .. **CLC 13, 52**
    See also CA 65-68; CAAS 9; CANR 10, 38, 59, 88; CN; DLB 14; SFW
Tenneshaw, S. M.
    See Silverberg, Robert
Tennyson, Alfred 1809-1892 ... **NCLC 30, 65; DA; DAB; DAC; DAM MST, POET; PC 6; WLC**
    See also BRW; CDBLB 1832-1890; DA3; DLB 32; EXPP; PAB; PFS 1, 2, 4, 11; RGEL; WLIT 4; WP

Turgenev, Ivan 1818-1883 .... NCLC 21, 37;
DA; DAB; DAC; DAM MST, NOV;
DC 7; SSC 7; WLC
See also DFS 6; DLB 238; RGSF; RGWL

Turgenev, Ivan Sergeevich
See Turgenev, Ivan

Turgot, Anne-Robert-Jacques
1727-1781 .... LC 26

Turner, Frederick 1943- .... CLC 48
See also CA 73-76; CAAS 10; CANR 12,
30, 56; DLB 40

Tutu, Desmond M(pilo) 1931- .... CLC 80;
BLC 3; DAM MULT
See also BW 1, 3; CA 125; CANR 67, 81

Tutuola, Amos 1920-1997 ...... CLC 5, 14, 29;
BLC 3; DAM MULT
See also BW 2, 3; CA 9-12R; 159; CANR
27, 66; CN; DA3; DLB 125; DNFS;
MTCW 1, 2; RGEL; WLIT 2

Twain, Mark TCLC 6, 12, 19, 36, 48, 59; SSC
34; WLC
See also Clemens, Samuel Langhorne
See also AAYA 20; AMW; BPFB 3; BYA 2;
CLR 58, 60, 66; DLB 11, 12, 23, 64, 74;
EXPN; EXPS; FANT; LAIT 2; NFS 1, 6;
RGAL; RGSF; SFW; SSFS 1, 7; YAW

Tyler, Anne 1941- . CLC 7, 11, 18, 28, 44, 59,
103; DAM NOV, POP
See also AAYA 18; AMWS 4; BEST 89:1;
BPFB 3; BYA 12; CA 9-12R; CANR 11,
33, 53; CDALBS; CN; CPW; CSW; DLB
6, 143; DLBY 82; EXPN; MTCW 1, 2;
NFS 2, 7, 10; RGAL; SATA 7, 90; YAW

Tyler, Royall 1757-1826 .... NCLC 3
See also DLB 37; RGAL

Tynan, Katharine 1861-1931 .... TCLC 3
See also CA 104; 167; DLB 153, 240; FW

Tyutchev, Fyodor 1803-1873 .... NCLC 34

Tzara, Tristan 1896-1963 ...... CLC 47; DAM
POET; PC 27
See also CA 153; 89-92; MTCW 2

Uhry, Alfred 1936- .. CLC 55; DAM DRAM,
POP
See also CA 127; 133; CAD; CD; CSW;
DA3; DFS 11; INT 133

Ulf, Haerved
See Strindberg, (Johan) August

Ulf, Harved
See Strindberg, (Johan) August

Ulibarri, Sabine R(eyes) 1919- .... CLC 83;
DAM MULT; HLCS 2
See also CA 131; CANR 81; DLB 82; HW
1, 2; RGSF

Unamuno (y Jugo), Miguel de
1864-1936 ..... TCLC 2, 9; DAM MULT,
NOV; HLC 2; SSC 11
See also CA 104; 131; CANR 81; DLB 108;
EW; HW 1, 2; MTCW 1, 2; RGSF;
RGWL

Undercliffe, Errol
See Campbell, (John) Ramsey

Underwood, Miles
See Glassco, John

Undset, Sigrid 1882-1949 .... TCLC 3; DA;
DAB; DAC; DAM MST, NOV; WLC
See also CA 104; 129; DA3; FW; MTCW
1, 2; RGWL

Ungaretti, Giuseppe 1888-1970 ... CLC 7, 11,
15
See also CA 19-20; 25-28R; CAP 2; DLB
114; RGWL

Unger, Douglas 1952- .... CLC 34
See also CA 130; CANR 94

Unsworth, Barry (Forster) 1930- .... CLC 76,
127
See also BRWS 7; CA 25-28R; CANR 30,
54; CN; DLB 194

Updike, John (Hoyer) 1932- . CLC 1, 2, 3, 5,
7, 9, 13, 15, 23, 34, 43, 70, 139; DA;
DAB; DAC; DAM MST, NOV, POET,
POP; SSC 13, 27; WLC
See also AAYA 36; AMW; AMWR; BPFB
3; BYA 12; CA 1-4R; CABS 1; CANR 4,
33, 51, 94; CDALB 1968-1988; CN; CP;
CPW 1; DA3; DLB 2, 5, 143, 227; DLBD
3; DLBY 80, 82, 97; EXPP; HGG;
MTCW 1, 2; NFS 12; RGAL; RGSF;
SSFS 3

Upshaw, Margaret Mitchell
See Mitchell, Margaret (Munnerlyn)

Upton, Mark
See Sanders, Lawrence

Upward, Allen 1863-1926 .... TCLC 85
See also CA 117; 187; DLB 36

Urdang, Constance (Henriette)
1922-1996 .... CLC 47
See also CA 21-24R; CANR 9, 24; CP;
CWP

Uriel, Henry
See Faust, Frederick (Schiller)

Uris, Leon (Marcus) 1924- .... CLC 7, 32;
DAM NOV, POP
See also AITN 1, 2; BEST 89:2; BPFB 3;
CA 1-4R; CANR 1, 40, 65; CN; CPW 1;
DA3; MTCW 1, 2; SATA 49

Urista, Alberto H. 1947- .... PC 34
See also Alurista
See also CA 45-48, 182; CANR 2, 32;
HLCS 1; HW 1

Urmuz
See Codrescu, Andrei

Urquhart, Guy
See McAlmon, Robert (Menzies)

Urquhart, Jane 1949- .... CLC 90; DAC
See also CA 113; CANR 32, 68; CCA 1

Usigli, Rodolfo 1905-1979
See also CA 131; HLCS 1; HW 1

Ustinov, Peter (Alexander) 1921- .... CLC 1
See also AITN 1; CA 13-16R; CANR 25,
51; CBD; CD; DLB 13; MTCW 2

U Tam'si, Gerald Felix Tchicaya
See Tchicaya, Gerald Felix

U Tam'si, Tchicaya
See Tchicaya, Gerald Felix

Vachss, Andrew (Henry) 1942- .... CLC 106
See also CA 118; CANR 44, 95; CMW

Vachss, Andrew H.
See Vachss, Andrew (Henry)

Vaculik, Ludvik 1926- .... CLC 7
See also CA 53-56; CANR 72; CWW 2;
DLB 232

Vaihinger, Hans 1852-1933 .... TCLC 71
See also CA 116; 166

Valdez, Luis (Miguel) 1940- .. CLC 84; DAM
MULT; DC 10; HLC 2
See also CA 101; CAD; CANR 32, 81; CD;
DFS 5; DLB 122; HW 1; LAIT 4

Valenzuela, Luisa 1938- .... CLC 31, 104;
DAM MULT; HLCS 2; SSC 14
See also CA 101; CANR 32, 65; CWW 2;
DLB 113; FW; HW 1, 2; RGSF

Valera y Alcala-Galiano, Juan
1824-1905 .... TCLC 10
See also CA 106

Valery, (Ambroise) Paul (Toussaint Jules)
1871-1945 ... TCLC 4, 15; DAM POET;
PC 9
See also CA 104; 122; DA3; EW; GFL 1789
to the Present; MTCW 1, 2; RGWL

Valle-Inclan, Ramon (Maria) del
1866-1936 .... TCLC 5; DAM MULT;
HLC 2
See also CA 106; 153; CANR 80; DLB 134;
EW; HW 2; RGSF; RGWL

Vallejo, Antonio Buero
See Buero Vallejo, Antonio

Vallejo, Cesar (Abraham)
1892-1938 .. TCLC 3, 56; DAM MULT;
HLC 2
See also CA 105; 153; HW 1; LAW; RGWL

Valles, Jules 1832-1885 .... NCLC 71
See also DLB 123; GFL 1789 to the Present

Vallette, Marguerite Eymery
1860-1953 .... TCLC 67
See also CA 182; DLB 123, 192

Valle Y Pena, Ramon del
See Valle-Inclan, Ramon (Maria) del

Van Ash, Cay 1918- .... CLC 34

Vanbrugh, Sir John 1664-1726 .... LC 21;
DAM DRAM
See also BRW 2; DLB 80; IDTP; RGEL

Van Campen, Karl
See Campbell, John W(ood, Jr.)

Vance, Gerald
See Silverberg, Robert

Vance, Jack CLC 35
See also Vance, John Holbrook
See also DLB 8; SCFW 2

Vance, John Holbrook 1916-
See Queen, Ellery; Vance, Jack
See also CA 29-32R; CANR 17, 65; CMW;
FANT; MTCW 1; SFW

Van Den Bogarde, Derek Jules Gaspard
Ulric Niven 1921-1999 .... CLC 14
See also CA 77-80; 179; DLB 19

Vandenburgh, Jane CLC 59
See also CA 168

Vanderhaeghe, Guy 1951- .... CLC 41
See also BPFB 3; CA 113; CANR 72

van der Post, Laurens (Jan)
1906-1996 .... CLC 5
See also AFW; CA 5-8R; 155; CANR 35;
CN; DLB 204; RGEL

van de Wetering, Janwillem 1931- ... CLC 47
See also CA 49-52; CANR 4, 62, 90; CMW

Van Dine, S. S. TCLC 23
See also Wright, Willard Huntington

Van Doren, Carl (Clinton)
1885-1950 .... TCLC 18
See also CA 111; 168

Van Doren, Mark 1894-1972 .... CLC 6, 10
See also CA 1-4R; 37-40R; CANR 3; DLB
45; MTCW 1, 2; RGAL

Van Druten, John (William)
1901-1957 .... TCLC 2
See also CA 104; 161; DLB 10; RGAL

Van Duyn, Mona (Jane) 1921- ...... CLC 3, 7,
63, 116; DAM POET
See also CA 9-12R; CANR 7, 38, 60; CP;
CWP; DLB 5

Van Dyne, Edith
See Baum, L(yman) Frank

van Itallie, Jean-Claude 1936- .... CLC 3
See also CA 45-48; CAAS 2; CAD; CANR
1, 48; CD; DLB 7

van Ostaijen, Paul 1896-1928 .... TCLC 33
See also CA 163

Van Peebles, Melvin 1932- .... CLC 2, 20;
DAM MULT
See also BW 2, 3; CA 85-88; CANR 27,
67, 82

van Schendel, Arthur(-Francois-Emile)
1874-1946 .... TCLC 56

Vansittart, Peter 1920- .... CLC 42
See also CA 1-4R; CANR 3, 49, 90; CN;
RHW

Van Vechten, Carl 1880-1964 .... CLC 33
See also AMWS 2; CA 183; 89-92; DLB 4,
9, 51; RGAL

van Vogt, A(lfred) E(lton) 1912-2000 . CLC 1
See also BPFB 3; CA 21-24R; 190; CANR
28; DLB 8; SATA 14; SATA-Obit 124;
SCFW; SFW

Varda, Agnes 1928- .... CLC 16
See also CA 116; 122

Waugh, Auberon (Alexander)
1939-2001 .... **CLC 7**
See also CA 45-48; 192; CANR 6, 22, 92;
DLB 14, 194

Waugh, Evelyn (Arthur St. John)
1903-1966 .. **CLC 1, 3, 8, 13, 19, 27, 44,
107; DA; DAB; DAC; DAM MST,
NOV, POP; SSC 41; WLC**
See also BPFB 3; BRW; CA 85-88; 25-28R;
CANR 22; CDBLB 1914-1945; DA3;
DLB 15, 162, 195; MTCW 1, 2; RGEL;
RGSF; WLIT 4

Waugh, Harriet 1944- .... **CLC 6**
See also CA 85-88; CANR 22

Ways, C. R.
See Blount, Roy (Alton), Jr.

Waystaff, Simon
See Swift, Jonathan

Webb, Beatrice (Martha Potter)
1858-1943 .... **TCLC 22**
See also CA 117; 162; DLB 190; FW

Webb, Charles (Richard) 1939- .... **CLC 7**
See also CA 25-28R

Webb, James H(enry), Jr. 1946- ...... **CLC 22**
See also CA 81-84

Webb, Mary Gladys (Meredith)
1881-1927 .... **TCLC 24**
See also CA 182; 123; DLB 34; FW

Webb, Mrs. Sidney
See Webb, Beatrice (Martha Potter)

Webb, Phyllis 1927- .... **CLC 18**
See also CA 104; CANR 23; CCA 1; CP;
CWP; DLB 53

Webb, Sidney (James) 1859-1947 .. **TCLC 22**
See also CA 117; 163; DLB 190

Webber, Andrew Lloyd **CLC 21**
See also Lloyd Webber, Andrew
See also DFS 7

Weber, Lenora Mattingly
1895-1971 .... **CLC 12**
See also CA 19-20; 29-32R; CAP 1; SATA
2; SATA-Obit 26

Weber, Max 1864-1920 .... **TCLC 69**
See also CA 109; 189

Webster, John 1580(?)-1634(?) ... **LC 33; DA;
DAB; DAC; DAM DRAM, MST; DC
2; WLC**
See also BRW 2; CDBLB Before 1660;
DLB 58; IDTP; RGEL; WLIT 3

Webster, Noah 1758-1843 .... **NCLC 30**
See also DLB 1, 37, 42, 43, 73

Wedekind, (Benjamin) Frank(lin)
1864-1918 .... **TCLC 7; DAM DRAM**
See also CA 104; 153; DLB 118; EW;
RGWL

Wehr, Demaris **CLC 65**

Weidman, Jerome 1913-1998 .... **CLC 7**
See also AITN 2; CA 1-4R; 171; CAD;
CANR 1; DLB 28

Weil, Simone (Adolphine)
1909-1943 .... **TCLC 23**
See also CA 117; 159; EW; FW; GFL 1789
to the Present; MTCW 2

Weininger, Otto 1880-1903 .... **TCLC 84**

Weinstein, Nathan
See West, Nathanael

Weinstein, Nathan von Wallenstein
See West, Nathanael

Weir, Peter (Lindsay) 1944- .... **CLC 20**
See also CA 113; 123

Weiss, Peter (Ulrich) 1916-1982 .. **CLC 3, 15,
51; DAM DRAM**
See also CA 45-48; 106; CANR 3; DFS 3;
DLB 69, 124; RGWL

Weiss, Theodore (Russell) 1916- ... **CLC 3, 8,
14**
See also CA 9-12R; CAAE 189; CAAS 2;
CANR 46, 94; CP; DLB 5

Welch, (Maurice) Denton
1915-1948 .... **TCLC 22**
See also CA 121; 148; RGEL

Welch, James 1940- ..... **CLC 6, 14, 52; DAM
MULT, POP**
See also CA 85-88; CANR 42, 66; CN; CP;
CPW; DLB 175; NNAL; RGAL; TCWW
2

Weldon, Fay 1931- . **CLC 6, 9, 11, 19, 36, 59,
122; DAM POP**
See also BRWS 4; CA 21-24R; CANR 16,
46, 63, 97; CDBLB 1960 to Present; CN;
CPW; DLB 14, 194; FW; HGG; INT
CANR-16; MTCW 1, 2; RGEL; RGSF

Wellek, Rene 1903-1995 .... **CLC 28**
See also CA 5-8R; 150; CAAS 7; CANR 8;
DLB 63; INT CANR-8

Weller, Michael 1942- .... **CLC 10, 53**
See also CA 85-88; CAD; CD

Weller, Paul 1958- .... **CLC 26**

Wellershoff, Dieter 1925- .... **CLC 46**
See also CA 89-92; CANR 16, 37

Welles, (George) Orson 1915-1985 .. **CLC 20,
80**
See also AAYA 40; CA 93-96; 117

Wellman, John McDowell 1945-
See Wellman, Mac
See also CA 166; CD

Wellman, Mac **CLC 65**
See also Wellman, John McDowell; Well-
man, John McDowell
See also CAD; RGAL

Wellman, Manly Wade 1903-1986 ... **CLC 49**
See also CA 1-4R; 118; CANR 6, 16, 44;
FANT; SATA 6; SATA-Obit 47; SFW

Wells, Carolyn 1869(?)-1942 .... **TCLC 35**
See also CA 113; 185; CMW; DLB 11

Wells, H(erbert) G(eorge)
1866-1946 . **TCLC 6, 12, 19; DA; DAB;
DAC; DAM MST, NOV; SSC 6; WLC**
See also AAYA 18; BPFB 3; BRW; CA 110;
121; CDBLB 1914-1945; CLR 64; DA3;
DLB 34, 70, 156, 178; EXPS; HGG;
LAIT 3; MTCW 1, 2; RGEL; RGSF;
SATA 20; SCFW; SFW; SSFS 3; SUFW;
WCH; WLIT 4; YAW

Wells, Rosemary 1943- .... **CLC 12**
See also AAYA 13; BYA 7; CA 85-88;
CANR 48; CLR 16, 69; CWRI; MAICYA;
SAAS 1; SATA 18, 69, 114; YAW

Welsh, Irvine 1958- .... **CLC 144**
See also CA 173

Welty, Eudora 1909-2001 .... **CLC 1, 2, 5, 14,
22, 33, 105; DA; DAB; DAC; DAM
MST, NOV; SSC 1, 27; WLC**
See also AMW; BPFB 3; CA 9-12R; CABS
1; CANR 32, 65; CDALB 1941-1968;
CN; CSW; DA3; DLB 2, 102, 143; DLBD
12; DLBY 87; EXPS; HGG; LAIT 3;
MTCW 1, 2; RGAL; RGSF; RHW; SSFS
2, 10

Wen I-to 1899-1946 .... **TCLC 28**

Wentworth, Robert
See Hamilton, Edmond

Werfel, Franz (Viktor) 1890-1945 ... **TCLC 8**
See also CA 104; 161; DLB 81, 124;
RGWL

Wergeland, Henrik Arnold
1808-1845 .... **NCLC 5**

Wersba, Barbara 1932- .... **CLC 30**
See also AAYA 2, 30; BYA 6; CA 29-32R,
182; CAAE 182; CANR 16, 38; CLR 3;
DLB 52; JRDA; MAICYA; SAAS 2;
SATA 1, 58; SATA-Essay 103; YAW

Wertmueller, Lina 1928- .... **CLC 16**
See also CA 97-100; CANR 39, 78

Wescott, Glenway 1901-1987 .. **CLC 13; SSC
35**
See also CA 13-16R; 121; CANR 23, 70;
DLB 4, 9, 102; RGAL

Wesker, Arnold 1932- ... **CLC 3, 5, 42; DAB;
DAM DRAM**
See also CA 1-4R; CAAS 7; CANR 1, 33;
CBD; CD; CDBLB 1960 to Present; DLB
13; MTCW 1; RGEL

Wesley, Richard (Errol) 1945- .... **CLC 7**
See also BW 1; CA 57-60; CAD; CANR
27; CD; DLB 38

Wessel, Johan Herman 1742-1785 .... **LC 7**

West, Anthony (Panther)
1914-1987 .... **CLC 50**
See also CA 45-48; 124; CANR 3, 19; DLB
15

West, C. P.
See Wodehouse, P(elham) G(renville)

West, Cornel (Ronald) 1953- .... **CLC 134;
BLCS**
See also CA 144; CANR 91

West, Delno C(loyde), Jr. 1936- .... **CLC 70**
See also CA 57-60

West, Dorothy 1907-1998 .... **TCLC 108**
See also BW 2; CA 143; 169; DLB 76

West, (Mary) Jessamyn 1902-1984 ... **CLC 7,
17**
See also CA 9-12R; 112; CANR 27; DLB
6; DLBY 84; MTCW 1, 2; RHW; SATA-
Obit 37; YAW

West, Morris L(anglo) 1916-1999 ..... **CLC 6,
33**
See also BPFB 3; CA 5-8R; 187; CANR
24, 49, 64; CN; CPW; MTCW 1, 2

West, Nathanael 1903-1940 .... **TCLC 1, 14,
44; SSC 16**
See also AMW; BPFB 3; CA 104; 125;
CDALB 1929-1941; DA3; DLB 4, 9, 28;
MTCW 1, 2; RGAL

West, Owen
See Koontz, Dean R(ay)

West, Paul 1930- .... **CLC 7, 14, 96**
See also CA 13-16R; CAAS 7; CANR 22,
53, 76, 89; CN; DLB 14; INT CANR-22;
MTCW 2

West, Rebecca 1892-1983 ... **CLC 7, 9, 31, 50**
See also BPFB 3; BRWS 3; CA 5-8R; 109;
CANR 19; DLB 36; DLBY 83; FW;
MTCW 1, 2; RGEL

Westall, Robert (Atkinson)
1929-1993 .... **CLC 17**
See also AAYA 12; BYA 2; CA 69-72; 141;
CANR 18, 68; CLR 13; FANT; JRDA;
MAICYA; MAICYAS; SAAS 2; SATA
23, 69; SATA-Obit 75; WYA; YAW

Westermarck, Edward 1862-1939 . **TCLC 87**

Westlake, Donald E(dwin) 1933- .... **CLC 7,
33; DAM POP**
See also BPFB 3; CA 17-20R; CAAS 13;
CANR 16, 44, 65, 94; CMW; CPW; INT
CANR-16; MTCW 2

Westmacott, Mary
See Christie, Agatha (Mary Clarissa)

Weston, Allen
See Norton, Andre

Wetcheek, J. L.
See Feuchtwanger, Lion

Wetering, Janwillem van de
See van de Wetering, Janwillem

Wetherald, Agnes Ethelwyn
1857-1940 .... **TCLC 81**
See also DLB 99

Wetherell, Elizabeth
See Warner, Susan (Bogert)

Whale, James 1889-1957 .... **TCLC 63**

Whalen, Philip 1923- .... **CLC 6, 29**
See also CA 9-12R; CANR 5, 39; CP; DLB
16; WP

Williams, Tennessee 1914-1983 . **CLC 1, 2, 5, 7, 8, 11, 15, 19, 30, 39, 45, 71, 111; DA; DAB; DAC; DAM DRAM, MST; DC 4; WLC**
See also AAYA 31; AITN 1, 2; AMW; CA 5-8R; 108; CABS 3; CAD; CANR 31; CDALB 1941-1968; DA3; DFS 1, 3, 7, 12; DLB 7; DLBD 4; DLBY 83; GLL 1; LAIT 4; MTCW 1, 2; RGAL

Williams, Thomas (Alonzo)
1926-1990 .... **CLC 14**
See also CA 1-4R; 132; CANR 2

Williams, William C.
See Williams, William Carlos

Williams, William Carlos
1883-1963 .... **CLC 1, 2, 5, 9, 13, 22, 42, 67; DA; DAB; DAC; DAM MST, POET; PC 7; SSC 31**
See also AMW; CA 89-92; CANR 34; CDALB 1917-1929; DA3; DLB 4, 16, 54, 86; EXPP; MTCW 1, 2; PAB; PFS 1, 6, 11; RGAL; WP

Williamson, David (Keith) 1942- ..... **CLC 56**
See also CA 103; CANR 41; CD

Williamson, Ellen Douglas 1905-1984
See Douglas, Ellen
See also CA 17-20R; 114; CANR 39

Williamson, Jack CLC 29
See also Williamson, John Stewart
See also CAAS 8; DLB 8; SCFW 2

Williamson, John Stewart 1908-
See Williamson, Jack
See also CA 17-20R; CANR 23, 70; SFW

Willie, Frederick
See Lovecraft, H(oward) P(hillips)

Willingham, Calder (Baynard, Jr.)
1922-1995 .... **CLC 5, 51**
See also CA 5-8R; 147; CANR 3; CSW; DLB 2, 44; IDFW 3, 4; MTCW 1

Willis, Charles
See Clarke, Arthur C(harles)

Willy
See Colette, (Sidonie-Gabrielle)

Willy, Colette
See Colette, (Sidonie-Gabrielle)
See also GLL 1

Wilson, A(ndrew) N(orman) 1950- .. **CLC 33**
See also BRWS 6; CA 112; 122; CN; DLB 14, 155, 194; MTCW 2

Wilson, Angus (Frank Johnstone)
1913-1991 . **CLC 2, 3, 5, 25, 34; SSC 21**
See also BRWS 1; CA 5-8R; 134; CANR 21; DLB 15, 139, 155; MTCW 1, 2; RGEL; RGSF

Wilson, August 1945- ... **CLC 39, 50, 63, 118; BLC 3; DA; DAB; DAC; DAM DRAM, MST, MULT; DC 2; WLCS**
See also AAYA 16; AFAW 2; AMWS 8; BW 2, 3; CA 115; 122; CAD; CANR 42, 54, 76; CD; DA3; DFS 3,7; DLB 228; LAIT 4; MTCW 1, 2; RGAL

Wilson, Brian 1942- .... **CLC 12**

Wilson, Colin 1931- .... **CLC 3, 14**
See also CA 1-4R; CAAS 5; CANR 1, 22, 33, 77; CMW; CN; DLB 14, 194; HGG; MTCW 1; SFW

Wilson, Dirk
See Pohl, Frederik

Wilson, Edmund 1895-1972 .. **CLC 1, 2, 3, 8, 24**
See also AMW; CA 1-4R; 37-40R; CANR 1, 46; DLB 63; MTCW 1, 2; RGAL

Wilson, Ethel Davis (Bryant)
1888(?)-1980 .... **CLC 13; DAC; DAM POET**
See also CA 102; DLB 68; MTCW 1; RGEL

Wilson, Harriet
See Wilson, Harriet E. Adams
See also DLB 239

Wilson, Harriet E. Adams
1827(?)-1863(?) .... **NCLC 78; BLC 3; DAM MULT**
See also Wilson, Harriet
See also DLB 50

Wilson, John 1785-1854 .... **NCLC 5**

Wilson, John (Anthony) Burgess 1917-1993
See Burgess, Anthony
See also CA 1-4R; 143; CANR 2, 46; DA3; DAC; DAM NOV; MTCW 1, 2

Wilson, Lanford 1937- .... **CLC 7, 14, 36; DAM DRAM**
See also CA 17-20R; CABS 3; CAD; CANR 45, 96; CD; DFS 4, 9, 12; DLB 7

Wilson, Robert M. 1944- .... **CLC 7, 9**
See also CA 49-52; CAD; CANR 2, 41; CD; MTCW 1

Wilson, Robert McLiam 1964- .... **CLC 59**
See also CA 132

Wilson, Sloan 1920- .... **CLC 32**
See also CA 1-4R; CANR 1, 44; CN

Wilson, Snoo 1948- .... **CLC 33**
See also CA 69-72; CBD; CD

Wilson, William S(mith) 1932- .... **CLC 49**
See also CA 81-84

Wilson, (Thomas) Woodrow
1856-1924 .... **TCLC 79**
See also CA 166; DLB 47

Wilson and Warnke eds. CLC 65

Winchilsea, Anne (Kingsmill) Finch
1661-1720
See Finch, Anne
See also RGEL

Windham, Basil
See Wodehouse, P(elham) G(renville)

Wingrove, David (John) 1954- .... **CLC 68**
See also CA 133; SFW

Winnemucca, Sarah 1844-1891 .... **NCLC 79; DAM MULT**
See also DLB 175; NNAL; RGAL

Winstanley, Gerrard 1609-1676 .... **LC 52**

Wintergreen, Jane
See Duncan, Sara Jeannette

Winters, Janet Lewis CLC 41
See also Lewis, Janet
See also DLBY 87

Winters, (Arthur) Yvor 1900-1968 .... **CLC 4, 8, 32**
See also AMWS 2; CA 11-12; 25-28R; CAP 1; DLB 48; MTCW 1; RGAL

Winterson, Jeanette 1959- .... **CLC 64; DAM POP**
See also BRWS 4; CA 136; CANR 58; CN; CPW; DA3; DLB 207; FANT; FW; GLL 1; MTCW 2; RHW

Winthrop, John 1588-1649 .... **LC 31**
See also DLB 24, 30

Wirth, Louis 1897-1952 .... **TCLC 92**

Wiseman, Frederick 1930- .... **CLC 20**
See also CA 159

Wister, Owen 1860-1938 .... **TCLC 21**
See also BPFB 3; CA 108; 162; DLB 9, 78, 186; RGAL; SATA 62; TCWW 2

Witkacy
See Witkiewicz, Stanislaw Ignacy

Witkiewicz, Stanislaw Ignacy
1885-1939 .... **TCLC 8**
See also CA 105; 162; DLB 215; RGWL; SFW

Wittgenstein, Ludwig (Josef Johann)
1889-1951 .... **TCLC 59**
See also CA 113; 164; MTCW 2

Wittig, Monique 1935(?)- .... **CLC 22**
See also CA 116; 135; CWW 2; DLB 83; FW; GLL 1

Wittlin, Jozef 1896-1976 .... **CLC 25**
See also CA 49-52; 65-68; CANR 3

Wodehouse, P(elham) G(renville)
1881-1975 .... **CLC 1, 2, 5, 10, 22; DAB; DAC; DAM NOV; SSC 2**
See also AITN 2; BRWS 3; CA 45-48; 57-60; CANR 3, 33; CDBLB 1914-1945; CPW 1; DA3; DLB 34, 162; MTCW 1, 2; RGEL; RGSF; SATA 22; SSFS 10; TCLC 108

Woiwode, L.
See Woiwode, Larry (Alfred)

Woiwode, Larry (Alfred) 1941- ... **CLC 6, 10**
See also CA 73-76; CANR 16, 94; CN; DLB 6; INT CANR-16

Wojciechowska, Maia (Teresa)
1927- .... **CLC 26**
See also AAYA 8; BYA 3; CA 9-12R, 183; CAAE 183; CANR 4, 41; CLR 1; JRDA; MAICYA; SAAS 1; SATA 1, 28, 83; SATA-Essay 104; YAW

Wojtyla, Karol
See John Paul II, Pope

Wolf, Christa 1929- .... **CLC 14, 29, 58, 150**
See also CA 85-88; CANR 45; CWW 2; DLB 75; FW; MTCW 1; RGWL

Wolfe, Gene (Rodman) 1931- .... **CLC 25; DAM POP**
See also AAYA 35; CA 57-60; CAAS 9; CANR 6, 32, 60; CPW; DLB 8; FANT; MTCW 2; SATA 118; SCFW 2; SFW

Wolfe, George C. 1954- .... **CLC 49; BLCS**
See also CA 149; CAD; CD

Wolfe, Thomas (Clayton)
1900-1938 ...... **TCLC 4, 13, 29, 61; DA; DAB; DAC; DAM MST, NOV; SSC 33; WLC**
See also AMW; BPFB 3; CA 104; 132; CDALB 1929-1941; DA3; DLB 9, 102; DLBD 2, 16; DLBY 85, 97; MTCW 1, 2; RGAL

Wolfe, Thomas Kennerly, Jr.
1930- .... **CLC 147; DAM POP**
See also Wolfe, Tom
See also CA 13-16R; CANR 9, 33, 70; DA3; DLB 185; INT CANR-9; MTCW 1, 2; TUS

Wolfe, Tom CLC 1, 2, 9, 15, 35, 51
See also Wolfe, Thomas Kennerly, Jr.
See also AAYA 8; AITN 2; AMWS 3; BEST 89:1; BPFB 3; CN; CPW; CSW; DLB 152; LAIT 5; RGAL

Wolff, Geoffrey (Ansell) 1937- .... **CLC 41**
See also CA 29-32R; CANR 29, 43, 78

Wolff, Sonia
See Levitin, Sonia (Wolff)

Wolff, Tobias (Jonathan Ansell)
1945- .... **CLC 39, 64**
See also AAYA 16; AMWS 7; BEST 90:2; BYA 12; CA 114; 117; CAAS 22; CANR 54, 76, 96; CN; CSW; DA3; DLB 130; INT CA-117; MTCW 2; RGAL; RGSF; SSFS 4, 11

Wolfram von Eschenbach c. 1170-c. 1220 .... **CMLC 5**
See also DLB 138; RGWL

Wolitzer, Hilma 1930- .... **CLC 17**
See also CA 65-68; CANR 18, 40; INT CANR-18; SATA 31; YAW

Wollstonecraft, Mary 1759-1797 ..... **LC 5, 50**
See also BRWS 3; CDBLB 1789-1832; DLB 39, 104, 158; FW; LAIT 1; RGEL; WLIT 3

Wonder, Stevie CLC 12
See also Morris, Steveland Judkins

Wong, Jade Snow 1922- .... **CLC 17**
See also CA 109; CANR 91; SATA 112

Woodberry, George Edward
1855-1930 .... **TCLC 73**
See also CA 165; DLB 71, 103

Literary Criticism Series
Cumulative Topic Index

This index lists all topic entries in Gale's *Classical and Medieval Literature Criticism, Contemporary Literary Criticism, Literature Criticism from 1400 to 1800, Nineteenth-Century Literature Criticism,* and *Twentieth-Century Literary Criticism.*

Topic Index

NCLC Cumulative Nationality Index

ISBN 0-7876-5237-7

90000

9 780787 652371